Southwest USA

Kim Grant,
Becca Blond, John A Vlahides

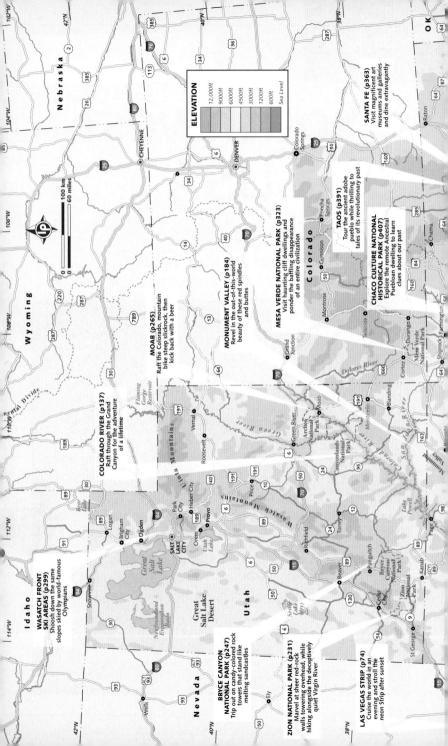

WASATCH FRONT SKI AREAS (p299)
Shoosh down the same slopes skied by world-famous Olympians

BRYCE CANYON NATIONAL PARK (p247)
Trip out on candy-colored rock towers that stand like melting sandcastles

ZION NATIONAL PARK (p231)
Marvel at sheer red-rock walls towering overhead, while hiking alongside the deceptively quiet Virgin River

LAS VEGAS STRIP (p74)
Cruise the world in an evening and stroll the neon Strip after sunset

COLORADO RIVER (p137)
Raft through the Grand Canyon for the adventure of a lifetime

MOAB (p265)
Raft the Colorado, mountain bike steep slickrock, then kick back with a beer

MONUMENT VALLEY (p184)
Revel in the out-of-this-world beauty of these red spindles and buttes

MESA VERDE NATIONAL PARK (p323)
Visit haunting cliff dwellings and ponder the baffling disappearance of an entire civilization

SANTA FE (p363)
Visit magnificent art museums and galleries and dine extravagantly

TAOS (p391)
Tour the ancient adobe pueblo while thrilling to tales of its revolutionary past

CHACO CULTURE NATIONAL HISTORICAL PARK (p407)
Explore the remote Ancestral Puebloan dwelling to learn clues about our past

ELEVATION

12,000ft
9000ft
6000ft
4500ft
3000ft
1200ft
600ft
Sea Level

100 km
60 miles

CARLSBAD CAVERNS NATIONAL PARK (p452)
Tour a massive cave system and watch bats fly out at dusk

BISBEE (p217)
Exudes perfectly preserved Victorian charm and an old mining town vibe

GRAND CANYON NATIONAL PARK (p131)
Marvel at the iconic canyon's sublime beauty from above or below its rim

Destination Southwest USA

The story of the American Southwest is as haunting, surreal and mysterious, as beautiful, wild and magical as the land on which it plays out. The legend of the Wild West has always been America's grandest tale, capturing the fascination and igniting the imagination of writers, photographers, singers, filmmakers and travelers the world around. It's taken on mythical proportions and enticed millions to visit.

And what a fascinating adventure story it is. Sometimes tragic but never dull, it's a tale of Ancestral Puebloans who built cliffside cities that mysteriously vanished; of persecuted Mormons who settled Utah; of rough-and-ready miners, cowboys, outlaws and trappers; of yuppie transplants, hippies, artists and New Agers who set up camp in abandoned mining towns and turned tourism into the new gold; and of the US military, which closed off vast stretches of land for nuclear testing, and whose antics ignited a flurry of alien conspiracy theories.

All these stories are set to a raw, ethereally beautiful, constantly changing backdrop of desolate deserts, rugged snowcapped mountains, dazzling red arches and mazelike canyons. Watch the sky smolder purple from a hilltop surrounded by majestic saguaro cacti in middle-of-nowhere Arizona. Get lost in Utah's canyon country, where the air is so quiet and still you can almost hear the ancestors whisper. Raft the Colorado River through the Grand Canyon for the thrill of your life. Get caught up in the nostalgia of Main Street America on a trip down Route 66. Or visit the fabulous cities. Play with the devil in decadent Las Vegas. Shop for world-class art in chic Santa Fe. Ski white powder bowls at ritzy resorts. Step back in time in old mining meccas. Whatever your whim, the region will indulge.

CURTIS MA

Scenes of the Southwest

RALPH LEE HOPKINS

Nature carves unusual sandstone sculptures in Zion National Park (p231), Utah

JIM WARK

A river runs through it – the confluence of the Colorado and Green Rivers, Canyonlands National Park (p279), Utah

Sunrise illuminates the majestic South Rim (p133), Grand Canyon National Park, Arizona

RALPH LEE HOPKINS

A monument in stone rises from the glassy surface of Lake Powell (p150), Arizona

The sphinx of Luxor (p75) crouches enigmatically beneath Mandalay Bay (p75), Las Vegas, Nevada

All the stars come out to shine along The Strip (p74) in the neon heart of Las Vegas

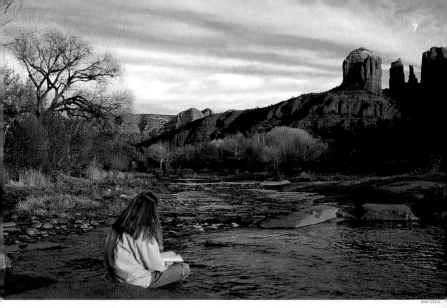

ANN CECIL

Pausing for pleasure in the distinctive red rock country around Sedona (p165), Arizona

Balcony House (p325) of the Ancestral
Puebloans, Mesa Verde National Park,
Colorado

CHRIS MELLOR

KRISTIN PILJAY

Scenes from traditional life adorn an adobe, Taos
(p391), New Mexico

Outdoor Adventures

Skiers survey the magnificent Wasatch Front (p299), Utah

Paddles plow the choppy waters of the Taos Box (p395) on Rio Grande, New Mexico

A hiker admires awe-inspiring stone contours at Antelope Canyon (p150), Arizona

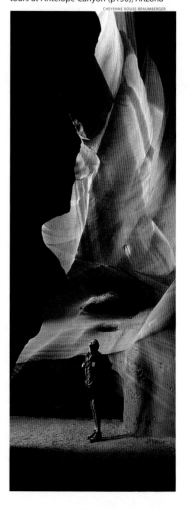

OTHER HIGHLIGHTS

- There's excellent mountain biking in the Southwest, especially on Moab's slickrock (p269).
- For a different perspective, check out the Southwest from a hot-air balloon (p64).

Native Americans

A solemn elder of the Navajo, Monument Valley Navajo Tribal Park (p184), Arizona

A bejewelled Navajo woman demonstrates weaving at the Indian Pueblo Cultural Center (p351), Albuquerque, New Mexico

Mystery lurks between the lines of ancient Hopi petroglyphs, Mesa Verde National Park (p323), Colorado

The Old West

Echos of cowboy boots and dancing shoes
at OK Corral (p215), Tombstone, Arizona

RICHARD CUMMINS

MARK & AUDREY GIB

An iconic road sign along Route 66 (p189),
Seligman, Arizona

Service with a six-shooter at the Copper Queen Hotel's saloon (p219), Bisbee, Arizona

RICHARD CUMMINS

Art

LEE FOSTER

Distinctive Pueblo turquoise worn at the Indian Pueblo Cultural Center (p351), Albuquerque, New Mexico

Silver and turquoise kachina doll (p186)

KARL LEHMANN

Native American blanket, pottery and rug on display in Sedona (p165), Arizona

ANN CECIL

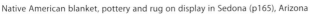

Fabulous Food

Ristras (handstrung ropes of chiles) at Black Mesa Winery (p390), New Mexico

A colorful serving of guacamole, beef and beans at the Phoenician (p125), Scottsdale, Phoenix, Arizona

Fresh produce is the center of attention at a market in Santa Fe (p363), New Mexico

Contents

Regional Map Contents

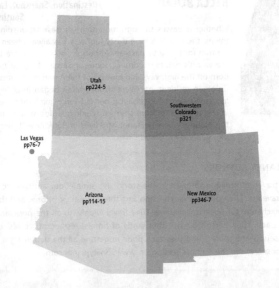

16

The Authors

KIM GRANT
Coordinating Author, New Mexico

Kim Grant has long considered New Mexico the wellspring of her original home. She began making quarterly pilgrimages in the early 1990s; by 2003 the frequency had almost tripled. A photographer drawn to the light, a tai chi practitioner drawn to her community, and a writer yearning to live a more simple and observant life, Kim is happiest in three places: cruising on wide open roads, scrambling along mountain trails and relaxing at sunset with a margarita. The Southwest is a natural fit. Over the course of this research she decided to leap and move to New Mexico. There's no denying the pull.

My Southwest

I thrive by camping in quiet places, blanketed by stars and awakened with sun (and by lounging at four-star resorts – but this isn't about that). I find springtime peace in the Sonoran Desert at Saguaro National Park (p209) and Organ Pipe Cactus National Monument (p211). I feel stillness in shifting sands at White Sands National Monument (p438), where an oasis changes perspectives. I find serenity on the back roads of Taos (p391), where the mountain radiates a strength worth seeking. I find calm in houseboating on Lake Mead (p192), where canyons whisper secrets long after darkness descends. And I find essence writ large at every single national park in southern Utah, but especially in delicate Arches National Park (p276), and quiet-as-a-pin Bryce Canyon National Park (p247).

BECCA BLOND
Destination, Snapshot, Las Vegas, Arizona, Southwestern Colorado

Whether it passes through mountains or deserts, bustling cities or ghost towns, the lure of a long dusty highway has always been too great an adventure for Becca to pass up. Although she's seen more than her share of the world's emptiest corners, some of Becca's favorite travel stories were born off the highways and byways of the American Southwest. A long-time Colorado resident, her Western love affair began in college when she put as many miles as possible on her old Tercel exploring the golden nuggets in this region's treasure chest of scenic goodies. When she's not traversing the globe for Lonely Planet, she lives in Boulder with her boyfriend and a big, goofy dog named Duke.

LONELY PLANET AUTHORS

Why is our travel information the best in the world? It's simple: our authors are independent, dedicated travelers. They don't research using just the Internet or phone, and they don't take freebies in exchange for positive coverage. They travel widely, to all the popular spots and off the beaten track. They personally visit thousands of hotels, restaurants, cafés, bars, galleries, palaces, museums and more – and they take pride in getting all the details right, and telling it how it is. For more, see the authors section on www.lonelyplanet.com.

JOHN A VLAHIDES   Utah
A freelance writer and member of the North American Snowsports Journalists Association, John is also a French-trained chef and former Clefs d'Or luxury-hotel concierge. He regularly writes about the West and lives in California, where he spends his free time touring the coast by motorcycle, sunning beneath the Golden Gate Bridge, skiing the Sierra Nevada and singing tenor with the San Francisco Symphony Chorus.

CONTRIBUTING AUTHORS

Lisa Dunford, who wrote the Mormons, Polygamy & the LDS boxed text (p40), moved through eight states and three countries before settling in Texas as a newspaper editor. Maybe it was the inherited pioneer spirit of her great-great-great-grandfather Brigham Young that brought her west, but no matter where she wanders now as a freelance writer and editor, she always returns to her homestead on the river.

David Goldberg MD completed his training in internal medicine and infectious diseases at Columbia-Presbyterian Medical Center in New York City, where he has also served as voluntary faculty. At present, he is an infectious diseases specialist in Scarsdale, NY, and the editor-in-chief of the website MDtravel-health.com. The Health chapter was adapted from his text.

David Lukas has been an avid student of the natural world since the age of five. Now a professional naturalist, David leads natural history tours, conducts biological surveys and writes about natural history. His articles have appeared in many national magazines, and he writes a weekly nature column for the *Los Angeles Times*. For this book David wrote the Environment chapter.

Mark Morford wrote the What Is Burning Man? boxed text (p110). A columnist for sfgate.com and the *San Francisco Chronicle*, he is also a yoga teacher and fiction writer, outstanding parallel parker, fervent wine devotee, former smoker, frequent skeptic and sporadic true believer. Mark has been to Burning Man four times.

Getting Started

How do you envisage your trip? As one-part desert pilgrimage and one-part high-rolling party, with a dash of Native American mysticism and a pinch of Wild West fables thrown in for good measure? How you answer these questions will begin to narrow your choices considerably. And in a place as far and wide as the American Southwest, as expansive as it is, narrow is better. Otherwise, without making some early key decisions, your trip could corkscrew into a chasm as deep as the Grand Canyon. You could cruise right by some 1000-year-old Ancestral Puebloan site or petroglyphs without realizing it. You could spin the wheel in Las Vegas, Nevada, and never get to Las Vegas, New Mexico.

WHEN TO GO

The best season to visit the Southwest is January to December. That's right – just go. Of course the timing depends on what you want to do.

In northern Arizona, New Mexico and Utah, high season equates to summertime – traditionally from Memorial Day (late May) to Labor Day (early September). Expect higher prices and more crowds, except in hot southern Arizona where luxury resorts cut their prices in half.

Wintertime visitors flock to the highlands for great skiing. Utah has world-class skiing; New Mexico is also pretty darn good. If you don't enjoy hurtling down snow-covered mountains, head to southern Arizona. Hotels in Phoenix, Tucson and other southern Arizona towns consider winter (Christmas to May) their high (and more expensive) season. While the rest of the country is buried under snowdrifts, southern Arizonans enjoy T-shirt weather most days.

See Climate Charts (p456) for more information.

Spring and fall are less crowded, but some services may not be available then. Fall is favored in the mountains of northern New Mexico and southwestern Colorado for watching golden-leaved aspen trees and cottonwoods. It's not like the foliage show staged in New England, but these beauties twinkle like a precious metal in glistening sunlight. Further, they rustle like nothing you've ever heard. In the springtime, the Sonoran desert near Tucson in Arizona comes alive with tiny wildflowers and blooming cacti.

The Southwest conjures up images of searing desert heat, and this is certainly true in many parts of the region. An excellent rule of thumb is to gauge the climate by the altitude. The lower you are, the hotter and drier it will be. Las Vegas, southwestern and south-central Arizona temperatures exceed 100°F (38°C) for weeks on end and occasionally surpass 120°F (49°C). The humidity is low, however, and evaporation helps to cool the body. Nighttime temperatures drop by 20°F or 30°F. Winter temperatures occasionally drop below freezing, but only for a few hours.

COSTS & MONEY

If you camp, share a rental car with another person and plan picnics, your daily expenses can be as low as $40 per person per day. Two people staying in budget motels, eating lunch in fast-food Mexican restaurants and enjoying moderate dinners can expect to spend between $70 and $85 per person per day.

If you spend ample time in cities (like Sedona, Santa Fe, Taos and Park City) and stay at a preponderance of historic hotels and character-filled B&Bs, costs edge up to about $110 per person per day. For those

TOP TENS

Festivals & Events

Southwesterners really know how to throw a party. Whether it involves food or dance (or probably both together), or aliens and music (probably not simultaneously), you're bound to find fun. For more comprehensive listings, check the individual towns and p459.

- Sundance Film Festival (Park City, p309), late January
- Winterfest (Park City, p309), early February
- Green Jell-O Sculpting Contest (Zion National Park, p237), mid-March
- World Series of Poker (Las Vegas, p90), mid-April to mid-May
- Telluride Bluegrass Festival (Telluride, p342), late June

- Solar Music Festival (Taos, p396), late June
- Santa Fe Indian Market (Santa Fe, p374), mid- to late August
- Jazz on the Rocks (Sedona, p169), late September
- International Balloon Fiesta (Albuquerque, p353), early October
- Helldorado Days (Tombstone, p216), mid-October

Landscapes & Photo Opportunities

Upon gazing at a crested butte silhouetted at sunset, or devouring dawn breaking over the Grand Canyon, you'll wish you'd never uttered the word 'awesome' until then. Only then will you understand its true meaning. It's no exaggeration to say that jaw-dropping scenery blankets the entire region, but for particularly scenic drives, check out each state's Scenic Byways section. And keep your camera ready.

- Grand Canyon National Park (p131)
- Monument Valley (p184 and p286)
- Canyon de Chelly National Monument (p182)
- Mesa Verde National Park (p323)
- White Sands National Monument (p438)

- Chaco Culture National Historical Park (p407)
- Bryce Canyon National Park (p247)
- Zion National Park (p231)
- Arches National Park (p276)
- Canyonlands National Park (p279)

Pit Stops for Foodies

From mild to hot and from rustic to refined, Southwestern cuisine will knock your socks off. Plan on dipping your blue corn chip into a few of these restaurants. For a thorough discussion of native and nouvelle cuisine, peruse the Food & Drink chapter (p66).

- Café Poca Cosa (Tucson, p207)
- Café Roka (Bisbee, p219)
- Medizona (Phoenix, p128)
- Jean Pierre Bakery (Durango, p334)
- Aureole (Las Vegas, p95)

- Sadie's (Albuquerque, p358)
- Monte's Chow Cart (Taos, p397)
- The city of Santa Fe (Santa Fe, p375)
- Cafe Diablo (Torrey, p261)
- Deer Valley Resort (Park City, p302)

occasions when nothing less than a famous resort or spa will suffice, and dining at the top celebrity-chef-owned eateries is *de rigueur,* two people will undoubtedly drop $250 per person per day. Staying in Vegas costs a bundle, especially on weekends. You can easily throw down $300 a day for a midrange hotel, a show and decent meals. None of these scenarios includes purchasing a Native American silver necklace or a Navajo rug.

Discounts abound; see p458. Most state tourism centers publish brochures with dining and lodging coupons. Also consider printing out Internet coupons before departing and bringing them along. Discounts on car rentals and accommodations are often available to members of American Automobile Association (AAA; see p473).

TRAVEL LITERATURE

Before heading off, pick up some books to help inspire your trip.

For engaging historical information, little else beats Michael S Durham's beautifully illustrated *The Smithsonian Guide to Historic America – The Desert States* (1998).

Jack Ruby's Kitchen Sink: Offbeat Travels Through America's Southwest (2001) by Tom Miller is a quirky read to accompany your own odyssey.

Stephen Trimble's remarkably satisfying *The People: Indians of the American Southwest* (1993) is derived from a decade of travel and includes interviews and photographs of the area's many tribes.

Barbara Kingsolver's novel *Animal Dreams* (1990) yields wonderful insights into a small Hispanic village near the Arizona–New Mexico border and from a Native American pueblo.

Traveler's Tales: American Southwest (2001), a collection of regional essays, will infuse your impending adventure with a forthcoming richness.

House Made of Dawn (1968), a Pulitzer Prize winner by Kiowa novelist and poet N Scott Momaday, is about a pueblo Native American's struggle to return home after fighting in WWII.

Ann Zwinger writes eloquently in *Down Canyon: A Naturalist Explores the Colorado River Through the Grand Canyon* (1995).

The Monkey Wrench Gang (1975), Edward Abbey's classic, is a fictional and comical account of real people who plan to blow up Glen Canyon Dam before it floods Glen Canyon.

The region doesn't suffer from a drought of inspired writers; for more on Southwestern literature, see p42.

DON'T LEAVE HOME WITHOUT...

- Comfortable footwear with good traction for scrambling over rocky surfaces
- Strong sunscreen, high-quality sunglasses and a wide-brimmed hat
- Plenty of layers of clothing
- A great set of road maps
- Gear for camping and hiking, and reading up on desert survival techniques
- A spiffy outfit if you're staying in Vegas
- Your favorite CDs for long drives
- A bathing suit (for swimming pools, rivers and lakes)
- Binoculars
- A copy of your passport, driver's license and phone numbers for your credit cards
- Packing your Swiss Army knife and traditional film in your checked luggage (not carry-on)

INTERNET RESOURCES

American Southwest (www.americansouthwest.net) Arguably the most comprehensive site for national parks and natural landscapes of the Southwest.

Arizona Highways (www.arizonahighways.com) Online version of the glossy magazine with weekend getaways and photography tips; information on local flora and fauna too.

Lonely Planet (www.lonelyplanet.com) Succinct summaries, travel news, links and the Thorn Tree bulletin board.

New Mexico CultureNet (www.nmcn.org) Articles about artists and writers of New Mexico, as well as a history of the region, with events listings and arts directories.

Notes from the Road (www.notesfromtheroad.com) Click on Desert Southwest to enter another world; it'll be hard to return.

Visit Las Vegas (www.visitlasvegas.com) An inclusive site as flashy as the city itself, brought to you by the Las Vegas Convention and Visitors Authority.

Itineraries
CLASSIC ROUTES

FOUR CORNERS LOOP
10 Days

Sure, it's the only spot where four states touch. But what states! What scenery! What history and culture! Take a photo of Four Corners, then high-tail it out to beautiful buttes and majestic mesas, ride narrow gauge railways and explore ruins, trading posts and great trails. This trip is 725 miles.

Start in **Durango** (p331) and spend a day exploring the historic old mining town. Ride the narrow gauge railway to **Silverton** (p336) the next afternoon; then spend the evening eating and drinking in one of the Durango's pleasant microbreweries. Next head to the haunting ruins at **Mesa Verde National Park** (p323), where you can hike and learn about the region's fascinating history. From Mesa Verde head toward Arizona and stop at the **Four Corners Navajo Tribal Park** (p183) to snap a picture with your hands and feet in four different states. Head into New Mexico to ogle at **Shiprock** (p406), a stunning and ragged red rock formation. Spend your fourth night here. Begin the dusty and rutted drive to isolated **Chaco Culture National Historical Park** (p407), arguably the most notable architectural sight in the entire region. Sleep near **Window Rock** (p180), the capital of the **Navajo Reservation** (p180), where you can visit the Navajo Nation Museum & Library. Stop at the old-world commercial hub of the region, the **Hubbell Trading Post National Historic Site** (p182), which served as the reservation's lifeline when it was established in the 1870s. Detour (65 miles each way) over to **Second Mesa** and the heart of the **Hopi Reservation** (p185), where you will find native artisans and the Hopi Cultural Center. Make your way into the relatively verdant **Canyon de Chelly National Monument** (p182), an inhabited and cultivated canyon complete with hogans and herds of sheep. Hold onto your hat and lift your jaw off the floor as you approach the out-of-this-world beautiful **Monument Valley** (p184 and p286). Continue driving north to **Mexican Hat** (p286) in Utah to drink in the grandeur.

GRAND TOUR
One Month

Throw a pair of cowboy boots, hiking boots and comfy walking shoes into the saddle bag, pardner, and get ready to ride. Suspend judgments and roll the dice on the **Las Vegas Strip** (p74) before receiving some kicks on **Route 66** (p189) between Kingman and Williams. Continue to kick back in funky **Flagstaff** (p154), before venturing deep into the **Grand Canyon National Park** (p131). Shine your spirit in **Sedona** (p165) before getting in touch with your shabby chic side in **Jerome** (p173). Visit the Heard Museum in **Phoenix** (p116), mellow out at **Saguaro National Park** (p209), and hang out in collegiate **Tucson** (p198). Fancy yourself a gunslinger in **Tombstone** (p214) before settling into charming **Bisbee** (p217). Head east for **White Sands National Monument** (p438), with sprawling dunes as pure as driven snow. Watch bats swoop from caves at **Carlsbad Caverns National Park** (p452). Ponder little green men landing near **Roswell** (p445) before sinking into **Santa Fe** (p363), a foodie haven and magnet for art mavens. Feel tomorrow's science at **Los Alamos** (p384) and yesterday's civilization at **Bandelier National Monument** (p386). Take the ultrascenic **High Road to Taos** (p388) to hang with hippies and ski with bums in **Taos** (p391), before driving the luscious **Enchanted Circle** (p402). Chill out in laid-back **Durango** (p331) before exploring ancient civilizations at **Mesa Verde National Park** (p323). Be prepared with plenty of film at **Monument Valley** (p184 and p286). Then head to the most stunning collection of national parks in the US. Visit a park a day or spend a few days in two or three parks, including **Canyonlands National Park** (p279) and **Arches National Park** (p276), for which **Moab** (p265) serves as a staging area. Then cruise **Highway 12** (p256) near **Capitol Reef National Park** (p261), **Grand Staircase-Escalante National Monument** (p251), the spires at **Bryce Canyon National Park** (p247) and the sheer red-rock walls at **Zion National Park** (p231), before returning to Las Vegas.

Gas up the car and assemble some good CDs for the best road trip in the entire USA. From the wildest national parks and the swankiest art colonies, to the most ancient Native cultures and woolly Western folklore, it's all here, connected by dozens of scenic byways. Expect to drive about 2750 miles.

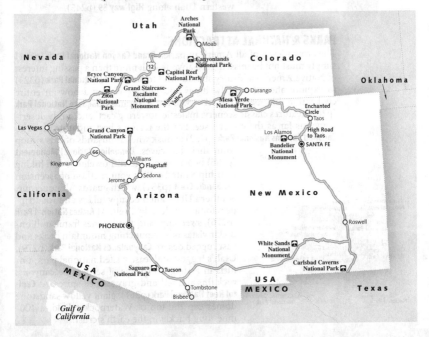

TAILORED TRIPS

OLD WEST

The drawl creeps in slowly: Howdy pardner. The swagger slows you down; don't let the saloon door hit you on your way out. These small towns have struck gold by mining our desire to relive the dusty days and retire to comfortable digs at night. **Jerome** (p173) was once known as the 'wickedest town in the old West.' Today it's a charming little artist's haunt with cool B&Bs and funky shops. Spend a few days in the beautiful, perfectly preserved **Bisbee** (p217). The bad old days are alive and kicking in touristy **Tombstone** (p214), where the famous shootout at the OK Corral

went down. Once saloon-swinging mining haunts, today towns like **Durango** (p331), **Silverton** (p336) and **Telluride** (p341) offer plenty of opportunities to explore the past (and the outdoors) amid stunning mountain scenery. Make your way up here and hit pay dirt. Silver mines and Victorian architecture draw history buffs to **Silver City** (p428). **Lincoln** (p444), where ranchers and shopkeepers fought the 1878 Lincoln County War (p31), looms large thanks to legendary Billy the Kid. Fans of the immortalized outlaw pay their respects at **Fort Sumner** (p448) where the Kid made his last stand, proving mortal after all. Retrace the boot prints and stomping grounds of legendary outlaw Butch Cassidy and Mormon pioneers through southwestern Utah along **Highway 89** (p245).

PARKS & NATURAL ATTRACTIONS

The crown jewel of all American parks, **Grand Canyon National Park** (p131) simply must not be missed. And anyone with more than a passing interest in Native American history should head to **Mesa Verde National Park** (p323) to explore ancient cliff dwellings and ponder why and how an entire civilization disappeared in AD 1300. For naturalists, **Saguaro National Park** (p209) features classic scenery: majestic, towering cacti and sandy desert-scapes as far as the eye can see. For the region's best nightlife, head to **Carlsbad Caverns National Park** (p452) at dusk when thousands of bats swoop

from their bat caves. **Bandelier National Monument** (p386) boasts accessible cliff dwellings and hiking near hip Santa Fe. Pick your method of ascension for **Sandia Crest** (p351), which guards Albuquerque. Southern Utah could occupy hikers and roadtrippers for a month all by itself. At **Arches National Park** (p276), sweeping sandstone arches frame million-dollar vistas of sky-punching mountain peaks and vast rugged desert. **Canyonlands National Park** (p279), Utah's biggest and least-visited national park, unfurls in a rugged expanse of serpentine canyons, rock fins and red-and-gray striped spires. At **Capitol Reef National Park** (p261), giant yellow sandstone domes cap the top of Waterpocket Fold, a 100-mile-long buckle in the earth's crust.

SOUTHWEST FOR KIDS

Fly into Phoenix, where you can immediately escape the heat and amuse the little ones at one of the city's numerous waterparks. Try **Waterworld Safari** (p123), which boasts a six-story-high waterslide. In Tucson, the educational **Arizona-Sonora Desert Museum** (p200) is home to local desert animals thriving in their natural habitat. Kids also love **Old Tucson Studios** (p201), once an actual film set and now featuring shootouts and Wild West events galore. In **Tombstone** (p214), kids delight at OK Corral shootouts and outrageous Boothill Graveyard tombstones. Culture reigns in New Mexico, beginning at Santa Fe's festive **Museum of International Folk Art** (p366), where learning and history are fun. Speaking of which, science has never been more interactive or relevant than at **!Explora! Children's Museum** (p354) in Albuquerque. The **Martínez Hacienda** (p392) in Taos gives kids a great idea of New Mexican life in the early 1800s. Family values are exalted in Mormon culture, which makes Utah a great spot for kids, especially **Salt Lake City** (p287). To keep kids in their bodies, head to Utah's self-styled adventure capital and go rafting down the **Colorado River** (p265) or biking around **Moab** (p265). The Olympic town of Park City is attractive for **nature walks** (p308) and **horseback rides** (p308) through meadows of wildflowers, as well as **skiing** at some of America's best ski resorts (p299).

HISTORIC ROUTE 66

Starting from Las Vegas, head south to little **Topock** (p190) on the California border. Savor the broad horizons of the old highway between here and **Seligman** (p189). Along the way pass through gun-slinging **Oatman** (p190), detour to the little western outpost of **Chloride** (p190) and cruise through the mining settlement of **Kingman** (p188). Head east to the windblown streets of **Winslow** (p186). Next up is the vintage 1940s downtown of **Williams** (p163). Ride the train to the **Grand Canyon** (p163), then cruise into funky **Flagstaff** (p154), where the old western heart beats strong. In **Holbrook** (p187), detour to the **Petrified Forest National Park** (p187). Onward to New Mexico and **Gallup** (p415), the trading epicenter for the Zuni and Navajo reservations. Despite David Cassidy's Partridge Family song singing its praises, **Albuquerque** (p349) is highly undersung. Head north to an oasis of art and culture, **Santa Fe** (p363), before detouring to the charming other **Las Vegas** (p419). Or from Albuquerque, cruise due east to **Santa Rosa** (p417) and its classic Route 66 Auto Museum. The last stop, **Tucumcari** (p418), fittingly upholds the mythology of Route 66 with perfection.

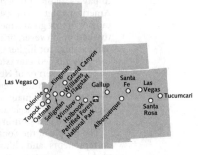

Snapshot

While in the Southwest, you may hear locals talking about a smattering of ongoing issues – the area's rapid growth, the lack of water, the drought that's left Lake Powell at its lowest level in 30 years, maybe even the emasculation of subsistence farming. Politicians are discussing the same issues. When the mines closed in the mid-20th century, towns turned tourism into the new gold, actively promoting their natural wonders, sunny skies and outdoor adventures. Their efforts paid off; tourists and transplants flocked to the region. Rebirth and reinvention became their mantra. But as the cities exploded, so did the problems. The fragile, arid environment is not equipped to handle the sheer volume of people now living inside its confines. With 37.5 million visitors in 2004, Las Vegas is one of the most popular US tourist traps, yet the city was built in the middle of a desert. The water it needs to sustain itself has to be drawn from somewhere else, taking the precious resource away from small farmers in Colorado's San Luis Valley, and from already struggling rural New Mexican towns.

At the same time old mining pits are leeching dangerous chemicals into the ground, polluting the water table. Mountains are being stripped of their timber to sustain rapid construction, making them prone to erosion. Conservationists are at war with Big Business, lawmakers are in a constant struggle to find a balance between development and preservation. Native Americans pushed onto barren reservations built gaudy casinos in hopes of cashing in on the capitalistic craze. But as cities expanded, residents found themselves living next to these glowing monoliths. Arguments still break out at city council meetings, with demands that casino construction be restricted and claims it deters the historic beauty of their towns and clogs their highways with drunken gamblers.

While slowly homogenizing, race relations still play an intricate role in the dynamics of the Southwest. With the exception of Mormon Utah, the region is commonly perceived as having a tricultural mix of Native Americans, Latinos and Anglos (see p40). Following the great Anglo migration in the late 19th century, Whites have dominated the top of the economic pyramid. Latinos, who had relied on subsistence farming for centuries, were slowly pushed off their land and forced to take jobs to pay escalating property taxes. Once the majority, Latinos and Native Americans found themselves minorities, swept up and often lost in the pursuit of that great American Dream. A national movement for affirmative action, however, brings new hope for the region's poorest residents. Scholarships for higher education, low-interest small business loans and federally funded grants are opening doors once firmly shut. The well-respected governor of New Mexico, Bill Richardson, is Latino. And traditionally conservative republican Colorado elected its first Latino – and first Democrat in many years – to the US senate in 2004, although some argue Ken Salazar's election had more to do with dislike for the opposing candidate than a shift in racial and political ideology.

The people of the Southwest have always been fighters, survivors and entrepreneurs, and although the region's future is rife with potholes of problems, we bet they'll come out on top.

History

THE FIRST AMERICANS

The first inhabitants of what is now the Southwest United States reached North America over 25,000 years ago from Asia by way of the Bering Strait. We know this partly because in the 1920s workers in Clovis, New Mexico, discovered stone spear points embedded in the bones of extinct mammals that dated to over 11,000 years ago. Archaeological sites near Cochise County in southeastern Arizona have also yielded the remains of baskets and stone cooking implements.

As game became extinct and the population grew, the earliest hunters augmented their diets with wild berries, seeds, roots and fruits. After 3000 BC, contacts with farmers in what is now central Mexico, led to the beginnings of agriculture in the Southwest. Primitive corn was grown, and by 500 BC beans and squash were also cultivated. Between 300 BC and AD 100, distinct groups began to settle in villages in the Southwest.

Pueblo Bonita at Chaco Canyon, which reached its nadir as a civilization in 1020, once had over 40 kivas and 600 rooms.

THE ANCESTRAL PUEBLOANS

By about AD 100, three dominant cultures were emerging in the Southwest: the Hohokam of the desert, the Mogollon of the central mountains and valleys, and the Ancestral Puebloans – formerly known as the Anasazi. (Anasazi, a Navajo word meaning 'enemy ancestors,' is a term to which many modern Pueblo people object; it's no longer used.)

The intrepid Hohokam culture existed in the deserts of Arizona from 300 BC to AD 1400, adapting to desert life by creating an incredible, river-fed irrigation system. In addition to using stone tools to dig miles and miles of 15ft-wide canals, they augmented farming by collecting wild desert foods and lived in simple mud or stick shelters over shallow depressions in the earth. The Hohokam developed low earthen pyramids (perhaps serving as temples) and sunken ball courts with earthen walls. Because they cremated their dead, archaeologists have been left with comparatively little information. Nonetheless, a rich heritage of pottery attests to Hohokam artistry; see Casa Grande Ruins National Monument (p210).

The Mogollon culture settled near the Mexican border from 200 BC to AD 1400. They lived in small communities, often elevated on isolated mesas or ridge tops, and built simple pit dwellings. Although they farmed, they depended more on hunting and foraging for food. Growing villages featured the kiva – a circular, underground chamber used for ceremonies and other communal purposes.

By about the 13th or 14th century, the Mogollon were likely being peacefully incorporated by the Ancestral Puebloan groups from the north. One indication of this is the beautiful black-on-white Mimbres pottery with its distinctive animal and human figures executed in a geometric style reminiscent of Puebloan ware. Good examples are found in Deming (p435) and Silver City (p429); the Gila Cliff Dwellings (p431) are a late-Mogollon site with Puebloan features.

The Ancestral Puebloans inhabited the Colorado Plateau, also called the Four Corners area (p183), which comprises parts of northeastern

10,000 BC	AD 100
Clovis culture hunts with spears in New Mexico	Hohokam, Mogollon and Ancestral Puebloan cultures emerge

Arizona, northwestern New Mexico, southwestern Colorado and south-eastern Utah. This culture left the richest archaeological sites and ancient settlements that are still inhabited in the Southwest.

The earliest Ancestral Puebloans gathered food in baskets and initially lived in pit houses but eventually used mud plastered brush called wattle-and-daub and fashioned more complex kivas with underground tunnels. The craftsmanship of their basket weaving has led archaeologists to refer to these as the Basket Maker periods. Ancestral Puebloans were the first to use looms to weave cotton cloth (decorated with turkey feathers) and the first to wear yucca sandals.

Important Ancestral Puebloan sites can be seen at Mesa Verde National Park (p323), Navajo National Monument (p183), Canyon de Chelly National Monument (p182), Bandelier National Monument (p386), Aztec Ruins National Monument (p408) and Chaco Culture National Historical Park (p407).

Today, descendants of the Ancestral Puebloans live in Pueblo Indian communities along New Mexico's Rio Grande, and in the Acoma (p411), Zuni (p415) and Laguna (p414) pueblos of New Mexico's northwestern corner. The oldest links with the Ancestral Puebloans are found among the Hopi tribe of northern Arizona (p185). Here, perched on a mesa top, the village of Old Oraibi (p186) has been inhabited since the 1100s, making it the oldest continuously inhabited settlement in North America. The New Mexican pueblos at Acoma (p411) and Taos (p400) may be as old.

By 1050, the Southwest had many trade routes – and items principally traded were treasures and ornaments in silver, turquoise and copper, sea-shells and exotic macaws.

By about 1400, the Hohokam had mysteriously disappeared, their villages abandoned. Most likely, a combination of factors including drought, overhunting, conflict among groups and disease contributed to their departure. The Mogollon people were more or less incorporated into the Ancestral Puebloans, who themselves began to leave many of their ancient pueblos in the 1400s and, by the 1500s, had mainly moved to the pueblos now found along the Rio Grande. In an impressive architectural triumph, but a minor note in their history, they began to build numerous cliff dwellings around 1200 (some are preserved in Mesa Verde National Park; see p323), after which the area was deserted until arrival of the Navajo in the 16th century.

From gunslingers and prospectors to Native Americans ancient and contemporary, www.desertusa.com deals the goods on people and places that call (and have called) the Southwestern desert home.

THE NAVAJO, HOPI & APACHE

Native American tribes living in the Southwest today are comparatively recent arrivals. The Navajo moved into the Four Corners area, especially northeastern Arizona. The Apache consisted of several distinct groups: the Jicarilla Apache in the north-central mountains of New Mexico, the Mescalero Apache in New Mexico's south-central mountains and the Western Apache in southeastern Arizona.

While these tribes skirmished and raided the Pueblo and Hopi descendants of the Ancestral Puebloans, the Pueblo people also took advantage of the hunting skills of the newcomers. Likewise, the Apache and Navajo learned about pottery, weaving and agriculture from the Pueblo tribes.

1300	1400–1500
Vibrant culture at Mesa Verde disappears	Most pueblos abandoned or moved to Rio Grande

Throughout the Southwest, Apache, Comanche, Navajo and Hopi were alternately fighting with one another and with the Spaniards, and it was this warfare that limited further Spanish expansion in the area during the 18th century.

When the Europeans did arrive in the Southwest they brought a lifestyle completely foreign to the Native Americans. Mother Earth and Father Sky, bows and arrows, ritual dances and sweat lodges, foot travel, spiritual oneness with the land – all these were to be challenged by the new concepts of Christ and conquest, gunpowder and sword, European civilization and education, horses and a grasping desire for land.

THE SPANIARDS ARRIVE

The initial Spanish incursion into the Southwest occurred after a shipwreck off the coast of Florida in 1528 sent four survivors journeying westward across the US through Texas and up the Rio Grande. Tales of their early sojourns launched the first major expedition, led by Francisco Vasquez de Coronado, in February 1540. It included 300 soldiers, hundreds of Native American guides and herds of livestock. It also marked the first major violence between Spanish explorers and the native people.

The expedition's goal was the fabled, immensely rich Seven Cities of Cibola. For two years, they traveled through what is now Arizona, New Mexico and as far east as Kansas, but instead of gold and precious gems, the expedition found adobe pueblos. During the harsh winters, the expedition expropriated some of the pueblos for its own use, burned one, and killed dozens of Native Americans. This ferocity was the hallmark of many Europeans to come.

Persistent fables of rich cities were periodically revived by small groups that made forays along the Rio Grande. In 1598, a large force led by Don Juan de Onate stopped near present-day El Paso, Texas. Declaring the land to the north New Mexico, he claimed it for Spain and became governor. Then he headed north through the desert, the Jornada del Muerto or 'Journey of the Dead.'

During the Spaniards' first few years in northern New Mexico, they tried to subdue the pueblos, resulting in much bloodshed. The fighting started in Acoma Pueblo (p411) when a Spanish contingent of 30 men led by one of Onate's nephews demanded tax payment in the form of food. The Acoma Indians responded by killing him and about half of his force. Onate retaliated with greater severity. Relations with the Native Americans, poor harvests, harsh weather and accusations of Onate's cruelty led to many desertions among the colonizers. By 1608, Onate had been recalled to Mexico. A new governor, Pedro de Peralta, was sent north to found a new capital in 1609 – Santa Fe (p363) remains the capital of New Mexico today, the oldest capital in what is now the USA. In 1610, Peralta built Santa Fe's Palace of the Governors (p366), the oldest non–Native American building in the US still in use today.

A particularly destructive Spanish campaign in 1675 was aimed at destroying the Pueblo kivas and powerful ceremonial objects such as prayer sticks and kachina dolls. In 1680, the united northern Pueblos rose up in retaliation in the Pueblo Revolt and succeeded in driving some 2400

Latter Days (2003) is a heart-felt story about a gay Mormon boy. (By the way, being gay in Mormonland is *not* okay – though elders apparently look the other way if you absolutely swear you never have sex.)

1598	1846–48
Onate declares land north of El Paso for Spain	Mexican American War; ends with signing of Guadalupe-Hildago treaty

Spaniards back down the Rio Grande to El Paso. The Pueblo people took over Santa Fe's Palace of the Governors and held it until 1692. The northern Pueblo people, a mix of many different tribes, languages and beliefs, didn't remain united for long, though. In 1692, the Spaniards again took over Santa Fe and eventually subdued the area's pueblos. During the 18th century, the colony grew and the Spaniards lived uneasily but relatively peacefully alongside the Pueblo peoples.

From Geronimo to Zane Grey and from historical structures to Native American sites, www.az historytraveler.org lives up to its tag line: 'come for the scenery, stay for the stories.'

Less brutal incursions were made into Arizona by the Jesuit priest Eusebio Kino, who garnered nearly mythical status as the one who brought God to southern Arizona. Beginning in 1687, he spent over two decades in the Arizona-Sonora area, establishing missions at Tumacácori (p212) and San Xavier del Bac (p210). After Kino's departure, conditions for the Native Americans deteriorated and led to the short-lived Pima Revolt of 1751 and the Yuma Massacre of 1781.

In an attempt to link Santa Fe with the newly established port of San Francisco and to avoid Native American raids, small groups of explorers pressed into what is now Utah, but were turned back by the rugged and arid terrain. The 1776 Dominguez-Escalante expedition was the first to survey Utah, but no attempt was made to settle there until the arrival of the Mormons in the 19th century.

In addition to armed conflict, Europeans introduced smallpox, measles and typhus, to which the Native Americans had no resistance, into the Southwest. Upwards of half of the Pueblo populations were decimated by these diseases, shattering cultures and trade routes and proving a destructive force that far outstripped combat.

THE TERRITORY YEARS

After the Mexican American War, most of present-day Arizona and New Mexico became the New Mexico Territory; Utah and Nevada became the Utah Territory; Nevada became a separate territory in 1861, Arizona in 1863. Territories, unlike states, could not elect senators and representatives to Congress but were headed by an elected governor, with little power in the nation's capital.

For decades, US forces pushed west across the continent, killing or forcibly moving whole tribes of Native Americans who were in their way. The most widely known incident is the forceful relocation of many Navajo in 1864. US forces, led by Kit Carson, destroyed Navajo fields,

THE WAR THAT RESHAPED AMERICA

As part of its fulfillment of 'Manifest Destiny,' which held that America should stretch from sea to sea, the US attempted to buy New Mexico and California. When the attempt proved unsuccessful, the US declared war on Mexico in 1846. After the US captured Mexico City, Mexico ceded all the land between Texas and the Pacific. The treaty of Guadalupe-Hidalgo, signed later that year in what is Las Cruces (p432), gave the US formal ownership of New Mexico, California and Texas, in return for $18.25 million. By contrast, Santa Fe was taken without violence when the Mexican governor was simply paid $50,000 to leave. In 1853 the Gadsden Purchase added land in Arizona. During the subsequent Civil War, efforts were made to reclaim the Gadsden lands for the Confederacy, to no avail.

1847	1864
Mormons arrive in Salt Lake City	Navajo, rounded up by Kit Carson, forced to march 'The Long Walk'

orchards and houses, and forced the people into surrendering or with-drawing into remote parts of Canyon de Chelly (p182). Eventually they were starved out. About 9000 Navajo were rounded up and marched 400 miles east to a camp at Bosque Redondo, near Fort Sumner (p448) in New Mexico. Hundreds of Native Americans died from sickness, starvation or gunshot wounds along the way. The Navajo call this 'The Long Walk,' and it remains an important part of their history.

The last serious conflicts were between US troops and the Apache. This was partly because raiding was the essential path to manhood for the Apache. As US forces and settlers moved into Apache land, they became obvious targets for the raids that were part of the Apache way of life. These continued under the leadership of Mangas Coloradas, Cochise, Victorio and, finally, Geronimo, who surrendered in 1886 after being promised that he and the Apache would be imprisoned for two years and then allowed to return to their homeland. As with many promises made during these years, this one, too, was broken.

Even after the wars were over, Native American people continued to be treated like second-class citizens for many decades. Non–Native Americans used legal loopholes and technicalities to take over reservation land. Many children were removed from reservations and shipped off to boarding schools where they were taught in English and punished for speaking their own languages or behaving 'like Indians' – this practice continued into the 1930s.

The history of the Southwest during the 19th century is strongly linked to the development of transportation. During early territorial days, movement of goods and people from the East to the Southwest was very slow. Horses, mule trains and stagecoaches represented state-of-the-art transportation at the time. Major routes included the Santa Fe Trail and the Old Spanish Trail, which ran from Santa Fe into central Utah and across Nevada to Los Angeles, California. Regular stagecoach services along the Santa Fe Trail began in 1849; the Mormon Trail reached Salt Lake City in 1847.

The arrival of more people and resources via the railroad led to further land exploration and the frequent discovery of mineral deposits. Many mining towns were founded in the 1870s and 1880s; some are now ghost towns like Santa Rita (p428), while others like Tombstone (p214) and Silver City (p428) remain active.

For a classic Hollywood depiction of western expansion in the US, look no further than *How the West Was Won* (1962).

THE WILD WEST
Romanticized tales of gunslingers, cattle rustlers, outlaws and train robbers fuel Wild West legends. Good and bad guys were designations in flux – a tough outlaw in one state became a popular sheriff in another. And gunfights were more frequently the result of mundane political struggles in emerging towns than storied blood feuds. New mining towns mush-roomed overnight, playing host to rowdy saloons and bordellos where miners would come to brawl, drink, gamble and be fleeced.

Legendary figures Billy the Kid and Sheriff Pat Garrett, both involved in the infamous Lincoln County War (p448), were active in the late 1870s. Billy the Kid reputedly shot and killed more than 20 men in a brief career as a gunslinger – he himself was shot and killed by Garrett at the

Pat Garrett's *The Authentic Life of Billy, the Kid* (2000) analyzes the myths and falsehoods defining and surround-ing one of the greatest Southwestern heroes.

1869	1936
John Wesley Powell leads expedition down the Colorado River	Hoover Dam built during Great Depression

---

TOP FIVE OLD WEST SITES

▪ **OK Corral, Tombstone** (AZ; p215) Home of the famous gunfight, where the Earps and Doc Holliday fought the Clantons and McLaurys in 1881.

▪ **Lincoln** (NM; p444) Historical home of Billy the Kid.

▪ **Jerome** (AZ; p173) Once known as the 'wickedest town in the old West,' brimming with brothels and gunfights galore.

▪ **Durango** (CO; p331) From Ancestral Puebloan roots to the arrival of the Denver and Rio Grande railroad in 1879, a town rich in Southwest heritage.

▪ **Silverton** (CO; p336) Old miners' spirit and railroad history with a historical downtown.

---

tender age of 21. In 1881, Wyatt Earp, along with his brothers Virgil and Morgan, and Doc Holliday, shot dead Billy Clanton and the McLaury brothers in a blazing gunfight at the OK Corral (p215) in Tombstone – the showdown took less than a minute. Both sides accused the other of cattle rustling, but the real story will never be known.

Butch Cassidy and the Sundance Kid (p248) once roamed much of Utah. Cassidy, a Mormon, robbed banks and trains with his Wild Bunch gang during the 1890s, but never killed anyone. For more on the Wild West, see p24.

TURN OF THE 20TH CENTURY

Las Vegas came onto the scene after the completion of a railroad linking Salt Lake City and Los Angeles in 1902. For Vegas history, see p73.

The struggle for an adequate supply of water for the growing desert population marked the early years of the 20th century, resulting in federally funded dam projects such as the 1936 Hoover Dam (p191) and, in 1963, the Glen Canyon Dam (p55) and Lake Powell (p150). Water supply continues to be a key challenge to life in this region, with 2001–02 the driest year on record. For more information, see p57.

GREAT DEPRESSION & WORLD WAR II

During the Depression, the region benefited from a number of federal employment projects, and WWII rejuvenated a demand for metals mined in the Southwest. In addition, production facilities were located in New Mexico and Arizona to protect those states from the vulnerability of attack. Migrating defense workers precipitated population booms and urbanization, which was mirrored elsewhere in the Southwest.

ATOMIC AGE

In 1943, Los Alamos (p384), then a boys' school perched on a 7400ft mesa, was chosen as the top-secret headquarters of the Manhattan Project – code name for the research and development of the atomic bomb. The 772-acre site, accessed by two dirt roads, had no gas or oil lines, only one wire service, and it was surrounded by forest.

Isolation and security marked every aspect of life on 'the hill.' Scientists, their spouses, army members providing security, and locals serving as domestic help and manual laborers, lived together in a makeshift

Although it covers everything west of the Mississippi, www .americanwest.com is a treasure trove of popularized information about cowboys, local heroes and pioneers.

1945	1996
First atomic bomb detonated in New Mexico	Utah's Grand Staircase-Escalante National Monument established

community. Surrounded by guards and barbed wire and unknown even to nearby Santa Fe, the residents' postal address was simply 'Box 1663, Santa Fe.'

Not only was resident movement restricted and mail censored, there was no outside contact by radio or telephone. Perhaps even more unsettling, most residents had no idea why they were living in Los Alamos. Knowledge was on a 'need to know' basis; everyone knew only as much as their job required.

In just under two years, Los Alamos scientists successfully detonated the first atomic bomb at the Trinity site (p439), now White Sands Missile Range.

Upon the US' detonation of the atomic bomb in Japan, the secret city of Los Alamos was exposed to the public and its residents finally understood why they were there. The city continued to be clothed in secrecy, however, until 1957 when restrictions on visiting were lifted. Today, the lab is still the town's backbone, and a tourist industry embraces the town's atomic history by selling T-shirts featuring exploding bombs and bottles of La Bomba wine.

Some of the original scientists disagreed with the use of the bomb in warfare and signed a petition against it – beginning the love/hate relationship with a nuclear development still in evidence in the Southwest today. Ongoing controversies stem from the locations of nuclear power plants and transport, and disposal of nuclear waste, notably at Yucca Mountain, 90 miles from Las Vegas.

> The National Park Service's website, www.cr.nps.gov/nr/travel /amsw/intro.htm, covers sites on the National Register of Historic Places and has maps as well as itineraries.

21ST-CENTURY SOUTHWEST

A booming tourist industry and a prosperous diversified economy help fuel growth in the Southwest, growth that's augmented by annual part-time residents who migrate seasonally to enjoy the warmer temperatures. Manufacturing, government and service industries have become increasingly important sectors in the Southwest's economy.

Traditionally, though, mining and ranching were the backbone of the economy and major factors in settling the region. Although some 19th-century laws regulating these industries are still in force, recently there have been moves to bring the industries into the 21st century. Perhaps not surprisingly, much of this legislation has been met with strong resistance from the industries involved. Miners and ranchers consider the old laws to be reasonable; others find that current concerns about fair prices for the use of public lands, conservation, water quality and pollution necessitate a modernization of the laws.

One of the most contentious issues is that of ranchers' traditional rights to graze on public land for a small fraction of the current cost of a grazing lease on private land. Modern ranching is a far cry from the rough-and-tumble 19th century, but still sparks the interest of many visitors who stay on 'dude ranches' or take part in cowboy-led horse packing trips.

The Culture

The uniquely tricultural Southwest rises from Native American, Spanish/Latino and Anglo ways of life, which developed historically in that order. At various times over the last millennium, each group has been at odds with the other, much of the time in extremely violent ways. But today, these three distinct groups exist in relative harmony, while retaining their individual identities. Still, each cannot help but be influenced by the others.

Although the region is geographically vast, more than anything, the groups are linked by the psychology and spirit of the land. New Age Anglo transplants appreciate the deeply profound spirituality of the Native Americans; Catholic feast days are celebrated by Native Americans on pueblos. The richness of the cultural triad rests squarely on each culture's ability to honor its own roots while opening the door (just enough) to the other. When civilizations scratch out an existence, and indeed thrive, in the harsh desert, they cannot do so alone. From mariachi to bluegrass, from blue corn to green chile, each is a distinctive element in the stew.

The Indian Pueblo Cultural Center's website, www.indianpueblo.org, features historical information and current events for New Mexico's 19 pueblos.

REGIONAL IDENTITY

Southwesterners are a tricky lot to characterize. Sure there are plenty of stereotypes – retirees, Native Americans, cowboys, transplants – and while many fit the bill, others can't be branded so easily. On the whole, you'll find the people in this region more laid-back and friendly than their counterparts on the East and West coasts. Even at glitzy restaurants in the biggest cities (with the exception of Las Vegas) you'll see more jeans and cowboy boots than haute couture. Chat with a local at a low-key pub in Arizona or Colorado, and they'll likely tell you they're from somewhere else. They moved out here for the scenery, unpolluted air, a slower pace of life.

People out here consider themselves environmentally friendly. Recycling is a big deal. So is a healthy lifestyle. They like to hike and mountain bike, ski and ride the rapids. They might have money, but you won't necessarily know it. It's sort of a faux pas to flaunt your wealth. Dogs are bigger assets than Louis Vuitton bags.

The Heard Museum's website, www.heard.org, touts specific Native American organizations, Arizona's 21 tribes and links to other informative websites.

Arizona is known for its retirement homes, and plenty of Americans are lured to the warm weather, dry air and abundant sunshine. You'll see villages of RV parks surrounding Phoenix and Tucson; early-bird specials are the plat du jour at many restaurants.

Colorado, Arizona and New Mexico are states with large Native American and Latino populations, and these residents take pride in maintaining their heritage. They were once isolated, both regionally and economically, but the last few decades have seen greater opportunities for immersion of these minority groups into the Southwest's major cities and universities. And although many now hold jobs that were once not available to them, they are still careful to maintain their cultural identities.

The concept of family and religion are important to these groups, and many work hard to eradicate the stereotypes surrounding their ethnicity. Family and religion are also core values in Mormon Utah, playing an intrinsic role in day-to-day life and shaping their ideological identity.

LIFESTYLE

In a region of such diversity and size, it's impossible to describe the 'typical' Southwestern home or family. What lifestyle commonalities, after all, can be seen in the New Age mystics of Sedona, the businesspeople, showfolk and casino workers of Las Vegas and the Mormon faithful of Salt Lake City? Half the fun of touring the Southwest is comparing and contrasting.

Utah's heavily Mormon population stresses traditional family values, and drinking, smoking and premarital sex are frowned upon. You won't see much fast fashion or hear much cursing here, although the 2002 winter Olympics in Salt Lake City brought more variety in food and nightlife.

Family and religion are also core values for Native Americans and Latinos throughout the region. For the Hopi, tribal dances are such sacred events they are mostly closed to outsiders. And although many Native Americans and Latinos are now living in urban areas, working as doctors and lawyers, large family gatherings and traditional customs are still important facets of daily life.

Because of its favorable weather and boundless possibilities for outdoor adventures, much of the Southwest is popular with East and West coast transplants. In cities like Santa Fe, Telluride, Tucson and Flagstaff, you'll find a blend of students, artists, wealthy retirees and adventure junkies. In urban centers throughout the region (with the exception of Utah) many people consider themselves 'spiritual' rather than religious, and forgo church for Sunday brunch. Women work as long hours as men, and many children attend daycare. Southwesterners on the whole expect the same quality of living as their counterparts on the East and West coasts, and take pleasure in dining out, drinking with friends or catching the latest gallery opening.

THE DESERT LIFE

Desert conditions comprise 70% of the Southwest, overwhelmingly shaping the people and lives of all who dwell there. Folks who survive under the harsh privation of these lands are often cast as mythical individualists. And Southwesterners do not disappoint.

Triculturalism presents difficulties to a homogenized understanding of the way each group sees the challenges of desert living within the context of their own culture and heritage. But the Southwestern ethos has been shaped by this very survival.

In a practical sense, the most compelling daily challenge is, quite simply, a lack of water. With some projections forecasting that Las Vegas will be completely out of water by the year 2010, this situation is far from abstract. From the time when the Hohokam dug primitive irrigation canals to the early 1900s when legislation allowed dam building – to the detriment of historical sites and natural ecological areas – the pursuit and control of water has shaped the history of the Southwest. Ongoing struggles persist today between Native American groups vying for land rights; legion battlelines are drawn between environmental groups and industry (see p57).

Mother Nature is not cooperating to alleviate the epic struggle for water. Drought and forest fires have been persistent. Conservation efforts have, at best, a cursory impact as cities like Albuquerque and Phoenix continue to spread like a horizontal mushroom cloud.

For the observant, the four deserts – Mojave, Chihuahuan, Great Basin and Sonoran – are far from a wasteland. Slow down to witness a complex ecosystem that's light-years from the ordinary, juicy with cacti, playful jackrabbits, reclusive desert sheep and radiant flowers. When spring snow melts, runoffs provide enough moisture for efficient and adaptive flora to survive the driest seasons. So too are human inhabitants efficient and matter-of-fact about desert living, accepting cyclical deprivations in exchange for bursts of drama – seen only by an initiated eye. For more on desert conditions, see p50.

RUGGED ICONOCLASTS

The Southwest has long drawn stout-hearted individualists and people pursuing slightly different agendas than American society as a whole.

Old mining towns like Jerome in Arizona were founded by fierce individualists – gamblers, mining company executives, storekeepers and prostitutes. As old ghost towns colorfully drift downhill, their unslick storefronts have been charmingly rebuilt and still attract renegades searching for what it means to be solitary, red-blooded and self-reliant.

Artists are attracted to the Southwest's clear light, cheap housing and wide-open spaces. Collectors, in turn, follow artists and gentrify towns like Santa Fe (p363), Taos (p391) and Prescott (see p175).

Then there are the mainstream dropouts who come to get lost and be left alone. The wide expansiveness of the landscape attracts thrill seekers looking to 'turn on, tune in and drop out.' The town of Madrid in New Mexico, on the Turquoise Trail (p361), attracts a motley crew of Harley Davidson aficionados. And Moab (p265), often called the 'extreme sports capital of America,' attracts bikers of a different ilk. Both groups come to enjoy the crispness of the desert air, spectacular scenery and the thrill of the ride – living with bravado, drinking the marrow of life.

POPULATION

The Southwest continues to be one of the fastest-growing regions in the USA. And who can blame the transplants? From young families to retirees, they're drawn by a lower cost of living, a more relaxed quality of life and warmer weather.

To hear Native American ethnic voices and learn about Mexican-American history, browse www .digitalhistory.uh.edu.

From 1990 to 2000, Nevada, Arizona, Colorado and Utah experienced the greatest population growth of all the US states. The metro areas of Las Vegas, Salt Lake City and Phoenix are the fastest-growing and densest cities by far. But despite this influx, the region as a whole is sparsely populated. Only Montana and Wyoming are less densely inhabited. Arizona's relatively high density is skewed by the greater Phoenix metropolitan area, which accounts for over 60% of the state's inhabitants. Similarly, the Salt Lake City region accounts for three-quarters of Utah's population.

Arizona has 10 times the population it had in the mid-1900s; New Mexico's population has tripled since the early 1950s. But Las Vegas beats them all: it's grown to over a million people since it was founded less than 100 years ago.

Along with Texas and California, New Mexico has the largest concentration of Latinos in the country – by far. Albuquerque, Santa Fe and the Tucson area are easily the country's most ethnically diverse areas (along with California). The Navajo and various Apache tribes make up a substantial part of Arizona's and New Mexico's populations, clustered in northeastern Arizona, northwestern New Mexico and central New Mexico.

Between AD 1000 and AD 1300, over 25,000 communities in the Four Corners region were established over a 60,000 sq mile area.

With the exception of Utah, households across the region are made up of about 57% married heterosexual couples; Utah's is a whopping 10% higher. Not surprisingly, Utah also has the lowest number of same-sex households (about 25% less than any other states).

SPORTS

Professional sports teams are based in Phoenix (p130) and Salt Lake City (p298). The Arizona Diamondbacks of Phoenix play major league baseball from mid-April through September; the only Southwestern major league football team, the Arizona Cardinals, play from September through December. Basketball (played November through April) is

ROUND 'EM UP

As much a spectator sport as a professional sport these days, rodeo (which means 'roundup' in Spanish) began in the 1880s. Its cast of characters – from cowboys and cowgirls to judges and clowns – all play important parts in the passion play that's a distinct show of Southwestern grit. While men are the main contenders in rodeo, women also compete, mainly in barrel racing, team roping and calf roping. Although the clowns perform amusing stunts, they have a serious role helping cowboys when they get into trouble.

Each rodeo follows the same pattern. The first order of the day is the Grand Entry, during which all contestants, clowns and officials parade their horses around the arena, raise the American flag and sing the national anthem. Actual events then begin; here's a primer.

- Bareback bronc riding: a rider must stay on a randomly assigned bucking bronco (a wild horse) for eight seconds. A good ride is one in which the horse bucks wildly and the rider stays on with style – a score of over 70 is good.

- Calf roping: a calf races out of a chute, followed closely by a mounted cowboy with a rope loop. When he reaches the calf, the cowboy throws the animal down, ties it and throws up his hands to show he's done. A good roper can do the whole thing in under eight seconds.

- Saddle bronc riding: this has similar rules to the bareback bronc riding event and is scored in the same way.

- Steer wrestling: in this event (also called bull-dogging), a steer that may weigh as much as 700lb runs out of a chute, tripping a barrier line, which is the signal for two cowboys to pursue the animal and try to wrestle it to the ground. The best cowboys can accomplish this feat in under five seconds.

- Barrel racing: three large barrels are set up in a triangle, and the rider must race around them in a cloverleaf pattern. Good times are around 15 to 17 seconds.

- Team roping: a team of two horseback ropers pursues and ropes a steer running out of the chute. Good times are under seven seconds.

- Bull riding: riding a bucking and spinning 2000lb bull is even wilder and more dangerous than bronc riding, and it is often the crowd's favorite event. Using only one – heavily gloved – hand, the cowboy holds on to a rope that is wrapped around the bull. And that's it – there's nothing else to hold on to, and there are no other rules apart from staying on for eight seconds and not touching the bull with your free hand. Bull riding scoring is the same as for bronc riding.

Great rodeos include:

Fiesta de los Vaqueros (p204) Tucson, late February.

Canyonlands Rodeo (p275) Moab, June.

Rodeo de Santa Fe (p373) Santa Fe, late June.

State Rodeo (p359) Albuquerque, September.

Annual Navajo Nation Fair (p181) Window Rock, early September.

Dixie Roundup (p229) St George, mid-September.

National Finals Rodeo (p90) Las Vegas, December.

A word of caution for some readers who may want to avoid rodeos: according to People for the Ethical Treatment of Animals (PETA, www.peta.org), these Wild West macho displays of man trumping animal often come at the expense of the animals and for the profit of big rodeo promoters.

more competitive; you can watch hoops with Salt Lake City's Utah Jazz (men), the Phoenix Suns (men) and the Phoenix Mercury (women). Because pro tickets are hard to get, you'll have a better rim shot with college sports. Albuquerque teams across the board are quite popular (p359). In fact, their minor league baseball team sells more merchandise

NATIVE AMERICAN CULTURE

From pueblo architecture to spirituality and religion, it's difficult to separate Native American influences from the rest of the Southwest. They infuse its spirit like the mesas dominate the horizon. One couldn't be without the other. From sculptor RC Gorman (p45) and the flute music of Carlos Nakai (a Navajo-Ute who has played his traditional cedar flute with classically trained musicians) to the writings of Louise Erdrich (a member of the Turtle Mountain Band of Chippewa whose novels *Love Medicine, The Beet Queen* and *Tales of Burning Love* explore cultural identity), their influences ride the cultural winds as easily as eagles soar.

See p181 for details on Navajo rugs and p186 for details on kachina dolls.

Zuni, Hopi & Navajo Silver Jewelry

Native silversmiths working on and near the Navajo reservation often come from multigenerational traditions of silver artisans. Anthropological finds show that the earliest natives adorned themselves with stone and shell bracelets and necklaces with representations of small animals. Silverwork didn't arrive in the Southwest until the Anglos arrived. The first Native American metalwork dates to the early 1800s and often featured designs and motifs also found in basketwork, cave drawings and other artifacts.

Native American jewelry is most commonly made of sterling silver and often features stamp work, shells or opaque stones like turquoise, lapis, onyx, coral or carnelian. Look for excellent craftsmanship, symmetry, snug settings and uniform stones. Check for a mark or signature from the artisan on the piece.

How to know if you're buying the 'genuine' thing? By federal law (thanks to the Indian Arts and Crafts Act of 1990), in order to be deemed Native American or Navajo jewelry, the objects must be made by a member of a state or federally recognized tribe or a Native American artisan. When it's authentic, reputable merchants will offer a detailed written description of your purchase. If you're buying an expensive item – and authentic jewelry can be pricey – ask if it comes with a certificate from the Indian Arts & Crafts Board (www.doi.gov/iacb/).

Fine authentic jewelry can be found at the Santa Fe Indian Market (p374).

Pueblo Pottery

Pottery traditions (www.pueblopottery.com) and their modern interpretations provide a fascinating journey through Native American culture. Creations in style and design are now almost endless, but knowing a bit about design traditions proves an excellent starting point to exploring their meanings and your preferences.

The color of the pottery was originally dictated by the type of clay available in the local area. Zia pottery is often of red clay, Acoma white and Hopi yellow. Design traditions at Santa Clara Pueblo (p384) often feature carved relief work; families within the Santa Clara Pueblo have developed specialized designs within the common motif. Cochiti pottery is distinctive by its use of a black finish and bold graphics. If a piece has a shiny base glaze with matte finish designs, it's likely from the San Ildefonso Pueblo (p383). Styles and techniques have been shared and augmented between pueblos and families, though, creating a rich array for modern pottery aficionados.

Maria Martinez (1887–1980) of the San Ildefonso Pueblo, the region's best-known potter, led a revival of traditional pottery making during the 1920s. Her 'black on black' pots are some of the finest ever made and are now worth thousands of dollars.

Hopi Culture & Spirituality

Treasure any opportunity to observe and learn about Hopi spirituality. And don't take it for granted – more and more Hopi believe that their religious practices should be shielded from

than most major league pro teams. But it's the University of Arizona Wildcats that consistently place among the best basketball teams in the nation.

Several major league baseball teams (like the Chicago White Sox) migrate from the cold, wintry north every February and March for training

the public eye and reserved for native audiences, or at least those highly respectful of its sacred nature. This reticence has been bred over time by those looking to exploit their traditions for money or self-aggrandizement, a practice at odds with Hopi spiritual values.

Hopi traditions are quite complex and best left to the Hopi to explain and demonstrate. In fact, the ceremony cycles vary so much that even most Hopi cannot claim complete knowledge. Hopi protectors warn that any group or individuals attempting to sell opportunities for a Hopi experience are probably illegitimate, since profiting from the religion is an anathema to Hopi spiritual practice – which dictates that Hopi rituals are for the good of all humankind.

Hopi life originated in a matriarchal society in which land and social status were passed on from the mother; villages were organized around agriculture. Hopi life now centers on their reservation in Second Mesa, Arizona (p185), where historical battles – dating from the mid-1500s with Coronado's arrival – to reclaim farmed land from Navajo and Anglos continue. The other chief focus of Hopi families is to keep Hopi tradition alive in their young people, while giving them the education and exposure needed to succeed in modern life.

Dance & Music

Swirling dancers bedecked in headdresses and facepaint, wearing intricately beaded clothing and stomping to the beat of a circle of drummers – this spectacle is one that many travelers to the region want to see. From the visitor's point of view, Native American dances can be grouped into three categories, although there is certainly overlap between them.

First, there are the ceremonial or ritual religious dances that take place on Indian reservations. Some are celebratory occasions that mark stages of life (for instance, a girl's puberty rite) and others, such as rain dances, revere specific gods. Because of the strong religious and traditional motives, access to ceremonial dances is usually strictly controlled.

Some ceremonials are open to the public, but photography or recording of any kind is completely prohibited. Occasionally, a tourist might try to sneak a quick and unobtrusive photo. In this case, a tribal police officer may confiscate the camera, or an irate tribal elder may simply grab the camera and hurl it over the nearest cliff! Refrain from applauding and asking many questions; follow instructions about where to stand or sit; wear appropriate clothing (no shorts or tank tops) and generally behave in a quiet and respectful way.

Social dances, the second category, can be very traditional or relatively modern, and are danced for competition, display, to tell a story, as an honor or just for the fun of getting together with other families, clans or tribes. The dancers are accompanied by drum groups and singers. Usually, songs are in one of the Native American languages, or they are vocables (songs made up of sounds that are not words). An emcee calls each dance, often with an inside joke or two, and usually at least some of the dances are called in English, especially the intertribals, when anyone, including members of the tourist tribe, can go out and dance.

Visitors best enjoy these dances because they can participate if they wish, and let go of their worries about interfering in a religious ceremony. Social dances occur during powwows, festivals, fairs, rodeos and other gatherings on Indian reservations.

Often a small admission fee is charged. Indian food, arts and crafts, and cassettes or CDs are sold, and photography may be permitted. Photographers can usually take general pictures of the festivities but should always ask permission to take photographs of individuals. A small tip may be requested in this case.

The third dance category is purely performance, where visitors sit in a theater (often outdoors) and watch. It's art, but it's also authentic. One of the best places to see dance performances is during the summer at Red Rock State Park just outside of Gallup in New Mexico (p416).

seasons in warmer Arizona. They play in what is aptly referred to as the Cactus League.

Since the 2002 Winter Olympics were held in and around Park City, Utah, you might pay homage to venues around town (p292 and p298) and at the Wasatch Front Ski Areas (p299).

MULTICULTURALISM

The Southwest has a tricultural mix of Native American, Latino and Anglo cultures.

New Mexico and Arizona have large populations of Native Americans, over half of whom are Navajo. Other tribes include various Apache groups, Havasupai, Hopi, Hualapai, various Pueblo tribes, Tohono O'odham, Ute and a host of smaller groups. Arizona and New Mexico have the third- and fourth-largest Native American populations of the 50 states. Utah is predominantly white.

Native Americans mostly live in the Four Corners area, especially on the Navajo (p180) and Hopi Reservations (p185). Large Apache reservations occupy eastern Arizona; the Tohono O'odham Reservation is set

---

MORMONS, POLYGAMY & THE LDS   Lisa Dunford

Tell someone in Europe you live in Chicago and you may hear a gangster joke; mention Dallas, you're a JR Ewing–style millionaire; say you're from Salt Lake City and likely as not the question of polygamy *will* come up. Throughout its history, Utah has been a predominately Mormon state. Approximately 70% of the current population has church affiliation. But as the president of the Church of Jesus Christ of Latter-day Saints (LDS), Gordon Hinckley, has said, the church today has nothing to do with those practicing polygamy.

Many of the American-born church's beliefs are easily recognizable to other Christian religions and to some New Age philosophies. The Saints believe that Jesus Christ is the only begotten son of God; he died so that sins may be forgiven through repentance. Every person is a child of God. We lived with the Heavenly Father before we were born and he sent us to Earth to learn and to grow more like Him before we return to heaven. Family is a big part of God's plan for us, as it creates the environment in which we learn. Members of the LDS believe the Bible is the word of God and – here's a departure – so is the *Book of Mormon: Another Testament of Jesus Christ.*

In the 1820s an angel named Moroni revealed the golden plates containing the *Book of Mormon* to LDS church founder Joseph Smith. It took several years and several scribes, to take down the translation that Smith – an uneducated farmer – read out from hieroglyphic-like inscriptions. The *Book of Mormon* tells the story of a family's exodus from Jerusalem in 600 BC and their subsequent lives, prophesies, trials, wars and visitations by Christ in the new world (Central America). The book is named for purported author Mormon, one of the last members of a dying clan. His son Moroni was the angel who revealed the text to Smith. After publication, a new church was created in Fayette, New York, in April 1830. Smith continued to receive revelations from God throughout his life.

When an 1843 visitation revealed the principle of plural marriage to prophet Smith, it was darn controversial even then. Critics said that Smith had the revelation because he'd already taken several wives in secret and he wanted to convince his legal wife that it was just fine. Believers said Smith got the call as early as 1831, but he knew the time had not come to make it public. Either way, it was not until after Smith's murder in 1844 that 'the principle' became church policy. Problems with neighbors drove the Saints to Ohio – to Missouri, to Illinois – and on to the Utah territory by 1846. Polygamy was formally established as the path to a righteous life in 1852 by the second church president, Brigham Young.

For all the impact plural marriage has had, it seems surprising that it was endorsed for less than 40 years. But by the 1880s a series of federal laws had made both polygamy and 'unlawful

in Arizona's southern desert. Reservation or 'rez' culture is definitely bicultural – Native American and Anglo – in most respects.

New Mexico (along with Texas and California) has the highest proportion of Latinos in the US, with the Rio Grande Valley and Santa Fe being historically the center. Southern Arizona, too, has much Latino influence. In the border areas, many Latinos are of Mexican-American heritage and proudly call themselves Chicano. Some still don't recognize the legality of the US claim of Mexican land in 1848 after the Mexican American War and the Gadsden Purchase in 1853; they refer to the land affected as Aztlan.

RELIGION

Even though they're more inclined towards spirituality than religion, New Age practitioners are prevalent in Arizona and New Mexico enclaves. Of the traditional groups, Catholics have the numerical edge in New Mexico, and Mormons are by far the majority in Utah. New Mexico and Utah have very few Jews, while Arizona's Jewish population is about 2%, which mirrors the national average.

---

cohabitation' crimes, banned church members from holding office, and made the seizure of church assets possible. Federal agents tracked down and imprisoned polygamous men, leaving multiple wives and even more multiple children, without financial support. In 1890, church president Wilford Woodruff received guidance from the Lord that the principle was no longer to be followed. Change took some time; in the ensuing few years some church leaders may have secretly given new plural unions the go-ahead. Excommunication of those in plural marriages didn't begin until 1910, and then members began testifying against their former brothers and sisters in court. Large-scale prosecution of polygamists in Utah died out in the 1960s, as alternative lifestyle tolerance grew. Once the Saints went mainstream, the community prospered.

Today the Church of the Latter-day Saints has more than 12 million members. Service to family and community is still big, even if families aren't as big. All church positions aside from those of the highest officials – the president, his council and the quorum of 12 apostles – are voluntary. There's no professional clergy. Sunday meetings are often held in chapels; temples are reserved for the performance of ordinances such as celestial marriage in which man and wife are joined, or sealed, for eternity. Extensive resources – monthly magazines in numerous languages, books, videos and websites, cultural and sporting activities, and church groups for different ages – support the larger family. Not everyone enjoys the expected amount of church involvement, but the membership can be a strong support network available around the world – and beyond the grave.

But what happened to polygamy? Well, fundamentalists continue to practice the principle: some are clans with a family patriarch as a spiritual leader, others are highly organized, cultlike groups such as the one in Canon City, Arizona, on the Utah border. Some polygamists are just doing their best to follow the righteous path they believe was given them. Others are child abusers at best and sociopaths at worst such as Ervil LaBaron's followers who shot opponents in the 1980s, the Lafferty brothers whose murderous story is told in *Under the Banner of God* and Jeremy Kingston who was prosecuted for the rape of a 15-year-old relative. The secretive nature of polygamous groups can conceal heinous crimes.

Though plural marriage has not been condoned by the Church of the Latter-day Saints for more than 100 years, it's had an undeniable impact on both the church and the state. Try to imagine how many Utah natives alone have ancestors who practiced polygamy – it's mind boggling. I know because my great-great-grandmother, Dora Young Dunford, was the daughter of Brigham Young and his 20th wife, Lucy Bigelow. Since Dora had 57 siblings (and 25 mothers), I figure that exponentially, I must be related to at least a third of the population of the Southwest. Now that's an extended family.

SPANGLISH & SILENCE

Particularly in New Mexico and Arizona, you are likely to hear 'Spanglish,' in which speakers switch smoothly between Spanish and English, even within the same sentence.

Visitors to Indian reservations should remember that silence is almost like a statement. If you say something to an Indian and are met by silence, this doesn't indicate that the person you are talking to is ignoring you. Indians speak their minds when they disagree with the speaker and may remain silent when they agree or have no special opinion. One word you might hear frequently in this area is the Navajo greeting 'ya'at'eeh.' For more on Navajo language, see p182.

Native American tribes practice the oldest North American religions. Some, like the Native American Church that uses hallucinatory peyote buttons as a sacrament, are partly pan–Native American responses to encroachment by Anglo culture. Generally, though, the Native American ways are beliefs that Native Americans feel and know essentially because they are Native Americans – it's not something that non–Native Americans can properly understand or convert to. Different tribes often have particular creation stories, rituals and practices, which means that there are dozens of unique and carefully prescribed spiritual ways of life. Additionally, Indians usually maintain a strict sense of privacy about their most important ceremonies and thus books written by even the most respected outsiders, such as anthropologists, usually contain some inaccuracies when describing Native American religion.

Pulitzer Prize winner Paul Horgan deftly elucidates the three dominant cultures in The Heroic Triad with exquisite lyricism.

ARTS

The rich history and cultural texture of the Southwest is a fertile source of inspiration for artists, writers, photographers and musicians alike. And because of that, the Southwest is loaded with options for observers to enjoy art in all its forms. As with all things in the Southwest, the experiences and perspectives of Native Americans, Latinos and Anglos are as varied as their cultural and personal experiences.

Literature

Literature of the Southwest is as varied as the culture is broad. From the classic western novels of Zane Gray, Louis L'Amour and Larry McMurtry to contemporary writers like eco-savvy Barbara Kingsolver and Native American Louise Erdrich (p38), authors imbue their work with the scenery and sensibility of the Southwest. Drawing from the mystical reality that is so infused in Latin literature, Southwestern style can sometimes be fantastical and absurdist, yet poignantly astute. The beauty, rich texture, tragedy and historical tension have provided inspiration and context for thousands of writers of fiction, poets and playwrights. The following writers are arguably the best-known.

Leslie Marmon Silko's novel, Ceremony, describes a young war-stricken Laguna Indian and his return to traditional ways after WWII. Silko, a Pueblo herself, unfurls the weblike story slowly, interspersing it with fragments of native myths.

DH Lawrence moved to Taos (p403) in the 1920s for health reasons, and went on to write the essay 'Indians and Englishmen' and the novel *St Mawr*. Through his association with artists like Georgia O'Keeffe, he found some of the freedoms from puritanical society that he longed for.

Tony Hillerman, an enormously bestselling author from Albuquerque, wrote *Skinwalkers, People of Darkness, Skeleton Man* and *The Sinister Pig*. His award-winning mystery novels take place on the Navajo, Hopi and Zuni Reservations.

Hunter S Thompson, who committed suicide in early 2005, wrote *Fear and Loathing in Las Vegas*, set in the temple of American excess in the desert; it's the ultimate road trip novel, in every sense of the word.

Edward Abbey (p280), a complex writer, created the thought-provoking and seminal works of *Desert Solitaire* and *The Journey Home: Some Words in Defense of the American West*.

John Nichols wrote *The Milagro Beanfield War*, the tale of a western town's struggle to take back its fate from the Anglo land barons and developers. A telling, brave and sometimes comical look at the region's tensions, hatreds and history, Robert Redford's movie of the novel was filmed in Truchas, NM (p389).

Cinema

With its sheer grandiose scenery and rich cultural history, is it any wonder that the Southwest has been fodder for hundreds and hundreds of films? The theme of good versus evil – whichever side of the complex equation one finds oneself straddling in the Southwest – played out in such grandeur is irresistible to the auteur.

A few sites have doubled as film and TV sets so often they are locked in the American consciousness as definitive views of the West. Picture Monument Valley (p184), where *Stagecoach* (1939), *The Searchers* (1956) and *Back to the Future III* (1990) were filmed; picture Moab (p265) for *Thelma and Louise* (1991), Dead Horse Point State Park (p284) for *Mission Impossible: 2* (2000), Lake Powell (p150) for *Planet of the Apes* (1968) and Tombstone (p214) for the eponymous *Tombstone* (1993).

Specific locations abound for specific scenes too. Snippets from *Casablanca* (1942) were filmed in Hotel Monte Vista (p160); *Butch Cassidy and the Sundance Kid* (1969) was shot at the ghost town of Grafton (p237); *City Slickers* (1991) was set at Ghost Ranch (p388) in Abiquiu, NM.

Also worth a visit, the Old Tucson Studios (p201) is now a Western theme park and the Moab Museum of Film & Western Heritage (p268) is chock full of local film paraphernalia.

Worthy film festivals include CineVegas (p90) and Colorado's Telluride Film Festival (p342). Robert Redford's Sundance Film Festival (p309) showcases innovative new filmmaking and supports efforts to preserve and protect the Southwestern environment.

Music

The larger cities of the Southwest offer titillating options for classical music. Choose among Phoenix' Symphony Hall (p130), which houses the Arizona Opera and the Phoenix Symphony Orchestra, the famed Santa Fe Opera

Martin Scorsese's movie, Casino (1995), charts the rise and fall of a Vegas casino magnate, with stunning performances by Robert De Niro and Sharon Stone.

Filmed in Utah, Footloose stars Kevin Bacon as a pugnacious city boy, displaced in a small western town where popular music and dancing are banned.

TOP 10 PLACES FOR ART & CULTURE

From ancient petroglyphs to stunning collections of modern art, the Southwest sizzles with cultural hotspots.

Tubac, AZ (p212) One of Arizona's largest art destinations with more than 80 shops and galleries.

Phoenix, AZ (p118) Full of intriguing museums.

Telluride, CO (p342) With the excellent Bluegrass Festival and Telluride Film Festival.

Santa Fe museums, NM (p365) An extraordinary confluence of fine art, folk art and native culture on Museum Hill.

Taos, NM (p391) One of the most influential art communities in America.

Indian Pueblo Cultural Center, NM (p351) With feast days and celebrations that provide a rare glimpse into pueblo life.

Canyonlands National Park, UT (p283) An unchanged ancient landscape of 2000-year-old Native American rock paintings.

Sundance Resort, UT (p315) Art lovers and film fanatics can rediscover their creative souls.

Salt Lake City, UT (p287) Hear the Mormon Tabernacle Choir's weekly rehearsal or radio broadcast.

For live broadcasts of Mormon Tabernacle Choir concerts, visit www.mormontabernacle choir.com.

(p379), the New Mexico Symphony Orchestra (p359) in Albuquerque and the Arizona Opera Company (p208) in Tucson and Phoenix.

Other offerings include the Telluride Bluegrass Festival (p342) and performances by the Mormon Tabernacle Choir (p291).

Nearly every major town attracts county, bluegrass and rock groups. A notable major venue is Flagstaff's Museum Club (p162), with a lively roster of talent. Surprisingly, Provo, UT (p315), has a thriving indie rock scene, which offers a stark contrast to the Osmond family image that Utah often conjures.

A mecca for entertainers of every stripe, Las Vegas' (p102) current headliners include popular icons like Céline Dion and Wayne Newton, but for a little gritty goodness head to Joint (p105).

Try and catch a mariachi ensemble (typically dressed in ornately sequined, body-hugging costumes) at El Taoseño Restaurant and Lounge (p399) and the International Mariachi Festival (p434).

Architecture

Not surprisingly, architecture has tricultural regional influences. First and foremost are the ruins of the Ancestral Puebloans – most majestically their cliff communities and Taos Pueblo (p400). These traditional designs and examples are echoed in the Pueblo Revival style of Santa Fe's Museum of Fine Arts (p366) and are speckled across the region today. Santa Fe overflows with them.

The most traditional structures are adobe – mud mixed with straw, formed into bricks, mortared with mud and smoothed with another layer of mud. This style dominates many New Mexico city- and landscapes.

You can catch examples of 17th- and 18th-century mission-style architecture – characterized by red tiled roofs, ironwork and stucco walls – in religious and municipal buildings like Santa Fe's State Capitol (p370). The domed roof and intricate designs of San Xavier del Bac (p210) embody the Spanish colonial style.

In the 1800s Anglo settlers brought many new building techniques and developed Territorial-style architecture, which often includes porches, wood-trimmed doorways and other Victorian influences.

Master architect Frank Lloyd Wright was also a presence in the Southwest, most specifically at Taliesin West (p119) in Scottsdale. More re-

---

EARTHSHIP ARCHITECTURE

Is that Mos Eisley Spaceport about two miles past the Rio Grande Gorge? No, it's the world's premier sustainable, self-sufficient community of earthships. Welcome home to this environmentally friendly architectural form, pioneered in northern New Mexico and consisting of auto tires packed with earth, stacked with rebar and turned into livable dwellings (p395; http://earthship.org).

This is the brainchild of architect Mike Reynolds, sometimes described as one-third visionary, one-third entrepreneur and one-third cult leader. Earthships are a form of biotecture (biology + architecture = buildings based on biological systems of resource use and conservation) that maximizes available resources so you'll never have to be on the grid again.

Walls made of old tires are laid out for appropriate passive solar use, packed with tamped earth, and then buried on three sides for maximum insulation. The structures are outfitted with photovoltaic cells and an elaborate gray-water system that collects rain and snow, which filters through several cycles that begin in the kitchen and end in the garden.

Though this is their home, earthships have landed in Japan, Bolivia, Scotland, Mexico and beyond, often organized into communities like at the Rio Grande Gorge, and more are being built using available kits ($10,000 to $60,000 total cost) every day.

cently, architectural monuments along Route 66 (p412) include kitschy motels lit by neon signs that have forever transformed the concept of an American road trip.

Painting, Sculpture & Visual Arts

The region's most famous artist is Georgia O'Keeffe (1887–1986; p389 and p388), whose Southwestern landscapes are seen in museums throughout the world. Also highly regarded is Navajo artist RC Gorman (born 1932), whose sculptures and paintings of Navajo women are becoming increasingly famous worldwide. Gorman has lived in Taos for many years. Both Taos (p391) and Santa Fe (p363) have large and active artist communities considered seminal to the development of Southwestern art (see p394 and p367). The area around Flagstaff (p154) has many thriving artist communities.

The vast landscapes of the region have long appealed to large-format black and white photographers like Ansel Adams whose *Moonrise, Hernandez New Mexico* (near Chimayo) can be seen at the Center for Creative Photography (p201) at the University of Arizona.

For something completely different, pop into art galleries and museums in Las Vegas, specifically the Bellagio (p80) and Venetian (p82).

Jewelry & Crafts

Latino and Native American aesthetic influences are evident in the region's pottery, paintings, weavings, jewelry, sculpture, woodcarving and leatherworking. See p181 for a discussion of Navajo rugs and p186 for Hopi kachina dolls; for Zuni silverware, see (p38). Excellent examples of Southwestern Native American art are displayed in many museums, most notably in Phoenix' Heard Museum (p119) and Santa Fe's Institute of American Indian Arts Museum (p370). Contemporary and traditional Native American art is readily available in hundreds of galleries.

Kitsch & Folk Art

The Southwest is a repository for kitsch and folk art – just look at the preponderance of roadside stands, antique and curio stores that fill countless small towns and big cities. In addition to the predictable Native American knock-offs and beaded everything (perhaps made anywhere but there), you'll find invariable UFO humor in Roswell (p445) and unexpected nuclear souvenirs at Los Alamos (p384). Perhaps you'd like to be the first on your block to own an Atomic City T-shirt, emblazoned with a red and yellow exploding bomb, or a bottle of La Bomba wine.

More serious cultural artifacts fill the Museum of International Folk Art (p366).

Of the 37 million annual visitors to Las Vegas, 100,000 couples say 'I do.'

Theater & Dance

First and foremost, the pueblos host numerous and extraordinary dances (p39).

Notable modern dance companies include the Phoenix-based Ballet Arizona (p130) and the Santa Fe–based Maria Benitez Spanish Dance Company (p381). Although some of the noteworthy dancing in Las Vegas is not a family affair (they don't call it The Strip for nothing), the Cashman Center Theatre (p104) features major touring shows; there are also endless cabaret clubs. In Utah, Park City's George S and Dolores Doré Eccles Center for the Performing Arts (p313) hosts varied events.

Environment David Lukas

The Southwest is a place of dramatic surprises and contrasts. While everyone thinks immediately of deserts and cacti, alpine tundra and verdant marshes also contribute to the fabric of life in this region. What's surprising is the close proximity of these contrasting habitats. In the Santa Catalina Mountains (p201) outside Tucson, for example, you can ascend from searing desert to snow-blanketed fir forests within 30 miles, the ecological equivalent of driving 2000 miles from southern Arizona to Canada.

Even the desert itself is anything but monotonous, look closely and you will discover everything from fleet-footed lizards to jewel-like wildflowers. Superimposed onto an astonishing complex of hidden canyons and towering mountains, the Southwest includes four distinct desert zones, each of which is home to its own unique mix of plants and animals. One of the best parts of the Southwest is that the land has an open and inviting feel – meaning that all of its components, geologic and ecological, may be readily enjoyed by attentive visitors.

To make reservations for any USDA Forest Service campground, go to www.reserveusa.com.

THE LAND
Geologic History

Although the Southwest is now an inland desert region, its geologic story is that of a coastal region along the young North American continent. Long washed by advancing and retreating seas, the region was eventually built up through uplift and an accumulation of sediments that pushed the ocean's edge westward to its modern location along the Pacific coast. This story is spectacularly told in the colorful, exposed layers of rock throughout Utah, Arizona and New Mexico. Most of the visitor centers in the region's national parks and monuments have excellent displays that help explain this geologic story.

It may be hard to imagine now but the Southwest once lay under a succession of seas that alternately left behind evidence of deepwater deposits, shallow mudflats and coastal sand dunes. During this time North America was a young continent on the move, revolving slowly and migrating northward from the southern hemisphere over millions of years. Extremely ancient rocks (among the oldest on the planet) exposed in the deep heart of the Grand Canyon show that the region was underwater two billion years ago, and younger layers of rocks in southern Utah reveal that this region was continuously or periodically underwater until about 60 million years ago.

The National Landscape Conservation Society's www.discovernlcs.org describes Southwestern monuments, historic trails, scenic rivers and conservation areas.

At the end of the Paleozoic era (about 286 million years ago), a collision of continents into a massive landmass known as Pangaea deformed the earth's crust and produced pressures that uplifted an ancestral Rocky Mountains. Though this early mountain range lay to the east, it formed rivers and sediment deposits that began to shape the Southwest. In fact, erosion leveled the range by 240 million years ago, with much of the sediment draining westward into what we now call Utah. Around the same time, a shallow tropical sea teeming with life, including a barrier reef that would later be sculpted into Carlsbad Caverns (p452), covered much of southern New Mexico.

For long periods of time (between episodes of being underwater), much of the Southwest may have looked like northern Egypt today: floodplains and deltas surrounded by expanses of desert. A rising chain of island mountains to the west apparently blocked the supply of wet storms and desert sand dunes piled up thousands of feet high. This piece of the story can be seen today in the famous Navajo sandstone cliffs of Zion National Park (p231).

This sequence of oceans and sand ended around 60 million years ago as North America underwent a dramatic separation from Europe, sliding westward over a piece of the earth's crust known as the East Pacific plate and leaving behind an ever-widening gulf that became the Atlantic Ocean. This collision, named the Laramide Orogeny, resulted in the birth of the modern Rocky Mountains and uplifted an old basin into a highland known today as the Colorado Plateau. Fragments of the East Pacific plate also attached themselves to the leading edge of the North American plate, transforming the Southwest from a coastal area to an interior region increasingly detached from the ocean.

In contrast to the compression and collision that characterized earlier events, the earth's crust began stretching in an east–west direction about 30 million years ago. The thinner, stretched crust of New Mexico and Texas cracked along zones of weakness called faults, resulting in a rift valley where New Mexico's Rio Grande now flows. These same forces created the stepped plateaus of northern Arizona and southern Utah.

Increased pulling in the earth's crust between 15 and eight million years ago created a much larger region of north–south cracks in western Utah, Arizona and Nevada known as the Basin and Range province. Here, parallel cracks formed hundreds of miles of valleys and mountain ranges that stretch from the Sierra Nevada to the Rocky Mountains.

During the Pleistocene glacial period, large bodies of water accumulated throughout the Southwest. Utah's Great Salt Lake (p294) is the most famous remnant of these mighty ice age lakes, but salty crusts remain in many other basins that formerly held vast lakes.

For the past several million years the dominant force in the Southwest has probably been erosion. Not only do torrential rainstorms readily tear through soft sedimentary rocks, but also the rise of the Rocky Mountains generates large powerful rivers that wind throughout the Southwest, carving mighty canyons in their wake. Nearly all of the contemporary features in the Southwest, from arches to hoodoos, are the result of weathering and erosion.

Geographic Makeup of the Land

If the Southwest could be said to have a geographic heart, many people would agree that it's the Colorado Plateau – an impressive and nearly impenetrable 130,000 sq mile tableland lurking in the corner where Colorado, Utah, Arizona and New Mexico join. Formed in an ancient basin as a remarkably coherent body of neatly layered sedimentary rocks, the plateau has remained relatively unchanged even as the lands around it were compressed, stretched and deformed by powerful forces in the earth's crust.

Perhaps the most powerful testament to the plateau's long-term stability is the precise layers of sedimentary rock stretching back two billion years. In fact, the science of stratigraphy – the reading of earth's history in rock layers – stemmed from work at the Grand Canyon, where an astonishing set of layers have been laid bare as the Colorado River worked its way downward. Throughout the Southwest, and the Colorado Plateau in particular, layers of sedimentary rock detail a history of ancient oceans, coastal mudflats and arid dunes.

Another powerful statement is that portions of the Colorado Plateau were among the last regions of continental United States to be mapped.

Naturalist Terry Tempest Williams' book *Refuge* is a compelling personal insight into Mormon culture and the natural history of the Great Salt Lake.

This land of deeply cut sandstone canyons has long been a refuge of wilderness seekers, criminals and iconoclastic hermits of all stripes. Even with the best of modern technology, the region remains scarcely traveled and poses a serious challenge for all adventurers.

All other geographic features of the Southwest seem to radiate out from the plateau. To the east, running in a north–south line from Canada to Mexico are the Rocky Mountains. Dominating the landscape of northern New Mexico, these towering mountains are a sanctuary for aspens and home to legends of grizzly bears. The most significant contribution of the Rocky Mountains is the mighty Colorado River that gathers on the mountains' high slopes and cascades down to cut through the Southwest's soft rocks. East of the Rocky Mountain line, the eastern third of New Mexico grades into the Llano Estacado – a local version of the vast grasslands of the Great Plains.

In Utah, a line of mountains known collectively as the Wasatch Line bisects the state nearly in half – with the eastern half on the Colorado Plateau, and the western half in the Basin and Range province. This western province is comprised of numerous north–south mountains and valleys formed by a stretching of the earth's crust. It encompasses western Arizona and the land from southern Arizona into the southwestern corner of New Mexico. Within these mountains and valleys there is scarcely any potable water, making this an extremely difficult region to cross for early explorers and wagon trains.

Northern Arizona is highlighted by a spectacular set of cliffs called the Mogollon Rim that run several hundred miles to form a boundary between the Colorado Plateau to the north and the highland region of central Arizona. The mountains of central Arizona decrease in elevation as you travel into the deserts of southern Arizona.

Landscape Features

Part of the fun of visiting the Southwest is learning to recognize diagnostic features of the landscape. In fact, it would be impossible to miss them because the area is mostly devoid of trees and rocks stick out like sore thumbs. Plus the Southwest is jam-packed with one of the world's greatest concentrations of remarkable rock formations.

One reason for this is that the area's widespread sedimentary layers are so soft that rain and erosion readily carve them into fantastic shapes. But the full story is a bit more complicated because not any old rain will do. It has to be hard rain that is fairly sporadic. Frequent rain would simply

---

CRYPTOBIOTIC CRUSTS

Only in recent years have cryptobiotic crusts begun to attract attention and concern. These living crusts cover and protect desert soils, literally gluing sand particles together so they don't blow away. Cyanobacteria, one of the earth's oldest life forms, start the process by extending mucous-covered filaments into the dry soil. Over time these filaments and the sand particles adhering to them form a thin crust that is colonized by algae, lichen, fungi, and mosses. This crust plays a key role in desert food chains, as well as absorbing tremendous amounts of rainwater and reducing erosion.

Unfortunately, this thin crust is easily fragmented under heavy-soled boots and tires. Once broken, the crust takes 50 to 250 years to repair itself. In its absence, winds and rains erode desert soils, and much of the water that would nourish desert plants is lost. Many sites in Utah, in particular, have cryptobiotic crusts. Visitors to the Southwest have an important responsibility to protect these crusts by staying on established trails.

wash the formations away. And between rain there have to be long arid spells that keep the eroding landmarks intact.

What makes landscape viewing so ultimately rewarding in the Southwest are the unbelievable ranges of colors. Scientists will tell you how the colors derive from the unique mineral composition of each rock type, but most visitors to the parks are content to stand on the rim of the Grand Canyon (p131) or Bryce Canyon (p247) and simply watch the breathtaking play of light on the orange and red rocks.

This combination of color and soft rock is best seen in badlands, where the rock crumbles so easily you can actually hear the hillsides sloughing away. The result is an otherworldly landscape of rounded knolls, spires and folds painted in outrageous colors. Excellent examples can be found in the Painted Desert of Petrified Forest National Park (p187), at Capitol Reef National Park (p261) or in the Bisti Badlands south of Farmington, New Mexico.

A more elegantly sculptured version are called hoodoos. These towering, narrow pillars of rock can be found throughout the Southwest, but are magnificently showcased at Bryce Canyon National Park (p247). Although formed in soft rock, these precarious spires differ from badlands because parallel joints in the rock create deeply divided ridges that weather into rows of pillars. The examples at Bryce are further accentuated when layers of resistant limestone cap the pillars and prevent them from crumbling.

Under special circumstances, sandstone may form fins and arches. At Arches National Park (p276), where there's a remarkable concentration of these features, it's thought they're the result of a massive salt deposit laid down by a sea 300 million years ago. Squeezed by the pressure of overlying layers, this salt body apparently domed up then collapsed, creating a matrix of rock cracked along parallel lines. Erosion along deep vertical cracks left behind fins and narrow walls of sandstone that can sometimes partially collapse to create freestanding arches.

The National Park Service has a website with links to sites for every park and monument at www.nps.gov.

Streams cutting through resistant sandstone layers form natural bridges, which are similar in appearance to arches. Three examples of natural bridges can be found in Natural Bridges National Monument (p286). These formations are the result of meandering streams that double back on themselves to cut at both sides of a rock barrier. At an early stage of development these meandering streams could be called goosenecks as they loop across the landscape. Perhaps the Southwest's most famous example can be found at the Goosenecks State Park (p286).

The Rio Grande of New Mexico flows along a unique formation called a rift valley. Like the famous Rift Valley in Africa, this formation is the result of divergent forces breaking apart the overlying earth's crust. In New Mexico, the rift originated about 30 million years ago and the area along this zone of stretching dropped by as much as 25,000ft. The rift has obviously filled in considerably since then, but it remains low enough to chart the river's course.

Many of the Southwest's characteristic features are sculpted in sandstone. Laid down in horizontal layers like stacks of pancakes, these rocks create distinctive features such as flat-topped mesas. Surrounded by sheer cliffs, mesas represent a fairly advanced stage of erosion where the original landscape has retreated to a few scattered outposts that tower over everything else. The eerie skyline at Monument Valley (p184 and p286) on the Arizona–Utah border is a classic example.

Where sandstone layers remain more intact, as in the ponderous walls of Zion National Park (p231), it's possible to see details of the ancient sand dunes that created the sandstone. As sand dunes were blown across the landscape millions of years ago they formed fine layers of cross-bedding that can still be seen in the rocks at Zion. Wind-blown ripple marks and tracks of animals that once walked the dunes are also preserved. Modern sand dunes include the spectacular dunes at White Sands National Monument (p438), where shimmering white gypsum crystals thickly blanket 275 sq miles. Here you can find living examples of features that are preserved in sandstone elsewhere in the Southwest.

For the most comprehensive introduction to the Arizona desert check out the excellent *A Natural History of the Sonoran Desert*, edited by Steven Phillips and Patricia Comus.

Although the sedimentary rocks of the Colorado Plateau are unique for their degree of horizontalness (a measure of the region's long-term stability), compression of the earth's crust also created some folds that are known as monoclines. Layers of folded rock are recognized by their tilted or even vertical appearance, and one of the best examples in the world is the 100-mile-long Waterpocket Fold (p262) in Capitol Reef National Park.

Looking beneath the surface, the 85-plus caves at Carlsbad Caverns National Park (p452) provide further proof that tropical seas once covered the region. These caves are chiseled deep into a massive 240-million-year-old limestone formation that was part of a 400-mile-long reef similar to the modern Great Barrier Reef of Australia.

Ecological Provinces

The Southwest includes all four divisions of the North American Desert, and although they look similar to the uninitiated, each of the four is remarkably different. Not only are the climatic conditions unique to each region, but the rugged, inhospitable nature of the landscape means that plants and animals often adapt to local conditions and have very limited ranges.

The western edge of the Southwest lies in the rain shadow of the Sierra Nevada and coastal ranges of California, which deprive the region of life-giving rainstorms. Located in the north the Great Basin Desert is a high, cold desert that receives much of its precipitation in the form of winter snows. Utterly dominated by vast stands of unpalatable shrubs like sagebrush and shadscale, this desert supports little life. The Great Basin Desert covers most of Utah (except for the mountains in the center and northeast corner of the state) and small portions of northern Arizona.

Lying just to the south, the closely related Mojave Desert barely extends into Arizona as a finger reaching upstream along the arid depths of the Grand Canyon. This desert includes some of the driest and hottest places in North America because it sits in a region where warm, descending air sucks up extra moisture. The Mojave Desert is home to drought-tolerant specialists like creosote bushes and yuccas.

Edward Abbey shares his desert philosophy and insights in his classic *Desert Solitaire: A Season in the Wilderness*, a must read for desert enthusiasts and conservationists.

Much of southern Arizona is occupied by the Sonoran Desert near Tucson (p198), the richest North American desert in terms of plants and animals. This is the land of giant saguaros and organ-pipe cacti. Perhaps because it receives rainfall during both the winter and summer seasons this region is able to support many forms of life.

The Chihuahuan Desert is a Mexican desert that extends northward into south-central New Mexico and the southwest borderlands of Texas. Unlike the Great Basin, this desert receives much of its precipitation from summertime monsoons that move inland from the Gulf of Mexico. Enclosed by two Mexican mountain ranges and sitting on an elevated plateau, this desert province is fairly distinct from the other three desert types. One of its most characteristic plants is the agave.

The Southwest offers more than just deserts. Numerous mountain ranges are scattered throughout the region, including some high elevation peaks and upland areas that have more in common with Canada than the deserts at their feet. Entire ranges are cloaked in aspen groves and verdant spruce-fir forests. Some mountains are even high enough to support alpine tundra.

Geology of the Grand Canyon

Arizona's Grand Canyon (p131) is the best-known geologic feature in the Southwest and for good reason: not only is it built on a scale so massive it dwarfs the human imagination, but it also records two billion years of geologic history – a huge amount of time considering the earth is just 4.6 billion years old. The canyon itself, however, is young, a mere five to six million years old. Carved by the powerful Colorado River as the land bulged upward, the 277-mile-long canyon reflects the differing hardness of the 10-plus layers of rocks in its walls. Shales crumble easily and form slopes, while resistant limestones and sandstones form distinctive cliffs.

The layers making up the bulk of the canyon walls were laid during the Paleozoic era, 570 to 245 million years ago. These formations perch atop a group of one- to two-billion-year-old rocks lying at the bottom of the inner gorge of the canyon. Between these two distinct sets of rock is the Great Unconformity, a several hundred million year gap in the geologic record where erosion erased 12,000ft of rock and left a huge mystery.

The oldest rocks in the canyon, dark gray Vishnu schist and pinkish Zoroaster granite, formed when sediments and volcanic ashes showered into a shallow tropical sea. These were later compressed into metamorphic rock as the earth buckled and uplifted into a mighty mountain range that eventually eroded away. Between 1.2 billion and 825 million years ago the area was covered once again by an ocean that rose and fell more than 18 times, leaving deposits that metamorphosed into a rock unit named the Grand Canyon Supergroup. Above the Supergroup lies the Great Unconformity, and above that 225 million years of rocks

A GEOLOGY PRIMER

All rocks are divided into three large classes – sedimentary, igneous and metamorphic. Sedimentary rocks dominate the landscape of the Colorado Plateau and elsewhere in the Southwest. They form when sediments and particles cement together over time. Borne by wind or water, sediments generally settle in horizontal layers that tell geologists a lot about the conditions under which they were formed. Limestone is a type of sedimentary rock that is little more than accumulated calcium carbonate, which acts like a strong cement until softened by water. Sandstone consists of sand particles that stack poorly, leaving lots of room for calcium carbonate to penetrate, making this a very hard and durable rock. At the opposite end of the spectrum from limestone, mudstone (which includes shale) consists of flaky particles that stack so closely together that they leave little room for binding cement. Thus mudstone is often very soft and breakable.

Igneous rocks originate underground as molten magma. They may cool deep underground or erupt to the surface as lava or volcanic ash. Across the Southwest, volcanic outcrops are typically recent in origin and the region's best-known volcanic feature, New Mexico's Shiprock (p406), is only 12 million years old. While rarely encountered among the monolithic sedimentary rocks of the Colorado Plateau, volcanic features reach their greatest diversity and number in New Mexico.

Metamorphic rocks start out as either sedimentary or igneous rocks, then are transformed by exposure to intense heat or pressure, especially where the earth's crust buckles and folds into mountain ranges. Metamorphic rocks usually remain underground except where overlying layers of rock have eroded away. Examples include recently exposed outcrops in the bottom of the Grand Canyon (p131), and mountain ranges in western Utah and Arizona known as turtlebacks because they rise to the surface after sediments slid off.

were laid down by a long succession of marine, freshwater and desert environments. Whenever deeper waters prevailed, fine-grained clays and deep-sea oozes settled to the ocean floor to become thinly layered shales and limestones. As sea levels fell, coastal deltas, mudflats and swamps collected sediments that transformed into siltstones and sandstones. Well-known examples of these particular layers include Redwall and Kaibab limestones, the Hermit and Bright Angel shales, and the Coconino and Tapeats sandstones. Unlike the dark-colored rocks of the lower canyon, these upper layers are distinct in being pale buff or orangish.

The North Rim of the Grand Canyon is 1200ft higher than the South Rim.

WILDLIFE

The Southwest's desolate landscape doesn't mean it lacks wildlife – on the contrary. However, the plants and animals of North America's deserts are a subtle group and it takes patience to see them, so many visitors will drive through without noticing any at all. While a number of species are widespread, many have adapted to the particular requirements of their local environment and live nowhere else in the world. Deep canyons and waterless wastes limit travel and dispersal opportunities for animals and plants as well as for humans, and all life has to hunker down carefully in order to survive this place. It's easy to hurtle through in the comfort of a modern, air-conditioned vehicle, but only when you leave the confines of your car will you fully encounter this landscape and its many inhabitants.

Animals

REPTILES & AMPHIBIANS

While most people expect to see snakes and lizards in a desert, it's less obvious that frogs and toads find a comfortable home here as well. But on a spring evening, the canyons of the Southwest may fairly reverberate with the calls of canyon tree frogs or red-spotted toads. With the rising sun, these are replaced by several dozen species of lizards and snakes that roam among rocks and shrubs. Blue-bellied fence lizards are particularly abundant in the region's parks, but visitors can always hope to encounter a rarity like the strange and venomous Gila monster. Equally fascinating, if you're willing to hang around and watch for a while (but never touch or bother), are the Southwest's many colorful rattlesnakes. Quick to anger and able to deliver a painful or toxic bite, rattlesnakes are placid and retiring if left alone (see also p480).

BIRDS

Over 400 species of birds can be found in the Southwest, bringing color, energy and song to every season. There are blue grosbeaks, yellow warblers and scarlet cardinals. There are massive golden eagles and tiny vibrating calliope hummingbirds. In fact, there are so many interesting birds that it's the number one reason many people travel to the Southwest. Springtime is particularly rewarding as songbirds arrive from their southern wintering grounds and begin singing in every nook and cranny. It's enough to make anyone's blood begin to race because spring is in the air.

One recent arrival at the Grand Canyon is at the top of everyone's list of must-see wildlife. With 9ft wingspans, the California condor looks more like a prehistoric pterodactyl than any bird you've ever seen. Kids squeal with delight and adults whoop with excitement as these birds swoop back and forth over canyon viewpoints. Pushed to the brink of extinction, these unusual birds are staging a minor comeback at the Grand

Canyon. After several decades in which no condors lived in the wild, a few wild pairs are now nesting on the Grand Canyon rim.

Fall provides another bird-watching highlight when sandhill cranes and snow geese travel in long skeins down the Rio Grande Valley to winter at the Bosque del Apache National Wildlife Refuge (p425). And although the Great Salt Lake looks like a salty wasteland, it is in fact one of North America's premier sites for migrating birds each fall, with millions of ducks and grebes stopping to feed on tiny brine shrimp before continuing their southward journey.

MAMMALS

Sadly, the Southwest's most charismatic wildlife species were largely exterminated by the early 1900s. First to go was the grizzly bear. Long gone are the thundering herds of buffalo. Silent are the nights when wolves would send shivers down your spine. Absent are the mysterious tropical jaguars that crossed the border out of Mexico. Vanished with hardly a trace are North America's most abundant mammals, the prairie dogs (actually small rodents) that numbered in the billions.

Like the California condor, however, some species are being reintroduced into their former ranges. A small group of Utah prairie dogs were successfully released in Bryce Canyon National Park (p247) in 1974. Mexican wolves were released in the midst of public controversy into the wilds of eastern Arizona in 1998. And bighorn sheep and elk are being reintroduced to new areas.

Mule deer still roam as widely as ever, and coyote are seen and heard nearly everywhere. Small numbers of elk, pronghorn antelope and bighorn sheep inhabit their favorite habitats, but it takes a lot of luck or some sharp eyes to spot these creatures. Even fewer people will observe a mountain lion, one of the wildest and most elusive animals in North America. These large cats are fairly common, but shy away from any human contact.

Collared peccaries can be found in the arid desert stretches of southern Arizona and New Mexico. These hairy, pig-like animals with tusks move in large packs, and females with young may aggressively charge humans. Long-tailed coatis, relatives of the raccoon, also travel in groups in the same region. They have long noses that help them track down small food items.

An estimated nine million free-tailed bats once roosted in Carlsbad Caverns (p452). Though reduced in recent years, the evening flight is still one of the premier wildlife spectacles in North America.

Plants

Although the Southwest is largely a desert region, the presence of many large mountain ranges creates a remarkable diversity of niches for plants. Perhaps the best way to begin understanding the plants of this region is to understand life zones and the ways each plant thrives in its favored zone. First developed in 1889 by C Hart Merriam after visiting the Grand Canyon, the life zone concept is now used worldwide.

At the lowest elevations, generally below 4000ft, high temperatures and lack of water create desertlike conditions where drought-tolerant desert plants like cacti, sagebrush and agave survive. Many of these species have greatly reduced leaves to reduce water loss, or hold water like a cactus to survive long, hot spells.

At mid-elevations, from 4000ft to 7000ft, conditions cool a bit and more moisture is available for woody shrubs and small trees. In much of Utah, northern Arizona and New Mexico, piñon pines and junipers blanket vast areas of low mountain slopes and hills. Both trees are short and stout to help conserve water. Piñon pines have short, paired needles

A fully hydrated giant saguaro can store more than a ton of water.

and pitchy cones loaded with nutritious seeds (pine nuts!). Junipers have leaves that are reduced to scales and bluish rounded cones that look like little berries.

Nearly pure stands of stately, fragrant ponderosa pine take over around 7000ft on many of the west's mountain ranges. In fact, this single tree best defines the western landscape and many animals rely on it for food and shelter; timber companies also consider it their most profitable tree. Ponderosa pines are easily recognized by their sweet-smelling bark, large cones and long needles in sets of three.

High mountain, or boreal, forests are composed of a mix of spruce, fir, quaking aspen and a few other conifers. This is a land of cool, moist forests and lush meadows where brilliant wildflower shows may erupt

CACTI OF THE SOUTHWEST

If your first encounter with a cactus is when one pokes a spine into your skin you'll never forget this unique plant. Nor will you forget them if your first encounter is during the flowering season when they burst forth with deeply colored blossoms of unsurpassed beauty.

The Southwest's 100 or so species of cacti are superbly adapted to arid environments. The succulent pads that form the body of the plant are actually modified stems, and their waxy 'skin' helps prevent water loss. Leaves have been transformed into spines that protect the plant from thirsty herbivores like deer. In order to save water, cacti also close their pores during the day and open them so the plant can breathe at night. And during every rainstorm, cacti drink up as much water as they can and store it in their succulent tissues – after a good rainfall you can actually see how swollen the cacti become.

It is fairly easy to identify the six most common types of Southwestern cacti: the prickly pear, pincushion, cholla, columnar, hedgehog and barrel cacti.

Prickly pears, mainly in the genus *Opuntia*, have flattened pads with clusters of spines. Watch out for this group because they have tiny glochids on their pads that break off painfully in the skin and are nearly impossible to remove.

Pincushion cacti, often in the genus *Mammilaria*, are small and cylindrical in cross-section, and don't have ribs running from top to bottom. The fishhook cactus in this group has hooked spines that are difficult to remove.

Cholla (*choy*-uh) are also cylindrical and lack ribs, but are much taller and have branches. Like the prickly pears, they belong to the genus *Opuntia*. They can range from pencil chollas (with extremely thin branches) and teddybear chollas (which look warm and fuzzy but have wickedly barbed spines) to jumping cholla (which have fruits hanging in loose chains which readily detach by burying their spines in your skin). Chollas have some of the most difficult spines to remove – if you are stuck, it may be easiest to cut the spines with scissors and then remove them one by one with forceps.

The remaining three types of cacti are all cylindrical in cross-section and ribbed. These include the towering (15ft to 50ft tall) giant saguaros of southern Arizona (see p209) that stand like massive columns in the desert. Other columnar cacti include the organ-pipe cacti, which branches from the ground (best seen in Organ Pipe Cactus National Monument, p211, though many other similar species live across the border in Mexico).

Hedgehog cacti, often in the genus *Echinocereus*, are less than four inches in diameter and flower from their sides. The claret-cup cactus in this group has deep red flowers and is one of the most beautiful cacti in the Southwest. Barrel cacti, mainly in the genus *Ferocactus*, are similar but grow to be more than five inches in diameter and have flowers emerging from the top of the plant. Some extraordinary examples have grown to 10ft in height.

Caution! All cacti are legally protected and cannot be collected no matter how tempting they look or how perfect they would fit on your windowsill back home. It is also illegal to damage or destroy a cactus. Southwestern states treasure these plants and enforce these laws rigorously.

after the snow melts. Quaking aspen is easily identified by its white, skin-like bark and shimmering leaves that turn fluorescent red and orange in the fall. Spruce is a Rocky Mountain tree that hopscotches into the Southwest on high mountaintops. To confirm this tree's identity, grasp a branch and feel for sharp, spiny-tipped needles that prick your hand.

Perhaps the biggest surprises of all are the incredibly diverse flowers that appear each year in the deserts and mountains of the Southwest. These include late winter flowers that begin blooming on the desert floor in February, and late summer flowers that fill mountain meadows after the snow melts or pop out after summer monsoons in New Mexico. At times, the displays of flowers can be more overwhelming than your first glimpse of the Grand Canyon – you just have to find them at the right moment and that's something that may happen only once in your whole life. Visitors' favorite flowers include red columbines with their bright yellow centers and red long-spurred tubes, crimson monkeyflowers that brighten remote desert oases with a flash of unexpected color, and yellow evening primroses whose four large papery petals emerge in the evening like delicate origami.

NATIONAL & STATE PARKS

One of the most fabulous concentrations of national parks, wildlife refuges, and monuments in all of North America can be found in the Southwest. While many visitors head for these stellar landmarks, equally interesting (though less crowded) attractions can be found in smaller state parks and wildlife sanctuaries throughout the region. Try to include a mix of both in your trip and learn more about what the Southwest has to offer.

GLEN CANYON DAM'S UNCERTAIN FUTURE John A Vlahides

In 1963 the gates of Glen Canyon dam closed and Lake Powell began to fill. Dubbed the 'Place No One Knew' by a (recommended) book of the same name, Glen Canyon was the heart of the largest roadless area in continental USA, part of the last-mapped area of the lower 48 states. The few old timers who ran the Colorado River through the canyon before it was flooded tell of a place that rivaled the Grand Canyon for scenic grandeur, full of ancestral Indian sites and stunning rock formations that only a few thousand people had seen since John Wesley Powell's 1869 expedition. Indeed, nothing had changed for centuries. Then came the dam.

Still controversial a half-century later, the dam blocks the passage of Colorado River mud downstream, clarifying and chilling the water before its transit into the Grand Canyon, drastically altering the river's ecosystem; invasive species have taken over. Lake Powell was mostly created for recreation. In the 1960s, there was no need for this reservoir or its electricity; the desert cities (such as Page) grew up because of the dam, not the other way around. And several feet of lake water are lost every year to evaporation in the hot, arid desert. Eventually the dam will entirely silt up with the mud. A fairly strong movement is afoot to decommission it and drain the lake; for more details, visit the Living Rivers website (www.livingrivers.org) or stop by their nonprofit ice cream store, Restoration Creamery (p268), in Moab.

But drought, more than anything else, may cause Lake Powell's eventual demise. Between 1999 and 2005, water levels dropped by about half, and marinas, such as Hite, sat closed, their docks suspended high above dry land (they've since been removed). The water rose following the wet winter of 2005, but the future remains uncertain. On the upside, you can now explore land that was formerly submerged. And there's still a lot of lake for boating. Don a foam baseball cap, throw a case of longnecks in the cooler, pump up your boom box, and you'll blend right in.

NATIONAL & STATE PARKS

Park	Features	Activities	Page
Arches NP	sandstone arches, diverse geologic formations	hiking, camping, scenic drives	p277
Bosque del Apache National Wildlife Refuge	cottonwood forest along Rio Grande, abundant cranes & geese each winter	birdwatching	p425
Bryce Canyon NP	eroded hillsides, red & orange hoodoos & pillars	camping, hiking, scenic drives, stargazing, cross-country skiing	p247
Canyon de Chelly NM	ancient cliff dwellings, canyons, cliffs	hiking and backpacking (guided only), horseback riding, scenic overlooks	p182
Canyonlands NP	sandstone formations at confluence of Green & Colorado Rivers	rafting, camping, mountain biking, backpacking	p279
Capitol Reef NP	buckled sandstone cliffs along the Waterpocket Fold	mountain biking, hiking, camping, wilderness solitude	p261
Carlsbad Caverns NP	underground cave system, limestone formations, bat flight in evening	ranger-led walks, spelunking (experienced only), backpacking	p452
Dinosaur NM	fossil beds along Yampa & Green Rivers, dinosaur fossils & exhibits	hiking, scenic drives, camping, rafting	p319
Grand Canyon NP	canyon scenery, geologic record, condors, remote wilderness	rafting, hiking, camping, mountain biking	p131
Grand Staircase-Escalante NM	desert wilderness, mountains, canyons, wildlife	mountain biking, hiking, camping, solitude	p251
Mesa Verde NP	Ancestral Puebloan sites	hiking, cross-country skiing	p323
Monument Valley Navajo Tribal Park	desert basin with sandstone pillars & buttes	scenic drive, guided tours, horseback riding	p184
Organ Pipe Cactus NM	Sonoran Desert, cactus bloom May-Jun	cactus viewing, scenic drives, mountain biking	p211
Petrified Forest NP	Painted Desert, fossilized logs	scenic drives, backcountry hiking	p187
Saguaro NP	desert slopes, giant saguaro, wild-flowers, gila woodpeckers, wildlife	cactus viewing, hiking, camping	p209
White Sands NM	white sand dunes, specially adapted plants & animals	scenic drives, limited hiking, moon-light bicycle tours, range of walks	p438
Zion NP	sandstone canyons, high mesas	hiking, camping, scenic drives, backpacking, rock climbing	p231

NP – National Park; NM – National Monument

ENVIRONMENTAL ISSUES

In an arid landscape like the Southwest, it comes as little surprise that many of the region's most important environmental issues revolve around water and that nature gets the short end of the deal when water is scarce (as has been happening in recent years). The construction of dams and manmade water features throughout the Southwest have radically altered the delicate balance of water that sustained life for countless millennia. Dams, for example, halt the flow of warm waters and force them to drop their rich loads of life-giving nutrients. The Glen Canyon Dam on the Colorado River now captures nearly all of the 380,000 tons of sediment that once flowed annually down the Grand Canyon. These sediments once rebuilt floodplains, nourished myriads of aquatic and riparian food chains, and sustained the life of ancient endemic fish that now flounder on the edge of extinction. In place of rich annual floods, dams now release cold waters in steady flows that favor the introduced fish and weedy plants that have overtaken the West's rivers.

In other areas, the steady draining of aquifers to provide drinking water for cows and sprawling cities is shrinking the water table, and drying up unique desert springs and wetlands that countless animals once depended on during the dry season (see p35). Cows further destroy the fragile desert crust with their heavy hooves, and also graze on native grasses and herbs that are soon replaced by introduced weeds. Unfettered development around the region's many cities and communities is increasingly having the largest impact as uniquely adapted habitats are bulldozed to make room for more houses. There are very few productive valley bottoms left in the Southwest that have not been dramatically altered by cows or development, and these were once the most important habitats for birds and mammals. Arizona's San Pedro River is a notable exception that shows what's possible – almost half of the bird species in North America have been recorded in this relatively tiny area!

On mountain slopes high above the desert floor, forests are being cut at an unsustainable rate. The region's stately pine and fir forests have been largely converted into thickets of scrawny little trees. The cutting of trees and building of roads in these environments can further dry the soil and make it harder for young trees and native flowers to thrive, plus injuries to an ecosystem in an arid environment take a very long time to heal.

Although there are too many examples of these issues to count, it's also worth noting a few triumphs. For instance the Malpais Borderlands Group, a handful of ranchers on the southern border of Arizona and New Mexico, has successfully pushed for sound ranching techniques. The group's leader William McDonald, a fifth-generation rancher from Douglas, Arizona, was honored with a MacArthur Foundation Genius Award in 1998. And (hope beyond hope) there is a serious, growing discussion about the possibility of taking down the Glen Canyon Dam (see p55). Local environmental groups continue to fight on behalf of these and other issues throughout the Southwest, but everything depends on how the waves of newcomers moving to the Southwest will vote and contribute to the future of this marvelous region.

Read Marc Reisner's *Cadillac Desert: The American West and Its Disappearing Water* for a thorough account of how exploding populations in the West have utilized every drop of available water.

Southwest USA Outdoors

Sure the Southwest encompasses five states, but chances are it's fixed in our collective consciousness as a blistering desert. Many of her mountains, though, are swathed in forests; the valleys are seamed with rivers; and, indeed, even the deserts are improbably brilliant with a collage of cactus flowers – if you know when and where to find them. Everything about this region is immense and it can often seem as though there is too much to choose from. It's true. But there are ways to hone in on the wild array of activities available, from hair-raising to serene. On foot or on skis, in the saddle of a horse or on a bike, in the middle of nowhere or close to a home-base: it's your choice. Kick up some dust (or powder), flex your physique, soothe your muscles, fill your eyes with more than you thought possible and allow the landscape to sweetly overwhelm you.

Adventures on America's Public Lands, edited by Mary Tisdale and Bibi Booth, flushes out the best-kept secrets of the American West.

SKIING & SNOWBOARDING

Endless vistas, blood-curdling chutes, sweet glades and ricocheting half-pipes: downhill skiing and boarding is epic whether you're hitting fancy resorts or local haunts. Generally if you can downhill ski at a resort, you're allowed to snowboard, but it's always best to double check. The ski season lasts from late November to early April, depending on where you are.

Salt Lake City and nearby towns hosted the 2002 Winter Olympics, and has rip-roaring routes to test your metal edges. Slopes are uncrowded at Snowbasin (p300), where the Olympic downhill races were held. The terrain here is, in turns, gentle and ultra-yikes. Nearby Alta (p303) is the quintessential Utah ski experience: unpretentious and packed with powder fields, gullies, chutes and glades (sorry, no boarders allowed). New Mexico's Taos Ski Resort (p401) is easily one of the most challenging mountains in the US.

Park City (p306), where the US Olympic ski team has its headquarters, is one of the few places where you can try the Olympic sports of ski jumping, bobsledding and luge.

Ski areas often offer full resort amenities, including lessons and equipment rentals (although renting in nearby towns can be cheaper). Got

---

OUTDOORS WITH KIDS

The Southwest is chock-full of outdoor adventures for the little ones. Let 'em loose at:

New Mexico Museum of Natural History & Science (p351) Be transported through 38 million years of New Mexico's geologic and evolutionary history.

Angel Fire Resort (p404) Kids can enjoy a park designed as a winter wonderland just for them.

Great American Duck Races (p436) Drawing tens of thousands to duck races, tortilla tosses, outhouse races and more.

Snow Canyon State Park (p231) A miniature sampler of Utah's famous land features: slot canyons, cinder cones, lava tubes and slickrock.

Grand Canyon (p139) It offers ranger-led activities including mule rides, hiking and hugely popular fossil walks. Rim Trail hikes are perfect for little legs. Kids can earn a Junior Ranger badge by completing self-guided activity books.

Grand Canyon Field Institute (p139) Offers excursions that may or may not include meals and lodging.

Arizona-Sonora Desert Museum (p200) One of the country's best living museums with displays of desert plants and live desert critters like javelinas, coyotes, scorpions and more.

TOP FIVE HOT SPRINGS

Communal bathing in natural springs is a long-held tradition in the Southwest. These pools are such a treasure that ancient peoples thought them god-sent. (Once you partake in healing waters, you may agree.) Occasionally, if you hike far enough, you can enjoy hot springs without a fee, but most springs these days have resorts built around them and charge you an hourly rate for a soak. Check out the following:

- Montezuma, NM (p420), reputed to have curative and therapeutic powers.

- Truth or Consequences, NM (p425), once called Hot Springs, a funky resort town with natural hot mineral springs. Nearby Geronimo Springs Museum shelters a natural spring in which Geronimo purportedly bathed.

- Pagosa Springs, CO (p335), the spot for soaking in one of the 17 glorious riverside pools.

- Ouray Hot Springs, CO (p338), with crystal-clear natural spring waters sweetly clear of sulphur smells.

- Glenwood Springs, CO (p340), the place for a hot soak after a long day of ice climbing or mountain biking.

kids? Don't leave them at home when you can stash them at a ski school for a day. For complete resort and tour package information, contact local tourist offices and order the Utah *Winter Vacation Planner* (p310) or pick it up in the Wasatch Mountains (p299).

In Utah, the National Ability Center (p308) has year-round sports programs. Ski (www.skimag.com) and Skiing (www.skiingmag.com) magazines give details on conditions, resorts and events.

Cross-Country & Backcountry Skiing

Backcountry and telemark skiing are joining cross-country skiing and snowshoeing as alternates for exploring the untamed Southwestern terrain.

A must-ski for cross-country aficionados? Head to Utah's serene Soldier Hollow (p306), the Nordic course used in the 2002 Winter Olympics. It's accessible to all skill levels.

It's hard to believe there's skiing in Arizona until you find yourself shushing along on the North Rim of the Grand Canyon (p148). The South Rim boasts 18 miles of easy to medium-difficulty, groomed and signed trails within the Kaibab National Forest (p144).

Colorado's Wolf Creek (p335) is laid-back and awesome; waist-high powder is packed in wide-open bowls and steep glades. The San Juan Hut Systems (p342) consist of a great series of shelters along a 206-mile route from Telluride to Moab, Utah.

If you're an advanced skier looking for knock-your-socks-off adventure, *definitely* consider a backcountry trek with Ski Utah Interconnect Adventure Tour (p299).

Search for wilderness areas, wildlife refuges and trails at www.public lands.org. You can also buy recreation permits, books and maps.

HIKING, CAMPING & BACKPACKING

Conveniently, it's always hiking season *somewhere* in the Southwest. When temperatures hit the 100s in Phoenix, cooler mountain trails beckon in Utah and New Mexico. When highland trails are blanketed in snow, southern Arizona tenders balmy weather. Parks near St George in southwestern Utah offer pleasant hiking possibilities well into midwinter. Of course, hardy and experienced backpackers can always don cross-country skis or snowshoes and head out for beautiful wintertime mountain treks.

CHOICE CAMPING & BACKPACKING SPOTS

Pine Valley Wilderness Area (p231) Offers relatively cool, quiet and challenging hiking in midsummer, when the pulsating desert heat blurs your vision, particularly along the 35-mile Summit Trail.

Zion National Park's (p231) Famous backpacking trip The Narrows traverses 16 miles of narrow canyons and spends half of its time in the North Fork of the Virgin River.

Canyonlands National Park (p282) The premier backpacking district here is the Needles. Chesler Park Loop and Joint Trail combine for an awesome 11-mile loop across desert grasslands, past towering red-and-white striped pinnacles and through deep, narrow fractures.

Grand Canyon National Park (p136) Adventure enthusiasts should camp in the inner gorge, walk the Colorado River's sandy banks, explore side canyons and sleep beneath a vast swath of stars.

Havasu Canyon (p145) This hidden valley with 200ft-high waterfalls on the Havasupai Reservation is a treasure.

Gila National Forest (p431) Perfect for backpackers, campers, anglers, birders and cross-country skiers seeking challenging solitude.

Planning

More and more people venture further from their cars and into the wilds these days, adding another reason beyond logistics for careful planning. Some places cap the number of backpackers due to ecological sensitivity or limited facilities. Reservations are essential in highly visited areas such as the Grand Canyon (p131), and during the busy spring and fall months in more seasonal areas like Canyonlands National Park (p279). Consider going to the less heavily visited Bryce Canyon National Park (p247), or Bureau of Land Management (BLM) lands and state parks, for a backpacking trip during busy months. Not only are they less restrictive than the national parks, but usually you can just show up and head out.

Along with archives that reach far and wide, www.cyberwest.com lists the region's best hiking, biking and skiing locations.

Backcountry areas are fragile and cannot support an inundation of human activity, especially insensitive and careless activity. The key is to minimize your impact, leave no trace of your visit (www.lnt.org) and take nothing but photographs and memories. To avoid erosion and, in many desert areas, damage to the delicate cryptobiotic crust (p48), stay on main trails and use common sense and responsible backcountry ethics.

Safety

The climate is partly responsible for the epic nature of the Southwestern landscape. The weather is extraordinary in its unpredictability and sheer, pummeling force – from blazing sun to blinding blizzards and deadly flash floods (p63). When there's too much water – the amounts necessary to scour slot canyons smooth – you'll drown. Too little water combined with unforgiving heat leads to crippling dehydration (p478). A gallon (3.8L) of water per person per day is the recommended minimum in hot weather. Sun protection (brimmed hats, dark glasses and sunblock) is vital to a desert hiker. Know your limitations, pace yourself accordingly and be realistic about your abilities and interests. If a hot shower, comfortable mattress and clean clothes are essential to your well-being, don't head out into the wilderness for five days – plenty of day hikes offer access to quite stunning locations.

Solo travelers should always let someone know where they are going and how long they plan to be gone. At minimum, use sign-in boards at trailheads or ranger stations. Travelers looking for hiking companions can inquire or post notices at ranger stations, outdoors stores, campgrounds and hostels.

MOUNTAIN BIKING & CYCLING

As with hiking and backpacking, perfect cycling weather can be found any time of year in different parts of the Southwest. Southern Arizona is a perfect winter destination; Tucson (p198), considered a bicycle-friendly city, has many bike lanes and parks with bike trails. In spring and fall, Moab (p269) is an incredibly popular destination for mountain bikers wanting to spin their wheels on scenic slickrock trails. During the searing heat of summer, the high elevations around Brian Head (p243) attract an increasing number of bikers looking for a scenic destination that beats the heat.

Local bike shops in all major and many minor cities rent bikes and provide maps and information. Visitor information offices and chambers of commerce usually have brochures with detailed trails maps.

Following are some choice mountain biking spots.

Four Corners Area

The area around Cortez offers outstanding mountain bike trails among piñon-juniper woodland over slickrock mesa. Be sure to try the 26-mile trail from Dove Creek to Slick Rock along the Dolores River. Another good ride begins at the Sand Canyon archaeological site west of Cortez and follows a downhill trail west for 18 miles to Cannonball Mesa near the state line.

- See p329
- Bike rental from Kokopelli Bike & Board is $20 per day
- Nearest town is Cortez
- Colorado Plateau Mountain Bike Trail Association ☎ 702-241-9561

Black Canyon of the Gunnison National Park

A dark, narrow gash above the Gunnison River leads down a 2000ft-deep chasm that's as eerie as it is spectacular. Head to the 6-mile-long South Rim Rd, which takes you to 11 overlooks. To challenge your senses, cycle along the smooth pavement running parallel to the rim.

- See p339
- $8 admission per vehicle for seven days
- Nearest town is Montrose
- Black Canyon of the Gunnison National Park ☎ 970-249-1915

San Juan Hut System

This runs along the 206-mile route stretching from Telluride west to Moab, and is very popular with mountain bikers. The peaks surrounding Telluride offer awesome single-track routes and stupendous scenery. Beginners should try the two-mile-long River Trail that connects Town Park with Hwy 145. For more of a workout, continue up Mill Creek Trail, west of the Texaco gas station near where River Trail ends, and turn around at the Jud Wiebe Trail (which is for hikers only).

- See p342
- San Juan Hut System ☎ 970-626-3033; www.sanjuanhuts.com
- Nearest town is Telluride
- Huts run at $25 a night

Kaibab National Forest

Ride all or part of the still-evolving Arizona Trail, a 24-mile (one-way) trip to the south boundary of the Tusayan Ranger District. It's an excellent, relatively easy ride. Tusayan Bike Trail is a moderate ride on an old logging road. The trailhead is 0.3 miles north of Tusayan on the west side of Hwy 64/180. Another 16 miles from the trailhead Grandview Lookout

Questions about critters, cacti and the best places to roam on the range are answered in the *Audubon Field Guide to the Southwestern States*.

has an 80ft fire tower with fabulous views. Three interconnected loops offer 3-, 8-, and 9-mile round-trips.

■ See p144
■ $20 per vehicle, $10 for bicyclists and pedestrians for a seven-day pass
■ Nearest town is Tusayan
■ Tusayan Ranger Station ☎ 928-638-2443; www.fs.fed.us/r3/kai

Carson National Forest

Carson contains an enormous network of mountain bike and multiuse trails between Taos, Angel Fire and Picuris Peak.

■ See p395
■ Rent bikes from Gearing Up Bicycle Shop for $35 per day
■ Nearest town is Taos
■ Carson National Forest ☎ 505-758-6200; www.fs.fed.us/r3/carson

Moab

This area attracts bikers from around the world to its steep slickrock trails and challenging 4WD roads that wind through woods and into canyon country. Legendary Slickrock Trail is for experts only. This 12.7-mile, half-day loop *will* kick your butt. Intermediate riders can learn to ride slickrock on Klondike Bluffs Trail, a 15.6-mile round-trip that passes dinosaur tracks. For a family-friendly ride, try the 8-mile Bar-M Loop.

■ See p269
■ Nearest town is Moab
■ The Needles Visitor Center ☎ 435-259-471; www.nps.gov/cany/needles
■ $10 for vehicles, $5 for motorcycles, pedestrians and cyclists; full-suspension bikes start at around $30 a day at Rim Cyclery (check out their museum)

ROCK CLIMBING

Although it only took six million years for the Colorado River to erode the Grand Canyon, some of the rocks on the bottom of the canyon are two billion years old.

If Dr Seuss had designed a rock-climbing playground, it would look a lot like the surreal Southwest, filled with enormous blobs, spires, blobs on spires and soaring cliffs. While southern Utah seems to have the market cornered on rock climbing, a peek into other sections yields the beta on the vertical scene. Just keep an eye on the thermometer – those rocks can sizzle during summer. Help keep climbing spaces open by respecting access restrictions, whether they are set by landowners harried by loud louts, or by endangered, cliff-dwelling birds that need space and silence during nesting season.

Otherwise, make a swift approach to central Arizona's Granite Mountain Wilderness (p175), which attracts rock climbers in warmer months. Pack your rack for the rocky reaches of Taos Ski Resort (p401), or pack your picks for the Ouray Ice Park (p338), where a two-mile stretch of the Uncompahgre Gorge has become world renowned for its sublime ice formations. Southwestern Utah's Snow Canyon State Park (p231) offers more than 150 bolted and sport routes. Zion Canyon (p236) has some of the most famous big-wall climbs in the country, including Moonlight Buttress, Prodigal Son, Touchstone and Space Shot. In southeastern Utah, Moab and Indian Creek (p271) make awesome destinations.

CAVING & CANYONEERING

Much of the Southwest's most stunning beauty is out of sight, sitting below the earth's surface in serpentine corridors of stone that make up miles of canyons and caves. Visit Carlsbad Caverns National Park (p452) and not

---

FLASH FLOODS – A DEADLY DESERT DANGER

Flash floods, which occur when large amounts of rain fall suddenly and quickly, are most common during the 'monsoon months' from mid-July to early September, although heavy precipitation in late winter can also cause these floods. They occur with little warning and reach a raging peak in a matter of minutes. Rainfall occurring miles away is funneled from the surrounding mountains into a normally dry wash or canyon, and a wall of water several feet high can appear seemingly out of nowhere. There are rarely warning signs – perhaps you'll see some distant rain clouds – but if you see a flash flood coming, the only recommendation is to reach higher ground as quickly as possible.

Floods carry a battering mixture of rocks and trees and can be extremely dangerous. And a swiftly moving wall of water is much stronger than it appears. At only a foot high, it will easily knock over a strong adult. A 2ft-high flood sweeps away vehicles.

Especially during the monsoon season, heed local warnings and weather forecasts. Avoid camping in sandy washes and canyon bottoms, which are the likeliest spots for flash floods. Campers and hikers are not the only potential victims; every year foolhardy drivers driving across flooded roads are swept away. Flash floods usually subside fairly quickly. A road that is closed will often be passable later on the same day.

---

only will you feel swallowed whole by the planet, but you'll be amply rewarded with a bejeweled trove of glistening, colorful formations.

Canyoneering adventures vary from pleasant day hikes to multiday, technical climbing excursions. Longer trips may involve technical rock climbing, swimming across pools, shooting down waterfalls and camping. Many experienced canyoneers bring inflatable mattresses to float their backpacks on as well as to sleep on.

Arizona and Utah offer some of the best canyoneering anywhere. The first canyoneers in the huge gashes of the Colorado Plateau were Native Americans, whose abandoned cliff dwellings and artifacts mark their passage. See for yourself at the many-fingered Canyon de Chelly (p182), accessible with a Navajo guide intimately familiar with its deep mazes.

The Grand Canyon (p131) is the mother of all canyoneering experiences, attracting thousands to its jaw-dropping vistas.

Then there are slot canyons, hundreds of feet deep and only a few feet wide. These must be negotiated during dry months because of the risk of deadly flash floods (above). Always check with the appropriate rangers for weather and safety information. The Paria Canyon (p255), carved by a tributary of the Colorado River on the Arizona-Utah border, includes the amazing Buckskin Gulch (p256), a 12-mile-long canyon, hundreds of feet deep and only 15ft wide for most of its length. Perhaps the best-known (though now highly commercialized) slot canyon is Antelope Canyon (p150), near Lake Powell. You can also drive through magical Oak Creek Canyon (p169), with dramatic red, orange and white cliffs sweetened with aromatic pine. A nimbus of giant cottonwoods crowd the creek.

Zion National Park (p235) offers dozens of canyoneering experiences for day hikers and extreme adventurers, with weeping rocks, tiny grottoes, hanging gardens and majestic, towering walls.

RAFTING, KAYAKING, CANOEING & BOATING

Few places in the US offer as much watery diversity as the Southwest. Bronco-busting rivers share the territory with enormous lakes and sweet trickles that open into great escapes. Whatever your interest, ability or experience, there are trips to fit your whim and watery toys of choice (raft, kayak or canoe). Busloads of people go white-water

---

TOP HOT-AIR BALLOONING SPOTS

Soaring spires and plunging canyons look amazing from the ground up, but from the perspective of a peregrine, the sight is simply over-the-top. Dozens of companies offer scenic flights that usually lift off in calm morning air, drift for about an hour and finish with a traditional champagne brunch; costs are in the low $100s per person. Most companies need a day's notice, and reserve the right to cancel flights during windy weather and during the summer. Consider these places and events for soaring:

- Albuquerque, NM, hosts the world's biggest hot-air ballooning festival (p353) held every October.
- Gallup, NM, draws over 200 balloonists for a rally (p416) in early December.
- Socorro, NM, lights up with hot-air balloons in the dusky skies over Main Street (p425).
- Panguitch, UT, celebrates with a huge June festival, Chariots in the Sky (p246).
- Park City, UT, is *the* place for a sunrise and champagne float (p308).
- Sedona, AZ, might spin your balloon (p169) in an invisible energy vortex, but the swirling canyon colors are intensely visible.

---

rafting at Taos Box (p371), the steep-sided canyon framing the Rio Grande, but there are also mellow float trips throughout New Mexico and overnight guided rafting trips. Tiny Pilar (p390) serves as a base for white-water rafting. Colorado's Animas River (p332) also boasts challenging white water.

In Utah, float through Dinosaur National Monument (p319) to see starkly eroded, dramatic canyons. Moab (p269) serves as a hub for the state's most bashing rapids; more than a dozen outfitters run trips here. Jet boat, kayak and canoe trips are also available, as are combo horseback riding/hiking/rafting trips. The long float along the gentle Green River (p264) is ideal for canoes and follows John Wesley Powell's 1869 route. And of course, rafting the Colorado River (p137) through the Grand Canyon is a must.

If you're disabled, book with Salt Lake City–based Splore (p270).

Near the California–Arizona state line, a series of dammed lakes on the lower Colorado River is thronged with boaters year-round. Area marinas rent canoes, fishing boats, speed boats, water-skiing boats, jet skis and windsurfers. On the biggest lakes – especially Lake Powell (p154) in the Glen Canyon National Recreation Area and Lake Mead (p192) in the Lake Mead National Recreation Area – houseboat rentals sleep up to six to 12 people and allow exploration of remote areas difficult to reach on foot.

Lake Powell contains about 8.5 trillion gallons of water and has 1960 miles of coastline, more than the coastline from Seattle to San Diego.

The thrill of speed mixed with alcohol makes high-use houseboat areas dangerous for kayakers and canoeists. If you're renting a big rig, take the same care with alcohol as you would when driving a car. Check speed limits because of high-traffic or erosion dangers. Carbon monoxide emitted by houseboat engines is a recently recognized threat. Colorless and odorless, the deadly gas is heavier than air and gathers at water level, creating dangerous conditions for swimmers and boaters. In recent years, several swimmers have drowned after being overcome by carbon monoxide.

HORSEBACK RIDING

Cowboys and Indians, the Pony Express, stagecoaches, cattle drives and rodeo riding – horse legends are legion in the Southwest. This continues to the present day with Bob Baffert, the horse trainer from Nogales, Arizona (p220).

OK. You probably aren't looking to win the Derby, but horseback riding is quite popular in the Southwest. Adventures range from one-hour rides for beginners (or experienced riders who just want to get on a horse again) to multinight horsepacking trips with wranglers, cooks, guides and backcountry camping. Another possibility is staying at a ranch where visitors go horseback riding on a daily basis, and the comforts of a bed and shower await at the end of each day.

Many towns have stables and offer horseback rides. In some, such as the South Rim of the Grand Canyon (p137), only mules are available; these must be booked months in advance. But next door in the Kaibab National Forest, Apache Stables (p144) offers the only horseback ride with a canyon-rim view. During the winter, southern Arizona has delightful riding weather. When the weather warms up, head up to Sedona's M Diamond Ranch (p167) to experience the town like cowboys in the movies did – with two-hour cattle drives, sunset dinner rides and horse-drawn-wagon dinners.

If your gang can't agree on what to do, combine your favorite activities with a customized horseback/rafting/camping trek near Taos with Rio Grande Stables (p395). While you're there, take a once-in-a lifetime tour through Taos Pueblo's vast Native American land, off-limits except with a guide from the Taos Indian Horse Ranch (p400).

For the best multiday trips into Grand Staircase-Escalante National Monument, you can't beat Escalante Canyon Outfitters (p255). Horses carry gear and packs; superb guides provide excellent interpretation *and* do the cooking. There's nothing quite like seeing the stunning Monument Valley (p184) just like John Wayne did: from the back of a horse.

The non-profit National Ability Center (p308) runs a horseback riding program for people with disabilities and their families. Other programs include skiing, rafting, climbing and biking.

If your idea of a Southwestern vacation leans more towards a week in a comfortable ranch in the country with excellent food and happy horses available for daily riding, check out www.ranchweb.com or www.dude ranches.com. Also contact the **Dude Ranchers' Association** (☎ 970-223-8440; www .duderanch.org), which lists dozens of ranches throughout the Southwest.

Ben Guterson's *Seasonal Guide to the Natural Year* details when and where to catch the peak periods for flowers blooming, flocks migrating and the rituals of mating.

Food & Drink

To foodies, the Southwest has not traditionally been considered a culinary mecca. But in the recent past, attention to raw ingredients and local preparations has created more of a food focus. Isolated geographically from Mexico and Spain, and culturally from the USA, the Southwest's cooking traditions are the result of a long line of unknown artists who have conjured up a distinctive cuisine from the simplest ingredients.

John Middelkoop's documentary, *Beans from God: The History of Navajo Cooking,* examines the significant role that food plays in Navajo spiritual life.

The signature cuisine consists of various combinations of Mexican, Spanish and Native American foods. Classic American offerings of meat and potatoes though – a staple in cowboy country – are universally available for less adventuresome palates.

Although the Southwest is no UN when it comes to food choices, there is more choice than ever. A development spurt occasioned by the 2002 Winter Olympics in Salt Lake City (p295) brought forth more ethnic restaurants than that city has ever seen. Las Vegas eateries (p95) run the gamut from sublime five-star dining experiences to gambler's bargain buffets (p96). Sophisticated menus in cities are increasingly commonplace, with Santa Fe (p375) leading the charge into haute cuisine thanks to the storied Coyote Cafe (p377). The best town for foodies in Southwestern Colorado is Durango (p333). No one will go hungry in Phoenix (p126), which offers the biggest selection in the state; Tucson (p206) is well-known for its Mexican food.

STAPLES & SPECIALTIES

Huevos rancheros are the quintessential Southwestern breakfast; eggs prepared to order are served on top of two fried corn tortillas, loaded with beans and potatoes, sprinkled with cheese, and served swimming in chile. Breakfast burritos are built by stuffing a flour tortilla with eggs, bacon or chorizo, cheese, chile and sometimes beans.

A Southwestern lunch or dinner will probably start with a big bowl of corn chips and salsa. Almost everything comes with beans, rice and your choice of warm flour or corn tortillas, topped with chile, cheese and sometimes sour cream. Blue corn tortillas are one colorful New Mexican contribution to the art of cooking.

For a collection of native recipes including ones for Navajo and Zuni breads, as well as Indian tacos and tamales, check out www.aniwaya.org.

Don't expect your Southwestern meal – often featuring the 'Three Sisters' of corn, beans and squash – to arrive at the table as a distinct main with a couple of neatly arranged side dishes. It's all piled together – richly seasoned rice or potatoes and beans (the pride of any serious cook) might flank a chile-and-cheese-covered burrito bursting with gooey goodness. Enjoy it as a symphony rather than a series of solos.

Steak & Potatoes

Home, home on the range, where the ranches and the steakhouses rule. Have a deep hankerin' for a juicy slab of beef with a salad, baked potato and beans? Look no further than the Southwest. In Utah, the large Mormon population influences culinary options – good, old-fashioned American food like chicken, steak, potatoes, vegetables, homemade pies and ice cream prevail.

Mexican Food

Mexican food is often hot and spicy, but it doesn't have to be. If you don't like spicy food, just go easy on the salsa and you should be fine.

There are some distinct regional variations in the Southwest. In Arizona, Mexican food is of the Sonoran type, with specialties such as *carne seca* (dried beef). Meals are usually served with refried beans, rice, and flour or corn tortillas; chiles are relatively mild. Tucsonans (p206) refer to their city as the 'Mexican food capital of the universe,' which, although hotly contested by a few other places, carries a ring of truth. Colorado restaurants serve Mexican food but they don't insist on any accolades for it.

New Mexico's food is different from, but reminiscent of, Mexican food. Pinto beans are served whole instead of refried; *posole* (a corn stew) may replace rice. Chiles aren't used so much as a condiment (like salsa) but more as an essential ingredient in almost every dish. *Carne adobada* (marinated pork chunks) is a specialty.

Native Foods

Modern Native American cuisine bears little resemblance to that eaten before the Spanish conquest, but it is distinctive from Southwestern cuisine. Navajo and Indian tacos – fried bread usually topped with beans, meat, tomatoes, chile and lettuce – are the most readily available. Chewy *horno* bread is baked in the beehive-shaped outdoor adobe ovens *(hornos)* using remnant heat from a fire built inside the oven, then cleared out before cooking.

Most other Native cooking is game-based and usually involves squash and locally harvested ingredients like berries and piñon nuts. Overall it's difficult to find, especially in southwestern Colorado, Utah and Las Vegas. Your best bets for good grub are festival food stands, powwows, rodeos, pueblo feast days, casino restaurants or people's homes at the different pueblos.

> Green chile is to New Mexicans what breath is to life – essential. McDonalds understands this and offers green chile throughout the region at its fast-food eateries.

HOT STUFF

From the sweet red bell pepper to the brutish jalapeño, smoky chipotle and potent serrano, chiles are carefully cultivated. Flourishing where lesser plants fail, they are revered as much for their health benefits as their bite.

None match Hatch green chiles, New Mexicans will tell you, although the Chimayó red chile (p389) is often preferred among discriminating critics for its more elegant flavor. Both are from the same plant but are harvested at different times. Chiles are picked green in September and October, an event that fills every town in New Mexico with the scent of the outdoor roast, done in special barrel-shaped contraptions.

Those chiles left on the plant are allowed to mature to a deep ruby red, then strung on the *ristras* which adorn walls and doorways throughout the Southwest. The red chiles are dried and laboriously ground into a paste that becomes the basis of rich red sauces, or a piquant spice for sprinkling atop almost anything. Waitstaff immediately offer you the choice: 'Red or green?' Each batch varies according to harvest and preparation. If you can't decide, say 'Christmas' and you'll get it half-and-half.

New Mexico harvests more than 30,000 acres of chiles annually, predominantly in the southwestern town of Hatch (p432), and just about every restaurant (including McDonalds) offers it. When you see it on a menu, it refers to either chopped-up fresh-roasted chile (served, for example, on a hamburger) or chile sauce, usually made with ground pork or beef (vegetarian options are usually just plain chile sauce) and most commonly drenching burritos, enchiladas and tamales. Unlike Tex-Mex or Mexican sauce, made predominantly with tomatoes and meat, chile (pureed or chopped) is the sauce's foundation. An unpretentious bowl of chile – basically a bowl of chopped chile and pinto beans served with a flour tortilla – is perhaps the quintessential New Mexican meal.

Exceptions include Albuquerque's Indian Pueblo Cultural Center (p351), the Metate Room (p328) in southwestern Colorado, Tewa Kitchen (p401) near Taos Pueblo and the Hopi Cultural Center Restaurant & Inn (p185) on the Hopi Reservation.

Fruits & Vegetables

Beyond the chile pepper, Southwestern food is characterized by its use of *posole, sopaipillas* (deep-fried puff pastry) and blue corn. *Posole,* Spanish for hominy, is dried or frozen kernels of corn processed in a lime solution to remove the hulls. It's served plain, along with pinto beans, as a side dish. Blue corn tortillas, have a heartier flavor than the more common yellow corn tortillas. Pinto beans, served either whole or refried, are a basic element of most New Mexican dishes.

Corn is ground and patted into tortillas or made into *masa* (slightly sweet corn dough), then elaborately folded into corn husks with a filling to make tamales. Or it's soaked in lye until tender and used in a rich stew called *posole.*

Beans, long the staple protein of New Mexicans, come in many colors, shapes and preparations. They are usually stewed with onions, chiles and spices and served somewhat intact or refried to a creamy consistency. They're just perfect for scooping with a corn chip.

Squash is no longer a real staple, but if you see *calabasas* (a variety of squash) on the menu, give it a try. Avocados are a delightful staple, made into zesty guacamole. 'Guac' recipes are as closely guarded and vaunted by cooks as their bean recipes.

Nouvelle Southwestern Cuisine

An eclectic mix of Mexican and Continental (especially French) traditions began to flourish in the late 1970s and it continues to mushroom. Try innovative combinations such as chiles stuffed with lobster or barbecued duck tacos. But don't expect any bargains here. Southwestern food

Homegrown in New Mexico, the last place you'd expect, Gruet (www.gruetwinery.com) produces arguably the best affordable champagne in the country.

GREEN CHILE STEW

Hungry ahead of your scheduled departure? Green chile stew is perhaps the ultimate expression of chile cuisine, and most certainly the pride of every New Mexican cook. It's also the only proven cure for the common cold. Although this recipe may be best saved for when you are more acclimated to the cuisine, the daring among us will go ahead and give it a try. Begin preparing your taste buds today.

½ lb ground beef, pork or turkey	1 clove garlic, minced
½ lb boneless sirloin, cubed	½ cup fresh cilantro, chopped
4 cups chicken broth	1½ tsp oregano
½ cup beer	2½ tsp cumin
2 lbs fresh green chiles, roasted, peeled and chopped	⅛ cup parsley, chopped
1 tomato, chopped	1 tsp salt
1 medium onion, chopped	1 tsp pepper

In a large pot, sauté ground meat and sirloin until done. Remove from pot. Add onions, garlic and cilantro to pot and cook for three to five minutes or until onions are soft. Add chicken broth, beer, green chiles and tomato. Bring to a boil and then reduce to a simmer. Add meat, oregano, cumin, parsley, salt and pepper. Simmer for two hours, stirring occasionally.

is usually inexpensive, but as soon as the chef tacks on a 'nouvelle' tag, the tab soars as high as a crested butte.

Generally speaking cities such as Phoenix (p128), Tucson (p207), Santa Fe (p375) and Albuquerque (p357) have the most nouvelle Southwestern restaurants. Stellar examples include Flagstaff's Josephine's (p161) and Santa Fe's SantaCafé (p376), but this only represents the tip of the menu.

DRINKS

There are three things a good wine grape needs: lousy soil, lots of sunshine and dedicated caretakers, all of which New Mexico has. For a full run-down of its 33 producers, contact the **New Mexico Wine Growers Association** (☎ 505-899-3815, 866-494-6366; www.nmwine.com). The bubbly star is Albuquerque's Gruet Winery (p354), with an outstanding brut and award-winning whites. Dixon's La Chiripada Winery (p390) is known for its Riesling and cabernet sauvignon.

Even though most of Utah is dry due to Mormon morals, whet your whistle with a microbrew at Ray's Tavern (p265) and Eddie McStiff's (p274). In Durango, Lady Falconburgh's (p334) boasts the largest selection in the Four Corners region and features beer from the Ska Brewing Company (p334). In Arizona, the Beaver Street Brewery (p161) serves handmade ales. New Mexico has lots of choices, including Embudo Station (p390) and Eske's Brew Pub & Eatery (p399), both of which make great green chile beers. Santa Fe's two entries, the Blue Corn Café & Brewery (p379) and Second Street Brewery (p379), offer quality selections. Keep a sharp lookout for Roswell Alien Amber, affixed with a loony label.

Finding a cocktail in Sin City is as easy as placing a five-dollar bet. But, if you're itching for something a little more cosmopolitan than the casino floor, head to the Ghost Bar (p101).

> In *The Red Chile Bible: Southwestern Classic & Gourmet Recipes,* authors Kathleen Hansel and Audrey Jenkins educate fellow gourmands about how best to utilize the fiery gem so that our palates can live to tell the story.

CELEBRATIONS

Santa Fe offers many upscale food-related events, including the Wine & Chile Fiesta (p374). Smaller New Mexico festivals, no less charming, include the Chile Fiesta (p413), Apple Festival (p428) and Cloudcroft's Cherry Festival (p439).

At Christmastime, though, the really good food comes rolling out. Families get together for big tamale-making parties, *biscochitos* (traditional cookies made with anise) are baked by the hundreds and specially spiced hot chocolate is served.

For centuries, pueblos have really known how to throw a ceremony. Feast days, replete with dances, pole climbs, races and whatnot, are topped off with great food. The biggest events are noted throughout the book; they're mostly in New Mexico.

For more unusual culinary happenings, visit Zion National Park's green Jell-O sculpture competition (p237) or Roswell's New Mexico Dairy Day (p446) with its cheese sculpting competition. In Las Cruces, they make the world's largest enchilada at the Whole Enchilada Fiesta (p434).

> Because they were considered such a hot commodity, chile peppers were once used as currency.

WHERE TO EAT & DRINK

From fine cafés to roadside trailers, you will find delicious regional food – for anywhere from $2 to $100 per person! Breakfast will run $3 to $10, depending on whether you're at a retro diner or a culinary hot spot. Lunch should be $4 to $10ish. You can get a good dinner in a pleasant, though not fancy, restaurant for $15 to $25 per person, without tax, tip or drinks. In posh big-city restaurants and swanky resorts, it's easy to fork out over $50 per person. For the breakdown of our price categories, see p460.

DOS & DON'TS

■ If you're lucky enough to be invited to eat with Native Americans, be sure to inquire about customs in advance – and don't chatter.

■ Don't smoke without asking if it's permissible.

■ Except when ordering room service, the gratuity is not included. Tip at least 15% to 20% at midrange and upper-end eateries.

■ Clear your own tray in fast-food restaurants.

Except deep in the desert or the mountains, you're never far from food. In cities and on highways, some fast-food restaurants are open 24 hours a day. For general restaurant opening and closing hours, see p456. There are variations on this theme, though. Some restaurants serve breakfast all day. Many places are open for lunch *and* dinner, continuing to serve meals through the afternoon. Some restaurants serve a lighter, less formal menu until midnight or 1am. Some restaurants close on Mondays. Utah restaurants are generally closed on the Lord's Day (that'd be Sunday).

If you're looking for quality regional grub, ask the locals where they're chowing down. Places that gussy themselves up are unlikely to be your best bets for authentic cuisine.

VEGETARIANS & VEGANS

Most metro area eateries offer at least one veggie dish, although few are devoted solely to meatless menus. These days, fortunately, almost every larger town has a natural food grocer. In fact, they're popping up throughout the Southwest faster than weeds in a compost pile. That said, you may go wanting in smaller hinterland towns, where beef still rules. In that case, your best bet is to assemble a picnic from the local grocery store.

'Veggie-heads' will be happiest in New Mexico and Arizona; go nuts (or more specifically, go piñon.) Thanks to the area's long-standing appeal to hippie-types, vegetarians and vegans will have no problem finding something delicious on most menus, even at drive-thrus and tiny dives. There's one potential pitfall, though: traditional Southwestern cuisine uses lard in beans, tamales, *sopaipillas* (deep-fried puff pastry) and flour (but not corn) tortillas, among other things. Be sure to ask – often, even the most authentic places have a pot of pintos simmering for vegetarians.

EATING WITH KIDS

All but the most upscale restaurants are kid-friendly, and generally have children's menus, high chairs and large booths for big families. Crayons or other toys are also sometimes available to amuse tots. Most waitstaff know to automatically omit the chile for younger kids, but tweens and teens should specifically ask for it on the side, if necessary.

Although Las Vegas (p95) has returned to its original mojo as a destination for gamblers and swingers – and is no Disney in the Desert – plenty of Sin City restaurants are still great for kids. Utah venues are invariably family-friendly.

If the kids are feeling cantankerous, avoid the crowds by eating between 2pm and 5pm (if the restaurant is open), just to give yourself a little more room. For more on traveling with kids, see p456.

The Santa Fe School of Cooking Cookbook, by Susan Curtis, shares recipes from the Southwest's seminal cooking school.

HABITS & CUSTOMS

Folks in the Southwest observe standard US habits, etiquette and customs regarding eating and serving food. Invariably, American-sized portions are 'super-sized.' If you're invited to dinner in someone's home, bring a gift (wine or chocolates) and don't overstay your welcome. Families eat dinner earlier than couples.

EAT YOUR WORDS

You'll probably encounter some different cuisine and preparations in the Southwest than you're accustomed to. Take a gander at this list so that you don't end up eating something meaty or deep-fried unless you want to.

From growing to roasting, www.chili-pepper-plants .com contains everything you need to know about how to cool it down and spice it up.

Main Dishes

Burrito (or burro) A soft flour tortilla folded around a choice of chicken, beef, chile, bean or cheese filling. A breakfast burrito is stuffed with scrambled eggs, potatoes and ham.

Carne adobada Pork chunks marinated in a spicy chile and herb sauce, then baked.

Carne seca Beef that has been dried in the sun before cooking.

Chile relleno Chile stuffed with cheese and deep-fried in a light batter.

Chimichanga A burrito that is deep-fried to make the tortilla crisp.

Enchilada A rolled corn tortilla stuffed with a choice of sour cream and cheese, beans, beef or chicken, and smothered with a red (or green) chile sauce and melted cheese.

Fajitas Marinated beef or chicken strips grilled with onions and bell peppers, and served with tortillas, salsa, beans and guacamole.

Flauta Similar to a burrito but smaller and tightly rolled rather than folded, and then fried.

Huevos rancheros Fried eggs on a soft tortilla, covered with chile sauce and melted cheese, and served with beans.

Mole A mildly spicy, dark sauce of chiles flavored with chocolate, usually served with chicken.

Posole A corn stew, which may be spicy and have meat.

Refried beans A thick paste of mashed, cooked pinto beans fried with lard.

Taco A crispy, fried tortilla, folded in half and stuffed with a combination of beans, ground beef, chiles, onions, tomatoes, lettuce, grated cheese and guacamole.

Tamale Slightly sweet corn dough (masa) stuffed with a choice of pork, beef, chicken, chile or olives (or nothing) and wrapped in a corn husk before being steamed.

Tortilla A pancake made of unleavened wheat or corn flour. They stay soft when baked, become crisp when fried, and form the basis of most Mexican dishes. Small pieces, deep-fried, become the crispy tortilla chips served with salsa as an appetizer in many Mexican restaurants.

Tostada A flat (ie, open-faced) taco.

Snacks & Dessert

Guacamole Mashed avocado seasoned with lime juice and cilantro, and optionally spiced with chopped chiles and other condiments.

Nachos Tortilla chips covered with melted cheese and other toppings.

Salsa A cold dip or sauce of chopped chiles, pureed tomatoes, onions and other herbs and spices.

Sopaipilla Deep-fried puff pastry served with honey as a dessert, or, in New Mexico, plain as an accompaniment to the main course.

Las Vegas

Fabulous Las Vegas is a walking contradiction. Where else can you traverse the globe in an afternoon? Take a gondola ride through Venice, stare at ancient Egypt's pyramids from atop of the Eiffel Tower?

In Sin City, fate is decided by the spin of a roulette wheel. Here, the poor feel rich and the rich lose thousands. In this high-octane desert oasis, all that glitters is gold. Glamour's sweet stench is thicker than the blue-haired grandmother's cigarette smoke. Feeding nickels into the slot machine, she's slugging gin-and-tonics in knee-high boots and a bosom-bearing top that seems so wrong yet so right. Seedy but decadent, Vegas is a puzzling paradox. Glitzy casinos boast art collections rivaling New York and celebrity-laden bars rivaling LA. At a strip joint the perky-breasted gal dancing on the pole tells you the money's so good she commutes from the West Coast. It's nearing dawn outside, but you wouldn't know it because the city is lit brighter than your neighbor's Christmas extravaganza on steroids.

Time is irrelevant here. There are no clocks, just never-ending buffets and ever-flowing drinks. There's a bum bumming cigarettes from a Gucci-clad starlet. A bible-toting Elvis and a giddy couple that just pledged eternity in the Little White Wedding Chapel. There's a drunken guy on his last fling, and another hawking his first hip-hop album. Give Vegas a day, and whatever your fantasy, it gives you the world.

HIGHLIGHTS

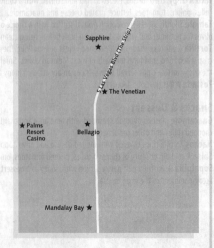

Most Spectacular Casino
The Bellagio (p80) is excessive, classy and stylish all at once.

Hottest Place to be Seen
The bars inside the Palms Resort Casino (p84) are celeb favs, exuding swank and skin.

Coolest Pool
The complex at Mandalay Bay (p75) includes a clothing-optional beach club and summer surfing competitions.

Best Place to be Sinful
Even if it ain't your style, cut loose and visit a world-famous strip club such as Sapphire (p105). It's a ritualistic Vegas must.

Best Place to Propose
Propose on the canals of Venice, on a romantic gondola ride for two at the Venetian (p82).

| POPULATION: 517,000 | AREA: 58 SQ MILES | www.lasvegas24hours.com |

HISTORY

What history, you ask. Looking around, you are to be forgiven. Unlike the rest of the ruin-laden Southwest, traces of early history are scarce in this town.

Contrary to Hollywood legend there was much more at the dusty crossroads than a gambling parlor and some tumbleweeds the day mobster Ben 'Bugsy' Siegel rolled in and erected a glamorous, tropical-themed casino under the searing sun.

Hearty Uto Aztecan–speaking Paiute people inhabited the Las Vegas Valley for a millennium before trappers and traders blazed the Spanish Trail. The completion of a railroad linking Salt Lake City to Los Angeles in 1902 speared Las Vegas into the modern era. The legalization of gambling in 1931 carried Vegas through the Great Depression, when bookmakers flocked to the newly minted Sin City. Lax divorce requirements, quickie weddings, legal prostitution and championship boxing bouts proved recession-proof bets for local boosters. New Deal dollars kept flowing into Southern Nevada's coffers right through WWII.

WWII brought a huge air-force base and big aerospace bucks, plus a paved highway to LA. Soon after, the Cold War justified the Nevada Test Site. It proved to be the textbook case of 'any publicity is good publicity': monthly above-ground atomic blasts shattered casino windows Downtown, while the city's official Miss Mushroom Cloud mascot promoted atomic everything in tourism campaigns.

A building spree sparked by the Flamingo in 1946 led to mob-backed tycoons upping the glitz ante at every turn. Big-name entertainers such as Frank Sinatra, Liberace and Sammy Davis Jr arrived on stage at the same time as topless French showgirls.

The high-profile purchase of the Desert Inn in 1966 by eccentric billionaire Howard Hughes gave the gambling industry a much-needed patina of legitimacy. Spearheaded by Hughes' spending spree, corporate ownership of casinos blossomed and publicly traded companies bankrolled another building bonanza in the late 1960s and early '70s. The debut of the MGM Grand in 1993 signaled the dawn of the era of the corporate 'megaresort.'

An oasis in the middle of a final frontier, Sin City continues to exist chiefly to satisfy the needs and desires of visitors. Hosting over 35 million visitors a year, Las Vegas is the engine of North America's fastest growing metropolitan area and the last liberty port of opportunity for countless people seeking their fortune.

ORIENTATION

Two interstate highways (I-15 and US Hwy 95) bisect the town. If it's your first visit, and you're driving, arrive at night so you can pull over before reaching city limits and admire the lights from afar. Then, take the first exit and cruise the length of The Strip.

In a very real sense, there are two Las Vegases. Downtown sits at the north end of the tourist corridor, with Glitter Gulch and the Fremont Street Experience streaking down its middle. The desolate area along Las Vegas Blvd (aka The Strip) links Downtown with the Upper Strip, which begins at the Stratosphere. Treasure Island and the Venetian mark the start of the Lower Strip, which runs south past Mandalay Bay to the airport.

Few short-term visitors venture beyond The Strip, where some of the best bars, live music and ethnic food await. The less glitzy Eastside and Westside (of The Strip) are locals' domains, while the area around the University of Nevada (UNLV) campus attracts more carpetbaggers.

The airport is just south of The Strip (see p109 for more information).

Maps are widely sold at hotels, gas stations and newsstands. Rand McNally's *Las Vegas* is very easy to use and contains several fold-out maps.

INFORMATION

Bookstores

Borders Book Shop (Map pp76–8; ☎ 702-258-0999; 2323 S Decatur Blvd) West of The Strip.
Waldenbooks (Map pp76–8; ☎ 702-733-1049; 3200 S Las Vegas Blvd) Inside the Fashion Show Mall.

Emergency

Police (non-emergency) (☎ 311 or 702-229-3111)
Gamblers Anonymous (☎ 702-385-7732)
Rape Crisis Hotline (☎ 702-366-1640)

Internet Access

Most hotels in Vegas have business centers that will charge you an arm and a leg for 24/7

Internet access. The cafés listed here are your best options if you don't have your own computer.

Cyber Stop (Map pp76-8; ☎ 702-736-4782; Hawaiian Marketplace, Polo Towers Plaza, 3743 S Las Vegas Blvd; per hr $12; ☽ 7am-2:30am)

Kinkos Downtown (Map p87; ☎ 702-383-7022; 830 S 4th St; per min 20¢; ☽ 7am-10pm Mon-Fri); The Strip (Map pp76-8; ☎ 702-951-2400; Tropicana, 395 Hughes Center Dr; per min 20¢; ☽ 24hr) Wi-fi (wireless Internet) hotspots.

Internet Resources

The Lonely Planet website (www.lonelyplanet.com) has Sin City links and details. Other good sites:

Vegas.com www.vegas.com
Las Vegas.com www.lasvegas.com
Las Vegas' official site www.ci.las-vegas.nv.us
Las Vegas Convention & Visitors Authority www.lasvegas24hours.com

Media

The conservative daily *Las Vegas-Review-Journal* (www.lvrj.com) is Nevada's largest. On Friday it publishes the *Neon* entertainment guide. The *Las Vegas Sun* (www.lasvegassun.com) is the afternoon rag. There are several free tabloid weeklies including *CityLife* (www.lasvegascitylife.com) and *Las Vegas Weekly* (www.lasvegasweekly.com).

Medical Services

Sunrise Hospital & Medical Center (Map pp76-8; ☎ 702-731-8000, emergency ☎ 702-731-8080; 3186 Maryland Pkwy) Twenty-four-hour emergency facilities.

University Medical Center of Southern Nevada (Map p87; ☎ 702-383-2000, emergency 702-383-2661; 1800 W Charleston Blvd) Twenty-four-hour emergency facilities.

CVS (Map pp76-8; ☎ 702-262-9028; 3758 S Las Vegas Blvd) Twenty-four-hour pharmacy.

Walgreens (☎ 702-739-9638; 3765 S Las Vegas Blvd) Twenty-four-hour pharmacy.

Money

Every hotel-casino, bank and most convenience stores have ATMs. Fees imposed by casinos to exchange foreign currency tend to be higher than banks but a bit lower than exchange bureaus.

American Express (Map pp76-8; ☎ 702-739-8474; Fashion Show Mall, 3200 S Las Vegas Blvd) Changes currencies at competitive rates.

Post

Post office (Map pp76-8; ☎ 702-735-8519; 3100 S Industrial Rd) Just west of The Strip.

Time Zone

Nevada is on Pacific Standard Time, which means Las Vegas is one hour behind Utah, New Mexico and Arizona (except from late spring to early fall, when Nevada and Arizona are in sync).

Tourist Information

Las Vegas Convention & Visitors Authority Visitor Information Center (Map pp76-8; ☎ 702-892-0711, 877-847-4858; www.lasvegas24hours.com; 3150 Paradise Rd; ☽ 8am-5pm) The city's official tourist office.

Las Vegas Convention & Visitors Authority hotline (LVCVA; ☎ 702-892-7575) Has helpful operators, and recorded entertainment and convention schedules.

DANGERS & ANNOYANCES

The major tourist areas are safe. However Las Vegas Blvd between Downtown and The Strip gets shabby and Fremont St east of Downtown is definitely unsavory – it's lined with great old neon signs but also loads of fleabag motels. If you're staying at USA Hostels Las Vegas (p95), which is east of Downtown, avoid walking alone at night.

On The Strip, beware of pickpockets in crowds and on buses. Police and private security officers are out in force and surveillance cameras are omnipresent. In-room safes are provided by most hotels.

Beware of businesses along The Strip advertising themselves as 'Official Tourist Bureaus.' They are actually low-rent agencies pushing overpriced helicopter and Grand Canyon tours.

SIGHTS & ACTIVITIES

The action in Vegas tends to center on the casinos, but if you're sick of the clinking of slots there are thrill rides and amusements guaranteed to get your adrenalin pumping.

The Strip & Around

As the cliché goes, The Strip is constantly reinventing itself. Every megaresort is an attraction, with plenty on offer besides gambling. This newer, brighter, shinier center of gravity is an adult Disneyland, dealing nonstop excitement. With each new development it becomes more spectacular (and more of a spectacle).

LAS VEGAS IN...

If you haven't visited Vegas recently, you can't claim to know America's fastest-growing metropolis. Most new must-sees front The Strip, but when you grow weary of all the glitz, it's worth checking out Downtown's vintage vibe.

One Day

Cruise The Strip, then hit the megaresorts for a taste of casino action. Ride the monorail between properties, with stopovers for noshing and shopping. After a gourmet dinner, catch a late **Cirque du Soleil show** (p103) then party until dawn.

Two Days

On your second day, wake up on The Strip with a spot of **brunch** (p96). Relax by the **pool** (p85) or luxuriate at a **spa** (p81) – it's going to be another late night. Rent a **convertible** (p110) and roll east to **Hoover Dam** (p191). After a catnap, dine with a celebrity chef then sup a nightcap at an **ultralounge** (p101) with a view.

Three Days

Follow the One Day and Two Days itineraries above, then sleep in and detour Downtown to see where it all began. Sidle up to a buffet at a classy carpet joint. Stroll Fremont St after sunset to experience the **Experience** (p86) and check out the illuminating **Neon Museum** (p88). After sunset, revisit The Strip to let it ride one last time and visit a **strip club** (p105) to put the *sin* back in sinful.

Unless otherwise noted, all megaresorts are open 24 hours a day, seven days a week, 365 days per year (many places in Vegas don't even have locks on their front doors!), don't charge admission, offer free valet (tip $2) and self-service parking, are on CAT's 301/302 bus lines and are wheelchair accessible.

Megaresorts are listed south to north, with off-Strip and noncasino sights at the end.

MANDALAY BAY

The best thing about **'M-Bay'** (Map pp76-8; ☎ 720-632-7777, 877-632-7800; www.mandalaybay.com; 3950 S Las Vegas Blvd) is that it doesn't try to be any particular fantasy. There's a tropical theme, but it's not a destination. You aren't forced through the casino to see the fantastic lobby (think high ceilings, marble and a giant aquarium). Instead the place feels like a classy resort, a pleasant escape from The Strip's pseudo-Parises and Egypts.

Standouts among M-Bay's attractions include the multilevel **Shark Reef** (☎ 702-632-7000, 877-632-7000; adult/child $15/10; ⏰ 10am-11pm), an aquarium complex home to thousands of submarine beasties and a shallow pool where you can pet pint-sized sharks. Other rare and endangered toothy reptiles are on display in the fun, if overpriced, compound. Rather save your money for the slots? Check out the two free and very impressive aquari-

ums, one near the registration desk and the other at the Coral Reef Lounge. Gamblers will appreciate the vast and classy casino, and race and sports book.

LUXOR

Named after Egypt's splendid ancient city, the landmark **Luxor** (Map pp76-8; ☎ 702-262-4000, 888-777-0188; www.luxor.com; 3900 S Las Vegas Blvd) just might be the most impressive resort on The Strip. The resort's designers chose a theme that easily could have ended up a pyramid of gaudiness, but instead resulted in an elegant Egyptian shrine. The pyramid houses the world's largest atrium, has 120,000 sq ft of smartly arranged gaming areas and hosts a diverse array of attractions.

The 30-story pyramid, cloaked in black glass from base to apex, is Luxor's focus. The atrium is so voluminous it could accommodate nine 747 jetliners and still have room for 50 Cessnas. At its apex a 40-billion-candle-power beacon – the world's most powerful – sends a shaft of blue and white light 10 miles into space that's visible by astronauts.

A 10-story-high crouching sphinx and a sandstone obelisk etched with hieroglyphics guard the pyramid. The interior is tastefully decorated with enormous Egyptian statues

(Continued on page 79)

Map features and labels:

Grid references (top): F1, F2, F3, F4, E1, E2, E3, E4, D1, D2, D3, D4, C1, C2, C3, C4, B1, B2, B3, B4, A1, A2, A3, A4

12th St
Cochran St
16th St
Chapman Dr
Phillips Ave
Exley Ave
E Oakey Blvd
Pardee Pl
Phillips Ave
Karen Ave
Del Mar Ave
La Jolla Ave
Izabela Ave
Vegas Valley Dr
Palora Ave
Raindance Way
Silver Mesa Way
E Desert Inn Rd
To Sunrise Hospital & Medical Center (0.3mi)
Commanche Ave
E Twain Ave
Boulevard Mall

To Las Vegas Motor Speedway (1mi); KOA (4mi)
Topanga St

Vegas Village Shopping Center
7

State St
Kendale St
Sherwood St
Van Patten St
Lynnwood St

Las Vegas Country Club

Rome St
Brussels St
Athens St
Cambridge St
Dumont Blvd
Sierra Vista Dr
Swenson St
Edison Cir
Elm Dr

Griffith Ave
E Oakey Blvd
Ellen Way
Barbara Way
8th St
St Louis Ave
Van Patten Dr
Beverly Way

56
S Las Vegas Blvd

Paradise Rd
Santa Clara Dr
47
E Sahara Ave
Karen Ave
Las Vegas Hilton
20
Las Vegas Convention Center
E Desert Inn Rd
Paradise Rd
3

W Wyoming Ave
New York Ave
Chicago Ave
Stratosphere
31
65
Industrial Rd

Sahara
29
Wet 'n' Wild Water Park
Riviera Blvd
Mel Ave
Convention Center Dr
Kishner Dr
46
Wynn Golf and Country Club
Country Club Ln

Baltimore Ave
Cleveland Ave
Cincinnati Ave
62
Fun Dr

604
Riviera
49
Riviera

Circus Circus Dr
Circus Circus
12
4
Westward Ho
Stardust
30
Convention Center Dr
Stardust Rd
35
Wynn Las Vegas
Burbank Ave
Sands Ave

S Las Vegas Blvd (The Strip)
37

15

Silver Ave
W Oakley Blvd
S Rancho Dr
Western St

See Downtown Las Vegas Map (p87)

To Bare Essentials (0.2mi); Borders Book Shop (1mi)

Desert Inn Road Super Arterial
58

Industrial Rd
Highland Dr
Westwood Dr
Rancho Dr

13
Fashion Show Dr
Fashion Show Mall
63
Frontier
Spring Mountain Rd
Treasure Island
33
The Venetian

59

Glinavy Ave
W Sahara Ave
Alcoa Ave
Merritt Ave
Kings Ave
Richfield Blvd
Winnington Way
Rigel Ave
Aldebaran Ave

Meade Ave
Sheridan St
Sirius Ave
Polaris Ave
Procyon Ave
Spring Mountain Rd
57
W Twain Ave
Schiff Dr
55

Industrial Rd

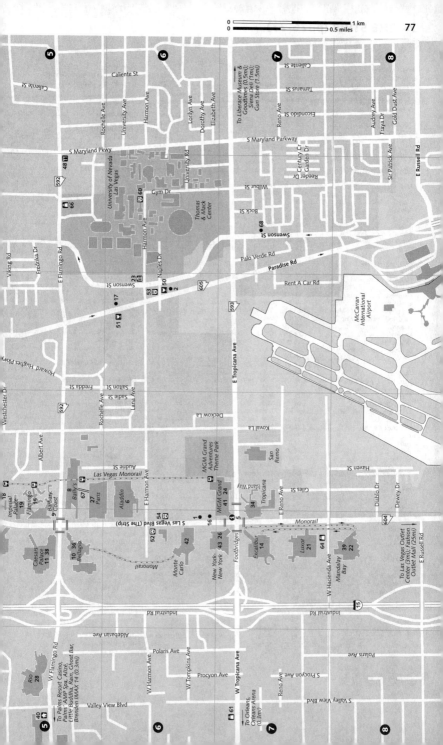

0 _____ 1 km
0 _____ 0.5 miles

5

Caliente St

Caliente St

Rochelle Ave

University Ave

Harmon Ave

Lorilyn Ave

Dorothy Ave

Elizabeth Ave

S Maryland Pkwy

48

592

66

University of Nevada Las Vegas

University Rd

Gym Dr

Harmon Ave

60

Naples Dr

Thomas & Mack Center

E Flamingo Rd

Viking Rd

Fredrika Dr

Swenson St

592

51

17

53 50

2

605

23

6

To Liberace Museum & Goodtimes (0.5mi); Siena Deli (1mi); Gun Store (1.5mi)

S Maryland Parkway

Reno Ave

Escondido St

Century Cr Garden Dr

Reeder Dr

Wilbur St

Bock St

Palo Verde Rd

Swenson St

68

Paradise Rd

Rent A Car Rd

593

7

Caliente St

Tamarus St

Audrey Ave

Flaya Dr

Gold Dust Ave

Sir Patrick Ave

E Russell Rd

8

McCarran International Airport

Howard Hughes Pkwy

Westchester Dr

592

Albert Ave

Fredda St

Salton St

Sadie St

Rochelle Ave

Lana Ave

E Tropicana Ave

Deckow La

Koval La

Island Way

San Remo

Giles St

Haven St

Diablo Dr

Dewey Dr

604

To Las Vegas Outlet Center (3mi); Fashion Outlet Mall (25mi)

E Russell Rd

Las Vegas Monorail

Audrie St

MGM Grand Adventures Theme Park

18

15

Imperial Palace

Flamingo

Birthday Coast

8

Bally's

27 Paris

Aladdin

6

E Harmon Ave

9

MGM Grand

41 24

Tropicana

34

E Reno Ave

5

Caesars Palace

11 38

10 36

Bellagio

S Las Vegas Blvd (The Strip)

54

52

1

16

Footbridges

5

Monorail

W Hacienda Ave

Luxor

21

64

Mandalay Bay

39

22

Monte Carlo

42

New York-New York

43 26

Excalibur

14

Monorail

Industrial Rd

Industrial Rd

15

Rio

28

40

5

W Flamingo Rd

To Palms Resort Casino, Palms' AMP Spa, Alizé, Little Buddha, Rain, Ghost Bar, Brenden IMAX 14 (0.3mi)

Aldebaran Ave

W Harmon Ave

Polaris Ave

Procyon Ave

Valley View Blvd

6

W Tropicana Ave

S Procyon Ave

Reno Ave

Polaris Ave

S Valley View Blvd

7

61

To Orleans, Orleans Arena (0.3mi)

8

(Continued from page 75)

of guards, lions and rams; sandstone walls adorned with hieroglyphic-inscribed tapestries and grand columns; a stunning replica of the great Temple of Ramses II and a pharaoh's treasure of polished marble.

The **King Tut Museum** (☎ 702-262-4000; admission $5; ☽ 9am-midnight) features exquisite reproductions of ancient artifacts that English archaeologist Howard Carter discovered on his apocryphal descent into the fabled tomb of an obscure Egyptian dynasty. The artifacts are explained during a 15-minute self-guided audio tour.

EXCALIBUR

Faux drawbridges and Arthurian legends aside, the caricature castle known as **Excalibur** (Map pp76-8; ☎ 702-597-7777, 877-750-5464; www .excalibur.com; 3850 S Las Vegas Blvd) epitomizes gaudy Vegas. In a moat near the entrance, a fire-breathing dragon does mock battle with Merlin on the hour. The dinner show, *Tournament of Kings*, is more demolition derby with hooves than flashy Vegas production.

TROPICANA

Built in 1957, the ˋTrop´ (Map pp76-8; ☎ 702-739-2222, 888-826-8767; www.tropicanalv.com; 3801 S Las Vegas Blvd) has had nearly half a century to lose its luster, but thanks to a few lifts and tucks, it's looking better than ever. There's a festive Caribbean village, exotic birds in the Wildlife Walk and a Polynesian longhouse that hosts Hawaiian musicians.

MGM GRAND

With over 5000 rooms, the $1 billion **MGM** (Map pp76-8; ☎ 702-891-1111, 877-880-0880; www .mgmgrand.com; 3799 S Las Vegas Blvd) retains the 'world's largest hotel' title, although there's mounting competition from the Genting Highlands resort complex in Kuala Lumpur. Despite its size, the shimmering emerald-green 'City of Entertainment' does a decent job of making its attractions seem intimate.

MGM (owned by movie mogul Metro Goldwyn Mayer) has accomplished this feat by co-opting themes from Hollywood movies. The most obvious example is the resort's nightclub, **Studio 54** (p103). The adjacent casino consists of one gigantic circular room with an ornate domed ceiling and replicated 1930s glamour replete with

a bandstand featuring live jazz and swing nightly. At 171,500 sq ft, MGM Grand's gaming area is equal in size to four football fields and offers a whopping selection of slots and the full spectrum of table games, plus the requisite race and sports book, a poker room and a keno lounge.

Out front, it's hard to miss the USA's largest bronze statue, a 100,000lb lion that's 45ft tall, perched atop a 25ft pedestal and ringed by lush landscaping, fountains and Atlas-themed statues. Other attractions include the **lion habitat** (see p88), two shopping concourses and the usual assortment of grand entertainment and eating establishments. There's so much to do here that many guests choose not to spend their time anywhere else.

NEW YORK-NEW YORK

Give me your tired, huddled (over a Wheel of Fortune slot machine) masses. Opened in 1997, the $485 million **New York-New York** (Map pp76-8; ☎ 702-740-6969, 888-693-6763; www .nynyhotelcasino.com; 3790 S Las Vegas Blvd) is a min-imegapolis featuring scaled-down replicas of the Empire State Building (47 stories or 529ft), the Statue of Liberty (ringed by a 9/11 memorial), a mini version of the Brooklyn Bridge, a Coney Island–style roller coaster called the Manhattan Express, and renditions of the Chrysler, AT&T and CBS buildings. Manhattan-a-phobes beware: it really can feel like Central Park on a sunny Sunday afternoon.

The attention to detail is remarkable, down to the whiffs of steam rising from faux manhole covers near the Chrysler elevator. This Disneyfied version of the Big Apple can get even more crowded than the real deal: around 200,000 pedestrians stride NYC's Brooklyn Bridge each year, but more than five million traverse Vegas' version.

CHUMP CHANGE

When the MGM opened in December 1993, $3.5 million in quarters were needed for its slot machines and to provide change. Thirty-nine armored cars were hired to transport the 14 million coins, which were delivered in 3600 sacks. Each sack weighed 60lb.

The highlight of the **Manhattan Express** (admission $12.50, re-ride $6; ⏰ 10am-midnight) is a heartline twist-and-dive maneuver, producing a sensation similar to the one felt by a pilot during a barrel roll in a fighter plane. The rest of the four-minute ride includes lots of stomach-dropping dipsy-dos, high-banked turns, a 540° spiral and good Strip views. Note that your head and shoulders may take a beating. Hold on tight and secure loose valuables in the lockers out front.

The crowded casino attracts a mélange of (mostly middle American) humanity. Slews of slots and gaming tables are set against a rich backdrop of famous landmarks. Down with off-track betting? The race and sports book offers electronic satellite wagering. Restaurants and retail shops hide behind colorful facades from Park Avenue, Greenwich Village and Times Square storefronts. Don't miss the ornate casino-level Rockefeller restrooms, they'll take you back in time and make you feel like royalty. The kids will dig the Coney Island Emporium arcade on the 2nd level.

ALADDIN

Retooled to target the Asian and European jet set, the $1.4 billion **Aladdin** (Map pp76-8; ☎ 702-785-5555, 877-333-9474; www.aladdincasino .com; 3667 S Las Vegas Blvd) reopened in 2000 after the 1950s original was dramatically imploded. Inside the appealing Moroccan facade are a multilevel casino, several restaurants, an impressive shopping arcade and a smart club catering to super high rollers.

PARIS

Napoleon once said, 'Secrets travel fast in Paris.' The same can be said for Las Vegas, where **Paris** (Map pp76-8; ☎ 702-946-7000, 877-796-2096; www.parislv.com; 3655 S Las Vegas Blvd), which opened in 1999, was one secret that made the rounds in record time. This $785 million Gallic caricature evokes the gaiety of the City of Light – right down to wandering minstrels playing accordion music. The 34-story replica of the Hotel de Ville strives to capture the essence of the grand dame by re-creating her landmarks. Fine likenesses of the Opéra, the Arc de Triomphe, Champs-Élysées, Parc Monceau and even the river Seine frame the property.

Just like in the French capital, the signature attraction is the **Eiffel Tower** (☎ 888-266-5687; adult/child $9/7; ⏰ 10am-1am). Ascend in a glass elevator to the observation deck for panoramic views overlooking The Strip. How authentic is the half-scale tower? Gustave Eiffel's original drawings were consulted, but the 50-story replica is welded rather than riveted together. It's also fireproof and engineered to withstand a major earthquake.

Surrounded by street scenes from the Seine's Left and Right Banks, the bustling 85,000-sq-ft, high-ceilinged casino is home to 100 games tables, a couple of thousand slot machines and a popular sports bar, and race and sports book. Don't miss the USA's only authentic French roulette wheel in the high-limit area (it has no '00'). Gourmet fare is dished up at a dozen French restaurants while live French-style entertainment is featured in the lounges.

BALLY'S

The only real theme at **Bally's** (Map pp76-8; ☎ 702-739-4111, 800-634-3434; www.ballyslv.com; 3645 S Las Vegas Blvd), one of The Strip's most cheerful megaresorts, is 'big.' There's a popular sports book and football field–sized casino and the epic **Sterling Sunday Brunch** (p95) is worth every dime, with top-shelf champagne and cracked crab legs galore. A walkway links Bally's with Paris.

BELLAGIO

Inspired by the beauty of the lakeside Italian village, the $1.6 billion **Bellagio** (Map pp76-8; ☎ 702-693-7111; www.bellagio.com; 3600 S Las Vegas Blvd) is Vegas' original opulent, if parvenu, pleasure palazzo. Built by Steve Wynn on the site of the legendary Dunes, its Tuscan architecture and eight-acre artificial lake are, in a word, elegant. Visitors strolling The Strip will be dazzled by the choreographed show of dancing fountains that spring from the blue-green waters every 15 minutes. Beyond the glass and metal porte-cochere, inside the 36-floor resort, are a stable of world-class gourmet restaurants, a swish shopping concourse, a European-style casino and the **Bellagio Gallery of Fine Art** (☎ 702-693-7871; admission $15; ⏰ 9am-9pm), which showcases temporary exhibits by world-class artists, including Monet.

The highlight of the hotel's stunning lobby is the 18ft ceiling, which is adorned with a backlit glass sculpture composed of

SPLENDID SPAS

There are some spas in Vegas just perfect for pampering. Day-use fees are $20 to $35; treatments run from $100 to $175 per hour. Some spas are reserved for hotel guests only.

- **Spa Bellagio** (Map pp76–8; ☎ 702-693-7472; Bellagio, 3600 S Las Vegas Blvd; ☼ 6am-8pm) The pinnacle of Euro-style pampering, this luxurious spa was recently expanded. It's perfect for groups of friends and offers services like Ashiatsu oriental bar therapy and Indian Head and Thai Yoga massages.

- **Canyon Ranch SpaClub** (Map pp76–8; ☎ 702-414-3600; Venetian, 3355 Las Vegas Blvd; ☼ 5:30am-10pm) Popular with couples for side-by-side treatments, this giant place offers more than 100 different activities and even features a three-story rock-climbing wall. Popular treatments include Abhyanga massage, mango sugar glo body scrubs and a soak in the Royal King's Bath, a custom made bronze tub.

- **Palms' AMP Spa** (Map pp76–8; ☎ 702-947-7777; Palms, 4321 W Flamingo Rd; ☼ 6am-8pm) Ultrasoft 'cashwear' robes, stone massage and a celebrity stylist – it's trendy to the max (the glam factor is super high here) and you can relax by the lushly landscaped pool with its signature lavender floor before enjoying a couple's massage or heading to the lighted tropical cabanas.

- **Oasis Spa** (Map pp76–8; ☎ 800-258-9038; Luxor, 3900 S Las Vegas Blvd; closed 11:30pm Tue-6am Wed) Receive a pampering fit for a queen, in this case ancient Egypt's Nefertiti. The theme is Egyptian, of course, and the place never closes (well except for Tuesday nights). All the usual treatments are on offer, but the reason to come is because you can, at any hour!

2000 hand-blown flowers in vibrant colors. Real flowers, cultivated in a gigantic on-site greenhouse, brighten countless vases throughout the property. Adjacent to the lobby, the **Conservatory and Botanical Gardens** host dazzling seasonal floral arrangements, which are installed by crane through the soaring 50ft ceiling.

In the courtyard the distinctive swimming pool area is surrounded by private cabanas and accented by artfully formed citrus and parterre gardens. The Mediterranean villa setting makes for a pleasant stroll, but use of the facilities by nonguests is limited. In 2005, a new luxury Spa Tower and expanded spa facilities will be the lavish icing atop the five-diamond cake. Baby strollers and unaccompanied children under 18 are not allowed at the Bellagio.

CAESARS PALACE

Vegas' first fully realized megaresort upped the luxury ante when it debuted in 1966. Thanks to ongoing megabucks renovations, **Caesars** (Map pp76–8; ☎ 702-731-7110, 877-427-7243; www.caesarspalace.com; 3570 S Las Vegas Blvd) is redefining its swanky self and is as impressive and quintessentially Vegas as ever.

The Greco-Roman fantasyland captured the world's attention with its full-size marble reproductions of classical statuary (including a not-to-be-missed 4-ton Brahma shrine near the front entrance), its Strip-side row of towering fountains and its cocktail waitresses costumed as goddesses. Bar girls continue to roam the gaming areas in skimpy togas, and the fountains are still out front – the same ones daredevil Evil Knievel made famous when he jumped over them on a motorcycle on December 31, 1967.

Two central casinos contain a hundred card tables and a couple thousand slots that will accept up to $500 chips. The state-of-the-art race and sports book has 90 video screens. Other attractions include a movie theater with a dome-shaped screen and the upscale **Forum Shops** (p107) concourse featuring an impressive aquarium and animatronic fountain shows, worthy of a wander even if you can't afford to purchase the designer purses and swanky shoes.

BARBARY COAST

Lavish Tiffany-styled stained glass, stately chandeliers and polished dark wood dominate **Barbary Coast** (Map pp76–8; ☎ 702-737-7111, 888-227-2279; www.barbarycoastcasino.com; 3595 S Las Vegas Blvd), a Victorian gem – only Main Street Station (p86) does turn-of-the-20th-century better. Don't miss the showpiece *Garden of Earthly Delights* stained-glass mural on the casino's west wall. At night a hip party-hearty crowd flocks in for late-night lounge acts and swanky dancing.

FLAMINGO

Back in 1946, the **Flamingo** (Map pp76-8; ☎ 702-733-3111, 800-732-2111; www.flamingolv.com; 3555 S Las Vegas Blvd) was the talk of the town. Today, it isn't quite what it was back when its janitorial staff wore tuxedos, but its magnificent gardens, 15 acres of pools, waterfalls and waterways are still a sight to behold. Stop by the hotel's bars and restaurants during happy hour (4pm to 7pm) to score some deals.

IMPERIAL PALACE

Though the pagoda facade is a bit hokey, the Oriental theme at the popular low-limit **Imperial Palace** (Map pp76-8; ☎ 702-731-3311, 800-634-6441; www.imperialpalace.com; 3535 S Las Vegas Blvd) is tastefully done. Plus, dealers in the casino do celebrity impersonations. Car buffs could easily pass an entire day viewing one of the world's largest privately owned **Auto Collections** (☎ 702-731-3311; www.autocollections .com; admission $7, free coupons on website; ⏰ 9:30am-9:30pm), located on the 5th floor. Among the wonderful vehicles on hand (all of which are for sale): Steve McQueen's 1923 Indian Big Chief; Tom Jones' 1981 Mercedes Benz 500 SEL sedan and more Rolls Royces than you can toss a chauffeur at.

HARRAH'S

Everywhere you look there's something playfully suggestive of Carnival or Mardi Gras at **Harrah's** (Map pp76-8; ☎ 702-369-5000, 800-392-9002; www.harrahs.com; 3475 S Las Vegas Blvd). Check out the enormous backlit mural over the main entrance that features Sin City's entertainment legends, then step inside one of the largest and brightest casinos in town. It's usually packed, as is the popular lounge.

VENETIAN

Impresario Sheldon Adelson broke ground on his replica of La Serenissima (Most Serene Republic) – reputed to be the home of the world's first casino – shortly after the controversial and dramatic implosion of the 44-year-old Sands in 1996.

His $1.5 billion, 35-story facsimile of a doge's **palace** (Map pp76-8; ☎ 702-414-1000; www .venetian.com; 3355 S Las Vegas Blvd; gondola rides adult/ child/private from $12.50/5/50), inspired by the splendor of Italy's most romantic city, features roaming mimes and minstrels in period costume, hand-painted ceiling frescoes and full-scale reproductions of Venetian landmarks. Flowing canals, vibrant piazzas and welcoming stone walkways capture the spirit of Venice in faithful detail.

A highlight is a romantic private gondola ride down the Grand Canal, or, for those with a little less cash, a group trip. A visit to the stunning **Guggenheim Hermitage Museum** (☎ 702-414-2440, 866-484-4849; www.guggenheimlas vegas.org; adult/child $15/7; ⏰ 9:30am-8.30pm) is another must. The austere gallery has a partnership with Russia's State Hermitage Museum of St Petersburg, which ensures the masterpieces keep on coming. Impressionism, postimpressionism and early modernism are the focus of the vast collection.

Even if you've had the good fortune of strolling the cobblestone pathways and plying the romantic canals of the one-and-only Italian port, you won't want to miss the Vegas version. In a city filled with spectacles, the Venetian is surely one of the most spectacular.

MIRAGE

When the **Mirage** (Map pp76-8; ☎ 702-791-7111, 800-374-9000; www.mirage.com; 3400 S Las Vegas Blvd) opened in 1989, then-owner Steve Wynn boasted he'd create a property 'so overriding in its nature that it would be a reason in and of itself for visitors to come to Las Vegas.' The $630 million Mirage is such a place. It captures the imagination with a tropical setting replete with a huge atrium filled with jungle foliage, meandering creeks and soothing cascades. Woven into this waterscape are scores of bromeliads enveloped in sunlight and fed by a computerized misting system. Circling the atrium is a huge Polynesian-themed casino, which places gaming areas under separate roofs to invoke a feeling of intimacy. Real and faux tropical plants add to the casino's elegant splendor.

Don't miss the awesome 20,000-gallon saltwater aquarium, with 90 species of tropical critters (including pufferfish, manta rays and pygmy sharks), in the registration area. Acclaimed impressionist Danny Gans and touring comedians like Jay Leno provide evening entertainment. Although the dynamic duo, otherwise known as Siegfried and

TOP 10 VEGAS EXPERIENCES

A beautiful woman with more than one story to tell, Vegas is a sensual being with a playful side. She's a globetrotting gal who's been around the block a time or two, a glamorous and sophisticated lady with a taste for caviar and Louis Vuitton. She's slightly edgy with a hint of danger in her sweet perfume. An intriguing contradiction, she's sassy one minute and standoffish the next. She's been to the top of the world, and tasted the grittiness at the bottom. She can throw back shots with the boys and scream her heart out at a boxing match, but the minute you get too near she'll slip away. She's a mysterious lady, Las Vegas, guarding her secrets closely, but if you dig deep enough she just might let them spill. To really get to know her, leave the slot machine and check out life through her eyes:

■ Rent a swinging zootsuit from **Valentinos' Zootsuit Collection** (p108) and strut your stuff on **The Strip** when the sun goes down.

■ Head to the **Hilton** (p90) for a *Star Trek* wedding on the bridge of the USS *Enterprise* with a Klingon as your witness.

■ Take a rollicking ride on the **Manhattan Express roller coaster** (p80).

■ Mingle with celebrities at the Palms Resort Casino's ultrahot **Ghost Bar** (p101), then get treated like one when you splash out on their $7500 per night Real World Suite (where the popular reality show gang lived).

■ Pretend it's Academy Awards night and try on a real movie star's diamond necklace at **Fred Leighton** (p108).

■ Spend an evening at an over-the-top **strip club** (p105).

■ Drop a few bucks in the slots while trapeze acts whiz overhead at **Circus Circus** (p84).

■ Indulge after-hours with a treatment or full-body tanning at Luxor's 24-hour **Oasis Spa** (p81).

■ Forget the cost and pull out the plastic for an all-out splurge at a renowned restaurant such as **Aureole** (p95) or **Picasso** (p98).

■ Experience the romance of Venice's canals on a gondola ride at the **Venetian** (opposite).

Roy, are no longer performing following Roy's near fatal tiger accident at a live show in October 2003 (p104), you can still visit **Siegfried & Roy's Secret Garden & Dolphin Habitat** (p88).

At the casino's south entrance, slanted glass at the **royal white tiger habitat** permits a glare-free view of a parade of big cats 24 hours a day. Out front in the 3-acre lagoon, the fiery trademark **faux volcano** erupts frequently with a roar, inevitably bringing traffic on The Strip to a screeching halt.

TREASURE ISLAND

Yo, ho, whoa: traces of **Treasure Island's** (TI; Map pp76-8; ☎ 702-894-7111, 800-944-7444; www .treasureisland.com; 3300 S Las Vegas Blvd) original swashbuckling skull-and-crossbones theme linger, but the new-look terracotta-toned resort now strives for an 'elegant Caribbean hideaway' feel – with 'leave the kids at home' implied. TI's shift away from family-friendly, to bawdy and naughty, epitomizes

Vegas' ongoing efforts to put the 'sin' back in 'casino.' One-armed Playboy bandits have replaced the playful pirates, plastic doubloons and chests full-o-booty.

Visitors approach the property via a wood-bottomed bridge with hemp-rope supporting sides (for that 'authentic' piratey feel!) that spans the artificial Sirens' Cove, beside which is a replica of an 18th-century sea village. The spiced-up **Sirens of Treasure Island** (admission free; ⊙ every 90 min 7-11:30pm Mon-Sat) is a mock sea battle that pits sultry temptresses against renegade free-booters. It takes place in the cove fronting the entryway. In the harbor, two ships – a privateer vessel and a British frigate – face off on schedule several times nightly.

STARDUST

Stuck in no-man's-land, the **Stardust** (Map pp76-8; ☎ 702-732-6111, 866-642-3120; www.stardustlv.com; 3000 S Las Vegas Blvd) has stuck to its Rat Pack roots and continues to lure fans of bygone

Vegas. You gotta love the landmark 188ft starry sign, which is cast in nearly every Hollywood establishing shot of Vegas. When completed in 1958, the $10 million Stardust was a 'real class joint,' as the mobsters used to say. With 1065 rooms, it was also the world's largest resort complex. The Dunes introduced bare-breasted showgirls to Vegas with *Minsky Goes to Paris* in 1957, but the Stardust countered by importing real French showgirls for *Lido de Paris*. Today, the Stardust's entertainment consists chiefly of a washed-up Wayne Newton.

CIRCUS CIRCUS

It's hard to miss the enormous clown-shaped marquee and the tent-shaped casino under the big top. Granted, this sprawling **resort** (Map pp76-8; ☎ 702-734-0410, 800-444-2472; www.circuscircus.com; 2880 S Las Vegas Blvd) looks pretty gaudy, but there's plenty of fun to be had by all ages.

Circus Circus' 5-acre indoor **Adventuredome amusement park** (☎ 702-794-3939, 877-224-7287; www.adventuredome.com; adult/child day pass $23/15, per ride $4-6; ☼ daily) is packed with thrills. Must-rides include the double-loop, double-corkscrew Canyon Blaster and the open-sided Rim Runner toboggan water ride. The tamer garden-variety carnival sideshow rides are popular with wee ones. Wandering clowns perform free shows throughout the day. Opening times vary seasonally; call or check the website for hours.

Above the casino is the Midway Arcade with the cacophonous **Slots-A-Fun** (p89) just a stumble away.

SAHARA

Courtesy of a $100 million face-lift, the Moroccan-themed **Sahara** (Map pp76-8; ☎ 702-737-2111, 888-696-2121; www.saharavegas.com; 2535 S Las Vegas Blvd) is one of the few old-Vegas carpet joints that have survived the mega-resort onslaught. The *Arabian Nights* theme continues inside the casino.

Most compelling, perhaps, are the Nascar Cafe's thrill rides at **Las Vegas Cyber Speedway & Speed** (☎ 702-733-7223; www.nascarcafélasvegas.com; Cyber Speedway $8, re-ride $4, Speed per ride $10, all-day pass $13; ☼ Cyber Speedway noon-9pm Sun-Thu, 11am-10pm Fri & Sat; Speed 11am-midnight Sun-Thu, to 1am Fri & Sat). Indy car simulators are so authentic that they excite real Formula One drivers. The faux racers are bolted to hy-

draulic platforms fronting 20ft wraparound screens that are scary in their realism. Speed is an electromagnetic roller coaster that slingshots to a top speed of 70mph.

STRATOSPHERE

Las Vegas has many buildings exceeding 20 stories, but only one that tops a hundred. At 1149ft, the white, three-legged $550 million **Stratosphere** (Map pp76-8; ☎ 702-380-7777, 800-998-6937; www.stratospherehotel.com; 2000 S Las Vegas Blvd) is the tallest building west of the Mississippi. At its base is a casino with all the trappings of a sprawling gaming room, but sadly lacking in the themes Vegas is famous for. What the place lacks in attitude, it makes up for in altitude. Atop the elegantly tapered tower you'll find a revolving restaurant, a circular bar, and indoor and outdoor viewing decks offering the most spectacular 360° panoramas in town.

To get you there, the Stratosphere boasts America's fastest elevators: they ascend and descend at 20.5mph, or about three times the speed of regular elevators, lifting you 108 floors in a mere 37 ear-popping seconds.

The casino boasts adrenalin-pumping **amusement park rides** (per ride $19; ☼ 10am-1am Sun-Thu, to 2am Fri & Sat): the Big Shot straps riders into completely exposed seats that zip up and down the tower's pinnacle for 12 seconds, exerting four Gs of force. Views from the High Roller are good, but the ride is a dud. The verdict is still out on the new X Scream.

You can also catch good-value, if rather cheesy, production shows – one featuring celebrity impersonators, another a long-running daytime cabaret. It's a down-to-earth resort that attracts a lot of families. Children (and even adults) will find the retro-futuristic 1964 World's Fair–themed Strat-O-Fair midway arcade particularly appealing.

PALMS RESORT CASINO

Still basking in MTV's *Real World* glow, the **Palms** (Map pp76-8; ☎ 702-942-7777, 866-725-6773; www.palms.com; 4321 W Flamingo Rd) attracts loads of big-name celebrities (hint to the celebrity obsessed: Paris Hilton, Tara Reid, Lindsey Lohan and Britney Spears are just a few of the famously beautiful people that like to shack up here) as well as a younger, mostly local crowd. Although there's no coherent theme, no expense seems to have been spared. Glamorous to the nines and hip to the max, its lounges and clubs are some of the hottest in town (it was at a club here that Britney Spears once gave an impromptu concert). And its restaurants hold their own with the best of the best. Other highlights include a fabulous spa and salon, a 14-screen cinema, an Imax theater, a 1200-seat showroom and a big casino.

RIO

Forget Carnival, the festive **Rio** (Map pp76-8; ☎ 702-777-7777, 800-752-9746; www.playrio.com; 3700 W Flamingo Rd) is positioning itself as bachelorette headquarters with its new **Chippendales Theater** (p106). There's a good mix of restaurants and buffets, shopping and gaming choices, plus loads of free entertainment. The free *Masquerade Show in the Sky* is a spectacle of floats, clowns, musicians and dancers. It's all rather corny, but then again you're not paying anything to see it.

HARD ROCK HOTEL & CASINO

The **Hard Rock** (Map pp76-8; ☎ 702-693-5000, 800-473-7625; www.hrhvegas.com; 4455 Paradise Rd) is home to one of the world's most impressive collections of rock 'n' roll memorabilia. The complex consists of an unremarkable Hard Rock Cafe and an über-trendy hotel-

casino. Inside, the Joint concert hall, the happening Center Bar and the nightclub **Body English** (p102) attract a done-up, sex-charged crowd as well as lots of celebrities. The pool complex is a constant throbbing (literally, there are underwater speakers!) meat-market party with a capital P.

GAMEWORKS

Developed by Sega and Universal Studios, this high-tech **arcade** (Map pp76-8; ☎ 702-432-4263; www.gameworks.com; 3785 S Las Vegas Blvd; unlimited play per hr/3hr $20/27; ☒ 10am-midnight Sun-Thu, to 2am Fri & Sat) attracts both teenagers and adults. The large underground space contains a popular eatery, full bar, 75ft climbing wall, pool hall and loads of virtual-reality games. It's most crowded – and fun – at night.

MARJORIE BARRICK MUSEUM OF NATURAL HISTORY

UNLV's hidden cultural gem is an anthropological treasure trove. The **museum's** (Map pp76-8; ☎ 702-895-3381; http://hrcweb.nevada.edu /museum/; UNLV, cnr Swenson St & Harmon Ave; admission free; ☒ 8am-4:45pm Mon-Fri, 10am-2pm Sat) exhibits include a Southwestern herpitarium (with regular feedings of native iguanas and gila monsters) and early Vegas history to modern art and a Xeriscape desert garden.

TOP FIVE COOL POOLS

Vegas is home to some truly spectacular aquatic hangouts, open to guests during the spring and summer (and sometimes even year-round). The coolest of the cool are:

Mandalay Bay (p75) There's an 11-acre pool complex here. Check out the wave pool, the lazy river, the sand-and-surf beach or the clothing-optional Moorea Beach Club. In the summer surfers compete for top honors on 6ft waves.

Hard Rock (above) At the Hard Rock, the music never stops. The pool complex features underwater speakers to keep you pumped as you swim the laps. There's also a hip beach club with a bar featuring swim-up blackjack and Tahitian-style cabanas for rent. The place draws a hip young crowd, especially on Sunday night when the pool area is turned into Rehab, a beach party focusing on relaxation and rejuvenation. There's even a built-in dance floor!

Mirage (p82) The lush tropical pool complex stays open 11 months out of the year (closes in December). It's a sight to behold with water tumbling off cliffs, deep grottos, palm-tree studded islands for sun bathing and almost a quarter-mile of faux beach shoreline! Pool rafts add to the paradise beach vibe and there are three waterslides. The pools are heated year-round.

Caesars Palace (p81) Classic marble statues, overflowing fountains and lushly manicured grounds make the four sapphire pools at the Garden of the Gods fit for a Roman emperor. The Temple Pool is the focal point and features fountains galore and a giant rotunda top. There are also two whirlpool spas and poolside cabanas for rent.

Tropicana (p79) With an island vibe and numerous swimming options, the Tropicana holds its own with glitzier resorts for its cool pool factor. Featuring one of Vegas' only indoor swimming places, it also has swim-up blackjack and an adults-only Lagoon Pool.

Downtown

Despite all its efforts to refashion itself into some sort of bedazzling, family-friendly neon amusement park, Downtown remains the heart and soul of old Vegas.

Fremont St was where all the action originated, and the smoky, low-ceilinged casinos have changed little over the years. As attractions they don't offer much to nongamblers, but their proximity to one another is a real plus. You can easily stroll between half a dozen gaming joints – a vast contrast to the challenges of navigating The Strip. Parking is never a problem, there's convenient public transportation and a monorail extension project is on the horizon.

MAIN STREET STATION

The most charming of Downtown's establishments, **Main Street Station** (Map p87; ☎ 702-387-1896, 800-465-0711; www.mainstreetcasino.com; 200 N Main St) re-creates Victorian opulence with detailed handiwork, old-fashioned elegance and an extensive collection of antiques, architectural artifacts and collectibles. Throughout the lovely hotel and 28,000-sq-ft casino are notable *objets d'histoire*, most keeping to the turn-of-the-20th-century theme; then there are the other pieces of history, such as a large graffiti-covered chunk of the Berlin Wall above the urinals in the men's room.

Other artifacts on display include Buffalo Bill Cody's private rail car, which he used

to travel the USA with his Wild West Show from 1906 until his death in 1917; three exquisite bronze chandeliers above the casino's central pit, which were originally installed in the 1890s at Coca Cola's headquarters in Austin, Texas, and the ornate mahogany woodwork that now graces the casino entry, lobby and the Company Store, which was removed from a 19th-century drugstore in Kentucky. The gorgeous Pullman Grille dining room was built around an ornate carved oak fireplace and wine storage cabinets taken from Preswick Castle in Scotland (the unique sideboard niche includes panels that depict the characters and morals of *Aesop's Fables*).

There are historic treasures at almost every turn. Pick up a free *Guide to Artifacts, Antiques & Artworks* pamphlet, which describes all the property's historic attractions, from the registration desk.

FREMONT STREET EXPERIENCE

A decade ago, Vegas' downtrodden Downtown had lost nearly all of its tourists to the rapidly developing Strip. It was headed downhill, fast. So, with no end in sight to development on The Strip, something had to be done.

Always ready for a gamble, city and business boosters came up with a plan, which was realized in December 1995: a $70 million, four-block **pedestrian mall** (Map p87; ☎ 702-373-5200; www.vegasexperience.com; Fremont St, btwn Main St & Las Vegas Blvd) topped by an arched steel canopy filled with computer-controlled lights. Five times nightly, the canopy becomes a six-minute light-and-sound show enhanced by 550,000 watts of wraparound sound. The latest addition is the Viva Vision super-big screen, featuring 12.5 million synchronized LEDs. What's more, the misting system built into the canopy provides welcome relief on hot days.

Has the newfangled mall helped business pick up Downtown? Absolutely.

GOLDEN NUGGET

The **Golden Nugget** (Map p87; ☎ 702-385-7111, 800-846-5336; www.goldennugget.com; 129 E Fremont St) has set the Downtown benchmark for total extravagance since opening in 1946. Thanks to an injection of chutzpah by Fox's *Casino* reality-show stars Tim and Tom, it's still at the top of its class. The luxurious rooms

---

TOP FIVE POKER HOTSPOTS

With the rules of Texas Hold 'em a frequent conversation starter these days, it's obvious poker is the hottest game in town.

Bellagio (p80) This is the biggest and best game in town for high-limit stakes. Just learning the rules? Try your hand at the lower-limit tables.

Mirage (p82) With 31 tables devoted to varying limits of Seven Card Stud, Texas Hold 'em, Omaha Eight and more, the Mirage is a good bet.

Palms Resort Casino (p84) Best known for hosting Bravo's *Celebrity Poker Showdown*, the Palms also hosts no-limit Texas Hold 'em 24/7.

Golden Nugget (right) A favorite with high-stakes players, the Nugget also has a nonsmoking room.

Binion's (p88) The old-school Binion's is the original home of the World Series of Poker.

INFORMATION
Kinkos...**1** C3
Marriage License Bureau....**2** C3
University Medical Center of
  Southern Nevada..............**3** A4

SIGHTS & ACTIVITIES
Binion's..**4** C2
Golden Nugget...............................**5** C2
Las Vegas Natural History
  Museum...**6** D1
Little White Wedding Chapel....**7** C4
Main Street Station.......................**8** C2
Neon Museum..................(see 9)
Neonopolis..**9** D2
Viva Las Vegas Wedding
  Chapel...**10** C4

SLEEPING
Golden Nugget....................(see 5)
Main Street Station...........(see 8)
USA Hostels Las Vegas.............**11** E3
Viva Las Vegas Villas..........(see 10)

EATING
Andre's...**12** D3
Binion's Ranch Steakhouse...(see 4)
Carson Street Café...............(see 5)
El Sombrero Café.....................**13** C3
Golden Gate Deli & Bay City
  Diner...**14** C2
Hugo's Cellar...........................**15** C2
Pullman Bar & Grille...........(see 8)

DRINKING
Triple Seven Brew Pub............(see 8)

ENTERTAINMENT
Cashman Center Theatre........**16** D1
Crown Neonopolis 14.............(see 9)
Girls of Glitter Gulch...........**17** C2

SHOPPING
A Slightly Sinful Adventure.....**18** C4
Attic...**19** C4
Funk House...............................**20** C4
Gypsy Caravan.........................**21** C4
Las Vegas Premium Outlets....**22** B3
Neonopolis..........................(see 9)
Valentino's Zootsuit Collection....**23** C4
Williams Costume Company....**24** C4
Yana's Junk..............................**25** C4

TRANSPORT
CAT Bus Station......................**26** C2
Downtown Bus Station............(see 27)
Greyhound..................................**27** C2

are good value and no brass or cut glass was spared in the Victorian casino. Don't miss the gigantic 61lb Hand of Faith nugget in the lobby or the free jazz in the bar at night.

BINION'S
The old-school **Binion's** (Map p87; ☎ 702-384-1574, 800-622-6468; www.binions.com; 128 E Fremont St) is best known for its 'zero limit' betting policy and as the host of the World Series of Poker (which is now shared with Harrah's, p82). It's worth a wander to see the action in the high-stakes room and free *Honky Tonk Cowgirls* show. Binion, a savvy horse trader, once quipped 'An honest deal makes its own friends.' Although Benny's gone to the great round up in the sky, Binion's still lives up to his motto.

NEONOPOLIS
The crown jewel of the Downtown redevelopment effort, **Neonopolis** (Map p87; ☎ 702-477-0470; www.neonopolis.com; 450 Fremont St; ⊙ 11am-11pm) is most notable for its collection of vintage neon signs. Twenty retail shops surround open courtyards full of alfresco dining options, a cinema complex and the **Neon Museum** (☎ 702-387-6366; www.neon museum.org; cnr Fremont & 3rd Sts; admission free ⊙ 24/7/365). Plaques tell the story of each sign at this alfresco vintage assemblage. Sparkling genie lamps, glowing martini glasses, 1940s motel marquees and more brighten up this otherwise bleak slice of Downtown. Look for the flashy 40ft-tall chap on horseback.

RICHARD PETTY DRIVING EXPERIENCE
Curious what it's like to be in high-speed pursuit? This **driving experience** (Map p87; ☎ 702-643-4343, 800-237-3889; www.1800bepetty.com; Las Vegas Motor Speedway, 7000 N Las Vegas Blvd; admission from $99; ⊙ varies, call for schedule) is your chance to ride shotgun during a Nascar-style qualifying run. Speeds in the 600-horsepower stock cars reach up to 160mph.

LAS VEGAS FOR CHILDREN
Now that sin is in fashion again, few places in Vegas bill themselves as family-friendly. State law prohibits people under 21 from loitering in gaming areas and the only mega-resorts that cater to children are **Circus Circus** (p84) and **Excalibur** (p79). Several proper-ties actively discourage kids by prohibiting strollers. That said, there are still plenty of things to see and do with the wee ones. But beyond arcades and amusement rides, teenagers will likely be bored out of their minds.

MGM Grand Lion Habitat
This multilevel **enclosure** (Map pp76-8; ☎ 702-891-1111; www.mgmgrand.com; MGM Grand, 3799 S Las Vegas Blvd; admission free; ⊙ 11am-10pm) showcases up to six adult lions daily. MGM owns eight of the magnificent felines, but only two are allowed in the enclosure simultaneously. Don't miss the see-through walkway tunnel, where the big cats roam around on-lookers.

Siegfried and Roy's Secret Garden & Dolphin Habitat
The Mirage's tropical **garden** (Map pp76-8; ☎ 702-791-7188; www.mirage.com; Mirage, 3400 S Las Vegas Blvd; admission $12, under 10 free; ⊙ 11am-7pm Mon-Fri, 10am-7pm Sat & Sun) features exotic and endangered lions, tigers, jaguars and an ele-phant in a lush zoo setting. The big cats are usually napping; late afternoon is the best chance to see them frolicking. Up-close-and-personal Atlantic bottlenose dolphin inter-actions and underwater viewing areas are the highlights of the super-sized aquarium.

Circus Circus Midway
Home to free circus acts, this **midway** (Map pp76-8; ☎ 702-734-0410, 800-444-2472; www.circus circus.com; Circus Circus, 2880 S Las Vegas Blvd; admission free; ⊙ 11am-midnight, shows every 30 min) features animals, acrobats and magicians perform-ing daily on center stage. Grab a seat; there's no admission charge or reserved seating. Nearby are loads of arcades – both the video variety and old-fashioned carnival games.

BABYSITTING & CHILD-CARE

The **Gold Coast** (p91) and **Orleans** (p91) have on-site child-care centers. Other ho-tels refer parents to nanny agencies such as **Around the Clock Childcare** (☎ 702-365-1040, 800-798-6768), which charges $52 per child for a four-hour minimum plus $11 for each additional hour. Employees have been fingerprinted by police and background-checked by the FBI.

Court Jesters Stage

The main draw at the **Court Jesters Stage** (Map pp76-8; ☎ 702-597-7777, 800-937-7777; www.excalibur-casino.com; Excalibur, 3050 S Las Vegas Blvd; admission free; ⊗ 10am-10pm Mon-Thu, 10am-1am Fri & Sat, shows every 30 min) is a variety of free high-quality circus acts. Musicians play period instruments while magicians perform feats that medieval alchemists never would have imagined possible. There are also jugglers and puppeteers.

Las Vegas Natural History Museum

There's heaps for the kids to do at this **museum** (Map p87; ☎ 702-384-3466; www.lvnhm.org; 900 N Las Vegas Blvd; adult/child $6/3; ⊗ 9am-4pm) that's divided into five themed rooms. Highlights include the marine-life aquariums, native Nevada wildlife taxidermy, fossils and animatronic tyrannosauruses, and the hands-on young scientist center.

ONLY IN LAS VEGAS
Liberace Museum

For connoisseurs of over-the-top extravagance, this **museum** (Map pp76-8; ☎ 702-798-5595; www.liberace.org; 1775 E Tropicana Ave; adult/child $12/8; ⊗ 10am-5pm Mon-Sat, 1-5pm Sun) is a must-do. The home of 'Mr Showmanship' houses the most flamboyant art cars, outrageous costumes and ornate pianos you'll ever see. There's a hand-painted Pleyel on which Chopin played; a red, white and blue Rolls-Royce convertible and a wardrobe exhibit full of feathered capes and million-dollar furs, darling.

Elvis-A-Rama Museum

The King may have left the building, but his impersonators and the largest private collection of his memorabilia are still very much in the house. This **museum** (Map pp76-8; ☎ 702-309-7200; www.elvisarama.com; 3401 Industrial Rd; admission $10, show packages $15-28; ⊗ 10am-8pm) is gaudy, cheesy and over-the-top, but then so was the man himself.

Slots-A-Fun

For cheap drinks, cheap eats and cheap thrills, it's tough to beat lowbrow **Slots-A-Fun** (Map pp76-8; ☎ 702-734-0410; 2890 S Las Vegas Blvd; admission free ⊗ 24hr). Grab a coupon book from neighboring Circus Circus (p84), a few 75¢ beers and $1 half-pound hot dogs. Then kick back, relax and enjoy the laughable lounge acts.

TOURS

Most tours appeal to seniors who prefer to leave the driving to others. It's easy enough to tour The Strip on your own via monorail, taxi, trolley, bus or car, but Hoover Dam package deals can save a lot of ticketing headaches and adventure outfitters can ease logistic hassles. Hotel pick-up and drop-off from The Strip are included in most rates. Check online for frequent promotions.

Black Canyon River Adventures

This **company** (☎ 702-294-1414, 800-455-3490; www.blackcanyonadventures.com; Hacienda Hotel, Boulder City; adult/child $73/45 plus $106 per person transport cost from Las Vegas) offers a 12-mile motor-assisted journey down the Colorado River. Boats launch from the base of Hoover Dam (p191), and visit several hot springs en route to Willow Beach Marina.

Escape Adventures

Escape the neon jungle for a single-track mountain-bike, road-bike or hiking **tour** (☎ 702-596-2953, 800-596-2953; www.escapeadventures.com; half/full-day from $89/149) of stunning Red Rock Canyon (p112). The packages include free hotel transfers.

Rocky Trails Adventure Tours

This one-stop shop for outdoor **adventure tours** (☎ 702-869-9991, 888-846-4747; www.adventurelasvegas.com; tours $99-499; ⊗ reservations 24hr) arranges everything from guided kayak floats below Hoover Dam and glider soaring rides to off-road ATV tours and 4WD ghost town explorations.

Papillon Grand Canyon Helicopters

Vegas' oldest helicopter flightseeing **tour operator** (☎ 702-736-7243, 888-635-7272; www.papillon.com; tour $55-75, with dinner $112-142; ⊗ departs 6-9pm) does luxury tours all over the Southwest, including the Grand Canyon. Its half-hour Neon Nights jetcopter flyover of The Strip and dinner-flight package are the most notable offerings.

FESTIVALS & EVENTS

For the full run-down on Vegas events, check www.vegasfreedom.com.

New Year's Reserve a year in advance; The Strip is *the* place to celebrate; January

Mardi Gras Fetes around town on the Saturday before Ash Wednesday; February

St Patrick's Day Parade Downtown turns green every March 17th

Sam's Town 300 One-hundred and forty-thousand Nascar dads descend on the Las Vegas Motor Speedway (p106); early March

World Series of Poker High rollers vie for millions at Binion's (p88) and Harrah's (p82) from mid-April to mid-May

Cinco de Mayo Fremont Street Experience (p86) hosts a Mexican Independence Day celebration; May 5

CineVegas Sin City's premier film festival lights up the Palms Resort Casino (p84) for a week in mid-June

High Rollers World's richest amateur bowling tourney at Sam's Town; late July

Professional Bull Riders World Finals Four days of gallopin' giddyup at Sam Boyd Stadium; October

Craftsman Truck Series More Nascar madness at the Las Vegas Motor Speedway (p106), November

National Finals Rodeo Ten days of steer wrestling at the Thomas & Mack Center; December

SLEEPING

With more than 130,000 guestrooms, there's no shortage of places to stay in the Vegas

Valley. Options range from filthy fleapits east of Downtown to exquisite penthouse suites overlooking The Strip. Accommodations range from $15 per night at a hostel to $10,000 for a private self-contained villa with butler service at one of The Strip's ritzy megaresorts.

Whatever you do, don't arrive without a reservation, at least for the first night. You'd be amazed how often every standard room in town is occupied. During the biggest conventions, even Laughlin (75 miles away, p194) is booked solid.

The Strip & Around
BUDGET

There are a few places on The Strip, and near it, where you can secure budget accommodation. The cheapest places also tend to be the most child-friendly.

Circus Circus (Map pp76–8; ☎ 702-734-0410, 877-224-7287; www.circuscircus.com; 2880 S Las Vegas Blvd; r from $40; P ☒) Most standard rooms at this family favorite have sofas and balconies.

GOING TO THE CHAPEL, GOING TO GET MARRIED

Spontaneous weddings have always been a Vegas trademark. It must be part of that slightly naughty, lose your inhibitions, what happens in Vegas stays in Vegas theme. Britney's done it, so has Nicky Hilton. The quickie drunken wedding even made for an episode of *Friends*. In fact, more than 100,000 couples choose to say their vows in Vegas each year! Whether it's a planned affair, or a spur-of-the-moment decision, Las Vegas offers more than 30 different places to tie the knot. These range from the traditional to the fantasy, from indoor to outdoor. You can be married by a minister or by an Elvis impersonator. There's no waiting period and you don't need a blood test. You just have to be at least 18 years old and show up at the **Marriage License Bureau** (Map p87; ☎ 702-455-4415; 200 S 3rd St; ☽ 8am-midnight Mon-Thu, 24hr Fri-Sun). Once you have the certificate, it's off to the chapel.

For an out-of-this world marriage experience, head to the **Las Vegas Hilton** (Map pp76–8; ☎ 702-697-8751; www.startrekexp.com/weddings.php; 3000 Paradise Rd; ☽ chapel 8am-5pm) where you'll be tying the knot Star Trek–style. Intergalactic music plays as you cross the bridge of the USS *Enterprise* and you'll even have a Klingon or Ferengi for your witness. If you want to keep it short-and-sweet you'll pay about $500. More elaborate packages cost between $1000 and $3000.

For something a little more traditional, try the **Little White Wedding Chapel** (Map p87; ☎ 702-382-5943; www.littlewhitechapel.com; 1301 S Las Vegas Blvd; ☽ 24hr). It's welcomed thousands of couples since opening in 1946, and is a favorite spot for celebs to say 'I do.' Demi Moore and Bruce Willis were hitched here. So was Michael Jordan. And who can forget Britney Spears? You can have an Elvis impersonator officiate your ceremony and even have the affair broadcast over the Internet. If you really can't wait to get married, the chapel will pick you up and take you to its sister property, the Tunnel of Vows Drive-Thru. Wedding ceremonies start at $60, while packages including everything from pictures and limos to flowers and videos cost between $200 and $800.

If you just want to watch, peek inside the **Viva Las Vegas Wedding Chapel** (Map p87; ☎ 702-384-0771, 800-574-4450; www.vivalasvegasweddings.com; 1205 S Las Vegas Blvd; admission free) to see if anyone is getting married – the public is welcome and ceremonies are broadcast live online. Call to check the current wedding schedule.

Suites, like clowns, come in varying shapes and sizes. The decor is tasteful and most of the well-maintained rooms are nonsmoking. Avoid the motel-style Manor rooms out back. Children under 18 stay free. The hotel also operates an RV park in conjunction with KOA.

Excalibur (Map pp76-8; ☎ 702-597-7777, 877-750-5464; www.excalibur.com; 3850 S Las Vegas Blvd; r from $50; P ⟁) Another child-friendly option (kids under 18 stay free), for better or worse, Excalibur's relentless Arthurian motif doesn't end in the casino. Two 28-story towers house 4000-plus rooms; all wallpapered to resemble a castle. Upsides are nonsmoking, family-friendly rooms, wide, wheelchair-friendly doors and Jacuzzi suites.

Orleans (Map pp76-8; ☎ 702-365-7111, 800-675-3267; www.orleanscasino.com; 4500 W Tropicana Ave; r from $60; P ⟁) The French-provincial rooms are good-value 450-sq-ft 'petite suites' with separate lounge, dining and bedroom. There's a spa, fitness center, arcade, on-site childcare and the best bowling alley in town.

Sahara (Map pp76-8; ☎ 702-737-2111, 800-634-6666; www.saharavegas.com; 2535 Las Vegas Blvd; r from $45; P ⟁) The last of The Strip casinos with a desert theme, this aging complex doesn't churn up a lot of excitement, but does contain simple, comfortable rooms that are among the city's better bargains. Rooms in the 'old' tower are slightly cheaper.

Gold Coast (Map pp76-8; ☎ 702-367-7111, 888-402-6278; www.goldcoastcasino.com; 4000 W Flamingo Rd; r from $35; P ⟁) Standard rooms are unremarkable, but they won't leave you feeling squeezed. You can do better elsewhere, but some folks (mostly cowboys and elders) prefer the tranquil off-Strip location and easy bowling and bingo access. Free childcare is an added plus.

KOA (Map pp76-8; ☎ 702-451-5527, 800-562-7782; 4315 Boulder Hwy; tent & RV sites for 2 people $24; P ⟁) A few miles east of town, it has tent and RV sites.

MIDRANGE
Many places listed here would fall into the luxury bracket elsewhere, but Vegas is a city so hell-bent on excess that even the lower-priced places have top-notch amenities and all the swank you can stomach.

Luxor (Map pp76-8; ☎ 702-362-4000, 888-777-0188; www.luxor.com; 3900 S Las Vegas Blvd; r from $75; P ⟁) Featuring Art Deco and Egyptian fur-

> ### NEW KID ON THE STRIP
> The Strip's famous skyline has a different look these days, thanks to the brand new $2.7 billion **Wynn Las Vegas** (Map pp76-8; ☎ 702-770-7100; www.wynnlasvegas.com; 3131 Las Vegas Blvd), which opened in May 2005. The most expensive hotel-casino built to date, it upholds the city's decadent reputation. With a 50-story curved tower covered in bronze glass, the facility is as swanky as it gets. The entire place exudes an air of secrecy – the entrance is obscured from the Strip by a $130-million artificial mountain, which rises seven stories tall. Inside, the Wynn resembles a natural paradise – with mountain views, tumbling waterfalls, fountains and other special effects. Perks include a golf course, 2716 guest rooms and 111,000-sq-ft of gaming space. Acclaimed director Franco Dragone has created a water-themed production show, *Le Reve,* in a specially constructed theater-in-the-round, which includes a 1-million-gallon pool doubling as the stage.

nishings and marble bathrooms (but no tub), Luxor's rooms are one of Vegas' best midrange deals. The newer tower often has better views than the ones in the pyramid, which have slanted windows.

Mandalay Bay (Map pp76-8; ☎ 702-632-7777, 877-632-7800; www.mandalaybay.com; 3950 S Las Vegas Blvd; r from $125; P ⟁) M-Bay's eclectic South Seas theme persists in its ornately appointed 515-sq-ft standard rooms. Amenities include floor-to-ceiling windows and luxurious bathrooms. Hip House of Blues rooms feature art naïf motifs. Many well-tanned guests feel it's worth a stay just to gain access to the sprawling pool complex (see p85).

Hard Rock Hotel & Casino (Map pp76-8; ☎ 702-693-5000, 800-473-7625; www.hardrockhotel.com; 4455 Paradise Rd; r from $125; P ⟁) Everything about this intimate boutique hotel-casino suggests stardom. French doors reveal expansive views, and portraits of rockers grace the stylish Euro-minimalist rooms. Suites are fitted with souped-up stereos, large-screen TVs, wi-fi and jet tubs. The action revolves around the lush pool area, with a sexy sandy beach, whirlpools and private cabanas.

GAY & LESBIAN LAS VEGAS

East of The Strip bordering the western edge of the UNLV campus (the area between Swenson St, Naples Dr and Paradise Rd), the Fruit Loop triangle is an island of flamboyance in a sea of straightness and ground zero for Vegas' cliquish queer community. See www.gaylasvegas.com, www.outlasvegas.com or www.outinlasvegas.com for the scoop on Sin City's active, if closeted, scene.

Apollo Spa (Map pp76-8; ☎ 702-650-9191; www.apollospa.com; Commercial Center, 953 E Sahara Ave) is the steamiest men's health club. Stop by **Get Booked** (Map pp76-8; ☎ 702-737-7780; www.getbookedlasvegas.com; 4640 S Paradise Rd) for party invites.

It's all about the pool and the parties at Sin City's first gay, clothing-optional getaway, **Blue Moon Resort** (Map pp76-8; ☎ 702-361-9099, 866-798-9194; www.bluemoonlv.com; 2651 Westwood Dr; r $90-200; 🐾). Amenities include in-room adult programming and unlimited use of the sultry steam room.

Buffalo (Map pp76-8; ☎ 702-733-8355; 4640 Paradise Rd) is a cruisy Levi's and leather boyz bar with pool tables, beer busts and tough-looking but friendly fellows out for a good time. It never closes.

Every night is a party at **Free Zone** (Map pp76-8; ☎ 702-794-2300; 610 E Naples Dr), a casual mixed queer hangout. Tuesday is ladies night, Wednesday brings an acoustic open mic, Thursday is boyz night, and Friday and Saturday nights feature *What a Drag* cabaret. Admission is free and the doors never shut.

Gipsy (Map pp76-8; ☎ 702-731-1919; 4605 S Paradise Rd; admission $5-10 after 10pm; 🕙 9pm-late) is by all accounts the premier gay dance club in town. There's a party every night, daily happy hour and everyone is welcome.

Goodtimes (Map pp76-8; ☎ 702-736-9494; Liberace Museum, 1775 E Tropicana Ave) is a mellow men's club where intimate conversation rules. There's a stainless-steel dance floor, pool tables and video poker. Happy hour runs from 5pm to 7pm daily, with a legendary Monday liquor bust from midnight to 3am.

New York-New York (Map pp76-8; ☎ 702-740-6969, 866-815-4365; www.nynyhotelcasino.com; 3790 S Las Vegas Blvd; r from $80; P 🐾) The Art Deco rooms are classy and freshly remodeled with black marble-topped bathroom sinks and comfy beds. The cheapest rooms are rather tiny (just what one would expect in NYC), but pay a few dollars more and you'll have enough legroom. Avoid noisy lower-level rooms facing the roller coaster. Just like the Big Apple, the charm awaits in public spaces.

Monte Carlo (Map pp76-8; ☎ 702-730-7777, 888-529-4828; www.monte-carlo.com; 3770 S Las Vegas Blvd; r from $125; P 🐾) It's hardly Monaco, but traditional European style permeates the spacious rooms. Suites are only medium size, but lovely retreats with large marble tubs. The swimming complex is cool (with a river pool and wave pool) and the spa is something to behold, with Chinese marble, Indian stone, Italian porcelain, Indonesian ceramics and Saudi Arabian granite.

Caesars Palace (Map pp76-8; ☎ 702-731-7110, 877-427-7243; www.caesarspalace.com; 3570 S Las Vegas; r from $125; P 🐾) Gone are the frosted glass and mirrors on the ceilings, but decadence still reigns. Caesars' standard rooms are some of the most luxurious in town. Subtle design accents such as Pompeian mural wall treatments enhance the spaciousness. A new 26-story all-suite tower overlooking the huge pool complex debuted in 2005.

Rio (Map pp76-8; ☎ 702-777-7777, 877-746-7153; www.playrio.com; 3700 W Flamingo Rd; ste from $125; P 🐾) The all-suite Rio is a great deal – if you don't mind being off-Strip. Most rooms (averaging 600 sq ft) boast floor-to-ceiling windows, separate vanity and dressing areas and a huge TV. For thrice the price 'masquerade suites' include a Jacuzzi tub and 180° panoramas. Some rooms are windowless.

MGM Grand (Map pp76-8; ☎ 702-891-7777, 877-880-0880; www.mgmgrand.com; 3799 S Las Vegas Blvd; r from $125; P 🐾) There's plenty to choose from at the world's largest hotel (5000-plus rooms in four 30-story towers), but is bigger better? Yes and no. Luxurious suites, with multiple bathrooms and patio whirlpools, can be a bargain. Standard rooms have plain Art Deco–themed Hollywood bungalow decor.

It's the casino and entertainment options that make the MGM shine.

Mirage (Map pp76-8; ☎ 702-791-7111, 800-374-9000; www.mirage.com; 3400 S Las Vegas Blvd; r from $125; P ⓧ) Standard digs here are elegant but smaller than most. All rooms have marble entryways and canopies over the headboard, with toned-down tropical colors. If space is a concern, upgrade to a suite – you can do better elsewhere, but the central location is tough to beat.

Paris (Map pp76-8; ☎ 702-946-7000, 877-796-2096; www.parislv.com; 3655 S Las Vegas Blvd; r from $125; P ⓧ) Standard rooms at this Hotel de Ville replica are a comfortable 450 sq ft, draped in rich royal-blue fabrics. An armoire serves as the closet, enhancing the regal Gallic feel. Rates climb steeply for upper-floor rooms with Strip views and the opulent suites. Above all else, the mid-Strip location is ace.

Bally's (Map pp76-8; ☎ 702-739-4111, 888-742-9248; www.ballyslv.com; 3645 S Las Vegas Blvd; r from $125; P ⓧ) Location, location, location. Two blissfully theme-free towers house spacious standard 450-sq-ft rooms and larger suites. All rooms have sofas and are pleasantly decorated in earthy tones. Extras include a top-notch health club, tennis courts and private poolside cabanas.

Tropicana (Map pp76-8; ☎ 702-739-2222, 888-826-8767; www.tropicanalv.com; 3801 S Las Vegas Blvd; r from $95; P ⓧ) World famous since its 1957 debut, the Trop is still going strong. The Island Tower retains a kitschy Polynesian theme, while the newer Paradise Tower tries for French provincial. Most of the rooms have floor-to-ceiling windows but are cramped. The huge pool complex (p85) with swim-up blackjack keeps things cool.

Las Vegas Hilton (Map pp76-8; ☎ 702-732-5111, 888-732-7117; www.lvhilton.com; 3000 Paradise Rd; r from $125; P ⓧ) The decor at the conventioneers' choice can only be described as upscale-contemporary American hotel. Standard digs are spacious, with automated drapes and deeper-than-usual tubs. Refined suites fetch thrice as much.

Treasure Island (Map pp76-8; ☎ 702-894-7111, 800-288-7206; www.treasureisland.com; 3300 S Las Vegas Blvd; r from $125; P ⓧ) The rooms here feel deceptively expansive, thanks to floor-to-ceiling windows and a soft earthy color scheme. Recent grown-up additions include deluxe poolside cabanas amid waterfalls and lush greenery, a huge party-friendly hot tub and the Strip-front Tangerine (p103), a burlesque lounge and nightclub. The casino has the easiest valet and self-service parking on The Strip. But unless you really dig the Caribbean, the class here just doesn't match the high admission fee.

Flamingo (Map pp76-8; ☎ 702-733-3111, 888-308-8899; www.flamingolasvegas.com; 3555 S Las Vegas Blvd; r $75-125; P ⓧ) The Flamingo attracts faithful flocks for two good reasons: price and

---

SLEEPING, WORTH A SPLURGE?

Everything in Las Vegas is so over-the-top glam, why shouldn't your room be as well? If you're going to splurge anywhere on your Southwestern vacation, Vegas is the place to do it. Even the midrange places feature lots of glamorous bang for the buck.

Best of all, if you're willing to spend some time searching, you'll likely score a suite room for less than you'd pay in a comparably sized city. Vegas is a buyer's market and rates fluctuate wildly according to demand. Arrive midweek and rooms go for as much as 50% less than on weekends. That said, rates triple during big conventions and even quadruple for major holidays like Valentine's Day and New Year's Eve.

The best way to find a deal is to first check the casino websites. Many properties lure customers during slow periods with discounted room rates, which are advertised online and in Sunday travel sections of major newspapers. Remember, Strip properties can offer rooms for the same price as a dumpy Downtown joint since they make their bucks back in the gaming areas.

Also check online hotel consolidators like www.travelocity.com, www.hotels.com and www.priceline.com. These companies buy large blocks of rooms, and if demand is low they'll re-sell them at a major discount. The rack rate at the Bellagio might be upwards of $300, but book through a consolidator and you might only pay $160.

If you arrive without a reservation, visit the Las Vegas Convention & Visitors Authority (LVCVA; ☎ 800-332-5333), which might be able to secure a discounted room.

AUTHOR'S CHOICE

Barbary Coast (Map pp76-8; ☎ 702-737-7111, 888-227-2279; www.barbarycoastcasino.com; 3595 S Las Vegas Blvd; r from $40; [P]) With cheap rooms smack bang mid-Strip, the Barbary is The Strip's worst kept secret. It's a great value and features charming Victorian-era decor, so it's often tough to secure a bed in the basic rooms.

Palms Resort Casino (Map pp76-8; ☎ 702-942-7777, 866-942-7770; www.palms.com; 4321 W Flamingo Rd; r from $125; [P] [R]) Off-Strip and originally aimed at young locals, the post–*Real World* Palms now attracts a flashier MTV-influenced crowd and has become a favorite with celebs like Paris Hilton and Britney Spears (she spent her *first* wedding night here). Standard rooms are generous (440 sq ft), as are the tech-savvy amenities. Request an upper floor to score a Strip view. The playpen suites are tailored for bachelor and bachelorette parties. For true luxury, rent the Real World Suite (from $7500), where the gang lived during filming. The 2900-sq-ft suite looks just like it did in the TV show, and is where Leonardo DiCaprio often sleeps when he's in town.

Bellagio (Map pp76-8; ☎ 702-693-7111; www.bellagio.com; 3600 S Las Vegas Blvd; r from $300; [P] [R]) If anything in Vegas is truly 'spectacular,' this luxe five-diamond destination is it. Over-size, lavish bathrooms feature Italian marble, plush robes and deep soaking tubs. Updated guestrooms are styled out with original artwork and picture windows overlooking the lush grounds. The stately new Spa Tower suites elevate luxury to a new level.

---

location. The tropical-themed abodes are tiny, but floor-to-ceiling windows compensate somewhat. For regulars, the location trumps the downsides.

Stratosphere (Map pp76-8; ☎ 800-998-6937; www.stratospherehotel.com; 2000 S Las Vegas Blvd; r from $75; [P] [R]) The main drawback (or attraction?) at the sky-high Stratosphere is its distance from the action. Size is average but the decor is more fetching than most, particularly in the newer tower. A mandatory $5 resort fee includes free Tower admission. Other plusses include a huge swimming complex and adults-only beach.

TOP END

True luxury comes cheaper here than almost anywhere else in the world. If you drop wads of cash around the casino, expect to be comped a sumptuous suite. Impeccable service, 24/7 can-do concierge pampering and expedited airport check-in are par for the course. Remember, booking online can score deep discounts.

Venetian (Map pp76-8; ☎ 702-414-1000; www.venetian.com; 3355 S Las Vegas Blvd; r from $300; [P] [R]) Fronted by flowing canals and graceful arched bridges, the Venetian's 700-sq-ft 'standard' rooms are anything but. In fact, they are the largest and most luxurious in town, with oversized Italian marble baths and canopy-draped bedchambers. The new 36-story Venezia luxury tower has a private garden pool and exclusive concierge level.

Four Seasons (Map pp76-8; ☎ 702-632-5000; www.fourseasons.com/lasvegas; Mandalay Bay, 3960 S Las Vegas Blvd; r from $300; [P] [R] [□]) Private elevators whisk guests away to the 424 exclusive rooms on Mandalay Bay's 35th through 39th floors. The nongaming resort emphasizes quiet comfort and 24/7 concierge coddling. Standard rooms are 500 sq ft, while suites reach 4400 sq ft. In-room high-speed Internet, a full-service spa and twice-daily housekeeping seal the deal.

THEhotel (Map pp76-8; ☎ 702-632-7777; www.mandalaybay.com; Mandalay Bay, 3950 S Las Vegas Blvd; ste from $300; [P] [R] [□]) From the moment you enter the intimate lobby adjacent Mandalay Bay, you feel a world away from The Strip's hustle-bustle. The expansive suites boast broadband Internet, wet bars, plasma TVs, separate living areas and cosmo NYC chic decor. Special business-friendly suites are adjacent to the convention center. Twenty non-suite rooms are slightly less expensive.

Downtown

Golden Nugget (Map p87; ☎ 702-385-7111, 800-846-5336; www.goldennugget.com; 129 E Fremont; r $75-125; [P] [R]) Downtown's crown jewel owes its elegance to ex-owner Steve Wynn and its newfound panache to Fox's *Casino* reality show. The ample standard rooms, with half-canopy beds and marble everywhere, are good value. The two-level luxury apartments are truly unique. A lavish spa and fitness center round out this class act.

Main Street Station (Map p87; ☎ 702-387-1896, 800-465-0711; www.mainstreetcasino.com; 200 N Main St; r from $75; (**P**)) Stay Downtown for an intimate experience. The 406 spacious rooms, as handsome as the rest of the casino and among Vegas' loveliest, are elegant, bright and cheery, with large plantation shutters. The 17-floor tower features marble-tile foyers, Victorian sconces and marble-trimmed hallways.

Viva Las Vegas Villas (Map p87; ☎ 702-484-0771, 800-574-4450; www.vivalasvegasvillas.com; 1205 S Las Vegas Blvd; r from $40; (**P**) (**⊠**) (**▣**)) Tying the knot? This wedding wonderland is the most inviting place between Downtown and The Strip. Themes include Blue Hawaii, Disco, Gangster and Gothic. Non-themed rooms have TV/VCRs and free videos. Continental breakfast is served in a 1950s diner with free DSL Internet. Watch weddings live online!

USA Hostels Las Vegas (Map p87; ☎ 702-385-1150; 1322 Fremont St; dm/s/d $15/35/45; (**⊠**)) It's on the not-so-nice outskirts of downtown, but top-notch facilities (including a pool, Jacuzzi and bar) and an incredibly accommodating staff redeem the location. Call for free pick-up from the Greyhound station.

EATING

Sin City is an unmatched eating adventure. Since Wolfgang Puck brought Spago to Caesars in 1992, celebrity Iron Chefs have taken up residence in nearly every megaresort. With so many star-struck tables to choose from, stakes are high and there are many overhyped eating gambles.

Cheap buffets and loss-leader meal deals still exist, mostly Downtown, but the gourmet quotient is high with prices to match. If you're arriving from other cities in the region you may be stunned by the cost of food in Las Vegas. Midrange places generally charge in the $20s for mains, while true luxury will set you back more than $30 per plate. It's slim pickings for vegetarians, with only a few options at most places – buffet salad bars are your best bet.

Make reservations for the fancier restaurants; book as far in advance as possible, especially if you're here on a weekend. Unless otherwise noted, the dress code at upscale eateries is business casual. At the most famous places, jackets are required for men.

Las Vegans are on the go 24/7, so it's always possible to get a meal. Every major casino has a 24-hour café and at least a couple of restaurants. Breakfast is often served nonstop and weekend champagne brunch buffets are served between 9am and 4:30pm. Vegas' restaurants alone could be fodder for an entire book; here are some favorites, organized by cuisine, but there are many, many more.

The Strip & Around
AMERICAN
Aureole (Map pp76-8; ☎ 702-632-7401; Mandalay Bay, 3960 S Las Vegas Blvd; dishes $30; (**⋎**) 6-10:30pm) Chef Charlie Palmer's inspired seasonal American dishes – such as spice-crusted tuna with foie gras – soar to new heights here. The prix fixe tasting menus ($95) are pure art and it's worth ordering wine just to watch the stewards ascend the four-story tower. There's an extensive wine list and formal dress is required. Reservations are essential but difficult.

Palm (Map pp76-8; ☎ 702-732-7256; Forum Shops, Caesars Palace, 3570 S Las Vegas Blvd; dishes $20-45) Vegas' premier surf-and-turf haven is lauded for its jumbo Nova Scotia lobster and gigantic portions – but prepare to be clawed by the prices. The $16 prix fixe lunch, however, is one of the best deals in town. The shrimp cocktails and prime steaks are fantastic.

Bally's Steakhouse (Map pp76-8; ☎ 702-967-7999; Bally's, 3645 S Las Vegas Blvd; brunch $58) Indulge at the best – and most expensive – Sunday brunch in town. Ice sculptures and lavish flower arrangements abound at the Sterling Brunch, as do food stations featuring roast duckling, steak Diane, seared salmon with beet butter sauce – you get the idea. Reservations suggested.

Michael's (Map pp76-8; ☎ 702-737-7111; ground fl, Barbary Coast, 3595 S Las Vegas Blvd; dishes from $30; (**⋎**) seatings 6pm, 6:30pm, 9pm & 9:30pm) Lavished with the Barbary Coast's signature Tiffany-styled stained glass, this top-drawer gourmet room does four dinner seatings daily. Prime à la carte delicacies include chateaubriand and live Maine lobster. It's old Vegas at its most rococo. Reservations essential, coats required.

Emeril's (Map pp76-8; ☎ 702-891-7374; MGM Grand, 3799 S Las Vegas Blvd; dishes $20-30) The Crescent City's most televised chef, Emeril Lagasse, cranks it up a notch at his New Orleans fish house with barbecued oysters and lobster cheesecake. The wine list is a *Wine*

BEST RABELAISIAN FEASTS

When it comes to groaning boards, the adage 'you get what you pay for' was never truer. Most buffets feature live-action stations specializing in sushi, seafood, pasta, stir-fries and so on. Among the standard mains at the upscale resorts: shrimp, lobster claws, antipasti, beef tenderloin, carved-to-order roast meats, fresh fruit, various soups and lots of salad material. Buffet prices, like hotel rates, fluctuate. Generally, expect to pay $7 to $15 for breakfast, from $15 to $60 for brunch, $10 to $20 for lunch and $15 to $25 or more for dinner. Following are some favorites.

Buffet at Bellagio (below) Competing for top honors in the class category, this buffet features a sumptuous all-you-can-eat spread including crowd-pleasers such as smoked salmon and creative dishes from around the world. Go for dinner.

Le Village Buffet (p99) Arguably one of the best buffets on The Strip, Le Village showcases selections from around France as well as a delicious Sunday brunch that includes unlimited champagne.

Bally's Steakhouse (p95) Indulge in the best – and most expensive – Sunday brunch in town. Ice sculptures and lavish flower arrangements add to the rich ambiance, while selections like roast duckling and steak Diane get your juices flowing.

Carnival World Buffet (p99) With dishes from China, Brazil, Mexico and Italy on offer, as well as loads of fresh seafood, some say this is the best buffet in town. It's pretty darn good, so it's hard to dispute that claim. It's certainly the best all-around buffet off The Strip.

House of Blues (below) Church might be an oxymoron in Sin City, but you can find holy redemption, Vegas style, at House of Blues' Gospel Brunch. It includes unlimited champagne and is the most uplifting (and unique) Sunday eating experience in town.

Spectator award-winner, and the banana cream pie drizzled with caramel is sumptin' else.

Café Bellagio (Map pp76-8; ☎ 702-693-7111; Bellagio, 3600 S Las Vegas Blvd; dishes $10) Bellagio's all-hours eatery is among the best in town. The menu features exciting twists on traditional American favorites. Big draws are the delicious coffee drinks, flowery setting and its gorgeous views of the swimming pool and garden areas.

House of Blues (Map pp76-8; ☎ 702-632-7600; Mandalay Bay, 3960 S Las Vegas Blvd; dishes $10-20) This homey roadhouse (burgers, salads, barbecue) is a good pit stop before a show and a pre-show dinner receipt whisks you past the show door line. The swampy bayou atmosphere and down home southern cuisine is enhanced by eccentric outsider folk art. Skip church: the uplifting Sunday Gospel Brunch includes unlimited champagne.

Delmonico Steakhouse (Map pp76-8; ☎ 702-414-3737; Venetian, 3355 S Las Vegas Blvd; dishes from $30) Bam: it's celeb chef Emeril Lagasse's greatest gourmet hits, as seen on TV. The cuts are ready for prime time, the influences are Creole and the chateaubriand-for-two is carved tableside. Big oak doors open into a vaulted ceiling space with a petite grand piano.

Valentino (Map pp76-8; ☎ 702-414-3000; Venetian, 3355 S Las Vegas Blvd; dishes $30; ☯ 5:30-11pm) James Beard award-winning chef Piero Selvaggio presides over the menu of contemporary takes on classics (scads of carpaccio and truffle essence). The wine cellar – 24,000 bottles, mostly from boutique Italian vintners – is enviable and the room is low-lit and romantic.

Buffet at Bellagio (Map pp76-8; ☎ 702-693-7111; casino level, Bellagio, 3600 S Las Vegas Blvd; breakfast $12, brunch $15, dinner $25-35) The Bellagio rightfully takes top honors for Vegas' best live-action buffet. The sumptuous all-you-can-eat spread includes such crowd-pleasers as smoked salmon, roast turkey and innumerable creative Chinese, Japanese and Italian dishes.

Prime Steakhouse (Map pp76-8; ☎ 702-693-7223; Bellagio, 3600 S Las Vegas Blvd; dishes $20-55; ☯ dinner) Luxurious contemporary chop house with stylistic nods to 1930s speakeasies. Trademark dishes include scallops with caper-raisin emulsion and caramelized cauliflower and Maine lobster with braised artichokes. Jackets preferred.

Victorian Room (Map pp76-8; ☎ 702-737-7111; Barbary Coast, 3595 S Las Vegas Blvd; dishes $5-10) Deep red leather booths, stained glass and polished brass add ambiance to this lively and central 24-hour coffee shop. Graveyard specialties like New York steak-and-eggs ($5.95) and 24/7 T-bone or prime rib deals make it a favorite after-hours hangout.

Charlie Palmer Steak (Map pp76-8; ☎ 702-632-5120; Four Seasons, Mandalay Bay, 3960 S Las Vegas Blvd; dishes from $30; ☺ 5-10:15pm) Artisan-aged beef is grilled to perfection at this classy hideaway. There's an impressive wine list and reservations are essential.

Nobhill (Map pp76-8; ☎ 702-891-7337; MGM Grand, 3799 S Las Vegas Blvd; dishes from $30; ☺ 5:30-10:30pm) James Beard award-winning chef Michael Mina brings the best of Northern California's gourmet cornucopia, including housemade sourdough breads, farmstead cheeses and Monterey Bay abalone. True to NoCal form, the ambiance is laid-back yet elegant. Five-course tasting menus and bar seating.

Gallagher's (Map pp76-8; ☎ 702-740-6450; New York-New York, 3790 S Las Vegas Blvd; dishes from $25; ☺ 4-11pm) You can't ignore the house specialty, dry aged sirloin, in the meat lockers out front. The rest of the USDA-choice menu's surf-and-turf offerings are justifiably famous. To whet your appetite, try the burgundy escargot.

Top of the World (Map pp76-8; ☎ 702-380-7711, 800-998-6937; Stratosphere, 2000 S Las Vegas Blvd; dishes $22-35) A dressy, revolving romantic roost perched atop the Stratosphere Tower. While taking in the cloud-level views, patrons enjoy impeccable service and delicious (if overpriced) mains such as veal, lobster and almond-crusted salmon. Reservations recommended. Good wine list.

Siena Deli (Map pp76-8; ☎ 702-736-8424; 2250 E Tropicana Ave; dishes $6-10; ☺ 8am-6:30pm Mon-Sat) Mama mia, Siena is the best deli in town, hands down. Make a meal out of Sicilian-style flat pizzas, Illy espresso and housemade tiramisu. Or grab a mouthwatering hot or cold deli sandwich. They only sell what they eat – *ho mangiato bene!*

Harrie's Bagelmania (Map pp76-8; ☎ 702-369-3322; 855 E Twain Ave; dishes $4-10; ☺ 7am-4pm Mon-Sat) This kosher deli and NYC-style bagelry is the real deal, right down to the chicken in a pot and matzo-ball soup. Harrie's is a great breakfast spot pulling in half the ex-Manhattanites in town.

Stage Deli (Map pp76-8; ☎ 702-893-4045; Forum Shops, Caesars Palace, 3570 S Las Vegas Blvd; dishes $6-10) Sky-high sandwiches, named after gourmand celebs such as Wilt Chamberlin

(corned beef with sauerkraut and Swiss), and a huge selection of heaping sides make this a cheap and filling option.

AJ's Steakhouse (Map pp76-8; ☎ 702-693-5500; Hard Rock, 4455 Paradise Rd; dishes from $30; ☺ 6-11pm Tue-Sat) The Rat Pack would feel right at home in this clubby, macho chop house. The superb steaks, filets and smooth martinis are almost overshadowed by the retro 1950s decor. Live piano jazz. Reservations essential.

Tony Roma's: A Place for Ribs (Map pp76-8; ☎ 702-732-6111; Stardust, 3000 S Las Vegas Blvd; dishes $10-27) An informal and very popular restaurant specializing in barbeque baby back ribs with a variety of sauces, as well as barbecue shrimp and chicken.

Grand Lux Café (Map pp76-8; ☎ 702-414-3888; Venetian, 3355 S Las Vegas Blvd; dishes from $10) A sophisticated quick bite if you don't want to stray too far from the tables. The plates of global comfort food are piled high and the ambiance is elegant yet casual. Don't miss a decadent dessert.

Mr Lucky's (Map pp76-8; ☎ 702-693-5000; Hard Rock, 4455 Paradise Rd; dishes $5-10) A casual all-hours diner overlooking the casino action. The full late-night comfort food menu doesn't list the $7.77 surf-and-turf special: a juicy 8oz steak, three jumbo shrimp and your choice of starches.

Rainforest Café (Map pp76-8; ☎ 702-891-1111; MGM Grand, 3799 S Las Vegas Blvd; dishes $9-20) This jungle-themed restaurant is a perfect place to bring the kids. The food is secondary to the lush faux-forest setting, a host of mechanized exotic animals and simulated tropical downpours. The elephant bellows loud enough to drown out any crying children.

Olives (Map pp76-8; ☎ 702-693-8181; Bellagio, 3600 S Las Vegas Blvd; dishes $20-30) Bostonian chef Todd English dishes up homage to the life-giving fruit. Flatbread pizzas, housemade pastas and flame-licked meats get top billing. Window seats face the open kitchen while patio tables overlook Lake Como. Good wine list.

America (Map pp76-8; ☎ 702-740-6451; New York-New York, 3790 S Las Vegas Blvd; dishes $8-15) A fanciful bas-relief US map hangs over this reliable, patriotic all-hours eatery. Many go red-white-and-blue in the face trying to pick something from the extensive menu of all-American fare. Extensive bi-coastal beer and wine selection.

ASIAN

Hyakumi (Map pp76-8; ☎ 877-346-4642; Caesars Palace, 3570 S Las Vegas Blvd; dishes from $30; ⏰ 5:30-10:30pm Sun-Thu, to 11pm Fri & Sat) One of Vegas' top Japanese joints, 'yah-*coo*-me' (literally '100 tastes') offers diners a choice of *teppanyaki* grill table or sushi bar seating. Gracious waitstaff don traditional obis and kimonos and the decor is rustic country village meets English garden.

Nobu (Map pp76-8; ☎ 702-693-5090; Hard Rock, 4455 Paradise Rd; dishes $20-30; ⏰ 6-11pm) Iron chef Matasuhisa's sequel to his NYC namesake is every bite as good as the original. The beats are down-tempo…the setting pure Zen. Andean influences surface in spicy offerings like *anticucho* chicken skewers. The Kobe beef is suave, the cocktails creative and dessert downright decadent. Feeling flush: try the Chef's Special *omakase* dinner. Reservations suggested.

Mizuno's (Map pp76-8; ☎ 702-739-2713; Tropicana, 3801 S Las Vegas Blvd; dishes from $20; ⏰ 5:30-10:45pm) Chefs prepare tempura, shrimp, lobster, chicken and steak tableside on *teppan* grills with swordsmen-like moves. The restaurant itself is a work of art, with gorgeous marble floors and many Japanese antiques. Reservations required.

Royal Star (Map pp76-8; ☎ 702-414-1888; Venetian, 3355 S Las Vegas Blvd; dishes $20-30) Feng shui principles guided LAX airport architect Lin Wa's design of this exquisitely appointed Hong Kong–style eatery. Tableside dim sum service utilizes traditional carts, while dinner features auspicious Mandarin and Cantonese delicacies like abalone with yellow morels. Full bar.

Jasmine (Map pp76-8; ☎ 702-693-8166; Bellagio, 3600 S Las Vegas Blvd; dishes $30-45; ⏰ dinner) An elegant lakefront eatery surrounded by lovely gardens. Executive chef Philip Lo offers modern takes on Cantonese, Sichuan and Hunan classics like braised superior shark fin with silver sprouts and Jin Wah ham.

Noodles (Map pp76-8; ☎ 702-693-7111; Bellagio, 3600 S Las Vegas Blvd; dishes $10-20) Doling out noodle bowls from across the Orient, this late-night joint features stylish modern decor. Dim sum and Hong Kong–style barbecue make guest appearances.

Todai Seafood & Sushi Buffet (Map pp76-8; ☎ 702-892-0021; Aladdin, 3663 S Las Vegas Blvd; lunch $16, dinner $27) This all-you-can-gorge 160ft Japanese seafood spread features 15 salads and 40 types of sushi. Lobster, shellfish and crab legs are added to the mix at dinner. Children under 12 eat for half-price.

FRENCH

Alizé (Map pp76-8; ☎ 702-951-7000; Palms, 4321 W Flamingo Rd; dishes from $30; ⏰ 5:30-10:30pm) André Rochat's top-drawer gourmet room is named after the gentle French Mediterranean trade wind. The panoramic floor-to-ceiling views (enjoyed by every table) are stunning, just like the haute cuisine. A huge wine-bottle tower dominates the middle of the room. Casual evening dress.

Lutèce (Map pp76-8; ☎ 702-414-2220; Venetian, 3355 S Las Vegas Blvd; dishes from $30; ⏰ 5:30-10:30pm) Impeccable modern renditions of classic gourmet French fare (sautéed foie gras with chocolate sauce) are presented in a sophisticated, austere setting. The wine cellar is top-notch, the superb seafood dishes as sought-after as canalside seats with Strip views. Reservations essential.

Le Cirque (Map pp76-8; ☎ 702-693-7223; Bellagio, 3600 S Las Vegas Blvd; dishes from $30; ⏰ dinner) Top toque Marc Poidevin pairs artful haute cuisine with world-class wines in a joyous, intimate setting. The signature dish at this modern French restaurant is rabbit fricassee with Riesling, chanterelles and fava beans. A three-ring tasting menu costs $85, five acts $115. Jacket and tie required.

Eiffel Tower Restaurant (Map pp76-8; ☎ 702-948-6937; 11th fl, Eiffel Tower, Paris, 3655 S Las Vegas Blvd; dishes from $30; ⏰ dinner) The adage about the better the view, the worse the food doesn't

---

AUTHOR'S CHOICE

Picasso (Map pp76-8; ☎ 702-693-7223; Bellagio, 3600 S Las Vegas Blvd; dishes from $30; ⏰ 6-9:30pm Wed-Mon) Five-star chef Julian Serrano delivers artistic Franco-Iberian fusion in a museum-like setting. Original eponymous masterpieces complement mains like the signature sautéed fallow deer medallions and seafood *boudin*. Vaulted ceilings and exposed wood beams create an unpretentious Mediterranean feel. Linger on the patio over a digestif. Prix fixe ($85) and degustation ($95) menus recommended. Jacket and tie suggested. Reservations are essential but difficult.

apply here. Views of The Strip and Bellagio's fountains are as breathtaking as the near-perfect renditions of haute classics like foie gras at this French masterpiece. Tasting menu recommended. Good wine list. Reservations required; dress business casual.

Le Village Buffet (Map pp76-8; ☎ 702-946-7000; Rue de la Paix, Paris, 3655 S Las Vegas Blvd; breakfast $13, lunch $18, Sunday brunch & dinner $25) Food selections from France's various regions are represented at distinct cooking stations, with an emphasis on seafood. Fresh fruit and cheeses, cracked crab legs and a wide range of pastries make the Village arguably the best value buffet on The Strip. The popular Sunday brunch includes unlimited champagne.

Pamplemousse (Map pp76-8; ☎ 702-733-2066; 400 E Sahara Ave; dishes $15-30; ☺ dinner Tue-Sun) A landmark romantic hideaway, famous for its French Riviera–style salad (a basket of fresh veggies and vinaigrette dip), appetizers like escargots and soft-shell clams, and mains like Wisconsin duckling with orange curry sauce. 'Nicely casual' dress code, jackets appreciated.

Mon Ami Gabi (Map pp76-8; ☎ 702-944-4224; Paris, 3655 S Las Vegas Blvd; dishes $12-22) Think charming Champs Élysées bistro. This elevated patio seating in the shadow of the Eiffel Tower is the only Stripside alfresco dining and is great for people-watching. There's a raw seafood bar and the steak frites are *parfait*. Good, reasonable wine list.

FUSHION & ECLECTIC

Red Square (Map pp76-8; ☎ 702-632-7407; Mandalay Bay, 3960 S Las Vegas Blvd; dishes $20-25; ☺ 5:30-10:30pm) How postperestroika: a headless Lenin invites you to join your comrades for a tipple behind the red curtain in this postmodern Russian restaurant. There's a solid ice bar, heaps of caviar, a huge selection of frozen vodkas and infusions – and loaner sable fur coats for when you step into the locker!

808 (Map pp76-8; ☎ 877-346-4642; Caesars Palace, 3570 S Las Vegas Blvd; dishes $15-35; ☺ 5:30-10:30pm Sun-Thu, to 11pm Fri & Sat) Chef Jean-Marie Josselin dials Hawaii ('eight-oh-eight') daily on the coconut wireless to procure the raw goods that fuel this tropical-island-themed delight. The result is a creative mingling of French, Mediterranean, Indian and Pacific

---

> **MEALS ON WHEELS**
>
> Can't stand to face the heat? **Restaurants on the Run** (☎ 702-735-6325, 888-447-6325; www.ontherun.cc) will deliver the goods to both sides of The Strip from a couple of dozen (mostly chain) eateries to your room for a $7 fee, plus the cost of your meal.

Rim elements. Many locals regard this as their city's top seafood stop.

Little Buddha (Map pp76-8; ☎ 702-942-7778; Palms, 4321 W Flamingo Rd; dishes $15-20; ☺ 5:30-11pm Sun-Thu, to 12:30am Fri & Sat) An offshoot of Paris' terribly popular Buddha Bar, it dishes super-fresh sushi and French-Chinese fusion at reasonable prices (well for Vegas that is). Recommended mains include the duck confit, tempura pizza and spicy tuna tartar. The music and interior will sweep you away.

Chinois (Map pp76-8; ☎ 702-737-9700; Forum Shops, Caesars Palace, 3570 S Las Vegas Blvd; dishes $20-30) Peripatetic chef Wolfgang Puck scores again with his signature Eurasian fusion served in a soothing, artistic far Eastern atmosphere. Pair the Shanghai lobster with a premium glass of cold sake. There's a trendy dance club upstairs.

Paymon's Mediterranean Café & Hookah Lounge (Map pp76-8; ☎ 702-731-6030; 4147 S Maryland Pkwy; dishes $5-10) One of the city's few veggie spots. It serves items such as baked eggplant with fresh garlic, baba ganoush, tabbouleh and hummus. Carnivores should try the kebab sandwich, gyros or rotisserie lamb. The adjacent Hookah Lounge is a tranquil spot to chill with a water pipe and fig-flavored cocktail.

Meskerem Ethiopian (Map pp76-8; ☎ 702-732-4250; 252 Convention Center Dr; dishes under $10) In the Somerset Shopping Center just east of The Strip, this small, pleasant spot serves Ethiopian meals in unassuming but relatively relaxed environs. There are a few vegetarian options. For something different, go at breakfast and try the Ethiopian-style egg dishes and espresso.

Carnival World Buffet (Map pp76-8; ☎ 702-252-7767; Rio, 3700 W Flamingo Rd; breakfast $12, lunch $15, dinner $20) Food from China, Brazil, Mexico, Italy and the United States is showcased at this lavish buffet, one of the town's best. Go for dinner.

Quark Bar & Restaurant (Map pp76-8; ☎ 702-697-8725; Las Vegas Hilton, 3000 Paradise Rd; dishes $10-17) *Star Trek* fans and other geek-pretenders should beam right into this surprisingly cool and moody eatery. Amid a futuristic setting you can indulge in 'Little Green Salads,' 'Hamborgers' and other 'exotic' dishes, perhaps with Klingons in a nearby booth.

ITALIAN

Circo (Map pp76-8; ☎ 702-693-7223; Bellagio, 3600 S Las Vegas Blvd; dishes $20-30) This whimsical big top–inspired *osteria* overlooks the dancing fountains on faux Lake Como. Rustic yet complex Tuscan mains such as pan-seared foie gras with mission fig compote perform well with an international cellar of 500 wines. Jacket and tie required.

Zeffirino (Map pp76-8; ☎ 702-414-3500; Grand Canal Shoppes, Venetian, 3355 S Las Vegas Blvd; dishes $12-15) Housemade breads and seafood prepared with Venetian techniques are the highlights. Handcrafted furnishings accent the elegant dining room, with porch seating overlooking the canal.

Antonio's (Map pp76-8; ☎ 702-252-7737; Rio, 3700 W Flamingo Rd; dishes from $20; ☯ 5-11pm) Sumptuous northern Italian cuisine is served in a stylish Mediterranean setting, replete with inlaid marble floors and a domed faux sky. Veal lovers should try the fork-tender osso buco, served on a bed of saffron-infused risotto.

Terrazza (Map pp76-8; ☎ 702-731-7568; Caesars Palace, 3570 S Las Vegas Blvd; dishes $20-30; ☯ 5:30-11pm Tue-Sat) Rustic, well-prepared northern Italian fare, such as wood-fired pizzas, are served in a delicious poolside setting. The plush lounge has live jazz Wednesday to Sunday.

MEXICAN & LATIN AMERICAN

rumjungle (Map pp76-8; ☎ 702-632-7408; Mandalay Bay, 3960 S Las Vegas Blvd; dishes $20-30; ☯ 5:30-10:30pm) It's like a culinary episode of *Survivor*, featuring all-you-can-eat *rodizio* skewers of all kinds of meats. A tower of 150 bottles of firewater looms over the open fire pit and dueling conga drums compliment the Brazilian menu. After hours, the joint turns into an animated dance club.

Border Grill (Map pp76-8; ☎ 702-632-7403; Mandalay Bay, 3960 S Las Vegas Blvd; dishes $12-17) Overlooking Mandalay Beach, this modern, stylish restaurant features fare as seen on the Food Network's *Too Hot Tamales*. The

tortilla soup, green corn tamales and sautéed rock shrimp pass for authentic Nayarit fare.

Pink Taco (Map pp76-8; ☎ 702-693-5000; Hard Rock, 4455 Paradise Rd; dishes $10-20) The *comida* is Californiafied but tasty at this Baja fish taco shack crossed with a low-rider-themed Sunset Strip tequila bar. Margaritas are two-for-one and appetizers half-price during the popular 4pm to 7pm happy hour.

Downtown

Andre's (Map p87; ☎ 702-385-5016; 401 S 6th St; dishes $30; ☯ 6-11pm) Chef André Rochat's Provençal-decorated 1930s home is proof that hotels don't hold a monopoly on haute cuisine. Seasonal menu highlights include roasted Provimi veal chops stuffed with king crab and wild mushroom–encrusted bison tournedos. Request a tour of the world-class wine cellar and try for patio seating. Reservations essential, dress to impress.

Hugo's Cellar (Map p87; ☎ 702-385-4011, 800-634-6045; Four Queens, 202 E Fremont St; dishes $30; ☯ 5:30-11pm) Ladies get roses on arrival at this romantic Downtown institution, a classic Vegas gourmet room. Meals start with an exceptional salad cart and end with fruit dipped in chocolate for dessert. In between, it's martinis and surf-and-turf, baby.

Pullman Bar & Grille (Map p87; ☎ 702-387-1896, 800-713-8933; Main Street Station, 200 N Main St; dishes from $20; ☯ 5-10:30pm Wed-Sat) A well-kept secret, the Pullman features the finest Black Angus beef and seafood specialties, and a good wine list, amid gorgeous carved wood paneling. The centerpiece namesake is a 1926 Pullman train car, now a cigar lounge.

El Sombrero Café (Map p87; ☎ 702-382-9234; 807 S Main St; dishes $5-10; ✗) High-viscosity beef

---

BIG BUCKS BURGER

Since when is a hamburger worth $60? When it's built with Kobe beef, sautéed foie gras, shaved truffles and Madeira sauce. Chef Hubert Keller (of San Francisco's famed Fleur de Lys) serves up his signature Rossini burger along with burger-themed desserts and other gourmet comfort treats daily at the **Burger Bar** (Map pp76-8; ☎ 702-632-9364; 3930 S Las Vegas Blvd) in Mandalay Place (p107), the shopping mall linking Luxor and Mandalay Bay.

chili colorado is a highlight at this humble Mexican adobe eatery that's light-years away from The Strip. It's family-run and intimate enough to be well served by a single friendly waitress. Ask for help with the vintage jukebox and try the sweet agave wine margaritas.

Binion's Ranch Steak House (Map p87; ☎ 702-382-1600, 800-622-6468; Binion's, 128 E Fremont St; dishes $30; ☷ 6-10:30pm) When high-rollers finish up in the poker room, they retire their Stetsons and ride the glass elevator to this classy old Vegas penthouse meatery for stunning 24th-floor views.

Carson Street Café (Map p87; ☎ 702-385-7111; Golden Nugget, 129 E Fremont St; dishes $4-10) Downtown's best 24-hour eatery slings surprisingly good grub. The Euro-style sidewalk café features sandwiches, Mexican fare, filet mignon and prime rib. For dessert, try one of the delectable sundaes. There's a full bar.

Golden Gate Deli & Bay City Diner (Map p87; ☎ 702-385-1906; Golden Gate, 1 E Fremont St; dishes $1-10) Cheap breakfasts, graveyard steak-and-eggs, succulent porterhouse steaks and the best 99¢ shrimp cocktail in town (it's tiny – super-size it for $2.99) are the draws at this inviting pair of eateries inside Downtown's historic San Francisco–themed hotel.

DRINKING

Most booze consumption in Vegas takes place while staring down slot machines and gaming tables. Sometimes though, you just need to step away and take solace in what the country singer Dick Curless called a 'loser's cocktail.' For this the casinos, and a few independent watering holes, offer plenty of diversity – from the trendy, celebrity-heavy club that just could be in Los Angeles to the quiet, low-lit romantic hideaway – you'll never be left out to dry in Vegas.

V Bar (Map pp76-8; ☎ 702-414-3200; Venetian, 3355 S Las Vegas Blvd) Celebs, agents and glam young thangs meet and greet in this beautiful minimalist lounge. The acid jazz and low-key house music are mere accoutrements since low lighting and secluded sitting areas (and sturdy martinis) encourage intimate behavior.

Hush (Map pp76-8; ☎ 702-261-1000; Polo Towers, 3745 S Las Vegas Blvd, 19th fl; cover $5-20 ☷ 8pm-4:30am) Tucked away high atop a timeshare condo complex, this lounge is best known by a

hip younger crowd for its 180° Strip view. The rooftop pool, private Moroccan cabanas and oversized elevated beds open up for uptempo DJ nights.

Venus (Map pp76-8; ☎ 702-414-4870; Venetian, 3355 S Las Vegas Blvd; lounge cover $10-20; ☷ bar 5pm-1am Mon-Sun, lounge 9:30pm-5am Wed-Sun) Exotic tropical cocktails, wine by the glass and close proximity to balconies overlooking The Strip make this tiki bar and retro lounge combo a favorite local hang-out. Weekly events include ladies night on 'Flirt' Wednesday and DJ dance parties on Saturday.

VooDoo Lounge (Map pp76-8; ☎ 702-247-7923; Rio, 3700 W Flamingo Rd; cover after 8pm $10) The 51st-floor views are fab from the patio at Rio's Masquerade Tower. The lounge boasts an extensive cocktail menu, nightly live lounge acts and spirited bartender antics. Strict dress code (dress to impress). Entry is free with dinner reservations.

Fireside Lounge at the Peppermill (Map pp76-8; ☎ 702-735-7635; Peppermill, 2985 S Las Vegas Blvd) The Strip's most unlikely romantic hideaway is inside a retro coffee shop. Courting couples flock here for the low lighting, sunken fire pit and cozy nooks built for cuddling. Skip the food – sup a Scorpion.

Hofbräuhaus (Map pp76-8; ☎ 702-853-3227; 4510 Paradise Rd) Opposite the Hard Rock, this new $12 million beer hall and garden is a replica of the original in Munich. Celebrate Oktoberfest year-round with premium imported suds, big Bavarian pretzels, fair *frauleins*, oom-pah bands and trademark *gemütlichkeit* (congeniality).

Bar at Times Square (Map pp76-8; ☎ 702-740-6969; New York-New York, 3790 S Las Vegas Blvd; cover Fri & Sat $10) Thirty- to fifty-somethings dig the sing-along vibe at this packed dueling piano bar. Show up early on weekends or risk waiting out in Greenwich Village. If you can't stand the queue, grab a pint nearby at Nine Fine Irishmen.

Triple Seven Brewpub (Map p87; ☎ 702-387-1896; Main Street Station, 200 N Main St) Locals and an older casino crowd flock to this spacious Downtown spot for Monday night football, happy hour and graveyard specials. The sushi and oyster bar, five draught homebrews and cheap pub grub satiate all comers.

Coyote Ugly (Map pp76-8; ☎ 702-740-6330; New York-New York, 3790 S Las Vegas Blvd; cover $10-20) It's a bar…a T-shirt and also a movie! A hangover-curing cereal can't be far off. The antics at this serial Southern saloon are contrived, but fun nonetheless. A rowdy mix of conventioneers and genXers worship gyrating babes in crop tops pouring shots from the bartop.

ENTERTAINMENT
Clubs & After Hours

Little expense has been spared to bring clubs at The Strip's megaresorts on par with New York and Los Angeles in the area of wildly extravagant hangouts. Surf www.vegasafter10.com for pics, VIP tips and passes, and current listings. Many venues have bottle service, which means you agree to purchase an entire bottle of liquor (usually top end) and in exchange you usually get a hot table at the venue.

Rain (Map pp76-8; ☎ 702-942-7777; Palms, 4321 W Flamingo Rd; cover $20-40; ☾ 11pm-late Thu-Sat) Britney Spears once threw an impromptu concert while partying at this hot, hot club. You enter through a bright futuristic tunnel and are immediately immersed in color and motion. The bamboo dance floor appears to float on a bed of fountains, thanks to a computer-programmed river featuring dancing

---

AUTHOR'S CHOICE

Ra (Map pp76-8; ☎ 702-262-4949; Luxor, 3900 S Las Vegas Blvd; cover $10-30; ☾ 10pm-dawn Wed-Sat) Vegas' most spectacular club is fit for the ancient Egyptian god of the sun, who inhabited the heavens by day and raged in the underworld at night. Wednesday's Pleasuredome/Flaunt brings fashion shows, deep house and an old-school mix. Other nights feature big-name house and hip-hop DJs. The dress code is fashionable and the crowd is young and sybaritic.

---

jets and fountains. Fog and pyrotechnics set the mood, and the place feels elegant but not outright pretentious.

Body English (Map pp76-8; ☎ 702-693-4000; Hard Rock, 4455 Paradise Rd; cover $20; ☾ 10:30pm-4am Fri-Sun) The Hard Rock's elegant new Euro-style club emphasizes posh and VIP pampering. Booth reservations require one bottle ($300 minimum) per foursome, but there's a big bar upstairs. Famous folk hang out in the VIP rooms, while the lesser knowns dance to mainstream house, hip-hop and rock tunes below.

Light (Map pp76-8; ☎ 702-693-8300; Bellagio, 3600 S Las Vegas Blvd; cover $25; ☾ 10:30pm-4am Thu-Sun) Intimate, sophisticated Light emphasizes socializing while professional hosts push the top-shelf bottle service – there's no bar. High-NRG dance mixes dominate the dance floor. If you want to chill, book a VIP booth. It's another celeb hangout and reservations are recommended.

Foundation Room (Map pp76-8; ☎ 702-632-7631; 43rd fl, Mandalay Bay, 3950 S Las Vegas Blvd; ☾ admission by invitation only) M-Bay's exclusive club hosts after-show parties in a luxurious dining room. Celebs such as Andre Agassi hold court in the exclusive Lodge, where DJ entertainment and special events liven up the vibe.

Drai's (Map pp76-8; ☎ 702-737-0555; Barbary Coast, 3595 S Las Vegas Blvd; cover $20; ☾ midnight-8am Wed-Sun) Feel ready for an after-hours scene straight outta Hollywood? Drai is an LA producer and gourmet restaurateur to the starlets. Things don't really get going until 3am, when DJs spinning progressive discs keep the fashion plates content. Dress to kill.

Club Seven (Map pp76-8; ☎ 702-739-7744; 3724 S Las Vegas Blvd; cover $10-30; ☾ 11pm-9am Wed-Sun) The vibe at this hip, spacious lounge is DJ driven, although there's occasional live tunes in the Stripside patio in summer. Bonuses include a fine dance floor and saddle-up sushi bar. After hours, it morphs into Alesium, a comfy spot to watch sunrise over a Red Bull.

Tabu (Map pp76-8; ☎ 702-891-7129; MGM Grand, 3799 S Las Vegas Blvd; cover $10-40; ☾ 10pm-dawn Tue-Sun) Stylish indulgence and sensual sophistication rule at MGM's latest ultralounge. DJs spin to an interactive backdrop while stunning model/hostesses mix cocktails tableside. Wednesday's Boutique night brings local designers out on the catwalk.

Club Rio (Map pp76-8; ☎ 702-777-7977; Rio, Scinta Showroom, 3700 W Flamingo Rd; cover $10-20 ☯ 11pm-dawn Thu-Sat) This hot and sweaty club lures a mixed young, well-dressed local singles crowd with its 30,000 sq ft, 3D laser lights and thumpin' sound system. Thursday's a hot Latin Libido frenzy while other nights feature hip-hop and high-energy dance music.

Curve (Map pp76-8; ☎ 702-290-9582; Aladdin, London Club, 3663 S Las Vegas Blvd; cover $20; ☯ Curve 10:30pm-dawn Fri & Sat, Living Room 6pm-dawn Wed-Sun) What exactly is 'nightlife evolved'? Just ask the small tuxedo-clad doorman to find out. Resident DJs spin cutting-edge progressive mixes in Curve's eight ultra-elegant rooms. The patio and lounging areas all overlook The Strip. The chilled-out Living Room has attentive premium bottle service and DJs play jazz tunes on Wednesday.

Tangerine (Map pp76-8; ☎ 702-992-7970; Treasure Island, 3300 S Las Vegas Blvd; cover $20-40; ☯ 10pm-4am Tue-Sat) Treasure Island turns up the heat with its new lounge and nightclub. DJs spin pop, house and hip-hop, while burlesque dancers heat up the bartop hourly from 10:45pm to 1:45am with 15-minute quickies. The outdoor patio overlooking Sirens' Cove is the place to sit and sip while the ships cruise by during the battle royale.

Studio 54 (Map pp76-8; ☎ 702-891-7254; MGM Grand, 3799 S Las Vegas Blvd; cover $10-40; ☯ 10pm-dawn Tue-Sat) Like a flawed remake of a great film, this huge three-story club fails to capture the magic that existed at New York's namesake nightspot. The decor is black, silver and industrial and the grooves are always chart toppers. Inside are mostly tourists wondering where all the glamorous people went. Thursday's Dollhouse fashion night is the best bet.

CIRQUE DU SOLEIL: AN ENDURING LEGACY

Cirque du Soleil was born on the streets of Baie-Sant-Paul, a small Canadian village outside Quebec City, in the early 1980s. Although the company is known today for its elaborate productions, its origins were much simpler – a small group of entertainers showcasing their circus skills, everything from stilt walking to fire breathing and dance, on the town streets. While their talented shenanigans gained local notoriety, national recognition did not arrive until 1984, when the group pitched a show concept to the Quebec City government that would tie in with Canada's 450th birthday celebration.

Mixing the visually stunning theatrics of the circus (minus the animals) with traditional aspects of street performance, the production featured elaborate costumes, original music and dazzling light displays. Over the decades, the troupe has created numerous productions incorporating everything from graceful water acrobatics and flirtatious eroticism to surrealism and mystery. In a constant state of metamorphosis and re-invention, over 20 years after its humble beginnings Cirque du Soleil's circus artistry continues to dazzle crowds around the world. Its three Las Vegas productions remain the hottest tickets in Sin City.

Zumanity (Map pp76-8; ☎ 702-740-6815, 800-963-9364; New York-New York, 3790 S Las Vegas Blvd; admission $65-125; ☯ 7:30pm & 10:30pm Fri-Tue) Billed as 'another side of Cirque du Soleil,' the Human Zoo shares the energized pulse, contorted acrobatics and flirtatious eroticism of the troupe's other risk-taking resident Strip shows. So what's the hook that's made it the hottest ticket in town? Maybe it's the curvilinear thrust stage, uninhibited costumes by Thierry Mugler…or the romantic red loveseats reserved for couples.

O (Map pp76-8; ☎ 702-693-7722, 888-488-7111; Bellagio, 3600 S Las Vegas Blvd; admission $99-150; ☯ 7:30pm & 10:30pm Wed-Sun) Cirque du Soleil's original venture into aquatic theater is truly a spectacular feat of imagination. 'Eau' (French for water) is 3D surrealism. A talented international cast – performing in, on and above the precious liquid – surveys drama through the ages.

Mystère (Map pp76-8; ☎ 702-894-7722, 800-392-1999; Treasure Island, 3300 S Las Vegas Blvd; admission $95, limited seats for $60; ☯ 7pm & 10pm Wed-Sun) Cirque du Soleil director Franco Dragone does for theater what Dali did for painting. His evocative celebration of life begins with a pair of babies making their way in a world filled with strange creatures. A misguided clown's humorous antics are interspersed with acrobats, aerialists and dancers performing one spectacular feat of strength and agility after another.

Production Shows

Vegas is one big show – a minimal plot production that typically includes a variety of song, dance and magic acts. Leaving town without seeing a show is like leaving Paris without seeing Notre Dame.

Rita Rudner (Map pp76-8; ☎ 702-740-6815, 866-606-7111; New York-New York, 3790 S Las Vegas Blvd; admission $60; ☽ 8pm Mon-Thu, 9pm Fri & Sat) The comedienne, whose trademark is telling stories and delivering one-liners with soft-spoken naiveté, delivers a real kick in the pants. Her shrewd observations about life are a hoot and the intimate theater (425 seats) lends itself well to her shtick.

Folies Bergère (Map pp76-8; ☎ 800-829-9034; Tropicana, 3801 S Las Vegas Blvd; admission $49 & $59; ☽ covered 7:30pm & topless 10:30pm Mon, Wed, Thu & Sat; topless 8:30pm Tue & Fri) Las Vegas' longest-running production is a tribute to the Parisian Music Hall. Appropriately, it contains some of the most beautiful showgirls in town. The theme is 'France through the years' and the song-and-dance numbers include a fashion show, a royal ballroom number and the inevitable can-can routine.

Blue Man Group (Map pp76-8; ☎ 702-362-4400, 800-557-7428; Luxor, 3900 S Las Vegas Blvd; admission from $82; ☽ 7pm & 10pm Mon & Wed-Sat, 7pm only Tue & Sun; inquire about additional matinees) A trio of non-speaking comedic percussionists mix mind-bending audiovisual displays with juvenile but fun behavior in an odd and bemusing show. Bring a jacket: the first six rows of the audience are the recipients of catapulted Jell-O tubs, flying marshmallows and paint splattered off the tops of snare drums.

La Femme (Map pp76-8; ☎ 702-891-7777, 800-929-1111; MGM Grand, 3799 S Las Vegas Blvd; admission $59; ☽ 8pm & 10:30pm Wed-Mon) Za, za, zoom. The classiest topless show in town defines sexy. The 100% red room's intimate bordello feel oozes amour. Onstage, balletic dancers straight from Paris' Crazy Horse Saloon perform provocative cabaret numbers interspersed with voyeuristic L'Art du Nu vignettes. *Zut alors* – it's a classy peep show par excellence.

Céline Dion: A New Day (Map pp76-8; ☎ 702-731-3110, 877-423-5463; Caesars, 3570 S Las Vegas Blvd; admission $95-242; ☽ 8:30pm Wed-Sun) Cirque du Soleil maestro Franco Dragone pushed Céline to expand her limits for her new spectacular, which routinely fills Caesars' purpose-built $95-million Colosseum to

capacity. She rips through 20 new ballads and greatest hits during 100 minutes, with plenty of backup from North America's biggest LED screen – and lots of hot male dancers.

Theater, Magic, Cabaret & Comedy

Big-name comedians headline the Golden Nugget, House of Blues, Hilton and MGM Grand.

Comedy Stop (Map pp76-8; ☎ 800-829-9034; Tropicana, 3801 S Las Vegas Blvd; admission $15-20; ☽ nonsmoking 8pm, smoking 10:30pm) A-list funny-men and -women crack up the Trop's mezzanine-level cabaret during two nightly shows.

Aladdin Theatre (Map pp76-8; ☎ 702-785-5055; Aladdin, 3667 S Las Vegas Blvd; admission $25-125) Acts at the Aladdin's upgraded 7000-seat performing-arts auditorium range from Broadway blockbusters like *Jesus Christ Superstar* to classic rock acts like Jerry Lee Lewis and comedy kingpins such as Sinbad.

Cashman Center Theatre (Map p87; ☎ 702-631-4748; 850 N Las Vegas Blvd; admission $20-55) Major touring productions like the *Vagina Monologues* stop at this 1950-seat performing-arts space Downtown at the Cashman Convention Center.

Improv (Map pp76-8; ☎ 702-369-5111; Harrah's, 3475 S Las Vegas Blvd; admission $25; ☽ 8:30pm & 10:30pm Tue-Sun) Harrah's well-established showcase spotlights touring stand-up headliners of the moment.

Las Vegas Little Theatre (Map pp76-8; ☎ 702-362-7996; 3920 Schiff Dr; admission $10-20) Local amateur troupes have presented 'remastered' classics like *I Hate Hamlet* at this lively community venue for three decades.

Classical Music, Opera & Dance

Watch for the debut of a new special-effects rendition of Andrew Lloyd Webber's *Phantom of the Opera* – complete with an onstage lake and an exploding replica of the Paris Opéra chandelier – in a purpose-built $25 million theater at the Venetian in early 2006.

Las Vegas Philharmonic (Map pp76-8; ☎ 702-895-2787; UNLV Performing Arts Center, 4505 S Maryland Pkwy; admission $25-66; ☾ shows 8pm) This 80-piece orchestra performs at UNLV's Artemus Ham Concert Hall and around town at casino grand openings.

Nevada Ballet Theatre (Map pp76-8; ☎ 702-243-2623; UNLV Performing Arts Center, 4505 S Maryland Pkwy; admission $20-65) Nevada's only professional dance company presents both classical and contemporary performances year-round at a variety of venues, primarily at UNLV's Judy Bayley Theatre. Call for the current schedule.

UNLV Performing Arts Center (Map pp76-8; ☎ 702-895-2787; 4505 S Maryland Pkwy; admission $10-80) The Performing Arts Center hosts over 600 events on three stages throughout the year. The 1870-seat Artemus Ham Concert Hall has great acoustics while the 550-seat Judy Bayley Theatre accommodates everything from ballet to experimental music fests. The intimate Black Box Theatre presents smaller theatrical productions.

Live Music

House of Blues (Map pp76-8; ☎ 702-632-7600; Mandalay Bay, 3950 S Las Vegas Blvd; admission $10-100; ☾ shows from 6pm) Blues is the tip of the hog at this Mississippi Delta juke joint. Capacity is 1900, but seating is limited, so show up early if you want to take a load off. The sight lines are good and the outsider folk art decor is übercool.

BOX OFFICES & INFO LINES

Allstate Ticketing (☎ 702-597-5970, 800-838-9383; www.showtickets.com) Twenty-one outlets around town.

Nevada Ticket Services (☎ 702-597-1588, 800-597-7469; www.lasvegastickets.com) Sold-out tickets source.

Ticketmaster (☎ 702-474-4000; www.ticketmaster.com) Broker for mainstream events.

Tickets2Nite (Map pp76-8; ☎ 888-484-9264; www.tickets2nite.com; 3785 S Las Vegas Blvd) Showcase Mall half-price, same-day tickets booth.

UNLV Tickets (☎ 702-739-3267, 866-388-3267; www.unlvtickets.com) Source for all university events.

Joint (Map pp76-8; ☎ box office 702-226-4650; info 702-693-5066; Hard Rock, 4455 Paradise Rd; admission $20-1000; ☾ shows from 7pm) Concerts at this intimate venue (capacity 1400) feel like private shows, even when Bob Dylan or the Rolling Stones are in town. Most shows are standing room only, with reservable VIP balcony seats upstairs.

Sand Dollar Blues Lounge (Map pp76-8; ☎ 702-871-6651; 3355 Spring Mountain Rd; cover $3-5 after 10pm) A few doors down from a Harley repair shop, this unpretentious club is the only one in town featuring live jazz and blues nightly. It's smoky, casual and nautical themed with video poker and pool tables and draws a mixed, mostly local crowd. The Ethiopian-run Italian café next door serves good grub until late.

Strip Clubs

Vegas is the original adult Disneyland. Prostitution may be illegal, but there are plenty of places offering the illusion of sex on demand. Lap dances cost $20.

Sapphire (Map pp76-8; ☎ 702-796-6000; 3025 S Industrial Rd; cover $20) The theme is big, big, big and just about everything here is bigger than life. Vegas' largest adult entertainment complex features a massive multilevel main stage and a story-high martini display. Famous folks flock to Sapphire, but you probably won't catch a glimpse – they have their own entrance with skybox seating.

Spearmint Rhino (Map pp76-8; ☎ 702-796-3600; 3344 Highland Dr; cover $20) The glam factor is high at this highly regarded topless club. The women are beautiful, but the place has a laid-back air and gals won't feel uncomfortable accompanying their boyfriends. Spearmint is a smallish place with an intimate vibe. It fills up fast, so arrive early for the best seating.

Girls of Glitter Gulch (Map p87; ☎ 702-385-4774; 20 E Fremont St; admission free, 2-drink min) As you experience Fremont Street (p86), you can't help but notice this topless joint that Downtown boosters wish would just go away. Inside you'll find friendly dancers and a mostly tourist crowd; unescorted women are welcome.

Olympic Garden (Map pp76-8; ☎ 702-385-9361; 1531 S Las Vegas Blvd; cover $20; ☾ 24hr) The OG wins high marks from topless club aficionados – and the nickname 'Silicone Valley' from the competition. Up to 50 dancers

GIRLS JUST WANNA HAVE FUN

Why should the boys have all the fun? Girls, if you're hot for a night of sexy male bods, Vegas is your town.

The dancers at Rio's (p85) 400-seat **Chippendales Theater** (Map pp76-8; $35-45; 10pm) are more about being in the spotlight than giving the girls a feel, so you won't feel uncomfortable if you're new at this strip-club thing. Private sky boxes, a spacious cocktail lounge and a plush bathroom complete with 'gossip pit' are perks.

If you're feeling a little naughtier, head to Excalibur (p79), where you can touch the lovely lads of **Thunder from Down Under** (Map pp76-8; admission $35-45; 8:30pm & 10:30pm). They provide nonstop fun and flirting. And we mustn't forget the down-and-dirty **Men of Olympus**, who strut their stuff upstairs Wednesday through Sunday at the Olympic Garden (p105).

work at any given time, thus there's something to please everyone. Studs strip upstairs Wednesday through Sunday.

Cinemas

Check **Moviefone** (702-222-3456; www.moviefone.com) for showtimes, trailers and music listings.

Brenden Imax 14 (Map pp76-8; 702-507-4849; Palms, 4321 W Flamingo Rd; admission $9) The swankest off-Strip movieplex is fitted with Imax and Lucasfilm THX digital sound, plus stadium seating for superior sightlines.

Crown Neonopolis 14 (Map p87; 702-383-9600; Neonopolis, 450 E Fremont St; admission $8) Vegas' newest theater is also the cheapest. All 14 screens sport digital THX sound and high-backed, stadium-style seating.

Luxor Imax Theatre (Map pp76-8; 702-262-4555, 800-557-7428; Luxor, 3900 S Las Vegas Blvd; admission $10-15) Luxor's theater projects onto a seven-story, wall-mounted – rather than curved overhead – screen, but the images (half 2D, half 3D) are 10-times more detailed than conventional cinemas. With only 312 seats, you're plenty close to the action.

Sports

Although Vegas doesn't have any professional sports franchises, it's a very sports-savvy town. Handicapping is one of the most

popular activities and you can wager on just about anything at race and sports books.

For auto racing, including Nascar, Indy racing, drag racing and dirt-track races check out the enormously popular **Las Vegas Motor Speedway** (Map p87; 702-644-4444, 800-644-4444; 7000 N Las Vegas Blvd).

World-class boxing draws fans from all over the globe. Venues include:

Mandalay Bay Events Center (Map pp76-8; 877-632-7800; www.mandalaybay.com; Mandalay, 3950 S Las Vegas Blvd) Twelve thousand seats: boxing, headliner concerts, bull riding!

MGM Grand Garden Arena (Map pp76-8; 877-880-0880; www.mgmgrand.com; MGM Grand, 3799 S Las Vegas Blvd) Seventeen thousand seats: boxing, motorsports, mega concerts, tennis.

Orleans Arena (Map pp76-8; 888-234-2334; www.orleansarena.com; Orleans, 4500 W Tropicana Ave) Nine thousand seats for boxing, ice hockey, motorsports and concerts.

SHOPPING

Las Vegas is a shopper's paradise. Consumption is as conspicuous as dancing fountains in the middle of the desert. Upscale international haute purveyors cater to the cashed-up – you can find almost anything (name brand, at least) that you'd see in London or Los Angeles. Plus a few unique high-roller items not likely to be sold anytime soon, like Ginger Rogers' 7.02-carat marquis diamond engagement ring and the world's largest carved emerald, both on display in Fred Leighton at the Bellagio.

Shopping Areas

The Strip is the focus of the shopping action, with upscale boutiques concentrated in the newer resorts fronting the southern half. Downtown and the Westside are the places to cruise for wigs, naughty adult goods and trashy lingerie. On the Eastside, near UNLV, Maryland Pkwy is chock-a-block with hip shops catering to the college crowd. Malls dominate the scene but upscale specialty shops at megaresorts stay open late. Trendy one-off boutiques are scarce, but are popping up on the fringes of The Strip.

Department Stores & Shopping Centers

Practically every casino includes some type of shopping mall. The following are places that stand out for their superb shops or interesting architectural design.

Forum Shops (Map pp76-8; ☎ 702-893-4800; Caesars Palace, 3500 S Las Vegas Blvd) Franklins fly out of Fendi bags faster than in high-roller casinos at the nation's most profitable consumer playground. Caesars' fanciful re-creation of an ancient Roman market houses 150 designer shops. Included in the mélange are one-name catwalk wonders like Armani, Escada, Versace, Fendi and MaxMara. Don't miss the new spiral escalator.

Desert Passage (Map pp76-8; ☎ 702-736-7114; Aladdin, 3663 S Las Vegas Blvd) Aladdin's upscale North African–themed marketplace has 130 retailers and a dozen restaurants, plus a rainy harbor and scads of wandering street performers. The emphasis is on jewelry, gifts and women's apparel. Cargo bikes await to transport baggage-laden shoppers to the remote parking garage.

Via Bellagio (Map pp76-8; ☎ 702-693-7111; Bellagio, 3600 S Las Vegas Blvd) Bellagio's swish indoor promenade is home to the who's who of fashion-plate designers: Armani, Chanel, Dior, Fred Leighton (p108), Gucci, Hermès, Prada, Tiffany and Yves Saint Laurent.

Grand Canal Shoppes (Map pp76-8; ☎ 702-414-4500; Venetian, 3355 S Las Vegas Blvd) Living statues and mezzo-sopranos lurk among 75 upscale shops and art galleries at this indoor mall. Cobblestone walkways wind past Ann Taylor, BCBG, Banana Republic, Godiva, Kenneth Cole, Jimmy Choo and Movado.

Mandalay Place (Map pp76-8; ☎ 702-632-7777; skybridge btwn Mandalay Bay & Luxor) M-Bay's new upscale commercial promenade houses 40 unique, fashion-forward boutiques, including Samantha Chang, Fornarina, Oilily, Sauvage, GF Ferré, Davidoff, Mulholland, Musette and Shoe Obsession.

MGM Grand Studio Walk & Star Lane Shops (Map pp76-8; ☎ 702-891-3300; MGM Grand, 3799 S Las Vegas Blvd) What to give the wannabe starlet who has everything? This Hollywood-themed mall may hold the answer. Designer luggage, costume jewelry and LV logo items are in the mix. At CBS TV City you can watch and rate TV pilots.

Fashion Show Mall (Map pp76-8; ☎ 702-369-0704; 3200 S Las Vegas Blvd) Unique shops are sparse at Nevada's biggest and flashiest – and The Strip's only – mall, but at least it's centrally located. There are 250 storefronts, plus Bloomingdale's, Dillard's, Neiman Marcus, Nordstrom, Saks Fifth Avenue, Robinsons-May and Macy's department stores. Models hit the runway in the afternoon Wednesday to Sunday. Good food court. Look for the Cloud (a multimedia canopy) out front.

Neonopolis (Map p87; ☎ 702-477-0470; 450 Fremont St) The crown jewel in the Downtown redevelopment effort is most notable for its collection of vintage neon signs. Twenty retail shops surround open courtyards along with the Crown cinema complex and alfresco dining options.

Paris' Le Boulevard (Map pp76-8; ☎ 702-946-4111; Paris, 3655 S Las Vegas Blvd) Bally's and Paris are connected via this chichi cobblestone replica

---

BLUE LIGHT SPECIALS: SHOP TIL' YOU POP

Brand-name bargain hunters can 'buy direct' at the following outlet malls:

Las Vegas Outlet Center (Map pp76-8; ☎ 702-896-5599; 7400 S Las Vegas Blvd) A five-minute drive south of the airport, with 130 stores, including lots of housewares (Dansk, Corning-Revere, Off 5th) and shoe shops (Famous Footwear, Nine West, Reebok). For the kiddies there's a full-size carousel.

Fashion Outlet Mall (Map pp76-8; ☎ 702-874-1400, 888-424-6898; 32100 S Las Vegas Blvd) Forty-five minutes southwest of Vegas, off I-15 (exit 1) in Primm, near the Nevada-California state line. There's a good mix of 100 high-end (Coach, Escada, Versace, Williams Sonoma, Neiman Marcus' Last Call) and every-day (Banana Republic, Gap, Old Navy, Nautica, Sketchers) brands. If you're not driving, it's accessible from The Strip via a shopper shuttle ($13) that departs daily from MGM Grand, Aladdin's Desert Passage and New York-New York. Call the toll-free number for shuttle reservations.

Las Vegas Premium Outlets (Map p87; ☎ 702-474-7500; 875 S Grand Central Pkwy) The most upscale of Vegas' outlets features 120 high-end names like Armani Exchange, Coach, Dolce & Gabbana, Guess, Kenneth Cole and Polo Ralph Lauren. There are also a few midrange options, such as Eddie Bauer and Levi's. The Downtown Shoppers Express shuttle serves the mall (from The Strip) every 20 minutes from 10am until 5pm.

of Rue de la Paix. The winding promenade features French restaurants, lounges and boutiques. Highlights include fashion-forward Lunettes eyewear, La Vogue designer lingerie, Clio Blue jewelry and La Cave gourmet food and wine.

Clothing & Jewelry

Buffalo Exchange (Map pp76-8; ☎ 702-791-3960; 4110 S Maryland Pkwy) Trade in your nearly new garb for cash or credit at this fashionable second-hand chain that runs a bit closer to the mainstream. They've combed through the dingy thrift store stuff and culled only the best 1940s to '70s vintage, clubwear, costuming goodies and contemporary dapper designer duds. A real find.

Fred Leighton: Rare Collectible Jewels (Map pp76-8; ☎ 702-693-7050; Via Bellagio, 3600 S Las Vegas Blvd) Many Academy Awards night adornments are on loan from the world's most prestigious collection of antique jewelry. And in Las Vegas, unlike at the uptight NYC outlet, they'll let anyone try on finery that once belonged to royalty.

Attic (Map p87; ☎ 702-388-4088; 1018 S Main St) A $1 'lifetime pass' (applied toward your first purchase) is required to enter this vintage emporium, but it's worth it, even if you don't buy. The 1st floor is mostly furnishings and hippie-chic clubwear. Upstairs, the 1960s and '70s are strengths, with a smaller pre-1960s selection and a cool retro coffee bar with Greek grub.

Retro Vintage Clothing (Map pp76-8; ☎ 702-877-8989; 1055 E Flamingo Rd; ⏰ noon-6pm Tue-Sat) Lots of timeless glam duds get cast off in this ahistorical town. Many end up at this upscale resale boutique, which specializes in men's and women's clothing from the 1920s through to the 1980s. Rentals available.

Valentino's Zootsuit Connection (Map p87; ☎ 702-383-9555; 906 S 6th St) A sweet (and stylish!) husband and wife team outfit partygoers with upscale vintage apparel: fringed Western wear, felt hats and custom dresses. Rentals and custom swinging zootsuits are a specialty.

Williams Costume Company (Map p87; ☎ 702-384-1384; 1226 S 3rd St) Williams has supplied The Strip's starlets with DIY costuming goods since 1957. Check out the headshots in the dressing rooms, then pick up some rhinestones, sequins, feathers, etc – you go girl. Friendly staff. Costume rentals available.

Jewelers (Map pp76-8; ☎ 702-893-9979; Hilton, 3000 Paradise Rd; ⏰ 24hr) Nevada's largest discount jewelry chain stocks a wide selection of rings and necklaces. The Hilton branch stays open around-the-clock to accommodate that 3am urge for a solid gold chain.

Specialist Shops

Downtown Arts & Antiques District (Colorado Ave btwn Main & 3rd Sts) A significant antiques district has taken shape just south of Downtown in a series of funky stores inside older homes. Places worth checking out include the **Funk House** (Map p87; ☎ 702-678-6278; 1228 S Casino Center Blvd), **Gypsy Caravan** (Map p87; ☎ 702-868-3302; 1302 S 3rd St) and **Yana's Junk** (Map p87; ☎ 702-388-0051; 201 E Colorado Ave).

Houdini's Magic Shop (Map pp76-8; ☎ 702-796-0301; Venetian, 3355 S Las Vegas Blvd) The legendary escape artist's legacy lives on at this shop packed with gags, pranks and magic tricks. Magicians perform and each purchase includes a free private lesson.

Wine Cellar (Map pp76-8; ☎ 702-777-7614; Rio, 3700 W Flamingo Rd; ⏰ 3pm-midnight Mon-Fri, noon-midnight Sat & Sun) Rio's classy subterranean tasting room stocks 45,000 bottles from 3000 vintners, assembled by an ex-president of the International Court of Master Sommeliers. Single malt Scotch tasting flights and exotic chocolates round out the amazing, must-taste collection.

Guggenheim Store (Map pp76-8; ☎ 702-414-2400; Venetian, 3355 S Las Vegas Blvd) The Venetian's museum shop stocks items that are as classy as the art collection. It's a discerning spot to find an aesthetically pleasing souvenir.

Metropolitan Museum of Art Store (Map pp76-8; ☎ 702-691-2506; Desert Passage, 3663 S Las Vegas Blvd) NYC's savvy Met is known for its reproductions and singular gift items. Sales of books, scarves, stationery, prints and jewelry support the museum's educational mission.

Naughty Novelties

In a town with as many strip clubs as gas stations, it should come as little surprise that the adult apparel business is ba-bah-booming. All those hard-working beefy guys and sultry women obviously don't have time to make their own G-strings and tasseled undies.

Adult Superstore (Map pp76-8; ☎ 702-798-0144; 3850 W Tropicana Ave; ⏰ 24hr) Popular with couples, this enormous, well-lit porn warehouse has more pussies than the SPCA: toys, books, magazines, videos, tasteful 'marital enhancement products' and titillating accessories. Single guys gravitate toward the XXX arcade upstairs.

Bare Essentials (Map pp76-8; ☎ 702-247-4711; 4029 W Sahara Ave) Pros swear by BE for business attire. It's heavy on theme wear – lots of cheerleader and schoolgirl outfits. There's a good selection of knee-high boots and many of the men's and women's fantasy fashions come in plus sizes.

A Slightly Sinful Adventure (Map p87; ☎ 702-387-1006; 1232 S Las Vegas Blvd) Many of the outfits here are layered: tiny outer garments followed by much tinier undergarments. For voyeurs, admiring the goods in the presence of the professional clientele can make a visit worth the effort.

Paradise Electro Stimulations (☎ 702-474-2991, 800-339-6953; 1509 W Oakey Blvd) The 'Tiffany's of Fetish Boutiques' is tucked discreetly away on the wrong side of the tracks. It's the exotic, erotic and invigorating home of owner Dante Amore's legendary Auto-Erotic Chair, which you must see (and feel) to believe. Yeow-ch.

Weird & Wonderful

Imperial Palace Auto Collection (Map pp76-8; ☎ 702-794-3174; Imperial Palace, 3535 S Las Vegas Blvd) The entire lot on display is for sale on consignment (sorry, no test drives) at this indoor antique and collectibles lot on the 5th floor of the parking garage.

Bonanza Gifts Shop (Map pp76-8; ☎ 702-385-7359; 2460 S Las Vegas Blvd; ☾ 11am-midnight) If it's not the 'World's Largest Gift Shop,' it's damn close. The amazing kitsch selection of only-in-Vegas souvenirs includes entire aisles of dice clocks, snow globes, sassy slogan T-shirts, shot glasses and XXX gags.

Gun Store (Map pp76-8; ☎ 702-454-1110; 2900 E Tropicana Ave) Attention wannabe Schwarzeneggers: this high-powered shop offers gun rentals, live submachine gun rounds in its indoor video training range and security, safety and concealed arms permit classes. Not to mention the massive cache of weapons for sale.

GETTING THERE & AWAY

Las Vegas is readily accessible from every major North American city and, by extension, from most of the world's metropolises.

Air

Thirty-five airlines offer non-stop service. Direct flights depart from London, Mexico City, Singapore, Toronto and Tokyo. Check the Web or Sunday travel sections in major newspapers for discounted flights and package deals.

Las Vegas is served by **McCarran International Airport** (LAS; Map pp76-8; general inquiries ☎ 702-261-5211, parking information ☎ 702-261-5121, flight information ☎ 702-261-4636; www.mccarran.com) and three general aviation facilities. Just south of The Strip, McCarran is one of the world's 10 busiest airports, yet very easy to navigate. Baggage handling is notoriously slow, but upgrades are in the works. Self-service kiosks ease check-in headaches. Domestic flights use Terminal 1; international and charter flights depart from Terminal 2. A free tram links outlying gates. Pastimes include slot machines, an aviation museum and a 24-hour fitness center.

Bus & Train

Long-distance **Greyhound** (Map p87; ☎ 800-231-2222; www.greyhound.com) buses arrive at the **Downtown bus station** (Map p87; ☎ 702-384-9561; 200 S Main St). Talk of reviving **Amtrak** (☎ 800-872-7245; www.amtrak.com) train service persists, but for now the closest stations are in Needles, CA (106 miles away), Kingman, AZ (123 miles) and Barstow, CA (159 miles). Greyhound provides daily connecting Thruway motorcoach service between Las Vegas and these three cities (all fares around $30).

Car & Motorcycle

If not flying, most visitors arrive in their own transport. There's ample free parking and the city's logical street grid is easy to navigate. It's a 145-mile drive (three hours) to Death Valley National Park, 155 miles (three hours) to Zion National Park, 267 miles (five hours) to Grand Canyon Village, 275 miles (five to six hours) to Los Angeles and 425 miles (seven to eight hours) to San Diego. Dial ☎ 877-687-6237 for recorded Nevada road condition updates, or ☎ 800-427-7623 for California conditions.

GETTING AROUND

Since the primary tourist areas are flat, the best way to get around Vegas is on foot, in conjunction with the occasional taxi, trolley, bus or monorail. While you're gumshoe-ing around town, make sure you stay well hydrated.

Due to exponential growth and stifling traffic congestion, public transit and regional planning are becoming civic priorities. Muggy bus routes serve the sprawling suburbs, but gridlock along The Strip makes navigating the city's core a chore. Air-con private monorails and trolleys also ply The Strip.

Unless otherwise noted, all attractions offer free valet (tip $2) and self-service parking.

To/From the Airport

Taxi fares to Strip hotels – 30 minutes maximum in heavy traffic – run between $10 and $20, cash only. Fares to Downtown average $15 to $25. Fares include a $1.20 airport tax.

Bell Trans (☎ 800-274-7433, 702-739-7990; www .bell-trans.com) offers shuttles for $5 per person to The Strip, $6.50 to Downtown. A limousine costs $34 per hour for a chartered sedan or $41 per hour for a luxury six-person stretch limo, a good deal for groups.

If you're traveling light, city bus No 109 ($1.25) runs 24/7 to the CAT bus station, a short walk from Downtown hotels.

Car & Motorcycle

In most instances, rental cars (p474) can be delivered to your hotel; most hotels also have rental desks. Ten percent in local fees are tacked onto rates, plus a 10% airport surcharge. For weekend use, reserve at least two weeks in advance. For something glamorous, ring **Rent-A-Vette** (Map pp76-8; ☎ 800-372-1981; www.rent-a-vette.com; 5021 Swenson St). Ferraris and exotic convertibles fetch $250 to $750 per day.

Las Vegas Motorcycle Rentals (Map pp76-8; ☎ 877-571-7174; www.lvhd.com; 2605 S Eastern Ave) rents a range of brand new Harleys, from Sportsters ($90 per day) to V-Rods ($200 per day), including unlimited mileage, a helmet and rain suit.

WHAT IS BURNING MAN? *Mark Morford*

Six thousand topless women covered in nothing but body paint, glitter and dust are riding vividly decorated bicycles around the center ring of an enormous, scorching desert campground, singing and whistling and laughing and calling themselves the Critical Tits brigade, as the crowd cheers and hopes they're all wearing lots of SPF 30 on their nipples.

And just over there, rising from the desert floor like a wicked steel flower, is the Hand of God, a 30ft metal appendage/sculpture that shoots colossal tongues of flame from its fingertips 300ft into the ink-black night sky, and you can feel the heat and hear the thunder and taste the smoke from a half-mile away.

There is a 25ft-high sculpture made of plaster and wire mesh and real animal bones called the Tree of Life. There is an intricate laser-light installation beaming unknowable messages to the cosmos. There are, well, all manner of sculpture, installation, maze, structure, lightshow or noisemaker, from the sacred to the deliciously profane, scattered around the desert floor like confetti tossed from the heavens.

And this is just the beginning. This is just a hint of what Burning Man is all about.

There are vehicles. There are semitrucks re-imagined as floating luminescent party wagons, enormous mobile pirate galleons, motorized couches on wheels, rolling art vehicles of every shape and size and twisted metal Mad-Maxish mutation, enormous neon animated sea creatures floating slowly like Fellini dreamscapes across the desert floor at night.

There are fully functioning bars. There are nightclubs powered by generators. There are pagan wedding chapels. There just may be a dust-choked casino. There are lounges and stages and huge dome tents filled with giant pillows for frolicking and chatting and then sleeping it all off afterwards.

And there is upwards of 30,000 people, a surprisingly mellow and reasonably organized spectacle of calmly euphoric individuals who, for one week per year, trek from all parts of the country (and world) to this same spot in the Nevada desert and use this oddly beautiful, inimitable event called Burning Man to strip away their everyday inhibitions and peel back the masks of 'normal' to discover themselves anew.

Limousine

If you want to see Vegas in true style, rent a limo for an hour or two, or even an entire night. Rates start at about $50 per hour for a regular limo, $70 per hour for a stretch. Try calling **Omni Limousine** (☎ 702-367-1000; 4440 E Cheyenne Ave, Suite A), which provides luxury transport any hour of the day or night.

Public Transport

The new private $650 million air-con **monorail system** (☎ 702-699-8200; www.lvmonorail.com; ☺ 6am-2am) links many properties along The Strip's resort corridor, shuttling between the MGM Grand and the Hilton, Convention Center and the Sahara. A one-way ride costs $3, or you can buy a 10-ride pass for $25. Unlimited-ride passes are $15 for one day, $40 for three.

A separate free tram system connects Treasure Island and the Mirage, and Excalibur, Luxor and Mandalay Bay. Most off-Strip hotel-casinos offer free shuttle service to and from The Strip.

Citizens Area Transit (CAT; ☎ 702-228-7433; www .catride.com) operates daily from 5:30am to 1:30am, with the most popular Strip and Downtown routes running 24/7; the fare is $2 (exact change required).

Taxi

Although expensive on a per-mile basis, taxis are reasonable on a per-trip basis. A 4.5 mile lift from one end of The Strip to the other runs $10 to $15, plus tip. Taxi stands are at every hotel-casino entrance. Fares (cash only) are metered: flagfall is $3 plus $1.80 per mile, or 40¢ per minute for waiting. By law, all companies must have at least one wheelchair-accessible van. Reputable companies include **Desert Cab** (☎ 702-386-9102), **Western** (☎ 702-736-8000) and **Yellow/Checker/Star** (☎ 702-873-2000).

Trolley

Private four-wheeled air-con **trolleys** (☎ 702-382-1404) ply the length of The Strip, stopping at most hotels. The only detour is to

---

Burning Man. It is that curious and famously impossible-to-describe event that takes place every year in a sun-baked, crusted, dusted, windblown, desperately stark slab of desert (aka 'the playa') about 100 miles northeast of Reno, Nevada (500 miles from Vegas) during the first week of September. It is that glittery, sun-soaked, sexed-up, free-form, profoundly liberating, often incredibly silly week-long experience that defies all attempts to characterize it but I'll try it anyway by saying it's one part survivalist camping experience, one part art festival, one part continuous rave party, one part moneyless community experiment, and all parts freedom of expression and costume and libido and self. At the end of it all everyone gathers to watch a massive, neon-lit, five-story wooden effigy of a man burn to the ground in a spectacular, cheering, energized roar of love and community and time.

If you go, you participate. Somehow, some way. You bring art, you decorate your camp, you share, you give. This is the only true rule. There are no spectators.

It started way back in 1986 with a handful of friends gathering on a San Francisco beach to erect an 8ft effigy of a 'man' to burn, just because. Within a few years their little ritual was drawing hundreds, then thousands. Its current home has been christened Black Rock City, the name given the enormous functioning 'city' that springs up in the Nevada desert, out of nowhere, for this one precious week every year, then vanishes completely and leaves no trace behind.

As of this writing, tickets to attend Burning Man are $250, each. They go on sale at the beginning of the year, and are available through the second official day of the event, in September, via www.burningman.com.

Burning Man. It is, all at once, extraordinary and dirty and dangerous and hilarious and annoying and raw and smelly and hot and deeply whimsical. It is for artists and alternative types and spiritual nomads, yuppie dads and receptionists and cubicle workers and lost souls and found spirits. It is for anyone. But it's definitely not for everyone.

You supply your own everything: food, water, camping gear, transportation, a bike (mandatory to get around the playa), inebriants, costumes, SPF 30. Laughter and euphoria and awe and the deep sense that you have, upon arrival, somehow transcended time and space and self, are, of course, free.

LAS VEGAS

the Hilton on Paradise Rd. Trolleys operate every 15 to 20 minutes daily from 9:30am to 1:30am; the fare is $1.75 and exact change is required. Frequent stops make them the slowest way to get around.

AROUND LAS VEGAS

Straddling the Arizona-Nevada state line, Hoover Dam and Lake Mead are popular excursions from Vegas. Both are covered in more detail on p191.

RED ROCK CANYON NATIONAL CONSERVATION AREA

Only 20 miles west of Vegas, this dramatic valley is noted for the steep Red Rock escarpment, rising 3000ft on its western edge. A 13-mile, one-way scenic loop starts at the Bureau of Land Management (BLM) **visitor center** (☎ 702-363-1921) near Hwy 159. It's especially impressive at sunset and sunrise. Day use is $5. Camping at the **Oak Creek campground** (campsites $10) is available year-round on a first-come, first-served basis.

TOIYABE NATIONAL FOREST

The Spring Mountains form the western boundary of the Las Vegas valley, with higher rainfall, lower temperatures and fragrant pine forests. The village of Mt Charleston has a USDA Forest Service (USFS) **ranger station** (☎ 702-872-5486) and gives access to several hikes, including the demanding 9-mile trail up to Charleston Peak (elevation 11,918ft).

Campgrounds (campsites $6) are open from mid-May to October.

VALLEY OF FIRE STATE PARK

Near the north end of Lake Mead National Recreation Area, easily accessible from Las Vegas, this **park** (admission $5) is a masterpiece of desert scenery, with psychedelic sandstone in wonderful shapes. Hwy 169 runs through the park, right past the **visitor center** (☎ 702-397-2088), which has hiking information and excellent exhibits. The winding side road to **White Domes** is especially scenic.

The valley is at its most fiery at dawn and dusk, so consider staying in one of the two year-round **campgrounds** (campsites $7).

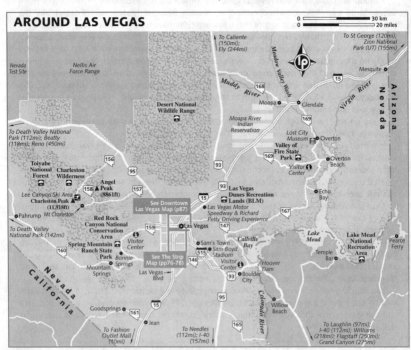

AROUND LAS VEGAS

Arizona

Ask an African school child, a Taiwanese businessman or London secretary what epitomizes the USA, and they'll likely mention the Grand Canyon. They'll describe a cowboy-and-Indian scene from a shoot-'em-up Western, or a car commercial featuring fiery red rocks and pale sandy deserts, big green cacti and galloping horses. They might not be able to pinpoint Arizona on a map, or even link the vivid images to the state, but the blockbuster scenery is so well known, so cliché Wild West, it easily holds its own. Like a young Hollywood starlet whose name you can't remember, identity is secondary, what's important is her famous face.

Ask an American about the Grand Canyon state and they'll talk about the stereotypes: silky golf courses and retirement communities, strip-mall cities and hotter-than-hell summer heat.

But ask an Arizonian about their state, and they'll wax lyrical on its hidden treasures. There'll be talk of tiny desert outposts where you expect nothing, but find everything. They'll say the Grand Canyon is certainly grand, but there's so much more – rivers to raft, mountains to ski, mining towns to explore. They'll talk about a historical legacy as proud as it is sad, tell you Arizona has the third largest Native American population in the 50 states. They'll speak about poverty and racism and how their ancestors were forced onto barren reservations. But there will be an upbeat tone when describing places where visitors can learn about Native American culture, taste mouth-watering fry-bread and shop for handcrafted turquoise jewelry.

HIGHLIGHTS

- **Best of the Best**
  The granddaddy of them all, it's the sight known around the world: visiting Arizona without seeing the Grand Canyon (p131) is like leaving your house without shoes.

- **Best Wild Adventure**
  Rafting the Colorado River (p137) through the Grand Canyon is a must-do-before-you-die experience.

- **Best Boomtowns that Never Busted**
  Perfectly preserved, beautiful Bisbee (p217) exudes Victorian charm. Artsy Jerome (p173) is Europe in the desert.

- **Best Reason to Visit the Navajo Reservation**
  Support local tourism and explore out-of-this-world beautiful Monument Valley (p184).

- **Best All Around Town**
  Sip microbrews, ski powder or drive an all-terrain vehicle (ATV) in fun and funky Flagstaff (p154).

Colorado River ★
Monument Valley Navajo Tribal Park ★
★ Grand Canyon National Park
★ Flagstaff
★ Jerome
Bisbee ★

| ■ POPULATION: 5.9 MILLION | ■ AREA: 182,487 MILES | ■ www.arizonaguide.com |

ARIZONA

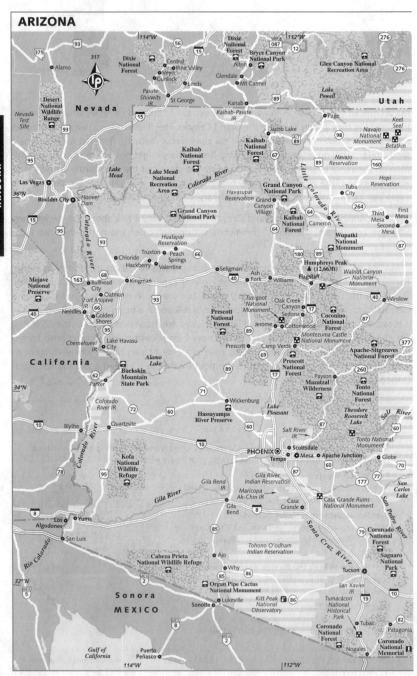

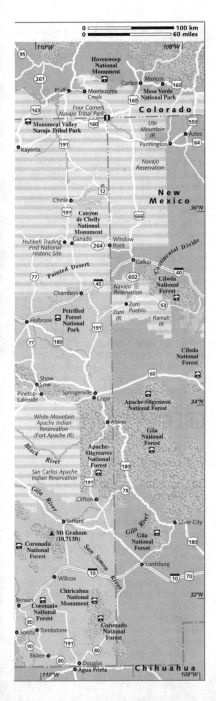

ARIZONA

Climate

While Arizona's mountains are capped with snow during winter (December through March), most of the state receives little annual rainfall. During summer (June to August), temperatures often soar above 100°F, and in places like Phoenix and Yuma it's not uncommon for daily temperatures to reach around 110°F. Locals often boast that it's a dry heat, but it's still uncomfortable. Nights are usually cooler, especially in the desert regions and around the Grand Canyon. Winters in the northern half of the state are cold. There's often snow on the ground in places like Flagstaff and Williams, and the North Rim of the Grand Canyon sees so much snowfall that roads close. In the southern half of the state, winters are milder. Daily highs of around 70°F are common in Phoenix, Yuma and even Tucson. Fall and spring see less extreme temperatures, and are great times to visit Arizona.

National & State Parks

From gaping canyons to towering cacti, Arizona has some of the most spectacular and well-known national parks in the USA, if not the world. The Grand Canyon (p131) is the most popular park in the country, and a not-to-be-missed attraction. In southern Arizona, Saguaro National Park (p209) and Organ Pipe Cactus National Monument (p211) preserve large stands of cacti amid stunning desert scenery. On and around the Navajo Reservation you'll find Petrified Forest National Park (p187), with millions-of-years-old trees and colorful sandscapes. Monument Valley Navajo Tribal Park (p184) is also here; filled with fabulous red buttes and mesas, it's a favorite location for film and TV commercial shoots.

Arizona State Park Headquarters (Map p122; ☎ 602-542-4174; www.pr.state.az.us; 1300 W Washington St, Phoenix, AZ 85007) are in Phoenix. The Website has loads of info on Arizona state parks.

ARIZONA SCENIC BYWAYS

Arizona has some fabulous byways to explore, many more than are listed here. For more information on scenic drives, check out www.byways.org.

Traversing some of Arizona's most rugged terrain, the **Apache Trail Historic Road** starts 15 miles east of Phoenix and follows Hwy 88 northeast from Apache Junction. It ends 71 miles later in Globe. At times steep, winding, narrow and unpaved (but OK for conventional vehicles), the road passes through the canyons, rock outcroppings and fantastic geological formations of the Superstition Wilderness Area. The section through Fish Creek Canyon is the most spectacular. Here the road hugs the edge of a high-walled canyon with 100ft sheer drop-offs. Once you reach Globe, you can return to Phoenix via the much faster paved Hwy 60.

For the **North Rim Parkway**, start in Jacob Lake and follow scenic Hwy 67 south past pine, fir and aspen trees in the Kaibab National Forest. You'll hit Grand Canyon National Park's North Rim entrance 30 miles later. The road continues another 13 miles through the park to the edge of the rim. The drive is outstanding in autumn, when the aspen trees blaze yellow. From the rim, you'll have to backtrack the way you came.

Hwy 163 travels north from Kayenta in the Navajo Reservation into stupendous **Monument Valley**. This is one of the most scenic drives in the state. See p184 for more details.

The **Sedona–Oak Creek Canyon Scenic Road** (Hwy 89A) winds northeast from Sedona into spectacular Oak Creek Canyon, with dizzyingly narrow walls and dramatic colored cliffs. For more info, see p169.

Called the Mother Road, a journey down historic **Route 66** takes you back in time; see p189.

Information

Arizona Department of Transportation (www.dot .state.az.us) Road closures and other transportation details.
Arizona Office of Tourism (Map pp120-1; ☎ 866-275-5816; www.arizonaguide.com; 1110 W Washington St, Suite 155, Phoenix, AZ 85007) Statewide travel information.
Arizona State Parks (www.pr.state.az.us) Information on state parks.
Arizona State Website (www.az.gov) The official website for Arizona.

TIME ZONE

Arizona is on Mountain Standard Time (seven hours behind Greenwich Mean Time, GMT). It is the only Western state that does not observe daylight-saving time. From late spring to early fall Arizona is eight hours behind GMT. The exception is the Navajo Reservation, which – in keeping with those parts of the Reservation in Utah and New Mexico – observes daylight-saving time.

Getting There & Around

Phoenix International Airport (Sky Harbor) and McCarran International Airport in Las Vegas are the region's main hubs. Tucson also has a large airport with multiple daily flights around the country. I-40 and I-10 are the major east–west veins through Arizona. Old Rte 66 runs parallel to I-40 across much of Arizona. I-17 runs north–south. Greyhound buses run several times a day along major highways (I-40, I-10), connecting big cities and stopping at smaller towns along the way. Arizona is best explored in your own vehicle, as public transport is limited in national parks and Native American reservations. The state has loads of fabulous drives, including long stretches of fabled Rte 66 (p189) that just aren't the same if seen from the back of a bus.

The Amtrak (www.amtrak.com) train service is more limited in Arizona than other parts of the country. The *Southwest Chief* travels between Chicago and Los Angeles daily and stops in Flagstaff. The *Sunset Limited* makes three trips a week between Los Angeles and Jacksonville, Florida with stops in Yuma and Tucson.

GREATER PHOENIX

pop 3.3 million / elev 1200ft
To an outsider, Greater Phoenix appears a tangled web of freeways and strip malls, golf courses and palm trees, mountains and tall buildings. Penetrating its urban – yet very suburban – fold seems daunting. Your hotel reservation is in Scottsdale, but you're driving through central Phoenix. Are you even in the right metropolis? When you follow the directions to that classy restaurant you heard was all the rage, you end up in a strip-mall parking lot. That can't be right, or can it? It's all rather disorienting at first, but don't lose faith. True, the hottest club in town just might be next to a K-Mart, but hidden away within the sprawl are more than a few great gems.

Easily the Southwest's largest city, the Greater Phoenix Metropolitan Area covers almost 2000 sq miles and incorporates dozens of bedroom communities, including popular Scottsdale, Mesa and Tempe. It's a city in constant flux, a victim of its own growing pains. Phoenix is in that chaotic adolescent phase where she can't decide whether to turn glam or just stay grunge. Known locally as the 'Valley of the Sun,' the city boasts more than 300 days of sunshine a year. It's searing hot in summer (above 110°F), but delightful in winter.

As the Southwest's most important gateway, many visitors choose to spend a few days here checking out the sights before moving on. Major museums, superlative shopping, relaxing resorts, delectable dining, spectator sports and golfing greens (where do they get that water?) abound. Re-laxed sophistication is the city's hallmark. A cowboy hat and jeans are rarely out of place, ties are seldom required.

ORIENTATION

Because metro Phoenix grew to engulf many small towns, there are several historical centers. Phoenix, Scottsdale, Tempe and Mesa are the most interesting.

Phoenix is the largest town and houses the state capitol, several important museums and professional sport facilities. Southeast of Phoenix, Tempe is home to Arizona State University and has an active student population. East of Tempe is Mesa, which has several museums as well as shops, hotels and restaurants. Scottsdale,

ARIZONA

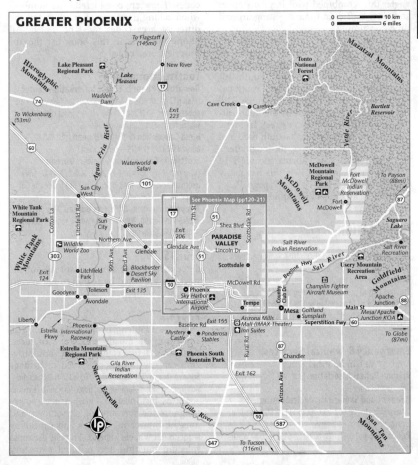

GREATER PHOENIX

northeast of Phoenix, is known for both its Western downtown area – now full of fine galleries, boutiques and crafts stores – and its many upscale resorts and restaurants.

Other towns, including Chandler to the southeast and Glendale and Peoria to the northwest, are thriving residential and manufacturing communities. Sun City and Sun City West, in the northwest of the valley, are among the largest retirement communities in the country, but offer little for tourists. Paradise Valley, nestled between the arms of Phoenix and Scottsdale, is the valley's most exclusive residential neighborhood.

Because the valley's roads run north–south or east–west, to get from one point to another you often have to take two sides of a triangle; this, combined with large distances and slow traffic, can make getting around time-consuming.

Central Ave runs north–south through Phoenix, dividing west addresses from east addresses. Washington St runs east–west dividing north addresses from south addresses. Scottsdale Rd runs north–south between Scottsdale and Tempe. In Tempe, Mill Ave runs north–south and is the main eating, drinking and shopping street. In Mesa, Center St is the main north–south road and Main St the main east–west thoroughfare.

Major freeways in Phoenix include I-17 North (Black Canyon Hwy; this has many motels along it), I-10 West (Papago Fwy), I-10 South (Maricopa Fwy) and Hwy 60 East (Superstition Fwy).

INFORMATION
Bookstores
Bookman's (☎ 480-835-0505; 1056 S Country Club Dr, Mesa) Great selection of used books.
Book Store (Map pp120-1; ☎ 602-279-3910; 4230 N 7th Ave) Lots of periodicals and magazines.
Wide World of Maps (Map pp120-1; ☎ 602-279-2323; 2626 W Indian School Rd) Fine selection of maps and guidebooks.

Emergency & Medical Services
Dial ☎ 911 in an emergency.
Arizona Dental Association (☎ 602-957-4777) Gives dental referrals.
Banner Good Samaritan Medical Center (Map pp120-1; ☎ 602-239-2000; 1111 E McDowell Rd) Emergency services 24 hours.
Police (Map pp120-1; ☎ 602-262-6151; 620 W Washington St)

Internet Access
Central Phoenix Library (Map p122; ☎ 602-262-4636; 1221 N Central Ave) Free Internet access.

Media
The local daily is the *Arizona Republic*.

Money
Foreign exchange is available at the airport and major bank branches.

Post
Post office (Map p122; ☎ 602-253-9648; 522 N Central Ave)

Telephone
The Phoenix area has three telephone area codes. These are considered local numbers when calling from one to another, but the different area codes must be dialed. All phone numbers in this book list the appropriate area code.

Tourist Information
Downtown Phoenix Visitor Information Center (Map p122; ☎ 602-254-6500, 877-225-5749; www.visit phoenix.com; 50 N 2nd St) The valley's most complete source for tourist information.
Mesa Convention & Visitors Bureau (☎ 480-827-4700, 800-283-6372; 120 N Center St, Mesa)
Scottsdale Convention & Visitors Bureau (Map pp120-1; ☎ 480-945-8481, 800-877-1117; www .scottsdalecvb.com; 4343 N Scottsdale Rd) Inside the Galleria Corporate Center.
Tempe Convention & Visitors Bureau (Map pp120-1; ☎ 480-894-8158, 800-283-6734; www.tempecvb.com; 51 W 3rd St, Suite 105)

SIGHTS
Since the Phoenix area is so spread out, attractions are listed by region to make your life a little simpler.

Phoenix
Downtown Phoenix is a relatively small area, consisting of mostly modern structures, though you'll find eight late-19th- and early-20th-century houses preserved in **Heritage Square** (Map p122; ☎ 602-262-5071; 115 N 6th St; admission free; ☼ 10am-4pm Tue-Sat, noon-4pm Sun). This is about as historical as Phoenix gets, so try to imagine the surrounding skyscrapers and imagine thundering hooves and squeaking stagecoach wheels instead. To visit the most splendid building, the restored two-story

1895 **Rosson House** (tour adult/child $3/1), you'll need to join a tour. Kids will dig the Square's **Arizona Doll & Toy Museum** (☎ 602-253-9337; cnr 7th & Monroe Sts; adult/child $2.50/1), where antique dolls study at desks in a 1912 schoolroom. The Square also features fine-arts and crafts shops and great places to grab lunch.

What Phoenix lacks in historical architecture it makes up for in museums. At the top of the list is the **Heard Museum** (Map pp120-1; ☎ 602-252-8840; www.heard.org; 2301 N Central Ave; adult/child $7/3; ☼ 9:30am-5pm). Emphasizing quality over quantity, it has outstanding presentations on Native American history and culture. Don't miss the fascinating kachina doll room and thought-provoking audio-visual displays.

The unique collection of fashions from the 18th century to the 20th century will be the highlight of a visit to the **Phoenix Art Museum** (Map p122; ☎ 602-257-1880; www.phxart.org; 1625 N Central Ave; adult/child $9/3, free Thu; ☼ 10am-5pm Tue-Sun). The museum also has permanent Asian, American and European art collections.

The **Arizona Science Center** (Map p122; ☎ 602-716-2000; www.azscience.org; 600 E Washington St; adult/child $9/7; ☼ 10am-5pm) is another popular attraction. With 350 hands-on exhibits, it encourages visitors to explore and experiment. Computers, bubbles, weather, physics and biology are just a few of the subjects and toys. Live demonstrations are held throughout the day.

The exhibit on the sinking of the USS *Arizona* at Pearl Harbor in 1941 and some 2000-year-old archaeological artifacts are highlights of the **Phoenix Museum of History** (Map p122; ☎ 602-253-2734; 105 N 5th St; adult/child $5/2.50; ☼ 10am-5pm Mon-Sat, noon-5pm Sun).

If you're all museumed out, head to the beautiful 145-acre **Desert Botanical Gardens** (Map pp120-1; ☎ 480-941-1225; 1201 N Galvin Pkwy; adult/child $7.50/4; ☼ 8am-8pm Oct-Apr, from 7am May-Sep) for a worthwhile urban getaway. There are thousands of arid-land plants and you'll learn about desert ecosystems. The surrounding **Papago Park** has picnic areas, jogging, biking and equestrian trails along with a children's fishing pond.

After being diagnosed with tuberculosis in 1927, Boyce Luther Gulley spent the last 15 years of his life building the one-of-a-kind 18-room fantasy he called **Mystery Castle** (Map p117; ☎ 602-268-1581; 800 E Mineral Rd; adult/child $5/3; ☼ 11am-4pm Tue-Sun). Stone, petroglyphs, adobe and automobile parts make up the walls of the three-story structure, held together by a mix of sand, cement, calcium and goat's milk. Always concerned about disturbing the natural landscape, Gulley employed some really strange architectural methods – a flight of stairs goes over a boulder so the builders wouldn't have to disturb it! After Gulley died in 1945, he left the castle to his daughter, Mary Lou, who conducts tours of the very odd property.

Scottsdale

Most visitors come to Scottsdale to wander through its popular downtown shopping district known as **Old Town** for its early-20th-century buildings (and others built to *look* old). Basically, though, it's home to many upscale galleries and gift stores.

During the mid-20th century, architect Frank Lloyd Wright built, lived in and taught at **Taliesin West** (Map pp120-1; ☎ 480-860-2700; www.franklloydwright.org; 12621 Frank Lloyd Wright Blvd; adult/child $18/5; ☼ 9am-5pm). A complex of mesmerizing, environmentally organic buildings are set on 600 acres at the eastern edge of Scottsdale's many subdivisions. It's a worthwhile tour.

Tempe

Arizona State University (ASU) is the heart and soul of Tempe. Founded in 1885 and home to some 46,000 students, it features a few museums and the **Gammage Auditorium** (Map pp120-1; ☎ 480-965-4050; cnr Mill Ave & Apache Blvd; admission free; ☼ 1-4pm Mon-Fri Oct-May). This was Frank Lloyd Wright's last major building and tours are offered. The tours are free, last about 30 minutes and are offered between 1pm and 3:30pm.

Mill Ave is Tempe's main drag: packed with restaurants, bars and other collegiate hangouts. It's a fun place to wander around and look for old vinyl or vintage dresses.

Mesa

Animated dinosaurs, dioramas of ancient Indians, an eight-cell territorial jail, gold panning near the Dutchman's Mine and changing art shows are just a few of the many displays and interactive exhibits at the **Mesa Southwest Museum** (☎ 480-644-2230; 53 N MacDonald St; adult/child $7/5; ☼ 10am-5pm Tue-Sat, 1-5pm Sun). One of the world's largest collections

ARIZONA

PHOENIX

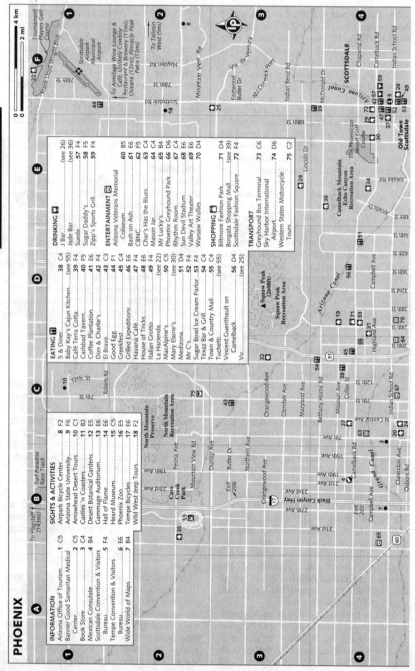

INFORMATION
Arizona Office of Tourism.........1	C5
Banner Good Samaritan Medical	
Center.................................2	C5
Book Store............................3	C4
Mexican Consulate.................4	B4
Scottsdale Convention & Visitors	
Bureau.................................5	F4
Tempe Convention & Visitors	
Bureau.................................6	E6
Wide World of Maps.............7	B4

SIGHTS & ACTIVITIES
Airpark Bicycle Center............8	F2
Arizona State University.........9	F6
Arrowhead Desert Tours........10	C1
Castles 'n Coasters................11	B2
Desert Botanical Gardens.......12	E5
Gammage Auditorium............13	E6
Hall of Flame.......................14	E6
Heard Museum.....................15	C5
Phoenix Zoo........................16	E5
Tempe Bicycles....................17	E6
Wild West Jeep Tours............18	F2

EATING 🍴
5 & Diner............................38	C4
Baby Kay's Cajun Kitchen......39	(see 55)
Café Terra Cotta...................39	F4
Carlsbad Tavern...................40	F5
Coffee Plantation................41	E6
Don & Charlie's....................42	F4
El Bravo..............................43	C3
Good Egg...........................44	F1
Greekfest............................45	C4
Grilled Expeditions...............46	E6
Havana Café.......................47	F4
House of Tricks....................48	E6
Italian Grotto.......................49	F4
La Hacienda........................(see 22)
MacAlpine's........................50	C5
Mary Elaine's......................(see 30)
Medizona...........................51	D4
Mr C's................................52	F4
Sugar Bowl Ice Cream Parlor...53	F4
Texaz Bar & Grill.................54	C4
Town & Country Mall............55	C4
Tuchetti.............................56	D4
Vincent Guerithault on	
Camelback.........................(see 55)
Vu.....................................(see 25)

DRINKING 🍸
J Bar..................................(see 26)
Jade Bar.............................(see 36)
Suede.................................57	F4
Sugar Daddy's.....................58	F5
Zipp's Sports Grill.................59	F4

ENTERTAINMENT 🎭
Arizona Veterans Memorial	
Coliseum............................60	B5
Bash on Ash........................61	E6
CBNC.................................62	F5
Char's Has the Blues............63	C4
Mason Jar...........................64	C4
Mr Lucky's...........................65	B4
Phoenix Greyhound Park.......66	D6
Rhythm Room......................67	C4
Sun Devil Stadium...............68	E6
Valley Art Theater...............69	E6
Warsaw Wallies...................70	D4

SHOPPING 🛍
Biltmore Fashion Park...........71	D4
Borgata Shopping Mall.........(see 39)
Scottsdale Fashion Square......72	F4

TRANSPORT
Greyhound Bus Terminal.......73	C6
Sky Harbor International	
Airport...............................74	D6
Western States Motorcycle	
Tours.................................75	C2

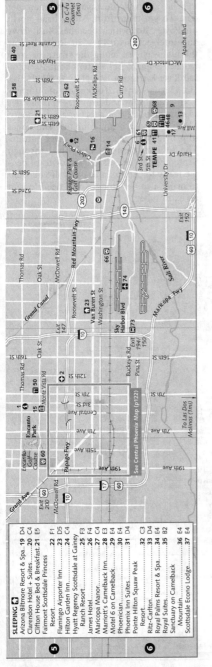

of fighter aircraft is on display at the **Champlin Fighter Aircraft Museum** (Map p117; ☎ 480-830-4540; Falcon Field Airport, 4800 E McKellips Rd; adult/child $7/5; ⊗ 8:30am-3:30pm Jun-Aug, 10am-5pm Sep-May). Extensive supporting exhibits complement the various bombers and fighters used from WWI to the Vietnam War.

ACTIVITIES
Hiking & Biking

Phoenicians live amid urban sprawl all week, so on weekends they like to lace up their boots and head to the hills. Mountains ring the city, and there are numerous city and regional parks to hike and bike through. **Phoenix South Mountain Park** (Map p117; ☎ 602-495-0222; 10919 S Central Ave), covering 25 sq miles, is the largest city park in the USA. With more than 40 miles of trails, great views and dozens of Native American petroglyph sites to admire, it's a favorite weekend escape.

For some serious desert views, especially at sunset, head to **Squaw Peak Recreation Area** (Map pp120-1; ☎ 602-262-7901; Squaw Peak Dr). The trek to the 2608ft summit of Squaw Peak is one of Phoenix' most popular outdoor endeavors. The park is crowded on winter weekends and parking can be difficult. Try the lots northeast of Lincoln Dr between 22nd and 24th Sts, but beware they fill early.

A little way out of town, **White Tank Mountain Regional Park** (Map p117; ☎ 623-935-2505; per vehicle $3; ⊗ dawn-dusk) offers hiking trails. A good choice is the trail to the top of the 4018ft White Tank Mountain. To reach the park, drive 10 miles northwest on Grand Ave (Hwy 60), then 15 miles west on Olive Ave (the western extension of Dunlap Ave).

Mountain- and road-biking is possible in all three parks, with many designated trails. If you need to pick up some pedals, try the following bike rental shops:

Adventure Bicycle Co (☎ 480-649-3394; 1110 W Southern Ave, Mesa; per day from $25)
Airpark Bicycle Center (Map pp120-1; ☎ 480-596-6633; 8666 E Shea Blvd, Scottsdale; per day from $25)
Tempe Bicycles (Map pp120-1; ☎ 480-966-6896; 330 W University Dr, Tempe; per day from $25)

Horseback Riding

Business owners quickly learnt that tourists liked to start their Western holidays with a few hours in the saddle, and today the town boasts dozens of riding outfits. Short rides, often combined with a country breakfast

ARIZONA

ARIZONA

or barbecue cookout, are the most popular excursions, although just about anything from sunrise rides to overnight pack trips can be arranged. Many places close during the summer, when it's just too darn hot.

Ponderosa Stables (Map p117; ☎ 602-268-1261; 10215 S Central Ave; ride from $25) is a well-known company that leads rides into South Mountain Park. For overnight trips into the mountains east of Phoenix, contact **Don Donnelly Stables** (☎ 480-982-7822, 800-346-4403; 6010 S Kings Ranch Rd, Apache Junction; ride from $30), located 15 miles west of town.

Tubing

Floating down the Salt River in an inner tube is loads of fun, and it's also a great way

to relax and cool down on a hot summer day. To get there from Mesa, head north on Power Rd, which becomes Bush Hwy and intersects with the Salt River. Follow the highway east along the river; the road reaches Saguaro Lake after about 10 miles. **Salt River Recreation** (Map p117; ☎ 480-984-3305; 1320 N Bush Hwy; tubes $12) offers lots of information, rents tubes and provides van shuttles to starting places for short or all-day floats. Make sure you bring sunblock and shoes to protect your feet from the river bottom. The tubing season is mid-April through September; weekends draw crowds of people ready to cool off and party. If you want to bring a cooler along, you'll need to rent an extra tube.

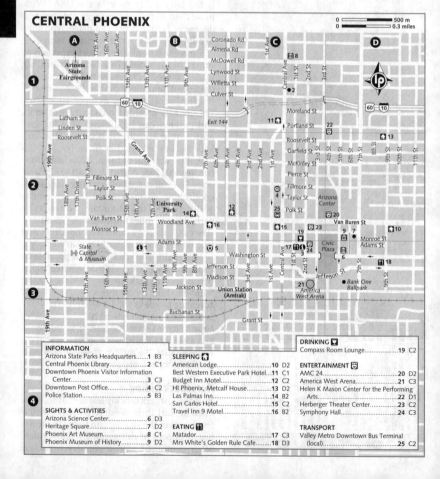

CENTRAL PHOENIX

INFORMATION	
Arizona State Parks Headquarters	1 B3
Central Phoenix Library	2 C1
Downtown Phoenix Visitor Information	
Center	3 C3
Downtown Post Office	4 C2
Police Station	5 B3

SIGHTS & ACTIVITIES	
Arizona Science Center	6 D3
Heritage Square	7 D2
Phoenix Art Museum	8 C1
Phoenix Museum of History	9 D2

SLEEPING	
American Lodge	10 D2
Best Western Executive Park Hotel	11 C1
Budget Inn Motel	12 C2
HI Phoenix, Metcalf House	13 D2
Las Palmas Inn	14 B2
San Carlos Hotel	15 C2
Travel Inn 9 Motel	16 B2

EATING	
Matador	17 C3
Mrs White's Golden Rule Cafe	18 D3

DRINKING	
Compass Room Lounge	19 C2

ENTERTAINMENT	
AMC 24	20 D2
America West Arena	21 C3
Helen K Mason Center for the Performing	
Arts	22 D1
Herberger Theater Center	23 C3
Symphony Hall	24 C3

TRANSPORT	
Valley Metro Downtown Bus Terminal	
(local)	25 C2

PHOENIX FOR CHILDREN

Phoenix is a great family town, with plenty to keep the little tykes occupied. If your child loves animals, head to the **Phoenix Zoo** (Map pp120-1; ☎ 602-273-1341; 455 N Galvin Pkwy; adult/child $10/5; ☼ 9am-5pm Sep-Jun). A wide variety of animals, including some rare ones, are housed in several distinct and natural-looking environments. Don't miss the petting zoo. For something a bit more exotic (and probably more interesting for adults), try the **Wildlife World Zoo** (Map p117; ☎ 623-935-9453; 16501 W Northern Ave; adult/child $12/5; ☼ 9am-5pm), which specializes in rare and exotic species – from white tigers to black jaguars. The aquarium with seahorses, piranhas and electric eels is pretty cool.

If your children want to be firefighters when they grow up, they shouldn't miss the **Hall of Flame** (Map pp120-1; ☎ 602-275-3473; 6101 E Van Buren St; adult/child $5/3; ☼ 9am-5pm Mon-Sat, noon-4pm Sun). It exhibits more than 90 fully restored fire-fighting machines and related paraphernalia from 1725 to present day.

To cool off in summer, visit **Waterworld Safari** (Map p117; ☎ 623-581-1947; 4243 W Pinnacle Peak Rd; adult/child $20/16; ☼ 10am-8pm Mon-Thu, 10am-9pm Fri & Sat, 11am-7pm Sun Jun-Aug), with a six-story-high water slide, acres of swimming pools and a wave-making machine. It's 2 miles west of I-17 at exit 217. In Mesa, **Golfland Sunsplash** (Map p117; ☎ 480-834-8319; 155 W Hampton Ave, Mesa; admission $21; ☼ 10am-10pm Mon-Thu, 10am-midnight Fri & Sat, noon-10pm Sun) offers the same watery attractions, along with tube floats, bumper boats, miniature golf and go-carts.

Castles 'n Coasters (Map pp120-1; ☎ 602-997-7575; 9445 E Metro Pkwy; admission $23; ☼ 10am-9pm Sep-May; 5-11pm Fri, noon-11pm Sat, 5-9pm Sun Jun-Aug), by the Metrocenter Mall, is a giant amusement park. The highlight is the 2000ft-long Desert Storm roller coaster, complete with two 360-degree loops, that's fun for kids of all ages. Smaller roller coasters are suitable for younger riders and there are a dozen other attractions, including four miniature golf courses, video arcades, go-carts and carousels.

TOURS

Several companies offer tours in and around Phoenix. **Vaughan's Southwest** (☎ 602-971-1381, 800-513-1381; www.southwesttours.com) offers 4½-hour city tours ($45), as well as a 14-hour

tour to the Grand Canyon ($115) for people with really limited time. They pick you up from your hotel.

Many companies offer 4WD tours into the surrounding desert. These last anywhere from four hours to all day and stress various themes: ghost towns, cookouts, Native American petroglyphs and ruins, natural history, sunset tours or even target shooting. Tours start at around $75. Two reputable companies are **Arrowhead Desert Tours** (Map pp120-1; ☎ 602-942-3361; www.azdeserttours.com; 841 E Paradise Lane, Phoenix) and **Wild West Jeep Tours** (Map pp120-1; ☎ 480-922-0144; www.wildwestjeeptours.com; 7127 E Becker Lane, Scottsdale).

FESTIVALS & EVENTS

Phoenix' most popular and well-known event is the **Fiesta Bowl football game** (☎ 480-965-8777; www.tostitosfiestabowl.com) held each year on New Year's Day at the ASU Sun Devil Stadium. It's preceded by one of the largest parades in the southwest. American football fans are known to be fanatical about their favorite teams, so expect hotels to fill months in advance.

The **Arizona State Fair** (☎ 602-252-6771; www.azstatefair.com) takes place the first two weeks of October and attracts folks from across the state. It offers the typical rodeo and midway action, deep-fried foods and cotton candy, along with lots of sheep and goat competitions.

SLEEPING

From basic motels to ritzy resorts, the valley's hundreds of places to stay have one thing in common – prices plummet in summer. Rates from January to April can be two or even three times more expensive than summer rates at top-end places. The seasonal price difference is not as great at cheaper motels.

Chain motels outnumber everything else in town, and many are represented by a dozen or more properties scattered around the valley. B&Bs are few and far between.

Budget

Central Phoenix has the region's best selection of cheap places to stay, concentrated along Van Buren St. The downtown area is OK, but east of 10th St the neighborhood deteriorates into blocks of boarded-up buildings, used-car lots and streetwalkers' turf (police patrols periodically scout the area). The neighborhood from around 24th to about 36th Sts, north of the airport, improves a bit, but still remains seedy.

In Tempe, Apache Blvd has a couple of nondescript budget motels, as well as some chains. Apache Blvd becomes Main St in Mesa, and continues for about 20 miles into and through Apache Junction. This long strip of ugly, modern Americana has a number of budget motels scattered along it – if you don't need to stay near the center, drive and see.

HI Phoenix, Metcalf House (Map p122; ☎ 602-254-9803; 1026 N 9th St; dm/d $17/35; **P** $3) Popular with young budget travelers, this friendly hostel occupies a nondescript house in a working-class residential neighborhood north of downtown (too far to walk). It has kitchen and laundry facilities, but does not accept reservations.

Motel 6 on Camelback (Map pp120-1; ☎ 480-946-2280; www.motel6.com; 6848 E Camelback Rd, Scottsdale; r $52; **P** **⊠**) Yes, it's a standard chain, but it's conveniently located smack dab in the middle of upscale Scottsdale, only a quick drive from Old Town.

Flamingo Airporter Inn (Map pp120-1; ☎ 602-275-6211; 2501 E Van Buren; r $40; **P**) The closest cheapie to the airport, this offers typical motel-style rooms.

McDowell Mountain Regional Park (Map p117; ☎ 480-471-0173; 15612 E Palisades Dr; campsites $15) Has about 70 campsites with water and electrical hookups, as well as showers.

Mesa/Apache Junction KOA (☎ 480-982-4015; www.koa.com; 1540 S Tomahawk Rd, Apache Junction; campsites $18, RV sites $22-27; **P** **⊠**) Closest KOA to the center of things. It has a pool and hot tub.

If you're looking for decent, clean lodging in the $30 to $45 range, the following are recommended:

Budget Inn Motel (Map p122; ☎ 602-257-8331; 424 W Van Buren St; **P**)

Travel Inn 9 Motel (Map p122; ☎ 602-254-6521; 201 N 7th Ave; **P**)

Las Palmas Inn (Map p122; ☎ 602-256-9161; 765 NW Grand Ave; **P**)

American Lodge (Map p122; ☎ 602-252-6823; 965 E Van Buren St; **P**)

Midrange

Chain hotels still dominate this price bracket, but a few independent options provide more color and character than most Phoenix hotels.

Clarendon Hotel + Suites (Map pp120-1; ☎ 602-252-7363; www.theclarendon.net; 401 W Clarendon Ave; r from $110; **P** **⊠**) A new boutique joint, rates are absurdly cheap for an establishment as classy as this (but it had just opened, so prices could skyrocket). Rooms are sparse with dark wood furniture and original art on the walls. There's a chocolate, blue and khaki color scheme. At the time of research, work was underway on Carson's at Clarendon with plans to turn it into a dark and sophisticated bar and restaurant.

San Carlos Hotel (Map p122; ☎ 602-253-4121, 800-528-5446; www.hotelsancarlos.com; 202 N Central Ave; r $140; **P** **⊠**) Unlike most Phoenix hotels, this 1928 downtown property has loads of character. It's a Renaissance–inspired beauty that's been nicely restored with early fixtures and wood trim. Rooms are small but atmospheric, and there's a café, restaurant, bar and exercise room. If you're trying to avoid a chain (and can't afford a resort), it's a solid choice.

Maricopa Manor (Map pp120-1; ☎ 800-292-6403; www.maricopamanor.com; 15 W Pasadena Ave; r from $130; **P** **▢** **⊠**) Located inside a well-maintained Spanish-style manor house, this small place has seven beautiful suites, many with French doors onto a deck overlooking the pool, garden and fountain areas. Others feature gas fireplaces or whirlpool tubs. An elegant atmosphere presides. If you're looking for a more intimate resort experience, this is *the* place to stay.

Clifton House Bed & Breakfast (Map pp120-1; ☎ 480-990-0682; www.bbonline.com/az/clifton; cnr Oak & 68th Sts, Scottsdale; ste $95; **P**) With just one suite in a private home (it has a separate entrance), this place offers the discriminating guest a very private stay. Indian screens, plush carpets, brass and glass tables and a Mexican-tiled bathroom make up the decor. Outside there's a cactus garden, along with a peaceful patio decked out with a fireplace and fountain. Rates include a full breakfast.

Hilton Garden Inn (Map pp120-1; ☎ 602-279-9811; www.hiltongardeninn.com; 100 W Clarendon Ave; r $80-130; **P** **⊠**) The best feature at this place north of downtown is the giant sports club, complete with aerobics and workout rooms, personal trainers, racquetball and basketball courts and a spa and sauna. The 180 rooms are standard, but perfectly comfortable. There's an on-site restaurant, busy sports bar and nightclub. If you're looking for resort-style amenities at lower prices, this is your hotel.

Phoenix Inn Suites (Map pp120-1; ☎ 602-956-5221, 800-956-5221; www.phoenixinn.com; 2310 E Highland Ave; r $130-170; Ⓟ ⚛) The 120 spacious rooms all come with refrigerators, coffee makers and microwaves. The pool, Jacuzzi, exercise room and airport transfers are bonuses.

Royal Suites (Map p117; ☎ 602-942-1000, 800-647-5786; 10421 N 33rd Ave; r $110-150; Ⓟ ⚛) North of town, this place offers 80 clean and modern mini-suites with kitchenettes. There are discounts for extended stays.

Inn Suites (Map p117; ☎ 480-897-7900, 800-842-4242; 1651 W Baseline Rd; r $110-150; Ⓟ ⚛) South of Tempe, this place near I-10 exit 155, has pleasant rooms of various sizes; all include kitchenettes, and some have sitting rooms or full kitchens. Continental breakfast, evening cocktail hour and airport transportation are included. With two tennis courts and an exercise room, you can get a workout while the kids are on the playground, or just relax in the spa.

Scottsdale Econo Lodge (Map pp120-1; ☎ 480-994-9461, 800-528-7396; 6935 5th Ave; r $70-110; Ⓟ ⚛) A chain option, but there is fashionable shopping within walking distance. Rooms are comfortable, if nondescript.

Best Western Executive Park Hotel (Map p122; ☎ 602-252-2100; www.bwexecutiveparkhotel.com; 1100 N Central Ave; r from $99; Ⓟ 💻 ⚛) This modern, clean-cut, business-oriented hotel north of downtown includes a complimentary shuttle to the airport and other locations. A solid, if rather sterile, midrange choice.

Top End

The most elegant and expensive places to stay in Phoenix are the resorts, of which the city has more than its share. These aren't just places to sleep, they are destinations within themselves (some make an entire vacation out of it). Expect attractively landscaped grounds with extensive communal areas. Spacious rooms or suites are supplemented by a variety of restaurants, bars and other entertainment venues, as well as several swimming pools, whirlpools, saunas, staffed gyms and (at extra cost) massage, beauty treatments, tennis, racquetball and golf. Most can provide babysitting and some have children's clubs (again, at extra cost). Activities may include anything from bicycle rental to basketball courts to horseback riding and hot-air ballooning. Peak-season rates are listed; prices plummet in the summer.

Phoenician (Map pp120-1; ☎ 480-941-8200, 800-888-8234; www.thephoenician.com; 6000 E Camelback Rd, Scottsdale; r from $450; Ⓟ 💻 ⚛) Almost overpoweringly opulent, this modern place holds its own against the best resorts in the world. Rooms are super-deluxe, of course, and there are numerous eating and drinking options, including the top-rated contemporary-French Mary Elaine's (p128). There are some unusual offerings such as archery, badminton and croquet, which set this place apart from other hotels in its class.

James Hotel (Map pp120-1; ☎ 480-308-1100; www.jameshotel.com; 7353 E Indian School Rd, Scottsdale; r from $160, ste $520; Ⓟ ⚛) Paris Hilton has slept here, along with a host of other celebs. It's a very hip place with bright modern decor and giant flat-screen TVs on the walls. Rooms have a stark 1960s vibe. Stay at this boutique masterpiece if you want to see and be seen.

Sanctuary on Camelback Mountain (Map pp120-1; ☎ 480-948-2100; www.sanctuaryoncamelback.com; 5700 E McDonald Dr, Paradise Valley; r from $300; Ⓟ ⚛) This swanky spa resort offers massage under the stars ($130), and accommodation in spa or mountain casitas. Some rooms are sleek and elegant, others clinically sparse. All feature very comfortable beds. It's a trendy and romantic choice.

Royal Palms Resort & Spa (Map pp120-1; ☎ 602-840-3610; www.royalpalmsresortandspa.com; 5200 E Camelback Rd, Scottsdale; r from $355; Ⓟ ⚛) President Bush chose to stay here twice in 2004. Rooms are done up in the Spanish Colonial style and range from minimalist to gilded, depending on how much you shell out. Homemade cookies, truffles or candy are part of the nightly turndown service.

Fairmont Scottsdale Princess Resort (Map pp120-1; ☎ 480-585-4848; www.fairmont.com; 7575 E Princess Dr, Scottsdale; r $470, casita & ste around $600; Ⓟ ⚛) A world-class option, this place is the home of the annual Professional Golfers' Association (PGA) Phoenix Open. With 450 beautifully landscaped acres, this is one of the valley's largest full-scale resorts. Service is impeccable, the restaurants are classy (see La Hacienda, p128), the rooms ornate and pristine.

ARIZONA

Arizona Biltmore Resort & Spa (Map pp120-1; ☎ 602-955-6600, 800-950-0086; www.arizonabiltmore. com; 24th St & E Missouri Ave; r $350-530, ste from $680; ⓟ ⓢ) Frank Lloyd Wright influenced much of the design for the city's first luxury resort. A beautiful and historically interesting place, it opened in 1929 and underwent extensive renovations and additions in the 1990s. Now boasting over 700 discerning units, many with private balconies, its modern facilities include two golf courses, several swimming pools (one with a long water slide) and tennis courts, an athletic club, health spa, children's program and two very good restaurants.

Hyatt Regency Scottsdale at Gainey Ranch Resort (Map pp120-1; ☎ 480-991-3388, 800-233-1234; www.hyatt.com; 7500 E Doubletree Ranch Rd, Scottsdale; r from $300; ⓟ ⓛ ⓢ) If you love to swim, you'll love this posh resort with 11 pools, an artificial beach, huge waterslide and numerous hot tubs. The rooms are modern with private porches, floor-to-ceiling windows and a soothing khaki and light-brown color scheme. The resort does a good job of positively promoting Native American heritage with an educational room and dance performances. The place features three great restaurants, including Vu (p128), as well as lounges with live music.

Ritz-Carlton (Map pp120-1; ☎ 602-468-0700, 800-241-3333; 2401 E Camelback Rd; r $300-400; ⓟ ⓢ) The ritziest nonresort hotel in Phoenix, it offers elegant and soothing rooms and suites. The place features superb dining, including the Grill – one of Arizona's top American restaurants. There's also a bar with nightly lounge entertainment. Other amenities include a fitness center with trainers and massage therapists, a spa, sauna, tennis courts and golf privileges with transport to the courses.

Marriott's Camelback Inn (Map pp120-1; ☎ 480-948-1700, 800-242-2635; www.camelbackinn.com; 5402 E Lincoln Dr, Scottsdale; r from $400, ste from $600; ⓟ ⓢ) Guests keep returning to this 120-acre place that opened in 1936. It's considered a world-class resort and highlights include 36 holes of excellent golf, a full-service spa and health club, several pools and tennis courts, and the highly rated Chaparral restaurant, serving continental fare.

Pointe Hilton Squaw Peak Resort (Map pp120-1; ☎ 602-997-2626; www.pointehilton.com; 7677 N 16th St; r $250; ⓟ ⓢ) With nine acres of pools, including water slides and a 'river' tubing

area, as well as a popular kids' program, this a good family choice. Rates include a complimentary evening beverage service. Rooms, however, are slightly less luxurious than similarly priced resorts.

EATING

Phoenix has the biggest selection of restaurants in Arizona: from fast food to ultrafancy, it's all here. About two-thirds of the places listed here are in the valley, and some of the very best are in the resorts, although you don't have to be a guest to dine there. Reservations are recommended at the fancier places. All addresses are in Phoenix, unless otherwise indicated.

Budget

Matador (Map p122; ☎ 602-254-7563; 125 E Adams St; dishes $6-10) A downtown favorite, this large and modern place serves Mexican breakfasts and hangover-curing *menudos* (tripe stew). Lunch and dinner are also south-of-the-border themed, although there are a few American options. Lunch lines are common, but they usually move quickly.

5 & Diner (Map pp120-1; ☎ 602-264-5220; 5220 N 16th St; dishes $5-10) A visit here is lots of fun, featuring inexpensive food, friendly service and a '50s setting. The menu is the predictable prenouvelle American cuisine: burgers, fries, tuna melts, shakes, etc. The diner's success has led to eight others opening in the valley.

Los Dos Molinos (dishes $7-12; ❤ lunch & dinner Tue-Sat) Phoenix (Map pp120-1; ☎ 602-243-9113; 8646 S Central Ave); Mesa (☎ 602-835-5356; 260 S Alma School Rd) Known for its cheap and tasty fare, the food at these New Mexican influenced restaurants is delicious, especially if you have a taste for chiles. Both restaurants are a family affair, with different generations working the stove and tables. Their slogan is 'some like it hot,' so ask them to hold the hot sauce if you're not a super-spicy chile fan.

Good Egg (Map pp120-1; ☎ 480-483-1090; 14046 N Scottsdale Rd, Scottsdale; dishes $5-8; ❤ breakfast & lunch) One of several locations around town, this congenial breakfast joint serves all sorts of benedicts, scrambles and omelets. Low-carb options and sandwiches are also on the menu.

Coffee Plantation (Map pp120-1; ☎ 480-829-7878; 680 S Mill Ave, Tempe; dishes $3-8; ❤ 6am to midnight) A Tempe institution for more than a decade, this espresso and cappuccino place is popular with ASU students, high-school kids and 20-something young professionals. It also serves light meals and a selection of tasty pastries. About 10 other Coffee Plantations have opened in the Greater Phoenix area.

MacAlpine's (Map pp120-1; ☎ 602-252-3039; 2303 N 7th St; dishes from $5; ☯ breakfast & lunch) The oldest diner in Phoenix, and perhaps Arizona, it serves up huge breakfasts and features an authentic soda fountain, genuine sundaes and other icy delights.

Mrs White's Golden Rule Cafe (Map p122; ☎ 602-262-9256; 808 E Jefferson St; dishes $8; ☯ noon-3pm Mon-Fri) A hole in the wall with hanging, hand-lettered menus, it serves home-style, well-prepared and tasty dishes (they aren't greasy, but not exactly low on calories).

El Bravo (Map pp120-1; ☎ 602-943-9753; 8338 N 7th St; dishes $5; ☯ lunch & dinner) Even though it's not centrally located, the Mexican food at this simple and genuine family restaurant has received great reviews. On the menu are combination plates, a choice of inexpensive à la carte Sonoran dishes and Navajo tacos.

Sugar Bowl Ice Cream Parlor (Map pp120-1; ☎ 480-946-0051; 4005 N Scottsdale Rd, Scottsdale; dishes $2-8; ☯ breakfast, lunch & dinner) When the kids get tired of shopping, bring them to this pink and white place specializing in cold, creamy ice cream cones and sundaes. It also serves light meals.

Tuchetti (Map pp120-1; ☎ 602-957-0222; 2135 E Camelback Rd; dishes $10; ☯ lunch & dinner) Families pack this place where the decor is Italy à la Disney. There's a large children's menu, and a wide selection of pizza and pasta dishes.

Midrange

Grilled Expeditions (Map pp120-1; ☎ 480-317-0600; cnr 7th St & Mill Ave, Tempe; dishes $10-20; ☯ lunch & dinner) Melt-in-your-mouth steaks as well as Cajun dishes and a large salad menu are served in bright, modern environs or on the packed patio. Anything beef is a good choice; the house specialty is the 1200 Series NY Strip ($25), which has been buried in 1200°F mesquite coals. Happy hour brings $3 martinis and half-price appetizers from 4pm to 7pm and 9:30pm to close.

Café Terra Cotta (Map pp120-1; ☎ 480-948-8100; 6166 N Scottsdale Rd, Scottsdale; dishes $12-20; ☯ lunch & dinner) After enjoying great success as a

Tucson favorite, the owners opened a second location in Scottsdale at the Borgata Mall. The menu is innovative, with a few wild choices, as well as standard steak and chicken choices for the less adventurous. Be sure to leave room for one of the heavenly desserts.

Italian Grotto (Map pp120-1; ☎ 480-994-1489; 3915 N Scottsdale Rd, Scottsdale; dishes $10-20; ☯ lunch & dinner) The lounge interior is dark and lit by candles. Modern art graces the brushed metal walls and comfy half-circle black leather booths abound, making it a romantic spot for an Italian meal. Try the lasagna; it's a steal at $11. The calamari *fra diavolo* is also a good pick; it's spicy and sumptuous.

Landmark (☎ 480-962-4652; 809 W Main St, Mesa; dishes $10-20; ☯ lunch & dinner) One of Mesa's best restaurants, this place has been serving good American food for about 25 years. Built as a Mormon church in the early 1900s, the restaurant is decorated with antiques and photos, and has a huge salad bar. The home-style, traditional American dinner mains draw crowds of knowing locals.

C-Fu Gourmet (Map pp120-1; ☎ 480-899-3888; 2051 W Warner Rd, Chandler; dishes $15-20; ☯ lunch & dinner) The seafood at this Asian restaurant is super fresh (you can even see it swimming before it's cooked). Selections vary depending on what's floating around, although fish, crab and shrimp are staples. Check out the recommended dim sum selection at lunch.

Carlsbad Tavern (Map pp120-1; ☎ 480-970-8164; 3313 N Hayden Rd, Scottsdale; dishes from $10; ☯ lunch & dinner) Popular with a younger adult crowd, this place serves good and inexpensive New Mexican fare. The patio is popular, even in summer when a pond and mist sprinkler system keeps temperatures bearable. Inside, a mischievous menu ('the Carlsbad Daily Guano') plays up to the batty cavernous interior.

House of Tricks (Map pp120-1; ☎ 480-968-1114; 114 E 7th St, Tempe; dishes $15; ☯ lunch & dinner) Enthusiastic diners gobble up the reasonably priced innovative meat, chicken and fish dishes on the shady patio. If you'd rather dine inside, there are two early-20th-century cottages ready to charm. A good deal.

Havana Cafe (Map pp120-1; ☎ 602-952-1991; 4225 E Camelback Rd, Scottsdale; dishes $7-15; ☯ lunch & dinner) Recommended for its Cuban fare, the mains are excellent, and the decor colorful

ARIZONA

and casual. If you're hankering for a giant sandwich, try the Cuban served on grilled bread with roast pork, Swiss cheese, mortadella and cured ham, and topped with *mojo* and pickles.

Texaz Bar & Grill (Map pp120-1; ☎ 602-248-7827; 6003 N 16th St, Phoenix; dishes $10-15) Not exactly a steak house, but it has huge, meaty meals – they don't skimp on potatoes and gravy. The 18oz T-bone steak is a winner, and burgers or chicken-fried steaks are also popular. This fun, down-home place pays homage to the 'Lone Star State,' with Texan 'stuff' filling all available wall space. It's popular with locals and visitors alike.

Pinnacle Peak Patio (Map pp120-1; ☎ 480-585-1599; 10426 E Jomax Rd, Scottsdale; dishes from $10) Evening meals are complemented with country music and dance lessons nightly. Steak is the star attraction on the menu. It's a fun spot, where the kids can cut loose on the dance floor.

Baby Kay's Cajun Kitchen (Map pp120-1; ☎ 602-955-0011; 2119 E Camelback Rd; dishes from $10; ☺ lunch & dinner) For Cajun catfish and crawfish try this place in the Town & Country Mall. It's gained local notoriety for its delicious 'dirty rice' (a mixture of rice with sausage, onions, peppers and seasonings) and a whole bunch of other Southern specials.

Mr C's (Map pp120-1; ☎ 480-941-4460; 4302 N Scottsdale Rd, Scottsdale; dishes $10-20; ☺ lunch & dinner) If you crave opulent surroundings with your Peking duck, Mr C's will indulge. The food is classic Cantonese, and many say the best in town.

Greekfest (Map pp120-1; ☎ 602-265-2990; 1940 E Camelback Rd; dishes $13-20; ☺ breakfast, lunch & dinner) Set back from the road, this is an excellent bet for Greek food. Both food and ambiance are delightful. The sign is small, so keep an eye out.

Don & Charlie's (Map pp120-1; ☎ 480-990-0900; 7501 E Camelback Rd, Scottsdale; dishes $15-20; ☺ dinner) Baseball fans pack this place filled with ballpark memorabilia and photos of sporting personalities. The food is meaty, with lots of barbecued options.

Top End

Medizona (Map pp120-1; ☎ 480-947-9500; 7214 E 4th Ave, Scottsdale; dishes $24; ☺ dinner) One of Phoenix's top restaurants, this place has won numerous local awards. It combines Mediterranean and Southwestern cuisine with

excellent results – the menu is unique, the food well presented and enchanting, the environs intimate and romantic.

Vu (Map pp120-1; ☎ 480-991-3388; 7500 E Doubletree Ranch Rd, Scottsdale; dishes $25-30; ☺ dinner) Inside the Hyatt Regency Scottsdale, this swanky and vibrant restaurant is mod to the max. Dishes are contemporary steak and seafood oriented, and the tables overlook a lagoon and lush gardens. There's a unique (and lengthy) wine list and designer martinis to get you nicely lubricated.

Mary Elaine's (Map pp120-1; ☎ 480-423-2530; 6000 E Camelback Rd, Scottsdale; dishes from $25; ☺ dinner) Posh and very elegant, this restaurant inside the Phoenician (p125) has earned a well-deserved stellar reputation for serving delicious and creative Southwestern and French cuisine. Jackets are required for men.

Vincent Guerithault on Camelback (Map pp120-1; ☎ 602-224-0225; 3930 E Camelback Rd, Scottsdale; dishes from $20; ☺ lunch & dinner) Considering the famous chef, prices remain reasonable at this classy Southwestern restaurant with a French touch. The haute cuisine menu includes some seriously sumptuous appetizers. Try the duck tamales stuffed with Anaheim chiles and raisins or the grilled shrimp and frizzled tortilla salad. Mains and desserts are just as tasty. Perfect for a romantic date.

La Hacienda (Map pp120-1; ☎ 480-585-4848; 7575 E Princess Dr, Scottsdale; dishes $25; ☺ dinner) Upscale Mexican cuisine is complemented by beautiful surroundings, strolling mariachis and top-notch service at this restaurant inside the Fairmont Scottsdale Princess Resort (p125). The food is as superb as the setting.

Oceana (Map pp120-1; ☎ 480-515-2277; 9800 E Pinnacle Peak Rd, Scottsdale; dishes $30; ☺ lunch & dinner) A must for the seafood lover. Fancy fresh fins, including sea urchins and sushi, are served at this classy place in the La Mirada shopping center.

DRINKING

Posh watering holes are found in the most unlikely of spots in the Phoenix area, hidden amid chain stores in strip malls. Scottsdale has the greatest concentration of trendy bars and clubs, while Tempe attracts the student crowd. Meander down Tempe's Mill Ave, between 3rd and 7th Sts, and see what strikes your fancy.

Jade Bar (Map pp120-1; ☎ 480-948-2100; 5700 E McDonald Dr, Paradise Valley) A luscious place inside the Sanctuary on Camelback Mountain (p125), this place overlooks the sparkling valley. Order a cantaloupe martini as the sun sinks low on the horizon.

J Bar (Map pp120-1; ☎ 480-308-1100; 7353 E Indian School Rd, Scottsdale) Swanky and seductive, this sleek joint is a big-city bar featuring a long list of specialty drinks. It's a place to see and be seen. Look for it inside the James Hotel (p125).

Suede (Map pp120-1; ☎ 480-970-6969; 7333 E Indian Plaza, Camelback Rd, Scottsdale) The walls are lined with suede, *of course*, at this ultrachic joint featuring a patio with a fireplace. It's a good spot to start or end an evening.

Sugar Daddy's (Map pp120-1; ☎ 480-970-6556; 3102 N Scottsdale Rd, Scottsdale; cover $2) Live music rocks this casual – and often rowdy – local pick nightly. If your ears are ringing make your way outside to one of the best patios in town. You'll be fighting for personal space, but that could be a good thing if you've come to flirt (as many have).

Armitage Wine Lounge & Café (Map pp120-1; ☎ 480-502-1641; 20751 N Pima Rd, Scottsdale) Folks from around the Valley flock to this great new wine bar to sip vintages on overstuffed couches and chairs made for sinking. It's a warm and classy place.

Unlikely Cowboy Restaurant & Brewery (Map pp120-1; ☎ 480-502-5557; 20751 N Pima Rd, Scottsdale) Award-winning hand-crafted brews are served at the foot of the McDowell mountains. The Cowboy specializes in German lagers and wheat ales, and also does some excellent pub grub.

Compass Room Lounge (Map p122; ☎ 602-252-1234; 122 N 2nd St) Spectacular 360-degree views of downtown are the reason to visit this rotating bar on the 24th floor of the Hyatt Regency Phoenix. It's great for a sunset drink, or to stare down at the twinkling lights of the city far below. The decor is richly posh, the lighting low. While the restaurant serves delicious American fare, it's really all about the views.

Zipp's Sports Grill (Map pp120-1; ☎ 480-970-9507; 7551 E Camelback Rd, Scottsdale) One of three Scottsdale locations, Zipp's is a neighborhood pub type of place with pool tables, nightly drink specials and patios for socializing. The kitchen serves juicy burgers and such until 1am.

ENTERTAINMENT

The free alternative weekly *New Times*, published every Thursday and available all over the city, lets you know what's going on around town. Published on the same day, the *Arizona Republic's The Rep* also has exhaustive entertainment listings, with an emphasis on popular music and nightlife.

Clubs & Live Music

Covers vary depending on the night of the week and type of act. Generally clubs charge between $5 and $10 to get in. Live music, especially big-name bands, mean you'll need to fork over between $10 and $40.

Rhythm Room (Map pp120-1; ☎ 602-265-4842; 1019 E Indian School Rd, Scottsdale) Live blues and jazz are spotlighted at this local favorite. It attracts a mixed, often eclectic crowd looking for a good time.

CBNC (Map pp120-1; ☎ 480-990-3222; 1420 N Scottsdale Rd, Scottsdale) DJs spin excellent hip-hop, R&B and dance tunes at this popular club. You may even spot a big-name celeb on the dance floor. Ladies get in free most nights.

Mr Lucky's (Map pp120-1; ☎ 602-246-0686; 3660 NW Grand Ave) Grab your boots and spurs, pardner, and ride-on down to Mr Lucky's for live country and western and dancing. The outside corral has bull-riding competitions on weekends (with real bulls, not the mechanical kind). Western wear is a must.

Char's Has the Blues (Map pp120-1; ☎ 602-230-0205; 4631 N 7th Ave) Have a hankering for the blues? Then stop by this often-packed place that showcases some excellent acts most nights of the week.

Warsaw Wallies (Map pp120-1; ☎ 602-955-0881; 2547 E Indian School Rd) A small, funky place, it often has exceptional blues bands with low or no cover.

Mason Jar (Map pp120-1; ☎ 602-956-6271; 2303 E Indian School Rd) This club used to be legendary for rocking out to heavy metal (Guns N' Roses and Nirvana played it in their early days), but it's branching out a bit these days to include hip-hop, Goth and salsa. That's right, Monday's salsa night. Tuesday is Goth night and Wednesday is hip-hop and all-ages night, which means no alcohol. The rest of the week you can expect a hard-hitting line up of touring rock bands.

Bash on Ash (Map pp120-1; ☎ 480-966-8200; 230 W 5th St, Tempe) This place hosts good rock bands and an 'all-ages area.'

Symphony Hall (Map p122; ☎ 602-262-7272; 225 E Adams) The Arizona Opera (☎ 602-266-7464) and the Phoenix Symphony Orchestra (☎ 602-495-1999) are based here.

Cinemas

There are dozens of cinema multiplexes throughout the valley showing the year's best and worst movies.

Valley Art Theater (Map pp120-1; ☎ 602-222-4275; 509 S Mill Ave, Tempe) Showcases a variety of foreign and alternative flicks.

Imax Theatre (Map p117; ☎ 480-897-1453; Arizona Mills Mall, cnr Priest & Baseline Rds) South of town, docu-movies are screened on an eight-times-larger-than-normal screen.

AMC 24 (Map p122; ☎ 602-244-2262; Arizona Center, 565 N 3rd St) This huge multiplex theater features armrests that fold up so you can cuddle with your date, and there's steep seating so you don't have to peer around people's heads.

Theater

The following are Phoenix's most acclaimed venues and companies. Not much goes on during summer.

Herberger Theater Center (Map p122; ☎ 602-252-8497; 222 E Monroe St) Two stages host productions by the Arizona Theater Company (☎ 602-256-6995), Ballet Arizona (☎ 602-381-0184), Actors Theater of Phoenix (☎ 602-253-6701) and others occasionally.

Helen K Mason Center for the Performing Arts (Map p122; ☎ 602-258-8128; 333 E Portland St) Home of the Black Theater Troupe, it also hosts other African American performers.

Gammage Auditorium (Map pp120-1; ☎ 480-965-3434; cnr Mill Ave & Apache Blvd, Tempe) On the ASU campus, it is the university's main center for the performing arts; see also p119.

Sports

Phoenix has some of the nation's top professional teams, and tickets for the best games sell out fast.

The **America West Arena** (Map p122; ☎ 602-379-7867; 201 E Jefferson St) hosts a number of teams including:

Phoenix Suns (☎ 602-379-7800; www.suns.com) This National Basketball Association (NBA) team plays professional basketball December to April.

Phoenix Mercury (☎ 602-252-9622) The women's NBA team plays professional basketball from June to September.

Arizona Rattlers (☎ 602-514-8383) An arena football team, the Rattlers were the 1994 world champions, and have games between May and August.

Phoenix Coyotes (☎ 480-473-5600) The National Hockey League (NHL) team plays ice hockey from December to March.

The **Phoenix Mustangs** (☎ 602-340-0001) are a West Coast Hockey League team that play at the **Arizona Veterans Memorial Coliseum** (Map p122; 1826 W McDowell Rd) in the State Fairgrounds. The National Football League (NFL) **Arizona Cardinals** (Map pp120-1; ☎ 602-379-0102; Sun Devil Stadium, ASU campus, Tempe) play professional football (fall to spring) at the ASU stadium – the site of the 1996 Super Bowl. **ASU student teams** (☎ 602-965-2381), such as the Sun Devils, also use the stadium. The **Arizona Diamondbacks** (Map p122; ☎ 602-462-6500; Bank One Ballpark, cnr E Jefferson & S 7th Sts) are a major-league baseball team.

Professional golfers compete for a seven-figure purse at the PGA Phoenix Open, held every January at the **Tournament Players Golf Course** (Map pp120-1; ☎ 480-585-3600; 17020 N Hayden Rd, Scottsdale).

You can watch horseracing at **Turf Paradise** (Map pp120-1; ☎ 602-942-1101; cnr 19th Ave & Bell St) from October to May, and see Greyhounds race year-round at **Phoenix Greyhound Park** (Map pp120-1; ☎ 602-273-7181; 3801 E Washington St). Nascar car racing takes place at **Phoenix International Raceway** (Map p117; ☎ 602-254-4622; 7602 S 115th Ave) at Baseline Rd, Avondale.

SHOPPING

The question is not so much what to buy (you can buy just about anything) but where to go. Scottsdale is the art gallery capital of Arizona. Apart from its stellar museum, the **Heard Museum** (Map pp120-1; ☎ 602-252-8840; www.heard.org; 2301 N Central Ave) has the best bookshop about Native Americans and the most reliable, excellent and expensive selection of Native American arts and crafts.

The valley has several notable shopping malls. You may not be a fan of malls, but the air conditioning does give them a certain allure when the mercury climbs in summer. For more upscale shopping, visit the **Scottsdale Fashion Square** (Map pp120-1; cnr Camelback & Scottsdale Rds, Scottsdale) and the even more exclusive **Biltmore Fashion Park** (Map pp120-1; cnr Camelback Rd & 24th St). Both provide a good selection of cheap to expensive restaurants, and the Biltmore is home to some of the valley's best eateries. One of the fancier outdoor malls, featuring lots of boutiques and galleries, **Borgata** (Map pp120-1; 6166 N Scottsdale Rd, Scottsdale) was designed to look like a medieval town.

GETTING THERE & AWAY

Sky Harbor International Airport (Map pp120-1; ☎ 602-273-3300) is 3 miles southeast of downtown. It's by far the largest airport in the Southwest, and its three terminals (illogically called Terminals 2, 3 and 4) contain all the standard features of any major airport. There are economy long-term parking lots ($5 or $8 a day) within a short walk or shuttle-bus ride of the terminals, and pricier short-term lots ($20 a day) next to the terminals.

Greyhound (Map pp120-1; ☎ 602-389-4200; 2115 E Buckeye Rd) runs regular buses to Tucson ($16, two hours), Flagstaff ($23, 3½ hours) and Los Angeles ($37, seven hours), among other cities.

GETTING AROUND

From the airport, **SuperShuttle** (☎ 602-244-9000) runs vans providing airport-to-your-door service at any time. Fares are lower than those of taxis, which add a $1 airport surcharge in addition to their metered rates.

Valley Metro (☎ 602-253-5000; www.valleymetro .org; fare $1.25) operates buses all over the valley, including service to and from the airport. During the week they also run the free Flash service around ASU and the free Dash service around the downtown Phoenix area.

Western States Motorcycle Tours (Map pp120-1; ☎ 602-943-9030; 9401 N 7th Ave) rents big bikes to riders aged 21 and over who're at least 5ft and 5in tall, with a motorcycle license and two years recent riding experience. Daily rates range from $75 for an 800cc Suzuki Intruder to $175 for an Electra-Glide Classic Harley. Weekly rates are available.

There are several 24-hour cab services, but with a $3 drop fee and fares of well over $1 per mile, you can rack up a pricey ride fairly rapidly in the large valley area. The main cab companies are **Ace Taxi** (☎ 602-254-1999), **Checker Cab** (☎ 602-257-1818) and **Yellow Cab** (☎ 602-252-5252).

GRAND CANYON REGION

A trip to Grand Canyon National Park is an iconic American experience. Initially dismissed as little more than an obstacle to exploration, the canyon first drew 19th-century miners bent on exploiting its rich natural resources. Native American resistance and the lack of water slowed development, but by the time Frederick Jackson Turner declared the end of the American frontier in 1893, entrepreneurs had transformed the canyon into one of the country's most celebrated destinations. At the dawn of the Industrial Revolution, people flocked to the canyon in search of the romanticized wilderness ideal and embraced its sublime beauty. They still do. Today, the park attracts 5 million visitors each year from around the world.

Perhaps the most obvious draw is the spectacular landscape. The Grand Canyon's dramatic scenery enthralls even the most jaded visitors and leaves all who witness it somehow changed. Its dimensions are mind-blowing. The Grand Canyon is a mile deep and averages 10 miles wide. Snaking along its floor are 277 miles of the Colorado River, which has carved the canyon over the past 6 million years, exposing rocks up to 2 billion years old – half of Earth's total life span.

The two rims of the Grand Canyon offer quite different experiences, and as they lie more than 200 miles apart by road, are rarely visited on the same trip. Most visitors choose the South Rim, which boasts easy access, the bulk of services and the panoramic vistas for which the park is famous. The quieter North Rim has its own charms; at 8200ft elevation (1000ft higher than the South Rim), its cooler temperatures support wildflower meadows and tall, thick stands of aspen and spruce.

Hiking trails from both rims descend into the canyon, and if you've got at least two days, you can hike from rim to rim. If you'd like to visit the inner canyon without hiking, consider a mule or rafting trip.

Despite the Grand Canyon's many riches, most visitors only spend a few hours in the park. It is possible to appreciate the canyon on a short stroll along the Rim Trail or an afternoon drive from viewpoint to viewpoint, but stay longer if you can. The more time

ARIZONA

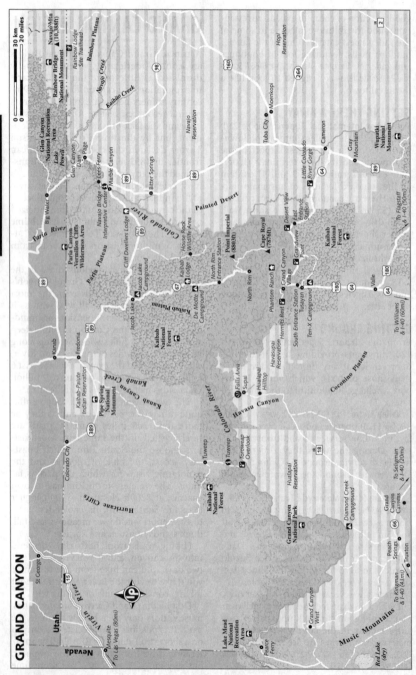

you have, the more you'll discover its subtle nuances and quiet charm – a fairyland of moss deep in the canyon, a teasing creek cascading over rocks, echoes of history at ancient Pueblo Indian sites, and a silence and stillness that seem to engulf you. Even a short hike beneath the rim forms an intimate connection to the land that adds to the grandeur. Take your time, and let the Grand Canyon reveal its secrets.

GRAND CANYON NATIONAL PARK – SOUTH RIM
elev 7200ft

The Grand Canyon's South Rim encompasses some of the park's best and worst aspects. Here, scenic drives along the rim offer ample opportunities to enjoy gorgeous canyon vistas. Accessible to visitors of all ages and abilities, the 13-mile Rim Trail skirts the edge of the gorge and connects with Grand Canyon Village. Those wanting to descend into the canyon can choose from more than a dozen trailheads spread out along the rim or join regular mule trains on day and overnight trips. Several museums and distinctive stone buildings illuminate the park's human history, and rangers lead a host of daily programs on subjects from geology to condors.

On the flip side, the South Rim sees the most crowds, especially in the peak summer season, when lines are long, shuttles are packed and trails are covered in boot prints. Even this, however, doesn't have to detract from your trip. Patience and a sense of humor go a long way, as does the right attitude. Despite the crowds, you'll still see deer and other wildlife, find a quiet spot to enjoy the canyon's sublime beauty and be able to hike in solitude.

Climate

On average, temperatures are 20°F cooler on the South Rim than at the bottom of the Grand Canyon. At the South Rim in summer, expect highs in the 80°Fs and lows around 50°F. Weather is cooler and changeable in fall, and snow and freezing overnight temperatures are likely by November. January has average overnight lows in the teens and daytime highs around 40°F. Winter weather can be beautifully clear, but be prepared for occasional storms that can cause havoc.

IF YOU ONLY HAVE A DAY AT THE GRAND CANYON

Encompassing 1,217,403 acres (more than 1900 sq miles), the Grand Canyon is a huge park. With so much to see, it's hard to know where to begin. If you only have a day, start very early (say 6am, there's a lot to see) and enter the park through the quieter East Entrance. Climb the **Watchtower** (p134) for great views, then head west along **Desert View Drive** (p139) to Grand Canyon Village and have lunch at historic **El Tovar** (p141). After lunch, take in an afternoon **ranger program** (p135), then walk along the rim to the **Kolb Studio** (p134). In the late afternoon head into the canyon on the South Kaibab Trail to **Cedar Ridge** (p135), a 2.8-mile round-trip hike that offers a glimpse of the canyon's depths. Then take the red **Hermits Rest Route** shuttle to Pima Point or Hopi Point for sunset views. Finish your day with dinner at the **Arizona Room** (p141) in Bright Angel Lodge. Either stay the night in the village, or exit via the South Entrance.

The inner canyon is much drier with about eight inches of rain annually, about half that of the South Rim. During summer, temperatures inside the canyon soar above 100°F almost every day and often exceed 110°F in midsummer, which can be potentially lethal for unprepared hikers. Strong hot winds often blow in summer. Even in midwinter, freezing overnight temperatures are rare in the inner canyon, with average lows around 37°F and highs around 58°F.

The peak season ranges from about April to November, and the park is busiest from Memorial Day to Labor Day.

Orientation

Most visitors enter the park via the **South Entrance**, 80 miles northwest of Flagstaff on Hwy 180. In summer be prepared to wait up to 30 minutes or more at the entrance station. A few miles north lies Grand Canyon Village, which sprawls over 3 sq miles and is the primary hub of activity. Here you'll find lodges, restaurants, two of the three developed campgrounds, the backcountry office, the visitor center, shuttles, the clinic, bank, grocery store and other services.

The **East Entrance** lies on Hwy 64, 32 miles west of Cameron and 25 miles east of the village. At this entrance you'll find a campground, a gas station and the Desert View service hub, which offers a snack bar, small information center and general store. If possible, choose this entrance. It's only 10 miles further from Flagstaff than the South Entrance, and your first views of the canyon will be much more dramatic and peaceful.

Information

BOOKSTORES

Books & More Store (☎ 928-638-0199; Canyon View Information Plaza, Grand Canyon Village) Most extensive bookstore in the park.
Desert View Information Center (☎ 928-638-7893; East Entrance) Regional books.
Grand Canyon Association (GCA; ☎ 828-638-2481; www.grandcanyon.org) Sells over 350 books, maps, trail guides and videos about the Grand Canyon. Stores are in the visitor centers, and profits benefit the national park.
Kolb Studio (☎ 928-638-2771; Grand Canyon Village) Small but excellent selection.

EMERGENCY & MEDICAL SERVICES

Dial ☎ 911 in an emergency. The nearest hospital to the canyon is 80 miles south in Flagstaff (p154).
Clinic (☎ 928-638-2552; Grand Canyon Village; ☼ 9am-7pm Mon-Sat, 10am-4pm Sun) Offers walk-in medical care.
Dental Service (☎ 928-638-2395; Grand Canyon Village; ☼ 9am-7pm Mon-Sat, 10am-4pm Sun) At the clinic.

FEES

The park entrance ticket (per vehicle $20, bicyclists and pedestrians $10) is valid for seven days and can be used at any entrance point, including the North Rim (p147). All passes are honored. Bus and train passengers either pay a lesser fee or may have the fee included in the tour.

TOURIST INFORMATION

Visitors can get assistance at ranger stations near the Grand Canyon Railway depot, Indian Garden below the South Rim, the River Ranger station and Phantom Ranch at the canyon bottom. Telephone the **park** (☎ 928-638-7888; www.nps.gov/grca) for recorded information on everything from weather conditions to applying for river-running permits.
Canyon View Information Plaza (☎ 928-638-7644) Six miles north of the South Entrance Station at the northeast-end Grand Canyon Village. Ranger-staffed info desk and bulletin boards with information about lodging, weather, tours, talks and a host of other things.
Desert View Information Center (☎ 928-638-7893; East Entrance) Staffed info center.

Sights

While the canyon itself is the primary attraction, several buildings and museums offer a fascinating historical perspective to enrich your park experience. You'll learn how Pueblo Indians carved out a living, why early explorers saw the canyon primarily as an obstacle, whether prospectors struck it rich, how artists interpreted the canyon, and how entrepreneurs and railways ultimately transformed it into one of the world's most famous tourist destinations.

KOLB STUDIO

Born in Pennsylvania, photographers Ellsworth and Emery Kolb first came to the Grand Canyon in 1902. The brothers built the **studio** (☎ 928-638-2771; Grand Canyon Village; ☼ 8am-7pm) in 1904 and made their living photographing parties traveling the Bright Angel Trail. In 1911 they filmed their own trip down the Green and Colorado Rivers, and visitors clamored to their small auditorium to see the film, in which both brothers repeatedly tumble into the water. Emery continued to show the film to audiences twice daily until his death at 95 in 1976. Today, their studio holds a small, well-stocked bookstore and an art-gallery with changing exhibits. You can still see clips of the original Kolb river picture, though it's no longer projected on a full screen.

WATCHTOWER

A scramble up this five-story stone **tower** (☎ 928-638-2736; Desert View; ☼ 8am-7:30pm summer, 9am-4:30pm winter) offers unparalleled views of the canyon and surrounding desert. Near the east entrance, it was built in 1932 and is the highest point on the South Rim. Inside, the walls are decorated with reproductions of ancient petroglyphs as well as contemporary Native American artwork.

YAVAPAI OBSERVATION STATION

Panoramic views of the canyon unfold behind plate-glass windows at this **station** (☼ 8am-7pm, to 5pm winter) at the northeast end of Grand Canyon Village. There is a geology museum and spectacular views all the way down to Phantom Ranch on the canyon bottom. Accompanying plaques identify the various landmarks and explain how they were formed.

Activities

RANGER-LED ACTIVITIES

Free ranger programs are one of the park's greatest treasures. Lasting from 30 minutes to four hours, the talks cover everything from fossils to birds to Native American history. Programs are held throughout the park and often involve a short walk. *The Guide* (given to tourists upon park entry) provides a complete listing of current ranger programs. A kiosk at Canyon View Information Plaza also clearly explains current programs.

The **Cedar Ridge Hike** is one regular offering. It involves a strenuous 3-mile hike (three to four hours round-trip) 1140ft below the rim on the South Kaibab Trail. While you can hike this trail by yourself, the ranger explains canyon geology and history. It departs from the South Kaibab Trailhead at 7am. Take the green Kaibab Trail Route shuttle from Canyon View Information Plaza to access the trailhead.

The daily one-hour **Fossil Walk** is an easy half-mile one-way walk to exposed fossil beds along the rim. Rangers teach you how to recognize fossils found about 10 minutes down the trail.

During the week following summer solstice, the Tucson Amateur Astronomy Association offers a **Star Party** nightly at Yavapai Point (opposite), featuring a slide presentation followed by telescope viewing of the June sky. Just show up.

Mather Amphitheater hosts evening programs examining significant aspects of the canyon's natural or cultural history. Subjects change nightly; check the kiosk at the **Canyon View Information Plaza** (☎ 928-638-7610).

HIKING

Hiking along the South Rim is among park visitors' favorite pastimes, with options for every skill level. Most trails start with a super steep series of switchbacks that descend quickly to a dramatic sandstone ledge of about 2 miles beneath the rim before hitting the sun-baked Tonto Platform 3 miles later. From the platform it's a fast and furious pitch to the canyon floor and Colorado River. Most day hikers will want to stay above the Tonto Platform, particularly in summer.

The **Rim Trail** is the most popular, and easiest, walk in the park. It connects a series of scenic points and historical sights over 13 miles and portions are paved. Every viewpoint is accessed by one of the three shuttle routes, which means you can walk to a vista and shuttle back. The 3 miles or so that wind through the village are usually packed, but crowds thin out the further west you venture. The mile east of Pima Point, where the trail is set far back from the road, offers stunning views and relative solitude. The viewpoints at Mohave and Hopi Points offer great views of the Colorado River, with three visible rapids.

The most popular of the corridor trails is **Bright Angel**, which can be done as either a short or long day hike. Equally attractive to first-time canyon hikers, seasoned pros and mule trains, it is a heavily trafficked route. But the din doesn't lessen the sheer beauty. The steep and scenic 8-mile descent to the Colorado is punctuated with four logical turnaround spots, including two well-appointed resthouses to seek shade and hydrate. Even though the trail offers shade and seasonal water, summer heat can be crippling – day hikers should either turn around at one of the two resthouses (a 3- to 6-mile round-trip) or hit the trail at dawn to safely make the longer hikes to Indian Garden and Plateau Point (9.2- and 12.2-miles round-trip). The trailhead starts at the Grand Canyon Village. Hiking to the Colorado for the day is not an option.

The **South Kaibab** is arguably one of the park's prettiest trails, combining stunning scenery and adventurous hiking with every step. The only corridor trail to follow a ridgeline, the red-dirt path traverses the spine of a crest, allowing for unobstructed 360-degree views. Blasted out of the rock by rangers in the mid-1920s, the South Kaibab is steep, rough and wholly exposed, making a summer ascent particularly dangerous. Rangers discourage all but the shortest of day hikes during summer. Turn around at Cedar Ridge, perhaps the park's finest short day hike, about a three-hour round-trip. It's a dazzling spot, particularly at sunrise, when the deep ruddy umbers and reds of

ARIZONA

each canyon fold seem to glow from within. During the rest of the year, the continued trek to **Skeleton Point**, 1.5 miles beyond Cedar Ridge, makes for a fine hike – though the climb back up is a beast in any season. The trailhead is 4.5 miles east of the village along Yaki Point Rd. Parking is only permitted between December and February. Take a shuttle at other times.

One of the steepest trails in the park, dropping 1200ft in the first three-quarters of a mile, **Grandview** is also one of the finest and most popular hikes. The payoff following the stunning (and grueling) descent is an up-close look at one of the inner canyon's sagebrush-tufted mesas and a spectacular sense of solitude. While rangers don't rec-

ommend the trek to **Horseshoe Mesa** (3 miles, four to six hours) in summer (there's no water on the very exposed trail, and the climb out is a doozy), it's not overly long and certainly doable for strong hikers strapped with a hydration system. For a shorter, but still rewarding option hike to **Coconino Saddle**. Though it's only 1.5 miles round-trip, it packs a quick and precipitous punch as you plunge 1600ft over less than a mile. With the exception of a few short level sections, the Grandview is a rugged, narrow and rocky trail. The trailhead is at Grandview Point, 12 miles east of the village on Desert View Dr.

The wilderness **Hermit Trail** descends into pretty Hermit Canyon by way of a cool spring. It's a rocky trip down, but if you set

---

BACKCOUNTRY ACCESS

The Grand Canyon's backcountry is an exhilarating place to explore. From the rim it's impossible to truly appreciate the rich wilderness that lies below. But dip down to the canyon floor along the main corridor trails and you'll quickly be immersed in scenes of otherworldly beauty. Adventure enthusiasts should plan to spend at least a night or two deep in the inner gorge – walking the sandy banks of the Colorado, exploring the side canyon tributaries, sleeping beneath the vast swath of stars and listening to the nightly serenade of chirping frogs.

Most overnight backpacking trips go from the South Rim to the river and then return because rim-to-rim trips involve a five-hour car shuttle. Typically, three days and two nights are spent below the rim, with a choice of spending two nights at either Bright Angel (in Grand Canyon Village) or Indian Garden Campground, or one night at each (normally Bright Angel on the first night). If you arrange a shuttle, you could add a night at Cottonwood Campground on the way up to the North Rim. If your time is limited, a two-day/one-night trip is also rewarding. Because the Kaibab Trail is steep, this is the usual descent route, with the longer but less steep Bright Angel Trail used for climbing out. These two trails are called the 'corridor trails' and are recommended for first-time visitors.

If you want to hike but prefer a bed to a sleeping bag, you can stay at the canyon-bottom Phantom Ranch Lodge (p140).

The backcountry is a vast land of extremes – over-the-top views, bone-dry conditions and scorching temperatures. For most, it's an entirely unfamiliar and inhospitable area, in terms of both terrain and climate, where rote situations can quickly turn dangerous. Hiking in the backcountry requires keen preparation and caution. Each year numerous canyon rescues involve both inexperienced hikers and strong backpackers.

Overnight hikes require a **backcountry permit**. Control of camper numbers is very tight, and demand often far exceeds available slots. If you're caught camping in the backcountry without a permit, expect a hefty fine and possible court appearance.

Permits cost $10, plus an additional $5 per person per night. The fee is nonrefundable and payable by check or credit card. Reservations are accepted in person or by mail or fax beginning the first day of the month, four months prior to the planned trip. Detailed instructions and the permit request form are available from the **Grand Canyon National Park Service Backcountry Reservations Office** (☎ 928-638-7875; fax 928-638-2125; www.nps.gov/grca; PO Box 129, Grand Canyon, AZ 86023; ☼ 8am-noon & 1-5pm). Once a permit is granted, itinerary changes are not permitted, except for emergencies. You're permitted to list three alternative dates and routes, which can markedly increase your chances of securing a permit. If you arrive without a permit, add your name to the waiting list, which can take anywhere from a day to a week to clear.

out early in the morning and take it slow, it offers a wonderfully serene hike and a peek into secluded nooks. The best destinations for day hikers are to **Santa Maria Spring** (5 miles round-trip) or to **Dripping Springs** via a spur trail (6.5 miles round-trip). The upper section of the Hermit is well shaded in the morning, making it a cool option in summer. The trailhead is 8 miles west of Grand Canyon Village.

MULE RIDES

One- and two-day mule trips into the canyon depart every day of the year from the corral west of Bright Angel Lodge. The seven-hour **day trip** ($130) takes riders down the Bright Angel Trail to Indian Garden, then follows the Plateau Point Trail to Plateau Point – an overlook of the Colorado River. Here you can hop down and stretch your legs while enjoying the view before the 6-mile return trip. Riders stop for lunch at Indian Garden. **Overnight trips** ($350) follow the Bright Angel Trail to the river, travel east on the River Trail and cross the river on the Kaibab Suspension Bridge to spend the night at Phantom Ranch. It's a 5½-hour, 10-mile trip to Phantom Ranch. **Two-night trips** (1/2 people $450/765) to Phantom Ranch are offered between mid-November and 31 March. Overnight trips include accommodations and all meals.

Don't plan a mule trip assuming it's the easiest way to travel below the rim. It's a bumpy ride on a hard saddle, and unless you are used to riding a horse regularly, you *will* be sore. Riders must be at least 4ft 7in tall, speak fluent English and weigh less than 200lbs. No personal bags are allowed on the mules. Anything that could possibly fall off and injure someone in the canyon below will be confiscated till your return.

When you arrive at the corral, the wranglers will give you a small bag (a 15lb ice bag) that is just big enough for a bathing suit, a change of clothes and a few personal items. These will be put in saddlebags for the trip – your bag will not necessarily be on your mule, so don't put anything in it you may need during the ride. Carry sunscreen and any medications in your pocket. You must wear a hat that secures to your head, a long-sleeved shirt and long pants (preferably jeans) or you will not be allowed on the mule. You should also wear sunglasses,

but they must also secure to your head. The wranglers will give each rider a water pouch and will provide additional water with meals. Be sure to eat something before you leave – it's a long, tiring ride to lunch.

To book a mule trip more than 24 hours and up to 23 months in advance, call **Xanterra** (☎ 303-287-2757, 888-297-2757; www.xanterra .com). If you arrive at the park and want to join a mule trip the following day (pending availability), stop by the transportation desk at Bright Angel Lodge (p140) in Grand Canyon Village. If the trips are booked, join a waiting list, then show up at the lodge at 6:15am on the day of the trip and hope there has been a cancellation. If riding a mule is important to you, reserve this trip well in advance.

If you're not planning a mule trip, just watching the wranglers prepare the mules can be fun, particularly for young children. In summer stop by the mule corral at 8am; in winter they get going at about 9am.

WHITE-WATER RAFTING

The King Kong of rivers, a run down the Colorado River is an epic, adrenaline-pumping adventure. 'Normal' rapids are rated I through V (with V being pretty damn tough), but the 160-plus rapids on the Colorado are rated I to X, with many V or higher. Two merit a X! The biggest single drop is at Lava Falls, which plummets 37 stomach-churning feet in just 300yd. The quick roller coaster thrills are only the beginning of a spiritual, exhilarating experience. The canyon's true grandeur is best grasped looking up from the river, not down from the rim. Glimpse the region's human history in ruins, wrecks and rock art. Hike to mystical grottos and waterfalls, up amazing slot canyons. View wildlife in its native habitat. Watch for subtle changes as light dances across canyon walls.

The Colorado is not a river to take for granted. People have died here before, and more will die in the future. Always wear your life vest, listen closely to your guide, and give this river the respect it deserves. If you do, you're likely to finish unscathed.

It's possible to run the Colorado on a private trip, but before throwing the raft in the pickup make sure you have serious experience (remember that 37ft drop?) and a permit. Over 22,000 people run the river

ARIZONA

each year, and many more want to. So many in fact, that the NPS has stopped adding people to the waiting list (which currently hovers around 20 years). This could change, however, so check with the **Grand Canyon River Trip Information Center** (River Permits Office; ☎ 928-638-7843; www.nps.gov/grca/river; c/o Grand Canyon National Park, PO Box 129, Grand Canyon, AZ 86023) if you're keen. If you're not already on the list, a commercial trip is going to be your only option. Here the biggest decision is picking a boat – oar, paddle or motorized. Motorized trips are generally the least scary option. The huge inflatable boats go twice as fast as oar or paddle boats, seat eight to 16 passengers and tend to be more stable (meaning you'll probably still fall out, but there is less chance of the boat flipping).

For more excitement take an oar boat (the most common raft on the river). It still provides stability, but feels more like a raft. The guide does all the rowing (thus retaining control on big rapids).

For heart-attack fun, take a paddle trip. You, your shipmates and a guide paddle in tandem. Flippage is almost guaranteed, and you're completely dependent on your shipmates' paddling skills (depending on your mindset, it's either bad news or very fun).

River nights are spent camping (gear provided) under the stars on sandy beaches. It's not as primitive as it sounds – guides are legendary for their combination of whitewater abilities, gastronomy and information.

Given two or three weeks, you can run the entire 279 miles of river through the canyon. Three shorter sections (each 100 miles or less) take four to nine days. Motorboats shorten the descent time. Oarpowered trips cost $200 to $300 per day, motorboats between $225 and $325. Book six to 12 months in advance. The following outfitters are recommended:

Arizona River Runners (☎ 602-867-4866; www.raftarizona.com; PO Box 47788, Phoenix, AZ 85068) Motorboat trips.

Grand Canyon Dories (☎ 209-736-0805; www.oars.com; PO Box 216, Altaville, CA 95221) Full length or upper and middle combo trips.

Oars (☎ 209-736-2924; www.oars.com; PO Box 67, Angels Camp, CA 95222) Oar-powered trips; paddle trips on request.

Outdoors Unlimited River Trips (☎ 928-526-454; www.outdoorsunlimited.com; 6900 Townsend Winona Rd, Flagstaff, AZ 86004) Specializes in paddle trips.

FISHING
Provided it's not your main source of food, fishing in the Grand Canyon can be a fun and peaceful activity. The Colorado is fairly well laden with trout and catfish, as are the permanent tributaries. Fishing is best during the winter months, when spawning trout make their way from the Colorado up Bright Angel Creek. To fish, you'll need an Arizona state fishing license, which you can pick up at Grand Canyon Village Marketplace on the South Rim or north of the park in Lees Ferry. For nonresidents a license costs $12.50 for one day, $26 for five days or $101 for the year; the Colorado River–only license (good for a year) is a bargain at $38.50.

To fish along the Colorado in the park, you'll also need an overnight backcountry permit; see Backcountry Access, p136. North of the park, there's excellent angling near Lees Ferry, especially along the 16-mile stretch from the outflow of Lake Powell at Glen Canyon Dam.

WINTER ACTIVITIES
In winter, the higher North Rim area offers more snow for better **cross-country skiing** than the South Rim area. However, the South Rim boasts 18 miles of easy- to medium-difficulty, groomed and signed skiing trails within the Kaibab National Forest, near the east entrance of the park. The plowed parking area and access to the trails is on East Rim Drive, about 10 miles north of the junction of Hwys 64 and 180, 2 miles east of Grandview Point.

About half a mile into the access trail is an information kiosk that describes routes and distances; the longest trail is 7.5 miles. One trail has a canyon-view overlook, but all trails stay in the national forest and do not go to the South Rim of the national park.

Skiers are free to tour the national forest regardless of trails and there are no restrictions on camping unless you enter the park. You'll need to bring your own skis. Rentals are available in the nearby town of Flagstaff (see p159).

SOUTH RIM SCENIC DRIVES
Two scenic drives follow the rim on either side of the village – Hermit Rd to the west and Desert View Drive to the east. The rim dips in and out of view as the road passes

through the piñon-juniper and ponderosa stands of Kaibab National Forest. Pullouts along the way offer spectacular views and interpretive signs explain the canyon's features and geology.

Resist the temptation to simply jump out of your car and snap a photo. It takes a while to absorb each view. If you're short on time, select a few choice overlooks to enjoy at length. Breathe in the desert air, watch for birds, peer down at the river and wonder at the forces that carved this canyon.

The 8-mile **Hermit Road Drive** offers several exceptional views. It begins at the west end of Grand Canyon Village, and ends at the distinctive **Hermits Rest**, built as a rest stop for early park tourists. Here you can peruse the small gift shop and snack bar or hike the Hermit Trail (see p136) into the canyon. If you just want to stretch your legs, hike down about 10 minutes and search the walls for exposed fossil beds.

The **Desert View Drive** begins at Mather Point and heads west for 25 miles to the park's East Entrance. Seven well-marked viewpoints, a small museum and an Ancestral Puebloan site line the road. A leisurely drive, with plenty of time for every stop, takes about four hours.

Grand Canyon for Children

The park offers plenty of cool kids' activities, including mule riding, hiking and fossil hunting. Scenic hikes along the Rim Trail involve minimal elevation change and are perfect for little legs.

Many of the ranger-led programs are designed with kids in mind, including the hugely popular fossil walks. During the summer, rangers host daily hour-long (4:30pm, Mather Campground) of educational activities geared toward seven- to 11-year-olds. Evening programs featuring astronomy, campfires and short walks are great end-of-the-day activities for youngsters.

The **Discovery Pack Program** begins with a 90-minute ranger talk, during which children (ages nine to 14) and their families are given a pack with binoculars, a magnifying lens, field guides and other naturalist tools. Families then take the day to leisurely explore the park and complete the activities in their field journal.

The **Junior Ranger Dynamic Earth Program** takes kids (ages nine to 14) on a 1-mile hike along an unpaved portion of the Rim Trail and explains the geology of the canyon through hands-on activities.

For younger kids (ages seven to 11), the **Way Cool Stuff for Kids** program uses hands-on activities to teach children about the park's plants and wildlife. Each ranger may choose a different activity. For example, one ranger builds a forest with the children, who pretend to be trees, grasses, bees and other plants and creatures.

In the park's most popular program, children aged four to 14 can earn a **Junior Ranger** badge. Achieving the honor involves attending a ranger program (see *The Guide* for a schedule) and completing a self-guided activity book, which includes wildlife detective work, drawing petroglyphs and jotting down different sensory experiences. To participate, pick up a free *Junior Ranger* booklet at the Canyon View Information Plaza.

Keep in mind that rangers are not babysitters – adults must accompany all children.

The **Grand Canyon Field Institute** (☎ 928-638-2485; www.grandcanyon.org/fieldinstitute) offers several family-oriented classes featuring naturalist-led hikes; some excursions include meals and lodging.

Tours

Tours inside the park are run by **Xanterra** (☎ 303-287-2757; 888-297-2757; www.xanterra.com), which operates in conjunction with the National Park Service (NPS). Xanterra has information desks at the Bright Angel, Maswik and Yavapai Lodges.

Narrated bus tours offer a good introduction to the canyon, as drivers stop at the best viewpoints, point out the various buttes, mesas and plateaus, and offer historical anecdotes. Tickets are available at each lodge's transportation desks or from the El Tovar (p140) concierge. Children under 16 ride for free when accompanied by an adult. Tours include a two-hour **Hermits Rest Route tour** (tour $15.75; ☉ 9am & 4pm) and a four-hour **Desert View Drive tour** (tour $28; ☉ 9am & 12:30pm). A combination tour ($34) combines both tours. There are also sunrise and sunset tours; ask at the lodges.

Sleeping

Visitors to the park's South Rim have six lodges and three campgrounds to choose from. If you don't find a spot in the park, you can always pitch your tent free of charge in the surrounding Kaibab National Forest (p144).

Xanterra (☎ 888-297-2757; www.xanterra.com) operates all park lodges, as well as the Trailer Village campground. You can make reservations up to 23 months in advance – and these are highly recommended, especially in the summer. Visit Xanterra's South Rim website (www.grandcanyonlodges.com) for more information. For same-day reservations you can call the **South Rim switchboard** (☎ 928-638-2631).

If you can't find a room within the park, consider a chain motel in Tusayan (p143).

Bright Angel Lodge & Cabins (Grand Canyon Village; r & cabins $50-240) Built in 1935, the log-and-stone Bright Angel offers historic charm and recently refurbished rooms. Unfortunately, the public spaces have neither the quiet elegance nor rustic Western character found at El Tovar (right). You will find two restaurants and a small, nondescript bar with a TV. But if you want to relax with a drink, you're much better off walking a few doors down to El Tovar. The least expensive doubles are very simple – no TV, just a bed, desk and sink – with bathrooms down the hall, but a great deal considering how close you are to the rim. More expensive rooms are brighter, airier and big on character (many are decorated in rustic Western style).

Kachina Lodge & Thunderbird Lodge (Grand Canyon Village; d $115-125) Standard motel-style rooms with two queen beds and TVs. Pay an extra $10 for a rimside room, some come with partial canyon views. The drab concrete buildings resemble elementary schools, but they're close to the rim. Neither lodge has a lobby or front desk – guests at Kachina check in at El Tovar (right), while those at Thunderbird check in at Bright Angel (above).

Maswik Lodge (Grand Canyon Village; r $67-119) A quarter-mile from the rim, Maswik Lodge (named for the Hopi kachina who guards the canyon) comprises 16 two-story wood-and-stone buildings set in the woods. Rooms at Maswik North are more expensive, and feature private patios, high ceilings and forest views. Rooms at the less expensive Maswik South are smaller and don't offer much of a view. There's less foot traffic and general bustling about here than

at the rim, but the rooms are of the standard motel variety. Amenities include a bar with pool table and big-screen TV.

Yavapai Lodge (Grand Canyon Village; r $90-105; Apr-Oct) Lying more than a mile from the central village, this motel offers a few hidden advantages. It's close to Canyon View Information Plaza and within walking distance of the grocery store, post office and bank in Market Plaza. The lodgings are stretched out amid a peaceful piñon and juniper forest and rooms are basic but spotless.

Phantom Ranch (dm/d $23/78) At the bottom of the canyon, this place offers basic cabins sleeping four to 10 people and segregated dorms. Most cabins are reserved for overnight mule tours, but hikers may make reservations if space is available. There are separate shower facilities. Meals are available in the dining hall by advance reservation only. They are nothing fancy but enough to feed hungry hikers. If you lack a reservation, try showing up at the Bright Angel Lodge transportation desk at 6am to snag a canceled bunk (some folks show up earlier and wait). Snacks, limited supplies, beer and wine are also sold. Postcards bought and mailed here are stamped 'Mailed by Mule from the bottom of the Canyon.'

Mather Campground (☎ 800-365-2267; http://reservations.nps.gov; Grand Canyon Village; campsites $15-40) Camp on well-dispersed sites in relative peace and quiet amid piñon and juniper trees. There's plenty of shade and the flat ground offers a comfy platform. There are pay showers, laundry facilities, drinking water, toilets and grills. A small general store stocks camping supplies, drinks and basic food items, and a full grocery store is a short walk away. Accepts reservations between April 1 and November 30. The 320 sites sleep between six and 40 people; disabled sites are closer to the facilities and on more level ground.

Desert View Campground (☎ 928-638-0105, 800-365-2267; http://reservations.nps.gov; campsites $10; ☽ mid-May–mid-Sep) Set back from the road, 25 miles east of Grand Canyon Village, in a quiet piñon juniper forest near the East Entrance, this first-come, first-served campground is a peaceful alternative to the more crowded Mather. Sites are spread out enough to ensure a bit of privacy. You'll find toilets and drinking water but no showers or hookups. A small cafeteria/snack shop serves breakfast, lunch and dinner, while nearby is a general store that offers basic camping supplies and staples like pasta, canned food, milk, beer and wine.

Trailer Village (☎ 928-638-2631; www.xanterra .com; Grand Canyon Village; camp & RV sites $24) As the name implies, this is basically a trailer park offering little in the way of natural surroundings. Expect RVs lined up tightly at paved pull-through sites amid a rather barren, dry patch of ground. Check for spots with trees on the far north side. You'll find picnic tables and barbecue grills, but showers are a quarter-mile away at Mather Campground.

Eating & Drinking

El Tovar and Bright Angel Lodge offer creative menus with surprisingly good food. Picnicking is a great way not only to save money, but also enjoy some quiet moments. If you're visiting the park for more than a day, bring a small cooler to stow picnic supplies and keep drinks cold. In-room refrigerators are a rarity in park lodges, but you can get ice at Canyon Village Marketplace, Desert View Marketplace and the North Rim General Store.

El Tovar Dining Room (☎ 928-638-2631; El Tovar Hotel; dishes $12-22; ☽ breakfast, lunch & dinner; ✗) If at all possible, take in at least one meal at the historic El Tovar Hotel (opposite). The memorable surroundings feature dark wood, tables set with china and white linen, and huge picture windows with views of the rim and canyon beyond. The service is excellent, the menu creative, the portions big and the food very good – much better than you might expect. Though you're welcome to dress up to match the elegant setting, you'll also feel perfectly comfortable in jeans. Reservations are required for dinner. El Tovar has a piano bar for après-dinner drinks or late afternoon cocktails.

Arizona Room (☎ 928-638-2631; Bright Angel Lodge; dishes $8-21; ☽ dinner) A wonderful balance between casual and upscale, this restaurant is one of the best options for dinner on the South Rim. Antler chandeliers hang from the ceiling, and picture windows overlook a small lawn, the rim walk and the canyon beyond. It's a bright, busy place. Doors open at 4:30pm, and by 4:40pm you may have an hour wait – reservations are not accepted. There is no indoor bar, but you can sit outside on the small deck, and enjoy views with your drink while you wait (a margarita costs $7.60). Mains include steak, chicken and fish dishes, while appetizers include such creative options as toasted cumin onion rings.

Phantom Ranch (☎ 928-638-2631; dishes $20-30) On the canyon floor, Phantom Ranch offers family-style meals that feature hearty stews, steaks and vegetarian fare, as well as picnic lunches ($9). There are two dinner sittings (5pm and 6:30pm), and breakfast ($18) is served predawn. Make reservations before your trip into the canyon.

Bright Angel Restaurant (☎ 928-638-2631; Bright Angel Lodge; dishes $8-13; ☽ breakfast, lunch & dinner) This family-style restaurant offers burgers, fajitas, lasagna, roast turkey and other simple dishes. Of the three South Rim restaurants with waiter service, this is the least inviting. With few windows and no canyon views, it's a bit dark and resembles a basic, nondescript coffee shop. Families with small children gravitate here, and it can be loud.

Maswik & Yavapai Cafeterias (☎ 928-638-2631; Grand Canyon Village; dishes $6-10; ☽ breakfast, lunch & dinner) Based in their respective lodges, expect cafeteria food, service and seating. Though fairly predictable, the food is pretty good – a nice variety and not too greasy. You'll find pizza, burgers, fried chicken, Mexican fare and other cooked dishes, as well as beer, soda and milk.

ARIZONA

NIGHTLIFE IN THE GRAND CANYON

The park isn't exactly nightlife central, but if you've still got energy at the end of the day, there are a few places to cut loose on the South Rim.

The patio off the bar at **El Tovar** (p140) is a great spot to sit with a prickly pear margarita and watch people pass by. Inside there's a dark and cozy lounge, with big, cushioned chairs and stained glass. Sports fans can catch a game on the big-screen TV at **Maswik Lodge Sports Bar** (p140). The dark, windowless bar at **Bright Angel** (p140) doesn't offer much in the way of character, but it's fun to look at the historic photos on the bar. All bars close at 11pm, and drinks are prohibited along the rim itself.

On Thursday nights park employees head to Tusayan, just outside the park's South Entrance, for dancing at the **Grand Hotel** (see opposite). Some opt to catch the latest scores at the popular sports bar in the **Best Western Grand Canyon Squire Inn** (opposite), which also features a video arcade, pool tables and a bowling alley.

At campground amphitheaters in summer, rangers on both rims offer evening talks on a variety of subjects. Check *The Guide* for program descriptions, times and locations.

Deli at Marketplace (☎ 928-631-2262; Grand Canyon Village; dishes $5-8; ☺ 7am-8pm) This counter in the village grocery store is the best place to find a fresh-made sandwich for a picnic. If you prefer, you can sit at one of the few indoor tables and enjoy such hot dishes as pizza and fried chicken. In the morning the deli offers donuts and coffee.

Desert View Trading Post Snack Bar (☎ 928-638-2360; dishes $2-6; ☺ breakfast, lunch & dinner) The only place to eat on the east end of the rim (aside from the general store), this small snack bar serves limited breakfast, lunch and dinner selections. Menu items include burgers, corn dogs, premade sandwiches and soda, as well as cereal, eggs and French toast in the morning.

Getting There & Away

Most people arrive at the canyon in private vehicle or on a tour. Las Vegas and Phoenix serve as regional air hubs, where most folks either pick up a rental car or catch a commuter flight to Tusayan or Flagstaff. Both **Air Vegas Airlines** (☎ 800-255-7474; www.airvegas .com) and **Scenic Airlines** (☎ 800-634-6801; www .scenicairlines.com) offer daily flights (about $200) from Las Vegas to Grand Canyon National Park Airport in Tusayan, 7 miles from the South Rim. **Canyon Airport Shuttle** (☎ 928-638-0821; one-way $5) leaves the airport in Tusayan every hour on the half-hour with several stops in Tusayan en route to the Grand Canyon Village.

There are several advantages to flying into Las Vegas (290 miles from the South Rim). For one, in order to attract the gambling set, airlines offer cheap flights and packages to the city year-round. Driving to the park from Vegas is also easy – aside from delays around Hoover Dam, traffic is minimal to either rim.

Phoenix is 220 miles from the South Rim and once you escape city traffic it's a beautiful drive to the canyon, passing through several mountain towns and Sedona's celebrated red rock country. Take Hwys 89 and 89A north and follow the signs to the canyon. You could easily spend a few leisurely days driving to the park.

Operated by **Amtrak** (☎ 928-774-8679, 800-872-7245; www.amtrak.com), the *Southwest Chief* makes a daily run between Chicago and Los Angeles, with stops at Flagstaff and Williams. In Williams you can connect with the historic **Grand Canyon Railway** (☎ 800-843-8724; www.thetrain.com), with original 1923 Pullman cars chugging the scenic 65 miles to the South Rim.

Greyhound (Map pp156-7; ☎ 928-774-4573, 800-229-9424; www.greyhound.com; 399 S Malpais Lane, Flagstaff) stops at Flagstaff to/from Albuquerque, Las Vegas, Los Angeles and Phoenix.

Open Road Tours (☎ 928-226-8060, 800-766-7117; www.openroadtours.com) offers shuttles from Phoenix Sky Harbor airport to Flagstaff (one-way $31, round-trip $56) continuing on to Williams and the Grand Canyon (one-way $20, round-trip $40). The fare from Williams to the park is $15.

Getting Around

Free shuttles operate along three routes: around Grand Canyon Village, west along Hermits Rest Route and east along Kaibab Trail Route. Buses run every 15 minutes during the day and every 30 minutes from one hour before sunrise until daylight and from dusk until one hour after sunset. Bus stops are clearly marked and free maps are available. Park your car and ride – it's easier.

Shuttles from rim to rim are available from May to October (when the North Rim is open), leave at 1:30pm, take five hours and cost $60 one-way or $100 round-trip. Call **Trans-Canyon Shuttle** (☎ 928-638-2820). Other services are available on request.

TUSAYAN
pop 562 / elev 6612ft
Its park proximity (just 7 miles south of Grand Canyon Village) keeps Tusayan's hotels booked and its restaurants packed. It makes a good base, especially during the summer months when park lodging is often completely booked out (although during these times Tusayan is equally busy and advance reservations are highly recommended). Considering the number of tourists that pass through town, Tusayan is not particularly memorable. Sprawling along Hwy 64, it's really just a half-mile strip of fast-food franchises, chain hotels and souvenir shops. the **chamber of commerce** (☎ 928-638-2901; Hwy 64) has a visitor information booth in the Imax Theater lobby.

Using a film format three times larger than normal 70mm movie frames, a screen up to eight times the size of conventional cinema screens and a 14-speaker stereo surround system, the **Imax Theater** (☎ 928-638-2468; Hwy 64; adult/child $10/7; ⏱ 8:30am-8:30pm Mar-Oct, 10:30am-6:30pm Nov-Feb) presents *Grand Canyon – The Hidden Secrets*. This 34-minute movie plunges you into the canyon's history and geology through the eyes of ancient Native Americans, John Wesley Powell and a soaring eagle. The effects are quite splendid (you get a great aerial perspective) and it's a great introduction to the canyon that adults will enjoy as much as the kids.

Sleeping
As with the Grand Canyon, reservations are recommended, especially in summer. Summer rates are pricey for what are basically motel rooms, but if you can't get a room on the South Rim and want to be near the canyon, this is what you're stuck with. Winter rates (November to March) are $30 to $50 lower. All motels are along Hwy 64, and there are many more than those listed here.

Grand Hotel (☎ 928-638-3333, 888-634-7263; www .visitgrandcanyon.com; r $150; 🖳) There's a distinct Western motif in this hotel's open public spaces, including a big fireplace, high ceilings, woven rugs, stone floors and faux pine beams. Though new, the decor has an old look, and it works. Tour buses come for the 7pm Native American dance show at the restaurant, and nightly country-music performances cap off the theme. While the rooms are nothing special, they are relatively big and the ones out back face the woods. The indoor pool and hot tub are winter-night plusses.

Best Western Grand Canyon Squire Inn (☎ 928-638-2681, 800-622-6966; r $110-190; 🖳) With plenty of stuff to keep kids and adults alike busy, this is the only resort-like accommodation in Tusayan. You'll find a restaurant, coffee shop, popular sports bar, bowling alley, beauty salon, pool tables, exercise room, tennis courts and much more. The rooms are spacious and clean.

Grand Canyon Quality Inn & Suites (☎ 928-638-2673, 800-228-5151; www.grandcanyonqualityinn.com; d/ste $128/178; 🖳) One of Tusayan's better options, this place features spacious rooms and suites, a bright, modern restaurant and an 8ft indoor hot tub set in an atrium.

Seven Mile Lodge (☎ 928-638-2291; r $70) The cheapest motel in town, this place has 20 basic rooms. It doesn't take reservations. Rooms open at 9am daily and are usually filled by early afternoon in summer, so show up early.

Grand Canyon Camper Village (☎ 928-638-2887; Hwy 67; camp/RV sites $18/23) A mile south of the park, this private campground has showers, a playground and mini-golf. Sites are on dirt with no shade or natural surroundings, so there's little to recommend it. However when everywhere else is full, it often has space, is safe and relatively quiet.

Eating
Mexican Kitchen (☎ 928-638-1105; Grand Canyon Village Shops; dishes $6-10; ⏱ breakfast) Sporting bright turquoise walls and Southwestern chairs, this tiny café offers decent Mexican food, including tacos and fajitas (no beer or wine). The friendly, low-key spot is a welcome alternative to bigger, tourist-oriented restaurants.

Jennifer's Coffeehouse & Bakery (☎ 928-638-3433; Grand Canyon Village Shops; dishes $2-7; ⏱ 7am-5pm; 🖳) Where USDA Forest Service (USFS) rangers come to grab a sandwich and escape the tourists. It's a small place with high tables, Internet access ($3 for 15 minutes), coffee, pastries and a limited menu. Breakfast items include Belgian waffles and eggs with bacon. Sandwiches are made to order, including a veggie sandwich. Ask the staff to pack a picnic for you if you'd rather enjoy your meal in the forest or at the park.

Quality Inn Restaurant (☎ 928-638-2673; Quality Inn, Hwy 64; dishes $8-15; ☒ 24hr) A great option for hungry families, this hotel serves daily buffets in its indoor atrium. Kids under 12 eat for half-price, and those under five eat for free. It's bright and airy and you can get a drink from the bar.

Canyon Star (☎ 928-638-3333; Grand Hotel; dishes $11-21) This spacious restaurant with high ceilings and faux wooden beams strives for a Western feel. To set the mood and attract tour-bus crowds, a Native American dance show is held every evening at 7pm followed by live country music. The food is overpriced and nothing special, though some options are more interesting than others, including Portobello mushroom lasagna.

Getting There & Away

See p142 for transport information throughout the region.

KAIBAB NATIONAL FOREST

Divided by the canyon into two distinct ecosystems, the Kaibab National Forest offers a peaceful escape from park crowds. With several great mountain-biking trails and unlimited opportunities for camping, hiking and cross-country skiing, the forest extends outdoor recreation options beyond the park. You won't find spectacular canyon views, but you won't find the crowds either. Bring plenty of water, as natural water sources are scarce in this arid region. You'll likely spot elk, mule deer, turkeys and coyotes, while on rare occasions you may encounter a mountain lion, black bear or bobcat.

The main road through the forest is Hwy 64/180, which connects Williams and Flagstaff with the canyon. Hwy 64 accesses the district's northeast corner. If you plan on hiking or camping in the forest, maps are available at the Williams visitor center (p163) and the park's Canyon View Information Plaza Books & More Store (p134).

Tusayan Ranger Station (☎ 928-638-2443; www.fs .fed.us/r3/kai) is just outside the canyon's South Entrance.

For mountain biking try the **Tusayan Bike Trail**, a moderate ride on an old logging road. The trailhead is 0.3 miles north of Tusayan on the west side of Hwy 64/180. It's 16 miles from the trailhead to the **Grandview Lookout** and 80ft fire tower with fabulous views. If you don't want to ride all that way, three interconnected loops offer 3-, 8- and 9-mile round-trips.

From the lookout you can hike or ride part or all of the still-evolving **Arizona Trail**, a 24-mile one-way ride to the south boundary of the Tusayan Ranger District. This is an excellent and relatively easy ride. Eventually, the Arizona Trail will span the state more than 750 miles from north to south.

Apache Stables (☎ 928-638-2891; www.apache stables.com; Hwy 64) offers horseback rides through the forest. The strenuous four-hour East Rim ride ($95, ages 14 and up) winds through the Kaibab to a canyon view on Desert View Drive; this is the only ride that offers rim views, though it does not go along the rim or into the canyon. The one-hour ride through the forest costs $30, while the two-hour ride costs $55. You can take a one-hour evening saunter to a campfire and return on a wagon ($41). For families with small children, the outfitter offers a campfire wagon ride ($12.50), where trailriders rendezvous with the wagon for a cookout beneath the stars. For both campfire trips you must bring your own food (think hot dogs and marshmallows) and drinks – if you bring a small cooler, the staff will put it on the wagon.

In the winter the USFS maintains a groomed **cross-country skiing** loop 0.3 mile north of Grandview Lookout.

The USFS **Ten-X Campground** (☎ 928-638-2887; campsites $10; ☒ mid-Apr–Sep) is set in the woods 2 miles south of Tusayan. You'll find picnic tables, water and toilets but no showers or hookups. This is a pleasant, quiet campground and an excellent alternative to the park's Mather campground.

Dispersed **camping** (free) is allowed in the national forest (put not in the park) as long as you refrain from camping in meadows, within a quarter-mile of the highway or any surface water, or within half a mile of any developed campground.

HAVASUPAI RESERVATION

pop 600

One of the canyon's true treasures is Havasu Canyon, a hidden valley with four gorgeous, spring-fed waterfalls and inviting, azure swimming holes in the heart of the 185,000-acre Havasupai Reservation. Because the falls lie 10 miles below the rim, most trips are combined with a stay at either Havasu Lodge in Supai or the nearby campground. Lying 8 miles below the rim, **Supai** is the only village within the Grand Canyon.

Orientation & Information

The Reservation lies south of the Colorado River and west of the park's South Rim. From Hualapai Hilltop, a three- to four-hour drive from the South Rim, a well-maintained trail leads to Supai and numerous waterfalls beyond. Information is available from the **Havasupai Tourist Enterprise** (☎ 928-448-2141; PO Box 160, Supai, AZ 86435). Visitors pay an entry fee of $20 when they arrive in Supai. The local post office distributes its mail by pack animals – postcards mailed from here bear a special postmark to prove it. Recreational drugs – including liquor – and nude swimming are not allowed. Trail bikes are not allowed below Hualapai Hilltop, and fires are prohibited – campers must cook with gas stoves. Be sure to purify your water. There is a small emergency clinic in Supai.

Sights & Activities

The 8-mile **Hualapai Trail** to Supai from Hualapai Hilltop is a serenely beautiful hike. Moderately challenging, it takes between three and five hours. Do not try to hike down and back in one day – not only is it dangerous, but it also doesn't allow enough time to see the falls, as they are further down in **Havasu Canyon**. The trail descends with steep switchbacks for 1.5 miles, levels off in a dry creek bed and winds through the canyon for 5 miles before meeting the Havasu Creek. Follow the trail downstream 1.5 miles to the village of Supai. Shade trees line the creek, and the sheer walls of the canyon rise dramatically on either side of the trail. You must secure reservations to camp or stay in the lodge (p146) before starting out.

After a night in Supai, you can continue through Havasu Canyon to the numerous waterfalls. First up is the 75ft-high **Navajo Falls**, just a mile beyond Supai. Next comes **Havasu Falls**, which drops 100ft into a sparkling blue pool surrounded by cottonwoods; it's a popular swimming hole. **Havasu Campground** sits a quarter-mile beyond Havasu Falls. Just past the campground, the trail passes **Mooney Falls**, which tumbles 200ft into another blue-green swimming hole. To get to the swimming hole, you must climb through two tunnels and descend a very steep trail (chains provide welcome handholds). Limestone walls tower over the creek and falls. After a picnic and a swim, continue about 2 miles to **Beaver Falls** and the Colorado River. The trail passes small pools and cascades and crosses the creek many times. The river lies 10.5 miles from Supai and 8 miles beyond the campground. Camping is prohibited beyond Mooney Falls, so it's a strenuous hike to the river and back. It's recommended that you don't attempt to hike to the river; in fact, the Reservation actively discourages it. Enjoy the waterfalls instead.

If you don't want to hike to Supai, you can arrange for a mule or horse to carry you in and out. It costs $120 per round-trip for rides to the lodge, and $150 per round-trip for rides to the campground. It's about half that price if you hike in and ride out, or vice versa. Mules depart Hualapai Hilltop at 10am year-round. Call the lodge or campground (wherever you'll be spending the night) in advance to arrange a ride.

On Thursday, Friday, Sunday and Monday from mid-March through October, a **helicopter** (one-way $85) shuttles between Hualapai Hilltop and Supai from 10am to 1pm. You can't call to make advance reservations; you just arrive at the parking lot and sign up. There's no hangar or anything – just a helicopter in the dirt. Call Havasupai Tourist Enterprise (left) before you arrive to be sure the helicopter is running. From November to mid-March the helicopter operates on Friday and Sunday only.

Sleeping & Eating

Remember: it's 8 miles to the lodge and more than 10 miles to the campground from Hualapai Hilltop. It is absolutely essential that you make reservations in advance; if you hike in without a reservation and they're full, you will have to hike all the way back up to your car at the trailhead.

ARIZONA

Havasupai Lodge (☎ 928-448-2111; PO Box 159, Supai, AZ 86435; r $80) In Supai, it offers motel rooms, all with canyon views. There are no TVs or telephones. Reservations are essential; the lodge is often booked months in advance for the entire summer, and unless you plan to camp, there's nowhere else to stay. A café serves breakfast, lunch and dinner, and a general store sells basic groceries and snacks.

Havasupai Campground (☎ 928-448-2121; Havasupai Camping Office, PO Box 160, Supai, AZ 86435; campsites $10) Two miles past Supai, campsites spread out along the creek between Havasu and Mooney Falls. There are picnic tables, pit toilets and a spring for drinking water (purify it first). There are no showers, but you can swim in the river and pools. Fires are not permitted. This campground is often packed in summer, so be sure to hike its length before choosing a spot to pitch your tent.

Getting There & Around

Seven miles east of Peach Springs on historic Rte 66, a signed turnoff leads to the 62-mile paved road to Havasu Canyon. At Hualapai Hilltop you'll find the parking area, stables and trailhead into the canyon. To get to Supai, park your car and then hike, ride or fly the 8 miles down to the village. If you plan on hiking or riding down, you must spend the night either in Peach Springs (ideally) or in one of the motels along Rte 66 (see right).

Don't let place names confuse you: Hualapai Hilltop is on the Havasupai Reservation, not the Hualapai Reservation as one might think.

HUALAPAI RESERVATION

This reservation borders many miles of the Colorado River northeast of Kingman and includes the only road to the river within the Grand Canyon. In 1988 the Hualapai opened 'Grand Canyon West,' and they market their section of the canyon as 'untouched by our 20th-century world. No buildings, no traffic, no noise.' As an alternative to the remote North Rim or the touristy South Rim, Grand Canyon West does indeed offer visitors a chance to enjoy the canyon with less chaos. You won't find the historic buildings or sublime views, and it's a bit of a drive to get here, but that's part of its charm.

The reservation covers the southwest rim of the canyon, bordering Havasupai Reservation to the east and Lake Mead National Recreation Area to the west. The **Hualapai Office of Tourism** (☎ 888-255-9550; www.hualapaitours .com; Hualapai Reservations, PO Box 538, Peach Springs, AZ 86434) staffs an office at Hualapai Lodge (below) in the blink-and-you'll-miss-it town of Peach Springs. The Reservation entrance fee is $6.30 per day per person. You can buy passes at Hualapai Lodge.

Sights & Activities

The 22-mile unpaved scenic **Diamond Creek Road** heads north from Peach Springs to the Colorado River. It's the only road to the river within the canyon. At its end you'll find picnic tables and a camping area. Don't forget to purchase an entrance permit from the Hualapai Lodge front desk before driving down the road.

If you don't have the time (or money) for the classic Grand Canyon rafting experience, head over to **Hualapai River Runners** (☎ 928-769-2219, 888-255-9550). This is the only company to offer one-day white-water rafting trips within the Grand Canyon. Its motorized rafts hold up to 10 people. Trips, at $265 per person, aren't cheap (by day-trip rafting standards), but then again this *is* the Grand Canyon. Trips leave Monday to Friday, May through October from Hualapai Lodge and package deals are available. Children must be at least 8 years old.

Sleeping & Eating

Hualapai Lodge & Diamond Creek Restaurant (☎ 928-769-2230, 888-255-9550; 900 Rte 66; r $75; dishes $5-10) This modern hotel is the only place to stay in Peach Springs. Rooms are clean and perfectly acceptable. The restaurant serves standard American fare breakfast, lunch and dinner.

Diamond Creek Campground (☎ 888-255-9550; per person $10) On the Colorado, at the end of Diamond Creek Rd, is this small but basic beach camping spot. The elevation here is 1900ft, so the campground is extremely hot in summer. You'll find toilets and a picnic table but no drinking water. The campground only holds about 10 people, so call to check availability.

Grand Canyon Caverns & Inn (☎ 928-422-3223; www.gccaverns.com; Rte 66; s/d $52/57; ☒) Thirteen miles east of Peach Springs, it offers basic motel rooms, a pool and a restaurant serving burgers and fried food (dishes $3 to $7).

Getting There & Around
There are no regular shuttles or buses to Peach Springs or the Hualapai Reservation. River trips include a shuttle to the Reservation from Hualapai Lodge in Peach Springs.

Driving to Grand Canyon West involves travel along dirt roads. Call or stop by Hualapai Lodge to check road conditions before heading out – roads may be impassable after a lot of rain. Three miles west of Peach Springs is Buck & Doe Rd, which leads about 50 miles to Grand Canyon West. Grand Canyon West can also be reached from Hwy 93. Head north from Kingman about 26 miles, northeast along the paved Pierce Ferry Rd (toward Lake Mead) for about 30 miles, then 21 miles along the dirt Diamond Bar Rd.

CAMERON
A tiny, windswept community 32 miles east of the park's East Entrance, Cameron sits on the western edge of the Navajo Reservation. There's not much to it – in fact the town basically comprises of the **Cameron Trading Post & Motel** (☎ 928-679-2231, 800-338-7385; RV sites/r $16/80). The spacious rooms, many with balconies, feature hand-carved furniture and a southwestern motif. There's also a restaurant serving decent meals (but no booze, you're on Reservation land) and a trading post selling a large selection of quality Native American crafts.

GRAND CANYON NATIONAL PARK – NORTH RIM
elev 8200ft
On the Grand Canyon's North Rim, solitude reigns supreme. There are no shuttles or bus tours, no museums, paved rim trails, shopping centers, schools or garages. Rugged and remote (it's only 10 miles from the South Rim, p133, as the crow flies, but a 215-mile, five-hour drive on winding desert roads from Grand Canyon Village), this rim boasts meadows thick with wildflowers and dense clusters of willowy aspen and spruce trees. The air is often crisp, the skies vast and blue. If the crowds on the South Rim make you cringe, this is where to head for beautifully wild isolation. In fact, the area is so remote it sees only 10% of park visitors.

Opportunities to enjoy the view are more limited here than on the South Rim – you won't be able to see the canyon from as many perspectives, as overlooks are scarce.

There are few amenities. The Grand Canyon Lodge, a large wood-and-stone hotel, sits on the canyon rim and guest cabins line either side of the road. Its horseshoe-shaped covered boardwalk offers a postal window, gift shop, small snack stand and saloon. A mile north is a one-story motel, a campground and general store. That's just about all you'll find.

At 8200ft, this rim is about 10°F cooler than the south – even on summer evenings you'll need a sweater. Several excellent trails, including the wonderful Widforss Trail, wind through the aspens and pines, offering subtle glimpses of the canyon.

Facilities on the North Rim are closed from mid-October to mid-May, although you can still drive into the park and stay at the campground until the first snow closes the road from Jacob Lake. Snow falls as early as late-October and as late as January.

Orientation & Information
The only entrance to the North Rim lies 30 miles south of Jacob Lake on Hwy 67. From the entrance it is 13 miles north to the rim. The park headquarters are at the South Rim. For general park info, including entrance fees and backcountry permits (required for overnight hikes), see p136.

Most visitor facilities are clustered around Grand Canyon Lodge, including the adjacent **North Rim Visitor Center** (☎ 928-638-9875). The general store, gas station and the **North Rim Backcountry Office** (☎ 928-638-7868) are beside the campground, 1.5 miles north of the lodge. To contact the Grand Canyon Lodge front desk, the saloon, gift shop or general store, call the **North Rim switchboard** (☎ 928-638-2612).

Sights & Activities
BRIGHT ANGEL POINT
Though it tends to be busy, this short and easy paved trail (0.3 miles) is a must for all ages. Beginning from the back porch of Grand Canyon Lodge, the trail wraps up, down and out along a narrow finger of an overlook that dangles between the Transept Trailand Roaring Springs Canyon. Breezes sometimes carry the echo of

rushing water up from Roaring Springs several thousand feet below. The sensation of being suspended in air above the canyon is exhilarating. Along the way, there are some nooks for private overlooks and even picnics – look for the spot right near the trail's end, off to the right.

From the oft-packed overlook at the trail's end, spectacular views branch out toward Bright Angel Canyon. You'll have unfettered views of mesas, buttes, spires and temples, as well as a straight shot of the South Rim, 11 miles away. This pretty trail is a good choice for a quick postarrival walk to stretch your legs. It's a very popular spot at both sunrise and sunset; but if you have a good flashlight or headlamp, visit the point after dusk for unparalleled stargazing.

HIKING & BACKPACKING

The 1.5-mile **Transept Trail** goes north from the lodge through forest to the North Rim Campground, where there are rim views. The **Widforss Trail** follows the rim for five miles, starting near the visitor center, and finishing at Widforss Point, which offers one of the best North Rim canyon views. Along the way you'll pass through stands of spruce, white fir, pine and aspen. The **North Kaibab Trail** plunges down to Phantom Ranch on the Colorado River, 5750ft below and 14 miles away. The trailhead is 2 miles north of Grand Canyon Lodge. There is a parking lot there. It is the only maintained rim-to-river trail from the North Rim and it connects with trails to the South Rim. The first 4.7 miles are the steepest, dropping well over 3000ft to **Roaring Springs** – a popular all-day hike and mule-ride destination. Drinking water is available at Roaring Springs from May to September only. If you prefer a shorter day hike below the rim, you can walk just three-quarters of a mile down to **Coconino Overlook** or a mile to the **Supai Tunnel**, 1400ft below the rim, to get a flavor of steep inner-canyon hiking.

Hikers wishing to continue to the river will normally camp. **Cottonwood Campground** is 7 miles and 4200ft below the rim and is the only campground between the North Rim and the river. Here, there are 14 backcountry campsites (available by permit only; see p136), drinking water from May through September and a ranger station.

About 1.5 miles below the campground a short side trail leads to pretty **Ribbon Falls** – a popular bathing spot. Phantom Ranch (p140) and the Bright Angel Campground are 7 and 7.5 miles respectively below Cottonwood. Because the river is twice as far from the North Rim than the South Rim, rangers suggest three nights as a minimum to enjoy a rim-to-river and return hike, staying at Cottonwood on the first and third nights and Bright Angel on the second. Faster trips, while technically feasible, would be an endurance slog and not much fun.

Hiking from North to South Rim requires a shuttle to get you back (see p143 for details).

MULE RIDES

Canyon Trail Rides (☎ 435-679-8665; www.canyonrides .com; Grand Canyon Lodge) offers one-hour mule trips ($20) along the rim and half- or full-day trips into the canyon. The full-day, seven-hour trip ($95, minimum age 12 years) departs at 7:25am and descends about 4000ft to Roaring Springs. Lunch and water are provided. Half-day trips ($45, minimum age 8 years) go to Supai Tunnel, 2000ft below the rim and leave at 7:25am and 12:25pm. If you're not used to riding, this trip is far gentler on your muscles and still lets you experience the inner gorge. Unlike mule trips on the South Rim, you can usually book a trip when you arrive at the park.

CROSS-COUNTRY SKIING

Once the first heavy snowfall closes Hwy 67 into the park (as early as late October or as late as January), you can cross-country ski the 44 miles from Jacob Lake to the rim and camp at the campground (no water, pit toilets). It's a serenely beautiful route that takes about three days. Make sure you are well prepared, fit and comfortable in severe weather conditions before setting out. Camping is permitted elsewhere on the North Rim during winter if you have a backcountry permit (see p136).

You can ski any of the rim trails, though none are groomed. Experienced skiers may descend into the canyon along the North Kaibab Trail (left). Be sure your skis are properly equipped; it can be a treacherous trek.

NORTH RIM SCENIC DRIVES

The drive on Hwy 67 through the Kaibab Plateau to Bright Angel Point takes you through thick forest. There are excellent canyon views from the point, but to reach other overlooks you need to drive north for almost 3 miles and take the signed turn east to Point Imperial and Cape Royal. It is 9 miles to **Point Imperial**, which is the highest overlook in the entire park and has stunning views.

Backtrack about 4 miles from Point Imperial and drive 15 miles south to **Cape Royal** where there are more great views and some short hiking trails.

With a high-clearance 4WD you can take unpaved roads to several other outlooks along the North Rim. One of the most spectacular of the remote overlooks is **Toroweap Overlook** at **Tuweep**, far to the west of the main park facilities. An unpaved road, usually passable to conventional vehicles, leaves Hwy 389 9 miles west of Fredonia and continues on for 55 miles to the Tuweep Ranger Station, which is staffed year-round. An alternative route is a 90-mile dirt road from St George, Utah. It is five more miles from Tuweep to the Toroweap Overlook, where there is primitive **camping** (permit required) but no water or other facilities – you must be totally self-sufficient.

Sleeping

North Rim accommodations are limited to one lodge and one campground. If these are booked, try your luck 80 miles north in Kanab, Utah (p244), or 84 miles northeast in Lees Ferry; both offer motel-style lodges.

Grand Canyon Lodge (☎ 928-638-2612, 888-297-2757; www.grandcanyonnorthrim.com; r & cabins $91-116; ⊙ mid-May–mid-Nov) Walk through the front door of Grand Canyon Lodge into the sunroom and there, framed by three huge picture windows, is the canyon in all its glory. You'll have driven for ages to get here, and this first view of the canyon is breathtakingly magical, unspoilt by traffic or masses of tourists. A small back porch with a stone fireplace and rough-hewn rocking chairs is perched directly on the rim. By far the best sleeping option in the park (perhaps in *any* US national park), this lodge made of wood, stone and glass featuring a 50ft-high lobby is the kind of place you imagine should be perched on the rim.

Rustic, yet modern, cabins comprise the majority of accommodations. Views and size vary depending on price – the largest sleep five. Reserve as far in advance as possible, the lodge is usually full.

North Rim Campground (☎ 800-365-2267; http://reservations.nps.gov; campsites $15) Set back from the road, 1.5 miles north of Grand Canyon Lodge, beneath ponderosa pines, this campground offers pleasant sites on level ground blanketed in pine needles. There is water, a store, snack bar and coin-operated showers and laundry, but no hookups. Reservations can be made up to five months in advance. Without a reservation, show up before 10am and hope for the best. The campground remains open once snow closes the road from Jacob Lake, but there are no services (pit toilets only), no water and you must have a backcountry permit.

Eating & Drinking

Grand Canyon Lodge Dining Room (☎ 928-638-2612; Grand Canyon Lodge; dishes $9-20) Some people get belligerent if they can't get a window seat at this wonderful spot with panoramic views. The windows are so huge, however, it really doesn't matter where you sit. The solid menu includes several vegetarian options. Dinner reservations are required.

Café on the Rim (☎ 928-638-2612; dishes $4-6) This small cafeteria beside the lodge serves surprisingly good food. The limited menu includes made-to-order sandwiches, pizza and ice cream. There are a few indoor tables, but you're better off taking your plate outside to enjoy the high-mountain air.

Rough Rider Saloon (☎ 928-638-2612) For a drink and a browse of the Teddy Roosevelt memorabilia, visit this popular drinking hole adjacent to the Grand Canyon Lodge. In nice weather take your drink to the stone patio where rough-hewn rocking chairs line the canyon rim, a fire blazes in the fireplace and rangers offer talks (sometimes providing telescopes for guests to stargaze). The place opens at 5:30am, so you can pick up a coffee (or if you're hardcore, a morning cocktail).

Getting There & Around

There is no public transport to the North Rim. The **Transcanyon Shuttle** (☎ 928-638-2820; Grand Canyon Lodge; one-way/round-trip $65/110) departs at 7am (cash only) for the South Rim. Reserve at least a week in advance. Children under 12 receive a discount. A hikers' shuttle (from $2) to the North Kaibab Trail departs at 5:20am and 7:20am from Grand Canyon Lodge. Sign up the night before at the front desk.

ARIZONA STRIP

Bordered to the north by Utah, to the south by the Grand Canyon, to the east by the Navajo Reservation and to the west the Kaibab Forest, traditionally and geographically this area has closer ties with Mormon Utah than Arizona. Large and wild with poor roads, it remains one of the last holdouts of the 19th-century practice of polygamy. The only reason to visit tiny Fredonia, the main town in the Arizona Strip located 74 miles north of the rim, is if you can't find lodgings closer to the park. Although, in that case you're probably better off staying in larger Kanab (p244), 7 miles further north in Utah. Apart from a few pricey motels, Fredonia has the **Kaibab National Forest District Headquarters** (☎ 928-643-7395; 430 S Main), which has lots of info on hiking and camping in the forest. Stone cabins, many with kitchenettes, surround a pleasant grassy courtyard at the **Grand Canyon Motel** (☎ 928-643-7646; 175 S Main; r from $40). The **Crazy Jug Motel** (☎ 928-643-7752; 465 S Main; r $50) boasts clean, new rooms and the town's only **restaurant** (dishes $5-12).

Fourteen miles southwest of Fredonia on Hwy 389 is **Pipe Spring National Monument** (☎ 928-643-7105; www.nps.gov/pisp; admission $4; ◷ 8am-5pm), once used by Native Americans and Mormon pioneers as a resting spot and cattle ranch. Literally an oasis in the desert, it is both lovely and interesting. Visitors can experience the Old West amid cabins and corrals, an orchard, ponds and a garden. In summer, rangers and costumed volunteers re-enact various pioneer talks. Tours of the stone **Winsor Castle** (built by Mormons in 1869 for church tithing and refuge from Native Americans) are offered every half-hour. There's also a small museum and half-mile ridge trail promising excellent views.

PAGE & LAKE POWELL

Popular with families and college kids alike, the **Glen Canyon National Recreation Area** (which includes Lake Powell, the country's second-largest artificial reservoir) is set amid striking red-rock formations, sharply cut canyons and dramatic desert scenery. It attracts water rats year-round, from the party-hearty kids in the houseboat to the family tearing up the water on jet skis.

Despite a hard fight by conservationists, work on Glen Canyon Dam began in 1956 and was completed seven years later. Glen Canyon slowly filled to become Lake Powell and in 1972 the lake and more than a million acres of surrounding desert were established as Glen Canyon National Recreation Area. Most of the lake lies in Utah; only the south tip dips into Arizona. The only paved roads to Lake Powell are at the marinas – thus the best way to explore its 1960-mile shoreline is by boat.

Orientation & Information

The region's central town is Page (population 6900), a drab tourist center on the southern tip of the recreation area. Hwy 89 (called N Lake Powell Blvd in town) forms the main strip. Services include the **chamber of commerce** (☎ 928-645-2741; 644 N Navajo Dam Plaza), the **library** (☎ 928-645-4270; 479 S Lake Powell Blvd), which offers free Internet, and the **hospital** (☎ 928-645-2424; Vista Ave at N Navajo Dr), which has emergency services.

The Recreation Area entrance fee is $10 per vehicle or $3 per individual entering on foot or bicycle.

Five marinas serve the lake. The largest, and only one in Arizona, is **Wahweap Marina** (☎ 928-645-2433), 6 miles north of Page. **Bullfrog Marina** (☎ 435-684-3000) in Utah, 290 miles from Page on Lake Powell's west shore, is linked to **Halls Crossing** (☎ 435-684-7000) in Utah, 238 miles from Page on the east shore, by a 30-minute ferry ride. Marinas rent boats, and host rangers and small supply stores.

As the Recreation Area's only licensed concessionaire, **Aramark** (☎ 800-528-6154; www.lakepowell.com) runs the marinas. You can call or visit its website to book rooms at one of two hotels on the lake, reserve a houseboat or other boats and arrange rafting trips and tours. Its website is also an excellent resource for Lake Powell.

Sights
ANTELOPE CANYON

Everywhere you look in Page, there seems to be another photo of Antelope Canyon, a scenic slot canyon (much higher than it is wide) on the Navajo Reservation a few miles east of Page. There are actually two canyons –

ARIZONA

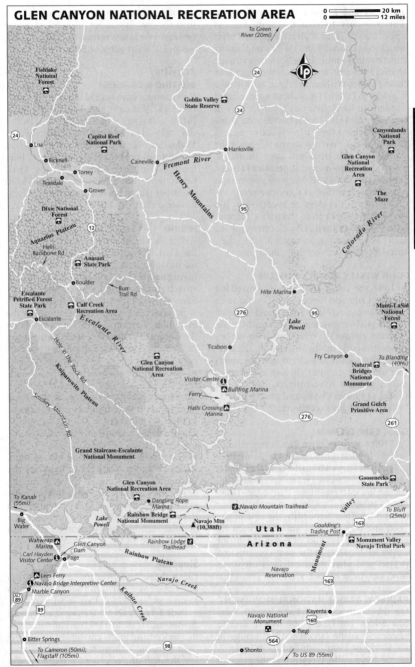

an upper and a lower Antelope Canyon. The only way to visit the more famous upper canyon is through an organized tour, which costs about $28 (1½ hours). Unfortunately, these tours have become a strange tourist attraction more about the process of taking a photo (where to take it, how to take it, when to take it) than about appreciating the canyon itself. Every day, particularly in summer, crowds of people pile into shuttles and schlep their tripods, cameras and film into the narrow canyon. Four tour companies offer trips into upper Antelope Canyon; Navajo-owned **Roger Ekis's Antelope Canyon Tours** (☎ 928-645-9102; www.antelopecanyon .com; 22 S Lake Powell Blvd) is recommended.

Though not as deep or spectacular, the lower canyon is open to the public (admission $5). To get there, take Coppermine Rd (Hwy 98) about 3 miles south of Page, then turn left on paved Antelope Point Rd.

JOHN WESLEY POWELL MUSEUM
In 1869 one-armed John Wesley Powell led the first Colorado River expedition through the Grand Canyon. This small **museum** (☎ 928-645-9496; www.powellmuseum.org; 64 N Lake Powell Blvd; admission $3; 🕑 9am-5pm mid-Feb–mid-Dec) is worth a peek, as anyone visiting the canyon should know a little something about this amazing explorer. It displays memorabilia of early river runners, including a model of Powell's boat, and photos and illustrations of his excursions.

GLEN CANYON DAM
At 710ft tall, **Glen Canyon Dam** is the nation's second-highest concrete arch dam. Free guided tours depart from the **Carl Hayden Visitor Center** (☎ 928-608-6404; 🕑 8am-7pm late-May–early-Sep, 8am-5pm rest of year) at the dam edge. Tours last 60 to 90 minutes, leave every half-hour in summer (less frequently the rest of the year) and take you deep inside the dam via elevators. Displays and videos in the visitor center tell the story of the dam-construction project and offer technical facts on water flow, generator output, etc.

RAINBOW BRIDGE NATIONAL MONUMENT
On the south shore of Lake Powell, **Rainbow Bridge** (☎ 928-608-6404; www.nps.gov/rabr; admission $4) is the largest natural bridge in the world at 290ft high and 275ft wide. A sacred Navajo site, it resembles the graceful

arc of a rainbow. Most visitors arrive on a tour (below). It's about 50 miles by water (at least four hours round-trip) from Wahweap, Halls Crossing or Bullfrog Marinas.

Activities
BOATING & CRUISES
You can rent kayaks ($52 a day), 18ft runabouts ($270 a day) and 14ft fishing boats ($138 a day), as well as water skis ($25 a day) and other 'toys' at the marinas. From Wahweap Marina, **Aramark** (☎ 800-528-6154; www.lakepowell.com) offers half- or full-day boat tours to Rainbow Bridge ($81 and $108, respectively) and a variety of cruises, from one-hour jaunts on Wahweap Bay ($11) to dinner cruises ($61).

HIKING
Ask at the chamber of commerce (p150) or the Carl Hayden Visitor Center (left) for information and maps of the area's many hiking and biking trails. If you just want to stretch your legs a bit in Page, a few easy day hikes venture into scenic red-rock country. A popular photograph around town is the incredible view from a ridge overlooking the Colorado at **Horseshoe Bend**. As the name implies, the river bends around a stone outcrop, forming a perfect horseshoe. The hike to the overlook is about 1.5 miles round-trip. Though it's short and relatively flat, the mostly sand trail can be a slog. You might want to tote toddlers in a backpack, as there are no guardrails at the viewpoint. The trailhead is south of Page off Hwy 89, just across from 541 mile marker.

The 8-mile **Rimview Trail**, a mix of sand, slickrock and other terrain, bypasses the town and offers views of the surrounding desert and Lake Powell. While there are several access points (pick up a brochure from the museum or chamber of commerce), a popular starting point is behind Lake View School at the end of N Navajo Dr.

Sleeping
Clean, basic and overpriced chain hotels line Lake Powell Blvd in Page. Expect rates to drop at least $25 dollars in winter.

Uncle Bill's (☎ 928-645-1224; www.canyon-country .com/unclebill; 117 8th Ave; r $40-150) The owners at this welcoming motel encourage you to feel right at home – throw a steak on the grill, leaf through one of several hundred books lining the shelves or just hang out. Uncle Bill, the self-professed 'mayor of 8th Ave,' and his wife, an accomplished artist, are well connected in Page and happy to suggest places to go and things to do. The cheapest rooms share a bathroom. The most expensive is a three-bedroom suite.

Lake Powell Resort (☎ 928-645-2433; www.lake powell.com; 100 Lake Shore Dr; d $140-160; ☒) The only hotel with a direct view of the lake. The small pool perches on red rocks and overlooks the water, and huge windows in the dining room offer panoramic views. The rooms are all basic; rates for lake-view rooms with tiny patios are about $15 more (and worth it). In the lobby you can book boat tours and arrange boat rental.

Courtyard by Marriott (☎ 928-645-5000, 800-321-2211; 600 Clubhouse Dr; d $80-120; ☒) Surrounded by a golf course away from the strip's noise and traffic, it offers a peaceful alternative to other chain hotels. A courtyard with a large pool makes it a good spot for families.

Lake Powell International Hostel (☎ 928-645-3898; 141 S 8th Ave; dm $13, r $18-24) Private rooms at this clean and quiet hostel share a kitchen and living room (with a TV), so it's akin to staying at a three-bedroom apartment. Dorms are clean and cozy.

Page-Lake Powell Campground (☎ 928-645-3374; 849 S Coppermine Rd; tent & RV sites $17-26; ☒) Just out of town, this offers RV sites with hookups, a few tent sites, an indoor pool and hot tub, laundry facilities and showers.

ARIZONA

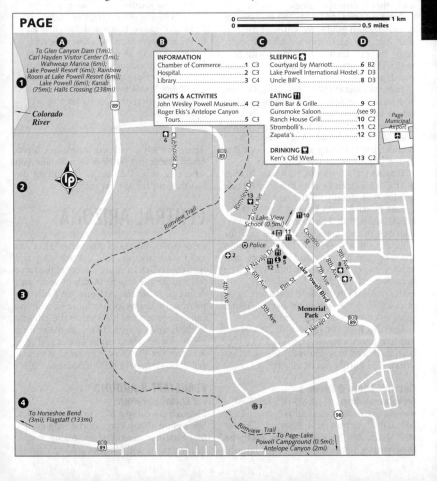

You can camp anywhere along the Lake Powell shoreline for free as long as you have a portable toilet or toilet facilities on your boat. Developed **NPS campgrounds** (tent sites $10-16, RV sites $22-26) are available at Wahweap, Bullfrog and Halls Crossing Marinas.

Eating & Drinking

Ranch House Grill (☎ 928-645-1420; 819 N Navajo Dr; dishes $4-9; ☺ 5am-3pm) *The* breakfast joint, it offers good food, huge portions and fast service. After a three-egg omelet and two huge pancakes ($5.65), you won't need to stop for lunch.

Stromboli's (☎ 928-645-2605; 711 N Navajo Dr; dishes $7-13) Popular for its low prices and large outdoor deck, this place serves pizza and other Italian specialties.

Dam Bar & Grille (☎ 928-645-2161; 644 N Navajo Dr; dishes $6-12) Raft guides recommend it for its pub fare and microbrewery vibe. If you're really hungry, try the 1lb burger with fries ($12). The patio is pleasant on summer evenings.

Gunsmoke Saloon (☎ 928-645-2161; 644 N Navajo Dr; dishes $6-19; ☺ dinner) This cavernous place serves barbecue dinners, from sandwiches to racks of ribs with salad, baked beans, corn, fries and bread. After dinner it's a popular bar featuring alternative rock and plenty of drunken revelers.

Zapata's (☎ 928-645-9006; 615 N Navajo Dr; dishes $7-11) For Mexican, head to this colorful café serving basic food with few surprises.

Lake Powell Resort's Rainbow Room (☎ 928-645-2433; dishes $9-18) The food is nothing special, but there's something to be said for a meal with a view. The lodge overlooks the lake, and picture windows frame dramatic views of red rock and blue water. The breakfast and lunch buffet ($8 to $12) are better value than the à la carte dinner. If nothing else, the adjoining bar is a good place to come for a sunset drink.

Ken's Old West (☎ 928-645-5160; 718 Vista Ave) For live country music, dancing and a big-barn feel, head here Thursday through Saturday. The party can last all night.

Getting There & Around

Great Lakes Airlines (☎ 928-645-1355, 800-554-5111; www.greatlakesav.com) offers flights between Page Municipal Airport and Phoenix, Denver and Moab. **Avis** (www.avis.com) and **Enterprise** (www.enterprise.com) rent cars from the airport.

HOUSEBOATING ON LAKE POWELL

Houseboats give water rats the opportunity not only to play in the lake, but also to sleep, eat and drink on it. Despite hosting hundreds of houseboats, Lake Powell is big enough to boat for several days and rarely see anyone else. If you're trying to decide whether to rent a houseboat here or on Lake Mead in Western Arizona, Lake Powell offers much more dramatic scenery and plenty of secluded inlets, bays and coves. Summer rates range from $1106 to $3354 for three days to $1854 to $6450 for a week, in boats ranging from 36ft to 59ft that sleep between eight and 12 people. Rates drop by 40% between October and April. The smallest boats have tiny to mid-size refrigerators, simple galleys, toilet and shower, gas barbeque and 150-quart ice chests. Larger boats may have an electric generator (for air-conditioning and small appliances), canopies, swim slides, ladders and much more space. Contact **Aramark** (☎ 800-528-6154; www.lakepowell.com) for details and reservations. Boats book up well in advance.

There are no scheduled buses, but **Greenhound Shuttle** (☎ 877-765-6840) will take you wherever you want to go (including the North Rim) for 95¢ per mile.

CENTRAL ARIZONA

In summer, droves of southern Arizonans head north to camp, fish, sightsee, shop and find cool relief. In winter, many of the same folks make the trip in search of snow and skiing. But central Arizona isn't just the province of canny locals; this area, with the fun college town of Flagstaff, is the gateway to the Grand Canyon. There are old mining towns, funky artists' communities and even a center for the New Age amid stunning red-rock scenery in offbeat Sedona.

FLAGSTAFF & AROUND

pop 57,600 / elev 6900ft

Flagstaff is a gal who likes to break the rules. She's good at mocking – redefining even – that Arizona stereotype of searing temps, sandy deserts and loads of golfing retirees.

She's got mountains, even winter snow. Heck, there's even skiing. Older folks? She doesn't know them all too well. She's not opposed; it's just she runs with a younger crowd. That would be the college crowd, the kids attending Northern Arizona University (NAU) – the school she hosts. She likes to party, sip microbrews at her many pubs, and dance the night away at her clubs. And she really digs the outdoors, from hiking to skiing.

Sheepherder Thomas Forsyth McMillan first settled Flagstaff in early 1876, but it was the arrival of the railroad in 1882 that really put the town on the map. Cattle and sheep ranching became economic mainstays, and the surrounding forests formed the basis of a small logging industry.

Today, tourism is Flagstaff's major economic stimulant. The cool summer temperatures attract Arizonans; it's 141 freeway miles north of Phoenix, 25 slow rural highway miles north of Sedona and under a two-hour drive from the Grand Canyon. With a pedestrian-friendly historic downtown, loads of great restaurants, leisurely coffeehouses and interesting hotels, along with fantastic scenery and proximity to myriad outdoor activities, Flagstaff is a wonderful place worth at least a few days of your time.

Orientation & Information

Approaching Flagstaff from the east, I-40 parallels old Rte 66. Their paths diverge at Enterprise Rd – I-40 veers southwest, while old Rte 66 curls northwest, hugging the railroad tracks and becoming the main drag through the historic downtown. NAU sites between downtown and I-40.

Biff's Bagels (☎ 520-226-0424; 15 Beaver St; per hr $5; ☼ 7am-3pm) Surf the Web in a convenient downtown location. Also does bagels and coffee.

Coconino National Forest Supervisor's Office (☎ 928-527-3600; 2323 Greenlaw Lane) For info on camping, hiking and biking in the forest.

Library (☎ 928-774-4000; 300 W Aspen Ave) Free Internet access.

Main post office (☎ 928-527-2440; 2400 Postal Blvd)

Medical Center (☎ 928-779-3366; 1200 N Beaver St) Twenty-four-hour emergency services.

Police (☎ 928-556-2316; cnr Butler & Lone Tree)

USFS Peaks Ranger Station (☎ 928-526-0866; 5075 N Hwy 89) Info on the Mt Elden, Humphreys Peak and O'Leary Peak areas north of Flagstaff.

Visitor center (☎ 928-774-9541, 800-842-7293; www .flagstaffarizona.org; 1 E Rte 66) Inside the historic Amtrak railway station; offers information on lodging and dining along with free maps and brochures.

Sights

The various sights and museums in and around Flagstaff are all interesting and well worth a visit.

MUSEUM OF NORTHERN ARIZONA

If you have time for only one sight in Flagstaff, come here. In an attractive stone building set in a pine grove, this small but excellent **museum** (☎ 928-774-5211; www .musnaz.org; 3001 N Fort Valley Rd; adult/student $5/3; ☼ 9am-5pm) features exhibits on local Native American archaeology, history and customs as well as geology, biology and the arts. Don't miss the wonderful collection of Hopi kachina dolls and a lovely display of Native American basketry and ceramics. Check the website for information on weekend craft demonstrations and one- to three-day workshops for children and adults.

LOWELL OBSERVATORY

On Mars Hill a mile west of downtown, the **observatory** (☎ 928-774-2096; www.lowell.edu; 1400 W Mars Hill Rd; admission $4; ☼ 9am-5pm Apr-Oct, noon-5pm Nov-Mar), a national historic landmark, was built in 1894 by Percival Lowell. In 1896 Lowell bought a 23in Clark refractor telescope for $20,000 ($6 million in today's currency) and spent the next 20 years looking for life on Mars. Though he never spotted a Martian, the observatory has witnessed many important events, including the first sighting of Pluto in 1920. In the '60s, NASA used the Clark telescope to map the moon. Visitors can stargaze through the telescope (9pm Monday to Saturday June to August, varying times the rest of the year). The short Pluto Walk climbs through a scale model of our solar system, providing descriptions of each planet. You can stroll the grounds on your own, but the only way to see the telescopes is on a tour (10am, 1pm and 3pm in summer, 1pm and 3pm in winter).

RIORDAN MANSION STATE HISTORIC PARK

Centered around a beautiful 13,000-sq-ft mansion, this **park** (☎ 928-779-4395; www.pr.state .az.us; 409 W Riordan Rd; adult/child $5/3; ☼ 8:30am-5pm May-Oct, 10:30am-5pm Nov-Apr) is a must for

ARIZONA

ARIZONA

FLAGSTAFF

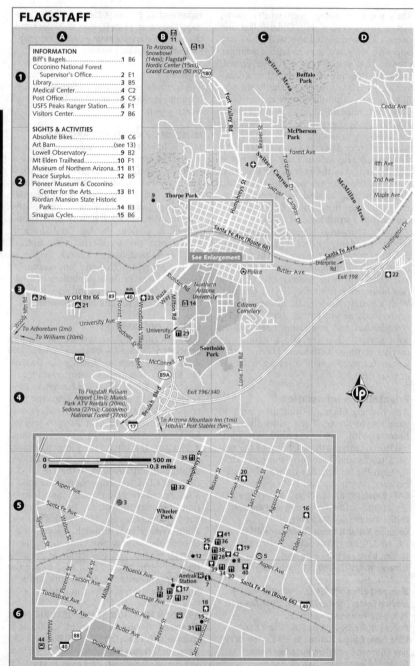

INFORMATION
Biff's Bagels.....................................1 B6
Coconino National Forest
  Supervisor's Office.........................2 E1
Library..3 B5
Medical Center................................4 C2
Post Office.......................................5 C5
USFS Peaks Ranger Station.............6 F1
Visitors Center.................................7 B6

SIGHTS & ACTIVITIES
Absolute Bikes.................................8 C6
Art Barn...................................(see 13)
Lowell Observatory..........................9 B2
Mt Elden Trailhead.........................10 F1
Museum of Northern Arizona........11 B1
Peace Surplus.................................12 B5
Pioneer Museum & Coconino
  Center for the Arts.......................13 B1
Riordan Mansion State Historic
  Park..14 B3
Sinagua Cycles...............................15 B6

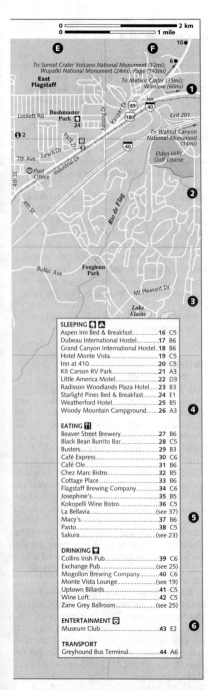

anyone interested in the Arts and Crafts movement. Having made a fortune from the Arizona Lumber Company, brothers Michael and Timothy Riordan had the house built in 1904. The exterior features hand-split wooden shingles, log-slab siding and rustic stone. Filled with Edison, Stickley, Tiffany and Steinway furniture, the interior is a shrine to Arts and Crafts. Visitors are welcome to peruse the grounds and picnic, but entrance to the house is by guided tour only (daily on the hour).

PIONEER MUSEUM & COCONINO CENTER FOR THE ARTS

Housed in the old 1908 county hospital, the **Pioneer Museum** (☎ 928-774-6272; 2340 N Fort Valley Rd; admission by donation; ✆ 9am-5pm Mon-Sat) preserves Flagstaff's early history in photographs and an eclectic mix of memorabilia ranging from vintage farm equipment to early medical instruments. Don't miss the 1920s permanent-wave machine – an early curling iron.

Behind the museum, the **Art Barn** (☎ 928-774-0822; 2320 N Fort Valley Rd; admission free) has been displaying and selling local artisans' work for three decades. Here you'll find a good selection of jewelry, photography, painting, pottery and kachina dolls, among other objects. Hours vary; you'll have to call or stop by.

ARBORETUM

Appealing to a wider audience than just plant lovers and gardeners, the **Arboretum** (☎ 928-774-1442; www.thearb.org; 4001 S Woody Mountain Rd; admission $4; ✆ 9am-5pm Apr–mid-Dec), about 2 miles west, has 200 acres of grounds and greenhouses dedicated to horticultural research and display. Two short wood-chip trails hug a meadow and wind beneath ponderosa pines, passing a herb garden, native plants, vegetables and wildflowers. Plan a picnic at one of the tables scattered throughout the gardens. The arboretum offers tours (11am and 1pm), as well as a summer adventure program for children age four to 12 (call or check the website for details).

WALNUT CANYON NATIONAL MONUMENT

The Sinagua cliff dwellings at **Walnut Canyon** (☎ 928-526-3367; www.nps.gov/waca; admission $3; ✆ 9am-6pm) are set in nearly vertical walls of a small limestone butte amid this forested

DETOUR: SUNSET CRATER VOLCANO NATIONAL MONUMENT & WUPATKI NATIONAL MONUMENT

For a great day-trip from Flagstaff head north on Hwy 89 for about 12 miles until you reach Park Loop Rd 545. Head east on this well-marked 36-mile loop for a trip back in time and a geology lesson or two. The first site you'll hit is **Sunset Crater Volcano National Monument** (☎ 928-526-0502; www.nps.gov/sucr; admission $5; ☺ 8am-6pm). In AD 1064 a volcano erupted on this spot, spewing ash across 800 sq miles, spawning the Kana-A lava flow and leaving behind the 8029ft-high Sunset Crater. The eruption forced farmers to vacate lands they had cultivated for 400 years and subsequent eruptions continued for more than 200 years. The visitor center, 2 miles from Hwy 89, houses a seismograph and other exhibits pertaining to volcanology, while a 1-mile interpretive trail through the **Bonito lava flow** (formed around 1180) grants visitors a firsthand look at volcanic features. A shorter 0.3-mile loop is wheelchair accessible, and there are a few other trails as well.

From the crater, continue on the loop until you reach the neighboring **Wupatki National Monument** (☎ 928-679-2365; www.nps.gov/wupa; admission $5, free if paid at Sunset Crater; ☺ 8am-6pm). The first volcanic eruptions enriched the surrounding soil so heartily that ancestors of today's Hopi, Zuni and Navajo returned to farm the land in the early 1100s. By 1180 thousands were living here in advanced, multistory buildings, but by 1240 their pueblos were mysteriously abandoned. About 2700 of these structures lie within the monument, although few are open to the public. A short self-guided tour takes you to the largest dwelling, **Wupatki Pueblo**. The trailhead starts behind the visitor center. Other dwellings sit within half a mile of the loop road just north of the visitor center, and a 2.5-mile road veers west from the center to **Wukoki Pueblo**, the best preserved of the buildings.

When you're finished exploring the monument continue on the Loop Rd until it rejoins Hwy 89, about 26 miles north of Flagstaff. The entire trip is about 80 miles round-trip.

canyon. The mile-long **Island Trail** descends 185ft (more than 200 stairs), passing 25 cliff-dwelling rooms; many more can be seen in the distance. A shorter, wheelchair-accessible **Rim Trail** affords several views of the rooms from a distance. The monument is 11 miles southeast of Flagstaff off I-40, exit 204.

METEOR CRATER

A huge meteor crashed into our planet almost 50,000 years ago and produced this crater, which is 570ft deep and almost a mile across. The **crater** (☎ 928-289-2362, 800-289-5898; www.meteorcrater.com; adult/child $10/6; ☺ 6am-6pm mid-May–mid-Sep, 8am-5pm mid-Sep–mid-May) is privately owned and operated, and national park passes aren't accepted. It has been used as a training ground for some of the Apollo astronauts; the on-site museum has exhibits about meteors and space missions. Descending into the crater isn't allowed, but you can walk the 3.5-mile Rim Trail. However, apart from a big hole in the ground, there's not much to see and several readers suggest that it is an overpriced attraction. The crater is off I-40, exit 233, 35 miles east of Flagstaff.

Activities
HIKING & BIKING

Ask at the USFS ranger station (p155) for maps and information about the many hiking and mountain-biking trails in and around Flagstaff. Tackle the steep, 3-mile one-way hike up 9299ft **Mt Elden**; the trailhead is just past the ranger station on Hwy 89. Arizona's highest mountain, the 12,663ft **Humphreys Peak** north of Flagstaff in the San Francisco Mountains is a reasonably straightforward though strenuous hike in summer. The trail begins at the Arizona Snowbowl (opposite) and winds through forest, coming out above timberline. The elevation, steepness and loose footing make for a breathless ascent, but the views make it worthwhile. It is 4.5 miles one-way; allow six to eight hours round-trip.

Absolute Bikes (☎ 928-779-5969; 18 N San Francisco St; half/full-day rental from $15/25) has the scoop on the biking scene. The shop offers mountain-, road- and children's-bike rentals, as well as trail maps and info. They also sell equipment and do repairs. **Sinagua Cycles** (☎ 928-779-1092; 113 S San Francisco St) offers similar services.

SKIING & SNOWBOARDING

Believe it or not, skiing is possible in the state, and Arizonans flock by the thousands each year to swoosh down the powdery stuff at the **Arizona Snowbowl** (☎ 928-779-1951, snow report ☎ 928-779-4577; www.arizonasnowbowl.com; Snowbowl Rd; half/full-day $34/42; ☺ mid-Dec–mid-Apr). It's small but lofty, with four lifts servicing 30 runs (beginner through expert) between 9200ft and 11,500ft. Day lodges offer rentals, lessons and meals, but no accommodations. The season is dependent on snowfall, and the resort sometimes opens or closes earlier. Arizona Snowbowl is 7 miles northwest of Flagstaff along Hwy 180, then another 7 miles on Snowbowl Rd; chains or 4WD may be required but ski buses are available.

If downhill isn't your style, cross-country skiing is offered at the **Flagstaff Nordic Center** (☎ 928-779-1951; Hwy 180; trail pass $10). The season is short (call to see if they are open), but there are 30 miles of groomed trails, skiing lessons, rentals and food. It's located 15 miles northwest of Flagstaff.

If you want to pick up skis before you reach the slopes, head to **Peace Surplus** (☎ 928-779-4521; 14 W Rte 66). The store offers rentals and is jam-packed with outdoor supplies.

HORSEBACK RIDING

The **Hitchin' Post Stables** (☎ 928-774-1719, 928-774-7131; 448 S Lake Mary Rd; rides from $25) is one of many companies in town offering hourly and day-long rides. Most trips head to Walnut Canyon; other destinations are available upon request. In winter it offers horse-drawn sleigh rides. The company is located about 5 miles southeast of town.

4WD & ATV TOURS

Self-guided 4WD tours through the Coconino National Forest are an exhilarating way to experience the scenery.

Munds Park ATV Rentals (☎ 928-286-2887; www.mundsparkatvrentals.com; 60 W Pinewood Blvd; rentals from $90; ☺ 9am-5pm Wed-Sat & Mon) rents two-rider ATVs, which are great for families. Insurance and helmets are included in the price; you must be 21 years old to rent. The company is 20 miles south of Flagstaff.

Festivals & Events

Flagstaff is busy throughout summer with many events, often held simultaneously. The visitor center has details. The **Festival of Native American Arts** (☎ 928-779-2300) is held between late June and mid-August at the Coconino Center for the Arts. It has performances and exhibits. The **Flagstaff Winter Festival** (☎ 928-774-9541) is also a big highlight, with sled-dog races, skiing excursions and races, and other snowy events. It takes place in February.

Sleeping

Flagstaff provides the best budget and moderately priced lodging in this region. Summer is the high season and hotel prices rise accordingly – a room that costs $30 in April can be $60 on an August weekend. **Flagstaff Central Reservations** (☎ 928-527-8333, 800-527-8388; www.flagstaffrooms.com) makes reservations for the midrange motels and B&Bs in northern Arizona.

BUDGET

Basic motels line Rte 66, especially the 3-mile stretch east of downtown and near NAU southwest of downtown. Rte 66 parallels the railway and the cheaper places don't have soundproof rooms. Almost anytime from September to May you can cruise along here and find 15 motels advertising rooms for about $30 or even less; prices rise dramatically during busy summer weekends. Check the room before you pay, though – some are worse than others.

Weatherford Hotel (☎ 928-779-1919; www.weatherfordhotel.com; 23 N Leroux St; r from $60) Dating from 1898, it was once northern Arizona's finest hotel and now is Flagstaff's most historic. It's also fantastic value, keeping its rates the same year-round. It's a charming place with a turn-of-the-19th-century feel in its eight rooms (no TV or phone). There are lounges for curling up with a book. Popular Charly's (restaurant and pub) downstairs and Zane Grey ballroom upstairs are attractive and authentic-looking old-fashioned places for a drink. It's a real find that's a nice change from corporate hotels.

Grand Canyon International Hostel (☎ 928-779-9421; www.grandcanyonhostel.com; 19 S San Francisco St; dm/d from $15/30; 🖳) Housed in a historic building with hardwood floors and Southwestern decor, dorms are clean, small four-person bunk rooms with linen included. There's a kitchen, laundry facilities, TV lounge and a host of backpacker-geared tours on offer, including one to the Grand Canyon.

Dubeau International Hostel (☎ 928-774-6731; www.grandcanyonhostel.com; 19 W Phoenix Ave; dm/d from $15/30) Owned by the same folks as the Grand Canyon International Hostel, this place offers similar facilities, as well as a nonsmoking lounge with fireplace, jukebox, foosball and pool table. It can get rowdy when busy.

Woody Mountain Campground (☎ 928-774-7727; 2727 W Rte 66; tent & RV sites $16-22; Apr-Oct;) Offers 146 sites for tents, as well as a playground and coin laundry.

Kit Carson RV Park (☎ 928-774-6993; 2101 W Rte 66; tent & RV sites $27) Nearby, this place has 265 RV sites with hookups amid ponderosa pines available all year.

MIDRANGE

Starlight Pines Bed & Breakfast (☎ 928-527-1912; www.starlightpinesbb.com; 3380 E Lockett Rd; r from $120;) Shadowed by Mt Elden, the four rooms here come with fireplaces, handmade soap and vintage clawfoot bathtubs. A romantic place, it even serves breakfast in bed.

Hotel Monte Vista (☎ 928-779-6971, 800-545-3068; www.hotelmontevista.com; 100 N San Francisco St; r $60-120) Scenes of the movie *Casablanca* were filmed at this c 1927 hotel, where many of the 50 rooms and suites are named after the film stars who slept in them. Rooms have been restored to their 1920s glory, and are comfortable and old-fashioned but not luxurious (though John Wayne and Humphrey Bogart handled it just fine).

Little America Motel (☎ 928-779-7900, 800-865-1401; www.littleamerica.com; 2515 E Butler Ave; r $110;) Set amid acres of lawns and pine trees, this is a wonderful find. The lobby is elegant and the spacious rooms are beautifully appointed with faux antique furniture, goose-down pillows and rich bedding. Small patios in each room open onto 500 acres of grass and woods. Amenities include a playground, pool with a small bar, coffeeshop and an upscale restaurant. This oasis in the most unexpected of places, minutes from downtown, is great for families – rooms even feature Nintendo.

Aspen Inn Bed & Breakfast (☎ 928-773-0295; www.flagstaffbedandbreakfast.com; 218 Elden St; r from $100;) In an elegant 1912 home restored to its original early-20th-century style, it has a European flair and three rooms, each decorated differently. Our favorite is the Peach Room, with hardwood floors and an antique king-sized brass bed.

Arizona Mountain Inn (☎ 928-774-8959; www.arizonamountaininn.com; 4200 Lake Mary Rd; r from $110;) Tucked back in the pines a mile south of town, this place offers 17 cabins with fireplaces and kitchens, and three rooms (including breakfast) in the main lodge. It's a good place to get away from all the hustle, is pet friendly and has handicapped access.

TOP END

Inn at 410 (☎ 928-774-0088, 800-774-2008; www.inn410.com; 410 N Leroux St; r $135-190;) Elegant and very romantic, this fully renovated 1907 house offers nine spacious, beautiful and unique bedrooms. Most come with a fireplace or whirlpool bath, and a full gourmet breakfast and afternoon snacks are included. Two units have adjoining rooms suitable for families with children. It's popular on weekends, so book in advance.

Radisson Woodlands Plaza Hotel (☎ 928-773-8888; 1175 W Rte 66; r $100-170;) This place tries hard to shake its chain roots. The ambiance is trans-Pacific, with a Japanese restaurant (Sakura, opposite) and Southwestern coffeeshop. The lobby features severely square chandeliers and tightly clipped plants; the guest rooms have a contemporary feel and a desert color scheme. Facilities include a pool, spa, sauna, steamroom and exercise equipment. Rates drop in winter.

Eating

Local laws prohibit smoking in all city restaurants (but not restaurant/bars).

BUDGET

Flagstaff is a student town, so budget places abound. Quality isn't sacrificed by low prices, however; all the following places serve delicious food.

La Bellavia (☎ 928-774-8301; 18 S Beaver St; dishes $6-8; breakfast & lunch) Breakfast options galore – Bellavia has benedicts to burritos, as well as a long list of sandwiches and espresso drinks. (Try one of the egg benedict dishes.) The atmosphere is old-school, no-frills dining, which makes the lack of charm almost charming. Service is friendly and quick.

Café Olé (☎ 928-774-8272; 119 S San Francisco St; dishes $5-11; dinner Tue-Sat) To taste some of the best Mexican food in the region, stop by this brightly colored joint (think chile peppers and wall murals). It's a friendly, family-run place – the Aguinaga family has been perfecting their recipes for more than a decade. The food veers toward New Mexican–style, featuring green and red chile sauce, and everything is fresh and healthy (no lard in the beans, minimal frying). For spice lovers, this is Mexican food with some serious kick.

Flagstaff Brewing Company (☎ 928-773-1442; 16 E Rte 66; dishes $8) Skis on the walls and a boat hanging from the ceiling give this low-key brewpub a fun outdoorsy vibe. The food is of the bar-staple variety – pizza, burgers, soup and salads – but quite tasty. There's a large selection of delicious microbrews (the best in town) and daily happy hour from 4:30pm to 6:30pm (pints go for just $2.50).

Cafe Express (☎ 928-774-0541; 16 N San Francisco St; dishes $8) In the heart of downtown, this place tempts the tastes with a whole café full of pastries. It also features various coffees, vegetarian and natural-food meals, and salads, juices, beer and wine. Dine on the outside deck or inside amid the red walls, exposed brick and local Western art. It's a congenial spot, perfect for lingering.

Macy's (☎ 928-774-2243; 14 S Beaver St; dishes $4-7) With chessboards on the tables and a cozy wooden ambiance, it's no wonder this place is a long-standing town favorite. Serving breakfast all day, lots of tasty coffee drinks, good pastries and eclectic light meals, it's popular with students, outdoorsy types and caffeine lovers.

Black Bean Burrito Bar (☎ 928-779-9905; 12 E Rte 66; dishes $3-6) The budget-conscious will appreciate this simple diner featuring big burritos with a great variety of fillings. You can eat in (no comfort here, but there's a good people-watching window) or take out.

MIDRANGE & TOP END

Eating is reasonably priced in Flagstaff, considering the quality of the food. Restaurants might not be as sophisticated as those in big cities, but there's plenty of atmosphere, attitude and pallet-pleasing cuisine.

Josephine's (☎ 928-779-3400; 503 N Humphreys St; dishes $15-20) Josephine's features a casual, yet elegant atmosphere in a 1911 Arts and Crafts bungalow with an outdoor patio and two fireplaces. The creative and eclectic food is made from only the freshest ingredients. At dinner try the seared *ahi* tuna with ginger mango salsa and *cilantro* rice or the tortilla-encrusted halibut. Crab cakes, pecan-encrusted fish tacos and a turkey and Brie sandwich are some of the stand-out choices at lunch.

Buster's (☎ 928-774-5155; 1800 S Milton Rd; dishes $10-18) For some of Flagstaff's best fresh seafood selections, including an oyster bar, try this place, which also offers steaks and prime rib. Inexpensive lunch fare includes good salads, sandwiches and burgers. The bar selection is excellent and Buster's is popular (and often noisy), filled with locals and tourists. Dine between 6:30pm and 7:30pm and receive a discount on dinner mains.

Pasto (☎ 928-779-1937; 19 E Aspen; lunch $9-12, dinner $20) With yellow walls, glittery chandeliers, faux ivy and a line out the door, this Italian pasta joint is a popular choice. The food is delicious, and the place emits an upmarket charm.

Chez Marc Bistro (☎ 928-774-1343; 503 N Humphreys St; dishes $16-30; ⏰ dinner) Classic French, complete with a French-born chef and a romantic, French-provincial atmosphere. Inside a lace-curtained 1911 house, dinner mains range from vegetarian to excellent seafood and meats. The extensive bar list includes French wines and single-malt scotches. It's a small, intimate place with blazing fireplaces in winter and an outdoor patio in summer. Reservations recommended.

Beaver Street Brewery (☎ 928-779-0079; 11 S Beaver St; dishes $8-11) Perfect on a chilly night, grab a pint and sit on a comfy chair by the pot-bellied stove. Grub is of the burger and pizza variety with a few eclectic twists like basil and sundried-tomato burgers, and margarita chicken sandwiches. A local fave for its excellent microbrews (five handmade ales are usually on tap), it's classier and more sophisticated than many brewpubs. You'll enjoy the beer garden in summer.

Sakura (☎ 928-773-9118; Woodlands Plaza Hotel, 1175 W Rte 66; dishes $15-23; ⏰ dinner) Austere ambiance and seating at communal tables (where the fresh seafood, steak and chicken is sliced, diced and flamed in front of you) is the name of the game at this recommended Japanese restaurant. Choose noodles or rice, then veggies, meat or seafood to accompany it and watch the chef light a giant fire to cook it tableside.

Kokopelli Wine Bistro (☎ 928-226-9463; 6 E Aspen Ave; dishes $7-12; ⏰ lunch & dinner) Reasonably priced lunches and dinners, along with wine and champagne tasting, make this a good choice. It has an Italian-bistro look with vintages lining the walls. Tastings cost $6 for six wines. Dinner is meat and pasta oriented, while lunch features paninis and salads.

Cottage Place (☎ 928-774-8431; 126 W Cottage Ave; dishes $16-26; ☺ dinner Tue-Sun) Eat in several intimate and pretty rooms in an early-20th-century house. The varied continental menu includes a few vegetarian options. The delicious appetizers pose a minor dilemma, competing with soups and salads on the mains menu; it's best to come hungry and with a reservation. There's a long wine list, linen table cloths and a romantic air.

Drinking & Entertainment

Flagstaff likes to party. It's a college town, so when school's in session the bars are packed with kids as well as skiers, locals and passers-through. From quiet bars to live-music joints and rowdy pubs, Flagstaff is as big on variety as the microbrews it produces. Read the *Sundial* (the Friday entertainment supplement to Flagstaff's *Arizona Daily Sun*), and the free *Flagstaff Live* (published on the first and third Thursday of the month, available from venues about town) to find out what's happening.

Exchange Pub (☎ 928-779-1919; 23 N Leroux St) Inside the Weatherford Hotel, this place has varied live music ranging from bluegrass to blues, folk to fusion, jazz to jive. It's historic, cozy and intimate with old posters adorning the exposed-brick walls and even has a fireplace.

Zane Grey Ballroom (☎ 928-779-1919; 23 N Leroux St) On the Weatherford's top floor, this fancy bar is worth checking out for…who knows? Jazz? Tango? Poetry? If nothing's going on, it's still a good place to mull over a book while enjoying a fine glass of wine.

Monte Vista Lounge (☎ 928-774-2403; 100 N San Francisco St) In the Hotel Monte Vista, this vintage basement bar has red vinyl stools and plenty of scarred wood. It showcases regional talent with a focus on alternative music.

Flagstaff Brewing Company (☎ 928-773-1442; 16 E Rte 66) Handcrafted brews and live music in a rustic ski lodge setting. What more could you ask for? Well, there's a daily happy hour (4:30pm to 6:30pm) when the kick-ass pints go for just $2.50, as well as decent food (p161).

Mogollon Brewing Company (☎ 928-773-8950; 15 N Agassiz St) The back room at the Mogollon has been turned into a club with a large stage and dance floor. There's live music on most nights of the week, including some national acts. The front section is a traditional brewpub, serving a variety of handmade ales.

Collins Irish Pub (☎ 928-214-7363; cnr Leroux St & Rte 66) Hundreds of dollar bills line the walls at this small and atmospheric place. There are wood tables on which to pound your empty Guinness pint.

Wine Loft (☎ 928-773-9463; 17 N San Francisco St) Photographs on the exposed-brick walls and lots of plants make this second-story place perfect for a sedate afternoon drink. It showcases wines from around the region and the world.

Museum Club (☎ 928-526-9434; 3404 E Rte 66) For a livelier time, dance to far-from-sedate country and western music at this popular barn-like place. It dates from the 1920s and '30s and used to house a taxidermy museum, which may account for its local nickname, 'the Zoo.'

Uptown Billiards (☎ 928-773-0551; 114 N Leroux St; ✗) To shoot some pool without the stench of cigarettes, head to this nonsmoking joint with a good beer selection.

Flagstaff Symphony Orchestra (☎ 928-523-5661; www.flagstaffsymphony.org) Holds eight annual performances in the Audrey Auditorium on the NAU campus. Check the website for the schedule.

Getting There & Around

Flagstaff Pulliam Airport is 3 miles south of town off I-17. **America West Express** (☎ 800-235-9292; www.americawest.com) offers several daily flights to and from Phoenix. **Greyhound** (☎ 928-774-4573; www.greyhound.com; 399 S Malpais Lane) stops in Flagstaff en route to/from Albuquerque ($56, seven hours, daily), Las Vegas ($50, six hours, daily), Los Angeles ($53, 11 hours, multiple daily) and Phoenix ($25, three hours, multiple daily). **Open Road Tours** (☎ 928-226-8060; www.openroadtours.com) offers shuttles to the Grand Canyon ($20) and Phoenix Sky Harbor Airport ($31). Call to arrange pickup.

Operated by **Amtrak** (☎ 928-774-8679; www.amtrak.com), the *Southwest Chief* stops in Flagstaff on its daily run between Chicago and Los Angeles.

Mountain Line Transit (☎ 928-779-662) services four local bus routes Monday through Saturday for 75¢ per ride. Pick-up a user-friendly map at the visitor center. Those with disabilities can use the company's on-call VanGo service.

If you need a taxi, call **Friendly Cab** (☎ 928-774-4444) or **Sun Taxi** (☎ 928-774-7400, 800-483-4488).

WILLIAMS

pop 2840 / elev 6762ft

With old Rte 66 running through its center (see p189), Williams epitomizes Main street America. Literally a two-street town, it seems like nothing much has changed here over the decades. It's the kind of place where you can dine on homemade pie or shop for trinkets in 1950s-era shops. Resilient to its core, Williams put up the good fight against 'progress': it was the last town to tear down its traffic light on the famous Rte 66, and residents are proud to tell you so. Mountain man Bill Williams passed through here several times before he died in 1849, and settlers in 1874 named the place after him. In 1901, the railway to the Grand Canyon opened, making Williams a tourist center. Today most folks come to ride this historic steam train to the South Rim, then stay to dine and sleep in its friendly establishments.

Orientation & Information

Rte 66 passes through the main historic district as a one-way street headed east; Railroad Ave parallels the tracks and Rte 66 and heads one-way west. Most businesses lie along these two roads.

Health Care Center (☎ 928-635-4441; 301 7th St) Offers emergency services.

Library (☎ 928-635-2263; 113 S 1st St) Free Internet.

Police (☎ 928-635-4461; 113 S 1st St) Dial ☎ 911 in an emergency.

Post office (☎ 928-635-4572; 120 S 1st St)

Visitor center (☎ 928-635-4061, 800-863-0546; 200 W Railroad Ave) Inside the historic train depot, this center offers a small bookstore with titles on the canyon as well as the usual maps, eating and lodging info. The USFS is also located here.

Sights & Activities

There are plenty of opportunities for hiking and biking in nearby Kaibab, Coconino and Prescott National Forests. Ask at the visitor center for maps and information.

Most tourists come to ride the historic **Grand Canyon Railway** (☎ 928-773-1976, 800-843-8724; www.thetrain.com; Railway Depot, 200 W Railroad Ave; adult/child round-trip from $58/25), which uses turn-of-the-19th-century steam locomotives to carry passengers to the canyon's South Rim. The train departs Williams at 10am, following a 9:30am Wild West shoot-out by the tracks (a slapstick performance to put you in the mood). You'll arrive at the Grand Canyon at 12:15pm and the return train pulls out at 3:30pm, arriving back at Williams by 5:45pm.

Even if you're not a train buff, this trip can be a lot of fun if you get into the spirit. A banjo player wanders the aisles, joking with passengers and strumming folk classics like 'I've Been Working on the Railroad.' Other characters in period costumes offer historical and regional narration. Robbers often hold up the train, but the sheriff usually takes care of them. There's something about riding the rails, waving your arms out the window or pretending to be Franklin D Roosevelt stumping on the rear platform, that brings out the kid in most people.

Passengers can choose from five classes of service. Check the website for more info.

Sleeping

Rates from mid-May to mid-September (given here) can halve in winter, or rise during special events and holidays. Summer reservations are advised unless you arrive by early afternoon.

BUDGET

In Williams itself, you'll see a number of motels offering rooms in the $20s in winter, and between $40 and $55 in summer.

Highlander Motel (☎ 928-635-2541, 800-800-8288; 533 W Rte 66; r from $35) The owners are out-of-their-way friendly at this very clean, good-value motel. The wood rafters on the ceiling give it a personal touch.

Red Lake Campground & Hostel (☎ 928-635-5321, 800-581-4753; redlake@azaccess.com; Hwy 64; camp/RV sites $10/14, dm/d $11/33) Eight miles north of I-40 exit 165, this welcoming place offers spots for campers and RVs, as well as a hostel with dorms and private rooms with three beds and shared bathroom. Amenities include coin showers, laundry and a grocery store.

Railside RV Ranch (☎ 928-635-4077, 888-635-4077; www.thegrandcanyon.com/railside; 877 Rodeo Rd; camp/RV sites $17/20) The closest campground to the center, this has 100 RV sites with hookups and four sites for tents. There are showers, a game room and laundry, but little shade. The sites are right on the railroad tracks, so it can get noisy.

MIDRANGE & TOP END
Sheridan House Inn (☎ 928-635-9441, 888-635-9345; www.grandcanyonbbinn.com; 460 E Sheridan Ave; d/ste $145/210; ☻ Mar-Dec; ✗) Steve and Evelyn Gardner are the gracious hosts at this pine-fringed hilltop inn. Included in the rate is a full hot breakfast and buffet-style dinner, served on the outdoor deck in summer. You're encouraged to help yourself to a fridge full of complimentary beer, soda, juice and water. Downstairs you'll find a pool table and fully stocked bar – fix a drink and relax on the adjacent flagstone patio. While not historic, the rooms are well appointed (nothing too cutesy) and offer CD players, TVs, VCRs and full marble baths. The inn's video library includes a selection of children's flicks.

Terry Ranch B&B (☎ 928-635-4171, 800-210-5908; www.terryranchbnb.com; 701 Quarter Horse Rd; r $115-155; ✗) The four rooms in this B&B boast antique oak and cherry furniture, clawfoot tubs and fireplaces. Terrycloth bathrobes and a basket of toiletries in the bathrooms are nice touches. A wraparound porch, quilt bedspreads, Southwestern rugs, log cabin–style walls and leather breakfast plates all add to the homey Old West vibe.

Red Garter Bed & Bakery (☎ 928-635-1484, 800-328-1484; www.redgarter.com; 137 W Railroad Ave; r from $90) Up until the 1940s, gambling and girls were the draw at this 1897 bordello-turned-B&B. The largest room was once reserved for the house's 'best gals,' who would lean out the window to flag down customers. Set back from the road, the other three rooms are smaller and less interesting, although the place underwent renovations in mid-2005. Innkeeper John Holst grew up around here and knows the area well. He's happy to get out the map, offer suggestions and relate the saucy history of the bordello and town.

Canyon Motel (☎ 928-635-2552, 800-482-3955; 1900 E Rodeo Rd; r $70-100) Stone cottages plus rooms in two railway cabooses and a former Grand Canyon Railway coach car offer a kitschy alternative to a standard motel. Resting on sections of old track, the train cars sport private decks, and even though they're a bit on the cramped side, kids love the experience. Several cars provide bunkbeds; campfires highlight the evenings. The little cottages feature white walls and wood floors, with kitchenettes and king or double beds.

Canyon Country Inn Bed & Breakfast (☎ 928-635-2349; 442 W Rte 66; r $45; ✗) A quaint little family home with teddy bears lining the stairs, and large homely rooms each decorated slightly differently. Good value.

Lodge (☎ 877-503-4366; www.thelodgeonroute66.com; 200 E Rte 66; r $90) A nice-looking motel with clever decor. The exterior has a Native American theme with lots of wooden posts. The spotless rooms feel distinctly non-motelish with lovely linens, wrought-iron fixtures and stucco walls. Prices drop by $30 in winter.

Fray Marcos Hotel (☎ 928-635-4010; 235 N Grand Canyon Blvd; r $120; ☙) This sprawling place caters primarily to Grand Canyon Railway passengers. While the spacious lobby, with a flagstone fireplace and paintings of the canyon, hints at the elegance of days past, the Southwestern-style rooms are standard hotel fare. The indoor pool, hot tub and fitness room are plusses. Ask about room/railway packages. Prices drop significantly in winter.

Eating & Drinking
Culinary masterpieces are not exactly Williams' strength. The food is as American-based as the town itself. If you're craving country cooking however (or have a really bad hangover), you'll be pleased with the fatty, fried choices.

Cruiser's Café 66 (☎ 928-635-2445; 233 W Rte 66; dishes $8-15; ☻ 4-10pm) Rte 66 fans will dig the eclectic decor – from the giant stuffed buffalo at the entrance to the vintage gas pumps, old signs and murals eulogizing America's most famous highway. It's a fun place, serving barbeque and other American fare inside a 1930s filling station.

Rod's Steak House (☎ 928-635-2671; 301 E Rte 66; dishes $8-20) Locals say the service here depends on owner Stella's mood, so don't count on lots of smiles. The place has been here for half a century, and is among the best in town. The food is consistently good. The cow-shaped sign and menus spell things out – if you want a steak and potatoes this is where to come.

Pine Country Restaurant (☎ 928-635-9718; 107 N Grand Canyon Blvd; dishes $4-10) Americana and country kitchen are well represented at this simple family restaurant. Good old American staples like chicken fried steak with mashed potatoes and country gravy, plus a large selection of creamy pies fill the menu. There are lots of greasy breakfast choices in the $5 range.

Pizza Factory (☎ 928-635-3009; 214 W Rte 66; dishes $5-10) You can't beat the $3.40 price tag for half a pitcher of beer (it's of the Budweiser variety) at this cheery pizza joint with a red checkered floor. The menu includes pizza (or course), along with calzones, pastas and salads.

Pancho McGillicuddy's (☎ 928-635-4150; 141 W Railroad Ave; dishes $8-15) If only walls could talk…this place would have a story to tell. On a block once known as 'Saloon Row' for its many bars, Pancho McGillicuddy's is housed in one of the town's oldest buildings, constructed in 1895. With an old-time feel and mounted animal heads on the walls, it serves Mexican grub as well as a gringo option or two. There are more than 30 tequilas on the menu, and margaritas come in every flavor possible – from pear cactus to guava.

Twisters (☎ 928-635-0266; 417 E Rte 66; dishes $2-6) Take the kids to this '50s-style 'Rte 66' soda fountain for ice-cream treats, hot dogs, burgers and more.

World Famous Sultana Bar (☎ 928-635-2028; 301 W Rte 66) Whet your whistle with a brew (or stiff drink) at this quirky bar. During prohibition it had a basement speakeasy providing bootleg liquor and gambling to invite-only guests. Today, it's a saloon from another era, where the smoke is thick, the talk boisterous and the stuffed mountain lion keeps watch over the pool table. Sometimes there's live music.

Getting There & Around

Greyhound (☎ 928-635-0870; www.greyhound.com; 1050 N Grand Blvd) stops at the Chevron gas station. **Amtrak** (☎ 800-872-7245; www.amtrak.com) stops on the outskirts of town. **Open Road Tours** (☎ 928-226-8060, 800-766-7117; www.openroad tours.com; Railway Depot, 200 W Railroad Ave) offers two daily shuttles to the canyon ($15) and Flagstaff ($10), as well as a connecting shuttle from Flagstaff to Phoenix airport ($30).

SEDONA
pop 11,300 / elev 4500ft

If the scenery looks familiar in picture-perfect Sedona, it's probably because you've seen it on the silver screen. With spindly towers, grand buttes and flat-topped mesas, it's easy to understand why Hollywood found these splendid crimson sandstone formations so enticing. Sitting at the south end of lovely Oak Creek Canyon, Sedona is one of the prettiest locations in Arizona. The drive into town from Flagstaff, to the north, is nothing short of breathtaking – the road curves through a narrow canyon with solid cliffs, crumbling rocks, verdant green trees and even a babbling brook.

Perhaps they'd seen the old Westerns shot here, because in the 1960s and '70s the surrounding beauty started attracting retirees, artists and tourists in large numbers, and town growth exploded. New Age types, who believe this area is the center of vortexes that radiate the Earth's power (see box, p168), were quick to follow. Today the combination of scenic beauty and mysticism attracts throngs of tourists year-round. You'll find all sorts of alternative medicine and practices, from psychic channeling, past-life regression, crystal healing, shamanism and drumming workshops to more traditional massages, yoga, tai chi and acupressure.

The surrounding canyons offer excellent hiking and mountain biking, and the town itself bustles with art galleries and schmick gourmet restaurants, along with more than one top-end resort. Unlike Flagstaff, Sedona's economy is almost entirely tourist driven, and in summer the traffic and crowds in town and on the trails can be oppressive. But just be patient and let Sedona's famous beauty soothe your soul.

Orientation & Information

The towns' main drag is Hwy 89A, which leads south to Prescott (57 miles) and north to Flagstaff (28 miles) through Oak Creek Canyon. It's best to have a car, as shops, restaurants and bars are widely spread along the highway, many in small shopping blocks. There's no real concentrated town center, so walking from one end to another isn't really feasible. Much of the surrounding area is national forest land, and you'll need to purchase a Red Rock Pass (per day/week $5/15), available from the visitor center, if you want to park anywhere on it. To the east is the 'Y', the junction of Hwys 179 and 89A. There are more restaurants, hotels and shops south on Hwy 179, heading towards the village of Oak Creek.

Gateway visitor center (☎ 928-282-9119; www.red rockcountry.org; Forest Rd at Hwy 89A) Oodles of tourist information; can provide lodging bookings. Sells Red Rock Passes.

Library (☎ 928-282-7714; 3250 White Bear Rd) Free Internet access.

Medical center (☎ 928-204-3000; 3700 W Hwy 89A) Twenty-four-hour emergency services.

Police (☎ 928-282-3100; 100 Road Runner Rd)

Post office (☎ 928-282-3511; Hwy 89A at Hwy 179)

USFS ranger station (☎ 928-282-4119; 250 Brewer Rd) Stop by for camping and hiking info or a Red Rock Pass.

Sights & Activities

From the wild to the mild, Sedona's got something for everyone.

JEEP & ATV TOURS

Sedona's stunning scenery is the backdrop for many a rugged adventure. And a long-time favorite way to experience it is from the back of a Jeep. Many companies offer 4WD tours, which range from mild to wild, but **Pink Jeep Tours** (☎ 928-382-5000, 800-873-3662; www.pinkjeep.com; 204 N Hwy 89A; tours from $95) is the

---

SEDONA

INFORMATION
Gateway Visitors Center	1	G2
Library	2	A3
Medical Center	3	A3
Police	4	B3
Post Office	5	G2
USFS Ranger Station	6	G3

SIGHTS & ACTIVITIES
Earth Wisdom Tours	7	H2
Institute of Ecotourism	8	G3
Mountain Bike Heaven	9	D3
Pink Jeep Tours	10	G2
Sedona ATV Adventures	11	B3
Sedona Sports	12	G3

SLEEPING
Inn on Oak Creek	13	G3
Lantern Light Inn	14	A3
L'Auberge de Sedona	15	H2
Matterhorn Lodge	16	H2
Rancho Sedona RV Park	17	H3
Sky Ranch Lodge	18	D4

EATING
Coffeepot Restaurant	19	C3
Cowboy Club	20	H2
Dahl & Di Luca	21	C3
Heartline Cafe	22	D3
Javelina Cantina	23	G3
L'Auberge de Sedona	(see 15)	
New Frontiers Natural Foods & Deli	24	E3
Oak Creek Brewing Company	25	D2
Pietro's	26	C3
Rene at Tlaquepaque	(see 8)	
Sedona Memories	27	H2
Shugrue's Hillside Grill	28	G4
Thai Spices	29	B3

DRINKING
Historic Rainbow's End Restaurant & Nightclub	30	A3
Laughing Coyote	31	B3
Oak Creek Brewing Company	(see 25)	

SHOPPING
Crystal Castle	32	G3
Garland's Navajo Rugs	33	H3
Tlaquepaque Village	(see 8)	

TRANSPORT
Sedona-Phoenix Shuttle	34	C3

To Boynton Canyon, Enchantment Resort & Yavapai Dining Room (5mi)

Kachina Dr

Road Runner Rd

Dry Creek Rd

White Bear Rd

Arroyo Dr

Juniper Dr

Piñon Dr

To Red Rock State Park (5.5mi)

Harmony Dr

Andante Dr

Carol Canyon Dr

Thunderbird Dr

Road Runner Rd

Madole Rd

Soldier Pass Rd

Sutz Bear Cat Dr

Shelby St

Sunset Dr

Coffee Pot Dr

Yavapai Dr

Pony Soldier Rd

Mountain Shadows Dr

Northview Rd

View Dr

Inspirational Dr

Oak Creek Blvd

West Sedona

89A

most esteemed. Since 1958 it has provided the most talked about off-road adventures in the Southwest, and has been featured on numerous TV shows and magazine covers. The tours take you alongside adrenaline-pumping drop-offs, past panoramic vistas and archeological sites. Tour guides are knowledgeable and provide lessons on Native American history and culture, along with weird geological facts and other local lore.

If you'd rather do the driving, check out **Sedona ATV Adventures** (☎ 928-204-2662; www.grand canyonatvadventures.com; 165b Coffeepot Dr; 2/4-hr tour $95/170). Explore the backcountry and learn about the history of the area on a guided ATV Tour. You'll be operating your own

vehicle, so it can prove even more exhilarating than a Jeep tour.

HORSEBACK RIDING

To experience Sedona the way the cowboys in the movies did, give **M Diamond Ranch** (☎ 928-592-0148; www.mdiamondranch.com; rides from $55; ☯ Mon-Sat) a call. This working cattle ranch just outside town picks up from your hotel and offers a variety of rides. The two-hour cattle drives, where you get to help corral the bovines, are popular, as are the sunset dinner rides. After a short trail ride, help load the horse-drawn wagon and head to a scenic overlook where cowboy entertainment will accompany your Arizona-style steak dinner.

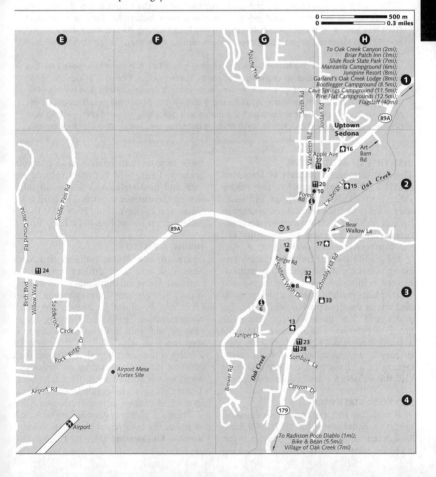

IN SEARCH OF THE NEW AGE

Sedona is the foremost New Age center in the Southwest and one of the most important any-where. The term 'New Age' loosely refers to a trend toward seeking alternative explanations or interpretations of what constitutes health, religion, the psyche and enlightenment. Drawing upon new and old factual and mystical traditions from around the world, New Agers often seek to transform themselves psychologically and spiritually in the hope that such personal efforts will eventually transform the world at large.

You can't miss the New Age stores in town – many of them have the word 'crystal' in their names. They sell books, crystals and various New Age paraphernalia, distribute free maps showing vortex sites, provide information, and may arrange various spiritual or healing events. The **Center for the New Age** (☎ 520-282-2085; www.sedonanewagecenter.com; 341 Hwy 179) is a good place to start your exploration. Sedona's offerings include mainstream services such as massages, nutrition counseling, acupressure, meditation, and yoga and tai chi classes, and the increasingly esoteric practices of herbology, psychic channeling, aura photography, astrology, palmistry, tarot card and runes reading, aromatherapy, past-life regressions, crystal healing, shamanism, drumming workshops, reflexology, hypnotherapy and more…

The four best-known vortexes, or high-energy sites, where the Earth's power is said to be strongly felt, are in Sedona's local red-rock mountains. These include Bell Rock near Village of Oak Creek east of Hwy 179, Cathedral Rock near Red Rock Crossing, Airport Mesa along the Air-port Rd, and Boynton Canyon. Local maps show these four main sites, though some individuals claim that others exist.

New Agers (for want of a better term) are generally gentle folk, but some have been criticized for performing rituals, such as chanting or offerings, in scenic areas. Chanting in a public scenic area can be as irritating as loud radio, revving motorcycle or droning aircraft, and leaving offer-ings of crystals or food is tantamount to littering. If you want to participate in such public rituals, please keep your vocal interactions with the planet to a peacefully personal level, pick up your offerings when you're through, and leave nothing but your love, energy and blessings behind.

INSTITUTE OF ECOTOURISM

The well-organized **Institute of Ecotourism** (☎ 928-282-2720; www.ioet.org; 91 Portal Lane; workshop $10-25) hosts loads of workshops and semi-nars. Topics include astronomy, geology of the red rocks, Sedona's vortex mystery, na-ture writing, wilderness photography and the Native American perspective. A visit to the facility itself is free and quite inter-esting. Check out the interactive natural-history exhibits, organic greenhouse and native plants garden. There's a theater mod-eled after a deserted pueblo, which displays photo and film presentations about the Southwest desert. The institute also runs a youth program ($25), where kids par-ticipate in various adventures from orien-teering to archeology excavation. Call or visit the website for a schedule of events.

RED ROCK STATE PARK

This park has an environmental education center, a **visitor center** (☎ 928-282-6907; Lower Red Rock Loop Rd; per vehicle $8; ☉ 8am-6pm, to 5pm in summer), picnic areas and six short hiking trails in a riparian habitat amid gorgeous scenery. Ranger-led activities include na-ture and bird walks and full-moon hikes during the warmer months. The park is 5.5 miles west of the Y along Hwy 89A, then 3 miles left on Lower Red Rock Loop Rd.

HIKING & BIKING

There are easy scenic trails in Red Rock State Park and more difficult ones in the national forest surrounding town. Hiking is possible year-round, though some higher trails may be closed in winter. The USFS ranger station (p166) sells hiking maps. One popular trail in Oak Creek Canyon is **West Fork Trail**, which follows the creek for 7 miles – the canyon walls rise more than 200ft in places. Wander up as far as you want, splash around a bit, then turn back. The trailhead is 3 miles north of Slide Rock, in the Call of the Canyon Recreation Area.

There are plenty of good biking trails; ask at any of the bike-rental places, including: **Mountain Bike Heaven** (☎ 928-282-1312; 1695 W Hwy 89A)

Sedona Sports (☎ 928-282-6956; 251 Hwy 179)
Bike & Bean (☎ 928-284-0210; 6020 Hwy 179) Just over 5 miles south of town.

Tours

Sedona offers numerous organized tours. The 4WD 'Jeep Tours' (p166) are some of the most popular, but there are plenty of others. You can join a tour to see and photograph scenery, experience energy vortexes, look at archaeological sites or visit the Grand Canyon or Hopi Reservation. Most companies expect a minimum of four passengers and charge more per person for smaller groups. Many also offer overnight tours.

Sedona Trolley (☎ 928-282-5400; 270 Hwy 89A; adult/child $8/3; ☺ 10am-5pm) One narrated tour, lasting 55 minutes, covers Tlaquepaque (a shopping and art-gallery center) and the Chapel of the Holy Cross. Another covers West Sedona and Boynton Canyon. Tours depart on the hour.

Crossing Worlds (☎ 928-649-3060, 800-350-2693; www.crossingworlds.com) Offers tours on Hopi, Navajo and other Native American cultures, and Sedona vortexes. Tours last anywhere from 2½ hours to multiple days. A four-hour vortex tour costs $85. Call to arrange pick-up.

Earth Wisdom Tours (☎ 928-282-4714, 800-482-4714; 293 N Hwy 89A) Vortexes and Native American lore. Tours last from two hours to all day and start at around $35.

Northern Light Balloon Expeditions (☎ 928-282-2274, 800-230-6222; www.sedona.net/fun/balloon) Daily sunrise flights ($170 per person). Hotel pickup.

Festivals & Events

The Gateway visitor center has information about the many events taking place in Sedona throughout the year; most are oriented toward the arts. The annual all-day **Jazz on the Rocks** (☎ 928-282-1985; www.sedonajazz.com) features big-name musicians on the last Saturday in September. The concert usually sells out, so buy your tickets in advance. Other noteworthy events include the **Sedona Arts Festival** (☎ 928-204-9456; www.sedonaartsfestival.org), held during the third weekend in October, and the 'lighting of the luminaries' at Tlaquepaque Village during the second weekend in December; both Tlaquepaque Village and the neighboring resort are fantastically lit up over this period.

Sleeping

Sedona hosts several beautiful B&Bs, creekside cabins as well as full-service resorts, but be prepared to spend a lot of money. Rates at chain motels range from $70 to $120, which is quite reasonable by Sedona standards.

BUDGET

Budget options are limited in Sedona.

Rancho Sedona RV Park (☎ 928-282-7255, 888-641-4261; 135 Bear Wallow Lane; RV sites $33-52) Has a laundry, showers and 30 RV sites, most with full hookups.

Dispersed camping is not permitted in Red Rock Canyon. The **USFS** (☎ 928-282-4119; 250 Brewer Rd; campsites $12) runs the following campgrounds along Hwy 89A in Oak Creek Canyon north of town; none have hookups.

DETOUR: OAK CREEK CANYON & SURROUNDING BACKCOUNTRY DRIVES

For something truly magical take Hwy 89A northeast into **Oak Creek Canyon**. It's a drive that won't soon be forgotten. The canyon is at its narrowest here, and the red, orange and white cliffs at their most dramatic. Forests of pine and sycamore cloak the canyon and the air smells sweet and romantic. Giant cottonwoods crowd the creek sides, providing a scenic shady backdrop for trout fishing and swimming. Stop at **Grasshopper Point** ($7), about 2 miles into the drive, to cool off; it's a great swimming hole.

Continue on for another 5 miles until you reach **Slide Rock State Park** (☎ 928-282-3034; admission per car $8; ☺ 8am-6pm, to 5pm in winter). Here you can unpack the picnic basket and watch for birds as you enjoy lunch. Afterwards jump into the creek and allow yourself to be swept down the natural rock shoot from which the park derives its name. It's fun for kids and adults alike.

At the end of the day head back into town and turn off at the paved **Airport Rd**, it's a short but fantastic late-afternoon route. The setting sun makes for a trippy picture – the rocks blaze a psychedelic red and orange against a bright pink and purple sky.

Unless otherwise stated, the season is May through September.

Manzanita (year-round) Eighteen sites, 6 miles north of town.

Bootlegger Ten sites; no water; 8.5 miles north of town.

Cave Springs Eighty-two sites; showers; 11.5 miles north of town.

Pine Flat East & Pine Flat West Fifty-seven sites; 12.5 miles north of town.

MIDRANGE

Lantern Light Inn (928-282-3419; www.lanternlight inn.com; 3085 W Hwy 89A; r from $125;) A charming little place with lovely garden areas and quaint rooms with courtyards, it's excellent value if you want to escape the big-hotel and resort market. The proprietors at this B&B are super friendly and cater to their guests' every whim. A large breakfast is included and will be tailored to your tastes (there is a big emphasis on healthy). Rooms come in a variety of sizes. The two-bedroom guesthouse (two/four people $195/295) is absolutely huge, and akin to having your own home. It comes with a giant kitchen, living room with fireplace, multiple bathrooms and even a private courtyard with lounge chairs and a pond with a waterfall. For something a little less extravagant, try the Ryan Room ($169), with cheery yellow walls and couches around a fireplace.

Sky Ranch Lodge (928-282-6400, 888-708-6400; www.skyranchlodge.com; Airport Rd; r $80-160;) With spectacular views of the town and surrounding country, this lodge offers spacious motel rooms on six landscaped acres. Some rooms include balconies, fireplaces, kitchenettes or refrigerators. Also available are cottages ($190) with vaulted ceilings, kitchenettes and private decks.

Garland's Oak Creek Lodge (928-282-3343; www.garlandslodge.com; Hwy 89A; r from $130; May–mid-Nov) Set back from Oak Creek, on eight secluded acres with broad lawns, an apple orchard and woods, this lodge offers nicely appointed Western log cabins, many with fireplaces. Rates include a full hot breakfast, 4pm tea and a gourmet dinner. It feels like a bit of a private club – guests stroll the grounds, drink in hand and speak in hushed tones. Catering to adults who crave quiet and service, Garland's is 8 miles north of Sedona. It's not particularly child friendly, charging $60 extra for any child over the age of two.

Matterhorn Lodge (929-282-7176; www.matter hornlodge.com; 230 Apple Ave; r from $90;) The 23 rooms at this place have balconies overlooking uptown Sedona and Oak Creek. Amenities include in-room coffeemakers and refrigerators, a pool and a whirlpool. It's within walking distance of many shops and restaurants.

Radisson Poco Diablo Resort (928-282-7333; www.radissonsedona.com; 1752 S Hwy 179; r $70-170;) A good place to bring the family, there's a game room and children's playground. Rooms are large and include balconies, couches and desks. There's a par-three golf course. You need to book online or through a consolidator to get the cheapest rates. It's not as posh as some resorts, and not bad value either.

TOP END

Sedona has a host of upscale resorts and inns offering luxurious amenities and total relaxation.

Inn on Oak Creek (928-282-7896; www.innonoak creek.com; 556 Hwy 179; r $195-290;) Casual elegance on the water is the theme at this charming B&B with fabulous views. Each of the eclectic rooms is unique, and lots of time was put into the decoration. Try the Restive Rooster Room, which has a tub with a view or the Bunkhouse Room, which is Western themed and features an old rifle and Wild West artwork. The included breakfast takes place over four courses and is as gourmet as it gets. Guests also enjoy an afternoon hors d'oeuvres hour. It's by far Sedona's most charming and intimate sleeping option.

Briar Patch Inn (928-282-2342, 888-809-3030; www.briarpatchinn.com; 3190 N Hwy 89A; r $170-325;) Nestled in nine wooded acres along Oak Creek, just north of town, this lovely inn offers 17 log cottages with Southwestern decor and Native American art on the walls. All cottages include patios and several lie beside the burbling creek. There's a small meadow with grazing sheep and a creek-side cottage for massages. Accompanied by a classical guitarist, a delicious breakfast buffet beckons from the stone patio overlooking the water. This friendly, relaxed, unpretentious spot is wonderfully rejuvenating.

Junipine Resort (928-282-3375, 800-742-7463; www.junipine.com; 8351 N Hwy 89A; r $125-225) In woodland 8 miles north of Sedona, this resort offers spacious, thoughtfully decorated one- and two-bedroom 'creekhouses,' with kitchens, living rooms, fireplaces and decks. Some come with lofts, others have creek-side views, hot tubs or both. Two-bedroom units sleep up to four people, a great option for families ($25 for each additional person, children under 12 free). The on-site restaurant serves good food, so you don't need to brave the windy roads to get a bite to eat.

L'Auberge de Sedona (☎ 928-282-1661, 800-272-6777; www.lauberge.com; 301 L'Auberge Lane; r $210-450; 🏊) The emphasis at this upscale country inn is romantic relaxation and gastronomic overindulgence. The restaurant serves fine French cuisine in an ultrafancy setting (jackets required for men), while the spacious rooms feature fireplaces and no TVs.

Enchantment Resort (☎ 928-282-2900, 800-826-4180; www.enchantmentresort.com; 525 Boynton Canyon Rd; r from $375; 🏊) This full-service world-class resort is so exclusive you can't even enter the driveway unless you're staying or have reservations at one of its three restaurants. Spectacularly located in Boynton Canyon, 5 miles off Hwy 89A northwest of Sedona, the rooms sprawl across the extensive grounds and include private balconies and great views. Hiking trails whisk you high above or far into the canyon, while several pools, tennis courts, saunas and even a croquet field provide other forms of exercise. For relaxation, the onsite spa Mii amo, offers dozens of massages and other treatments. A children's program provides activities for four- to 12-year-olds.

Eating

Sedona has plenty of upscale restaurants and even the budget places serve fresh, innovative dishes. In fact, some visitors consider the cuisine as much of an attraction as the scenery. Reputable chefs are drawn to the town, rewarded both by the lovely setting and by an appreciative and (sometimes) discerning audience of food-loving travelers. Reservations are a good idea.

BUDGET
Thai Spices (☎ 928-282-0599; 2986 W Hwy 89A; dishes from $6; 🕐 lunch & dinner) Despite its unpretentious exterior, this popular restaurant serves good, spicy and inexpensive Thai food, including a wonderful coconut soup and some macrobiotic dishes.

Coffeepot Restaurant (☎ 928-282-6626; 2050 W Hwy 89A; dishes $5-8; 🕐 6am-2pm) For breakfast and lunch, this has been the place to go for decades. It's always busy and service can be slow, but meals are inexpensive and the selection is huge – it offers more types of omelets than most restaurants have menu items (it claims 101, including peanut butter and jelly!).

New Frontiers Natural Foods & Deli (☎ 928-282-6311; 1420 W Hwy 89A; sandwiches $5; 🕐 breakfast, lunch & dinner) This natural foods grocery store is a good place to stop for picnic supplies or to grab a fresh sandwich from the deli.

Sedona Memories (☎ 928-282-0032; 321 Jordan Rd; dishes $5-7; 🕐 10am-2pm Mon-Sat) This low-key sandwich joint features several vegetarian options, homemade bread and a quiet outdoor patio.

MIDRANGE
Oak Creek Brewing Company (☎ 928-204-1300; 2050 Yavapai Dr; dishes $9-15; 🕐 lunch & dinner) There's an American menu featuring burgers, pizzas, sandwiches, and hot and delicious wings. Food is served inside a casual light-wood themed environment with copper brewing vessels at the bar. There are nine beers on tap, many of which were gold-medal winners at the Great American Beer Festival. If you're not in the mood for brew, the mango frozen margarita is simple divine.

Heartline Cafe (☎ 928-282-0785; 1610 W Hwy 89A; dishes $9-15; 🕐 lunch & dinner) This restaurant's name refers to the Zuni symbol for good health and long life, and indeed the imaginative menu offers the kind of fresh, clean and tasty food you might expect. Options include Thai-style vegetables, barbecued pork with apple-and-onion chutney, pecan-encrusted trout and tea-smoked duck salad. Enclosed in a blue wall covered with flowering vines, the pleasant outdoor patio holds eight tables around a small clay fireplace.

Cowboy Club (☎ 928-282-4200; 241 Hwy 89A; lunch dishes $8-12, dinner mains $20; 🕐 lunch & dinner) From the outside it looks like a saloon, but step inside and you'll find a large and determinedly Southwestern restaurant split into two sections. The Grille Room offers primarily steaks, though you'll also find chicken, fish and veggie options. The more adventurous can even try the rattlesnake. Pricier fine dining is offered in the Silver Saddle Room.

ARIZONA

Javelina Cantina (☎ 928-203-9514; 671 Hwy 179; dishes $12-16; ☾ lunch & dinner) There's a tropical sunset scene painted on one wall and a giant picture window with fantastic rock views occupying another. It's a bustling and popular place that does a slightly more Americanized version of Mexican food. Make dinner reservations or prepare for an hour's wait.

Pietro's (☎ 928-282-2525; 2445 W Hwy 89A; dishes $14-20; ☾ dinner) A small pasta and meat-based menu is served in elegant Victorian surroundings done up in romantic reds with flouncy table clothes and drapes. The Italian food is delicious, and the place gets very busy.

Dahl & Di Luca (☎ 928-282-5219; 2321 W Hwy 89A; dishes $11-20; ☾ lunch & dinner) Vying with Pietro's for the title of best Italian, this place is slightly larger with more pasta options on the menu. The vibe is Italian wine cellar meets grotto with dim lighting and a cozy bar. It's a romantic place where folks keep their voices low.

TOP END

Shugrue's Hillside Grill (☎ 928-282-5300; 671 Hwy 179; dishes $25-30; ☾ lunch & dinner) Promising panoramic views, an outdoor deck from which to enjoy them and consistently excellent food, this restaurant is a great choice for an upscale meal. If it's too chilly to sit outside, don't fret – the walls are mostly glass so you can still enjoy the scenery. The menu offers everything from steak to ravioli, but is best known for its variety of well-prepared seafood. A jazz ensemble plays on the weekends. Meals are cheaper at lunch and feature lots of sandwiches ($10). Reservations are recommended.

Rene at Tlaquepaque (☎ 928-282-9225; Tlaquepaque Village, Hwy 179; dishes from $20; ☾ lunch & dinner; ☒) Long considered one of Sedona's best, this restaurant offers upscale continental cuisine (lamb is a specialty) and some unusual meats (pronghorn antelope and ostrich). Plenty of art on the walls adds to the appeal.

L'Auberge de Sedona (☎ 928-282-1667; 301 L'Auberge Lane; dishes $30; ☾ breakfast, lunch & dinner) It's beautiful, elegant, romantic and very French. The high prices, small portions and formal dining are irresistible to many visitors; reservations and dinner jackets are required. The best value is the prix-fixe dinner menu, which changes daily and runs at about $60 for six courses. Dinner mains include French delicacies such as frog legs, pheasant, veal and escargot.

Yavapai Dining Room (☎ 928-282-2900; Enchantment Resort, 525 Boynton Canyon Rd; dishes $20-30; ☾ breakfast, lunch & dinner) This place serves superb food in a jaw-dropping setting (make a reservation or you won't even make it up the driveway). The Southwestern cuisine has all sorts of interesting twists and the menu changes regularly. It's fair value for the food (seafood, meat and pasta based) and a bargain considering the location. The Sunday champagne brunch ($29) is stellar and expansive.

Drinking & Entertainment

Read the monthly *Red Rock Review* for local events. Nightlife is fairly quiet, consisting mainly of lounge entertainment at the resorts.

Oak Creek Brewing Company (☎ 928-204-1300; 2050 Yavapai Dr) With a long cocktail menu and nine homemade brews on tap this is a popular spot day or night. There's a large outdoor patio and nightly live music – from rock to blues to reggae.

Historic Rainbow's End Restaurant & Nightclub (☎ 928-282-1593; 3235 W Hwy 89A) Locals dig the scarred-wood bar and pool tables in this smoky old saloon. There's a small jukebox and neon beer signs on the walls. Live music rocks the place Friday and Saturday nights – everything from country to rock – and there's room for dancing.

Laughing Coyote (☎ 928-282-1842; 2575 W Hwy 89A) A dive bar with a few pool tables, this place is small and smoky and sometimes has live music.

Shopping

Shopping is a big draw in Sedona, and visitors will find everything from exclusive boutiques to T-shirt shops. Uptown along Hwy 89A is the place to go souvenir hunting. Just south of 89A on Hwy 179, **Tlaquepaque Village** (☎ 929-282-4838) is home to dozens of high-end art galleries. Across the street is **Crystal Castle** (☎ 928-282-5910); it's one of several stores selling New Age books and gifts. Continuing south, **Garland's Navajo Rugs** (☎ 928-282-4070; 411 Hwy 179) has the area's best selection of rugs, as well as other Native American crafts.

Getting There & Around

The **Sedona-Phoenix Shuttle** (☎ 928-282-2066, 800-448-7988; www.sedona-phoenix-shuttle.com; one-way/round-trip $40/65) runs between Phoenix Sky Harbor airport and Sedona eight times daily. It drops off and picks up at the Super 8 Motel (2545 W Hwy 89A). Call to make reservations. **Sedona Taxi Airporter & Tours** (☎ 928-282-5545) offers cab service to Flagstaff. **Greyhound** (☎ 800-229-9424; www.greyhound.com) stops in Camp Verde, about 30 minutes south of Sedona, and in Flagstaff, about 40 minutes north. **Bob's Taxi** (☎ 928-282-1234) offers local cab service. **Sedona Jeep & Car Rentals** (☎ 928-282-8700; www.sedonajeeprentals.com; 3009 W Hwy 89A) can outfit you with a jeep for backcountry exploration.

JEROME

pop 330 / elev 5400ft

Precariously perched on a steep hillside, Jerome is by far the most unique-looking small town in the region. The tiny place has a European feel, as if someone took a small French country village and transported it to the Arizona desert. The buildings are in various stages of decay. Some feature old weathered-wooden shop fronts, others are completely abandoned with rotting porches, boarded windows and peeling paint. Still others have been restored to their former glory, all tidy brick and veneered wood fronts with cheery signs. In short, Jerome is shabby chic and eclectically enticing. The landscape is barren but hauntingly beautiful. Old mine pits scar the distant red rock mesa and mountain views, but their presence only adds to the appeal. The air is fresh, the vibe un-touristy and altogether romantic. In fact, once you arrive, it's very hard to leave.

Rich in copper, gold and silver, this area was mined by Native Americans before Europeans took the land away. And Jerome retains as colorful a past as any Old West town. The first mine opened in 1876 and by the time it shut in 1952 it had produced enough copper to put 13 pounds a piece into the hands of every citizen in the world. During its late-1800s heyday, Jerome was known as the 'wickedest town in the west.' Two dozen saloons operated around-the-clock and gunfights and brawls were daily occurrences. The 1929 stock market crash brought the party to a screeching halt and many mines shut their shoots. When the

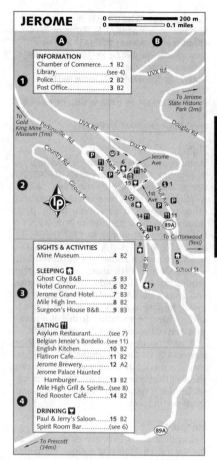

JEROME

0 _____ 200 m
0 _____ 0.1 miles

INFORMATION
Chamber of Commerce......1 B2
Library.........................(see 4)
Police.............................2 B2
Post Office......................3 B2

SIGHTS & ACTIVITIES
Mine Museum.....................4 B2

SLEEPING
Ghost City B&B..................5 B3
Hotel Connor.....................6 B2
Jerome Grand Hotel............7 B3
Mile High Inn....................8 B2
Surgeon's House B&B...........9 B3

EATING
Asylum Restaurant...........(see 7)
Belgian Jennie's Bordello..(see 11)
English Kitchen.................10 B2
Flatiron Cafe....................11 B2
Jerome Brewery................12 A2
Jerome Palace Haunted
    Hamburger..................13 B2
Mile High Grill & Spirits...(see 8)
Red Rooster Café...............14 B2

DRINKING
Paul & Jerry's Saloon........15 B2
Spirit Room Bar...............(see 6)

last closed, it looked like Jerome was fated to disappear into the desert dust.

Hope came in the form of hippies, artists and retirees in the late 1960s. Folks looking to live outside the mainstream, to escape the constraints of the Cold War, bought up the empty late-19th- and early-20th-century buildings and lovingly turned them into art galleries, souvenir shops, restaurants, saloons and even a few B&Bs. Many of the antique shops and art galleries feature unique high-quality pieces, and shopping here is a real joy.

Orientation & Information

To reach Jerome from Prescott follow Hwy 89A for 34 miles. This is the main drag through town. The drive is slow and windy and not recommended for large trailers.

Chamber of Commerce (☎ 928-634-2900; www .jeromechamber.com; Hull Ave; ☺ 10am-4pm summer) Offers tourist information.

Library (☎ 928-639-0574; 111 Jerome Ave) Free Internet access.

Police (☎ 928-634-8992; Main St) Inside the town hall building.

Post office (☎ 928-634-8241; 120 Main St)

Sights

If you're interested in Jerome's wild history, stop by the **Mine Museum** (☎ 928-634-5477; 200 Main St; adult/child $1/free; ☺ 9am-4:30pm), which displays old photos, documents, tools and other memorabilia pertaining to the past. Another must for the history buff is a visit to the **Jerome State Historic Park** (☎ 928-634-5381; adult/child $2.50/1; ☺ 8am-5pm). Two miles beyond Jerome en route to Cottonwood, it surrounds the 1916 mansion of colorful mining mogul 'Rawhide' Jimmy Douglas and gives a thorough understanding of the town's mining legacy. View models, exhibits and a video presentation inside the mansion and old mining equipment outside.

A mile north of town, the **Gold King Mine Museum** (☎ 928-634-0053; adult/child $4/2; ☺ 9am-5pm) is a miniature ghost town. Adults can check out antique mining equipment demos, while kids explore the walk-in mine and small petting zoo.

Sleeping

Accommodations here are as eccentric as the town itself, featuring antique flourishes and quaint decor.

Ghost City B&B (☎ 928-634-4678, 888-634-4678; www.ghostcityinn.com; 541 Main St; d from $80; ✖) In a crumbly old 1898 building, this is the kind of place that looks like it would have a resident ghost or two (you'll have to stay to find out!). It has a creaky front porch, a veranda with great views and a hot tub for relaxing. The four cheapest rooms share a bathroom, while two others have private facilities. All are unconventional, featuring either Victorian or early American furnishings. There's a full breakfast included and cookies on arrival.

Surgeon's House B&B (☎ 928-639-1452, 800-639-1452; 101 Hill St; r $100-150; ✖) Built in 1917 at the top of the town, this is a very funky looking place covered in gnarled old vines. The

three suites all come with great views (one has a huge picture window) and include full breakfast. The coolest asset is the back garden, with lounge chairs, fountains and even a beach motif. The garden is perched high on a hill with fabulous mesa views.

Jerome Grand Hotel (☎ 928-634-8200; www.jer omegrandhotel.com; 200 Hill St; r $95-145) Built as a hospital in 1926, the hotel is aging gracefully and remains full of charm. The original elevator still operates, and many of the 30 simple rooms have balconies and excellent views.

Mile High Inn (☎ 928-634-5094, 800-634-5094; 309 Main St; r $55-95) This place was remodeling when we stopped by, so prices could go up. The rooms are each decorated differently, one comes with a four-poster lodge pole bed; another sports cowboy memorabilia. One features 1940s-style Art Deco, while another features early-20th-century furnishings. The cheapest share a bathroom. There's a Victorian parlor with a fireplace made for unwinding.

Hotel Conner (☎ 928-634-5006, 800-523-3554; 164 Main St; r $75-125) This 1898 place has 10 restored bedrooms with period furniture. The hotel is over the popular Spirit Room Bar (opposite) with live music on weekends; rooms 1 to 4 get the worst (or best) of the bar noise.

Eating & Drinking

Asylum Restaurant (☎ 928-639-3197; 200 Hill St; dishes $10-20; ☺ lunch & dinner) Serving nouveau American fare at dinner and sandwiches at lunch, Asylum (inside the Jerome Grand Hotel) exudes atmosphere with deep-red walls, lazy fans, gilded artwork, jazz music and views, views, views. There's a very long wine list, including a decent selection of bubbly. The old hotel bar is the perfect place for a quiet drink.

Jerome Palace Haunted Hamburger (☎ 928-634-0554; 410 Clark St; dishes $6-13; ☺ breakfast, lunch & dinner) The glass-enclosed deck offers fantastic views, as does the cozy interior. The restaurant is perched high on a hill and serves a mix of burger and Mexican fare, along with pricier rib, steak and chicken dishes. There's a full bar with a long margarita and cocktail menu.

Red Rooster Café (☎ 928-634-7087; 363 Main St; dishes $5-10; ☺ lunch) A popular lunch spot, it serves soups, salads and sandwiches. The bright yellow walls and pressed-tin ceiling make it an inviting choice.

Belgian Jennie's Bordello (☎ 928-639-3141; 412 Main St; dishes $10-20; ☽ Wed-Sun; ☒) Pizzas, pastas and salads pack the menu. There are daily four-course dinner specials and the decor is Victorian-era. It doubles as a teahouse, with a large selection.

Jerome Brewery (☎ 928-634-8477; 111 Main St; dishes $7; ☽ lunch & dinner) They don't brew their own beer anymore (although the icy cold microbrews from across the country are altogether tasty), but it's a fun place for a sandwich or pizza – the food is quite good. Modern art on the walls and sturdy wood tables give it its cozy charm, and there's even an old foosball table to play on.

English Kitchen (☎ 928-634-2132; 119 Jerome Ave; dishes $5-8; ☽ breakfast & lunch) Meals have been served here since 1899, and it claims it's Arizona's oldest restaurant. Eat standard inexpensive breakfasts and lunches inside or on the outside deck. Day-trippers often pack the place.

Flatiron Cafe (☎ 928-634-2733; 416 Main St; dishes $3-8; ☽ breakfast & lunch) A tiny, cheery place with a large selection of coffees and pastries as well as interesting sandwiches made from the freshest ingredients.

Mile High Grill & Spirits (☎ 928-634-5094; 309 Main St; dishes $6-10) This casual restaurant serves American fare. Big greasy hangover-curing breakfasts and over-stacked sandwiches are the norm.

Spirit Room Bar (☎ 928-634-5006; 164 Main St) Under the Hotel Connor, this is the town's liveliest watering hole with live music on weekends. It's a dark and smoky old-time joint that takes you back a century or two.

Paul & Jerry's Saloon (☎ 928-634-2603; 206 Main St) Opened in 1899, it bills itself as the oldest saloon in Arizona. It's a low-key place for a drink with a pressed-tin ceiling, pool tables and a long wood bar. There's live music on weekends.

PRESCOTT

pop 40,200 / elev 5346ft

Untypical Arizona, Prescott doesn't quite fit the state persona. Sure it boasts Old West saloons, hotels and a historic Victorian-era downtown with a colorful history (think hard-core drinking, brothels and gunfights). But the shaded tree-lined square, European-style sidewalk cafés and strange, yet beautiful, landscape surrounding it defies the typecast. Founded by gold prospectors in 1864, Prescott, 60 miles north of Wickenburg, became Arizona's first territorial capital. President Abraham Lincoln preferred the progressive mining town to conservative Tucson, which he considered to have Confederate ties. Vestiges of early territorial life are found in Prescott's many historic buildings. And today its character, heritage, recreational opportunities, two colleges and small artists' community give the town a bohemian air that consistently wins over tourists.

Orientation & Information

Chamber of Commerce (☎ 928-445-2000, 800-266-7534; www.prescott.org; 117 W Goodwin St) Tourist office.

Library (☎ 928-445-8110; 215 E Goodwin St) Free Internet.

Main post office (☎ 928-778-1890; 442 Miller Valley Rd)

Medical Center (☎ 928-445-2700; 1003 Willow Creek Rd)

Police (☎ 928-778-1444; 222 S Marina St)

Prescott National Forest office (☎ 928-771-4700; 344 S Cortez St) Info on camping, hiking and more in the national forest.

Sights & Activities

Montezuma St west of Courthouse Plaza was once the infamous **Whiskey Row**, with 40 drinking establishments serving thirsty cowboys and miners. A devastating 1900 fire destroyed 25 saloons, five hotels and the red-light district, but many early buildings remain and you can still finish a bottle on colorful Whiskey Row.

The **Sharlot Hall Museum** (☎ 928-445-3122; www.sharlot.org; 415 W Gurley St; suggested donation $5; ☽ 10am-5pm Mon-Sat, 1-5pm Sun) is Prescott's most important museum. It displays historical artifacts and old photographs. See the boxed text (p177) for more on the woman behind the museum.

The Prescott National Forest office (above) offers suggestions on hikes, climbs, picnic areas and fishing holes. Local lakes are stocked with trout, bluegill, bass and catfish. **Thumb Butte Lake** (Gurley & Thumb Butte Rds) is a fishing spot 3 miles from town. **Lynx Lake**, 4 miles east on Hwy 69 then 3 miles south on Walker Rd, offers fishing, hiking, camping and small-boat rental (summer only).

The **Granite Mountain Wilderness** attracts rock climbers in the warmer months. It also has a fishing lake, campgrounds and hiking trails. To reach it bear left on Iron Springs Rd from Grove Ave downtown then turn right on unpaved USFS Rd 347 and continue another 4 miles. To ride the rocks or cruise through the forest, visit **Ironclad Bicycles** (☎ 928-776-1755; 710 White Spar Rd; rentals from $20), which rents mountain bikes. For horseback riding try **Granite Mountain Stables** (☎ 928-771-9551; 2400 Shane Dr; rides from $35), about 10 miles northwest of town.

Sleeping

Rates on summer weekends are much higher than weekdays or during the off-season. Chain and independent motels are found on Gurley and Montezuma Sts on the outskirts of town. Rooms start at $40 a night, but make sure the heating or air-con work before taking one.

Hassayampa Inn (☎ 928-778-9434, 800-322-1927; www.hassayampainn.com; 122 E Gurley St; r $100-200) One of Arizona's most elegant hotels when it opened in 1927, today the restored inn has a vintage hand-operated elevator, many original furnishings, hand-painted wall decorations and a lovely dining room. The 68 rooms vary, but all include decent linens and sturdy dark-wood furniture. The cheapest are on the smallish side, while the most expensive come with spa tubs. A full breakfast and evening cocktail are included.

Hotel Vendome (☎ 928-776-0900, 888-463-3583; www.vendomehotel.com; 230 S Cortez St; d from $80) With charm dating back to 1917, this his-

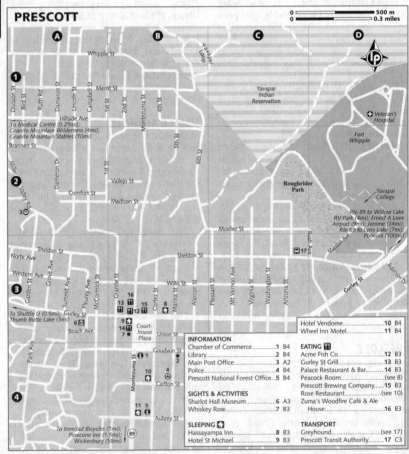

INFORMATION				TRANSPORT	
Chamber of Commerce	1 B4				
Library	2 B4				
Main Post Office	3 A2				
Police	4 B4				
Prescott National Forest Office	5 B4				

SIGHTS & ACTIVITIES		
Sharlot Hall Museum	6 A3	
Whiskey Row	7 B3	

SLEEPING		
Hassayampa Inn	8 B3	
Hotel St Michael	9 B3	

Hotel Vendome	10	B4
Wheel Inn Motel	11	B4

EATING		
Acme Fish Co	12	B3
Gurley St Grill	13	B3
Palace Restaurant & Bar	14	B3
Peacock Room	(see 8)	
Prescott Brewing Company	15	B3
Rose Restaurant	(see 10)	
Zuma's Woodfire Café & Ale House	16	B3

TRANSPORT		
Greyhound	(see 17)	
Prescott Transit Authority	17	C3

toric hotel features quaint, homey rooms with quilts. Try for the room with the sunset tub. The hosts are friendly and the cozy wooden bar is an inviting place for a drink.

Hotel St Michael (☎ 928-776-1999, 800-678-3757; 205 W Gurley St; r from $59) You're paying for location at this popular hotel on the edge of Whiskey Row. Rebuilt in 1900, the 72 older but clean rooms are nothing special, featuring mismatched furniture and thin sheets. Rates include a continental breakfast.

Wheel Inn Motel (☎ 928-778-7346, 800-717-0902; 333 S Montezuma St; r from $40) Convenient to Whiskey Row and downtown, rooms are ordinary no-frills affairs with microwaves, large baths and porches.

Willow Lake RV Park (☎ 928-445-6311; Willow Lake Rd; camp/RV sites $14/20; ☀) Offering 170 RV sites with hookups and 30 places to pitch a tent, as well as showers, a playground and coin laundry, this is a popular place. It's located 4 miles north of town off Hwy 89 (turn west on Willow Lake Rd).

Eating & Drinking

Peacock Room (☎ 928-778-9434; Hassayampa Inn, 122 E Gurley St; dishes $10-20; ☾ lunch & dinner) Serving cocktails and a wide range of American cuisine, this is a highly recommended and elegant dining spot that sometimes showcases live music.

Rose Restaurant (☎ 928-777-8308; 235 S Cortez St; dishes from $20; ☾ dinner Wed-Sun) This tiny restaurant features Prescott's most celebrated

chef. Seafood, meat and pasta make up the menu and the place is as gourmet as it comes in town. Reservations recommended.

Prescott Brewing Company (☎ 928-771-2795; 130 Gurley St; dishes $7-20; ☾ lunch & dinner) Very crowded with a large bar and a separate dining room, it features its own microbrews and beers from around the world. A charismatic place, serving decent English- and American-style pub food, the bar walls are plastered with beer labels. happy hour, from 4pm to 6pm and 10pm to close, sees $2 pints, $3 tacos, 20¢ wings and half-price appetizers. Not a bad deal.

Palace Restaurant & Bar (☎ 928-541-1996; 120 S Montezuma St; dishes $8-20; ☾ lunch & dinner) Step through the swinging carved wooden doors and back in time at this old-fashioned place (check out their pressed-tin ceilings and tiled bathrooms). It's big, airy and classy. Waitstaff in late-19th-century garb serve tasty lunches and hearty dinners that are heavy on the steak. It's worth a bite.

Zuma's Woodfire Café & Ale House (☎ 928-541-1400; 124 N Montezuma St; dishes $10-20; ☾ lunch & dinner) A funky and quite cozy spot, this place serves wood-fired pizzas, decent Italian food and an above-average selection of libations (the margaritas are sure to get you drunk). Happy hour runs from 4pm to 6pm Tuesday to Friday and features $2.50 beer and wine, half-price appetizers and $5 pizzas. When it's warm, dine on the outdoor patio.

Pinecone Inn (☎ 928-445-2970; 1245 White Spar Rd; dishes from $8) Prescottians drive out from

ARIZONA

SHARLOT HALL

Twelve-year-old Sharlot Mabrith Hall arrived in Prescott in February 1882 after an arduous horseback trip from Kansas with her family. During the journey she was thrown by her horse, causing a back injury that plagued her for the rest of her life.

While helping run her family's ranch, she became fascinated with life on the frontier. Largely self-schooled, she began describing the gold miners, Native Americans and ranchers around her in a series of stories and poems that soon gained local admiration. In 1909 she was appointed Territorial Historian, the first woman to hold a political office in Arizona.

In 1924 she traveled to Washington, DC, to represent Arizona in the Electoral College. She caused a stir in the capital with her outfit that included a copper mesh coat provided by a local mine. There was no mistaking that Arizona was the 'Copper State.' During her visit to the east, she toured several museums; these inspired her to found a museum of Arizona history.

On her return to Prescott, Hall leased the first territorial capitol building and restored the governor's mansion. In 1928, she moved her extensive personal collection of historical artifacts into the mansion and opened it as a museum. She lived on the property, expanding and adding to the collection until her death in 1943. The museum bearing her name (p175) has continued to flourish since then. In 1981, Sharlot Hall was elected to the Arizona Women's Hall of Fame.

town to enjoy the large breakfasts and tasty American lunches and dinners. There's frequent live music and dancing. It's a good spot for a change of pace.

Gurley St Grill (☎ 928-445-3388; 230 W Gurley St; dishes $9-12) This popular place has an industrial decor featuring exposed pipe. The menu is burger, sandwich, pasta, pizza and salad oriented.

Acme Fish Co (☎ 928-541-0221; 220 Gurley St; dishes $9-20; ☺ lunch & dinner) With a fish motif throughout (what else would you expect?), this place serves fish (of course) along with sandwiches and salads. Happy hour, from 4pm to 7pm, features a raw bar with $1 oysters and peel-and-eat shrimp for $5 a pound.

Getting There & Away

America West (☎ 800-235-9292) flies daily to Phoenix from Prescott's Ernest A Love airport, located 9 miles north of town on Hwy 89.

Prescott Transit Authority/Greyhound (☎ 928-445-5470, 800-445-7978; 820 E Sheldon St) has buses to Phoenix ($24, 2½ hours, 13 daily) and Flagstaff ($22, 1½ hours, daily). **Shuttle U** (☎ 800-304-6114; www.shuttleu.com; 1505 W Gurley St) runs several vans a day ($26, 2½ hours) to Phoenix airport.

WICKENBURG

pop 5080 / elev 2093ft

In the 1860s Wickenburg was a thriving community surrounded by gold mines. Today the main draw is several dude ranches offering cowboy-style vacations from fall to spring. Coming from the north, Wickenburg is a real change in climate. Casual visitors will be greeted with Western buildings constructed between the 1860s and the 1920s, cacti, palms and big blue skies.

The **chamber of commerce** (☎ 928-684-5479, 800-942-5242; www.wickenburgchamber.com; 216 N Frontier St) offers info and walking maps. The friendly **library** (☎ 928-684-2665; 160 N Valentine St) has free Internet.

The 1863 **Trinidad House** is said to be Arizona's oldest home. Locals like to point out the 19th-century **Jail Tree**, where outlaws were chained in the late-1800s.

Those hoping to strike it rich, especially kids, will enjoy a visit to the **Vulture Mine** (☎ 928-859-2743; Vulture Mine Rd; adult/child $7/5; ☺ 8am-4pm). Henry Wickenburg found gold

nuggets lying on the ground here in 1863. Today you can rent a gold pan ($4) and look for treasure. To reach the mine take US 60 west out of town and turn left on Vulture Mine Rd, from here it's 12 miles.

If you'd rather explore the backcountry, **BC Jeep Tours** (☎ 928-684-7901; www.bcjeeptours.com; 295 E Wickenburg Way; tours from $50) offers a variety of tours from 1½ hours to three hours.

Sleeping & Eating

Wickenburg's guest ranches usually close in summer. During the cooler months they offer all-inclusive packages that include horseback riding, meals and other activities. Rates depend on occupancy, dates, rooms and activities.

Flying E Ranch (☎ 928-684-2690; www.flyingeranch .com; 2801 W Wickenburg Way; r from $250; ☺ Nov-Apr; ☒) A down-home working cattle ranch set on 20,000 beautiful acres. It's particularly appealing to families, and sees a lot of repeat business. Rooms are Western themed and the price includes activities and three hearty meals a day. There's no bar, so you'll need to bring your own liquor.

Rancho de los Caballeros (☎ 928-684-5484; www .sunc.com; 1551 S Vulture Mine Rd; r from $370; ☺ mid-Oct–mid-May; ☒) It feels a bit more like an exclusive resort than a dude ranch, but this place is very popular nonetheless. The focus here is on relaxation and golf, although there is also horseback riding. Rates include all meals, but you'll pay extra for golfing and riding. The main lodge is a joy, with a flagstone floor, colorfully painted furniture and copper fireplace. Rooms feature Indian rugs, handcrafted furniture and exposed-beam ceilings. Dinner is a formal affair, and you'll need to dress accordingly. There's live cowboy music in the saloon at night.

Los Viajeros (☎ 928-684-7099; 1000 N Tegner St; r from $80; ☒) If you just want to spend the night try Los Viajeros, which offers simple but large rooms with nicer-than-usual motel furniture (it's made of matching pale-colored wood). There's a table and chairs, fridge, patio and calming stucco walls.

Rancho 7 Restaurant (☎ 928-684-2492; 111 E Wickenburg Way; dishes $10-20) Locally popular for decades, Rancho 7 features home-style American and Mexican cooking. Play darts, pool and shuffleboard in the adjoining bar.

Pony Espresso (☎ 928-684-0208; 223 E Wickenburg Way; dishes $5; ☺ breakfast, lunch & dinner) Superb for an afternoon sandwich, coffee or ice-cream cone. It's a funky little coffeeshop with red walls, comfy couches and lots of books and chess tables.

House of Berlin (☎ 928-684-5004; 169 E Wickenburg Way; dishes $12-15; ☯ lunch & dinner) Perfect if you're just itching for German haute cuisine. Delicious smells waft out. The menu is heavy on the Wiener schnitzel.

Sangini's Pizza (☎ 928-684-7828; 107 E Wickenburg Way; dishes $8-17; ☯ lunch & dinner) A meal here is a strange dining experience. There's an Italian motif with fountains, wine bottles and bright walls on a bleak floor amid cheap tables. But the food's not half bad.

Getting There & Away
Wickenburg is one hour northwest of Phoenix off US 60. There is no public transport to the town.

PAYSON & AROUND
pop 14,800 / elev 5000ft
Payson's nearly perfect climate (coolish summers and not too cold winters) has made the town a popular retirement spot. Just 94 miles north of Phoenix, it attracts Phoenicians by the thousands hoping to seek relief from stifling summer heat. Founded by gold miners in 1882, Payson was once a ranching and logging center but today considers tourism its main draw. The main drags are a curious, but unappealing, mix of strip malls and antique shops. However, the surrounding Tonto National Forest provides numerous opportunities for hiking, swimming, fishing and hunting and is the reason to visit.

Hwy 87, the Beeline Hwy, connects Payson to Phoenix and you'll find many businesses along it. Contact the **Rim Country Regional Chamber of Commerce** (☎ 928-474-4515; www.rimcountrychamber.com; 100 W Main St) and the **Tonto National Forest Payson Ranger Station** (☎ 928-474-7900; 1009 E Hwy 260) for regional information.

The **Tonto Natural Bridge State Park** (☎ 928-476-4202; per vehicle $6; ☯ 8am-6pm May-Sep, 9am-5pm Oct-Apr) is the area's biggest tourist attraction. The largest travertine bridge in the world, it spans a 150ft-wide canyon and measures over 400ft in width. Formed from calcium carbonate deposited over the years by mineral-laden spring waters, the bridge actually resembles a tunnel more than a freestanding arch. The park offers hiking opportunities under, over and around the bridge. To reach the park, take Hwy 87 north for 11 miles and look for the turn-off.

For something different, try hiking in the forests surrounding Payson in the company of llamas, which carry your gear. **Fossil Creek Llamas** (☎ 928-476-5178; www.fossilcreekllamas.com; hikes from $40) offers two-hour to all-day llama treks. The place also offers wellness courses and retreats, and for something different you can sleep in a teepee B&B.

Sleeping & Eating
Majestic Mountain Inn (☎ 928-474-0185, 800-408-2442; www.majesticmountaininn.com; 602 E Hwy 260; r $80-130; ☒) Set in landscaped lawns amid pines, this is the best option in town. A modern place built to resemble an attractive mountain lodge, it features a large stone chimney and fireplace in the lobby. Deluxe rooms have fireplaces of their own, and luxury units include double whirlpool tubs facing the fireplace.

Rim Country Inn (☎ 928-474-4526; 101 W Phoenix; r from $60) One of the nicest cheaper places, offering basic and clean rooms.

Ponderosa (campsites $12) There are several developed USFS campsites, with drinking water but no showers along Hwy 260 east of Payson. Try Ponderosa, 15 miles east.

Cucina Paradiso (☎ 928-468-6500; 500 N Hwy 87; dishes $7-15; ☯ lunch & dinner) It's not a fancy place, but the food here is the best in town. Italian is the genre and calamari the specialty of the house. Try the calamari Caesar salad or the spicy calamari *fra diavolo*.

NAVAJO & HOPI RESERVATIONS

Some of Arizona's most beautiful and photogenic landscapes lie in the northeastern corner of the state. Between the fabulous buttes of Monument Valley Navajo Tribal Park on the Utah state border and the fossilized logs of the Petrified Forest National Park are lands locked in ancient history. Here, mesas are topped by some of the oldest continuously inhabited villages on the continent. Traditional and modernized Navajo hogans dot the landscape that's also nestled with Hopi kivas (ceremonial spaces).

ARIZONA

ARIZONA

Native Americans have inhabited the region for centuries; it is known today as the Navajo and Hopi Reservations. The story of these Native Americans is as tragic as it is hopeful. Pushed off their land by pioneering settlers, thousands were slaughtered before the government relocated them to the harsh landscape on which they now reside. Poverty, depression and alcoholism ravished communities in the 20th century, and these problems continue today. Somehow, however, these hearty people managed to survive and even forgive humanity's nastiest prejudices, personal intrusions and brutality. Today, many are fiercely proud and patriotic citizens. Both tribes have turned to tourism for survival, and tourists come in droves to witness tribal dances and purchase fine crafts – from turquoise jewelry to Hopi kachina dolls and Navajo rugs.

At 27,0000 sq miles the Navajo Reservation is the country's largest, spilling over into the neighboring states of Utah, Colorado and New Mexico. It's the biggest reservation, partly because its harsh landscape didn't seem to offer much when reservations were doled out. The 2410-sq-mile Hopi Reservation inhabits the tops of three mesas and is completely surrounded by the Navajo Reservation.

Tribal laws take precedence over state laws, although both tribes accept federal laws. The sale or consumption of alcohol is strictly forbidden on Navajo and Hopi land, as are other drugs. Both tribes maintain their own police forces, and if you're caught doing something illegal, you'll have to go through their justice system (it's almost like being in a foreign country). When visiting a Native American reservation, please be respectful and keep in mind certain rules of etiquette. Many tribes ban all forms of recording, be it photography, videotaping or drawing. Others permit these activities if you pay a certain fee, and others still allow them only in certain places or at certain times. Ask permission before taking any pictures, recordings or videos. Kivas are always off-limits to visitors. Ceremonials and powwows are religious events; many do not have a fixed date and are arranged a couple of weeks ahead of time. The Navajo Tourism Office can inform you of upcoming public events. Do not applaud, chat or ask questions during ceremonials and powwows. Activities such as camping, fishing, hunting and backpacking require tribal permits – be sure to get the appropriate permits before engaging in any activities. When in doubt, ask. Also see p466.

NAVAJO RESERVATION
pop 88,000

The wounds are slowly healing but the scars remain, a searing testament to the nastiest, most embarrassing part of US history (p30). From the rusting trailers and social services buildings in small nowhere towns to the hand-made roadside signs promising handicrafts sold by 'Friendly Indians,' the evidence of hard times is everywhere, as innocuous as the copper sand that lines the desolate highways.

At times the Navajo Nation resembles a barren wasteland. But somewhere amid all the nothingness is some of North America's most spectacular scenery. Monument Valley's eye-catching fiery red buttes and twisty spindles are awe-inspiring. Canyon de Chelly and Navajo National Monuments, dotted with ancient abandoned pueblos, are hauntingly beautiful.

A visit to the reservation is more than just personally rewarding. The Navajo rely on tourist dollars to survive; help to keep their heritage alive by choosing to stay on reservation land or purchasing their world-renowned crafts.

Over half of the approximately 175,000 members of the Navajo Nation live on the reservation. About one in seven Native Americans in the USA are Navajo, making it the country's largest tribe.

The Navajo Reservation, unlike Arizona, observes mountain daylight-saving time: during summer, the reservation is one hour ahead of Arizona; on the same time as Utah and New Mexico.

Window Rock
pop 3500 / elev 6900ft

The tribal capital is at Window Rock, a bustling little place at the intersection of Hwys 264 and 12. Most businesses are clustered around the FedMart shopping plaza, within a few hundred yards of each other. Information about the whole Reservation is available from the **Navajo Tourism Office** (☎ 928-871-6436; www.navajo.org) in the center of town.

Backcountry use (including camping) anywhere on the Navajo Reservation requires a permit. Pick one up at the **Navajo Parks & Recreation Department** (☎ 928-871-6647; 36A E Hwy 264). Permits cost $5 per person for backcountry hiking. If you want to camp it's another $5 per person. The office is at the junction of Hwy 264 and Rte 12, next to the Zoo & Botanical Park on the east side of Window Rock. Note that the campgrounds mentioned in this chapter are not considered 'backcountry' and don't require a tribal permit.

The **Navajo Nation Museum & Library** (☎ 928-871-7941; cnr Hwy 264 & Post Office Loop Rd; admission free; ☻ 8am-5pm Mon, Tue & Thu-Sat, to 8pm Wed) features permanent collections, changing shows and the tribal library. A gift shop has an excellent selection of books about the Navajo and other tribes.

During tribal council sessions you can hear the 88 elected council delegates representing 110 Navajo chapters (communities) discussing issues in the Navajo language at the **Navajo Nation Council Chambers** (☎ 928-871-6417). Full council sessions are held at least four times a year, usually on the third Monday of January, April, July and October. At other times visitors can tour the chambers' colorful murals. The chambers are located north of town, below the Window Rock Arch for which the town was named.

The **Annual Navajo Nation Fair**, held for several days in early September, is one of the world's largest Native American events and features an intertribal powwow, Indian rodeo, traditional song and dance displays and competitions, and a barbecue with Navajo food.

ARIZONA

NAVAJO WEAVING

The Navajo are the best-known rug-weavers of the Native American tribes. A Navajo rug requires many months of labor and can involve several family members. Children tend the sheep, and various people participate in shearing, washing, carding, spinning and dyeing the wool before it even touches the loom. All is done by hand. The loom is a simple upright wooden frame, and the designs and colors are passed down from generation to generation, usually to the women. Legend has it that Spider Woman taught the women how to weave. You can watch weavers at work at some museums and trading posts; the Hubbell Trading Post (p182) at Ganado is a good place for this.

Navajo weavings were originally heavy blankets used in winter. When Anglos became interested in the work as a folk craft, they found that the origin of the rug could be recognized by its various designs and colors. For instance, a Ganado Red was a rug with a red background coming from the settlement of Ganado. Rugs with geometrical designs in earth colors bordered by black were from the Two Grey Hills region from the eastern part of Navajo lands. And the Shiprock area was known for Yei rugs, depicting supernatural beings revered by the Navajo. Several other regional styles can easily be detected with a little experience.

Today, weavers from any part of the Reservation can produce designs that were once specific to a particular area. While traditionally the designs have been geometric, some weavers currently use figurative designs. Such rugs are technically as valuable as the traditional ones.

Tips on Buying a Rug

Whether used as a floor covering or displayed on a wall, a good quality rug can last a lifetime. Given the cost of purchasing a good quality rug, buying one is not for the average souvenir-seeker. It can take months of research, or can be bought on a whim if you see one you really love. If you're a more cautious shopper, visit museums, trading posts and crafts stores in Indian country. Talk to weavers, exhibitors and traders to learn about the various designs. Don't just look at the rugs – feel them. A good rug will be tightly woven and have an even width. Prices of rugs vary from the low hundreds to thousands of dollars. This reflects the size of the rug, the weeks of work involved, the skill of the weaver and whether the yarn is store-bought or hand-spun.

Be aware that cheap imitation rugs are available. These may look nice, but they aren't handmade by Navajos. Some are mass-produced in Mexico using Navajo designs. The staff at a reputable store can show you the difference.

Rooms at the **Navajo Nation Inn** (☎ 928-871-4108; www.navajonationinn.com; Hwy 264; r from $70; 🖥), east of Hwy 12, feature Southwestern motifs. They're comfortable, but could do with a little fixing up. The place has a reasonably priced restaurant serving Navajo and American fare breakfast, lunch and dinner. If you'd rather stay at a chain motel, the **Days Inn** (☎ 928-871-5690; Hwy 264; r from $70; 🐾) features clean, nondescript digs along with an indoor pool, sauna and exercise room.

Window Rock is the headquarters of the Navajo Arts and Crafts Enterprise (NACE), which runs a **jewelry and crafts store** (☎ 928-871-4090; Hwy 264) next to the Navajo Nation Inn. The NACE was established in 1941 and is wholly Navajo operated. It guarantees the authenticity and quality of its products.

The **Navajo Transit System** (☎ 928-729-4002) runs buses from Window Rock to Gallup, New Mexico ($2.50 one hour, four daily Monday to Saturday) and Tuba City ($13, four hours, daily Monday to Friday), via the Hopi Reservation.

Hubbell Trading Post National Historic Site

Widely respected by Native Americans and Anglos alike for his honesty and passion for excellence, John Lorenzo Hubbell established this **trading post** (☎ 928-755-3475; admission free; 🕒 8am-6pm May-Sep, 8am-5pm Oct-Apr) at Ganado, 30 miles west of Window Rock, in 1878 and worked there until his death in 1930. The NPS operates the post today, and it looks much as it would have a century ago. It continues to sell local crafts, specializing in top-quality Navajo weavings worth thousands of dollars. Navajo women often give weaving demonstrations inside the visitor center, and rangers are on hand to answer questions. Tours of Hubbell's house, with a superb collection of early Navajo rugs and period furniture, are given several times a day.

Canyon De Chelly National Monument

This many-fingered canyon contains several beautiful historically significant Ancestral Puebloan (p27) sites. Families still farm the land, wintering on the canyon rims then moving to hogans on the canyon floor in spring and summer. The canyon is private Navajo property administered by the NPS.

Only enter hogans with a guide and don't take photographs without permission.

The canyon begins near the village of **Chinle**, where you'll find the **visitor center** (☎ 928-674-5500; 🕒 8am-5pm), which has information on guides and tours. The canyon walls start at just a few feet but rise dramatically, topping out at about 1000ft. Several side canyons connect with the canyon's two main arms, creating a maze-like effect.

For a great **scenic drive**, take the paved road that follows the southernmost and northernmost rims of the canyon complex. It affords excellent views of the splendid scenery below. It you look closely you'll see uninhabited pueblos scattered inside the canyon walls. Only rough tracks enter the canyon, so you need a 4WD. With your own vehicle you can hire a guide for $15 an hour (one guide can accompany up to five vehicles; three-hour minimum). Most of the bottom of the canyon is off-limits to visitors unless on a **guided hike** ($15, 4½hr, twice daily May-Sep). Find out more at the visitor center. The exception is a trail to the **White House**, a pueblo dating back to AD 1040. The trailhead is 6 miles east of the visitor center and makes for a pleasant

---

THE NAVAJO LANGUAGE

Navajo belongs to the Athapaskan language family, a group of languages that also includes Apache. Other tribes speaking Athapaskan languages live in Alaska, northwest Canada and coastal Oregon and California. The distribution of these tribes is considered as evidence of migration patterns across the continent.

Some Navajo, especially the elders, speak only the Navajo language, but most speak both Navajo and English. All members of the tribe have a deep respect for the Navajo language whether they are fluent or not.

Navajo and English have very different sentence structures and Navajo is not an easy language for outsiders to learn. During WWII, the Navajo Code Talkers spoke a code based on Navajo for US military radio transmissions. The code was never broken. The Code Talkers are now famous for their wartime contribution and the remaining members of this unit are frequently honored at tribal functions.

hike. **Justin Tso's Horseback Tours** (☎ 928-674-5678), near the visitor center, has horses available year-round for $10 per person per hour, plus $10 an hour for the guide.

Near the visitor center, **Cottonwood Campground** has 96 free sites on a first-come, first-served basis. There is water but no hookups or showers. Camping here is very popular, so in summer get there early.

A more remote option is the Navajo-run **Spider Rock Campground** (☎ 928-674-8261; campsites $10), 10 miles east of the visitor center along South Rim Drive. Surrounded by piñon and juniper trees, it offers peaceful respite from summer crowds. There is no water or electricity, but the owner sells bottled water and provides lanterns.

Featuring comfortable rooms of varying size, the **Thunderbird Lodge** (☎ 928-674-5841, 800-679-2473; www.tbirdlodge.com; d $100-150) is an attractive place. Try for a room in the old lodge, built in the late 1800s. An inexpensive cafeteria serves tasty Navajo and American food. Rates drop in winter.

Other options:

Holiday Inn (☎ 928-674-5000; www.holidayinnchinle .com; r $100-120; 🏊) Half a mile west of the visitor center. Restaurant and modern rooms.

Best Western Canyon de Chelly Inn (☎ 928-674-5875; www.canyondechelly.com; r $80-140; 🏊) In Chinle, just east of Hwy 191. Indoor pool, inexpensive restaurant.

Four Corners Navajo Tribal Park

Put a foot into Arizona and plant the other in New Mexico. Slap a hand down in Utah and place the other in Colorado. Now wiggle your butt for the camera, everyone's doing it! This is the only place in the USA where four states come together at one point, although you'll have to cough up a $3 admission fee if you want to say 'done it'. Flags and a slab mark the site, and vendors sell Native American souvenirs, crafts and food. It's all a bit cheesy, but you're coming for the photo after all!

There's a small **visitor center** (☎ 928-871-6647; www.navajonationparks.org; 🕐 7am-7pm, shorter in winter), picnic tables and toilets, but no water.

Kayenta & Around
pop 4500 / elev 5641ft
It's big country out here. Skies and barren land stretch out in all directions, and the air reeks of desolate isolation. If you're alone it's either slightly depressing or altogether exhilarating, depending on your persona. Established as a trading post in 1908, the area around Kayenta serves as a good lodging base for exploring stupendous Monument Valley, 24 miles away. The town's made news in recent decades for supplementing tourism with strong (and controversial) uranium- and coal-mining industries.

Roland's Navajoland Tours (☎ 928-697-3524) and **Sacred Monument Tours** (☎ 435-727-3218; www .monumentvalley.net) offer vehicle, hiking and horseback riding tours through Monument Valley. These last anywhere from two hours to overnight trips and start at around $60 per person. Call the company to see when tours are running (times vary depending on how many people have booked) and to arrange pick-up.

Pricey chain motels, scattered around the junction of Hwys 160 and 163, are your main lodging options. The **Holiday Inn** (☎ 928-697-3221; junction Hwys 160 & 163; r $80-150; 🏊) is a good bet. The Reservation's largest hotel, it has a kids' pool and a decent restaurant.

The **Anasazi Inn** (☎ 928-697-3793; Hwy 160; r $40-80) is about 10 miles west of Kayenta on Hwy 160. Rooms are simple and slightly shabby with wood paneling. The 24-hour restaurant serves cheap and tasty Navajo tacos and American fare. Prices vary according to the season.

The **Golden Sands Cafe** (☎ 928-697-3684; Hwy 163; dishes $4-10) serves American and Navajo food in casual environs. It's 1.5 miles north of Hwy 160 from Kayenta. The nearby **Amigo Cafe** (☎ 928-697-8448; Hwy 163; dishes $5-8) does Mexican.

About 70 miles east of Kayenta on Hwy 160, way out in the middle of nowhere, you'll find the village of Teec Nos Pos and the **Navajo Trails Motel** (☎ 928-674-3618; r $49). Rooms are basic, but it's the cheapest hotel in Navajoland. Rates drop even more in winter.

Navajo National Monument
The Ancestral Puebloan sites (p27) of Betatkin and Keet Seel are open to the public, exceptionally well preserved and altogether impressive. Due to the effort it takes to reach them (it's a 5-mile round-trip hike to Betatkin and a 17-mile round-trip slog to Keet Seel), the sites don't attract busloads of tourists. If you're looking to mix hiking

ARIZONA

with history and view ruins in relative solitude, a trip to the **Navajo National Monument** (☎ 928-672-2700; Hwy 564; admission free; ☺ 8am-5pm late-May–Sep) should not be missed.

Daily hiking permits are free, but limited. Call to reserve one in advance or stop at the visitor center, 9 miles north of Hwy 160 along Hwy 564. Both sites can only be visited on ranger-guided tours. Trips to Betatkin depart from the visitor center at 9am and last five hours. The 900ft drop means the return can be strenuous, so carry plenty of water.

You're on your own for the sometimes grueling 8.5-mile hike to Keet Seel, one of the Southwest's largest and best-preserved ancient pueblos. Once there you'll need to check in at the ranger station, as a ranger must accompany you into the site. Visitation is limited to 20 people per day, five people at a time, so there could be a wait. Entrance requires using a very long ladder, so it's not for people afraid of heights. Although the 17-mile round-trip can be done in a day, most visitors backpack in and stay at the primitive **campsite**. There's no drinking water, so carry your own. Camping is limited to one night and fires are prohibited. The 20 daily permits are free, but often taken early. Call ahead to reserve. There's a second free campground, with 31 first-come, first-served sites and water, at the visitor center.

Tuba City

pop 7300 / elev 4936ft

A small outpost in nowhere land, at the intersection of Hwys 160 and 264, Tuba City is technically the largest town in the western half of the Navajo Reservation. You wouldn't guess as much driving through. It's a down-and-out looking place trying hard to revitalize itself, but tough times are evident everywhere. The brand spanking new motel stands in stark contrast to the decrepit trailers and fast-food joints. A trip down the main drag yields an aging social-services building and large detention center. But the place feels real, and business owners make an extra effort to please.

The **Tuba Trading Post** (☎ 928-283-4545; cnr Main St & Moenave Ave) dates back to the 1880s and sells authentic Indian arts and crafts, as well as food. The adjacent 80-room **Quality Inn** (☎ 928-283-4545, 800-644-8383; cnr Main St & Moenave Ave; r $75-130) is upmarket and well maintained. On its premises is the **Hogan Restaurant** (☎ 928-283-5260; dishes $6-10), which serves Southwestern, Navajo and American fare.

The Navajo-run **Diné Inn Motel** (☎ 928-283-6107; Hwy 160 at Peshlakai Ave; r $40-70; ☒) looks brand new. The rooms are spotless with modern furniture, quality linens and a fridge and microwave.

DETOUR: MONUMENT VALLEY NAVAJO TRIBAL PARK

If the scenery here feels like serious déjà vu, it's probably because you've seen it a hundred times before. Like a classic movie star, Monument Valley has a face known round the world. Only the Grand Canyon is more famous. Her fiery red spindles and grand buttes have starred in movies and commercials, and featured in magazines and picture books. You might not know her name, but you've likely seen her photo framed on your neighbor's wall.

Like an ingenue in a sea of nondescript faces, Monument Valley's beauty is heightened by the drab landscape surrounding it. One minute you're in the middle of nowhere, just sand and rocks and endless sky, then suddenly you're transported to a fantasyland of crimson sandstone towers. It's a surreal experience not to be missed.

There are great views to be had from the **scenic drive** along Hwy 163, but to really get up close and personal, you'll need to visit the **Monument Valley Navajo Tribal Park** (☎ 435-727-3287; admission per person $5; ☺ 7am-7pm May-Sep, 8am-4:30pm Oct-Apr). Most of the park is in Arizona, but the area code is for Utah where there are more sights (p286). A 4-mile paved road leads to a visitor center with information, exhibits, a restaurant and tour companies. From the visitor center, a rough unpaved loop road covers 17 miles of stunning valley views. You can drive it in your own vehicle (ordinary cars can just get by) or take a **tour** ($30, 2½ hr). The advantage here is tours enter areas that private vehicles can't, and the money goes back into the community. Tours leave frequently in summer, less so in winter, inquire at the visitor center. If you want to play John Wayne in your own Western, take a **horseback ride** ($30). There's nothing quite like seeing the valley from the back of a horse. To sign up, head to the visitor center.

Kate's Café (☎ 928-283-6773; cnr Main St & Edgewater Dr; dishes $3-10) is a popular diner in an adobe building. It serves very cheap seafood, steak and pasta plates at dinner, features a large breakfast menu and lots of sandwich selections at lunch.

HOPI RESERVATION
pop 11,000 / elev 7200ft

Arizona's oldest and most traditional tribe, the Hopi have continuously inhabited three mesas in the high deserts of northeastern Arizona for centuries. Deeply religious and agricultural, they revere privacy and would just as soon be left alone to celebrate their cycle of life on the mesa tops. Because of their isolated location, they have received less outside influence than other tribes and have limited facilities for tourism.

Dance plays an integral role in Hopi life. Part of a ceremonial cycle, the dances are expressions of prayer and performed to create harmony with nature. If you are offered a chance to witness a Hopi dance, take it. Most of the annual ceremonies were closed to the non–Native American public in 1992. This was in part due to the private, sacred nature of the dances, and in part because the remote location did not have the infrastructure to support scores of visitors. Each individual village determines the attendance of non–Native American visitors at dances. Ask discreetly and perhaps you'll be invited. Remember that an invitation is an honor and to respect local customs.

Today, about 11,000 Hopi live on the 2410-sq-mile reservation, of which more than 1400 sq miles are partitioned lands used by the Navajo. A US Senate bill officially resolved a complicated century-old legal conflict between the two tribes about the boundaries of the reservations in 1996, but there are still disagreements between the two tribes.

Hwy 264 crosses the reservation and passes the three mesas forming its heart. Hwys 87, 77 and 2 enter the reservation from the south, giving access from the I-40 corridor. Hiking or driving off these main highways is prohibited without a permit (available from the tourist office at First Mesa, right).

The Hopi are not interested in having their culture dissected by outsiders, and all villages strictly prohibit any form of recording, be it camera, video- or audiotape or sketching. Alcohol and other drug use is also prohibited. Also see p466.

First Mesa
The first village on the mesa is **Hano**. It's inhabited by Tewa-speaking Pueblo Indians, now integrated into the Hopi tribe, who arrived in 1696 after fleeing from the Spaniards. Hano merges into the Hopi village of **Sichomovi** (you can't tell the difference).

At the end of First Mesa is the tiny village of **Walpi**, the most dramatic of the Hopi enclaves. In a spectacular setting that appears to jut out into space, it was built around AD 1200. The mesa is so narrow at this point that you can't drive in; cars must be left in a parking area near the entrance to the village. There is no water or electricity, so the handful of year-round residents have to walk into Sichomovi to get water. Hopi guides offer 45-minute walking tours (adult $8, child $5) of the village that depart from the **tourist office** (☎ 928-737-2262; village entrance parking area; ⌚ 9:30am-4pm). Guides speak excellent English and the tour is a highlight of a visit to Hopiland. Artisans living on First Mesa sell pots, kachina dolls and other crafts at fair prices. Look for the stalls in front of the tourist office.

Second Mesa
Called 'the center of the universe' by the tribe, Second Mesa is 10 miles west of First Mesa and has the Reservation's only hotel, the **Hopi Cultural Center Restaurant & Inn** (☎ 928-734-2401; www.hopiculturalcenter.com; r $95; ☒). It has 33 modern rooms and a restaurant (dishes $6 to $8) serving American fare and a few Hopi dishes. The **Hopi Cultural Center** (☎ 928-734-2401; adult/child $3/1; ⌚ 8am-5pm) is next door. The small but informative museum has exhibits on Hopi culture, including many historical photos. Ask here about attending the few village dances open to the public. To browse for excellent silverwork and other crafts, visit the nearby **Hopi Arts and Crafts Guild** (☎ 928-734-2463). Other villages on Second Mesa include **Shungopavi**, **Mishongnovi** and **Sipaulovi**. Shungopavi is the oldest village on the mesa and famous for its snake dances, where dancers carry live rattlesnakes in their mouths (although tourists are banned from viewing the ceremony). The latter two villages sometimes have social or butterfly dances open to the public.

ARIZONA

KACHINAS

Kachinas are several hundred sacred spirits that live in the San Francisco Mountains north of Flagstaff. At prescribed intervals during the year they come to the Hopi Reservation and dance in a precise and ritualized fashion. These dances maintain harmony among all living things and are especially important for rainfall and fertility.

Some Hopi who carefully and respectfully perform these dances prepare for the events over many days. They are important figures in the religion of the tribe, and it can be said that the dancers are the kachinas that they represent. This is why the dances have such a sacred significance to the Hopi and why the tribe is reluctant to trivialize their importance by turning a religious ceremony into a tourist spectacle. The masks and costumes used by each kachina are often spectacular.

One of the biggest kachina dances is the Powamuya, or 'Bean Dance,' held in February. During this time, young Hopi girls are presented with kachina dolls that incorporate the girls into the religious cycle of the tribe. The dolls are traditionally carved from the dried root of a cottonwood tree, a tree that is an indicator of moisture. Over time, these dolls have become popular collectors' items and Hopi craftsmen produce them for the general public as an art form. Not all kachinas are carved for the tourist trade: some are considered too sacred. Other tribes, notably the Navajo, have copied kachina dolls from the Hopi.

In March 1992, Marvel Comics, the well-known comic-book publisher, issued an NHL Superpro comic book in which there was a story about kachinas trying to violently capture a Hopi ice-skating champion who was not living a traditional lifestyle. The Hopi people considered this an inaccurate and blasphemous portrayal of the sacred nature of the kachina's role in Hopi life. It was also the last straw in many years of inappropriate actions regarding Hopi religious practices, and most kachina dances are now closed to tourists.

Third Mesa

The village of **Kykotsmovi** (☎ 928-734-2474), founded in the late 1800s and now the tribal capital, is located here. On top of the mesa is **Old Oraibi** village, which Hopi say has been continuously inhabited since the early 12th century. Oraibi is a couple of miles west of Kykotsmovi. The roads are unpaved and dusty, so park next to crafts shops near the village entrance and visit on foot. There are picnic areas off Hwy 264 just east of Oraibi and just east of Kykotsmovi on Oraibi Wash. On the highway leading to Oraibi is the **Monongya Gallery** (☎ 928-734-2344), which has a good crafts selection.

AROUND THE RESERVATIONS

On the I-40 corridor south of the Navajo and Hopi Reservations are several small towns that act as jumping-off points for exploring the Native American lands.

Winslow

pop 10,000 / elev 4880ft

'Standing on a corner in Winslow, Arizona, such a fine sight to see…' Sound familiar? Thanks to the Eagles catchy '70s tune 'Take It Easy,' otherwise nonmemorable Winslow has gained some serious name recognition. A small plaza on Rte 66 at Kinsley Ave, in the heart of old downtown, pays homage to the band. There's a life-sized bronze statue of a hitchhiker backed by a trompe l'oeil wall mural of the girl in a flatbed Ford that always attracts a posse of photographers.

If pop-culture's not your thing, you might consider Winslow as a lodging base. Just 60 miles south of the Hopi mesas, it provides the closest off-reservation accommodations.

The **chamber of commerce** (☎ 928-289-2434; www.winslowarizona.org; I-40, exit 253) has the usual tourist info. The **library** (☎ 928-289-4982; 420 W Gilmore St) offers free Internet.

About a dozen old motels, some run-down, are found along Rte 66. Rates range from $20 in winter to $40 in summer. The historic hacienda-style **La Posada** (☎ 928-289-4366; www.laposada.org; 303 E 2nd St; r/ste $79/99) is the best choice for many miles around. Opened in 1930, it was one of a chain of grand Fred Harvey hotels along the Santa Fe Railroad line, and numbered Harry Truman and Howard Hughes among its guests. Rooms are equipped with period furnishings and named after Western dignitaries and desperadoes. It's fabulous value. Its **Turquoise Room restaurant** (dishes $10-20) has an eclectic menu focusing on regional specialties, and offers the best food in town.

Mexican lunches and dinners have been served at the **Casa Blanca Café** (☎ 928-289-4191; 1201 E 2nd St; dishes $5-10) for half a century. Plates are large and tasty. Locals head to **Sue's Family Restaurant** (☎ 928-289-1234; 723 W 3rd; dishes $4-11) for some basic home-cooked diner fare.

Greyhound (☎ 928-289-2171; www.greyhound.com; cnr 4th & Williamson Sts) stops at the Circle K.

Holbrook

pop 4900 / elev 5080ft

Named after a railroad engineer, Holbrook was established in 1881 when the railroad reached this point. It soon became an important ranching center and the Navajo County seat. The proximity of the Petrified Forest National Park has added tourism to the town's economic profile.

The **chamber of commerce** (☎ 928-524-6558, 800-524-2459; 100 E Arizona St), housed inside the county courthouse, is the information center. You'll also find the **Old West Museum** here. Old and dusty, it has local history exhibits. The old city jail cells are the highlight of a visit. Admission is free. Native American dancers perform for free (tips appreciated) outside the 1898 county courthouse at 7pm during summer. Photography is permitted.

Seventeen miles from town, **Rock Art Canyon Ranch** (☎ 928-288-3260) is a working ranch with tours of Chevelin Canyon, brimming with petroglyphs. Horseback riding and other activities are offered at reasonable prices. Call for directions and rate info.

It's illegal to collect petrified wood inside the Petrified Forest National Park (right), but there are several rock shops in Holbrook where you can purchase pieces of the fossilized wood. The biggest and best of these shops is **Jim Gray's Petrified Wood Co** (☎ 928-524-1842; 147 Hwy 180; 🕐 7:30am-7pm). Featuring pieces of wood in various shapes and sizes (including a $24,000 petrified-wood coffee table), it also has a great display of minerals and fossils. This shop is worth a stop.

Most motels and hotels line Hopi Dr (east of I-40, exit 285) or Navajo Blvd, north of Hopi Dr intersecting with I-40, exits 286

and 289. Devotees of historic Rte 66 schlockabilia won't want to miss the **Wigwam Motel** (☎ 928-524-3048; clewis97@cybertrails.com; 811 W Hopi Dr; s/d $36/42). The 'village' has 15 concrete wigwams, which double as simple rooms, each with restored 1950s furniture. Quite a sight! Full of Western memorabilia, the **Butterfield Stage Co Steak House** (☎ 928-524-3447; 609 W Hopi Dr; dishes from $10) delivers the region's best steaks at good prices. You'll find reasonably authentic Italian fare at the locally recommended **Mesa Grande Italiano** (☎ 928-524-6696; 2318 Navajo Blvd; dishes $7-15).

Greyhound (☎ 928-524-3832; www.greyhound.com; 101 Mission Lane) stops at the Circle K.

Petrified Forest National Park

Despite the name, **Petrified Forest National Park** (☎ 928-524-6228; www.nps.gov/pefo; per vehicle $10) is not actually comprised of little glades of trees, eerily frozen in time (although that would be way cooler). In actuality, the 'forest' is really just a bunch of broken, horizontal fossilized logs, scattered over a vast area. The wood is impressive, however, and pre-dates the dinosaurs. Some logs are as much as 6ft in diameter, and one spans a ravine to form a fossilized bridge. The park's appeal is heightened by the stunning landscape of the **Painted Desert**, where colors are constantly changing depending on the location of the sun. The kaleidoscope of reds, pinks and oranges combined with the 225-million-year-old pieces of wood is a stunningly beautiful, almost haunting sight.

The conifer trees were washed into the area by floods. Logs were buried by sediment faster than they could decompose and groundwater dissolved silica and other elements, which then crystallized as colorful quartzes in the logs. Erosion eventually exposed them. Thousands of tons of petrified wood were taken by souvenir seekers and entrepreneurs until 1906, when the area became a national monument and later a national park. All collecting is now strictly prohibited (punishable by fines and imprisonment).

The park straddles I-40 at exit 311, 25 miles east of Holbrook. From this exit, a 28-mile paved park road offers a splendid **scenic drive**. Apart from short trails at some of the pullouts, there are no maintained hiking trails.

WESTERN ARIZONA

Western Arizona is not only the hottest part of the state; it is often the hottest area in the nation. The low-lying towns along the Colorado River (Bullhead City, Lake Havasu City and Yuma) boast average maximum daily temperatures of more than 100°F from June to September, and temperatures exceeding 110°F are not unusual. Balmy weather during the rest of the year attracts thousands of winter visitors, many of whom end up staying – western Arizonan cities have some of the fastest growing populations in the USA.

KINGMAN

pop 24,400 / elev 3345ft

There's not a lot going on in Kingman these days. Back when Rte 66 was still the Mother Road, Kingman was a bigger deal. Today it's just another fast-fading relic, a few decades past its prime. Run-down motels, ugly billboards and lots of gas stations and thrift stores grace its main drag. But several turn-of-the-19th-century buildings remain, and the wagon-wheel tracks of an old mining route are visible off White Cliffs Rd. If you're following the Rte 66 trail, or looking for cheap lodging, it's worth a stroll.

Rte 66 follows Business 40 (Andy Devine Blvd) through downtown, then veers left onto Beale St. Pick up self-guided driving tour maps at the **Powerhouse Visitor Center** (☎ 928-753-6106, 866-427-7866; 120 W Andy Devine Ave; ✆ 9am-6pm Mar-Nov, to 5pm Dec-Feb), which has a **Route 66 museum** (admission $3) opposite Locomotive Park. Further west, the **Mojave Museum of History and Arts** (☎ 928-753-3195; 400 W Beale St; admission $3; ✆ 10am-5pm Mon-Fri, 1-5pm Sat & Sun) chronicles Hualapai tribal traditions.

Sleeping & Eating

Most motels on Kingman's east side have rooms from $35.

Hotel Brunswick (☎ 928-718-1800; www.hotel -brunswick.com; 315 E Andy Devine Ave; r $30-60) The 1909 Hotel Brunswick has atmospheric downtown digs. Twelve old-fashioned cowboy/girl rooms with single beds share four bathrooms. More expensive rooms have larger beds, TVs and private bathrooms.

Hilltop Motel (☎ 928-753-2198; 1901 E Andy Devine Ave; r $40; ▢ ✆), A friendly, family-run place where Timothy McVeigh stayed before the Okalahoma City bombing (he wasn't a guest the owners care to remember). Rooms are smallish, but come with four movie channels.

Hualapai Mountain Park (☎ 928-757-3859, 877-757-0915; Hualapai Mountain Rd; tent/RV sites $10/17, cabins $35-75) About 15 miles south of town, it offers short trails, camping and 1930s stone-and-wood cabins.

Dambar Steak House (☎ 928-753-3523; 1960 E Andy Devine Ave; dishes $8-18) The classiest joint in town serves giant steaks in old-bad-boy West environs. Don't miss the saloon full of character with cow-skin tablecloths and daily happy hour.

Hubbs Café (dishes $15-19, ✆ dinner) The Hotel Brunswick onsite restaurant is a genteel Southwest bistro, serving pasta, steaks and a few international plates, such as Indonesian chicken curry. It's bottoms up at the adjacent bar.

The popular **Silver Spoon Family Restaurant** (☎ 928-753-4030; 2011 E Andy Devine Ave; dishes $7) features everything from gyros to hot roast beef. It's the kind of place where old-timers in cowboy hats crowd around the counter, sucking down cigarettes between bites of pie. Contemplate life while staring at the large Marlins mounted on the wall.

House of Chan (☎ 928-753-3232; 960 W Beale St; dishes $7-25; ✆ lunch & dinner). Generic on the outside, but it's quite cozy once you step inside; big windows and red vinyl chairs create the ambiance. Chinese and American dishes are served, and lunch specials go for just $5.

Mr D'z Route 66 Diner (☎ 928-718-0066; 105 E Andy Devine Ave; dishes $4-12) is about as kitschy as it gets. The bright turquoise and hot-pink exterior color scheme carries on inside. Grab the blue-plate special or thick-and-creamy milkshake at this '50s-style diner.

Getting There & Away

Kingman Airport (☎ 928-757-2134; Rte 66) is 6 miles northeast of town. **America West** (www .americawest.com) flies between Kingman and Phoenix three times a day Monday to Friday. Buses to Phoenix ($37, 3½ hours, daily), Las Vegas ($29, 2½ hours, daily), Flagstaff ($33, three hours, daily) and Los Angeles ($60, 11 hours, daily), among other cities depart from the **Greyhound Bus Depot** (☎ 928-757-8400; 3264 E Andy Devine Ave).

ROUTE 66, SELIGMAN TO TOPOCK

As if the Grand Canyon and Monument Valley aren't enough, Arizona also boasts the country's longest uninterrupted stretch of Rte 66, running from Seligman to Topock.

Seligman is a town that takes its Rte 66 heritage seriously! **Angel Delgadillo's Barbershop** (☎ 928-422-3352; www.route66giftshop.com; 217 E Rte 66) is more a nostalgic visitor center than anything else. The owner likes to reminisce about the Dust Bowl era and is active in statewide Rte 66 preservation efforts. His eccentric brother, Juan, runs the wacky **Snow Cap Drive-In** (☎ 928-422-3291; 301 E Rte 66; dishes from $5) down the street. Ironically the **Roadkill Café & Steakhouse** (☎ 928-422-3554; 502 W Rte 66; dishes $10-20) has an all-you-can-eat salad bar. Seligman has motels aplenty, with rooms from $30. The best of the bunch is the inviting **Deluxe Inn** (☎ 928-422-3244; 203 E Chino Ave; r from $40). After dark, shoot some stick or pop quarters in the jukebox at the **Black Cat** (☎ 928-422-3491; Rte 66), a favorite with bikers.

After Seligman the miles upon miles of open road slide past rolling hills and through canyon country. At the artificially

---

KICKIN' IT DOWN ROUTE 66 IN ARIZONA

Inspiring a strange blend of patriotism, nostalgia and melancholy in most Americans, Rte 66 is emblematic of the enduring restless nature of the USA. Beckoning connoisseurs of the open road or anyone searching for folklore on 'Main Street America,' a trip down this oft-forgotten highway just might be the highlight of your holiday. From kitschy souvenir shops to old-time diners to long abandoned mining outposts, there's always something to see. And between the towns and cities, you'll find big blue skies and wide-open spaces perfect to lose yourself in.

Rte 66 enthusiasts will find 400 miles of pavement stretching across Arizona – including the longest uninterrupted portion of old road left in the country, between Seligman and Topock (above). In Arizona, the Mother Road connects the dots between Winslow's windblown streets, Williams' 1940s-vintage downtown, Kingman's mining settlements and gunslinging Oatman: each a snapshot of a different era. Unpaved dirt segments, long forgotten towns and notorious bits of old highway provide a taste of old-school motoring. It's a blast from the past all right, where decades collide and time often seems to stand still.

In towns like Kingman (opposite) it's as if the clock stopped somewhere in the mid-1950s and never started ticking again. Aging motels with fading paint, classic American diners where they still make milkshakes the way they did half a century ago and rusting, long abandoned gas pumps line the broad streets. And the place gives a feel for what life was like when the highway, not the skyway, was the way to travel. In towns like Oatman (p190) you'll slide even further back in time. Wander the unpaved roads past weathered buildings. Have a smoke on a creaky old porch with a leathery old-timer and listen to his yarns, or down whiskey with the locals in the one saloon. A trip here is a bizarre experience that's about as close to 1880 as you can get in the early 21st century. And just when you're thoroughly confused as to what year it is, the road zips you right back to modern day. With funky pubs, classy restaurants, restored buildings and plenty of activities to keep you busy, Flagstaff (p154) reminds you this nostalgia tour doesn't just have to be about the old days. For more info on the old highway, visit the **Historic Route 66 Association of Arizona** (☎ 928-753-5001; www.azrt66.com; PO Box 66, Kingman, AZ 86402), which also organizes an annual 'Fun Run' motorcade from Seligman to Golden Shores. See also p412 and p25.

ARIZONA

lit **Grand Canyon Caverns** (☎ 928-422-3223; 45min tour adult/child $12/8; r $45-60; ☺ 8am-6pm May-Sep), 23 miles west of Seligman, an elevator drops 21 stories underground to caverns as big as a football field. Further west, **Peach Springs** is a jumping-off point for tribal-led river rafting (see p146). A bit further west are the blink-or-you'll-miss-them towns of **Truxton** and **Valentine**. In tiny **Hackberry** you'll find the eccentric and much loved **Old Route 66 Visitor Center** (☎ 928-769-2605). Built in 1934 as the Hackberry General Store, it's now run by a Rte 66 memorialist, and chock-full of highway knick-knacks.

Next up is Kingman (see p188). From here the road heads southwest. It's a long, dusty stretch of pavement eventually corkscrewing into the rugged Black Mountains. Watch for fluorescent-orange tumbleweeds, saguaro cacti and falling rocks as you travel along Gold Hill Grade over **Sitgreaves Pass** (3523ft). Afterward, the road twists and turns, heading past the century-old **Goldroad Mine** (☎ 928-768-1600; 1hr mine tours adult/child $12/6; ☺ 10am-6pm), where you can see actual gold veins. **Oatman**, 2 miles past the mine and 25 miles from Kingman, features old Wild West schlock for tourists. Wild donkeys, descendants of early mine prospectors' pack animals, crowd the town's main street of false-front buildings. Gunfight re-enactments are held at 1:30pm and 3:30pm on Saturday and Sunday. Every 4 July there's a sidewalk egg-frying contest. Yes, it's that hot here. Squeezed among antiques shops, the 1902 **Oatman Hotel** (☎ 928-768-4408; 181 N Main St; r from $40) is where Clark Gable and Carole Lombard honeymooned in 1939. Drop by and peruse historical exhibits (donation $1), or order a few tacos and a cold beer at the saloon downstairs.

A couple of miles west of Oatman, veer left onto the 20-mile historic byway that leads through breathtaking high-desert landscape. In spring, the region comes alive with wildflowers, but watch for flash floods. Keep going through **Golden Shores** – a few cafés, gas stations and watering holes – then curve around through **Havasu National Wildlife Refuge** (☎ 760-326-2853) for migratory- and water-bird habitats, and desert trails along the Colorado River. Further along is **Topock**, where you'll find the **Topock Gorge Marina** (☎ 928-768-2325; 14999 Hwy 95). It's in a lovely rocky location, and offers boat rent-als and pub-style food. The gorge straddles the Arizona/California state line and is 20 miles long.

CHLORIDE
pop 250 / elev 4200ft

This semi–ghost town, 20 miles northwest of Kingman, is a delightful place to get lost for a few hours. Sure it puts on the requisite Old West shoot-'em-up tourist shows, just like every other Arizona mining town, but Chloride's just seem less touristy. Maybe it's because the town is quieter than places like Tombstone or Oatman. Maybe it's because many roads here are still not paved. Or maybe it's because a visit to Arizona's oldest mining town (founded in 1862) really feels like stepping back a century or two. OK, so many of the buildings have been reconstructed to bring in tourist dollars, and the place sort of resembles a Hollywood set, but it's a charming one. Shoot-ups take place every Saturday at High Noon in front of the Dead Ass Saloon (we're not kidding). Snap a picture in front of its sign – 'Beer 5 cents, Whisky 25 cents, Hangings free.' There are a few antique and art stores to peruse and the original jail has two tiny, grimly barred cells flanking the woodstove-heated guard's room.

Jackass RV Tours (☎ 928-565-5036; adult/child $20/10) offers 1½-hour tours to Native American petroglyphs and huge murals painted by artist Roy Purcell on a rocky hillside. Drivers tell cowboy and Indian stories as you explore the area from the back of a strangely outfitted RV. It's a different experience. The company doesn't have an office or set hours, just give them a call to arrange a tour.

To really experience small town country America, you'll have to stay the night. When the sun goes down and the stars come out, you'll feel centuries away from modern day. **Sheps Miners Inn B&B** (☎ 928-565-4251; 9827 2nd St; r $35-65) has 12 homey rooms. Next door, **Yesterdays** (☎ 928-565-4251; 9827 2nd St; dishes $6-15) is where to spend the evening. A true Western saloon, it features creaky wooden stairs, vintage gas pumps and hand-painted murals. There's music nightly, from karaoke to live bands, on the small stage. Theme nights stir things up a bit – from Friday night fish fries to $3.95 pasta nights, there's always something going on.

LAKE MEAD & HOOVER DAM

Even those who challenge, or at least question, America's commitment to damming the American West have to marvel at the engineering and architecture of the Hoover Dam. Set amid the almost unbearably dry Mohave Desert, the dam towers over Black Canyon and provides electricity for the entire region. Lake Mead National Recreation Area is a popular boating, swimming and weekend camping destination for Las Vegas residents, and much of it is in Nevada.

Orientation & Information

Hoover Dam created Lake Mead, which boasts 700 miles of shoreline, while Davis Dam created the much smaller Lake Mohave. Black Canyon, the stretch of the Colorado River just below Hoover Dam, links the two lakes. All three bodies of water are included in the recreation area, created in 1964. The Colorado feeds into Lake Mead from Grand Canyon National Park, and rafting trips through the canyon finish on the east end of the lake.

Heading north from I-40 at Kingman, Hwy 93 crosses **Hoover Dam** (per vehicle $5, valid 5 days) about 30 minutes southeast of Las Vegas. Traffic across the dam can be terrible; expect delays of at least 30 minutes. The main cities on the south tip of Lake Mead are Bullhead City and Laughlin (see p193). Visitors to the lake will find most services in Boulder City, Nevada, a small town with a pleasant historic downtown about 7 miles west of the dam and 7 miles south of the visitor center.

Alan Bible Visitor Center (☎ 702-293-8990; www .nps.gov/lame; US Hwy 93) In Nevada, 5 miles west of Hoover Dam. Main visitor center.

Katherine Landing Visitor Center (☎ 928-754-3272) In Arizona, 3 miles north of Davis Dam.

Park Superintendent (☎ 702-293-8906, 800-680-5851; 601 Nevada Hwy, Boulder City, Nevada) Regional info. Assistance in emergencies.

Sights & Activities
HOOVER DAM

A statue of bronze winged figures stands atop Hoover Dam, memorializing those who built the massive 726ft concrete structure, one of the world's tallest dams. Originally named Boulder Dam, Hoover was built between 1931 and 1936 and was the first major dam on the Colorado River.

Thousands of men and their families, eager for work in the height of the Depression, came to Black Canyon and worked in excruciating conditions – dangling hundreds of feet above the canyon in 120°F desert heat. Hundreds lost their lives. A 25-minute film at the **Hoover Dam Visitor Center** (☎ 702-293-8321; www.hooverdam.usbr.gov; US Hwy 93; per vehicle $5; ☯ 9am-5pm), east of Boulder City, features original footage of the construction and is an interesting look at the history of not just Hoover Dam, but the sentiments and values that motivated American dam building.

BOATING

You can rent just about any type of watercraft imaginable at the **Lake Mead Resort & Marina** (☎ 702-293-3484). Twenty-foot ski boats cost $260 a day or $50 an hour, while patio boats that seat 10 people and travel up to 10mph cost $195 a day.

Desert River Outfitters (☎ 928-763-3033; www .desertriveroutfitters.com; 9649 Hwy 95, Bullhead City; per person $55) runs kayak trips down the Black Canyon from the base of Hoover Dam. There's a four-person minimum and you must reserve in advance.

FISHING

Fishing for striped largemouth bass is a popular sport on Lake Mead. While fly-fishing is possible, it's difficult and only recommended at certain times of year. For current conditions contact Michael Swartz of **FishVegas** (☎ 702-293-6294; www.fishvegas.com), an expert on Lake Mead fishing. He also offers guided trips for $250 for one or two people, and can also direct you to guides in the area (he's located in Las Vegas).

You must carry a state fishing license ($12.50), available from the marinas. If your license is from Nevada and you plan on fishing from a boat on Lake Mead, Lake Mohave or from the Arizona shores, you must also have a 'use stamp' from Arizona (and vice versa). A trout stamp is required if you intend to catch and keep trout.

CRUISES

If you want to see the lake but don't want to rent a boat, consider a sightseeing tour with **Lake Mead Cruises** (☎ 702-293-6180; www .lakemeadcruises.com; adult/child $19/9). Its boat is a triple-decker, air-conditioned Mississippi-style paddle wheeler. Daily tours leave at noon, 2pm and 4pm from Hemenway, a couple of miles north of the Alan Bible Visitor Center. The company offers a Sunday breakfast cruise ($29), dinner cruises ($35) and a Saturday dinner/dance cruise ($51). No meal-inclusive cruises are offered from mid-December through February.

SWIMMING

Given the dry heat of the surrounding desert, swimming in Lake Mead is understandably popular. Because water levels vary, what's a beach one year may be a desert the next. Call or stop by a visitor center (p191) for a list of beaches, and consider renting a boat to reach suitable water. Two miles north of the Alan Bible Visitor Center, the aptly named **Boulder Beach** (comprising pebbles and stone, not sand) is one good wading spot. Be sure to ask about pollution levels before swimming – houseboat owners sometimes dump raw sewage into the water rather than using pump-out stations.

Sleeping

Aside from campgrounds and houseboats, the only lodgings on Lake Mead are three properties owned by **Seven Crown Resorts** (☎ 800-752-9669; www.sevencrown.com). You must call Seven Crown Resorts, rather than the motels themselves, to make reservations. Don't expect a resort in the classic sense of the word – these are more like motels.

Temple Bar Resort (☎ 928-767-3211; r $55-115) The only lodging on the Arizona side, this resort is pleasant and remote. Rooms vary widely; some are simple cabins with separate bathrooms and no lake views, others are motel rooms with kitchenettes and views. If lake levels are high enough, a beach materializes. The resort is 47 miles east of Hoover Dam. To get here, head 20 miles south of Hoover Dam on Hwy 93 and look for a marked, paved northbound road.

Lake Mead Lodge (☎ 702-293-2074; d $65-85, ste $139; 🕸) A quiet place with grassy grounds on the Nevada side, it's just a five-minute drive north from Boulder City's restaurants and bars. The best feature is the pool overlooking the lake.

Echo Bay Resort (☎ 702-394-4000; r $90-115) About an hour's drive north from Boulder City, in Nevada. The resort sits amid a large marina and gets rather loud and busy. Not great value.

> **HOUSEBOATING ON LAKE MEAD**
>
> One of the most popular ways to explore Lake Mead is to rent a houseboat, available through **Forever Resorts Houseboats** (☎ 800-255-5561; www.foreverresorts.com) and **Seven Crown Houseboats** (☎ 800-752-9669; www.sevencrown.com). Rates vary widely depending on the season and size of boat. Early September mid-June is 'value season,' when rates are about $300 less than the rest of the year. Seven Crown rents the Grand Sierra (six nights for $3050), which has two bathrooms and officially sleeps 13 (though it's rather tight); the smaller, more basic Sierra (six nights for $2050) sleeps 10. Check the websites for complete information.

Cottonwood Cove Motel (☎ 702-297-1464; www.cottonwoodcoveresort.com; r $90-115) On Lake Mohave in Nevada, the resort here features a swimming beach and rooms with sliding glass doors overlooking the water.

Boulder Beach (☎ 702-293-2340; campsites $10) The nicest of the Nevada shore campgrounds, it overlooks the water and is quieter than other camping spots. Grounds feature cottonwoods and flowering trees, and you can swim. The campground is just a few miles north of the Alan Bible Visitor Center.

The NPS maintains eight campgrounds for tents and RVs (no hookups) in the recreation area ($10, first-come first-serve). All are in or near marinas and offer fire-grills and toilets.

Eating

You'll find basic restaurants at the Temple Bar, Boulder Beach and Echo Bay marinas on Lake Mead, and at Cottonwood Cove and Katherine Landing on Lake Mohave. The other marinas merely provide small convenience stores with snacks and drinks.

Best Cellars (☎ 702-293-9540; 538 Nevada Way, Boulder City; dishes $7-15) Outdoor seating, eclectic sandwiches and an extensive wine list give this place a great vibe. Try the Grecian Vegetarian (avocado, sprouts, roasted red pepper, baby greens and garlic mayonnaise served with chips) or one of the cheese plates (Spanish Machego, Italian Asiago, smoked Gouda and olives). Fresh salads are also on the menu.

Happy Days Diner (☎ 702-294-2653; 512 Nevada Way, Boulder City; dishes $4-7) This diner features a soda fountain and greasy diner classics like corn dogs, grilled Reubens and hot turkey sandwiches.

Getting There & Around

There are no shuttles to or around the recreation area. The only way to travel is by car. You'll find major car rental agencies in nearby Las Vegas.

BULLHEAD CITY & LAUGHLIN

combined pop 38,000 / elev 540ft

On the banks of the Colorado River, Laughlin, Nevada is the poor man's Las Vegas. The casinos lining the strip sport some fam-iliar names – such as Flamingo and Harrah's – but the look is more blue jeans than bling bling. You'll have to head west for heady opulence, marble and gold. Laughlin's a down-home riverboat gambling type of place. Think burgers, Budweiser and penny slots. It attracts an older, more sedate crowd than Vegas, the kind of folks looking to gamble in the city without all the sin.

Just across the river from Laughlin, back in Arizona, Bullhead City, or 'Bull' as some locals call it, is just south of the south end of Lake Mohave. It's a popular destination for Arizonans wanting to spend time on the water, a necessity in summer when temperatures often top 120°F!

ARIZONA

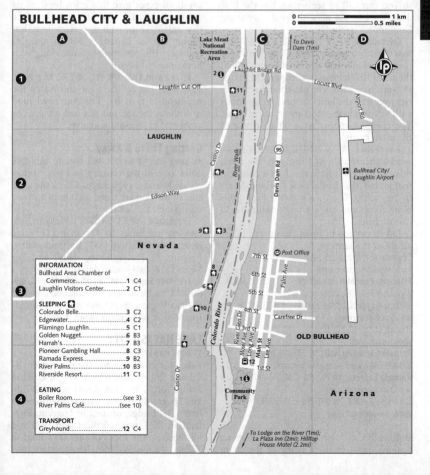

BULLHEAD CITY & LAUGHLIN

0 ___ 1 km
0 ___ 0.5 miles

Lake Mead National Recreation Area

Laughlin Bridge Rd

2 ℹ

Laughlin Cut-Off

🏨11

🏨5

LAUGHLIN

To Davis Dam (1mi)

Locust Blvd

Casino Dr

River Walk

95

Davis Dam Rd

🏨4

Edison Way

Airport Rd

Bullhead City/ Laughlin Airport

9🏨 🏨3

Nevada

7th St

⊗ Post Office

8🏨

6th St

6🏨

5th St

🏨10

4th St

3rd St

Carefree Dr

OLD BULLHEAD

Palm Ave

River Glen Dr

Moet Ave

Long Ave

Main St

Lee Ave

🏨12

1st St

1 ℹ

Community Park

Arizona

Colorado River

Casino Dr

INFORMATION
Bullhead Area Chamber of
   Commerce...........................1 C4
Laughlin Visitors Center............2 C1

SLEEPING 🏨
Colorado Belle.........................3 C2
Edgewater...............................4 C2
Flamingo Laughlin....................5 C1
Golden Nugget.........................6 B3
Harrah's..................................7 B3
Pioneer Gambling Hall..............8 C3
Ramada Express.......................9 B2
River Palms..............................10 B3
Riverside Resort.......................11 C1

EATING
Boiler Room...........................(see 3)
River Palms Café....................(see 10)

TRANSPORT
Greyhound..............................12 C4

To Lodge on the River (1mi);
La Plaza Inn (2mi); Hilltop
House Motel (2.2mi)

Information

The **Bullhead Area Chamber of Commerce** (☎ 928-754-4121; 1251 Hwy 95) and the **Laughlin visitor center** (☎ 702-298-3321, 800-227-5245; www.visit laughlin.com; 1555 S Casino Dr) both have area info.

Nevada time is one hour behind Arizona in winter but on the same time zone in summer (Arizona doesn't observe daylight-saving time).

Sleeping

From Sunday to Thursday, the Laughlin casinos are fantastic value with spacious modern double rooms in the low $20s; even on weekends they're still a good deal with rates around $40. The Laughlin visitor center has a free phone that connects to the casinos so you can call to see which has the best deal. The casinos, all with hotels, are along Laughlin's Casino Dr.

Colorado Belle (☎ 702-298-4000, 800-477-4837; www.coloradobelle.com; r from $20; 🖳 🛋) This very pleasant casino has a Mississippi riverboat theme, with Victorian wallpaper and a large slot-machine area. The old-time theme carries over into the hotel. Rooms are spacious with nifty wallpaper and are excellent value. The cheapest rooms are a bit of a hike to the main casino.

River Palms (☎ 702-298-2242, 800-835-7903; www .rvrpalm.com; r from $20; 🛋) Right on the river, this place doesn't have much of a coherent theme, but the drinks flow fast and freely in the casino. There's a non-smoking gambling room and quite a few restaurants to choose from.

Other casinos in town (room prices are all about the same):

Edgewater (☎ 702-298-2453, 800-677-4837; www.edgewater-casino.com)

Flamingo Laughlin (☎ 702-298-5111, 800-352-6464; www.laughlinflamingo.com)

Golden Nugget (☎ 702-298-7111, 800-237-1739; www.gnlaughlin.com)

Harrah's (☎ 702-298-4600, 800-447-8700; www.harrahs.com)

Pioneer Gambling Hall (☎ 702-298-2442, 800-634-3469; www.pioneerlaughlin.com)

Ramada Express (☎ 702-298-4200, 800-272-6232; www.ramadaexpress.com)

Riverside Resort (☎ 702-298-2535, 800-227-3849; www.riversideresort.com)

Bullhead City also has lots of sleeping options, most of them being of the chain variety. The following places are recommended.

La Plaza Inn (☎ 928-763-8080; 1978 Hwy 95; r from $30; 🛋) Has some suites and mini-suites.

Hilltop House Motel (☎ 928-753-2198; 2037 Hwy 95; r from $30; 🛋) Clean and simple.

Lodge on the River (☎ 928-758-8080; 1717 Hwy 95; r from $30; 🛋) Pleasant. Features kitchenettes in some rooms.

Eating & Drinking

All casinos feature multiple restaurants, at least one of which will have 24-hour service, along with bars and lounges. Food is cheap and decent, but don't expect haute cuisine.

Boiler Room (☎ 702-298-4000; Colorado Belle, Casino Dr; dishes $7-15) Copper-topped tables and overhead pipes give this microbrewery its pseudo-industrial vibe. It's a funky place that might seem ordinary elsewhere, but stands out in Laughlin. Salads, burgers and tasty ribs are on the menu, along with home-brewed beer.

River Palms Café (☎ 702-298-2242; River Palms; dishes $3-10) Eat by the river and watch the paddleboats float by. The American food is nothing special, but not bad either. The ambiance is pleasant and airy.

Getting There & Away

Air Laughlin (☎ 866-359-3486) flies to multiple cities around the country and often offers cheap fly-and-stay packages. Check the website, or the Sunday travel section of a major newspaper, for deals.

Greyhound (☎ 928-754-5586; 125 Long Ave, Bullhead City) has buses to Kingman ($11, one hour, daily), Flagstaff ($37, 3½ hours, daily), Phoenix ($43, 4½ hours, daily) and Las Vegas ($18, two hours, daily) and more.

Tri-State Super Shuttle (☎ 928-704-9000, 800-801-8687) has buses between Bullhead City and the Las Vegas airport (one-way $37, round-trip $64). It picks up at major hotels.

LAKE HAVASU CITY

54,800 / elev 575ft

Lake Havasu City made the news after developer Robert McCulloch bought London Bridge for $2,460,000, disassembled it into 10,276 granite slabs, and reassembled it here. The bridge, opened in London, England, in 1831, was rededicated in 1971 and has become the focus of the city's English Village – a touristy complex of restaurants, hotels and shops built in pseudo-English style. Students flock to town for water sports and loads of sunshine during spring break in March. It's a festive time; hotels are packed, streets are crowded with drunken revelers and live bands play late into the night.

The **tourism bureau** (☎ 928-453-3444, 800-242-8278; www.golakehavasu.com; 314 London Bridge Rd) has all the need-to-know info.

Sights & Activities

Once you've walked over London Bridge, you'll find that most of your options are water related. Plenty of companies provide boat tours (from around $35) from English Village. Options include one-hour narrated jaunts, day trips and sunset tours. Check at the tourism bureau or just show up and you can usually reserve a tour leaving within an hour or two.

The best beach in town is **London Bridge Beach**, in the county park off West McCulloch Blvd (look for it behind the Island Inn hotel). The park has lots of palm trees, a sandy beach and views of the bridge and distinct-looking mountains.

Lake Havasu Marina (☎ 928-855-2159) and **Blue Water Rentals** (☎ 928-453-9613), both in the English Village, rent a variety of boats from paddle craft ($16 per day) to 220ft pontoon boats ($220 a day). Canoes and kayaks can be rented (from $15 a day) from **Western Arizona Canoe & Kayak Outfitter** (Wacko; ☎ 928-855-6414; www.azwacko.com; 770 Winston Pl).

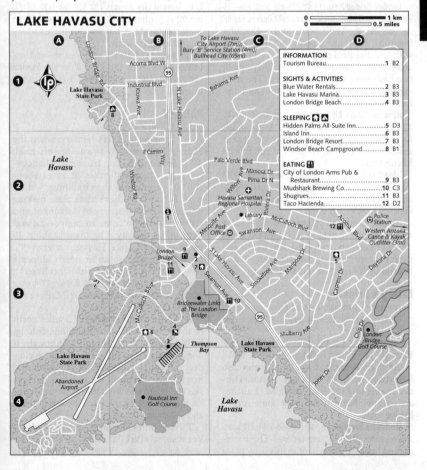

LAKE HAVASU CITY

0 — 1 km
0 — 0.5 miles

INFORMATION
Tourism Bureau.............................1 B2

SIGHTS & ACTIVITIES
Blue Water Rentals.......................2 B3
Lake Havasu Marina......................3 B3
London Bridge Beach....................4 B3

SLEEPING
Hidden Palms All-Suite Inn................5 D3
Island Inn.....................................6 B3
London Bridge Resort......................7 B3
Windsor Beach Campground...........8 B1

EATING
City of London Arms Pub &
  Restaurant..................................9 B3
Mudshark Brewing Co...................10 C3
Shugrues....................................11 B3
Taco Hacienda.............................12 D2

The company also offers tours ($40). The river is mild and sedate here, and paddling along a desert river, past cacti and rocky crags is a relaxing way to spend an afternoon (especially if you dip into the cool water every so often!). If you'd rather spend your time four-wheeling through the desert, check out **Outback Off-Road Adventures** (☎ 928-680-6151; www.outbackadventures.us; half/full-day tour $65/130), which offers a 4WD trips.

Sleeping

Rates vary tremendously from summer weekends to winter weekdays. The cheapest places, offering doubles for around $40 in winter but about $60 or more during summer, are found on Acoma Blvd.

London Bridge Resort (☎ 928-855-0888, 888-503-9148; www.londonbridgeresort.com; 1477 Queens Bay Rd; ste $100-300; 🏊) With pools and nightclubs, hot tubs, bars and restaurants, this resort with London Bridge views attracts a playful crowd. Over 120 units feature either one or two bedrooms with kitchenettes. The most expensive have whirlpool bathtubs and dining areas.

Hidden Palms All-Suite Inn (☎ 928-855-7144; 2100 Swanson Ave; ste $60-130; 🏊) A good bet for families or folks craving more sedate, upscale lodging. All rooms are suites with kitchenettes.

Island Inn (☎ 928-680-0606, 800-243-9955; 1300 McCulloch Blvd; r $65-120; 🏊) Rooms are pleasant, many sporting balconies and lake views. There's also a spa.

Windsor Beach Campground (☎ 928-855-2784; day use per vehicle $7; tent & RV sites $12) Two miles north of London Bridge Rd, this beach and camping area in a state park has showers and boat-launch facilities, but no hookups.

Eating & Drinking

Restaurants and bars line a half-mile stretch of McCulloch Blvd between Smoketree Ave and Acoma Blvd.

Shugrues (☎ 928-453-1400; 1425 McCulloch Blvd; dishes $10-30; 🕑 lunch & dinner) Fresh seafood is the main draw, but the large menu also advertises steak, chicken and pastas. Dinner mains include soup or salad. Lunches are cheaper. Many tables have some sort of bridge view.

Mudshark Brewing Co (☎ 928-453-2981; 210 Swanson Ave; dishes $8-18; 🕑 lunch & dinner) The hand-crafted brews are excellent at this busy place

a few blocks south of London Bridge. The menu features classic pizzas and burgers, as well as some unique mains: the cranberry-brandy pork tenderloin is a winner.

City of London Arms Pub & Restaurant (☎ 928-855-8782; 422 English Village; dishes $5-15) Catering to homesick Brits, or anyone craving decent pub grub like fish and chips, this wannabe authentic English watering hole also serves imported British brews. It gets rowdy at night.

Taco Hacienda (☎ 928-855-8932; 2200 Mesquite Ave; dishes $5-12) It's been around for decades and is locally popular for its inexpensive Mexican fare.

Getting There & Away

Lake Havasu City Airport (☎ 928-764-3330; 5600 N Hwy 95) is 7 miles north of town. **America West** (www.americawest.com) has several flights a day to and from Phoenix.

Greyhound (☎ 029-764-4010; www.greyhound.com) buses leave from the **Busy 'B' Service Station** (☎ 928-764-2440; 3201 N Hwy 95), 4 miles north of town.

PARKER

pop 3100 / elev 417ft

Parker gets wild in late January, when the Score 400 comes to town. An off-road, 4WD Jeep and pickup truck race that covers more than 300 miles, it lures about 100,000 people into the city limits. Otherwise, Parker's a rather sedate place making its money off the scores of Arizonans and Californians who come to camp, boat and swim in its vicinity. The town is about 30 miles south of Lake Havasu on Hwy 95. Most businesses are on or near California Ave (Hwy 95/62) or Riverside Dr (Hwy 95). The **chamber of commerce** (☎ 928-669-2174; www.coloradoriverinformation.com/parker; 1217 California Ave) has race info.

Locals head to **Parker Dam**, 15 miles north of town, for water- and jet-skiing, fishing, boating and inner-tubing. Although it doesn't appear as such, this is the world's deepest dam, with 70% of its structural height buried beneath the riverbed. To rent skis and boats, check out the numerous shops lining the stretch of road between town and the dam.

Twelve miles north of Parker, **Buckskin Mountain State Park** (☎ 928-667-3231; www.pr.state.az.us; day use $7; camp/RV sites $19/22) is a great place to take the kids. There's a playground and picnic area, as well as a swimming beach, boat ramp, recreation room, laundry facilities and grocery store. Rangers lead activities on weekends. For quieter, more scenic desert camping try the **River Island Unit** (☎ 928-667-3386; day use $6; campsites $12-20), a mile north of Buckskin.

In town, the pleasant **Kofa Inn** (☎ 928-669-2101; 1700 California Ave; r $40; 🔀) has clean, cozy American motel–style rooms. It is adjacent to **Coffee Ern's** (☎ 928-669-8145; 1720 California Ave; r from $40), which features a decent 24-hour family restaurant and simple, but clean, rooms. For casual home-style breakfasts (think diner coffee and fried eggs) head to the **Hole-in-the-Wall** (☎ 928-669-9755; 612 California Ave; dishes $4-8; 🕑 breakfast, lunch & dinner).

YUMA

pop 84,300 / elev 200ft

The sun is always blazing in Arizona's sunniest, driest and third-largest metropolitan area. With winter temps in the 70°Fs, and just three inches of rain per year, Yuma lures retirees by the thousands to winter in the scores of trailer parks around town. They're packing up the RVs by late spring, as summer here is hotter than hell. But despite its popularity with snowbirds (retired winter visitors), Yuma's been struggling to keep itself on the tourist map. Today it's working hard to restore its historic Colorado River downtown, with a new visual arts center and restored movie house as star attractions. If it's freezing and gray in Tucson, and you're in desperate need of a tan, you might just want to shack up here for a few days.

The **Medical Center** (☎ 928-344-2000; 2400 Ave A; 🕑 24hr) handles emergencies. The **Convention & Visitors Bureau** (☎ 928-783-0071; www .visityuma.com; 377 S Main St) provides information on the area.

Sights & Activities
YUMA TERRITORIAL PRISON STATE HISTORIC PARK

Between 1876 and 1909, this prison housed 3069 of Arizona's most feared criminals, including 29 women. Today the **prison** (☎ 928-783-4771; www.pr.state.az.us; 1 Prison Hill Rd; adult/child 4/2; 🕑 8am-5pm) is a slightly gruesome, mildly historical, definitely offbeat attraction suitable for the whole family. The

existing buildings, notably the guard tower and the rock-wall cells fronted by gloomy iron-grille doors, give an idea of what inmates' lives were like. The small museum displays interesting artifacts, including many photographs of the men and women incarcerated here.

RIVER & RAIL TRIPS

Brush up on local history and Native American lore while your jet boat glides past petroglyphs and mining camps. **Yuma River Tours** (☎ 928-783-4400; www.yumarivertours.com; 1920 Arizona Ave; tour adult/child from $56/46) offers informative day-trips, sunset cruises and custom charters. Guides are knowledgeable, and the tours fun. Boats depart from Fisher's Landing: from Yuma head north on Hwy 95 to Martinez Lake Rd, where you'll turn left and continue on for another 11 miles until you hit Fisher's Landing.

Kids will dig a trip on the vintage **Yuma Valley Railway** (☎ 928-783-3456; cnr 1st St & 2nd Ave; admission $15; 🕑 1pm Sat & Sun Nov-Mar, Sun only Apr-May & Oct), which leaves from the west end of 8th St, 6 miles west of downtown. The two-hour trips follow the Arizona-Sonora border, and a local historian provides interesting facts and folklore as the train chugs along.

Sleeping

Winter rates (usually January to April) can be up to $30 higher than summer rates and vary substantially according to demand. There are over 70 campgrounds, mainly geared to RVs on a long-term basis during the winter. Most have age restrictions (no children, sometimes only for people over 50) and prohibit tents. People planning a long RV stay should contact the visitors bureau for lists.

La Fuente Inn & Suites (☎ 928-329-1814, 800-841-1814; www.lafuenteinn.com; 1513 E 16th St; r $80-100; 🖳 🔀) In a modern, Spanish Colonial–style building surrounded by landscaped gardens, the spacious rooms are mainly one- or two-room suites. A continental breakfast, evening cocktail hour and exercise room are plusses.

Shilo Inn (☎ 928-782-9511, 800-222-2244; 1550 Castle Dome Ave; r $100-160; 🔀) Yuma's most classy hotel, it has a giant pool along with an exercise room, spa, sauna and steam bath. Some rooms have kitchenettes; others feature a

ARIZONA

balcony opening onto the courtyard. All have refrigerators and interior corridors. The restaurant and lounge are appealing.

Yuma Cabaña (☎ 928-783-8311, 800-874-0811; 2151 4th Ave; r $30-60; ⚲) Well recommended and well maintained, this place has Yuma's best budget rooms. A few have kitchenettes. Continental breakfast is included.

Best Western Coronado Motor Hotel (☎ 928-783-4453; www.bwcoronado.com; 233 4th Ave; r $70-135; ⚲) The picture of 1950s-style American motels, this attractive chain hotel on the edge of downtown features red-tiled roofs, whitewashed walls and lots of archways. The rooms are modern and clean, and the location is convenient.

Eating

Restaurants can be fairly dead midweek in summer but bustling during the busy winter season.

Lutes Casino (☎ 928-782-2192; 221 Main St; dishes $3-5) You won't find slots or poker anymore, just serious domino players, pool tables and arcade games. Serving the best hamburgers in town, order a cheeseburger and smother it with Lutes' own secret-recipe hot sauce. Eclectically decorated, this dark bar is a local favorite. Kids are welcome.

River City Grill (☎ 928-782-7988; 600 W Third St; dishes $8-20) Straight out of the big city, this hip and funky place is usually packed. Seafood is what to order, try the crab cakes to start and the tequila snapper as a main. The menu takes you around the globe, from Vietnam to Louisiana.

Garden Café (☎ 928-783-1491; 250 Madison Ave; dishes $7-13; ⚅ 9am-2:30pm Tue-Sun) Singing birds and quiet terraced gardens make this place a favorite with retirees. It serves sumptuous sandwiches, quiches and salads, as well as the usual breakfast offerings. The pancakes with lingonberry sauce are the specialty of the house.

Drinking & Entertainment

Historic Yuma Theater (☎ 928-783-4566; 254 Main St) Recently renovated, this old movie house sports 1930s Art Deco decor. It hosts theater productions and touring musical groups most evenings from November to March, with more sporadic performances in summer.

Red's Bird Cage Saloon (☎ 928-783-1050; 231 Main St) Next door to Lutes Casino, this place

is for pool, darts and drinking after Lutes closes. It's a funky joint that sometimes has live music.

Getting There & Away

Yuma Airport (☎ 928-726-5882; 2191 32nd St) has daily flights to Phoenix and Los Angeles.

The **Greyhound Bus Terminal** (☎ 928-783-4403; 170 E 17 Place) has buses to Phoenix ($25, four hours, daily) and Tucson ($53, six hours, daily) among other destinations.

SOUTHERN ARIZONA

Way down south by the Mexican border the skies are big and blue. This is a land of Stetsons and spurs, where cowboy ballads are sung around the campfire and thick steaks sizzle on the grill. It's big country out here, beyond the confines of bustling college-town Tucson, where long, dusty highways slide past rolling vistas and steep, pointy mountain ranges. A place where majestic saguaro cacti, the symbol of the region, stretch out as far as the eye can see. Some of the Wild West's most classic tales were begot in small towns like Tombstone and Bisbee, which still attract tourists by the thousands for their Old West vibe. The desert air here is hot, sweet and dry by day, cool and crisp at night. This is a land of stupendous sunsets, a place where coyotes still howl under starry, black-velvet skies.

TUCSON

pop 518,800 / elev 2500ft

A bustling college town where the Old West meets south-of-the-border, Tucson is attractive, fun and one of the most culturally invigorating places in the Southwest. Set in a flat valley surrounded by craggy, odd-shaped mountains, it's Arizona's second-largest city, but has a distinct small-town vibe. Rich in Latino heritage (more than 20% of the population is of Mexican or Central American descent), Spanish slides easily off most tongues and high-quality Mexican restaurants abound. Travelers looking to get a feel for the feisty flavor of the region will find Tucson easier to navigate and a more satisfying base than Phoenix, 116 miles to the north. The eclectic shops toting vintage garb, scores of funky restaurants and dive bars don't let you forget Tucson is a college town at heart, home turf to the 35,000-strong University of Arizona (U of A).

The city is set in a Sonoran Desert Valley, and its 2500ft elevation gives it a milder climate than Phoenix, although summers are still hot, with days frequently exceeding 100°F. Although it's fun to wander around the colorful historic buildings and peruse the shops, Tucson's best perks are found outside town. Whether you yearn to hike past giant cacti in the beautiful Saguaro National Park, watch the sun set over the ragged Santa Catalina mountains or check out the world-class Arizona-Sonora Desert Museum, a stray beyond city limits is bound to please just about anyone.

Orientation

Tucson lies mainly to the north and east of I-10 at its intersection with I-19, which goes to the Mexican border at Nogales. Downtown Tucson and the main historic districts are east of I-10 exit 258 at Congress St/Broadway Blvd, the major west–east thoroughfare. The downtown is compact and best visited on foot.

About a mile northeast of downtown is the University of Arizona campus. Just over a mile south of downtown is South Tucson, a separate town inhabited mainly by a traditional Latino population with few tourist sights (but it does have some cheap and funky restaurants with tasty Mexican food).

ARIZONA

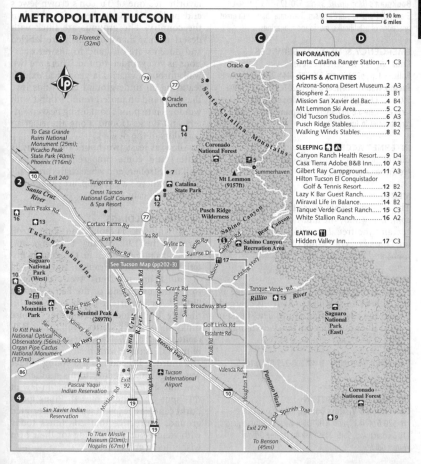

METROPOLITAN TUCSON

0 ___ 10 km
0 ___ 6 miles

INFORMATION
Santa Catalina Ranger Station....1 C3

SIGHTS & ACTIVITIES
Arizona-Sonora Desert Museum..2 A3
Biosphere 2..................................3 B1
Mission San Xavier del Bac........4 B4
Mt Lemmon Ski Area.................5 C2
Old Tucson Studios.....................6 A3
Pusch Ridge Stables....................7 B2
Walking Winds Stables..............8 B2

SLEEPING
Canyon Ranch Health Resort.....9 D4
Casa Tierra Adobe B&B Inn......10 A3
Gilbert Ray Campground.........11 A3
Hilton Tucson El Conquistador
  Golf & Tennis Resort..........12 B2
Lazy K Bar Guest Ranch..........13 A2
Miraval Life in Balance.............14 B2
Tanque Verde Guest Ranch.....15 C3
White Stallion Ranch...............16 A2

EATING
Hidden Valley Inn...................17 C3

The rest of the city is mainly an urban sprawl of shopping malls and residential areas interspersed with golf courses and parks. The main section of the city, between Campbell Ave and Kolb Rd, is known as midtown. The south end of town is the industrial area with Tucson International Airport and the Davis-Monthan Air Force Base. The steep and rugged Catalina Foothills dominate the north, home to the pricier residential districts, resorts and country clubs. East and west of town are wilderness areas, parts of which are protected by Saguaro National Park.

Information
BOOKSHOPS
Bookman's (Map pp202-3; ☎ 520-325-5657; 1930 E Grant Rd) Flagship store in a small Arizona chain with great selections of used books, music and magazines.

EMERGENCY & MEDICAL SERVICES
Dial ☎ 911 in emergencies.
Police (Map pp202-3; ☎ 520-791-4444; 270 S Stone Ave)
Tucson Medical Center (Map pp202-3; ☎ 520-327-5461; 5301 E Grant Rd; ⏱ 24hr) Offers emergency services. There are 10 hospitals and many smaller health care facilities in Tucson.

INTERNET ACCESS
Library (Map pp202-3; ☎ 520-791-4393; 101 N Stone Ave) Free Internet access.

MEDIA
The local newspapers are the morning *Arizona Daily Star,* the afternoon *Tucson Citizen* and the free *Tucson Weekly* published on Thursday, chock-full of great entertainment and restaurant listings.

MONEY
ATMs are abundant. Foreign exchange is available at most banks; a $5 fee is charged if you don't have an account. The Tucson airport does not offer currency exchange.

POST
Post office (Map pp202-3; ☎ 800-275-8777; 141 S 6th Ave)

TOURIST INFORMATION
Convention & Visitors Bureau (Map pp202-3; ☎ 520-624-1817, 800-638-8350; www.visittucson.org; 110 S Church Ave, Suite 7199) Ask for its free *Official Visitors Guide.*

Coronado National Forest Supervisor's Office (Map pp202-3; ☎ 520-670-4552; Federal Bldg, 300 W Congress)
Santa Catalina Ranger Station (Map p199; ☎ 520-749-8700; 5700 N Sabino Canyon Rd) At the entrance to Sabino Canyon.

Sights & Activities
ARIZONA-SONORA DESERT MUSEUM
Javelinas, coyotes, bobcats and snakes, hummingbirds, scorpions and just about every other local desert animal are displayed in natural-looking outdoor settings at this excellent living **museum** (Map p199; ☎ 520-883-2702; www.desertmuseum.org; 2021 N Kinney Rd; adult/child $10/2; ⏱ 8:30am-5pm) off Hwy 86, about 12 miles west of Tucson. A perennial local favorite, it's one of Tucson's crown jewels and perhaps even the best of its kind in the country. The grounds are thick with desert plants, many of which are labeled and docents are on hand to answer questions as you wander around. There are two walk-through aviaries, a geological exhibit featuring an underground cave (kids love that one) and an underground exhibit with windows into ponds containing beavers, otters and ducks (found along the riparian corridors of the desert).

Allow at least two hours (half a day is better) and come prepared for outdoor walking. Strollers and wheelchairs are available, and there's a gift shop, art gallery, restaurant and café.

HISTORIC BUILDINGS
In downtown Tucson, you can stroll through the 19th-century buildings and arts and craft galleries in the **Presidio Historic District**, between Franklin and Alameda Sts and Main and Court Aves. Cushing St forms the north end of the **Barrio Historico District**. An important business district in the late 1800s, today the buildings house funky shops and galleries. Don't miss **El Tiradito** (cnr Cushing St & Main Ave), a quirky, crumbling little shrine with a story of passion and murder. Legend has it a young herder was caught making love to his mother-in-law and shot dead by his father-in-law at this spot where he is buried. Pious locals burnt candles because it was unconsecrated ground, a practice that continues today with candle-burners praying for their own wishes to be granted.

CENTER FOR CREATIVE PHOTOGRAPHY

The University of Arizona campus houses some excellent museums and several notable outdoor sculptures. At the top of the heap is the internationally renowned **Center for Creative Photography** (Map pp202-3; ☎ 520-621-7968; www.creativephotography.org; 1030 N Olive Ave; admission free; ☯ 9am-5pm Mon-Fri, noon-5pm Sat & Sun). It houses a great collection of works by American photographers, interesting gallery shows and a remarkable archive (including most of Ansel Adams' and Edward Weston's work). It's a must for anyone with even a passing interest in photography.

REID PARK ZOO

Animals from around the world are showcased in this small but excellent **zoo** (Map pp202-3; ☎ 928-791-4022; Reid Park north of 22nd St; adult/child $4/1; ☯ 9am-4pm). Its compact size makes it a great children's excursion, and kids will love the well-constructed themed exhibits. Unusual offerings like giant anteaters and pygmy hippos complement all the standard favorites. Outside the zoo, the surrounding Reid Park provides picnic areas, playgrounds and a duck pond with paddleboat rentals in summer.

PIMA AIR & SPACE MUSEUM AND DAVIS-MONTHAN AIR FORCE BASE

The history of aviation is explained with more than 250 aircraft at this extensive **museum** (Map pp202-3; ☎ 520-574-0462; www.pimaair.org; 6000 E Valencia Rd; adult/child $9.75/6; ☯ 9am-5pm), a must for aircraft buffs. Once you've finished exploring, head to the nearby **Davis-Monthan Air Force Base** (Map pp202-3; ☎ 520-618-4806; adult/child $6/3) to check out nearly 5000 mothballed aircraft. Bus tours of the aircraft 'graveyard' are given several times a day Monday through Friday starting at 9:30am. Reserve in advance.

SANTA CATALINA MOUNTAINS

The best loved and most visited of Tucson's many mountain ranges, the Santa Catalinas are crowned by 9157ft Mt Lemmon. Head to the area around Sabino Canyon, where you'll find the USFS **Santa Catalina ranger station** (Map p199; ☎ 520-749-8700; 5700 N Sabino Canyon Rd; per vehicle $5; ☯ 8am-4:30pm Mon-Fri, 8:30am-4:30pm Sat & Sun). Maps, hiking guides and information are available here, and there is a short nature trail nearby. From here you

can join a narrated shuttle bus tour (adult $6, child $3), which departs every half-hour from 9am to 4:30pm. The buses spend 45 minutes doing a round-trip loop and stop at nine points along the way, including riverside picnic spots. You can get on and off at your whim.

If you want to hike, head to the Bear Canyon trailhead, 2.5 miles from the ranger station on a marked road. From the trailhead a 2.3-mile (one-way) hike leads to Seven Falls, a scenic and popular spot for picnics and swimming, with no facilities (allow 3½ hours round-trip). From the falls, the trail continues up as high as you want to go. This is only one of many trails in the Santa Catalinas. For more information, particularly on the popular hike to the summit of Mt Lemmon, inquire at the ranger station.

OLD TUCSON STUDIOS

Once an actual film set, used in the production of hundreds of Westerns, **Old Tucson** (Map p199; ☎ 520-883-0100; www.oldtucson.com; 201 S Kinney Rd; adult/child $15/10; ☯ 10am-6pm) is now a Western theme park. One of Tucson's most popular tourist attractions, it's a great place to bring the kids. Shootouts, stagecoach rides, saloons, sheriffs and Wild West events galore are all part of the hoopla visitors experience upon entering. The studios are a few miles southeast of the Arizona-Sonora Desert Museum off Hwy 86.

SKIING

Believe it or not, you can ski near Tucson. The **Mt Lemmon Ski Area** (Map p199; ☎ 520-576-1400; Catalina Hwy; adult/child $32/14; ☯ mid-Dec–Mar) is the most southerly ski area in the USA, catering mainly to intermediate and experienced skiers. Rentals, lessons and food are available, but don't expect world-class conditions (this is practically on the Mexican border after all). The season depends on snowfall, so call to make sure the lifts are running before heading up.

HORSEBACK RIDING

To ride amid cacti and scrub brush, or up into the rocky mountains, head to one of several stables in the area offering excursions by the hour, half-day or longer. Summer trips tend to be short breakfast or sunset rides because of the heat. Desert

ARIZONA

ARIZONA

TUCSON

ARIZONA

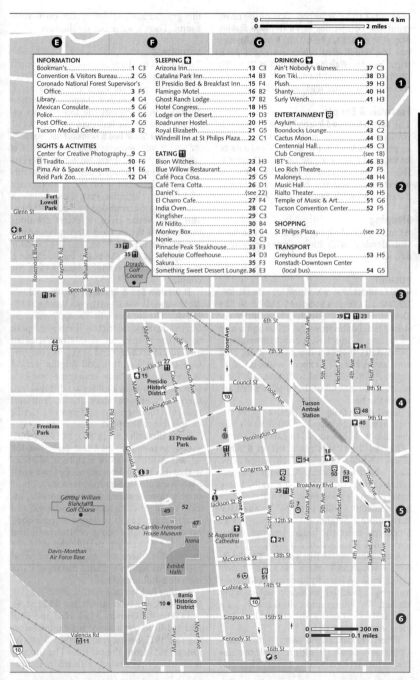

INFORMATION
Bookman's...................................**1** C3
Convention & Visitors Bureau........**2** G5
Coronado National Forest Supervisor's
  Office.......................................**3** F5
Library..**4** G4
Mexican Consulate......................**5** G6
Police...**6** G6
Post Office..................................**7** G5
Tucson Medical Center................**8** E2

SIGHTS & ACTIVITIES
Center for Creative Photography...**9** C3
El Tiradito..................................**10** F6
Pima Air & Space Museum..........**11** E6
Reid Park Zoo............................**12** D4

SLEEPING
Arizona Inn................................**13** C3
Catalina Park Inn........................**14** B3
El Presidio Bed & Breakfast Inn.....**15** F4
Flamingo Motel...........................**16** B2
Ghost Ranch Lodge.....................**17** B2
Hotel Congress...........................**18** H5
Lodge on the Desert...................**19** D3
Roadrunner Hostel......................**20** H5
Royal Elizabeth..........................**21** G5
Windmill Inn at St Philips Plaza....**22** C1

EATING
Bison Witches.............................**23** H3
Blue Willow Restaurant................**24** C2
Café Poca Cosa...........................**25** G5
Café Terra Cotta.........................**26** D1
Daniel's..................................(see 22)
El Charro Cafe............................**27** F4
India Oven.................................**28** C2
Kingfisher..................................**29** C3
Mi Nidito...................................**30** B4
Monkey Box...............................**31** G4
Nonie..**32** C3
Pinnacle Peak Steakhouse...........**33** F3
Safehouse Coffeehouse...............**34** D3
Sakura.......................................**35** F3
Something Sweet Dessert Lounge..**36** E3

DRINKING
Ain't Nobody's Bizness................**37** C3
Kon Tiki....................................**38** D3
Plush...**39** H3
Shanty.......................................**40** H4
Surly Wench...............................**41** H3

ENTERTAINMENT
Asylum......................................**42** G5
Boondocks Lounge......................**43** C2
Cactus Moon..............................**44** E3
Centennial Hall...........................**45** C3
Club Congress........................(see 18)
IBT's...**46** B3
Leo Rich Theatre........................**47** F5
Maloneys...................................**48** H4
Music Hall..................................**49** F5
Rialto Theater.............................**50** H5
Temple of Music & Art.................**51** G6
Tucson Convention Center...........**52** F5

SHOPPING
St Philips Plaza.......................(see 22)

TRANSPORT
Greyhound Bus Depot.................**53** H5
Ronstadt-Downtown Center
  (local bus)...............................**54** G5

cookouts can be arranged. One of the most reputable companies is **Pusch Ridge Stables** (Map p199; ☎ 928-825-1664; 13700 N Oracle Rd; rides from $25), which also offers overnight pack trips. Nearby, **Walking Winds Stables** (Map p199; ☎ 928-742-4422; 10811 N Oracle Rd; rides from $25) specializes in Catalina State Park rides.

Festivals & Events

The **Tucson Gem and Mineral Show** (☎ 520-332-5773; www.tgms.org), in early February, is the largest of its kind in the world. The **Fiesta de los Vaqueros** (Rodeo Week; ☎ 520-741-2233, 800-964-5662; www.tusconrodeo.com) is held the last week of February, and the huge nonmotorized parade is a locally famous spectacle.

Sleeping

As in Phoenix, lodging prices here can vary considerably, with higher rates in winter and spring.

BUDGET

Hotel Congress (Map pp202-3; ☎ 520-622-8848, 800-722-8848; 311 E Congress St; dm/s/d $42/62/72; P 🖳) Downtown's very popular, beautifully restored hotel dates from the 1920s and many of its fine rooms have period furnishings. Downstairs there's a hip music club, café and bar (p208), so expect some noise at night; if you can't deal with that, ask for a room at the far end of the hotel. Dorms are above the bar.

   Ghost Ranch Lodge (Map pp202-3; ☎ 520-791-7565; www.ghostranchlodge.com; 801 W Miracle Mile; r from $55; P 🐾) Designed in part by Georgia O'Keeffe, this 1940s place sits in 8 acres of cactus-filled desert and citrus gardens. Rooms have lots of character, with wooden-rafter ceilings and art on the walls. Some have private patios or kitchenettes. Rates are excellent value, perhaps because the surrounding neighborhood is run-down. Once you enter the lodge, you can forget about that. Plus, security is really tight.

   Roadrunner Hostel (Map pp202-3; ☎ 520-628-4709; www.roadrunnerhostel.com; 346 E 12th St; dm/d $16/35; P 🖳) A friendly place in an old adobe building, amenities include a self-cooking kitchen, TV lounge and coin laundry. It's a light and roomy hostel with clean dorms and pleasant common areas.

   Gilbert Ray Campground (Map p199; ☎ 520-883-4200; Kinney Rd; campsites $12; P) A couple of miles east of the Arizona-Sonora Desert Museum,

this ground has 152 desert sites open year-round. There's water but no showers.

MIDRANGE

Tucson has its share of chains, which you'll find scattered throughout town. The places listed here provide a bit more character. Rates drop in summer; if you're here then consider checking out the top-end places, rooms often go for less than $150.

Casa Tierra Adobe Bed & Breakfast Inn (Map p199; ☎ 520-578-3058; www.casatierratucson.com; 11155 W Calle Pima; r from $135; 🌙 mid-Aug–mid-Jun; P) For those seeking secluded desert abodes, this modern adobe home on the western edge of Saguaro National Park is well worth considering. Surrounded by 5 acres of cacti and Palo Verde trees, it offers fabulous views across the saguaro-strewn landscape. Sunsets are breathtaking, and the outdoor whirlpools is just the place for stargazing. It's a romantic, relaxing place perfect for couples.

   El Presidio Bed & Breakfast Inn (Map pp202-3; ☎ 520-635-6151, 800-349-6151; 297 N Main Ave; r $105-135; P) The location, in Tucson's most attractive historic district, is the biggest perk to staying at this inn. A mix of Victorian and adobe architectural styles, rooms feature antique furniture and original art on the walls. The shady courtyard boasts a Mexican fountain. Besides a full breakfast, there are complimentary drinks, fruit and snacks in the afternoon and evening. Credit cards are not accepted.

   Royal Elizabeth (Map pp202-3; ☎ 520-670-9022; www.royalelizabeth.com; 204 S Scott Ave; r $100-180; P 🐾) A mishmash of architectural styles makes this 1878 Victorian adobe inn a great place for a classic Southwestern stay. Thoroughly unpretentious from the outside, inside you'll find elaborate woodwork and beautiful antique furnishings. Rooms open off a large high-ceiling central hall, and while the downtown neighborhood is not memorable, there are museums and good restaurants within walking distance. Rates include a full breakfast

   Catalina Park Inn (Map pp202-3; ☎ 520-792-4541, 800-792-4885; www.catalinaparkinn.com; 309 E First Ave; r from $135; P) Owners Mark Hall and Paul Richard have put a lot of time into restoring this 1927 home, resembling a Mediterranean villa from the outside. The interior is classically decorated, with many unique and creative touches. Try for the basement Catalina room. It's giant, resembles a classic adobe and has a whirlpool in a former cedar closet. Two units in a separate cottage have more modern decor, while two upstairs rooms in the main inn come with balconies. A full breakfast is included. No children under 12.

Lodge on the Desert (Map pp202-3; ☎ 520-325-3366, 800-456-5634; www.lodgeonthedesert.com; 3-6 N Alvernon Way; r from $130; ⓟ ⓢ) A classic old Arizona resort, this place is set amid flower gardens and manicured lawns. A lush retreat that focuses on relaxation, rooms are in hacienda-style adobe buildings amid cacti and citrus trees. The decor is modern Southwestern and many units have beamed ceilings or fireplaces. The pool has great mountain views.

Flamingo Motel (Map pp202-3; ☎ 520-770-1910, 800-330-3533; www.flamingohoteltucson.com; 1300 N Stone Ave; r $75; ⓟ ⓢ) Quiet off-street rooms surround a nice pool at this fantastic old courtyard motel. The place is decorated everywhere you turn with vintage movie posters. Some rooms, though otherwise very basic, have cool movie-star themes (ask for your favorite celeb).

Windmill Inn at St Philips Plaza (Map pp202-3; ☎ 520-577-0007, 800-547-4747; www.windmillinns.com; 4250 N Campbell Ave; r from $130; ⓟ ⓛ ⓢ) Located in the St Philips Plaza shopping center, this good value place at the edge of the foothills has spacious rooms decorated in the Southwestern style. Business travelers will like the multiple phones and work desks, everyone will enjoy the in-room bars. A paved pathway along the Rillito River (dry most of the year) is just outside the hotel's backdoor. Bikes are provided for guests. An array of upscale shops is just across the parking lot.

TOP END

Tucson's ranches and resorts are often destinations in themselves, rivaling those in the Valley of the Sun for beauty, comfort and diversity of facilities. From golfing to horseback riding to rejuvenation, they offer something for everyone. We've listed just a few, there are many more. Rates can drop dramatically in summer and the months leading up to it, so if you're around during this time give these places a ring, you might score a serious deal.

AUTHOR'S CHOICE

Tanque Verde Guest Ranch (Map p199; ☎ 520-296-6275, 800-234-3833; www.tanque verderanch.com; 14301 E Speedway Blvd; r $290-480; ⓟ ⓢ) Far and away the most luxurious ranch in Tucson, it allows you to play cowboy by day and debutante by night. Fifteen miles east of town in the Rincon Mountains, it offers cookout rides, along with pools, tennis courts and a spa, sauna and exercise room. Digs are big and comfy, with fireplaces and patios in many units. The newest casitas are some of the most luxurious lodging in the state. Dinners are impressive buffet affairs, served in the dining room overlooking the mountains. Rates include all meals and activities.

Arizona Inn (Map pp202-3; ☎ 520-325-1541, 800-933-1093; www.arizonainn.com; 2200 E Elm St; r from $260; ⓟ ⓢ) The grand dame of Tucson hotels, this sedate and beautiful pink-stucco place provides tranquil respite from city life. The 14-acre grounds are attractively landscaped and the whole place is full of grace, character and a kind of old-Arizona charm you won't find elsewhere. Sip coffee on the porch, or take high tea in the library, lounge by the small pool surrounded by flowering trees and vines or join a game of croquet in the garden. Whatever your whim, the relaxing ambiance will make you feel right at home. Rooms are spacious, with a mix of original antiques and well-done reproductions. The service is friendly and unpretentious, yet professional. Rates drop by about $100 in summer.

Hilton Tucson El Conquistador Golf & Tennis Resort (Map p199; ☎ 520-544-5000, 800-325-7832; www .hiltonelconquistador.com; 10000 N Oracle Rd; r $220-420; ⓟ ⓢ) Magnificent sunsets, spectacular Santa Catalina views and three golf courses make this a favorite golfing resort in the region. Rooms are swanky to the max, with Southwestern-influenced furniture, marble bathrooms and balconies. Most units are built around a central courtyard featuring manicured grounds and a large pool with a waterslide (the kids will love this). If you're looking for more privacy, try a room in the separate casita area, which has its own pool. This is a family-friendly resort with children's programs and babysitting services. If you don't want to golf, there are plenty of other options – from horseback riding and racquetball to spa treatments.

Lazy K Bar Guest Ranch (Map p199; ☎ 520-744-3050, 800-321-7018; www.lazykbar.com; 8401 N Scenic Dr; r $240-385; ☼ Sep-Jun; P ☂) The style is very family oriented with plenty of activities for children. Ranch activities include horseback rides, guest rodeos, cookouts, hayrides and stargazing. The sit-down meals are of the hearty American ranch variety. Rooms vary in size and look, try for one of the newest units, which are splendidly comfortable. Rates include all meals and activities.

White Stallion Ranch (Map p199; ☎ 520-297-0252, 888-977-2624; www.wsranch.com; 9251 W Twin Peaks Rd; r $220-350; ☼ Sep-Jun; P ☂) With a more authentic vibe than any other ranch in the area, this place is great for those who crave quiet and wide-open space. Children will enjoy grooming their horse before a ride, or roaming free in the petting zoo. If you'd rather explore on foot, there are nature trails and guided walks through the surrounding desert. Rooms vary; ask for one of the recently renovated ones. Rates include all meals and activities.

Canyon Ranch Health Resort (Map p199; ☎ 520-749-9000, 800-742-9000; www.canyonranch.com; 8600 E Rockcliff Rd; 4-night inclusive packages from $4160; P ▣ ☂) One of America's premier health spas, this place offers the kind of pampering found at only a few resorts across the country. On staff are doctors, psychotherapists, fitness instructors and massage therapists. Services include health, fitness, nutrition and stress management consultations, along with fitness classes and activities (think pilates and golfing lessons), massage therapy, body and facial treatments, and manicures and pedicures. You can even arrange a makeup consultation or art class. Three gourmet low-calorie meals are served each day. Children are discouraged. Rates include meals and most services and activities.

Miraval Life in Balance (Map p199; ☎ 520-825-4000, 800-824-4000; www.miravalresort.com; 500 E Via Estancia; r $770-1100; P ☂) One of the country's most exclusive health spas, Miraval focuses more on alternative healing, stress management and self-discovery than on manicures and facials. Activities include yoga, meditation and tai chi as well as horseback riding, tennis and swimming. The resort strives to teach guests how to balance their lives, with

relaxation the primary objective. Classes include everything from equine therapy and ayurveda to cooking demonstrations. Rates include all meals and classes along with a $95 per day spa credit. No children. The highly recommended resort is about 20 miles north of Tucson.

Eating

Tucson has a well-deserved reputation for Mexican food, and you'll likely be pleasantly surprised by the caliber of cooking. This isn't a city for refried beans or enchiladas, instead you'll find freshly prepared and creative spice-infused dishes from across the country. If you're not in the mood for Mexican, the city has its share of excellent American and international restaurants, many rivaling those found in better known eating destinations such as New York, Los Angeles and San Francisco. Note that smoking is not allowed in Tucson's restaurants. All resorts listed (p205) have their own top-notch restaurants (open to nonguests).

BUDGET

Bison Witches (Map pp202-3; ☎ 520-740-1541; 526 4th Ave; dishes $6; ☼ lunch & dinner) College students pack this small sandwich shop daily, and for a good reason. The sandwiches are humongous, excellent value and filled with all sorts of tasty and imaginative ingredients. Try the half-sandwich/soup bread bowl combo. It's big enough to feed a small army. The environs are trendy, with bright walls and TVs showing sports. There's a good microbrew selection.

Monkey Box (Map pp202-3; ☎ 520-623-3500; Pioneer Plaza, 100 N Stone Ave; dishes $8; ☼ lunch & dinner) A small place with bright yellow walls, it attracts a young dressed-to-impressed professional crowd. On weekend nights they come to dine and groove to live jazz. The menu is simple, featuring salads, unique sandwiches and plenty of desserts. Try the roast beef and blue cheese quesadilla. There's a small, but decent, wine list.

Mi Nidito (Map pp202-3; ☎ 520-622-5081; 1813 S 4th Ave; dishes $6-10; ☼ lunch & dinner) Frequently gets rave reviews for its Mexican fare. There's often a wait; no reservations. Bill Clinton ate here when he was president.

Safehouse Coffeehouse (Map pp202-3; ☎ 520-318-3090; 4024 E Speedway Blvd; dishes from $2; ☼ breakfast, lunch & dinner) A great place to just chill, this locally recommended coffeeshop attracts artsy folks to its alternative environs. It serves a variety of coffee and espresso drinks, as well as pastries and snacks.

Something Sweet Dessert Lounge (Map pp202-3; ☎ 520-881-7735; 5319 E Speedway Blvd; desserts from $5; ⊙ lunch & dinner) The local choice for dessert, there's a giant list of sweet temptations to choose from. It's the sort of place to play Scrabble while devouring a giant sundae. It also has great Mexican coffee.

Blue Willow Restaurant (Map pp202-3; ☎ 520-795-8736; 2616 N Campbell Ave; dishes $6-10; ⊙ breakfast, lunch & dinner) A little bit of everything is served here, including plenty of veggie options. Although the menu isn't long, it's quite varied – from greasy breakfasts to fresh pastas, fish and overstuffed sandwiches. Dine outside amid the greenery on the patio, which is heated in winter.

India Oven (Map pp202-3; ☎ 520-326-8635; 2727 N Campbell; dishes $8; ⊙ lunch & dinner) Serves great Punjab food and has an inexpensive lunch buffet ($7). It's very popular and casual with lots of vegetarian options. Service can be slow.

MIDRANGE & TOP END

El Charro Cafe (Map pp202-3; ☎ 520-622-1922; 311 N Court Ave; dishes $15-20; ⊙ lunch & dinner) The oldest place in town, they say it has been in the same family since 1922. Its *carne seca* used to be dried on the roof in the old days. Today the Mexican food is innovative, mouthwatering and fresh, making it popular with tourists and locals alike.

Kingfisher (Map pp202-3; ☎ 520-323-7739; 2564 E Grant Rd; dishes $20; ⊙ lunch & dinner) Modern and

---

AUTHOR'S CHOICE

Café Poca Cosa (Map pp202-3; ☎ 520-622-6400; Clarion Hotel, 88 E Broadway Blvd; dishes $20; ⊙ lunch & dinner) Dark and intimate with red walls, fun art and trees with lights, this place serves Nuevo Mexican, or Mexican fine dining, to rave reviews. The excellent food incorporates many regions of Mexico, and the menu changes twice daily. Choices at this award-winning place are freshly prepared, innovative and beautifully presented. Try the chef's choice, it changes with each plate but features three different mains. The mole dishes and margaritas are also superb.

---

sophisticated with great decor, this is the kind of place where you'll want to linger. The menu is short, but everything is creative and delicious. Try the baby back ribs with prickly pear barbeque sauce; they're mouthwatering. The wine list is decent, the service efficient.

Nonie (Map pp202-3; ☎ 520-319-1965; 2526 E Grant Rd; dishes $12-15; ⊙ lunch & dinner) A New Orleans bistro serving authentic French Creole and Cajun cuisine, it's classy, cozy and comfortable. If crawfish, jambalaya, alligator and fried pickles are your idea of good food, the cooks know how to prepare them here. They also have the world's hottest hot sauce – available on special request only. There's also a children's menu.

Cafe Terra Cotta (Map pp202-3; ☎ 520-577-8100; 3500 E Sunrise Dr; dishes $12-24) Fine dining abounds in Tucson, but this restaurant gets consistently high ratings for its wood-fired pizzas, spicy pork tenderloin and other upscale Southwestern fare. The appetizers sound so appetizing that many people order two and forgo a main.

Sakura (Map pp202-3; ☎ 520-298-7777; 6534 E Tanque Verde Rd; dishes $15-20) A popular Japanese restaurant with pictures of the celebs that have dined here on the walls, it serves a varied menu including sushi and *teppan* (fun table-side chopping and pyrotechnics).

Daniel's (Map pp202-3; ☎ 520-742-3200; 4340 N Campbell Ave; dishes $12-25; ⊙ dinner) Italian-food lovers will like this elegant place in St Philips Plaza, which specializes in Tuscan-style meals. The pasta dishes are good value.

Pinnacle Peak Steakhouse (Map pp202-3; ☎ 520-296-0911; 6541 E Tanque Verde Rd; dishes $9-17; ⊙ dinner) Located in the touristy Trail Dust Town, done up to look like the grand old frontier (think streetside gunfights and wagon wheels) this place is great for kids. Wooden sidewalks pass dance halls and saloons as you swagger into the dining room. The sign outside warns 'Stop! No Ties Allowed'; if you have one on, you can donate it to the rafter decorations. The food is of the meat-and-potatoes variety, with plenty of options for the little ones. It's not exactly high class, but it's good family fare.

Hidden Valley Inn (Map p199; ☎ 520-299-4941; 4825 N Sabino Canyon Rd; dishes $8-20; ⊙ lunch & dinner) Its Old Wild West look brings in the tourist crowds for burgers and big steaks. It's a great family place with hundreds of animated models of the Old West around the walls – kids can wander around and look at them while waiting for a meal.

Drinking

The free alternative *Tucson Weekly*, published every Thursday, has the most detailed club and bar listings. Also read the Friday 'Starlight' section of the *Arizona Daily Star*. Downtown 4th Ave, near 6th St is a good place to barhop.

Plush (Map pp202-3; ☎ 520-798-1298; cnr 4th Ave & 6th St; club cover $5) One half is a chill lounge and wine bar with multicolored low lights, plush couches and funky art. It emits a fun, quiet-enough-to-talk vibe. The other half is a dark, smoky club showcasing live music. It has a mix of tables and standing room.

Surly Wench (Map pp202-3; ☎ 520-882-0009; 424 4th Ave) A classic dive with black walls, pinball and video games, it has cheap drink specials like $1.50 Schlitz. There's sometimes live music, but when bands play the small place is deafeningly loud.

Shanty (Map pp202-3; ☎ 520-623-2664; cnr 4th Ave & 9th St) The beer menu takes you around the world, from Africa to Asia to Europe, at this light and airy pub with copper pillars, pool tables and free popcorn. If it's warm, sit outside on the patio with the fountain.

Kon Tiki (Map pp202-3; ☎ 520-323-7193; 4625 E Broadway Blvd) For the ultimate kitschy pseudo-Tahitian experience, head to this very popular bar in a strip mall complex. Slurp down the house special – the scorpion. It's served in a punch bowl with long straws and contains enough booze (mixed with fruit juice) to get you and your friends really sloppy. An assortment of other tropical-themed drinks are offered, all served under a faux reed roof amid fake palm fronds. It's an experience all right.

Ain't Nobody's Bizness (Map pp202-3; ☎ 520-318-4838; 2900 E Broadway Blvd, Suite 118) In a shopping plaza, this has been Tucson's favorite lesbian bar for years now. Escape the chaos around the pool tables and on the dance floor by heading to the quiet smoke-free room. It's a good place for a long get-to-know-you chat.

Entertainment

Tucson's a college town, and it hosts loads of clubs showcasing everything from DJs to live music.

CLUBS & LIVE MUSIC

Club Congress (Map pp202-3; ☎ 520-622-8848; Hotel Congress, 311 Congress St) Live and DJ music are found at this very popular dance club. It attracts everyone from college kids to well-dressed professionals to guests staying at the hotel upstairs.

Asylum (Map pp202-3; ☎ 520-882-8949; 121 E Congress St; cover $5) DJs spin most nights at this popular downtown dance club. The decor is dark and edgy, with gothic art and photos on the walls. Black is the color du jour on the dance floor.

Cactus Moon (Map pp202-3; ☎ 520-748-0049; 5470 E Broadway Blvd) Loud and brash, it's the place to see and be seen if you're into two-stepping to recorded music. Come dressed in the latest Western garb for the ultimate country dancing experience.

Rialto Theater (Map pp202-3; ☎ 520-798-3333; 318 E Congress St; cover $10-35) This renovated 1919 vaudeville theater is Tucson's main venue for big-name bands drawing crowds too big for nearby Club Congress to accommodate. Expect acts on national tours.

IBT's (Map pp202-3; ☎ 520-882-3053; 616 N 4th Ave) Tucson's best gay dance club, the theme changes nightly – everything from drag shows to dance mixes to karaoke.

Boondocks Lounge (Map pp202-3; ☎ 520-690-0991; 3360 N 1st Ave; cover up to $10) Once a dive bar, it's now a well-respected venue for live blues and reggae. To find it, look for the giant Chianti bottle out front.

Maloneys (Map pp202-3; ☎ 520-338-9355; 213 N 4th Ave) A large bar with a big dance club playing Top 40 DJ-spun tunes. It's a dark joint drawing a mix of college students and 30- or 40-somethings. Locals say it's a bit of a meat market pick-up joint.

PERFORMING ARTS

Although it's not a huge scene, Tucson has a few venues to catch a symphony, theater or ballet performance.

Temple of Music & Art (Map pp202-3; ☎ 520-884-4875; 330 S Scott Ave) In a renovated 1920s building, it is the home of the Arizona Theatre Company (www.aztheatreco.org), which produces shows from October to May.

Tucson Convention Center (Map pp202-3; ☎ 520-791-4101; 110 S Church Ave) Has a Music Hall, the Leo Rich Theatre and a convention area that hosts the Arizona Opera Company (☎ 520-293-4336; www.azopera.com) and the Tucson Symphony Orchestra (☎ 520-882-8585; www.tucsonsymphony.org) during the winter months.

Centennial Hall (Map pp202-3; ☎ 520-621-3364; www.uapresents.org; 1020 E University Blvd) On the U of A campus, it hosts excellent international acts throughout the academic year, including ballet performances.

Shopping

Some of the best stores for Southwestern arts and crafts are in the **Presidio Historic District** (p200). **St Philips Plaza** (Map pp202-3; cnr River Rd & Campbell Ave) is another good place to look for high-end artwork. Prices are high, but so is the quality. Standouts here include the **Obsidian Gallery** (☎ 520-577-3598) for art and jewelry, **Bahti Indian Arts** (☎ 520-577-0290) for Native American wares, and the **Turquoise Door** (☎ 520-299-7787) for stunning jewelry.

For fun shopping in eclectic shops, from vintage jewelry to used CDs to weird and wonderful knick-knacks, you can't beat 4th Ave between S University Blvd and Congress St.

Getting There & Away

Tucson International Airport (☎ 520-573-8000) is 9 miles south of downtown. **Arizona Stagecoach** (☎ 520-889-1000; www.azstagecoach.com; transfers $8-35) offers door-to-door, 24-hour van service to anywhere in the metropolitan Tucson area. **Greyhound** (Map pp202-3; ☎ 520-792-3475; 2 S 4th Ave) runs buses to Phoenix ($16, two hours, daily) among other destinations. **Amtrak** (Map pp202-3; ☎ 800-872-7245; www.amtrak.com; 400 E Toole Ave) has trains to Los Angeles ($32, 9½ hours; three weekly).

Getting Around

The **Ronstadt-Downtown Center** (Map pp202-3; cnr Congress St & 6th Ave) is the major local transit center. From here **Sun Tran** (☎ 520-792-9222) buses serve metropolitan Tucson ($1). There are no night buses. The company also runs an old-fashioned-looking trolley (fit with air conditioning) linking U of A (it leaves from Old Main) with the 4th Ave shopping area, Congress and the Arts District, historical downtown and the Ronstadt-Downtown Center. Trolleys ($1) run two or three times an hour from about 10am to 6:30pm on weekdays and less frequently on Saturday (no Sunday service).

A taxi from the airport to downtown costs around $15. Companies include **Yellow Cab** (☎ 520-624-6611), **Allstate Cab** (☎ 520-798-1111) and **Checker Cab** (☎ 520-623-1133). Apart from the cab rank at the airport, you need to phone to get a cab – they don't cruise the streets.

AROUND TUCSON

There are many historically interesting, sometimes quirky, sights to the south, north and west of Tucson. The places listed here are less than an hour's drive from town and make great day trips.

Saguaro National Park

Although you see these towering succulents throughout the region, large stands of the majestic saguaro and their associated habitat and wildlife are protected in this **national park** (Map p199; ☎ 520-733-5153; www.nps.gov/sagu; admission $6; ⊙ 8.30am-5pm).

The park has two separate units, east and west of Tucson. The **Saguaro East visitor center** (☎ 520-733-5153; 3693 S Old Spanish Trail) is 15 miles east of downtown along Old Spanish Trail (take E Broadway Blvd). It has information on day hikes, horseback riding and park camping (free permits must be obtained by noon on the day of your hike). This section of the park boasts about 130 miles of trails, including the **Tanque Verde Ridge Trail**, which climbs to the summit of Mica Mountain (8666ft). If you'd rather see the cacti from the comfort of a vehicle, try the **Cactus Forest Drive**. This paved, one-way, 8-mile loop gives access to picnic areas, nature trails of varying lengths and views of the saguaro forest. The road is accessible to all vehicles, including bicycles. A 2.5-mile trail off the drive is suitable for mountain bikes only.

Two miles northwest of the Arizona-Sonora Desert Museum is the **Saguaro West visitor center** (☎ 520-733-5158; 2700 N Kinney Rd). Although night hiking is permitted in this portion of the park, camping is not. The **Bajada Loop Drive** is an unpaved 6-mile loop that begins 1.5 miles west of the visitor center and provides fine views of cactus forests, several picnic spots and access to trailheads. It's accessible to cars. There are short, paved nature trails near the visitor center. Longer trails climb several miles into the Tucson Mountains. These offer fine views and the chance to see Native American petroglyphs.

The **King Canyon trailhead**, just outside the park boundary (almost opposite the Arizona-Sonora Desert Museum), stays open until 10pm and is a great hike if you want to see the sunset or stargaze.

Saguaro seedlings are vulnerable to intense sun and frost, so they often grow in the shade of Palo Verde or mesquite trees, which act as 'nurse trees.' Saguaros grow slowly, taking about 15 years to reach a foot in height, 50 years to reach 7ft and almost a century before they begin to take on their typical many-armed appearance.

Late April is a good time to visit the park, when the saguaros begin blossoming with lovely white flowers – Arizona's state flower. By June and July, the flowers give way to ripe red fruit that has been traditionally picked by desert Indians; they use them both for food (as fruit and jam) and to make saguaro wine.

Biosphere 2

Built to be completely sealed off from Biosphere 1 (that would be earth), **Biosphere 2** (Map p199; ☎ 520-896-6200; www.bio2.edu; 32540 S Biosphere Rd; adult/child $13/9; ⓨ 8:30am-5pm) is a 3-acre glassed dome housing seven separate microhabitats designed to be self-sustaining. In 1991, eight bionauts entered Biosphere 2 for a two-year tour of duty, during which they were physically cut off from the outside world. They emerged thinner but in pretty fair shape. Although this experiment could be used as a prototype for future space stations, it was a privately funded endeavor and was engulfed in controversy. Heavy criticism came after the dome leaked gases and was opened to allow a bionaut to emerge for medical treatment. The facility is now operated by Columbia University and the public can tour the strange site and enter parts of the biosphere. Biosphere 2 is about 30 miles north of Tucson on Hwy 77.

Picacho Peak State Park

The westernmost 'battle' of the American Civil War was fought at Picacho Peak (3374ft), with Confederate forces killing two or three Union soldiers. The Confederates retreated to Tucson, 40 miles to the southeast, and dispersed, knowing their forces would soon be greatly outnumbered.

The **state park** (☎ 520-466-3183; day use per vehicle $5; camp/RV sites $10/15) is north of Tucson

off I-10 at exit 219. It provides year-round camping, picnicking and two steep hiking trails to the peak's summit. Fixed ropes and ladders are used to aid hikers, but no technical climbing is involved. It's about 2 miles and 1500ft up to the top.

Casa Grande Ruins National Monument

Once a major Hohokam village covering about 1 sq mile, this site was abandoned around AD 1350. Little remains today except for the Casa Grande (big house), preserved as a **national monument** (Map p199; ☎ 520-723-3172; per vehicle $3; ⓨ 8am-5pm). The monument is about 20 miles north of Tucson off I-10 (take exit 212). It's an imposing, impressive building, and the most unusual Hohokam structure standing today. About 30ft or 40ft high, Casa Grande has mud walls several feet thick. The mud was made from caliche, the rock-hard soil of the area that is the bane of the modern gardener. A huge amount of work went into constructing the building, and although rain and human intrusion have caused some damage, the general structure remains clear. To prevent further erosion, Casa Grande has been capped by a large metal awning, an effective, if incongruous, preservation tool. You cannot enter the building itself, though the outside makes for an impressive photo. The visitor center (located at the entrance-ticket station) has a small museum explaining the general history of the Hohokam, with special attention paid to the ruin.

Mission San Xavier del Bac

Dating back to 1692, **Mission San Xavier del Bac** (☎ 520-294-2624; 1950 W San Xavier Rd; admission by donation; ⓨ 7am-5pm) is Arizona's oldest European building still in use. One of 20-something missions in southern Arizona founded by Father Eusebio Francisco Kino, it was mostly destroyed in the Pima Indian uprising of 1751. Rebuilt in the late 1700s, today it looks much like it did 200 years ago. A graceful blend of Moorish, Byzantine and late Mexican Renaissance architecture, the building has been restored but work is always continuing on the frescoes inside. Just 9 miles south of downtown, a visit to San Xavier is one of the highlights of a trip to Tucson.

Nicknamed 'the white dove of the desert,' its dazzling white walls are a splendid sight as you drive south on I-19 (take exit 92). The mission is on the San Xavier Indian Reservation (part of the Tohono O'odham tribe), and the plaza by the mission parking lot has stores selling Native American jewelry, arts and crafts, and snacks. Inside you'll find a series of domes and arches and a colorful gilded altar. Catholic masses are held daily. Colorful religious ceremonies take place on the Friday after Easter, during the Fiesta of San Xavier in early December and on Christmas. Call the mission for details.

Titan Missile Museum

Anyone interested in Cold War history will enjoy a visit to this **museum** (Map p199; ☎ 520-574-9658; 1580 W Duval Mine Rd; adult/child $7.50/4; 🕑 9am-5pm daily Nov-Apr, Wed-Sun May-Oct). During the 1950s and '60s, the USA amassed a giant fleet of Intercontinental Ballistic Missiles armed with nuclear warheads ready to fly within seconds of receiving a launch order. Once an underground launch site for these missiles, today the nuclear warhead has been removed but the site remains much as it was during the tense Cold War, when a push of a button could have started a cataclysmic chain of devastating events. Guided tours of the site leave every half-hour November through April, less frequently in summer. These are both informative and interesting. This national historic monument is south of Tucson off I-19 (take exit 69).

DETOUR: HIGHWAY 86 TOWARDS ORGAN PIPE CACTUS NATIONAL MONUMENT

From Tucson, Hwy 86 heads west into some of the driest and emptiest parts of the Sonoran Desert. It's a great drive for anyone craving for the lure of the open road. Listen for the sounds of the desert – the howl of a coyote, the rattle of a snake. The skies are big, the land vast and barren. Away from the clutter of the city, the only manmade noise comes from the soft hum of your car wheels sliding across smooth pavement.

Fifty-six miles southwest of Tucson, just west of Sells, is the **Kitt Peak National Optical Observatory** (☎ 520-318-8726; www.noao.edu/kpno; Hwy 86; admission $2; 🕑 9am-3:45pm), the largest optical observatory in the world. It features 22 telescopes, one of which is used to study the sun via a series of mirrors. The largest telescope has a diameter of 4m and is housed in a 19-story-high dome. Guided tours (10am, 11:30am and 1:30pm) last about an hour and visit two or three telescopes. The three-hour nightly stargazing sessions ($36) are a real treat. These are very popular, limited to 20 people, and should be booked weeks in advance.

From the observatory, continue west on Hwy 86 to the town of Why. From here turn off on Hwy 85 and continue for 22 miles to **Organ Pipe Cactus National Monument** (☎ 520-387-6849; Hwy 85; admission $5; 🕑 8am-5pm). Anyone seeking solitude in stark, quiet and beautiful desert surroundings won't be disappointed by the undisturbed Sonoran habitat at this park. Here you can enjoy the succulents without the crowds. The park is home to three species of cacti, including saguaro. A giant columnar cactus, the organ pipe differs from the saguaro in that it branches from its base. The succulents are common in Mexico, but this national monument is one of the few places to see them in the USA. The monument is the *only* place in the USA to see the senita cactus. Its branches are topped by hairy white tufts, which give it the nickname 'old man's beard.'

The monument offers six hiking trails ranging from a 200-yard paved nature romp to strenuous climbs of over 4 miles. Cross-country hiking is also possible, but have a topographical map and a compass and know how to use them – a mistake out here could be deadly. Two scenic drives (21 and 53 miles) create loops from near the visitor center. The roads are steep, winding and unpaved, but passable to cars if it's dry. Both offer a chance to really experience the majesty of this incredible landscape.

Winter is the most pleasant season to visit the monument. Summer temperatures soar above 100°F on most days. There is a campground ($10) by the visitor center. The 200 sites are first-come, first-served and are often full by noon from mid-January through March. There is drinking water but no showers or RV hookups. Free backcountry camping (no water) is only allowed with a permit (obtainable for free at the visitor center).

When you're finished in the park, you'll need to backtrack the way you came – otherwise you'll be heading straight for Mexico.

TUBAC & AROUND

pop 1200 / elev 3200ft

Once a Pima Indian village and then a Spanish fort, today Tubac's historic buildings are filled with more than 80 shops and galleries selling fine arts, crafts, unique gifts and touristy Southwestern souvenirs. In the fertile Santa Cruz River valley, 45 miles south of Tucson, the town has become one of the state's largest art communities, and one of southern Arizona's most popular tourist destinations. It's just off I-19, exit 34.

Tubac is a small place, easily seen on foot. Visit the **Tubac-Santa Cruz Visitor Center** (☎ 520-398-0007; www.toursantacruz.com; 4 Plaza Rd) for gallery and walking maps.

Once you've perused the shops, head south for 3 miles to the well-preserved ruins of the Tumacácori Franciscan Church, now part of the **Tumacácori National Historic Park** (☎ 520-398-2341; www.nps.gov/tuma; I-19 exit 29; admission $5; ☺ 8am-5pm). Founded in 1691 by Jesuit missionary and explorer Father Eusebio Francisco Kino, the mission was one of Arizona's first Anglo settlements. Father Kino's task was to convert the Pima Indians. It was considered a success for the first 60 years until the 1751 Pima Revolt destroyed the mission. In the 1820s an adobe mission church was constructed at the site, much of which is still standing. Today the ruins are a haunting testament to the role Spanish missionaries played in settling the region. A small museum has exhibits on mission life and the history of the region. Native American and Mexican artists give demonstrations of indigenous crafts on weekends between September and May.

Sleeping & Eating

Amado Territory Inn (☎ 520-398-8684, 888-398-8684; www.amado-territory-inn.com; 30001 E Frontage Rd, Amado; r $95-135; ✗) In the nearby town of Amado (I-19, exit 48). Capturing the feel of a 19th-century ranch house, rooms feature rustic Mexican furnishings and reproduction antiques. They look much the way they would have 100 years ago.

Tubac Golf Resort (☎ 520-398-2211, 800-848-7893; www.tubacgolfresort.com; 1 Otero Rd; r $100-200; ☻) The low-key resort is built on the grounds of the 1789 Otero Ranch, the oldest Spanish land grant in the Southwest. The place has undergone extensive renovations in recent years (hoping to compete with larger golf resorts in Tucson), but still maintains a relaxed air. With red-tile roofs and graceful archways, the place has a charming old Spanish feel. The rooms are modern and spacious, and the grounds expansive and well maintained. There's even an excellent restaurant tucked back in the old stable block. The resort is a mile north of Tubac.

Amado Café (☎ 520-398-9211; E Frontage Rd; dishes $8-20) Next to the Amado Territory Inn, the Amado Café serves sandwiches and salads at lunch and more-filling steak and fish plates at dinner. The few Greek dishes are always a good choice. Contemplate country life from the rustic patio with the pretty fountain and mountain views.

Shelby's Bistro (☎ 520-398-8075; 19 Tubac Rd; dishes $10-25) Usually crammed with tourists at lunch, this is one of the few places to eat in Tubac. It's a casual restaurant serving upscale American cuisine – from designer pizza to tender pork loin.

Wisdom's Café (☎ 520-398-2379; 1931 E Frontage Rd; dishes $7) A roadside diner in operation since 1944, Wisdom's is a local institution. There's a cement floor, cowboy memorabilia on the walls and a big TV playing old Westerns in the corner. The menu is short, sweet and Mexican themed. Make sure to leave room for dessert; the place is famous for its fruit burros (basically a fruit pie). You'll pass it on the way to Tumacácori from Tubac (look for the giant chicken statues).

PATAGONIA & AROUND

pop 880 / elev 4050ft

To get away from it all, and perhaps taste a bit of Arizona wine (didn't know they grew grapes down here?), head south on Hwy 82 to tiny Patagonia. The countryside around here is a surprising change from the region's desertscapes. Tall grass blows in the wind, tumbleweeds cascade across one-lane highways and old windmills make for pretty pictures, especially when the clouds roll in. You may think you've been transported to the Great Plains; the look is so authentic the movie-version of the musical *Oklahoma!* was shot here.

Once an important stop on a western railway line, Patagonia's population has been declining since the trains stopped running in 1962. Today it's a sleepy little ranching center with tree-lined streets and old adobe buildings. It's trying hard to become an art destination, although so far there's not that much art. But with quaint B&Bs, good restaurants and a handful of nearby wineries, Patagonia is fast becoming a favorite weekend getaway for Tucsonans looking to spend a few days in the quiet countryside.

To find out what's going on, visit the **Patagonia Visitor Center** (☎ 520-394-0060; www .patagoniaaz.com; 307 McKeown Ave; ⊙ 10am-5pm Mon & Wed-Fri, 11am-4pm Sun). It's in the Mariposa Book & Gift shop, one block off Hwy 82.

Exploring the country roads on a quest for wine makes a great day trip. From Patagonia it's a 20-mile drive to **Callaghan Vineyards** (☎ 520-455-5322; www.callaghanvineyards .com; 336 Elgin Rd; ⊙ 11am-3pm Fri-Sun), which produces the best wine in the state. You can taste its seven reds and three whites. Make sure to try the Zinfandel, the wine it's known for. To get here, head north on Hwy 82 to the village of Sonita, where you'll head south on Hwy 83 and then east on Eglin Rd. A few miles back in the ghost town of Elgin is the **Village of Elgin Winery** (☎ 520-455-9309; www.elginwines.com; 471 Elgin Rd; ⊙ 10am-5pm). The quality of the varietals isn't as good, but tastings take place in an 1898 brothel.

Back in Patagonia, stay at the **Duquesne House** (☎ 520-394-2732; 357 Duquesne St; r $75) inside one of Patagonia's oldest buildings. This long established B&B has six old-fashioned units each with its own entrance, sitting room and porch. Try for the room with the woodstove and clawfoot tub. The owner also runs a gallery, so the artsy crowd will fit right in.

Another good option is the recently renovated **Stage Stop Inn** (☎ 520-394-2211, 800-923-2211; 303 W McKeown; r $90; ⊗). It's a modern motel with an Old West facade – think swinging doors and wooden ceilings. Arizona steaks and other American fare are served at its restaurant (dishes from $7), and it's bottoms-up at the adjoining saloon.

The **Velvet Elvis** (☎ 520-394-2102; 292 Hwy 82; dishes $8-15; ⊙ 11:30am-8:30pm Thu-Sun) serves designer pizzas, soups and salads amid funky artwork (including a velvet Elvis, of course). Drink selections include microbrews and organic wine.

A favorite with locals, the tiny **Café Sonita** (☎ 520-455-5278; 3280 Hwy 82; dishes $10-20), in Sonita, serves the best food in the area. The small menu changes daily, and offerings are chalked up on a blackboard. The choices are imaginative and everything is made from scratch, using only the freshest ingredients. Local wines accompany the meals. Hours vary, so call first.

BENSON
pop 4700 / elev 3580ft
A late 1800s railway halt, today rural Benson is a quiet travelers' stop. The famous Kartchner Caverns, 9 miles south, are the reason to visit. While in town, don't miss the **Singing Wind Bookshop** (☎ 520-568-2425; 700 W Singing Wind Rd; ⊙ 9am-5pm), 2.5 miles north of Benson along Ocotillo Ave. This ranch-house/bookshop has thousands of books with mainly Southwest themes.

Discovered in 1974, but not opened to the public until 1999 (the location was kept secret until state park protection could be assured), the **Kartchner Caverns State Park** (☎ 520-586-4100; Hwy 90; per vehicle $10, tour adult/child $23/13; ⊙ 7:30am-6pm) are among the largest and most spectacular caves in the USA. Almost completely undamaged and unexplored when discovered, the moist 2.5-mile long limestone cave's geological features are still growing. To ensure the protection of this fragile ecosystem – which includes stalactites, stalagmites and soda straws – all tours pass through airtight locks. The caverns feature two huge rooms, each larger than a football field with ceilings more than 100ft high. Two tours are offered. The shorter tour takes you past thousands of delicate soda straws, including the longest soda straw formation in the USA, measuring more than 21ft. It also visits the Throne Room, with a 58ft-tall crown jewel of a column in its center. The longer tour visits the other large room, aptly named the Big Room, and twists past hundreds of strange and fabulous formations. The caves are very popular and tours can sell out months in advance, so reservations are strongly recommended.

Sleeping options around Benson are generally of the chain motel variety. These are found between exits 302 and 304 on I-10. By far the best sleeping option around town is the **Skywatcher's Inn** (☎ 520-615-3886; 1311 S Astronomers Rd; r $75-110; ⊗). A four-room B&B at the Vega-Bray Observatory a few miles southeast of Benson, each room has a different theme. There's the Egyptian room, with a marble Jacuzzi and elaborate brass furnishings. And then there's a sort of intergalactic room with *Star Wars* toys and a domed ceiling. The observatory has a planetarium and eight telescopes. It offers four-hour guided introductory astronomy sessions ($85) along with other sky-watching packages. Reservations are necessary.

The **Benson Motel** (☎ 520-586-3346; 185 W 4th St; r from $35) is one of six old motels along 4th St (Hwy 80). It offers basic rooms and old-fashioned car garages. If you want to camp, try the **KOA** (☎ 520-586-3977; campsites from $19; 🔊), just off Ocotillo Rd, north of I-10 at exit 304. It has a hot tub and minigolf.

For grub, the **Chute-Out Steakhouse** (☎ 520-586-7297; 161 S Huachuca St; dishes from $10) is locally popular, even though the steaks aren't great. Stick with the tasty ribs. Italian and American fare is dished up at **Galleano's** (☎ 520-586-3523; 601 W 4th St), a homey little place that's good for breakfast (or lunch and dinner).

Greyhound (☎ 520-586-3141; 680 W 4th St) buses stop in town on their runs along I-10.

TOMBSTONE
pop 1500 / elev 4539ft

Stories this good just can't be made up. The year was 1877 and a rip-roaring, brawling, silver-mining town was about to be born. Despite friends' warnings that all he would find was his own tombstone, prospector Ed Schieffelin braved the dangers of Apache attack and struck it rich. He named the strike Tombstone and a legend was born. You've heard the stories, Doc Holliday and the shootout at the OK Corral, ladies of the night and hard-drinking, quick-to-draw miners. Rags to riches to rags tales of fortunes won and just as quickly spent. It's the stuff Hollywood makes movies about, and the tourists eat it up. There are hundreds of old mining towns scattered throughout the southwest, but Tombstone's always been the sweetheart; the most famous of them all.

In 1881, when the population reached 10,000, 110 saloon licenses were sold and there were 14 dance halls for the entertainment of the get-rich-quick miners. While saloons, gambling halls and bordellos accounted for a good portion of town businesses, there were, as always, a sprinkling of sober citizens running newspapers, banks

and general stores. The shootout at the OK Corral, when Wyatt Earp, his brothers Virgil and Morgan and their friend Doc Holliday gunned down outlaws Ike Clanton and Tom and Frank McLaury, also took place in 1881. This was one of dozens of gunfights in Tombstone, but it so caught people's imagination it's the one that made the history books (and movies).

Conjuring up the bad old frontier days takes some creative thinking when you're staring at boarded-up buildings and rusting mineshafts, but in Tombstone you taste it and touch it. When most boomtowns were going bust, Tombstone declared itself 'too tough to die.' The silver mining days were all but done when the 19th century ended, but the town never quite faded. When someone decided tourism was the new silver and the Old West was suddenly in vogue, Tombstone didn't have to reconstruct its past with quite as many wannabe replicas. Sure a few new structures were built in the style of the old days, but plenty of original buildings remained. The old county courthouse was turned into a museum in the 1950s. By 1962 the entire town was a National Historic Landmark. Today the Wild West is alive and kicking in Tombstone, and the town is one of Arizona's most popular tourist attractions. You'll have to visit to decide if it lives up to its reputation.

Orientation & Information

Tombstone is 181 miles southeast of Phoenix and 70 miles southeast of Tucson. The downtown is small. You'll find most businesses along Fremont, Allen and Toughnut Sts between 3rd and 6th Sts.

Library (☎ 520-457-3612; cnr 4th & Toughnut Sts) Free Internet access.

Police (☎ 520-457-2244; 313 E Fremont St)

Post office (☎ 520-457-3479; 100 Haskell St) Prove you've visited with a Tombstone postmark on your letter.

Tombstone Chamber of Commerce (☎ 520-457-3929, 800-457-3423; cnr 4th & Allen Sts) The scoop on what's happening.

Sights

Walking around town is free, but you'll pay to visit most attractions. The fees are small, but they quickly add up. If you're short on cash, decide what's most important. If you're traveling with the kids, make the OK Corral (and its corresponding attractions) and the Staged Shootouts your top priorities.

OK CORRAL

The gunfight at the **OK Corral** (☎ 520-457-3456; www.ok-corral.com; Allen St btwn 3rd & 4th Sts; admission $5.50; ❂ 9am-5pm) only lasted 30 seconds, but like all compelling stories it's grown some epic legs. Thanks in part to Hollywood's efforts, shootouts have become the symbols of the Wild American West, and Tombstone is all too happy to cash in on the phenomena. A first stop for many visitors, the OK Corral has models of the gunfighters and numerous other Western exhibits. The most interesting is CS Fly's early photography studio. Next door is **Tombstone's Historama** (admission $2.50). It's a 26-minute presentation where the town's checkered past is brought to life using animated figures, movies and narration. Shows take place on the hour between 9am and 4pm. The gunfight is a re-enacted daily at 2pm and costs another $1.50 to watch. Pay $7.50 to catch all three attractions.

TOMBSTONE COURTHOUSE STATE HISTORIC PARK

Built in 1882, abandoned in 1931 and rehabilitated in the 1950s, the **courthouse** (☎ 520-457-3311; cnr 3rd & Toughnut Sts; adult/child $4/1; ❂ 8am-5pm) displays thousands of artifacts relating to the town's history, including a 19th-century gallows, which will (for better or worse) pique children's interest. Staffed by knowledgeable state-park rangers, this museum deserves a visit.

STAGED SHOOTOUTS

A prime attraction, the **shootouts** (adult/child $4/1) are re-enacted by various acting troupes. Apart from the 2pm show at the OK Corral (which sells out early on weekends and holidays), there are daily shows at Helldorado (11:30am, 1pm and 3pm; downtown). Enjoy your shootout over an outdoor lunch at the Crazy Horse Restaurant (p217). The fight takes place several times per day; call for times. Other shootouts, some for free, occur spontaneously throughout the day (you'll just have to visit to see, although special events always call for extra gunfire...).

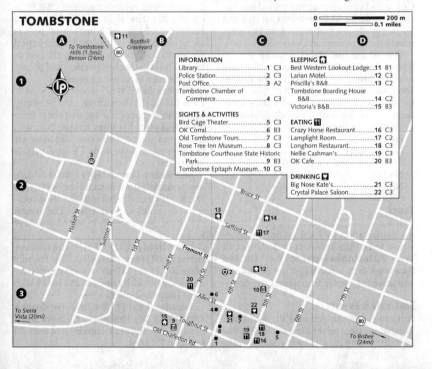

TOMBSTONE

| 0 | 200 m |
| 0 | 0.1 miles |

INFORMATION
Library..1 C3
Police Station...............................2 C3
Post Office....................................3 A2
Tombstone Chamber of
    Commerce................................4 C3

SIGHTS & ACTIVITIES
Bird Cage Theater.........................5 C3
OK Corral......................................6 B3
Old Tombstone Tours....................7 C3
Rose Tree Inn Museum..................8 C3
Tombstone Courthouse State Historic
    Park...9 B3
Tombstone Epitaph Museum...10 C3

SLEEPING
Best Western Lookout Lodge...11 B1
Larian Motel..............................12 C3
Priscilla's B&B............................13 C2
Tombstone Boarding House
    B&B......................................14 C2
Victoria's B&B...........................15 B3

EATING
Crazy Horse Restaurant............16 C3
Lamplight Room........................17 C2
Longhorn Restaurant................18 C3
Nellie Cashman's......................19 C3
OK Cafe.....................................20 B3

DRINKING
Big Nose Kate's.........................21 C3
Crystal Palace Saloon...............22 C3

To Tombstone Hills (1.5mi); Benson (24mi)

Boothill Graveyard

Bruce St

Haskell St
Summer St
1st St
2nd St
3rd St
4th St
5th St
6th St
7th St

Safford St
Fremont St
Allen St
Toughnut St
Old Charleston Rd

To Sierra Vista (20mi)

To Bisbee (24mi)

ARIZONA

OTHER SIGHTS

Once used by prostitutes to entertain clients, the **Bird Cage Theater** (☎ 520-457-3421; 517 E Allen St; admission $6; ☙ 8am-6pm) got its name from the 14 bed-sized, draped cages suspended from the ceiling. A bordello, gambling den, dance hall and saloon during the 1880s, this was once the wildest place in the West. All the original furnishings (except the prostitutes) remain, and once you slip inside you'll quickly feel the centuries slide back.

Antique 1880s furniture and the world's largest rosebush can be seen at the **Rose Tree Inn Museum** (☎ 520-457-3326; cnr 4th & Toughnut Sts; admission $3; ☙ 9am-5pm). The White Banksia rosebush arrived as a shoot sent from Scotland to a young emigrant wife in 1885; now over 8600 sq ft, the bush is especially pretty in April when the white flowers bloom.

The **Tombstone Epitaph Museum** (☎ 520-457-2211; cnr 5th & Fremont Sts; admission free; ☙ 9:30am-5pm) houses the presses of the town's first newspaper. It costs $1 for a replica of the 27 October, 1881 edition of the *Tombstone Epitaph*, which reports the gunfight at OK Corral and contains various period ads, including one for **GF Spangenberg** (cnr 4th & Allen Sts), a gun dealer that still operates today, selling both modern and antique weapons.

One of the few places you can see for free in this tourist town (though you have to enter through a gift shop!) is the **Boothill Graveyard** (off Hwy 80), just north of town, with the graves of many of Tombstone's early desperadoes. Some of the headstones make interesting reading:

Here lies
Lester Moore
Four slights from a 44
No Les
No More.

Tours

Ride a stagecoach around town while listening to narration by local guides, many of whom trace their ancestors back to the Old West. **Old Tombstone Tours** (☎ 520-457-3018; Allen St btwn 4th & 5th Sts; adult/child $5/4) last 20 minutes and leave frequently throughout the day.

Festivals & Events

Not much has changed over the years, and Tombstone likes celebrating as much today as it did during its wild years. Many weekends are reserved for lots of Western hooha with shootouts (of course!), stagecoach rides, fiddling contests, 'vigilette' fashion shows, mock hangings and melodramas. The biggest event is **Helldorado Days** (third weekend in October). Other events include **Territorial Days** (variable dates in March), **Wyatt Earp Days** (Memorial Day weekend), **Vigilante Days** (second weekend in August) and **Rendezvous of the Gunfighters** (Labor Day weekend).

Sleeping

Motels raise their rates during special events, when reservations are recommended. Summer rates drop a bit, but Tombstone is a year-round destination, so don't expect much of a change.

Victoria's B&B (☎ 520-457-3677, 800-952-8216; 211 Toughnut St; r $65-75; ✗) Dating from 1880, this place has a checkered past featuring gamblers, judges and ghosts. Nowadays, it has a private wedding chapel and the owner will arrange for a minister if you bring a partner and the wedding license.

Tombstone Boarding House B&B (☎ 520-457-3716; www.tombstoneboardinghouse.com; 108 N 4th St; r $70-90; ✗) The eight bedrooms, in two restored 1880s adobe homes, have private entrances and are furnished with period pieces. Its breakfast is reputedly the best in town – it includes champagne – and dinner is sometimes available on request.

Priscilla's B&B (☎ 520-457-3844; 101 N 3rd St; r from $60; ✗) A lacy-curtained, two-story Victorian clapboard house that dates from 1904, this place has three rooms, each with a sink and shared bathroom. Pay more for the two-room suite with TV and private bathroom.

Best Western Lookout Lodge (☎ 520-457-2223; www.tombstone1800.com/bwlookoutlodge; Hwy 80; r $60-190; ☖) It's a chain, but also the most comfortable motel around town. The rooms area good size, decently outfitted and have nice views.

Larian Motel (☎ 520-457-2272; www.tombstonemotels.com; 410 E Fremont St; r $40-60) This friendly place has 14 very clean rooms with coffeemakers, most with two beds and many with mini-fridge and microwave.

Tombstone Hills (☎ 520-457-3829; Hwy 80; camp & RV sites $22-28; ☖) This place, 1.5 miles north of town, has showers, laundry and over 80 tent and RV sites.

Eating

Most eating establishments are located in historic buildings. In keeping with its Old West theme, the cuisine is mostly standard American and Mexican.

Lamplight Room (☎ 520-457-3716; 108 N 4th St; dishes $11-17; ⊗ lunch & dinner) The best food in Tombstone is served in the living room of an 1880s home. Big on character, it's also the most charming place to eat. The menu is short but varied. It includes spicy Mexican fare and classics like chicken cordon bleu. On Friday and Saturday nights a classical guitarist provides a background serenade.

Nellie Cashman's (☎ 520-457-2212; cnr 5th & Toughnut Sts; dishes $9-19; ⊗ breakfast, lunch & dinner) Nellie was a tough Irishwoman who stood no nonsense but helped out many a down-and-out miner. This no-alcohol establishment, dating from 1882, serves home-style meals in a quietly charming dining room. Huge hamburger plates are around $6.

Crazy Horse Restaurant (☎ 520-457-3827; cnr 5th & Toughnut Sts; dishes $8-15; ⊗ breakfast, lunch & dinner) Dine to the clatter of gunfire at this wild place, where lunch is served outside during daily shootouts. Considering the major tourist draw, the reasonably priced Western food is surprisingly tasty. Dinners are more sedate indoor affairs.

Longhorn Restaurant (☎ 520-457-3405; cnr Allen & 5th Sts; dishes $5-15; ⊗ breakfast, lunch & dinner) Lunchtime lines are common at this popular place serving American and Mexican fare. Breakfasts and dinners are quieter.

OK Cafe (☎ 520-457-3980; 220 E Allen St; dishes $5-9; ⊗ breakfast & lunch) Whether you're craving something a little exotic (think buffalo, ostrich and emu burgers) or just some down-home American cooking (think burgers and BLTs), this café is sure to please. It's right on the tourist strip, but the food is decent.

Drinking

Sticking to their wild roots, several bars along Allen St flaunt loads of old-time ambiance. Now that the bordellos and gambling joints are gone, there's little to do in the evening but go on a pub crawl – or make that a saloon stagger.

Crystal Palace Saloon (☎ 520-457-3611; cnr 5th & Allen Sts) This lively saloon was built in 1879 and has been completely restored. It's a favorite end-of-the-day watering hole with Tombstone's costumed actors or anyone wanting to play outlaw for a night.

Big Nose Kate's (☎ 520-457-3107; 417 E Allen St) Full of Wild West character, this is another favorite drinking spot. It's also the place for dancing.

Getting There & Around

There is no public transport to Tombstone. You'll need your own wheels to visit.

BISBEE & AROUND

pop 6100 / elev 5300ft

Built into the steep walls of Tombstone Canyon, Bisbee is one of Arizona's most endearing towns. Oozing old-fashioned ambiance, its elegant Victorian buildings line narrow twisting streets. The rotting miners' shacks sprawled across the blazing red hills above town are potent reminders of Bisbee's copper boomtown days. Between 1880 and 1975, Bisbee's mines produced more than $6 billion worth of metals. By 1910 the population had climbed to 25,000, and with nearly 50 saloons and bordellos crammed along Brewery Gulch it quickly gained a reputation as the liveliest city between El Paso, Texas, and San Francisco, California.

When the copper mines went bust, it seemed Bisbee was doomed to become just another Arizona ghost town. But its place as the county seat ensured its survival. Today Bisbee is one of the best-preserved historic towns in the Southwest, and a darling of the movie-producing crowd. Not only has it played its Old West self, it's even doubled for New York and Greece! The residents here are an intriguing mix of aging miners, hippies and artists, and folks just wanting to leave big-city life behind. They've done a great job of seamlessly blending the rough-and-ready past with the trendy cosmopolitan, and the restored buildings now house charming B&Bs, hip galleries and funky restaurants. In the 21st century, there's no question that Bisbee is very much alive.

Orientation & Information

Hwy 80 runs through the center of town. Most businesses are found in the Historic District (Old Bisbee), along Subway and Main Sts and near the intersection of Howell and Brewery Aves. Warren is a suburb

3 miles southeast of town. It has many Victorian homes and the local hospital.

Dial ☎ 911 in an emergency.

Chamber of Commerce (☎ 520-432-5421, 866-224-7233; www.bisbeearizona.com; 31 Subway St) Staff can reserve space and sell tickets for a mine tour, and they keep track of available lodging.

Copper Queen Hospital (☎ 520-432-5383; cnr Bisbee Rd & Cole Ave, Warren)

Library (☎ 520-432-4232; 6 Main St) Free Internet access.

Police (☎ 520-432-2261)

Post office (☎ 520-432-2052; 6 Main St)

Sights & Activities

Housed in the 1897 office building of the Phelps Dodge Copper Mining Co, the **Bisbee Mining & Historical Museum** (☎ 520-432-7071; Copper Queen Plaza; adult/child $4/free; ☺ 10am-4pm) has a fine display depicting the first 40 years of Bisbee's history, along with exhibits about mining. It also has a history and mining research library associated with the Smithsonian Institute.

Bisbee owes its existence to the ore found in the surrounding hills. To learn how it was collected take an underground tour of the **Queen Mine** (☎ 520-432-2071; 119 Arizona St; adult/child $12/5; ☺ 9am-3:30pm). Retired miners give the hour-long tours, which descend deep underground (it's a chilly 47°F down here so bring warm clothes).

OK St is high on the hill above the southern edge of town and a good place to stroll, affording excellent views. A path at the top

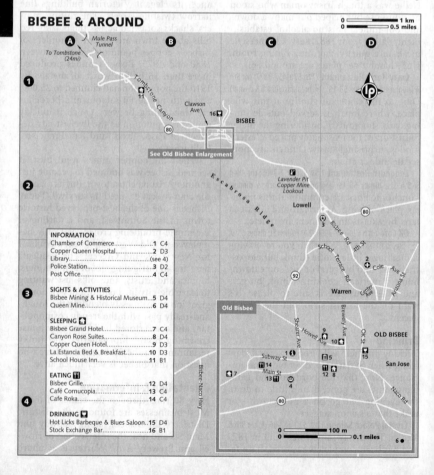

BISBEE & AROUND

0 ——————— 1 km
0 ——————— 0.5 miles

INFORMATION	
Chamber of Commerce	1 C4
Copper Queen Hospital	2 D3
Library	(see 4)
Police Station	3 D2
Post Office	4 C4

SIGHTS & ACTIVITIES	
Bisbee Mining & Historical Museum	5 D4
Queen Mine	6 D4

SLEEPING	
Bisbee Grand Hotel	7 C4
Canyon Rose Suites	8 D4
Copper Queen Hotel	9 D3
La Estancia Bed & Breakfast	10 D3
School House Inn	11 B1

EATING	
Bisbee Grille	12 D4
Café Cornucopia	13 C4
Cafe Roka	14 C4

DRINKING	
Hot Licks Barbeque & Blues Saloon	15 D4
Stock Exchange Bar	16 B1

Mule Pass Tunnel

To Tombstone (24mi)

Tombstone Canyon

Clawson Ave

BISBEE

See Old Bisbee Enlargement

Escabrosa Ridge

Lavender Pit Copper Mine Lookout

Lowell

Bisbee Rd

School Terrace Rd

4th St

Warren

Cole Ave

Center Ave

Arizona St

Bisbee-Naco Hwy

Old Bisbee

Brewery Ave

Shearer Ave

Howell Ave

OK St

OLD BISBEE

San Jose

Subway St

Main St

Naco Rd

0 ——————— 100 m
0 ——————— 0.1 miles

6 ●

of the street takes you up a hill for even better panoramic vistas. Locals have built colorful shrines into the rocks on the top of the hill. They're filled with candles, plastic flowers and pictures of the Virgin Mary. It's a sobering sight.

Sleeping

Most beds are full on weekends; reservations are recommended. Bisbee is refreshingly void of chain hotels; accommodation is in historic hotels or B&Bs.

Copper Queen Hotel (☎ 520-432-2216, 800-247-5829; www.copperqueen.com; 11 Howell Ave; r $85-200; ⊠ ⊋) This 1902 place was once Bisbee's most famous hotel. It's still a great find, retaining a casually elegant late-19th-century feel. The 47 rooms have modern amenities and antique furnishings, and vary in size and comfort. The old-fashioned saloon is a good place to pass an evening. Ask for a recently renovated room.

La Estancia Bed & Breakfast (☎ 520-432-5882; www.laestancia.biz; 7 Howell Ave; r from $95; ⊠) Chock-full of artwork and collectibles, you can tell much love went into decorating this refurbished Victorian home. Each room is unique and all have private entrances. A full breakfast is included. No children.

School House Inn (☎ 520-432-2996, 800-537-4333; 818 Tombstone Canyon; r $65-95; ⊠) Built in 1918 as a school, this place has nine attractive rooms with themes pertaining to its past. You can sleep in the Principal's Office or dream in the Writing Room. There are great views and a delicious full breakfast is included.

Canyon Rose Suites (☎ 520-432-5098; www.canyonrose.com; 27 Subway St; ste $75-200; ⊠) An all-suites place on the second floor of a commercial business, each unit comes with a full kitchen and hard-wood floors. The suites are spacious with a blend of rustic and contemporary furnishings.

ARIZONA

AUTHOR'S CHOICE

Bisbee Grand Hotel (☎ 520-432-5900, 800-421-1909; www.bisbeegrandhotel.com; 61 Main St; r $75-150) Of the Victorian red-velvet and stuffed-peacock school of elegance, this charming old hotel is by far a favorite place to sleep. The six suites, all with different themes, provide for a truly memorable stay. An ornate Chinese wedding bed, skylight and clawfoot tub are highlights of the swanky Oriental Suite. In the plush Victorian Suite you'll sleep under a red-velvet canopy. The Old Western Suite features the most unique bed around – it's a converted covered wagon. The African-themed Safari Suite is as wild as it sounds. Even the ordinary rooms are far from ordinary, featuring carefully selected antiques and comfy sheets. Grab a drink at the Western saloon, with a pressed-tin ceiling and 1880s bar, before retiring to the billiards room for a game of pool.

Eating & Drinking

Bisbee has some fine food and lively bars: say no more.

Cafe Roka (☎ 520-432-5153; 35 Main St; dishes $13-25; ⊗ dinner Wed-Sat) A very hip joint with local art on the walls, this place serves excellent and innovative gourmet American fare. All meals are four-course dinners, including salad, soup, sorbet and a main of your choice. Live jazz plays on Friday and Saturday night.

Bisbee Grille (☎ 520-432-6788; 2 Copper Queen Plaza; dishes $8-11) This is one of Bisbee's best casual dining restaurants. It's an attractive place adorned with old photographs. The menu changes frequently, but is pasta, meat and salad oriented. Try the Bisbee-style fajitas.

DETOUR: CORONADO NATIONAL MEMORIAL

Once you've finished exploring Bisbee, head west on Hwy 92 towards the Mexican border and **Coronado National Memorial** (☎ 520-366-5515; Hwy 92; www.nps.gov/coro; admission free; ⊗ 8am-5pm), which commemorates the first major European expedition into the Southwest. Francisco Vásquez de Coronado, accompanied by hundreds of Spanish soldiers and Mexican Indians, passed through here in 1540 on his way from Mexico City, where he was searching for gold in the Seven Cities of Cibola. Coronado is credited with introducing horses to the Native Americans. The memorial, right on the Mexican border, has a visitor center featuring exhibits on Coronado's expedition and the area's wildlife. It makes for an interesting day trip.

Café Cornucopia (☎ 520-432-4820; 14 Main St; dishes $5-10; ☻ 10am-5pm) This quaint café serves fresh squeezed juices and smoothies along with homemade soups, salads and sandwiches in the heart of old downtown.

Hot Licks Barbeque & Blues Saloon (☎ 520-432-7200; 37 OK St) Perched high above town in a historic building overlooking Brewery Gulch, this bar has live music several nights a week. Be sure to try the locally brewed OK Ale.

Stock Exchange Bar (☎ 520-432-9924; 15 Brewery Gulch) It's a fun place to shoot some pool, listen to live music or sing your heart out on the karaoke machine. The bar boasts the original stock board from Bisbee's heyday. The outside porch is perfect for sipping cocktails on a balmy evening.

NOGALES

pop 20,700 / elev 3865ft

There's something slightly hard and edgy about this border town; a whiff of danger permeates the air. Unless you have business down here, or are using it as a jumping-off point for a trip into Mexico, there's little reason to visit.

The town is Arizona's most important gateway into Mexico, and a constant flow of foot and vehicular traffic slides across the border separating Nogales, Arizona from Nogales, Sonora, Mexico. US citizens slip into Mexico to shop for bargains on handicrafts, pharmaceuticals and tequila, while Mexican citizens cross over to buy products not available in their country. Although a constructed line is all that separates the towns, they feel distinctly different. Shabby shacks clutter the steep hillsides on the Mexican side. The potholed streets are narrow and chaotic, crammed with handicraft stalls and taco stands, pharmacies and booze shops. Pimps and prostitutes often proposition foreign men; solo women may feel uneasy. But if you look like you know where you're going and walk authoritatively, you shouldn't run into much trouble.

There's a heavy police presence on the American side, and officers carry intimidatingly large guns. As long as you're not smuggling drugs, they'll likely ignore you. The main drag is typical border town Americana – fast food joints, aging motels and loads of cheap shops and duty free stores.

Orientation & Information

Steep hills, a dividing railroad, one-way roads, a confusing street system and poor local maps make getting around Nogales difficult for visitors. It's not a big town, though, so relax and you'll eventually find where you want to go.

Hospital (☎ 520-287-2771; 1171 W Target Range Rd) Emergency services.

Library (☎ 520-287-3343; 518 Grand Ave) Free Internet access.

Nogales-Santa Cruz County Chamber of Commerce (☎ 520-287-3685; www.nogaleschamber.com; 123 W Kino Park) Tourist information.

Police (☎ 520-287-9111; 777 Grand Ave)

Post Office (☎ 520-287-9246; 300 N Morley Ave)

US Immigration (☎ 520-287-3609) At the border.

Sleeping & Eating

Chain motels are found off I-19 at exit 4. Mariposa Rd east of I-19 has the usual assortment of fast-food restaurants and a supermarket. You can eat authentically (well, relatively, this is a border town) on the Mexican side at one of the numerous *taquerías*. Places come and go, so have a wander and see what looks good.

Rio Rico Resort & Country Club (☎ 520-281-7132; www.rioricoresort.com; 1069 Camino Caralampi; r $85-150; ▨ ▧) A secluded golf resort on a hilltop a few miles north of town, Rio Rico recently underwent extensive renovations and is the best bet in town. The place is decorated in the Spanish Colonial style with lots of colorful tile work. Rooms are tasteful and cozy. The restaurant serves great food with even better views. The 18-hole golf course is a short drive away and there are opportunities for horseback riding in the mountains.

La Hacienda de Sonita (☎ 520-455-5208; 34 Swanson Rd; r from $110; ✗) Great distant mountain views are found at this small B&B. Built in the hacienda style around a central courtyard, there's a cascading fountain and wood covered porches. Rooms are colorful with Southwestern or country themes.

Americana Motor Hotel (☎ 520-287-7211; 639 Grand Ave; r from $40; ▧) The best of the town's motels, this place is an old-school 1950s place. Rooms are aging, but clean and decent sized. There's an attached restaurant, so you won't have to wander around at night.

La Roca Restaurant (☎ 011-52-631-312-0760; Calle Elias 91; dishes $10-20) Built into a cliff on the Mexican side of the border, this place is a great find. Stone walls are lined with Mexican folk art; white-jacketed waiters serve big plates of food. At night candles provide a tranquil glow. Guaymas shrimp and chicken mole are always good choices. Make sure to try a margarita. To get here walk through the border checkpoint and cross the railroad tracks to your left. Look for a narrow street along the base of a cliff. The restaurant is about 100ft down this road. Solo travelers might not want to venture here after dark.

Mr C's Supper Club (☎ 520-281-9000; 282 W View Point Dr; dishes $15-20) Skip the American and go for Mexican at Mr C's. Guaymas shrimp is the house specialty; order it with Mexican flank steak. Mains include a visit to the salad bar.

Getting There & Away

Greyhound (☎ 520-287-5628; www.greyhound.com; 35 N Terrace Ave) operates frequent bus services from Nogales to Tucson ($6.50, one hour, hourly).

CROSSING THE MEXICAN BORDER

If you just want to visit Mexico for the day, it's best to cross the border on foot. Park on the US side (many lots around Crawford and Terrace Aves charge about $5 a day) and walk through immigration. US citizens must show at least a drivers license, although a passport is better, everyone else needs a passport. You'll have to pass through immigration again on your way back. US dollars and credit cards are accepted on the Mexican side of the border, and prices for Mexican handicrafts are good (though not much cheaper than in Arizona). Quality varies, so shop around.

Driving across the border is a serious hassle in this post-9/11 era, and shouldn't be attempted unless you're planning a longer sojourn in Mexico. Expect long lines and tight security, especially crossing back into the USA. To enter Mexico for more than a border day trip, bring a passport and a Mexican tourist card, which will be checked a few miles inside the country. The tourist card is available for free at the border upon producing a passport. Mexican tourist cards are valid for up to 180 days, but normally much less time is given. A few nationalities require a Mexican visa; recently, these included some European, African and Asian nationals, but the situation changes. Check with the Mexican consul in your home country or in Nogales (p459).

You can bring almost anything bought in Mexico back into the USA duty free as long as it's worth a total of less than $400 and doesn't include more than a quart of booze or 200 cigarettes. Fresh food is prohibited, as are fireworks, which are illegal for personal use in Arizona. Importing weapons and drugs is also illegal, except for prescribed drugs, which are cheaper in Mexico – some visitors without health insurance fill their prescriptions in Mexico. If you're purchasing prescription drugs in Mexico, be warned a prescription from a US doctor is not enough. You'll also need a prescription from a Mexican doctor to avoid being busted by Mexican police. In recent years Mexican authorities have raided border pharmacies and arrested folks without Mexican prescriptions. Pharmacies make their money off tourists, however, and many now boast next-door clinics where doctors quickly write prescriptions for a small fee.

Traveling by Mexican public transport is a little more adventurous than the equivalent in the USA. However, it's also much more far-reaching and you can get almost anywhere on a bus at reasonable cost. If you prefer to bring your own car, you should get Mexican car insurance, as US insurance is not normally valid in Mexico. Car insurance can be purchased at one of many places at the border for $10 to $15 a day. If you buy insurance for a week or month, rates drop substantially. Remember: Mexico's legal system is Napoleonic, that is, you are guilty until proven innocent, and you are likely to be arrested and held after a car accident unless you can show Mexican car insurance covering the accident.

Nogales is the main Arizona/Mexico border crossing and also the safest. Along the southeastern Arizona border, drug smuggling and international car theft are frequent occurrences, and illegal immigration is a concern. While it's most likely you won't have any problems, travelers should be aware that a small percentage of officials on both sides of the border are corrupt. The best defense is to make sure that your documents are perfectly in order, to travel by day and to not allow officials to intimidate you for any reason.

CHIRICAHUA NATIONAL MONUMENT

The strangely eroded volcanic pinnacles and balanced rocks of the Chiricahua Mountains are unlike any others in Arizona. And the **Chiricahua National Monument** (☎ 520-824-3560; Hwy 181; per vehicle $6; ✪ 24hr) contains the wildest and weirdest of these formations. One of the smaller and more remote NPS areas in the Southwest, its scenery and solitude makes it an enticing destination. There are no gas stations, food or lodging services (except camping) inside the monument, 40 miles southeast of Wilcox off Hwy 186. The remoteness makes Chiricahua attractive to wildlife: mountain lions, bobcats and bears are often sighted on the hiking trails. Keep a lookout for deer, coatis and javelinas.

If you're short on time, take the 8-mile paved **Bonita Canyon Scenic Drive**. The road climbs from the park entrance gate (at about 5000ft) to Massai Point at 6870ft, with several scenic pullouts and trailheads along the way. The views from the point are spectacular. The **visitor center** (☎ 520-824-3560) is 2 miles along this road from the entrance station. It has a slide show about the Chiricahuas, a small exhibition area and a bookstore. Ranger-led programs are offered March to October but may be curtailed in mid-summer.

To explore in greater depth, lace up your boots and hit the trails. Seventeen miles of hiking trails range from easy, flat 0.2-mile loops to strenuous 7-mile climbs. The short, flat trails west of the visitor center and campground are the easiest and are good for birding and wildlife observation. The trails east of the visitor center lead into rugged mountain country with the most spectacular geology. A hikers' shuttle bus leaves daily from the visitor center at 8:30am, going up to Massai Point for $2. Hikers return by hiking downhill.

The **Bonita Campground** (campsites $8), with 24 sites just north of the visitor center, has water but no hookups or showers. During the cooler months, the campground is often full by noon. Sites are on a first-come, first-served basis. No wilderness camping is permitted.

Utah

Towering mountain peaks, plunging canyons, sweeping sandstone domes, and seemingly endless expanses of undulating desert define the Utah landscape. Straddling the Great Basin's eastern edge and the Rocky Mountains' western front, the wild and rugged terrain never looks the same from any two angles, forever begging further exploration. From Brigham Young (who in 1847 declared, 'This is the place!') to the International Olympic Committee (which picked Salt Lake City – or SLC – to host the 2002 Winter Olympics), every story in Utah begins with the land. Moab is the mountain-biking capital of the world, Park City is home to the US ski team. And there are five stunning national parks to see.

The culture, by contrast, lacks diversity. There's not much multiculturalism in Utah: you're either a Mormon or a minority. This is the reddest of the red states, the most conservative in the USA, where George W Bush is welcomed with open arms and Michael Moore is not. If you're a leftie, don't sweat it. There are splotches of blue here and there. And Mormons are nothing if not nice: if you don't bring up politics, neither will they. Indeed, you'll get a warm reception everywhere you go.

UTAH

HIGHLIGHTS

- **Top Scenic Drive**
  Utah Hwy 12 (p256) curves past plummeting red-rock canyons, giant cream-colored domes and deep-green alpine forests.

- **Best Spot for Solitude**
  Grand Staircase-Escalante National Monument (p251) unfurls in two million acres of vast, uninhabited desert, as far as the eye can see.

- **Best All-Round Splurge**
  Sundance Resort (p315) is a rustic mountain artists' retreat that Ralph Lauren couldn't have designed better.

- **Hippest Small Towns**
  Park City (p306) tops the list, with the tiny side-by-side towns of Torrey (p259) and Boulder (p258) tying for second.

- **Easiest-to-Reach Jaw-Dropping Viewpoint**
  Dead Horse Point (p284) overlooks serpentine river canyons, with 2-mile-high mountain ranges looming on the horizon.

★ Park City

Sundance ★
Resort

Dead Horse
Point State Park
★

Torrey ★

Highway 12 ★   ★ Boulder

Grand Staircase-
★ Escalante National
Monument

- POPULATION: 2.4 MILLION   - AREA: 82,144 MILES   - www.utah.com

UTAH

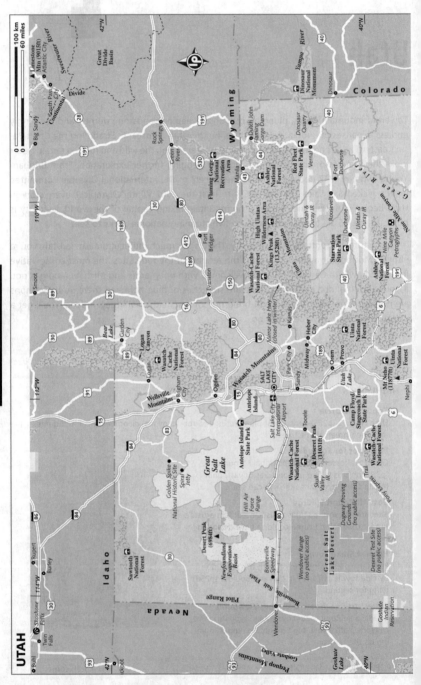

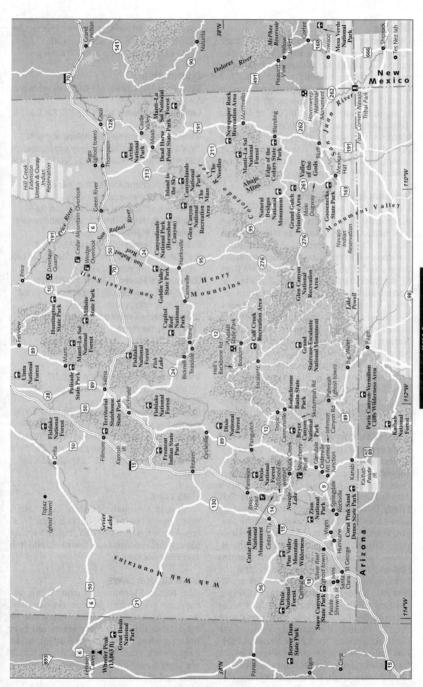

Climate

Utah has a high-mountain-desert climate with four seasons. The state's average elevation of 6100ft keeps summertime temperatures from scorching – except near the Grand Canyon. July temperatures run in the 80°Fs and 90°Fs, dropping 20°F to 30°F at night. January highs run 20°F to 40°F; at night, temperatures fall 10°F to 30°F. Fog blankets the state's valleys for extended periods in winter (to rise above the gray gloom, ascend the mountains). Most precipitation falls in winter and spring.

National & State Parks

Utah is chock-full of parks. National parks make a patchwork across the south. From west to east, they include: the towering rock faces of Zion and spindly sherbet-colored hoodoos of Bryce Canyon, the sandstone domes and chunky red rock of Capitol Reef, to the rock arches and natural bridges at Arches and winding canyons of Canyonlands. Between them lie national forests, Bureau of Land Management (BLM) lands as well as the vast Grand Staircase-Escalante National Monument, and various state parks, notably Dead Horse Point.

In Utah's northeastern-most reaches, the red-rock canyons of Flaming Gorge National Recreation Area are popular with boaters and hikers; kids and paleontologists love Dinosaur National Monument.

UTAH SCENIC BYWAYS

Scenic Byway 12 (p256), arguably Utah's most diverse and stunning route, winds through rugged canyons on a 124-mile journey from Bryce Canyon to Capitol Reef; for a detailed route guide, contact the **Garfield County Travel Council** (☎ 800-444-6689; www.bryce canyoncountry.com). **Hwy 95** (p286), also in canyon country, runs from southeastern Utah, past Natural Bridges National Monument, across Lake Powell and the Glen Canyon National Recreation Area, and behind the last-mapped mountains in the lower 48. **Hwy 261** (p286), aka **Moki Dugway**, follows a twisting route, dropping 1000ft in 3 miles for drop-dead desert views to Arizona; take the side route to the stunning Valley of the Gods. Ascending from Zion National Park, **Hwy 9** climbs above the park's sheer red-rock faces to swirls of yellow Navajo sandstone. In northeastern Utah, **Mirror Lake Hwy** (Rte 150,

p317) is one of the state's most spectacular high-alpine roads, winding beneath 12,000ft peaks before dropping into Wyoming.

Information

BLM (Map pp292-3; ☎ 801-539-4001; www.ut.blm.gov; 324 S State St, Suite 400)
Camping reservations (☎ 801-322-3770, 800-322-3770; www.nr.utah.gov)
Natural Resources Map & Bookstore (Map p290; ☎ 801-537-3320, 888-882-4627; www.maps.state.ut.us; 1594 W North Temple St, Salt Lake City) Sells US Geological Survey maps.
Public Lands Information Center (Map p288; ☎ 801-466-6411; www.cottonwoodcanyons.org; 3285 E 3300 South, Salt Lake City; ⏱ 10:30am-7pm Tue-Sat) Inside REI's Salt Lake City store, this is the central source of information for all public lands in Utah.
USDA Forest Service (USFS; Map pp292-3; ☎ 801-236-3400; www.fs.fed.us/r4/wcnf; 125 S State St, Salt Lake City, UT 84138) Sells maps and passes.
US Geological Survey (USGS; ☎ 303-202-4700, 888-275-8747; www.usgs.gov) The best topographic and satellite maps; order by phone or online.
Utah Avalanche Center (www.avalanche.org/~uac) Snow and weather reports.
Utah Public Library (http://pioneer.utah.gov)
Utah State Government's official website (www.utah.gov)
Utah State Parks & Recreation (Map p290; ☎ 801-538-7220; www.stateparks.utah.gov; 1594 W North Temple St, Salt Lake City)
Utah Travel Council (Map pp292-3; ☎ 801-538-1030, 800-200-1160; www.utah.com; Council Hall, Capitol Hill, Salt Lake City, UT 84114; ⏱ 8am-5pm Mon-Fri, 10am-5pm Sat & Sun) Publishes the free *Utah Travel Guide;* the council's bookstore (☎ 801-538-1398) sells guides and maps.

TIME ZONE

Utah is on Mountain Standard Time (MST, seven hours behind GMT), as is New Mexico. Arizona is also on MST, but late spring to early fall Arizona is an hour behind Utah and New Mexico.

UTAH LIQUOR LAWS

Due to the Mormon influence, Utah has the strangest liquor laws in the country. As everywhere in the USA, you must be aged 21 to drink. Grocery stores sell beer not exceeding 3.2% alcohol content, seven days a week. State-run liquor stores, which are closed on Sundays, sell stronger beer, wine and spirits.

Lounges and taverns sell only 3.2% beer – stronger drinks are available only in restaurants or 'private clubs.' To enter a private club, you must be a member; a temporary membership costs $4 and is valid three weeks, allowing you to invite seven guests.

In restaurants (which don't require membership), servers aren't permitted to offer drinks or show you a cocktail menu unless you specifically ask. You must order food too, but it can be just a snack. Nowhere can you buy two drinks for yourself at any one time (known as Utah's 'slammin' rule,' since you must throw it all back before ordering again). Alcohol is prohibited on Native American reservations.

Getting There & Around

Most highways have 65mph speed limits. Three major freeways – speed limit 75 mph – run through Utah. Exit numbers correspond with mileage markers. I-15 links Utah to Idaho, Arizona, Las Vegas, and southern California. I-80 connects Cheyenne, Salt Lake City, Reno and San Francisco. I-70 originates in central Utah and connects Denver with Moab via Green River.

Outside metropolitan areas public transportation is inadequate, so plan to drive. Note that most towns in Utah follow a typical Mormon grid, in which numbered streets radiate from a central hub (or zero point), usually the intersection of Main and Center Sts. Compass points indicate where you are in relation to that hub: thus, 100

E 300 S is one block east and three blocks south of Main and Center. It's easy once you get used to it.

SOUTHWESTERN UTAH

Locals call it 'color country,' but the cutesy label hardly does justice to the eye-popping hues that saturate the landscape. From the deep-crimson canyons of Zion National Park, to the delicate pink and orange minarets at Bryce Canyon, to the swirling yellow-white domes of Capitol Reef, the land is so spectacular that it encompasses three national parks *and* the gigantic Grand Staircase-Escalante National Monument (GSENM).

Ancestral Puebloans (p27) inhabited the area from about 1400 years ago, and you can still see their rock art. The Spanish Domínguez-Escalante missionaries passed through in 1776, but not till the Mormons arrived in 1851 did White settlement occur.

This section follows US Hwy 89 and I-15, the region's main thoroughfares, then heads east from Bryce Canyon along gorgeous Hwy 12, skirting the northern boundary of the GSENM. It ends at Capitol Reef. See p150 for Lake Powell and Glen Canyon National Recreation Area.

ST GEORGE

pop 54,050 / elev 2880ft

Jagged red-rock peaks tower over suburban subdivisions at the state's southernmost city, where summers sizzle, with highs exceeding 100°F. Nicknamed 'Utah's Dixie' for the Mormon pioneers who once grew cotton here, St George is a retirement and golf community. You'll be lucky to get dinner after 10pm, and there ain't much nightlife.

Travelers on a shoestring like the city's cheap lodging and proximity to Zion National Park. There's also golf, well-preserved Mormon buildings and Pine Valley Mountain Wilderness nearby, where you can escape summer's heat into an oasis of green.

Orientation

St George is on I-15 just north of the Arizona border, 120 miles or two hours from Las Vegas, and 305 miles or 4½ hours from Salt Lake City. The town lies about 35 miles (40 minutes) from Zion National Park's south

ORIENTATION

A grid map showing streets radiating from Zero Point (Town Centre): 500 North, 400 North, 300 North, 200 North, 100 North to the north; 100 South, 200 South, 300 South, 400 South, 500 South to the south. West streets: 400 West, 300 West, 200 West, 100 West. East streets: 100 East, 200 East, 300 East, 400 East.

entrance, 30 miles (25 minutes) from the Kolob Canyons' entrance on I-15, and 57 miles (45 minutes) from Cedar City to the north.

St George's center is the intersection of Main and Tabernacle Sts. The city's main commercial streets are St George Blvd and Bluff St, which with I-15 form a triangle that encompasses most of town.

Information

Chamber of Commerce (☎ 435-628-1658; www .stgeorgechamber.com; 97 E St George Blvd; ☼ 9am-5pm Mon-Fri, 10am-2pm Sat) The main source for town information. Also useful is the city's Convention & Visitors Bureau website (www.utahsdixie.com) and the City of St George website (www.sgcity.org).

Dixie Regional Medical Center (☎ 435-251-1000; 700 S & River Rd)

Interagency Information Center (☎ 435-688-3246; 345 E Riverside Dr; ☼ 7:45am-5pm Mon-Fri, 10am-3pm Sat) Provides information on USFS and BLM lands, state parks and the Arizona Strip (p150). It sells topographical and other maps and has a great selection of guides and regional histories.

Library (☎ 435-634-5737; 50 S Main St; ☼ 9am-9pm Mon-Thu, 9am-6pm Fri & Sat) With Internet access ($1 per hour).

Little Professor Books (☎ 435-674-9898; 15 N Main St) A convenient general-interest bookstore.

Police (☎ 435-634-5001; 175 E 200 North)

Post office (☎ 435-673-3312; 180 N Main St)

Utah Welcome Center (☎ 435-673-4542; ☼ 8:30am-5:30pm, later in summer) Two miles south of St George on I-15, with statewide information.

Zions Bank (☎ 435-673-4867; 40 E St George Blvd) With currency exchange and a 24-hour ATM.

Sights

HISTORIC MORMON SITES

The following offer free admission and guided tours.

The 1877 **Mormon Temple** (☎ 435-673-5181; 440 S 300 East; ☼ 9am-9pm) was Utah's first. The pretty **Mormon Tabernacle** (☎ 435-628-4072; cnr Tabernacle & Main Sts; ☼ 9am-5pm) is open to the public and hosts free music programs.

St George's **Daughters of Utah Pioneers (DUP) Museum** (☎ 435-628-7274; 145 N 100 East; ☼ 10am-5pm Mon-Sat) is the best of its kind outside Salt Lake City.

Dating from 1871, the **Brigham Young Winter Home** (☎ 435-673-2517; 67 W 200 North; ☼ 9am-5pm, to 7pm summer) was the Mormon leader's seasonal headquarters.

Just north in Santa Clara, the 1863 **Jacob Hamblin Home** (☎ 435-673-2161; Santa Clara Dr; ☼ 9am-5pm, to 7pm summer) gives a more evocative idea of the Mormon pioneer experience and mission.

PIONEER CENTER FOR THE ARTS

This collection of historic buildings contains the **St George Art Museum** (☎ 435-634-5942; 47 E 200 North; ☼ 10am-5pm Tue-Sat), which focuses on local and Western art, in modern and traditional styles.

DINOSAUR DISCOVERY SITE

St George's oldest residents aren't retirees from Idaho, but Jurassic-era dinosaurs. A **museum** (☎ 435-574-3766; www.dinotrax.com; 2200 E Riverside Dr; adult/child $2/1; ☼ 10am-5pm Mon-Sat) was constructed in 2005 to house the growing collection of tracks and other evidence first discovered here in 2000. Rare paleontological discoveries continue to be made, and scientists have only scratched the surface. Soon this will rank as one of America's most important dinosaur sites. Take 700 S east to Riverside Dr.

ROSENBRUCH WORLD WILDLIFE MUSEUM

More than 300 species are displayed in this **museum** (☎ 435-656-0033; www.rosenbruch.org; 1835 Convention Center Dr; ☼ noon-9pm Mon, 10am-6pm Tue-Sat; adult $8, child 3-12 $4), a tribute to wildlife and the art of taxidermy. Faux storms provide atmosphere; the bug room is gnarly.

Activities

Walking and biking trails crisscross St George. Eventually, they'll be connected, and the trail along the Virgin River will extend to Zion. Find maps at the chamber of commerce. For good views, visit **Pioneer Park** on Skyline Dr.

Paragon Climbing (☎ 435-673-1709; www.paragon climbing.com) offers excellent beginner and intermediate climbing courses (from $80 per half-day) and guided mountain biking ($35 to $45 per hour).

MOUNTAIN BIKING

There's first-rate slickrock mountain biking galore, particularly at **Gooseberry Mesa** and the **Green Valley Loop** (also called Bearclaw Poppie Trail).

Rentals run about $35. Call **Red Rock Bicycle Company** (☎ 435-674-3185; www.redrockbicycle

.com; 446 W 100 South; 9am-6pm Mon-Fri, 9am-5pm Sat) and **Bicycles Unlimited** (435-673-4492, 888-673-4492; www.bicyclesunlimited.com; 90 S 100 East; 8am-7pm Mon-Sat).

SWIMMING
In Santa Clara, **Sand Hollow Aquatic Center** (435-634-5938; www.ci.st-george.ut.us; 1144 N Lava Flow Dr; adult $6, child 4-17 $5.50; 1-9pm Mon-Fri, noon-6pm Sat) has a 25m lap pool and a 5800-sq-ft leisure pool with water slides. The facilities satisfy everyone from adult swimmers to teens and frolicking toddlers.

GOLF
The following courses are open to the public. The first three charge $17 for nine holes or $28 for 18 holes in winter (cheaper the rest of the year); Sunbrook charges $24 and $45, respectively. Reserve up to two weeks in advance. For online information, see www.sgcity.org/golf.

Dixie Red Hills (435-634-5852; 1250 N 645 West) Nine holes, par 34.

Southgate (435-628-0000; 1975 S Tonaquint Dr) Eighteen holes, par 70.

St George Golf Club (435-634-5854; 2190 S 1400 East) Eighteen holes, par 73.

Sunbrook (435-634-5866; 2366 Sunbrook Dr) Twenty-seven holes, par 36 each nine.

Tours
The chamber of commerce publishes a good self-guided walking tour of the Mormon historic district. Or take a guided tour with **Historic St George Live!** (435-634-5942; www.stgeorgelive.org; adult $2, child under 12 free) at 9am and 10:30am, Tuesday through Saturday from Memorial Day to Labor Day.

Festivals & Events
Avoid St George around Easter, when it becomes Utah's spring-break capital. Mid-September ropes in the **Dixie Roundup** (435-628-8282), a Professional Rodeo Cowboys Association (PRCA) rodeo, and the **St George Marathon** (www.stgeorgemarathon.com), which descends from the Pine Valley Mountains. October welcomes the **World Senior Games** (www.seniorgames.net).

Sleeping
Lodgings are plentiful and affordable in St George. Head to St George Blvd and Bluff St near I-15 for chain motels.

BUDGET
Prices are more attractive than the rooms: look before you buy. The following are among the best and are acceptably clean.

Sullivan's Rococo Inn (435-628-3671, 888-628-3671; www.rococo.net; 511 S Airport Rd; s $31-40, d $45-50;) On a bluff by the municipal airport, this scruffy hotel has gorgeous views.

Dixie Palm Motel (435-673-3531; 185 E St George Blvd; r midweek $34-45, weekend $40-70;) It may not look like much from the outside, but regular maintenance and TLC put this ahead of the pack. The 15 rooms have refrigerators and microwaves.

Best Value Inn (435-673-4666, 800-864-6882; www.bestvalueinn.com; 60 W St George Blvd; r midweek $30-35, weekend $35-40;) Rooms are dull but well kept; some have kitchenettes.

Other acceptable but rough-around-the-edges choices:

Chalet Motel (435-628-6272; 664 E St George Blvd; r midweek/weekend $38/44;)

Sands Motel (435-673-3501; 581 E St George Blvd; s/d $35/40;)

Sun Time Inn (435-673-6181, 800-237-6253; www.suntimeinn.com; 420 E St George Blvd; d midweek/weekend $40/70;) Overpriced on weekends.

Snowbirds fill the RV parks every winter. Tent-campers will do better at Snow Canyon State Park (see p231) or in Springdale (see p237).

Settler's RV Park (435-628-1624, 800-628-1624; www.settlersrvpark.com; 1333 E 100 South; tent $16.50, RV hookup $28;) Over 150 RV sites, several tent sites and full facilities.

MIDRANGE
St George Inn & Suites (435-652-3030, 800-718-0297; www.stgeorgeinnsuites.com; 245 N Red Cliffs Dr; d midweek/weekend $50/60;) This attractive chain motel also has coin laundry.

Singletree Inn (435-673-6161, 800-528-8890; www.singletreeinn.com; 260 E St George Blvd; d $50-60;) Clean and comparable to the chains.

Coronada Vacation Village (435-628-4436; www.coronadainn.com; 559 E St George Blvd; d midweek/weekend $50/75;) Though faded and worn, rooms are big, with full kitchens. Weekly rates are best.

Best Western Coral Hills (435-673-4844; www.coralhills.com; 125 E St George Blvd; r midweek/weekend $71/85;) Reliable comfort and two nice pools make this a good pick.

UTAH

TOP END

Green Gate Village (☎ 435-628-6999, 800-350-6999; www.greengatevillageinn.com; 76 W Tabernacle; r weekday $80-180, r weekend $100-200; 🔊 ❎) Grassy lawns separate nine historic buildings that comprise this attractive B&B inn. All rooms feature lovely antiques, TVs and refrigerators.

Seven Wives Inn (☎ 435-628-3737, 800-600-3737; www.sevenwivesinn.com; 217 N 100 West; r $80-180; 🔊 ❎) An eclectic and historic B&B, Seven Wives has 13 rooms, all individually decorated. 'Sarah' is playfully idiosyncratic and worth a splurge, with its own private hot tub inside an actual Model T Ford. 'Ada' is a free-standing, separate cottage with mismatched furniture and a kitchenette.

Olde Penny Farthing Inn (☎ 435-673-7755; www.oldepenny.citysearch.com; 278 N 100 West; r $70-120; ❎) This restored pioneer house has six rooms and full breakfast.

St George has two top-flight destination spas. Summer is cheaper than winter; ask about packages.

Red Mountain Spa (☎ 435-673-4905, 800-407-3002; www.redmtn.com; 1275 E Red Mountain Circle; s $249-279, d per person $209-239; 🔊 ❎ 🖵) The first choice for outdoor enthusiasts, rooms have a Zen-chic sensibility; rates include all meals.

Green Valley Spa (☎ 435-628-8060, 800-237-1068; www.greenvalleyspa.com; 1871 W Canyon View Dr; s $200-300, d per person $125-200; 🔊 ❎ 🖵) Ultracushy, it's the top choice for pampering luxury, with tennis, golf and five pools.

Eating & Drinking

St George's dining scene is mediocre. Springdale, an hour away at Zion, has better choices. Here are the best of the lot. Many places close Sunday.

Bean Scene (☎ 435-574-6434; 511 E St George Blvd; sandwiches $4.50; 🕑 6am-7pm Mon-Fri, 7am-4pm Sat, 8am-1pm Sun) Well, whadya know, a bohemian coffeehouse in St George, with occasional Saturday night happenings.

Jazzy Java (☎ 435-674-1678; 285 N Bluff St; items $2.50-8; 🕑 6am-5pm Mon-Fri, 7am-4pm Sat, 8am-2pm Sun) St George's other funky coffeeshop features a larger food selection, with full breakfasts, sandwiches and salads.

Bear Paw Coffee Company (☎ 435-634-0126; 75 N Main St; items $7-9; 🕑 breakfast & lunch) Tops for breakfast, the Bear Paw has a wide-ranging menu. Belgian waffles are a specialty.

Ancestor Square (cnr Main St & St George Blvd) Head here for family-friendly eateries (ie Formica tables and cheap eats). Pizza, pasta, Mexican and Chinese (all closed on Sunday).

Golden Corral (☎ 435-673-5700; 42 S River Rd; lunch/dinner $7/9; 🕑 11am-9:30pm Mon-Sat, 8am-8:30pm Sun) A surprisingly good all-you-can-eat buffet for hungry budgeteers.

Las Palmeras (☎ 435-674-3759; 929 W Sunset Blvd, Phoenix Plaza; dishes $6; 🕑 10am-9pm Sun-Thu, to 10pm Fri & Sat) The Salvadorean and Mexican cooking here is some of the best around.

Alvaro's (☎ 435-656-5746; 471 N 1680 East; items $2.50-6; 🕑 24hr) For late-night munchies, head here for Mexican fast food from an all-night drive-through.

Samurai 21 (☎ 435-656-8628; 245 N Red Cliff Dr; mains $15-20; 🕑 lunch & dinner Mon-Sat, dinner Sun) A shimmering oasis in a land of Applebee's, Samurai's Japanese chefs put on a great show at the tableside grills. There's also regular waiter service and a sushi bar.

Sullivan's Rococo Steak House (☎ 435-628-3671; 511 S Airport Rd; mains $18-31; 🕑 lunch & dinner Mon-Fri, dinner Sat & Sun) Sullivan's has great city views to go with its prime rib and steaks.

Scaldoni's (☎ 435-674-1300; www.scaldonis.com; 929 W Sunset Blvd, Phoenix Plaza; mains $11-28; 🕑 11:30am-10pm Mon-Sat, dinner Sun) This straightforward American-Italian restaurant's menu runs from veal marsala to the requisite pastas with red sauce. Full bar.

Painted Pony (☎ 435-634-1700; 2 W St George Blvd, Ancestor Square; sandwiches $8, dinner mains $17-25; 🕑 11:30am-10pm Mon-Sat) You won't find better in St George, with subtlety and nuance gracing most of the Southwestern-style dishes; standouts include rib-eye steak, pan-roasted escolar and the grilled portobello sandwich. The decor complements the cooking, with Navajo prints, tin sconces and colorful contemporary art. Make reservations.

Entertainment

The **St George Musical Theater** (☎ 435-628-8755; www.sgmt.org; 37 S 100 West) puts on musicals year-round. The outdoor **Tuacahn Amphitheater** (☎ 435-652-3300, 800-746-9882; www.tuacahn.org), 10 miles northwest in Ivins, hosts musicals in summer and other performances year-round.

October to May, **Dixie State College** (☎ 435-652-7994; www.dixie.edu/concerts) hosts a Celebrity Concert Series at the **Fine Arts Center Theater** (☎ 435-628-3121; 225 S 700 East).

There are several **cinemas** (☎ 435-673-1994) in town.

Getting There & Around

St George Municipal Airport (☎ 435-673-3451; 444 S River Rd) sits above town. **Skywest Airlines** (☎ 435-634-3000, 800-453-9417; www.skywest.com) operates five daily flights to Salt Lake City for Delta Airlines, and two to Los Angeles for United. A new airport is planned.

Greyhound (☎ 435-673-2933, 800-231-2222; www .greyhound.com) leaves from McDonald's at 1235 S Bluff, with buses to Salt Lake City ($55, six hours) and Las Vegas ($30, two hours).

St George Shuttle (☎ 435-628-8320, 800-933-8320; www.stgshuttle.com) runs vans to Las Vegas Airport ($25) and Salt Lake City ($55) by reservation. Also try **Red Rock Shuttle** (☎ 435-635-9104), which also serves Brian Head (from $65).

SunTran (☎ 435-673-8726) is St George's public transit system. Its three routes run from 6am to 8pm Monday through Friday, and 8am to 6pm on Saturday. Fare is $1; buses have bike racks.

For a taxi, call **Taxi USA** (☎ 435-656-1500).

AROUND ST GEORGE
Snow Canyon State Park

Red and white swirls of sandstone flow like lava, and lava lies broken like sheets of smashed marble in this small, accessible park. **Snow Canyon** (☎ 435-628-2255; www .stateparks.utah.gov; per car $5) is a miniature-size sampler of southwest Utah's famous land features. Easy trails lead to tiny slot canyons, cinder cones, lava tubes and vast fields of undulating slickrock, perfect for kids.

There's also great **rock climbing**, particularly for beginners, with over 150 bolted and sport routes, plus top roping. Recommended 1- to 3-mile **hiking** routes include Jenny's and Johnson Canyons, Petrified Dunes and Hidden Pinyon. **Cycling** is popular on the main road through the park, a 17-mile loop from St George.

Summers are blazing hot; visit in early morning, or come in spring or fall.

Outside of summer, the scenic **campground** (☎ 800-322-3770; tent/RV $14/17) is great. The park provides showers; campers can reserve 20 of its 33 sites.

From downtown St George, take Hwy 18 north for 1.5 miles to Snow Canyon Pkwy and follow signs past Ivins' gated communities to the park.

Oh, and for the record, it does snow here.

Silver Reef Ghost Town

This abandoned 19th-century silver-mining town is at exit 23 off I-15, 13 miles northeast of St George, near Leeds. The restored Wells Fargo building houses a museum and **art gallery** (☎ 435-879-2254; ☽ 9am-5pm Mon-Sat). Dioramas of the rough-and-tumble town and mine gives a feel of what it was like.

Pine Valley Mountain Wilderness

Laced with rushing streams, the mountainous 70-sq-mile **Pine Valley wilderness area** (day use $2; ☽ May 15–Oct 1) is Utah's second largest, after the High Uintas (p319). The mountains rise sharply, and the highest point, Signal Peak (10,365ft), remains snow-capped till July.

When the pulsating desert heat blurs your vision, Pine Valley offers cool, challenging **hiking**. Many begin as strenuous climbs. The 5-mile Mill Canyon Trail and the 6-mile Whipple Trail are most popular, each linking with the 35-mile Summit Trail. The best guide is *Loving the Laccolith* by Bridget McColville.

A small trout-stocked reservoir attracts local **anglers**.

Campgrounds (to reserve ☎ 877-444-6777; campsites $8-11) have water but no showers; bring mosquito repellent. Most sites are first-come, first-served, though you can reserve some. The Interagency Information Center (p228) in St George provides details and free backcountry permits.

Outside the wilderness area is the bucolic, tiny town of Pine Valley. The **Pine Valley Heritage Center** (☎ 435-574-2463; E Main St) theoretically provides information Monday through Saturday, but it's unreliable. The **Pine Valley Chapel** (cnr Forest Rd & E Main St; ☽ 10am-6pm Mon-Sat, noon-6pm Sun) was built in 1868 by Ebenezer Bryce. At the time of writing, the Pine Valley Lodge and its café, general store and camp showers had closed. Bring supplies.

Take Hwy 18 to the town of Central and head east to Pine Valley (32 miles); the wilderness area lies a few miles further, within Dixie National Forest.

ZION NATIONAL PARK

Towering red and white cliffs, sheer as bookends, lord half a mile high over the Virgin River, which carved southern Utah's most famous canyon, one of the Southwest's most dramatic natural wonders. But for all its initial awe-inspiring majesty, the park holds more delicate beauties as well – weeping rocks, tiny grottoes, hanging gardens, lush riverbanks and meadows of mesa-top wildflowers – that lend a meditative quality to the magnificent rock formations. The hiking is fantastic: there's nothing like the adrenaline rush from peering over the edge of one of Zion's 2000ft-high sandstone lips, or the thrill of negotiating a slot canyon.

High season runs April to November, and most of the park's 2.5 million annual visitors come May to September. Arrive early to secure campsites. Summers are hot (100°F is common); nighttime temperatures drop into the 60°Fs. Beware sudden cloudbursts July to September. Autumns are beautiful,

with warm days and cool nights. Winter brings snow, but daytime temperatures rise to 50°F. Wildflowers bloom in May, as do the bugs; bring repellant.

Zion is remarkably quiet, even in summer, because there are no cars. Plan to ride the shuttle (see p234).

Orientation

Zion occupies 147,000 acres between I-15 to the northwest and Hwy 9 to the south. No road within the park directly connects the northern and southern sections.

Three roads access the park. To the northwest, Kolob Canyons Rd branches east off I-15 and continues past an entrance gate and visitor center. To the south, Hwy 9

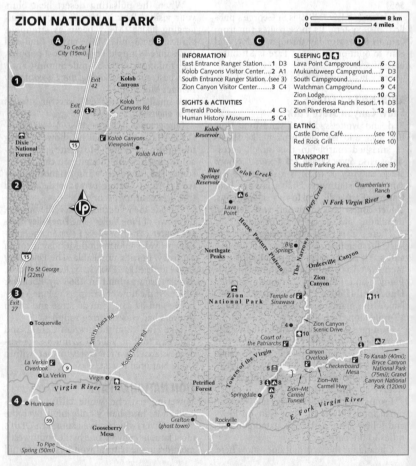

ZION NATIONAL PARK

INFORMATION	
East Entrance Ranger Station	1 D3
Kolob Canyons Visitor Center	2 A1
South Entrance Ranger Station	(see 3)
Zion Canyon Visitor Center	3 C4

SIGHTS & ACTIVITIES	
Emerald Pools	4 C3
Human History Museum	5 C4

SLEEPING	
Lava Point Campground	6 C2
Mukuntuweep Campground	7 D3
South Campground	8 C4
Watchman Campground	9 C4
Zion Lodge	10 C3
Zion Ponderosa Ranch Resort	11 D3
Zion River Resort	12 B4

EATING	
Castle Dome Café	(see 10)
Red Rock Grill	(see 10)

TRANSPORT	
Shuttle Parking Area	(see 3)

links I-15 with Hwy 89 (passing the visitor center and services), Zion Canyon Scenic Drive and the Zion-Mt Carmel Tunnel. I-15 and Hwy 9 are open year-round. The middle road, Kolob Terrace Rd, goes 35 miles north from Hwy 9 to Hwy 14 near Cedar City. The road lacks services, is paved only halfway and closes in winter.

Regarding the Zion-Mt Carmel Tunnel: if your vehicle is 7ft, 10in wide or 11ft, 4in high or larger, it must be escorted through, since vehicles this big need both lanes. Motorists requiring an escort must pay $10 over the entrance fee, good for two trips. Between April and October, rangers are stationed at the tunnel from 8am to 8pm daily; at other times, ask at the entrance stations. Vehicles prohibited at all times include those more than 13ft, 1in tall, single vehicles more than 40ft long and combined vehicles more than 50ft long.

Springdale sits on Hwy 9, outside the park's south entrance. A friendly community full of hotels, restaurants and services, Springdale is 3 miles long, but its center is a walkable quarter-mile stretch, a mile southwest of Zion.

Other small towns line Hwy 9 further west, including Rockville, Virgin, La Verkin and Hurricane, the largest. If you can't find what you need in Springdale, go to St George (p227), 40 minutes southwest of both Zion Canyon and Kolob Canyons. Cedar City (p240), another sizeable town, lies 15 minutes north of Kolob Canyons.

East of Zion, a few towns dot Hwy 89; the largest, Kanab (p243), is 40 minutes away.

There's so much to see in Zion that entire books have been written about it. The following descriptions are necessarily brief. Find more at the visitor center, or pick up Lonely Planet's *Zion & Bryce Canyon National Parks*.

Information

BOOKSTORES
Zion Natural History Association (ZNHA; ☎ 435-772-3264, 800-635-3959; www.zionpark.org) Runs the main visitor center's excellent bookstore.
Human History Museum (☎ 435-772-0168; ☯ 8am-6pm) Has a smaller bookstore to Zion Natural History Association.
Zion Rock & Mountain Guides (☎ 435-772-3303; www.zionrockguides.com; 1458 Zion Park Blvd; ☯ 8am-7pm) Stocks activity-specific guides.

EMERGENCY & MEDICAL SERVICES
In emergency, dial ☎ 911 or ☎ 435-772-3322. For Washington County police, fire and ambulance, call ☎ 800-624-9447.
Zion Canyon Medical Clinic (☎ 435-772-3226; 120 Lion Blvd; ☯ 9am-5pm Tue-Sat in summer; 1 day only in winter) is a walk-in urgent care clinic. The nearest 24-hour emergency room is in St George (p227).

INTERNET ACCESS
Springdale Library (☎ 435-772-3676; 898 Zion Park Blvd, Springdale; ☯ 10am-6pm Mon, Wed & Fri, 10am-9pm Tue & Thu, 10am-5pm Sat) Internet terminals ($1 per 30 minutes). In 2006, the library will move to Lion Blvd beside Town Hall.
Sol Foods Market & Deli and **Best Western Zion Park Inn** (p238) Internet access (per five minutes $1).

TOURIST INFORMATION
Zion Canyon Visitor Center (☎ 435-772-3256; www.nps.gov/zion; ☯ 8am-7pm summer, to 6pm spring & fall, to 5pm winter) The central source for information. Outside there's drinking water and restrooms; inside find books and maps, weather and river conditions and campground info. Ask about ranger-led activities, which include nature walks, interpretive talks on flora, fauna, ecology and geology.
Backcountry Desk (☎ 435-772-0170; ☯ 7am-7pm summer, to 6pm spring & fall) Housed in the visitor center, it dispenses permits.
Kolob Canyons Visitor Center (☎ 435-586-0895; ☯ 8am-4:30pm summer & winter, 7am-4:30pm spring & fall) At the northwest entrance. It has information and permits.
Zion Canyon Visitors Bureau (☎ 888-518-707; www.zionpark.com) It maintains a good website.

Dangers & Annoyances
Stay hydrated (p478), keep track of your kids, don't jump off rocks and watch for signs of heat exhaustion (p479). Flash floods occur year-round, particularly in July and August. Before hiking in river canyons, check weather and water conditions with rangers. If you hear thunder, if water rises suddenly or goes muddy, or if you feel sudden wind accompanied by a thunderous roar, immediately seek higher ground. Climbing a few feet can save your life, but if you can't, get behind a rock fin. You can't outrun a flash flood (p63).

Sights & Activities
Hiking is the primary activity. Hikes are listed in their respective geographic areas.

ZION SHUTTLE

From April 1 to October 31, the park operates two free, linked shuttle loops. The Zion Park Shuttle makes nine stops along Zion Canyon, from the main visitor center to the Temple of Sinawava at the end of the Zion Canyon Scenic Drive (a 90-minute round-trip). The Springdale Shuttle makes six regular stops and three flag stops along Hwy 9 from the park's south entrance to the Majestic View Lodge (p238) in Springdale, the hotel furthest from the park. Park visitors take the Springdale Shuttle to Zion Canyon Giant Screen Theatre (p239) and walk across a footbridge to a kiosk where rangers collect fees. The visitor center and the first Zion Canyon Shuttle stop lie just on the other side. It couldn't be easier.

The wheelchair-accessible shuttle buses accommodate large backpacks and carry up to two bicycles or one baby jogger. Pets aren't allowed. Shuttle stops have a shaded wood bench with schedule and route descriptions.

In summer shuttles operate from 5:45am to 11pm, in spring and fall from 6:45am to 10pm. Shuttles run every six to 10 minutes, from 9am to 8pm, and every 15 to 30 minutes early and late in the day.

Even in summer, when crowds ply the trails, remember solitude is just a few thousand feet away, straight up. The visitor center has an extensive selection of maps to get you there.

ZION CANYON

Spring to fall, the shuttle (above) stops at all major trailheads along the 7-mile road through Zion Canyon, the park's centerpiece. In low season, you can only park at these shuttle stops and several scenic pullouts.

In order of increasing difficulty, the best trails accessible from Zion Canyon Scenic Drive are listed following; distances are one-way. All have thrilling views.

The paved **Pa'rus Trail** parallels the road for almost 2 miles from Watchman Campground to the main park junction. It's the only trail that allows bicycles and dogs. The ever-wonderful, paved, mile-long **Riverside Walk** begins at the end of the road. From the trail's end, you can continue along (and in) the Virgin River for several miles; this is the final portion of the Narrows (opposite) – a difficult backpacking trip. The quarter-mile-long **Weeping Rock Trail** climbs 100ft to hanging gardens. **Emerald Pools** is another favorite; a paved half-mile-long trail leads to the lower pool and waterfall, while a mile-long unpaved trail leads to the upper pool.

Among the harder trails, **Hidden Canyon Trail** has several drop-offs and climbs 850ft in just over a mile to a narrow, shady canyon. More strenuous, but leading to great views, are the 2.5-mile **Angels Landing Trail** (1490ft ascent) and the 4-mile **Observation Point Trail** (2150ft ascent). For longer hikes and overnights, see opposite.

All can be slippery when wet; inquire about trail conditions before setting out.

ZION–MOUNT CARMEL HIGHWAY (HIGHWAY 9)

It's 10 miles from Zion Canyon to the park's east exit. The road east of the mile-long Zion-Mount Carmel Tunnel (see p233 for restrictions) leads quickly into dramatically different terrain – a landscape of etched slickrock, culminating at the top at the mountainous Checkerboard Mesa. The only marked trail is **Canyon Overlook Trail**, a moderately easy half-mile walk, yielding thrilling views 1000ft down into Zion Canyon.

For a sunset perch, head to the **La Verkin Overlook**, 20 miles west of Zion on Hwy 9 between Virgin and La Verkin. Take the signed turnoff up the 1.5-mile gravel-and-dirt road for a 360° overlook.

KOLOB CANYONS ROAD

This 5-mile-long road, which penetrates the Finger Canyons area, sees one-tenth the visitors that the south entrance does, though the scenery and hiking are stupendous. Enter off I-15, from exit 40; it's 40 miles from the visitor center on Hwy 9.

The road has parking and picnic areas. At the end, the easiest trail is a half-mile-long **Timber Creek Overlook Trail**, a 100ft ascent to a small peak with great views. The main hike is the 2.7-mile-long **Taylor Creek Trail**, which crisscrosses the creek. The hike to **Kolob Arch** has a big payoff: the arch vies with Landscape Arch in Arches National Park (p276) as 'biggest arch in the world.' Fit hikers can do the 14.4-mile round-trip in a day.

KOLOB TERRACE ROAD

This 11-mile road climbs to Lava Point (7890ft) and relief from the heat. Not as crowded as the main park, it's still busy in high season and just as scenically rewarding. The **Hop Valley Trail** is an alternate route to Kolob Arch, about 7 miles and 1100ft down. The 6-mile **Wildcat Canyon Trail** goes between Kolob Terrace Rd and Lava Point. The **West Rim Trail** heads 14.5 miles to Zion Canyon.

ZION CANYON SCENIC DRIVE

Zion's three main roads – Kolob Canyons Rd to the northwest, Kolob Terrace Rd in the middle, and Hwy 9 to the south – pass through fabulous scenery. But the most spectacular is the Zion Canyon Scenic Drive, which pierces the heart of Zion Canyon. This is most visitors' primary destination; if you've time for only one activity, tour this road (in the shuttle from April to October).

HUMAN HISTORY MUSEUM

Under a mile into the park is the air-conditioned **Human History Museum** (☎ 435-772-0168; admission free; ☽ 8am-6pm). Exhibits present the geological and human history of Zion and its birth as a park. There's also a good 22-minute introductory film, much better than Springdale's *Treasure of the Gods* (p239). The building is part of an original Mormon homestead.

BACKPACKING

Zion has 100 miles of backcountry trails with wilderness camping and enough quiet to hear the whoosh of soaring ravens overhead. You can hike the entirety of Zion north to south (a traverse of 50-plus miles); rangers can suggest shorter options.

The most famous trip is through the **Narrows**, a 16-mile journey into narrow canyons along the Virgin River's north fork. The easiest and busiest of the backcountry hikes, it's unforgettable. Plan on getting wet: about 50% of the hike is in the river. The trip takes 12 hours; split it into two days (if not, finish the hike in time to catch

the last park shuttle), spending the night on one of the designated campsites (box, p236). Move with the current: begin at Chamberlain's Ranch (outside the park); the trail ends at Riverside Walk at the north end of Zion Canyon. This hike is limited to between June and October, and may close late July to early September because of flash floods. Day hikers are allowed to wade upriver as far as Big Springs, so the final miles can get distressingly crowded.

The visitor center in Zion Canyon has a 'Ride Board' where you can connect with other backpackers. Or book van service (box, p236) in advance to pick you up anywhere you want.

CANYONEERING

If there's one sport that makes Zion special, it's canyoneering. Rappel over the lip of a sandstone bowl, swim icy pools, trace a slot canyon's curves – canyoneering is beautiful, dangerous and sublime all at once. And it's easy to learn. The park service sets dayuse limits. Zion's slot canyons are the park's most sought-after backcountry experience; reserve long in advance.

Take a course first. Guided trips are prohibited in the park; courses are held outside Zion, after which students can try out their newfound skills in the park. Among the easiest routes are The Subway and Orderville Canyon, which ends at the Narrows.

If you can use a harness, Pine Creek Canyon and Mystery Canyon are gorgeous, popular routes with moderate challenges and rappels of 50ft to 100ft. Pine Creek has easy access. Mystery Canyon lets you be a rock star – the last rappel drops into the Virgin River before admiring crowds hiking the Narrows.

Zion Rock & Mountain Guides (☎ 435-772-3303; www.zionrockguides.com; 1458 Zion Park Blvd, Springdale; ☽ 8am-7pm) rents and sells gear and has great guides. Guided trips near the park and courses start around $100. **Zion Adventure Company** (☎ 435-772-1001; www.zionadventures.com; 36 Lion Blvd, Springdale; ☽ 8am-8pm) and its sister location at **Zion Outdoor** (☎ 435-772-0990; 868 Zion Park Blvd, Springdale; ☽ 9am-9pm) both sell and rent equipment, lead trips and teach classes.

BIKING

Cycling is allowed only on Zion Canyon Rd and the Pa'rus Trail (opposite). No cars on

---

BACKCOUNTRY ACCESS

The longest trip within park borders is the four-day trans-park journey, but most hikes require only one overnight. The Backcountry Desk (p233) has details. Generally backcountry hikes are one-way and require a shuttle ride back (see end of this box). Zion's backcountry is hot, dry and remote; be prepared.

You'll need a permit for overnights. Half the permits can be reserved online (www.nps.gov/zion; $5); the remaining permits are distributed on a first-come, first-served basis a day ahead. Trying to get a next-day walk-in permit on a busy weekend is like getting tickets to see Madonna; lines form at the Backcountry Desk by 6am.

A permit lottery is held four months in advance for the most sought-after routes. Look online for details.

Trails limited to designated campsites include West Rim, La Verkin Creek, Hop Valley and The Narrows. Dispersed camping is allowed with restrictions on East Rim, Southwest Desert and sections of Wildcat Canyon Trail; ask rangers. Campsites can only be reserved online for one night; arrange multinight stays in person. Designated backcountry campsites are primitive.

Three shuttle companies operate vans to trailheads. Rates vary; typical high-season fares run $25 to $35 per person, with a two-person minimum. Make reservations, and reconfirm the day before your trip: **Red Rock Shuttles** (☎ 435-635-9104), **Zion Canyon Transportation** (☎ 877-635-5993), **Zion Rock & Mountain Guides** (☎ 435-772-3303).

Carry bug dope in spring. And don't forget entertainment: Yahtzee fits neatly in a tiny pocket, as does a harmonica.

Zion Canyon Rd in summer makes cycling there great. Mountain biking is prohibited, but nearby areas provide awesome single-track slickrock trails as good as Moab's. Try **Gooseberry Mesa**, **Hurricane Cliffs** and **Rockville Bench**; Springdale bike shops can provide information.

Zion Cycles (☎ 435-772-0400; www.zioncycles.com; 868 Zion Park Blvd, Springdale; ☻ 9am-9pm) rents and repairs. Rentals per hour/half-/full day cost $10/22/35. **Springdale Cycle Tours** (☎ 435-772-0575, 800-776-2099; www.springdalecycles.com; 1458 Zion Park Blvd, Springdale; ☻ 9am-6pm), rents, repairs and operates a **rental hut** (☻ 9am-1pm, 3-6pm) in front of Sol Foods Market, beside the park. Rentals per half-/full day cost $25/35. They also lead day trips from around $100 per person.

HORSEBACK RIDING

Canyon Trail Rides (☎ 435-679-8665, 435-772-3810; www.canyonrides.com) is Zion's official horseback-riding concessionaire, and operates across from Zion Lodge. March through November, it offers one- ($30) and three-hour ($55) rides. Kids must be seven or older. Rides follow the Sand Bench Trail along the Virgin River.

If you have your own horse, contact the Backcountry Desk (p233) for permits.

ROCK CLIMBING

Zion Canyon has some of the most famous big-wall climbs in America. However, there's not much for beginners or those who like sport climbs and bolted routes. For these head to Snow Canyon State Park (p231).

Overnight trips and bivouacs require permits. Contact the Backcountry Desk (p233), which also has route descriptions written by climbers.

Both outfitters listed under Canyoneering (p235) offer rock climbing courses for beginners and intermediates; Zion Rock & Mountain Guides has more climbing gear and route books more up-to-date than the park's route books.

SWIMMING & TUBING

Though too cold for swimming, Virgin River warms to 55°F to 65°F from June through September. The river is swift and generally only knee-deep. Tubing is prohibited within Zion but popular outside the park mid-May to August. **Zion Canyon Campground** (☎ 435-772-3237; www.zioncamp.com; 479 Zion Park Blvd) in Springdale rents tubes ($10) but doesn't provide return transportation. **Zion Tubing** (☎ 435-772-8823; www.ziontubing.com; 180 Zion Park Blvd, Springdale; ☻ 8am-8pm), inside Tsunami Juice & Java (p239) does both.

OUTSIDE THE PARK

In Springdale, **Zion Canyon Elk Ranch** (☎ 435-619-2424; 792 Zion Park Blvd; admission free; ☼ sunrise to sunset;) lets you pet elk, buffalo, Texas long-horns, horses and miniature donkeys; a bag of feed costs $2.

In nearby Rockville, **Grafton ghost town** includes a restored 1886 meeting house, a crumbling general store, cemetery and pio-neer log homes (on private property) – all standing empty. The bicycle scene in *Butch Cassidy and the Sundance Kid* was filmed here. In Rockville, take Bridge Rd, cross the bridge and turn right on Grafton Rd. In 0.5 mile, the road bears left and becomes gravel. A mile further, bear right at the dead end sign. In 2 miles, pass the cemetery, then drive a quarter mile to the ghost town. Park at the red gate.

Tours

There are no organized tours into Zion in summer; ride the shuttle (p234). Novem-ber through March, **Red Rock Shuttle & Tour** (☎ 435-635-9104) and **Southern Utah Scenic Tours** (☎ 435-867-8690, 888-404-8687; www.discover-the-west .com) offer Zion tours for groups, starting at $100 per person. **ATV Wilderness Tours** (☎ 888-656-2887; www.atvadventures.com/atv2/) and **Zion Outback Safaris** (☎ 866-946-6494; www.zionjeeptours .com) offer guided ATV tours or Jeep tours from $50.

Festivals & Events

On St Patrick's Day (mid-March) in Spring-dale is the hilarious green Jell-O sculpture competition. July 4 brings a parade and fireworks; the festivities continue with Utah's Pioneer Day (July 24), the Zion Can-yon Jazz & Arts Festival (August), and in November the Butch Cassidy 10km Mara-thon. Contact the **Zion Canyon Visitors Bureau** (☎ 888-518-7070; www.zionpark.com).

Sleeping

IN SPRINGDALE & ZION NATIONAL PARK

April through November, it's difficult to find lodging under $50 in the adjacent town of Springdale. (Budgeteers: head to St George.) Rates plummet in winter. The lower the number on Zion Park Blvd ad-dresses following, the closer the park en-trance; all are near shuttle stops. The website of the **Zion Canyon Visitors Bureau** (www.zionpark .com) lists links to area accommodations.

Budget

El Rio Lodge (☎ 435-772-3205, 888-772-3205; www.elrio lodge.com; 995 Zion Park Blvd; s/d $48/53) A great bar-gain, the 10 well-kept, plain rooms are clean, with TV and microwave but no phone.

Terrace Brook Lodge (☎ 435-772-3932, 800-342-6779; www.terracebrooklodge.com; 990 Zion Park Blvd; s/d $50/63, f $80-94; ⊠) Basic and pleasant, there's also a tiny pool.

Watchman (☎ 800-365-2267; http://reservations.nps .gov; campsites $16, RV hookup $18; ☼ year-round) A Park Service campground near South en-trance, with 170 sites. There's drinking water and toilets, but no showers. A few sites are reservable; book five months ahead. The campground's cottonwoods spew pollen in May.

South (campsites $16; ☼ Mar-Oct) A Park Serv-ice campground near South entrance, with 170 sites. There are no showers, but there are toilets and drinking water. Sites are non-reservable, so arrive early to secure one. The campgrounds' cottonwoods spew pol-len in May.

Lava Point (☼ summer) A free six-site camp-ground (no water) at the end of Kolob Ter-race Rd.

Zion Canyon Campground (☎ 435-772-3237; www .zioncamp.com; 479 Zion Park Blvd; day/week tent sites $20/120, RV hookup $24/144; ⊠) In Springdale, this place has riverside tent and RV sites and full facilities. Campsites are dusty and close together, but shaded.

Midrange

Under-the-Eaves Bed & Breakfast (☎ 435-772-3457, 866-261-2655; www.under-the-eaves.com; 980 Zion Park Blvd; r $75-95, ste $145; ⊠) Individually styled rooms in this historic home range from fun-ctional to palatial, with great views. Breakfast included.

Red Rock Inn (☎ 435-772-3139; www.redrockinn .com; 998 Zion Park Blvd; r $92-96, ste $150; ⊠) Five ro-mantic rooms feature art, rich color schemes, pretty quilts and jetted tubs. In-room break-fast included.

Harvest House (☎ 435-772-3880; www.harvesthouse .net; 29 Canyon View Dr; r $90-110; ⊠) This modern B&B has four spacious, bright, comfortable rooms and a hot tub. Breakfast included.

Canyon Ranch Motel (☎ 435-772-3357; www.cany onranchmotel.com; 668 Zion Park Blvd; s $64-82, d $74-92; ⊠ ⊠) Detached plain but comfy cottages surround a shaded lawn with swinging benches. Some have full kitchens (add $10).

UTAH

Pioneer Lodge (☎ 435-772-3233, 888-772-3233; www.pioneerlodge.com; 838 Zion Park Blvd; r midweek $72-82, weekend $82-92, ste $131-171; ☒) The decor needs updating, but rooms are well kept. 'Canyon-view' rooms share a massive deck.

Bumbleberry Inn (☎ 435-772-3224, 800-828-1534; www.bumbleberry.com; 897 Zion Park Blvd; s/d $68/78, ste $90; ☒) The quietest rooms are in the rear, with good views.

Also worth considering:

Zion Park Motel (☎ 435-772-3251; www.zionpark motel.com; 855 Zion Park Blvd; r/ste $70/130; ☒ ☒)

Driftwood Lodge (☎ 435-772-3262, 888-801-8811; www.driftwoodlodge.net; 1515 Zion Park Blvd; r $82, ste $120; ☒ ☒)

Top End

Zion Lodge (☎ 435-772-3213, 888-297-2757, reservations ☎ 303-297-2757; www.zionlodge.com; r/cabins/ste $125/133/147; ☒ ☒) Smack in the middle of Zion Canyon, the park's only lodge has 81 well-appointed motel rooms and 40 cabins with gas fireplaces. All have wooden porches with stellar views. There are no TVs, but there's a good restaurant. Book up to 23 months in advance, or try for a same-day reservation (☎ 928-638-2631).

Desert Pearl Inn (☎ 435-772-8888, 888-828-0898; www.desertpearl.com; 707 Zion Park Blvd; r poolside/riverside from $103/115; ☒ ☒) The romantic Desert Pearl is Springdale's most stylish property. Its 61 amenity-laden, earth-tone rooms have handwoven Oaxacan bedspreads, suede sofas, pressed-tin tables, wet bars and vaulted ceilings. Bathrooms have bidets, balconies have Adirondack chairs, and the pool deck is a flagstone masterpiece.

Flanigan's Inn (☎ 435-772-3244, 800-765-7787; www.flanigans.com; 428 Zion Park Blvd; r $100-120, ste $120-210; ☒ ☒) Rooms have vaulted ceilings, bold color schemes, good art and aromatherapy bath products. Bathrooms are small, but the onsite **Deep Canyon Adventure Spa** (☎ 800-765-7787; www.deepcanyonspa.com; 1hr massages & treatments $80-90) compensates.

Majestic View Lodge (☎ 435-772-0665, 866-772-0665; www.majesticviewlodge.com; 2400 Zion Park Blvd; r/ste $120/200; ☒ ☒) Epitomizing the varnished-log-furniture-and-antlers school of design, this lodge achieves genuine kitsch, but has comfortable rooms. There's also a restaurant, saloon and taxidermy-wildlife museum.

Also consider:

Best Western Zion Park Inn (☎ 435-772-3200, 800-934-7275; www.zionparkinn.com; 1215 Zion Park Blvd;

r $105-115, ste $115-180; ☒ ☒) Has the town's only liquor store and two pools.

Cliffrose Lodge (☎ 435-772-3234, 800-243-8824; www.cliffroselodge.com; 281 Zion Park Blvd; r $110-130, ste $135-165; ☒ ☒) Five gorgeous acres of lawn and gardens.

Novel House Inn (☎ 435-772-3650, 800-711-8400; www.novelhouse.com; 73 Paradise Rd; r $105-125; ☒) Romantic, formal B&B; no kids.

LODGING BEYOND SPRINGDALE & ZION NATIONAL PARK

About 25 miles west of the park, Hurricane (pronounced 'her-kin') has chain motels ($50 to $70).

Pah Tempe Hot Springs (☎ 435-635-2879; 825 N 800 East) The coolest place to stay, a hot spring on the Virgin River, hopes to reopen in early 2006; call ahead.

Zion River Resort (☎ 435-635-8594, 800-838-8594; www.zionriverresort.com; tent sites $30, RV hookup $38-43, cabins $60-70, teepees $35; ☒) This pristine RV park, 10 miles east of Hurricane on Hwy 9, has only eight tent sites but 114 RV sites; cabins have air-conditioning.

Mukuntuweep (☎ 435-648-3011; www.xpressweb.com/zionpark; tent sites $15, RV hookup $19, cabins $25) This will do in a pinch; cabins are beat up. Facilities include coin laundry, showers ($1 for guests, $3 for nonguests), gasoline, so-so Mexican restaurant and gift shop.

Zion Ponderosa Ranch Resort (☎ 435-648-2700, 800-293-5444; www.zionponderosa.com; tent $69, cabins $105, ste $145, child 3-11 $69; ☒ ☒ ☒) This all-inclusive resort is the ideal destination for activity-hungry families. Rates are per person and include all meals and scores of activities, including canyoneering, hiking, biking, ATV tours, horseback rides, basketball, tennis, swimming and lots more. Comfy cabins share spotless bathroom facilities. They also rent homes ($130 to $250 per person). The turnoff is 2 miles from Zion's east entrance.

Five miles west of Zion, Rockville has several B&Bs:

Serenity House (☎ 435-772-3393, 800-266-3393; www.serenity-house.com; 149 E Main St; r $40-50; ☒ ☒) Two rooms in a private home; organic breakfast.

Dream Catcher Inn (☎ 435-772-3600, 800-953-7326; www.dreamcatcherinnzion.com; 225 E Main St; r $70-100; ☒ ☒) Six pretty rooms; children are welcome.

Lyon's Inn (☎ 435-772-6881; www.lyonsinn.com; 125 E Main St; r $65-105; ☒ ☒) Four contemporary rooms; outdoor hot tub.

Amber Inn (☎ 435-772-0289, 866-370-1515; www .amber-inn.com; 244 W Main St; r $75-85; 🈁 ⊠) Plain but modern rooms; individually cooked breakfast.

Eating
IN ZION NATIONAL PARK
Zion Lodge (opposite) has the only in-park dining.

Castle Dome Café (Zion Lodge; dishes $3-6, pizza $11-15; 🕑 11am-5pm) Sandwiches, burgers, pizza, salads, soups, Asian-ish rice bowls and ice cream.

Red Rock Grill (Zion Lodge; ☎ 435-772-3213; lunch mains $6-8, dinner $12-21) The window-lined Zion Lodge dining room has a big deck with magnificent views. Breakfast is a buffet; at lunch expect sandwiches and wraps. Dinners are best, with solidly good, but not great, steaks and grilled fish; make reservations.

IN SPRINGDALE
Sol Foods Market & Deli (☎ 435-772-0277; 95 Zion Park Blvd; items $6-8; 🕑 8am-9pm, till 6pm in winter) For quick eats, this place has falafel and gyros, fish and chips, burgers and wraps, and a great patio with occasional live music.

Springdale Fruit Company Market (☎ 435-772-3222; 2491 Zion Park Blvd; sandwiches $5; 🕑 8am-8pm Apr-Oct) Come here for focaccia sandwiches and smoothies. There's also a lovely picnic area.

Zion Park Gift & Deli (☎ 435-772-3843; 866 Zion Park Blvd; sandwiches $6-10; 🕑 8am-9:30pm Mon-Sat) Serves fat sandwiches and ice cream.

Tsunami Juice & Java (☎ 435-772-3818; 180 Zion Park Blvd; wraps $6; 🕑 8am-8pm) Specializes in to-go wraps and fruit smoothies.

Mean Bean (☎ 435-772-0654; 932 Zion Park Blvd; dishes under $6; 🕑 6:30am-5pm) Great coffee, sandwiches, breakfast burritos and beer.

Zion Pizza & Noodle Company (☎ 435-772-3815; www.zionpizzanoodle.com; 868 Zion Park Blvd; pizza $10-14, pasta $11; 🕑 4-10pm) Families like this order-at-the-counter place, which serves up Utah microbrews.

Oscar's Café (☎ 435-772-3232; 948 Zion Park Blvd; mains $6-14; 🕑 8am-10pm) Meet fellow travelers on the patio at Oscar's, where the menu features Mexican standards and sandwiches. The specials are best; try the fresh fish tacos and huge rib-eye steaks ($27).

Bit & Spur Restaurant & Saloon (☎ 435-772-3498; 1212 Zion Park Blvd; mains $10-14, specials $18-24; 🕑 dinner) A local institution and the liveliest spot in town – with Springdale's only bar – the Bit rates among the region's best. Southwest-influenced seafood and steak specials are worth the splurge. There's occasional live music.

Spotted Dog Café (☎ 435-772-3244; 428 Zion Park Blvd; mains $12-25; 🕑 breakfast & dinner) Some prefer this place to the Bit & Spur. The high-end, Western-style cooking includes buffalo and elk meatloaf, blackened ahi, local trout and steaks; there's a full bar. There's also breakfast.

Pentimento (☎ 435-772-0490; 1515 Zion Park Blvd; mains $9-20; 🕑 breakfast & dinner) Inside the Driftwood Lodge (opposite), this is possibly the best in town, with a simple, classic menu – done *really* well – of rib-eye steaks, rack of lamb, wild game and lasagna. The twice-whipped potatoes are delish; save room for pie. There's also breakfast ($3 to $7).

Also consider the following:
Dolce Vita Bistro (☎ 435-772-0481; Paradise Rd; crepes $9-10, salads $13; 🕑 dinner Thu-Sun) Behind Zion Pizza & Noodle; fancy crepes and salads; live music.
Pioneer Restaurant (☎ 435-772-3009; 828 Zion Park Blvd; breakfast & lunch $4.50-8, dinner $7-16) Country diner food.
Switchback Grille (☎ 435-772-3700; 1149 Zion Park Blvd; lunch $6-13, dinner $14-30) All-American fare with wine.
Majestic View Lodge Restaurant (☎ 435-772-0665, 866-772-0665; www.majesticviewlodge.com; 2400 Zion Park Blvd; lunch $6-8, dinner $15-25; 🕑 7am-10pm) Wall-mounted trophy heads preview what's cooking.
Bumbleberry Restaurant (☎ 435-772-3224; 897 Zion Park Blvd; breakfast $5-8.50, sandwiches $5-7.50, dinner mains $9-13; 🕑 7:30am-9pm Mon-Sat summer, to 6pm or 7pm winter) Nothing-special family dining, but very special bumbleberry pie.

Entertainment
You can hear live music at the Bit & Spur (left), Dolce Vita Bistro (above) and Sol Foods Market (left). The outdoor **OC Tanner Amphitheater** (☎ 435-652-7994; www.dixie.edu /tanner; 300 Lion Blvd, Springdale; adult $9, child under 18 $5) hosts live concerts mid-May to August, from symphonic to country-western; pack a picnic.

The **Zion Canyon Giant Screen Theatre** (☎ 888-256-3456, 435-772-2400; www.zioncanyontheatre.com; 145 Zion Park Blvd, Springdale; adult/child $8/5) shows the 40-minute *Zion Canyon: Treasure of the Gods* on a six-story screen. Much of it is pure hokum, with some scenery from other parks, but it's still beautiful. They screen

UTAH

a mainstream movie at 8pm. Or catch a nostalgia-heavy variety show at **Bumbleberry Playhouse** (☎ 866-478-4854, 435-772-3611; www .bumbleberrytheatre.com; 897 Zion Park Blvd; adult $17.50, child 6-14 $10).

CEDAR CITY

pop 21,500 / elev 5800ft

Southern Utah's second-largest town is a well-placed stopover between Vegas and Salt Lake City, and one of the Southwest's cultural centers – at least in summer and fall, when its annual Shakespearean Festival stages plays so good you'll wonder if you're in Utah. Outdoors enthusiasts hit the trails at Cedar Breaks National Monument (p243), and ski or bike at Brian Head Resort (p243). If you're just driving through, note that Cedar City is 3000ft higher than St George, which means it's deliciously cool.

Locals work in agriculture or at the university. Old timers whistle the 'c' in Cedar, which makes it sound like 'Sheedar.'

Orientation & Information

Cedar City is on I-15, 55 miles from St George, 180 miles from Las Vegas and 260 miles from SLC. Bryce Canyon and Zion's South Entrance are 90 minutes away. Most businesses front Main St.

BLM (☎ 435-586-2401; 176 E DL Sargent Dr; ☯ 7:45am-4:30pm Mon-Fri) Manages the land west of I-15, known for its wild horses.

Cedar City & Brian Head Tourism & Convention Bureau (☎ 435-586-5124, 800-354-4849; www .scenicsouthernutah.com; 581 N Main St; ☯ 8am-5pm Mon-Fri year-round, 9am-1pm Sat summer) Offers free Internet access.

Chamber of Commerce (☎ 435-586-4484) Same building as the Cedar City & Brian Head Tourism & Convention Bureau.

Dixie National Forest Cedar City Ranger Station (☎ 435-865-3200; 1789 N Wedgewood Lane; ☯ 8am-5pm Mon-Fri) Provides information on the forest along Hwy 14.

Library (☎ 435-586-6661; 303 N 100 East; ☯ 9am-9pm Mon-Thu, 9am-6pm Fri & Sat) Free Internet.

Mountain West Books (☎ 435-586-3828; 77 N Main St; ☯ 9am-7pm Mon-Fri, 9am-6pm Sat) Has good books.

Police (☎ 435-586-2956; 10 N Main St)

Post office (☎ 435-586-6701; 333 N Main St)

Valley View Medical Center (☎ 435-868-5000; 1303 N Main St)

Zions Bank (☎ 435-586-7614; 3 S Main St; ☯ 9am-5pm Mon-Fri, 9am-1pm Sat) Currency exchange.

Sights & Activities

Iron Mission State Park (☎ 435-586-9290; 635 N Main St; per person/family $2/6; ☯ 9am-6pm, closed Sun in winter) is an attractive museum about Mormon pioneers and their early mining attempts. There are also 19th-century stagecoaches and buggies and a model-train diorama of Cedar City.

Southern Utah University (SUU; ☎ 435-586-7700; www.suu.edu; 351 W Center St) has a pleasant campus that hosts the annual Shakespearean Festival (opposite). It also contains the intimate **Braithwaite Fine Arts Gallery** (☎ 435-586-5432; admission free; ☯ noon-7pm Mon-Fri), open during the school year.

Downtown's mom-and-pop shops around Main and Center Sts are good for a quick stroll; refuel on ice-cream sodas at the vintage 1940s soda fountain at **Bulloch Drug** (☎ 435-586-9651; 91 N Main St; ☯ 9am-9pm Mon-Fri, 9am-7pm Sat). Popularly called the Rock Church, the **Mormon Tabernacle** (75 E Center St) was built in 1931; hours are variable.

Hiking and biking abound. At the foot of 300 E, the recommended 8-mile, unpaved **C Trail** is strenuous. **Canyon Park** (400 E at College Ave) marks the start of the paved **Canyon Walking Trail**, past painted cliffs along Hwy 14. Hwy 14 (p242) itself has great trails. **Cedar Cycle** (☎ 435-586-5210; www.cedarcycle.com; 38 E 200 South; ☯ 9am-5pm Mon-Fri, 9am-2pm Sat) repairs and rents bikes ($20 to $30 a day) and has trail information.

Festivals & Events

The play's the thing at Cedar City's main event, held annually at SUU since 1962. The Tony Award–winning **Utah Shakespearean**

WHADJA SAY?

Utahns have four ways of greeting each other. To talk like a local, don't just say 'hello'. Try one of these:

- How ya doin?
- Heck are ya? (Contraction of 'How the heck are you?')
- Howdy!
- Chupta?

The last is a contraction of 'What are you up to?,' which becomes 'Whatcha up to?,' which reduces to 'Chupta?' – to which your new friend might reply 'nunmuch.'

Festival (☎ 435-586-7878, 800-752-9849; www.bard.org)
presents three of the Bard's plays, plus three
other stage classics late June to September.
In the fall (mid-September to late October),
they present three more chestnuts, one
Shakespearean, one straight and one musical. Productions are top quality, but it's the
extras that draw the crowds. In summer,
there are free seminars discussing the plays,
free 'Greenshows' with Elizabethan minstrels, backstage tours, classes for credit,
child care and more. In fall, there's a pump-
kin festival, quilt gathering and more.

Shakespeare's plays are performed in
the roofless Adams Memorial Theater, an
excellent reproduction of London's Globe
Theater. The other plays are performed in
Randall Jones Theater; all stages are at SUU.
Reservations are recommended one to two
weeks in advance. Or ask about returned
tickets at the **Courtesy Booth** (☎ 435-586-7790),
near the Adams Theater. A few last-row
gallery tickets ($14, but good seats) go on
sale the day of the performance; come early.
Tickets cost $20 to $46.

The **Utah Summer Games** (☎ 435-865-8421;
www.utahsummergames.org), mid- to late June, are
styled as a mini-Olympics and attract 7600
amateur athletes competing in 50 events.

The free **Midsummer Renaissance Fair** (☎ 435-
586-3711; www.umrf.net) in early July features
more Renaissance entertainment. The **Neil
Simon Festival** (☎ 435-327-8673; www.simonfest.org)
presents works by contemporary American
playwrights, mid-July to mid-August. For
more events, contact the tourism bureau.

Sleeping
BUDGET
Rates tend to be high in summer, particularly during the Shakespearean Festival and
on weekends.

Cedar City KOA (☎ 435-586-9872; 1121 N Main St;
tent/RV sites $23/31, 1-/2-room cabins $43/60; ☒ ☐)
This clean, full-service KOA provides many
extras including a movie theater.

The following are basic, clean motels.
Cedar Rest Motel (☎ 435-586-9471; 479 S Main St;
r $45)
Best Value Inn (☎ 435-586-6557, 888-315-2378;
www.bestvalueinn.com; 323 S Main St; r $55; ☒)
Super 7 Motel (☎ 435-586-6566; 190 S Main St;
s/d from $45/55)

More motels are at exit 59 off I-15. USFS
campgrounds are near Hwy 14 (p242).

MIDRANGE
Cedar City's midrange options are limited
to chain-style hotels. All are reliably clean
and many of them have microwaves and
fridges.

Abbey Inn (☎ 435-586-9966, 800-325-5411; www
.abbeyinncedar.com; 940 W 200 North; midweek/weekend
$86/100; ☒) Richer decor and full breakfast
make this a good choice.

Stratford Court Hotel (☎ 435-586-2433, 877-688-
8884; www.stratfordcourthotel.com; 18 S Main St; r from $90;
☒ ☐ ☒) Includes coin laundry.

Best Western Town & Country Inn (☎ 435-586-
6518, 800-688-6518; www.bwtowncountry.com; 189 N
Main St; r $70-95; ☒) Two pools, one indoor.

Crystal Inn (☎ 435-586-8888, 888-787-6661; www
.crystalinns.com; 1575 W 200 North; r from $70; ☒ ☐)
Has a family restaurant (meals $8 to $20).

Ramada Limited (☎ 435-586-9916, 800-272-6232;
www.ramada.com; 281 S Main St; r from $60; ☒)
Standard-issue plain chain.

TOP END
To do Cedar City right, stay in one of its
romantic B&Bs. Most don't allow pre-teens.
Ask at the visitor center for a full list, or
visit the website www.lodgingcedarcity.com.
Reservations are essential.

Big Yellow Inn (☎ 435-586-0960; www.bigyellow
inn.com; 234 S 300 West; r $90-190; ☐ ☒) This
beautiful Georgian Revival–style home
features 11 sumptuous rooms with private
bathrooms; the tasteful decor ranges from
Oriental to full Victorian. A second house
has five more rooms ($100).

Garden Cottage B&B (☎ 435-586-4919, 866-586-
4919; www.thegardencottagebnb.com; 16 N 200 West; r
$100-110; ☒) An air of nostalgia infuses the
five charming rooms, which feature private baths, antiques, handmade lace, floral
wallpaper, quilts and historic photos of the
owner's Mormon forebears. The gardens
are stunning.

Iron Gate Inn (☎ 435-867-0603, 800-808-4599;
www.theirongateinn.com; 100 N 200 West; r $95-120;
☒ ☐) A rickety iron gate and big front
porch surround the 1897 house whose
oversize rooms have extra-spacious baths.
The charming innkeeper serves breakfast
in the garden.

Bard's Inn B&B (☎ 435-586-6612; www.bardsbandb
.com; 150 S 100 West; r $80-95; ☒) An easy walk
to the Shakespearean Festival, the seven attractive, if modest, rooms have beautiful
antiques.

UTAH

Baker House B&B (☎ 435-867-5695, 888-611-8181; www.bakerhouse.net; 1800 W Royal Hunte Dr; r $110-160; ⊠) The five rooms in this Queen Anne–style home are another cushy choice; all have Jacuzzis and fireplaces.

Eating

How wonderful it would be if Cedar City had dining on par with its B&Bs and top-notch theater. But unfortunately, it does not. Restaurants here feed the masses, not the cognoscenti. Main St has affordable choices.

Pastry Pub (☎ 435-867-1400; 86 W Center St; dishes $3-6; ☽ 7:30am-10pm Mon-Sat) This friendly spot serves pastries, salads and sandwiches, plus good coffee and yummy espresso shakes. During the festival, it's open till midnight.

Market Grill (☎ 435-586-9325; 2290 W 400 North; dishes $4-10; ☽ 6am-9pm Mon-Sat) Meet the core community of pick-up-truck-driving cowboys, farmers and students at this Wild West diner; on Thursdays, there's a live-stock market outside.

Garden House (☎ 435-586-6110; 164 S 100 West; lunch mains $6-10, dinner $13-22; ☽ lunch & dinner Mon-Sat) Inside a lovely former house, the chef-owned Garden House serves decent food, like French-dip sandwiches at lunch and surf-and-turf at dinner. But the atmosphere's what's best; upstairs tables are most romantic.

Sulli's Steakhouse (☎ 435-586-6761; 301 S Main St; mains $13-27; ☽ dinner) It's neither fancy nor romantic, but the menu covers the classic American-Italian and meat-and-potatoes basics. Full bar.

Along Hwy 14 there are two unpretentious, popular steakhouses: **Rusty's Ranch House** (☎ 435-586-3839; ☽ dinner Mon-Sat) is 2 miles from Cedar City, and **Milt's Stage Stop** (☎ 435-586-9344; ☽ dinner) is 5 miles. Both serve dinner only ($12 to $20). Rusty's leans toward steaks and barbecue; Milt's has more charm (read: fireplace and trophy heads) and serves steaks and seafood.

Drinking & Entertainment

Heritage Center (☎ 435-865-2882, 866-882-3327; www.heritagectr.org; 105 N 100 East) This place hosts performances and live theater year-round, and displays rotating art exhibits.

Sportsman's Lounge (☎ 435-586-6552; 900 S Main St; ☽ 1pm-1am) The hangout for billiards, foosball, TV, beer and Friday karaoke.

Groovacious Music Store (☎ 435-867-9800; 171 N 100 West; ☽ 10am-9pm Mon-Sat) A record store (with awesome vinyl) that hosts bands, Tuesday-evening open-mic shows and other events; call for schedules.

Grind Coffeehouse (☎ 435-867-5333; 19 N Main St; ☽ 7am-9pm Mon-Sat, later on show nights) Friday-night comedy performances (adults only) and occasional cabaret acts. Attention heathens: Evangelical Christians run the place (but not the performances); there's no booze. Unless you're into Jesus, stay away Sunday.

Getting There & Around

Cedar City Regional Airport (☎ 435-867-9408; www.cedarcity.org/city_government/airport.html; 2281 W Kittyhawk Dr) is a mile from town; **Skywest** (☎ 435-586-3033, 800-453-9417; www.skywest.com) flies daily to SLC.

The closest Greyhound stop is Parowan, 20 miles north on I-15. The **St George Shuttle** (☎ 435-628-8320, 800-933-8320; www.stgshuttle.com) can take you to SLC ($55), but not to St George.

CATS bus system (☎ 435-559-7433; www.cedarcity.org/city_government/cats.html; ☽ 7am-5:30pm Mon-Fri, 10am-6:30pm Sat) runs a single loop through town ($1).

For taxis call **Iron County Shuttle** (☎ 435-865-7076).

HWY 14 EAST OF CEDAR CITY

As scenic drives go, Hwy 14 is awesome. It leads 42 miles over the Markagunt Plateau, cresting at 10,000ft for stunning vistas of Zion National Park and Arizona. Along the way stop for hiking, trout fishing lakes and campgrounds ($10, with water). Visit the Cedar City Ranger Station (p240) for information. Four-wheel-drive or chains may be required November through April.

Hiking and biking trails with tremendous views, particularly at sunset, include the short **Cascade Falls** and **Bristlecone Trails** and the 32-mile **Virgin River Rim Trail**. A signed turnoff 24.5 miles from Cedar City leads to jumbled **lava beds**.

Half a mile further, pretty **Navajo Lake** has a marina with boat rentals, fishing, a **lodge** (☎ 702-646-4197; www.navajolakelodge.com), store and campgrounds, all open May to October.

Thirty miles from Cedar City, **Duck Creek** has a seasonal USFS **ranger station** (☎ 435-682-2432; ☽ 10am-5pm Memorial Day to Labor Day), campground, gasoline, groceries, diners, fishing and several lodges, including **Falcon's Nest Cabins** (☎ 435-682-2556, 800-240-4930; www.falconsnestcabins.com; cabins $75-90).

A couple of miles east, a passable dirt road leads 10 miles to **Strawberry Point**, for possibly the best views of all.

CEDAR BREAKS NATIONAL MONUMENT

Sculpted cliffs and towering hoodoos glow like neon tie-dye in a wildly eroded natural amphitheater, a majic kaleidoscope of magenta, salmon, plum, rust and ochre, rising to a height of 10,450ft atop the Markagunt Plateau.

Snow closes the tiny park and its only road, Hwy 148, October through May, but you can snowshoe or snowmobile in (see Brian Head Resort, below). The **visitor center** (☎ 435-586-9451; www.nps.gov/cebr; ☺ 8am-6pm) opens Memorial Day through Labor Day; rangers hold hourly talks. Entrance costs $3. The first-come, first-served **campground** (campsites $12) has water and restrooms, but no showers; it rarely fills. Summer temperatures range from 40°F to 70°F; brief storms drop rain, hail and even snow.

The park has five viewpoints off Hwy 148 and two 4-mile round-trip trails along the rim; no trails descend into the breaks. The **Ramparts Trail** – one of southern Utah's most magnificent trails – leaves from the visitor center. It only drops 400ft, but it's tiring because of the high elevation.

The **Alpine Pond Trail** is lovely, though less dramatic. Experienced hikers should consider the difficult 9-mile **Rattlesnake Creek Trail**, which skirts the adjacent national forest and drops to the canyon floor.

Take Hwy 14 to Hwy 148 and Cedar Breaks, 22 miles from Cedar City, or take Hwy 143 from I-15.

BRIAN HEAD

pop 118 / elev 9700ft

The highest town in Utah, Brian Head towers over Cedar City. The **chamber of commerce** (☎ 435-677-2810, 888-677-2810; www.brianheadutah .com; PO Box 190325, Brian Head, UT 84719) has information. Altitude sickness (p478) can be a problem; a hasty descent provides relief.

Brian Head **ski resort** (☎ 435-677-2035; www .brianhead.com; Hwy 143; lift ticket adult/child $39/26) is the closest resort to Vegas (four hours).

It's good for beginners, intermediates and free-riders, but advanced skiers might grow impatient with the short trails and slow lifts (except on a powder day). Still, it's the only resort in Utah within sight of the red-rock desert. There's also snow-biking and a kickin' six-lane snow-tubing area. **Night skiing** costs $10. The lodge rents snowshoes and cross-country skis for the semigroomed trails to Cedar Breaks. Take a snowmobile tour with **Thunder Mountain Sports** (☎ 866-677-2386; www.brianheadthunder.com; 1½hr tour $70).

The resort lowdown is as follows: 1320ft-vertical drop, base elevation 9600ft; 500 acres, six chairlifts.

In summer, the elevation keeps temperatures deliciously cool. Aside from hiking, there's weekend lift-served **mountain biking** ($16) and **scenic chair-lift rides** ($8).

The resort has great ski packages – two nights in Vegas, two nights in Brian Head – for under $200 per person. Otherwise, there's no budget lodging, but prices drop in summer. **Cedar Breaks Lodge & Spa** (☎ 888-282-3327, 435-677-4242; www.cedarbreakslodge.com; r $100-120, ste $130-190; ☒ ☒ ☒) has up-to-date time-share units in a hotel-style complex. For condos ($85 to $450), call **Brian Head Reservation Center** (☎ 435-677-2042, 800-845-9781; www.brianheadtown.com/bhrc/) and **Brian Head Condo Reservations** (☎ 435-677-2045, 800-722-4742; www.brianheadcondoreservations.com).

Brian Head Mall has cheap eats. In the Cedar Breaks Lodge, **Cedar Breaks Cafe** (☎ 435-677-4242; mains $9-23; ☺ breakfast & dinner) serves sit-down American meals; there's also a good **steakhouse** (mains $16-29; ☺ dinner Fri & Sat).

Brian Head is on Hwy 143. Take exit 75 off I-15 (near Parowan).

KANAB

pop 3500 / elev 4925ft

Vast expanses of rugged desert extend everywhere around the remote outpost of Kanab. Don't be surprised if it all looks familiar. Hollywood Westerns were shot here, and John Wayne and other gun-slingin' celebs helped earn Kanab the nickname 'Utah's Little Hollywood.'

Founded by Mormon pioneers in 1874, the town's economic mainstay was traditionally ranching, but tourism is the big money-maker now.

Orientation & Information

The town sits at a major crossroads: Grand Staircase-Escalante National Monument (GSENM) is 20 miles away, Zion 40 miles, Bryce Canyon 80 miles, Grand Canyon's North Rim 81 miles and Glen Canyon 74 miles.

Most businesses lie along Hwy 89. South of Kanab, the highway continues east along 300 S, to GSENM and eventually Page, Arizona (73 miles); Alt Hwy 89 leads south down 100 E to Arizona (3 miles) and the Grand Canyon.

Kanab has a grocery store and bank with 24-hour ATMs.

BLM Kanab Field Office (☎ 435-644-4600; 318 N 100 East; ☺ 8am-4:30pm Mon-Fri) Provides information and issues permits for Paria Canyon–Vermilion Cliffs Wilderness Area (p255).

Hospital (☎ 435-644-5811; 355 N Main St)

Kanab Visitor Center (☎ 435-644-4680; www.ut.blm .gov/monument; 745 E Hwy 89; ☺ 8am-4:30pm, closed weekends Nov-Mar) The GSENM's visitor center provides road, trail and weather updates.

Kane County Office of Tourism (☎ 435-644-5033, 800-733-5263; www.kaneutah.com; 78 S 100 East; ☺ 8am-8pm Mon-Fri, 9am-5pm Sat, 9am-1pm Sun summer; 8:30am-5pm Mon-Sat, 1-5pm Sun winter) This is the main source for area information; it hosts a special kids' website: www.kane4kids.com.

Library (☎ 435-644-2394; 374 N Main St; ☺ 9am-5pm Mon & Fri, 9am-7pm Tue-Thu, 10am-2pm Sat) Free Internet access.

Police (☎ 435-644-5807; 140 E 100 South)

Post office (☎ 435-644-2760; 39 S Main St)

Sights

Pick up the self-guided walking tour of historic houses. The best known is **Heritage House** (☎ 435-644-3506; 100 South at Main St; ☺ 4-8pm Mon-Fri summer).

Frontier Movie Town (☎ 435-644-5337, 800-551-1714; 297 W Center St; ☺ 8am-10pm summer, 10am-5pm winter) stages gunfights in summer in a cluster of actual Western movie sets ($16 to $20 with dinner); a costume shop can doll you up for $20 for a photo. The grill serves steaks and burgers ($7 to $14) and cold beer, a rarity in Kanab. It's free to walk through.

A classic tourist trap, **Moqui Cave** (☎ 435-644-8525; www.moquicave.com; adult/teen $4/2.50, child 6-12 $2; ☺ 9am-7pm Mon-Sat summer) has an odd collection of fluorescent minerals, dinosaur tracks, and cowboy and Indian artifacts inside a real cave. Head 5 miles north on Hwy 89.

Also off Hwy 89, 0.25 mile from Moqui Cave, is the nation's largest no-kill sanctuary, **Best Friends Animal Sanctuary** (tours ☎ 435-644-2001 ext 115; www.bestfriends.org; ☺ 8:30am-5pm). Free tours last 45 to 90 minutes; longer tours let you meet some of the 1500 animals. This could be your trip's feel-good highlight, especially if you adopt a pet. You can spend the night in one of eight cottages with kitchenettes (Best Friends members $107, nonmembers $125).

In late August Kanab's big annual event, **Western Legends Roundup** (☎ 800-733-5263; www .westernlegendsroundup.com), celebrates all things cowboy.

Sleeping

Kanab has a surplus of indie budget motels. High season lasts from mid-May to October. For a full list, see www.kaneutah.com.

Crazy Horse Campark (☎ 435-644-2782, 866-830-7316; www.crazyhorsecampark.com; 625 E 300 South; tent/RV sites $15/20; ☒) The spruced-up 80-site campground has coin laundry, showers, pool and playground.

Hitch'n Post Campground (☎ 435-644-2142, 800-458-3516; 196 E 300 South; tent sites $18, cabins $22-26) This friendly, 17-site campground is near the town center.

Bob-Bon Inn Motel (☎ 435-644-3069, 800-644-5094; www.bobbon.com; 236 N 300 West; r $36-59; ☒) The 16 rooms here are Kanab's best deal; they're small but spotless, with a modest Western feel.

Parry Lodge (☎ 435-644-2601, 800-748-4104; www .parrylodge.com; 89 E Center St; r $51-73; ☒) Back in the day, all the actors stayed here, but the rambling motel has become a faded dowager of the leading lady she once was. Rooms are clean and well kept, but the only thing special is the aura of days gone by. The **restaurant** (☺ 7-11am summer) only serves breakfast; the barn quit doing shows years ago.

Shilo Inn (☎ 435-644-2562, 800-222-2244; www .shiloinns.com; 296 W 100 North; r $86-96; ☒) Kanab's biggest hotel has dependably comfortable minisuites with refrigerators, microwaves and coffeemakers.

Treasure Trail Motel (☎ 435-577-2645, 800-603-2687; www.treasuretrailmotel.com; 150 W Center St; r $44-70; ☒) For those not interested in style, this motel provides 30 clean, sizeable rooms.

Clarion Victorian Suites (☎ 435-644-8660, 800-738-9643; www.victoriancharminn.com; 190 N Hwy 89; r $100-120; ☒ ☐) Every room has a gas fireplace and a jetted tub at this faux-Victorian hotel, Kanab's finest. Full breakfast is included in the price.

Eating & Drinking

Vermilion Café (☎ 435-644-3886; 4 E Center St; dishes $4-6; ☯ 7am-2:30pm Mon-Sat, 8:30am-1:30pm Sun) This unexpectedly hip coffeehouse serves breakfast burritos, sandwiches and espresso. There's also Internet access.

Three Bears Creamery Cottage (☎ 435-644-3300; 210 S 100 East; dishes under $5; ☯ 7am-8pm Mon-Sat, to 10pm summer) An old-fashioned ice cream parlor with build-your-own sundaes and banana splits, Three Bears also grinds wheat for house-baked bread, which it serves with savory homemade soups. It serves good breakfasts, too.

Rocking V Café (☎ 435-644-8001; 97 W Center St; dinner mains $15-23; ☯ 11:30am-9pm) The food and decor blend rustic and modern Southwest style. At lunch there are tasty burgers and wraps, but dinner is the draw, with great seafood and pasta, made all the better with margaritas. The upstairs gallery is packed with work by talented local artists.

Houston's Trail's End Restaurant (☎ 435-644-2488; www.houstons.net; 32 E Center St; mains $10-19; ☯ 6am-9:30pm, closed Jan-Feb) The waitresses wear six-shooters at this fun Kanab institution, which specializes in down-home chicken-fried or rib-eye steaks, barbecued ribs and fried chicken. They don't serve beer, but they do make breakfast.

Nedra's Too (☎ 435-644-2030; 310 S 100 East; mains $6-10; ☯ 7am-11pm summer, 8am-9pm winter) After a day on the trail, fill up on big plates of cheesy, greasy Mexican cooking and Navajo tacos. The salsa is delicious – even if it is only Utah-hot.

Entertainment

The **Crescent Moon Theater** (☎ 435-644-2350; 150 S 100 East) hosts nightly shows in summer, including the cowboy band Bar G Chuckwagon; in winter it shows classic movies. The **Kanab Theatre** (☎ 435-644-2344; 29 W Center St; ☯ Wed-Sun) screens first-run movies.

ALONG HIGHWAY 89

In the days before freeways, US Hwy 89 was Utah's main north–south artery. If you like driving but hate the interstate, you'll love Hwy 89. From the Grand Canyon, the well-paved road heads to Kanab, then at the junction with Hwy 9 – the road to Zion. Further north it follows Sevier River Valley, the route of Mormon pioneers. The following sights are north of Kanab.

Coral Pink Sand Dunes State Park

Restless winds shift giant, pink Sahara-like sand dunes across half this 3700-acre park. For lovers of the strange, it's worth the 24-mile, 90-minute round-trip off Hwy 89 to see the nearly shocking-pink dunes. NB: 1200 acres are devoted to ATVs.

A half-mile interpretive dune hike enters a 265-acre conservation area that's closed to off-highway vehicles (OHV). Day use is $5; there's a 22-site **campground** (campsites $14) with toilets and hot showers and pull-through RV sites. **Reservations** (☎ 800-322-3770) are essential weekends. The same winds that shift the dunes can make tent camping unpleasant.

A **visitor center** (☎ 435-648-2800; ☯ 9am-9pm, to 4pm winter) has displays and water.

Glendale & Around

pop 350 / elev 5500ft

Four small, historic towns dot Hwy 89 north of Hwy 9: Mt Carmel Junction, Mt Carmel, Orderville and Glendale. Few people ever stop, and that's part of their charm. For information, contact **East Zion Tourism Council** (☎ 435-648-2174; www.eastziontourismcouncil.org).

In Mt Carmel, the beautiful **Maynard Dixon Home & Studio** (☎ 435-648-2653; www.maynarddixon .com; ☯ May-Oct) is where Western artist Maynard Dixon (1875–45) lived and worked with artist Edith Hamlin, from 1939 until his death in 1945. Docent-led tours ($20 per person) are by appointment only; the buildings house works by Dixon and Hamlin, plus photos by his first wife, Dorothea Lange, and his friend Ansel Adams. If the red gate is open, take a self-guided tour ($5) of the grounds. It's at mile marker 84 on Hwy 89 and easy to miss. The Maynard Dixon Country Art Show is in August.

In Glendale, **Glendale Bench Rd** accesses Johnson Canyon and Skutumpah Rds (p253) in GSENM. Turn onto 300 North from Hwy 89; the intersection is marked by a faded sign.

The **Glendale KOA** (☎ 435-648-2490; campsites $20-24, cabins $35; ☯ May-Oct), 5 miles north on Hwy 89, has complete facilities including bike and horse rentals and a restaurant.

The seven-room **Historic Smith Hotel** (☎ 435-648-2156, 800-528-3558; www.historicsmith hotel.com; 295 N Main St; r $44-80; ✗) in Glendale offers true country hospitality, The comfy and homey rooms have bunk beds, antiques, quilts, handwoven rugs, family photos and framed needlepoint. Children are welcome. Breakfast is delicious, and owners Bunny and Rochelle are charming.

Next door, the **Buffalo Bistro** (☎ 435-648-2778; 305 N Main St; burgers $7, mains $17-28; ❤ 1-8pm Thu-Mon) conjures an Old West spirit with its breezy porch and outdoor grill sizzling with buffalo, wild boar, elk ribs, rabbit-and-rattlesnake sausage and, yes, rocky mountain oysters. Attend its over-the-top Testicle Festival in June.

If you just need a bed, Mt Carmel Junction has two options. The **Best Western Thunderbird Resort** (☎ 435-648-2203, 888-848-6358; www .bestwesternthunderbird.com/bw.htm; r $88; 🐾) provides dependable chain rooms and a bland restaurant. **Golden Hills Motel** (☎ 435-648-2268, 800-648-2268; www.goldenhillsmotel.com; r $38-52; 🐾) is just clean enough for the price.

Panguitch
pop 1500 / elev 6624ft

Founded in 1864, Panguitch was formerly a ranching and lumber town, but tourism is now the number-one industry. A popular stopover, the town is the seat of Garfield County and gateway for Bryce Canyon National Park (24 miles east). In June the Quilt Walk Festival celebrates pioneer history; Chariots in the Sky is a huge hot-air balloon festival. In July Pioneer Days includes a rodeo. The Garfield County Fair happens in August.

Visit **Garfield County Travel Council** (☎ 435-676-1160, 800-444-6689; www.brycecanyoncountry.com; 55 S Main St; ❤ 9am-5pm) and **Dixie National Forest Powell Ranger Station** (☎ 435-676-8815; www .fs.fed.us/dxnf; 225 E Center) for information.

Other services include the **library** (☎ 435-676-2431; 25 S 200 East), with free Internet access; **post office** (☎ 435-676-8853; 65 N 100 West); **hospital** (☎ 435-676-8811; 224 N 400 East); and **police** (☎ 435-676-8807; 45 S Main St). Showers are at the Big 4 Travel Center (right).

The **Paunsagaunt Wildlife Museum** (☎ 435-676-2500; www.brycecanyonwildlifemuseum.com; 250 E Center St; adult/child $4/2.50; ❤ 9am-8pm May-Oct) is the town's best attraction, with over 400 taxidermy animals and a butterfly and bug room.

SLEEPING

Big Fish KOA (☎ 435-676-2225, 800-562-1625; www .koa.com; 555 S Main St; campsites $19-23, cabins $44; 🐾) This campground has complete facilities.

Hitch-n-Post (☎ 435-676-2436; 420 N Main St; tent/RV sites $16/18) Has both tent and RV sites.

Paradise Campground (☎ 435-676-8348; 2153 N Hwy 89; tent/RV sites $16/18) Two miles north of Hitch-n-Post.

Red Brick Inn (☎ 435-676-2141, 866-732-2745; www.redbrickinnutah.com; 11161 N 100 West; d $79; ✗) Panguitch's only B&B is lovingly tended by on-site owners with an expansive world view. Rooms are cozy and comfortable. Outdoor hot tub.

Big 4 Travel Center (☎ 435-676-8986; 445 E Center St; r $38; ✗) Essentially a truckstop.

Bryce Canyon Motel (☎ 435-676-8441; 308 N Main St; r $40; ❤ Apr-Oct) A cheap motel.

Purple Sage (☎ 435-676-2659, 800-241-6889; www .purplesagemotel.biz; 132 E Center St; r $35-65; ❤ Mar-Oct; ✗) The most comfortable in Panguitch, rooms have pillow-top mattresses and upgraded furnishings. Outdoor hot tub.

Horizon Motel (☎ 435-676-2651, 800-776-2651; www.horizonmotel.net; 730 N Main St; r $55-60; ❤ Mar-Nov; ✗) The Horizon is an old-fashioned motel showing pride of ownership.

Canyon Lodge (☎ 435-676-8292, 800-440-8292; www.colorcountry.net/~cache; 210 N Main St; r $45-50; ❤ Mar-Oct; ✗) This immaculately kept motel has a hot tub and in-room massage.

Color Country Motel (☎ 435-676-2386, 800-225-6518; www.colorcountrymotel.com; 526 N Main St; r $45-60; 🐾) Color Country has the best pool in town, hot tub and well-kept rooms.

Other recommended motels:

Hiett Lamplighter Inn (☎ 435-676-8362, 800-322-6966; www.lamplighterinn.biz; 581 N Main St; r $40-60; ✗)

Blue Pine (☎ 435-676-8197, 800-299-6115; 130 N Main St; r $48-55; ✗)

Adobe Sands (☎ 435-676-8874, 800-497-9261; www .adobesands.com; 390 N Main St; r $42-52; ❤ May-Oct)

Bryce Way Motel (☎ 435-676-2400, 800-225-6534; 429 N Main St; r $45-55)

Best Western New Western (☎ 435-676-8876, 800-528-1234; 200 E Center St; r $65-85; ✗ 🐾) Unnecessarily expensive.

EATING

Panguitch's selection of restaurants is neither wide nor notable. Surprisingly, though, Panguitch has a 24-hour diner (April to November), the **Big 4 Travel Center** (☎ 435-676-8986; 445 E Center St; dishes $4-15; ❤ 24hr Apr-

Nov, 6:30am-9:30pm Dec-Mar). The **C-Stop Pizza and Deli** (☎ 435-676-8366; 561 E Center St; pizzas $5-14; ☺ 10:30am-10pm, shorter in winter) serves pizza and sandwiches. **Foy's Country Corner Cafe** (☎ 435-676-8851; 80 N Main St; dishes $5-12; ☺ 7am-9pm Mon-Sat) and **Flying M Restaurant** (☎ 435-676-8008; 580 Main St; dishes $5-12; ☺ 7am-10pm, to 9pm winter) are run-of-the-mill diners. **Cowboy's Smokehouse BBQ** (☎ 435-676-8030; 95 N Main St; dinner mains $18-28; ☺ 11:30am-9pm Mar-Oct) sometimes has good steaks; quality is erratic. **Grandma Tina's** (☎ 435-676-2377; 523 N Main St; dishes $5-15; ☺ 7am-10pm summer, closed Mon-Wed winter) serves Italian sausages and vegetarian pastas.

BRYCE CANYON NATIONAL PARK

Graceful spires of pink, yellow, white and orange hoodoos stand like sentinels at the eroding edges of the vast plateau that is Bryce Canyon National Park. Though the smallest of southern Utah's national parks, Bryce is the most visually stunning, particularly at sunrise and sunset, when an orange wash sets the otherworldly rock formations ablaze with color, an awe-inspiring sight. Down on the canyon floor, hike among vanilla-scented cedar trees and towering pines while marveling at the elegant, ancient rock above, one of the earth's most striking geological spectacles.

Crowds come May to September, clogging the park's main road. For solitude, visit in winter; though nighttime temperatures drop below freezing for over 200 consecutive nights, days are mild and sunny.

Orientation

Bryce is a compact 55 sq miles, shaped roughly like a seahorse. The park has one entrance, 3 miles south of Utah Hwy 12, via Hwy 63. The park's 18-mile-long main road climbs from 8000ft at the entrance to 9115ft at Rainbow Point. The route gets jammed on summer weekends. To alleviate congestion mid-May to late September, the park operates a shuttle (p251); board inside the park or just north of the entrance, at the junction of Hwys 12 and 63. Trailers are allowed only as far as Sunset Campground, 3 miles south of the entrance. Vehicles over 25ft-long are restricted beyond Paria View in summer. Snow blankets the park in winter, but most roads are plowed. Several are designated for cross-country skiing and snowshoeing.

Information

Admission is $20 per car, $10 on foot or motorcycle. The park's newspaper, *Hoodoo*, lists hikes, activities and ranger-led programs.

In an emergency call ☎ 911 or ☎ 435-676-2411. Bryce sits at 8000ft and stays relatively cool (80ºFs and 90ºFs) on summer days, but beware altitude sickness (p478).

Bryce Canyon Natural History Association (☎ 435-834-4600; www.brycecanyon.org) Operates the bookstore. Check out their online shop.

Garfield Memorial Hospital (☎ 435-676-8811; 200 North 400 East, Panguitch) The nearest clinic and emergency room.

Post office At Ruby's Inn (p250) and at Bryce Canyon Lodge (p249).

Ruby's Inn (p250) Just north of the park entrance, with free wireless Internet access; terminals cost $1 for five minutes.

Showers The general store (p251) has showers; in winter shower at Ruby's.

Visitor center (☎ 435-834-5322; www.nps.gov/brca; Hwy 63; ☺ 8am-8pm May-Sep, 8am-4:30pm Nov-Mar, 8am-6pm Apr & Oct) Just past the gate. Maps and books, a great introductory film and information on weather, road and campsite availability. Park headquarters are also here.

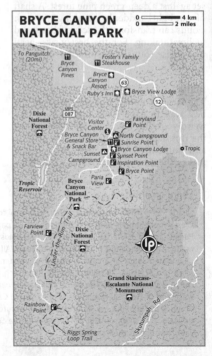

BRYCE CANYON NATIONAL PARK

0 — 4 km
0 — 2 miles

To Panguitch (20mi)
Bryce Canyon Pines
Foster's Family Steakhouse
Bryce Canyon Resort
Ruby's Inn
Bryce View Lodge
Dixie National Forest
USFS 087
Visitor Center
Bryce Canyon General Store & Snack Bar
Fairyland Point
North Campground
Sunrise Point
Bryce Canyon Lodge
Sunset Campground
Sunset Point
Inspiration Point
Bryce Point
Tropic
Tropic Reservoir
Bryce Canyon National Park
Paria View
Farview Point
Dixie National Forest
Under-the-Rim Trail
Grand Staircase-Escalante National Monument
Rainbow Point
Riggs Spring Loop Trail
Skutumpah Rd

Sights & Activities

The park's most famous sights are at Bryce Amphitheater, just south of the visitor center.

RIM ROAD SCENIC DRIVE

The park's 18-mile-long main road roughly parallels the canyon rim. Navigate using the park brochure you receive at the entrance gate.

It takes 30 minutes to drive the road's length. Because scenic overlooks lie on the east side (the left, as you head south), drive all the way to Rainbow Point, then turn around and work your way back, stopping at the pullouts as you come to them on your right. Traffic is heaviest at the overlooks into Bryce Amphitheater. If you stop nowhere else, see the stunning Bryce Point.

BRYCE AMPHITHEATER

Bryce Amphitheater stretches from Bryce Point to Sunrise Point, where hoodoos stand like platoons of soldiers or melting sandcastles, all painted endless shades of coral and magenta, ochre and white, and set against a deep-green pine forest. A shaft of sunlight suddenly breaking through clouds can transform the scene from grand to breathtaking. For the best views, head to Sunrise, Sunset, Inspiration or Bryce Point.

HIKING

The views from the rim are great, but the best way to experience the canyons and weirdly eroding hoodoos is to hike below the rim. Descents and ascents can be long and sometimes steep, and the altitude makes them strenuous. Allow extra time,

wear sturdy boots and carry extra water. Most trails skirt exposed drop-offs.

The easiest hike is along the 5.5-mile-long (one way) **Rim Trail**, which skirts Bryce Amphitheater from Fairyland Point to Bryce Point. Several sections are paved and wheelchair accessible; the most level is the half-mile section between Sunrise and Sunset Points. At Rainbow Point, the 1-mile **Bristlecone Loop** is an easy walk past 1600-year-old bristlecone pines, with 100-mile vistas. Outside main park boundaries (east of the entrance), off Hwy 12 at mileage-marker 17, take the easy half-mile walk to the year-round waterfall off **Mossy Cave Trail**, a summertime treat.

Many moderate trails descend below the rim. One of the most popular is **Queen's Garden**, which drops 320ft from Sunrise Point. Combine this with the **Navajo Loop Trail**, which descends 521ft from Sunset Point and passes through the famous narrow canyon 'Wall Street.' This 2.4-mile combined hike sees lots of traffic; it's among the few that may remain open in winter.

Two half-day hikes include the 8-mile **Fairyland Trail**, which leaves from Fairyland Point north of the visitor center, and the 7-mile-long **Peekaboo Trail**, which leaves from Bryce Point. Both have superb scenery and require 800ft elevation changes, plus many additional ups and downs. Peekaboo Trail allows horses.

The backcountry Under-the-Rim Trail, south of Bryce Amphitheater, can be broken into several athletic day hikes. The 11-mile stretch between Bryce Point and Swamp Canyon (which includes the 'Hat Shop') is one of the hardest and best. Check with rangers.

STICK 'EM UP!

Nearly every town in southern Utah claims a connection to Butch Cassidy (1866–?), the Old West's most famous bank and train robber. As part of the Wild Bunch, Cassidy (né Robert LeRoy Parker) pulled 19 heists from 1896 to 1901. Most accounts describe him with a breathless romanticism, comparing him with Robin Hood. All stories usually have one thing in common: a dilapidated shack or a canyon, just over yonder, that served as his hideout. But the itty-bitty town of Circleville, 28 miles north of Panguitch, is the honest-to-goodness boyhood home of the gun-slingin' bandit. The house still stands, partially renovated, 2 miles south of town on the west side of Hwy 89. Nobody is sure to where Cassidy fled, but most believe he died in South America in 1908. But ask around, and you're sure to hear a lot of conflicting, tall tales. For the Hollywood version, rent *Butch Cassidy and the Sundance Kid* (1969), with Robert Redford and Paul Newman at their sexiest.

HORSEBACK RIDING

The park's only licensed outfitter is **Canyon Trail Rides** (☎ 435-679-8665; www.canyonrides .com; 2hr/half-day ride $40/55), which operates out of Bryce Canyon Lodge (right); rides head into Bryce Amphitheater, past dramatic hoodoos, on horses and mules (mules give a smoother ride).

For horseback rides into the Dixie National Forest or the BLM lands surrounding Bryce, call **Scenic Rim Trail Rides** (☎ 435-679-8761, 800-679-5859; www.brycecanyonhorseback.com; Ruby's Inn, 1000 S Hwy 63; 1 hr/2hr ride $21/27, half-day $47, full day $77-92).

RANGER-LED ACTIVITIES

Summer to early fall, rangers lead canyon-rim walks, hoodoo hikes, geology lectures, campfire programs, kids' ecology walks and astronomy talks. On full moon, when skies are clear, take the **Moonlight Hike**, a two-hour stroll among the hoodoos; register at the visitor center the same day, but book early.

Tours

Rangers lead hikes in summer (and in spring and fall depending on the weather). **Bryce Canyon Scenic Tours** (☎ 435-834-5200, 800-432-5383; www.brycetours.com; adult/child $26/12) leads two-hour minibus tours. There's no commercial guided hiking at Bryce, but several companies lead **bicycle tours** in and around Bryce, usually dropping down to Zion. Try **Backroads Bicycle Adventures** (☎ 800-462-2848, 510-527-1555; www.backroads.com), **Rim Tours** (☎ 435-259-5223, 800-626-7335; www.rimtours.com) and **Western Spirit Cyclery** (☎ 435-259-8732, 800-845-2453; www.westernspirit.com).

Festivals & Events

The park hosts no events, but Ruby's Inn (p250) does. In February, **Bryce Canyon Winterfest** includes everything from cross-country skiing and snowmobiling to archery and snow sculpting. In August, the **Bryce Canyon Rim Run** follows a six-mile course partially along a portion of the Bryce Canyon rim that's outside park boundaries. Contact Ruby's (p250) or the **Garfield County Travel Council** (☎ 435-676-1160, 800-444-6689, www.bryce canyoncountry.com).

Sleeping

The park has one lodge and two campgrounds. Most visitors stay just north of

---

THE BEST OF BRYCE

- Best short hike into the canyon – Navajo Loop Trail (opposite).

- Best view for colored rock – Bryce Amphitheatre (opposite) at sunrise or early morning.

- Best views up, from inside the canyon – Wall of Windows and Silent City from the Peekaboo Trail (opposite).

- Best long hike for solitude, without leaving the hoodoo amphitheatres – Fairyland Trail (opposite).

- Best and most stunning hoodoos, as viewed from the rim – Silent City from Inspiration Point (see map p247).

- Best, most overlooked sight – 1600-year-old bristlecone pine trees on Bristlecone Loop trail (opposite).

- Best sunset viewpoint – the west-facing Paria View (see map p247).

---

the park near the Hwy 12/63 junction or 7 miles east in **Tropic**. Also consider **Panguitch** (p246), 24 miles west, or **Kodachrome Basin State Park** (p257), 19 miles east.

INSIDE THE PARK

Bryce Canyon Lodge (summer ☎ 435-834-5361, winter ☎ 435-772-3213, reservations ☎ 888-297-2757; www .brycecanyonlodge.com; r $108-136, cabins $126; ✷ Apr-Oct; ✗) The 1920s Bryce Lodge exudes rustic mountain charm. Rooms are in satellite buildings and range from modern hotel-style units with up-to-date furnishings and balconies, to romantic, slightly dated, free-standing cabins with gas fireplaces and front porches. If you can secure a reservation, it's worth every penny.

North Campground (reservations ☎ 877-444-6777; www.reserveusa.com; Bryce Canyon Rd; campsites $10, reservation fee May 15–Sep 30 $9) NPS operated campground near the visitor center. It offers laundry, showers, groceries, toilets and water. During summer, sites fill by noon.

Sunset Campground (2 miles south of visitor center; campsites $10; no reservations; ✷ late spring–fall) NPS operated. Sunset is more wooded than North Campground, but has fewer amenities (for laundry, showers, and groceries, visit North Campground). It has toilets and water. During summer, sites fill by noon.

UTAH

BACKCOUNTRY ACCESS

Only 1% of all visitors venture into the backcountry, virtually guaranteeing backpackers peace and solitude. You won't walk among many hoodoo formations, but you will pass through forest and meadow, with distant views of rock formations. And oh, the quiet.

Backpackers must register and purchase permits ($5) at the visitor center, between 8am and 2 hours before sunset. Make reservations in person up to 48 hours ahead. Rangers will discuss your route and show you where to camp and find water. Campgrounds are primitive. You must be self-sufficient: water below the rim must be purified; no fires are allowed (but campstoves are); and you must bury your waste and carry out all trash, including toilet paper (bring resealable plastic bags). When snow falls November to April, camping is difficult but still possible. Check with rangers.

The 23-mile Under-the-Rim Trail from Bryce Point to Rainbow Point is the park's longest, and it can be combined with the 9-mile Riggs Spring Loop Trail (also a good, strenuous day hike) at Rainbow Point for a one-way trip of over 30 miles. All backcountry campsites are along these trails. Connecting trails lead up the rim, allowing shorter trips.

Most backcountry trails are covered with snow late October to March or April; even in May, water sources along the trail may be frozen. June and September are ideal; in July and August be prepared for thunderstorms and mosquitoes. Bring bug dope and, if you have room, binoculars: the skies above Bryce are some of the darkest in America.

OUTSIDE THE PARK

Ruby's Inn (☎ 435-834-5341, 866-866-6616; www.rubys inn.com; 1000 S Hwy 63; r $100-130; 🖳 🖭) A gargantuan motel complex a mile north of the park, Ruby's has 369 standard-issue rooms; all have two beds. The attraction is the facilities (open to non-guests), including grocery and supply store, gasoline, laundry, currency exchange and liquor store (a rarity around here). Ruby's also rents bicycles and ATVs. In summer, there's a nightly rodeo Monday to Saturday.

Bryce View Lodge (☎ 435-834-5180, 888-279-2304, www.bryceviewlodge.com; r $65) Run by Ruby's, this place is geared for budget travelers, with smaller rooms and fewer extras, but you'll have access to Ruby's pool and hot tub.

Bryce Canyon Resort (☎ 435-834-5351, 800-834-0043; www.brycecanyonresort.com; junction Hwy 12/63; r $65-85, cabins $55-105; 🖭) Four miles from the park, this is a great alternative to Ruby's. Remodeled rooms have upgraded furnishings and extra amenities, but economy rooms are standard-issue and have neither air-conditioning nor phones. Some units have kitchenettes. There's also a small campground and restaurant (opposite).

Bryce Canyon Pines (☎ 435-834-5441, 800-892-7923; www.brycecanyonmotel.com; Hwy 12; r $65-85; 🍸 Apr-Nov; 🗙 🖭) This place has clean, plain rooms, a restaurant (opposite), and small campground. It's four miles west of the Hwy 12/63 junction.

The following are all in Tropic.

Bryce Country Cabins (☎ 435-679-8643, 888-679-8643; www.brycecountrycabins.com; 320 N Main St, Tropic; cabins $65; 🗙) These six cozy cabins on the western edge of Tropic have knotty-pine walls and lots of charm – among the best simple accommodations near Bryce.

Bryce Canyon Inn (☎ 435-679-8502, 800-592-1468; www.brycecanyoninn.com; 21 N Main St, Tropic; r $55-65, cabins $75-90; 🗙) Choose a motel room or knotty-pine cabin with refrigerator. Cabins are larger, but closer together, than at Bryce Country Cabins.

Stone Canyon Inn (☎ 435-679-8611, 866-489-4680; www.stonecanyoninn.com; 1220 Stone Canyon Lane, Tropic; r $120-155; 🍸 Feb-Nov; 🗙) The top choice for savvy travelers, Stone Canyon Inn sits on the outskirts of Tropic and has five rooms with ultracomfortable beds and gorgeous views. Delicious breakfasts include homemade breads and imaginative mains. The charming, urbane innkeeper also guides hikes on foot, horseback or ATV.

Bullberry Inn (☎ 435-679-8820; www.bullberryinn .com; 412 S Hwy 12, Tropic; r $65-85; 🗙) Built in 1998 this well-run, farmhouse-style inn has great views and is an excellent alternative to motels. The owners make their own bullberry jam, which you'll have with breakfast.

Bryce Trails B&B (☎ 435-679-8700, 866-215-5043; www.brycetrails.com; 1001 W Bryce Way, Tropic; r $80-130; 🗙) If the previous places are booked, try this B&B.

KOA of Canonville (☎ 435-679-8988; www.koa .com; Hwy 12, Canonville; tent/RV sites $20/28, cabins $46; ☺ Mar-Dec; ☒) A terrific campground for families with kids, with lots of amenities and spotlessly clean bathrooms and showers. Five miles east of Tropic in Canonville.

Also recommended:

Bryce Valley Inn (☎ 435-679-8811, 800-442-1890; www.brycevalleyinn.com; 199 N Main St, Tropic; r $65-80)

Bryce Pioneer Village (☎ 435-679-8546, 800-222-0381; www.bpvillage.com; 80 S Main St, Tropic; r $55-$75) Fourteen acres and an RV campground.

Eating

INSIDE THE PARK

Bryce Canyon Lodge (☎ 435-834-5361; breakfast & lunch dishes $7-11, dinner mains $15-22; ☺ Apr-Oct) Windows line the walls of the casual, rustic dining room at Bryce Canyon Lodge. At breakfast and lunch, expect standard American fare. At dinner the ambitious menu sometimes tries hard to be 'gourmet' and occasionally ends up being heavy-handed. Stick to simple dishes. This is by far the best place to eat. Dinner reservations are essential. Beer and wine, no liquor.

Bryce Canyon General Store and Snack Bar (☎ 435-834-5361; near Sunrise Point; dishes $3-5; ☺ 8am-8pm summer, 8am-6pm spring & fall; closed winter) Sells hot dogs, drinks, sandwiches, chile, soup and pizza.

OUTSIDE THE PARK

Nobody comes to Bryce for the food. Expect chicken-fried steak, canned gravy, frozen peas, gluey pie and pale watery coffee. If you're vegetarian, BYOV or subsist on iceberg lettuce and soggy fries.

Bryce Canyon Pines (☎ 435-834-5441; Hwy 12; breakfast & lunch $5-8, dinner mains $10-16; ☺ 6:30am-9:30pm) Marked only by a yellow sign reading 'Restaurant,' the Pines serves meat-and-potatoes meals. It's known for its homemade soups and pies, which are heavy but pretty good. It's 4 miles west of the Hwy 12/63 junction.

Bryce Canyon Resort (☎ 435-834-5351; junction Hwy 12/63; breakfast & lunch $5-9, dinner $6-14; ☺ 7am-9pm) The only Mexican restaurant near Bryce serves the usuals; they also make breakfast and have a small sports bar (beer and wine, no margaritas).

Foster's Family Steakhouse (☎ 435-834-5227; Hwy 12; dinner mains $9-18; ☺ 7am-10pm summer, 4-9pm spring & fall; closed winter) The beef-heavy menu at this diner-cum-steakhouse (2 miles west of junction Hwy 12/63) is satisfactory, despite the thin-cut steaks and iceberg-lettuce salads.

Ruby's Inn (☎ 435-834-5341; 1000 S Hwy 63; breakfast & lunch dishes $5-10, dinner mains $12-29; ☺ 6:30am-10pm, to 9:30pm in winter) Ruby's has two restaurants, a full-service dining room and buffet, and a diner with pizza, burgers and fried food. Both serve mediocre assembly-line cooking that's overpriced, but convenient. Expect a wait at dinner.

Bryce Canyon Inn and Pizza (☎ 435-679-8888; 21 N Main St, Tropic; dishes $5-12; ☺ 7:30-9pm Mon-Sat, 2pm-9:30 Sun; no breakfast in spring, Apr-Oct) Good pizza at lunch and dinner and outdoor seating make this Tropic's top spot for simple dining.

Hoodoo's (☎ 435-679-8600; 141 N Main St, Tropic; lunch & dinner mains $7-16; ☺ 11:30am-10pm summer, to 8pm spring & fall, closed winter) If you want a hot meal in Tropic, Hoodoo's serves steaks and fish, burgers and sandwiches. There's beer, but no wine.

Getting There & Around

A car is the only way around from fall through spring. Ruby's Inn sells gas, but it's cheaper in Tropic, 7 miles east.

If you're towing a trailer, leave it at your campsite, in the trailer turn-around lot in summer or in the visitor center parking lot in winter. No trailers are permitted south of Sunset Point.

If you arrive during peak summer periods, ride the voluntary summer-only **shuttle**, lest you find yourself unable to park. Just south of the Hwy 12/63 junction, leave your car at the terminus, and ride the bus into the park. But, if you arrive at the park, pay your fee, then find nowhere to park, you can easily turn around and drive five minutes back up the road to the shuttle-staging area. Carry your receipt to avoid paying again!

Tune to AM 1610 as you approach Bryce to learn about current shuttle operations. The *Hoodoo* newspaper shows routes. Shuttle information changes annually; check with rangers.

GRAND STAIRCASE-ESCALANTE NATIONAL MONUMENT

Nearly twice the size of Rhode Island, the 1.9-million-acre Grand Staircase-Escalante National Monument (GSENM) is the largest park in the Southwest and has some of the least visited, most spectacular scenery in the US. Its name refers to the 150-mile-long geological strata that begins at the bottom of the Grand Canyon and rises 3500ft to Bryce Canyon and the Escalante River canyons. Together the layers of rock reveal 260 million years of history in a riot of color. Sections of the GSENM have so much red rock that the reflected light casts a pink hue onto the bottoms of clouds above.

Established in 1996 by President Bill Clinton, the monument is unique for a BLM-managed area. It allows some uses that would be banned in a national park (like hunting and grazing – with permits), but allows fewer uses than other BLM lands to maintain its 'remote frontier' quality. Tourist infrastructure is thus minimal and limited to the park's edges.

Orientation

The park encompasses three major areas, broken up by geological significance. The **Grand Staircase** is in the westernmost region, south of Bryce Canyon and west of Cottonwood Canyon Rd. The **Kaiparowits Plateau** runs north–south in the center of the monument, east of Cottonwood Canyon Rd and west of Smoky Mountain Rd. The **Escalante Canyons** lie at the easternmost sections, east of Hole-in-the-Rock Rd and south of the Burr Trail.

The GSENM links the area between Bryce Canyon, Capitol Reef National Park and Glen Canyon National Recreation Area. Highway 12 (p256) skirts the northern boundaries between Tropic, Escalante and Boulder. Hwy 89 arcs east of Kanab into the monument's southwestern reaches. For info on roads into the GSENM, see opposite.

The visitor centers have good maps. To hike the backcountry, you'll need USGS 7.5 minute quadrangle maps, available at visitor centers and Escalante Outfitters (p257). Also consider the excellent guidebook *Hiking the Escalante* by Rudi Lambrechtse.

Information

There are no fees for the GSENM.

Obtain park information from **BLM Grand Staircase-Escalante National Monument** (☎ 435-826-5499; www.ut.blm.gov/monument, http://gsenm.az .blm.gov; PO Box 225, Escalante, UT 84726), or stop by one of five year-round visitor centers.

On the north side, the **Escalante Interagency Office** (☎ 435-826-5499; www.ut.blm.gov /monument, http://gsenm.az.blm.gov; 775 W Main St, Escalante; ⊙ 7:30am-5:30pm) is jointly operated by the BLM, the USFS and NPS and provides information about public lands throughout southern Utah.

In an emergency, dial ☎ 911. The nearest hospitals are in Panguitch (p246) and Kanab (p243).

Anasazi State Park (p259) Rangers here in Boulder can also answer questions.

Big Water Visitor Center (☎ 435-675-3200; 100 Upper Revolution Way, Big Water; ⊙ 9am-5:30pm spring-fall) To the south.

Cannonville Visitor Center (☎ 435-826-5640; 10 Center St, Cannonville; ⊙ 8am-4:30pm spring-fall) Five miles east of Tropic.

Kanab Visitor Center (☎ 435-644-4680; 745 E Hwy 89, Kanab; ⊙ 8am-4:30pm, closed weekends Nov-Mar) In the southwestern section, this is also park headquarters.

Paria Contact Station (Hwy 89, 44 miles east of Kanab; ⊙ 8:30am-4:15pm mid-Mar–mid-Nov) Just west of Big Water.

Dangers & Annoyances

Always check with rangers about weather and road conditions before driving or hiking. After heavy rain or snow, roads may be impassable, even with a high-clearance 4WD. After even light rains, the clay surface becomes dangerously slippery. If it starts to rain while you're driving, *stop*. Storms pass and roads dry quickly, sometimes even within 30 minutes. Never park

---

PARK POLITICS

The Grand Staircase-Escalante National Monument (GSENM) was created over the vehement objections of some local residents and legislators, who had hoped to develop the area's mining potential, and court challenges continue in earnest to overturn Democratic former president Bill Clinton's decision. (Remember, Utah is heavily Republican; lots of people 'round here hate Clinton.) Smart locals are learning to exploit the new tourist economy, but expect occasionally to see a bumper sticker that says, 'If it's tourist season, why can't we shoot 'em?' Fret not: such vituperations are uncommon. Nobody's gonna shoot you. Just to be safe, don't bring up politics.

in a wash. Be sure to carry extra water and food. Help in case of an emergency may be hard to find.

Water sources must be treated or boiled; campfires are permitted only in certain areas (use a stove instead); and biting insects are a problem in spring and early summer. Watch for scorpions and rattlesnakes.

Sights & Activities
SKUTUMPAH & JOHNSON CANYON ROADS
The most westerly route through the monument, the unpaved Skutumpah Rd heads southwest from Kodachrome Basin State Park, around the southern end of Bryce Canyon's Pink Cliffs. After 35 miles (two hours), Skutumpah Rd intersects with the 16-mile paved Johnson Canyon Rd, and passes the White Cliffs and Vermilion Cliffs areas en route to Hwy 89 and Kanab. For the best sightseeing, drive south to north. Four-wheel drive or high-clearance 2WD recommended.

COTTONWOOD CANYON ROAD
This 46-mile scenic backway heads east, then south, from Kodachrome Basin State Park, emerging at Hwy 89 near **Paria Canyon** (p255). It's the closest entry into GSENM from Bryce and an easy, sometimes rough drive, passable for 2WD vehicles (RVs not recommended). Twenty miles south of Hwy 12 you'll reach **Grosvenor Arch**, a yellow-limestone double arch, with picnic tables and restrooms.

The road continues south along the west side of the **Cockscomb**, a long, narrow monocline in the earth's crust. The Cockscomb divides the Grand Staircase from Kaiparowits Plateau to the east; there are superb views. The most scenic stretch lies between Grosvenor Arch and **Lower Hackberry Canyon** (p254). The road then follows the desolate Paria River valley toward Hwy 89.

SMOKY MOUNTAIN ROAD
A 78-mile dirt-and-gravel road (ATV or high-clearance 4WD only), this route takes over six hours. From Escalante, it crosses the rugged **Kaiparowits Plateau** and emerges at the Big Water Visitor Center on Hwy 89, just west of Glen Canyon. The prime destination is **Alstrom Point**, 38 miles from Hwy 89, a plateau-top vantage with stunning Lake Powell views.

HOLE-IN-THE-ROCK ROAD
The scenery and history are wild along this 57-mile dirt-and-gravel road, from 5 miles east of Escalante to Lake Powell (allow four to five hours one way). It's passable by 2WD when dry, except for the last 7 miles, which may require 4WD.

In 1879 to '80, Mormon pioneers followed this route on their way to settle new lands in southeast Utah. Little did they know the precipitous walls of Glen Canyon on the Colorado River would block their path. More than 200 pioneers blasted and hammered through the cliff, creating a route wide enough to descend with 80 wagons; look for historic markers. The final stretch now lies submerged beneath Lake Powell.

If you don't drive the entire route, visit **Devils Garden** (12 miles in), where rock fists, orbs, spires and fingers rise 40ft above the desert floor. A short walk from the car leads atop giant sandstone slabs – kids love it. There's also good hiking.

Dry Fork (26 miles in, p254) has great slot canyons. It has no campgrounds or facilities, but dispersed camping is permitted, with a free backcountry permit. The main road stops short of **Hole-in-the-Rock**, but hikers can descend to **Lake Powell**, a scrambling route doable in under an hour – but you have to climb out, too.

BURR TRAIL
The region's most immediately gratifying, dramatic drive, the initially paved Burr Trail heads east from Boulder, crosses GSENM's northeast corner and, after about 30 miles, reaches **Waterpocket Fold** (p262) in Capitol Reef National Park, where the road becomes loose gravel. Along the way are two trailheads: **Deer Creek** and the **Gulch**; check with rangers about these spectacular hikes.

Just past Deer Creek, the road enters **Long Canyon** beneath towering vertical red-rock slabs. At the end of the canyon, stop for views of the **Circle Cliffs**, hanging like curtains above the undulating valley. The **Henry Mountains** rise 11,000ft on the horizon. In Capitol Reef, the road meets the giant, angled buttes of hundred-mile-long Waterpocket Fold. Just ahead, the **Burr Trail Switchbacks** follow an original wagon route through the fold. You can drive to

> **BACKCOUNTRY ACCESS**
>
> Grand Staircase-Escalante National Monument (GSENM) is a mecca for hardcore backcountry adventurers. Hiking requires significant route-finding skills – GPS skills don't count. Know how to use a compass and a topographical map, or risk getting lost, even with an electronic route finder. If you got turned around and come to a wash, remember: it's always easier to walk downstream. Talk to rangers before leaving, and don't take unnecessary risks. For information on shuttles, see opposite.
>
> The waterproof *Trails Illustrated/National Geographic map* ($10) is great, but carry 7.5 minute quadrangle US Geological Survey (USGS) maps. Check with rangers about finding water; plan to carry and drink at least a gallon per day.
>
> To camp overnight you'll need a free backcountry permit from any visitor center (p252), information kiosk or major trailhead. Talk to rangers about regulations regarding dispersed camping. Pack out trash, and use a camp stove. Fires are allowed only in certain places and firewood is scarce. Bury human waste in catholes (6in deep, at least 200ft from water sources), or consider using human-waste containment bags.
>
> GSENM offers outstanding treks for serious hikers with advanced abilities. Ask rangers about Coyote Gulch, off Hole-in-the-Rock Rd; Escalante River Canyon; Boulder Mail Trail; and the Gulch, off the Burr Trail.

Notom-Bullfrog Rd (p263) and north to Hwy 24 or south to Glen Canyon. If returning to Boulder, first drive to the base of the switchbacks – the scale of the landscape will blow your mind.

PARIA VALLEY ROAD & MOVIE SET

The Paria (pa-*ree*-uh) Movie Set gives a quick taste of GSENM. The signed turnoff is 33 miles from Kanab on Hwy 89; a 5-mile dirt road (which is passable with a 2WD when dry) follows the Vermilion Cliffs to the site.

The original buildings were washed away; today, three rebuilt, plank-walled structures evoke the town-cum-movie set, with creaky swinging doors, raised sidewalks and hitching posts. The real set – the magnificently banded, painted cliffs surrounding you – needs no dressing. Informative signs tell the history of the set and the nearby **Pahreah ghost town**, which the river polished off. The town cemetery is 0.5 miles past the set; the river and townsite lie 0.5 miles further, where the road deteriorates. There's little left of the stone buildings.

HIKING

Carry a gallon of water per person, wear a hat and sunscreen, and carry food, maps and a compass. Check the weather, especially if you're planning to hike slot canyons or along washes, which are both flash-flood prone (p63).

Avoid walking on cryptobiotic crusts (p48), the chunky black soil that looks like burnt hamburger meat; it fixes nitrogen into the ground, changing sand to soil.

Along Hwy 12, **Calf Creek Falls** (p258) is one of the GSENM's most accessible day hikes and slogs through sand to a 126ft-tall waterfall. Just west, an easy trail heads to **Escalante Natural Bridge** (2 miles), crisscrossing the Escalante River (wear sturdy footwear) and arriving at a 130ft-high, 100ft-long sandstone arch.

The most easily accessible slot canyons are at **Dry Fork**, 26 miles down Hole-in-the-Rock Rd (p253) from Hwy 12. Check with rangers for directions to the four slots: the Narrows, Peekaboo Gulch, Spooky Gulch and Brimstone Gulch. Don't climb up and out of slots, then jump down the other side, lest you get trapped below the smooth face you've descended.

Off Cottonwood Canyon Rd (p253), 14 miles from Hwy 89, **Lower Hackberry Canyon** is a sculpted narrow gorge that continues 26 miles along an easy-to-hike wash. Expect several minor stream crossings; bring bug dope. The first few miles of canyon are the narrowest and prettiest.

Ask rangers about others, such as **Sheep Creek**, **Willis Creek** and the **Box**, all easy treks; or **Phipps Wash**, **Willow** and **Wolverine**, which are harder. Also check out the postcard-perfect hiking at **Paria Canyon-Vermilion Cliffs Wilderness Area** (opposite).

Tours

For the best multiday trips, you can't beat **Escalante Canyon Outfitters** (☎ 435-335-7311, 888-326-4453; www.ecohike.com; 4- to 6-day all-inclusive treks $770-1175; ☼ spring-fall). Horses carry gear and packs; superb guides provide excellent interpretation – and do the cooking.

For top-notch, custom-tailored, all-day adventure hikes, **Excursions of Escalante** (☎ 435-826-4714, 800-839-7567; www.excursions-escalante.com; Trailhead Café, 125 Main St, Escalante; $65-100; ☼ spring-fall) offers everything from easy photo walks to hard-core canyoneering.

Looking for fantastic geologic interpretation? Hook up with **Earth Tours** (☎ 435-691-1241; www.earth-tours.com; half-/full-day tours $50/75; ☼ spring-fall). Stop by the Burr Trail Outpost (p259) in Boulder for information.

Learn how to survive in GSENM's forbidding wilderness by studying with the **Boulder Outdoor Survival School** (☎ 303-444-9779; www.boss-inc.com).

In the GSENM's southern reaches, **Paria Outpost & Outfitters** (☎ 928-691-1047; www.paria .com; $60-175) leads guided 4WD trips, hikes and all-day tours.

Canyon Country Outback Tours (☎ 435-644-3807, 888-783-3807; www.ccobtours.com; $90-250) guides daytrips to slot canyons in GSENM; it's also one of only two guides permitted into Coyote Buttes in Vermilion Cliffs (right).

Sleeping & Eating

Sleep in Escalante (p257), Boulder (p258) Kanab (p243) or Kodachrome Basin State Park (p257). Eat in Escalante, Boulder or Kanab.

There are two developed campgrounds in the monument, both near Boulder. Beside a year-round creek, 15 miles east of Escalante, **Calf Creek Campground** (Map p262; ☎ 435-826-5499; www.ut.blm.gov/monument; Hwy 12; campsites $7) is surrounded by red-rock canyons (hot in summer) and has 13 non-reserveable sites with seasonal water. **Deer Creek Campground** (Map p262; www.ut.blm.gov /monument; Burr Trail; campsites $4; ☼ mid-May–mid-Sep), 6 miles southeast of Boulder, has four sites and no water, but sits beside a year-round creek beneath tall trees.

In the GSENM's southern reaches, **Paria Outpost & Outfitters** (☎ 928-691-1047; www.paria .com; r $65) has B&B rooms at its kick-back lodge and a campground near Big Water, off Hwy 89.

At Paria Contact Station (p252), the primitive **White House Campground** has walk-in tent camping. For information on campgrounds outside the monument, such as on Boulder Mountain (Hwy 12, between Boulder and Torrey; summer only), contact the visitor centers (p252) or **Dixie National Forest** (☎ 435-676-8815; www.fs.fed.us/dxnf).

Getting Around

The only way around is on foot or by private vehicle. High-clearance 4WD vehicles are best, since many roads are unpaved and only occasionally bladed. (Most off-the-lot SUVs and light trucks are *not* high-clearance vehicles.) Heed all warnings about road conditions.

Buy gasoline whenever you see it. Find stations in Tropic, Escalante, Boulder and Kanab.

Book hiker shuttles in advance. In Escalante contact **Excursions of Escalante** (☎ 435-826-4714, 800-839-7567; www.excursions-escalante.com; 125 Main St); if it's booked, call **Escalante Outback Adventures** (☎ 435-826-4967; www.escalante -utah.com; 325 W Main St). **Paria Outpost & Outfitters** (☎ 928-691-1047; www.paria.com), at mile marker 21 on Hwy 89, runs shuttles in the south.

PARIA CANYON–VERMILION CLIFFS WILDERNESS

Straddling the Utah–Arizona state line, this is one of the region's best and most popular wilderness areas for day hikers, serious canyoneers and photographers. Pick any six postcards from a southern Utah gift shop, and two will be from here. With endless slot canyons and miles of weathered, swirling slickrock, it's no wonder hiking permits here are so tough to get.

Check out www.az.blm.gov/paria, contact the **BLM Field Office** (p244) in Kanab or visit the **Paria Contact Station** (p252) on the Utah side of the wilderness area, which has water, and road and trail information; it also sells topographical maps and guidebooks. Beside the contact station is the **White House Campground** (campsites $5), with six primitive sites for walk-in tent camping only.

Day hikers can fight like dogs for a day-hike permit for **North Coyote Buttes** (a trailless expanse of slickrock that includes one of the Southwest's most famous formations, the Wave) or day hike the upper portions of three slot canyons (Wire Pass, Buckskin

UTAH

THE STORY OF EVERETT RUESS

Artist, poet, writer and adventurer Everett Ruess (1914–34) is a local legend in southern Utah. At 20 years old, he set out into the desert on his burro, somewhere near the Escalante River Canyon, never to be seen again. But he left behind scores of letters detailing his 'restless fascination' with the land, letters that paint a vivid portrait of life in canyon country before man and his machines forever altered the landscape. Most people have never heard of Everett Ruess, but in many ways he is to the Southwest what John Muir is to the Sierra Nevada – explorer, chronicler and ardent lover of nature.

Born into a well-placed California family and raised by his mother to participate in art in all its forms, Everett eschewed society and set off to explore the wilderness. His gift was perception and an ability to describe, in disarming prose, the astounding beauty he witnessed as he tramped through the red-rock deserts. He was a visionary, both in words and in his artwork, and gushed in wonderment, 'I have seen more beauty than I can bear.' Indeed, it eventually killed him: the very desert he so desperately loved swallowed him up without a trace. His disappearance remains a mystery, only adding to his modern-day mystique.

Pick up a copy of *Everett Ruess: A Vagabond for Beauty*, which includes his letters and an afterword by Edward Abbey. Find this and all of Ruess' posthumously published works at Escalante Outfitters (opposite), where you can also inquire about the October Everett Ruess Days festival (www.everettruessdays.org), which includes plein air art shows, speakers and workshops.

Gulch and Paria Canyon), for which you don't need a permit. All are nearly magical and shouldn't be missed. Slot canyons' accessibility changes annually; check with rangers. Beware of flash floods.

Wire Pass (3.4-mile round-trip, about two hours) is the most popular slot-canyon day hike. The pass dead-ends where Buckskin Gulch narrows, where you can continue along slots. From the **Buckskin Gulch** trailhead, you'll hike 3 miles to its narrow section. Both trailheads lie along House Rock Valley Rd (4.7 miles west of the contact station), a passable dirt road in dry weather.

It's about 4 miles from the **Paria Canyon** trailhead to its narrow section; the trail starts from the White House Campground.

Serious canyoneers can tackle the five-day trek along unforgettable 38-mile Paria Canyon to Lees Ferry, Arizona, with numerous stretches of knee-deep muddy water, some swims and many obstacles. Spring and fall are best; permits required.

All trails require a $5 fee per person per day. For slot canyons, self-pay and register at the trailhead. For North Coyote Buttes day-hiking permits, reserve online (www.az.blm.gov/paria) seven months ahead. Ten walk-in next-day permits are also given out by lottery at the Paria Contact Station (p252) at 9am every morning; arrive by 8:30am with fingers crossed. The walk-in system may change; call ahead.

Overnight permits are easier to get and can be reserved online. Use of human-waste carryout bags is encouraged; the contact station provides them for free.

See p255 for hikers' shuttles and p255 for guided trips.

HIGHWAY 12 TO TORREY

The 125-mile-long Highway 12 is one of the most spectacular roads in America. It begins south of Panguitch at Hwy 89, heads east past Bryce Canyon (p247) and along the northern boundaries of the GSENM (p251) before terminating in Torrey, just west of Capitol Reef National Park (p261).

Stop at the numerous pullouts and scenic viewpoints to see how quickly and dramatically the land changes from wooded plateau to red-rock canyon, and from slickrock desert to alpine forest. The *pièce de résistance* lies along a razor-thin ridge between Escalante and Boulder, called the **Hogback**.

Information and visitor centers in Panguitch (p246), Red Canyon (opposite), Bryce Canyon (p247), and the GSENM (p252) stock maps and a route guide.

Red Canyon

Aptly named Red Canyon provides the first glimpse of magnificent rock formations. Legend has it that outlaw Butch Cassidy once rode in this area; a tough hiking route, Cassidy Trail, bears his name.

The excellent **visitor center** (☎ 435-676-2676; Hwy 12; ◷ 9am-6pm summer, 10am-4pm spring & fall, closed Oct-Apr) has information and displays. Red Canyon is in **Dixie National Forest, Powell Ranger District** (☎ 435-676-8815; www.fs.fed.us/dxnf; 225 E Center St, Panguitch; ◷ 8am-4:30pm Mon-Fri).

Hiking, mountain biking, horseback riding and ATV riding are the primary activities. Pick up the trail-map brochure at the visitor center.

Several moderately easy **hiking** trails begin near the visitor center: the 0.7-mile, 30-minute Arches Trail passes 15 arches as it winds through a canyon; the 1-mile, 30-minute Pink Ledges Trail winds through red-rock formations. For a harder hike, try the 2.8-mile, two- to four-hour Golden Wall Trail.

Take a guided horseback ride with **Red Canyon Trail Rides** (☎ 435-834-5441, 800-892-7923; brycecanyonmotel.com; Hwy 12; 2hr $30, half-day $40, day $85), 5 miles west of the Hwy 12/63 junction, or with **Ruby's Red Canyon Horseback Rides** (☎ 435-834-5341, 800-468-8660; www.rubysinn.com; 1000 S Hwy 63; 1.5hr $28, half-day $45, day $79). There are also excellent **mountain-biking** trails. The best is Thunder Mountain Trail. Rent a bike at **Ruby's Inn** (p250; half-/full day $20/35); they also rent racks for cars but operate no shuttle.

Red Canyon Campground (☎ 435-676-8815; www .fs.fed.us/dxnf; campsites $9; ◷ mid-May–Sep) is scenic and beautifully maintained. They don't take reservations. There are 37 tent and RV sites, flush toilets, showers, drinking water and a dump station.

On Hwy 12, just east of Hwy 89, **Harold's Place** (☎ 435-676-2350; www.haroldsplace.net; cabins $65; ✗) has cozy, modern, knotty-pine-paneled cabins and a restaurant (breakfast and dinner); the specialty is trout. **Western Town Resort** (☎ 435-676-8770, 866-231-2956; www .silveradowildwest.com; Hwy 89 at Hwy 12; r $89-120; ✗ ▣) has 80 standard-issue motel rooms behind faux Wild West shop fronts; there's also a restaurant and square dancing.

Kodachrome Basin State Park

Petrified geysers and dozens of red, pink and white sandstone chimneys – some nearly 170ft tall – stand clustered together and resemble everything from a sphinx to a snowmobile at **Kodachrome Basin** (☎ 435-679-8562; www.stateparks.utah.gov; off Cottonwood Canyon Rd; admission $5), 9 miles south of Cannonville. Visit in the morning or afternoon, when shadows play on the red rock. Most sights are along **hiking** and **mountain-biking trails**. The moderate-easy 3-mile Panorama Trail gives the best overview; Sentinel Trail (0.5 miles, strenuous) and Sentinel Trail (1.25 miles, moderate) have great desert views from on high. **Ride horseback** in summer and inquire about stagecoach rides with **Scenic Safaris** (☎ 435-679-8536, 435-679-8787) at its Trail Head Station, which also sells groceries and basic supplies. Charming, charismatic proprietors Bob and Miraloy Ott will help you discern shapes in the rock.

April to November, Trail Head Station rents six knotty-pine **cabins** (☎ 435-679-8536, 435-679-8787; www.brycecanyoninn.com; cabins $65; ◷ Apr-Nov; ✗) with fridge, microwave and bath; cabins sleep four. The **campground** (☎ 801-322-3770, 800-322-3770; www.stateparks.utah .gov; campsites incl park admission $14) has 26 partially shaded sites, hot showers and flush toilets. Make reservations.

Escalante

pop 820 / elev 5600ft

The largest town on Hwy 12, Escalante lies halfway between Bryce and Capitol Reef. If you're spending time in the GSENM (p251), Escalante makes a good base.

Long populated by radical drop-outs and conspiracy theorists, Escalante is undergoing a transformation. Outsiders are moving in, taking over businesses and making the town safe for tourists. And the townspeople seem OK with it. You'll find more expansive thinkers and better lodging in Boulder (p258), but Escalante is on the rise.

The **Escalante Interagency Office** (p252) is at 75 W Main St. There is also a city information booth near Main and Center Sts, which has brochures detailing local historic buildings; it's open erratically, in summer only.

Find books, maps, camping and hiking supplies, USGS 7.5 minute quadrangle maps, high-speed Internet access and liquor (both rarities 'round here) at **Escalante Outfitters** (☎ 435-826-4266; 310 W Main St). In emergency, dial ☎ 911; the nearest medical care is in Panguitch (p246).

Pitch a tent or rent a cozy, heated camping cabin (shared bath) at oh-so-cute **Escalante Outfitters Bunkhouse Cabins** (☎ 435-826-4266; www.escalanteoutfitters.com; 310 W Main St; tent sites $14, cabins $40; ✗ ▣).

The single-story **Circle D Motel** (☎ 435-826-4297; www.utahcanyons.com/circled.htm; 475 W Main St; r $35-55) has cheap and clean – if dated – rooms; some have a fridge and microwave. The modern, ugly two-story **Prospector Inn** (☎ 435-826-4653; www.prospectorinn.com; 380 W Main St; r $57) has standard-issue rooms; skip the restaurant.

The best B&B in town is **Escalante's Grand Staircase B&B/Inn** (☎ 435-826-4890, 866-826-4890; www.escalantebnb.com; 280 W Main St; r $70-115; ✕ ▣) which has attractively styled rooms.

For a house rental, consider **Wild West Retreat** (☎ 435-826-4849, 866-292-3043; www.wildwestretreat.com; 200 East at 300 South; d/q $100/120; ✕), a refurbished 1930s barn with hot tub; **La Luz Desert Retreat** (☎ 435-826-4967, 888-305-4705; www.laluz.net; up to six people $125; ✕), a contemporary adobe home at the desert's edge (call for directions); or the **Vagabond Inn** (☎ 435-826-4266, 866-455-0041; www.vagabondbnb.com; 115 W Main St; up to six people $225-275; ✕), a three-bedroom 1890s brick house.

For groceries, visit **Griffin's** (☎ 435-826-4226; 300 W Main St).

The two best places to hang out and eat have **Internet access.** For coffee, croissants, sandwiches and burgers, visit **Trailhead Café** (☎ 435-826-4714, 800-839-7567; 125 E Main St; ☯ 8am-8pm, closed Tue & Nov-Apr). For granola and yogurt at breakfast and pizza and beer at lunch and dinner, visit **Esca-Latte Café** (☎ 435-826-4266; 310 W Main St; dishes $5-12; ☯ 8am-10pm Mar-Nov; 10am-6pm Tue-Sat Dec-Feb).

Head of the Rocks

At mileage-marker 69.8, 8 miles east of Escalante, pull off the highway for one of Utah's most arresting roadside views. The Aquarius Plateau lords over giant mesas, towering domes, deep canyons, and undulating slickrock that unfurl in an explosion of color. At mileage-marker 73, stop at the must-see **Kiva Koffeehouse** (☎ 435-826-4550; www.kivakoffeehouse.com; dishes $2-5; ☯ 8am-4:30pm, Apr-Nov; ✕) built into the cliff with floor-to-ceiling glass walls. They rent two cushy hideaway **cottages** (r $160-175), also in the cliff.

Calf Creek Recreation Area

Calf Creek (☎ 435-826-5499; www.ut.blm.gov/monument; Hwy 12; day-use $2), 15 miles east of Escalante between mileage-markers 75 and 76, has a **year-round running creek** and the only maintained hiking trail in the GSENM. The sandy **Calf Creek Falls Trail** (6 miles round-trip, moderately difficult) follows the creek through canyons, past an 800-year-old Native American granary and pictographs, before arriving at a 126ft-high waterfall. Leashed dogs are allowed.

Stop here when driving between Escalante and Boulder, and wade in the cool waters of the creek beneath shady cottonwoods, a refreshing treat, especially for kids who are tired of being in the car. Watch your footing: the moss-covered rocks are slippery. Picnic here; choose a table by the stream. There's also a good campground (p255).

Boulder

pop 180 / elev 6593ft

Until 1940, when Hwy 12 connected it to Escalante, Boulder received its mail by mule. After Salt Lake City, Boulder is the second largest – but least populated – town site in Utah. It's so remote that the federal government has classified it not as a rural town, but as a 'frontier community.' Nonetheless, it has one of the most sophisticated populations anywhere in southern Utah. Progressively minded and more expansive in its world-view than Panguitch or Escalante, Boulder has a diverse population of down-to-earth folks – from artists and farmers to geologists and cowboys – and everybody gets along.

Lorded over by Boulder Mountain and surrounded by the GSENM, Boulder makes a great home base, but has fewer services than Escalante or Torrey. To learn more, visit www.boulderutah.com. Town shuts down in winter; call ahead.

Stop at the **BLM information desk** (opposite) at the Anasazi State Park for information about the surrounding lands, including the ruggedly beautiful **Box-Death Hollow Wilderness Area** (box, opposite), up Hell's Backbone Rd. The stunning **Burr Trail** (p253) originates in Boulder. In an emergency, dial ☎ 911; for the nearest medical care, see Panguitch (p246) or Capitol Reef (p261).

Go horseback riding or drive cattle at **Boulder Mountain Ranch** (☎ 435-335-7480; www.boulderutah.com/bmr; rides $35-110), call for directions, or go fishing with **Boulder Mountain Fly-fishing** (☎ 435-335-7306, 435-231-1823; www.bouldermountainflyfishing.com; ☯ Mar-Nov).

Equal parts gallery, outfitter, café, and gathering place, the **Burr Trail Outpost** (☎ 435-335-7565; Burr Trail & Hwy 12; ☾ 8am-8pm Mar-Oct) is worth a visit.

SLEEPING & EATING

Pole's Place (☎ 435-335-7422, 800-730-7422; www .boulderutah.com/polesplace; d $52-66; ✗) The single -story, mom-and-pop motel is lovingly and immaculately maintained.

Circle Cliffs Motel (☎ 435-335-7333; www.boulder utah.com/lodge.html; 225 N Hwy 12; d $50-60; ✗) Three rooms with microwave, fridge and coffeemakers.

Boulder Mountain Lodge (☎ 435-335-7460, 800-556-3446; www.boulder-utah.com; Hwy 12 at Burr Trail; d $89-149; ✗) With the kick-back feel of a ranch but the amenities of a hotel, the lodge is the ideal place for day-hikers who want high-thread-count sheets and plush terry robes at night. Outside there's a hot tub, croquet lawn and bird sanctuary. Some rooms have a fridge and microwave.

Boulder Mountain Ranch (☎ 435-335-7480; www .boulderutah.com/bmr; cabins $60-82, lodge rooms $55-60; ✗) On a 160-acre working ranch in a lush green valley with a running creek, Boulder Mountain Ranch has freestanding log cabins that sleep four to six people; all have baths, woodstoves and fire rings. Up the hill, rent rooms in the giant log house, whose loft sleeps up to 14 people for a mere $150. Call for directions.

Hills and Hollows Country Store (☎ 435-335-7349; Hwy 12; store ☾ 9am-7pm, gas 24hr) Sells groceries, supplies, beer and gasoline. West of town.

Burr Trail Grill and Deli (☎ 435-335-7503; Hwy 12 at Burr Trail; sandwiches $6-8, pizzas $12-15; ☾ 7am-9pm Mar-Oct) For deli sandwiches, draft beer and pizza (after 5pm).

Boulder Mesa Restaurant (☎ 435-335-7447; 155 E Burr Trail; dishes $4-8, dinner mains $12-18; ☾ 7:30am-9pm) For biscuits and gravy and home-made French fries.

Hell's Backbone Grill (☎ 435-335-7464; Boulder Mountain Lodge, Hwy 12 at Burr Trail; breakfast dishes $4-8, dinner mains $12-22; ☾ breakfast & dinner spring-fall) If you've given up on eating well in southern Utah, take heart: the must-visit Hell's Backbone serves soulful, earthy preparations of locally raised meats and organically grown produce from its own garden. Save room for lemon-chiffon cake. Make reservations. Breakfasts are delish.

DETOUR: HELL'S BACKBONE ROAD

To get a sense of just how remote Boulder actually is, take a drive up Hell's Backbone Rd toward the Box-Death Hollow Wilderness Area. Just west of town, at mileage-marker 84, turn north off Hwy 12. Climbing steadily uphill for 14 miles along a gravel-and-dirt route, the sometimes-rough road reaches Hell's Backbone Bridge, a death-defying one-lane crossing above a plunging, yellow-and-orange slickrock canyon sure to give you vertigo. Cut the engine and get out. Wind funnels up the canyon, whistling through the pines, while giant crows float silently on the thermals. To the east, Boulder Mountain is carpeted with deep-green forests and stands of quaking aspen trees; in fall the aspens turn gold – a gorgeous sight. The rest of the drive passes mainly through woods as it continues 28 miles to Escalante, but the treat is the bridge. The road is open late spring to fall; check road conditions at the BLM Information Desk (below).

Anasazi State Park

The centerpiece of this **park** (☎ 435-335-7308; www.stateparks.utah.gov; Main St/Hwy 12, Boulder; per person/car $2/6; ☾ 8am-6pm spring & summer, 9am-5pm fall & winter) is a major outdoor **archaeological site** dating from AD 1130 to 1175. The museum includes a re-created six-room pueblo, a gallery and exhibits about the Anasazi (or Ancestral Puebloan) peoples. There's also a **BLM desk** (☎ 435-335-7382; ☾ 9am-5pm Apr-Oct) where you can talk to rangers and get permits and road updates. On weekends, local hippie dudes hang out here, carving arrowheads.

TORREY

pop 170 / elev 6843ft

After traversing 11,328ft-high Boulder Mountain (where you can camp, hike and fish), Hwy 12 drops into Torrey, 37 miles from Boulder. A quiet town built along a main street (Hwy 24), Torrey's primary industry has shifted from logging and ranching to tourism. They'll come for Capitol Reef National Park (p261), 11 miles east. In winter, Torrey shuts down, but in summer there's a whiff of countercultural sophistication in the air. If you're here the third weekend in July, don't miss the Bicknell International Film

Festival (BIFF), just up Hwy 24. This wacky spoof on Sundance includes films, parties and the 'fastest parade in America.'

Note: the town center lies just west of the ugly prefab chain motels and gas stations at the junction of Hwys 24 and 12 (aka 'malfunction junction').

The **Wayne County Travel Council** (☎ 435-425-3365, 800-858-7951; www.capitolreef.org; Hwy 24/12 junction; ☼ noon-7pm Apr-Oct) has information. For national forest information, head 3 miles west to the **Dixie National Forest Teasdale Ranger Station** (☎ 435-425-3702; www.fs.fed.us/dxnf; 138 E Main St, Teasdale; ☼ 9am-5pm Mon-Fri). For emergency and medical information, see Capitol Reef (opposite).

For horseback riding call **Cowboy Homestead Cabins** (☎ 435-425-3414, 888-854-4871; www.cowboyhomesteadcabins.com; half-day $85, all day $150). **Boulder Mountain Adventures & Alpine Angler's Flyshop** (☎ 435-425-3660, 888-484-3331; www.fly-fishing-utah.net; 310 W Main St) will show you where to fish; they also lead horseback-riding and fishing tours.

Sleeping

Some of the lodging listed here is 5 miles west in Teasdale. Area campgrounds open April to October.

Thousand Lakes RV Park (☎ 435-425-3500, 800-355-8995; www.thousandlakesrvpark.com; Hwy 24; tent/RV sites $10/18, cabins $29; ☒) One mile west of Torrey, with good facilities.

Sandcreek RV Park (☎ 435-425-3577; www.sandcreekrv.com; 540 Hwy 24; tent/RV sites $10/18, dm $12, cabins $28) This friendly place has camping, cabins and an exceptional one-room, eight-bed hostel. There are showers, laundry, gifts and espresso.

Sunglow Campground (☎ 435-836-2800; www.fs.fed.us/r4/fishlake; campsites $10) The Fishlake National Forest campground 6 miles west of Torrey (then east on USFS Rd 143) amid red-rock cliffs.

Boulder Mountain Dixie National Forest runs Oak Creek, Pleasant Creek ($9) and Singletree campgrounds ($10), with drinking water. All are above 8000ft (Map p262).

Austin's Chuckwagon Motel (☎ 435-425-3335, 800-863-3288; www.austinschuckwagonmotel.com; 12 W Main St; r $42-64, cabins $100-125; ☼ Apr-Oct; ☒ ☒) The best motel for service and value, Austin's has spacious rooms and cabins with kitchens. There's also satellite TV, hot tub, laundry and camper showers ($4).

Capitol Reef Inn & Cafe (☎ 435-425-3271; www.capitolreefinn.com; 360 W Main St; r $48; ☼ Apr-Oct; ☒) Ten comfortable rooms off the road are outfitted with hand-crafted wood furniture. Climb the giant kiva to watch the sunset. Hot tub.

Rim Rock Inn (☎ 435-425-3398; 2523 East Hwy 24; r $59; ☼ Mar-Nov; ☒) East of Torrey, surrounded by red-rock cliffs, this family-owned motel has standard-issue rooms with great views.

Pine Shadows Cabins (☎ 435-425-3939, 800-708-1223; www.pineshadowcabins.net; 195 W 125 South, Teasdale; cabins $69-75; ☒) Tucked between piñon pines beneath white cliffs, these five spacious cabins have vaulted ceilings and kitchenettes – a great hideaway just outside Torrey. Each has two beds. Great value.

None of the overpriced chain motels – Best Western, Days Inn, Holiday Inn Express and Super 8 – provides a sense of place, except in the views from their prefab windows. Skip the Wonderland Motel. Bicknell, 9 miles west, has more budget motels.

Torrey and Teasdale have several B&Bs and one top-end lodge.

Skyridge Inn (☎ 435-425-3222; www.skyridgeinn.com; 950 E Hwy 24; r $115-172; ☒) Every window of the immaculately kept inn has gorgeous views. Decked out in dressed-down country elegance, rooms have local art and down comforters; two have private hot tubs. Guests gather by the fire.

Muley Twist (☎ 435-425-3640, 800-530-1038; www.muleytwistinn.com; 249 W 125 South, Teasdale; r $99-109; ☼ Apr-Oct; ☒) The big wooden farmhouse looks small against the towering domes rising behind it, but inside, the down-to-earth inn has bright, airy and comfy rooms.

Lodge at Red River Ranch (☎ 435-425-3322, 800-205-6343; www.redriverranch.com; 2900 W Hwy 24, Teasdale; r $125-175; ☒) In the grand old tradition of Western lodges, the great room has a three-story-high open-beam ceiling, giant fireplace and exposed timber walls adorned with Navajo rugs. Details are flawless, from the country quilts on high-thread-count sheets to the masonry of each room's wood-burning fireplace. Breakfast is included (and open to nonguests).

Accommodation also worth a look:

Cactus Hill Motel (☎ 435-425-3578, 800-507-2624; www.cactushillmotel.com; State Rd 112, Teasdale; d/tr/q $48/52/56, cabins $75/85/95; ☼ Mar-Nov; ☒) Motel rooms on a ranch, and a cozy cabin on Boulder Mountain.

Torrey Pines Inn (☎ 435-425-3401; www.torreypines inn.com; Hwy 12; r $89-98, cottage $110; ✗) B&B rooms and a cottage with kitchen, 0.25 miles south of Torrey.

Cowboy Homestead Cabins (☎ 435-425-3414, 888-854-5871; www.cowboyhomesteadcabins.com; Hwy 12; cabins $64; ✗) Four knotty-pine-paneled cabins with kitchenettes, 3 miles south of Torrey.

Boulder View Inn (☎ 435-425-3800, 800-444-3980; www.boulderviewinn.com; 385 W Main St; s/d $45/48; ✗) Spotless motel rooms.

Torrey Trading Post (☎ 435-425-3716; www.torrey tradingpost.com; 75 W Main St; cabins $28; ✗) Two year-round tidy cabins with shared bathroom, but no air-conditioning.

Eating

Robber's Roost Books & Beverages (☎ 435-425-3265; 185 W Main St; ✆ May-Nov) Linger over coffee on a comfy couch by the fire at Torrey's hip bookstore café.

Capitol Reef Cafe (☎ 435-425-3271; 360 W Main St; breakfast $5-9, lunch & dinner mains $7-16; ✆ 7am-9pm Apr-Oct) Torrey's best for breakfast and lunch has vegetable-heavy dishes, salads and sandwiches; good dinners, too.

Rim Rock Restaurant (☎ 435-425-3398; 2523 East Hwy 24; mains $10-25; ✆ dinner daily Mar-Nov, Thu-Sun Nov & Dec, closed Jan-Feb; ✗) Every table has a million-dollar view. On the straightforward meat-heavy menu, choose from good grilled steaks, pastas and fish. Full bar. Come before sunset.

Cafe Diablo (☎ 435-425-3070; 599 W Main St; mains $17-28; ✆ dinner Apr-Oct; ✗) One of southern Utah's best, Diablo serves outstanding, highly stylized Southwestern cooking – including succulent vegetarian dishes – bursting with flavor and towering on the plate. For something you won't find back home, try the rattlesnake cakes. Save room for dessert. Sample from 23 tequilas (request a free ride home). Budgeteers: order appetizers ($7 to $9) and dessert; you won't leave hungry. Don't miss this one.

Drinking & Entertainment

Saturday afternoon **Robber's Roost** hosts an open mic and farmers' market. The **Rim Rock Patio** (☎ 435-425-3398; 2523 E Hwy 24; ✆ noon-10pm Mar-Nov) serves beer, pizza and ice cream; play darts or volleyball while you chugalug. Kids welcome. The **Wayne Theater** (☎ 435-425-3123; www.waynetheater.com; 11 E Main St, Bicknell) shows movies (weekends) for a pittance and hosts the **Bicknell International Film Festival** in July.

CAPITOL REEF NATIONAL PARK

Giant slabs of chocolate-red rock and sweeping yellow sandstone domes lord over the forbidding landscape of Capitol Reef, which Fremont Indians called the 'Land of the Sleeping Rainbow.' The park's centerpiece is Waterpocket Fold, a 100-mile-long monocline – a buckle in the earth's crust – that blocked explorers' westward migration like a reef blocks a ship's passage. Known also for its enormous sandstone domes, one of which resembles the Capitol Dome, the park has fantastic desert-hiking trails, 800-year-old petroglyphs and a verdant 19th-century Mormon settlement with prolific fruit trees.

Orientation & Information

There is no fee to enter Capitol Reef. The narrow park runs north–south along Waterpocket Fold. Hwy 24 traverses its northern section. Scenic Drive ($5) runs 10 miles south from the visitor center. Torrey is 10 miles west.

Capitol Reef's central region is the Fruita Historic District. To the far north lies Cathedral Valley and its moonscape, the least-visited section. To the south, the park narrows around the Fold.

Several unpaved roads access the northern reaches around Cathedral Valley; the easiest route Caineville Wash Rd, though portions require high-clearance 4WD. Notom-Bullfrog Rd heads south from Hwy 24 roughly paralleling Waterpocket Fold. Beyond the Burr Trail Switchbacks (p253), Notom-Bullfrog Rd merges with the Burr Trail Rd to Glen Canyon.

The **visitor center** (☎ 435-425-3791; www.nps.gov /care; Hwy 24 & Scenic Dr; ✆ 8am-4:30pm, longer in summer) is park headquarters and the only in-park source for information. Watch the short film, then ooh and aah over the

UTAH

WATER, WATER EVERYWHERE

Hidden inside Capitol Reef's towering jumble of rocks and winding canyons are giant natural cisterns full of water. These caches are rare in this arid landscape. John Wesley Powell, the first Western explorer to encounter the reef, found the precious resource and nicknamed the monocline Waterpocket Fold.

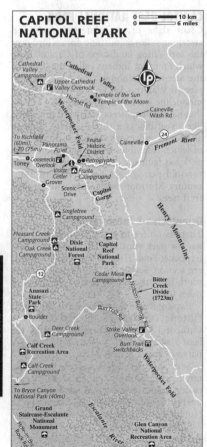

CAPITOL REEF NATIONAL PARK

0 ——— 10 km
0 ——— 6 miles

64-sq-ft park relief map, carved with dental instruments. Staff help plan hikes. Inquire about ranger-led programs.

In emergency, dial ☎ 911. For **police**, dial ☎ 435-425-3791. The nearest clinic is the **Wayne Community Health Center** (☎ 435-425-3744; 128 S 300 W, Bicknell; ☼ 9am-5pm Mon-Fri, 9am-1pm Sat), 19 miles west on Hwy 24; the closest hospital is **Sevier Valley Hospital** (☎ 435-896-8271; 1000 N Main St, Richfield), 75 miles west of the park via Hwy 24 to I-70. For other services, head to Torrey (p259).

Occasional summer thunderstorms pose a serious risk of flash floods. Always check weather with rangers at the visitor center. Bugs bite in May and June. Summer temperatures can exceed 100°F at the visitor

center (5400ft), but it's cooler than Moab! If it's too hot, ascend to Torrey (10°F cooler) or Boulder Mountain (30°F cooler).

Sights & Activities
FRUITA HISTORIC DISTRICT
Fruita (*froo*-tuh) is a cool green oasis, where shade-giving cottonwoods and fruit-bearing trees line the Fremont River's banks. The first Mormon homesteaders arrived in 1880; Fruita's final resident left in 1969.

The NPS maintains 2700 cherry, apricot, peach, pear and apple trees planted by early settlers. Visit between June and October, and pluck ripe fruit from the trees, for free, from any unlocked orchard. Ask rangers or call the **fruit hotline** (☎ 435-425-3791). Pick only mature fruit; leave the rest to ripen. Near the orchards is a wonderful **picnic area**, with roaming deer and birds in the trees, a desert rarity.

Among the historic buildings, check out the blacksmith shop, though it's just a shed with period equipment. Across the road is the **Ripple Rock Nature Center** (☼ 10am-3pm summer), a family-oriented learning center. The **Gifford Homestead** reveals the day-to-day world of pioneer homesteads.

East of the visitor center on Hwy 24, look for the Fremont Indian **petroglyphs**; these carvings convinced archaeologists that the Fremont were distinct from the Anasazi.

WATERPOCKET FOLD
Park boundaries roughly follow **Waterpocket Fold**. Hwy 24 crosses it; Scenic Drive parallels it. But the best way to see it within is to ascend the **Burr Trail Switchbacks** (p253), then drive north for 3 miles to **Strike Valley Overlook**. Domes along Hwy 24, such as Navajo and Capitol Domes, are actually part of the fold.

SCENIC DRIVES
Two main roads access the park: Hwy 24 and Scenic Drive. Other routes follow dirt roads bladed only four times a year. Always check weather and road conditions with rangers before heading out.

To drive beyond Fruita on **Scenic Drive** costs $5, payable at the self-serve kiosk. Numbered roadside markers correspond to a driving tour the park once published. There's talk of reprinting it; ask the visitor center. The best of the 9-mile-long route is its last 2 miles between the narrow sandstone walls of **Capitol Gorge**. It'll knock your socks off. Plan to hike (below).

The park sells guides ($1) to two excellent drives: **Loop-the-Fold** and **Cathedral Valley Loop**.

The 100-mile Loop-the-Fold tour offers a comprehensive overview of **Waterpocket Fold**; half the trip is on dirt roads generally accessible to 2WD passenger cars. For perspective on the size and scale of the park's centerpiece, this is the drive to take. Part of the route follows the Burr Trail, part of it Hwy 12, and part of it Hwy 24.

The much rougher, 58-mile Cathedral Valley Loop takes in otherworldly landscapes. You can usually drive a 2WD vehicle the first 15.5 miles of Caineville Wash Rd from Hwy 24 to the striking 400ft monoliths, **Temple of the Sun** and **Temple of the Moon**, and to **Glass Mountain**, a 20ft mound of fused selenite. This short in-and-out trip offers a taste of Cathedral Valley without 4WD. The turnoff from Hwy 24 to Caineville Wash Rd is at mile marker 98.4. NB: Unless you're driving a high-clearance 4WD vehicle, do not attempt the 58-mile loop along **Hartnet Rd**, which fords the Fremont River just before rejoining Hwy 24.

If you have time for only one backroad trip, head up the **Burr Trail Switchbacks** or drive the complete Loop-the-Fold tour. To reach Burr Trail, take **Notom-Bullfrog Rd**, a so-so dirt road – the prettiest stretch lies south of Bitter Creek Divide.

HIKING

Capitol Reef has little shade. Drink at least one quart of water every two hours of hiking,
increase your electrolyte intake (sodium and potassium) and wear a hat. If you're short on time and want variety, see the Goosenecks Overlook, and hike Grand Wash and Hickman Bridge Trails. Distances listed are one-way.

Just two miles west of the visitor center off Hwy 24, a short unpaved road reaches **Panorama Point** and **Gooseneck Overlook**, a dizzying 800ft-high viewpoint above serpentine Sulphur Creek. Afternoon light is best. Along Scenic Drive, a good dirt road leads to **Grand Wash Trail** (2.25 miles, easy) a flat hike between canyon walls that, at one point, tower 80 stories high but are only 15ft apart. **Hickman Bridge Trail** (1 mile, moderate), the park's most popular walk, includes a canyon walk, a stunning natural bridge and spring wildflowers. Mornings are coolest; it starts about 2 miles east of the visitor center.

At the end of Scenic Drive, the road dead-ends at **Capitol Gorge Trail** (1 mile, easy), which leads past petroglyphs; spur trails lead to **Pioneer Register**, where names carved in the rock date back to 1871, and the **Tanks**, giant water pockets.

The visitor center has a complete list of hikes. Ask about **Cassidy Arch** (off the Grand Wash Trail) and the **Golden Throne** (off the Capitol Gorge Trail).

ROCK CLIMBING

Technical climbing is allowed without permits. Note that Wingate sandstone can flake unpredictably. Follow clean-climbing guidelines, and take all safety precautions. For details, check with rangers or see www.nps.gov/care.

BACKCOUNTRY ACCESS

For a sense of the vastness of Waterpocket Fold, there's no better activity than backcountry hiking. Capitol Reef gets extremely hot in summer, and dehydration is a serous concern, so plan carefully. Wear a wide-brimmed hat and plan to carry all your water – don't count on finding water pockets.

Talk to rangers before setting out. Pick up a free backcountry permit and check conditions at the visitor center. Ground fires are prohibited; bring a stove. There are no established campgrounds. Never camp in a wash.

Upper Muley Twist Canyon has expansive views from atop Waterpocket Fold. Lower Muley Twist Canyon follows a dramatic, flash-flood-prone canyon that twists and turns between 800ft-high walls that are only 10ft apart at their narrowest. Also inquire about Halls Creek Narrows, a 22-mile round-trip canyon trek. Wherever you go, stay on trails, don't shortcut switchbacks, and avoid stepping on cryptobiotic crusts (p48).

BIKING
Scenic Drive works well for beginners and intermediates; experienced riders love Cathedral Valley, though it's a muddy mess when wet. Check with rangers. Rent bikes from **Capitol Reef Backcountry Outfitters** (☎ 435-425-2010; www.capitolreefoutfitters.com; 677 E Hwy 24 at Hwy 12, Torrey; per day $38-55), which also guides.

SWIMMING & WADING
Only wade in wide sections of calm water – and only if there's no flash-flood threat; ask rangers. Across the highway from Chimney Rock parking area (about 2 miles west of the visitor center), an easy trail leads to **Sulphur Creek**. Near the visitor center, hike up Sulphur Creek a mile to a large, shaded wading pool. Also wade along **Pleasant Creek**, at the end of Scenic Dr; get directions from rangers.

Do not swim at the waterfall on the north side of Hwy 24, 4 miles east of the petroglyphs. Rocks are slippery and currents strong. More accidents happen here than anywhere else in the park (usually compound fractures).

Tours
One of the best guides in southern Utah, **Hondoo Rivers & Trails** (☎ 435-425-3519, 800-332-2696; www.hondoo.com; 90 E Main St, Torrey) operates one-day and multiday hikes, and fantastic horseback and vehicle trips. For super-smart interpretation, **Earth Tours** (☎ 435-691-1241; www.earth-tours.com; half-/full-day tours $50/75; ☼ spring-fall) is run by a PhD in geology who can speak in lay terms. There's also **Wild Hare Expeditions** (☎ 435-425-3999, 800-304-4273; www .color-country.net/~thehare; 116 W Main St, Torrey).

Sleeping & Eating
Apart from camping in or around the park, the nearest lodging and dining are in Torrey (p260).

East on Hwy 24, stop in Caineville, 18 miles east of Capitol Reef between mileage-markers 102 and 103, at **Mesa Market** (☎ 435-456-9146; Hwy 24; ☼ 7am-3pm Easter till the first frost) for straight-from-the-garden organic salads and freshly baked artisanal bread from an outdoor stone-hearth oven. That's all they serve and it's delicious. Next door **Luna Mesa Oasis** (☎ 435-456-9122; dishes $5-15; ☼ 8am-8pm Mon-Sat) serves Mexican food.

Getting Around
Buy gasoline in Torrey or Boulder. Bicycles are allowed on all park roads but not trails. For shuttles, contact **Hondoo Rivers & Trails** (☎ 435-425-3519, 800-332-2696; www.hondoo.com; 90 E Main St, Torrey) or **Wild Hare Expeditions** (☎ 435-425-3999, 800-304-4273; www.color-country.net/~thehare; 116 W Main St, Torrey), both in Torrey.

SOUTHEASTERN UTAH

Soaring snow-capped peaks lord over blue-hued mesas and plunging red-rock river canyons in the most desolate corner of Utah, appropriately nicknamed Canyonlands. The terrain is so forbidding that it was the last region to be mapped in the continental USA.

Over 65 million years, water carved sheer-walled gorges along the course of the Colorado and Green Rivers, which define the borders of Canyonlands National Park, Utah's largest. Nearby Arches National Park encompasses more rock arches than anywhere else. Between the parks lies Moab, the state's premier destination for mountain biking, river-running and four-wheeling. South of Moab, Ancestral Puebloan sites are scattered among wilderness areas and parks, most famously Monument Valley (extending into Arizona, p184).

This section is organized in a clockwise fashion. It begins at I-70 and Green River, then heads south, then northwest, ending at the San Rafael Reef and I-70.

GREEN RIVER & AROUND
pop 970 / elev 4100ft
The only town of note along I-70 between Salina, Utah (108 miles west), and Grand Junction, Colorado (102 miles east), Green River is a river-running base and has cheaper accommodations than Moab. Settled in 1878, the town now relies mainly on tourism. It's also the 'world's watermelon capital' and celebrates the harvest with Melon Days in September.

The I-70 business loop north of the freeway between exits 158 and 162 becomes Main St. The **Emery County Travel Bureau** (☎ 435-564-3600, 888-564-3600; www.greenriver-utah .com; 885 E Main St; ☼ 8am-8pm daily summer, 8am-4pm Tue-Sun winter) sells river-running and hiking maps and guides.

Sights & Activities

The Colorado and Green Rivers were first explored in 1869 and 1871 by the legendary one-armed Civil War veteran, geologist and ethnologist John Wesley Powell. Learn about his amazing travels at **John Wesley Powell River History Museum** (☎ 435-564-3427; www.jwprhm.com; 885 E Main St; ☉ 8am-8pm Apr-Oct, 8am-4pm Nov-Mar; adult/child/family $2/1/5), which also has exhibits on the Fremont Indians, geology and local history.

Shady **Green River State Park** (☎ 435-564-3633; www.stateparks.utah.gov; per car $5; ☉ 8am-10pm), 1 mile south of Main St on Green River Blvd, borders the river. There's a **boat launch** and nine-hole **golf course** (for tee times ☎ 435-564-8882; 9/18 holes $9/16) with pro shop.

Crystal Geyser erupts unpredictably from near the east bank of the Green River every 13 to 17 hours, shooting sometimes 100ft in the air for 30 minutes. Ask the visitor center for directions. Also ask for directions to the dilapidated ghost town of **Sego**, 30 miles east-northeast of Green River at **Thompson and Sego Canyons**, where you can also see prehistoric rock art.

If you have **river-running** experience, you can start from the state park or Gray Canyon, 10 miles north. The river is flat between Green River and the confluence of the Colorado River for float-it-yourself rafting and canoeing. The current is deceptively strong; swim only with a life jacket.

Local outfitters run **whitewater-rafting** day trips for about $60 for adults and $40 for kids, including lunch and transportation; ask about multiday excursions. Call **Holiday Expeditions** (☎ 435-564-3273, 800-624-6323; www.bikeraft.com; 1055 E Main St) or **Moki Mac River Expeditions** (☎ 435-564-3361, 800-284-7280; www.mokimac.com; 100 Silliman Lane). Moki Mac also rents canoes and runs shuttles. **Green River Shuttles** (☎ 435-564-8292) also runs shuttles.

Sleeping

There are year-round campsites with water and showers at **Green River State Park** (for reservations ☎ 800-322-3770; www.reserveamerica.com; campsites $14; ☉ Mar-Nov). You'll find full facilities at **United Campground** (☎ 435-564-8195; 910 E Main St); and **Shady Acres RV Park** (☎ 435-564-8290, 800-537-8674; 350 E Main St). A tent site costs $17 and an RV site $24.

Motels are costliest in summer. Chains run $50 to $100. From cheapest to most expensive: Motel 6, Rodeway Inn, Super 8 and Comfort Inn.

Budget choices include **Robbers Roost Motel** (☎ 435-564-3452; www.robbersroost-motel.com; 225 W Main St; r $30-50; ☒), **Budget Inn** (☎ 435-564-3441; 60 E Main St; r $35-45; ☒), **Bookcliff Lodge** (☎ 435-564-3406, 800-493-4699; www.bookclifflodge.com; 395 E Main St; r $40-45; ☒ ☒) and **Green River Inn** (☎ 435-564-8237; 456 W Main St; r $40-60).

The nicest are **Best Western River Terrace** (☎ 435-564-3401, 800-528-1234; www.bestwestern.com; 880 E Main St; r $80-90; ☒ ☒) and **Holiday Inn Express** (☎ 435-564-4439, 877-531-5084; www.holidayinn.com; 965 E Main St; r $65-75; ☒ ☒ ☒).

Eating

Buy groceries at **Melon Vine Food Store** (☎ 435-564-3228; 76 S Broadway; ☉ 8am-7pm Mon-Sat).

Ray's Tavern (☎ 435-564-3511; 25 S Broadway; steaks $11-20) is far and away the best in town, Ray's serves burgers worth stopping for, plus great steaks and pizza. Microbrews and a pool table round out the fun.

Ben's Cafe (☎ 435-564-3352; 115 W Main St; dishes under $8) serves Mexican; the more upscale, river-view **Tamarisk Restaurant** (☎ 435-564-8109; 870 E Main St; mains $9-16) makes steaks and homemade desserts. The **Fairway** (☎ 435-564-3674; 118 W Main St; ☉ to 1am) is a smoky, locals' bar with light sandwiches.

Getting There & Around

Greyhound (☎ 435-564-3421, 800-231-2222; www.greyhound.com), in the Rodeway Inn (525 E Main St), goes to Grand Junction, Colorado ($28, 1 hour and 40 minutes); Salt Lake City ($37, four hours); and Las Vegas ($64, 7½ hours). **Bighorn Express** (☎ 888-655-7433; www.bighornexpress.com) also stops at the Rodeway Inn; it runs vans to Salt Lake City ($46, 3½ hours), Moab ($26, one hour) and Monticello ($36, two hours).

Amtrak (☎ 435-872-7245, 800-872-7245; www.amtrak.com; 250 S Broadway, at Green River Ave) runs daily to SLC ($27 to $52, five hours) and Denver, Colorado ($42 to $78, 11 hours). It's the only stop in southeastern Utah.

MOAB

pop 4780 / elev 4000ft

If you've been jonesing for civilization, Moab is a sight for sore eyes. Shop for groceries till midnight, browse the shelves at *two* indie bookstores, buy nail polish, and sit down for dinner at 9pm and still find several places open for a beer afterward. All this culture comes at a price: chain motels line Main St, T-shirt shops abound, and neon signs blot out the stars. If you're coming from the wilderness, Moab is jarring.

But there's a distinct sense of fun in the air. Moab bills itself as Utah's recreation capital, and it delivers. From the hiker to the four-wheeler, recreational enthusiasm borders on fetishism.

Southeastern Utah's largest town, Moab has almost lost its small-town rural roots, and some fear it's becoming the next Vail, Colorado. It won't ever become a sprawling suburb (it's surrounded by state and federal lands), but it gets overrun spring through fall, and the impact of all those feet, bikes and 4WDs on the fragile desert is a serious concern. People disagree on what to do. Talk to anyone and you'll fast learn that Moab's polarized political debates are yet another high-stakes extreme sport.

One thing is certain: people here love the land – even if they don't always agree about how to protect it. And if all that neon and traffic irritate you, remember that you can disappear into the vast desert, without a trace, in no time flat. But stock up on tequila before you leave 'cause there's no place else for miles.

History

Tucked beneath high rock walls in a fertile green valley, along an important Colorado River wildlife corridor, Moab was founded by Mormon farmers in the late 1870s after the Native Americans' repeated attempts to get rid of them failed. Nothing changed until the 1950s and the Cold War era, when the federal government subsidized uranium mining, and the population tripled in three years. In search of 'radioactive gold,' miners bladed a network of Jeep roads, which laid the groundwork for Moab to become a 4WD mecca 50 years later. (The miners also left radioactive tailings ponds.) Though uranium mining bottomed out in the 1980s when the feds quit paying premiums, salt and potash mining continue, as does drilling for natural gas, a contentious issue.

Hollywood loves Moab and shot hundreds of Westerns here, from the 1950s to the '70s. But neither the mining boom nor Hollywood has had as much influence on the current character of Moab as has the humble mountain biker. In the mid-1980s, an influx of fat-tire enthusiasts discovered the challenging and scenic slickrock desert and triggered a massive surge in tourism and youth culture that continues unabated.

Orientation & Information

Hwy 191 becomes Main St through town.

Refill water jugs at the Phillips 66 Station (Main St & 300 South), which provides a spigot. Alternatively go to Matrimony Springs (Hwy 128, 100yd east of Hwy 191 on the right).

BOOKSTORES & MEDIA

Back of Beyond Books (☎ 435-259-5154; 83 N Main St; ◷ 9am-10pm) Ultralefty bookstore that carries guides, histories and nonfiction.

Arches Book Company (☎ 435-259-0782; 78 N Main St; ◷ 7:30am-9pm) A general bookstore with good fiction; carries the *New York Times* and serves pretty-good coffee.

Newspapers Free newspapers include *Moab Happenings*, geared to visitors, and the iconoclastic *Canyon Country Zephyr*.

Moab Community Radio (89.7FM & 106.1FM) Tune in for alternative-programming, folk to funk.

EMERGENCY & MEDICAL SERVICES

In emergency dial ☎ 911. Cell phones work here, but not in canyons, where a satellite phone is essential.

Police (☎ 435-259-8938; 115 W 200 South)

Allen Memorial Hospital Emergency Room (☎ 435-259-7191; 719 W 400 North). For emergency medical care.

Moab Immediate Care & X-Ray (☎ 435-259-5276; 267 N Main St; ◷ noon-8pm) For nonemergency care.

Grand County Emergency Coordinator (☎ 435-259-8115) For search and rescue.

POST

Post office (☎ 435-259-7427; 50 E 100 North)

INTERNET ACCESS

Grand County Public Library (☎ 435-259-1111; www.grand.lib.ut.us; 25 S 100 East; ◷ 9am-9pm Mon-Wed, 9am-7pm Thu-Fri, 9am-5pm Sat) Provides T1 Internet service (per five minutes $1). Also visit Red Rock Bakery (p274), Slickrock Café (p274), Mondo Café (p276).

LAUNDRY & SHOWERS

Moab Speed Cleaners (☎ 435-259-7456; 702 S Main St; ◷ 8am-7pm). Do your laundry here.

Showers Archview Campground, Canyonlands Campground (p272) or Poison Spider Bicycles (p269).

UTAH

MOAB

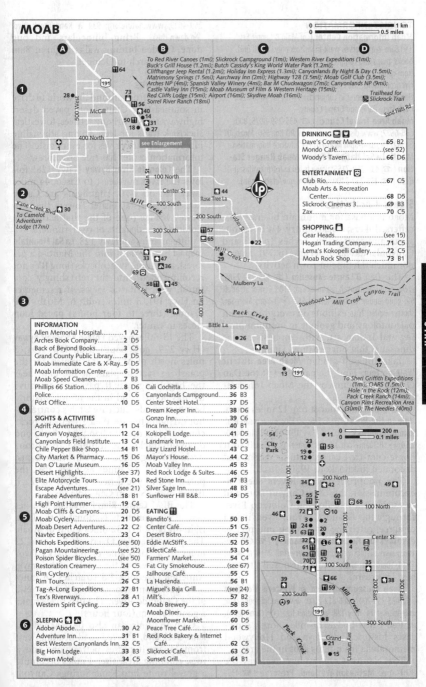

0 _____ 1 km
0 _____ 0.5 miles

To Red River Canoes (1mi); Slickrock Campground (1mi); Western River Expeditions (1mi);
Buck's Grill House (1.2mi); Butch Cassidy's King World Water Park (1.2mi);
Cliffhanger Jeep Rental (1.2mi); Holiday Inn Express (1.3mi); Canyonlands By Night & Day (1.5mi);
Matrimony Springs (1.5mi); Aarchway Inn (2mi); Highway 128 (3.5mi); Moab Golf Club (3.5mi);
Arches NP (4mi); Spanish Valley Winery (4mi); Bar M Chuckwagon (7mi); Canyonlands NP (9mi);
Castle Valley Inn (15mi); Moab Museum of Film & Western Heritage (15mi);
Red Cliffs Lodge (15mi); Airport (16mi); Skydive Moab (16mi);
Sorrel River Ranch (18mi)

Trailhead for
Slickrock Trail

Sand Flats Rd

DRINKING 🍺 🍷
Dave's Corner Market..............**65** B2
Mondo Café...................(see 52)
Woody's Tavern..................**66** D6

ENTERTAINMENT 🎭
Club Rio......................**67** C5
Moab Arts & Recreation
    Center....................**68** D5
Slickrock Cinemas 3............**69** B3
Zax.........................**70** C5

SHOPPING 🛍
Gear Heads...................(see 15)
Hogan Trading Company.......**71** C5
Lema's Kokopelli Gallery......**72** C5
Moab Rock Shop...............**73** B1

UTAH

To Sheri Griffith Expeditions
(1mi); OARS (1.5mi);
Hole 'n the Rock (12mi);
Pack Creek Ranch (14mi);
Canyon Rims Recreation Area
(30mi); The Needles (40mi)

INFORMATION
Allen Memorial Hospital...........**1** A2
Arches Book Company...............**2** D5
Back of Beyond Books..............**3** C5
Grand County Public Library......**4** D5
Moab Immediate Care & X-Ray..**5** D5
Moab Information Center...........**6** D5
Moab Speed Cleaners..............**7** B3
Phillips 66 Station..................**8** D6
Police...............................**9** C6
Post Office.........................**10** D5

SIGHTS & ACTIVITIES
Adrift Adventures................**11** D4
Canyon Voyages..................**12** C4
Canyonlands Field Institute.....**13** C4
Chile Pepper Bike Shop..........**14** B1
City Market & Pharmacy.........**15** D6
Dan O'Laurie Museum............**16** D5
Desert Highlights...............(see 37)
Elite Motorcycle Tours...........**17** D4
Escape Adventures..............(see 21)
Farabee Adventures.............**18** B1
High Point Hummer..............**19** C4
Moab Cliffs & Canyons..........**20** D5
Moab Cyclery....................**21** D6
Moab Desert Adventures.........**22** C2
Navtec Expeditions..............**23** C4
Nichols Expeditions............(see 50)
Pagan Mountaineering..........(see 52)
Poison Spider Bicycles.........(see 50)
Restoration Creamery...........**24** C5
Rim Cyclery......................**25** C5
Rim Tours.........................**26** C3
Tag-A-Long Expeditions.........**27** B1
Tex's Riverways..................**28** A1
Western Spirit Cycling..........**29** C3

SLEEPING 🏠 🏕
Adobe Abode.....................**30** A2
Adventure Inn...................**31** B1
Best Western Canyonlands Inn..**32** C5
Big Horn Lodge...................**33** B3
Bowen Motel.....................**34** C5

Cali Cochitta....................**35** D5
Canyonlands Campground......**36** B3
Center Street Hotel.............**37** D5
Dream Keeper Inn...............**38** D6
Gonzo Inn.......................**39** C6
Inca Inn..........................**40** B1
Kokopelli Lodge.................**41** D5
Landmark Inn....................**42** D5
Lazy Lizard Hostel..............**43** C3
Mayor's House..................**44** C2
Moab Valley Inn.................**45** B3
Red Rock Lodge & Suites.......**46** C5
Red Stone Inn...................**47** B3
Silver Sage Inn.................**48** B3
Sunflower Hill B&B.............**49** D5

EATING 🍴
Bandito's.........................**50** B1
Center Café.....................**51** C5
Desert Bistro..................(see 37)
Eddie McStiff's.................**52** D5
EklecticCafé....................**53** D4
Farmers' Market................**54** C4
Fat City Smokehouse..........(see 67)
Jailhouse Café..................**55** C5
La Hacienda....................**56** B1
Miguel's Baja Grill............(see 24)
Milt's.............................**57** B2
Moab Brewery...................**58** B3
Moab Diner......................**59** D6
Moonflower Market.............**60** D5
Peace Tree Café................**61** C5
Red Rock Bakery & Internet
    Café..........................**62** C5
Slickrock Cafe..................**63** C5
Sunset Grill....................**64** B1

City Park

0 _____ 200 m
0 _____ 0.1 miles

TOURIST INFORMATION

Moab Information Center (cnr Main & Center Sts; 8am-8pm) Serves walk-in visitors only. You'll find books, maps and comprehensive information on everything from campgrounds and permits to astronomical data and river conditions. The Canyonlands Natural History Association staffs the center in conjunction with the NPS, BLM, Utah State Parks and Grand County.

Moab Area Travel Council (☎ 435-259-8825, 800-635-6622; www.discovermoab.com; PO Box 550, Moab, UT 84532; 8am-5pm Mon-Fri) For advance information.

Manti–La Sal National Forest Moab Ranger Station (☎ 435-259-7155; www.fs.fed.us/r4/mantilasal)

BLM (☎ 435-259-2100; www.blm.gov/utah/moab)

Sights & Activities

Moab is a base for mountain bikers, river-rafters, hikers, backcountry-4WD enthusiasts and visitors to Arches (p277) and Canyonlands National Parks (p279). There's not much daytime in-town activity.

UTAH

The **Dan O'Laurie Museum** (☎ 435-259-7985; www.grandcountyutah.net/museum; 118 E Center St; adult $2, child under 12 free, family $5; 1-8pm Mon-Sat, shorter winter) has exhibits on everything from paleontology and geology to uranium mining and Indian art, with emphasis on the dinosaurs that once roamed Utah.

Take the self-guided **Moab Area Historic Walking Tour**. Find the pamphlet at the Dan O'Laurie Museum or the Moab Information Center.

An unabashed tourist trap 12 miles south, **Hole 'n the Rock** (☎ 435-686-2250; www.moab-utah.com/holeintherock; 11037 S Hwy 191; adult/child $4.50/2.50; 8:30am-7pm, shorter winter) is a 5000-sq-ft home-cum-cave carved into sandstone and decorated in knockout 1950s kitsch.

The nonprofit Living Rivers seeks to decommission the Glen Canyon Dam and re-establish a free-flowing Colorado River through the Grand Canyon. Even if you disagree, catch the fascinating interpretive displays at **Restoration Creamery** (☎ 435-259-1063; www.livingrivers.org/creamery.cfm; 21 N Main St; 1-10pm Mar-Oct), which also sells town's best ice cream.

Moab Museum of Film & Western Heritage (☎ 435-259-2002, 866-812-2002; www.redcliffslodge.com; mile-marker 14, Hwy 128; admission free; 8am-10pm), at Red Cliffs Lodge 15 miles north, showcases historical displays and Hollywood memorabilia from films shot in the area.

The Nature Conservancy oversees the 890-acre **Matheson Wetlands Preserve** (☎ 435-259-4629; www.nature.org; 934 W Kane Creek Blvd; dawn-dusk). Bring binoculars and bug dope. Guided birding walks begin at 8am Saturday, March to October.

SCENIC DRIVES

People come from around the world to drive in southeastern Utah. From paved desert highways for RV-driving retirees, to vertical slickrock trails for Jeep-driving adrenaline junkies, there are drives for every taste. The information center has free brochures.

The **Colorado River Byway** (Hwy 128) follows the river northeast to Cisco, 44 miles away just off I-70. Highlights are Castle Rock, the 900ft-tall Fisher Towers, the 1916 Dewey Bridge (one of the first across the Colorado), and sights of river-runners.

Fifteen miles up Hwy 128, **La Sal Mountain Loop Rd** heads south into the Manti–La Sal forest, ascending switchbacks (long RVs not recommended) into the refreshingly cool forest, with fantastic views. It re-emerges on Hwy 191, 8 miles south of Moab. The 67-mile (three to four hours) paved loop closes in winter.

The 15-mile, paved **Potash Rd Scenic Byway** (Hwy 279) goes south from Hwy 191, 3 miles north of Moab. It's named for the potash extraction plant at the end; near the beginning, you'll pass a radioactive tailings pond – and in the middle, natural beauty abounds. Such are Utah's contradictions. Highlights are Wall Street (the rock-climbers' favorite), Indian petroglyphs and dinosaur tracks, the trailhead to Corona Arch, and Jug Handle Arch, which is just 3ft wide, but 15 times as high. Past the potash plant, you'll need a 4WD to reach Island in the Sky, in Canyonlands.

The BLM **Canyon Rims Recreation Area** lies east of Canyonlands National Park. Turn right off Hwy 191, 32 miles south of Moab. The paved Needles Overlook Rd leads 22 miles to a panorama of the park. Two-thirds of the way to the overlook, the gravel Anticline Overlook Rd stretches 16 miles north to a promontory with awesome views of the Colorado River. The two roads make a good day trip (four hours).

Canyon Rims can also be reached via **Kane Creek Blvd,** a paved road heading west from Moab. It passes petroglyphs and a rock-climbing area, after 4 miles becoming a gravel route into Kane Springs Canyon.

After 10 miles, you ford the creek, which, depending on weather, may be impassable. After 14 miles you reach 4470ft Hurrah Pass, after which only 4WD vehicles can continue. The stupendous scenery includes views *up* to Dead Horse Point. At the base of the pass is Camelot Adventure Lodge (p273), where you can play disc golf (reservations required). From here, 4WD is mandatory and the route confusing, eventually ending 50 miles beyond at Hwy 211, east of the Needles area of Canyonlands National Park. Contact the BLM for maps and information.

MOUNTAIN BIKING

Moab's mountain biking is world-famous. Challenging trails ascend steep slickrock, wind through woods and up 4WD roads into wild canyon country. There's no place like it. Considering the numbers of riders, it's essential to protect the surrounding desert. Avoid all off-trail riding and pack everything out (including cigarette butts).

Spring and fall are busiest. In summer, start by 7am, otherwise it's too hot. Pick up *Above & Beyond Slickrock*, by Todd Campbell, or *Rider Mel's Mountain Bike Guide to Moab*. For bicycle shuttles, see p276.

Be sure to reserve rentals in advance. Full-suspension bikes start around $30 per day. **Rim Cyclery** (☎ 435-259-5333; www.rimcyclery.com; 94 W 100 North), Moab's longest-running shop, includes a museum of mountain-bike technology. Also consider **Moab Cyclery** (☎ 435-259-7423, 800-451-1133; www.moabcyclery.com; 391 S Main St;), **Poison Spider Bicycles** (☎ 435-259-7882, 800-635-1792; www.poisonspiderbicycles.com; 497 N Main St; ⏲ 8am-8pm spring & fall, shorter off-season) and **Chile Pepper Bike Shop** (☎ 435-259-4688, 888-677-4688; www.chilepepperbikeshop.com; 550-1/2 N Main St). Chile Pepper also does repairs.

Full-day tours (including rentals) start around $100. **Rim Tours** (☎ 435-259-5223, 800-626-7335; www.rimtours.com; 1233 S Hwy 191) leads half-, one- and multiday trips, as do **Escape Adventures** (☎ 435-259-7423, 800-451-1133; 391 S Main St; www.moabcyclery.com), **Nichols Expeditions** (☎ 435-259-3999, 800-648-8488; www.nicholsexpeditions.com; 497 N Main St) and **Western Spirit** (☎ 435-259-8732, 800-845-2453; www.westernspirit.com; 478 Mill Creek Dr). Diehards: ask about the Maze.

Road biking is also becoming popular; rent from Poison Spider.

RIVER RUNNING

Whatever your interest, be it bashing through rapids or studying canyon geology, rafting may prove the highlight of your vacation.

Rafting season runs from April to September; jet-boating season lasts longer. Water levels crest in May to June. Partial-day trips cost $35 to $50; full-day trips start at $125. Multiday excursions run $350 to $800. Jet-boat trips cost about $70. Kids cost less. Many outfitters combine rafting with hiking, 4WD or mountain-biking trips.

Day trips are often available on short notice, but book overnight trips well ahead. Know the boat you want. An oar rig is a rubber raft that a guide rows. A paddle boat is steered by the guide and paddled by passengers. Motor rigs are large boats driven by a guide (such as jet boats).

Do-it-yourselfers can rent canoes, inflatable kayaks or rafts. Canoes and kayaks run $30 to $40 per day, rafts $65 to $130 per day, depending on size. Advance permits are required for trips within the national parks and certain other areas.

Rapids are rated one (I) to six (VI), with Class I being still water and Class VI an unnavigable waterfall. Class II is good for

TOP FIVE MOUNTAIN-BIKING TRAILS

- Slickrock Trail – Moab's legendary trail will kick your ass! The 12.7-mile round-trip, half-day route is for experts only (as is the practice loop).
- Moonlight Meadow Trail – Beat the heat by ascending the La Sal Mountains to 10,600ft elevation for a moderate 10-mile loop, among aspens and pines (take it easy; you will get winded).
- Gemini Bridges – A moderate, full-day downhill ride past spectacular rock formations, this 13.5-mile one-way trail follows dirt, sand and slickrock.
- Klondike Bluffs Trail – Intermediates can learn to ride slickrock on this 15.6-mile round-trip trail, past dinosaur tracks to Arches National Park.
- Bar-M Loop – Bring the kids on this easy 8-mile loop skirting the boundary of Arches, with great views and short slickrock stretches.

families with tots. Class III is thrilling; Class IV is scary, depending on your perspective. Class V rapids are technical and dangerous.

Most rafting is on the **Colorado River**, northeast of town, including the Class-III-to-IV rapids of Westwater Canyon, near Colorado; the wildlife-rich 7-mile Class-I float from Dewey Bridge to Hittle Bottom (no permit required); and the Class I-to-II Moab Daily, the most popular stretch near town (no permit required; expect a short stretch of Class III rapids). South of town, below the Confluence, the Class V rapids of Cataract Canyon are legendary (NPS permit required).

The 68-to-124-mile Class-I float along the **Green River** is ideal for canoes and follow John Wesley Powell's 1869 route; start at Green River State Park (p265).

Guided Rafting

Outfitters take care of everything, from permits to food to setting up camp to transportation. It's impossible to say who's best, but **Canyon Voyages** (☎ 435-259-6007, 800-733-6007; www.canyonvoyages.com; 211 N Main St) and **OARS** (☎ 435-259-5919, 800-342-5938; www.oars.com; 2540 S Hwy 191) are great, as are **Sheri Griffith Expeditions** (☎ 435-259-8229, 800-332-2439; www.griffithexp.com; 2231 S Hwy 191) and **Adrift Adventures** (☎ 435-259-8594, 800-874-4483; www.adrift.net; 378 N Main St).

For large groups, call **Tag-A-Long Expeditions** (☎ 435-259-8946, 800-453-3292; www.tagalong.com; 452 N Main St), **Navtec Expeditions** (☎ 435-259-7983, 800-833-1278; www.navtec.com; 321 N Main St) or **Western River Expeditions** (☎ 435-259-7019, 888-622-4097; www.westernriver.com; 1371 N Hwy 191).

For educational trips, you can't beat **Canyonlands Field Institute** (☎ 435-259-7750, 800-860-5262; http://canyonlandsfieldinst.org; 1320 S Hwy 191). If you're disabled or traveling with someone with a physical or mental disability, book with **Splore** (☎ 801-484-4128; www.splore.org).

For canoe excursions, call the excellent **Red River Canoe** (☎ 435-259-7722, 800-753-8216; www.redrivercanoe.com; 1371 N Hwy 191).

For jet boat trips, call Adrift Adventures, Navtec or Tag-A-Long (above).

Without a Guide

Good outfitters will provide all information to help you plan a trip. Reserve equipment, permits and shuttles far in advance. Without permits, you'll be restricted to mellow

stretches of the Colorado and Green Rivers, but if you want to run Westwater Canyon or enter Canyonlands on either river, you'll need a permit. Contact the **BLM** (☎ 435-259-2100; www.blm.gov/utah/moab) or **NPS** (☎ 435-259-4351; www.nps.gov/cany/permits.htm). Strict rules govern sanitation and fires, depending on where you raft; confirm regulations.

To rent rafts, canoes and kayaks, contact **Canyon Voyages** (☎ 435-259-6007, 800-733-6007; www.canyonvoyages.com; 211 N Main St). For canoes, call **Red River Canoe** (☎ 435-259-7722, 800-753-8216; www.redrivercanoe.com; 1371 N Hwy 191) or **Tex's Riverways** (☎ 435-259-5101; www.texsriverways.com; 691 N 500 West).

See p276 for rafting shuttles.

HIKING

Carry lots of water and bug dope spring to early summer.

Contact **Hike Moab!** (☎ 435-260-8208; www.hikemoab.com) or **Moki Treks** (☎ 435-259-8033, 866-352-6654; www.mokitreks.com) for guided walks.

For overnight hikes, visit Canyonlands National Park (p279). Otherwise consider the brilliantly empty Dark Canyon Primitive Area (ask the BLM, p268).

For a moderate to difficult rim hike above Moab, try **Hidden Valley Trail**, which meanders through a pristine hanging valley. The trailhead is at the end of Angel Rock Rd. Above the switchbacks, you'll emerge in a grassy valley for a mellow 2-mile walk. Plan four to six hours.

To see petroglyphs and two spectacular arches, hike the moderately easy **Corona Arch Trail**; the trailhead is 6 miles up Potash Rd (p268). Follow cairns along slickrock to Bowtie and Corona Arches. You may recognize Corona from a well-known photograph in which an airplane is flying through it – this is one big arch! Plan two hours for the 3-mile walk.

The moderately easy **Negro Bill Canyon Trail** is a 2.5-mile walk along a stream. Scoot down a shaded side canyon to find petroglyphs, then continue to 243ft-wide Morning Glory Natural Bridge, at a box canyon. Plan three to four hours. The trailhead is at the BLM-information kiosk, 3 miles up Hwy 128, on the right.

The **Fisher Towers Trail** takes you past towering sandstone monoliths, the tallest 900ft. They get hot in the afternoon, so wait for sunset, when rays turn the rock orange and cast long shadows. (Caution: many hikers linger long and end up stuck in the dark. Bring a flashlight!) The moderate-to-difficult 2.2-mile (one-way) trail lies off Hwy 128, 21 miles northeast of Moab.

If you're short on time, take the easy 1-mile round-trip hike along **Moonflower Canyon**, a shaded stroll that ends at a sandstone bowl beneath hanging gardens. A perennial stream keeps dust down. The trailhead lies 1.2 miles along Kane Creek Blvd. Look for the petroglyphs.

To escape summer's heat, head to the **La Sal Mountains** east of Moab, and hike through white-barked aspens and Ponderosa pines. There are developed **campgrounds** along La Sal Mountain Loop Rd, including one at Warner Lake. Contact the Manti–La Sal National Forest rangers (p268).

FOUR-WHEEL DRIVING

Four-wheel driving is huge in Moab. If you go four-wheeling, stay on established routes. The desert looks barren, but it's a fragile landscape of complex ecosystems. Crypto-biotic soil crusts (p48) may take a century to regenerate after one tire track (really). You'll find plenty to keep you busy without off-roading.

For route details, visit the Moab Information Center (p268), ask a tour operator, or inquire at a rental agency.

For a guided two- to four-hour thrill ride up the slickrock in a Hummer, or to rent an ATV, call **Highpoint Hummer** (☎ 435-259-2972, 877-486-6833; www.highpointhummer.com; 281 N Main St; adult $65-89, child 39-55). Nobody knows the backcountry routes like **Dan Mick** (☎ 435-259-4567; www.danmick.com), but if you're a knee-jerk liberal, he'll push your buttons.

Several good companies lead 4WD and combination land/river trips.

Adrift Adventures (☎ 435-259-8594, 800-874-4483; www.adrift.net; 378 N Main St)

Canyon Voyages (☎ 435-259-6007, 800-733-6007; www.canyonvoyages.com; 211 N Main St)

OARS (☎ 435-259-5919, 800-342-5938; www.oars.com; 2540 S Hwy 191)

Navtec Expeditions (☎ 435-259-7983, 800-833-1278; www.navtec.com; 321 N Main St)

Tag-A-Long Expeditions (☎ 435-259-8946, 800-453-3292; www.tagalong.com; 452 N Main St)

If you rent a 4WD vehicle, read the insurance policy – it may not cover damage from off-roading and will likely carry a $2500 deductible. Whenever possible, rent a new vehicle. Reputable companies include **Farabee's** (☎ 435-259-7494, 888-806-5337; www.moab-utah.com/farabee; 401 N Main St) and **Cliffhanger Jeep Rental** (☎ 435-259-2599; www.moab-utah.com/cliffhanger; 1551 N Hwy 191).

Rent motorcycles from **Elite Motorcycle Tours** (☎ 435-259-7621, 888-778-0358; www.moab.net/elitetours; 1310 Murphy Lane).

ROCK CLIMBING & CANYONEERING

Moab has great **rock climbing**. West of town off Potash Rd, Wall Street (Moab's El Capitan) gets crowded; it's the spot to meet other climbers. Advanced climbers: check out the BLM-administered Indian Creek, off Hwy 211 on the way to Canyonlands' Needles.

For information and gear, the first choice is **Pagan Mountaineering** (☎ 435-259-1117; www.paganmountaineering.com; 59 S Main St, Suite 2), then **Gear Heads** (☎ 435-259-4327, 888-740-4327; www.gearheadsoutdoorstore.com; 471 S Main St; ⊗ 8:30am-10pm, shorter winter).

Rappel into canyons and hike through cascading water on a **canyoneering** expedition. Arguably the best, **Desert Highlights** (☎ 435-259-4433, 800-747-1342; www.deserthighlights.com; 50 E Center St; $80-120) leads outstanding trips to Arches' Fiery Furnace. For rock-climbing or canyoneering trips, call **Moab Desert Adventures** (☎ 435-260-2404, 877-765-6622; 801 Oak St; www.moabdesertadventures.com; trips $110-195). Also check out **Moab Cliffs & Canyons** (☎ 435-259-3317, 877-641-5271; www.cliffsandcanyons.com; 63 E Center St; guided rock climbing $90-190).

HORSEBACK RIDING

Rates generally range from $30 for two hours, $60 for half a day to $95 for a day (including lunch). If you want to combine riding and river-running, contact **Adrift Adventures** (☎ 435-259-8594, 800-874-4483; www.adrift.net; 378 N Main St), **Sheri Griffith Expeditions** (☎ 435-259-8229, 800-332-2439; www.griffithexp.com; 2231 S Hwy 191) or **Tag-A-Long Expeditions** (☎ 435-259-8946, 800-453-3292; www.tagalong.com; 452 N Main St).

Cowboy Adventures (☎ 435-259-7410; cowboyadventures@hotmail.com) leads trips year-round in the desert and La Sal Mountains; it also books horseback-rafting expeditions.

Red Cliffs Lodge (☎ 435-259-2002, 866-812-2002; www.redcliffslodge.com; mile marker 14, Hwy 128) guides half-day rides (March to November) around Castle Valley, north of town.

UTAH

WINTER ACTIVITIES

The La Sal Mountains, which lord over Moab, receive tons of powder, just perfect for cross-country skiing. For weather, road and avalanche-risk information, call ☎ 435-259-SNOW (435-259-7669) or visit www .avalanche.org.

The La Sals provide a hut-to-hut ski system, accessible also via snowmobile. To book the huts, contact **Tag-A-Long Expeditions** (☎ 435-259-8946, 800-453-3292; www.tagalong.com; 452 N Main St). **Rim Cyclery** (☎ 435-259-5333; 94 W 100 North; www.rimcyclery.com) rents equipment. **Gear Heads** (☎ 435-259-4327, 888-740-4327; www.gearheads outdoorstore.com; 471 S Main St; ☒ 8:30am-10pm, shorter in winter) rents snowshoes.

OTHER ACTIVITIES

Two companies run one-hour air tours ($99): **Slickrock Air Guides** (☎ 435-259-6216; www .slickrockairguides.com) and **Redtail Aviation** (☎ 435-259-7421; www.moab-utah.com/redtail).

Go skydiving or base-jumping with **Skydive Moab** (☎ 435-259-5867; www.skydivemoab.com; Canyonlands Field Airport; tandem jump $189-229).

The only red-rock disc golf (Frisbee) course in America, **Camelot Adventure Lodge** (☎ 435-260-1783; www.camelotlodge.com; per player $5) maintains an 18-hole, par-61 course over canyons, slickrock and cactus-strewn meadows; reservations essential. Call for directions.

The **Moab Golf Club** (☎ 435-259-6488; 2750 S E Bench Rd; 9/18 holes $25/37) has an 18-hole course.

Sleeping

Rates are for March to October. Some places close in winter.

Cyclists: ask whether a property provides *secure* bike storage, not just bike storage. Many rooms have refrigerators; some have microwaves. Also try **Moab Central Reservations** (☎ 435-259-5125, 800-748-4386).

BUDGET

Center Street Hotel (☎ 435-259-7615, 888-530-3134; http://moab-utah.com/hotel; 96 E Center St; s/d $35/39, ☒) Part hostel, part hotel, Center Street has rooms decorated in thrift-store chic, clean shared bathrooms and a kitchen. Great for long stays.

Kokopelli Lodge (☎ 435-259-7615, 888-530-3134; www.kokopellilodge.com; 72 S 100 East; d $56-63; ☒) Carefully tended, tiny old-fashioned motel. Hot tub and secure bike storage.

Inca Inn (☎ 435-259-7621; www.incainn.com; 570 N Main St; d $55; ☒) The service is good and the utilitarian rooms clean at this mom-and-pop motel.

Silver Sage Inn (☎ 435-259-4420, 888-774-6622; www.silversageinn.com; 840 S Main St; s/d $45/48) Clean and barebones.

Lazy Lizard Hostel (☎ 435-259-6057; www.lazy lizardhostel.com; 1213 S Hwy 191; dm/s/d/tr/q $9/22/24/ 30/36, cabins $35-47; ☒ ☐) Rough around the edges.

Up the Creek Campground (☎ 435-259-6995; www.moab-utah.com/upthecreek; 210 E 300 South; campsites per person $10) Twenty grassy tent-only, walk-in sites, showers included; walkable to downtown.

Canyonlands Campground (☎ 435-259-6848, 800-522-6848; www.canyonlandsrv.com; 555 S Main St; campsites $18, RV sites $25-27, cabins $35; ☒) Walkable from downtown; 140 shaded sites for tent or RV (with hookups); showers and swimming pool; camping cabins have aircon.

Slickrock Campground (☎ 435-259-7660, 800-448-8873; www.moab-utah.com/slickrock/campground .html; 1301-1/2 N Hwy 191; sites $18-22, cabins $30; ☒) A short drive to town; 200 shaded sites, RV hookups and dump station, camping cabins with air-conditioning, pool, hot tubs and groceries.

Hwy 128/River Rd BLM campgrounds (☎ 435-259-2100; www.blm.gov/utah/moab; Hwy 128; campsites $10) Vegetation and canyons provide shade at these 10 BLM campgrounds along a 28-mile stretch of the Colorado River. Each includes fire rings and vault toilets, but no water. No reservations. Bring bug dope.

Canyon Rims Recreation Area (☎ 435-259-2100; www.blm.gov/utah/moab; Hwy 191; campsites $10) Thirty miles south of town; two developed campgrounds with vegetation and well-spaced sites; water (March through October), fire rings and pit toilets. No reservations.

La Sal Mountains/Manti–La Sal National Forest (☎ 435-587-2041, 888-444-6777; www.fs.fed.us/r4 /mantilasal, www.reserveusa.com; off La Sal Mountain Loop Rd; campsites $8) Twenty to thirty degrees cooler than Moab; Warner Lake sits at 9400ft, one of several developed campgrounds with water.

Make reservations if possible. For more info, visit the **Moab Information Center** (p268), www.moab-utah.com or www.discover moab.com. **Canyon Voyages** (☎ 435-259-6007, 800-733-6007; www.canyonvoyages.com; 211 N Main St) rents gear; **Tag-A-Long Expeditions** (☎ 435-259-

8946, 800-453-3292; www.tagalong.com; 452 N Main St) rents tents and sleeping-bags.

MIDRANGE
Hotels
Caveat emptor: some of Moab's hotels are substandard. Stick to those listed here.

Adventure Inn (☎ 435-259-6122, 866-662-2466; www.adventureinnmoab.com; 512 N Main St; d $58-69; ☒) A great indie motel, it has clean rooms, decent linens and laundry facilities.

Red Stone Inn (☎ 435-259-3500, 800-772-1972; www.redstoneinn.com; 535 S Main St; d $55-70; ☎) The small pine-paneled rooms here are decorated with rustic wood furniture, lending a cozy feel to their otherwise utilitarian boxiness. Pets allowed.

Landmark Inn (☎ 435-259-6147, 800-441-6147; www.landmarkinnmoab.com; 168 N Main St; d $62-78; ☒ ☎) Kids love the waterslide at this motel, walkable to downtown. Rooms are scrupulously maintained and slightly kitsch. Amenities include great bathtubs and hot tub.

Big Horn Lodge (☎ 435-259-6171, 800-325-6171; www.moabbighorn.com; 550 S Main St; d $60-80; ☎) The old-fashioned knotty-pine paneling is at odds with the modern floor-to-ceiling black glass windows at this well-maintained motel on Main St, but service is great. Pets allowed.

Best Western Canyonlands Inn (☎ 435-259-2300, 800-528-1234; www.canyonlandsinn.com; 16 S Main St; d $100-110; ☎) At the crossroads of downtown, this well-maintained hotel has spacious rooms, expanded continental breakfast, hot tub and laundry. Don't confuse it with the Best Western Greenwell Inn across the street.

Holiday Inn Express (☎ 435-259-1150, 800-465-4229; www.hiexpress.com/moabut; 1653 Hwy 191 North; d $89-108; ☎) On the north end of Moab, this boxy prefab provides some of town's most comfortable midrange rooms, expanded continental breakfast and a hot tub.

Aarchway Inn (☎ 435-259-2599, 800-341-9359; www.aarchwayinn.com; 1551 Hwy 191 North; d $89-95; ☒ ☎) Another boxy prefab, the Aarchway has Moab's best pool. Rooms are spacious, but ho-hum looking; some accommodate six people. Amenities include kitchenettes, grills, fitness room and hot tub.

Also try:

Moab Valley Inn (☎ 435-259-4419; www.moabvalley inn.com; 711 S Main St; d $80-85; ☎)

Bowen Motel (☎ 435-259-7132, 435-874-5439; www.bowenmotel.com; 169 N Main St; d $60-80; ☒ ☎)

Red Rock Lodge & Suites (☎ 435-259-5431, 877-207-9708; www.red-rocklodge.com; 51 N 100 West; d $55-85; ☒)

B&Bs
Castle Valley Inn (☎ 435-259-6012; www.castlevalley inn.com; La Sal Mountain Loop Rd; r $95-125, bungalow $160-175; ☒) Moab's top midrange B&B lies 15 miles northwest of downtown. Choose a standard room or a freestanding bungalow with kitchen. The setting is idyllic, the reception warm and the style relaxed. Breakfasts include fruit picked fresh from on-site trees. Hot tub.

Cali Cochitta (☎ 435-259-4961, 888-429-8812; www.moabdreaminn.com; 110 S 200 East; r $95-125; ☒) The cozy rooms at this charming brick B&B are decorated with antiques. The innkeepers live off-site.

Dream Keeper Inn (☎ 435-259-5998, 888-230-3247; www.dreamkeeperinn.com; 191 S 200 East; r $100-125, cottage $145; ☒ ☎) This immaculate one-story midcentury-ranch-house B&B is surrounded by lush lawns. For more privacy book a cottage. Hot tub.

Other midrange B&Bs:

Adobe Abode (☎ 435-259-7716; www.adobeabode moab.com; 778 W Kane Creek Blvd; r $89-109; ☒) Southwestern-style.

Mayor's House (☎ 435-259-6015, 888-791-2345; www.mayorshouse.com; 505 Rose Tree Lane; r $80-130; ☒)

TOP END
Camelot Adventure Lodge (☎ 435-260-1783; www.camelotlodge.com; per person $125-145; ☒) On 50 rugged riverside acres beneath Hurrah Pass, the five-room Camelot is a bona fide backcountry lodge, unlike any place else. The only way here is via 4WD or boat. Ride camels, play disc golf, hike and mountain bike without driving anywhere. Leave your high heels at home. Rates include three down-home meals (BYOB). It's an unforgettable retreat for athletically inclined friends. Stay at least two nights.

Gonzo Inn (☎ 435-259-2515, 800-791-4044; www.gonzoinn.com; 100 W 200 South; d $129; ☒ ☎) Smack downtown, Moab's hippest hotel features such stylized furnishings like brushed-metal-and-wood headboards, concrete shower stalls and '50s-retro patio furniture. Laundry facilities and hot tub. Pets are OK.

UTAH

Sunflower Hill (☎ 435-259-2974, 800-662-2786; www.sunflowerhill.com; 185 N 300 East; r $125-175; ✗) The top choice for an in-town B&B, Sunflower Hill has rooms in two inviting buildings – an early-20th-century home and a 100-year-old farmhouse, both surrounded by manicured gardens. The 12 rooms range from dressed-down country to sophisticated elegance. Hot tub.

Pack Creek Ranch (☎ 435-259-5505; www.pack creekranch.com; cabins $95-225; ✗ 🐾) It used to be a wonderful resort, but its cottages have been sold off piecemeal. Still, the 11 log cabins at this little Shangri-La in the mountains are worth investigating. Bring groceries. Hot tub.

Red Cliffs Lodge (☎ 435-259-2002, 866-812-2002; www.redcliffslodge.com; Hwy 128; r $129-169; ✗ 🐾) Part dude ranch, part luxury motel, Red Cliffs (at mile marker 14) has exceptionally comfy rooms with vaulted ceilings, kitchenettes and private patios, some overlooking the river. It's perfect for families; some rooms sleep six. Hot tub.

Sorrel River Ranch (☎ 435-259-4642, 877-359-2715; www.sorrelriver.com; Hwy 128; d $209-239, ste 269-329; ✗ 🖳 🐾) Southeast Utah's only full-service luxury resort sits smack on the Colorado River (mile marker 17). Every in-room detail is perfect, from handmade log beds to custom-crafted lighting. There's an on-site spa, fitness center, salon and hot tub, kitchenettes and horseback riding. Families are welcome.

Eating

Many of Moab's restaurants close in winter; call ahead.

BUDGET

Jailhouse Café (☎ 435-259-3900; 101 N Main St; dishes $5-7; ⊙ 7am-noon) Moab's top breakfast spot serves fluffy omelets and delicious Benedicts. Expect a wait.

Moab Diner (☎ 435-259-4006; 189 S Main St; breakfast $5-7, dinner $7-15; ⊙ 6am-9pm) The diner has the fastest service in town, serving classic greasy-spoon fare. Great breakfasts.

EklectiCafé (☎ 435-259-6896; 352 N Main St; dishes $5-7; ⊙ breakfast & lunch year-round, dinner Sat & Sun summer) Sit outside at this homey café with a grown-up hippie feel that serves organic coffee, granola, quiche and salads.

Peace Tree Café (☎ 435-259-8503; 20 S Main St; dishes $4-6; ⊙ 8am-6pm) Sit outside and people-watch while savoring great salads, wraps and fresh-squeezed juice.

Red Rock Bakery & Internet Café (☎ 435-259-5941; sandwiches $4-6; ⊙ 7am-6pm) Come for real bagels and organic coffee, check your email and order a fat sandwich on homemade bread to take hiking.

Milt's (☎ 435-259-7424; 300 South at 400 East; ⊙ 6am-8pm Mon-Sat) Pull up a stool at this tiny 50-year-old diner for scratch pancakes, chile cheeseburgers, fries and milkshakes.

Bandito's (☎ 435-259-3894; 467 N Main St; burritos $5-8; ⊙ 11am-7pm) Head here for the fattest burritos.

MIDRANGE

The following have full bars. Some close in winter.

Buck's Grill House (☎ 435-259-5201; 1393 N Hwy 191; mains $9-24; ⊙ dinner) The best in its class, Buck's serves good steaks and Southwestern specialties like duck tamales, buffalo meatloaf and elk stew. Portions are huge, and they make good burgers. There's also a kids' menu.

Eddie McStiff's (☎ 435-259-2337; 59 S Main St; dishes $7-15; ⊙ 5:30pm-midnight Mon-Fri, 11:30am-midnight Sat & Sun) Moab's biggest restaurant has pizza, steaks, pastas, salads, burgers and bar food. Eddie McStiff's also brews tasty microbrews.

Fat City Smokehouse (☎ 435-259-4302; 100 W Center St; dishes $11-18; ⊙ 11am-9:30pm) Behind Club Rio, Fat City serves big plates of Texas-style barbecue and great beef tri-tip (a boneless cut of bottom sirloin steak). Caveat: smoke from the bar wafts into the dining room.

La Hacienda (☎ 435-259-6319; 574 N Main St; dishes $6-14; ⊙ 11am-10pm) For big plates of straightforward Tex-Mex, 'La Ha' is Moab's long-running favorite. Try the sour-cream sauce.

Moab Brewery (☎ 435-259-6333; 686 S Main St; dishes $6-15; ⊙ 11:30am-10pm) Serving frosty mugs of house microbrews and everything from tri-tip to tacos and stir-fry to salads, the cavernous brewery is good for families with kids and groups with diverse tastes.

Miguel's Baja Grill (☎ 435-259-6546; 51 N Main St; dishes $8-12; ⊙ 5-10pm) Miguel's makes great fish tacos like in Baja – good margaritas too.

Slickrock Café (☎ 435-259-8004; cnr Center & Main Sts; dishes $6-17; ⊙ 8am-10pm) At the crossroads of town Slickrock serves three meals a day.

Sit near the windows to people-watch. The vaguely Southwestern menu lists everything from sandwiches to steaks.

Red Cliffs Lodge (☎ 435-259-2002; mile marker 14, Hwy 128; dinner mains $12-24) Every table has a stunning view of red-rock buttes and the mighty Colorado. The Western-style dinner menu includes prime rib and steaks; lunch features salads and sandwiches. In nice weather sit outside. Come before sunset.

Sunset Grill (☎ 435-259-7146; 900 N Hwy 191; mains $13-21; ❧ dinner Mon-Sat) On a hill over-looking Moab, the Sunset serves straight-forward shrimp cocktail and filet mignon; the view is the draw.

TOP END

Make reservations.

Desert Bistro (☎ 435-259-0756; 92 E Center St; mains $16-29; ❧ dinner) Stylized preparations of game are the specialty at this convivial white-tablecloth restaurant, where every-thing is made in-house. Service is attentive, and there's a great wine list.

River Grill (☎ 435-259-4642; Sorrel River Ranch, Hwy 128; dinner mains $21-30) Sit on the veranda and watch the sunset over red-rock canyons at Moab's only luxury resort (at mile marker 17). The New American–menu changes frequently based on seasonal ingredients, but expect delicious steak, succulent rack of lamb and fresh seafood from the coast. Come before sunset.

GROCERIES

Moab's big grocery store is **City Market & Pharmacy** (☎ 435-259-5181; 425 S Main St; ❧ 6am-midnight, shorter in winter). For health food, visit the non-profit **Moonflower Market** (☎ 435-259-

---

AUTHOR'S CHOICE

Center Café (☎ 435-259-4295; 60 N 100 West; mains $16-28; bistro dishes $6-11; ❧ dinner) Hands down southern Utah's best restau-rant, the Center Café is what you'd expect of Mendocino, not Moab. The chef-owner cooks with confident style, drawing inspi-ration from regional American and Medi-terranean cuisine: there's everything from grilled prawns with cheddar-garlic grits to pan-roasted lamb with balsamic-port reduc-tion. Desserts are superb. Budgeteers: see the bistro menu.

5712; 39 E 100 North; ❧ 9am-8pm Mon-Sat, 10am-3pm Sun). There's a **farmers' market** (400 N 100 West; ❧ 8am-11:30am Sat May-Oct) at Swanny City Park.

Festivals & Events

Moab loves a party. For calendars, contact the **Travel Council** (☎ 435-259-8825, 800-635-6622; www.discovermoab.com).

Jeep Safari (www.rr4w.com) The week before Easter, more than 2000 4WD vehicles overrun town for this, the year's biggest event.

Skinny Tire Festival (☎ 435-259-2698; www.skinny tirefestival.com) Road cycling in spring.

Moab Arts Festival (www.moabartsfestival.org) May.

Canyonlands Rodeo (☎ 435-259-7089) June.

Moonshadows in Moab (☎ 435-259-2698; www .moonshadowsinmoab.com) Bike riding by moonlight; July.

Grand County Fair (☎ 435-259-5386) August/September.

Rumble in the Red Rocks Motocross (☎ 435-259-7814; www.racemoab.com) Motocrossers rev up in September.

Moab Music Festival (☎ 435-259-7003; www.moab musicfest.org) Featuring chamber music; September.

24 Hours of Moab Mountain Bike Race (☎ 435-259-5533; www.grannygear.com) Mountain biking post–Labor Day.

Moab Century Tour (☎ 435-259-2698; www.skinny tirefestival.com) Road bikes tour; October.

Gem & Mineral Show (☎ 304-259-2762; www .geocities.com/moabrockclub) October.

Moab Fat Tire Festival (☎ 435-260-1182; www .moabfattirefest.com) One of Utah's biggest biking events with tours, workshops, lessons, competitions and plenty of music; October.

Moab Folk Festival (☎ 435-260-2488; www.moabfolk festival.com) November.

Drinking & Entertainment

Moab has lots of bars. Hear live music on Friday and Saturday or sing karaoke on weeknights at raucous **Club Rio** (☎ 435-259-6666; 100 W Center St). Frat boys shoot pool at **Zax** (☎ 435-259-6555; 96 S Main St). Rough-cut drink-ers go to **Woody's Tavern** (☎ 435-259-9323; 221 S Main St). Chugalug pitchers at **Eddie McStiff's** (opposite) or **Moab Brewery** (opposite); both also serve good bar food.

Unlike many places in Utah, you can get good coffee in Moab. Get the skinny from locals along with great shade-grown espresso at **Dave's Corner Market** (☎ 435-259-6999; 401 Mill Creek Dr; ❧ 6am-10pm), owned by the mayor.

UTAH

At **Mondo Café** (☎ 435-259-5551; McStiff's Plaza, 59 S Main St; ☑ 6:30am-7pm) you can get jacked on caffeine, check email, then play Hacky Sack with the dudes.

The **Moab Arts & Recreation Center** (☎ 435-259-6272; www.moabcity.state.ut.us/marc; 111 E 100 North) holds everything from yoga to special events. Kids love **Butch Cassidy's King World Water Park** (☎ 435-259-2837; www.butchcassidyskingworldwaterpark.com; 1500 N Hwy 191).

Great fun for kids and grandparents, **Canyonlands by Night & Day** (☎ 435-259-2628, 800-394-9978; www.canyonlandsbynight.com; 1861 N Hwy 191, north of the river bridge; adult with/without dinner $44/34, child $32/26; ☑ Apr-Oct) runs a two-hour sunset boat trip on the Colorado (lighting the canyon walls), with an optional barbecue beforehand.

For unapologetic tourist fun, **Bar-M Chuck wagon** (☎ 435-259-2276, 800-214-2085; www.barmchuckwagon.com; Hwy 191; adult/child $23/12; ☑ Apr-Oct), 7 miles north of Moab, starts with a gunfight in the faux-Western town, followed by a cowboy dinner and Western-music show. Reservations recommended.

See movies at **Slickrock Cinemas 3** (☎ 435-259-4441; 580 Kane Creek Blvd).

Shopping

For camping gear, visit **Gear Heads** (☎ 435-259-4327, 888-740-4327; 471 S Main St; ☑ 8:30am-10pm, shorter winter).

Of the Native American crafts and galleries, the best are the **Hogan Trading Company** (☎ 435-259-8118; 100 S Main St; ☑ 9am-10pm, shorter winter) and **Lema's Kokopelli Gallery** (☎ 435-259-5055; 70 N Main St; ☑ 9am-10pm, shorter winter).

The **Moab Rock Shop** (☎ 435-259-7312; 600 N Main St) is a rock hound's paradise.

For some no-frills wine tasting, visit surprisingly good **Spanish Valley Winery** (☎ 435-259-8134; www.moab-utah.com/spanishvalleywinery; ☑ noon-7pm Mon-Sat, shorter winter); call for directions. Also worth a look, the **Castle Creek Winery** at Red Cliffs Lodge (p274).

Getting There & Around

Moab is 235 miles (4½ hours) from SLC via I-15, US Hwy 6 and US Hwy 191.

Salmon Air (☎ 800-448-3413, 435-259-0566; www.salmonair.com) flies from SLC to **Canyonlands Airport** (CNY; ☎ 435-259-7421; www.moabairport.com), 16 miles north of town, via Hwy 191. Alternatively, fly to Grand Junction, Colorado (115 miles northeast).

Bighorn Express (☎ 888-655-7433; www.bighornexpress.com) operates a scheduled van service to and from SLC. **Roadrunner Shuttle** (☎ 435-259-9402; www.roadrunnershuttle.com) operates on-demand service.

Greyhound (☎ 435-564-3421, 800-229-9424; www.greyhound.com) and **Amtrak** (☎ 435-872-7245, 800-872-7245; www.amtrak.com) serve Green River (p264), 53 miles northwest of Moab. From there, ride Roadrunner Shuttle or Bighorn Express.

For hiker-biker shuttles, contact **Acme Bike Shuttle** (☎ 435-260-2534); **Atomic Transfer** (☎ 435-259-6475); **Coyote Shuttle** (☎ 435-259-8656); or **Roadrunner Shuttle** (☎ 435-259-9402).

For rafting shuttles, call Roadrunner Shuttle, Acme Bike Shuttle, Coyote Shuttle or **River Runner Shuttle** (☎ 435-259-3512, 800-241-2591; www.rr-ss.com; 3885 Spanish Valley Dr). Roadrunner and River Runner provide the best long-distance service. To get from the Confluence, you must book a jet-boat shuttle in advance. Two companies book permits: Tex's Riverways (p270) and Tag-A-Long Expeditions (p270). Slickrock Air Guides (p272) and Redtail Aviation (p272) operate air shuttles for river trips.

ARCHES NATIONAL PARK

Giant windows and sweeping arcs of chunky sandstone frame snowy peaks and desert landscapes at Arches National Park. The park boasts the highest density of rock arches anywhere on earth – more than 2500 in a 116-sq-mile area. An easy drive (some say too easy) makes the most spectacular arches accessible to all.

You'll lose perspective on size, especially at the thin and graceful Landscape Arch, which stretches more than 300ft across; it's one of the largest in the world. Others are tiny – the smallest only 3ft across – but once you train your eye, you'll spot them everywhere, like in a game of 'Where's Waldo?' Arches are forever in flux, and eventually all break and disappear. The same forces of erosion that create them also cause their demise.

As you stroll beneath these monuments to nature's power, listen carefully, especially in winter, and you may hear spontaneous popping noises in distant rocks – it's the sound of arches forming. (If you hear popping noises *overhead*, however, run like the dickens!)

UTAH

Orientation & Information

Enter off Hwy 191, 5 miles north of Moab. Admission is $10 per car, or $5 by motorcycle, bicycle or on foot.

Crowds are often unavoidable, and parking areas overflow on weekends, spring to fall. The NPS may eventually institute a shuttle. For now, to keep drivers from parking in dangerous or sensitive areas, rangers have stepped up ticketing for illegally parked cars.

Arrive by 9am, when crowds are sparse and temperatures bearable; or visit after 7pm. If you can't find parking, continue to the next viewpoint. Drive carefully; accidents occur when drivers focus on the scenery, not the road.

There is no food in the park. For services, drive to Moab (p265).

Stop first at the **visitor center** (☎ 435-719-2299; www.nps.gov/arch; ☉ 8am-4:30pm, longer spring-fall) for schedules on ranger-led activities, books, maps and tickets for the Fiery Furnace hike (p278).

To buy books about the area in advance, contact the **Canyonlands Natural History Association** (☎ 435-259-6003, 800-840-8978; www.cnha.org; 3031 S Hwy 191, Moab UT 84532).

In emergency, dial ☎ 911 or contact **Grand County Emergency Coordinator** (☎ 435-259-8115). For medical services, see p266.

July highs average 100°F; carry at least one gallon of water per person.

Sights & Activities

SCENIC DRIVES

There's one main road, with two short spurs that lead to more major sights. The most popular stops lie closest to the visitor center. If you're tight on time, visit the **Windows Section**, off the first spur.

ARCHES AND BRIDGES

What's the difference between an arch and a bridge? Both form through erosion of sandstone. An arch forms when water freezes and expands in cracks, causing portions of the rock to break away. A bridge forms when water passes beneath sandstone, causing its erosion. But rivers dry up or change course, and it can sometimes become difficult to tell a bridge from an arch.

The park includes three unpaved roads. **Salt Valley Rd** is generally accessible to conventional vehicles (but not when wet). It leaves the main road a mile before Devils Garden and heads 9 miles west to **Klondike Bluffs**. You'll get away from the crowds, but you won't be alone. A moderate to difficult 3-mile round-trip hike leads to **Tower Arch**.

From Klondike Bluffs, an unnamed, 10-mile 4WD dirt road doubles back to the scenic drive at Balanced Rock. Drive north to south (the northbound route tackles a steep and sandy climb that may be impassable).

From Balanced Rock, **Willow Flats Rd** leads west 8 miles to Hwy 191. Formerly the main route into the park, it requires a high-clearance or 4WD vehicle. The road doesn't offer any important features, just distant views and solitude.

Check with rangers about up-to-date road conditions.

HIKING & BACKPACKING

Many short hikes originate near the main park road. Just over 2 miles from the entrance is **Park Avenue**, a mile-long trail past a

TOP FIVE PHOTO OPS

The light is best in the early morning and late afternoon. For a good shot, place something in the foreground, middle ground, and background. Consider *not* centering the subject.

■ Delicate Arch – You may not know till you're looking at it, but you've seen it in ads for years. Now take your own shot of the park's signature arch. Best in the morning.

■ North and South Windows – The two arches are part of one continuous wall; step back just far enough to frame them both.

■ Courthouse Towers – You might recognize these giant towers from the movie *Thelma and Louise*, the part where they locked the cop in the trunk.

■ Balanced Rock – To capture the giant boulder atop its spindly pedestal, get back just far enough to fill the frame, leaving a bit of sky above.

■ Double Arch – Head to the Windows Section when the sky is deep blue, and frame the twin spans so that you get three distinct areas of blue between the arcing rock.

giant fin of rock reminiscent of a New York skyscraper. The trail emerges 1.4 miles up the road at Courthouse Towers Viewpoint.

The gravity-defying **Balanced Rock** is accessible via a 0.3-mile-loop trail; the 3577-ton boulder sits atop a spindly pedestal, like a fist shooting out of the earth.

The Windows Section has stunning arches. The 0.6-mile-round-trip **Windows Trail** brings you smack dab to North and South Windows. If you see only one, stand beneath North Window; the views are awesome!

Sand Dune Arch and **Broken Arch** share the same trailhead. Both are moderately easy walks; kids love running through the sand to Sand Dune Arch (0.4-mile round-trip). Walk across grassland for 1 mile to reach 60ft Broken Arch.

The park's most famous hike is **Delicate Arch Trail**. About 2.5 miles beyond Balanced Rock, a spur road leads 2 miles to **Wolfe Ranch**, a well-preserved 1908 pioneer cabin.

A footbridge crosses Salt Wash (near Indian rock art) and marks the beginning of the moderate trail. The trail ascends slickrock, culminating in a wall-hugging ledge to Delicate Arch, one of the most famous in the world and well worth the 3-mile-round-trip hike. Views of the La Sal Mountains are fantastic. Tip: ditch the crowds by passing beneath the arch and dropping down the other side several yards; bring a picnic.

Nineteen miles from the visitor center, at the end of the paved road, **Devils Garden** marks the beginning of several hikes, from 2- to 7-miles round-trip, that pass nearly a dozen arches. The easy, 2-mile round-trip to **Landscape Arch** gets busy, but ahead, the trail gets less crowded and grows rougher.

Fiery Furnace is a maze of spectacularly narrow canyons and giant fins, accessible on a guided hike or by permit. Buy tickets in person (adult $8, child $4) at the visitor center. Reserve up to seven days in advance for the two- to three-hour walks, offered morning and afternoon, April to October. Hikes fill two days ahead. If you're an accomplished hiker and want to go it alone, you must pay a fee, watch a video and discuss with rangers how to negotiate this confusing jumble of canyons before they'll grant you a permit.

Backpacking isn't popular here, but if you're determined get a backcountry permit, available in person from the visitor center. There are neither trails nor campsites. Due to the fragility of cryptobiotic crusts (p48), the park discourages backcountry treks. The closest you'll come is the **Devils Garden Primitive Loop**. Check with rangers.

ROCK CLIMBING

Rock climbing is allowed only on unnamed features. Routes require advanced techniques. No permits are necessary. Ask about current regulations and route closures. For guided canyoneering into the Fiery Furnace, contact **Desert Highlights** (p271).

Sleeping & Eating

Devils Garden Campground (☎ 877-444-6777, 518-885-3639; www.reserveusa.com) The park's only campground sits 18 miles from the visitor center. Amenities include water, picnic tables, grills and toilets, but no showers. From March to October, half the sites are available by reservation only; for same-day availability, check at the visitor center, not the campground.

There's no place to eat in Arches, but it's only 10 minutes up the road from Moab. Pack a picnic lunch (see p275).

CANYONLANDS NATIONAL PARK

Vast serpentine canyons tipped with white cliffs loom high over the Colorado and Green Rivers, their waters a stunning 1000ft below the rim rock. Sweeping arches, skyward-jutting needles and spires, deep craters, blue-hued mesas and majestic buttes define the landscape. Canyonlands is Utah's largest, most rugged national park, a crumbling beauty, a 527-sq-mile vision of ancient earth.

For more than a casual day trip to the overlooks, you must be self-sufficient. Discounting the inaccessible rivers, most areas are completely waterless, including visitor centers (which sell bottled water) and campgrounds (only one of which has water in summer). Dirt roads are difficult to navigate, distances great, the summer heat brutal and many trails are steep. It's not hard to understand why, despite its beauty, this is the least visited of all the major Southwestern national parks.

Orientation

The Colorado and Green Rivers divide the park into three completely separate districts. The river canyons form a Y – the

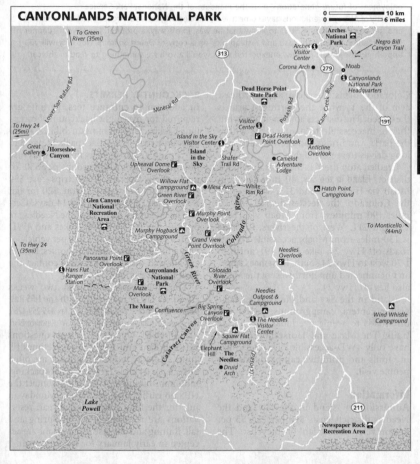

CANYONLANDS NATIONAL PARK

UTAH

THE BARD OF MOAB

Edward Abbey (1927–89), one of America's great Western prose writers, worked as a seasonal ranger at Arches National Monument in the 1950s, before it became a national park. In his essay collection, *Desert Solitaire: A Season in the Wilderness*, Abbey wrote of his time here and describes the simple beauty and subtle power of the vast landscape. In perhaps the book's most famous essay, he bemoaned what he dubbed 'Industrial Tourism,' the exploitation of the natural environment by big business acting in cahoots with government, turning the National Monument into a 'Natural Money-Mint.'

At the core of the problem: the automobile industry and its paving of the wilderness. Abbey believed passionately in the holiness of the land and felt that tourists who never got out of their cars ('upholstered mechanized wheelchairs') were robbing themselves of the chance to transcend the mundane, to experience the sanctity of the land and, in so doing, to liberate their consciousness. But some blame Abbey for contributing to the very thing he decried: by so unerringly evoking in his writing the stark beauty of life in the canyonlands of southern Utah, Abbey inadvertently helped attract to the Southwest thousands of people seeking that very remoteness he described. Nonetheless, his polemic lays out a clear, viable plan for ridding the parks of vehicles, which would make plenty of room for everyone and leave the parks 'unimpaired for the enjoyment of future generations' as is the mandate of the National Park Service.

Many of Abbey's predictions have come true – you need only arrive at Arches on a busy weekend and get stuck in a line of SUVs to know that he was, in his way, a prophet. Leave your summer beach reading in your suitcase and instead pick up a copy of *Desert Solitaire*. Not only will you apprehend the desert in new, unexpected ways, you'll also have something to read in the car.

Colorado forms the stem and northeast arm of the Y, while the northwest arm is the Green. The districts abut each other, but they're inaccessible to one another within the park – no bridges and few roads mean long drives to see the sights.

Cradled atop the Y is the most developed district, **Island in the Sky**, 40 minutes from Moab via Hwys 191 and 313. Southeast of the Colorado, the **Needles** district lies 75 miles (90 minutes) from Moab via Hwys 191 and 211. West of the rivers, the **Maze** is 130 miles from Moab, accessible via dirt roads off Hwy 24; take Hwy 191 north to I-70 west to Hwy 24 south. **Horseshoe Canyon**, an unconnected unit northwest of the Maze, also lies off Hwy 24.

Island in the Sky and the Needles have visitor centers, campgrounds, paved and dirt roads to scenic overlooks and hiking trails. The Maze and Horseshoe Canyon have only 4WD-accessible dirt roads, hiking trails and primitive campgrounds; few people visit.

Information

Admission to Island in the Sky and the Needles districts costs $10 per car, $5 per motorcycle, pedestrian or bicyclist. The Maze is free.

BACKCOUNTRY PERMITS

In addition to entrance fees, permits are required for overnight backcountry camping, backpacking, mountain biking, 4WD trips and river trips. Backpackers pay $15 per group (call for size limits). Day-use mountain bike or 4WD groups pay $30 for up to three vehicles. River trips cost $30 per group in Cataract Canyon, $20 for flat water trips. Permits are valid 14 days. Certain backcountry sections of the Needles are open to day use by horses, bikes and 4WD vehicles; permits cost $5 a day per vehicle or group of up to seven bikes or horses. Horses are allowed on all 4WD trails; contact the park for restrictions.

You must reserve at least two weeks ahead, by fax or mail only, with the **NPS Reservations Office** (☎ 435-259-4351, fax 435-259-4285; www.nps.gov/cany/permits.htm; 2282 SW Resource Blvd, Moab, UT 84532). Operators answer questions between 8am and 12:30pm (sometimes till 4pm), Monday to Friday (phones are often busy; keep trying). To reserve backpacking, mountain-biking or 4WD trips, contact the NPS no earlier than the second Monday in July for the following calendar year; reservations are recommended for spring and fall. Rafting and day-use reservations are accepted in early January for the same year.

Without reservations, you can get permits on a space-available basis the day before or the day of your trip from the visitor center in the district where your trip begins. Though you can call ahead to check availability, phone reservations aren't accepted.

EMERGENCY & MEDICAL SERVICES

Cell phones work up high, but only satellite phones work in canyons. Dial ☎ 911 in emergency. For search and rescue, contact **Grand County Emergency Coordinator** (☎ 435-259-8115). For medical services, see p266.

REGULATIONS

Four-wheel-drive vehicles, mountain bikes and street-legal motorbikes are permitted on dirt roads, but no ATVs. In the backcountry, campfires are allowed only along river corridors; use a fire pan, burn only driftwood or downed tamarisk, and pack out unburnt debris. Rock climbing is allowed (no permit needed), but under specific regulations; ask rangers.

TOURIST INFORMATION

Canyonlands Natural History Association (☎ 435-259-6003, 800-840-8978; www.cnha.org) Sells books for the NPS; operates from the Moab Information Center.
Canyonlands NPS Headquarters (☎ 435-259-7164, 435-719-2313; www.nps.gov/cany) For information only.
Island in the Sky Visitor Center (☎ 435-259-4712; www.nps.gov/cany/island; Hwy 313; ☼ 8am-4:30pm, longer spring-fall) Features exhibits, an excellent introductory video, books, maps, activities schedules, and permit and campground information.
Moab Information Center (p268) Get maps, books and information here.
Needles Visitor Center (☎ 435-259-4711; www.nps .gov/cany/needles; Hwy 211; ☼ 8am-4:30pm, extended Mar-Oct) Does the same as the Island in the Sky Visitor Center.
Ranger station (☎ 435-259-2652; www.nps.gov/cany /maze; Hans Flat Rd; ☼ 8am-4:30pm) At Hans Flat, three to six hours west of the Maze, with books and maps, but no other services.

Sights & Activities

For details about rafting, kayaking and canoeing the Green and Colorado Rivers, see p269.

Rock-climbing is allowed, but not in Horseshoe Canyon, on any archaeological site or on any feature marked on USGS maps, except Washerwoman Arch. All climbing must be free or clean-aid climbing. The Needles' soft rock is unsuitable for climbing. Check with rangers.

ISLAND IN THE SKY

You'll apprehend space in new ways atop the appropriately named Island in the Sky, a narrow, 6000ft-high flat-topped mesa that drops precipitously on all sides, providing some of the longest, most enthralling vistas of any park in southern Utah. The panoramic views are bookended in the west by the 11,500ft Henry Mountains, and in the east by the sky-punching 12,700ft La Sal Mountains, both still capped with snow in early summer. You can stand beneath a sparkling-blue sky and watch multiple thunderheads, miles apart, inundating far-off regions with gunmetal-grey sheets of rain, while you contemplate applying more sunscreen.

This is the most easily accessible and popular district of Canyonlands NP, welcoming 260,000 visitors a year. The island sits atop a sandstone bench called the **White Rim**, which indeed forms a white border 1200ft below the mesa top. Cliffs below the rim drop another 1500ft into the river canyons.

The Island in the Sky Visitor Center (left) sits 2 miles beyond the entrance station. From the visitor center, the road heads 12 miles to Grand View Point. Halfway there, a paved spur leads northwest 5 miles to Upheaval Dome. Overlooks and trails line each road.

Bring water – Island in the Sky lacks any water sources. And if one of those spectacular thunderheads comes your way, get in your car or seek shelter immediately.

Hiking & Backpacking

Most trails follow cairns (piles of rocks) over slickrock. Watch for cliff edges!

Several easy trails pack a lot of punch. The **Mesa Arch Nature Trail**, an easy half-mile loop, passes Mesa Arch, dramatically hung over the very edge of the rim; come at sunrise, when the arch's underside glows fiery red. A mile before Grand View Point, the **White Rim Overlook Trail** is a good spot for a picnic and an easy, 1.8-mile round-trip hike. At the end of the road, the **Grand View Trail** follows a 2-mile round-trip course at the edge of the rim. The latter two trails provide some of the best views in the park; even if you don't hike, Grand View Point Overlook is a must-see.

At **Upheaval Dome**, an easy half-mile spur leads to an overlook at one of the park's geological wonders, possibly the site of a meteorite strike 60 million years ago. Back near the 'Y' in the road, the moderate 2-mile round-trip **Aztec Butte Trail** climbs slickrock for stellar views and an ancient granary.

Longer hikes off the mesa to the White Rim are strenuous, steep and require advance planning. Choose from seven trails; ask rangers. There's one major backpacking route, the **Syncline Loop** (8.3 miles, five to seven hours). However, in summer the exposed trail gets blazingly hot. Most park rescues occur here, because day hikers underestimate the route, get turned around and/or run out of water. Talk to rangers before setting out. The park issues one permit a day for the **Murphy Hogback** campsite. An easy flat hike across grasslands takes you to this solo site with stunning views.

Four-Wheel Driving & Mountain Biking
Blazed by uranium prospectors in the 1950s, primitive **White Rim Rd** circles Island in the Sky. Accessible from the visitor center via Shafer Trail Rd, this 70-mile route is the top choice for 4WD and mountain-biking trips. It generally takes two to three days in a 4WD vehicle, or three to four days by bike. Since the route lacks any water sources, bicyclists should team up with a 4WD support vehicle or travel with an outfitter (see p269).

The NPS limits the number of vehicles. If you haven't got a permit, call the visitor center about cancellations. Rangers patrol the route and provide help in a pinch; they also check permits. Stay on trails.

Pick up *A Naturalist's Guide to the White Rim Trail* by David Williams and Damian Fagon.

THE NEEDLES
Named for its spires of orange-and-white sandstone jutting skyward from the desert floor, the Needles District's otherworldly terrain is so different from Island in the Sky, it's hard to believe they're part of the same park. Despite paved access roads, only half as many people come here as the Island. Why? It takes 90 minutes to drive

from Moab, and once you arrive, you have to work harder to appreciate the wonders – in short, you have to get out of the car and walk. But expend a little energy, and the payoff is huge: peaceful solitude and the opportunity to participate in, not just observe, the vastness of canyon country.

The Needles Visitor Center (p281) lies 2.5 miles inside park boundaries and provides drinking water. (If you've visited Island in the Sky, bring your receipt to avoid paying again.) If you have kids, ask about renting a Discovery Pack, which contains binoculars, magnifying lens and nature guide. From the visitor center, the paved road continues almost 7 miles to the **Big Spring Canyon Overlook**. Parking areas along the way access several sights, including arches, Ancestral Puebloan ruins and petroglyphs. Morning light is best for viewing the rock spires.

Hiking
The Needles has four short trails, totaling 4 miles, off the main road and easily doable in a day. They provide an overview of the region's human and geologic history. None are wheelchair accessible. Cairns mark sections across slickrock. **Roadside Ruin Trail** (0.3-mile loop, easy) leads to an Anasazi granary. Kids love **Cave Spring Trail** (0.6-mile loop, easy to moderate), which leads to an abandoned cowboy camp and climbs ladders up slickrock. **Pothole Point Trail** (0.6-mile loop, easy) might bore kids, but brainiacs love the biology of the potholes, which contain microorganisms that come to life after rainstorms, and complete their lifecycles before the water evaporates. (Keep fingers out of water-filled potholes; oils from your hand kill the critters.) **Slickrock Trail** (2.4-mile loop, easy to moderate) scampers across slickrock to fabulous views; on the return route, you'll face the district's namesake needles and spires in the distance.

For longer hikes, see box (opposite).

Four-Wheel Driving & Mountain Biking
Fifty miles of 4WD and mountain biking roads crisscross the Needles. Stay on designated routes. Motorists and bicyclists must obtain a permit for overnight trips (p280), but not for day use, with the exception of Lavender and Horse Canyons, which require a $5 day-use permit; book in advance or check at the visitor center for cancellations.

BACKCOUNTRY ACCESS

The Needles is Canyonlands' premier backpacking destination, and it's hard to secure an overnight permit. Fret not: strong hikers can do the best trails in a day. If you venture off-trail, stay in washes or on slickrock to avoid trampling fragile cryptobiotic crusts.

Carry and drink at least one gallon of water per person per day – more if you're backpacking – and balance the increased fluid intake with extra electrolytes (potassium and sodium). Leave your itinerary with someone. Designated campsites abut most trails; you can request specific sites when applying for your permit. At-large camping is permitted in side canyons lacking designated sites. Human waste must be carried out or buried in a 6in to 8in hole 300ft from water sources; consider using human-waste containment bags. Carry out used toilet paper.

Canyonlands' most popular treks, **Chesler Park Loop** and **Joint Trail** combine for an awesome 11-mile loop across desert grasslands, past towering red-and-white-striped pinnacles and between deep, narrow fractures, some only 2ft across. Elevation changes are mild, but the distance makes it a moderate to difficult day hike. Also consider the **Confluence Overlook Trail**, a moderate four- to six-hour round-trip from Big Spring Canyon trailhead to see the silty Green River flow into the muddy-red Colorado. Many hikes connect in a series of loops, some requiring routefinding skills. Among the best are the **Big Spring Canyon** and **Lost Canyon Trails**. For gorgeous scenery, the **Elephant Canyon Trail** to Druid Arch is hard to beat. Archaeology junkies love the rock art along the **Salt Creek Canyon Trail**. Ask rangers.

The *Trails Illustrated* map ($3) should suffice, but if you're inclined to wander, carry a 7.5 minute quadrangle USGS map.

Four-wheel drive roads here require high-clearance vehicles (most off-the-lot SUVs don't have high clearance). Know what you're doing, or risk damaging your vehicle and endangering yourself. Towing fees run about $1000. If you're renting a 4WD vehicle, check the insurance policy; you might not be covered here. For more info, including 4WD routes and road conditions, check with rangers when booking your permit.

Elephant Hill is the most technically challenging route in the district, with steep grades and tight turns. The route to the **Colorado River Overlook** is easy in a vehicle and moderately easy on a mountain bike; park and walk the final, steep 1.5-mile descent to the overlook. Following the district's main drainage, the **Salt Creek Trail** is moderately easy for vehicles, moderate for bikes.

HORSESHOE CANYON

West of Island in the Sky, Horseshoe Canyon shelters millennia-old Native American rock art. The centerpiece is the **Great Gallery** and its superb Barrier Canyon–style pictographs from between 2000 BC and AD 500. The heroic, life-size figures are magnificent. Artifacts recovered here date back as far as 9000 BC. Damaging the rock art is a criminal offense. Don't touch it. Even the oils from your skin can harm the paintings.

The Great Gallery lies at the end of a 6.5-mile round-trip hiking trail descending 750ft from the main dirt road. Plan six hours. Rangers lead hikes on Saturday and Sunday, from April to October; contact the **Hans Flat Ranger Station** (☎ 435-259-2652; www .nps.gov/cany/horseshoe; ☉ 8am-4:30pm).

You can camp on BLM land at the trailhead, though it's not a campground per se, but a parking lot. There is a single vault toilet, but no water. Alternatively make a long day trip from Moab (two hours). Take Hwy 191 north, to I-70 west, to Hwy 24 south. About 25 miles south of I-70, past the turnoff for Goblin Valley State Park, turn east (left) and follow the gravel road 30 miles.

THE MAZE

A 30-sq-mile jumble of high-walled canyons, the Maze is a rare preserve of true wilderness for hardy backcountry veterans. The colorful canyons are rugged, deep and sometimes inaccessible. Many of them look alike; it's easy to get turned around – hence the district's name. Plan on spending at least three days, though a week is ideal.

The Maze lies west of the Confluence. From Moab, it's 133 miles to the **Hans Flat Ranger Station** (☎ 435-259-2652; www.nps.gov/cany /maze; ☉ 8am-4:30pm). Take Hwy 191 north, to

I-70 west, to Hwy 24 south. About 25 miles south of I-70, just past the paved turnoff for Goblin Valley State Park, head southeast on the gravel road, 46 miles to Hans Flat. En route you'll cross Glen Canyon National Recreation Area (p150) and Orange Cliffs; if you plan to stop at Orange Cliffs, get a permit at Hans Flat.

The few roads into the district are poor and often closed with rain or snow; bring tire chains from October to April. You'll need a short-wheelbase, high-clearance 4WD vehicle. If you're inexperienced at four-wheeling, stay away. Be prepared to repair your Jeep and, at times, the road. For pre-departure advice and necessities, contact the ranger station.

The **Maze Overlook Trail** requires hikers to carry at least a 25ft-long rope to raise and lower packs. Camping is at-large; you'll find reliable water sources (ask a ranger). You can drive a 2WD vehicle to the North Point Rd junction, 2.5 miles south of Hans Flat, then hike 15 miles to the Maze Overlook.

Sleeping & Eating

ISLAND IN THE SKY

Seven miles from the visitor center, the non-reservable **Willow Flat Campground** (☎ 435-719-2313, 435-259-4712; www.nps.gov/cany; tent sites $5) has vault toilets but no water. Bring firewood and don't expect shade. Arrive early to claim a site during spring and fall. Alternatively, head to Dead Horse Point State Park (right) or Moab (p272).

THE NEEDLES

The non-reservable **Squaw Flat Campground** (☎ 435-719-2313, 435-259-4711; www.nps.gov/cany; tent sites $10), 3 miles west of the visitor center, fills every day spring to fall. It has flush toilets and cold water; many sites are shaded by juniper trees. If they're full, ask rangers about BLM lands.

Just outside the park, the **Needles Outpost** (☎ 435-979-4007; www.canyonlandsneedlesoutpost.com; Hwy 211; campsites $15; ☿ Apr-Nov) is an excellent alternative. Rock walls provide morning shade. Amenities include flush toilets, hot showers ($3 for campers, $5 for non-campers) and dump station. They accept reservations. An **on-site store** sells limited supplies, firewood, groceries, beer, ice, gasoline and propane. The **lunch counter and grill** (☿ 9am-5pm) serves sandwiches and burgers.

Getting There & Around

Driving between districts takes two to six hours. Carry extra fuel in the backcountry. For guided trips, outfitters and shuttles, see p269 and p276.

DEAD HORSE POINT STATE PARK

The views at Dead Horse Point pack a wallop, extending 2000ft down to the serpentine Colorado River, up to the La Sal Mountains' 12,700ft peaks, and out 100 miles across Canyonlands' mesmerizing stair-step landscape. (You might remember it from the final scene of the film *Thelma & Louise*.) If you thrive on rare, epic views, you're gonna love Dead Horse.

Leave Hwy 313, 4 miles north of Island in the Sky, 30 miles from Moab. Toward the end of the drive, the road traverses a narrow ridge just 30yd across. (Ranchers once herded horses across these narrows – some were forgotten and left to die, hence the park's name.) A rough footpath skirts the point for panoramic vistas. To escape the small (but sometimes chatty) crowds, take the short hikes that rim the mesa. Visit at dawn or dusk for best lighting.

The **visitor center** (☎ 435-259-2614; www.stateparks.utah.gov; admission $7; ☿ 8am-5pm winter, to 6pm summer) has great exhibits, shows on-demand videos and sells books and maps. Rangers lead walks and talks in summer. The 21-site **Kayenta Campground** (☎ 801-538-7220, 800-322-3770; www.stateparks.utah.gov; tent & RV sites $14), south of the visitor center, provides limited water, RV hookups and dump station. Reservations are accepted from March to October, but you can often secure same-day sites by arriving early. Fill RVs with water in Moab.

MONTICELLO & BLANDING

Monticello (pronounced 'mon-ti-*sell*-o'; population 1960, elevation 7069ft), the San Juan County seat, sits in the foothills of the Abajo Mountains. The best reason to stop is the multi-agency information center.

The Abajo Mountains rise to 11,360ft in the Manti–La Sal National Forest, offering camping, hiking and snowsports. The paved Harts Draw Rd (closed in winter), heads 17 miles through to **Newspaper Rock Recreation Area** on Hwy 211, a giant petroglyph panel. If you like backpacking way off the beaten path, ask the BLM about

Dark Canyon Wilderness Area. Befitting the area's religiosity, in 2004 US Hwy 666, which goes to Colorado, was officially renamed US Hwy 491.

The multi-agency **San Juan Visitor Center** (☎ 435-587-3235, 800-574-4386; www.southeastutah .com; 117 S Main St, Monticello; ☻ 10am-4pm Mon-Fri Nov–mid-Mar, 8am-5pm daily mid-Mar–Oct) has books and extensive information on all public lands in southeastern Utah. The **USFS Manti–La Sal Forest Ranger Station** (☎ 435-587-2041; 496 E Central St, Monticello), and the **BLM** (☎ 435-587-2141; 435 N Main St, Monticello) open Monday to Friday to walk-in visitors.

In Blanding (population 3162, elevation 6000ft), 25 miles south, **Edge of the Cedars State Park** (☎ 435-678-2238; www.stateparks.utah.gov; 660 W 400 North, Blanding; per person/car $2/6; ☻ 8am-7pm mid-May–mid-Sep, 9am-5pm mid-Sep–mid-May) is worth a stop. It preserves excavated Anasazi ruins, including a ceremonial kiva; the museum displays ancient artifacts.

The Manti–La Sal National Forest has two basic **campgrounds** (campsites $10; ☻ May-Sep) with water, 6 miles west of Monticello. Otherwise there's no reason to stay, but if you have to, chain motels (try the Best Western) cost $60 to $70. The best bargain is the clean, quiet **Triangle H Motel** (☎ 435-587-2274, 800-657-6622; 164 E Central St, Monticello; s/d $35/45). The dull, alcohol-free town of Blanding, has motels in the $30s. The 19th-century **Rogers House** (☎ 435-678-3932, 800-355-3932; www .rogershouse.com; 412 S Main St, Blanding; s $57-69, d $69-89; ✗) has lovely rooms and breakfast. The **Four Corners Inn** (☎ 435-678-3257, 800-574-3150; www.fourcornersinn.com; 131 E Center St, Blanding; s/d $45/60) has motel rooms.

In Monticello, **MD Ranch Cookhouse** (☎ 435-587-3299; 380 S Main St, Monticello; mains $7-18) makes good burgers and steaks. For pasta, steaks and seafood, head to **Lamplight Restaurant** (☎ 435-587-2170; 655 E Central St, Monticello; mains $7-17; ☻ dinner Mon-Sat). Food in Blanding is, well…bland.

HOVENWEEP NATIONAL MONUMENT

Beautiful, little-visited **Hovenweep** (☎ 970-560-4282; www.nps.gov/hove; admission $6) means 'deserted valley' in Ute. It straddles the Utah–Colorado border and contains six prehistoric, Ancestral Puebloan sites, five of which require long hikes to reach. There's a **visitor center** (☻ 8am-5pm), water, ranger station and basic **campground** (campsites $10), but

no facilities. The main access is east of Hwy 191 on Hwy 262 via Hatch Trading Post, over 40 miles from Bluff or Blanding. Roads are dangerous when wet.

BLUFF

pop 320 / elev 4380ft

Surrounded by red rock, tiny Bluff was founded by the 'Hole-in-the-Rock' Mormon pioneers in 1880 (p253). Make this cool little town your base for exploring the region. It's at Hwys 191 and 163, along the San Juan River. There's no visitor center, but business owners will direct you; ask for the walking-tour pamphlet. Check out www.bluff-utah .org. Bluff has no streetlights to preserve the night sky. Carry a flashlight.

One of town's main draws is floating the canyons of the San Juan River. **Wild Rivers Expeditions** (☎ 435-672-2244; www.riversandruins.com; 101 Main St; day trip adult/child $125/75) has been guiding educational river trips since 1957. The wonderful folks at **Far Out Expeditions** (☎ 435-672-2294; www.faroutexpeditions.com; 7th & Mulberry St) know every rock and twig in the area and have the trust of the Navajo; they consequently lead fantastic off-the-beaten-path trips to Monument Valley ($105) and other area locations.

Bluff has good lodgings, from motels to B&Bs. A favorite is the hospitable **Recapture Lodge** (☎ 435-672-2281; www.bluffutah.org/recapture lodge; Hwy 191; r $46-60; ☜), a rustic, cozy property pleasantly shaded behind trees between the highway and the river. **Far Out Bunkhouse** (☎ 435-672-2294; www.faroutexpeditions.com; 7th East & Mulberry St; r $65-85; ✗), run by Far Out Expeditions, has a terrific kitchen and two cozy private rooms, each with six bunks and private bathroom. The charming 1898 **Decker House Inn** (☎ 435-672-2304, 888-637-2582; www.deckerhouseinn.com; 189 N 3rd St; r with bathroom $50-100; ☐ ✗) has homey, inviting B&B rooms in a two-story Victorian. The nicest digs are at **Desert Rose Inn** (☎ 435-672-2303, 888-475-7673; www.desertroseinn.com; 701 W Hwy 191; r $74-84, cabins $84-94).

Be sure to stop by friendly **Cow Canyon Trading Post** (☎ 435-672-2208; Hwys 191 & 163; mains $11-18; ☻ dinner Thu-Mon Apr-Oct), which serves terrific regionally inspired meat and vegetarian dinners, with good salads, wine and beer. The trading post, open year-round, has rugs, baskets, pottery, jewelry and good books. Otherwise, for straightforward

UTAH

American with a view, visit **Twin Rock** (☎ 435-672-2341; 913 E Navajo Twin Dr; mains $7-14; ☺ 7am-9pm). For steaks, head to the Wild West–style **Cottonwood Steakhouse** (☎ 435-672-2282; Main St & 4th West; mains $11-22; ☺ dinner Mar-Nov).

MOKI DUGWAY & VALLEY OF THE GODS

The **Moki Dugway** (Hwy 261) goes south from Hwy 95 to connect with Hwy 163 at Mexican Hat. Along the way it cuts through the rugged, 650,000-acre **Cedar Mesa**, and past the wild and twisting canyon of **Grand Gulch Primitive Area**, hugely popular with backcountry trekkers (contact the BLM).

Take the turnoff to **Muley Point Overlook** – don't miss this cliff-edge viewpoint, one of the country's most sweeping and spectacular, looking out to Monument Valley and other stunning landmarks. Back on Hwy 261, the pavement ends and the Moki Dugway suddenly descends (going south) a whopping 1100ft along a series of fist-clenching hairpin turns. At the bottom, a dirt road heads east into the **Valley of the Gods**, a 17-mile drive through monoliths of sandstone for more mind-blowing scenery. Locals call it 'mini–Monument Valley.' Near the southern end of Hwy 261, a 4-mile paved road heads west to **Goosenecks State Park**, a small lookout with yet more jaw-dropping views, this time of the serpentine San Juan River, 1100ft below.

Spend a romantic night at the stone-and-wood **Valley of the Gods B&B** (☎ 970-749-1164; www.valleyofthegods.cjb.net; off Hwy 261; d $115; ✗), 6.5 miles north of Hwy 163.

MEXICAN HAT

pop 88 / elev 4244ft

The tiny settlement of Mexican Hat is named after a sombrero-shaped rock, 3 miles northeast on Hwy 163. A stopping point for travelers, the town lies on the north banks of the San Juan River; the south bank marks the northern edge of the Navajo Reservation.

Mexican Hat has a handful of rustic and simple lodgings ($45 to $70) and places to eat. **San Juan Inn** (☎ 435-683-2220, 800-447-2022; www.sanjuaninn.net; Hwy 163; r $70-80) is the nicest place. It has a year-round **restaurant** (☺ 7am-10pm) and the only full-liquor license within 100 miles. **Mexican Hat Lodge** (☎ 435-683-2222; www.mexicanhat.net; Hwy 163; r $65-72) has rooms and an outdoor steakhouse in summer (dinners $10 to $27).

MONUMENT VALLEY

From Mexican Hat, Hwy 163 winds southwest and enters the Navajo Reservation and, after about 30 miles, **Monument Valley**. Though you'll recognize it instantly from Hollywood movies and TV commercials, nothing compares to seeing the sheer chocolate-red buttes and colossal mesas for real. To get close, you must visit the Monument Valley Navajo Tribal Park (p184), just across the border in Arizona.

Just inside the Utah border, **Goulding's Lodge** (☎ 435-727-3231; www.gouldings.com; r $170; ☐ ☒) is the only hotel near Monument Valley; each room has a balcony with a million-dollar view of the colossal red buttes. Stay in the main motel, not the satellite buildings, and verify that your room is entirely, not partially, air-conditioned. A full-service outpost, Goulding's also has a restaurant, museum, tours, store, gas and **campground** (tent sites $18, RV sites $26-32).

HIGHWAY 95 TO SAN RAFAEL REEF & INTERSTATE 70

Hwy 95 from Blanding sees little traffic, but it's one of the most scenic drives in all of Utah, passing cracked, stained, ever-eroding layers of rock. Carry water and food.

Forty miles west of Blanding, **Natural Bridges National Monument** (☎ 435-692-1234; www.nps.gov/nabr; admission $6; ☺ 7am-sunset) became Utah's first NPS land in 1908. The highlight is a dark-stained, white sandstone canyon with three easily accessible natural bridges. The oldest, the Owachomo Bridge, spans 180ft but is merely 9ft thick. Trails to the bridges are short (half a mile one-way) but steep. Pick up maps and water at the **visitor center** (☺ 8am-5pm). Basic **camping** costs $10.

Just north of the monument, the **Fry Canyon Lodge** (☎ 435-259-5334; www.frycanyon.com) is the *only* building on Hwy 95 between Blanding and Hanksville. The restaurant and hotel are closed for remodeling till 2006. Fingers crossed that it reopens: it's a cool place. Continuing northwest, a bridge crosses Lake Powell; stop at the Hite overlook for otherworldly scenery.

In the west the majestic 11,000ft **Henry Mountains**, the last explored range in the lower 48, dominate the view. Between milemarkers 15 and 16, the 10-mile-long dirt road Burr Point Trail leads into the Robbers Roost area – famous as a hiding place for outlaws – and dead-ends at a panoramic overlook.

Sixteen miles past the Burr Point turnoff, Hwy 95 ends with a whimper at Hwy 24 in **Hanksville** (population 240, elevation 4300ft), a convenient stopping place. The **BLM** (☎ 435-542-3461; 406 S 100 West; ☷ 7:45am-4:30pm Mon-Fri) has maps and information about the surrounding lands, particularly the Henry Mountains. If you want to stay, the **Red Rock Campground & Restaurant** (☎ 435-542-3235; 226 E 100 North; campsites $10-16; ☷ mid-Mar–Oct) has 60 sites and a nothing-special diner. **Fern's Place** (☎ 435-542-3251; 99 E 100 North; r $30-55) has budget rooms. **Whispering Sands Motel** (☎ 435-542-3238; www.hanksville.com/whisperingsands /motel.html; 132 S Hwy 95; s/d $50/60; ☐) is town's nicest.

From Hanksville, Hwy 24 goes west 30 miles to Capitol Reef National Park (p261), and northeast 44 miles to I-70. En route to the freeway, Hwy 24 parallels the 2000ft-high, 65-mile-long **San Rafael Reef**, which some would like to see become a national park; for details, contact the BLM. For guided treks into this remote wilderness, contact **Hondoo Rivers & Trails** (☎ 435-425-3519, 800-332-2696; www.hondoo.com).

Twenty miles northeast of Hanksville via Hwy 24, drive 12 miles west to **Goblin Valley State Park** (per car $5), where Entrada-sandstone mounds look like goblins and giant mushrooms in a coliseum-like valley, right out of a Salvador Dalí fantasy; kids love it! The year-round **campground** (☎ 800-322-3770; www.stateparks.utah.gov; campsites $14) has water and showers.

NORTHERN UTAH

Northern Utah is huge. Vast, barren salt flats extend 100 miles west from the Great Salt Lake into Nevada. Civilization lies east, clinging to the skirts of the Wasatch Mountains and their lifeline to fresh drinking water. Salt Lake City (SLC) is but one of several cities that make up an 80-mile-long patchwork in the valley along the Wasatch Front, with Ogden in the north, SLC in the middle and Provo in the south. Giant saw-toothed peaks lord majestically above and in winter they get blanketed with feathery-light snow, drawing skiers

from across the globe to the world-famous resorts that hosted the 2002 Winter Olympics. In summer, the spectacular forested canyons and craggy summits become a wildflower-studded playground for hikers, mountain bikers and city dwellers seeking refuge from the valley's scorching heat.

Ute and Shoshone Native Americans roamed this valley, and it became the first region to be settled by mid-19th-century Mormon pioneers. Today 75% of the state's population lives along the Wasatch Front, but only 25% of Utah's state legislature is comprised of representatives from these districts. The rest are from rural areas, which explains the archaic statewide laws like those governing liquor. Contrary to popular belief, SLC's population is fairly open-minded; they even twice elected the current liberal-Democrat mayor, Rocky Anderson.

This section zigzags in and out of the mountains, first covering SLC, then the Wasatch Front ski areas, Park City and environs, then Provo in the south. At the end, it jumps north again, from Ogden to Utah's northern reaches.

SALT LAKE CITY
pop 1.7 million / elev 4330ft
Don't be lulled by your preconceptions about Salt Lake City (SLC). Ever since the Olympics came to town, Utah's state capital has become ever so slightly cosmopolitan. There's even a hint of counterculturalism in the air – albeit faint. Though Salt Lake is headquarters of the Mormon Church, only about half its citizens are LDS (Latter-day Saints; see p40). The result is a broader public discourse than in other Utah cities and towns. Sure, SLC is conservative by coastal standards, but at least there's an ongoing conversation about identity.

Be sure to see Temple Square, but remember there's a big secular city beyond the church walls, with enticing museums, a thriving university and dynamic arts scene. And when the trail beckons, you're only 45 minutes from the Wasatch Mountains' brilliant hiking and world-class skiing.

Orientation
Salt Lake City is laid out in a spacious grid with streets aligned north–south or east–west. (Streets were originally built 132ft wide, so that four oxen pulling a wagon could turn

METROPOLITAN SALT LAKE CITY

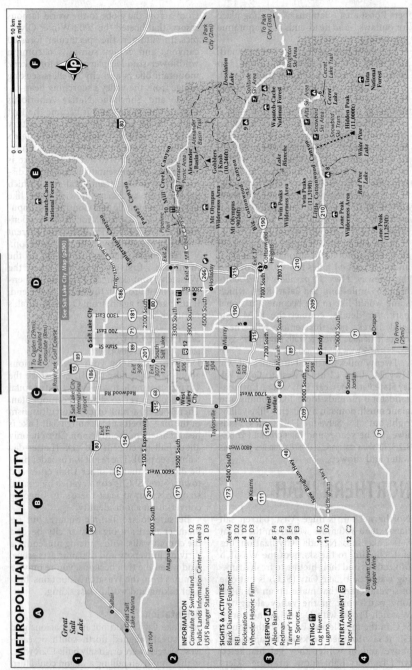

INFORMATION
Consulate of Switzerland........................1 D2
Public Lands Information Center..........(see 3)
USFS Ranger Station.............................2 D3

SIGHTS & ACTIVITIES
Black Diamond Equipment.................(see 4)
REI...3 D2
Rockreation..4 D2
Wheeler Historic Farm..........................5 D3

SLEEPING
Albion Basin..6 F4
Redman..7 F3
Tanner's Flat..8 E4
The Spruces..9 E3

EATING
Log Haven...10 E2
Lugano..11 D2

ENTERTAINMENT
Paper Moon...12 C2

around.) Everything radiates from Temple Square. The corner of South Temple St (east–west) and Main St (north–south) is the zero point for streets and addresses (see p227). North Temple St, westbound, goes to the airport, 6 miles from downtown. Eight blocks equals one mile.

Two major interstates cross at SLC: I-15 runs north–south, I-80 east–west. I-215 loops the city.

Because streets are so wide, there are mid-block pedestrian crossings downtown. Carry the orange flags, available at these crossings, for increased visibility.

Information

BOOKSTORES

Sam Weller Books (Map pp292-3; ☎ 801-328-2586, 800-333-7269; 254 S Main St) The best selection of travel books, guides and maps at SLC's biggest independent bookstore.

King's English (Map p290; ☎ 801-484-9100, 800-658-7928; 1511 S 1500 East) First-rate indie bookseller, staffed by enthusiastic bookworms.

Ken Sanders Rare Books (Map pp292-3; ☎ 801-521-3819; 268 S 200 East) Specializes in Western authors, Utah history and the Colorado Plateau. The epicenter of SLC's counterculture.

BiblioTect (Map pp292-3; ☎ 801-236-1010; 329 W Pierpont Ave) Southwestern art and architecture books.

EMERGENCY & MEDICAL SERVICES

In an emergency, call ☎ 911.

Police (Map pp292-3; ☎ 801-799-3000; 315 E 200 South)

Salt Lake Regional Medical Center (Map p290; ☎ 801-350-4111/4631; 1050 E South Temple St) Twenty-four-hour emergency.

University Hospital (Map p290; ☎ 801-581-2121/2291; 50 N Medical Dr) Twenty-four-hour emergency.

University of Utah Redwood Center (Map p290; ☎ 801-887-2499; 1525 W 2100 South; ☽ by appointment 8am-5pm; walk-in clinic 5-8pm Mon-Fri, 9am-8pm Sat & Sun) For non-emergency care.

LIBRARIES

City Library (Map pp292-3; ☎ 801-524-8200; www .slcpl.lib.ut.us; 210 E 400 South) Free Internet access, excellent periodicals. Five branch libraries scattered across town.

MEDIA

City Weekly (☎ 801-575-7003; www.slweekly.com) Free alternative weekly with good restaurant and entertainment listings; twice-annually it publishes the free, useful *City Guide*.

Salt Lake Metro (☎ 801-323-9500; www.slmetro.com) SLC's free, gay newspaper.

Salt Lake Tribune (☎ 801-257-8742; www.sltrib.com) Utah's largest-circulation paper; not Mormon-owned, but conservative.

Deseret Morning News (☎ 801-236-6000; www.des news.com) Ultraconservative, church-owned newspaper.

MONEY

It's difficult to change currency outside SLC. On weekends visit the airport.

Wells Fargo (Map pp292-3; ☎ 801-246-2677; 79 S Main St)

POST

Post office (Map pp292-3; ☎ 800-275-8777; www.usps .com; 230 W 200 South)

Post office (320 N 3700 West) At the airport; 24-hour service.

TOURIST INFORMATION

Visitor Information Center (Map pp292-3; ☎ 801-521-2822, 800-541-4955; www.visitsaltlake.com; 90 S West Temple St; ☽ 8:30am-5pm Mon-Fri year-round, 9am-5pm Sat & Sun summer) Inside the Salt Palace Convention Center. Publishes the free *Salt Lake Visitors Guide*. Good website.

Salt Lake Ranger Station (☎ 801-733-2660; www .fs.fed.us/r4/wcnf/unit/slrd) Covers the Wasatch-Cache National Forest. No walk-ins but telephone information provided.

Sights

If you're spending more than a few days here, the Visitor Information Center has a comprehensive list of sights. Also see p293 for more options.

TEMPLE SQUARE & AROUND

The city's most famous sight, **Temple Square** (Map pp292-3; ☎ 801-240-2534, 800-537-9703; www .visittemplesquare.com; admission free; ☽ 9am-9pm) occupies a 10-acre block surrounded by 15ft-high walls. Stop at the visitor centers inside the two entrances, on South and North Temple St. LDS docents give free, 30-minute tours. The **Tabernacle** is the highlight of Temple Square, but it is regrettably closed until 2007 for renovations.

Lording over the square is 210ft-tall **Salt Lake Temple**. Atop the tallest spire stands a golden statue of the angel Moroni who appeared to LDS-founder Joseph Smith. Temple ceremonies are secret and open only to LDS in good standing.

UTAH

SALT LAKE CITY

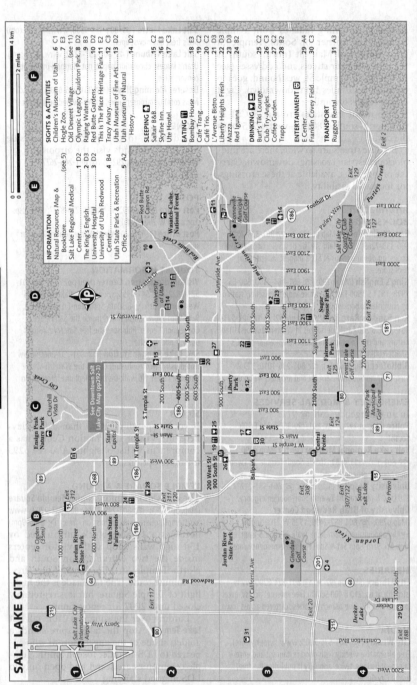

South of the Tabernacle lies **Assembly Hall**, a lovely 1877 Gothic hall, where you can hear noontime organ concerts Monday to Saturday; in summer there's another performance at 2pm. Inquire about the **concert series** (☎ 801-240-3323); this is a brilliant place to hear strings.

Adjoining Temple Square, the **Museum of Church History and Art** (Map pp292-3; ☎ 801-240-3310; 45 N West Temple St; admission free; ☺ 9am-9pm Mon-Fri, 10am-7pm Sat & Sun) has impressive exhibits of pioneer history and fine art. You can research your genealogy at the **Family History Library** (Map pp292-3; ☎ 801-240-2331; 35 N West Temple St; ☺ 7:30am-10pm Tue-Sat, to 5pm Mon).

On Main St at South Temple St the **Brigham Young Monument** marks the zero point for the city. East of the monument is the **Joseph Smith Memorial Building** (Map pp292-3; ☎ 801-240-1266; 15 E South Temple St; admission free; ☺ 8am-10pm Mon-Sat), which was, until 1987, the elegant Hotel Utah. Inside there's a **large-screen theater** (☎ 801-240-4383) with free, nine-daily screenings of the 65-minute-long *The Testaments*, about Mormon beliefs.

Built in 2000, the 21,000-seat **LDS Conference Center** (Map pp292-3; ☎ 801-240-0075; 60 W North Temple St; ☺ 9am-9pm Mon-Sat) is the largest auditorium in the world. Ascend to the rooftop garden for killer views.

Brigham Young lived in the **Beehive House** (Map pp292-3; ☎ 801-240-2671; 67 E South Temple St; admission free; ☺ tours 9:30am-4:30pm Mon-Sat, later summer, 10am-1pm Sun), until his death in 1877, and it has been meticulously maintained with period furnishings and artwork. Next door the 1855 **Lion House** (Map pp292-3; 63 E South Temple St) was built for Young's many wives. The building is closed to the public, but the Lion House Pantry Restaurant (p296) is open for dining.

Just north of Temple Square, the walls of the impressive **Utah State Capitol** (☎ 801-538-1563; ☺ 8am-8pm) are normally covered with historical murals, but the building is being renovated until 2007.

You'll find Daughters of Utah Pioneers (DUP) museums throughout Utah, but the **Pioneer Memorial Museum** (Map pp292-3; ☎ 801-532-6479; 300 N Main St; admission free; ☺ 9am-5pm Mon-Sat year-round, 1-5pm Sun summer) is by far the best – a vast four-story treasure trove of thousands of pioneer artifacts displayed in 38 rooms, filled with everything from furniture to a fire truck.

SING PRAISES

The **Mormon Tabernacle Choir** (☎ 801-240-4150; www.mormontabernaclechoir.com) is one of the world's foremost choirs. It's also one of the biggest. When they sing fortissimo, the sheer power of the 360-voice ensemble will blow you away. Alas, the 1867 Tabernacle, the acoustically bright, ringing hall where they normally sing, is being renovated until 2007. In the meantime, you can attend their famous Sunday morning radio broadcast, *Music and the Spoken Word* (the oldest continuous radio broadcast in America), in the LDS Conference Center at Temple Square at 9:30am; arrive by 9am. Or else attend their Thursday evening rehearsal at 8pm. Note that the sound in the cavernous auditorium (the biggest in the world) is flat and lacks the Tabernacle's 'ping,' so sit close to the stage. Pray for a speedy renovation.

DOWNTOWN

Clark Planetarium (Map pp292-3; ☎ 801-456-7827; www.clarkplanetarium.org; 110 S 400 West; adult/child $8/5, matinee $5; ☺ 11:30am-9pm Mon-Thu, 11:30am-11pm Fri & Sat, 11:30-7:45pm Sun) has the latest and greatest 3D skyshows and Utah's only Imax theater. Museum-exhibit halls are free. Adjoining the planetarium, the **Gateway** is a combination indoor-outdoor shopping center and dynamic memorial to the 2002 Olympics. The centerpiece is the **Olympic Snowflake Fountain**, which you can play in!

South Temple St is lined with historic buildings, from the grand 1909 **Union Pacific Railroad Depot** (Map pp292-3; 400 W South Temple St), which anchors the Gateway, to the **Kearns Mansion** (Map pp292-3; ☎ 801-538-1005; 603 E South Temple St), the governor's official residence (call about tours from April to November). The south end of the Gateway is anchored by the 1910 Denver-Rio Grande Depot, which is open to the public

One of the best things to do on Sunday is visit the **City Library** (Map pp292-3; ☎ 801-524-8200; www.slcpl.lib.ut.us; 210 E 400 South), where you can meander through dramatic glass-walled architecture (it looks like a giant comma) and stroll the roof garden; downstairs, stop by the indie shops, which focus on the humanities, from gardening to comic-book publishing. There's a good kids' area, too.

UTAH

The **Salt Lake Art Center** (Map pp292-3; ☎ 801-328-4201; 20 S West Temple St; admission by donation; 🕙 10am-5pm Tue-Sat, to 9pm Fri, 1-5pm Sun) has changing contemporary-art exhibits, lecture and gallery walks. The **Gallivan Center** (Map pp292-3; ☎ 801-535-6110; www.thegallivancenter.com; 200 S btwn State & Main Sts) has sculpture gardens, an amphitheater, and in winter an **ice skating rink** (☎ 801-535-6117; adult/child $5/4). In summer, bring a picnic to the outdoor concert and movie series (arrive early!).

AROUND DOWNTOWN

The **University of Utah** (Map p290; ☎ 801-581-7200; www.utah.edu; 200 South), or 'U of U,' 2 miles east of downtown, was the site of the Olympic Village in 2002. The **Olympic Legacy Cauldron Park** (☎ 801-581-8849, 866-659-7275; www.olyparks .com) has giant panels detailing the games; see the heavy-handed, but heartfelt **film** (adult/child $3/2; 🕙 10am-6pm Mon-Sat), with artificial fog and booming sound effects.

SLC's best art museum, **Utah Museum of Fine Arts** (Map p290; ☎ 801-581-7332; www.umfa.utah .edu; 410 Campus Center Dr; adult/child $4/2; 🕙 10am-5pm Tue-Fri, 10am-8pm Wed, 11am-5pm Sat & Sun) has soaring galleries, cherry-wood floors and permanent collections of tribal, Western and modern art; it also gets important international traveling shows.

The **Utah Museum of Natural History** (Map p290; ☎ 801-581-6927; www.umnh.utah.edu; President's Circle; adult/senior/child $6/3.50/3.50; 🕙 9:30am-5:30pm Tue-Sat, to 8pm Mon) features paleontology (dinosaurs!) and hands-on activities for kids.

Dedicated to the 1847 arrival of the Mormons, **This is the Place Heritage Park** (Map p290; ☎ 801-582-1847; www.thisistheplace.org; 2601 E Sunnyside Ave/800 South; 🕙 9am-6pm), encompassing **Old Deseret Village** (Map p290; adult/child $6/4; 🕙 tours 10am-5pm Memorial Day–Labor Day), is a 450-acre living-history museum with costumed docents depicting life in the mid-19th century. Some of the 41 buildings are replicas, others originals, including Brigham Young's farmhouse. September to May, self-guided tours cost $2.

Nearby, in the Wasatch Foothills, the lovely **Red Butte Gardens** (Map p290; ☎ 801-581-4747; Wakara Way; adult/senior/child $5/3/3; 🕙 10am-5pm, 9am-8pm May-Oct) has 150 acres with trails, 25 acres of gardens and gorgeous valley views.

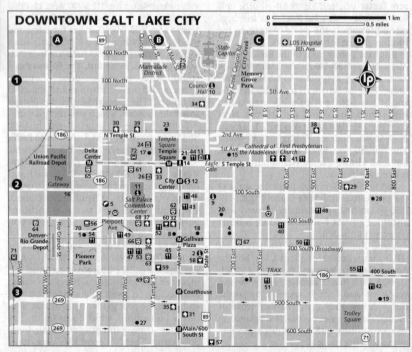

DOWNTOWN SALT LAKE CITY

Activities

The best of SLC's activities are in the Wasatch Front (see box, p296). For details on skiing, see p303. For fly-fishing, see Park City (p308).

The well-regarded **Guthrie Bicycle** (Map pp292-3; ☎ 801-363-3727; www.guthriebicycle.com; 156 E 200 South) rents road and mountain bikes (per day $30); ask about in-town trails. **Wasatch Touring** (Map pp292-3; ☎ 801-359-9361; www.wasatch touring.com; 702 E 100 South) rents bikes, kayaks, climbing shoes and ski equipment. **REI** (Map p288; ☎ 801-486-2100, 800-426-4840; www.rei.com; 3285 E 3300 South) rents camping equipment, climbing shoes, kayaks, and most winter-sports gear.

If you're into rock climbing, check out **Rockreation** (Map p288; ☎ 801-278-7473; www.rock reation.com; 2074 E 3900 South; admission $15; ☒ noon-9pm), which has 7000 sq ft of climbing terrain with bouldering, top rope and lead rope. Opening hours vary, so call ahead. Next door, **Black Diamond Equipment** (Map p288; ☎ 801-278-5552; www.bdel.com) manufactures climbing and backcountry-ski gear; take the very cool tour to see how it's done (call for times). The retail store is like a candy store for gearheads.

SLC's municipal 18-hole **golf courses** (for tee times ☎ 801-484-3333; www.slcgov.com/publicservices /golf; $24-27) are easily accessible. Try **Bonneville** (Map p290; ☎ 801-583-9513; 954 Conner St); **Glendale** (Map p290; ☎ 801-974-2403; 1630 W 2100 South);

Mountain Dell (☎ 801-582-3812), which has two courses in Parleys Canyon (Map p288); or **Rose Park** (Map p288; ☎ 801-596-5030; 1386 N Redwood Rd). Rent equipment from **Utah Ski & Golf** (Map pp292-3; ☎ 801-355-9088; www.utahskigolf .com; 134 W 600 South).

The **Parks & Recreation Department** (☎ 801-972-7800) has information about activities in the city's many parks. Liberty Park (Map p290) has the most **tennis courts** (☎ 801-328-4711; 1100 South & 550 East) and rents racquets at its pro shop, April to October; call ahead to reserve courts (per hour $4).

Salt Lake City for Children

There's lots for tots in SLC. The Visitor Information Center (p289) has an A-to-Z list.

The wonderful hands-on exhibits at the **Children's Museum of Utah** (Map p290; ☎ 801-328-3383; www.childmuseum.org; 840 N 300 West; admission $4; ☒ 10am-5pm Mon-Sat, to 8pm Fri, closed Mon winter) stimulate imaginations and senses. **Wheeler Historic Farm** (Map p288; ☎ 801-264-2241; www .wheelerfarm.com; 6351 S 900 East; admission free, tour & wagon ride $2; ☒ dawn-dusk, visitor center 9:30am-5:30pm), in South Cottonwood Regional Park, dates from 1886. Farmhands milk cows, churn butter, feed animals – and kids can help. There's also blacksmithing, quilting and hay rides in summer. The **Hogle Zoo** (Map p290; ☎ 801-582-1631; 2600 E Sunnyside Ave; adult/senior/child $7/5/5; ☒ 9am-6:30pm Jun-Sep, 9am-5:30pm Oct-May) takes you face-to-face with tigers,

UTAH

wolves, gorillas and even elephants (well, sort of face-to-face). Kids love the petting zoo and miniature-train rides ($1).

For a sure-to-please treat, cool off on the water slides at **Raging Waters** (Map p290; ☎ 801-972-3300; www.ragingwatersutah.com; 1700 S 1200 West; adult/child $18/14; ◷ 10:30am-7:30pm Mon-Sat, noon-7:30pm Sun May-Sep).

The **Tracy Aviary** (Map p290; ☎ 801-322-2473, 801-596-8500; 589 E 1300 South; adult/child $5/3; ◷ 9am-4:30 winter, to 6pm summer) delights bird lovers with displays of winged creatures from around the world. Kids can feed ducks, colorful lories and parrots.

Only in Salt Lake City

The **Pioneer Memorial Museum** (p291) is like Utah's attic, with a taxidermy two-headed lamb, human-hair artwork and other weird artifacts. At **Gilgal Garden** (Map pp292-3; ☎ 801-519-0871; www.gilgalgarden.org; 749 E 500 South; admission free; ◷ 8am-8pm Apr-Sep, 9am-5pm Oct-Mar) see a giant stone sphinx with Joseph Smith's face. Tucked behind private homes, this weird rock garden features giant biblical characters crafted by a Mormon stonemason.

Tours

Utah Heritage Foundation (☎ 801-533-8058; www.utahheritagefoundation.com) Terrific historic tours.

Grayline (☎ 801-534-1001; www.saltlakecitytours.org) Four-hour sightseeing tours cost $30.

Festivals & Events

The **Utah Arts Festival** (www.uaf.org) happens in June. July's **Days of '47** (☎ 801-254-4656; www.days of47.com), affectionately nicknamed 'Mormon Mardi Gras,' brings everything from a rodeo to an enormous parade.

Sleeping

SLC's lodgings are primarily chain properties. Many are clustered on W North Temple St near the airport; others are along S 200 West near 500 South and 600 South. Rates are lowest in spring and fall, and spike when there's a convention. At high-end hotels, rates are lowest on weekends. Summertime prices plunge at ski resorts (p299) and Park City (p309), both within 45 minutes of downtown.

BUDGET

Skyline Inn (Map p290; ☎ 801-582-5350; www.skylineinn.com; 2475 E 1700 South; r $55-69; P ⚲ 🖳) South of the university overlooking downtown, this modest, well-maintained hotel is a great off-the-beaten-path choice. Near Big and Little Cottonwood Canyons, it's especially good for skiers and hikers. Hot tub too.

City Creek Inn (Map pp292-3; ☎ 801-533-9100, 866-533-4898; www.citycreekinn.com; 230 W North Temple St; r $48-58; P) One of SLC's best budget choices is located right downtown, next to Temple Square. It's simple, attractive and family owned.

Travelodge Temple Square (Map pp292-3; ☎ 801-533-8200; 144 W North Temple St; r $45-60; P) Though it's not the most exciting place to stay, this standard chain is also right downtown and has friendly owners.

THE GREAT SALT LAKE

The Great Salt Lake is the largest lake west of the Great Lakes. How big is it? Well, that's hard to answer. Since 1873 the lake has varied from 900 to 2500 sq miles. Maximum depths have ranged from 24ft to 45ft – it's wide and shallow, like a plate. Spring runoff raises levels; summer's sweltering heat lowers them. Evaporation is also why the lake is so salty. But its salinity varies drastically, from 6% to 27%, depending on location and weather (compared to only 3.5% for seawater!).

Prehistoric variations in lake levels were much greater. Sixteen thousand years ago the lake was part of Lake Bonneville, which was 900ft higher and covered almost 20,000 sq miles. Then it burst through Red Rock Pass and drained into the Snake River (in present-day Idaho), dropping 350ft. Today's lake, a puddle by comparison, receded to its present size 8000 years ago. Look at the mountains, and you'll see terraces, marking the ancient levels, etched into the skirts of the Wasatch Front, about 900ft and 550ft above present lake levels.

The Great Salt Lake is a Unesco World Heritage site for its importance to millions of migratory birds. The height of the fall and spring migrations are not-to-be-missed wildlife pageants. The best place to see the lake (and the birds) is at Antelope Island State Park (see box, p317).

Avenues (Map pp292-3; ☎ 801-359-3855, 888-884-4752; www.hostelhandbook.com/slc; 107 F St; dm $14, d $25-40; Ⓟ ⌨ ⊗) A no-frills hostel in a lovely tree-lined residential neighborhood, the Avenues caters mostly to international travelers.

Ute Hostel (Map p290; ☎ 801-595-1645; www.info bytes.com/utehostel; 21 E Kelsey Ave; dm/d $15/35; Ⓟ) South of downtown, Ute Hostel is smaller and homier than the Avenues and is set among attractive hand-fashioned houses.

USFS campgrounds (Map p288; ☎ 801-236-3400, 877-444-6777; www.reserveusa.com; campsites $14) There are four basic, seasonal, reservable USFS campgrounds in Big and Little Cottonwood Canyons, high in the Wasatch Mountains.

MIDRANGE
Business-class chains (eg Marriott and Hilton) cost $100 on weekends, but nearly double on weekdays.

Peery Hotel (Map pp292-3; ☎ 801-521-4300, 800-331-0073; www.peeryhotel.com; 110 W 300 South; r $80-120; Ⓟ ⌨ ⊗) If you like historic hotels, this one's a charmer. The small but impeccably maintained rooms have thick bedspreads, gilt-framed mirrors, heavy wooden furniture and up-to-date bathrooms with pedestal sinks and aromatherapy soaps.

Inn on the Hill (Map pp292-3; ☎ 801-328-1466; www.inn-on-the-hill.com; 225 N State St; s $90, d $104-134; Ⓟ ⌨ ⊗) Maxfield Parish Tiffany glass adorns the entryway of this 1906 Renaissance Revival mansion overlooking Temple Square. Rooms are understatedly elegant, with no space-occupying froufrou diminishing their functionality. Some have fireplaces; all have jetted tubs. Play billiards or read by the fire in one of three parlors. The two-story carriage house ($150) sleeps six and has a kitchenette. Full breakfast.

Inn at Temple Square (Map pp292-3; ☎ 801-531-1000, 800-843-4668; www.theinn.com; 71 W South Temple St; r $100-155; Ⓟ ⌨ ⊗) A stately 1930 Edwardian building across the street from its namesake, this 'inn' is actually a 90-room hotel (no booze allowed). Rooms have thick carpeting and Colonial American furnishings; many have views of the square. Buffet breakfast.

Anton Boxrud (Map pp292-3; ☎ 801-363-8035, 800-524-5511; www.antonboxrud.com; 57 S 600 East; r $78-140; Ⓟ ⊗) You'll feel like a guest in a friend's home at this seven-room, meticu-lously restored 1901 Victorian on a tree-lined street, walkable to downtown. The charming innkeeper always has cookies and drinks on hand. Full breakfast.

Saltair B&B (Map p290; ☎ 801-533-8184, 800-733-8184; www.saltlakebandb.com; 164 S 900 East; r $80-110, cottages $130-150; Ⓟ ⊗) Inside a 1903 Victorian on a pretty (but busy) residential street, this B&B provides a range of rooms and cottages. B&B rooms include full breakfast; cottages have kitchens.

Shilo Inn (Map pp292-3; ☎ 801-521-9500, 800-222-2244; 206 S West Temple St; r $80-140; Ⓟ ⓡ) It's ugly outside, but its upper-end tourist-class rooms are surprisingly comfortable – but not worth over $100.

TOP END
Hotel Monaco (Map pp292-3; ☎ 801-595-0000, 877-294-9710; www.monaco-saltlakecity.com; 15 W 200 South; r $100-180; Ⓟ ⌨) Tops in town for splash and panache, the Monaco's sexy rooms are a riot of color – gold, red, yellow, green – with all the requisite bells and whistles, and shagadelic touches like leopard-print robes. They'll even send a goldfish to your room to keep you company.

Little America Hotel (Map pp292-3; ☎ 801-363-6781, 800-453-9450; www.littleamerica.com/slc; 500 S Main St; r $85-170; Ⓟ ⓡ ⌨ ⊗) The demure sister to the opulent Grand America, this oh-so-correct, full-service, 850-room hotel gets everything just right, without any fuss. For views, request an upper floor in the 17-story tower. Downstairs there's a classic American coffeeshop.

Grand America (Map pp292-3; ☎ 801-258-6000, 800-621-4505; www.grandamerica.com; 555 S Main St; r $210-330; Ⓟ ⓡ ⌨ ⊗) SLC's only true luxury hotel towers over the city like a 24-story wedding cake. The retro-fancy lobby sports over-the-top custom fixtures including Murano-glass chandeliers. Rooms are decked out with Italian-marble bathrooms, English-wool carpeting, tasseled damask draperies and other cushy touches. Sunday brunch (adults $32, kids $16) is equally lavish.

Eating
Foodies will be surprised to learn how well one can eat in SLC. Make reservations. Also see the Eating listings under each resort in the Wasatch Front Ski Areas section (p299); they're only 40-minutes drive away.

UTAH

EXPLORING THE WASATCH FRONT

When the mercury soars and the desert sizzles, beat the heat by ascending the Wasatch Front. Within an hour, you can be hiking deep-green forests to icy alpine lakes, or riding a tram up a mountainside for top-of-the-world vistas. Grab a jacket and head to Mill Creek, Little Cottonwood or Big Cottonwood Canyons (Map p288). (Because the latter two are watersheds, you can't bring your dog.)

Mill Creek is most intimate and has no resorts, only hiking and picnic areas; take exit 4 from I-215. **Big and Little Cottonwood** have ski resorts (p303) with lift-served hiking and mountain-biking; take exit 17 off I-215. Snowbird has an alpine slide, bungee-trampoline, tram rides, biking, hiking and music festivals. Solitude has biking and hiking. Ski-resort lodges and inns drop rates dramatically in summer; for ideas on sleeping and eating, see p303. For camping, see p295.

For a nifty full-day excursion, consider a loop tour. Hwy 190 through Big Cottonwood Canyon becomes a rough dirt road (summer only) at Brighton, crosses a 9800ft pass, then forks and drops into Park City (p306) or Heber City (p314). On a clear summer day, have a morning hike, picnic lunch, afternoon scenic drive and dinner in the mountains, and be back in SLC by eight.

The **Public Lands Information Center** (p226) has detailed information on the mountains. For a guide, John Veranth's *Hiking the Wasatch* is terrific. If you have no car **Canyon Transportation** (☎ 800-255-1841; www.canyontransportation.com) operates shuttles by reservation. UTA buses run in ski season.

BUDGET

Tony Caputo's Deli and Italian Market (Map pp292-3; ☎ 801-531-8669; 308 W 300 South; sandwiches $5-7; ☺ 9am-7pm Mon-Fri, 9am-5pm Sat, 11am-3pm Sun) Crowds line up for Tony Caputo's mouth-watering meatball sandwiches; save some room for the cannoli too. The big deli sandwiches are also good.

Red Iguana (Map p290; ☎ 801-322-1489; 736 W North Temple St; dishes $7-12; ☺ lunch & dinner) You'll find no better *mole* sauce than at this top pick for Mexican. The room ain't much, but with food this good, who cares. Great margaritas.

Lamb's Restaurant (Map pp292-3; ☎ 801-364-7166; 169 S Main St; mains $5-15; ☺ breakfast, lunch & dinner) Lamb's has been open since 1919, and everything on its blue-plate-style Americana menu is made in-house, from soup to mayonnaise to pie. Good breakfasts.

Mazza (Map p290; ☎ 801-484-9259; 1515 S 1500 East; mains $5-8; ☺ 11am-9pm Mon-Sat; Ⓟ) Order at the counter for delicious kebabs, shawarma and house-made falafel at SLC's best Mediterranean.

Cafe Trang (Map p290; ☎ 801-539-1638; 818 S Main St; mains $5-11; ☺ lunch & dinner) Come for rice-noodle bowls and aromatic Vietnamese specialties at this hole-in-the-wall with table service.

Lion House Pantry Restaurant (Map pp292-3; ☎ 801-363-5466; 63 E South Temple St; meals $6-10; ☺ 11am-8pm Mon-Sat) The down-home, carb-rich cookin' is just like your Mormon grandmother used to make, only it's served cafeteria-style in a historic house.

Hong Kong Teahouse (Map pp292-3; ☎ 801-531-7010; 565 W 200 South; mains $6-9; ☺ 11am-9:30pm Tue-Sun) Come Sunday before 3pm for great dim sum; other times, it's a respectably good Chinese joint.

Bombay House (Map p290; ☎ 801-581-0222; 1615 S Foothill Dr; mains $8-16; ☺ dinner Mon-Sat) East of downtown, Bombay's Indian cooking is vibrant and fiery. Arrive early; it gets packed.

Hires Big H (Map pp292-3; ☎ 801-364-4582; 425 S 700 East; meals $8; ☺ lunch & dinner) This classic '50s-style drive-in makes great burgers, fries and root beer.

Squatter's Pub Brewery (Map pp292-3; ☎ 801-363-2739; 147 W 300 South; meals $8-14; ☺ lunch & dinner) The classic brewpub, Squatters crafts Utah's best beer to accompany its Asian stirfries, juicy burgers, and bangers and mash. Fireplaces blaze in winter.

Red Rock Brewing Company (Map pp292-3; ☎ 801-521-7446; 254 S 200 West; dishes $8-15; ☺ lunch & dinner) Also vying for best-brewpub honors, Red Rock gets jammin' on weekends. The extensive menu includes good salads and wood-fired pizzas.

Salt Lake Roasting Company (Map pp292-3; ☎ 801-363-7572; 320 E 400 South; ☺ to midnight Mon-Sat) For pastries, soups, quiches, sandwiches, and room to spread out, you can't beat this two-story café.

MIDRANGE

Lugano (Map p288; ☎ 801-412-9994; 3364 S 2300 East; mains $10-20; ☺ dinner; Ⓟ) Bright, dynamic flavors are the hallmarks at this *bellissimo* chef-owned, modern-northern-Italian trattoria, where there's nary a tourist. Share specialties from the wood-fired oven. Well worth the 15-minute drive from downtown; great après-ski location.

Martine (Map pp292-3; ☎ 801-363-9328; 22 E 100 South; tapas $8-10, 2-course dinner $25-28, 3-course dinner $32; ☺ lunch Mon-Fri, dinner Tue-Sat) The chef is a proponent of the Slow Food movement at this soulful downtowner that serves small plates of earthy cooking, spiked with infused oils and flavor-packed sauce reductions. Come for dinner, not lunch.

Takashi (Map pp292-3; ☎ 801-519-9595; 18 W Market St; lunch $9-12, dinner $14-19; ☺ lunch & dinner Mon-Sat) Tops in town for sushi, Takashi's hip-and-happening scene means there's always a wait, unless you call ahead. Bring earplugs.

Café Trio (Map p290; ☎ 801-533-8746; 680 S 900 East; mains $8-16; ☺ 11am-10pm) This stylin' neighborhood fave for the under-40 set fires up flatbreads and roasted meats in its wood-burning oven. Killer martinis and sexy waiters too.

Avenues Bakery & Bistro (Map pp292-3; ☎ 801-746-5626; 481 E South Temple St; lunch $7-9, dinner $10-18; ☺ 6:30am-10pm Tue-Sat, no dinner Sun-Mon; Ⓟ) The owner is passionate about bread-making. Enjoy a crusty loaf with soup, salad or a tasty sandwich; at dinner there's bistro fare like lamb shanks and seared salmon.

L'Avenue Bistro (Map p290; ☎ 801-485-4494; 1355 E 2100 South; mains $16-23; ☺ lunch & dinner; Ⓟ) Francophiles flip over this big, bustling French brasserie's classic cassoulet, superb sauces and perfect *pomme frites*.

AUTHOR'S CHOICE

Metropolitan (Map pp292-3; ☎ 801-364-3472; 173 W Broadway; mains $18-28; ☺ dinner Mon-Sat) If Salt Lake had celebs, they'd hang out at Metropolitan, where the culinary skills are so good and the flavors so sparkling they merit comparison with big-city restaurants in California. The sexy concrete-and-velvet dining room complements the chef's artistry. Budget gourmands: order small plates from the bistro menu ($8 to $12) while swilling martinis at the bar.

Oasis Café (Map pp292-3; ☎ 801-322-0404; 151 S 500 East; lunch $6-9, dinner $16-20; ☺ 8am-9pm; Ⓟ) Fresh-faced bohemians flock here for French-press coffee, pastries, veg-heavy meals and organic-chicken dishes. Sit outside in nice weather.

Sage's Café (Map pp292-3; ☎ 801-322-3790; 473 E Broadway; mains $12-15; ☺ dinner Wed-Fri, 9am-9pm Sat & Sun) Everything at this café is vegan, organic and made in-house (including the root beer) at this comfy spot in a former home.

TOP END

Market Street Grill & Oyster Bar (Map pp292-3; ☎ 801-322-4668, 801-331-0644; 48 W Market St; breakfast $5-10, mains $13-30; ☺ breakfast from 6:30am, lunch & dinner) Fresh-from-the-coast seafood is the specialty at always-bustling Market Street, SLC's favorite, cosmopolitan fish house. The adjoining oyster bar gets packed with the city's bon vivants. It does good breakfasts too.

Cucina Toscana (Map pp292-3; ☎ 801-328-3463; 307 W Pierpont Ave; mains $15-25; ☺ dinner Mon-Sat) Osso buco and homemade pasta are the house specialties at this white-tablecloth dining room inside a converted warehouse; the charming, oh-so-Italian owner brought his recipes from Italy.

Log Haven (Map p288; ☎ 801-272-8255; mains $26; ☺ dinner) If you've been wondering lately where to pop the question, look no further than this ever-so-romantic log-cabin-style lodge, 4 miles up Mill Creek Canyon. On the plate, the highly stylized, architectural presentations are as memorable as the room.

Also consider:

Bambara (Map pp292-3; ☎ 801-364-5454; Hotel Monaco, 202 S Main St; mains $20-30; Ⓟ) Swank and happening, for 40-somethings on expense accounts.

Spencer's (Map pp292-3; ☎ 801-238-4748;, 255 S West Temple St; mains $20-33; Ⓟ) Old-guard, Scotch-and-cigar steakhouse. Tops for beef.

GROCERIES

SLC's best indie grocer, **Liberty Heights Fresh** (Map p290; ☎ 801-467-2434; 1242 S 1100 East) carries organic produce, fresh-baked bread and gourmet cheeses. For chain groceries go to **Albertson's** (Map pp292-3; ☎ 801-364-5594; 370 E 200 South), closest to downtown, or **Wild Oats Community Market** (Map pp292-3; ☎ 801-355-7401; 645 E 400 South), fabulous but pricey.

Drinking

See p226 to understand the slightly confusing rules about alcohol consumption.

Port O' Call (Map p292-3; ☎ 801-521-0589; 78 W 400 South) has sports downstairs, a main-floor neighborhood bar and giant dance floor and outdoor patio upstairs. **Bayou** (Map pp22-3; ☎ 801-961-8400; 645 S State St; ☽ Mon-Sat) has over 150 kinds of beer and good Cajun cookin' too. Swill gin in high heels at **Circle Lounge** (Map pp292-3; ☎ 801-531-5400; 328 S State St; ☽ Tue-Sat) where there's live jazz Thursday to Saturday. Martinis are the house drink at **Red Door** (Map pp292-3; ☎ 801-363-6030; 57 W 200 South; ☽ Mon-Sat); weekends get packed – and loud. Next door, **Bambara** (Map pp292-3; ☎ 801-364-5454; 202 S Main St), at the Hotel Monaco, is great for cocktails; it's popular with the khakis crowd. Show off your latest tattoos and piercings at **Burt's Tiki Lounge** (Map p290; ☎ 801-521-0572; 726 S State).

Sip lattes, play chess or read alongside SLC's indie-culture mavens in **Coffee Garden** (Map p290; ☎ 801-355-3425; 898 S 900 East; ☽ 6am-11pm) in the hip 9th and 9th neighborhood.

In the arts district, **Cup of Joe** (Map pp292-3; ☎ 801-363-8322; 353 W 200 South; ☽ 7am-midnight Mon-Sat; 9am-8pm Sun) has good coffee, gelato and weekend performances (right).

Entertainment

The **Salt Lake City Arts Council** (☎ 801-596-5000; www.slcgov.com/arts) has a complete cultural-events calendar, which lists theater, dance, opera, symphony and free outdoor concerts. The historic **Capitol Theater** (Map pp292-3; ☎ 801-355-2787; 50 W 200 South), dramatic **Rose Wagner Performing Arts Center** (Map pp292-3; 138 W 300 South), and acoustically rich **Abravenel Hall** (Map pp292-3; ☎ 801-533-6683; 123 W South Temple St) are primary venues. For tickets call **ArtTix** (☎ 801-355-2787, 888-451-2787; www.arttix.org).

Major dance clubs and live-music venues change frequently; check *City Weekly* for listings. **Club Sound** (Map pp292-3; ☎ 801-328-0255; 579 W 200 South; ☽ Wed-Sat) is 18 and over and has a huge dance floor and live bands; Friday is gay. **Club Naked** (Map pp292-3; ☎ 801-521-9292; 326 S West Temple St; ☽ Wed-Sat) has a big dance floor and DJ beats; Saturday is gay. Dance to house, hip-hop and R&B at **Vortex** (Map pp292-3; ☎ 801-548-1834; 404 S West Temple St; ☽ Wed-Sat); Friday's go-go dancers fire up the crowd. The **Velvet Room** (☎ 801-478-4310; 155 W 200 South) gets occasional headliners

such as Jimmy Cliff; otherwise there's dancing to DJ grooves. From dueling pianos to karaoke and comedy, there's always something happening at neighborhoody **Tavernacle Social Club** (Map pp292-3; ☎ 801-519-8900; 201 E Broadway); great martinis too. For coffeehouse cool, Friday is acoustic night and Saturday open-mic-poetry night (8pm to 10pm) at **Cup of Joe** (left).

Utah Jazz (www.nba.com/jazz), the men's professional basketball team, play at the **Delta Center** (Map pp292-3; ☎ 801-355-3865; 301 W South Temple St). The International Hockey League's **Utah Grizzlies** (☎ 801-988-7825) play at the **E Center** (Map p290; ☎ 801-988-8888; 3200 South Decker Lake Dr, West Valley City), which hosted most of the men's ice hockey competitions during the Olympics.

Franklin Covey Field (Map p290; ☎ 801-485-3800; 77 W 1300 South), hosts the **Salt Lake Stingers** baseball team, the AAA minor-league affiliate of the **Anaheim Angels**.

Shopping

The best downtown major-label shopping is at the diverse indoor-outdoor **Gateway** (☎ 801-456-0000; www.shopthegateway.com; 200 South to 50 North, 400 West to 500 West). Nearby, find artists' studios, indie boutiques and funky second-hand stores at **Artspace** (Map pp292-3; Pierpont Ave, btwn 300 & 400 West) in SLC's warehouse district. **Sugarhouse** (Map p290; 2100 South, btwn 900 & 1300 East) looks like Main Street USA and has a good mix of indie shops and mall stores. For more brand names, head to the 100 stores inside the converted trolley barns at **Trolley Square** (Map pp292-3; ☎ 801-521-9877; 600 South at 700 East).

Getting There & Around

AIR

Salt Lake City International Airport (Map p290; ☎ 801-575-2400; www.slcairport.com) is 6 miles west of downtown. Numerous door-to-door **shuttle vans** are available at the airport; a trip downtown costs $10 to $15. Call the airport's **transportation desk** (☎ 801-575-2477) for details.

BUS

Greyhound (☎ 801-355-9579; 160 W South Temple St) has several daily buses south through Provo and St George to Las Vegas, Nevada ($53, 8½ hours); west to San Francisco ($79, 16 hours); east to Denver ($61, 10 to 12 hours); and north to Seattle ($101, 20 to 24 hours).

CAR

National rental agencies have city and airport offices, see p474.

Rugged Rental (Map p290; ☎ 801-977-9111, 800-977-9111; www.ruggedrental.com; 2740 W California Ave) specializes in 4WDs and SUVs and has good service and better rates than the majors.

PUBLIC TRANSPORTATION

UTA (☎ 801-743-3882, 888-743-3882; www.rideuta.com; $1.30) buses serve Salt Lake City and the Wasatch Front area until about midnight (limited service Sunday). **TRAX** ($1.25), UTA's light-rail system, runs east from the Delta Center to the university; a second suburban line runs south to Sandy. The center of downtown Salt Lake is a free-fare zone.

UTA buses also go to Provo, Tooele, Ogden and other Wasatch Front–area cities

---

and suburbs ($2.50); during ski season they serve the four local resorts and Sundance, near Provo (all $6, round-trip).

Yellow Cab (☎ 801-521-2100) is a 24-hour taxi service.

TRAIN

Amtrak's (☎ 801-322-3510, 800-872-7245; www.amtrak .com) *California Zephyr* stops daily at the **station** (Map pp292-3; 340 S 600 West) going east to Chicago ($112 to $219, 35 hours) and west to Oakland, California ($59 to $115, 18 hours).

WASATCH FRONT SKI AREAS

Utah has awesome skiing, some of the best in North America. Its fabulous low-density, low-moisture snow – 300in to 500in of it a year – and thousands of acres of high-altitude terrain helped earn Utah the honor of hosting the 2002 Winter Olympics.

Resorts are clustered atop the peaks of the Wasatch Mountains. Most areas lie within 45 to 60 minutes of the SLC airport, so you can leave New York or Los Angeles in the morning and be skiing by noon. Saturday is busiest; Sunday ticket sales drop by a third because the Mormons are in church.

Ski season runs mid-November to mid-April. Snowbird is the last to close and sometimes stays open through Memorial Day. You don't need to rent a car to reach most areas. For transportation and resort information, contact **Ski Utah** (☎ 800-754-8724; www.skiutah.com).

Advanced skiers looking for knock-your-socks-off adventure should definitely consider a backcountry ski-trek with **Ski Utah Interconnect Adventure Tour** (☎ 801-534-1907; www.skiutah.com/resorts/interconnect; mid-Dec–mid-April), a guided, out-of-bounds tour of four to six resorts in one day. The $150 fee includes lunch, lift ticket and return transportation. The four-resort trip, versus the six, allows for more off-piste skiing.

Backcountry enthusiasts: heed avalanche warnings! Take a course at a resort, carry proper equipment and check conditions with the **Utah Avalanche Center** (☎ 801-524-4304; www.avalanche.org/~uac; ☺ 4am-noon). For **road conditions**, dial ☎ 511. All resorts rent equipment. Save by renting off-mountain (but if there's a problem with the equipment, you're stuck). Drink plenty of fluids: dehydrated muscles injure easily.

DETOUR: BINGHAM CANYON MINE

Twenty-five miles south of SLC, visit the reputedly only construction on earth, other than the Great Wall of China, that's visible from outer space: **Bingham Canyon Copper Mine** (☎ 801-252-3234; car/motorcycle $4/2; ☺ 8am-8pm Apr-Oct). Six *billion* tons of rock have been removed since 1906 from this humongous copper mine. It's an environmental disaster – and whadya know, it's a tourist attraction. The **visitor center** (☺ 8am-dusk Apr-Oct) includes a museum, film presentation and overlook. Take I-15 south to exit 301, then Hwy 48 west.

UTAH

The following resorts (downhill and cross-country) are laid out from north to south. Lodging options follow each listing.

Ogden Valley Resorts

Because the Ogden Valley is an hour's drive from Salt Lake City, most SLC metro area residents head to Park City or to the Cottonwood Canyons to ski. Consequently Ogden Valley's slopes are luxuriously empty.

The itty-bitty towns of Huntsville and Eden are nearest the resorts and have an inviting alpine feel; see right for sleeping and eating listings. If you're on a budget, the cheapest rooms are about 20 miles away, just out of the mountains, near the freeway in the not-so-pretty city of Ogden (p316).

SNOWBASIN

Between 1998 and 2001, **Snowbasin** (☎ 801-620-1000, 888-437-5488; www.snowbasin.com) shot to high-end resort status, when the owner spent $125 million to attract the Olympic downhill races. There's everything from gentle slow-skiing zones to wide-open groomers and boulevards, to jaw-dropping steeps and gulp-and-go chutes. Hotshots: check out the butterfly-inducing 73%-grade Olympic run, which dumps into a course with double fall lines. The exposed-timber-and-glass lodges are nothing short of magnificent, one decked out with marble bathrooms and a $750,000 chandelier of red Murano glass. The summit lodge (accessible to non-skiers) has a towering four-sided fireplace and a deck overlooking daredevil steeps. In 20 years the resort will be the next Vail, but for now Snowbasin remains a hidden gem with fantastic skiing, top-flight service and nary a lift line, even on Saturday. Snowbasin also grooms 25km of **Nordic skiing,** both classic and skating.

TOP FIVE RESORTS TO ESCAPE
SATURDAY CROWDS

■ Snowbasin (above)
■ Solitude (p304)
■ Sundance (p306)
■ Powder Mountain (right)
■ The Canyons (p303)

The Snowbasin lowdown: 2950ft vertical drop, base elevation 6400ft; 2660 acres, 20% beginner, 50% intermediate, 30% expert; one high-speed tram, three high-speed chairs, five fixed-grip chairs.

There's no on-mountain lodging yet, but the resort has package rates with the Little America Hotel (p295) in Salt Lake City (50 miles). Huntsville is 10 miles away.

POWDER MOUNTAIN

If you're someone who likes to don a backpack and spend the day in solitude, you'll groove on old-fashioned mom-and-pop **Powder Mountain** (☎ 801-745-3772; www.powder mountain.net; adult/senior/child $43/35/25). There's no snowmaking, but Mother Nature provides 500in annually. With 5500 skiable acres, this is America's largest area, but only 2900 acres are lift-served by just four chairs and three rope tows, none high-speed. You can also ski down to a shuttle bus that runs every 15 minutes back to the lodge. There's also cat-skiing (per ride $7). Best of all, two weeks after a storm, you'll still find powder. There's also **night skiing** till 10pm.

The Powder Mountain lowdown: 3005ft vertical drop, base elevation 6895ft; 10% beginner, 60% intermediate; 30% advanced.

Lodging in on-mountain motel rooms runs $85 to $110; condos range from $220 to $280. Eden is 8 miles away.

SLEEPING & EATING

Ask about ski packages at all the following places. Eden is closest to Powder Mountain; Huntsville is closest to Snowbasin.

Red Moose Lodge (☎ 801-745-6667, 866-996-6673; http://theredmooselodge.com; 2547 N Valley Junction Dr, Eden; r $80-110; ⊠ ☒ 🖳) This log-front place has good rates and big rooms in a modern, tin-roofed lodge.

Snowberry Inn (☎ 801-745-2634, 888-334-3466; www.snowberryinn.com; 1315 N Hwy 158, Eden; r $130-190; ⊠ 🖳) Seven theme-decorated rooms with private bathroom and spa; rates include full breakfast.

Wolf Lodge (☎ 801-745-2621, 800-345-8824; www .wolflodgecondos.com; 3615 N Wolf Creek Dr; r $120-165; ⊠) Just north of Eden, near Powder Mountain. You can rent condos with kitchens.

Wolf Creek Resort (☎ 801-745-3787, 800-301-0817; www.wolfcreekresort.com; 3900 N Wolf Creek Dr; condos with kitchen $175-250; ⊠ 🖳) The valley's nicest condos are here.

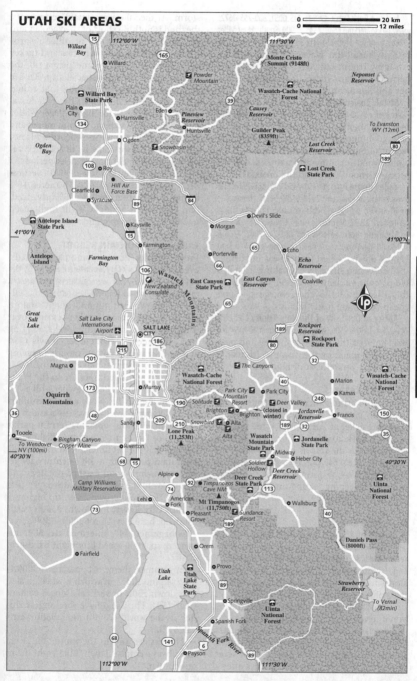

Jackson Fork Inn (☎ 801-745-0051, 800-255-0672; www.jacksonforkinn.com; 7345 E 900 South, Huntsville; $70-85, with spa $120-130) In Huntsville, nearest to Snowbasin, this place has seven simple, attractive rooms upstairs in a converted barn. Downstairs there's a restaurant (dinner and Sunday brunch).

Atomic Chalet B&B (☎ 801-745-0538; www.atomic chalet.com; r $110-150; ✕ 🖳) During the Olympics, the men's US downhill team stayed here, 10 minutes from Snowbasin (call for directions). Super-comfy modern rooms with blond-wood furniture and extras like bathrobes, in-room VCRs and full breakfast.

Valley House Inn (☎ 801-745-8259, 888-791-8259; www.valleyhouseinn.com; 7318 E 200 South, Huntsville; ste $100-170; ✕ 🐾) B&B theme rooms in a restored 1872 Victorian.

Shooting Star Saloon (☎ 801-745-2002; 7350 E 200 South, Huntsville; burgers $5; ☖ noon-8pm Wed-Sun) Hands-down the best place to eat and drink. It's been open since 1879, making it Utah's oldest continuously operating saloon. Seek this place out: the cheeseburgers – and cheap beer – are justly famous.

Abbey of Our Lady of the Holy Trinity (☎ 801-745-3784; 1250 S 9500 East; ☖ 10am-noon & 1:15-5pm Mon-Sat) For a treat, pick up honey and peanut butter made by the Trappist Monks at this abbey, 3 miles east of Huntsville.

Park City Resorts

By advance arrangement, trade your airline boarding pass for a same-day, free afternoon lift ticket at Park City's three resorts; see www.parkcityinfo.com for details. Rent equipment at the resorts or in town at **Jans** (Map p307; ☎ 801-649-4949, 800-745-1020; www.jans .com; 1600 Park Ave; ☖ 8am-9pm); make reservations. For sleeping, eating and transportation listings, see p309.

DEER VALLEY

A resort of superlatives, **Deer Valley** (☎ 435-649-1000, 800-424-3337; www.deervalley.com; adult/senior/child $73/51/41) is famous for superb dining, white-glove service and uncrowded slopes as meticulously groomed as the gardens of the Château de Versailles. Every trail perfectly follows the fall line, which means you'll never skate a single cat-track.

Because the genteel, fur-clad regulars stick to easy-does-it intermediate trails, powder hounds can find hundreds of acres of untracked glades and steeps, days after a storm. At the 10 on-mountain restaurants, the food is nothing short of spectacular, and no more expensive than at other resorts. From cilantro-glazed spare ribs and turkey chile, to ahi-tuna tartar and prime rib, the cuisine alone merits a special trip. To see a parade of haute-alpine drag that would make Isaac Mizrahi blush, head to Royal Street Cafe (p312) for lunch. Deer Valley hosted the 2002 Olympic slalom, mogul and freestyle-aerial events. Snowboarding is not allowed. The resort caps its ticket sales; reserve tickets in advance for peak periods.

The Deer Valley lowdown: 3000ft vertical drop, base elevation 6570ft; 1750 acres, 15% beginner, 50% intermediate, 35% advanced; one high-speed gondola, eight high-speed quads, 12 fixed-grip chairs.

PARK CITY MOUNTAIN RESORT

From boarder dudes to moms and dads, everyone skis **Park City Mountain Resort** (☎ 435-649-8111, 800-222-7275; www.parkcitymountainresort. com; adult/senior/child $71/40/42), host of the Olympic snowboarding and giant slalom events. The awesome terrain rises right over downtown and covers nine peaks, ranging from groomers to wide-open bowls (750 acres of them!), to cotton-mouth-inducing super steeps. Experts: make a beeline to Mt Jupiter; the best open trees are in the Black Forest. For untracked powder, hike up Pinecone Ridge. Test your aerial technique on an Olympic-worthy boarding and freestyle course at four amazing terrain parks; there's also a huge superpipe. **Night skiing** lasts till 7:30pm. At lunch, head to the mid-mountain Snowhut, a 19th-century lodge, for its mm-mm-good mashed potatoes and gravy. Avoid the mountain Saturday; it gets packed. To avoid crowds, stay up high.

Park City Resort lowdown: 3100ft vertical drop, base elevation 6900ft; 3300 acres, 18% beginner, 44% intermediate, 38% advanced; six high-speed lifts, eight fixed-grip chairs.

In summer, the resort operates a 3000ft-long 'alpine slide,' in which a wheeled sled flies down 550ft of vertical along a cement track ($9). They also have the longest zipline in the world (2300ft long, 550ft vertical; $17).

The easiest way to the mountain is via the always-empty Town Lift, right from downtown.

THE CANYONS

The **Canyons** (☎ 435-649-5400; www.thecanyons .com; adult/senior/child $71/42/42) transformed into Utah's largest resort in 1997, with an explosion of new lifts and acreage, and it continues to grow. Consequently its identity is evolving too. The 146 trails include varied terrain for all levels, with wide groomers for beginners and intermediates. Experts: head to Ninety-nine Ninety. There's a liberal open-boundary policy (heed avalanche warnings) as well as seven natural half-pipes, one of them a whopping mile long, perfect for boarding. The resort sprawls across eight aspen-covered peaks, and has lots of freshies on a powder day. To avoid skiing through an ugly real-estate subdivision, stay away from the area marked on maps as 'the Colony.' The resort is 4 miles outside of town, close to the freeway. On Saturday, when Park City Mountain Resort is teeming with people, you'll find more shoulder room here. On weekends in summer and winter, live-music concerts rock the base area; call for schedules.

The lowdown: 3190ft vertical drop, base elevation 6800ft; 3500 acres, 14% beginner, 44% intermediate, 42% advanced; one high-speed gondola, five high-speed chairs, seven fixed-grip chairs.

If you want to set up a home base at the mountain, the resort is booming with development and includes a pedestrian village, condos and the Grand Summit, a cushy hotel. Call the resort for details. (But it's more fun to stay in town.)

Salt Lake City Resorts

The four resorts east of Salt Lake City sit at the end of two canyons, Little Cottonwood and Big Cottonwood. (To remember which is which, the big resorts, Alta and Snowbird, are in Little Cottonwood, and the little resorts, Solitude and Brighton, are in Big Cottonwood.)

The USFS offers ranger-led skiing programs at Alta, Brighton and Snowbird; contact the **Cottonwood Canyons Foundation** (☎ 801-947-8263; www.cottonwoodcanyons.org). For a major splurge, go helicopter skiing with **Wasatch Powderbird Guides** (☎ 801-742-2800; www.powderbird.com; per day from $525).

Reach the resorts for $6 round-trip via SLC's public transit system, **UTA** (p299). For shuttle service, contact **Canyon Transportation**

(☎ 801-255-1841, 800-255-1841; www.canyontransport .com), which also goes to Park City and between Big and Little Cottonwood Canyons. Or call **All Resort Express** (☎ 801-457-9457; www .allresort.com). For ski-package deals, see www .visitsaltlake.com/ski or the specific resorts' websites.

ALTA SKI AREA

Dyed-in-the-wool skiers pilgrimage to **Alta** (☎ 801-359-1078, 888-782-9258; www.alta.com; Little Cottonwood Canyon; adult $47, child under 12 $20) for its legendary high-altitude snow, thrilling steeps and jaw-dropping terrain. This is one of the pinnacles of Utah skiing. A throwback to pre-Reagan days, Alta doesn't attract see-and-be-seen types, rather the see-and-say-hello crowd, an old-guard troop for whom change is *not* good.

Snowboarders aren't allowed, which keeps the snow cover from deteriorating, especially on groomers. Hook up with a local to find the best of the wide-open powder fields, gullies, chutes and glades that make Alta famous (among them, East Greeley, Devil's Castle and High Rustler). Warning: you may never want to ski anywhere else again. Get the $66 Alta-Snowbird pass, which permits access to both areas for a stunning 4700 acres of skiing. Beginners ski for free after 3pm ($5 rentals). Ask about off-piste snowcat skiing for expert powder hounds.

The lowdown: 2020ft vertical drop, base elevation 8530ft; 2200 acres, 25% beginner, 40% intermediate, 35% advanced; three high-speed chairs, four fixed-grip chairs.

Lodging at Alta is like the ski area: simple and just as it's been for decades. If you want glitz, head to Snowbird. Every place listed here offers ski-in, ski-out access and a

---

TOP 5 BEST ALPINE SKI AREAS

- Alta – the quintessential Utah ski experience.
- Deer Valley – impeccable grooming, incredible food.
- Snowbird – mind-blowing steeps and vast bowls.
- Snowbasin – Utah's best-kept secret.
- Solitude – lives up to its name.

hot tub. Breakfast and dinner are included. Room rates in the Alta section are per person, based on double occupancy; dorm rooms are a bargain.

Alta Lodge (☎ 801-742-3500, 800-707-2852; www .altalodge.com; dm $123, r per person $140, with bathroom $160-230; ☒ 🖳) Generations of families return annually to this mid-century-modern hotel, designed by a student of Mies van der Rohe. Favored by gray-at-the-temples East Coast ivy leaguers who read the *Times* by the fireplace and play backgammon in the cozy knotty-pine attic bar (open to nonguests), the lodge provides the classic Alta experience, a perfect blend of comfort and simplicity – with no TVs. The sense of community is marvelous; expect to meet new friends at the family-style dinners.

Alta Peruvian (☎ 801-742-3000, 800-453-8488; www.altaperuvian.com; dm $157, per person $170, with bathroom $210-222; 🖭 🖳) The spacious knotty-pine-paneled common areas make up for the tiny rooms at this sometimes-raucous, always-fun lodge, popular with university-age dudes, reunion groups and families with teenagers embarrassed by their parents. The bar has Alta's most happening après-ski scene. No TVs. Lift ticket included.

Snowpine Lodge (☎ 801-742-2000; www.thesnow pine.com; dm $106, per person $120-135, with bathroom $145-175; ☒) Built of granite blocks and exposed timbers, Alta's smallest and coziest lodge has basic accommodations and inviting common areas. The die-hard skier's first choice, it's also good for small families. No TVs.

Rustler Lodge (☎ 801-742-3333, 888-532-2582; www.rustlerlodge.com; dm $114, r per person $175-290; ☒ 🖳 🖭) Alta's top-end lodge has the most creature comforts and the feel of a city hotel; there's also a good spa.

Goldminer's Daughter (☎ 801-742-2300; www .goldminersdaughterlodge.com; dm $133, s $191, d per person $151; ☒ 🖳) In the middle of the parking lot, this midrange '60s-vintage hotel with cookie-cutter rooms has zero personality, but it's got an on-site day spa.

Collin's Grill (☎ 801-799-2297; mains $8-15; 😋 lunch) Book sit-down lunch mid-mountain and trade your ski boots for fuzzy slippers.

Shallow Shaft Restaurant (☎ 801-742-2177; mains $17-37; 😋 dinner) If you're not staying overnight, wait out the traffic here over dinner, across from the ski area. Great steaks and chops; make reservations.

SNOWBIRD SKI & SUMMER RESORT

If you can see it, you can ski it at **Snowbird** (☎ 801-933-2222, 800-453-3000; www.snowbird.com; Little Cottonwood Canyon; tickets $59) the industrial-strength resort with extreme steeps, long groomers, wide-open bowls (one of them an incredible 500 acres across) and a kick-ass terrain park.

The resort is particularly popular with speed demons and testosterone-driven snowboarder dudes. If you like to ski like a teenager, you'll flip out when you see this mountain. The 125-passenger tram ascends 2900-vertical ft in only six minutes; die-hards do 'tram laps,' racing back down the mountain to re-ascend in the same car they just rode up. Skiers (not boarders) can get a $66 Alta-Snowbird pass, which permits access to both areas, for a total of 4700 skiable acres. Up to two kids under 12 can ski for free with one paying adult. There's also **ice-skating** and **snow tubing** for non-skiers.

The lowdown: 3240ft vertical drop, base elevation 7760ft; 2500 acres, 27% beginner, 38% intermediate, 35% advanced.

Snowbird has four lodges; call **Central Reservations** (☎ 801-742-2222, 800-453-3000; www .snowbird.com) for package deals. In summer, rates drop precipitously, making this a bargain resort for families. Winter rates are listed.

The splashy Reagan-era black-glass-and-concrete 500-room **Cliff Lodge** (r $119-359; 🖭 🖳) is like a cruise ship in the mountains, with every possible destination-resort amenity, from a cushy full-service spa and dramatic 10-story glass-walled view bar, to kids' programs and a rooftop swimming pool. Come before sunset for the splurge-worthy 10th-floor **Aerie Restaurant** (mains $24-30); there's also a good, albeit pricey, **sushi bar**.

At the other end of the spectrum, the **Inn** (r $99-289), Snowbird's most affordable, homey and inviting property, has rooms and condos with kitchens; all have wood-burning fireplaces. Bring groceries and save a bundle. In winter you can get lift-ticket-and-room packages for about $100 per person.

SOLITUDE

You'll feel you've got the mountain to yourself at **Solitude** (☎ 801-534-1400; www.ski solitude.com; Big Cottonwood Canyon; adult/senior /child $47/10/26). Not only is it a great place to learn, but there's lots of speedy, roller-coaster-like corduroy to look forward to, once you've gotten your ski legs. If you're an expert, you'll dig the cliff bands, gullies, over-the-head powder drifts and super-steeps at Honeycomb Canyon. But it's the attitude-free vibe that makes Solitude so cool. There are no corporate tie-ins, hardly any show-offs, and practically nobody's here. Ask about guided backcountry tours.

Solitude's **Nordic Center** has 20km of groomed classic and skating lanes and 8km of snowshoeing tracks through enchanting forests of aspen and pine. Ask about guided owl-watching walks.

The lowdown: 2047ft vertical drop, base elevation 7988ft; 1200 acres, 20% beginner, 50% intermediate, 30% advanced.

Book on-mountain rooms through the **resort** (☎ 801-534-1400, 800-748-4754; www.skisolitude .com), which often has packages that cut room rates by as much as 50%. Summer rates drop significantly.

The **Village at Solitude** (r from $200) has studios, one-, two- and three-bedroom condos, with kitchens. The **Inn at Solitude** (r from $180) has comfy, slope-side hotel-style accommodations; there's an on-site spa, hot tub and pool.

If you splurge on only one meal, make it the **Yurt** (☎ 801-536-5709; www.skisolitude.com/yurt .cfm; mains $75; ☽ dinner Tue-Sun). Cross-country ski or snowshoe by lantern light a mile into the woods for a sumptuous, but unpretentious, five-course dinner in a bona fide canvas yurt with an open-kitchen and a European-trained chef running the show. BYO wine and reserve way ahead. (NB:

there's another yurt dinner at the Canyons in Park City, but it's fussy; this is the original and the best.)

Cozy up fireside at **St Bernard's** (☎ 801-535-4120; mains $19-25; ☽ breakfast & dinner), in the Inn at Solitude, for an unexpectedly good, French-inspired dinner.

For the best après-ski and bar scene, head to **Molly Green's Pub** (p306) at Brighton.

A classic mountain roadhouse a mile west of Solitude, the rustic dining room at **Silver Fork Lodge** (☎ 801-533-9977, 888-649-9551; www.silver forklodge.com; 11332 E Big Cottonwood Canyon; r winter/summer $135/80; lunch $7-10, dinner $13-25) feels like a cozy log cabin with a crackling fireplace. In summer sit outside and watch hummingbirds buzz across gorgeous alpine scenery. The American menu features pancakes and eggs Benedict at breakfast; hot sandwiches at lunch, and always-delicious ribs, steaks and seafood at dinner. The five knotty-pine lodge rooms include full breakfast.

BRIGHTON

Slackers, truants and bad-ass boarders rule **Brighton** (☎ 801-532-4731, 800-873-5512; www.bright onresort.com; adult/senior $41/10, child under 10 free), the mountain where many Salt Lake residents first learned to ski. The low-key resort remains a good first-timers spot, especially if you want to snowboard. Thick stands of pines line sweeping groomed trails and wide boulevards, and from the top, the views are gorgeous. There's a half-pipe and terrain park, a liberal open-boundary policy on non-avalanche-prone days, and good **night skiing** until 9pm, Monday to Saturday.

DETOUR: BONNEVILLE SALT FLATS

Ancient Lake Bonneville once covered all of northern Utah and beyond. Today, all that remains are the Great Salt Lake and thousands of acres of shimmering white salt flats, which create a super-smooth surface for car racing. Unfortunately problems of salt deterioration (partly due to mining activities) have caused the flats to shrink. To combat this, the **BLM** (☎ 801-977-4300; www .ut.blm.gov/saltlake_fo), along with Reilly Industries, have been pumping salty wastewater onto the flats since 1997, an effort that has been successful.

On October 15, 1997 (50 years and a day after the first aircraft broke the sound barrier) Englishman Andy Green caused a sonic boom on the salt flats by driving the jet-car *ThrustSSC* to 763.035mph, setting the first-ever supersonic world land-speed record. Most racing happens between August and October; for a complete calendar contact the BLM.

You can see the flats from I-80 a few miles northeast of the Nevada border. A paved side road leads to a parking area (no facilities), and you can drive on the hard-packed salt during late summer and fall (it's too wet otherwise). Obey posted signs: parts of the flats are thin and can trap vehicles. And remember, salt is corrosive. If you drive on the flats, wash your car afterward.

The lowdown: 1745ft vertical drop, base elevation 8755; 1050 acres, 21% beginner, 40% intermediate, 39% advanced; three high-speed chairs, four fixed-grip chairs.

The simple cinder-block rooms at **Brighton Lodge** (☎ 801-532-4731, 800-873-5512; www .brightonresort.com; dm $95, r $125-165; 🖳) are a good deal and have ski-in, ski-out access within spitting distance of the lifts. Also check out Silver Fork Lodge (p305).

For après-ski drinks and pub grub in an A-frame right on the hill, **Molly Green's Pub** (mains under $10) has a roaring fire, an old-school vibe and great slope-side views.

Heber City–Provo Area Resorts

SUNDANCE RESORT
Towering Mount Timpanogos, the second-highest peak in the Wasatch, lords over **Sundance** (☎ 801-225-4107; www.sundanceresort.com; adult/senior/child $40/12/18), a terrific little resort, great for families and newbies. From the top, the views over Utah Lake are mesmerizing. The crowd couldn't be nicer. The hill is primarily an amenity for the resort; if you're an accomplished skier or rider, you'll groove on the super-steeps, but you'll see the whole place in two hours.

The **Nordic Center** is where it's at. Cross-country ski 26km of groomed classic and skating lanes, on all-natural snow. You can also snowshoe 10km of trails past frozen waterfalls (ask about nighttime owl-watching walks). The woods are a veritable fairyland.

The lowdown: 2150ft vertical drop, base elevation 6100ft; 450 acres, 20% beginner, 40% intermediate, 40% advanced; three fixed-grip chairs.

For more details on Sundance, see p315. UTA buses (p299) serve Sundance from SLC in winter (round-trip $6).

SOLDIER HOLLOW
A must-ski for cross-country aficionados, **Soldier Hollow** (☎ 435-654-2002; www.soldierhollow .com; adult/senior/child $17/14/9; off Hwy 113), 2 miles south of Midway, was the Nordic course used in the Olympics. Its 31km of stride-skiing and skating lanes are groomed every night. Tucked in a valley beneath 7000ft ridgelines, the course is outstanding and accessible for all skill levels. You can even participate in your own biathlon – a combo of skiing and target shooting using the actual Olympic targets. For non-skiers, there's a

1201ft-long **snow-tubing hill** (for 2hr child aged 3-6 $9, child over 7 $15), open till 8pm; book in advance on weekends, since they cap tubing-ticket sales. If you dislike any of the conditions, return tickets within 30 minutes for a no-questions-asked refund.

PARK CITY
pop 7370 / elev 6900ft
Utah's only true resort town lives up to its reputation. Park City skyrocketed to international fame when it hosted the downhill, jumping and sledding events at the 2002 Winter Olympics. The Southwest's most important ski town, it's also home base for the US Ski Team. (For details on skiing, see p302). Come spring, the town gears up for hiking and mountain-biking season in the high peaks towering over town.

A silver-boom town that went bust a century ago, Park City is booming again. The Olympics have forever transformed the town. Subdivisions sprawl across hillsides, and the ultrarich build $15 million vacation homes above Deer Valley. SLC residents flock here in winter to escape the 'winter inversion' (when dark, gloomy smog looms above the valley for weeks) and to kick it in the sun at ultraconservative Utah's unapologetically liberal-minded town – full of raucous bars, great food and charming century-old buildings.

Orientation & Information
Downtown is 5 miles south of I-80 exit 145, and 32 miles west of SLC. Bypass Main St's traffic by driving on Park Ave.

There's snow all winter. Summer averages are in the 70°Fs; nights are chilly.

The local weekly newspaper is *Park Record*. KRCL FM96.5 is the indie radio station with the best programming.

In an emergency, dial ☎ 911.
Dolly's Bookstore (☎ 435-649-8062; 510 Main St)
Library (☎ 435-615-5600; 1255 Park Ave; 🕙 10am-9pm Mon-Thu, 10am-6pm Fri & Sat, 1-5pm Sun) Free Internet access.
Park City Family Health & Emergency Center (☎ 435-649-7640; 1665 Bonanza Dr) Urgent care and 24-hour emergency room.
Police (☎ 435-615-5500; 445 Marsac Ave)
Post office (☎ 435-649-9191; 450 Main St)
Visitor Information Centers (☎ 800-453-1360, 435-649-6104; www.parkcityinfo.com; 🕙 variable, generally 9am-6pm Mon-Sat, 11am-4pm Sun; later summer) Main St

(☎ 435-615-9559; Park City Museum, 528 Main St);
Kimball Junction (☎ 435-658-9616; Kimball Junction, Hwy
224 & Olympic Blvd) Request a vacation-planner brochure;
Kimball Junction location is at I-80.

Sights & Activities

The Park City visitor center has self-guided
walking-tour brochures of the downtown

area. For a comprehensive list of activities, visit www.parkcityinfo.com. In summer, Park City's three ski resorts (p302) keep
some lifts open for **scenic rides** and special
events. Be sure to keep your eyes peeled
for moose!

For cross-country and downhill skiing,
see p309.

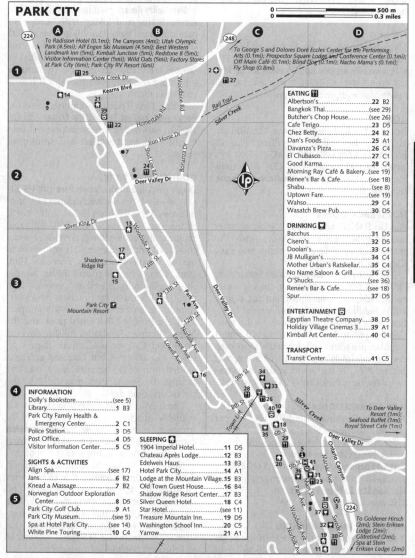

PARK CITY

0 — 500 m
0 — 0.3 miles

To Radisson Hotel (0.1mi); The Canyons (4mi); Utah Olympic
Park (4.5mi); Alf Engen Ski Museum (4.5mi); Best Western
Landmark Inn (5mi); Kimball Junction (5mi); Redstone 8 (5mi);
Visitor Information Center (5mi); Wild Oats (5mi); Factory Stores
at Park City (6mi); Park City RV Resort (6mi)

To George S and Dolores Doré Eccles Center for the Performing
Arts (0.1mi); Prospector Square Lodge and Conference Center (0.1mi);
Off Main Café (0.1mi); Blind Dog (0.1mi); Nacho Mama's (0.1mi);
Fly Shop (0.8mi)

Snow Creek Dr
Kearns Blvd
Woodbine Rd
Rail Trail
Silver Creek
Homestake Rd
Iron Horse Dr
Deer Valley Dr
Silver King Dr
Woodside Ave
14th St
Shadow Ridge Rd
Park City Mountain Resort
13th St
Park Ave
12th St
Norfolk Ave
Empire Ave
Lowell Ave
Deer Valley Dr
9th St
8th St
Town Lift
Silver Creek
Deer Valley Dr
Ontario Canyon
Main St
Swede Alley
Park Ave
Woodside Ave
Norfolk Ave
224

To Deer Valley
Resort (1mi);
Seafood Buffet (1mi);
Royal Street Cafe (1mi)

To Goldener Hirsch
(2mi); Stein Eriksen
Lodge (2mi);
Glitretind (2mi);
Spa at Stein
Eriksen Lodge (2mi)

EATING 🍴
Albertson's...........................**22** B2
Bangkok Thai......................(see 29)
Butcher's Chop House.......(see 26)
Cafe Terigo........................**23** D5
Chez Betty.........................**24** B2
Dan's Foods........................**25** A1
Davanza's Pizza..................**26** C4
El Chubasco........................**27** C1
Good Karma.......................**28** C4
Morning Ray Café & Bakery..(see 19)
Renee's Bar & Cafe...........(see 18)
Shabu..................................(see 8)
Uptown Fare.....................(see 19)
Wahso................................**29** C4
Wasatch Brew Pub..............**30** D5

DRINKING 🍸
Bacchus..............................**31** D5
Cisero's...............................**32** D5
Doolan's..............................**33** C4
JB Mulligan's......................**34** C4
Mother Urban's Ratskellar...**35** C4
No Name Saloon & Grill.......**36** C5
O'Shucks.............................(see 36)
Renee's Bar & Cafe..............**18**
Spur...................................**37** D5

ENTERTAINMENT 🎭
Egyptian Theatre Company.....**38** D5
Holiday Village Cinemas 3.......**39** A1
Kimball Art Center..............**40** C4

TRANSPORT
Transit Center......................**41** C5

INFORMATION
Dolly's Bookstore......................(see 5)
Library...................................**1** B3
Park City Family Health &
Emergency Center.................**2** C1
Police Station.........................**3** D5
Post Office............................**4** D5
Visitor Information Center........**5** C5

SIGHTS & ACTIVITIES
Align Spa...............................(see 17)
Jans.......................................**6** B2
Knead a Massage....................**7** B2
Norwegian Outdoor Exploration
Center...................................**8** D5
Park City Golf Club.................**9** A1
Park City Museum...................(see 5)
Spa at Hotel Park City............(see 14)
White Pine Touring................**10** C4

SLEEPING 🛏
1904 Imperial Hotel................**11** D5
Chateau Après Lodge..............**12** B3
Edelweiss Haus......................**13** B3
Hotel Park City.......................**14** A1
Lodge at the Mountain Village.**15** B3
Old Town Guest House............**16** B4
Shadow Ridge Resort Center...**17** B3
Silver Queen Hotel.................**18** C4
Star Hotel.............................(see 11)
Treasure Mountain Inn............**19** D5
Washington School Inn...........**20** C5
Yarrow.................................**21** A1

UTAH

MUSEUMS

The free **Park City Museum** (☎ 435-649-6104, 435-615-9559; www.parkcityhistory.org; 528 Main St; ☺ 10am-7pm Mon-Sat, noon-6pm Sun) has photos and historical exhibits.

The **Alf Engen Ski Museum** (☎ 435-658-4200; www.engenmuseum.org; adult $10, child aged 12-17 & senior $9, child aged 3-12 $8; ☺ 9am-6pm), at the Utah Olympic Park (right), has cool exhibits on skiing.

FISHING

Fly-fish for trout on the Provo and Weaver Rivers. Call **Fly Shop** (☎ 435-645-8382, 800-324-6778; www.pcflyshop.com; 2065 Sidewinder Dr) or **Jans** (☎ 435-649-4949, 800-745-1020; www.jans.com; 1600 Park Ave) for equipment and guides.

GOLF

Because the ball flies so far in the thin air at 7000ft, they call it 'ego golfing.' Play 18 holes at **Park City Golf Club** (☎ 435-615-5800; www.parkcity.org; 1541 Park Ave). Park City Mountain Resort (p302) operates a **miniature-golf course** (admission $6).

HORSEBACK RIDING

Park City Stables (☎ 435-645-7256; www.rockymtnrec.com/pcstab.htm) leads trail rides into the mountains, including Deer Valley and Park City Mountain Resorts.

The nonprofit **National Ability Center** (NAC; ☎ 435-649-3991; www.nac1985.org) runs a year-round adapted sports program for people with disabilities and their families; the facilities, trails and lessons are open to the non-disabled public. Horseback riding is the most popular program; call for details on others, including skiing, rafting, climbing and biking. NAC is the world leader in recreational therapy; Park City is its headquarters.

HOT-AIR BALLOONING

Hot-air ballooning costs $100 to $175 per person; inquire about specials. Balloon rides occur at sunrise and include champagne breakfast afterward.

Park City Balloon Adventures (☎ 435-645-8787, 800-396-8787; www.pcballoonadventures.com)

Morning Star Balloons (☎ 435-608-7433, 877-685-8555; www.morningstarballoons.com)

MOUNTAIN BIKING & HIKING

You'll feel on top of the world in the peaks over Park City, where over 300 miles of trails crisscross the mountains. The visitor center has trail maps. The **Mid-Mountain Trail** follows the ridgelines at 8000ft, connecting Deer Valley to the Olympic Park. The **Rail Trail** is an easy, popular route from town. **Jans** (☎ 435-649-4949, 800-745-1020; www.jans.com; 1600 Park Ave) and **White Pine Touring** (☎ 435-649-8710; www.whitepinetouring.com; 1685 Bonanza Dr) rent bikes and accessories and guide tours.

Deer Valley Resort (p302) has 50 miles of lift-served hiking and biking trails, and hosts major national mountain-biking events. **Park City Mountain Resort** (p302) also has lift-served biking and hiking, via the Town Lift. The **Canyons** (p303) runs its gondola in summer for hiking and mountain biking. All resorts rent equipment.

White Pine Touring (opposite) and the **Norwegian Outdoor Exploration Center** (☎ 435-649-5322, 800-649-5322; www.outdoorcenter.org) lead terrific backcountry hikes and wildflower walks.

UTAH OLYMPIC PARK

Don't miss the **Utah Olympic Park** (☎ 435-658-4200, 866-659-7275; www.utaholympicpark.com; adult/senior/teen/child $8/6/6/4; Hwy 224), 4 miles north of town at I-80, site of the 2002 Olympic ski jumping, bobsledding, skeleton, Nordic combined and luge events. It continues to host national competitions. There are 10m, 20m, 40m, 64m, 90m and 120m Nordic ski-jumping hills as well as a bobsled-luge run. The US Ski Team practices here year-round – in summer, the freestyle jumpers land in a bubble-filled jetted pool, and the Nordic jumpers land on a hillside covered in plastic! Call for a schedule; there's no fee to just observe, but take the excellent guided tour ($2). Because it's a training facility, the Sports Park may close to the public on some days.

Three-hour **Nordic ski-jumping** lessons are available in winter for $65. BYO skis. In summer, one-day **aerial freestyle-jumping** camps cost $65, including skis, coaching and a dozen-or-so jumps into the pool.

November to March, Park City's biggest thrill is an 80mph **bobsled** ride ($200) with an incredible 4Gs of centrifugal force. You can also take an introductory class to the **luge** and **skeleton** (3Gs), and sail at 60mph feet-first on your back (luge) or head first on your stomach (skeleton) for $150 each, November to February. Book long in advance.

Summertime 'rocket rides' – on wheels, down the de-iced Olympic bobsled run – are $65. For a cheaper thrill, clip on a harness and ride the world's steepest **ziplines** (33% grade; $7 to $12), a high-speed ride down a 0.25-mile-long cable, dropping nearly 500ft in elevation (you must weigh between 55 and 275 pounds).

SNOWMOBILING

If you'd rather motor than glide over the snow, two-hour rides cost about $100.

Park City Snowmobile Adventures (☎ 435-645-7256, 800-303-7256; www.rockymtnrec.com/pcsnomo.htm)

Red Pine Adventures (☎ 435-649-9445, 800-417-7669; www.redpinetours.com)

All Seasons Adventures (☎ 435-649-9619; www.allseasonsadventures.com)

CROSS-COUNTRY SKIING

White Pine Touring (☎ 435-649-8710; www.whitepinetouring.com; 1685 Bonanza Dr; day passes adult/senior/child $18/free/8) grooms an 18km course, with 3km, 5km and 10km loops of classic and skating lanes. They also rent skis, provide cross-country and telemark lessons, and guide snowshoe treks and overnight backcountry adventures.

The **Norwegian Outdoor Exploration Center** (☎ 435-649-5322, 800-649-5322; www.outdoorcenter.org; 333 Main St Mall) is a nonprofit educational guide service that leads customized crosscountry ski and snowshoe trips in the Uinta Mountains with top-notch interpretation. They're great fun, too! Rates include equipment rental; groups of three or more cost $20 per person. Smaller groups cost more.

SPAS & MASSAGE

When you've overdone it on the slopes, a spa treatment may be just what the doctor ordered.

Align Spa (☎ 435-647-9300; 50 Shadow Ridge Rd) has a down-to-earth Zen-like calm, is short on glitz, but long on relaxation.

Knead a Massage (☎ 435-615-8440; 875 Iron Horse Dr) has quiet, massage-only studios and reasonable prices.

The **Spa at Stein Eriksen Lodge** (☎ 435-645-6475; 7700 Stein Way) is discreet-chic and offers topnotch therapies in a small and swanky spa.

The **Spa at Hotel Park City** (☎ 435-940-5000; 2001 Park Ave) offers over-the-top indulgence in their 100,000-sq-ft spa with all the latest treatments.

Festivals & Events

Besides skiing, nothing has brought more attention to Park City than the **Sundance Film Festival** (☎ 801-328-3456; http://institute.sundance.org). In late January, town becomes the premiere showcase for independent film. Tickets sell out; watch the website for details.

In January or February, 10-day-long **Winterfest** (☎ 435-649-6100) commemorates the 2002 Olympics, with concerts, competitions, ice-sculpture contests and other events at Park City's biggest party. During ski season, major international competitions occur regularly at the resorts. Symphony, chamber music, bluegrass, jazz and other musical events happen throughout summer.

The **Art Festival** (☎ 435-649-8882), in early August, features 200 artists and draws 100,000 visitors. **Miners Day**, with a parade and contests, happens Labor Day weekend. For more details, contact the visitor centers or visit www.parkcityinfo.com.

Sleeping

Most Park City lodging is in individually owned condominium units in complexes run like hotels. The upside: you get a kitchen (which significantly cuts your food bill) and space for extra people. The downside: some condo owners have bad taste. Clarify whether the kitchen has an oven; otherwise it's a kitchenette. Most condo complexes have hot tubs; ask when you book.

Prices in this section are for the ski season; Christmas and New Year cost more. Summer rates drop significantly, sometimes by more than half. If you're on a budget, consider staying 19 miles south in Heber City (p314) or in SLC.

VACATION PACKAGES

A dozen or so companies can assemble packages, including accommodations, lift tickets, ski rentals, flights, car rental, transfers and other services. Among them:

Canyons Central Reservations (☎ 435-615-8040, 888-226-9667; www.thecanyons.com)

Deer Valley Central Reservations (☎ 435-649-1000, 800-558-3337; www.deervalley.com)

Lynx Ski and Golf Vacations (☎ 303-355-4775, 800-422-5969; www.lynxskivacations.com)

Park City Mountain Vacations (☎ 435-649-0493, 800-222-7275; www.parkcitymountain.com)

Park City Reservations (☎ 435-649-9598, 800-453-5789; www.parkcityres.com)

Park City Travel and Lodging (☎ 801-487-1300, 800-421-9741; www.parkcitytravel.com)

Premier Resorts (☎ 435-649-6493, 800-882-4754; www.premier-resorts.com)

RESERVATION SERVICES

Park City has no central reservations service with access to all accommodations. The **Visitor Information Centers** (p306) make suggestions, but not bookings. The following services specialize in Park City. Ask about packages with lift tickets. Skiers: verify distance from the resorts. 'Walk to the lifts' doesn't mean 'ski-in, ski-out.' Be precise about what you want.

The following list isn't comprehensive; the Park City Winter Vacation Planner and **Ski Utah** (☎ 800-754-8724; www.skiutah.com) list dozens more.

ABC Reservations (☎ 435-649-2223, 800-820-2223; www.abcreservations.com)

David Holland's Resort Lodging (☎ 435-649-0800, 800-754-2002; www.davidhollands.com)

Identity Properties (☎ 435-649-5100, 800-245-6417; www.pclodge.com)

R&R Properties (☎ 435-649-6175, 800-348-6759; www.parkcitylodging.com)

ResortQuest (☎ 435-649-6606, 800-519-4764; www.parkcityski.com)

BUDGET

There's a dearth of budget lodging in Park City in winter.

Chateau Après Lodge (☎ 435-649-9372, 800-357-3556; www.chateauapres.com; 1299 Norfolk Ave; dm/d/tr/q $30/85/95/105; ✕ P) Stay within walking distance of Park City Mountain Resort's lifts for under $100. Private rooms are clean and bare-bones basic. Segregated dorms have 15 bunks each. Best deal in town.

Star Hotel (☎ 435-649-8333; www.rixey.net/star hotel; 227 Main St; per person $95; ✕) Main St's last-remaining old-fashioned boarding house has 11 rooms with shared bathrooms, soft beds, creaky floors and mismatched furniture, but the owner is charming, and the price is right and includes breakfast and dinner.

Park City RV Resort (☎ 435-649-8935; 2200 Rasmussen Rd; tent $20, RV $30-35; ☻ year-round; ☐) The nearest campsite is 6 miles from town, 1 mile northwest of I-80 exit 145, along the north frontage road. Showers, playground, exercise room and fishing opportunities.

Also consider the campgrounds and state parks near Heber City (p314).

> **AUTHOR'S CHOICE**
>
> **Washington School Inn** (☎ 435-649-3800, 800-824-1672; www.washingtonschoolinn.com; 543 Park Ave; r $255-285; P ☐ ✕) Occupying a stately 1889 stone building that was once a schoolhouse, this inn above Main St feels like a country manor, with elegant, unfussy touches, such as Italian linens and sumptuous feather beds. For history and charm, you won't find better. Full breakfast. Hot tub and sauna.

MIDRANGE

Yarrow (☎ 435-649-7000, 800-927-7694; www.yarrow resort.com; 1800 Park Ave; r $140-190; ☻ ☐ P) This 180-room full-service hotel has well-appointed, spotlessly clean rooms, convenient to golf, skiing, cinema and grocery store. The town bus stops right outside.

Radisson Hotel (☎ 435-649-5000, 800-333-3333; www.radisson.com/parkcityut; 2121 Park Ave; r $120-240; ☻ ☐ P) Better-than-average chain rooms. Skier shuttle.

Best Western Landmark Inn (☎ 435-649-7300, 800-548-8824; www.bwlandmarkinn.com; 6560 N Landmark Drive; r $120-170; ☻ ☐ P) Save by staying near the freeway. Hot tub. Free skier shuttle.

1904 Imperial Hotel (☎ 435-649-1904, 800-669-8824; www.1904imperial.com; 221 Main St; r $150-225; ✕) Like a night at grandma's house, the Imperial has cozy and homey B&B rooms with private bathrooms. Great Main St location. Friendly innkeeper.

Old Town Guest House (☎ 435-649-2642, 800-290-6423; www.oldtownguesthouse.com; 1011 Empire Ave; r $145-200; ☐ ✕) This comfy B&B on the flanks of Park City Mountain Resort has cozy, homey touches such as quilts, lodgepole beds and paperback books. The owner also guides ski tours, trail runs and mountain biking and knows everything about the great outdoors. Great for active adventurers.

Treasure Mountain Inn (☎ 435-658-1417, 800-344-2460; www.treasuremountaininn.com; 255 Main St; studio $175, 1-/2-bedroom condo $225/350) Step right outside to Main St's nightlife and shopping. Great for families.

Lodge at the Mountain Village (☎ 435-649-0800, 800-824-5331; www.thelodgepc.com; 1415 Lowell Ave; r $180, studio $175-310, condo from $375; ☻ P ✕) Ski-in-ski-out condos smack at the base of Park City Mountain Resort's lifts.

Shadow Ridge Resort Center (☎ 435-649-4300, 800-451-3031; www.shadowridgeresort.com; 50 Shadow Ridge Rd; r $175-225, condo $285-335; ☒ Ⓟ ☒) A hundred yards from Park City Mountain Resort's lifts. Save by booking a living room/kitchen unit with pull-out sofa (instead of a bed) for $125 to $175.

Edelweiss Haus (☎ 435-649-9432, 800-245-6417; www.pclodge.com/edelweiss.htm; 1482 Empire Ave; 1-bedroom condo $170-280, 2-bedroom condo $215-360; ☒ ☒ Ⓟ ☒) Seventies-vintage condos two blocks from Park City Mountain Resort; big pool.

Prospector Square Lodge and Conference Center (☎ 435-649-7100, 800-453-3812; www.prospectorsquare lodge.com; 2200 Sidewinder Drive; r $135, studio $150-160, 3-bedroom condo $325; ☒ Ⓟ ☒) Save money by staying five minutes from downtown.

TOP END
There's no shortage of expensive lodging in Park City, particularly at Deer Valley. Rates bottom out in summer, putting the rarefied world of luxury lodging within reach of many travelers.

Stein Eriksen Lodge (☎ 435-649-3700, 800-453-1302; www.steinlodge.com; 7700 Stein Way; r from $375; ☒ Ⓟ ☒) Giant timber beams and a towering stone fireplace dominate the lobby at Deer Valley's signature, ultracushy, full-service luxury slopeside lodge. Rooms have deluxe amenities, from marble baths to big-screen TVs. Ski out the door and down the hill to the lifts.

Goldener Hirsch (☎ 435-649-7770, 800-252-3373; www.goldenerhirschinn.com; 7570 Royal St; r from $395; Ⓟ ☒ ☒) The demure step-sister to next-door Stein Eriksen Lodge, the Goldener was fashioned after a lodge in Salzburg. Rooms sport hand-painted Austrian furniture, private decks, wood-burning fireplaces, feather-light duvets and 400-thread-count Frette linens. Rates include sumptuous breakfast. In summer, stay for $100.

Hotel Park City (☎ 435-940-5000; www.hotelpark city.com; 2001 Park Ave; r $300-650; ☒ Ⓟ ☒ ☒) The lobby looks like a grand, national park lodge at Park City's only in-town full-service luxury hotel. Rooms have all the latest gadgets (eg Bose sound systems, triple-headed showers), with unexpected touches like rose petals on the feather bed to greet your arrival, perfect for a honeymoon or kiss-and-make-up weekend. The spa is tops in town.

Silver Queen Hotel (☎ 435-649-5986, 800-447-6423; 632 Main St; 1-/2-bedroom ste $425/525; ☒ ☒) Leopard-print carpets line the hallways at this all-suites right on Main St; every unit sports plush fabrics, fireplace, washer-dryer, full kitchen and room for four to six people. Great rooftop hot tub.

Eating
Unlike the rest of Utah (SLC excluded), Park City has dozens of good – and several great – restaurants. Make reservations in winter. Some places close in summer; call ahead. Expect to pay resort prices.

BUDGET
Morning Ray Café & Bakery (☎ 435-649-5686; 268 Main St; breakfast $5-9, dinner $11-19; ☺ 7am-2pm & 5-9:30pm Wed-Sun) Locals call it the 'Morning Wait,' but it's worth it for the strong coffee, veggie scrambles, homemade granola and bona fide New York bagels, flown in par-boiled and baked on site. Dinners are good (pot roast, pasta), but breakfasts are best.

Off Main Café (☎ 435-649-6478; 1782 Prospector Ave, Parking Lot H; dishes $5-8; ☺ breakfast) If the 'Morning Wait' lives up to its nickname, ditch downtown for this cute café that serves one mean breakfast.

Uptown Fare (☎ 435-615-1998; 227 Main St; dishes $5-7; ☺ lunch) Only your mom could fix a more comforting meal than you'll find at this cozy spot for homemade soups, sandwiches (try the house-roasted turkey) and chocolatey scratch brownies.

El Chubasco (☎ 435-645-9114; 1890 Bonanza Dr, mains $4-7; ☺ lunch & dinner) Serious aficionados agree the hands-down-best Mexican is at this order-at-the-counter hole-in-the-wall joint; heed the degree-of-spiciness warnings on the salsas!

Good Karma (☎ 435-658-0958; 817 Park Ave; dishes $7-9; ☺ 11:30am-9pm Mon-Sat) Tibetan prayer flags greet you at this fab little curry shop, owned by a hip, young couple who make everything fresh daily using halal meats. All curry dishes come with rice and nan; there's also soba and ramen noodles. The Indian-made chutney is delish.

Davanza's Pizza (☎ 435-649-2222; 690 Park Ave) At the base of the Town Lift, Davanza's doesn't make America's best pizza, just Park City's. Ask for the 'high-school special': pizza, french fries and soda for $5.

UTAH

Nacho Mama's (☎ 435-645-8226, 888-845-8226; 1821 Sidewinder Dr; meals $10-14; ☾ dinner) Kids love the gooey yellow cheese smothering their big plates of Mexican food; parents love the margaritas and waiter service.

Wasatch Brew Pub (☎ 435-649-0900; 250 Main St; meals $8-16; ☾ from 4pm Mon-Fri, from 11am Sat & Sun) The Polygamy Porter goes down easy with good pub grub. Stick around for TV sports, billiards and darts.

MIDRANGE

Shabu (☎ 435-645-7253; 333 Main St; mains $17-26; ☾ dinner) Park City's bon vivants flock to this happenin', 2nd-floor pan-Asian for fiery-hot popcorn shrimp, sake-steamed bass, fresh-from-the-coast sushi, teriyaki sizzle platters and the namesake *shabu shabu*, a hotpot of flavorful broth with meat or veggies. There's live music most nights.

Renee's Bar & Cafe (☎ 435-615-8357; 136 Heber Ave; lunch mains $7-11, dinner $10-14) You don't have to be vegetarian to appreciate the menu at Park City's top spot for herbivores. Among the standout savory options are the portobello-mushroom Rueben, gruyere cannelloni and macaroni and cheese. (If you're still waffling about the veg thing, let killer martinis and live jazz make up your mind.)

Cafe Terigo (☎ 435-645-9555; 424 Main St; lunch $12-15, dinner 17-28; ☾ Mon-Sat) Tops for lunch (especially on the flower-festooned patio in summer), Terigo makes terrific salads and pastas, meats and seafood.

Royal Street Cafe (☎ 435-645-6724; Silver Lake Lodge, Deer Valley; lunch $10-20, dinner $14-29; ☾ 11:30am-9pm, Dec-Mar & Jun-Aug) If you're a foodie, you'll love Deer Valley's slopeside lodge, where you can ooh and ah over such dishes as crawfish bisque, duck-confit-and-butter-lettuce wraps, wild-salmon napoleon, and perfect pulled-pork sandwiches. Sit upstairs. Prices drop in summer.

Bangkok Thai (☎ 435-649-8424; 605 Main St; mains $12-18; ☾ dinner) Though pricey for Thai, the curries and noodle dishes hit the spot. There are early-bird specials (4pm to 6pm) and delivery, too.

Butcher's Chop House (☎ 435-647-0040; 751 Main St; lunch $9-13, dinner $16-29; ☾ lunch & dinner) Right under the Town Lift, Butcher's has a solidly masculine feel, befitting its prime steaks and chops. The big granite bar is a good spot for cocktails, mac 'n' cheese and steak sandwiches.

TOP END

Glitretind (☎ 435-645-6455; dinner mains $22-34; ☾ breakfast, lunch & dinner; ℗) The romantic dining room at Stein Eriksen Lodge (p311) is one of the best. On the seasonally changing menu, expect superb presentations of European-inspired cooking, with an emphasis on game meats in winter. The wine cellar is among the finest in Utah, as is Sunday brunch (adult $29, child $19). Desserts are just as impressive: the lodge even has its own chocolatier.

Chez Betty (☎ 435-649-8181; 1637 Short Line Rd; mains $20-32; ☾ dinner; ℗) Hold hands by candlelight at this off-the-beaten-path indie charmer, where the deliciously simple, soulful menu draws inspiration from both French-provincial and California cuisine. The owner is one of Park City's greatest chefs.

Seafood Buffet (☎ 435-645-6632; adult/child $50/22; ☾ 6:30-9:30pm Mon-Sat Dec-Apr; ℗) Fish in the mountains? You betcha. If you like seafood, don't miss this stunning buffet in the cavernous Snow Park Lodge at Deer Valley. Have your fill of ahi sushi, Dungeness crab, Pacific oysters, poached salmon, prime rib and dozens of other hot and cold dishes, all perfectly prepared. Save room for dessert – if you can. Reservations required.

Blind Dog (☎ 435-655-0800; 1781 Sidewinder Dr; sushi $6-13, lunch $8-16, dinner $20-36; ☾ lunch Mon-Fri, dinner nightly; ℗) Meet the locals at the Blind Dog, a combination steakhouse and sushi bar. The steaks are tops (as is the wine list), but the super-fun, kinda-sexy, always-good sushi bar is where it's at.

Chimayo (☎ 435-649-6222; 368 Main St; mains $26-36; ☾ dinner) Every plate is perfect at Chimayo, combining the earthy flavors of Southwestern cooking with European-culinary technique. The room is one of the prettiest in town, adorned with wrought-iron chandeliers, carved wooden beams and Mexican tiles.

Goldener Hirsch (☎ 435-649-7770; 7570 Royal St; mains $23-35; ☾ dinner; ℗) Hand-painted Austrian furniture, a low beamed ceiling and roaring fireplace complement the Alpine-Swiss-French specialties, like fondue and Wiener schnitzel. If you ski Deer Valley, the bar is a sweet spot for après-ski fondue. Call for directions.

Wahso (☎ 435-615-0300; 577 Main St; mains $25-36; ☾ dinner) Reminiscent of colonial Indo-China, the visually stunning dining room at Wahso matches the heady aroma of its stellar French-Asian cooking; bring your checkbook.

GROCERIES
Mid-June to October, the Canyons Resort hosts a **farmers market** (☎ 435-649-6100; ⏰ 2-7pm Wed). Two blocks south of I-80 on Hwy 224, **Wild Oats** (☎ 435-575-0200; 1748 W Redstone Dr) has the best-quality meats and produce. **Albertson's** (☎ 435-649-6134; 1760 Park Ave) is the best in-town grocery, but it gets packed. **Dan's Foods** (☎ 435-645-7139; 1500 Snow Creek Dr) has no queues.

Drinking
Bars quiet *way* down in summer.

Mother Urban's Ratskellar (☎ 435-615-7200; 625 Main St) Town's hottest bartenders mix drinks for 20- and 30-somethings who come here for live jazz and blues and open mic nights.

Renee's Bar & Cafe (☎ 435-615-8357; 136 Heber Ave; ✗) Drink martinis with laid-back locals while tapping your toe to live music. Tuesday is Tecate-and-tacos night.

Spur (☎ 435-615-1618; 350 Main St; ✗) Bands play weekends at the Spur, a favorite of fresh-faced 30- and 40-somethings.

No Name Saloon & Grill (☎ 435-649-6667; 447 Main St) Rugby players and bikers get hammered on Jaeger here. It's famous for its buffalo burgers.

O'Shucks (☎ 435-645-3999; 427 Main St) The floor crunches with peanut shells at this hard-drinkin' bar for snowboarder dudes.

Bacchus (☎ 435-940-9463; 442 Main St; ✗) Wine aficionados swoon over smoked salmon and 100 vintages by the glass.

JB Mulligans (☎ 435-658-0717; 804 Main St) An Irish pub with a fireplace, darts and acoustic sets; Monday beers cost 50¢.

Doolan's (☎ 435-649-0888; 738 Main St) For sports head to Doolan's, which has a dozen screens.

Cisero's (☎ 435-649-6800; 306 Main St) Frat boys play foosball and shoot pool. There's entertainment Thursday through Sunday; Wednesday is locals night.

Entertainment
During the summer, concerts take place at the three resorts and other venues around town; many are free. Call the visitor center, see www.parkcityinfo.com, or contact **Moun-tain Town Stages** (☎ 435-901-7664; www.mountain towntages.com). Also check out the 'Scene' section in the *Park Record*, or pick up a copy of the pretty-good free monthly, Park City's *EAR* for entertainment, arts and recreation news.

Egyptian Theatre Company (☎ 435-649-9371; www.egyptiantheatrecompany.org; 328 Main St) The restored 1926 theatre is a primary venue for Sundance; the rest of the year it hosts plays, musicals and concerts.

George S and Dolores Doré Eccles Center for the Performing Arts (☎ 435-655-3114; www.ecclescenter .org; 1750 Kearns Blvd) From movies to ballet, the center hosts an eclectic program year-round.

Kimball Art Center (☎ 435-649-8882; www.kimball -art.org; 638 Park Ave) An exhibition space for Utah artists and the main resource for fine-arts information in Park City. The center hosts a gallery walk on the first Friday of every month through downtown's commercial galleries.

Park City Film Series (☎ 435-615-8291; www.park cityfilmseries.com) Screens first-run foreign and independent movies at the library, 8pm Friday and Saturday.

Redstone 8 (☎ 435-575-0221; Kimball Junction) Across from Utah Olympic Park. Stadium seating.

Holiday Village Cinemas 3 (☎ 435-649-6541; 1776 Park Ave) Next to Albertson's.

Shopping
Main St is chock-a-block with shopping, from antiques and art to chocolate and custom perfume. The **Factory Stores at Park City** (☎ 435-645-7078), near I-80 exit 145, have dozens of factory-outlet stores.

Getting There & Around
Several companies run vans from SLC's airport and hotels to Park City. Make reservations. **Park City Transportation** (☎ 435-649-8567, 800-637-3803; www.parkcitytransportation.com) operates shared rides ($30). **Powder for the People** (☎ 435-649-6648, 888-482-7547; www.powder forthepeople.com) has private-charter vans ($87 for one to three people, $29 for each additional passenger); reservations required. **All Resort Express** (☎ 435-649-3999, 800-457-9457; www.allresort.com) runs shared rides ($30 per person), 4WDs and sedans. **Park City Cabs & Shuttles** (☎ 800-724-7767, 435-658-2227; www .parkcityshuttle.com; 1/2/3/4+ passengers $40/28/27/25)

operates shared vans; it also operates charters to Alta and Snowbird ($100 per van, not per person).

Free buses operated by **Park City Transit** (☎ 435-615-5350) run three to six times an hour from 8am to 11pm, with diminished service from 6am to 8am and 11pm to 2am. The excellent system covers most of Park City, including the three ski resorts, and makes it easy not to rent a car. Pick up schedules and maps at the Visitor Information Center (p306), **Transit Center** (558 Swede Alley) or ask bus drivers.

Parking is difficult. Meter regulations are strictly enforced; carry quarters. Free lots are available off Main St; follow signs.

Taxis are easy to hail on Main St. Otherwise, you can call **Ace Transportation** (☎ 435-649-8294) or **Advanced Transportation Services** (☎ 435-647-3999).

HEBER CITY & MIDWAY
elev 5593ft

Twenty miles south of Park City, in the vast Heber Valley on the eastern side of the Wasatch Mountains, Heber City (population 7290) makes an affordable base for exploring the surrounding mountains. Midway (population 2121) is prettier – it's tucked against the mountains – and has nicer places to stay.

Orientation & Information

Main St (Hwy 40), Heber City's main commercial street, runs north–south; 100 South westbound goes to Midway.

Pick up information at the **Chamber of Commerce** (☎ 435-654-3666; www.hebervalleycc.org; 475 N Main St; ☯ 8am-5pm) or **Uinta National Forest Heber Ranger Station** (☎ 435-654-0470; 2460 S Hwy 40). Log onto the Internet over coffee and sandwiches at **Sidetrack Café** (☎ 435-654-0563; 94 S Main St; ☯ 6:30am-5pm Mon-Fri, 7:30am-5pm Sat & Sun).

Sights & Activities

The 1904 **Heber Valley Historic Railroad** (☎ 435-654-5601; www.hebervalleyrr.org; 450 S 600 West, Heber City; adult/senior/child $26/21/16), makes scenic trips through gorgeous Provo Canyon.

In Midway, swim in a beehive-like limestone cave at way-cool **Homestead Crater** (☎ 435-654-1102, 800-327-7220; www.homesteadresort .com; admission Mon-Fri $10, Sat & Sun $15; 700 N Homestead Dr, Midway), a 65ft-deep geothermal pool that stays 90°F year-round; make reservations.

Fifteen miles southwest of Heber City along Hwy 189 is the beginning of beautiful and steep-walled **Provo Canyon**. On the north side of Provo Canyon, take the paved, 16-mile **Alpine Loop Road** (Hwy 92) an incredibly scenic, twisting road past 11,750ft **Mt Timpanogos**, as well as two campgrounds and hiking trails.

The three spectacular caverns at **Timpanogos Cave National Monument** (☎ 801-756-5239/8; www.nps.gov/tica; per car $3; ☯ May-Sep) can only be visited on a ranger-led hike; call ahead. The middle of Alpine Loop is closed in winter; for details contact the USFS (p226), **Provo** (☎ 801-342-5100) or **Pleasant Grove** (☎ 801-785-3563) for maps, camping regulations and hiking information.

In summer the ski tracks at Soldier Hollow (p306) are used for **mountain biking** and **equestrian events**; the course is wheelchair accessible. Immediately adjacent there's a gorgeous 36-hole **golf course** (☎ 435-654-0532, 888-927-2824).

Sleeping & Eating

Camp in the surrounding national forest and nearby state parks; the campgrounds easiest to reach are off the Alpine Loop Rd. In summer, chain motels in Heber City cost between $50 and $90; the Holiday Inn costs $90 to $110. For something nicer, stay in Midway.

Swiss Alps Inn (☎ 435-654-0722; www.swissalps inn.com; 167 S Main St, Heber City; r $65-80; ☒) This quaint motel is one of the best in town.

Homestead Resort (☎ 435-654-1102, 800-327-7220; www.homesteadresort.com; 700 N Homestead Dr, Midway; r $110-220, ste $190-250, condo from $280; ☐ ☒ ☒) Most destination family resorts of this caliber faded into obscurity a generation ago, but the Homestead endures as a classic American inn with terrific food.

Blue Boar Inn (☎ 435-654-1400, 800-650-1400; www.theblueboarinn.com; 1235 Warm Springs Rd, Midway; r $150-295; ☐ ☒) European-country antiques fill this charming B&B. Its romantic dining room (mains cost between $24 and $30) is a hidden gem.

Snake Creek Grill (☎ 435-654-2133; 650 W 100 South/Hwy 113, Heber City; mains $14-20; ☯ Thu-Sun) One of northern Utah's best restaurants looks like a saloon from an old Western. The all-American Southwest-style menu features blue-cornmeal-crusted trout and finger-lickin' ribs.

AROUND HEBER CITY

Sundance Resort

Art and nature blend seamlessly at **Sundance** (☎ 801-225-4107, 800-892-1600; www.sundanceresort .com; Hwy 92), a magical resort-cum-artists' colony founded by Robert Redford, where day-trippers and bedraggled urbanites connect with the land and rediscover their creative souls. Aside from skiing and snowshoeing (p306), ride horseback, fly-fish, do yoga, write, climb or hike Mt Timpanogos.

Every building is a discrete, rough-hewn beauty, including the way-cool art shack, where you can throw pottery and make jewelry. Sundance hosts numerous year-round cultural events, from its namesake film festival and screen-writing and directing labs, to writers' workshops and music seminars. In summer there are outdoor films and music series, one with the Utah Symphony. Call for the calendar. Shoppers love the general store and its artisanal handicrafts and home furnishings.

The **cottages** (from $255; ☒ ▣) are the perfect place to honeymoon or write your next novel. Tucked among the trees, they've got pine walls and ever-so-comfy country-style furnishings such as quilts, paperback books and board games in crushed cardboard boxes; some have kitchens.

The **Deli** carries tasty picnic supplies. The **Foundry Grill** (lunch mains $9-16, dinner $11-31) cooks up sizzling burgers and steaks, *real* salads and a scrumptious Sunday-brunch buffet (adult $28, child $14). A massive pine-tree trunk stands in the middle of the **Tree Room** (mains $25-35) at Sundance's top-flight restaurant, a study in rustic-mountain chic (reservations essential). The artfully presented, sophisticated menu emphasizes game meats. You'll be hard pressed to find a better meal this side of San Francisco.

The **Owl Bar** looks like a Wild West roadhouse, but it's full of art freaks, mountain hipsters and local cowboys drinking by a roaring rock fireplace. Built of cast-off barn wood, the Owl's centerpiece is a century-old bar at which the real Butch Cassidy once drank. On Friday and Saturday there's good live music.

PROVO

pop 105,440 / elev 4490ft

The reddest of the reds, Provo is a right-wing Republican's dream city – the third largest city in Utah. The most compelling reason to visit the city is to see Brigham Young University (BYU) and hear indie bands (really). The town shuts down on Sunday.

Orientation & Information

University Ave (Hwy 189), north off I-15, exit 266, is Provo's main drag. Center St, running east from I-15, exit 268, crosses University Ave (don't confuse with University Pkwy) at Provo's meridian (or zero) point.

Get information at the **Utah Valley Visitors Bureau** (☎ 801-370-8393, 800-222-8824; www.utah valley.org/cvb; 51 S University Ave; ☽ Mon-Sat year-round, Sun Jun-Aug) inside the beautiful courthouse. For forest information, contact the **Uinta National Forest Ranger Station** (☎ 801-377-5780; 88 W 100 North). The **library** (☎ 801-852-6650; 550 N University Ave) has free Internet access.

The **BYU campus** (☎ 801-378-4636; www.byu.edu) is enormous and known for its squeaky-clean student dress codes. Drive 450 East north toward the **visitor center** (☎ 801-422-4431; tours by reservation). The campus has three worthwhile museums, particularly the what's-this-doing-here **Museum of Art** (☎ 801-378-2787; ☽ 10am-6pm Mon-Fri, to 9pm Mon & Thu, noon-5pm Sat). BYU also sponsors major arts and sporting events.

Sights & Activities

Ice skate at the Olympic hockey rink, **Peaks Ice Arena** (☎ 801-377-8777; www.peaksarena.com; 100 N Seven Peaks Blvd; adult/child $4/3.50; ☽ Mon-Sat).

In summer, cool off at **Seven Peaks Resort Water Park** (☎ 801-373-8777; www.sevenpeaks.com; 1330 E 300 North; adult/child $18.50/14.50, after 4pm $10.50; ☽ 11am-8pm Mon-Sat Memorial Day–Labor Day), the state's largest.

Watch birds and swim at 6ft-deep, 150-sq-mile **Utah Lake State Park** (☎ 801-375-0731, for reservations ☎ 800-322-3770; www.stateparks.utah.gov; 4400 W Center St; per car $6, campsites $15).

Sleeping & Eating

If you're staying the night, chain motels run in the $40s to $50s at University Ave and 300 South. Try the **Best Western Columbian Inn** (☎ 801-373-8973; www.bestwestern.com; 70 E 300 South; r $42-50; ☒ ☒). The nicest digs are at the **Hines Mansion B&B** (☎ 801-374-8400, 800-428-5636; www.hinesmansion.com; 383 W 100 South; r $120-220; ▣ ☒).

UTAH

DETOUR: GOLDEN SPIKE NATIONAL HISTORIC SITE

On May 10, 1869, the westward Union Pacific Railroad and eastward Central Pacific Railroad met at Promontory Summit. With the completion of the transcontinental railroad, the face of the American West changed forever. This **National Historic Site** (☎ 435-471-2209; www.nps.gov/gosp; admission $7; ☺ 9am-5pm, closed Mon-Tue Oct-Apr), about 55 miles northwest of Ogden, on Hwy 83, has auto tours, walks and demonstrations using replicas of the original steam engines. Aside from Golden Spike National Historic Site, few people visit Utah's desolate northwest corner. But while you're here...

At the end of a dirt road (4WD recommended but not required), 15 miles west of the visitor center, there's a wonderfully unique outdoor art installation, the **Spiral Jetty** (www.spiraljetty.org). Created by Robert Smithson in 1970, it's a 1500ft coil of rock and earth spinning out into the water. Often submerged, it became visible recently due to low water level; contact Golden Spike or the **BLM** (☎ 801-977-4300) for directions and a map.

Restaurants line Center St. For quick eats **Guru's** (☎ 801-377-6980; 45 E Center St; dishes $5-9; ☺ 11am-9pm Mon-Sat) serves tasty rice bowls and big salads. For Italian, head to **Otavio's** (☎ 801-377-9555; 77 E Center St; mains $11-16; ☺ Mon-Sat) for pizza and pasta.

Drinking

Surprise, surprise: Provo has underground alternative culture and great young bands. (The Used sprang from Provo.) The best spots are **Starry Night** (☎ 801-427-3169; 198 W Center St) and the **Muse** (☎ 801-377-6873; 145 N University Ave); hours vary. Neither serves alcohol; there's no age minimum.

Getting There & Away

Greyhound (☎ 801-373-4211, 800-231-2222; www.grey hound.com; 124 N 300 West) serves SLC ($10, 55 minutes). **UTA** (☎ 801-743-3882, 888-743-3882; www.rideuta.com) runs frequent services to SLC ($2.50), with diminished service Sunday. **Amtrak** (☎ 800-872-7245; www.amtrak.com; 300 West & 600 South) runs the *California Zephyr* once a day in both directions.

OGDEN

pop 77,230 / elev 4300ft

After the completion of the transcontinental railway in 1869, Ogden became a major railroad town. Today its restored, 19th-century downtown is a big draw, as are hiking and skiing (p300).

During its heyday, historic 25th St between Union Station and Grant Ave was lined with brothels and raucous saloons; now it has the best selection of restaurants and bars – and great neon signs. Ogden is 38 miles north of SLC.

The restored **Union Station** houses the **visitor center** (☎ 801-627-8288, 866-867-8824; www .ogdencvb.org; 25th St & Wall Ave) and three detour-worthy **museums** (☎ 801-629-8535; adult/senior/ child $5/4/3; ☺ 10am-5pm Mon-Sat). Don't miss the vintage locomotives, model trains and impeccably restored early-20th-century antique automobiles; upstairs there's a firearms collection. Also in Union Station is the **Outdoor Information Center** (☎ 801-625-5306; ☺ Mon-Fri year-round, Sat Jun-Sep), operated by the USFS, with maps and information on hiking, biking and kayaking the Ogden and Weber Rivers. Ask about ice skating at Olympic venues. Snowbasin ski resort (p300; 19 miles) has lift-served mountain-biking in summer.

For motels in the $30s, head to Washington Blvd, but see the room before you pay (some are nasty). The best is vintage-1940s **Mill Street Inn** (☎ 801-394-9425; 1450 Washington Blvd; s/d $33/40; 🖳), on five acres with a stream; see the terrific car museum. The best places are downtown. The once-glorious **Ben Lomond Historic Suite Hotel** (☎ 801-627-1900, 877-627-1900; www.benlomondsuites.com; 2510 Washington Blvd r $50-100) needs a fluff job, but it's adequate. The top spot is the spiffy **Hampton Inn & Suites** (☎ 801-394-9400, 800-426-7866; www .ogdensuites.hamptoninn.com; 2401 Washington Blvd; r $90-100; 🖳), an ersatz boutique hotel.

Karen's (☎ 801-392-0345; 242 25th St; dishes under $8; ☺ breakfast & lunch) serves stick-to-your-ribs comfort food. Inside Union Station, the **Union Grill** (☎ 801-621-2830; 2501 Wall Ave; mains $9-15; ☺ 11am-10pm Mon-Sat) gains kudos for its reliably good pastas, seafood and chops. Find high-end pub grub and tasty microbrews at **Roosters 25th Street Brewing Co**

(☎ 801-627-6171; 253 25th St; mains $9-18; ⏲ lunch & dinner). For well-cooked steaks in an over-done room, head to the **Prairie Schooner** (☎ 801-392-2712; 445 Park Blvd; meals $13-26; ⏲ dinner) where you can eat in faux Conestoga wagons. For steaks and trout, 5 miles east of town, **Gray Cliff Lodge** (☎ 801-392-6775; 508 Ogden Canyon; mains $15-24; ⏲ dinner Tue-Sun) is postcard pretty when it's snowy outside.

Greyhound (☎ 801-394-5573, 800-231-2222; www .greyhound.com; 2393 Wall Ave), north of Union Station, has daily buses to SLC ($10.50, 45 minutes). **UTA** (p299) has frequent service to SLC ($2.50).

LOGAN & AROUND
pop 42,670 / elev 4775ft

Logan is a quintessential old-fashioned American community with strong Mormon roots. Situated 80 miles north of Salt Lake City in bucolic Cache Valley, it offers year-round outdoor activities – hiking, camping, snowmobiling and cross-country skiing. Founded in 1859, it's home to Utah State University. Get oriented at the **Cache Valley Tourist Council** (☎ 435-752-2161, 800-882-4433; www.tourcachevalley.com; 160 N Main St; ⏲ 9am-5pm Mon-Fri).

The **Wellsville Mountain range** is reputedly one of the highest in the world to rise from such a narrow base. Get information and maps from the **Logan Ranger Station** (☎ 435-755-3620; 1500 E Hwy 89; ⏲ 8am-4:30pm Mon-Fri).

The 40-mile drive through **Logan Canyon** (Hwy 89 to Garden City) is beautiful year-round, but in fall the brilliant foliage is jaw-dropping. Enjoy hiking and biking trails, rock climbing, fishing spots and seasonal campgrounds.

Perhaps the best of its kind, the **American West Heritage Center** (☎ 435-245-6050; www.awhc.org; adult/child/family $6/4/25; ⏲ 10am-5pm Mon-Sat Memorial Day–Labor Day), on Hwy 89 south of town, recreates 19th-century frontier communities with plenty of hands-on activities. It hosts the popular weeklong **Festival of the American West** in July, a must for frontier buffs.

For accommodation, midrange chains are your best choice.

Beaver Creek Lodge (☎ 435-946-3400, 800-946-4485; www.beavercreeklodge.com; Hwy 89, mileage-marker 487; r summer $80-90, winter $100-130; ⊠) This lodge in Logan Canyon has TVs but no phones, and offers horseback riding and snowmobiling packages.

Bluebird Restaurant (☎ 435-752-3155; 19 N Main St; dishes $4-8) For a meal, try the 1920s-style Bluebird.

Caffe Ibis (☎ 435-753-4777; 52 Federal Ave; dishes under $6; ⏲ 8am-4pm) Popular with the university crowd, this café serves gourmet coffees and sandwiches.

NORTHEASTERN UTAH

Despite being hyped as 'Utah's Dinosaur-land,' the main attraction is actually the high wilderness terrain. All towns are a mile above sea level and the rugged Uinta Mountains make for gorgeous outdoor trips.

Mirror Lake Highway

This alpine route (Hwy 150) begins in **Kamas**, about 12 miles east of Park City, and covers 65 miles as it climbs to elevations of more than 10,000ft into Wyoming. The road provides beautiful vistas of the western Uintas and passes by scores of lakes, campgrounds and trailheads. Contact the **Kamas Ranger Station** (☎ 435-783-4338; 50 E Center St, Kamas; ⏲ 8am-4:30pm Mon-Fri) for information on the Wasatch-Cache National Forest.

WHERE THE BUFFALO ROAM

Tens of millions of bison once roamed the West. Today, Antelope Island's 700-strong herd is one of the biggest that remains.

Calves are born March to May on this island in the Great Salt Lake, when the herd is at its largest. But because of the finite natural food supply, the bison are rounded up in late October and corralled for veterinary inspection. Some are removed for the overall good of the herd, and the rest roam free. The fall roundup is one of the area's most thrilling wildlife spectacles.

In spring and fall, hundreds of thousands of migratory birds, en route to distant lands, descend on the island to feast on tiny brine shrimp along the Great Salt Lake's shore. The island is home to burrowing owls, raptors and numerous other birds. Also keep your eyes peeled for pronghorn antelope, bighorn sheep and deer, which all share the terrain with badgers, porcupines, coyotes and jackrabbits – a veritable menagerie. If you're into spotting wildlife, or if you want to see the Great Salt Lake up close, don't miss Antelope Island.

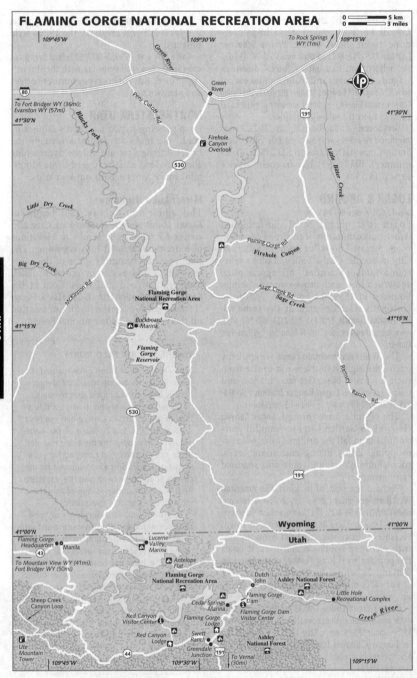

FLAMING GORGE NATIONAL RECREATION AREA

Uinta Mountains

The only way to access the 800-sq-mile, east–west-trending High Uintas Wilderness Area is by foot or horse – tough going, but the rewards are great. The high country has hundreds of lakes, most of which are stocked annually with trout and whitefish. Come for the excellent fishing and the rare experience of wild, remote wilderness. The Ashley National Forest's **Roosevelt Ranger Station** (☎ 435-722-5018; www.fs.fed.us/r4/ashley /recreation; 244 W Hwy 40, Roosevelt; ☯ 8am-5pm Mon-Fri) has information.

Basic **campgrounds** (campsites $8-10) are in the national forest surrounding the wilderness area, and there are several interesting lodging options, too. On Hwy 35 in Hanna, **Defa's Dude Ranch** (☎ 435-848-5590; www.defasdude ranch.com; cabins $30-40; ☯ May-Oct; ☒) has rustic cabins in a beautiful, remote setting; bring your own bedding (or request it). There's also a café, saloon and horseback riding ($20 per hour).

Flaming Gorge National Recreation Area

Named for its fiery red sandstone, Flaming Gorge provides 375 miles of shoreline around Flaming Gorge Reservoir. Along with fantastic scenery, there's fly-fishing and rafting upon the Green River, trout fishing, hiking and cross-country skiing. Information is available from the USFS **Flaming Gorge Headquarters** (☎ 435-784-3445; www.fs .fed.us/r4/ashley/recreation; ☯ 8am-4:30 Mon-Fri year-round, Sat & Sun summer), the **Flaming Gorge Dam Visitor Center** (☎ 435-885-3135; US 191; ☯ 10am-4pm winter, 9am-5pm spring & fall, 8am-6pm summer) at Flaming Gorge Dam; or the **Red Canyon Visitor Center** (☎ 435-889-3713; ☯ 10am-5pm May-Sep), 4 miles west of Greendale Junction. Day-use of Flaming Gorge costs $2.

Sheep Creek Canyon, a dramatic 13-mile paved loop through the Sheep Creek Canyon Geological Area, leaves Hwy 44 about 15 miles west of Greendale Junction.

The reservable **campgrounds** (☎ 877-444-6777, www.reserveusa.com; campsites $14-18) in and around Flaming Gorge are mostly open May to October, and have several nonreservable sites. **Red Canyon Lodge** (☎ 435-889-3759; www.redcanyon lodge.com; 790 Red Canyon Rd; cabins $95-125; ☐) provides rustic and luxury cabins without TVs;

Flaming Gorge Lodge (☎ 435-889-3773; www.fglodge .com; 155 Greendale, Hwy 191; r/condo $83/123; ☒) rents motel rooms and modern condominiums. Both are open year-round.

Vernal

pop 7720 / elev 5331ft

This town is the region's largest and has plenty of motels and services. The local **visitor center** (☎ 435-789-3799; www.dinoland.com; 496 E Main St ☯ 9am-5pm) includes a good **natural history museum** (with a garden full of life-size dinosaurs) and has brochures on driving tours; the Red Cloud Loop & Petroglyphs tour is a highlight. The **Vernal Ranger Station** (☎ 435-789-1181; 355 N Vernal Ave; ☯ 8am-5pm Mon-Fri) has details on camping and hiking.

Red Fleet State Park (☎ 435-789-4432; www.state parks.utah.gov; admission $5), 12 miles northeast of Vernal on Hwy 191, has boating, camping ($11) and an easy hike to a series of fossilized dinosaur tracks.

The Green and Yampa Rivers are the main waterways in the area and both have rapids to satisfy the white-water enthusiast, as well as calmer areas for gentler float trips. Trips run from $65 to $800 for one to five days; the visitor center has a list of outfitters.

Sage Motel (☎ 435-789-1442, 800-760-1442; www .vernalmotels.com; 54 W Main St; s/d $49/55) is a simple, but friendly and welcoming place to stay.

Greyhound (☎ 435-789-0404; www.greyhound.com; 72 S 100 West) runs buses to SLC (4¼ hours).

Dinosaur National Monument

One of the largest dinosaur fossil beds in North America was discovered here in 1909. The quarry was enclosed and hundreds of bones were exposed but left in the rock. Visitors now come to marvel at the find. Apart from the quarry, you can drive, hike, backpack and raft through the national monument's dramatic, starkly eroded canyons.

The monument straddles the Utah–Colorado state line. Headquarters are in tiny Dinosaur, Colorado, while the **dinosaur quarry** (☎ 435-789-2115; www.nps.gov/dino; admission $10; ☯ 8am-6pm daily summer, 8am-4:30pm Mon-Fri winter) is in Utah, about 15 miles east of Vernal via Hwys 40 and 149. There are several basic **campgrounds** (campsites up to $12) with water (in summer).

Southwestern Colorado

The story of Southwestern Colorado is a timeless classic. Part ghost story, part swash-buckling adventure, it's set to a spectacular backdrop of table-topped mesas and crumbling ruins, rugged peaks and big, big skies. Spanning centuries and blurring the line between past and present, the plot is schizophrenically complex, but never dull.

Cowboys and Indians, yuppies and ski-bums, leathery-skinned mountain folk and mink coated fast-talking transplants are the heroes and heroines. Their lives are the intertwined threads of a tightly woven tapestry, as colorful and varied as the landscape they live in.

In the ruins of Mesa Verde National Park there's a mystery without conclusion, a tale of a civilization of Ancestral Puebloans who vanished without a trace in 1300. It's a disappearance so intriguing that eight centuries later, historians and tourists flock to the cliff-side empires in search of puzzle-solving clues.

There's fodder for a grand adventure story in the mining haunts of Telluride, Durango and Ouray. It begins with fortune-seekers riding the rails west and ends with world-class ski resorts and charming towns determined to keep their historical legacy alive. Yesteryear's bordellos may now be swanky restaurants and tourism may be the new gold, but step into an old saloon, where smoke and ragtime fill the air, and time will slip away.

Yes, the Four Corners region, the only place in the USA where four states meet, has a story that visitors deem worth its weight in gold. To know for sure, you'll just have to visit.

HIGHLIGHTS

■ **Best Place to Hear the Ancestors Whisper**
Mesa Verde National Park (p323), where an entire civilization of Ancestral Puebloans (Ancestral Puebloans) vanished in 1300.

■ **Best All Around Town**
Laid-back Durango (p331) features outdoor adventures galore, charming old-world hotels, mouthwateringly good restaurants and even a steam-driven choo-choo train.

■ **Most Spectacular Drive**
Travel to the top of the world and back in time on the jaw-dropping beautiful San Juan Skyway (p336).

■ **Best Place to Get Lost**
Sandwiched between imposing peaks, tiny Ouray (p338) is a little slice of heaven.

■ **Best Kept Secret**
Wolf Creek Ski Area (p335) gets Colorado's best snow, yet crowds are unheard of and lift tickets are well priced.

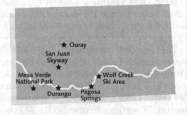

■ POPULATION: 4.7 MILLION ■ AREA: 166,568 SQ MILES ■ www.colorado.com

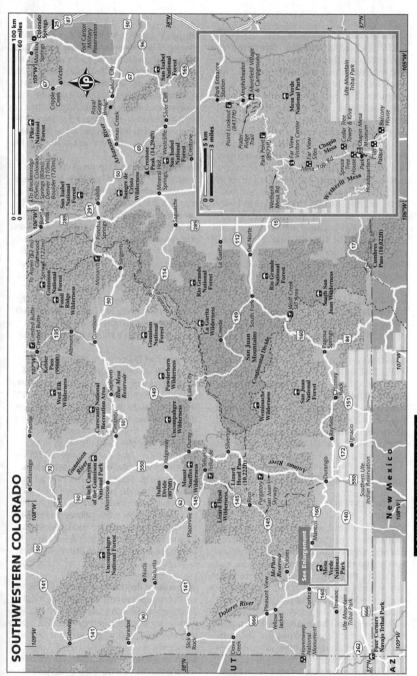

SOUTHWESTERN COLORADO

Climate

Like elsewhere in the state, Southwestern Colorado's weather is fickle and changeable. The weather bureau might report snow, but you'll wake up to blue skies and warm temperatures. The San Juan Mountains dominate the region, and winter comes early. Temperatures drop dramatically in mid-September and higher elevations will usually see their first snowfall then. The heaviest snow begins to fall in mid-November and continues through April, when the mercury starts rising, although it can snow anytime – even in July. Summer temperatures can rise into the 80°F range at lower elevations, although you should always carry a sweater because nights are cool, no matter what the time of year. Southwestern Colorado sees plenty of sunshine, and though it may snow in July, you also get January days warm enough for a T-shirt!

National & State Parks

Mesa Verde National Park (opposite) is one of the southwest's largest tourist draws. It's primarily an archeological preserve with elaborate cliff dwellings abandoned by a civilization of Ancestral Pueblo Indians in 1300. Just outside the Four Corners 'official' boundaries is **Black Canyon of the Gunnison National Park**. One of the country's newest, and most eerie, parks Black Canyon features a 2000ft chasm over the Gunnison River. Sheer walls, dizzying depths and narrow openings are all exhibited here. The region has numerous state parks as well as thousands of acres of land ripe for exploration in the **San Juan National Forest**.

SOUTHWESTERN COLORADO SCENIC BYWAYS

Venturing off the beaten path is easy in the southwestern portion of the state. The Four Corners area yields the greatest concentration of old mining roads in Colorado, and exploring these back roads is more than just visually stunning. You'll also glean a deeper understanding of the region's complex, often colorful, history, which stretches back more than 10 centuries. A few suggestions for great drives follow, but for more information on scenic byways visit www.coloradobyways.org.

Alpine Loop A demanding but fantastic drive, this 63-mile loop begins in Ouray (p338), travels east to Lake City, then takes you back to its starting point. Along the way you'll cross two 12,000ft mountain passes, swap pavement and people for solitude and stunning scenery and traverse the remote and rugged heart of the San Juan Mountains. You'll need a high-clearance 4WD vehicle and some four-wheeling skill to conquer this drive – but if you're up for the challenge, you'll reap great rewards. Abandoned town sites and mining haunts abound, and the Alpine Loop is perfect for anyone craving a little quiet time and the chance to visit with the ghosts of Colorado's past. Allow at least four to six hours.

Trail of the Ancients It's been more than eight centuries since the Ancestral Puebloan Indians, or Anasazi, disappeared without a trace from the cliffside dwellings they built in and around Mesa Verde National Park (opposite), and yet their mysterious disappearance is still pondered today. If you're searching for clues, this 114-mile drive along Hwy 145, Hwy 184 and US 160 might be a good place to start. Begin your journey in Cortez (p328) and either head northwest toward Hovenweep National Monument (p285) on the Utah border (which, like Mesa Verde, contains dense clusters of Anasazi dwellings) or southwest toward the meeting point of Colorado, Utah, Arizona and New Mexico: Four Corners. Either way, you'll travel through arid and broken terrain and pass cliff dwellings, pottery shreds and rock art. Allow three hours for the drive.

Imogene Pass This spectacular 4WD route connects Ouray (p338) with Telluride (p341). The road is only 16 miles long, but requires a high-clearance vehicle and takes about three hours to drive in each direction. Built in 1880, the old mining road is one of the highest in the San Juan Mountains (the pass summits at 13,114ft) and takes you by two important mining sites. In Ouray, head south on Main St and turn right on Bird Camp Rd (City Rd 361). You'll pass the Bird Camp Mine, once one of the San Juan's most prolific, before climbing high into the mountains. Along the way you'll have to cross a stream or two, and at times the road snakes precariously close to sheer cliff drops, which can be a thrilling adrenaline rush if you're an experienced four-wheeler. Eventually the route opens up into high alpine meadows before reaching the summit of Imogene Pass. Traveling down, towards Telluride, you'll pass the abandoned Tomboy Mine. Still littered with old mining paraphernalia, it once had a population as large as present-day Ouray.

Million Dollar Hwy Passing old mine head-frames and extraordinary alpine scenery, this breathtaking stretch of US 550, between Silverton (p336) and Ouray (p338), got its name from the valuable ore in the roadbed fill. It can be scary when raining or snowing, so take caution. See p338 for more info.

San Juan Skyway The region's most publicized drive, and for good reason, this 236-mile loop takes you past old mines and 14,000ft peaks, over high alpine passes and into lively towns including Telluride (p341), Durango (p331), Ridgeway (p341) and Ouray (p338). Allow at least two days to drive the entire loop. For more information see p336.

Information

Colorado is on Mountain Standard Time and observes daylight savings.

Colorado Bureau of Land Management (☎ 303-239-3600; www.co.blm.gov) The state's plentiful natural beauty makes camping one of its best accommodation options. This site offers information on booking public campgrounds.

Colorado State Parks (☎ 303-470-1144; www.parks .state.co.us) Information on state parks.

Colorado Travel & Tourism Authority (☎ 800-265-6723; www.colorado.com; PO Box 3524, Englewood, CO 80155) Provides state-wide tourism information along with free state highway maps.

National Park Service (NPS; ☎ 303-969-2500; www .nps.gov; Intermountain Region, 12795 Alameda Pkwy, Denver, CO 80225) Comprehensive website with state-by-state listings of national parks.

Getting There & Around

Southwestern Colorado is best seen by private vehicle. US 160 is the main east–west vein through the region, while US 550 runs north–south and connects Durango with Silverton, Ouray and Ridgeway to the north. If you're arriving from central or northern Utah, take I-70 east to US 50 south. In Montrose, Colorado, US 50 intersects with US 550. Denver International Airport (DIA; see p468) is Colorado's main hub, although it's 300-plus miles northeast of Durango. However, from DIA you can catch a commuter plane to regional destinations such as Durango and Telluride.

Greyhound (☎ 800-231-2222; www.greyhound.com) has fixed routes throughout the region. **TNM&O** (☎ 719-635-1505; www.greyhound.com) is affiliated with Greyhound and serves the same lines through Colorado.

For more information on transportation throughout the Southwest, see p472.

MESA VERDE NATIONAL PARK

Shrouded in mystery, Mesa Verde is a fascinating, if slightly eerie, national park to explore. It is here that a civilization of Ancestral Puebloans (p27) appears to have vanished into thin air in 1300. Mesa Verde is unique among parks for its focus on preserving this civilization's cultural relics so that future generations may continue to interpret the puzzling settlement, and subsequent abandonment, of the area.

Ancestral Puebloan sites are found throughout the canyons and mesas of the park, perched on a high plateau south of Cortez and Mancos. If you have time for only a short visit, check out the Chapin Mesa Museum (p324) and try a walk through the Spruce Tree House (p325), where you can climb down a wooden ladder into the cool chamber of a kiva.

Mesa Verde rewards travelers who set aside a day or more to take the ranger-led tours of Cliff Palace and Balcony House (p325), explore Wetherill Mesa (p325), to simply linger in the museum or to participate in one of the campfire programs run at Morefield Campground (p328).

Preserving the Ancestral Puebloan sites while accommodating ever-increasing numbers of visitors continues to challenge the National Park Service (NPS). The NPS strictly enforces the Antiquities Act, which prohibits the removal or destruction of any antiquities and also prohibits public access to many of the approximately 4000 known Ancestral Puebloan sites.

History

A US army lieutenant recorded the spectacular cliff dwellings in the canyons of Mesa Verde in 1849–50. The large number of sites on Ute tribal land, and their relative inaccessibility, protected the majority of these antiquities from pothunters.

The first scientific investigation of the sites in 1874 failed to identify Cliff Palace, the largest cliff dwelling in North America. Discovery of the 'magnificent city' occurred only when local cowboys Richard Wetherill and Charlie Mason were searching for stray cattle in 1888. The cowboys exploited their 'discovery' for the next 18 years by guiding both amateur and trained archaeologists to the site, particularly to collect the distinctive black-on-white pottery.

The shipping of artifacts overseas motivated Virginia McClurg of Colorado Springs to embark on a long campaign to preserve the site and its contents. McClurg's efforts led Congress to protect artifacts on federal land with passage of the Antiquities Act and to establish Mesa Verde National Park in 1906.

Orientation

The North Rim summit at Park Point (8571ft) towers more than 2000ft above the Montezuma Valley. From Park Point the mesa gently slopes southward to a 6000ft elevation above the Mancos River in the Ute Mountain Tribal Park. Parallel canyons, typically 500ft below the rim, dissect the mesa-top and carry the drainage southward. Mesa Verde National Park occupies 81 sq miles of the northernmost portion of the mesa and contains the largest and most frequented cliff dwellings and surface sites.

The park entrance is off US 160, midway between Cortez and Mancos. From the entrance it's about 21 miles to Park Headquarters, Chapin Mesa Museum and Spruce Tree House. Along the way are Morefield Campground (4 miles), the panoramic viewpoint at Park Point (8 miles) and the Far View Visitor center opposite the Far View Lodge and restaurant (about 11 miles). Towed vehicles are not allowed beyond Morefield Campground.

Chapin Mesa (right) contains the largest concentration of sites in the area. South from Park Headquarters, Mesa Top Rd consists of two one-way circuits. Turn left about one-quarter mile from the start of Mesa Top Rd to visit Cliff Palace and Balcony House on the east loop. Take the west loop by continuing straight to mesa-top sites and many fine cliff-dwelling vantages. Taking this loop first allows you to roughly follow the Ancestral Puebloan chronology in proper sequence.

At Wetherill Mesa (opposite), the second-largest concentration of sites, visitors may enter stabilized surface dwellings and two cliff dwellings. From the junction with the main road at Far View Visitor center, the 12-mile mountainous Wetherill Mesa Rd snakes along the North Rim, acting as a natural barrier to tour buses and indifferent travelers. The road is open only from Memorial Day in late May to Labor Day in early September.

Information

Park roads are open 8am to sunset, except Wetherill Mesa Rd, which closes at 4:30pm. Winter vehicle travel on Mesa Top Rd is subject to weather conditions. You may snowshoe or cross-country ski on the roadway when conditions permit.

Chapin Mesa Museum (☎ 970-529-4475) Provides information on weekends when Park Headquarters is closed.
Far View Visitor center (☎ 970-529-5036) More comprehensive information is available at the Chapin Mesa Museum, but visitors must first stop at Far View to obtain the required tickets ($2.75) for tours of Cliff Palace, Long House or Balcony House.
Mesa Verde Museum Association (☎ 970-529-4445; Chapin Mesa Museum) Has an excellent selection of materials on the Ancestral Puebloan and modern tribes in the American Southwest.
Morefield Village (showers 10¢, washers per load $1; ☯ 24hr May–mid-Oct) Near the Morefield Campground turnoff; has showers and washing machines.
Park Headquarters (☎ 970-529-4461; www.nps.gov /meve; 7-day park entry per vehicle $10, bicyclists, hikers & motorcyclists $5; ☯ 8am-4:30pm Mon-Fri) Provides brochures and maps to each visitor. These are also available in French, Spanish and German.

Sights & Activities

CHAPIN MESA

If you only have time to visit one area of the park, don't miss Chapin Mesa. There is no other place where so many remnants of Ancestral Puebloan settlements are clustered together, providing an opportunity to see and compare examples of all phases of construction – from pithouses to Pueblo villages to the elaborate multiroom cities tucked into cliff recesses. Pamphlets describing most excavated sites are available at either Far View Visitor center or Chapin Mesa Museum (below).

On the upper portion of Chapin Mesa are the **Far View Sites**, which are perhaps the most densely settled area in Mesa Verde after 1100. The large-walled pueblo sites at Far View House enclose a central kiva and planned room layout that was originally two stories high. To the north is a small row of rooms and an attached circular tower that likely used to extend just above the adjacent 'pygmy forest' of piñon pine and juniper trees. This tower is one of 57 in Mesa Verde that may once have served as a watchtower, a religious structure or an astronomical observatory for agricultural schedules.

The **Chapin Mesa Museum** (☎ 970-529-4475; admission free; ☯ 8am-6:30pm spring-fall, to 5pm winter) has exhibits pertaining to the park. It makes a good first stop, especially if you want to learn a bit more about the history behind the dwellings you are about to visit.

CLIFF PALACE & BALCONY HOUSE

Tickets are required for the one-hour guided tours of either **Cliff Palace** or **Balcony House** (admission $2.75; ☉ 9am-5pm Mar-Nov), on the east loop of Mesa Top Rd.

Foot access to Cliff Palace, the largest site in the park, resembles the approach taken by the Ancestral Puebloans – visitors must climb a stone stairway and four 10ft ladders. This grand representative of engineering achievement, with 217 rooms and 23 kivas, provided shelter for 250 people. Its inhabitants were without running water – springs across the canyon, below Sun Temple, were the most likely water sources. Use of small 'chinking' stones between the large blocks is strikingly similar to Ancestral Puebloan construction at distant Chaco Canyon.

A visit to Balcony House is quite an adventure and will challenge any fears you might have of heights or small places, but you'll be rewarded with outstanding views of Soda Canyon, 600ft below the sandstone overhang that served as the ceiling for 35 to 40 rooms. The Balcony House tour requires you to descend a 100ft-long staircase into the canyon, then climb a 32ft-tall ladder, crawl through a 12ft-long tunnel and climb an additional 60ft of ladders and stone steps to get out. It's the most challenging tour in the park, but might just be the most rewarding, not to mention fun!

SPRUCE TREE HOUSE & MESA TOP ROAD

Near the Park Headquarters, an easy walk without ladders or steps leads to Spruce Tree House. This sheltered alcove, more than 200ft wide and almost 90ft deep, contains about 114 rooms and eight kivas once housing about 100 people. One kiva has a reconstructed roof and ladder for entry. During winter, when many portions of the park are closed, access to this site is by ranger-led tours only; see p326.

South from Park Headquarters, the 6-mile Mesa Top Rd circuit connects 10 excavated mesa-top sites, three accessible cliff dwellings and many vantages of inaccessible cliff dwellings from the mesa rim. It's open 8am to sunset.

WETHERILL MESA

The less frequented western portion of Mesa Verde offers a comprehensive display of Ancestral Puebloan relics. The **Badger House Community** consists of a short trail connecting four excavated surface sites depicting various phases of Ancestral Puebloan development. For a complete chronological circuit, continue on the trail to **Long House**, the second largest cliff dwelling in Mesa Verde National Park (for this you will first need to purchase a $2.75 ticket at the Far View visitor center). The nearby **Step House**, which was initially occupied by Modified Basketmaker peoples residing in pithouses, later became the site of a Classic Pueblo–period masonry complex with rooms and kivas. Stairways and indentations in the rocks provided access to the partially irrigated crops in the terraces on the mesa top.

PHOTOGRAPHING MESA VERDE

Almost anywhere you travel in Mesa Verde is worthy of a picture or two, but perhaps the most photographed site in the park is the secluded four-story **Square Tower House** on the west loop of Mesa Top Rd. The ruin is closed to the public but can be viewed from a southwest overlook. Looking down on the ruins makes for a powerful photo, especially in the late afternoon.

Cliff Palace, the largest of the ruins with 217 rooms, also makes a great picture. The ruin faces southwest, so the best light is in the late afternoon or early evening. Try to join a later tour, when you'll have the best light and fewest companions.

Balcony House is one of the few eastern-facing ruins, and is best photographed early morning when the warm light makes the structures glow. Try to join an early tour and travel as light as possible – a visit here requires climbing ladders and crawling through tunnels. If you're shooting film, pick a faster speed (at least 400ISO) for sharper pictures. Digital shooters should set their cameras to a higher ISO.

There are many other photogenic spots around the park, including good late-afternoon views of many cliff dwellings from **Sun Point** or mesa-top sights on the west loop of Mesa Top Rd, where you'll also find the astronomically aligned **Sun Temple**.

PARK POINT

The fire lookout at Park Point (8571ft) is the highest elevation in the park and offers panoramic views. To the north are the 14,000ft peaks of the San Juan Mountains; in the northeast are the 12,000ft crests of the La Plata Mountains; to the southwest, beyond the southward sloping Mesa Verde plateau, is the distant volcanic plug of Shiprock; and to the west is the prone humanlike profile of Sleeping Ute Mountain.

HIKING

Hiking is a great way to explore the park, but follow the rules. Backcountry access is specifically forbidden and fines are imposed on anyone caught wandering off designated trails or entering cliff dwellings without a ranger. Please respect these necessary regulations, so that the fragile and irreplaceable archeological sights and artifacts remain protected for centuries to come.

When hiking in Mesa Verde always carry water and avoid cliff edges. Trails can be muddy and slippery after summer rains and winter snows, so wear appropriate footwear. Most park trails, except the Soda Canyon Trail, are strenuous and involve steep elevation changes. Hikers must register at the respective trailheads before venturing out.

The 2.8-mile **Petroglyph Loop Trail** is accessed from the Spruce Tree House (p325). It follows a path beneath the edge of a plateau before making a short climb to the top of the mesa, where you'll have good views of the Spruce and Navajo Canyons. This is the only trail in the park where you can view petroglyphs.

The 2.1-mile **Spruce Canyon Loop Trail** also begins at the Spruce Tree House (p325) and descends to the bottom of Spruce Tree Canyon. It's a great way to see the canyon bottoms of Mesa Verde.

The easy 1.5-mile **Soda Canyon Overlook Trail** takes you to the canyon edge and offers views of Balcony House and other archeological sites along Soda Canyon. It begins at a parking area on the Cliff Palace Loop Rd just past the Balcony House parking area.

Starting at the Morefield Campground (p328), the 1.5-mile **Knife Edge Trail** does not require a permit and makes a great end-of-day hike. It provides fabulous views of the Montezuma Valley and excellent spots to watch the sun set.

BIKING

Finding convenient parking at the many stops along Mesa Top Rd is no problem for those with bikes. Only the hardy will want to enter the park by bike and immediately face the grueling 4-mile ascent to Morefield Campground (p328), quickly followed by a narrow tunnel ride to reach the North Rim. An easier option is to unlimber your muscles and mount up at Morefield, Far View Visitor center or Park Headquarters.

If you choose to cycle, note that the NPS prohibits bicyclists on Wetherill Mesa Rd and secure bicycle parking is rare. Ride only on paved roadways.

WINTER ACTIVITIES

Winter is a special time in Mesa Verde. The crowds disperse and the cliff dwellings sparkle in the snow. The skies are often blue and sunny and you may be the only person around. In recent years there has been enough snow to ski or snowshoe on most winter days after a snowstorm (although Colorado's dry climate and sunshine cause the snow to melt quickly). Before setting out, check the current snow conditions by calling ☎ 970-529-4461.

Two park roads have been designated for cross-country skiing and snowshoeing when weather permits. The **Cliff Palace Loop Rd** is a 6-mile relatively flat loop located off the Mesa Top Loop Rd. The road is closed to vehicles after the first snowfall, so you won't have to worry about vehicular traffic. Park at the closed gate and glide one mile to the Cliff Palace overlook, then continue on past numerous other scenic stopping points.

The **Morefield Campground Loop Rds** offer multiple miles of relatively flat terrain. The campground (p328) is closed in winter, but skiers and snowshoers can park at the gate and explore to their heart's content.

Tours

The park concessionaire, **Aramark Mesa Verde** (☎ 970-529-4421; www.visitmesaverde.com; PO Box 277, Mancos, CO 81328), offers guided tours to excavated pit homes, cliff dwellings and the Spruce Tree House daily from May to mid-October.

Introductory three-hour tours (adult/child $36/25) depart from Morefield Campground (p328) at 8:30am and from Far View Lodge (p328) at 9am. Afternoon tours (adult/

child $39/28) include the Balcony House and depart the Far View Lodge only at 1pm.

A full-day tour (adult/child $56/44), leaving at 9:30am from the Far View Lodge, includes the morning-tour sites and goes on to examine later architecture and social developments, also taking in the Cliff Palace and with lunch provided along the way.

Sleeping & Eating

Nearby Cortez (p329) and Mancos (p330) have plenty of midrange places to stay; Farmington, NM (p406) also has accommodation options and is only 1½ hours' drive away. Within the national park, visitors must choose between two extremes: camping or staying at a high-end lodge.

MYSTERIES OF THE ANCESTRAL PUEBLOANS

Why the Ancestral Puebloans entered Mesa Verde is a subject of much speculation. Habitations in Mesa Verde evolved greatly between 450 – when the earliest simple structures were constructed – and 1300 – when the great cities were mysteriously left behind.

The earliest period of settlement, the so-called Modified Basketmaker phase that extended to about 750, found the Ancestral Puebloans dispersed across the mesa tops in small clusters of permanent pithouse dwellings – semi-subterranean structures with posts supporting low-profile roofs.

During the Developmental Pueblo Period, up to 1100, Ancestral Puebloans built surface houses with simple shared walls – like row-house apartments – forming small hamlets surrounded by fields of maize, beans and squash.

The following Classic Pueblo phase, to 1300, saw the Mesa Verde Ancestral Puebloans elaborate on the earlier structures using masonry building materials. Their efforts housed a peak population of perhaps several thousand in Pueblo villages, the precursors to cities. Greater clusters of people created opportunities for united accomplishments and perhaps a rudimentary division of labor, social organization, political control and even organized raids on neighboring villages. During this period the Ancestral Puebloans created subsurface roundrooms or kivas – for decades believed by archaeologists to be only for ceremonial use, but more recently seen to also have more basic functions, such as a place to hold tribal meetings. Hydraulic schemes to irrigate crops and provide villagers with water were developed during this time as well.

There is mounting evidence of regular communication between Mesa Verdeans and Chaco Canyon peoples in northwestern New Mexico during this period. Some researchers suggest the political, economic and social influences extended even further afield into Mesoamerica (present-day Mexico and Central America).

The Puebloans suddenly moved to the alcoves of the cliff faces around 1200. Community size depended on available cliff space, so while small cavities may have contained only a few compartments, there were many larger communities with more than 200 compartments, including elaborate blocks or rooms, cantilevered balconies, sunken round rooms and even tower structures – many connected with internal passageways.

Ancestral Puebloans inhabited the cliff dwellings for less than a century before disappearing in accord with a regional demographic collapse that is the greatest unexplained event of the era. Death, disease, invasion, internal warfare, resource depletion and climatic change are among the hardships that these peoples faced. Tree-ring chronologies offer proof of a widespread drought from 1276 to 1299, yet this explanation fails to account for the earlier population decline at Chaco Canyon or Mesa Verde's survival of earlier droughts. Population movements did occur and it is probable that many Ancestral Puebloans migrated south to the pueblos of present-day New Mexico and Arizona.

Period	Chronology
I Basketmaker	AD 1–550
II Modified Basketmaker	550–750
III Developmental Pueblo	750–1100
IV Classic Pueblo	1100–1300

SOUTHWESTERN COLORADO

An overnight stay in the park allows convenient access to the many sites during the best viewing hours, participation in evening programs and the sheer pleasure of watching the sun set over Sleeping Ute Mountain from the quiet of the mesa top.

Far View Lodge (☎ 970-529-4421; r $100; ◐ mid-Apr–Oct; ✗) Perched on the mesa top 15 miles from the park entrance, this lodge has rooms with Southwestern furnishings, private balconies and great views. It's good value and offers a memorable visit. There are no TVs or phones to disturb guests.

Morefield Campground (☎ 970-529-4421; campsites $19, RV hookups $25; ◐ May–mid-Oct) With 445 campsites only 4 miles from the park entrance, this place has plenty of capacity for the peak season. Grassy tent sites at Navajo Loop are conveniently located near Morefield Village (which offers a general store, gas station, restaurant, showers and laundry). Free evening campfire programs take place nightly from Memorial Day (late May) to Labor Day (early September) at the Morefield Campground Amphitheater.

Metate Room (☎ 970-529-4421; Far View Lodge; dishes $15-25; ◐ dinner) This restaurant has an innovative menu inspired by Native American food and flavors. Native American artwork and spectacular views of the park and Four Corners region provide the ambiance, while palates are titillated with mains like oven-roasted chicken breast with green chile stuffing and buffalo fajitas. A special experience.

Spruce Tree Terrace (☎ 970-529-4421; dishes $5-10) Near the Chapin Mesa Museum, this laid-back restaurant serves sandwiches, salads and the like, inside or out.

Far View Terrace (☎ 970-529-4421; dishes from $5; ◐ Apr-Oct) Immediately south of the visitor center, this self-service place offers reasonably priced meals. Don't miss their special – the Navajo Taco.

Getting There & Around

Mesa Verde is best seen by private vehicle. There is no public transport in the park.

CORTEZ

pop 8900 / elev 6200ft

There's nothing particularly stunning or outright unique about Cortez, but it's location, 10 miles west of Mesa Verde National Park, makes it a good lodging base for exploring the area. Typical of small-town Colorado, the downtown is lined with squat buildings housing shops selling hunting rifles, trinkets and surprisingly eclectic clothing; family-style restaurants dishing up homemade delicacies; and even an excellent microbrewery. The outer edges of the town are jam-packed with independent motels and fast-food outlets. Far-off mountain vistas complete the picture.

Orientation & Information

Colorado Welcome Center (☎ 970-565-4048; 928 E Main St) Maps, brochures and some excellent pamphlets on local activities like fishing and mountain biking are available here.

M&M Truckstop (☎ 970-565-6511; 7006 US 160/666; showers $5) South of town; offers refreshing showers.

Post office (☎ 800-275-8777; 35 S Beech St)

Quality Book Store (☎ 970-565-9125; 34 W Main St) Sells travel books and maps and offers a good selection on local history and Native American cultures.

Southwest Memorial Hospital (☎ 970-565-6666; 1311 N Mildred Rd) Provides emergency services.

Sights & Activities

CROW CANYON ARCHAEOLOGY CENTER

The **center** (☎ 970-565-8975, 800-422-8975; www.crow canyon.org; 23390 Rd K; adult/child $50/25; ◐ 9am-5pm Wed & Thu Jun–mid-Sep), about 3-miles north of Cortez, offers a day-long educational program that visits an excavation site west of town. Programs teach the significance of regional artifacts and are an excellent way to learn about Ancestral Puebloan culture first-hand.

The center also offers a more extensive one-week adult research program ($900), which includes Southwestern meals and log cabin lodging for the duration. Classroom time culminates with visits to the dig site and active participation in excavation. Reservations are required for both programs.

CORTEZ COLORADO UNIVERSITY CENTER & MUSEUM

Exhibits on the Ancestral Puebloans, as well as visiting art displays, make this **museum** (☎ 702-565-1151; 25 N Market St; admission free; ◐ 10am-9pm Mon-Sat May-Oct, to 5pm Nov-Apr) worthy of a visit if you have a few hours to kill.

Its **Cultural Park** is an outdoor space where Ute, Navajo and Hopi tribe members share their cultures with visitors through dance and craft demonstrations. Weaving demonstrations and Ute Mountain art also are displayed, and visitors can check out a Navajo hogan.

Summer evening programs feature Native American dances six nights a week at 7:30pm, followed at 8:30pm by cultural programs that often feature Native American storytellers.

BIKING

The Four Corners area around Cortez offers some outstanding mountain-bike trails among piñon-juniper woodland and over 'slickrock' mesa. The dispersed sites at Hovenweep National Monument (p285) are ideal riding destinations. In fact the roads are often better suited to bikes than cars.

A good ride begins at the Sand Canyon archaeological site west of Cortez and follows a downhill trail west for 18 miles to Cannonball Mesa near the state line. If you're looking for a shorter ride, at the 8-mile mark the Burro Point overlook of Yellow Jacket and Burro Canyons is a good place to turn back. Mountain-bike enthusiasts should be sure to try the 26-mile trail from Dove Creek to Slick Rock along the Dolores River.

Pick up a copy of *Mountain and Road Bike Routes for the Cortez-Dolores-Mancos area*, available at the Colorado Welcome Center (opposite) and at local chambers of commerce. It provides maps and profiles for several road and mountain-bike routes. You can contact the **Colorado Plateau Mountain Bike Trail Association** (☎ 702-241-9561) for more route recommendations and other pertinent information.

Kokopelli Bike & Board (☎ 702-565-4408; 30 W Main St; per day $20) rents mountain bikes. The price includes helmet, air pump, water bottle and tools. Staff can also provide information about trails in the area.

Sleeping

Cortez has a plethora of sleeping options. With one exception, places are of the lower budget-motel variety (good for the wallet, bad if you're searching for lots of charm). In winter rates drop by almost 50%. If none of the following places seem appealing, there is the eclectic Old Mancos Inn (p330) in tiny Mancos 18 miles to the east. Durango (p332) is 42 miles east and offers lodging for all tastes.

Kelly Place (☎ 970-565-3125; www.kellyplace .com; 14663 Montezuma County Rd; r & cabins $75-145) This unique adobe-style guest lodge is situated on a 100-acre archaeological and horticultural preserve, 15 miles west of Cortez in McElmo Canyon. The lodge was founded by the late George Kelly, who was a botanist and the author of several outstanding guides to Rocky Mountains plants. The rooms are tastefully appointed and rates include breakfast. The cabins all have kitchenettes and one even has a Jacuzzi. Apart from horseback riding, cultural tours and archaeological programs are also offered.

Aneth Lodge (☎ 970-565-3453; 645 E Main St; r $60) Funky turquoise and pink baths and mismatched posters (Smokey the Bear meets Mesa Verde) give this cheapy its ramshackle character. Clean and almost spacious, rooms feature sinks both inside and outside the bathroom.

Sand Canyon Inn (☎ 970-565-8562, 800-257-3699; 301 W Main St; r $60; ⬛) Smack in the center of town, this is a pleasant spot with a sundeck and laundry facilities. Rooms are spotless and quite large with a table and chairs. It's pet friendly.

Tomahawk Lodge (☎ 970-565-8521, 800-643-7705; 728 S Broadway; r $60; ⬛) Friendly hosts welcome you at this clean place. It feels more personable than the average motel with unique Native American art on the walls. A few rooms allow pets.

Travel Lodge (☎ 970-565-7778, 800-578-7878; 440 S Broadway; r $80; ⬛) Rooms are typical, but it's a friendly place. It offers laundry service and you can soak in the hot tub after a day of exploring.

Ute Mountain Motel (☎ 970-565-8507; 531 S Broadway; r $64) Nothing fancy, but the basic rooms are clean and decent value. Plus, the proprietor is welcoming.

Anasazi Motor Inn (☎ 970-565-3773; 640 S Broadway; r $64) Slightly overpriced but a decent winter option when it offers ski deals (stay and get a half price lift ticket) at Telluride (p341).

Cortez-Mesa Verde KOA (☎ 970-565-9301; www .koa.com; 27432 E Hwy 160; campsites $21, full RV hookups $28, extra person $3; ☽ Apr–mid-Oct) This is the only campground in Cortez that's not situated right next to a highway or dedicated to RVs. Tent sites for parties of two are a bit pricey.

Eating & Drinking

Main Street Brewery & Restaurant (☎ 970-544-9112; 21 E Main St; dishes $7-12; ☾ lunch & dinner) The excellent German-style house-brewed beers are listed on the wall, right next to the cheery hand-painted murals at this cozy place. The large menu features everything from Southwestern cuisine to Mexican and Italian and includes the requisite burgers and pizzas. After dinner kick it up a notch in the downstairs game room, where you can enjoy a beer and some pool.

Nero's Italian Restaurant (☎ 970-565-7366; 303 W Main St; dishes $12-20; ☾ dinner Mon-Sat) An award-winning Italian restaurant, the large and interesting menu is served in intimate environs. Eat between 5pm and 6pm to receive the $7 early bird special.

Francisca's (☎ 970-565-4093; 125 E Main St; dishes $5-8; ☾ lunch & dinner Tue-Sat) Locals nominate this place for the best Mexican food in town. The inexpensive dishes are served in unique environs – white wicker chairs meet Tecate and Corona signs.

Homesteaders (☎ 970-565-6253; 45 E Main St; lunch $5, dinner $7-13; ☾ lunch & dinner) A good bet for standard American family fare, this place has barbecue dinners and fresh-baked pies and breads. The lunch menu includes lots of omelets – but don't stop by before 11am, it's not technically a breakfast joint.

Dry Dock Lounge & Restaurant (☎ 970-564-9404; 200 W Main St; dishes $15; ☾ lunch & dinner) Southwestern cuisine along with pasta and seafood are served in a ship-themed casual atmosphere. The menu is large and varied and offers a few lighter choices.

Getting There & Around

Cortez Municipal Airport (☎ 970-565-7458) is served by **United Express** (www.united.com), which has daily flights to Denver. The airport is 2 miles south of town off US 160/666.

Cortez is easier to reach by car from Phoenix, Arizona, or Albuquerque, New Mexico, than from Denver (379 miles away by the shortest route). East of Cortez, US Hwy 160 passes Mesa Verde National Park on the way to Durango – the largest city in the region.

MANCOS

pop 900 / elev 7000ft

A quick sprint through tiny Mancos and you'll think you've stumbled upon yet an-

other Colorado ghost town. But slow down for a minute and wander amid the historic homes and landmark buildings and you'll be pleasantly surprised. Sleeping and eating options are limited, but the ones that exist are charming and eclectic. Mesa Verde National Park is just 7 miles to the west, so if visiting the park is on your itinerary, Mancos makes an appealing alternative to Cortez's nondescript motels.

Historic displays and a walking tour map are available at the **visitor center** (☎ 702-533-7434; www.mancos.org; cnr Main St & Railroad Ave). It also has information on outdoor activities and local ranches that offer horseback rides and Western-style overnight trips.

Sleeping

Old Mancos Inn (☎ 970-533-9019; www.oldmancosinn .com; 200 W Grand Ave; r $30, with bathroom $50) This is the best bet in town, and happens to be one of the few truly gay-friendly hotels in Colorado. The hotel's warm owners, Dean and Greg, have worked hard to renovate the place and provide unique, pleasant rooms for reasonable prices. The inn has 12 rooms that share bathrooms; three with en-suite bathroom. The outside deck adds yet more value.

Bauer House (☎ 970-533-9707, 800-733-9707; 100 Bauer Ave; r $75-125; ☾ mid-Apr–Oct; ✗) In a historic 1880s brick Victorian mansion on manicured lawns, this B&B has four rooms, one with a kitchen and bar. Refreshments are served under an apple tree on the back lawn and croquet-, bocce- and a putting-green also grace the grounds. The interior environs are filled with antiques.

Jersey Jim Lookout (☎ 970-533-7060; per night $40, 2-night min stay; ☾ mid-May–mid-Oct) How about spending the night in a former fire lookout tower? Standing 55ft above a meadow 14 miles north of Mancos at an elevation of 9800ft, this place is on the National Historic Lookout Register and comes with an Osborne Fire Finder and topographic map. The tower accommodates up to four adults (bring your own bedding) and must be reserved long in advance: The reservation office opens on the first work-day of March (1pm to 5pm) and the entire season is typically booked within days.

Enchanted Mesa Motel (☎ 970-533-7729; 862 W Grand Ave; r from $45) Hipper than most independent motels, rooms come with shiny lamps and pleasant furniture. There's a big playground out front for the kids and the laundry room has a pool table.

Eating & Drinking

Absolute Baking Co (☎ 970-533-1200; 110 S Main St; dishes $7; ❤ breakfast & lunch) The most happening spot in town, this café serves healthy and delicious homemade meals including wraps, salads, pastas and sandwiches. The congenial owners are rightly justified in advertising 'sublime breads…food with integrity.' Only organic flours and grains go into the fresh-baked breads and pastries. If you're in the market for a new book, the café has a decent collection of used ones for sale. Grab a cup of coffee and just chill out.

Millwood Junction (☎ 970-533-7338; cnr Main St & Railroad Ave; dishes $10-20; ❤ 4-10.30pm) This is a popular steak and seafood dinner joint. Folks from miles around come to Mancos on Friday night for the $14 seafood buffet. The restaurant often doubles as a club, showcasing live music.

Columbine Bar (☎ 970-533-7397; 123 W Grand Ave; dishes $5) More of a local drinking joint than a restaurant, this smoky old wooden saloon serves booze and burgers. The mounted animal heads keep watch as you shoot pool.

DOLORES

pop 1100 / elev 7000ft

Scenic Dolores, sandwiched between the walls of a narrow canyon by the same name, offers history buffs a hearty meal of American Indian artifacts and romantics a charming place to rest theirs heads. Housed in a replica of the town's old railroad depot, the **Dolores Visitor Center** (☎ 702-882-4018, 800-807-4712; 421 Railroad Ave) has regional information on lodging and outdoor activities.

One reason to visit is for a stop at **Anasazi Heritage Center** (☎ 702-882-4811; 27501 Hwy 184; admission $3; ❤ 9am-5pm, to 4pm Dec-Feb), 3 miles to the west. The center offers hands-on exhibits including weaving, corn grinding, tree-ring analysis and an introduction to the way in which archaeologists examine potsherds. One of the largest archaeological projects in the Four Corners region was undertaken along the Dolores River between 1978 and 1981, and the center offers modern displays of Ancestral Puebloan artifacts uncovered during the project, as well as other regional archaeological finds. The Bureau of Land

Management operates the museum and its nonprofit shop has a wide variety of books, maps and nature guides ranging from professional reports to introductory materials geared toward the general public.

By far the best sleeping option in town is the graceful **Rio Grande Southern Hotel** (☎ 970-882-7527; www.riograndebandb.com; 101 S Fifth St; ste $75; ❤ Mar–mid-Dec). Step back in time at this National Historic Landmark, where Norman Rockwell prints and an old-world front desk beckon guests. A cozy library and antique-filled guestrooms add to the charm. Bedrooms are small, but all four units are multiroom suites, so there's enough legroom. Try for Room 4, where Zane Gray is rumored to have stayed while writing *Riders of the Purple Stage*. A full breakfast is included.

At the east end of town, the **Outpost Motel** (☎ 970-882-7271, 800-382-4892; 1800 Central Ave; s/d $43/49, cabins $95) has small but clean rooms, as well as cabins. Some rooms have kitchenettes and the courtyard features a pleasant little wooden deck overlooking the Dolores River.

Dolores Mountain Inn (☎ 702-882-7203, 800-842-8113; 701 Railroad Ave; r $60-120) has immaculate modern rooms and the motel's genial owner offers bike rentals, shuttle service and guided tours.

If you want to camp, you can find out about nearby sites in the San Juan National Forest from the USDA Forest Service (USFS) **Dolores Ranger Station** (☎ 970-882-7296; cnr 6th St & Central Ave; ❤ 8am-5pm Mon-Fri). Otherwise the **Dolores River RV Park** (☎ 970-882-7761; 18680 Railroad Ave; campsites $12, RV hookups $20), located about 1.5 miles east of town, has pleasant sites.

For some hearty German cuisine, visit the **German Stone Oven Restaurant** (☎ 702-882-7033; 811 Railroad Ave; dishes $9-15; ❤ lunch & dinner), which dishes up platters of bratwurst and Wiener schnitzel.

Dolores is 11 miles north of Cortez on Hwy 145, also known as Railroad Ave.

DURANGO

pop 14,800 / elev 6580ft

The region's most happening and attractive attraction, Durango is nothing short of delightful. It's one of those archetypal old Colorado mining towns that are filled with graceful old hotels, and Victorian-era saloons, with mountains as far as the eye can see. It's a place seemingly frozen in time. The waitress slinging drinks at the scarred wooden bar is dressed straight out of the early-19th century. The antique-laden inn and the musician pounding ragtime on worn ivory keys add to the surrealism.

It's only after stepping into the classy stores and restaurants that you'll remember it's modern day. There's a dining option poised to charm the most critical of palates and a store for any desire, from outdoor apparel to fancy jewelry or funky retro garb. But if you're appetite is still not whet, dip into Durango's goody bag of adventures to get the glands really salivating. Meander through the historic district and listen for a shrill whistle, then watch the steam billow as the old train pulls in (below). Rent a bike and explore the trails, or get out the skis and head up the road for miles upon miles of powdery white bowls and tree-lined glades (right).

Orientation & Information

Most visitors' facilities are along Main Ave, including the 1882 Durango & Silverton Narrow Gauge Railroad Depot (at the south end of town). Motels are mostly north of the town center. The downtown is compact and easy to walk in a few hours.

Maria's Bookshop (☎ 970-247-1438; 960 Main Ave) A good general bookstore.

Mercy Medical Center (☎ 970-247-4311; 375 E Park Ave) Outpatient and 24-hour emergency care.

Post Office (☎ 970-247-3968; 222 W 8th St)

Public Library (☎ 970-385-2970; 1118 E 2nd Ave) Free Internet access.

San Juan-Rio Grande National Forest Headquarters (☎ 970-247-4874; 15 Burnett Ct) Offers camping and hiking information and maps. It's about a half-mile west on US Hwy 160.

Visitor Center (☎ 800-525-8855; www.durango.org; 111 S Camino del Rio) South of town, at the Santa Rita exit from US Hwy 550.

Sights & Activities

DURANGO & SILVERTON NARROW GAUGE RAILROAD

Climb aboard this steam-driven **train** (☎ 970-247-2733, 888-872-4607; www.durangotrain.com; adult/child $65/31) for a scenic 45-mile trip north to Silverton, a National Historic Landmark. The journey is best in fall, when the trees put on a magnificent color show. The train has

been in continuous operation for 123 years, carrying passengers behind vintage locomotives and allowing them to relive the sights and sounds of yesteryear. The dazzling trip takes 3½ hours each way, and allows two hours for exploring Silverton. It is only offered from May through October (8:15am and 9am). In winter the train runs to Cascade Canyon (adult/child $45/22), where you will learn about native flora and fauna.

SKIING & SNOWBOARDING

The town's other main draw is **Durango Mountain Resort** (☎ 970-247-9000, 800-693-0175; www.durangomountainresort.com; lift ticket adult/child $55/28; ⏱ mid-Nov–Mar), 25 miles north on US 550. The resort, also known as Purgatory, is one of the state's least expensive and offers 1200 skiable acres and boasts 260in of snow per year. Eleven lifts carry skiers and boarders to 85 different trails of varying difficulty, while two terrain parks offer plenty of opportunity to catch some big air. There's a 400ft half-pipe as well as rails, hits, drops and tabletops. Those interested in cross-country skiing can check out the Nordic Center across Hwy 550 from the main base. There are 10 miles of groomed trails for all levels. The cost is $8.50 for adults, $6.50 for kids.

RAFTING

Rivers West (☎ 970-259-5077; 520 Main St; half-/full-day from $40/60) One of numerous companies that offer a variety of trips down the Animas River. Beginners should check out the one-hour introduction to rafting, while the more adventurous can try the combination trip. It includes a ride to Silverton on the narrow gauge railroad (left) and a run down the upper Animas, which boasts Class III to V rapids.

Sleeping

In town, summer rates (the ones quoted here) are depressingly high and you'll be hard pressed to find much for less than $100. Rooms fill quickly, so it's best to book ahead. Visit in winter, however, and you're in for a treat – some rates drop by 50%. There is a string of cheap motels north of town on Hwy 550 that go for around $60 in summer, as little as $30 in winter. All have similar lower-budget facilities, but most are clean and comfortable enough.

BUDGET

Siesta Motel (☎ 970-247-0741; 3475 N Main Ave; s/d from $45/55) This family-owned hotel is one of the town's cheapest options. It's a welcoming place offering spacious and comfortable rooms. There's a little courtyard with a barbecue grill.

Adobe Inn (☎ 970-247-2743; 2178 Main Ave; r from $30) A cheapie just north of town, it has pleasant rooms that will do for a night if other places are full.

United Campground (☎ 970-247-3853; 1322 Animas View Dr; campsites $20; 🏊) The nicest camping option near town, United has a riverside setting and very decent tent sites. The city trolley, part of Durango's public transport system, makes a stop here.

MIDRANGE & TOP END

General Palmer Hotel (☎ 970-247-4747; www.general palmer.com; 567 Main Ave; r from $105) A Victorian landmark built in 1898, the hotel features pewter, brass or wood four-poster beds along with quality linens and a teddy bear for snuggling. Rooms are small, but elegant, and if you tire of TV there's a collection of board games at the front desk. The entire place is reminiscent of a time long past. Check out the cozy library or the relaxing solarium.

Leland House (☎ 970-385-1920; www.rochester hotel.com; 721 E Second Ave; r from $150) The 10 charming rooms in this 1927 restored brick

---

AUTHOR'S CHOICE

Strater Hotel (☎ 970-247-4431; www.strater .com; 699 Main St; r $200) A lovely old-world place with courteous staff and a museum-like interior: check out the Stradivarius violin or the gold-plated commemorative Winchester. In fact the hotel boasts the largest collection of Victorian walnut furniture in the country. Romantic and peaceful rooms are furnished with antiques, crystal and lace. Beds are super comfy and the linens impeccable. It's a fantastic deal in winter, when rooms with king sized beds can go for as little as $79. The Strater runs summertime melodrama theatre and operates the historic Diamond Belle Saloon – perfect for a late-afternoon cocktail. The hot tub is a major romantic plus, it can be reserved by the hour.

---

apartment house are named after historic figures associated with the building, and decked out with their memorabilia and biographies. All rooms have kitchen facilities and a gourmet breakfast is included.

Rochester House (☎ 970-385-1920; www.rochester hotel.com; 721 E Second Ave; r from $150) Next door to Leland House and run by the same folks, this newly renovated place features spacious rooms with high ceilings. The decor is influenced by old Westerns, with movie posters and marquee lights adorning the hallways. It's a little bit of old Hollywood in the new West.

Durango Lodge (☎ 970-247-0955; www.durango lodge.com; 150 5th St; r $100; 🏊) One of the cheapest options in town, this place offers large rooms with big TVs, matching oak furniture, fridge and coffeemaker. It's not quite as charming as other downtown establishments, but more than OK. The hot tub and swimming pool are a plus.

Eating

If you're looking for a good meal, Durango is the place to be. From the budget diner to the high-end steak house to mouthwatering microbreweries, Durango offers a surprisingly diverse collection of restaurants for a town its size.

BUDGET

Sizzling Siam (☎ 970-385-9470; 519 Main Ave; dishes $6; 🕐 lunch & dinner) This tiny place emits a delicious aroma upon stepping inside. It offers cheap, tasty and large Thai staples from *pad thai* to green curry. Eat in or take it away.

Durango Bagel (☎ 970-385-7297; 106 Main Ave; dishes $2-5; 🕐 breakfast & lunch) Grab a bagel on the way to the slopes. The place has more varieties of cream cheese than you can imagine, as well as more substantial bagel-based sandwiches bursting with goodies.

MIDRANGE

East by Southwest (☎ 970-247-5533; 160 E College Dr; sushi $4-13, dishes $12-20; 🕐 lunch & dinner) Thai, Vietnamese, Indonesian and Japanese cuisine, including a full sushi bar, is served in a congenial low-key setting. The food is delicious and can be washed down with a creative martini or sake cocktail. Locals rave.

Steamworks (☎ 970-259-9200; 801 E 2nd Ave; dishes $9-15; 🕐 lunch & dinner) Industrial meets ski lodge at this popular microbrewery with high sloping rafters and metal pipes. There's a large bar area, separate dining room and a Cajun influenced menu. The house specialty is the Cajun Bowl (one/two person $17/30), which features crab, shrimp, sausage, corn and potatoes boiled into a gigantic stew. The homemade brews are excellent. At night there are DJs and live bands.

Carver Brewing Co (☎ 970-259-2545; 1022 Main Ave; lunch $5-7, dinner $10-15; ⊙ lunch & dinner) This relaxed brewery churns out 1000 barrels of beer annually; enjoy a pint with burgers and sandwiches in the outdoor beer garden. A local institution.

Mama Boy's Italian Ristorante (☎ 970-247-0060; 2659 Main Ave; dishes $10-20; ⊙ lunch & dinner) Slightly out of town, this local fave serves authentic and hearty Italian meals – from New York pizzas to lasagna to eggplant parmigiana. There is an extensive wine list and a host of pastries to choose from.

TOP END

Randy's (☎ 970-247-9083; 152 E College Dr; dishes $20-25; ⊙ dinner) A fine-dining establishment serving an eclectic menu of mainly seafood and steak, it's an intimate place just perfect for that special meal. Eat between 5pm and 6pm and get the same menu for $12 to $14. Happy hour runs from 5pm to 7pm and offers drinks and appetizers specials in the bar. Locals say this is the finest restaurant in town for top-end dining.

Ore House (☎ 970-247-5707; 147 E College Dr; dishes $20-30; ⊙ dinner; ✗) The best steakhouse in town, food is served in casual and rustic environs. Order a hand-cut aged steak or the Ore House grubsteak ($40) with steak,

---

AUTHOR'S CHOICE

Jean Pierre Bakery (☎ 970-385-0122; 601 Main Ave; dishes $5-12; ⊙ breakfast & lunch) Visit this charming patisserie on a cold winter day (or any day for that matter) for a taste of France in Colorado. The mouthwatering delicacies are made from scratch. Don't miss the soup and sandwich lunch special ($12), which includes a sumptuous French pastry chosen from the large counter display. Service could use a little improvement, but once you taste the food you'll forget how long it took to arrive. Well worth at least one meal.

---

crab leg and lobster; it's easily big enough for two. There's also a large wine cellar.

Palace (☎ 970-247-2018; 505 Main Ave; lunch $10, dinner $20-25; ⊙ lunch & dinner) Serving seafood, meats, pastas and some more unique delicacies like elk tenderloin, this restaurant next to the train tracks is done up in a cozy old wooden-saloon style. There's lots of stained-glass fixtures and low lighting. Lunch is great value – the same dishes go for about half the price.

Drinking

With a mix of college students and ski bums, it's little surprise that Durango has an active night scene. Both Carver Brewing Co (left) and Steamworks (p333) are popular after-dark watering holes. Live and DJ music is featured nightly at Steamworks.

Ska Brewing Company (☎ 970-247-5792; 545 Turner Dr) Big on flavor and variety, these are the best beers in town. Mainly a production facility, this small friendly place has a tasting-room bar. It's usually jam-packed with locals catching up on gossip over an end-of-the-day pint. The brewmaster often doubles as the bartender, and the atmosphere is refreshingly relaxing. When you're done trying the brews, pick up a few bottles to take back to your hotel room.

Diamond Belle Saloon (☎ 970-376-7150; 699 Main Ave) This is a period place right down to the waitress dressed in Victorian-era garb – fishnets and a garter with a feather in her hair. Cozy and elegant, the piano player pumps out ragtime tunes and takes requests. There are half-price appetizers and drink specials from 4pm to 6pm. The perfect place to start (or end) an evening.

Lady Falconburgh's (☎ 970-582-9664; 640 Main Ave) With the largest selection of microbrews and imports in the Four Corners region, it's no secret that this place is popular. There's a brick and brass theme with original murals on the walls and more than 100 beers on offer – 38 of which are on tap. Voted Durango's best pub by locals, it's a great place for mingling. You won't feel out of place going here alone.

El Rancho (☎ 970-259-8111; 975 Main Ave) Locals like to drink here after work. A dive with attitude, the long bar is made for serious boozing. There are pool tables in the back. El Rancho gets progressively rowdier as the night progresses.

Pongas (☎ 970-382-8554; 121 W Eighth St) Stop by to shoot some pool, or take a lesson in snooker or golf on the 10ft-by-5ft table. A local fave.

Scoot 'n Blues (☎ 970-259-1400; 900 Main Ave) There's live music nightly upstairs. Downstairs is Club Liquid, where DJs spin. The entire place has a biker-bar feel with vintage Harley and Indian cycles. If you need to sop up all the booze, barbecue ribs, chicken sandwiches and burgers are on the menu.

Getting There & Around

Durango-La Plata County Airport (☎ 970-247-8143) is 18 miles southwest of Durango via US 160 and Hwy 172. **American Airlines** (www.aa .com) offers daily jet service to Dallas during ski season. Otherwise you are on commuter turbo-prop equipment. **United Express** (www.united.com) has daily flights to Denver, while **America West** (www.americawest.com) serves Phoenix, Arizona.

Greyhound/TNM&O (www.greyhound.com) buses run daily from the **Durango Bus Center** (☎ 970-259-2755; 275 E 8th Ave) north to Grand Junction and south to Albuquerque, New Mexico.

Durango lies at the junction of US Hwy 160 and US Hwy 550, 42 miles east of Cortez, 49 miles west of Pagosa Springs and 190 miles north of Albuquerque in New Mexico.

PAGOSA SPRINGS & AROUND

pop 1620 / elev 7079ft

West of Durango, on US 160 at the junction with US 84 south to New Mexico, the open ponderosa pine forests give way to the tourist billboards of Pagosa Springs. The town isn't Colorado's most memorable, but no one really comes to sightsee. They come to ski some of the state's best powder, to hike and mountain bike or just to sit and soak in the rich mineral springs locals swear by. Pagosa is a Ute term for 'boiling water,' which is the town's biggest tourist card. The San Juan River flows past volcanic rock formations in the center of town and steam billows up in many spots along the way.

The **Pagosa Springs Area Chamber of Commerce** (☎ 970-264-2360; www.pagosaspringschamber .com; 402 San Juan St) operates a large visitor center located across the bridge from US Hwy 160.

Sights & Activities

HOT SPRINGS

For visitors to Pagosa Springs, soaking in the glorious riverside pools at the **Springs** (☎ 970-264-2284; 165 Hot Springs Blvd; admission $13; ☽ 7am-11pm Sun-Thu, to 1am Fri & Sat) is de rigueur. The healing, mineral-rich waters are drawn from the Great Pagosa Aquifer and the 17 different outdoor soaking tubs overlook the San Juan River. The pools vary in temperature from 94°F to 111°F, with the hottest of them appropriately named 'the lobster pot.'

WOLF CREEK SKI AREA

With more than 450in of snow per year, **Wolf Creek** (☎ 970-264-5629; www.wolfcreekski.com; lift ticket $45; ☽ Nov–mid-Apr) is a powder hound's dream. Located 25 miles north of Pagosa Springs on US 160, this family-owned ski area is one of Colorado's best-kept secrets. Never crowded and lacking the glitz and glamour of larger resorts, it's simply a laid-back and awesome place to ride. The powder can be waist-high after a big storm blows through, and the five lifts service 50 trails, from wide-open bowls to steep tree glades.

CHIMNEY ROCK ARCHAEOLOGICAL AREA

Stunning rock spires house Ancestral Puebloan ruins overlooking the Piedra River at this **archaeological area** (☎ 970-883-5359; tours $6; ☽ mid-May–Oct) 18 miles west of Pagosa Springs on Hwy 131. Recent research suggests the site was a Chacoan outlier that may have furnished timber to more southern communities. Another recent discovery suggests the twin pinnacles were used to observe lunar events. By 1125 the site, like others in the southwest, was abandoned, possibly as a consequence of drought.

Guided tours are the only way to visit the hundreds of structures, including the Great Kiva that once housed between 1200 and 2000 inhabitants. A fire lookout tower offers views of the excavated Chacoan sites perched high on the rock formation. Two-hour walking tours leave daily in-season at 9.30am, 10.30am, 1pm and 2pm.

Sleeping & Eating

Oso Grande Ranch (☎ 970-751-9548; www.osogrande ranch.com; r from $90) Five rustic guestrooms are located in a large ranch style log home.

The wraparound porch offers sweeping mountain views and there are horses on the premises for guests to ride and a hot tub to soak in afterwards. Rates include a full breakfast and a turndown service at night. Hiking and mountain biking are popular activities and there are trails within walking distance.

Springs Resort Hotel (☎ 970-264-4168; www.pago sahotsprings.com; 165 Hot Springs Blvd; r $100-180, ste $200; ☻ ☒) Guests here enjoy all-you-can-soak privileges in the hotel's top-notch hot springs, along with amenable rooms. The cheapest are nothing special, but you're paying for the healing waters. The deluxe rooms feature thicker mattresses, higher thread-count sheets, more floor space and kitchenettes. The resort also features a spa, offers ski packages and welcomes pets.

San Juan Motel (☎ 970-264-2262; 191 E Pagosa St; r from $40, cabins from $60, campsites $16) This economical place has rooms in all shapes and sizes, as well as cabins with or without kitchens, plus places to pitch a tent. A family oriented option, facilities include a game room, laundry, a hot tub and ski packages at Wolf Creek.

Davidson's Country Inn (☎ 970-264-5863; 2763 US 160; r $75-100) On a 32-acre working ranch, the inn is just north of town and surrounded by mountains. The three-story log cabin offers comfortable rooms crammed with family treasures. The cheapest share

bathrooms, the largest can accommodate an entire family. There's a game room with a pool table and a full country breakfast is included.

Elkhorn Café (☎ 970-264-2146; 438 Main St; dishes $5-8) Serving Mexican fare that is as spicy as it is filling, this is a popular spot with locals. Stop by for a breakfast burrito before hitting the slopes. The restaurant also serves the usual burger and sandwich fare.

JJ's Upstream Restaurant (☎ 970-264-9100; 356 E Hwy 160; dishes from $8) Right on the San Juan River, it has a great vibe and a varied menu. There are nightly dinner specials, including early bird cheap meals. Full bar service and a nightly happy hour complete the picture.

SILVERTON
pop 500 / elev 9318ft

The air is fresh and thin at almost 10,000ft, just the way the locals like it. A throwback to another era, the entire town was designated a National Historic Landmark in 1966. Today tiny Silverton is a charming place to explore. Towering peaks, shimmering lakes and well-preserved Victorian buildings provide the backdrop, while friendly residents and an easy-going atmosphere envelop you upon arrival.

Silver and gold miners invaded the area after the Brunot Agreement removed the Ute bands in 1873. Mining activity peaked in the early 1900s, but since 1991, when

---

DETOUR: SAN JUAN SKYWAY

Drive the San Juan Skyway in late September or early October, when the Aspen trees glow yellow, when there's a hint of snow and pine and cedar in the crisp, crisp air and you'll feel your stress drift right out the window. Life's day-to-day tensions will get lost somewhere among the towering peaks, picturesque towns and old mines around each bend, or melt into the bright sun and intense blue Colorado sky.

The 236-mile route takes you to the top of the world as it twists and turns past a series of 'fourteeners' (a Colorado term for peaks exceeding 14,000ft). The present blends into the past as you descend through rotting mines and ghost towns where time has worn away the meat, leaving just the bones behind. The air is heavy with history. Places like Telluride (p341), Durango (p331) and Silverton (above) tell a thousand colorful yarns of yesteryear, while an air of mystery and intrigue lingers over the ancestral homes of the Puebloan Indians at Mesa Verde (p323). The San Juan Skyway will take you past bubbling rapids ripe for rafting and quiet fishing spots on the Animas River. Bluegrass, jazz and folk music provide a summer soundtrack, when local towns host renowned festivals.

From Ridgeway take US 550 south to Ouray and then over Red Mountain Pass to Silverton. Continue heading south of US 550 until you hit Durango. From here you can head west on US 160 to the ruins at Mesa Verde, then head north on Rte 145 toward Telluride before following Rte 62 back to Ridgeway. To drive the entire byway allow at least one or two days.

Sunnyside mine closed, the economy has depended on tourists riding the seasonal Durango & Silverton Narrow Gauge Railroad (p332). If you arrive in winter, you just might find the place practically void of tourists.

The **Silverton Chamber of Commerce & Visitor center** (☎ 970-387-5654; Hwy 550 & Hwy 110) provides information about the town. Check your e-mail for free at the **public library** (☎ 970-387-5770; 1111 Reese St; ⊙ 11am-8pm Tue-Thu, 10am-5pm Fri & Sat). The **post office** (☎ 970-387-5420; 138 W 12th St) has the usual services.

Sights & Activities

To see the region from the open back of a truck (don't worry there are seats), contact **Historic San Juan Tours** (☎ 970-387-5716; historic sanjuantours@earthlink.com; 1148 Empire St; adult/child from $35/25; ⊙ Mar-Nov). The company offers a variety of tours that take you over the top of 13,000ft peaks, past ghost towns and historic mines, and through meadows of wildflowers. If you want to explore the area's numerous back roads on your own, quite a few companies offer Jeep rentals. **Triangle Jeep Rental** (☎ 970-387-9990; www.trianglejeeprental .com; 864 Greene St; per day $140) will provide you with a Jeep, map and operating instructions. They're also happy to talk routes and tailor a trip to your comfort level. Popular routes include four-wheeling over high mountain passes to the towns of Telluride (p341) or Ouray (p338). Other trails take you past well-persevered ghost towns and near historic mines.

In the winter, **Silverton Mountain** (☎ 970-387-5706; www.silvertonmountain.com; per day $100), 6 miles from town on Hwy 110, is a playground for advanced and expert skiers. The new kid on the block, it offers guided-only high-elevation skiing. The facility is an innovative and unusual offering at a base of 10,400ft. Included in the price are a guide, avalanche beacons, probe poles and shovels. Again, you really need to know your stuff before heading out – the easiest terrain here is comparable to skiing double blacks at other resorts.

Sleeping & Eating

Wyman Hotel & Inn (☎ 970-387-5372; www.the wyman.com; 1371 Greene St; r 105-180; ⊙ mid-Dec–Oct; ⊠) In a handsome red sandstone building, this hotel is on the National Register of

Historic Places. Rooms are uniquely decorated with late-19th-century antiques and feature Victorian-era wallpaper and top-quality beds and linens. High ceilings and arched windows are the norm throughout the place. The price includes a full breakfast and an afternoon wine and cheese tasting.

Teller House Hotel (☎ 970-387-5466; www.teller househotel.com; 1250 Greene St; r from $64-90; ⊠) A Victorian-era throwback, Teller House offers an interesting and enjoyable stay and gives a real feel for what a late-19th-century boarding house was like. Rooms are filled with antiques and quite spacious. A full breakfast is included.

Inn of the Rockies (☎ 970-387-5336; www.innof therockies.com; 220 E Tenth St; r $75-150 incl breakfast; ⊠) This 1898 inn has nine unique rooms furnished with Victorian antiques. The hospitality is first-rate and its New Orleans–inspired breakfasts (included in the price) and baked treats merit special mention. There's also a hot tub for soaking after a long day.

Silverton Hostel (☎ 970-387-0115; 1025 Blair St; dm/r $12/30) In a restored 1911 grocery store and bordello, this is not the most inspiring hostel in town. It's rather small, slightly dank and doesn't have a lot going on, but if you're on a budget it should do.

Triangle Motel (☎ 970-387-5780; www.triangle motel.com; 864 Greene St; s/d from $50/60) Clean, modern and comfortable rooms are offered at this motel. Some come with kitchenettes. Rates drop by almost half in the winter.

Avalanche Coffee House (☎ 970-387-5282; 1067 Blair St; dishes $8-12; ☺ lunch daily, dinner Fri & Sat) When the snow starts falling, pick up a paper and head to this cozy hangout for a steaming cup of fresh coffee and delicious baked goods. A local favorite, all the food is made from scratch. The menu features sandwiches, soups and quiches. Dinner sees more substantial offerings.

Teki's Place (☎ 970-387-5630; 1124 Greene St; dishes $5-9) Locals pour in here early every morning to fill up on the hearty American breakfasts. You should too.

Getting There & Around
TNM&O (www.greyhound.com) buses stop in front of **Teki's Place** (1124 Green St). One-way train tickets to Durango or Weminuche Wilderness trailheads on the Durango & Silverton Narrow Gauge Railroad (p332) can be purchased at the **Silverton Depot** (☎ 970-387-5416; cnr 10th & Animas Sts; ☺ May-Oct). **Durango Transportation** (☎ 800-626-2066) operates a bus to Durango ($15, one hour, twice daily).

By car, Silverton is 45 miles north of Durango via US 550.

OURAY & THE MILLION DOLLAR HIGHWAY
pop 840 / elev 7760ft
Between Silverton and Ouray, US 550 is known as the Million Dollar Hwy because the road-bed fill contains valuable ore. One of the state's most memorable drives, it's a breathtaking stretch of pavement that passes old mine head-frames and larger-than-life alpine scenery – at some points the spectacular peaks are so close they seem ready to grab you. The road is scary when raining or snowing, so take extra care.

Sandwiched between imposing peaks, Ouray just might be that little bit of paradise John Denver waxes lyrical about in 'Rocky Mountain High.' Here the mountains don't just tower over you, they embrace you – the peaks surrounding Ouray leave barely a quarter-mile of valley floor in town. 'Awesome' doesn't do the place justice.

The **visitor center** (☎ 970-325-4746; www.ouray colorado.com) is at the hot springs pool and has lodging and recreation information.

Sights & Activities
Ouray's stunning scenery isn't the only ace up the town's sleeve. The **Ouray hot springs**

(☎ 970-325-4638; 1220 Main St; pool admission $8; ☺ 10am-10pm) is the perfect place for a healing soak. The crystal-clear natural spring water is free of the sulphur smells plaguing other hot springs, and the giant pool features a variety of soaking areas at temperatures ranging from 96°F to 106°F.

Climbing the face of a frozen waterfall can be a sublime experience. To try it, head to the **Ouray Ice Park** (☎ 970-325-4061; www.ouray icepark.com; admission free; ☺ 7am-5pm mid-Dec–March), a 2-mile stretch of the Uncompahgre Gorge that has been dedicated to public ice climbing. The first of its kind in the world, the park draws enthusiasts from around the globe to try their hand on climbs for all skill levels. **San Juan Mountain Guides** (☎ 970-325-4925; www.ourayclimbing.com; 2-/3-day courses $305/455) offers a weekend two-day introduction to climbing course and a three-day advanced course at the park. All equipment is included, but check their website for dates. If you already know your stuff and just need to pick up some gear, stop by **Ouray Mountain Sports** (☎ 970-325-4284; 722 Main St).

Festivals & Events
Every year in mid-January Ouray holds the **Ouray Ice Festival** (☎ 970-325-4288; www.ourayice festival.com), which doubles as a fundraiser for the Ouray Ice Park (above). The festival features four days of climbing competitions, dinners, slide shows and clinics. You can watch the competitions for free, but to check out the evening events you'll need to make a $15 donation. Once inside, however, you'll get free brews from popular Colorado microbrewer New Belgium.

Sleeping & Eating
Some of Ouray's lodges are destinations within themselves.

Beaumont Hotel (☎ 970-325-7000; www.beaumo nthotel.com; 505 Main St; r $180-350) Ouray's classiest lodging option, this small hotel offers 12 rooms elegantly appointed with period furnishings. Established in 1886, the hotel was closed for more than 30 years before undergoing extensive renovations and reopening five years ago. The Beaumont also boasts a spa and three unique boutiques.

Box Canyon Lodge & Hot Springs (☎ 970-325-4931; www.boxcanyonouray.com; 45 3rd Ave; s/d from $70/80) This place offers geothermally heated rooms that are spacious and accommodating. The real treat here, however, are the four wooden spring-fed hot tubs for guests – just perfect for a romantic star-gazing soak.

Wiesbaden (☎ 970-325-4347; www.wiesbadenhotsprings.com; cnr 6th & 5th Aves; r from $120; 🏊) This hotel's star lure is a natural indoor vapor cave, free for guests. It's a cozy spot to spend the night, with hot springs just outside.

Historic Western Hotel, Restaurant & Saloon (☎ 970-325-4645; www.historicwesternhotel.com; 210 Seventh Ave; r $35-95) Old Wild West meets Victorian elegance at this place, one of the largest remaining wooden structures on Colorado's western slope. It offers rooms for all budgets; the cheapest have shared bathrooms. The open-air second-floor veranda commands stunning views of the Uncompahgre Gorge, while the Old West Saloon serves affordable meals and all sorts of drinks in a timeless setting.

DETOUR: CRESTED BUTTE & BLACK CANYON OF THE GUNNISON NATIONAL PARK

If the Four Corners region has whet your appetite for Colorado's splendors and you're craving a bigger bite, then drive north on US 550 to US 50. Head east for 12 miles to Hwy 347 north and continue on for 7 miles to **Black Canyon of the Gunnison National Park** (☎ 970-249-1915; 7-day admission per vehicle $8). Here a dark narrow gash above the Gunnison River leads down a 2000ft-deep chasm that's as eerie as it is spectacular. No other canyon in America combines the narrow openings, sheer walls and dizzying depths of the Black Canyon, and a peek over the edge evokes a sense of awe (and vertigo) for most. Head to the 6-mile long South Rim Rd, which takes you to 11 overlooks at the edge of the canyon, some reached via short trails up to 1.5 miles long (round-trip). To challenge your senses, cycle along the smooth pavement running parallel to the rim's 2000ft drop off. You definitely get a better feel for the place than if you're trapped in a car.

From the park continue east on US 50 for about 80 miles until you reach remote and beautiful **Crested Butte**, your destination for the night (or two or three). As far as towns go, Crested Butte feels real. Despite being one of Colorado's best ski resorts (some say *the* best) it doesn't put on airs. There's nothing haughty, or even glossy, about the place – just fresh mountain air, a laid-back attitude and friendly folk.

Crested Butte Mountain Resort (☎ 970-349-2333, 800-544-8448; www.skicb.com; lift tickets $60) sits 2 miles north of the town and caters mostly to intermediate and expert skiers. Surrounded by forests and the rugged peaks of the West Elk, Raggeds and Maroon Bells–Snowmass Wilderness Areas, the scenery is wet-your-pants beautiful.

Crested Butte is also a **mountain-biking** mecca, full of excellent high-altitude singletrack trails. For maps, information and mountain-bike rentals visit the **Alpineer** (☎ 970-349-5210; 419 6th St). The attractive **Crested Butte International Hostel** (☎ 970-349-0588, 888-389-0588; www.crestedbuttehostel.com; 615 Teocalli Ave; dm $20-27, r from $60) is one of Colorado's nicest. Rooms share a bathroom and bunks come with reading lamps and lockable drawers.

For more privacy try the handsome cedar-flavored **Inn at Crested Butte** (☎ 970-349-1225, 800-949-4828; www.innatcrestedbutte.com; 510 Whiterock Ave; r from $70). It has comfy doubles and triples, an outdoor hot tub and a free shuttle to the ski resort. There's a wheelchair-accessible room on the ground floor.

Certainly not a secret, the **Secret Stash** (☎ 970-349-6245; 21 Elk Ave; pizzas $13-17; ☽ dinner) is an enticing pizza place with a joyful interior. Sit on the floor upstairs, or park yourself in a velvety chair.

Cheap meals are served at the pleasant **Paradise Cafe** (☎ 970-349-6233; cnr 4th St & Elk Ave; mains $4-7; ☽ breakfast & lunch). If you have a hankering for Thai or Vietnamese head to **Ginger Cafe** (☎ 970-349-7291; 313 3rd St; mains $8-12; ☽ lunch & dinner). Crested Butte has an interesting music scene year-round and the lively **Eldo** (☎ 970-349-6125; 215 Elk Ave) is where most out-of-town bands play. From the great outdoor deck you can peep at street life below. The **Princess Wine Bar** (☎ 970-349-0210; 218 Elk St) is an intimate joint perfect for sitting and chatting. First-rate live music of the local singer/songwriter flavor is on show nightly.

The trip from Ouray (opposite) to Crested Butte takes a little less than three hours. Leave early, however, as you'll want at least a few hours in the national park.

Amphitheater Forest Service Campground (☎ 877-444-6777; US 550; campsites $12) A mile south of town, this USFS campground has pleasing tent sites.

Tundra Restaurant at the Beaumont (☎ 970-325-7040; 505 Main St; dishes from $20; ☼ dinner daily, brunch Sun) This elegant restaurant has won several awards for its wine cellar and does Thursday evening tastings. Billing itself as serving 'high altitude' cuisine, it focuses on regional specialties with great results.

Outlaw Restaurant (☎ 970-325-4366; 610 Main St; dishes $14-22; ☼ lunch & dinner) Appetizing steaks and seafood, and a host of other dishes –

IF YOU'VE GOT A FEW EXTRA DAYS IN COLORADO

So you've covered the southwestern corner of the state, but the place has entranced you so much you're just not quite ready to leave. If you're keen to explore a little further, much of the rest of the state (with the exception of the eastern plains, sorry, but they just can't compete with the adventure-laden mountains) is equally fabulous. Following are a few favorite destinations.

■ **Boulder** Tree-hugging hippies, trust funders, well-heeled young professionals and hard-drinking college kids give this city its unique independent vibe. A long ways from the con-servative mind-set found in much of Colorado, residents here take pride in saying they live in the 'People's Republic of Boulder.' The city has an ongoing love affair with the outdoors, and you'll see a constant slew of mountain bikers pedaling the main roads. Hang out on the pedestrian-only Pearl St Mall – packed with boutiques, restaurants and bars – and catch a street performance. Down a pint or two at one of the microbreweries or grab an inner tube and float down Boulder Creek on a hot summer day. Despite the city's reputation for party-ing, those not interested in over-indulgence won't feel at odds. There are family-friendly places to sleep and eat, intimate dining options for that special night and loads of quiet hiking trails for afternoon escapes. Plus, the ever-popular Rocky Mountain National Park is an easy daytrip away. Boulder is 30 miles north of Denver on Hwy 36.

■ **Breckenridge** This resort town with a 19th-century mining feel is full of young people look-ing to party (many migrate to 'Breck' after university to spend a few years 'ski bumming'). In fact the motto seems to be 'ride hard all day, drink hard all night.' But it's also a great place to bring the family. There's beginner terrain at the ski resort, the restaurants are kid-friendly and many hotels offer babysitting services. With four of Colorado's best snow riding resorts less than an hour's drive away, Breckenridge, 80 miles west of Denver off I-70, makes an ideal regional base.

■ **Colorado Springs** A very popular family vacation spot, Colorado's second-largest city sits in a picture-perfect location below famous Pikes Peak. It's a rather bizarre amalgamation of evangelical conservatives, tourists and military installations, but it offers loads of tourist activities. Take a stroll through Garden of the Gods, with its towering red rock spires; ride the cog railroad to the top of Pikes Peak, where Katherine Lee Bates was inspired to write *America the Beautiful;* or wander the streets of historic Manitou Springs, home to scores of New Age shops and even a penny arcade. Colorado Springs is on I-25, 60 miles south of Denver.

■ **Aspen** Home to great skiing and beautiful alpine scenery, Aspen is Colorado's glitziest high-octane resort and plays host to some of the wealthiest skiers in the world – where else in Colorado can you shop at Prada or Gucci? The scenery, especially in the fall when the trees put on a spectacular display, is just extra sugary eye-candy. The historic town is charming, and the rock stars that vacation here must like to party, because the bars are happening. It's a romantic place, perfect for a weekend getaway with a loved one. Aspen is 150 miles south-west of Denver on Hwy 82.

■ **Glenwood Springs** Located just outside a spectacular canyon, Glenwood Springs is a pleas-urable place to kick up your heels. Aside from its world-famous hot springs, it offers tip-top road- and mountain-biking and loads of hiking trails. In the summer raft Glenwood Canyon's Class III to IV white-water. Whether you're traveling solo, with the kids or with a significant other, Glenwood Springs will accommodate. The town is 150 miles west of Denver on I-70.

from pasta to nightly specials – are served in a relaxing atmosphere. There's live piano music, a full bar and loads of regional memorabilia on the walls.

Silver Nugget Café (☎ 970-325-4100; 746 Main St; lunch dishes $6-9, dinner dishes $7-20; ☯ breakfast, lunch & dinner) A busy, contemporary eatery in a historic building, Silver Nugget features a large breakfast menu as well as deli-style sandwiches at lunch. Dinner offerings include deep-fried Rocky Mountain rainbow trout and liver and onions.

Getting There & Around
Ouray is 24 miles north of Silverton along US 550 and reached by private vehicle.

RIDGEWAY
pop 720 / elev 6895ft

More than a few classic Westerns were shot in and around this enticing 19th-century railway town, including *How the West Was Won* and *True Grit*. But don't let the rustic vibe fool you; Ridgeway has its share of swanky ranches, including one owned by fashion designer Ralph Lauren.

Fishing aficionados should head to **Ridgeway State Park & Recreation Area** (☎ 970-626-5822; 2855 US 550; admission free; ☯ dawn-dusk), 12 miles north of town. The reservoir here is stocked with loads of rainbow trout, as well as German brown, kokanee, yellow perch and the occasional large-mouth bass. There are also hiking trails and campsites.

Decorated in a Southwestern adobe style, the **Chipeta Sun Lodge & Spa** (☎ 970-626-3737; www.chipeta.com; 304 S Lena St; r $160-215) is the best sleeping option. The friendly owners can give you loads of local advice, a hearty breakfast is included in the price and there are hot tubs for soaking. Rooms feature hand-painted Mexican tiles, rough hewn log beds and decks with a view.

Scenes from the movie *True Grit* were filmed at the appropriately named **True Grit** (☎ 970-626-5739; 123 N Lena Ave; dishes $8-15). This popular neighborhood pub is sort of a shrine to John Wayne – pictures and memorabilia grace the walls. Burgers, sandwiches and tasty chicken fried steaks are on the menu.

Ridgeway is at the crossroads of US 550 and Rte 62 and a good spot from which to start a circular drive on the San Juan Skyway (see p336).

TELLURIDE
pop 2000 / elev 8750ft

It's been a hunting ground for the Utes, a saloon-swinging mining mecca and a ghost town. But nowadays, folks flock to this archetypal mountain town for outdoor adventures galore, fantastic festivals and an all round laid-back feel. Easy on the eyes, Telluride boasts not only a well-preserved Victorian downtown, but also picture-perfect Colorado mountain views.

Orientation & Information
Colorado Ave, also known as Main St, is where you'll find most of the restaurants, bars and shops. The town's small size means you can get everywhere on foot, so leave your car at the intercept parking lot at the south end of Mahoney Dr (near the visitor center) or wherever you are staying.

From town you can reach the ski mountain via two lifts and the gondola. The latter also links Telluride with Mountain Village, the true base for the Telluride ski area. Located 7 miles from town along Hwy 145, Mountain Village is a 20-minute drive east, but only 12 minutes away by gondola (free for foot passengers).

Ajax Peak, a glacial headwall, rises up behind the town to form the end of the U-shaped valley that contains Telluride. To the right (or south) on Ajax Peak, Colorado's highest waterfall, Bridal Veil Falls, cascades 365ft down; a switchback trail leads to a restored Victorian powerhouse atop the falls.

Bookworks (☎ 970-728-0700; 191 S Pine St) The town's biggest bookstore.

Telluride Medical Center (☎ 970-728-3848; 500 W Pacific Ave) Handles skiing accidents, medical problems and emergencies.

Telluride Sports (☎ 970-728-4477; 150 W Colorado Ave) Has topographical and USFS maps, sporting supplies and outdoor information.

Visitor center (☎ 970-728-3041, 800-525-3455; www .telluride.com; 398 W Colorado Ave) It has loads of area information.

Sights & Activities
Covering three distinct areas, **Telluride Ski Resort** (☎ 970-728-6900, 866-287-5015; www.telluride skiresort.com; lift tickets $70) is served by 16 lifts. Much of the terrain is for advanced and intermediate skiers, but there's still ample choice for beginners.

There are public cross-country trails in Town Park, as well as along the San Miguel River and the Telluride Valley floor west of town. Instruction and rentals are available from the **Telluride Nordic Center** (☎ 970-728-1114; 800 E Colorado Ave). Experienced Nordic skiers will appreciate the **San Juan Hut Systems'** (☎ 970-626-3033; www.sanjuanhuts.com; hut per night $25) series of crude huts along a 206-mile route stretching from Telluride west to Moab in Utah. In the summer these huts, which are equipped with bunks and cooking facilities, are popular with mountain bikers. Book well in advance, huts fill quickly.

While on the subject, **mountain biking** is big news in Telluride. The surrounding peaks offer awesome single-track routes and of-course stupendous scenery. Beginners should try the easy and smooth gravel **River Trail** that connects Town Park with Hwy 145 for a total trail distance of about 2 miles. If you want a bit more of a workout continue up **Mill Creek Trail**, west of the Texaco near where the River Trail ends. After the initial climb, the trail follows the contour of the mountain and ends at the Jud Wiebe Trail (hikers only) where you'll have to turn back. To rent some gear, visit **Easy Rider Mountain**

Sports (☎ 970-728-4734; 101 W Colorado Ave). The shop has a variety of bikes to choose from, as well as maps and information.

Hiking is also popular in the region. The **Jud Wiebe Trail**, a 2.7-mile loop from town, offers views after a 1300ft climb and is the only trail near Telluride dedicated to foot travel. Take Oak St north to Tomboy Rd and continue on the gated road on your left to reach the signed trailhead. The return portion of the loop ends at Aspen St.

The **Bear Creek Trail** is 2 miles and ascends 1040ft to a beautiful cascading waterfall. From this trail you can access the strenuous Wasatch Trail, a 12-mile loop that heads west across the mountains to **Bridal Veil Falls**. The Bear Creek trailhead is at the south end of Pine St, across the San Miguel River.

Sleeping

Camel's Garden (☎ 970-728-9300; www.camelsgarden .com; 250 W San Juan; r from $275) This modern and luxurious choice is located at the base of the gondola. The lobby is filled with local artwork and the large rooms feature custom-crafted furniture and Italian marble bathrooms with oversized tubs. Don't miss the giant 25ft outdoor hot tub. The complex also features restaurants, bars and

---

TELLURIDE'S FABULOUS FESTIVALS

Telluride has two giant festivals each year. The **Telluride Bluegrass Festival** (☎ 800-624-2422; www.planetbluegrass.com; admission per day $55; ☺ late Jun) sells out months in advance and attracts thousands for a weekend of top-notch rollicking bluegrass in a fantastic outdoor setting. It's an awesome party. Arrive early to scope out a grassy spot and set up the blanket and picnic basket. Stalls sell all sorts of food and local microbrews to keep you happy. When the sun goes down revelers kick it up a notch, dancing wildly to the day's most anticipated acts. Many folks choose to camp, and if you purchase your ticket early enough you can get a four-day festival and camping pass for $240. This combo allows you to pitch your tent at Warner Field, within walking distance of the festival. If this option is sold out, you can camp at Ilium Campground, a beautiful site on the river 7 miles west of Telluride. During the festival a four-day pass costs $45 per person and includes frequent shuttle service between the site and festival. There are numerous other campgrounds within 15 miles of Telluride that cost about $12 per site (see opposite). All campgrounds fill up quickly during festival week, so arrive early. Tickets and camping passes can be purchased on the festival website.

Telluride's other blow out event is the increasingly popular and esteemed **Telluride Film Festival** (☎ 603-433-9202; www.telluridefilmfestival.com; admission $20-650; ☺ early Sep). National and international films are premiered at venues throughout the town, and the event attracts big-name stars. The only way to guarantee you'll see your first choice film is to purchase a pass. These start at $325 and include priority entrance to numerous screenings. Admission to individual films costs $20, however these tickets are only made available right before show time and passholders get first dibs. For more information on the relatively complicated pricing scheme visit the film festival website.

AUTHOR'S CHOICE

Hotel Columbia (☎ 970-728-0660; www
.columbiatelluride.com; r from $135) A real gem,
each of the hotel's rooms has a balcony,
fireplace and a mountain view. Baths are
larger than average and breakfast is included. Other highlights include a rooftop Jacuzzi, library and fitness room. Plus,
the hotel is right across the street from the
gondola.

spa treatments. You may be able to find a
deal at this pricey place by booking through
a consolidator like www.hotels.com.

Victorian Inn (☎ 970-728-6601, 800-611-9893; www
.tellurideinn.com; 401 W Pacific Ave; r from $80) It's exte-
rior doesn't look very Victorian, but this inn
has comfortable rooms (some with kitchenettes) emitting a hint of the era. There's a
hot tub and sauna outside.

Oak Street Inn (☎ 970-728-3383; 134 Oak St; r from
$66) Rooms are rather spartan, but it's the
cheapest option in town and not bad value
if you're on a budget. The cheapest rooms
share bathrooms.

Telluride Town Park Campground (☎ 970-728-
2173; 500 W Colorado Ave; campsites $10; ☾ mid-May–
mid-Sep) Right in the center of town, this place
has 20 sites with shower access ($1.50 for a
hot shower). It fills up quickly in the peak
season.

Matterhorn Campground (☎ 970-327-4261; Hwy
145; campsites from $12, vehicle pass $6; ☾ mid-May–
mid-Sep) Ten miles south of Telluride, this
USFS campground has well-maintained
sites as well as shower and toilet blocks. It's
a good option if you arrive during a festival
and other lodging options are full.

Eating

Baked in Telluride (☎ 970-728-4775; 127 S Fir St;
mains $6-10; ☾ breakfast, lunch & dinner) For a fill-
up on pizza, sandwiches, salads and calzones head to this very casual place. The
front deck is where to sit if you're looking
to see or be seen.

221 South Oak (☎ 970-728-9505; 221 S Oak St;
dishes $25; ☾ dinner) An intimate restaurant in
a historic home, this place has a small but
innovative menu mixing world flavors with
excellent results. Dishes are meat-, fish- and
seafood-based and incorporate lots of fresh
vegetables. There's a long wine list and a

sumptuous dessert selection. Vegetarians
shouldn't be frightened by all the meaty
choices – a veggie menu is available upon
request.

Fat Alley (☎ 970-728-3985; 128 S Oak St; mains $6-9;
☾ lunch & dinner) For barbecue, bourbon and
beer try this low-key restaurant. Barbecue
is the specialty of the house, but there are
also burgers, Southwestern dishes and veggie options. It's a good place to bring the
kids, the restaurant bills itself as 'family
oriented.'

Drinking

Last Dollar Saloon (☎ 970-728-4800; 100 E Colorado
Ave) For a splash of local color with your
cocktail, head to this town favorite. With
the best selection of imported beers in
town, as well as pool tables and darts, it's
no wonder this creaky wooden bar is so
popular.

Fly Me to the Moon Saloon (☎ 970-728-6666; 132
E Colorado Ave) Let your hair down and kick up
your heels to the tunes of live music at the
Fly Me to the Moon Saloon, the best place
in Telluride to groove.

Smugglers Brewpub & Grille (☎ 970-728-0919;
225 South Pine St) Beer lovers will feel right at
home at casual Smugglers, a great place to
hang out in any season. With at least seven
beers on tap, this brewpub is big on variety. And with the pint of the day only $2
between 3pm and 5pm, you can afford to

AUTHOR'S CHOICE

Cosmopolitan (☎ 970-728-1292; 300 W San
Juan Ave; dishes from $20; ☾ dinner) Can you
resist a menu that includes Himalayan yak
ribeye and lobster corn dogs? Chef Chad
Scothorn has won numerous awards for
his culinary aptitude, and his restaurant,
inside the Hotel Columbia, certainly boasts
the most unique menu in town. Influenced
by the cuisines of France, the Southwest and
Thailand, the menu changes weekly, but the
food is always excellent. Complement your
meal with a bottle of fine wine – there are
200 vintages to choose from. For something
special, dine in the intimate tasting cellar,
where 2000 bottles line the walls and the
floors are travertine. Here you'll be served
a six-course meal paired with five different
wines.

sample the best they have. Try the chocolaty Two Plank Porter or the Smuggler's Scottish Strong Ale.

Sheridan Bar (☎ 970-728-3911; 231 W Colorado Ave) Most of this historic bar survived the waning mining fortunes even as the adjoining hotel was busy selling off chandeliers and finely carved furnishings to help pay the heating bills. These days, overdressed visitors occupy stools and chat about upcoming film releases next to the occasional old-timer or young hippy girl. Despite the air of pretentiousness, it's still worth stopping by for the yesteryear atmosphere.

Getting There & Around

Commuter aircraft serve the mesa-top **Telluride Airport** (☎ 970-778-5051; www.telluride airport.com) 5 miles east of town, weather permitting. At other times planes fly into Montrose, 65 miles north. **Telluride Express** (☎ 970-728-6000; www.tellurideexpress.com) runs shuttles to Montrose airport (adult/child $42/20), call to arrange pick-up.

New Mexico

'Land of Enchantment,' indeed. Although it's an apt marketing moniker, you won't read that word-weary phrase again here. Not because it's false. There are simply too many other descriptors for this tricultural powerhouse. New Mexico looms large with legendary Anglo counter culture, dynamic pueblo traditions and a potent Hispanic presence.

Santa Fe, Taos and Albuquerque offer enough diversions to keep jaded Manhattanites happy, and enough outdoor pursuits to keep active Boulder residents from gathering moss. From valleys bursting with brilliant yellow cottonwood trees to dirt roads leading to red rocks and pine forests, spectacular byways won't disappoint. Northwestern New Mexico is dominated by Navajo lands, as well as the mysterious Chaco Cultural National Historical Park. Follow the Santa Fe Trail through the northeast to Las Vegas or follow Rte 66 through Tucumcari and Santa Rosa, with the Southwest's best diving site. Then belly up an Old West bar in Cimarron. For roads less traveled, head to Southwestern New Mexico, where the Gila National Forest offers untrammeled hiking trails and remote cliff dwellings. Watch wildlife at the Bosque Del Apache National Wildlife Refuge; chill out in Truth or Consequences hot springs; or kick some tumbleweed in ghost towns. Southeastern New Mexico boasts the world's largest gypsum dunes at White Sands National Monument, the world's most prominent UFO site at Roswell and one of the world's largest cave systems at Carlsbad Caverns. It's the most diverse part of the state and it just doesn't get any better.

HIGHLIGHTS

■ **Hottest Springs**
The waters of Ojo Caliente (p387) are classic, but the luxe digs at Sierra Grande Lodge & Spa (p426) in Truth or Consequences will get your blood boiling.

■ **Coolest Drinks**
There's just something about those margaritas at the Adobe Bar (p399) at the Taos Inn.

■ **Best Spot for Solitude**
Sit out the precious pre-dawn and post-dusk moments at White Sands National Monument (p438).

■ **Most Spectacular Drive**
It's a toss-up between the High Road to Taos (p388) and the Turquoise Trail (p361) since both have more than their share of historic churches and quaint villages.

■ **Best High Flying Nightlife**
Watch the bats fly out for a dusky dinner at Carlsbad Caverns National Park (p452).

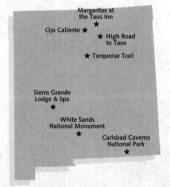

■ POPULATION: 1.8 MILLION ■ AREA: 121,356 SQ MILES ■ www.newmexico.org

NEW MEXICO

NEW MEXICO

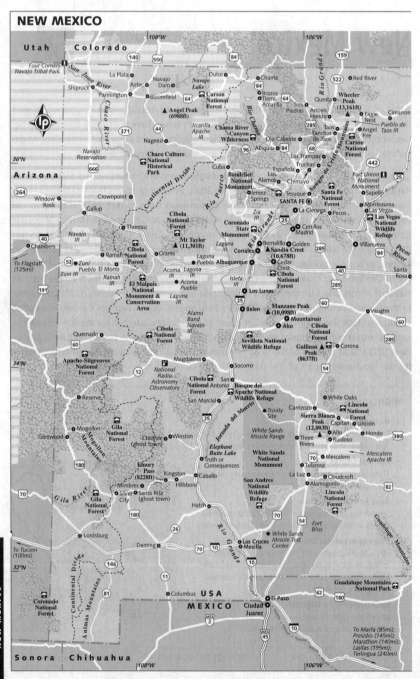

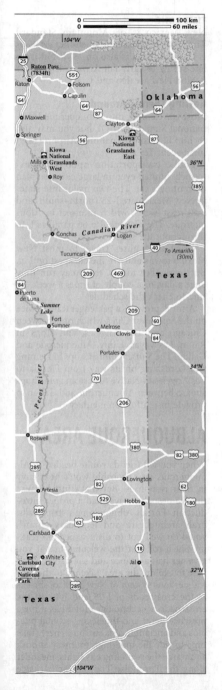

Climate

Because the altitude in New Mexico ranges from 3000ft to 13,000ft, temperatures can vary wildly. What you can depend on, no matter the season, is about 300 days a year of sun and dry air. The southern desert receives less than 10in of rain annually, but when it rains (usually in late summer), thunderstorms are intense. Mountainous areas near Taos receive quite a bit of snow (anywhere from about 200in to 300in per winter), while the Sacramento Mountains in Southern New Mexico average about 180in.

National & State Parks

Unique geologic features and ancient ruins pepper the New Mexico landscape, often cascaded in crystalline light against the backdrop of a bright blue sky. Southeastern New Mexico boasts the stark rolling dunes of **White Sands National Monument** (p438) and the cave system of **Carlsbad Caverns National Park** (p452). In the Southwest, **Gila National Forest** (p431) offers backpackers a natural playground and a springboard to visit cliff dwellings and hot springs. Nearby **Bosque del Apache National Wildlife Refuge** (p425) is a winter home for endangered whooping cranes. To the north, **Bandelier National Monument** (p386) offers 50 sq miles of canyons and hiking trails. Northwestern New Mexico holds some of the country's most inspiring ancient Indian sites, including the massive Puebloan buildings at **Chaco Culture National Historical Park** (p407) and **Aztec Ruins National Monument** (p408), connected to Chaco by a 30ft-wide ancient road.

NEW MEXICO SCENIC BYWAYS

New Mexico is laced with dozens of beautiful and beckoning byways, but four in particular have been designated National Scenic Byways. For more information, visit www.byways.org.

The **Santa Fe Trail** made it possible for wagon trains to roll westward, and their wagon ruts still remain at Fort Union National Monument. From Santa Fe (p363), travel north on Hwy 25 to lovely Las Vegas (p419), then take Hwy 518 east to Hwy 161, south to Hwy 25 and north to Hwy 21 to gunslinging Cimarron (p421). From here take Hwy 64 north to the ranching center of Raton (p422) and Colorado. The eastern spur heads through Clayton (p423) and into Oklahoma. Allow a couple of days to explore this route.

The **Jemez Mountain Trail** makes for a picturesque day trip from Santa Fe through its National Forest. Take Hwy 4 east past the famous labs at Los Alamos (p384) and past Bandelier National Monument (p386) before taking Hwy 126 west toward mountainous Cuba (p411). Then head east on Hwy 44 through the Jemez Indian Reservation, and east on Hwy 4 back to Santa Fe.

The looped **Billy the Kid** byway pays tribute to the Wild West (allow at least two days). Travel from Capitan (p442), home of the original Smokey Bear, east on Hwy 48 to Ruidoso (p440), west on Hwy 70 past the famous raceway at Ruidoso Downs (p440) and east on Hwy 380 towards Lincoln (p444), where Billy the Kid made his last stand.

Referred to as the 'Royal Highway of the Interior Land,' **El Camino Real** follows the Rio Grande from Santa Fe through Bernalillo (p360), down Hwy 47 south to San Miguel Mission and Socorro (p424), past the startling beauty of Elephant Butte Lake (p427), to the hot-springs haven of Truth or Consequences (p425), past chile-laden Hatch (p432), the university town of Las Cruces (p432) and onward to the Texas border. Allow a few days for this drive.

Two more official Scenic Byways worth checking out are the **Turquoise Trail** (p361) and **Route 66** (p412).

Information

All About New Mexico (www.psych.nmsu.edu/~linda/chilepg.htm) Links to practically everything imaginable about New Mexico, from outdoor recreation to where to buy chile products.

New Mexico Culture (www.nmculture.org) Includes a historical timeline, a calendar of events and an index of museums, parks and monuments.

New Mexico Net (www.nmnet.org) Not the most elegant site, but certainly comprehensive.

New Mexico State Parks (www.nmparks.com) Search by park to find a list of facilities, fishing guides and other resources.

New Mexico Tourism Bureau (☎ 505-827-7400, 800-545-2040; www.newmexico.org; 491 Old Santa Fe Trail, Santa Fe; ☉ 8am-6pm) The official site for the Land of Enchantment.

Public Lands Information Center (www.publiclands.org) A convenient consolidation providing camping and recreation information for all New Mexico public lands and waters.

TIME ZONE

New Mexico is on Mountain Standard Time (MST; seven hours behind GMT), as is Utah. Arizona is also on MST, but from late spring to early fall Arizona is an hour behind New Mexico and Utah.

Getting There & Around

Most travelers fly into Albuquerque International Sunport (ABQ), but you may also fly into El Paso International Airport (ELP) in adjacent Texas.

Public transportation options are extremely limited even in large cities, so plan on renting a car. The two major interstates in New Mexico are I-25 (north–south) and I-40 (east–west), which intersect in Albuquerque. The historic Rte 66 parallels I-40 throughout the state.

Greyhound buses travel to most New Mexico towns and are the cheapest option. But in smaller towns, they may run only once a day, or a couple of times a week. Be sure to check the schedule.

Amtrak provides a passenger train service on the *Southwest Chief,* which runs between Chicago and Los Angeles, and stops in Raton, Las Vegas, Lamy, Albuquerque and Gallup. The *Sunset Limited* stops in Deming and Lordsburg on its way from Florida to Los Angeles. A Native American guide hops aboard between Albuquerque and Gallup to provide insightful commentary.

ALBUQUERQUE AREA

When you tell friends you're headed to Albuquerque, you probably won't hear envy in their responses. But that's just because they've probably never had a proper introduction. For all Albuquerque's strip malls, drab architecture and legendary sprawl, you'd do well not to dismiss her too readily. She'll roll out the welcome mat if you give her half a chance and she makes a fine base to explore the area. Likened to the central nervous system of New Mexico, she sits at the crossroads of I-25 and I-40, at the crossroads of technology (Intel has a huge presence here) and timelessness (vital pueblos and ancient forests surround her). Take time to ride the mile-high tramway at dusk and watch the twinkling city lights, meander along the Turquoise Trail up the backside of the Sandias (where former mining towns have turned into funky outposts), camp and mountain bike in the Manzanos and hike at Tent Rocks, a dramatic landscape that looks imported from southern Utah.

ALBUQUERQUE

pop 712,700 / elev 5285ft

Depending on your perspective, New Mexico's most populous city is simply another dot on the map of Rte 66, or it's a distinctive and vibrant mix of university students, Native Americans, Hispanics and gays and lesbians. You'll find square dances and tai chi classes flyered with equal enthusiasm. You'll find cowboys and chiropractors chowing down at hole-in-the-wall taquerías as well as retro cafés. Albuquerque may not knock your socks off with sparkle, but it'll get under your skin with sincerity. It exudes a 'realness' that's hard to find in Santa Fe anymore and a 'normalcy' that somehow bypassed Taos.

Positioned in the valley between the Sandia Mountains and the Rio Grande, Albuquerque possesses a magical setting that connects mountains and desert. Like tethered hot-air balloons waiting to be unleashed at dawn, Albuquerque is bristling with energy and diversity – it just may not be as obvious as balloons tacking to and fro. From dark downtown bars to touristy Old Town (albeit one with a quintessential plaza), from hip university shops to a fantastic pueblo cultural center, Albuquerque truly offers something for everyone. And its modesty is refreshing.

Orientation

Two interstate highways, I-25 (north–south) and I-40 (east–west), intersect in Albuquerque. An approximate grid surrounds that intersection, the major boundaries of which are Paseo del Norte Dr to the north, Central Ave (old Rte 66) to the south, Rio Grande Blvd to the west and Tramway Blvd to the east. Central Ave is the main street, passing through Old Town, downtown, the university, Nob Hill and state fairground.

Street addresses often conclude with a directional designation, such as Wyoming NE. The center point is where Central Ave crosses the railroad tracks, just east of downtown. For instance, locations north of Central Ave and east of the tracks would have a NE designation.

Information

BOOKSTORES

Page One (Map p350; ☎ 505-294-2026; www.page1 books.com; 11018 Montgomery Blvd NE; ☺ 9am-10pm Mon-Sat, 9am-8pm Sun) Huge and comprehensive.

Page One Too (Map p350; ☎ 505-294-5623; 11200 Montgomery Blvd NE; ☺ 9am-10pm Mon-Sat, 9am-8pm Sun) Sells used books across the street from its parent shop.

UNM Bookstore (Map pp354-5; ☎ 505-277-5451; Central Ave; ☺ 8am-6pm Mon-Fri, 10am-5pm Sat) On the south side of the campus on Central at Cornell.

EMERGENCY

Police (Map pp354-5) Roma Ave (☎ 505-768-2020; 400 Roma Ave NW); Central Ave (☎ 505-256-8368; 2901 Central Ave NE)

INTERNET ACCESS

Kinko's (Map pp354-5; ☎ 505-255-9673; 2706 Central Ave SE) Open 24 hours; Internet usage costs 20¢ per minute.

Main Library (Map pp354-5; ☎ 505-768-5140; 501 Copper Ave NW; ☺ 10am-6pm Mon-Sat, until 7pm Tue & Wed) Unlimited Internet access after you purchase a $3 library card.

INTERNET RESOURCES

Albuquerque.com (www.albuquerque.com) Attraction, hotel and restaurant information.

Albuquerque Online (www.abqonline.com) Exhaustive listings and links for local businesses.

City of Albuquerque (www.cabq.gov) Information on public transport, area attractions and more.

MEDICAL SERVICES

Presbyterian Hospital (Map pp354-5; ☎ 505-841-1234, emergency 505-841-1111; 1100 Central Ave SE; ☺ 24hr emergency)

University Hospital (Map pp354-5; ☎ 505-272-2411; 2211 Lomas Blvd NE; ☺ 24hr emergency) Head here if you don't have insurance.

Walgreens (Map pp354-5; ☎ 505-265-1548, 800-925-4733; 6201 Central Ave NE; ☺ 24hr)

POST

Downtown post office (Map pp354-5; ☎ 800-275-8777; 201 5th St SW)

Main post office (Map pp354-5; ☎ 800-275-8777; 1135 Broadway Ave NE)

TOURIST INFORMATION

Albuquerque Convention & Visitors Bureau (Map pp354-5; ☎ 505-842-9918, 800-733-9918; www.itsa trip.org; 20 First Plaza; ☺ 8am-5pm Mon-Fri)

Old Town Information Center (Map p352; ☎ 505-243-3215; www.itsatrip.org; 303 Romero Ave NW; ☺ 9:30am-5pm, until 4:30pm Oct-Apr)

NEW MEXICO

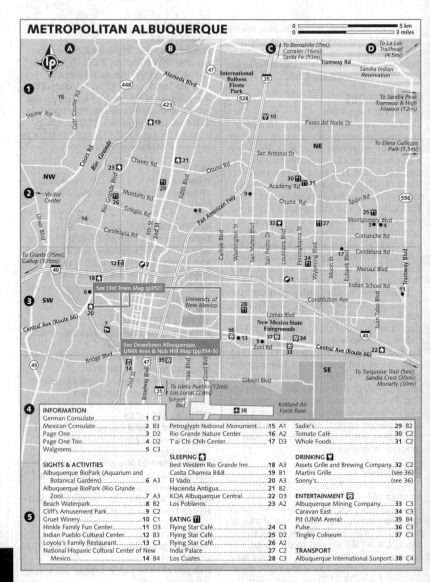

METROPOLITAN ALBUQUERQUE

INFORMATION		
German Consulate	1	C3
Mexican Consulate	2	B3
Page One	3	D2
Page One Too	4	D2
Walgreens	5	C3

SIGHTS & ACTIVITIES		
Albuquerque BioPark (Aquarium and Botanical Gardens)	6	A3
Albuquerque BioPark (Rio Grande Zoo)	7	A3
Beach Waterpark	8	B2
Cliff's Amusement Park	9	C2
Gruet Winery	10	C1
Hinkle Family Fun Center	11	D3
Indian Pueblo Cultural Center	12	B3
Loyola's Family Restaurant	13	C3
National Hispanic Cultural Center of New Mexico	14	B4
Petroglyph National Monument	15	A1
Rio Grande Nature Center	16	A2
T'ai Chi Chih Center	17	D3

SLEEPING		
Best Western Rio Grande Inn	18	A3
Casita Chamisa B&B	19	B1
El Vado	20	A3
Hacienda Antigua	21	B2
KOA Albuquerque Central	22	D3
Los Poblanos	23	A2

EATING		
Flying Star Café	24	C3
Flying Star Café	25	D2
Flying Star Café	26	A2
India Palace	27	C2
Los Cuates	28	C3
Sadie's	29	B2
Tomato Café	30	C2
Whole Foods	31	C2

DRINKING		
Assets Grille and Brewing Company	32	C2
Martini Grille	(see 36)	
Sonny's	(see 36)	

ENTERTAINMENT		
Albuquerque Mining Company	33	C3
Caravan East	34	C3
Pit (UNM Arena)	35	B4
Pulse	36	C3
Tingley Coliseum	37	C3

TRANSPORT		
Albuquerque International Sunport	38	C4

Sights

OLD TOWN

From its founding in 1706 until the arrival of the railroad in 1880, Old Town Plaza was the hub of Albuquerque. These days it is the city's most popular tourist area, with many original buildings, and museums and galleries within walking distance.

From mid-April to mid-November, the Albuquerque Museum (opposite) offers informative and free guided **Old Town walking tours** (☎ 11am Tue-Sun). Alternatively, the Information Center publishes *Old Town: A Walking Tour of History and Architecture* that guides you to 17 historically significant structures.

NEW MEXICO

SANDIA CREST

Albuquerqueans always know which way is east thanks to 10,678ft Sandia Crest, sacred to Sandia Pueblo and well-named for the way its granite cliffs glow at sunset (*sandia* is Spanish for 'watermelon'). There are three ways to the top.

Beautiful 8-mile (one-way) **La Luz Trail** (FR 444; parking $3) is the most rewarding, rising 3800ft from the desert, past a small waterfall to pine forests and spectacular views. It gets hot, so bring lots of water.

Sandia Peak Tramway (Map p350; ☎ 505-856-7325; www.sandiapeak.com; Tramway Blvd; adult/child $15/10; ☺ 9am-8pm Wed-Mon, 5-8pm Tue), the world's longest at 2.7 miles, is the most extravagant route. You can hike up and take the tram down, trekking two more miles at the bottom on Tramway Trail to your car. The breathtaking ride starts among desert cholla cacti and soars to the pines of the 10,300ft Sandia Peak in 18 minutes. To reach the tram, take Tramway Blvd north on the east side of town, or take I-25 exit 234 and head east on Hwy 556.

Or you can drive all the way to the top. From Albuquerque, take I-40 east to exit 175, and head 6 miles north on Hwy 14 to Hwy 536. Or go north on I-25 to exit 242 and take Hwy 165 east past Placitas; this bumpy dirt road through Las Huertas Canyon connects with Hwy 536 just north of the ski base and a few miles south of the peak. Along the way, stop at **Sandia Man Cave**, where the oldest human encampment in North America was discovered in 1936. It's a beautiful drive, though it may be closed in winter due to snow. The helpful **Sandia Ranger Station** (☎ 505-281-3304; 11776 Hwy 337; ☺ 8am-5pm, closed Sun Oct-Apr), about a mile south of I-40 exit 175, has maps and information.

Atop the mountain, another **ranger station** (☎ 505-248-0190; NM 165; ☺ 9:30am-sunset May-Oct) offers nature programs; **Sandia Crest House** (☎ 505-243-0605; NM 165; dishes $3-7; ☺ 9:30am-sunset), in the same building, serves burgers and snacks. This is the jumping off point for exquisite **Sandia Crest Trail**, which heads 11 miles north and 16 miles south with incredible views; hike north along the ridgeline to appreciate the best of them.

Take the trail 2 miles south to the tram terminal and **High Finance Restaurant** (Map p350; ☎ 505-243-9742; 40 Tramway Rd; lunch dishes $6-15, dinner dishes $16-42; ☺ 11am-9pm), which has mediocre food but fabulous views.

Built in 1706 (though it has been renovated several times since), the adobe **San Felipe de Neri Church** (Map p352; ☎ 505-243-4628; 2005 N Plaza; admission free; ☺ 7am-7pm summer, 9am-5:30pm winter) is Old Town's most famous sight. A Spanish mass is held at 8:15am on Sunday.

The **Albuquerque Museum** (Map p352; ☎ 505-242-4600; www.albuquerquemuseum.com; 2000 Mountain Rd NW; adult $4, child 4-12 $1; ☺ 9am-5pm Tue-Sun), which exhibits changing shows of New Mexican artists, explores the city's Indian, Hispanic and Anglo history.

The teen-friendly **New Mexico Museum of Natural History & Science** (Map p352; ☎ 505-841-2800; www.nmnaturalhistory.org; 1801 Mountain Rd NW; adult $6, seniors & students $5, child under 11 $3; ☺ 9am-5pm) features the so-called Evolator (evolution elevator), which transports visitors through 38 million years of New Mexico's geologic and evolutionary history through the use of video technology. The museum also houses a huge-screen **DynaTheater** (adult $6, child 3-12 $3), which screens films about dinosaurs.

The **Turquoise Museum** (Map p352; ☎ 505-247-8650; 2107 Central Ave NW; adult $4, child 6-18 $3; ☺ 9.30am-4pm Mon-Fri, until 3pm Sat) will help you to recognize the real stuff. Why is that important? Because less than 10% of the state's multibillion-dollar turquoise businesses create products using natural turquoise. It's small but worth a visit.

INDIAN PUEBLO CULTURAL CENTER

Operated by New Mexico's 19 pueblos, this **center** (Map p350; ☎ 505-843-7270; www.indianpueblo .org; 2401 12th St NW; adult/child $4/2; ☺ 9am-5pm) is a must for anyone planning to visit Indian pueblos. A historical museum traces the development of Pueblo cultures; exhibits compare cultures through languages, customs and crafts; an art gallery features changing exhibits and a restaurant serves Pueblo fare. It's great one-stop shopping, so to speak.

NEW MEXICO

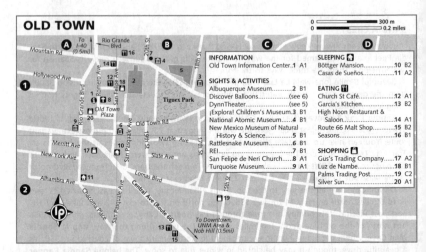

OLD TOWN

INFORMATION	
Old Town Information Center..1	A1

SIGHTS & ACTIVITIES	
Albuquerque Museum..........2	B1
Discover Balloons...............(see 6)	
DynnTheater.....................(see 5)	
¡Explora! Children's Museum.3	B1
National Atomic Museum......4	B1
New Mexico Museum of Natural	
History & Science...............5	B1
Rattlesnake Museum............6	B1
REI...........................7	B1
San Felipe de Neri Church.....8	A1
Turquoise Museum..............9	A1

SLEEPING	
Böttger Mansion................10	B2
Casas de Sueños................11	A2

EATING	
Church St Café..................12	A1
Garcia's Kitchen.................13	B2
High Noon Restaurant &	
Saloon........................14	A1
Route 66 Malt Shop............15	B2
Seasons.............................16	B1

SHOPPING	
Gus's Trading Company......17	A2
Luz de Nambe..................18	B1
Palms Trading Post.............19	C2
Silver Sun.........................20	A1

DOWNTOWN

Recently rejuvenated with a few trendy restaurants, galleries and clubs, downtown has a few less 1950s department stores and sleepy diners than it used to. Built in 1927 and preserved as a historic landmark, the renovated **KiMo Theater** (Map pp354-5; ☎ 505-768-3544; 423 Central Ave NW; ☎ theatre tours 9am-4pm Mon-Fri) serves as a community arts center (p359). Architect Carl Boller has created a kind of pueblo–Art Deco in the KiMo, using impressions gathered on visits to Indian pueblos and reservations.

The small **New Mexico Holocaust & Intolerance Museum** (Map pp354-5; ☎ 505-247-0606; www.nmholocaustmuseum.org; 415 Central Ave NW; donations accepted; ☎ 11am-3:30pm Tue-Sat) houses powerful exhibits on genocides worldwide, from Armenia to Acoma (p411).

UNM AREA

With about 18,000 full-time students in some 125 fields, the University of New Mexico is the state's leading university. Redondo Dr loops around the campus; maps are available at the University Bookstore on Central Ave; and tours are given through **Recruitment Services** (Map pp354-5; ☎ 505-277-2260; www.unm.edu; Student Union Bldg, Redondo & Stanford Drs; ☎ 9am & 2pm).

The **Maxwell Museum of Anthropology** (Map pp354-5; ☎ 505-277-4404; off University Blvd; ☎ 9am-4pm Tue-Fri, 10am-4pm Sat) has an interesting 'People of the Southwest' exhibit depicting 11,000 years of the region's cultural history.

A fabricated dig demonstrates the painstaking methods of archaeology.

The smallish **University Art Museum** (Map pp354-5; ☎ 505-277-4001; Center for the Arts Bldg, cnr Redondo & Cornell Drs; ☎ 9am-4pm Tue-Fri, 5-8pm Tue, 1-4pm Sun), renowned for its photographs, is also crammed with paintings, prints and sculptures, many of which highlight New Mexico's rich Hispanic tradition.

METRO ALBUQUERQUE

Rich with bird life, the 270-acre **Rio Grande Nature Center** (Map p350; ☎ 505-344-7240; www.nmparks.com; 2901 Candelaria Rd NW; per car $3; ☎ park 8am-5pm, visitor center 10am-5pm) also offers gentle hiking and biking trails that wind through meadows and groves of trees.

The **Petroglyph National Monument** (Map p350; ☎ 505-899-0205; www.nps.gov/petr; per car $1 Mon-Fri, $2 Sat & Sun) offers trails of varying degrees of difficulty set around rock etchings dated from AD 1300. Head west on I-40 across the Rio Grande and take exit 154 north.

The huge adobe-style **National Hispanic Cultural Center of New Mexico** (Map p350; ☎ 505-246-2261; www.nhccnm.org; 1701 4th St SW; adult/child $3/free; ☎ 10am-5pm Tue-Sat) houses a visual arts building, a performance center and three galleries of Hispanic art, history and culture. The library offers tons of records of Hispanic genealogy.

In the Sandia foothills, the tranquil **Elena Gallegos Park** (Map p350; ☎ 505-857-8334; per car $1 Mon-Fri, $2 Sat & Sun; ☎ 7am-9pm Apr-Oct, 7am-7pm Nov-Mar) offers several miles of biking and

NEW MEXICO

hiking trails. It's clearly located on Tramway Blvd NE, north of Academy Ave.

The **Albuquerque Bio Park** (Map p350; ☎ 505-843-7413; www.cabq.gov/biopark; adult $7, child 2-12 $3; ☻ 9am-5pm) includes a zoo, aquarium and botanical gardens (combo ticket for all three costs $10 for adults, $5 for kids). The 60-acre **Rio Grande Zoo** (903 10th St SW) is home to more than 1300 animals from around the world, while the **aquarium** and **botanical gardens** (2601 Central Ave NW) feature a 285,000-gallon shark tank and several conservatories housing an array of desert species.

Activities

The omnipresent Sandia Mountains offer opportunities galore for hiking, skiing, picnicking, biking and camping.

Sandia Peak Ski Area (☎ 505-242-9052; www .sandiapeak.com; full-/half-day lift tickets adult $40/29, child & senior $30/22) rents downhill skis at the ski base ($18). There's no ski rental where the tram drops you off at the top, so if you want to rent skis at the mountain you have to drive. (See box on p351 for ways to reach the mountaintop.)

Cross-country trails atop the mountain are maintained by the Cibola National Forest. In town, rent equipment at **REI** (Map p352; ☎ 505-247-1191; 1905 Mountain Rd NW) and **Mountains and Rivers** (Map pp354-5; ☎ 505-268-4876; www.mountains-and-rivers.com; 2320 Central Ave SE), across from UNM.

Extensive **mountain-biking** trails criss-cross the Sandias and the Rio Grande Bosque. From late May to mid-October, the Ski Area operates a **chairlift** (one round-trip ride with bike $8, 1-day unlimited rides $14; ☻ 10am-4pm). Rent bikes at the top of the lift (accessed by the tram, see box on p351) or at the ski base for $35 a day, including unlimited lift rides. Bikes are not allowed on the tram.

Albuquerque's best hikes are the La Luz Trail (box on p351) and the Crest Trail, but there are many shorter hikes throughout the Sandias, too, including several easily accessed by the tram.

Only in Albuquerque

The **T'ai Chi Chih Center** (Map p350; ☎ 505-299-2095; www.taichichihassociation.org; Scottsdale Village, 3107 Eubank St NE; ☻ call for class schedule) is the only one of its kind in the country to teach tai chi chih, a moving meditation originated by Albuquerque resident Justin Stone in 1974 that activates, balances and circulates the *chi* (life force). Maybe you'll get lucky and meet the originator, who often drops into the center to offer his wisdom.

The **Rattlesnake Museum** (Map p352; ☎ 505-242-6569; www.rattlesnakes.com; 202 San Felipe St NW; admission $2.50; ☻ 10am-5pm), Old Town's most interesting diversion – exhibiting some 45 live snakes – claims to be the world's largest public collection of different species of rattlesnakes.

A LOT OF HOT AIR

Because of particularly conducive air currents, Albuquerque has been famous for hot-air ballooning since the early 1970s. Since then, the **International Balloon Fiesta** (☎ 505-821-1000, 888-422-7277; www.balloonfiesta.org) has grown into the largest balloon festival in the world. You just haven't lived until you've seen a three-story-tall Tony the Tiger land in your hotel courtyard, which is exactly the sort of thing that happens for nine days between the first and second weekends in October. Almost a million spectators pour into town, and yeah, everything's packed and parking is tough, but witnessing the 'mass ascension', with hundreds of colorful balloons fluttering and inflating like living, breathing beings is amazing. And being in the air? Even better! During the fiesta hundreds of hot-air balloon pilots show their skills in a variety of events and competitions. Daily morning mass ascensions lure photographers. Finding accommodations is a big problem, with most hotels booked months in advance. Last-minute visitors will likely have difficulty finding accommodations, even in Santa Fe or beyond.

Several companies offer rides over the city and the Rio Grande, including **Discover Balloons** (Map p352; ☎ 505-842-1111; www.discoverballoons.com; 205b San Felipe NW; per person $140); **World Balloon** (☎ 505-293-6800, 800-351-9588; per person $150, with 2-week advance reservation $140); and **Enchanted Winds** (☎ 505-293-0000, 888-246-6359; www.rainbowryders.com). You get the ride, hotel pickup and a traditional champagne breakfast upon landing. Reserve at least two days in advance. For more about ballooning elsewhere in the Southwest, see p64.

The **National Atomic Museum** (Map p352; ☎ 505-284-3243; www.atomicmuseum.com; 1905 Mountain Rd NW; adult $5, child 6-17 $4; ◷ 9am-5pm) displays a range of atomic weaponry, including replicas of Little Boy and Fat Man – the bombs that destroyed Hiroshima and Nagasaki. A theatre runs *Ten Seconds That Shook the World*, an hour-long film about the development of the atomic bomb, and *Commitment to Peace*, about the Cold War.

Gruet Winery (Map p350; ☎ 505-821-0055; www.gruetwinery.com; 8400 Pan American Fwy NE; ◷ 10am-5pm Mon-Fri, noon-5pm Sat), known across the country for award-winning sparkling wine, the Gruet family also produces a rich and oaky chardonnay and a pinot noir with hints of black cherry and plum.

Tours

New Mexico native Christy Rojas runs **Aventura Artistica** (☎ 800-808-7352; www.newmexicotours.com), which specializes in three- and four-day tours of the Albuquerque–Santa Fe area.

Albuquerque for Children

Kids can easily stay entertained for a couple of days in Albuquerque. Although many attractions are suitable for adults too, they are primarily aimed at kids.

The **iExplora! Children's Museum** (Map p352; ☎ 505-224-8300; www.explora.mus.nm.us; 1701 Mountain Rd NW; adult $7, child under 12 $3; ◷ 10am-6pm Mon-Sat, noon-6pm Sun) has programs and exhibits designed to and encourage creativity

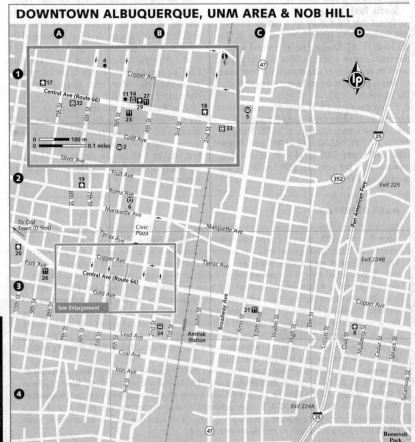

DOWNTOWN ALBUQUERQUE, UNM AREA & NOB HILL

and imagination. With demonstrations involving light, electricity, sound, motion, anatomy and more, the center teaches kids scientific principles with a dose of fun.

Cliff's Amusement Park (Map p350; ☎ 505-881-9373; www.cliffsamusementpark.com; 4800 Osuna NE; adult/child $21/18; ☽ Apr-Sep, with widely varying hr) is a great reward for the kids being so patient and cooperative in the back seat. The park has about 25 rides, including a roller coaster, the Water Monkey, a play area and other traditional favorites.

Adults might enjoy the **Beach Waterpark** (Map p350; ☎ 505-345-6066; www.thebeachwaterpark .com; 1600 Desert Surf Circle; adult $27, child 5-9 $11; ☽ May-Sep) as much as kids. There are seven water slides and a giant pool that creates

5ft swells for body surfers. If you're timid, tired or just a toddler, float down the Lazy River or have a splash in one of the kiddie pools.

Hinkle Family Fun Center (Map p350; ☎ 505-299-3100; www.hinklefamilyfuncenter.com; 12931 Indian School Rd NE; 5hr pass $35, per ride $6; ☽ noon-10pm Sun-Thu, noon-midnight Fri & Sat) keeps little ones of all ages amused with bumper cars, laser tag, mini-golf and a huge 'jungle play area' where kids can crawl and climb and slide around. Burn off some energy, especially if it's too hot or cold or wet to play outside.

Festivals & Events
Friday's *Albuquerque Journal* (www.abqjournal.com) includes a venue section with

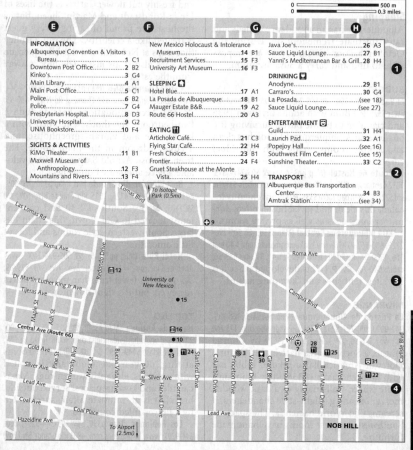

an exhaustive listing of festivals and activities. The following are most notable.

Gathering of Nations Powwow (☎ 505-836-2810; www.gatheringofnations.com; late Apr) Features dance competitions, displays of Native American arts and crafts, and the 'Miss Indian World' contest.

Gay/Lesbian/Bisexual/Transgender Pride (☎ 505-873-8084; mid-Jun) All-inclusive, just like Albuquerque and Santa Fe.

New Mexico Arts & Crafts Fair (late Jun) A three-day event at the fairgrounds.

Summerfest (Sat evenings throughout the summer) With different foods and entertainment featured each week.

Bernalillo Wine Festival (☎ 505-867-3311; admission $10; ⏱ early Sep) Locally produced wine and live music, staged about 15 minutes north of Albuquerque.

New Mexico State Fair (☎ 505-265-1791; www.expo nm.com; 16 days in Sep) A biggie rodeo with live music.

Sleeping

Albuquerque has an abundance of beds and rates fluctuate tremendously. During the October balloon fiesta, rooms are impossible to find and carry a 30% premium.

BUDGET

El Vado (Map p350; ☎ 505-243-4594; 2500 Central Ave SW; r $32; P) Built with adobe bricks in 1936 and claiming to be the purest surviving Rte 66 motel in Albuquerque, El Vado has clean and simple rooms, many with individual carports.

Route 66 Hostel (Map pp354-5; ☎ 505-247-1813; 1012 Central Ave SW; dm HI members/nonmembers $17/16, s/d $22/28, r with bathroom $33; P) Conveniently located, this clean and jovial hostel offers dormitory bunk beds as well as private rooms.

KOA Albuquerque Central (Map p350; ☎ 505-296-2729, 800-562-7781; www.koakampgrounds.com; I-40 exit 166, 1200 Skyline Rd NE; tent sites $21-41, RV sites $33-56, cabins $40-70; ☒ P) This developed place has RV sites, tent sites and 'kamping kabins.'

MIDRANGE

La Posada de Albuquerque (Map pp354-5; ☎ 505-242-9090, 800-777-5732; www.laposada-abq.com; 125 2nd St NW; r $70-90; P) Built in 1939 by Conrad Hilton, a Socorro-area native, this Historic Hotel of America has a relaxed lobby bar with weekend jazz (p358), tile fountains, white stucco walls rising to a dark-wooded mezzanine and gaslight-style chandeliers. It screams Old World hacienda. The spacious Southwestern guest rooms have handmade furniture.

Mauger Estate B&B (Map p354-5; ☎ 505-242-8755, 800-719-9189; www.maugerbb.com; 701 Roma Ave NW; r $89-179; ☒ ☐) This restored Queen Anne house (Mauger is pronounced 'major'), whose rooms have stocked refrigerators and freshly cut flowers, attracts the likes of Linda Rondstadt and Martin Sheen, but as the hosts are proud of saying 'every guest is treated like a celebrity.' The same trolley that stops at Nob Hill and the Albuquerque Bio Park also stops just a few blocks away from the estate.

Casita Chamisa B&B (Map p350; ☎ 505-897-4644; www.casitachamisa.com; 850 Chamisal Rd NW; r $80-95; ☒ ☒) Accommodations here include a two-bedroom guesthouse equipped with a kitchenette and vibrant greenhouse, and a large bedroom in the main house. The friendly host, Arnold Sargeant, offers valuable advice about area offerings.

Best Western Rio Grande Inn (Map p350; ☎ 505-843-9500, 800-959-4726; 1015 Rio Grande Blvd NW; s/d $93/103; ☒ P) South of I-40 and conveniently located to Old Town, this chain has large, Southwestern-style rooms and lots of little amenities.

Hotel Blue (Map pp354-5; ☎ 505-924-2400; www .thehotelblue.com; 717 Central Ave NW; s/d $79/89; ☒ P) It has fewer frills than the other places reviewed, but it's right downtown.

TOP END

Hacienda Antigua (Map p350; ☎ 505-345-5399, 800-201-2986; www.haciendantigua.com; 6708 Tierra Dr NW; r incl breakfast $149-199; ☒ ☒ ☐) The rooms at this 200-year-old adobe are decorated with antiques, elegantly woven rugs, Mexican tiles and kiva fireplaces. Served outside, breakfast is an intimate affair, surrounded by a flower-filled courtyard.

Los Poblanos (Map p350; ☎ 505-344-9297, 866-344-9297; www.lospoblanos.com; 4803 Rio Grande Blvd NW;

r $135-250; (⊠ ⬛ ⬜) Set on 25 acres of the Los Poblanos ranch, this place has a conference center, walking trails and a community organic garden.

Böttger Mansion (Map p352; ☎ 505-243-3639, 800-758-3639; www.bottger.com; 110 San Felipe St NW; r incl breakfast & extras $110-169; (P)) Built in 1912, this friendly place retains its original Victorian style – there's no Old West or Southwestern feel here! Perhaps you'll get lucky and arrive on a first or third Thursday of the month. That's when the B&B serves a delightful high tea that may include lemon sorbet, melon soup, cheese and leek quiche and dessert.

Eating

Albuquerque offers the region's widest variety of international cuisines while serving up some of the best New Mexican food anywhere.

OLD TOWN

High Noon Restaurant & Saloon (Map p352; ☎ 505-765-1455; 425 San Felipe St NW; dishes $11-27; ⓨ lunch & dinner) For grilled contemporary fare and excellent margaritas in a rough-hewn, 18th-century adobe, this is your place.

Seasons (Map p352; ☎ 505-766-5100; 2031 Mountain Rd NW; lunch $7-14, dinner $14-28; ⓨ lunch Mon-Fri, dinner daily) With bright-yellow walls, high ceilings, fresh flowers and a creative menu, this contemporary place provides welcome relief from the usual Old Town atmosphere. Try the hearty red-chile-dusted chicken burgers or Baja tacos inside or on the rooftop cantina.

Church St Café (Map p352; ☎ 505-247-8522; 2111 Church St NW; dishes $6-12; ⓨ breakfast & lunch daily, dinner Thu-Sat) Historic Casa Ruiz, home to one of Albuquerque's founding families for over 250 years, now houses this cozy café serving New Mexican fare.

Route 66 Malt Shop (Map p352; ☎ 505-242-7866; 1720 Central Ave SW; dishes $5; ⓨ lunch & dinner Mon-Sat) This nostalgic and friendly place only has a tiny counter with four stools, one table and one booth. But it serves great green-chile cheeseburgers, hot pastrami and other sandwiches.

Garcia's Kitchen (Map p352; ☎ 505-842-0273; 1736 Central Ave SW; dishes $4-9; ⓨ lunch & dinner) A family restaurant that draws crowds of locals with its homemade specialties, Garcia's is popular for its *carne adobada* (pork marinated in red chile and spices), fajitas and chile stew.

DOWNTOWN

Artichoke Café (Map pp354-5; ☎ 505-243-0200; 424 Central Ave SE; dishes $9-29; ⓨ dinner) The unpretentious service here belies the fact that the place has been voted an Albuquerque favorite many times. The back outdoor patio offers relief from Central Ave traffic.

Java Joe's (Map pp354-5; ☎ 505-765-1514; 906 Park Ave SW; dishes $3-6; ⓨ breakfast & lunch) This low-key place caters to a young, earthy crowd with scrambled tofu as well as the usual breakfast burrito and pastries.

Sauce Liquid Lounge (Map pp354-5; ☎ 505-242-5839; 405 Central Ave NW; dishes $7-9; ⓨ 4pm-2am Tue-Sat) A popular and trendy spot, Sauce primarily serves very tasty gourmet pizza. The funky lounge in the back is a busy spot to hang out with a late-night drink (p358).

Fresh Choices (Map pp354-5; ☎ 505-242-6447; 402 Central Ave SW; dishes $5-8; ⓨ lunch & dinner) This brick-walled place has a soup, salad, pizza and pasta bar for $7.

UNM AREA & NOB HILL

Flying Star Café (ⓨ 6:30am-11pm Sun-Thu, to midnight Fri & Sat) Central Ave (Map pp354-5; ☎ 505-255-6633; 3416 Central Ave SE); Juan Tabo Blvd (Map p350; ☎ 505-275-8311; 4501 Juan Tabo Blvd NE); Rio Grande Blvd (Map p350; ☎ 505-344-6714; 4026 Rio Grande Blvd NW); Menaul Blvd (Map p350; ☎ 505-293-6911; 8001 Menaul Blvd NE) With four locations, the always-packed Flying Star is *the* place to go for homemade soups, muffins, breads, desserts and ice cream. It also serves innovative mains and gourmet sandwiches, beer and wine.

Frontier (Map pp354-5; ☎ 505-266-0550; 2400 Central Ave SE; dishes $3-7; ⓨ 24hr) An Albuquerque tradition for delicious but inexpensive meals, the Frontier boasts enormous cinnamon rolls and the best *huevos rancheros* ever. The food, people-watching and Western art collection are all outstanding.

Yanni's Mediterranean Bar & Grill (Map pp354-5; ☎ 505-268-9250; 3109 Central Ave NE; lunch dishes $11-25, dinner dishes $12-30; ⓨ lunch & dinner) This pleasant and bright place prepares perfect Atlantic salmon, yellow-fin sole encrusted in parmesan and the best calamari in Albuquerque. Start with a light lemon chicken or red lentil soup and make sure you save room for a baklava sundae. It also has more traditional Greek platters.

NEW MEXICO

Gruet Steakhouse at the Monte Vista (Map pp354-5; ☎ 505-256-9463; 3201 Central Ave NE; lunch dishes $8-16, dinner dishes $15-32; ⏰ lunch & dinner) Owned by the Gruet winery family (p354), this Nob Hill steakhouse specializes in steak (try the steak salad), of course, but it also has a fair amount of seafood. Upstairs, the popular bar spills onto a balcony overlooking the nighttime scene.

METROPOLITAN ALBUQUERQUE

Whole Foods (Map p350; ☎ 505-856-0474; 5815 Wyoming Blvd) This organic grocery store has a large selection of ready-made dishes, sandwiches and a large salad bar.

Los Cuates (Map p350; ☎ 505-255-5079; 491 Lomas Blvd; dishes under $8; ⏰ 11am-9pm) Serving up huge and excellent plates of Southwestern specialties, this place is not for tender palates, as the salsa and chile are full strength. If the place is packed, try the restaurant across the street – same name, same owners.

India Palace (Map p350; ☎ 505-271-5009; 4410 Wyoming Blvd NE; dishes $7-12; ⏰ lunch & dinner) Locally favored for spicy East Indian cuisine, the tandooris, curries, seafood and vegetarian dishes are custom-made to suit anyone's heat tolerance.

Tomato Café (Map p350; ☎ 505-821-9300; 5901 Wyoming Blvd NE; buffet $7-9; ⏰ lunch & dinner) For the city's most consistently fresh and bountiful buffets, this place rules. Start at the varied salad bar and move on to six different pizzas and three different pasta dishes. Stay healthy with the green beans with garlic and perfectly steamed broccoli.

High Finance (Map p350; ☎ 505-243-9742; Sandia Peak; lunch dishes $7-10, dinner dishes $17-45; ⏰ lunch Wed-Mon, dinner nightly) For a so-so meal with a wow-wow view, take the tramway up here

or drive up the eastern side of the Sandias and walk about a half-mile along the crest to the restaurant. Lunch is more reasonably priced. Their bar opens for early birds; plan to arrive before dusk.

Loyola's Family Restaurant (Map p350; ☎ 505-268-6478; 4500 Central Ave SE; dishes $3-8; ⏰ 6am-2:30pm Tue-Sun) For pure Rte 66–style and Denny's-style New Mexican fast-food, Loyola's has been serving no-frills fare since before there was even a song about the Mother Rd.

Drinking

Sauce Liquid Lounge (Map pp354-5; ☎ 505-242-5839; 405 Central Ave NW; ⏰ 4pm-2am Tue-Sat) This hip little place with a bit of a New York–lounge feel, is part airy restaurant (p357), part dark bar with plush chairs. A DJ plays house music Friday and Saturday, but it's not so loud that you can't just hang and talk.

Assets Grille & Brewing Company (Map p350; ☎ 505-889-6400; 6910 Montgomery Blvd NE; dishes $6-14; ⏰ lunch & dinner Mon-Sat, bar open nightly) Serving fresh-brewed micro beer along with a broad menu, this fun bar is brimming with young professionals.

La Posada (Map pp354-5; ☎ 505-242-9090; 125 2nd St NW), a historic and genteel downtown hotel (p356), the lobby features a happy hour between 5pm and 7pm Wednesday to Friday with finger foods and a piano bar. A jazz combo entertains every Friday and Saturday night.

Anodyne (Map pp354-5; ☎ 505-244-1820; 409 Central Ave NW) This is an excellent spot for a game of pool. The huge space has book-lined walls, wood ceilings, plenty of overstuffed chairs, more than a hundred bottled beers and great people-watching on Central Ave.

Martini Grille (Map p350; ☎ 505-255-4111; 4200 Central Ave SE; ⏰ Mon-Sat) A Nob Hill piano bar that attracts all ages.

Sonny's (Map p350; ☎ 505-255-5932; 4214 Central Ave SE; ⏰ from 11am) This is a low-key bar, with a mixed crowd and live rock music on weekends.

Carraro's (Map pp354-5; ☎ 505-268-2300; 108 Vassar Dr SE; ⏰ from 5pm) This is a popular Nob Hill place, great for unwinding with brews, pool, pizza and pals.

Entertainment

For a comprehensive list of Albuquerque's diverse nightspots and a detailed calendar of upcoming events, get *Alibi* (www.alibi

---

AUTHOR'S CHOICE

Sadie's (Map p350; ☎ 505-345-5339; 6230 4th St NW; lunch dishes $5-7, dinner dishes $7-11; ⏰ lunch & dinner) A massive place with a barn-like atmosphere (and a big-screen TV in the bar), Sadie's is a local institution. One author makes this her first stop in Albuquerque – bar none. Recite along with us: 'a carafe of grand gold margaritas and the enchilada dinner, please, with blue corn, rolled, chicken, green vegetarian, no onions and a side of guac. Great. Thanks.'

NEW MEXICO

.com), a free weekly published every Tuesday. The entertainment sections of Thursday evening's *Albuquerque Tribune* and the Friday and Sunday *Albuquerque Journal* are helpful, too.

CINEMAS

Guild (Map pp354-5; ☎ 505-255-1848; 3405 Central Ave NE) Situated about a mile east of the university, the Guild screens foreign films and Hollywood fringe.

Southwest Film Center (Map pp354-5; ☎ 505-277-5608; Rodondo & Stanford Drs; UNM campus; ◯ Sep-Apr) Runs several series concurrently in the basement of the Student Union Building in the SUB Theater.

NIGHTLIFE

Many live-music clubs and bars are concentrated downtown, including **Launch Pad** (Map pp354-5; ☎ 505-764-8887; 618 Central Ave SW), a retro-modern place grooving to alternative sounds and punk (both local and national bands). It serves a full menu at the contemporary diner in the front.

At **Caravan East** (Map p350; ☎ 505-265-7877; 7605 Central Ave NE) practice your two-step or line dancing with live country and western bands while enjoying a complimentary happy hour buffet.

The **Albuquerque Mining Company** (Map p350; ☎ 505-255-4022; 7209 Central Ave NE; ◯ from 6pm), a venerable institution, and the more hip **Pulse** (Map p350; ☎ 505-255-3334; 4100 Central Ave SE; ◯ from 9pm) are the two most popular gay and lesbian nightclubs.

PERFORMING ARTS

Popejoy Hall (Map pp354-5; ☎ 505-277-4569; www.unmtickets.com; Central Ave at Cornell St SE) and the historic **KiMo Theater** (p352) are the primary places to see big-name national acts, as well as local opera, symphony and theater. The **Pit** (Map p350; ☎ 505-925-5626; www.unmtickets.com; 1111 University Blvd SE) and **Tingley Coliseum** (Map p350; ☎ 505-265-1791; 300 San Pedro NE) host Albuquerque's major events. **Sunshine Theater** (Map pp354-5; ☎ 505-764-0249; 120 Central Ave SW) stages alt-rock shows.

The **New Mexico Ballet Company** (☎ 505-292-4245; www.nmballet.org; tickets $15-20) performs from October to April. The **New Mexico Symphony Orchestra** (☎ 505-881-8999; www.nmso.org; tickets $10-50) performs at various venues, including at the zoo (p353).

SPORTS

About those **Albuquerque Isotopes** (Map pp354-5; ☎ 505-924-2255; www.albuquerquebaseball.com; Isotopes Park, Av Cesar Chavez & University SE). First of all: yes, the city's baseball team really was named for the *Simpsons'* episode 'Hungry, Hungry Homer,' when America's favorite TV dad tried to keep his beloved Springfield Isotopes from moving to Albuquerque. It didn't work, and now the 'Topes sell more merchandise than any other minor (and most major) league team. They sometimes win, too.

Albuquerque Scorpions (☎ 505-265-1791; www.scorpionshockey.com) play hockey at Tingley Coliseum (left). The **State Rodeo** (☎ 505-265-3976; www.exponm.com) is held in September at the New Mexico State Fairgrounds.

The **UNM Lobos** (☎ 505-277-4569; www.unm.edu) football squad packs the Pit, but it's the women's basketball and volleyball teams that carry the banner to playoffs and national championships.

Shopping

For Native American crafts and informed salespeople, stop by the **Palms Trading Post** (Map p352; ☎ 505-247-8504; 1504 Lomas Blvd NW; ◯ Mon-Sat), or **Gus's Trading Company** (Map p352; ☎ 505-843-6381; 2026 Central Ave SW). **Luz de Nambe** (Map p352; ☎ 505-242-5699; 328 San Felipe St NW; ◯ Mon-Sat) sells discounted and famed Nambeware (p381). **Silver Sun** (Map p352; ☎ 505-242-8265; 2042 South Plaza NW) is a reputable spot for turquoise.

Another good spot to stroll, without the touristy feel of Old Town, is around the university and in Nob Hill. If you walk east from the university down and around Central Ave, you'll find an eclectic mix of shops (from a tattoo parlor to a herbal medicine shop to a toy store) until you reach the Nob Hill Shopping Center at Carlisle.

Getting There & Around

Though the **Albuquerque International Sunport** (Map p350; ☎ 505-244-7700; www.cabq.gov/airport; 2200 Sunport Blvd) is New Mexico's biggest, it's still relatively small. It's served by major airlines, car rental companies and private shuttles that run to downtown Albuquerque, Santa Fe and points north.

SunTran (☎ 505-243-7433; www.cabq.gov/transit; adult/child $1/35¢; ◯ 6am-9pm, some lines run until 6pm), the public bus system, covers most of Albuquerque on weekdays and hits the tourist spots daily. The airport, four miles south of downtown, is served by the No 50 SunTran bus weekdays from 7am to 8:30pm and Saturday from 9am to 7pm. Three **trolleys** (adult/child $1/35¢; 🕑 9am-6pm) serve downtown, Central Ave and Nob Hill.

Cabbies patrol the airport, train and bus stations and the major hotels, but are rarely roaming the streets to hail down. **Yellow Cab** (☎ 505-247-8888) has 24-hour service. A taxi takes 10 minutes to get downtown from the airport and charges about $8. Most hotels and motels offer free shuttles.

The **Albuquerque Bus Transportation Center** (Map pp354-5; 300 2nd St SW) houses **Greyhound** (☎ 505-243-4435, 800-231-2222; www.greyhound.com), which serves destinations throughout New Mexico.

Sandia Shuttle (☎ 505-243-3244; www.sandiashuttle .com) runs daily shuttles to many Santa Fe hotels, from 8am to 5pm ($23), as does **Fausts Transportation** (☎ 505-758-3410, 888-830-3410), which leaves the airport at 1:30pm daily. **Twin Hearts** (☎ 505-751-1201, 800-654-9456) leaves four times daily for Santa Fe, Taos, Red River and Angel Fire.

Amtrak's *Southwest Chief* stops daily at the **Amtrak Station** (Map pp354-5; ☎ 505-842-9650; www.amtrak.com; 214 1st St SW).

Wheelchair Getaways (☎ 505-247-2626, 800-642-2042) rents wheelchair-accessible vans.

AROUND ALBUQUERQUE
Corrales
pop 7300 / elev 5015ft

Squished between ever-expanding Albuquerque, the developing west mesa and the suburban sprawl of Rio Rancho, the rural village of **Corrales** (☎ 505-897-0502) is about 20 minutes from downtown Albuquerque, along the Rio Grande. Horses, llamas, sheep and other animals live side by side with million-dollar homes and traditional working farms. The main thoroughfare is Corrales Rd (Hwy 448), a New Mexico Scenic Byway; most other roads are dirt. Corrales offers easy access to the Rio Grande and walks along the bosque. Stop by the **Old San Ysidro Church** (off Corrales Rd), built between 1776 and 1778 and a beautiful example of Spanish colonial architecture.

For sleeping, the warm and friendly **Nora Dixon Place** (☎ 505-898-3662, 888-667-2349; www .noradixon.com; 312 Dixon Rd; r from $80) has three

rooms that look out onto a peaceful courtyard with spectacular views of the Sandias.

Excellent pizza is served at **Village Pizza** (☎ 505-898-0045; Corrales Rd; pizzas $11-21; 🕑 11am-9pm); order your pie with green chile.

Bernalillo
pop 7000 / elev 5052ft

Just north of Corrales in Bernalillo, the **Coronado State Monument** (☎ 505-867-5351; adult/child $3/free; 🕑 8:30am-5pm Wed-Mon) is a multitiered Kuaua pueblo (c 1300) that served as the explorer Coronado's winter dwelling in 1540. It features a restored kiva (a circular, underground ceremonial chamber) and 15 original kiva paintings. The adjacent **campground** (☎ 505-980-8256; tent sites $8-11, RV sites $18-20) has cottonwoods for shade. Sites beneath the trees attract the higher fee. The ground has views of the Sandia Mountains and the Rio Grande.

Serving hearty Southwestern food and burgers, the **Range Cafe & Bakery** (☎ 505-867-1700; 925 Camino del Pueblo; dishes $6-13) is an open, airy, bustling place with delicious food and excellent service. Take exit 240 off I-25 and turn north onto Camino del Pueblo for 1 mile.

Next door, **Silva's Saloon** (☎ 505-867-9976; 955 Camino del Pueblo; 🕑 10am-late Mon-Sat, noon-5pm Sun) is a quintessential Old West bar, a family-run spot "setting 'em up since '33." The walls and ceiling are packed with posters, photos, dollar bills, memorabilia and whatever else someone happens to donate, hence its claim to be a 'historical museum.' Stop by for a classic margarita and great conversation – you may have to knock, since it's sometimes locked to keep out ruffians!

The excellent **Prairie Star** (☎ 505-867-3327; Tamaya Blvd; dishes $16-34; 🕑 dinner Tue-Sun), west of I-25 at exit 242, has spectacular views of the bosque and Sandia mountains. Dishes like bison tenderloin in horseradish aioli are served in a romantically appointed historic adobe. It's also an ideal spot for a sunset patio drink.

¡Traditions! Festival Marketplace within the **Legends of New Mexico Museum** (☎ 505-867-8600; I-25 exit 257; adult/child $5/free; 🕑 10am-4pm Thu-Mon), north of Bernalillo, spotlights the state's most famous visitors and residents – from Billy the Kid to Bill Gates, from Roswell aliens to Smokey Bear. When they say it's a tribute to multiculturalism, they mean it.

Area Pueblos

SANDIA PUEBLO

About 13 miles north of Albuquerque, this **pueblo** (☎ 505-867-3317; www.sandiapueblo.nsn.us; I-25 exit 234) was established around AD 1300. It opened one of the first casinos in New Mexico and subsequently used its wealth to successfully lobby for legislation preventing further development of Sandia Crest, the Sandia people's old sacred lands, appropriated by Cibola National Forest. The **Sandia Casino** (☎ 800-526-9366; www.sandiacasino.com;

DETOUR: TURQUOISE TRAIL

The Turquoise Trail, a National Scenic Byway, has been a major trade route since at least 2000 BC, when local artisans began trading Cerrillos turquoise with communities in present-day Mexico. Today it's the scenic back road between Albuquerque and Santa Fe, lined with quirky communities and other diversions.

In **Cedar Crest**, just a bit up Sandia Crest Rd (NM 165), don't miss the highly recommended **Tinkertown Museum** (☎ 505-281-5233; www.tinkertown.com; 121 Sandia Crest Rd; adult/child $3/1; ☑ 9am-6pm Apr-Nov). Woodcarver and wisdom collector Ross J Ward built this inspiring assortment of towns, circuses and other scenes. They come alive with a quarter and are surrounded with antique toys, junque and the suggestion that you eat more mangoes naked.

The nearby **Museum of Archaeology** (☎ 505-281-2005; 22 Calvary Rd, off NM 14; adult/child $3/2; ☑ noon-7pm May-Oct) has an 'archaeological site' outdoors (kids dig this) and local Indian artifacts inside. They also run the adjacent **Turquoise Trail Campground** (tent/RV sites $13/22, cabins $50-100), with hot showers and cool shade.

Sandia Mountain Hostel (☎ 505-281-4117; 12234 N Hwy 14; dm $15) is a great independent hostel, with passive solar-designed common areas, four friendly donkeys, one horse and lots of classic cars (in various states of disrepair) on the expansive and woodsy grounds. Give them a day's notice and they'll pick you up at the end of the SunTran trolley line in Albuquerque.

Continue up the Turquoise Trail, which winds through **Golden**, with an art gallery and lots of gorgeous desert scenery.

A bustling coal mining–company town in the 1920s and '30s, **Madrid** (pronounced *maa*-drid) was all but abandoned after WWII. In the mid-1970s, the company's heirs sold land lots cheaply to tie-dyed wanderers who have built a thriving arts community with galleries and wacky shops. It's not nearly as mellow as you'd think, attracting more bikers than New Agers, but that's just part of the appeal.

The **Old Coal Mine Museum** (☎ 505-438-3780; 2846 NM 14; adult/child $4/1; ☑ 9:30am-5pm, shorter hr in winter) preserves old mining equipment, pretty much right where the miners left it, and hosts the **Madrid Melodrama & Engine House Theatre** (☎ 505-438-3780; www.madridmelodrama .com; adult/child $10/5; ☑ 3pm & 7pm Sat, 3pm Sun May-Oct) starring a steam locomotive and lots of Wild West desperados, scoundrels and vixens. Marshmallows are included in the price of admission.

There are a couple of nice B&Bs in the area, including **Java Junction** (☎ 505-438-2772; www .java-junction.com; 2855 NM 14; r $69) and **Madrid Lodging** (☎ 505-471-3450; www.madridlodging.com; 14 Opera House Rd; d $85-100).

The 1919 **Mine Shaft Tavern** (☎ 505-473-0743; 2846 NM 14; dishes $5-8; ☑ lunch daily, dinner Fri-Sun) has live music on weekends and the 'longest stand-up bar in New Mexico' (built in 1946). **Mama Lisa's Cafe** (☎ 505-471-5769; NM 14; snacks $5-9; ☑ 11am-5pm Wed-Mon summer, Sat & Sun winter) serves good *quesadillas* and a great red-chile chocolate cake.

A photographer's dream, with unpaved streets and an Old West adobe town relatively unchanged since the 1880s, **Cerrillos** is home to the first mine in North America, built to extract turquoise around AD 100.

The top-drawer **Cerrillos Turquoise Mining Museum & Petting Zoo** (☎ 505-438-3008; 17 Waldo St; admission $2; ☑ 9am-5pm) packs five rooms with mining equipment dating back to 3000 BC; bottles and antiques excavated from an abandoned area hotel; Chinese art, pioneer-era tools and anything else the owners thought was worth displaying. For $2 more you can feed the goats, llamas and unusual chickens.

Continue north on NM 14 until you hit I-25, which takes you into Santa Fe.

NEW MEXICO

8am-4am Mon-Thu, 24hr Fri-Sun) boasts an elegant outdoor venue, the Sandia Casino Amphitheater, hosting everything from symphony orchestras to boxing matches to Bill Cosby.

Bien Mur Marketplace (☎ 800-365-5400; www.bienmur.com; 100 Bien Mur Dr NE), across the road from the casino, claims to be the largest Native American–owned trading post in the Southwest, which is probably true. The tribe invites visitors to **Marketfest** (late Oct), when Native artists show their stuff, as well as to corn dances during **Feast Day** (Jun 13).

SAN FELIPE PUEBLO

Though best known for the spectacular **San Felipe Feast Green Corn Dances** (May 1), this conservative Keres-speaking **pueblo** (☎ 505-867-3381; I-25 exit 252) now has a couple more claims to fame. The **Casino Hollywood** (☎ 505-867-6700; www.sanfelipecasino.com; I-25 exit 252; 8am-4am Sun-Wed, 24hr Thu-Sat) isn't just for gambling – this themed venue takes full advantage of its location to pull in acts like Los Lobos and Julio Iglesias. Visitors are also invited to **San Pedro Feast Day** (Jun 29); occasionally the pueblo hosts an **Arts & Crafts Fair** (Oct).

SANTA ANA PUEBLO

This **pueblo** (☎ 505-867-3301; www.santaana.org; US 150) is *posh*. Really posh. It boasts two great **golf courses** (☎ 505-867-9464, 800-851-9469; www.santaanagolf.com; greens fees $32-100), the Santa Anna Golf Club, with three nine-hole courses, and extravagant Twin Warriors Golf Club, with 18 holes and waterfalls.

DETOUR: TENT ROCKS NATIONAL MONUMENT

If you're driving I-25 between Albuquerque and Santa Fe, make the time for the bizarre and beautiful Tent Rocks. When volcanic ash erupted from the nearby Jemez Mountain volcanoes, it was sculpted into teepee-like formations and steep sided, narrow canyons. Visitors can hike up a dry riverbed through the piñon-covered desert to the formations, where sandy paths weave through the rocks and canyons. You'll need a couple of hours to drive the desert dirt road to get here and to hike around a bit, but it's well worth it. Take I-25 exit 264; follow Hwy 16 west to Hwy 22.

Santa Ana Star Casino (☎ 505-867-0000; US 150; 8am-4am Sun-Wed, 24hr Thu-Sat) has a staggering buffet, 36 lanes of bowling and the opportunity to challenge Rocko the Rooster to a $25,000 game of tic-tac-toe (watch out, he's good).

The **Stables at Tamaya** (☎ 505-771-6037; 9:30am-3:30pm) offer trail rides and lessons ($65) through the bosque, into which the pueblo has recently pumped millions of dollars for cleanup and restoration. And, lest you forget that this is not Beverly Hills west, there are **Corn Dances** (Jun 24 & Jul 26).

The luxurious **Hyatt Tamaya** (☎ 505-867-1234; www.tamaya.hyatt.com; 1300 Tayuna Trail; d from $189;), hidden in the desert landscape with expansive views, has three pools, three restaurants and a small spa.

SANTO DOMINGO PUEBLO

This nongaming **pueblo** (☎ 505-465-2214; Hwy 22; 8am-dusk) has long been a seat of Pueblo government – the All Indian Pueblo Council still meets here annually. Several galleries and studios at the pueblo abut the plaza in front of pretty 1886 **Santo Domingo Church**, with murals and frescos by local artists. The tribe is most famous for *heishi* (shell bead) jewelry, as well as the huge **Corn Dances** (Aug 4) and a wildly popular **Arts & Crafts Fair** (early Sep).

This pueblo is on Hwy 22, 6 miles northwest from I-25 exit 259, about halfway between Albuquerque and Santa Fe.

COCHITI PUEBLO

About 10 miles north of Santo Domingo on NM 22, this **pueblo** (☎ 505-465-2244) is known for its arts and crafts, particularly ceremonial bass drums and storyteller dolls. Several stands and shops are usually set up around the plaza and mission built in 1628; dances are held on the **Feast Day of San Buenaventura** (Jul 14 & Dec 25). There's no photography allowed here, but visitors can snap away at the **golf course**, considered the state's most challenging, or **Cochiti Lake**, favored by nonmotorized boaters and swimmers.

ISLETA PUEBLO

This **pueblo** (☎ 505-869-3111), 16 miles south of Albuquerque at I-25 exit 215, is best known for its church, the **San Augustine Mission** (☎ 505-869-3398). Built in 1613, it's been in constant use since 1692. A few plaza shops sell local pottery, and there is gambling at the **Isleta Casino and Resort** (☎ 505-724-3800; www.isleta-casino.com; ☯ 8am-4am Mon-Thu, 24hr Fri-Sun). On **Saint Augustine's Day** (Sep 4 & Aug 28), ceremonial dancing is open to the public.

Manzano Mountains

Often overlooked in favor of the Sandias, the Manzano Mountains are easily accessible from Albuquerque and offer great camping, hiking (including the breathtaking 22-mile crest trail with several access trails), biking and cross-country skiing. Tiny **Mountainair** is the central town, where you'll find **Cibola National Forest Mountainair Ranger District** (☎ 505-847-2990; Beal St), with wilderness maps of the Manzanos for $7.

Nestled in the foothills 12 miles north of Mountainair, **Manzano Mountains State Park** (☎ 505-847-2820; day-use fee $5, tent/RV sites $10/14; ☯ Apr-Dec) affords spectacular views of the distant easterly mountains. You can also camp at **Red Canyon Campground** (tent/RV sites $10/14; ☯ Apr-Oct), off Forest Rd 253 (follow signs in Manzano), or **Fourth of July Campground** (tent/RV sites $10/14; ☯ Apr-Nov), signposted on Hwy 55 from Tajique. In Mountainair, **Tillies** (☎ 505-847-0248; Hwy 60; tent/RV sites $10/16, r with kitchenettes up to 4 people $54) and **El Rancho Motel** (☎ 505-847-2577; Hwy 60; d around $30) have basic accommodations.

To reach the Manzanos from Albuquerque, drive east on I-40 to Tijeras Canyon/Cedar Crest (exit 175) and south on Hwy 337, which becomes Hwy 55 after 30 miles. From Belen, take Hwy 47 southeast to Hwy 60, go east till you reach Hwy 55 at Mountainair, and then go north.

Salinas Pueblo Missions National Monument

This relatively tourist-free monument, well worth a visit, consists of three separate pueblos and their accompanying 17th-century Spanish missions, which were each abandoned in the late 17th century. The small museum at the **headquarters** (☎ 505-847-2585; www.nps.gov/sapu; Hwy 60, Mountainair; admission free; ☯ 9am-5pm) gives a good overview, but each site has a little visitor center.

The biggest of the three sites is **Gran Quivira**, 25 miles south of Mountainair along Hwy 55. Around 300 rooms and several kivas have been excavated here. You can also visit the ruins of two churches, dating

from 1630 and 1659. Eight miles north of Mountainair on Hwy 55, **Quarai** highlights the 40ft-high remains of a 1630 church. **Abo**, 9 miles west of Mountainair along Hwy 60, features the remains of a ruined 1620 church and a large Tompiro pueblo.

SANTA FE & TAOS

The rugged beauty of New Mexico's most visited region is downright compelling. But it can't be separated from the mix of people who have settled here over the last 400 years (and more). Native Americans, Hispanic settlers, traders, mountain men, artists and hippies have all passed through, leaving indelible, living marks on the region. There are dozens of opportunities to feel its pulse: through art museums and historical houses to spirited festivals and real-world pueblo visits.

To get your physical pulse racing, consider river running on the Rio Grande (p371), mountain biking near Santa Fe (p372), skiing north of Taos (p401) and hiking in Bandelier. To get your artistic pulse racing, search for the ghosts of Georgia O'Keeffe in the Abiquiu hills (p387) and DH Lawrence around Taos (p391), or visit as many studios and galleries as your eyes can take. To get your cultural pulse racing, watch low-rider cars cruise the strip in Española (p386) and visit the outstanding Museum of International Folk Art (p366) in Santa Fe. And as you're hanging out in the hot springs at Ojo Caliente (p387), don't forget to ponder the birth of nuclear energy at Los Alamos (p384).

SANTA FE
pop 62,200 / elev 7000ft

In the last decade Santa Fe–style has become synonymous with laid-back sophistication, abstract adobe architecture, and carved wooden furniture and doorways. No matter where you're from, you've probably already encountered the ubiquitous, iconic images: howling coyotes and flute-playing Kokopellis; well-to-do Anglo women (probably from either US coast) with graying hair wearing long black skirts and silver necklaces; art, art and more art – everywhere you look. These images are certainly ever present and they might seem like clichéd

NEW MEXICO

SANTA FE

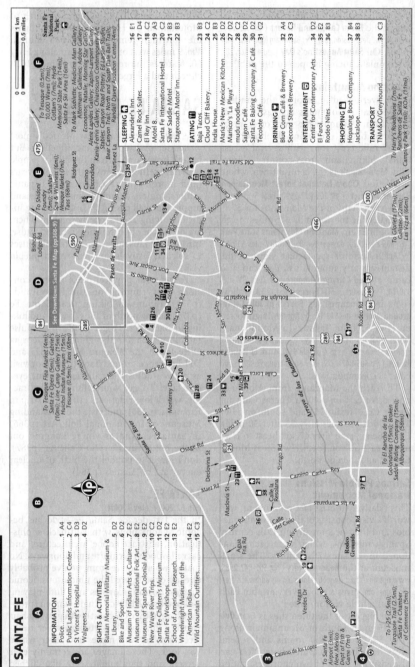

INFORMATION
Police..	1 A4
Public Lands Information Center..........	2 C4
St Vincent's Hospital........................	3 D3
Walgreens.......................................	4 D2

SIGHTS & ACTIVITIES
Bataan Memorial Military Museum &	
Library..	5 D2
Bike and Sport................................	6 D2
Museum of Indian Arts & Culture........	7 E2
Museum of International Folk Art........	8 E2
Museum of Spanish Colonial Art.........	9 C2
New Wave River Trips.......................	10 C2
Santa Fe Children's Museum..............	11 D2
Santa Fe Workshops.........................	12 E2
School of American Research.............	13 E2
Wheelwright Museum of the	
American Indian.............................	14 E2
Wild Mountain Outfitters..................	15 C3

SLEEPING
Alexander's Inn................................	16 E1
Camel Rock Suites............................	17 D4
El Rey Inn.......................................	18 C2
Motel 8..	19 A3
Santa Fe International Hostel.............	20 C2
Silver Saddle Motel..........................	21 B3
Stagecoach Motor Inn......................	22 B3

EATING
Baja Tacos......................................	23 B3
Cloud Cliff Bakery............................	24 C2
India House.....................................	25 B3
Maria's New Mexican Kitchen............	26 D2
Marisco's 'La Playa'..........................	27 D2
mudu noodles.................................	28 C2
Saigon Café....................................	29 D2
Santa Fe Baking Company & Café......	30 D2
Tecolote Café..................................	31 C2

DRINKING
Blue Corn Café & Brewery.................	32 A4
Second Street Brewery......................	33 C3

ENTERTAINMENT
Center for Contemporary Arts............	34 D2
El Farol...	35 E2
Rodeo Nites....................................	36 B3

SHOPPING
Hopalong Boot Company..................	37 B4
Jackalope..	38 B3

TRANSPORT
TNM&O/Greyhound........................	39 C3

To Tesuque (0.5mi);
100 West;
Cottam's (7mi); Hyde
Memorial State Park (10mi);
Santa Fe Ski Area (16mi)

To Mark Sublette; Medicine Man Gallery;
Aftermann Galleries; Adobe Gallery;
Economos; Natalie; Morning Star Gallery;
Alene Lapides Gallery; Zaplin-Lampert Gallery;
Kania/Ferrin Gallery; Ichabod Gallery; Frank Howell
Gallery; Canyon Road Pottery; Ed Larson Studio;
Stables; Canyon Road Trail;
Bear Canyon Trail; North and South Dale Ball Trails;
Randall Davey Audubon Center (4mi)

To Tesuque Flea Market (4mi);
Santa Fe Opera (5mi); Gabriel's
(10mi); Line Camp Gallery (15mi);
Huichol Indian Museum (15mi);
Tesuque (0.5mi); Taos (68mi)

To Shidoni
Foundry
(5mi); ShaNah
Spa & Wellness (6mi);
Taos (68mi)

To Santa Fe
Airport (3mi);
New Mexico
Dept of Fish &
Game (7mi)

To Harry's Roadhouse (7mi);
Rancheros de Santa Fe
Camping Park (11mi); KOA (11mi)

To I-25 (2.5mi);
Turquoise Trail (2.5mi);
Santa Fe Chamber
of Commerce (5mi)

To El Rancho de las
Golondrinas (15mi); Broken
Saddle Riding Company (15mi);
Albuquerque (58mi)

To Glorieta (17mi);
Galisteo (22mi);
Las Vegas (66mi)

0 — 1 km
0 — 0.5 miles

Santa Fe
National
Park

See Downtown Santa Fe Map (pp368-9)

images, but take heart – there's no greater aesthetically alluring cliché in America. Enjoy them. But also stroll down the narrow streets behind the plaza and across the railroad tracks to find a place rich with Hispanic influence, a colorful place bursting with a life force as red as *ristras* and as fiery as a New Mexico sunset.

Santa Fe's riches are an embarrassment. From extraordinary dining (to suit all budgets) and world-class opera to a dozen excellent museums celebrating everything and everyone with ties to New Mexico's rich cultural heritage, a visitor could spend two weeks here and still leave treasures to unearth.

Orientation

Cerrillos Rd (I-25 exit 278), a 6-mile strip of hotels and fast-food restaurants, enters town from the south; Paseo de Peralta circles the center of town; St Francis Dr (I-25 exit 282) forms the western border of downtown and turns into US 285, which heads north toward Española, Los Alamos and Taos. Alameda follows the canal east–west through the center of town, and Guadalupe St is the main north–south street through downtown. Most downtown restaurants, galleries, museums and sites are either on or east of Guadalupe St and are within walking distance of the plaza, in the center of town.

Information

BOOKSTORES

Borders Books & Music (Map pp368-9; ☎ 505-954-4707; Sambusco Market Center, 500 Montezuma Ave) An expansive selection of Southwestern reading.

Collected Works (Map pp368-9; ☎ 505-988-4226; 208B W San Francisco St) Though small, this independently owned store has a good selection of regional, travel and general interest books.

Travel Bug (Map pp368-9; ☎ 505-992-0418; www .mapsofnewmexico.com; 839 Paseo de Peralta) For travel books or practically every map you could ever need.

EMERGENCY

Police (Map p364; ☎ 505-955-5000; 2515 Camino Entrada)

INTERNET ACCESS

CD Café (Map pp368-9; ☎ 505-986-0735; 301 N Guadalupe St) Sip coffee or listen to CDs while you surf for $10 per hour.

Santa Fe Public Library (Map pp368-9; ☎ 505-955-6781; 145 Washington Ave) Make reservations for a free half-hour of Internet access.

MEDICAL SERVICES

St Vincent's Hospital (Map p364; ☎ 505-983-3361; 455 St Michael's Dr) 24-hour emergency care.

Walgreens (Map p364; ☎ 505-982-4643; 1096 S St Francis Dr) 24-hour pharmacy.

MONEY

It's a tourist town, and all-too-convenient ATMs are everywhere.

Wells Fargo (Map pp368-9; ☎ 505-984-0424; 241 Washington Ave) changes foreign currency.

POST

Post office (Map pp368-9; ☎ 800-275-8777; 120 S Federal Place)

TOURIST INFORMATION

Chamber of Commerce (Map p364; ☎ 505-983-7317; www.santafechamber.com; ☼ 8am-5pm) Inconveniently located at the Cerrillos exit from I-25, in the Premium Outlet Mall, this chamber has information for residents and visitors.

New Mexico Tourism Bureau (Map pp368-9; ☎ 505-827-7336; www.newmexico.org; 491 Old Santa Fe Trail; ☼ 8am-5pm) Housed in the historic 1878 Lamy Building (site of the state's first private college), this friendly place has flyers, information, a hotel reservation line, free coffee and even free Internet access on one slow computer.

New Mexico State Parks (Map p364; ☎ 505-476-3355; www.nmparks.com; 141 E De Vargas St; ☼ 8am-4pm Mon-Fri) This office has information on all state parks and recreation areas, but doesn't reserve campsites.

Public Lands Information Center (Map p364; ☎ 505-438-7542; www.publiclands.org; 1474 Rodeo Rd; ☼ 8:30am-4:30pm Mon-Fri) This place is very helpful, with maps and information on public lands throughout New Mexico.

Visitor Center (Map pp368-9; ☎ 505-955-6200, 800-777-2489; www.santafe.org; 201 W Marcy St; ☼ 8am-5pm Mon-Fri) Conveniently located at the Sweeny Convention Center.

Sights

Museum Hill has four excellent museums, a research library and a recommended café, all linked by a sculpture-lined trail. Almost 3 miles southwest of the plaza, take the M Line – a Santa Fe Trails (p382) bus geared toward visitors – that winds through historic neighborhoods.

PLAZA

The plaza dates back to the city's beginning in 1610, and from 1821 to 1880 it was the end of the Santa Fe Trail. Traders from as far away as Missouri drove here in their wagons laden with goods. Today, Native Americans sell their jewelry and pottery along the wall of the Palace of the Governors, kids skateboard and play hacky-sack and tourists weighed down with cameras and purchases flock into the square.

MUSEUMS OF NEW MEXICO

A collection of four very different **museums** (☎ 505-827-6463; $7 for one museum, $15 for a four-day pass to all four, children under 16 free; ☒ 10am-5pm Tue-Sun), two of them on Museum Hill, also offer seminars, musical events and a variety of guided tours with historic or artistic focuses, many designed for children. Both the Palace of the Governors and Museum of Fine Arts, the two located on the plaza, are free on Friday from 5pm to 8pm. All the museums have fabulous gift shops.

The **Museum of International Folk Art** (Map p364; ☎ 505-476-1200; www.moifa.org; 706 Camino Lejo) houses more than 100,000 objects from more than 100 countries and is arguably the best museum in Santa Fe. The exhibits aren't simplistically arranged behind glass cases; the historical and cultural information is concise and thorough; and a festive feel permeates the rooms. The Hispanic wing displays religious art, tin work, jewelry and textiles from northern New Mexico and throughout the Spanish colonial empire, dating from the 1600s to the present.

The **Museum of Fine Arts** (Map pp368-9; ☎ 505-476-5072; www.museumofnewmexico.org; 107 Palace Ave; ☒ tours 1:30pm) features works by regional artists and sponsors regular gallery talks and slide lectures. Built in 1918, the architecture is an excellent example of the original Santa Fe–style adobe. With more than 20,000 pieces – including collections of the Taos Society of Artists, Santa Fe Society of Artists and other legendary collectives – it's a who's who of the geniuses who put this dusty town on par with Paris and New York.

The **Palace of the Governors** (Map pp368-9; ☎ 505-476-5100; www.museumofnewmexico.org; 100 Palace Ave) is one of the oldest public buildings in the country. Built in 1610 by Spanish officials, it housed thousands of villag-ers when the Indians revolted in 1680 and was home to the territorial governors after 1846. Since 1909 the building has been a museum, with more than 17,000 historical objects reflecting Santa Fe's Indian, Spanish, Mexican and American heritage. Volunteers lead free, highly recommended palace tours throughout the day; call for exact times.

The **Portal Program** (www.newmexicoindianart.org) allows artisans with tribal enrollment to sell jewelry and art in front of the palace. It's a tradition that began in the 1880s, when Tesuque artisans began meeting the train with all manner of wares. Today up to 1200 members representing almost every New Mexican tribe draw lots for 76 spaces beneath the vigas each morning; the rest fan out across downtown to ply their work.

The **Museum of Indian Arts & Culture** (Map p364; ☎ 505-476-1250; www.miaclab.org; 710 Camino Lejo) opened in 1987 to display artifacts unearthed by the Laboratory of Anthropology, which must confirm that any proposed building site in New Mexico is not historically significant. Since 1931 it has collected over 50,000 artifacts. Rotating exhibits explore the historical and contemporary lives of the Pueblo, Navajo and Apache cultures.

GEORGIA O'KEEFFE MUSEUM

The renowned painter first visited New Mexico in 1917 and lived in Abiquiu, a village 45 minutes northwest of Santa Fe, from 1949 until her death in 1986 (p389). Possessing the world's largest collection of her work, this **museum** (Map pp368-9; ☎ 505-946-1000; www.okeeffemuseum.org; 217 Johnson St; adult/child $8/free; ☒ 10am-5pm, until 8pm Fri, galleries closed Wed Nov-Jun) showcases the thick brushwork and luminous colors that don't always come through on ubiquitous posters; relish them here firsthand. Housed in a former Spanish Baptist church, its adobe walls have been renovated to form 10 skylighted galleries. Tours of O'Keeffe's home in Abiquiu (p387) require two months advance notice.

ST FRANCIS CATHEDRAL

Jean Baptiste Lamy was sent to Santa Fe by the Pope with orders to tame the wild western outpost town through culture and religion. Convinced that the town needed a focal point for religious life, he began

NEW MEXICO

EXPLORING CANYON ROAD

At one time Canyon Rd was a dusty street lined with artists' homes and studios, but today most of the artists have fled to cheaper digs and the private homes have been replaced with a flock of upscale galleries. Today it's a can't-miss attraction: over 90 galleries at the epicenter of the nation's healthiest art scene display rare Indian antiquities, Santa Fe School masterpieces and wild contemporary work. It's a little overwhelming, but sooth your battered brain with wine and cheese on Friday (at 5pm or so), when glittering art openings clog the narrow street with elegant collectors. Here are just a few favorites on the strip; also see Top Museum-Like Galleries (p382) and Shopping (p381). Bring your walking shoes (and credit cards), but leave your expectations about finding a parking space at home.

Alene Lapides Gallery (Map pp368-9; ☎ 505-984-0191; 558 Canyon Rd) Shows amazing New Mexican contemporary artists.

Chiaroscuro Contemporary Art (Map pp368-9; ☎ 505-986-9197; 708 Canyon Rd) This sophisticated and often abstract collection features modernism in every medium.

Kania-Ferrin Gallery (Map pp368-9; ☎ 505-982-8767; 662 Canyon Rd) Though pottery has enjoyed a renaissance, Native American basketry is rare – but not here.

Stables (Map pp368-9; 821 Canyon Rd) This cool collection of studio/galleries showcases real live artists at work; standouts include the **Canyon Road Pottery** (Map pp368-9; ☎ 505-983-9426) with excellent and affordable hand-thrown pottery, and the amazing **Ed Larson Studio** (Map pp368-9), with illustrated political poetry.

---

construction of this cathedral in 1869. Lamy's story has been immortalized in Willa Cather's book *Death Comes for the Archbishop*. Inside the **St Francis Cathedral** (Map pp368-9; ☎ 505-982-5619; 131 Cathedral Place; ⏰ 8am-5pm; mass 7am & 5pm Mon-Sat, 8am, 10am, noon & 5pm Sun) is a small chapel, Capilla de Nuestra Señora la Conquistadora, Reina de la Paz, where the oldest Madonna statue in North America is housed. The statue was carved in Mexico and brought to Santa Fe in 1625, but when the Indians revolted in 1680, the villagers took it into exile with them. When Don Diego de Vargas retook the city in 1692, he brought the statue back, and legend has it that its extraordinary powers are responsible for the reconquest of the city.

LORETTO CHAPEL

The gothic **chapel** (Map pp368-9; ☎ 505-982-0092; www.lorettochapel.com; 207 Old Santa Fe Trail; admission $2.50; ⏰ 9am-6pm summer, 9am-5pm winter) is modeled on St Chapelle in Paris, and was built between 1873 and 1878 for the Sisters of Loretto, the first nuns to come to New Mexico. St Chapelle has a circular stone staircase, but when the Loretto Chapel was being constructed, no local stone masons were skilled enough to build one and the young architect didn't know how to build one of wood. The nuns prayed for help and a mysterious traveling carpenter, whom the nuns believed afterward to be St Joseph, arrived. He built what is known as the Miraculous Staircase, a wooden spiral staircase with two complete 360-degree turns and no central or visible support. He left without charging for his labors and his identity remains unknown.

SAN MIGUEL MISSION

The original construction of this **mission** (Map pp368-9; ☎ 505-983-3974; 401 Old Santa Fe Trail; admission $1; ⏰ 9am-5pm Mon-Sat, 10am-4pm Sun; mass 5pm Sun) was started in 1625, and it served as a mission church for the Spanish settlers' Tlaxcalan Indian servants, who had been brought from Mexico. Though considered the oldest church in the United States, much of the original building was destroyed during the Pueblo Revolt of 1680, and it was rebuilt in 1710, with new walls added to what remained. The current square tower was added in 1887 and the interior was restored in 1955.

SANTUARIO DE GUADALUPE

The adobe **church** (Map pp368-9; ☎ 505-988-2027; 100 Guadalupe St; admission free; ⏰ 9am-4pm Mon-Sat) is the oldest extant shrine to Our Lady of Guadalupe, the patroness of the poor in Mexico. It was constructed between 1776 and 1796 near the end of the Camino Real, a 1500-mile trading route from Mexico that

DOWNTOWN SANTA FE

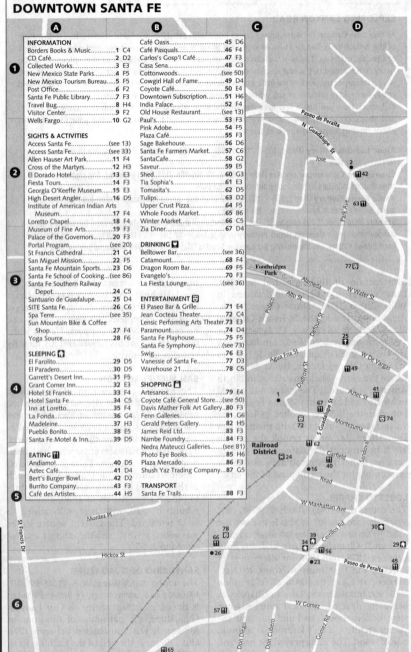

INFORMATION

Borders Books & Music	1 C4
CD Café	2 D2
Collected Works	3 E3
New Mexico State Parks	4 F5
New Mexico Tourism Bureau	5 F5
Post Office	6 F2
Santa Fe Public Library	7 F3
Travel Bug	8 H4
Visitor Center	9 F2
Wells Fargo	10 G2

SIGHTS & ACTIVITIES

Access Santa Fe	(see 13)
Access Santa Fe	(see 33)
Allen Hauser Art Park	11 F4
Cross of the Martyrs	12 H3
El Dorado Hotel	13 E3
Fiesta Tours	14 F3
Georgia O'Keeffe Museum	15 E3
High Desert Angler	16 D5
Institute of American Indian Arts Museum	17 F4
Loretto Chapel	18 F4
Museum of Fine Arts	19 F3
Palace of the Governors	20 F3
Portal Program	(see 20)
St Francis Cathedral	21 G4
San Miguel Mission	22 F5
Santa Fe Mountain Sports	23 D6
Santa Fe School of Cooking	(see 86)
Santa Fe Southern Railway Depot	24 C5
Santuario de Guadalupe	25 D4
SITE Santa Fe	26 C6
Spa Terre	(see 35)
Sun Mountain Bike & Coffee Shop	27 F4
Yoga Source	28 F6

SLEEPING

El Farolito	29 D5
El Paradero	30 D5
Garrett's Desert Inn	31 F5
Grant Corner Inn	32 E3
Hotel St Francis	33 F4
Hotel Santa Fe	34 C5
Inn at Loretto	35 F4
La Fonda	36 G4
Madeleine	37 H3
Pueblo Bonito	38 E5
Santa Fe Motel & Inn	39 D5

EATING

Andiamo!	40 D5
Aztec Café	41 D4
Bert's Burger Bowl	42 D2
Burrito Company	43 F3
Café des Artistes	44 H5
Café Oasis	45 D6
Café Pasquals	46 F4
Carlos's Gosp'l Café	47 F3
Casa Sena	48 G3
Cottonwoods	(see 50)
Cowgirl Hall of Fame	49 D4
Coyote Café	50 E4
Downtown Subscription	51 H6
India Palace	52 F4
Old House Restaurant	(see 13)
Paul's	53 F3
Pink Adobe	54 F5
Plaza Café	55 F4
Sage Bakehouse	56 D6
Santa Fe Farmers Market	57 C6
SantaCafe	58 G2
Saveur	59 E5
Shed	60 G3
Tia Sophia's	61 E3
Tomasita's	62 D5
Tulips	63 D2
Upper Crust Pizza	64 F5
Whole Foods Market	65 B6
Winter Market	66 C5
Zia Diner	67 D4

DRINKING

Belltower Bar	(see 36)
Catamount	68 F4
Dragon Room Bar	69 F5
Evangelo's	70 F3
La Fiesta Lounge	(see 36)

ENTERTAINMENT

El Paseo Bar & Grille	71 E4
Jean Cocteau Theater	72 C4
Lensic Performing Arts Theater	73 E3
Paramount	74 D4
Santa Fe Playhouse	75 F5
Santa Fe Symphony	(see 73)
Swig	76 E3
Vanessie of Santa Fe	77 D3
Warehouse 21	78 C5

SHOPPING

Artesanos	79 E4
Coyote Café General Store	(see 50)
Davis Mather Folk Art Gallery	80 F3
Fenn Galleries	81 G6
Gerald Peters Gallery	82 H5
James Reid Ltd	83 F3
Nambe Foundry	84 F3
Nedra Mateucci Galleries	(see 81)
Photo Eye Books	85 H6
Plaza Mercado	86 F3
Shush Yaz Trading Company	87 G5

TRANSPORT

Santa Fe Trails	88 F3

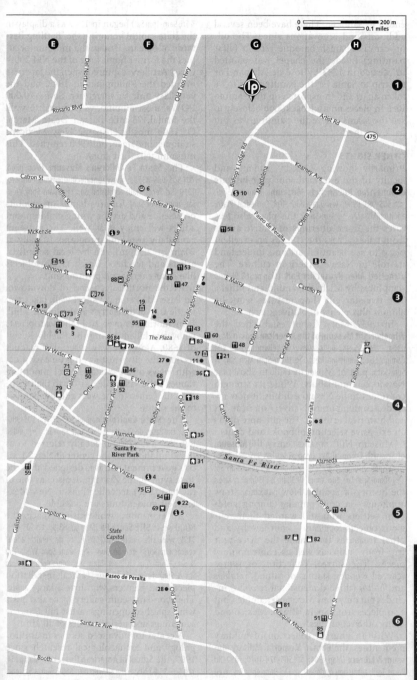

ended in Santa Fe. There have been several additions and renovations since. The oil-on-canvas Spanish baroque *retablo* (altar painting) inside the chapel was painted in Mexico in 1783 by José de Alzíbar. For the trip to Santa Fe, the painting had to be taken apart and transported up the Camino Real in pieces on muleback. Look closely to see the seams where the painting was put back together.

OTHER SIGHTS

Primarily showing work by students and faculty of the esteemed four-year **Institute of American Indian Arts Museum** (Map pp368-9; ☎ 505-983-8900; www.iaia.edu; 108 Cathedral Place; adult/child $4/2; ☾ 9am-5pm), this place also features the finest offerings of Native artists from tribes across the US. It's an excellent place to see beautiful art and understand its role in Native American culture. The attached **Allen Hauser Art Park** (Map pp368-9) has sculptures by Michael Naranjo and others. The five-star gift shop features work by alumni plus plenty of Native kitsch.

In 1937 Mary Cabot established the **Wheelwright Museum of the American Indian** (Map p364; ☎ 505-982-4636; www.wheelwright.org; 704 Camino Lejo; admission free; ☾ 10am-5pm Mon-Sat, 1-5pm Sun), part of Museum Hill, to showcase Navajo ceremonial art. While its strength continues to be Navajo exhibits, it now includes contemporary Native American art and historical artifacts. The gift store offers an extensive selection of books and crafts.

Museum Hill's smallest entry, the **Museum of Spanish Colonial Art** (Map p364; ☎ 505-982-2226; www.spanishcolonial.org; 750 Camino Lejo; admission $6; ☾ 10am-5pm Tue-Sun; tours 10:30am & 2:30pm) traces the history of Spanish New Mexico. Straw appliqué – a craft popular among gold-poor settlers who still wanted their religious objects to gleam – join jewelry and other treasures that made the three-year trip from Spain, as well as contemporary pieces. The surreal collection of *santos* (carved wooden statues of saints), *retablos* and *bultos* (three-dimensional *retablos*) includes not only New Mexican examples, but also pieces from Spain, Brazil, Mexico and many other countries.

With an unusual collection of military mementoes, the **Bataan Memorial Military Museum & Library** (Map p364; ☎ 505-474-1670; 1050 Old Pecos Trail; admission by donation; ☾ 9am-4pm Tue, Wed & Fri, 9am-1pm Sat) began in 1947 as a display in the state capitol honoring the 'Battling Bastards of Bataan.' Today the museum occupies the former home base of the NM 200th Coast Artillery, captured when the Japanese invaded the Philippines in 1942, and the very last unit to surrender. Some 70,000 POWs, most Filipino, were forced to walk the brutal, 75-mile Bataan Death March. Of 1800 mostly Hispanic New Mexicans stationed in Bataan, only 900 returned. This museum tells their story.

The **Santa Fe Children's Museum** (Map p364; ☎ 505-989-8359; www.santafechildrensmuseum.org; 1050 Old Pecos Trail; admission $4; ☾ 10am-5pm Wed-Sat, noon-5pm Sun) features hands-on exhibits on science and art for young children, but adults will enjoy it as well. The museum runs daily two-hour programs (usually at 10am or 2:30pm), led by local scientists, artists and teachers, which tackle subjects like solar energy and printmaking.

At the northeastern end of downtown, on Paseo de Peralta, a short walk takes you to the **Cross of the Martyrs** at the top of a hill. It memorializes over 20 Franciscan priests who were killed during the Pueblo Revolt of 1680. Along the way, a series of plaques recount the city's history. It is an easy walk, with views of the city and three mountain ranges – the Sangre de Cristos to the northeast, the Jemez to the west and the Sandias to the south.

The **State Capitol** (Map pp368-9; ☎ 505-986-4589; cnr Paseo de Peralta & Old Santa Fe Trail; ☾ guided tours 10am & 2pm Mon-Fri), locally referred to as the Roundhouse, is the center of New Mexico's government and was designed after the state symbol, the Zia sign. It also has one of the best (free) art collections in New Mexico. Self-guided tours are possible.

An enormous, whitewashed space, the 8000 sq ft **SITE Santa Fe** (Map pp368-9; ☎ 505-989-1199; www.sitesantafe.org; 1606 Paseo de Peralta; adult/concession $6/3, free on Sun; ☾ 10am-5pm Wed, Thu & Sat, 10am-7pm Fri, noon-5pm Sun; tours 6pm Fri, 2pm Sat & Sun) is perfect for radical installation pieces and painters who love a large scale. The hybrid museum-gallery space also hosts wine-splashed openings, artist talks, movie screenings and performances of all kinds.

A center for advanced studies in anthropology and archaeological research since 1907, the **School of American Research** (Map p364; ☎ 505-954-7205; www.sarweb.org; 660 E Garcia St; tours

$15; ☻ tours 2pm Fri) has a vaulted comprehensive collection of textiles and Indian art in its Indian Arts Research Center. Reservations are required for the tour.

Five miles north of Santa Fe in Tesuque, the **Shidoni Foundry** (Map p364; ☎ 505-988-8001; Bishop's Lodge Rd) is an 8-acre apple orchard devoted to bronze sculptures. Founded in 1971, it has evolved into a world-renowned fine art casting facility and showplace. A gallery hosts changing exhibits, and there is a year-round outdoor sculpture garden on the lawn. Every Saturday, you can watch 2000°F molten bronze being poured into ceramic shell molds, one of several steps in the complex lost-wax casting technique.

About 15 miles north of Santa Fe, the bizarre **Line Camp Gallery** and **Huichol Indian Museum** (Map p364; ☎ 505-455-3600; www.tribesgallery .com; US Hwy 84/285; admission $1; ☻ 10:30am-6pm Tue-Sun) claims the largest collection of Huichol Indian art in North America. *Nearika* (unbroken strands of colorful yarn coiled into tales of life and death) and *chaquira* (sculptures of animals covered in tiny, obsessively patterned beads) are said to depict the understandably bizarre dreams of the 'People of Peyote.'

In La Cienega, 15 miles south of Santa Fe, **El Rancho de las Golondrinas** (Map p364; ☎ 505-471-2261; www.golondrinas.org; 334 Los Pinos Rd; adult/child $5/2; ☻ 10am-4pm Wed-Sun Jun-Sep) consists of a 200-acre ranch with 70 restored and original buildings. It's a veritable living-history museum that shows what life was like for Spanish settlers in the 18th and 19th centuries. Take I-25 southwest to exit 276.

Activities
Although Santa Fe's museums, churches, galleries and shops are absolutely top notch, visitors do not live by art appreciation alone. Get thee to the great outdoors. Several sporting shops dispense information, provide guides and rent equipment for outdoor activities, including **Santa Fe Mountain Sports** (Map pp368-9; ☎ 505-988-3337; 607 Cerrillos Rd) and **Wild Mountain Outfitters** (Map p364; ☎ 505-986-1152; 815 St Michaels Dr).

SKIING
The **Santa Fe Ski Area** (Map p364; ☎ 505-982-4429, snow report 505-983-9155; www.skisantafe.com; lift tickets adult/child $47/34; ☻ 9am-4pm end Nov-Apr) is a half-hour from the plaza up Hwy 475. From the

summit (12,000ft), you can admire 80,000 sq miles of desert and mountains. On weekends from June through August and for a couple weeks during fall foliage, the chairlift is open (one way/round-trip $4/6). There's also an expansive system of hiking trails.

Cottam's (Map p364; ☎ 505-982-0495; Hyde Park Rd), on the way to the slopes, has reasonable prices on ski gear packages (adult/child $22/13) and also rents snowshoes ($10).

There are numerous cross-country ski trails in the Jemez Mountains and the Santa Fe National Forest. Contact the **Public Lands Information Center** (Map p364; ☎ 505-438-7542; www.publiclands.org; 1474 Rodeo Rd; ☻ 8:30am-4:30pm Mon-Fri).

RAFTING
Busloads of people head up to the Taos Box, around the Rio Grande, for white-water river running, but there are also mellow float trips throughout New Mexico and overnight guided rafting trips. Contact **New Wave River Trips** (Map p364; ☎ 505-984-1444, 800-984-1444; www.newwaverafting.com; 1101 Cerrillos Rd). Stay cool on day trips through the Rio Grande Gorge (adult/child half-day $47/44, full day $84/77) or Taos Box ($100), or go for a three-day Rio Chama float ($400). Here's a bonus: You can ride the white-water in a 'funyak,' an inflatable kayak that leaves the driving up to you.

HIKING
Just walking around Santa Fe can be quite strenuous because of the 7000ft elevation. Spend a day or two acclimatizing before rushing off into the mountains of the **Santa Fe National Forest**, immediately to the east of town. The heart of the national forest is the undeveloped **Pecos Wilderness**, with trails leading to several peaks over 12,000ft. Nearly 1000 miles of trails, forming a complex web, are suitable for short hikes and multiday backpacks.

Weather changes rapidly in the mountains and summer storms are frequent, especially in the afternoons, so check weather reports; hike prepared. The trails are usually closed by snow in winter, and higher trails may be closed through May.

Maps and thorough area hiking information is available from the very helpful **Public Lands Information Center** (Map p364; ☎ 505-438-7542; 1474 Rodeo Rd; ☻ 8:30am-4:30pm Mon-Fri).

The most immediately accessible trail-heads are northeast of Santa Fe and near the ski base, within **Hyde Memorial State Park** (Map p364; ☎ 505-983-7175; Hwy 475; per car per day $5). Short loops are possible – the 5-mile Borrego-Bear Wallow Loop to Tesuque Creek, which starts at the north end of Hyde Memorial State Park, is a good one. These trails connect with the popular Winsor Trail (Trail 254), which offers access to a huge network of trails in the Pecos Wilderness.

Protecting 135 acres along the acequias of Santa Fe Canyon, just 4 miles from the plaza, the **Randall Davey Audubon Center** (Map pp368-9; ☎ 505-983-4609; www.nm.audubon.org; 1800 Upper Canyon Rd; trail use $2; ☺ 9am-4pm Mon-Fri, 9am-2pm Sat) has information on the juniper and piñon forest's coyotes, bobcats and other wildlife. It's near the trailhead for the 3-mile **Bear Canyon Trail** (Map pp368-9), which leads into the steep-sided canyon.

A great opportunity for day hikers and intermediate mountain bikers, the **North and South Dale Ball Trails** (Map pp368-9; ☎ 505-827-7173) run more than 20 miles to circumnavigate some of Santa Fe's most exclusive neighborhoods, eventually winding past the 'no trespassing' signs to views of unspoiled mountains and deserts. To get here, follow Upper Canyon Rd north to the well-signed parking lot at Cerro Gordo Rd.

FISHING
High Desert Angler (Map pp368-9; ☎ 505-988-7688, 888-988-7688; www.highdesertangler.com; 435 S Guadalupe St) rents and sells rods, reels, flies and other fishing gear, gives classes for all levels and provides area guide services. In addition to private casting lessons ($35 per hour), guided excursions to private streams (s/d $275/300) and a variety of multiday trips, they also supply independent souls with a one-day license ($18 to $25).

For regulations and licenses, ask High Desert Angler or call the **New Mexico Department of Game and Fish** (☎ 505-476-8000).

MOUNTAIN BIKING
Sun Mountain Bike & Coffee Shop (Map pp368-9; ☎ 505-982-8986; www.sunmountainbikeco.com; 102 E Water St) has information about regional trails, rents bikes and can drop you off at trailheads. **Bike & Sport** (Map p364; ☎ 505-820-0809; www.nmbikensport.com; 542 W Cordova Rd) rents mountain bikes starting at $22 a day.

HORSEBACK RIDING
Broken Saddle Riding Company (Map p364; ☎ 505-424-7774; www.brokensaddle.com; 1hr/2hr $50/65; 26 Vicksville Rd, Cerrillos; ☺ 8am-sunset) offers day-rides around a forested property and in Cerrillos, as well as sunset ($70) and moonlight ($85) options.

Courses
If you develop a love for New Mexican cuisine, try cooking lessons at the **Santa Fe School of Cooking** (Map pp368-9; ☎ 505-983-4511; www.santafeschoolofcooking.com; Plaza Mercado). Classes, with over 20 options, including traditional New Mexican and Southwestern breakfast, are 2½ hours long and range from $58 to $75, including the meal.

Santa Fe Workshops (Map p364; ☎ 505-983-1400; www.santafeworkshops.com; Mt Carmel Rd) help you develop your inner Ansel Adams awareness at week-long traditional photography and digital imagery workshops (classes $795 to $1200). Meals and lodging are extra.

Yoga Source (Map pp368-9; ☎ 505-982-0990; www.yogasource-santafe.com; 518 Old Santa Fe Trail; 1 class $15, 4 classes $52) can stretch your horizons with five different styles of yoga and classes for every level.

Santa Fe for Children
Check the 'Pasatiempo' section of Friday's *New Mexican* for its 'Bring the Kids' column, with a rundown on area events for children.

The Santa Fe Children's Museum (p370) is wonderful, with interactive and educational activities for kids up to 10 years or so. Kids of all ages shouldn't miss the amazing Museum of International Folk Art (p366). Expose your children to the diversity of cultures that Santa Fe is so proud of. El Rancho de las Golondrinas (p371) shows off Spanish colonial history made real. The Santa Fe Opera (p379) does backstage tours during opera season and it's free for folks under 17. A visit to the Wheelwright Museum of the American Indian (p370) will introduce them early to Native culture.

Several hiking trails, particularly those at Randall Davey Audubon Center (left), are perfect for active children; just be sure to coat them with sunscreen and make sure they don't get dehydrated.

Magical Happenings Babysitting (☎ 505-982-9327) can have sitters stay with your kids in your hotel room or take them out on excursions; it's $15 an hour for one child (four-hour minimum), plus a $5 travel fee. Make reservations in advance, particularly during high season.

Tours

Several companies offer walking and bus tours of Santa Fe and northern New Mexico. Others organize guided trips to the pueblos, as well as air tours and biking, hiking, rafting and horseback-riding trips. **Access Santa Fe** (Map pp368-9; ☎ 505-988-2774; www.accesssantafe .com; adult $10, child under 12 free; ⊙ 9:30am & 1:30pm), a 'destination management company' departs from the lobbies of the **El Dorado Hotel** (W San Francisco St) and **Hotel St Francis** (see p375) for a two-hour walking city tour.

Fiesta Tours (Map pp368-9; ☎ 505-983-1570; 118 Old Santa Fe Trail; adult/child $7/4; ⊙ 10am, noon & 2pm, more frequently in summer) has open-air tour buses departing from the corner of Lincoln and Palace Ave. These one-hour city tours take in the cathedral, plaza, Canyon Rd and historic neighborhoods of Santa Fe.

Outback Tours (☎ 888-772-3274; www.outback tours.com) focuses on the region's geology, ecology and history on its backroad 4WD day, overnight, and evening tours to Taos ($96), Jemez ($85) and Abiquiu ($85). They do pick-ups at downtown hotels and the Santa Fe Visitor Center.

Stefanie Beninato (☎ 505-988-8022; www.nmtours .com) offers garden, art and ghost tours of Santa Fe ($12 to $18) and different regional day tours.

Though the Santa Fe Railroad doesn't run through town, the old **Santa Fe Southern Railway** (Map pp368-9; ☎ 505-989-8600, 888-989-8600; www.sfsr.com; 410 S Guadalupe St; ⊙ 9am-5pm Mon-Sat, 11am-5pm Sun) offers several scenic rides using the old spur line. The most popular run, a four-hour day trip (adult $32 to $55, child $18 to $42), takes you past the Galisteo Basin and to the fairly ghostly town of Lamy. But there are several other themed trips offered.

Festivals & Events

The **Santa Fe Visitors Bureau** (www.santafe.org) provides an excellent list of events, musical and theatrical productions and museum shows. But some of the biggies include the following.

Pride on the Plaza (www.santafehra.org; mid-Jun) Drag queens, parades, floats, a film festival, music, comedy and more; area bars and restaurants throw special bashes for a full week when everyone flies the rainbow flag.

Rodeo de Santa Fe (☎ 505-471-4300; www.rodeode santafe.org; admission $8-30; late Jun) For more than half a century, wranglers, ranchers and cowpokes, along with plenty of rhinestone cowpersons, have been gathering to watch those bucking broncos, clowns in barrels, lasso tricks and fancy shooting. A pre-Rodeo parade takes it all downtown.

Spanish Market (☎ 505-982-2226; www.spanish market.org; late Jul) Traditional Spanish colonial arts, from retablos and *bultos* to handcrafted furniture and

---

WRAPPED, RUBBED & SCRUBBED

Visitors from faster-paced places (which means almost everywhere else) sometimes feel frustrated with New Mexico's relaxed approach to life: 'Isn't this restaurant supposed to be open on Tuesdays? We had reservations! What do you *mean*, they've gone fishing?' When this starts to happen, it's time to head to a spa, to indulge in hot-stone massages or blue-corn facials, to soak your cares away. Many of the following and other spas have accommodations that offer spa packages.

10,000 Waves (Map p364; ☎ 505-982-9304; www.tenthousandwaves.com; 3451 Hyde Park Rd; communal tubs $14, private tubs per person $19-27; ⊙ 9:15am-10pm Wed-Mon, 4-10pm Tue) It's true Japanese style, with landscaped grounds concealing 10 attractive tubs in smooth Zen design: some with waterfalls, cold plunges, hot and dry saunas, and two swimsuit-optional tubs, one of which is reserved for women (noon-8pm).

ShaNah Spa & Wellness (Map p364; ☎ 505-983-6377; www.bishopslodge.com; 1297 Bishops Lodge Rd; ⊙ 7am-8pm) Enjoy the view with an outdoor massage overlooking the piñon forested property of Bishop's Lodge. Outdoor hot tubs and *dosha*-balancing Ayurvedic treatments designed to stimulate your Third Eye make this a fine place to regenerate.

Spa Terre (Map pp368-9; ☎ 505-988-5531; 211 Old Santa Fe Trail; ⊙ 9am-9pm) Within the Inn at Loretto (p375), this spiritually aware spa has Native American–themed decor and exotic offerings like the Balinese massage followed by a yogurt bath.

SANTA FE INDIAN MARKET

This world-famous event, sponsored by the **Southwest Association for Indian Arts** (☎ 505-983-5220; www.swaia.org), takes place the weekend after the third Thursday in August, and packs the plaza with the finest Native American juried artisans from all over North America. Tours of studios, galleries and museum archives run throughout the week. Rooms are packed, parking is tough, jet-setters snag all the best tables...and it's all worth it, at least once in your life. You won't see art like this at your local museum. Get there Friday or Saturday to see pieces competing for the prestigious top prizes (they get snapped up by collectors), but try your bargaining skills on Sunday.

---

metalwork, make this juried show an artistic extravaganza, second only to the Indian Market (above). Another Spanish Market is held in early December at the Sweeny Convention Center.

Santa Fe Fiestas (☎ 505-988-7575; www.santafefiesta.org; early Sep) Two weeks of events celebrating the September 4, 1692, resettlement of Santa Fe, including concerts, a carnival, parades and a candlelight procession.

Wine & Chile Fiesta (☎ 505-483-8060; www.santafewineandchile.org; late Sep) It's a gourmet's fantasy fiesta, with wine tastings and fine cuisine; dinner events sell out early.

Las Posadas (December 24) All of Santa Fe is illuminated with *farolitos*; carolers and revelers chow *biscochitos*, drink hot chocolate and make merry.

Sleeping

Rates vary from week to week, day to day and mood to mood, so always bargain if you're up to it. Generally, January and February offer the lowest rates and September, October, March and April are midrange; prices listed here are for May through August (high season). Rates can be reduced by as much as half or more during low season. Many agencies can help with reservations, including **Santa Fe Stay** (☎ 505-820-2468, 800-995-2272; www.santafestay.com), specializing in home stays, ranch resorts and casitas, and **All Santa Fe Reservations** (☎ 877-737-7366; www.all-santafe.com) with condo and ski packages.

BUDGET

Silver Saddle Motel (Map p364; ☎ 505-471-7663; www.motelsantafe.com; 2810 Cerrillos Rd; s/d $59/65; P)

One of the rustic subjects of the 1988 documentary film *Motel*, Silver Saddle is your best budget bet. Inspired Southwestern comfy-rustic decor, including some with attractively tiled kitchenettes and lots of kitschy appeal, make this Americana at its finest.

Motel 8 (Map p364; ☎ 505-471-8811; 3358 Cerrillos Rd; r $50-68; P) This excellent budget option offers a great deal on rooms that are much nicer than those in many supposedly nicer properties near the plaza.

Santa Fe International Hostel (Map p364; ☎ 505-988-1153; santafehostel@quest.net; 1412 Cerrillos Rd; dm $15, s/d $25/35, s/d with bathroom $33/43; P) A cherry tree shades the outdoor patio and grill here, and many of the slightly tatty rooms (with private and same-sex dorms) feature murals by visiting artists. Throw in a free continental breakfast, communal kitchen, linen and no lockout, and it all adds up to one fine hostelling experience.

The Santa Fe National Forest (p371) and the Pecos Wilderness (p371) have numerous camping sites. Stop by the **Public Lands Information Center** (Map p364; ☎ 505-438-7542; 1474 Rodeo Rd) for maps and detailed information.

KOA (Map p364; ☎ 505-466-1419, 800-562-1514; www.koa.com; Frontage Rd; tent sites $24-30, RV sites $28-40, 'kamping kabin' $40-50; Mar-Nov; P)Eleven miles southeast of town (off exit 290 from I-25 North), campsites have lots of amenities.

Rancheros de Santa Fe Camping Park (Map p364; ☎ 505-466-3282; www.rancheros.com; Frontage Rd; tent/RV sites $20/32; Mar-Nov; P) Nice views and a convenience store.

MIDRANGE

El Rey Inn (Map p364; ☎ 505-982-1931, 800-521-1349; www.elreyinnsantafe.com; 1862 Cerrillos Rd; r $79-119, ste $120-199; P) A highly recommended classic courtyard hotel, with super rooms, a great pool and even a kid's playground scattered around 5 acres of greenery.

Pueblo Bonito (Map pp368-9; ☎ 505-984-8001, 800-461-4599; www.pueblobonitoinn.com; 138 W Manhattan Ave; r $130-165) All rooms at this pleasant adobe complex (c 1900) have kiva fireplaces, and some have kitchenettes. Rates include a cold breakfast buffet and tasty afternoon margaritas and wine.

Camel Rock Suites (Map p364; ☎ 505-989-3600, 877-989-3600; www.camelrocksuites.com; 3007 S St Francis Dr; ste $109; P) Sure, it's like vacationing in a gated community right off I-25, but huge suites – apartments, really – with full kitchens, dining room and fold-out sofas make this place a fantastic deal. It also offers free shuttles downtown.

Garrett's Desert Inn (Map pp368-9; ☎ 505-982-1851, 800-888-2145; www.garrettsdesertinn.com; 301 Old Santa Fe Trail; r $99-139, ste $119-149; P ⊠ ⛺) Because it's next to the plaza and has been sprayed with stucco, the basic rooms and spacious suites seem far more attractive than their counterparts on Cerrillos Rd.

Alexander's Inn (Map p364; ☎ 505-986-1431, 888-321-5123; 529 E Palace Ave; r $85-130, casita $150-240; ⊠) In a historic neighborhood five blocks from the plaza, this beautiful 1903 Arts and Crafts home is decorated for a frilly romantic escape, while casitas (small houses; some are located several blocks away) boast fireplaces and full kitchens.

Hotel St Francis (Map pp368-9; ☎ 505-983-5700, 800-529-5700; www.hotelstfrancis.com; 210 Don Gaspar Ave; r $129-239, ste $230-425; P ⊠ ⛤) Built as a luxury property in 1923, this great plaza hotel is elegant in a decadently decrepit sort of way. Basic rooms are small but you can upgrade for a few dollars, and the lovely lobby does a famous afternoon tea.

El Paradero (Map pp368-9; ☎ 505-988-1177; www.elparadero.com; 220 W Manhattan Ave; r $95-160; P ⊠) Interesting for its architecture alone – the historic building's brick facade predates the city's adobe-only laws – this very traditional B&B has small but airy rooms along with suites (with TVs and kitchenettes) and a lovely courtyard.

Madeleine (Map pp368-9; ☎ 505-986-1431, 888-321-5123; www.madeleineinn.com; 106 Faithway St; r $160-220; ⊠ ⛤) Come here for the full B&B experience, complete with Victorian architecture, Queen Anne antiques, decadent homemade snacks, lovely gardens and even private cottages. The less expensive rooms are tiny but just as sweet.

Santa Fe Motel & Inn (Map pp368-9; ☎ 505-982-1039, 800-930-5002; 510 Cerrillos Rd; r $109, casita $139;

AUTHOR'S CHOICE

El Farolito (Map pp368-9; ☎ 505-988-1631, 888-634-8782; www.farolito.com; 514 Galisteo St; r $180-225; P ⊠ ⛺) Intimate and elegant, each comfy adobe casita (some including patios) comes with a stocked fridge, VCR and all the amenities you expect from a fine B&B.

P ⊠) With far more stylish rooms (some with fireplaces) than the exterior would suggest, this motel has great weekly rates that make it an even better deal. Kitchenettes are about $15 extra.

Stagecoach Motor Inn (Map p364; ☎ 505-471-0707; 3360 Cerrillos Rd; r incl breakfast $78-150; P ⊠) With heaps more character than most Cerrillos Rd entries, this has huge, beautifully decorated rooms and a shady courtyard.

TOP END

Grant Corner Inn (Map pp368-9; ☎ 505-983-6678, 800-964-9003; www.grantcornerinn.com; 122 Grant Ave; r $145-240; P ⊠) The elaborate gourmet breakfast – voted among the best in Santa Fe – is worth the trip, but the comfortable, antique-filled rooms and every adorable amenity invite you to stay a while.

Hotel Santa Fe (Map pp368-9; ☎ 505-982-1200, 800-825-9876; www.hotelsantafe.com; 1501 Paseo de Peralta; r $139-259; P ⊠ ⛤ ⛺) This sprawling adobe in the Guadalupe district is majority-owned by the Picuris Pueblo (p390). Rooms are spacious and tasteful, some with a terrace and all with a refrigerator. The outdoor hot tub is nice. Rates change seven times a year and can be as low as $85.

Inn at Loretto (Map pp368-9; ☎ 505-988-5531, 800-727-5531; www.hotelloretto.com; 211 Old Santa Fe Trail; r $175-360; P ⊠ ⛤ ⛺) It looks as gorgeous as Taos Pueblo and is filled with obsessively luxurious rooms and suites. It's also home to Spa Terre (p373).

La Fonda (Map pp368-9; ☎ 505-982-5511, 800-523-5002; www.lafondasantafe.com; 100 E San Francisco St; r $219-299, ste $349-529; P ⊠ ⛤ ⛺) More than just another stylish pueblo-revival hotel, the original 'Inn at the end of the Santa Fe Trail,' which claims to have been here since 1610, is an institution. Its eclectic art collection adorns boutiques, restaurants and bars, including one atop the Belltower Bar (p379), with the best sunsets in town. The lobby is alive with folks selling jewelry, reading tarot cards, strumming guitars and enjoying life – all of which makes up for the smallish, sometimes weird rooms.

Eating

The sheer number of dining options in Santa Fe can be overwhelming and exhausting to even think about. Fortunately, very few places are downright bad, although quite a few are over-priced.

THE PLAZA & CANYON RD
Budget

Burrito Company (Map pp368-9; ☎ 505-982-4453; 111 Washington Ave; dishes $3-9; ☺ breakfast & lunch) This popular plaza-side favorite lets you spend more money on art and enjoy budget blue corn enchiladas and chorizo burritos that can compete with the best of 'em.

Downtown Subscription (Map pp368-9; ☎ 505-983-3085; 376 Garcia St; snacks $2-7; ☺ 6am-7pm) Excellent coffee, 31 types of tea, pastries and a few savory offerings are complimented by a truly spectacular newsstand and flagstone patio.

Tia Sophia's (Map pp368-9; ☎ 505-983-9880; 210 W San Francisco St; dishes $3-7; ☺ breakfast & lunch Mon-Sat) The plaza workforce joins knowledgeable collectors for this top spot's fabulous lunch specials and other great New Mexican offerings.

Carlos' Gosp'l Café (Map pp368-9; ☎ 505-983-1841; 125 Lincoln Ave; dishes $3-9; ☺ breakfast & lunch Mon-Fri, lunch Sat) Chill with hipsters and mellow businesspeople listening to gospel tunes in the sunny courtyard while enjoying vegetarian hangover stew or the Alice B Toklas turkey-Swiss sandwich.

Upper Crust Pizza (Map pp368-9; ☎ 505-982-0000; 329 Old Santa Fe Trail; dishes $6-10, pizza $10-24; ☺ 11am-10pm) Relax on the patio or in the cozy interior over pizza piled with pesto, piñon or pepperoni. It's considered by many to be Santa Fe's best; the sausage roll is a staff favorite.

Café des Artistes (Map pp368-9; ☎ 505-820-2535; 223b Canyon Rd; dishes $4-8; ☺ 8:30am-5pm) Yes, you can fortify yourself on Canyon Rd without breaking the bank. For French-inspired dishes, like flaky almond croissants and brie-and-berry salads, head to this sunny patio.

Midrange

Cottonwoods (Map pp368-9; ☎ 505-983-1615; 132 Water St; dishes $7-11; ☺ 7:30am-8pm Thu-Mon) Downstairs and downscale from its famed sister restaurant, the Coyote Café (opposite), this unpretentious pub welcomes budget gourmets to sample Mark Miller's cut-rate creations, from steak burritos to green-chile potato chowder. Kids love the blue corndog while adults appreciate the full bar, which serves the Coyote's signature cocktails.

India Palace (Map pp368-9; ☎ 505-986-5859; 227 Don Gaspar Ave; dishes $8-14) Cloth napkins and stemware add ambiance, but it's the recommended lamb *sagwala, baingan bartha* (tandoori eggplant) and buffet lunch ($9) that pack those pretty tables with locals and tourists.

Paul's (Map pp368-9; ☎ 505-982-8738; 72 W Marcy St; lunch dishes $7-9, dinner dishes $15-20; ☺ lunch Mon-Fri, dinner nightly) A definite date spot with ambiance more suited to the top-end category than the prices reflect, Paul's early nightly $22 prix fixe menu adds an award-winning chocolate ganache and appetizer to mains like pecan-crusted baked salmon.

Shed (Map pp368-9; ☎ 505-982-9030; 113½ E Palace Ave; lunch dishes $7-10, dinner dishes $9-19; ☺ Mon-Sat) Serving superb New Mexican cuisine since 1953, the Shed allows you to order anything – it's all fantastic – but get it red. You'll be set with an order of *calabasas* on the side and the rich chocolate mocha cake for dessert.

Pink Adobe (Map pp368-9; ☎ 505-983-7712; 406 Old Santa Fe Trail; dishes $14-24; ☺ lunch Mon-Fri, dinner daily) A Santa Fe classic, the Pink Adobe has been packing 'em in since 1944 with hearty and hailed cuisine like enchiladas and steak Dunigan (cooked with green chile), their signature dish.

Plaza Café (Map pp368-9; ☎ 505-982-1664; 54 Lincoln Ave; breakfast & lunch dishes $7-14; dinner dishes $8-22) Serving hearty meals since before the roads were paved, this Formica-furnished 1918 establishment still makes one of the best breakfasts around, great New Mexican food and a mean gyro. And while you're here, give your favorite New Mexico politician a ring (numbers are posted) to let them know what you think.

AUTHOR'S CHOICE

SantaCafé (Map pp368-9; ☎ 505-984-1788; 231 Washington Ave; lunch dishes $8-16, dinner dishes $19-37; ☺ lunch Mon-Sat, dinner nightly; ℗) Chef David Sellars is practically an international celebrity for dishes like goat cheese–stuffed free-range chicken with confit tamales (get the green-chile mashed potatoes on the side). To boot, they're served in an 1850s adobe built by the infamous Padre Gallegos. Lunch is a deal, the wine list flawless and the dining room historic. You want more? Give up wanting; there's nothing more to want.

Top End

Coyote Cafe (Map pp368-9; ☎ 505-983-1615; 132 Water St; dishes $21-42; ✹ dinner Fri-Mon & Thu) Chef Mark Miller ascended to superstar status years ago, and his high-quality interpretations of New Mexican cuisine – try the buttermilk corncakes with *chipotle* prawns or pecan-wood grilled rib chop – remain a highlight of any foodie's visit.

Casa Sena (Map pp368-9; ☎ 505-988-9232; 125 E Palace Ave; lunch dishes $10-14, dinner dishes $23-36) Housed in an 1880s-era adobe and fronted by an idyllic patio, this restaurant serves four-star cuisine with Southwestern flair, like the trout baked in adobe with asparagus-leek risotto, with a choice of 1100 wines (no, that's not a typo).

Cafe Pasqual's (Map pp368-9; ☎ 505-983-9340; 121 Don Gaspar Ave; lunch dishes $8-14; dinner dishes $18-35; ✹ lunch Mon-Sat, dinner nightly) Make reservations for dinner if you like, but definitely wait in line to enjoy the famous breakfasts, including *huevos motuleños*, featuring eggs with black beans, sautéed bananas, feta cheese and more; tamale *dulce*, a sweet-corn tamale with fruit, beans and chocolate; or the enormous Durango ham-and-cheese omelet. It's all served up in the festive, if claustrophobic, interior. Jump ahead in line by sitting at the community table, where tourists and locals mix it up daily.

GUADALUPE ST AREA

Budget

Whole Foods Market (Map pp368-9; ☎ 505-992-1700; 753 Cerrillos Rd) A shrine to the organic economy's success in a capitalist world, this expansive store has all things natural, including an outrageous deli and salad bar, plus enough free samples that you won't even bother with the rest.

Zia Diner (Map pp368-9; ☎ 505-988-7008; 366 S Guadalupe St; dishes $7-12; ✹ 11am-10pm; [P]) Voted 'Best Comfort Food' by locals, this cozy diner is known for its meatloaf, liver and onions, and homemade pies. Have a beer and watch pink-haired hipsters and graying progressives coo over their blue-plate specials (served weekdays only).

Bert's Burger Bowl (Map pp368-9; ☎ 505-982-0215; 235 N Guadalupe St; dishes $3-5; ✹ 8am-7pm; [P]) Despite its grubby veneer, this humble outlet has a devoted following on par with any four-star restaurant for its burgers and *carne adovada*.

Santa Fe Farmers Market (Map pp368-9; ☎ 505-983-4098; cnr Cerrillos Rd & Guadalupe St; ✹ 7am-noon Sat & Tue Apr-Nov; [P]) Local produce, much of it heirloom and organic, is on sale at these spacious digs alongside homemade goodies, inexpensive food and a fair number of arts and crafts offerings.

Winter Market (Map pp368-9; 1614b Paseo de Peralta; ✹ 9am-1pm Sat Nov-Apr; [P]) Held at the nearby El Museo Cultural de Santa Fe.

Midrange

Saveur (Map pp368-9; ☎ 505-989-4200; 204 Montezuma; $9 per pound; ✹ 8am-4pm Mon-Sat; [P]) Basically a foodie's dream salad bar, this innovative entry serves everything from mixed greens to steamed fish and noodle salads, buffet style. Bonus: at 3:15pm, soups and salads go for 30% off, and 50% off at 3:30pm.

Andiamo! (Map pp368-9; ☎ 505-995-9595; 322 Garfield St; dishes $8-20; ✹ dinner) Hipsters to hippies will tell you this place is more than just another extensive, award-winning wine list and fresh and fabulous antipasto, pan-seared pork tenderloin, grilled polenta with gorgonzola cheese and tiramisu. It's an excuse to dress up (or down), to see and be seen – make reservations.

Sage Bakehouse (Map pp368-9; ☎ 505-820-7243; 535c Cerrillos Rd; sandwiches $3-6; ✹ 7am-5pm Mon-Sat; [P]) Coffee, pastries and light lunches are served on a pleasant patio, or while watching bakers remove excellent pecan-raisin and extra-sour sourdough bread from the ovens.

Cafe Oasis (Map pp368-9; ☎ 505-983-9599; 526 Galisteo; dishes $7-11; ✹ 9:30am-midnight Sun-Thu, 9am-2am Fri & Sat; [P]) With built-in lofts that you can sit in, organic eclectic dishes and friendly service, you can't go wrong here. As one fan says 'it's like walking into *Alice in Wonderland*.'

Aztec Café (Map pp368-9; ☎ 505-820-0025; 317 Aztec St; sandwiches $6; ✹ 7am-'dark' Mon-Sat, from 8am Sun) This cozy café keeps the tattoos-and-climbing-gear crowd caffeinated and fed with sandwiches and malteds, all served beneath local art that pales in comparison to the fabulous people-watching.

Tomasita's (Map pp368-9; ☎ 505-983-5721; 500 S Guadalupe St; dishes $7-15; ✹ 11am-10pm Mon-Sat; [P]) Locals hate to admit it, but they love this tourist standby for its outstanding green chile, served atop excellent burritos, enchiladas and the huge $10 blue-plate specials (served weekdays only). It's raucous – perfect for families hauling even the most exuberant kids.

Cowgirl Hall of Fame (Map pp368-9; ☎ 505-982-2565; 319 S Guadalupe St; dishes $8-13; ⊗ lunch Mon-Fri, 8:30am-2am Sat, 8:30am-midnight Sun, kitchen closes at 11pm) Winning both Best Bar and Best Place for Kids in a local survey, thanks to a great playground outside and live music inside after 9pm (p380), the Hall of Fame has fabulous food too. Try the salmon tacos, butternut squash casserole or anything mesquite grilled – they're all served with Texas caviar (black-eyed pea salsa) and wacky Western-style feminist flair.

Top End

Tulips (Map pp368-9; ☎ 505-989-7340; 222 N Guadalupe St; dishes $18-32; ⊗ dinner Tue-Sat) California-French cuisine and the perfect accompanying decor make you feel like you're in Napa Valley or Provence. The rooms are intimate and the short, fabulous menu changes often. Make reservations and prepare to linger.

Old House Restaurant (Map pp368-9; ☎ 505-988-4455; 309 W San Francisco St; dishes $26-32; ⊗ dinner) The El Dorado Hotel's flagship restaurant, the Old House, has won every award around with Southwestern-style gourmet grub like the red pepper soup, aged angus beef and the signature warm liquid-centered chocolate cake. It boasts more wines by the glass than anywhere in town.

CERRILLOS RD
Budget

Santa Fe Baking Company & Café (Map p364; ☎ 505-988-4292; 504 W Cordova Rd; dishes $4-10; ⊗ 6am-8pm; P) This lively local spot rocks for a quick sandwich on homemade bread.

Saigon Café (Map p364; ☎ 505-988-4951; 501 W Cordova Rd; dishes $8-11; ⊗ 11am-9pm Mon-Sat; P) Lauded as the best Asian food in Santa Fe, Saigon Café serves huge portions of authentic Vietnamese hot and sour soup and vermicelli salad.

Cloud Cliff Bakery (Map p364; ☎ 505-983-6254; 1805 2nd St; dishes $6-11; ⊗ 7am-5pm Mon-Fri, 8am-3pm Sat & Sun) Slip on your Birkenstocks and drop by for a loaf. Rainbow trout wraps, grilled polenta breakfasts, soups and sandwiches are served alongside organic wines and microbrews. Plenty of lefty commentary (and sometimes live evening music) keeps folks on their toes.

Baja Tacos (Map p364; ☎ 505-471-8762; 2621 Cerrillos Rd; dishes $2-6; ⊗ 7am-9pm Mon-Sat, 8am-8pm Sun; P) Grab some New Mexican classics (including good *carne adovada*) from their extensive vegetarian menu inside the cramped interior or at the drive-thru. Even if you don't eat here, check this out: the amazing mural outside, *Her Story is a Part of Our History*, by noted area artists Julia Coyne and Amberleigh, uniquely depicts Santa Fe's cultural heritage, showing potter Maria Martinez, flamenco maestra Maria Benitez and painter Georgia O'Keeffe.

Tecolote Café (Map p364; ☎ 505-988-1362; 1203 Cerrillos Rd; dishes $4-8; ⊗ 7am-2pm Tue-Sun; P) Start your morning with the sheepherder's breakfast (new potatoes, chile and onions topped with eggs and cheese), excellent eggs Benedict (with Santa Fe's best hollandaise sauce) or any other enormous main at the finest hole-in-the-wall on the strip.

Midrange

mudu noodles (Map p364; ☎ 505-983-1411; 1494 Cerrillos Rd; dishes $12-19; ⊗ dinner Mon-Sat; P) Pan-Asian organic dishes like salmon dumplings, Vietnamese spring rolls and tofu laksa inspire lines out the door of this lovely spot; the noodles (of course) and specials are always recommended, and almost everything has a vegan version.

Maria's New Mexican Kitchen (Map p364; ☎ 505-983-7929; 555 W Cordova Rd; dishes $6-18; ⊗ 11am-10pm Mon-Fri, noon-10pm Sat & Sun; P) Huge portions of New Mexican standards, prepared with locally grown ingredients and topped off with great *natillas* (a type of custard), would make this 1952 Santa Fe standby a winner anyway, but with more than 100 margaritas ($5 to $45, made with lemon, not lime), it's a must.

Mariscos 'La Playa' (Map p364; ☎ 505-982-2790; 537 Cordova Rd; dishes $8-16; ⊗ 11am-9pm Wed-Mon; P) Mexican-style seafood, including justly famed *ceviche, cocteles* and *caldo* 'El Mejor' – a soup with shrimp, octopus, scallops, clams, crab and calamari – all go well with an agave wine margarita.

India House (Map p364; ☎ 505-471-2651; 2501 Cerrillos Rd; dishes $7-13; ⊗ 11:30am-2:30pm Mon-Sat, 5-10pm daily; P) Excellent lamb *sagwala*, lamb-stuffed *keema nan* and everything vindaloo. Or just show up for the abundant lunch buffet ($7), one of the best deals in town.

METRO SANTA FE

Harry's Roadhouse (Map p364; ☎ 505-989-4629; 96b Old Las Vegas Hwy; breakfast & lunch dishes $5-8, dinner $8-15) The attractive setting and elegant cuisine far surpass what the prices imply, and dishes like Moroccan vegetable stew over couscous (offered in winter), turkey meatloaf and Cajun blackened catfish, are overshadowed only by the specials.

Gabriel's (Map p364; ☎ 505-455-7000; US Hwy 84/285; lunch dishes $7-8, dinner dishes $10-20; ☼ 11:30am-9pm; ℗) The scenic patio and beautiful interior, hung with Miguel Martinez's art, are fabulous spots to enjoy fresh guacamole, made to order at your table, excellent New Mexican cuisine and even better ribs. Plan to drop by if you're headed to the flea market or points north.

Tesuque Flea Market (Map p364; ☎ 505-988-8848; cnr Bishops Lodge Rd & NM 591; dishes $7-14) In the upscale village of Tesuque (sometimes described as 'the Beverly Hills of Santa Fe'), grab gourmet groceries or an excellent lunch – from Frito pies to steak fajitas – and enjoy them on the pleasant porch outside.

Drinking

Talk to 10 residents and visitors and you'll get 10 different responses about where to find the best margarita. Here are three top places: the Shed (p376), La Fonda (p375) with good people watching and Maria's New Mexican Kitchen (opposite) with more than 100 varieties.

Belltower Bar (Map pp368-9; ☎ 505-982-5511; 100 E San Francisco St; ☼ 5pm-sunset Mon-Thu, 2pm-sunset Fri-Sun May-Oct) Atop La Fonda, you can enjoy a cold beer or killer margarita while watching one of those patented New Mexico sunsets. In the lobby of La Fonda, **La Fiesta Lounge** (dishes $10-23; ☼ 11am-11:30pm) serves a popular lunch buffet and the same great margaritas alongside good New Mexican cuisine. You can hear live music almost nightly.

Blue Corn Café & Brewery (Map p364; ☎ 505-438-1800; 4056 Cerrillos Rd; dishes $7-15; ☼ 11am-10pm Sun-Thu, until 11pm Fri & Sat) This cavernous brewpub has won awards for its Atomic Blonde Ale and Cold Front Coffee Stout, served alongside tapas, burgers and Chuy's *chalupas*.

Second Street Brewery (Map p364; ☎ 505-982-3030; www.secondstreetbrewery.com; 2nd St; dishes $6-10; ☼ 11am-11pm) After a hard day hiking (or perhaps shopping for hiking equipment) stop by this microbrewery and pair a Cream Stout with their fish and chips, or an Otowi Pale Ale with the Danish *bleu* and walnut salad. There's often live music in the evenings.

Dragon Room Bar (Map pp368-9; ☎ 505-983-7712; 406 Old Santa Fe Trail; pub grub $8-24; ☼ 11:30am-2am Mon-Fri, 5pm-midnight Sat & Sun) Stop and sit for a spell in this warm and weathered adobe, which has provided shelter, sustenance and stiff drinks to conversationalists since WWII. There's live music – usually flamenco guitar, Latin jazz or the like – almost nightly, starting around 9pm.

Evangelo's (Map pp368-9; 200 W San Francisco St) It's rowdy, it's smoky, and one of these days the floor is probably going to cave in during a packed classic rock show. In short, it's the perfect escape from plaza couture. Drop in, put on some Patsy Cline, grab a draft beer and have a blast.

Catamount (Map pp368-9; ☎ 505-988-7222; 125 E Water St) It's got pool tables, a nice dark bar and a brighter patio.

Entertainment

Check the *Santa Fe Reporter* and the 'Pasatiempo' section of Friday's *New Mexican* for a thorough listing of what's going on in Santa Fe.

SANTA FE OPERA

Opera fans (and those who've never seen or heard an opera in their life) come to Santa Fe for this and this alone: an architectural marvel, with views of wind-carved sandstone wilderness crowned with sunsets and moonrises, and at center stage (and what a stage!) internationally renowned vocal talent performing humanity's masterworks of aria and romance. Best of all? You can wear jeans! The show begins two hours before the curtain rises, when you can enjoy a preperformance buffet and tour ($40) or bring your own dinner and eat in the parking lot. You'll see everything from pizza on the roof of someone's car to elegant meals with crystal, linen and candles in the bed of a pickup truck. **Backstage tours** (adult/child $5/free; ☼ 1pm Mon-Sat Jul & Aug) offer opportunities to poke around the sets. Purchase tour and opera tickets at the **box office** (Map p364; ☎ 505-986-5900, 800-280-4654; www.santafeopera.org; tickets $24-142; late Jun-late Aug). The opera grounds are 5 miles north of Santa Fe on Hwy 84/285.

NEW MEXICO

CINEMAS

Jean Cocteau Theatre (Map pp368-9; ☎ 505-988-2711; www.transluxmovies.com; 418 Montezuma Ave; adult/child $8.25/4.75, matinee $5.50) shows selected independent flicks alongside coffee from their café.

The **Center for Contemporary Arts** (Map p364; CCA; ☎ 505-982-1338; 1050 Old Pecos Trail; adult/child $8/5; ☉ 10am-9pm Mon-Fri, noon-8pm Sat & Sun) screens old and/or artsy films; plus it puts on a popular film noir festival.

LIVE MUSIC

Several restaurants and bars in town offer all kinds of live music; call first to see who is playing when and ask if there are cover charges.

Cowgirl Hall of Fame (Map pp368-9; cover $1-5) In addition to being a fine and rustic-with-a-vengeance venue for catching live shows (despite the name, rarely country), it also has microbrews, great food (p378) and non-smoking events.

El Paseo Bar & Grille (Map pp368-9; ☎ 505-992-2848; 208 Galisteo St; dishes $5-8; ☉ 11:30am-1:30am Mon-Sat, 11:30am-midnight Sun, kitchen closes at 10pm) This seemingly sedate wood-paneled pub with microbrews, cigars and green-chile cheese steak sandwiches is an excellent place to catch a show.

La Fonda (Map pp368-9; ☉ 11:30am-1:30am) The small lounge at this hotel (p375) offers surprisingly good country and folk music; the terrific Bill and Bonnie Hearne, Santa Fe folk musicians of the Nancy Griffith mold, play here.

El Farol (Map p364; ☎ 505-983-9912; 808 Canyon Rd; tapas $7-10; ☉ 11:30am-late) Billed as the 'oldest bar in Santa Fe,' built in 1835, this cool, dark adobe features music Wednesday through Saturday, murals by artist Alfred Morang (who painted them in the 1950s to pay off his tab) and lots of tapas. Make reservations to enjoy the latter while taking in **flamenco** ($45; ☉ 7:30pm on the first & third Wed of month).

Vanessie of Santa Fe (Map pp368-9; ☎ 505-982-9966; 434 W San Francisco St; dishes $15-32; ☉ 5:30-10:30pm) You don't really come to Vanessie for the food, though there's nothing wrong with it. No, the attraction here is the piano bar, featuring blow-dried lounge singers who bring Neil Diamond and Barry Manilow classics to life in their own special way.

DANCE CLUBS

Paramount (Map pp368-9; ☎ 505-982-8999; 331 Sandoval; cover varies) This place not only has a dance floor where you can move to reggae, Trash Disco and local hip-hop DJs, but it also hosts national recording artists, musical theater, and jazz and acoustic performances. The adjacent **Bar B** (☉ 5pm-2am) is more relaxed, with local performers of the highest caliber, and karaoke nights known to turn into impromptu comedy routines.

Swig (Map pp368-9; ☎ 505-955-0400; 135 W Palace Ave; cover $5 on Fri & Sat, tapas $13-20; ☉ 5pm-2am, from 6pm Sun) OK, so there's not really much of a dance floor (and the scantily clad male go-go dancers take up much of it), but with killer DJs imported from all over the country, lots of fancy martinis, a dress code reading 'appropriate attire' (translation: white hot) and some seriously groovy South Beach–style surroundings, it's just got that vibe. This isn't specifically a gay club, but it's quite gay friendly.

Warehouse 21 (Map pp368-9; ☎ 505-989-4423; 1614 Paseo de Peralta; cover $5-10) This all-ages club and art center in a 3500 sq ft warehouse is the perfect alcohol-free venue for edgy local bands, plus a fair number of nationally known acts, or for just showing off the latest in multihued hairstyles.

Rodeo Nites (Map p364; ☎ 505-473-4138; 2911 Cerrillos Rd; cover $5 on Fri; ☉ 6pm-1:30am) It's so big and so packed that it may be a little daunting if you're not already hip to the two-step scene. But it's still the best of its ilk in town, with live music almost nightly, including ranchero and salsa.

PERFORMING ARTS

Santa Fe enjoys an incredible variety of music, theater and dance, much of which is recognized internationally. It is not only the quality of the performances but also the variety of venues – cathedrals, chapels and outdoor theaters – that make the scene particularly interesting. *Four Seasons Santa Fe* (www.santafeevents.org) maintains an exhaustive listing of highbrow events.

Santa Fe Symphony (Map pp368-9; ☎ 505-983-3530, 800-480-1319; www.sf-symphony.org; tickets $15-44) Mounts eight concerts and many more special-event performances at the Lensic Performing Arts Center (opposite).

Santa Fe Chamber Music Festival (☎ 505-982-1890; www.sfcmf.org; tickets $10-50, free open rehearsals;

Jul & Aug) Highly acclaimed, this festival draws internationally renowned classical, folk and jazz musicians to Santa Fe.

Maria Benitez Spanish Dance Company (☎ 505-982-1237, 800-982-9198; www.mariabenitez.com; tickets $24-49; Jun-Sep) Perhaps the best flamenco troupe in North America, this company hosts intensely focused and festively garbed protégées who have earned every accolade with their impressive performances of the ultimate Spanish dance.

Desert Chorale (☎ 505-988-2282, 800-244-4011; www.desertchorale.org; tickets $15-50, some free events) Offers 15 eclectic programs at various venues during the summer; Christmas holiday performances are also popular.

Santa Fe Playhouse (Map pp368-9; ☎ 505-988-4262; www.santafeplayhouse.org; 142 E DeVargas St; tickets $12-$20; 8pm Thu-Sat, 2pm Sun) The state's oldest theater company performs avant-garde and traditional theater and musical comedy.

Lensic Performing Arts Theater (Map pp368-9; ☎ 505-984-1370; www.lensic.com; 1050 Old Pecos Trail) A beautifully renovated 1930 movie house, the theater hosts eight different performance groups and a weekly classic film series. It's open for touring productions as well.

Shopping

You can spend weeks shopping in Santa Fe, and some people do. Native American jewelry (predominantly silver and turquoise), basketry, pottery and textiles are for sale at every other store along the Palace of the Governors and in the plaza. Quality and prices vary considerably, and though the choices can be overwhelming, it is worth shopping around. Santa Fe is also a mecca for art collectors, and the town is full of galleries; pick up the *Wingspread Collectors Guide* at most big hotels. Galleries line Canyon Rd (p367), but downtown is also packed with fine art. Don't forget the two biggest shopping extravaganzas: the juried shows of Spanish Market (p373) and Indian Market (p374).

Nambe Foundry Outlet (Map pp368-9; ☎ 505-988-3574; www.nambe.com; 104 W San Francisco St) A unique metal alloy that contains no silver, lead or pewter (but looks like silver), was discovered in 1951 to the north of Santa Fe, near Nambé. Fashioned into gleaming and elegant pieces, Nambeware designs are individually sandcast and have won national and international recognition. There's also

an **outlet** (☎ 505-988-5528; 924 Paseo de Peralta) near Canyon Rd.

Plaza Mercado (Map pp368-9; ☎ 505-988-5792; www.plazamercado.com; 112 W San Francisco St) Just steps from the plaza is this swish spot packed with art galleries, antique stores and Santa Fe–style clothing, some feng shuied.

If you're looking for Mexican-style tiles, go to **Artesanos** (Map pp368-9; ☎ 505-983-1743; 222 Galisteo St), which also has other Mexican folk art. In the fall, you can send *ristras* (wreaths of chile peppers) directly from the store. **Coyote Café General Store** (Map pp368-9; ☎ 505-983-1615; 132 W Water St) stocks a variety of Southwestern salsa, hot sauces, chiles, tortilla and *sopaipilla* mixes and other local food items, as well as cookbooks. **Jackalope** (Map p364; ☎ 505-471-8539; 2820 Cerrillos Rd) is filled with a seemingly endless kaleidoscope of kitsch: cow skulls, kiva ladders, ceramic chickens, Navajo pot holders and much, much more.

James Reid Ltd (Map pp368-9; ☎ 505-988-1147; 114 E Palace Ave) has some beautiful hand-crafted silver jewelry and an exceptional collection of belt buckles. **Natalie** (Map pp368-9; ☎ 505-982-1021; 503 Canyon Rd) carries the finest cowboy and cowgirl gear. **Hopalong Boot Company** (Map p364; ☎ 505-471-5570; 3908 Rodeo Rd) sells secondhand Western wear, including lots of broken-in boots; it's a must for the rhinestone cowperson on a budget.

The **Shush Yaz Trading Company** (Map pp368-9; ☎ 505-992-0441; 1048 Paseo de Peralta) has an amazing collection of fine silver and turquoise jewelry, as well as outstanding kachinas. Of all the Canyon Rd shops dealing Native American antiquities, **Morning Star Gallery** (Map pp368-9; ☎ 505-982-8187; 513 Canyon Rd) is the best. You can buy Santa Fe–style folk art at the **Davis Mather Folk Art Gallery** (Map pp368-9; ☎ 505-983-1660; 141 Lincoln Ave). For photography books, including first editions and out-of-print books, go to **Photo Eye Books** (Map pp368-9; ☎ 505-988-4955; 376 Garcia St).

Perhaps more a museum than a gallery, **Fenn Galleries** (Map pp368-9; ☎ 505-982-4631; 1075 Paseo de Peralta) is one of Santa Fe's best known. The outdoor garden features larger-than-life bronze sculptures, and the low-ceilinged adobe interior is filled with masterpieces. The **Gerald Peters Gallery** (Map pp368-9; ☎ 505-954-5700; 1011 Paseo de Peralta) carries a collection of fine art (and all the Southwest masters) that few museums can

---

TOP MUSEUM-LIKE GALLERIES

When is a gallery more like a museum? Check out these places (and the Gerald Peters Gallery, p381) for the answer to that burning cultural question.

Zaplin-Lampert Gallery (Map pp368-9; ☎ 505-982-6100; www.zaplinlampert.com; 651 Canyon Rd) The renowned collection of Santa Fe and Taos School masters is nothing short of phenomenal.

Economos (Map pp368-9; ☎ 505-982-6347; 500 Canyon Rd) This is where museums come to purchase fantastic retablos, ancient Native American art, pre-Columbian Mexican pieces and much, much more.

Altermann Galleries (Map pp368-9; ☎ 505-820-1644; www.altermanngalleries.com; 203 Canyon Rd) This is the classic venue for legendary Southwestern fine art – cowboys, Indians and landscapes from (art) household names.

Adobe Gallery (Map pp368-9; ☎ 505-955-0550; www.adobegallery.com; 221 Canyon Rd) This gallery includes pieces by the 'Five Matriarchs' of the pueblo pottery renaissance: Maria Martinez, Margaret Tofoya, Maria Nampeyo, Lucy Lewis and Helen Cordero, among many other famed Indian artisans.

Mark Sublette: Medicine Man Gallery (Map pp368-9; ☎ 505-820-7451; www.medicinemangallery .com; 200 Canyon Rd) It's got more Maria Martinez pottery than her San Ildefonso museum, quality antique retablos, Navajo blankets and $5000 kachinas.

---

touch. Its back room is filled with treasures the Museum of Fine Arts can't even afford. **Nedra Mateucci Galleries** (Map pp368-9; ☎ 505-982-4631; 1075 Paseo de Peralta) displays top works from the Taos Society.

There aren't many fleas at the **Tesuque Flea Market** (Map p364; US Hwy 84/285; ☿ 9am-4pm Fri, 8am-5pm Sat & Sun Mar-Nov), a tiny outdoor market a few minutes north of Santa Fe at Tesuque Pueblo (opposite). But there are definitely deals on high-quality rugs, jewelry, art and clothing – for significantly less than you'll find them in town.

Getting There & Around

Great Lakes (☎ 505-473-4118, 800-554-5111) has daily flights from Denver. **Roadrunner Shuttle** (☎ 505-424-3367) provides transportation from the airport to local hotels ($13).

Santa Fe Trails (Map pp368-9; ☎ 505-955-2001; www.santafenm.gov; per ride adult/child $1/50¢, day pass $2; ☿ 6am-11pm Mon-Fri, 8am-8pm Sat, 10am-7pm Sun) is the country's first natural-gas city bus system. The bus depot is on Sheridan Ave between Palace and Marcy Aves. **Capital City Cab** (☎ 505-438-0000) provides a taxi service throughout town.

TNM&O/Greyhound (Map p364; ☎ 505-471-0008; St Michael's Dr) has four buses daily to Albuquerque ($11, 80 minutes) and two daily buses to Taos ($16-18, 1½ hours). **Sandia Shuttle** (☎ 505-474-5696, 888-775-5696) runs from the major hotels 10 to 12 times a day to Albuquerque International Airport ($23).

Twin Hearts Shuttle (☎ 800-654-9456; www.twin heartsexpress.com) runs between Santa Fe and the Albuquerque Sunport ($20), Taos ($25), Española ($15), Red River ($30) and Questa ($25) daily; make reservations in advance. **Faust** (☎ 505-758-3410) offers similar services.

The **Amtrak** (☎ 800-872-7245; www.amtrak.com) *Southwest Chief* stops at Lamy; from here, buses continue 17 miles to Santa Fe.

From Albuquerque, there are three routes to Santa Fe. The quickest is straight up I-25, which takes about 50 minutes. You can also drive up the east of the Sandias on the Turquoise Trail (p361). Without stopping, this drive takes roughly 1½ hours. The longest route is through the Jemez Mountains into Los Alamos (p384) and south on Hwy 84/285 into Santa Fe. This makes a great day trip; leave Albuquerque early enough to drive leisurely through the mountains, stopping at Bandelier National Monument (p386) and Los Alamos. From Los Alamos, it's another 40-minute drive to Santa Fe.

AREA PUEBLOS

A quick glance at most maps reveals the region north of Santa Fe to be the heart of Pueblo Indian lands. The **Eight Northern Pueblos** (ENIPC; ☎ 505-852-4265) all lie within 40 miles of Española, some of which is on long-term lease from Santa Clara Pueblo (p384). Together they publish the excellent *Eight Northern Indian Pueblos Visitors Guide*, available free at area visitor centers.

Many pueblos operate casinos, usually several miles from the main pueblo, which are generally open 8am to 4am Monday to Thursday morning, then stay open 24 hours through Sunday. Slots, craps, poker, shows and endless buffet tables are the big draws, but unlike casinos in Las Vegas, there's usually a gift shop selling high-quality pottery and other work by local artisans.

The pueblos themselves aren't really tourist attractions – they're towns, with schools, modern houses, post offices and whatnot. They are certainly a must-see, as you'll learn (or unlearn) a lot about Native culture, and area artists in particular appreciate the traffic.

Begin by purchasing the required camera permits from either the visitor center, if there is one, or Governor's Office, where they may be able to point you toward galleries, guided tours and other areas of interest, if they aren't too busy.

Tesuque Pueblo
pop 800 / elev 6000ft

Nine miles north of Santa Fe along Hwy 285/84 is **Tesuque Pueblo** (☎ 505-983-2667, 800-483-1040; Rte 5), whose members played a major role in the Pueblo Revolt of 1680. Today, the Reservation encompasses more than 17,000 acres of spectacular desert landscape, including Aspen Ranch and Vigil Grant, two wooded areas in the Santa Fe National Forest. **San Diego Feast Day** (Nov 12) features dancing, but no food booths or vendors are allowed.

Pojoaque Pueblo
pop 2700 / elev 7000ft

Although this pueblo's history predates the Spaniards, it is known that a smallpox epidemic in the late 19th century killed many inhabitants and forced the survivors to evacuate. No old buildings remain. The few survivors intermarried with other Pueblo people and Hispanics, and their descendants now number about 200. In 1932, a handful of people returned to the pueblo and they have since worked to rebuild their people's traditions, crafts and culture.

The **Poeh Cultural Center & Museum** (☎ 505-455-3334; www.poehcenter.com; ☾ 10am-4pm Mon-Sat), on the east side of Hwy 84/285, features exhibits on the history and culture of the Tewa-speaking people. Next door, check out the large selection of top-quality crafts from the Tewa pueblos at the **visitor center** (☎ 505-455-9023; 96 Cities of Gold Rd).

The pueblo public buildings are 16 miles north of Santa Fe on the east side of Hwy 84/285, just south of Hwy 502. The annual **Virgen de Guadalupe Feast Day** (Dec 12) is celebrated with ceremonial dancing.

San Ildefonso Pueblo
pop 1500 / elev 6000ft

Eight miles west of Pojoaque along Hwy 502, this ancient **pueblo** (☎ 505-455-3549; per car $3, camera/video/sketching permits $10/20/25; ☾ 8am-5pm) was the home of Maria Martinez, who in 1919, along with her husband, Julian, revived a distinctive traditional black-on-black pottery style. Her work, now valued at tens of thousands of dollars, has become world famous and is considered by collectors to be some of the best pottery ever produced.

Several exceptional potters (including Maria's direct descendants) work in the pueblo, and many different styles are produced, but black-on-black remains the hallmark of San Ildefonso. Several gift shops and studios, including the **Maria Poveka Martinez Museum** (admission free; ☾ 8am-4pm Mon-Fri), sell the pueblo's pottery. The **Pueblo Museum**, with exhibits on the pueblo's history and culture and a small store, is next to the visitor center.

Visitors are welcome to **Feast Day** (Jan 23) and **corn dances** (throughout the summer).

Nambé Pueblo
pop 1750 / elev 6200ft

Just driving into this **pueblo** (☎ 505-455-2036), through dramatically sculpted, multihued sandstone, is fantastic. NM 503, which leaves US Hwy 285/84 just north of Pojoaque to head into hills speckled with piñon, makes for a scenic addition to the High Rd to Taos (p388).

Perhaps because of the isolated location (or inspirational geology), Nambé has long been a spiritual center for the Tewa-speaking tribes, a distinction that attracted the cruel attentions of Spanish priests intent on conversion by any means necessary. After the Pueblo Revolt and Reconquista wound down, Spanish settlers annexed much of their land.

NEW MEXICO

Nambé's remaining lands have a couple of big attractions; the loveliest are two 20-minute hikes to **Nambé Falls** (per car per day $5). The steep upper hike has a photogenic overlook of the falls, while the easier lower hike along the river takes in ancient petroglyphs. The most popular attraction, however, is **Lake Nambé** (☎ ranger station 505-455-2304; Hwy 101; per car per day $10; ☯ 7am-7pm Apr-Oct), created in 1974 when the US dammed the Rio Nambé, flooding historic ruins but creating an important reservoir that attracts nonmotorized boaters and trout lovers.

Public events include **San Francisco de Asis Feast Day** (Oct 4) and the **Catholic Mass and Buffalo Dance** (Dec 24).

Santa Clara Pueblo
pop 1000 / elev 6800ft

The pueblo entrance is 1.3 miles southwest of Española on Hwy 30. Several galleries and private homes sell intricately carved black pottery. Stop first at **Singing Water Gallery** (☎ 505-753-9663; www.singingwater.com; Hwy 30; ☯ 11:30am-5pm), right outside the main pueblo. In addition to representing 213 of some 450 Santa Clara potters, owners Joe and Nora Baca also offer tours of the pueblo on weekends ($10), pottery demonstrations ($30) and classes, and can arrange feast meals ($12) with 48 hours notice.

On the Reservation at the entrance to Santa Clara Canyon, 5.7 miles west of Hwy 30 and southwest of Española, are the **Puye Cliff Dwellings**. Ancestors of today's Santa Clara Indians lived here until about 1500. The original carvings were cut into the Puye Cliffs on the Pajarito Plateau, and structures were later added on the mesas and below the cliffs. Because of a fire back in 2000, the cliff dwellings are not opened to the public but it's always subject to change.

Santa Clara Feast Day (Aug 12) and **St Anthony's Feast Day** (Jun 13) feature the Harvest and Blue Corn Dances. All are open to the public; the **Governor's Office** (☎ 505-753-7330; Hwy 30; ☯ 8am-4:30pm Mon-Fri) issues photo permits ($5).

San Juan Pueblo
pop 6750 / elev 5600ft

Drive a mile north of Española on Hwy 68 and 1 mile west on Hwy 74 to get to **San Juan Pueblo** (☎ 505-852-4400), which is really no more than a bend in the road with a compact main plaza surrounded by cottonwoods. The

pueblo was visited in 1598 by Juan de Oñate, who named it San Gabriel and made it the short-lived first capital of New Mexico. The original Catholic mission, dedicated to St John the Baptist, survived until 1913 but was replaced by the adobe, New England–style building that faces the main plaza. Adjacent to the mission is the **Nuestra Señora de Lourdes Chapel**, built in 1889. The kiva, shrines and some of the original pueblo houses are off-limits to visitors. There is a $5 fee for photography and for video cameras.

The **Oke Oweenge Crafts Cooperative** (☎ 505-852-2372; Hwy 74; ☯ 9am-4:30pm Mon-Sat) has a good selection of traditional red pottery, seed jewelry, weavings and drums. The onsite **Silver Eagle Lounge** serves alcohol and has live music nightly, while the **Harvest Cafe** (dishes $1-12, buffet $6-9; ☯ 6:30am-10pm Sun-Thu, to midnight Fri & Sat) has a great salad bar and $1 breakfast specials.

Public events include the **Basket Dance** (Jan), **Deer Dance** (Feb), **Corn Dance** (Jun 13), **San Juan Feast Day** (Jun 24) and a series of Catholic and traditional dances and ceremonies from December 24 to 26.

LOS ALAMOS
pop 18,300 / elev 7400ft

Los Alamos, hugging the national forest and set on mesas overlooking the desert, offers a fascinating dynamic in which souvenir T-shirts printed with atomic explosions and 'La Bomba' wine are sold next to books on Pueblo history and wilderness hiking.

Orientation

Built on long thin mesas separated by steep canyons, Los Alamos has a confusing layout. The main entrance from the east is Hwy 502, which branches into the east–west streets of Canyon Rd, Central Ave and Trinity Dr – these are the main streets of town. Central Ave and Canyon Rd form an oval enclosing the heart of town. Canyon and Central merge on the west side of town as Canyon Rd and meet back up with Trinity at Hwy 501. The highway veers around past the Los Alamos National Laboratory towards Bandelier National Monument and turns into Hwy 4. Got that?

Information

Chamber of Commerce (☎ 505-662-8105, 800-444-0707; www.visit.losalamos.com; 109 Central Park Sq; ☯ 9am-5pm Mon-Fri, 9am-4pm Sat, 10am-3pm Sun)

Forest Service (☎ 505-667-5120; 475 20th St; 🕑 8am-4pm Mon, Wed & Fri)
Hospital (☎ 505-662-4201; 3917 West Rd; 🕑 24hr)
Library (☎ 505-662-8250; 2400 Central Ave) Free Internet access.
Otowi Station Museum Shop and Bookstore (☎ 505-662-9589; 1350 Central Ave; 🕑 8am-5pm Mon-Fri, 9am-6pm Sat, 11am-6pm Sun) A fine selection of science and regional books.
Post Office (☎ 505-662-2071; 1808 Central Ave)

Sights & Activities

On July 16, 1945 a flash in the New Mexico desert forever changed the world. In that single moment, later said to be the most important event of the 20th century, scientists released energy equal to all the bombs dropped on London by Nazi Germany. Soon thereafter, on August 6 and August 9, 1945 the cities of Hiroshima and Nagasaki were destroyed by the first atomic bombs used in warfare.

You can't actually visit the Los Alamos National Laboratory, where the first atomic bomb was conceived, but you can visit the well-designed **Bradbury Science Museum** (☎ 505-667-4444; www.lanl.gov/museum; Central Ave; admission free; 🕑 10am-5pm Tue-Sat), which covers atomic history. The **Los Alamos Historical Museum** (☎ 505-662-4493; www.losalamos.com/historicalsociety; 1921 Juniper St; admission free; 🕑 9:30am-4:30pm Mon-Sat, 11am-5pm Sun) features atomic age popular culture artifacts and exhibits on the social history of life 'on the hill' during the secret project. Pick up one of their self-guided downtown walking-tour pamphlets. The **Art Center at Fuller Lodge** (☎ 505-662-9331; www.artfulnm.org; Central Ave; 🕑 10am-4pm Mon-Sat) mounts mixed-media shows of local and national artists. Fuller Lodge, built in 1928 to serve as the dining hall for the local boys' school, was purchased by the US government for the Manhattan Project. Inside are two small but good museums.

Pajarito Mountain Ski Area (☎ 505-662-5725, 888-662-7669; www.skipajarito.com; lift tickets adult/child 13-17/child 7-12 $39/31/25; 🕑 Fri-Sun), 7 miles west of downtown, offers challenging skiing.

Sleeping

Canyon Inn B&B (☎ 505-662-9595, 800-662-2565; www.canyoninnbnb.com; 80 Canyon Rd; r $70) Catering to folks working at the labs, this B&B provides breakfast fixings so that guests can prepare the meals whenever they rise.

Holiday Inn Express (☎ 505-661-1110; www.hiexpress.com; 2455 Trinity Dr; r $65-100; 💻) This is the nicest hotel in town and includes an exercise room with a sauna.

Quality Inn & Suites (☎ 505-662-7211; www.choicehotels.com; 2201 Trinity Dr; r incl breakfast $89-99; ⊠ 🅿) Recently refurbished, these 79 rooms and eight mini-suites represent some of the best value in Los Alamos; many rooms have microwaves and refrigerators.

Eating

Canyon Bar & Grill (☎ 505-662-3333; 163 Central Park Sq; mains $5-12; 🕑 11am-2am Mon-Sat, to midnight Sun) The best place in town for a beer and basic

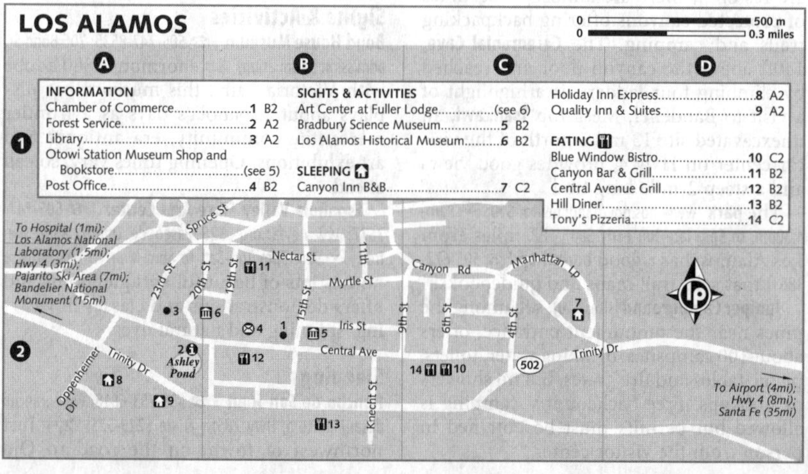
LOS ALAMOS
0 500 m
0 0.3 miles
A
B
C
D
1
2
INFORMATION
Chamber of Commerce....1 B2
Forest Service....2 A2
Library....3 A2
Otowi Station Museum Shop and Bookstore....(see 5)
Post Office....4 B2
SIGHTS & ACTIVITIES
Art Center at Fuller Lodge....(see 6)
Bradbury Science Museum....5 B2
Los Alamos Historical Museum....6 B2
SLEEPING
Canyon Inn B&B....7 C2
Holiday Inn Express....8 A2
Quality Inn & Suites....9 A2
EATING
Blue Window Bistro....10 C2
Canyon Bar & Grill....11 B2
Central Avenue Grill....12 B2
Hill Diner....13 B2
Tony's Pizzeria....14 C2
To Hospital (1mi); Los Alamos National Laboratory (1.5mi); Hwy 4 (3mi); Pajarito Ski Area (7mi); Bandelier National Monument (15mi)
Spruce St
Nectar St
Myrtle St
Iris St
Central Ave
Canyon Rd
Manhattan Lp
Trinity Dr
Oppenheimer Dr
23rd St
20th St
19th St
15th St
11th
9th St
6th St
4th St
Knecht St
Ashley Pond
502
To Airport (4mi); Hwy 4 (8mi); Santa Fe (35mi)

bar fare has a great green-chile cheeseburger. The local hangout has a long bar, pool table, live music and dancing on Friday and karaoke on Thursday. You won't find any glitz or Southwestern affectations here.

Central Avenue Grill (☎ 505-662-2005; 1789 Central Ave; dishes $7-18) For a more upscale and contemporary setting, with high ceilings and big windows that open onto downtown Los Alamos, this place serves satisfying dishes like shrimp fajitas, green-curry chicken and Asian-spiced salmon.

Blue Window Bistro (☎ 505-662-6305; 813 Central Ave; lunch dishes $8-9, dinner dishes $8-21; ☼ lunch & dinner) On the north side of the shopping center, this brightly colored café offers lunchtime gyros and poached salmon, and dinners like Southwestern chicken and double-cut pork chops.

Hill Diner (☎ 505-662-9745; 1315 Trinity Dr; dishes $8-10) An adequate array of American diner fare is served daily at this popular and inexpensive place. Chicken-fried steak aficionados won't be disappointed here.

Tony's Pizzeria (☎ 505-662-7799; 723 Central Ave; pizzas $13-17; ☼ lunch & 4-8pm Mon-Sat) They have the best pizza in town, but their pasta dishes are pretty good too; hold off on dessert.

BANDELIER NATIONAL MONUMENT

Because of its convenient location and spectacular landscape, Bandelier is an excellent choice for folks interested in ancient pueblos. Rio Grande Puebloans lived here until the mid-1500s. Although none of the sites are restored, there are almost 50 sq miles of protected canyons offering backpacking trails and camping. The **Ceremonial Cave**, 140ft above the canyon floor and reached by climbing four ladders, is a highlight of a visit to Bandelier. Mesa-top **Tsankawi**, an unexcavated site 13 miles north of the visitor center on Hwy 4, provides good views and a steep 2-mile long trail.

The **park** (www.nps.gov/band; per car $10; ☼ 8am-4:30pm, to 5pm late Jun-early Sep), 12 miles from Los Alamos, has a good **bookshop** (☎ 505-672-3861) that sells trail maps and guidebooks.

Juniper Campground (sites $10), set among the pines near the monument entrance, offers about 100 campsites, drinking water, toilets, picnic tables and fire grates, but no showers or hookups. Free backcountry camping is allowed but permits must be obtained in person from the visitor center.

ESPAÑOLA

pop 9700 / elev 5595ft

In some ways Española is the gateway to the real New Mexico, separating the tourist-choked wonderland of Santa Fe from the reality of the rural. The Rio Grande, Rio Chama and Santa Cruz River converge near the city. Much of the surrounding area is farmland, and much has been deeded to Hispanic land-grant families since the 17th century. Though the town itself doesn't offer much beyond a strip with fast-food restaurants and a disproportionate number of hair salons, its central location and abundance of good budget restaurants make it a convenient (though not particularly pleasant) place from which to explore northern New Mexico. There has been an increase in violent crime in the area, so be careful walking at night and lock up your valuables.

Orientation & Information

Hwy 84/285 runs through Española and is the main north–south road, splitting north of town into Hwy 84 heading northwest toward Abiquiu and Hwy 285 heading north toward Ojo Caliente. Hwy 30 runs southwest toward Los Alamos. Española is 24 miles north of Santa Fe and 44 miles south of Taos. Contact the **Chamber of Commerce** (☎ 505-753-2831; www.espanolanmchamber.com; 710 Paseo de Oñate; ☼ 9am-5pm Mon-Fri) for maps and the **Española Ranger Station** (☎ 505-753-7331; 1710 N Riverside Dr; ☼ 7:30am-4:30pm Mon-Fri) about area trails and campsites.

Sights & Activities

Bond House Museum (☎ 505-747-8535; 706 Bond St; admission by donation) An enormous 1880 adobe with Victorian airs, this museum displays about Española's days as a frontier mercantile community, era antiques and art exhibitions. Opening times vary, so call ahead.

Española Valley Fibre Arts Center (☎ 505-747-3577; www.evfac.org; 325 Paseo de Oñate; admission free; ☼ 9am-5pm Tue-Sat, to 8pm Mon) This place houses lots of beautiful antique looms and offers demonstrations and classes in weaving, spinning and natural dyes.

Sleeping

Rancho de San Juan (☎ 505-753-6818, www.ranchodesanjuan.com; Hwy 285; r & ste $225-525; ✖) Just northwest of town, on the road to Ojo

Caliente, this small gem has first-class rooms and service and a spectacular setting for dining (below).

Inn at the Delta (☎ 505-753-9466, 800-995-8599; 304 Paseo de Oñate; r incl buffet breakfast $100-150; ✖) The nicest place in town has huge rooms with hot tubs, Mexican tile-work, a fireplace, high ceilings with vigas and locally carved Southwestern furniture.

Ranchito San Pedro B&B (☎ 505-753-0583; www .janhart.com; Hwy 581; cabins $95; ✖) This adobe 'art dude ranch,' in a surprisingly pastoral neighborhood, is about as relaxing as they come.

Eating

Rancho de San Juan (☎ 505-753-6818; www.rancho desanjuan.com; Hwy 285; breakfast dishes $8-17, prix fixe dinner $55) Want an excuse to dress up in Española? This four-star place gets a good nod for New Mexican classics, at two nightly seatings. The property also has first-class accommodations including a spa, as well as a sandstone shrine carved into a nearby mesa that's well worth the $5 admission.

'Original' La Cocina Taqueria (☎ 505-753-3486; 310 Old Los Alamos Hwy; dishes $4-7; ✾ breakfast & lunch Mon-Fri) This beloved hole in the wall does legendary stuffed *sopaipillas*, while their **'New' Cocina Taqueria** (☎ 505-753-3016; 411 Santa Clara Bridge Rd; dishes $5-9; ✾ 11am-8:30pm) has nicer digs and a bigger menu, including a great fajita salad.

Angelina's (☎ 505-753-8543; 1226 N Railroad Ave; dishes $8-28) Serving some of the area's best *sopaipillas,* delicious beans and green chile, this is a great place for simple New Mexican fare.

Getting There & Away

Greyhound (☎ 505-753-8617, 800-231-2222; www .greyhound.com) buses stop at **Box Pack Mail** (1227A N Railroad Ave), across from Angelina's (above), and head to Albuquerque ($17.50, two hours), Santa Fe ($9, 45 minutes), Taos ($10.50, one hour) and beyond.

OJO CALIENTE

Billed as America's oldest health resort, **Ojo Caliente** (☎ 800-222-9162; www.ojocalientespa.com; 50 Los Baños Dr; s/d $74/110, cottage s/d $90/145; ✖), which means 'hot eye' in Spanish, offers five springs, plus a charmingly tattered, family-owned resort with pleasant if not luxurious rooms and casitas. The onsite **Artesian**

Restaurant (dishes $5-25) prepares organic and local ingredients with aplomb, including fresh trout encrusted with pine nuts in a cilantro-jalapeño butter.

The springs, considered sacred by Pueblo Indians, are an unusual trick of hydrogeology: each of the beautiful pools is fed by a different water source with different mineral contents. The Lithia spring has a kick – bring a bottle so you can take some home. Drop by for a visit (weekday/weekend $16/20) and consider indulging in one of their **spa treatments** (massage $44-125, wraps $9-85, facials $45-89, luxury packages $120-350), a yoga class (Wednesday through Sunday) or hiking along one of their trails.

Other accommodations within walking distance include the **Inn at Ojo** (☎ 505-583-9131; www.ojocaliente.com; Los Baños Dr; r incl breakfast $95; ✖), with a ping-pong table and nicer rooms than the resort. For eats, stop at the **Mesa Vista Cafe** (☎ 505-583-2245; Hwy 285; dishes $4-7; ✾ 8am-8pm), serving New Mexican diner food with lots of veggie options and a recommended red-chile cheeseburger.

PECOS

When the Spanish arrived, this five-story pueblo with almost 700 rooms was an important center for trade between the Pueblo Indians of the Rio Grande and the Plains Indians to the east. The Spaniards completed a church in 1625, but it was destroyed in the Pueblo Revolt of the 1680s. The remains of the rebuilt mission, completed in 1717, are the major attraction. The pueblo itself declined, and in 1838 the 17 remaining inhabitants moved to Jemez Pueblo.

At the **Pecos National Historical Park Visitor Center** (☎ 505-757-6414; www.nps.gov/peco; adult/child $3/free; ✾ 8am-5pm), a museum and short film explain more about the area's history. From Santa Fe, take I-25 east and follow signs; it's about 25 miles southeast.

The nearby town of Pecos is home to the **Pecos Benedictine Monastery** (☎ 505-757-6415; www.pecosabbey.org; Hwy 63; s $65; ✖), which has small hermitage rooms perfect for the aspiring ascetic.

ABIQUIU

pop 500 / elev 6800ft
The tiny community of Abiquiu (sounds like bar-b-que) is famous because the renowned artist Georgia O'Keeffe (p389) lived

and painted here. With the Rio Chama flowing through farmland and spectacular rock formations, the ethereal landscape continues to attract artists, and many live and work in Abiquiu.

Sights & Activities

Georgia O'Keeffe died in 1986, at age 98, and her adobe house is open for limited visits. Her **foundation** (www.georgiaokeeffe.org) offers one-hour **tours of O'Keeffe's home** (☎ 505-685-4539; www.abiquiuinn.com/Tour.htm; $22; ☽ Tue, Thu & Fri Apr-Nov), often booked months in advance, so plan ahead.

The spiritual landscape lures more than artists, two religious sanctuaries are perched in the hills. Muslims worship at **Dar Al Islam Mosque** (☎ 505-685-4515), an adobe mosque that welcomes visitors. From Hwy 84, take Hwy 554 (southeast of Abiquiu) towards El Rito, cross the Rio Chama, take your first left onto County Rd 155 and follow it for 3 miles. The mosque is up a dirt road on the right. Day visitors are welcome to join the monks in prayer at the **Christ in the Desert Monastery** (right); take Forest Service Rd 151, a dirt road off of Hwy 84 just south of Echo Amphitheater or 5 miles north of Ghost Ranch (right), and drive 13 beautiful miles.

The **Ghost Ranch Living Museum** (☎ 505-685-4333; www.ghostranch.org; US Hwy 84; ☽ 8am-5pm Tue-Sat), founded amid the colorful canyonlands as the former 1766 Serrano Land Grant, was later dubbed Rancho de los Brujos (Ranch of the Witches) because of various eerie *X-Files*–style supernatural activity. This Presbyterian retreat offers lodging (right), classes and other activities for folks of any or no faith. Take the recommended 4-mile round-trip trek into **Box Canyon** or the popular 3-mile round-trip to **Chimney Rock**, with views of the Piedra Lumbre basin.

Surrounded by red rock and high-desert terrain, **Abiquiu Lake & Dam** (☎ 505-685-4371; Hwy 84; ☽ dawn-dusk) is a beautiful swimming spot.

Sleeping & Eating

Abiquiú Inn (☎ 505-685-4378, 800-447-5621; www .abiquiuinn.com; US Hwy 84; RV sites $18, r $89-149, 4-person casitas $189; ☒) An area institution, this sprawling collection of shaded adobes is peaceful and lovely; some spacious rooms have kitchenettes. The very professional

staff also runs the onsite **Abiquiú Cafe** (dishes $7-16). Stick to the Middle Eastern menu – falafel, dolmas and gyros are all winners – and you can't go wrong.

Ghost Ranch (☎ 505-685-4333; www.ghostranch .org; US Hwy 84; tent/RV sites $16/23, dm incl board $45-70, dm with bathroom & board $80; ☒) This spectacular spot is where *City Slickers* was filmed. When space is available (seminar participants get first dibs), you can get a dorm bed here, including cafeteria-style meals made with locally raised meat and organic veggies grown on their farm.

Old Abiquiu B&B (☎ 505-685-4784; www.oldabi quiu.com; Hwy 84; r $55-95) This property, adjacent to the church ruins and near a wildlife refuge on the south end of Hwy 84, offers three rooms (two with a kiva fireplace) nestled in the woods overlooking the river.

Christ in the Desert Monastery (www.christdesert .org; off US Rte 84; r incl board $50-75; ☒ ☒) When you really want to get away from it all, head west from US Hwy 84 onto the rough dirt Forest Service Rd 151, then follow it along the meandering Rio Chama for 13 inspirational miles to this isolated Benedictine monastery. Rates for the simple rooms, outrageous trails and peace and quiet include vegetarian meals served without conversation – special medallions indicate your silent retreat. Chores are requested (not required) and include minding the gift shop or tending the garden.

Bodes (☎ 505-685-4422; US Hwy 84; dishes $5-7; ☽ 6:30am-7pm Mon-Sat, to 6pm Sun) Hang out with the locals at this good deli and small grocery store across from the village plaza. On winter nights, this may be the only place in town to eat.

El Farolito (☎ 505-581-9509; 1212 Hwy 554; dishes $5-12; ☽ Tue-Sun) In the tiny oasis of El Rito, north of Abiquiu on Hwy 554, El Farolito is definitely recommended for good New Mexican fare.

HIGH ROAD TO TAOS

Go on, take the High Rd. It certainly has a nice ring to it. From Española take Hwy 76 as it winds through river valleys, skirts high sandstone cliffs reminiscent of Roadrunner cartoons, and edges past high mountain pine forests. Along the way you can pop into weaving and wood-carving studios, and linger in charming villages like Chimayo (with a fabulous restaurant and a healing sanctuario), Truchas (partially gentrified but rife with old adobe farms) and Las Trampas (with one of the loveliest churches in the country). If you don't stop at all, which would defeat the purpose, you can make it to Taos in 2½ hours. But plan on spending a long, leisurely afternoon.

Chimayo

pop 2900 / elev 6200ft

Originally established by Spanish families with a land grant, Chimayo is famous for its 1816 **Santuario de Chimayo** (☎ 505-351-4889; NM 76; admission free; ❧ 9am-5pm, mass 11am Mon-Sat & noon Sun). Legend has it that the dirt from the church has healing powers, and the back room is a shrine to its miracles, with canes, wheelchairs, crutches and other medical aids hanging from the wall. Kneel into a hole in the ground and smear some dirt on your ailing body. As many as 30,000 people make an annual pilgrimage to the church every spring on Good Friday.

The Oviedo family has been carving native woods since 1739, and today the **Oviedo Gallery** (☎ 505-351-2280; www.oviedoart.com; Hwy 76; ❧ 10am-6pm) is housed in the 270-year-old family farm. If you're interested in handloomed weaving, head to **Centinela Traditional Arts** (☎ 505-351-2180, 877-351-2180; www.chimayo weavers.com; NM 76; ❧ 9am-6pm Mon-Sat, 10am-5pm Sun). Irvin Trujillo, a seventh-generation Rio Grande weaver, whose carpets are in collections at the Smithsonian in Washington, DC, and the Museum of Fine Arts (p366) in Santa Fe, works out of and runs this cooperative gallery of 20 weavers. Naturally dyed blankets, vests and pillows are sold, and you can watch the artists weaving on handlooms in the back.

The most famous place for dinner is **Rancho de Chimayó** (☎ 505-351-4444; www.ranchodechimayo .com; 300 County Rd 98; dishes $8-16; ❧ 11:30am-9pm Mon-Fri, 8:30am-10:30am Sat & Sun, closed Mon Nov-Apr), serving classic New Mexican cuisine, courtesy of the Jaramillo family's famed recipes, and the perfect margarita. Guestrooms are fine, but it's the location and old-school ambiance that packs 'em in.

Also highly recommended, the unpretentious **Casa Escondida** (☎ 505-351-4805; www.casa escondida.com; 64 County Rd 100; r $99-149) has eight rooms and a hot tub.

Truchas

pop 950 / elev 8400ft

Continue up Hwy 76 to Truchas, originally settled by the Spaniards in the 18th century. Robert Redford's *Milagro Beanfield War* was filmed here, and with the town's dusty New Mexican feel, small farms and spectacular views, it's easy to see why. Twelve

---

GEORGIA O'KEEFFE

Although classically trained as a painter at art institutes in Chicago and New York, 21-year-old Georgia O'Keeffe was always uncomfortable with traditional European style. For four years after finishing school, she did not paint, and instead taught drawing and did graphic design.

However, after studying with Arthur Wesley Dow, who shared her distaste for the provincial, O'Keeffe began developing her own style. She drew abstract shapes with charcoal, representing dreams and visions, and eventually returned to oils and watercolors. These first works caught the eye of her future husband and patron, photographer Alfred Steiglitz, in 1916.

In 1929 she visited Taos' Mabel Dodge Luhan Ranch and returned to paint 'The Lawrence Tree,' still presiding over **DH Lawrence Ranch** (p403). O'Keeffe tackled the subject of the **San Francisco de Asis Church** (p395) in Ranchos de Taos, painted by so many artists before her, in a way that had never been considered: only a fragment of the mission wall, contrasted against the blue of the sky.

It was no wonder she loved New Mexico's expansive skies, so similar to her paintings' negative spaces. As she spent more time here, landscapes and fields of blue permeated her paintings. During desert treks, she collected the smooth white bones of animals, subjects she placed against that sky in some of her most identifiable New Mexico works.

Telltale scrub marks and bristle impressions divulge how O'Keeffe blended and mixed her vibrant colors on the canvas itself. This is in direct contrast to photographs of her work, which convey a false, airbrush-like smoothness. At the **Georgia O'Keeffe Museum** (p366), you can experience her work first hand.

galleries, including the **Cordovas Handweaving Workshop** (☎ 505-689-2437; www.la-tierra.com/busyles; Main Truchas Rd; ⏰ sporadic), are nestled in the tiny village.

Rancho Arriba B&B (☎ 505-689-2374; www.rancho arriba.com; Main Truchas Rd; s/d $50/70, d with bathroom & breakfast $100; ☒ 🖳), in a rustic adobe farmhouse on the edge of Pecos Wilderness, has horses and wood stoves, and will arrange to cook you dinner in advance.

If you drive through town, rather than taking the turn for Taos, you'll find yourself winding into a mountain river valley, a creek and the trailhead to Truchas Peak (at 13,101ft, the second-highest peak in New Mexico) and the Carson Wilderness Area.

There are no restaurants, but you can grab snacks and beer at **Tofoya's General Store** (☎ 505-689-2418; Main Truchas Rd; snacks $3-5; ⏰ 8am-7pm Mon-Sat, 11am-4pm Sun), serving Truchas since 1915.

Las Trampas

Built in 1760 and constantly defended against Apache raids, the **Church of San José de Gracia** (Hwy 76; ⏰ 9am-5pm Mon-Sat Jun-Aug) is considered one of the finest surviving 18th-century churches in the USA. Original paintings and carvings remain in excellent condition, and self-flagellation bloodstains from the Los Hermanos Penitentes (a 19th-century secretive religious order with a strong following in the northern mountains of New Mexico) are still visible.

Picuris Pueblo
pop 86 / elev 7500ft

Once among the largest and most powerful pueblos, the Pikuri built adobe cities at least seven-stories tall and boasted a population approaching 3000. After the Pueblo Revolt and Reconquista, when many retreated to Kansas rather than face DeVargas' wrath, the returning tribe numbered only 500. Between raids by the Spanish and Comanches, that number continued to dwindle.

The **Governor's Office** (☎ 505-587-2519; photo/video permits $5/10; ⏰ 8am-5pm Mon-Fri) can, with advance notice, help arrange guided pueblo tours that include their small buffalo herd, organic gardens, ruins from the old pueblo site and the exquisite 1770 **San Lorenzo de Picuris Church**. The unique tower kiva is off-limits to visitors but makes an impression even from the outside. The tribe's **Picuris**

Pueblo Museum (☎ 505-587-1099) displays tribal artifacts and local art. The best time to visit the pueblo is during the popular **San Lorenzo Feast Days** (August 9 & 10), with food and crafts booths, dances, races and pole climbs.

From Picuris Pueblo, follow Hwy 75 east and go north on Hwy 518 to connect with Hwy 68, the main road to Taos.

LOW ROAD TO TAOS

People talk about the High Rd being so much more scenic than the so-called Low Rd that no one can fault you for having depressed expectations about this route. Fortunately, you'll be quite surprised at how scenic it is. If you don't have an afternoon to spare in getting from Santa Fe to Taos, take Hwy 68 from Española for 37 miles as it turns into a winding, two-lane road that follows the Rio Grande. Much of the road cuts through the river valley, with steep rocks to one side and the river on the other.

Fifteen miles north of Española, the **Black Mesa Winery** (☎ 505-852-2820, 800-852-6372; www .blackmesawinery.com; 1502 NM 68, Velarde; ⏰ 10am-6pm Mon-Sat, noon-6pm Sun) offers tastings before the highway cuts through the apple orchards of Velarde and into the Rio Grande Canyon.

Eight miles further, **Embudo Station** (☎ 505-852-4707, 800-452-4707; www.embudostation.com; NM 68; dishes $6-20; ⏰ 11:30am-9pm Tue-Sun May-Sep, noon-9pm Fri-Sun Oct-Apr; ☒) is situated along a particularly lovely stretch of the Rio Grande. Surrounded by cottonwoods, this pleasant brewery and restaurant serves New Mexican fare and sandwiches, as well as specialties like smoked ham and trout. You can also rent a large and nicely appointed river-view **cabin** ($100 incl breakfast) behind the restaurant.

Take a slight detour east on Hwy 75 to the small farming community of **Dixon**, where there are a couple of galleries as well as the excellent **La Chiripada Winery** (☎ 505-579-4437, 800-528-7801; www.lachiripada.com; NM 75; ⏰ 10am-5pm Mon-Sat, noon-5pm Sun), which offers tastings.

Seven miles further north, tiny **Pilar** is the base for summer white-water rafting. **Big River Raft Trips** (☎ 505-758-9711, 800-748-3746; www.bigriverrafts.com; cnr NM 68 & CR 570) offers full-day and half-day floats ($50 to $105). The **Rio Grande Gorge Visitor Center** (☎ 505-751-4899; NM 68; ⏰ 9am-4.30pm most days mid-Jan–Nov) has information on campsites and area hikes.

TAOS

pop 4700 / town elev 6950ft / ski-base elev 9207ft

This tiny town has a big reputation. Isolated Taos boasts – with a pleasant but ever-so-disinterested tone – a long history of luring storied artists, fabled clear light, a stunning multistory adobe pueblo inhabited by dignified souls and a magnificent mountain setting.

It's an eccentric place, full of bohemians and mainstream drop-outs, solar-energy-enthusiasts, fine chefs, acculturated B&B owners and old-time Hispanic families who still farm hay fields. It's rural *and* worldly, a place where grazing horses *and* a disproportionate number of artists hold equal sway.

Taoseños carry on a time-honored tradition of honoring the present by enjoying it; whatever needs to get done can always get done tomorrow. You can be as active (skiing, fly fishing, white-water rafting and hiking) or as laid-back (drinking coffee, nursing a margarita or conversing with locals) as you'd like. You can spend as much or as little money as you want. No one cares much. Embrace Taos on her terms – casual, charming and unhurried to the core – and she'll quickly return the favor.

Orientation

Entering from the south, Hwy 68 turns into Paseo del Pueblo Sur, a strip of motels and fast-food chains. It changes briefly into

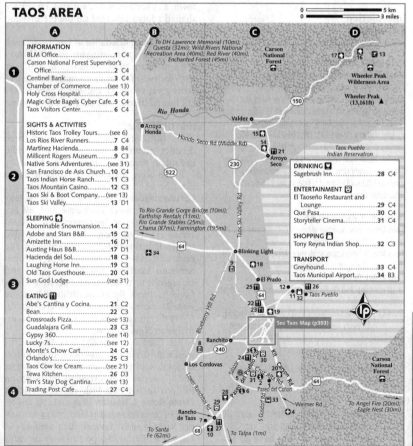

TAOS AREA

INFORMATION	
BLM Office..........................1 C4	
Carson National Forest Supervisor's	
Office..............................2 C4	
Centinel Bank.....................3 C4	
Chamber of Commerce.........(see 13)	
Holy Cross Hospital..............4 C4	
Magic Circle Bagels Cyber Cafe.5 C4	
Taos Visitors Center...........6 C4	
SIGHTS & ACTIVITIES	
Historic Taos Trolley Tours......(see 6)	
Los Rios River Runners...........7 C4	
Martínez Hacienda................8 B4	
Millicent Rogers Museum.........9 C3	
Native Sons Adventures........(see 31)	
San Francisco de Asis Church..10 C4	
Taos Indian Horse Ranch.........11 C3	
Taos Mountain Casino...........12 C3	
Taos Ski & Boot Company.....(see 13)	
Taos Ski Valley.....................13 D1	
SLEEPING	
Abominable Snowmansion.......14 C2	
Adobe and Stars B&B............15 C2	
Amizette Inn........................16 D1	
Austing Haus B&B.................17 D1	
Hacienda del Sol..................18 C3	
Laughing Horse Inn...............19 C3	
Old Taos Guesthouse............20 C4	
Sun God Lodge...................(see 31)	
EATING	
Abe's Cantina y Cocina..........21 C2	
Bean...................................22 C3	
Crossroads Pizza..................(see 13)	
Guadalajara Grill..................23 C3	
Gypsy 360..........................(see 14)	
Lucky 7s.............................(see 12)	
Monte's Chow Cart...............24 C4	
Orlando's.............................25 C3	
Taos Cow Ice Cream.............(see 21)	
Tewa Kitchen......................26 D3	
Tim's Stay Dog Cantina........(see 13)	
Trading Post Cafe.................27 C4	

DRINKING	
Sagebrush Inn.....................28 C4	
ENTERTAINMENT	
El Taoseño Restaurant and	
Lounge.............................29 C4	
Que Pasa............................30 C4	
Storyteller Cinema................31 C4	
SHOPPING	
Tony Reyna Indian Shop.........32 C3	
TRANSPORT	
Greyhound...........................33 C4	
Taos Municipal Airport............34 B3	

Map labels:
0 — 5 km
0 — 3 miles

To DH Lawrence Memorial (10mi); Questa (32mi); Wild Rivers National Recreation Area (40mi); Red River (40mi); Enchanted Forest (45mi)

Carson National Forest

Wheeler Peak Wilderness Area

Wheeler Peak (13,161ft)

Rio Hondo

Valdez

Arroyo Hondo

Hondo-Seco Rd (Middle Rd)

Taos Ski Valley Rd

Taos Pueblo Indian Reservation

Arroyo Seco

Taos Ski Valley Rd

To Rio Grande Gorge Bridge (10mi); Earthship Rentals (11mi); Rio Grande Stables (25mi); Chama (87mi); Farmington (195mi)

Blinking Light

El Prado

Taos Pueblo

See Taos Map (p393)

Blueberry Hill Rd

Ranchito

Los Cordovas

Lower Ranchito Rd

Kit Carson Rd

Carson National Forest

Paseo del Cañon

Weimer Rd

To Angel Fire (20mi); Eagle Nest (30mi)

Rancho de Taos

To Santa Fe (62mi)

To Talpa (1mi)

NEW MEXICO

Santa Fe Rd and then into Paseo del Pueblo Norte, the main north–south street in the town. One mile north of town, Paseo del Pueblo Norte forks: to the northeast it becomes Camino del Pueblo and heads toward Taos Pueblo, and to the northwest it becomes Hwy 64 and goes toward the Ski Valley. Kit Carson Rd begins at Paseo del Pueblo Sur near the center of town at the Taos Plaza and runs east, turning into Hwy 64 as it heads toward Angel Fire. The 'blinking light' north of town is a focal point for directions (though it now functions as a regular traffic light); from it, Hwy 64 heads west to the Rio Grande Gorge Bridge, Hwy 522 heads northwest to Arroyo Hondo and Questa, and Hwy 150 heads northeast to Arroyo Seco and the Taos Ski Valley.

Information

EMERGENCY
Police (Map p393; ☎ 505-758-2216; 107 Civic Plaza Dr)

INTERNET ACCESS
Magic Circle Bagels Cyber Cafe (Map p391; ☎ 505-758-0045; 710 Paseo del Pueblo Sur; per hr $6; ☺ 6:30am-4pm Mon-Fri, 7am-2pm Sat & Sun) Three fairly fast computers go well with lattes, soups and 19 different bagels ($3 to $6), right in the Raley's shopping center.

Public library (Map p393; ☎ 505-758-3063; 402 Camino de la Placita; ☺ noon-6pm Mon, 10am-6pm Tue-Fri, 10am-5pm Sat) Internet access costs $2 an hour without a library card. You can purchase a temporary (four-month) card without residency for $1 plus a $25 refundable deposit.

INTERNET RESOURCES
Taos Guide (www.taosguide.com) Click for an exhaustive list of easy-to-navigate links.

Taos Webb (www.taoswebb.com) Access links and information, including sites covering north-central New Mexico.

Taos Is Art Online (www.taosis.com) Check the schedule of art openings and studio tours, plus links and articles on local galleries.

Taos Link (www.taoslink.com) It's a tad intimidating, with links to every website even remotely associated with Taos.

MEDICAL SERVICES
Holy Cross Hospital (Map p391; ☎ 505-758-8883; 1397 Weimer Rd; ☺ 24hr)

MONEY
First State Bank (Map p393; ☎ 505-758-6600; 120 W Plaza) and **Centinel Bank** (Map p391; ☎ 505-758-6700; 512 Paseo del Pueblo Sur) both have ATMs.

POST
Main post office (Map p393; ☎ 505-758-2081; Paseo del Pueblo Norte at Brooks)

TOURIST INFORMATION
Taos Visitor Center (Map p391; ☎ 505-758-3873, 800-732-8267; www.destinationtaos.com; Paseo del Pueblo Sur at Paseo del Cañon; ☺ 9am-5pm)

Bureau of Land Management Office (BLM; Map p391; ☎ 505-758-8851, 888-882-6188; www.nm.blm.gov; 226 Cruz Alta Rd; ☺ 7:45am-4:30pm Mon-Fri)

Carson National Forest Supervisor's Office (Map p391; ☎ 505-758-6200; www.fs.fed.us/r3/carson; 208 Cruz Alta Rd; ☺ 8am-4:30pm Mon-Fri)

Sights
For a village that gets as much tourist traffic as Taos, there aren't that many sights to see. Wander historic Ledoux St and downtown, a collection of ancient and irregularly shaped adobes centered on the picturesque plaza.

The **Museum Association of Taos** (www.taosmuseums.org) offers a six-museum pass ($20) and a six-museum ticket (adult/child $10/7 or $8/5 for two) for area museums that represents great value. All museums have different hours, themes and single-entry prices.

HISTORIC HOMES
Three influential local figures reflect three distinct elements of Taos' history: the mountain man, the artist and the trader.

Resembling an adobe fortress with no exterior windows and massive walls, the **Martínez Hacienda** (Map p391; ☎ 505-758-1000; www.taoshistoricmuseums.com/martinez.html; NM 240; adult/child $6/3; ☺ 9am-5pm summer, shorter in winter) served as a refuge for neighbors and valuable livestock during the Comanche and Apache raids of the late 18th century. Don Antonio Severino Martínez bought it in 1804 and enlarged it to accommodate his flourishing trade business. By his death in 1827, there were 21 rooms and two interior courtyards; today the museum focuses on colonial family life in New Mexico.

Kit Carson (1809-68) was the Southwest's most famous mountain man, guide, trapper, soldier and scout, and his home and life serve as an excellent introduction to Taos in the mid-19th century. The **Kit Carson Home & Museum** (Map p393; ☎ 505-758-4945; Kit Carson Rd; adult/child $5/3; ☺ 9am-5pm summer, shorter in winter) houses such artifacts as Carson's rifles, telescope and walking cane.

Built in 1825 with 30in adobe walls and traditional territorial architecture, the home's 12 rooms are today furnished as they may have been during Carson's days, with exhibits on all periods of Taos history and mountain-man lore.

The 1797 **Blumenschein Home & Museum** (Map p393; ☎ 505-758-0505; www.taoshistoricmuseums .com/blumenschein.html; 222 Ledoux St; adult/child $6/3; ☒ 9am-5pm summer, shorter in winter) was the home of artist Ernest Blumenschein (one of the founding members of the Taos Society of Artists, see boxed text, p394) in the 1920s. Today it's maintained much as it would have been when the Blumenscheins lived here. While the period furniture is interesting, the art is spectacular.

HARWOOD FOUNDATION MUSEUM

Housed in a historic mid-19th-century adobe compound, the **Harwood Foundation Museum** (Map p393; ☎ 505-758-9826; www.har woodmuseum.org; 238 Ledoux St; adult/senior $7/6; ☒ 10am-5pm Tue-Sat, noon-5pm Sun) features paintings, drawings, prints, sculpture and photography by northern New Mexican artists, both historical and contemporary. If the Taos Society of Artists (see boxed text, p394) is the village's Barbazon, then this museum is its Louvre. Founded in 1923, the Harwood has been run by the University of New Mexico since 1936 and underwent a major renovation in 1997. It is the second-oldest museum in New Mexico.

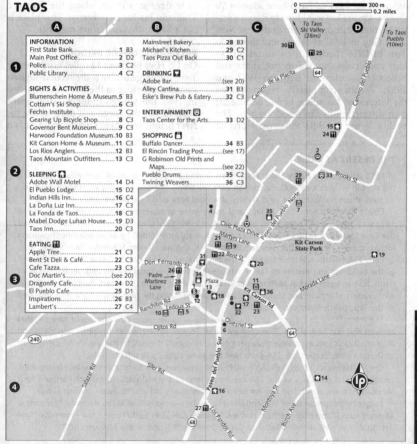

TAOS

0　　　300 m
0　　　0.2 miles

INFORMATION
First State Bank................................1 B3
Main Post Office...............................2 D2
Police...3 C2
Public Library...................................4 C2

SIGHTS & ACTIVITIES
Blumenschein Home & Museum....5 B3
Cottam's Ski Shop.............................6 C3
Fechin Institute.................................7 C2
Gearing Up Bicycle Shop..................8 C3
Governor Bent Museum...................9 C3
Harwood Foundation Museum.......10 B3
Kit Carson Home & Museum..........11 C3
Los Rios Anglers.............................12 B3
Taos Mountain Outfitters...............13 C3

SLEEPING
Adobe Wall Motel...........................14 D4
El Pueblo Lodge..............................15 D2
Indian Hills Inn...............................16 C4
La Doña Luz Inn..............................17 C3
La Fonda de Taos...........................18 C3
Mabel Dodge Luhan House.............19 D3
Taos Inn...20 C3

EATING
Apple Tree......................................21 C3
Bent St Deli & Café.........................22 C3
Cafe Tazza......................................23 C3
Doc Martin's...............................(see 20)
Dragonfly Cafe...............................24 D2
El Pueblo Cafe................................25 D1
Inspirations....................................26 B3
Lambert's.......................................27 C4

Mainstreet Bakery..........................28 B3
Michael's Kitchen...........................29 C2
Taos Pizza Out Back.......................30 C1

DRINKING
Adobe Bar.................................(see 20)
Alley Cantina..................................31 B3
Eske's Brew Pub & Eatery...............32 C3

ENTERTAINMENT
Taos Center for the Arts.................33 D2

SHOPPING
Buffalo Dancer................................34 B3
El Rincón Trading Post................(see 17)
G Robinson Old Prints and
　Maps.......................................(see 22)
Pueblo Drums.................................35 C2
Twining Weavers............................36 C3

To Taos Ski Valley (28mi)
To Taos Pueblo (10mi)

Camino de la Placita
Camino del Pueblo
Brooks St
Paseo del Pueblo Norte
Civic Plaza Drive
Martyrs Lane
Bent St
Kit Carson State Park
Don Fernando St
Padre Martinez Lane
Plaza
Kit Carson Rd
Morada Lane
Ranchitos Rd
Ledoux St
Ojitos Rd
Quesnel St
(240)
Siler Rd
Salazar Rd
Paseo del Pueblo Sur
Montoya St
Burch Ave
Los Pandoy Rd
(68)

NEW MEXICO

MILLICENT ROGERS MUSEUM

This **museum** (Map p391; ☎ 505-758-2462; www.milli centrogers.org; Millicent Rogers Museum Rd; adult/child $7/6 10am-5pm, closed Mon Nov-Mar), about 4 miles from the plaza, is filled with pottery, jewelry, baskets and textiles from the private collection of Millicent Rogers, a model and oil heiress who moved to Taos in 1947 and acquired one of the best collections of Indian and Spanish colonial art in the USA. You want to know what a top-quality squashblossom necklace is supposed to look like? Look no further. Also displayed are contemporary Native American and Hispanic artworks.

FECHIN INSTITUTE

This **museum** (Map p393; ☎ 505-758-2690; www .fechin.com; 227 Paseo del Pueblo Norte; admission $5; 10am-4pm Wed-Sun) was home to Russian artist Nicolai Fechin, who emigrated to New York City in 1922 at age 42 and moved to Taos in 1926. Today his paintings, drawings and sculptures are in museums and collections worldwide. Between 1927 and 1933, Fechin completely reconstructed the interior of his adobe home, adding his own distinctly Russian woodcarvings. The Fechin house exhibits the artist's private

collection, including much Asian art, and hosts occasional chamber music events. Five-day watercolor, sculpture and other arts workshops are offered from May to October at the nearby ranch.

GOVERNOR BENT MUSEUM

When New Mexico became a US territory after the Mexican American War in 1846, Charles Bent was named the first governor. Hispanics and Indians did not appreciate being forced under US rule, and on January 19, 1847, they attacked the governor in his home. Bent's family was allowed to leave, but he was scalped and killed. Today his home is a small **museum** (Map p393; ☎ 505-758-2376; 117 Bent St, adult/child $2/1; 9am-5pm summer, shorter in winter) with memorabilia from his early days as a trader along the Santa Fe Trail and his life as governor. This place is not a Museum Association member.

RIO GRANDE GORGE BRIDGE

On US Hwy 64 about 12 miles northwest of Taos, the gorge bridge is the second-highest suspension bridge in the USA. Constructed in 1965 the vertigo-inducing steel spans 500ft across the gorge and 650ft above the river below, and there's a walkway across it

---

THE DESERT AS MUSE

In 1893 artist Joseph Henry Sharp first visited Taos to produce a group of illustrations depicting the pueblo for publication. Quite smitten with the scene, Sharp spread the word among his colleagues about his 'discovery,' and shortly afterward relocated here permanently.

Ernest Blumenschein, Bert Phillips and many more of his contemporaries followed, and in 1912 they, along with Oscar Berninghaus, Eanger Irving Couse, and Herbert Dunton, established the Taos Society of Artists (TSA). The original six were later joined by other prominent painters including Lucy Harwood, the only female member, and Juan Tafiho Mirabol, a Taos Indian.

Early TSA paintings were inspired by the backdrop of the Sangre de Cristo Mountains as well as the buildings and people of Taos Pueblo. Set against the tonal shapes and neutral colors of earth, human figures act as anchors of color seen nowhere else in the desert. Pueblo architecture, with clusters of organic and sculptural block shapes reflecting the high desert light, also appealed to the Taos painters' artistic sensibilities.

The artists' styles were as diverse and experimental as the many philosophies of painting that defined the first half of the 20th century. From Sharp's illustrative and realistic approach and Blumenschein's impressionistic treatment of Southwestern themes, to the moody Art Deco spirit of Dunton's landscapes, the TSA portrayed the same subjects in infinite ways.

Only in later years would the TSA's contribution to modern art's development be fully recognized. Historically the paintings of the TSA are recognized as a visual documentary of northern New Mexican cultures, which had not yet been so dramatically influenced by the industrial age.

Larger collections of these influential works can be viewed in Taos at the Harwood Foundation Museum (p393) and Blumenschein Home & Museum (p393). In Santa Fe, visit the Museum of Fine Arts (p366) as well as the galleries of Gerald Peters (p381) and Nedra Mateucci (p382).

all. The views west over the emptiness of the Taos Plateau and down into the jagged walls of the Rio Grande are incredible.

SAN FRANCISCO DE ASIS CHURCH

Four miles south of Taos in Ranchos de Taos, this oft-photographed **church** (Map p391; ☎ 505-758-2754; St Francis Plaza; ☑ 9am-4pm Mon-Fri) was built in the mid-18th century and opened in 1815. It's been memorialized in numerous Georgia O'Keeffe paintings (p389) and Edward Weston photographs. Mass is held at 6pm the first Saturday of the month, and usually at 7am, 9am and 11:30am every Sunday (call to confirm).

EARTHSHIPS

These innovative (or wacky, depending on your perspective) **structures** (Map p391; ☎ 505-751-0462; http://earthship.org; US Hwy 64; tour $5; ☑ 10am-4pm) are the brainchild of architect Michael Reynolds, whose idea was to develop a building method that 'eliminates stress from both the planet and its inhabitants.' The Earthships are constructed of used automobile tires and cans into which earth has been pounded. Buried on three sides by earth, they are designed to heat and cool themselves, make their own electricity and catch their own water. Sewage is decomposed naturally, and dwellers grow their own food. They are open daily for tours and are available for rental (p397). The tour office is located 1.5 miles past the Rio Grande Gorge Bridge on US Hwy 64 West.

Activities

The variety of outdoor activities in the Taos area is exhaustive; consult www.taosoutdoorrecreation.com for an online rundown of all your options.

Native Sons Adventures (Map p391; ☎ 505-758-9342, 800-753-7559; www.nativesonsadventures.com; 1033 Paseo del Pueblo Sur; ☑ 7am-6pm) is a good source of information; they rent equipment and guide various trips. The huge **Taos Mountain Outfitters** (Map p393; ☎ 505-758-9292; www.taosmountainoutfitters.com; 114 S Plaza) rents and sells everything you need to get out and play.

HIKING

There is no shortage of nearby hiking trails, ranging from easy day hikes to overnight backcountry trips, from alpine mountain trails along rivers to awesome hikes along and through the Rio Grande Gorge. Start at the Carson National Forest Supervisor's Office (p392) or BLM (p392), both of which offer information on most area excursions. Many hikes begin near the Taos Ski Valley (p401).

RAFTING

The major summertime attraction is white-water rafting in the Taos Box, the steep-sided cliffs that frame the Rio Grande. Busloads of rafters from Santa Fe go up to Pilar (p390), which can become a flurry of sunburned and screaming tourists. The best time to go is in May and June, when snowmelt keeps the rivers rapid, but it's warm enough to enjoy the splash. In town, contact **Los Rios River Runners** (Map p391; ☎ 505-776-8854, 800-544-1181; http://losriosriverrunners.com; Hwy 68; ☑ 8am-6pm).

HORSEBACK RIDING

Rio Grande Stables (Map p391; ☎ 505-776-5913; www.lajitasstables.com/taos.htm; ☑ mid-May–mid-Sep), on the road to the ski valley, offers one-to three-hour trips ($40 to $130), all-day rides (including one to the top of Wheeler Peak) and combination horseback-rafting-camping treks they'll customize just for you. Rates start at $40 for one hour. Also see Taos Indian Horse Ranch, p400.

FISHING

There's lots of area fly-fishing, and **Los Rios Anglers** (Map p393; ☎ 505-758-2798, 800-748-1707; www.losrios.com; 126 W Plaza) provides guided trips. If you're a hardcore angler, know what you're doing and are willing to pay for a local guide (one/two/three people $250/275/350), this is a fine place, but it's not for beginners. Or do it yourself – they've got all the tackle you could possibly need.

BIKING

An enormous network of mountain-bike and multiuse trails threads the region of the Carson National Forest between Taos, Angel Fire and Picuris Peak. Pick up maps and information at the Carson National Forest Supervisor's Office (p392).

Gearing Up Bicycle Shop (Map p393; ☎ 505-751-0365; www.gearingupbikeshop.com; 129 Paseo del Pueblo Sur; ☑ 9:30am-6pm summer, shorter in winter) rents mountain and hybrid bikes (per hour/day/week $10/35/110) plus gear.

SKIING

Of course Taos Ski Valley (p401) is the main draw, but check out others nearby, including Angel Fire (p404), Red River (p403) and Enchanted Forest (p403), with 25 miles of groomed nordic trails.

Cottam's Ski Shop (Map p393; ☎ 505-758-2822, 800-322-8267; www.cottamsskishops.com; 207a Paseo del Pueblo Sur; ☺ 7am-6pm) rents ski packages for high-performance shooshers ($35 to $40) and casual skiers ($20 to $25).

Tours

Historic Taos Trolley Tours (Map p391; ☎ 505-751-0366; www.taostrolleytours.com; cnr Paseo del Pueblo Sur & Paseo del Cañon; adult/child $33/10; ☺ 10:30am & 2pm) offers two different tours aboard red trolleys from the visitor center. One visits Taos Pueblo, San Francisco de Asis and the plaza (where they'll also pick you up); the other takes in Millicent Rogers Museum and the Martinez Hacienda.

Festivals & Events

There are numerous athletic and cultural events all year, as well as visual arts workshops; the visitor center (p392) has details. The **Solar Music Festival** (☎ 800-732-8267; www.solarmusicfest.com; Kit Carson Park, 1-/3-day pass $20/65, kids under 10 free; late Jun), a three-day festival with exhibits and camping, features a solar stage packed with performers like Michelle

Shocked, Los Lobos and Harry Belafonte. **Christmas Holidays** (late Dec) feature dances at Taos Pueblo (p400) and mass at San Francisco de Asis Church (p395). Christmas carolers and *farolitos* everywhere help keep everyone's spirits bright.

Sleeping

Taos offers a wide variety of accommodations, from free camping in national forests to gourmet B&Bs in historic adobes. The village attracts visitors all year, though December to February and June to August are generally the high seasons.

Reservation services include the **Taos Association of Bed & Breakfast Inns** (☎ 800-939-2215; www.taos-bandb-inns.com), **Accommodations Taos** (☎ 800-257-7720; www.accommodationstaos.com) and **Taos Vacation Rentals** (☎ 800-788-8267; www.taosvacationrentals.com).

BUDGET

El Pueblo Lodge (Map p393; ☎ 505-758-8700, 800-433-9612; www.elpueblolodge.com; 412 Paseo del Pueblo Norte; r $54-107; ☒ ☲) This place is right downtown, with big, clean rooms, some with kitchenettes and/or fireplaces, a pool, hot tub and fresh pastries in the morning. What's not to love?

Adobe Wall Motel (Map p393; ☎ 505-758-3972; 227 E Kit Carson Rd; r $56-66; ☒) For almost 100 years, this shady courtyard motel has been

---

GOOD DAY SUNSHINE

Just as the Rio Grande Gorge opens up to engulf US Hwy 68 for the scenic climb into Taos, your radio will start to sputter. Don't put on that tired old CD; flip to KTAO 101.9 FM (www.ktao.com), broadcasting shows like 'Trash and Treasures' (where callers describe their wackiest for-sale items), Larry Torres' news and views from Taos Pueblo, and lots of great music.

KTAO has been doing it all with solar power since 1991, when station owner Brad Hockmeyer installed 50,000 watts worth of photovoltaic cells atop Mount Picuris. The station broadcasts all that good stuff, 100% terrorism-, Texas oil- and Clear Channel–free.

The station sponsors events throughout the year, but the biggest bash is the Solar Music Festival (above; www.solarmusicfest.com), held as a benefit for the New Mexico Solar Energy Association (www.nmsea.org). A free Solar Village sets up outside, showcasing everything from the Los Alamos National Laboratory's solar-powered supercomputer to homemade solar cookers. Grab a cup of solar-percolated coffee and chat up alternative-energy lovers pitching straw-bale construction, solar cars that fool the UFO-watchers down in Roswell, passive solar design ('used at Taos Pueblo for a thousand years!'), and of course the Taos Earthships (p395).

You may even spot a protester or two outside carrying signs that ask, 'Solar energy is free, why does this cost admission?' Talk to them about the radical New Mexico solar scene – folks who seceded from the US government–affiliated Solar Energy Industries Association (www.seia.org) to protest US subsidies of fossil fuel technologies. Ah, Taos, where there's even a counter-counterculture.

accommodating travelers in big, slightly tattered rooms with wonderful fireplaces.

Sun God Lodge (Map p391; ☎ 505-758-3162, 800-821-2437; www.sungodlodge.com; 919 Paseo del Pueblo Sur; r $54-74; ✗) These nice-enough adobe rooms are arranged around a green courtyard; they're a little threadbare but original.

MIDRANGE

Laughing Horse Inn (Map p391; ☎ 505-758-8350, 800-776-0161; www.laughinghorseinn.com; 729 Paseo del Pueblo Norte; r $54-118, ste $130-160; ✗) Narrow adobe rooms are furnished with chile-shaped Christmas lights, piñon incense and hand-hewn furniture – it's how Taoseños actually live! The communal atmosphere continues with a hot tub under the stars, kitchen privileges and a huge penthouse. The vibe reminds you why you travel in the first place.

La Doña Luz Inn (Map p393; ☎ 505-758-4874, 800-758-9187; www.ladonaluz.com; 114 Kit Carson Rd; r $60-199; ✗) The fabulous location is just the beginning at this historic 200-year-old inn. Rooms range from the tiny La Luz (guests should be under 6'2") to the three-level Rainbow Room suite, which features a hot tub on the rooftop sundeck. All are decorated in colorful Spanish colonial style and with a cheerful clutter of amazing art. Lots of it is sacred, most of it antique and all of it beautiful.

Old Taos Guesthouse (Map p391; ☎ 505-758-5448, 800-758-5448; www.oldtaos.com; 1028 Witt Rd; r $83-165; ✗ ▣) Outdoorsy types enchanted with this wilderness wonderland can stay here in spacious, Southwestern-style rooms wrapped around a shady lawn and hot tub, hidden away in a quiet residential neighborhood. The proprietors are seasoned adventurers and can point you toward excursions of every sort.

Mabel Dodge Luhan House (Map p391; ☎ 505-751-9686, 800-846-2235; www.mabeldodgeluhan.com; 240 Morada Lane; r $95-220; ✗) You may have stayed at plusher B&Bs, but not one of them has a story like this. The 'Patroness of Taos,' Mabel Dodge Luhan – by equal measures graceful and grand, scandalous and unbearable – built this fabulous mansion to bring in everyone from Emma Goldman and Margaret Sanger to Carl Jung and Ansel Adams for a nice chat…after which they would find somewhere less stressful to stay.

Indian Hills Inn (Map p393; ☎ 505-758-4293, 800-444-2346; 233 Paseo del Pueblo Sur; r $69-99; ✗ ▣) This inexpensive, independently run option offers pleasant, fairly basic rooms within walking distance of the plaza.

Earthship Rentals (Map p391; ☎ 505-751-0462; US Hwy 64; r $150-200) Want to experience life off the grid (ie forgoing TV and phone)? Stay in an Earthship (p395), which is 100% solar powered with a gray-water system, beautifully biotectured interior and reduced rates for multiple-night stays.

TOP END

Hacienda del Sol (Map p391; ☎ 505-758-0287, 866-333-4459; www.taoshaciendadelsol.com; US 64; r $105-240; ✗ ▣) The foothills retreat where Mabel Dodge and beau Tony Luhan first shacked up is still one of the most romantic spots in town, with fireplaces, Jacuzzis and those gorgeous mountains right out back.

Taos Inn (Map p393; ☎ 505-758-2233, 800-826-7466; www.taosinn.com; 125 Paseo del Pueblo Norte; r $85-225; ✗ ▣) Parts of this landmark date to the 17th century, which is why it's on the National Register of Historic Places – and why it's not exactly the plushest place in town. But it's fabulous, despite the gradually settling adobe architecture, with a cozy lobby, heavy wood furniture, a sunken fireplace and lots of live local music at its famed Adobe Bar (p399).

La Fonda de Taos (Map p393; ☎ 505-758-2211, 800-833-2211; www.hotellafonda.com; 108 S Plaza; r $139-169; ✗) Though it's been completely renovated in upscale Southwest style, this plaza-side hotel, formerly owned by notorious playboy Saki Karavas, just can't shake its sexy vibe – even the kiva gas fireplaces in the smallish, angled suites seem like they're up to illuminate no good. Perhaps it's the 'forbidden art' of DH Lawrence (p403), banned in 1929 Europe and displayed here to consenting adults ($3), depicting, and perhaps inspiring, all sorts of sinful fun.

Eating

Eating out in Taos can be pricey, but there are excellent inexpensive options as well. Here, even the fanciest of places is casual.

BUDGET

Monte's Chow Cart (Map p391; ☎ 505-758-3632; 402 Paseo del Pueblo Sur; dishes $3-7; ☼ Mon-Sat) Skip the chains and drive through this independently owned joint, with great breakfast burritos and a quality chile *relleno* burrito (ask for the 'Trujillo'). Many burritos are available as meal deals with fries and a large drink.

Cafe Tazza (Map p393; ☎ 505-758-8706; 122 Kit Carson Rd; organic goodies $3-7; ⏱ 7am-5pm, later in summer) The outdoor patio and courtyard make it a pleasant place to enjoy an espresso and pastry. Menu items include homemade soups and tamales and a wide selection of coffee drinks, all served in a bohemian atmosphere. Live entertainment, including acoustic folk-pop and poetry readings, takes place on most weekend evenings.

Dragonfly Cafe (Map p393; ☎ 505-737-5859; 402 Paseo del Pueblo Norte; dishes $5-11; ⏱ 7am-3pm Mon-Thu, 7am-9pm Fri, 8am-9pm Sat & Sun) With the atmosphere exuding eternal Sunday brunch, this fine spot serves all manner of baked goods and egg dishes. But the real star is a gravlax (Scandinavian-style salmon) plate and curried chicken salad served on their excellent bread. For something different, try the recommended *bibimbop* (eggs, veggies and rice with kimchie).

Bent Street Deli & Cafe (Map p393; ☎ 505-758-5787; 120 Bent St; breakfast & lunch dishes $4-10, dinner dishes $11-21; ⏱ 8am-9pm Mon-Sat) Build your own sandwich (or order one of its 21 recommended combinations), grab a side of cucumber salad or tabbouleh, then kick back. Dinner is gourmet comfort food and breakfast is grand, but it's really all about the sandwiches.

Mainstreet Bakery (Map p393; ☎ 505-758-9610; Guadalupe Plaza; dishes $4-7; ⏱ 7am-2pm Mon-Fri, 7am-noon Sat & Sun) Their bread and butter is baking for natural grocers, but grab some toast with a side of scrambled tofu or perhaps more traditional (and huge) breakfast treats. Or try the lunch special, a bowl of black beans, green chile, red onions, tomatoes and cornbread.

Bean (Map p391; ☎ 505-758-5123; 1033j Paseo del Pueblo Sur; dishes $4-7; ⏱ breakfast & lunch) The best lattes in town come with pastries, breakfast burritos and other breakfasty snacks.

Michael's Kitchen (Map p393; ☎ 505-758-4178; 304c Paseo del Pueblo Norte; breakfast & lunch dishes $5-7, dinner dishes $8-13; ⏱ 7am-8:30pm) OK, so it's a little touristy. But that doesn't make the gigantic cinnamon rolls any less gooilicious or the huge plates of New Mexican and pork-chops-and-mashed-potatoes-type comfort food any less grubbing. Hidden

between the ski bunnies and art collectors you'll find plenty of Taoseños willing to suffer the mob too.

MIDRANGE

Orlando's (Map p391; ☎ 505-751-1450; NM 522; dishes $7-11; ⏱ 10:30am-3pm & 5-9:30pm) This is it, the best New Mexican food in town, period. Those chicken enchiladas and huge burritos, all dressed to perfection and served up in the packed and beautiful dining room can't be beat.

Taos Pizza Out Back (Map p393; ☎ 505-758-3112; 712 Paseo del Pueblo Norte; slices $4-6, medium pies $15-25; ⏱ 11am-9pm) Enjoy every possible ingredient under the sun as pizza pies or slices the size of a small country. For example, the recommended Vera Cruz has chicken breast and veggies marinated in a honey-*chipotle* sauce. This kid-friendly spot has crayons at the table and a great back patio.

Guadalajara Grill (Map p391; ☎ 505-751-0063; 1384 Paseo del Pueblo Sur; dishes $4-14; ⏱ 11:30am-9pm) Right next to the car wash, this Mexican (*not* New Mexican) favorite serves everything from Mazatlan shrimp and fresh oysters to basic but bombastic burritos, with white wine sangria on the side.

El Pueblo Cafe (Map p393; ☎ 505-751-9817; 625 Paseo del Pueblo Norte; dishes $4-11; ⏱ 7am-late) With four wines on tap, great Frito pies, late hours and recommended *huevos rancheros* (the pitched debate about which was better on top, red or green, soon involved every table – go Christmas: half-and-half), it's no wonder folks love El Pueblo.

Inspirations (Map p393; ☎ 505-751-0959; 114 Doña Luz St; dishes $5-8; ⏱ 9:30am-5:30pm Mon-Fri, 11am-5pm Sat & Sun) Can't decide what to eat? When's your birthday? Order meals designed for your astrological sign at this New Agey outpost, with wheatgrass, lattes and the best salad bar in town (⏱ 11am-3pm). Should your Cancer moon ache for the avocado and cheese sandwich, Gemini sun debate the meze platter's merits and Taurus ascendant insist on the tempeh burger glazed with peanut sauce, there's still hope: Tarot-card readers (per minute $1) are usually available to assist you in these and other decisions.

TOP END

Doc Martin's (Map p393; ☎ 505-758-2233; 125 Paseo del Pueblo Norte; breakfast & lunch dishes $5-11, dinner dishes $14-24) It's won every award, charmed every tourist and been a top spot for locals since Blumenschein came up with the TSA here. Duck tamales, grilled trout *primavera*, wild mushroom ravioli and spectacular *huevos rancheros* are just a prelude to the great desserts; try a prix fixe dinner ($18 to $23) with four heavenly courses.

Apple Tree (Map p393; ☎ 505-758-1900; 123 Bent St; lunch dishes $6-10, dinner dishes $13-25; ⏰ 11:30am-3pm & 5pm-10pm) It's fancy, taking full advantage of its fabulous location and historic adobe with fine art, candles, a lovely patio, a huge wine list and gourmet twists on New Mexican classics like mango chicken (or tempeh) enchiladas. The real deal is at lunch, when an abbreviated to-go menu wraps up simpler but still stunning fare picnic-style for a few dollars less than you'd pay to eat inside.

Trading Post Cafe (Map p391; ☎ 505-758-5089; cnr NM 68 & NM 518; lunch dishes $7-11, dinner dishes $7-22; ⏰ 11:30am-9:30pm Tue-Sat, dinner Sun) White tablecloths and stemware evoke an ambiance improved only by their amazing art – there'll be no lack of conversation starters, that's for sure – plus a divine *torta* Cubana and recommended fresh fettuccini carbonara.

Lambert's (Map p393; ☎ 505-758-1009; 309 Paseo del Pueblo Sur; dishes $15-32; ⏰ dinner) Everyone in town has their favorite dish, which they simply must describe in mouthwatering detail after gushingly recommending this as their second-favorite restaurant *ever* (after Orlando's), or first-favorite if someone else is paying. The seafood paella, red chile rubbed buffalo loin, and especially the pepper-crusted lamb get 'em all starry-eyed.

Drinking

Eske's Brew Pub & Eatery (Map p393; ☎ 505-758-1517; 106 Des Georges Lane; pub grub $6-10; ⏰ 4-10pm Mon-Thu, 11am-10pm Fri-Sun) This crowded hangout rotates more than 25 microbrewed ales, from Taos Green Chile to Doobie Rock Heller Bock, to compliment hearty bowls of Wanda's green-chile stew and sushi on Tuesday. Live local music, from acoustic guitar to jazz, is usually free but national acts might charge a cover.

Alley Cantina (Map p393; ☎ 505-758-2121; 121 Terracina Lane; pub grub $6-14; ⏰ from 11:30am) It figures that the oldest building in Taos is a comfy bar, built in the 1500s by forward-thinking Native capitalists as the Taos Pueblo Trading Post. Nowadays you can catch

live music ranging from zydeco to rock and jazz almost nightly, but don't miss the Cullen Winter Blues band.

Adobe Bar (Map p393; ☎ 505-758-2233; 125 Paseo del Pueblo Norte; ⏰ from noon) There's something about this place. There's something about the chairs, the Taos Inn's history, the casualness, the vibe and the tequila. It's true, the packed streetside patio has some of the state's finest margaritas, along with an eclectic line-up of great live music like Manzanares and Madi Soto – and there's almost never a cover.

Sagebrush Inn (Map p391; ☎ 505-758-2254; 1508 Paseo del Pueblo Sur; ⏰ from 3pm) Live music almost nightly focuses on classic rock and country, which may well lure people onto the dance floor. Look for the huge 1929 mission-style building with giant wooden portals and an outdoor patio and then settle into the great long bar.

Entertainment

Que Pasa (Map p391; ☎ 505-758-7344; 338 Paseo del Pueblo Sur; ⏰ 10am-6pm Mon-Sat, noon-5pm Sun) This music store keeps a calendar of area events, and sells tickets to most of them.

El Taoseño Restaurant and Lounge (Map p391; ☎ 505-758-4142; 819 Paseo del Pueblo Sur; ⏰ 6am-9pm, to 2pm Sun) Mexican and Spanish performers, including mariachi, norteños, flamenco and more, liven up this top spot (also loved as a splurge for authentic New Mexican cuisine).

Taos Chamber Music Group (☎ 505-758-0150; http://taoswebb.com/tcmg; advance tickets adult/child $15/7.50, $16 at door) For classical and jazz, this group performs at venues throughout the region.

Taos Center for the Arts (TCA; Map p393; ☎ 505-758-2052; www.taoscenterforthearts.org; 133 Paseo del Pueblo Norte; tickets $5-30) In a remodeled 1890s adobe mansion, the TCA stages local and international performances of everything from chamber music to belly dancing to theater.

Storyteller Cinema (Map p391; ☎ 505-758-9715; 110 Old Talpa Cañon Rd; tickets adult/child $7.25/5) A few mainstream flicks and lots of artsy ones show at Taos' only movie house, right off Paseo del Pueblo Sur.

Shopping

Taos has historically been a mecca for artists, and the huge number of galleries and

NEW MEXICO

studios in and around town are evidence of this. Unfortunately, there are also a lot of T-shirt and coffee-mug shops (generally around the plaza).

Twining Weavers (Map p393; ☎ 505-758-9000; 133 Kit Carson Rd) Features handwoven rugs, tapestries and pillows.

El Rincón Trading Post (Map p393; ☎ 505-758-9188; 114 Kit Carson Rd) Dates back to 1909 when German Ralph Meyers, one of the first traders in the area, arrived. Even if you're not looking to buy anything, stop in here to browse through the dusty museum of artifacts, including Indian crafts, jewelry and Old West memorabilia.

Buffalo Dancer (Map p393; ☎ 505-758-8718; 103a East Plaza Taos) One of the older outlets for Native American jewelry on the plaza, this store carries Rodney Concha's fine pieces plus other work in silver and semiprecious stones.

Pueblo Drums (Map p393; ☎ 505-758-7929, 888-412-3786; www.pueblodrums.com; 110 Paseo del Pueblo Norte) Offers handmade drums by Phillip Martinez.

G Robinson Old Prints & Maps (Map p393; ☎ 505-758-2278; www.johndunnshops.com; 124d Bent St) The star of the Dunn House Shops carries a unique assortment of original maps of the American West, including railroad, geological and army surveys, plus collectable cartography from all over the world, dating as far back as the 1500s.

Getting There & Around

Tiny **Taos Municipal Airport** (Map p391; ☎ 505-758-4995; Hwy 64) simply serves as a landing strip for personal planes.

Greyhound (Map p391; ☎ 505-758-1144, 800-231-2222; www.greyhound.com; 1386 Paseo del Pueblo Sur) has daily bus services to Albuquerque ($28-30, 2¼ hours) and Santa Fe ($16-18, 1½ hours), with stops at Pilar and Española.

Faust (☎ 505-758-3410, 888-830-3410; one-way $45) leaves the Albuquerque Sunport daily at 1:30pm; the return shuttle leaves Taos for Albuquerque at 8am. Times are subject to change.

The **Chile Line** (☎ 505-751-4459; one way/round-trip 50¢/$1; ☽ 7am-7pm Mon-Sat) runs north–south along NM 68 between the Rancho de Taos post office and Taos Pueblo every 30 minutes, connecting to Greyhound buses. It also serves the Ski Valley and Arroyo Seco in winter. All buses are handicap-accessible.

Taos is about 90 minutes from Santa Fe via the Low Rd (p390); and about three hours on the more scenic High Rd (p388), though with recommended stops it could easily take all day.

TAOS PUEBLO

pop 2200 / elev 7100ft

Whatever you do, don't miss it. Built around 1450 and continuously inhabited ever since, **Taos Pueblo** (Map p391; ☎ 505-758-1028; www.taospueblo.com; Taos Pueblo Rd; adult/child $10/5, photography or video permit $5; ☽ 8am-4pm, closed for 10 weeks around Feb & Mar) is the largest existing multi-storied pueblo structure in the USA and one of the best surviving examples of traditional adobe construction. It's what all that pueblo-revival architecture in Santa Fe wants to be when it grows up.

One of New Mexico's largest and most spectacular Indian celebrations, **San Geronimo Day** (Sep 29 & 30) is celebrated with dancing and food. The huge **Taos Pueblo Pow-wow** (☎ 505-758-1028; www.taospueblopowwow.com; Taos Pueblo Rd; admission $5; ☽ 2nd week in Jul) features Plains and Pueblo Indians gathering for dancing and workshops as this centuries-old tradition continues. Of all the pueblos in northern New Mexico, Taos Pueblo has the most events and celebrations open to the public.

Sights & Activities

Taos Mountain Casino (Map p391; ☎ 505-737-0777, 888-946-8267; www.taosmountaincasino.com; Taos Pueblo Rd; ☽ 8am-1am Sun-Wed, 8am-2am Thu-Sat) has less razzle-dazzle – not to mention smoke – than some casinos. In fact, this cozy alcohol- and cigarette-free spot is one of the nicest places around to blow your cash.

Several craftspeople sell fine jewelry, *micaceous* (an aluminum mineral found in local rocks) pottery and other arts and crafts at the main pueblo, which you can peruse after touring the place. You can also grab tacos, chewy *horno* bread and other snacks ($3 to $5).

Just outside the pueblo, stop at the **Tony Reyna Indian Shop** (Map p391; ☎ 505-758-3835; Taos Pueblo Rd; ☽ 8am-noon & 1-6pm), which has a vast collection of arts and crafts from Taos and other tribes. Also see Shopping (p399) for more galleries that carry local artists' work.

Taos Indian Horse Ranch (Map p391; ☎ 505-758-3212, 800-659-3210; 1-/2hr easy rider $45/85, 2hr experienced rider $115) offers riding trips through Indian land, and a 24-hour rafting/riding/camping trip; call for details.

Eating

Tewa Kitchen (Map p391; ☎ 505-751-1020; Taos Pueblo Rd; dishes $5-13; ☻ 11am-5pm Wed-Mon, to 7pm Jun-Aug) It's one of the few places in the state where you can sit down to a plate of Native treats like *phien-ty* (blue-corn fry-bread stuffed with buffalo meat), *twa chull* (grilled buffalo) or a bowl of heirloom green chile grown on pueblo grounds.

Grab some green-chile stew or an ice-cream cone at surprisingly good **Lucky 7s** (Taos Mountain Casino; snacks $3-5; ☻ 10am-9pm Sun-Thu, to 10pm Fri & Sat) settle into some blackjack or slots, and stay a while.

ARROYO SECO

pop 1150 / elev 7100ft

For an unprocessed local flavor, a groovy plaza and a growing art scene, Arroyo Seco fills the bill. Just 10 minutes north of Taos, there's not much to do in the center of town but you'll find plenty of ways to not do anything.

Adobe and Stars B&B (Map p391; ☎ 505-776-2776, 800-211-7076; www.taosadobe.com; 584 Hwy 150; r incl breakfast $110-185; ✗ 🖳) Amazing rooms with real fireplaces and private entrances, fabulous mountains visible through huge windows, and simply wonderful vibes; this could well be the best B&B in New Mexico.

Abominable Snowmansion (Map p391; ☎ 505-776-8298; 476 Ski Valley Rd; dm $15-22, s/d campsites $12/16, teepees & cabins $34-38, r $45-52; ✗ 🖳) This HI hostel boasts a cozy lodge, with clean (if a tad threadbare) private rooms, a wonderful campground with an outdoor kitchen, fun teepees, surprisingly nice cabins and a sweet and simple dorm room.

Gypsy 360° (☎ 505-776-3166; 'downtown' Arroyo Seco; dishes $6-12; ☻ 8am-4pm Tue-Sat, 9am-3pm Sun) Right on the tiny plaza, with a sundrenched patio and relaxing interior, these folks cater to the traveler in everyone – serving Vietnamese spring rolls, Japanese sushi, Indonesian satay, and beer from all over the world. They're still getting things rolling but plan to have later hours and live music in the very near future.

Abe's Cantina y Cocina (Map p391; ☎ 505-776-8516; NM 150; dishes $3-8; ☻ 7am-5:30pm Mon-Fri, 7am-2pm Sat, cantina 10am-close) Predating the hipsters by a few decades, this small grocery store and deli is renowned for its tamales and cantina. It's a good place to throw one back and chat up folks.

Taos Cow Ice Cream (Map p391; ☎ 505-776-5640; 485 Hwy 150; dishes $3-6; ☻ 7am-7pm) On the way to Taos Ski Valley, this place has tasty all-natural ice cream, baked goods, breakfasts and deli sandwiches.

TAOS SKI VALLEY

If you're coming here to ski, you already know what awaits: one of the USA's most challenging mountains, one which even gets folks from Colorado all excited. And jealous.

Summer visitors to the village, which was once the rough-and-tumble gold mining town of Twining, will find an alpine wilderness with great hiking and cheap lodging. They won't find a gas station or grocery store though.

To reach the valley, take Hwy 64 north out of Taos to the blinking light, and veer right on Hwy 150 toward Arroyo Seco. The 20-mile drive winds along a beautiful mountain stream, but during the winter, the **Chile Line** (opposite) runs several times a day from downtown Taos.

Contact the **Taos Ski Valley** (Map p391; ☎ 505-776-2291, 800-776-1111; www.skitaos.org, www.taosski valley.com) for details on accommodations, ski school and ski packages.

Skiing

With more than 300in of all-natural powder annually, a peak elevation of 11,819ft and a 2612ft vertical drop, seasoned skiers are already stoked that more than half of the ski area's 72 trails are ranked experienced.

The valley's **Chamber of Commerce** (Map p391; ☎ 505-776-2291; 505-776-2233, 800-992-7669; www .taosskivalley.com; Village Office, Firehouse Rd; ☻ 8am-5pm) offers lots of skiing-lodging-dining-lessons packages. Rates for basic lift tickets vary throughout the season (adult $28-57, child $22-45). Week-long ski packages, including room, board, lessons and lift tickets, average $1,800 per person.

Hiking

Several trailheads are located along Hwy 150 to Taos Ski Valley and at the northern end of the Ski Valley parking lot. If you just want to romp, get tickets for the **chairlift**

(☎ 505-776-2291; adult/child $7/5; ⏱ 10am-4:30pm Thu-Mon late Jun-Sep) at **Taos Ski & Boot Company** (☎ 505-776-2292; NM 150) in the village, then walk on down the mountain along any of the super scenic and well-marked trails. No mountain bikes are allowed on the lift.

Sleeping & Eating

High season is Thanksgiving to Easter but there are dips in March and November and peaks during the holidays. From March to October, many lodges are closed and others offer excellent discounts.

Amizette Inn (Map p391; ☎ 505-776-2451, 800-446-8267; www.amizette.com; NM 150; r incl breakfast $75-160; ✗) With cabins and your choice of breakfast, this is a sweet spot to alight.

Austing Haus B&B (Map p391; ☎ 505-776-2649, 800-748-2932; www.austinghaus.com; NM 150; r incl breakfast $59-210; ✗) Two miles from the slopes, this claims to be the tallest wood-framed structure in the US; it definitely has the nicest dining room around.

Tim's Stray Dog Cantina (Map p391; ☎ 505-776-2894; 105 Sutton Place; dishes $3-11; ⏱ 8am-9pm winter, 11am-9pm summer) Head here for beer, chile *rellenos* and a mean breakfast burrito.

Crossroads Pizza (Map p391; ☎ 505-776-8866; 6 Thunderbird Rd; dishes $10, pizzas $16-20; ⏱ 11am-9:30pm) They deliver.

ENCHANTED CIRCLE

This 84-mile loop around Wheeler Peak, New Mexico's highest mountain at 13,161ft, passes a few small towns, hiking trails, camping sites and two ski basins (though Taos Ski Valley is by far the best). Take Hwy 64 north out of downtown Taos to Hwy 522, stopping by the DH Lawrence Memorial (opposite) before heading north to Questa. Detour west on Hwy 378 to Wild Rivers National Recreation Area and then retrace your steps back to Questa. Head east on Hwy 38 to Red River and follow the circle south to quiet Eagle Nest and Angel Fire, a ski resort plastered on a mountainside. Then take Hwy 64 west over the winding roads and through the woods of Carson National Forest you go – back to Taos following the streambed.

Questa

pop 1850 / elev 7670ft
Unlike other communities on the Enchanted Circle, Questa is primarily a mining town.

It also has a good-sized contingent of artists, subsistence farmers and other organic types. Everyone appreciates the view: an alpine bowl glittering with lakes and bright wildflowers, spectacularly torn by the great chasm just north. Stop at the **Questa Ranger Station** (☎ 505-586-0520; Hwy 38; ⏱ 8am-4:30pm Mon-Fri), about a mile east of Questa, before exploring any of the area wilderness.

Kachina Motel (☎ 505-586-0640; 2306 Hwy 522; s/d $45/65; ⏱ summer only; ✗) is cute, clean and pretty basic. There are a handful of restaurants in town, but the **Questa Cafe** (☎ 505-586-9631; 2422 NM 522; dishes $3-9; ⏱ 6am-10pm Mon-Sat, 6am-3pm Sun) is an expansive diner beloved for its Frito pie, chile-cheese fries (go for red) and homemade desserts.

Wild Rivers National Recreation Area

Awe-inspiring camping and hiking are available year-round at the beautiful and desolate Wild Rivers National Recreation Area, 26 miles north of Taos. The Wild Rivers Backcountry Byway (Hwy 378) is a 13-mile scenic loop through the area. Flat mesas covered in sagebrush surround the deepest part of the Rio Grande Gorge. Though the area can be relatively busy from May to August, it is easy to get away from the crowds.

Red River

pop 500 / elev 8750ft
There, on the edge of the vast alpine plains, you see it: a cluster of cheerfully painted shops and chalets, gleaming in the high desert sun. Red River, a ski resort for the masses, is decked out in German-peasant style with an Old West theme. It was founded as a mining town in the late 1800s and by the early 1900s was a bustling community of hard-drinking gold miners, with high hopes that were subsequently dashed by difficult-to-process ore. The view kept things cheerful, however, and hangers-on realized that their outdoor paradise might appeal to flatlanders with income.

Fortunately, the national forest prevents further development and protects its Old West feel. The buildings, in fact, look like they're right out of a movie set. Small-town family fun and outdoor recreation are the focus here. You won't find a wild nightlife or the post-hippie and ski clientele characteristics of Taos.

DETOUR: DH LAWRENCE RANCH & MEMORIAL

A pilgrimage-worthy destination for many reasons, **DH Lawrence's former home** (☎ 505-776-2245; off Hwy 522; admission free; ☉ sunrise-sunset), administered by UNM, allows folks to pay their respects to the famed author of such classics as Lady Chatterley's Lover.

Lawrence lived here for only a few months from 1924 to 1925, chopping wood, hiking trails and (with the help of his wife, Frieda) fighting off the attentions of typist Lady Dorothy Brett and patron Mabel Dodge Luhan. He somehow managed to complete the novella St Mawr in between. Relax beneath the Lawrence Tree, which attracts O'Keeffe fans (yep, it looks just like her painting) and contemplate what he called 'the best experience he ever had.'

Lawrence returned to Europe in 1925 and succumbed to tuberculosis in 1930. After Frieda moved back to Taos in 1934, she ordered his body exhumed and incinerated, and had the ashes brought to the ranch. Luhan and Brett both showed up uninvited to help scatter the said ashes which, according to legend, prompted Frieda to finally dump the remains into a wheelbarrow full of wet cement, saying, 'Let's see them try to steal this!'

Ascend the meandering paved walkway to the memorial, designed by Frieda's third husband, where the lump of concrete has been inscribed with DHL's initials and pressed leaves. It's heart-warming, with a scandalous giggle, just like Lawrence would have wanted.

To get to the memorial, drive past the farming village of Arroyo Hondo on Hwy 522 and follow signs down a dirt road on the right.

The **Chamber of Commerce** (☎ 505-754-2366, 800-348-6444; www.redrivernewmex.com; 100 E Main St; ☉ 8am-5pm Mon-Fri) publishes a comprehensive visitors guide to this tiny town and has great information on the surrounding wilderness.

ACTIVITIES

Frye's Old Town Shootout (☎ 505-754-6165; Main St; admission free; ☉ 9am-8pm Jun-Sep, hrs vary Oct-May) showcases the Second Amendment in all its 10-gallon-hatted, buckskin-jacketed glory as cowboys hold a faux showdown right in the center of town.

The area around Red River offers great hiking through the Carson National Forest's mountain meadows, lakes and streams. Pick up trail maps at the Chamber of Commerce. Trails vary from 2 to 16 miles and all levels of difficulty, and weave through Columbine Canyon, including one to the top of Wheeler Peak. The trailhead for Red River Nature Trail, an easy 2-mile trail along the stream that hugs the town, starts at the ski base. Beaver Ponds Trail and Middle Fork Lake Trail start at the end of Upper Valley Rd. You can either take an easy half-day hike to the Beaver Ponds, or park at the Middle Fork Trail lot and hike 2 miles, ascending 2000 vertical feet, to a high mountain lake.

The fishing here is also spectacular; several lakes and the Red River itself are stocked with rainbow and German brown trout. **Jeff Fagan** (☎ 505-754-2504; half/full day $100/150, each extra person $25) leads guided fly-fishing expeditions and supplies all your gear.

Though there aren't high-terrain mountain trails at **Red River Ski Area** (☎ 505-754-2223, 800-331-7669; www.redriverskiarea.com; Hwy 38; lift tickets adult/child $49/43; ☉ 9am-4pm Nov-Mar), it's a great place for beginners or if you find the intensity of Taos intimidating. Call for package rates, which include lifts and lesson.

With 1400 acres and 30km of groomed trails through the national forest and alpine fields, the **Enchanted Forest** (☎ 505-754-2374, 800-966-9381; www.enchantedforestxc.com; NM 38; adult/child $10/3; ☉ 9am-4:30pm Nov-Mar) is New Mexico's biggest cross-country ski area. Snowshoes and cross-country ski rentals are available for $12 a day. **Miller's Crossing** (☎ 505-754-2374; 417 W Main St) maintains the trails and runs a small shop.

SLEEPING & EATING

Reservations Unlimited (☎ 505-754-6415; www.red riverreservations.com; r $85-220; ✗) Ask them to arrange a stay for you in a vacation home, cabin or condominium.

Copper King Lodge (☎ 505-754-6210, 800-727-6210; http://redrivernm.com/copperking; Main St; r $69-169; ✗) Rough-hewn wood, rustic furnishings and a great backyard make these cabins and condos with kitchenettes a great deal.

NEW MEXICO

Lodge at Red River (☎ 505-754-6280, 800-915-6343; http://redrivernm.com/lodgeatrr; Main St; s/d $42/84, f $106-165; ✖) This huge prefab resort hotel has some of the nicest rooms in town, plus an onsite bar and restaurant with fresh trout all summer long.

Shotgun Willies (☎ 505-754-6505; cnr Main St & Pioneer Rd; dishes $3-10; ☺ 7am-3pm) Come here for enormous artery-clogging breakfasts for just $4, and barbecue by the pound.

Der Market (☎ 505-754-2974; 307 W Main; ☺ 7am-8pm) Not only is it adorable, it's the best place to resupply in the Enchanted Circle.

You can catch live acts all over town on weekends at **Bull o' the Woods Saloon** (☎ 505-754-2593; Main St; ☺ 1pm-2am).

Eagle Nest
pop 300 / elev 8300ft

This windswept high plains town is a better place to explore the great outdoors if you can't take the tourist overkill of Red River. The tiny **Chamber of Commerce** (☎ 505-377-2420, 800-494-9117; www.eaglenest.org; Therma Dr; ☺ 10am-4pm Tue-Sat) has reams of information.

Three miles north of Eagle Nest on US 64, **Cimarron Canyon State Park** (☎ 888-667-2757; tent/RV sites $10/14) runs alongside a dramatic 8-mile stretch of scenic Cimarron River, hued in pine greens and volcanic grays. It also encompasses Horseshoe Mine, beaver ponds, lots of wildlife and fishing, and plenty of hikes.

A graceful **Vietnam Veterans Memorial** (☎ 505-377-6900; Hwy 64; donations welcome), overlooking the vast and lonely plains, was the first US monument to honor troops in Vietnam. Dr Victor Westphall built the shrine in the memory of his son, David Westphall III, who died in battle in 1968. The **visitor center** (☺ 9am-5pm) displays artifacts, exhibits and personal items that attempt to convey the experience of being a soldier, or family member, during that conflict.

SLEEPING & EATING
Laguna Vista Lodge (☎ 505-377-6522, 800-821-2093; www.lagunavistalodge.com; 51 Therma Dr; r $80-100, f $150-200; ✖ ▢) This place has spacious, beautiful rooms and amenities galore, including kitchenettes in the family suites, while the neighboring **restaurant and saloon** (lunch dishes $10, dinner dishes $12-25; ☺ 11am-2am-ish Mon-Sat, noon-midnight Sun) serves burgers, salads and trout.

D&D Motel (☎ 505-377-2408, 800-913-9548; 116 Therma Dr; r $45-85, cabins with kitchenette $85-175) Don't expect a cookie-cutter experience here. This wonderful place – basically prefab trailers that they call cabins – is brightly decorated, and the 'large cabin,' which sleeps seven comfortably, is so much like landing in a comfy country home that you almost expect to find a pot of beans simmering in the kitchen.

ANGEL FIRE
pop 1050 / elev 8382ft

Twenty-two miles east of Taos, this ski resort is condominium heaven, sprawling on the edge of a plateau, and consisting of a few monotonous restaurants and motels and lots of condos.

The Angel Fire **Chamber of Commerce** (☎ 505-377-6661; 800-446-8117; www.angelfirechamber.org; 3407 Mountain View Blvd; ☺ 9am-5pm Mon-Fri) has lots of information.

Angel Fire Resort (☎ 505-377-6401, 800-633-7463; www.angelfireresort.com; NM 434; lift tickets 1-day adult/child $45/33; ☺ 9am-4pm Oct-Mar) As if the 2077ft vertical drop and 450 acres of trails weren't enough, the resort poured $40 million into a retrofit, adding lifts, trails, snowbiking (on bikes with skis), snowboarding and a ski park just for kids, making this one serious winter wonderland.

The resort takes advantage of the Taos Ski Valley snowboard ban with **Liberation Park**, featuring the state's only half-pipe: a Chris Gunnarson–designed, 400ft-long, competition-quality monster with a wicked 26% grade. You can, like, totally take advantage of this with a 'Learn to Snowboard, Keep the Gear' deal, including two days of lessons, boots and board for $349. Dude.

Conveniently, you can rent **skis** (☎ 800-633-7463; 1-day adult/child $22/13) and snowboards (adult/child $32/28), snowshoes ($12), snow bikes ($38), and just about anything else you might need for fun at the resort. But you may get better prices on rentals from **Bump's Ski Shop** (☎ 800-993-4754; N Angel Fire Rd).

Sleeping & Eating
There are some 2000 vacation homes in and around Angel Fire, and **Advantage Property Management** (☎ 505-377-2442, 888-924-2442; www.angelfirenightlyrentals.com) can set you up in one.

Angel Fire Resort (☎ 505-377-6401, 800-931-7001; www.angelfireresort.com; NM 434; r summer/winter $129/ 209, ste summer/winter $200/349; ☒ ▯ ☏) is comprehensive and self-contained, with three restaurants, package deals, childcare (☎ 505-377-4213; per day $50-60) and much more. Summer means empty rooms, so if you're coming at this time, bargain. With all the activities for children, it's a good deal for families, especially if the kids need a break from being cooped up in the car.

Red Cloud Ranch (☎ 505-751-0015; www.redcloud ranch.com; 250 Valle Escondido Rd; r incl breakfast $125-155; ☺ Jun-Sep) A cluster of rustic cabins at the epicenter of hiking and biking trails throughout adjacent Carson National Forest. The property offers a hot tub, trout pond and four-course dinner ($45).

Roasted Clove (☎ 505-377-0636; 48 N Angel Fire Rd; dishes $15-28; ☺ 5:30pm-9:30pm Wed-Mon) This is everyone's favorite fine-dining experience: maple-pecan pork tenderloin and mesquite-grilled filet are just a few gourmet dishes you'll be scarfing with the perfect fine-wine accompaniment.

Early Bird Cafe & Bakery (☎ 505-377-3992; 3420 NM 434; dishes $4-8; ☺ 6:30am-2pm Mon-Fri) This is the place for pastries, big breakfasts and excellent lunchtime sandwiches.

Willies Smokehouse (☎ 505-377-2765; NM 434; dishes $5-12; ☺ 11am-7:30pm) The place for barbecued chicken, beef and pork.

NORTHWESTERN NEW MEXICO

Dubbed 'Indian Country' for good reason – huge swaths of land fall under the aegis of the Navajos, Pueblo, Zuni, Apache and Laguna tribes – this quadrant of New Mexico showcases remarkable ancient Indian sites alongside modern, solitary Native American settlements. Since about 1075, the mesa-top Acoma Pueblo has commanded a simply spectacular site; starting around the mid-1500s, the Zunis (the most populous tribe in New Mexico) have carved out homes around their pueblo. From excavated dwellings at Chaco Culture National Park to unexcavated ones at Aztec Ruins National Monument, the mysteries of the land are carried on the wind. While Farmington may serve as the regional business

hub, Gallup reigns as its heart, a crossroads trading center for tribes and tourists.

It's not all Native Americans all the time, though. In Chama, it's all aboard. The Cumbres & Toltec Scenic Railroad transports travelers to the mid-19th century on a classic locomotive train trip through the mountains. And for driving fans, Hwy 64 east to Tres Piedras is hard to beat, as is Hwy 44 south of Cuba, part of the Jemez Mountain Trail (p348).

FARMINGTON & AROUND
pop 40,000 / elev 5400ft
Well sited for an overnight, the region's largest town serves as a pleasant base for excursions to nearby sites. Farmington itself has nice parkland on the San Juan River, a quaint downtown and some good trading posts, but most visitors hang around because they're visiting Shiprock, Salmon Ruin and Aztec Ruins (p408), just a few miles from Farmington. It's also the best place to stay when visiting the remote and desolate Chaco Culture National Historical Park (p407), located about two hours' drive south of Farmington.

Information
Bureau of Land Management (☎ 505-599-8900; 1235 La Plata Hwy; ☺ 7:45am-4pm Mon-Fri) Take Hwy 64 west across La Plata River and head north on La Plata Hwy.
Carson National Forest Ranger Station (☎ 505-632-2956; Hwy 64, Bloomfield; ☺ 8am-4:30pm Mon-Fri) Fourteen miles east of town.
Hospital (☎ 505-325-5011; 801 W Maple St)
Library (☎ 505-599-1270; 2101 Farmington Ave; ☺ 9am-9pm Mon-Thu, 9am-5pm Fri-Sun) Free Internet access.
Post office (☎ 505-325-5047; 2301 E 20th St)
Visitors Bureau (☎ 505-326-7602, 800-448-1240; www.farmingtonnm.org; Farmington Museum at Gateway Park, 3041 E Main St; ☺ 8am-5pm Mon-Fri)

Sights & Activities
IN FARMINGTON
Farmington proper won't hold your interest for long, but there are a few things worth a few moments. If it's foul weather or Junior is tired of the long drives, the **Children's Museum & Science Center** (☎ 505-599-1425; www.farmingtonmuseum.org/childrens.html; 302 N Orchard St; suggested donation $2; ☺ noon-5pm Tue-Sat) features fun hands-on exhibits pertaining to the region's culture and geology. There's no easier immersion.

The **Farmington Museum at Gateway Park** (☎ 505-599-1174; www.farmingtonmuseum.org; 3041 E Main St; suggested donation $2; ☻9am-5pm Mon-Sat) mounts national and juried regional art shows, and houses a permanent exhibit on the cultures and history of Farmington. After the Ancestral Puebloans departed the area, the Navajos and Utes moved in and were eventually followed by Anglo beaver-trappers and ranchers.

The Animas River waterfront and surrounding bosque has a developed 5-mile **River Corridor** that's pleasant to explore on foot or bike. Want to get your feet wet? Rent **fishing** and **river-rafting** gear for the Animas, La Plata and San Juan Rivers at the Outdoor Equipment Rental Center at **San Juan Community College** (☎ 505-566-3221; 4601 College Blvd; ☻3-6pm Tue-Thu, noon-6pm Mon & Fri). To find it, take 30th St east just past Hutton Rd to College Blvd and turn north.

You might not expect to play **golf** in these parts, but **Pinon Hills** (☎ 505-326-6066; www.farmington.nm.us) is one of the few public courses in the country with a five-star rating. To get here, take Butler Ave north to Sunrise Pkwy and head west.

NEARBY

Shiprock, a 1700ft-high volcanic plug and a lofty landmark for Anglo pioneers, is also a sacred site to the Navajo. It rises eerily over the landscape west of Farmington. It's certainly visible from Hwy 64, but there are better views from Hwy 666 and Indian Hwy 13, which almost skirts its base.

An ancient pueblo similar to Aztec Ruins (p408), **Salmon Ruin & Heritage Park** (☎ 505-632-2013; adult/child 6-16 $3/1; ☻8am-5pm Mon-Fri & 9am-5pm Sat & Sun) features a large village built by the Chaco people in the early 1100s. Abandoned, resettled by people from Mesa Verde (p323) and again abandoned before 1300, the site is named after George Salmon, an early settler who protected the area. Visit the adjoining park, which has remains of the Salmon homestead, petroglyphs, a Navajo hogan, an early Puebloan pithouse, a teepee and a *wickiup* (a rough brushwood shelter). Take Hwy 64 east toward Bloomfield.

Festivals & Events

Farmington likes to celebrate. Watch for the **Invitational Balloon Festival & Riverfest** (late May); the week-long **Connie Mack World Series**

Baseball Tournament (☎ 505-327-9673; 1101 N Fairgrounds Rd; mid-August), featuring top amateur ballplayers and scouts from college and professional teams; the **Totah Festival** (Labor Day weekend), with juried Native American arts and crafts and a Navajo rug auction; and the **Northern Navajo Nation Fair** (late Sep or early Oct), featuring a rodeo, powwow and traditional dancing. This fair is perhaps the most traditional of the large Indian gatherings and begins with the Night Way, a complex Navajo healing ceremony, and the *Yei Bei Chei* chant, which lasts for several days.

Sleeping

Kokopelli's Cave (☎ 505-325-7855; www.bbonline.com/nm/kokopelli; r $220-260; ☒) For something truly unique, this incredible 1650 sq ft cave is carved 70ft below the surface into the sandstone above La Plata River. Equipped with a kitchen stocked for breakfast and lunch, a VCR with videos and a hot tub, this spacious cave dwelling offers magnificent views over the desert and river. The isolation is magnificent. A 3-mile drive on dirt roads and a short hike is required to reach it.

Silver River Spa Retreat & Adobe B&B (☎ 505-325-8219, 800-382-9251; www.silveradobe.com; 3151 W Main St; r $115) Three miles from downtown, this lovely two-room place offers a peaceful respite among the trees on the San Juan River. Fall asleep to the sound of the river, wake to organic blueberry juice and enjoy a morning walk to the prairie-dog village. The additional guest house is attractively rustic, and is made of adobe and timbers.

Knights Inn (☎ 505-325-5061; 701 Airport Dr; r $40) This place, with 21 large rooms and weekly rates, has the cheapest, simplest and cleanest rooms in town. It fits the bill, nothing more, nothing less.

Mom & Pop RV Park (☎ 800-748-2807; 901 Illinois Ave; RV sites $17) Tent campers would be better off at Navajo Lake State Park (p409), but RVers will be perfectly happy here.

Eating & Drinking

Three Rivers Eatery & Brewhouse (☎ 505-324-2187; 101 E Main St; dishes $5-12; ☒) Managing to be both trendy *and* kid-friendly, this hippish place has good food and its own microbrews. Try the homemade potato skins or artichoke and spinach dip, but keep in mind that the steaks are substantial. Plenty of spiffy sandwiches (like a Thai turkey wrap) and soups (broccoli cheddar) are served at lunchtime.

Main Street Bistro (☎ 505-334-0109; 122 N Main St; dishes under $10; ☉ 7am-4pm Mon-Fri, to noon Sat) Yes! It seems like such a simple request: great coffee and a muffin to match. But it's all too rare outside Santa Fe, Taos and Albuquerque. This wonderful place has vegetarian sandwiches, good quiches and creative soups. You might just want to move in.

Something Special Bakery & Tearoom (☎ 505-325-8183; 116 N Auburn Ave; dishes $5; ☉ breakfast & lunch Tue-Fri) This cute Victorian, complete with a back patio, has healthy pastries, imaginative lunch dishes and a whopping selection of desserts. It never disappoints.

El Charro Cafe (☎ 505-327-2464; 737 W Main St; dishes $5-8) Small and homey, this café offers good Mexican food. The enchiladas are worthy of a drive.

Clancy's Pub (☎ 505-325-8176; 2703 E 20th St; dishes $7-14; ☉ lunch & dinner) Popular with 20- and 30-somethings, Clancy's offers imported beers to wash down hamburgers, Mexican food and other pub grub. Get more exotic at the dinnertime sushi bar. Dine inside where the rock music is loud, or on their patio (unfortunately overlooking a strip).

Sonya's Cookin' USA (☎ 505-327-3526; 2001 Bloomfield Hwy; dishes $6-13) This popular diner serves good inexpensive blue-plate lunch specials. You may wait in line for breakfast, but it'll be worth it.

Entertainment

Sandstone Productions (☎ 877-599-3331; tickets $6-11; ☉ Wed-Sat mid-Jun–mid-Aug) Mounts upwards of 30 annual shows at the Lions Wilderness Park Amphitheatre, a natural sandstone outdoor theatre 3 miles out of town.

Clancy's Pub (left) is always popular, but try testing your country two-stepping skills at the busy **Top Deck Lounge** (☎ 505-327-7385; 515 E Main St; ☉ 11am-1:30am Mon-Sat). Wednesday is the decidedly un-PC 'Ladies' Night,' when there's no cover charge. Karaoke takes center stage on Thursday, while country-western bands ($5 cover) perform on Friday and Saturday.

Shopping

Several trading posts offer high-quality Indian crafts (including Navajo rugs, p181). **Fifth Generation Trading Company** (☎ 505-326-3211; 232 W Broadway; ☉ 9am-5:30pm Mon-Sat), founded in 1875, displays a big selection.

DETOUR: CHACO CULTURE NATIONAL HISTORICAL PARK

Chaco, the center of a culture that extended far beyond the immediate area, was connected to Aztec (p408) and Salmon Ruins (opposite) by carefully engineered 30ft-wide roads. Very little of the road system is easily seen today, but about 450 miles have been identified from aerial photos and ground surveys. Clearly, this was a highly organized and integrated culture.

The **park** (per vehicle/bike $8/4; ☉ sunrise-sunset) contains massive and spectacular Puebloan buildings, evidence of 5000 years of human occupation, set in a remote high desert environment. The largest building, Pueblo Bonito, towers four stories tall and may have had 600 to 800 rooms and kivas. None of Chaco's sites have been reconstructed or restored. If you like isolation and using your imagination, few places compare. If you're also visiting Mesa Verde (p323), you may be disappointed here, especially considering how long it takes to reach the site. You'll need a whole day for a trip here.

All park routes involve rough and unpaved dirt roads, which can become impassable after heavy rains or snow. Park rangers prefer that visitors enter via Hwy 44/550 on the north side. About 3 miles south of the Nageezi Trading Post on Hwy 44/550 and about 50 miles west of Cuba, turn south at mile marker 112.5 on CR 7900, which is paved for 5 miles. Continue on the marked unpaved county road for 16 miles to the park entrance.

Park facilities are minimal – there's no food, gas or supplies. The nearest provisions are along Hwy 44, 21 miles from the **visitor center** (☎ 505-786-7014; www.nps.gov/chcu; ☉ 8am-5pm early Sep–late Jun, until 6pm late Jun-early Sep), where free backcountry hiking permits (no camping) are available. Inquire here about night-time astronomy programs (April to October).

The **Gallo Campground** (campsites $10) operates on a first-come, first-served basis. There are no hookups, but toilets, grills and picnic tables are available. Bring your own wood or charcoal. Water is available at the visitor center parking lot only.

About 15 miles west of town on Hwy 64, look for **Hogback Trading Company** (☎ 505-598-5154; 3221 Hwy 64; ☼ 8am-5pm Mon-Sat) and **Bob French's Navajo Rugs** (☎ 505-598-5621; 3459 Hwy 64; ☼ 8am-5pm Mon-Sat).

Getting There & Away

Mesa Airlines (☎ 800-637-2247; www.mesa-air.com) flies from Albuquerque; **America West Express** (☎ 800-235-9292; www.americawest.com) flies from Phoenix, and **United Express** (☎ 800-241-6522; www.united.com) flies from Denver.

TNM&O/Greyhound (☎ 505-325-1009; www.greyhound.com; 101 E Animas) has one or two daily buses to Albuquerque ($33, four hours) and Durango, Colorado ($13, 1¼ hours).

AZTEC

pop 6000 / elev 5600ft

Although Aztec is primarily on the traveler's map because of the reconstructed Great Kiva at Aztec Ruins, the old downtown of Aztec still has several interesting turn-of-the-19th-century buildings, many on the National Register of Historic Places. Cruise the pleasant tree-lined residential district, too. If you're in the area, time a visit with the annual **Aztec Fiesta Days** (first weekend in Jun), with arts and crafts, food booths and a bonfire during which 'Old Man Gloom' is burned to celebrate the beginning of summer.

Hwy 516 from Farmington (14 miles northeast) becomes Aztec Blvd in town and continues as Hwy 173 toward Navajo Dam State Park. For more details, visit the **visitor center** (☎ 505-334-9551, 888-838-9551; www.aztecnm.com; 110 N Ash; ☼ 8am-5pm Mon-Fri).

If you're in the area to explore ancient sites, consider hooking up with **Aztec Archaeological Consultants** (☎ 505-334-6675; 210 Main St; ☼ 8am-5pm Mon-Fri), which offers guided half- and full-day tours to nearby sites. Half-day tours cost $95 for one or two people and $25 for each additional person ($15 for children under 12).

Sights & Activities

An alternative to the bigger and more visited sites like Chaco Culture National Historical Park (p407) and Mesa Verde National Park (p323), the 27-acre **Aztec Ruins National Monument** (☎ 505-334-6174; www.nps.gov/azru; adult $4, child 17 & under free; ☼ 8am-5pm, to 6pm Jun-Aug) features the largest reconstructed kiva in the country, with an internal diameter of al-

most 50ft. Let your imagination wander as you sit inside the Great Kiva. Rangers give early-afternoon talks at the site (c 1100) about ancient architecture, trade routes and astronomy during the summer months. They're very informative.

The small but excellent **Aztec Museum & Pioneer Village** (☎ 505-334-9829; 125 N Main Ave; adult $3, child 11-17 $1; ☼ 9am-5pm Mon-Sat Jun-Aug, 10am-4pm Mon-Sat Sep-May) features an eclectic collection of historical objects, including telephones, barbershop chairs and a great display of late-19th-century regional photographs. Outside, a small 'pioneer village' shows off original or replica early buildings, such as a church, jail and bank.

If you've been racing around looking at ancient sites, perhaps you'd like to sit still at the **Aztec Speedway** (☎ 505-334-2023; off Hwy 544; ☼ races 7pm most Sat Apr-Sep), which resounds with the roar of automobile engines. It sure breaks the silence.

Sleeping & Eating

Enchantment Lodge (☎ 505-334-6143; 1800 W Aztec Blvd; s/d $32/48; ☒) When you need shelter from the elements, this basic motel has 20 rooms.

Miss Gail's Inn (☎ 505-334-3452, 888-534-3452; www.cptnet.com/~missgail; 300 S Main St; s/d incl breakfast $60/70; ☐) Built in 1907 as 'The American Hotel,' this historic and ramshackle two-storey brick structure is decorated with early photographs and period pieces. Rooms may be too frilly and Victorian for some folks; others may think them charming and sweet.

Ruins Road RV Park (☎ 505-334-3160; 312 Ruins Rd; tent/RV sites $10/20) Though not recommended for tent campers, this place is only a few minutes' walk from the national monument.

Aztec Restaurant (☎ 505-334-9586; 107 E Aztec Blvd; lunch dishes $3-7, dinner dishes $7-15; ☼ 6am-9pm) Stop by for big portions of reasonably priced Mexican and American fare.

NAVAJO DAM

Trout are jumpin' and visitors are floating. Navajo Lake, which stretches over 30 miles northeast and across into Colorado, was created by damming the San Juan River. At the base of the dam, there's world-class **trout fishing** from late June through September. You can fish year-round (although you'll need a permit), but catch-and-release

NEW MEXICO

regulations protect the stocks. The tiny community of Navajo Dam has several outfitters providing equipment, information and guided trips. Talk to the folks at **Born-n-Raised on the San Juan River, Inc** (☎ 505-632-2194; Hwy 173), based at Abe's Motel & Fly Shop, and **Rizuto's Fly Shop** (☎ 505-632-3893, 800-525-1437; www.rizutos.net).

River floating is also popular around here. Rent boats at the **Navajo Lake Marina** (☎ 505-632-3245) or the **Sims Mesa Marina** (☎ 505-320-0885) and put in at the Texas Hole parking lot at milepost 12 on Hwy 511. Then lazily float 2.5 miles to Crusher Hole. Ahhh. The Enchanted Hideaway Lodge (below) also rents a couple of drift boats ($125 daily).

Three recreation areas at the **state park** (☎ 505-632-2278; www.nmparks.com; NM 511; per car per day $5) offer boating, hiking, fishing and camping. Head 25 miles east of Aztec via US 550 and Hwy 173.

Sleeping & Eating

Enchanted Hideaway Lodge (☎ 505-632-2634; www .enchantedhideawaylodge.com; Hwy 173; ste & houses $55-150) This friendly and low-key place has several highly recommended and pleasant suites as well as a private house and condos with kitchens and gas grills. The spacious Stone House, with a heavenly outdoor hot tub set in a grove of trees, is particularly nice, is furnished with Southwestern flair and sleeps up to eight (each additional person over two costs $15).

Soaring Eagle Lodge (☎ 505-632-3721, 800-866-2719; Hwy 173; r per person incl board $120) Nestled under the cliffs against the river, this beautiful and peaceful place has simple suites with kitchenettes. Try to get one of the units unit right on the river, and while you're at it, ask about their multinight guided fishing tours too.

El Pescador (☎ 505-632-5129; Hwy 173; dishes $5-10) Every town has one and this is it: a place serving standard Mexican and American food.

The BLM runs three campgrounds with hookups ($14) and without ($10). The biggest one is **Lake Pine River**, just past the dam on Hwy 511, with a visitor center and marina. About 10 miles south of the lake, **Cottonwood Campground** (Hwy 511) occupies a lovely spot under the cottonwoods on the river. It has drinking water and toilets but no showers.

JICARILLA APACHE INDIAN RESERVATION

pop 3200

The Apache were relatively late arrivals in the Southwest, migrating from the north in the 14th century. The hawkish group took advantage of the more peaceful Pueblo peoples already living here. Indeed, the Zuni Indian word for 'enemy,' *apachu*, led to the Apache's present name. Jicarilla (pronounced hic-a-*ree*-ya) means 'little basket,' reflecting great skill in basket weaving and other crafts. Apache crafts generally draw visitors to the 1360-sq-mile reservation, home to about 3200 Native Americans.

Tiny **Dulce**, on Hwy 64 in the northern part of the reservation, is the **tribal capital** (☎ 505-759-3242 ext 218; ☯ 8am-5pm Mon-Fri). Unlike at most reservations, alcohol is available. No permits or fees are needed to drive through the reservation; photography is permitted.

CHAMA

pop 1200 / elev 7880ft

Only recently has the small mountain community of Chama been ever-so-slightly rediscovered. Even with first-ever sidewalks, it still feels like an outpost. Sure, Indians lived and hunted here for centuries, and Spanish farmers settled the Chama River Valley in the mid-1700s, but it was the arrival of the Denver & Rio Grande Railroad in 1880 that really put Chama on the map. Although the railroad closed, the prettiest part later reopened as one of the most scenic train trips in the Southwest.

Orientation & Information

East of the Jicarilla Reservation, Hwy 64 joins Hwy 84, crosses the Continental Divide and drops into Chama. Downtown is 1.5 miles north of the so-called Y-junction of Hwy 84/64 and Hwy 17. The main street is variously called Main, Terrace Ave or Hwy 17; the intersection, known as the Y, is the main reference point in town. A handy **information center** (☎ 505-756-2235; 2375 Hwy 17; ☯ 8am-6pm) is located at the Y.

Sights & Activities

The **Cumbres & Toltec Scenic Railway** (☎ 505-756-2151, 888-286-2737; www.cumbresandtoltec.com) is both the longest (64 miles) and highest (over the 10,015ft-high Cumbres Pass) authentic narrow-gauge steam railroad in the USA. It's a beautiful trip, particularly in September and October during fall foliage, through mountains, canyons and high desert. Some carriages are fully enclosed, but none are heated. Dress warmly.

The train runs between Chama and Antonito, Colorado, every morning from late May to mid-October. Several options for riding the train are offered. You can take a van to Antonito (a 1½ hour drive) and then ride the train back to Chama (adult $70, child 2-11 $37; six hours). Alternatively, go to the midpoint of Osier, Colorado, then return to your starting point (adult/child $70/37, six hours). Whatever you do, make reservations two weeks in advance. There is a snack bar and rest room on board, and the train makes a lunch stop in Osier.

Want to go backpacking and fishing in the San Juan Mountains? It's also possible to get off at Osier and be picked up at a later date. About 13 miles from Osier (on foot), the HI/AYH **Conejos River Hostel** (☎ 719-376-2518; dm members/nonmembers incl breakfast $12/15; ♡ usually closed in winter) is remote and uncrowded, except in July and on holiday weekends. Reservations are required and credit cards are not accepted. To shorten the hike, get off the train at the sublet water station (between Osier and Antonito) and hike 6 miles downhill to the hostel. If you're driving, the hostel is 10 miles west of Antonito; call for directions.

Although based in Taos, **Los Rios River Runners** (☎ 505-776-8854, 800-544-1181; www.losriosriverrunners.com) runs raft trips on the Rio Chama, which are great fun.

Several outfitters specialize in winter activities, including **Chama Ski Service** (☎ 505-

756-2492; www.cvn.com/~porters), which can outfit you with skis and provide information on ski touring. It can also provide back-country touring equipment including snowshoe rentals. **Cumbres Nordic Adventures** (☎ 505-756-2746, 888-660-9878; www.yurtsogood.com) offers back-country ski tours in the snowy San Juan Mountains and deluxe back-country yurt rentals for $100 to $115 per night.

Festivals & Events
Chama has a few events worth dropping in for, including the **Chama Chile Classic Cross-Country Ski Race** (early or mid-Feb), which attracts hundreds of competitors to 3.1-mile and 6.2-mile races; the **Chama Valley Music Festival** (every Fri & Sat in Jul), which features national and international acts; and **Chama Days** (early Aug), which features a rodeo, firefighters' water fight and chile cook off.

Sleeping & Eating
Gandy Dancer B&B (☎ 505-756-2191, 800-424-6702; www.gandydancerbb.com; 299 Maple Ave; r $99-129; ✕) Ensconced in an early-1900s house, this ultra tasteful place offers seven pristine and stylish rooms, an outdoor hot tub and views. The helpful hosts provide information, breakfast, reservations and dinners (November to March) or box lunches on request.

Chama Trails Inn (☎ 505-756-2156, 800-289-1421; www.chamatrailsinn.com; 2362 Hwy 17; r $61-70) More than a roadside motel, this place has 16 rooms with character – thanks to an abundance of handmade Southwestern furniture, local artwork and hand-painted tiles. A few rooms are further warmed with a gas fireplace. A communal hot tub and sauna come in handy after hiking.

DETOUR: ONWARD TOWARD TRES PIEDRAS
From Chama take Hwy 84/64 about 11 miles south to see the spectacular cliffs in scenic **Brazos Canyon**. Stay a while in extreme privacy. Set on 400 acres heading into the canyon, the handsome **Timbers at Chama** (☎ 505-588-7950; www.thetimbersatchama.com; 131 Hwy 512; d $100-175, cabins $200; ✕) has double rooms and a private cabin; rates include a hearty breakfast.

Just south of Los Brazos in Los Ojos, visit **Tierra Wools** (☎ 505-588-7231, 888-709-0979; www.handweavers.com; 91 Main St; r $65-85), a 100-year-old weaving cooperative in a rustic, century-old building. On weekends, village artisans carry on the Hispanic weaving tradition, with hand spinning, dying and weaving. In addition to a two-bedroom guesthouse, Tierra Wools also offers weaving classes (April to October).

From tiny TA (as Tierra Amarilla is locally know), head east on scenic Hwy 64 over a 10,000ft pass in the Tusas Mountains to Taos, 80 miles away. This road is closed in winter.

Foster Hotel (☎ 505-756-2296; 393 S Terrace Ave; s/d $45/53) If you're looking for local culture, look no further. Built in 1881 as a bordello, the hotel is the only building in Chama that wasn't wiped out by a massive fire in the 1920s. A few of the rooms are said to be so haunted that the management doesn't rent them.

Elkhorn Lodge & Café (☎ 505-756-2105, 800-532-8874; www.elkhornlodge.net; Hwy 84; s/d $65/79, cabins $89-125) Choose a simple but spacious motel room in the main log cabin or a freestanding cabin with a kitchenette (especially great for families) and then join 'em for a riverside chuckwagon barbecue dinner on Saturday night during the summer (adult $18, child $9). Evenings include old-time cowboy music.

Village Bean (☎ 505-756-1663; 425 Terrace Ave; dishes under $8; ☸ 7am-2:30pm Mon-Fri, 7am-3:30pm Sat & Sun) This lively space is a welcome addition to Chama's dining and hanging-out scene. Excellent coffee and tasty baked goods are a hallmark. Lunchtime sandwiches are served with homemade bread; soups and salads are made with equally fine attention. Kudos to them.

High Country Restaurant & Saloon (☎ 505-756-2384; 2289 S Hwy 17; breakfast buffet $8, lunch dishes $5-10, dinner dishes $8-22; ☸ lunch & dinner Mon-Sat, breakfast Sun) This Wild West saloon dishes up burgers, Mexican food, steak and seafood.

Rio Chama RV Campground (☎ 505-756-2303; tent sites $12, RV sites $19-24; ☸ May–mid-Oct) Situated on the Rio Chama, this camping area has views of the railroad bridge; you can watch (and hear) the steam train. There's a separate tenting area with covered picnic shelters.

CUBA

pop 600 / elev 6200ft

Mountainous Cuba is a convenient stop on the way to or from Chaco Culture National Historical Park (p407), since accommodation closer to Chaco is limited. Cuba is still about 50 miles to the turnoff for Chaco. Look for the **ranger station** (☎ 505-289-3265; ☸ 7am-4:30pm Mon-Fri) and **visitor center** (☎ 505-289-3808; ☸ 9am-1pm & 2-4pm Mon-Fri), both on Hwy 44.

Set in 360 beautiful acres in the Nacimiento Mountains, the friendly and recommended **Circle A Ranch Hostel** (☎ 505-289-3350; www.circlearanch.info; off Hwy 550; dm $20, r $35-55;

☸ May–mid-Oct) is a gem. The lovely old adobe lodge, which has exposed beams, grassy grounds, hiking trails and a classic kitchen, is a peaceful and relaxing place to hang out. Choose between private bedrooms (some with quilts and iron bedsteads) and shared bunk rooms.

Frontier Motel (☎ 505-289-3474; 6474 Main St; s $32-40, d $45-60) is the best choice of all the cheap motels in town.

El Bruno's Cantina y Restaurante (☎ 505-289-9429; Hwy 44; lunch dishes $5-7, dinner dishes $6-17) is an unexpected delight, easily one of the best restaurants in northwest New Mexico. With a beautiful outdoor patio and a handsome and artsy interior, El Bruno's serves absolutely delicious New Mexican food, with plenty of creative variations on the fajitas, *carne asada* and *chimichangas* theme.

For campers, Hwy 126 east of Cuba leads 11 miles to **Clear Creek** and **Rio Las Vacas campgrounds** (sites $5; ☸ May-Oct), operated by the USDA Forest Service (USFS).

ACOMA PUEBLO

Journeying to the top of 'Sky City' is journeying into another world. There are few more dramatic mesa-top locations; the village sits 7000ft above sea level and 367ft above the surrounding plateau. One of the oldest continuously inhabited settlements in North America, people have lived in Acoma Pueblo since the later part of the 11th century. In addition to a singular history and a dramatic location, it's also famous for pottery, which is sold by individual artists on the mesa. There is a distinction between 'traditional' pottery (made with clay dug on the Reservation) and 'ceramic' pottery (made elsewhere with inferior clay and simply painted by the artist), so ask the vendor.

Visitors can only reach Sky City on guided tours, which leave from the **visitor center** (☎ 505-469-1052, 800-747-0181; tours adult $10, child 6-17 $7) at the bottom of the mesa. These tours are offered daily every 45 minutes, except for July 10 to July 13 and either the first or second weekend in October, when the pueblo is closed to visitors. Though you must ride the shuttle to the top of the mesa, you can choose to walk down the rock path to the visitor center on your own. Definitely do this.

Festivals and events include a **Governor's Feast** (February), a Harvest Dance on **San Esteban Day** (September 2) and festivities at the **San Esteban Mission** (December 25 to 28). Photography permits cost $10; no videos are permitted.

The Sky City visitor center is about 13 miles south of I-40 exit 96 (15 miles east of Grants) or I-40 exit 108 (50 miles west of Albuquerque).

Sky City Hotel (☎ 505-552-6123, 888-759-2489; www.skycityhotel.com; exit 102 off I-40; r $70-80; ☒), the pueblo's modern casino, has 132 motel-style rooms and suites dressed up in Southwestern decor. Amenities include live entertainment, dining options, room service and a pool.

KICKIN' IT DOWN ROUTE 66 IN NEW MEXICO

Never has a highway been so symbolic as Rte 66. Snaking across the belly of America, this fragile ribbon of concrete pavement first connected the prairie capital of Chicago with the California dreamin' of Los Angeles in 1926. Along the way, lightning-bug towns sprouted up with neon signposts, motor courts and drive-ins, all providing the simple camaraderie of the road.

Called the 'Mother Road' in John Steinbeck's novel *The Grapes of Wrath*, Rte 66 came into its own during the Depression years, when hundreds of thousands of migrants escaping the Dust Bowl slogged westward in beat-up old jalopies painted with 'California or Bust' signs. Meanwhile unemployed young men were hired to pave the final stretches of muddy road. They completed the job, as it turns out, just in time for WWII.

Hitchhiking soldiers and factory workers rode the road next. Then, amid the jubilant postwar boom, Americans took their newfound optimism and wealth on the road, essentially inventing the modern driving vacation. And so the era of 'getting your kicks on Rte 66' was born. Traffic flowed busily in both directions.

But just as the Mother Road hit her stride, President Dwight Eisenhower, a US army general who had been inspired by Germany's autobahn, proposed a new interstate system for the USA. Slowly but surely, each of Rte 66's more than 2200 miles was bypassed. Towns became ghosts and traffic ground nearly to a halt. The highway was officially decommissioned in 1984.

A movement for preservation of the Mother Rd resulted in the National Historic Route 66 Association (www.national66.com), a nonprofit alliance of federal, state and private interests. Every year another landmark goes up for sale, but more are rescued from ruin.

Today this phoenix-like highway relies on travelers daring enough to leave the interstate behind for a combination of blue-line highways and gravel frontage roads. You can still spy relics of the original road, stay in a jewel of a 1930s motor court, revel in sunsets over the Painted Desert or splash in the Pacific Ocean. This is not just your mother's Mother Road. It's yours.

New Mexico revels in all 475 miles of its Rte 66 legacy. From east to west, cruise through the yesteryear towns of Tucumcari (p418), Santa Rosa (p417) and Las Vegas (p419); sophisticated Santa Fe (p363); quirky Albuquerque (p349); detour to Acoma Pueblo (Sky City; p411); stop in Grants (opposite) and hard-edged Gallup (p415), the unofficial capital of Indian country. In addition to publishing a quarterly magazine, the active New Mexico Route 66 Association (h505-224-2802; www.rt66nm.org; 1415 Central Ave NE, Albuquerque) has archives, news and event calendars on its website.

For complete information on this classic route consult Lonely Planet's excellent *Road Trip Route 66* guidebook. For Arizona locales, see p189 and for a classic itinerary, see p25.

GRANTS

pop 8800 / elev 6400ft

You can hear the sounds – boom, bust, bust, boom – if you listen carefully. They are the sounds of Grants' up-and-down history. These days it's simply a strip, with several motels that make it a convenient, albeit uninteresting, base from which to explore the region. Originally an agricultural center and railway stop founded in the 1880s, Grants experienced a major mining boom when uranium was discovered here in 1950.

Santa Fe Ave (business I-40, Hwy 118 or Rte 66) is the main drag through town. It runs parallel and north of I-40 between exits 81 and 85.

The Grants **Chamber of Commerce** (☎ 505-287-4802, 800-748-2142; www.grants.org; 100 N Iron St; 🕑 9am-4pm Mon-Sat) and **Cibola National Forest Mount Taylor Ranger Station** (☎ 505-287-8833; 1800 Lobo Canyon Rd; 🕑 8am-noon & 1-5pm Mon-Fri) provide more detailed information if you need it.

Sights & Activities

The **New Mexico Mining Museum** (☎ 505-287-4802; adult $3, child 7-18 $2; 🕑 9am-4pm Mon-Sat) bills itself as the only uranium-mining museum in the world. Although the mine no longer operates because of decreased demand, it remains America's largest uranium reserve. You can go underground by elevator in a miner's cage.

The 11,301ft peak of **Mt Taylor** is the highest in the area, and the mountain offers great views and hiking. Head northeast on Lobo Canyon Rd (Hwy 547) for about 13 miles to where it changes into gravel USFS Rd 239. For a great view follow 239 and then USFS Rd 453 for another 3.3 miles to **La Mosca Lookout** at 11,000ft, about a mile northeast of Mt Taylor's summit.

Festivals & Events

The **Mt Taylor Quadrathlon** (mid-Feb) between Grants and Mt Taylor combines cycling, running, cross-country skiing and snowshoeing. Individuals and teams of two to four athletes compete. Then there's the **Fire & Ice Route 66 Bike Rally** (Jul), a two-day Harley Davidson festival with motorcycle rodeo events and live music. The **Chile Fiesta** (early Oct) celebrates chile with a chile cook off and other events.

Sleeping & Eating

Cimarron Rose (☎ 505-783-4770, 800-856-5776; www .cimarronrose.com; 689 Oso Ridge Rd; ste $80-120) Although it's 30 miles southwest of Grants, this B&B is conveniently located on Hwy 53 between El Malpais and El Morro in the Zuni Mountains. With hiking in the Cibola National Forest just off the 20-acre property, it's a peaceful and pleasant rural alternative to the chain hotels in Grants or Gallup. Cimarron Rose offers two Southwestern-style suites, with tiles, pine walls and hardwood floors (one has a kitchen).

Coal Mine Campground (Lobo Canyon Rd; $5 🕑 mid-May–late Sep) This pleasantly wooded place is 10 miles northeast of town and has a nature trail and flush toilets, but no showers.

Blue Spruce RV Park (☎ 505-287-2560; Hwy 53; tent/RV sites $8/12) For tent and RV sites with showers and flush toilets, get off I-40 at exit 80.

Uranium Café (519 W Santa Fe Ave; dishes $4-7; 🕑 breakfast & lunch Mon-Sat) Across from the Mining Museum this funky place, complete with an old Chevy parked in the middle of the restaurant, serves up the town's best green chile. They certainly have a sense of humor about their status in town: 'our food will blow your mine.'

El Cafecito (☎ 505-285-6229; 820 E Santa Fe Ave; breakfast dishes $3-5, lunch & dinner dishes $5-8; 🕑 7am-9pm Mon-Fri, to 8pm Sat) This great local hangout is lively with families chowing down on enchiladas and burgers in a comfortable setting. You want to know where the locals go, now you know.

Four B's Restaurant (☎ 505-285-6697; Santa Fe Ave; dishes $6-10) Four B's dishes up burgers, New Mexican cuisine, pasta and steaks almost around the clock.

Getting There & Away

Greyhound (☎ 505-285-6268; www.greyhound.com; stops at 1700 W Santa Fe Ave) offers several daily buses to Albuquerque ($15.50, 1¼ hours), Flagstaff, Arizona ($46.50, 5½ hours) and beyond. Pay the driver in cash.

EL MALPAIS NATIONAL MONUMENT

Volcanic badlands in New Mexico? El Malpais (pronounced el mahl-pie-*ees*; meaning 'bad land' in Spanish) consists of almost 200 sq miles of lava flows abutting adjacent sandstone. All tolled, five major flows

DETOUR: LAGUNA PUEBLO

From Albuquerque you can zoom along I-40 for 150 miles to the Arizona border in a little over two hours. But don't. Stop at the Indian Reservation of Laguna, about 40 miles west of Albuquerque or 30 miles east of Grants. Founded in 1699, it's the youngest of New Mexico's pueblos and consists of six small villages. Since its founders were escaping from the Spaniards and came from many different pueblos, the Laguna people have a very diverse ethnic background.

The imposing stone and adobe **San José Mission** (☎ 505-552-9330; 9am-3pm Mon-Fri), visible from I-40, was completed in 1705 and houses fine examples of early Spanish-influenced religious art. It will beckon you off the interstate.

Main **feast days** include San José's (March 19 and September 19), San Juan's (June 24) and San Lorenzo's (August 10 and Christmas Eve). Contact **Laguna Pueblo** (☎ 505-552-6654) for more information.

have been identified; the most recent one is pegged at 2000 to 3000 years old. Prehistoric Native Americans may have witnessed the final eruptions since local Indian legends refer to 'rivers of fire.' Scenic Hwy 117 leads modern-day explorers past cinder cones and spatter cones, smooth *pahoehoe* lava and jagged aa lava, ice caves and a 17-mile-long lava tube system.

El Malpais is a hodgepodge of National Park Service (NPS) land, private land, conservation areas and wilderness areas administered by the BLM. Each area has different rules and regulations, which change from year to year. The **BLM** (☎ 505-287-7911) in Grants and the **BLM Ranger Station** (☎ 505-528-2918; Hwy 117; 8:30am-4:30pm), 9 miles south of I-40, have permits and information for the Cibola National Forest. **El Malpais Information Center** (☎ 505-783-4774; www.nps.gov/elma; Hwy 53; 8:30am-4:30pm), 22 miles southwest of Grants, and **El Malpais National Monument** (☎ 505-285-4641; www.nps.gov/elma; 123 E Roosevelt Ave, Grants; 8am-4:30pm Mon-Fri) have permits and information for the lava flows and NPS land. Backcountry camping is allowed, but a free permit is required.

Though the terrain can be difficult, there are several opportunities for hiking through the monument. An interesting but rough hike (wear sturdy footwear) is the 7.5-mile (one-way) Zuni-Acoma Trail, which leaves from Hwy 117 about 4 miles south of the ranger station. The trail crosses several lava flows and ends at Hwy 53 on the west side of the monument. Just beyond **La Ventana Natural Arch**, visible from Hwy 117 and 17 miles south of I-40, is the Narrows Trail, about 4 miles (one-way). Thirty miles south of I-40 is Lava Falls, a 1-mile loop.

County Rd 42 leaves Hwy 117 about 34 miles south of I-40 and meanders for 40 miles through the BLM country on the west side of El Malpais. It passes several craters, caves and lava tubes (reached by signed trails) and emerges at Hwy 53 near Bandera Crater. Since the road is unpaved, it's best to have a high-clearance 4WD. If you go spelunking, the park service requires each person to carry two sources of light and to wear a hard hat. Go with a companion – this is an isolated area.

At the privately owned **Bandera Ice Cave** (☎ 505-783-4303, 888-423-2283; adult $8, child 5-12 $4; 8am-4:30pm), 25 miles southwest of Grants on Hwy 53, a large chunk of ice (tinted green because of Arctic algae) stays frozen year-round. The ice cave, known to the Pueblo Indians as Winter Lake, is located in part of a collapsed lava tube.

EL MORRO NATIONAL MONUMENT

Throughout history travelers have liked to leave their mark, as in 'Kim was here.' El Morro is proof positive of that. Also known as Inscription Rock, it's been a travelers' oasis for a few millennia. Well worth a stop, this 200ft sandstone outcrop is covered with thousands of carvings, from pueblo petroglyphs at the top (c 1250) to inscriptions by Spaniard conquistadors and Anglo pioneers.

To reach **El Morro** (☎ 505-783-4226; www.nps .gov/elmo; adult/child $3/free; 9am-5pm, until 7pm in summer), head 43 miles southwest of Grants or 52 miles southeast of Gallup on Hwy 53. Of the two trails that leave the visitor center, the paved, half-mile loop to **Inscription Rock** is wheelchair accessible. The unpaved, 2-mile **Mesa Top loop trail** requires a steep climb to the pueblos. Trail access stops one hour before closing.

El Morro RV Park & Cabins (☎ 505-783-4612; Hwy 53; tent/RV sites $10/18; cabins $65-75) This NPS campground, with drinking water and pit toilets, is about a mile east of the visitor center and offers 26 sites and six cabins. Call ahead in the winter since it may be closed from October through April.

Ancient Way Café (☎ 505-783-4612; 4018 Hwy 53; dishes $6-10; ⏰ 10am-6pm Mon-Sat, to 4pm Sun) The only real area dining option is in pleasant little Ramah, a few miles west of El Morro. It's a no-frills place, somewhere to sustain your metabolism rather than fill your soul. Think along the lines of hash browns, fry bread, pork chops and chicken strips.

ZUNI PUEBLO

This pueblo, 35 miles south of Gallup, is well-known for its jewelry, and you can buy beautiful pieces at little shops throughout the town along Hwy 53. Other than that, there's not much going on, which is precisely why you might want to spend a little time driving around its housing developments. It'll give you a bare bones hint of modern reservation life, albeit from the outside looking in. Information is available from the extremely helpful **Zuni Tourism Program Office** (☎ 505-782-7238; ⏰ 8am-5:30pm), which dispenses photography permits. The office also offers daily tours, walking past stone houses and beehive-shaped mud ovens to the massive **Our Lady of Guadalupe Mission**, featuring impressive locally painted murals of about 30 life-size kachinas (p186). The church dates from 1629, although it has been rebuilt twice since then.

The **Ashiwi Awan Museum & Heritage Center** (☎ 505-782-4403; Ojo Caliente Rd; admission by donation; ⏰ 9am-5pm Mon-Fri) displays early photos and other tribal artifacts. They'll also cook traditional meals for groups of 10 or more ($10 per person) with advance reservations. Next door, **Pueblo of Zuni Arts & Crafts** (☎ 505-782-5531) sells locally made jewelry, baskets and other crafts.

The most famous ceremony at Zuni is the all-night **Shalak'o ceremonial dance** (last weekend in Dec). The **Zuni Tribal Fair** (late Aug) features a powwow, local food, and arts-and-crafts stalls. To participate in any ceremony hosted by the Zuni community, you must attend an orientation; call the program office for more information.

The friendly **Inn at Halona** (☎ 505-782-4547, 800-752-3278; www.halona.com; 1 Shalaka Dr; r $79, incl breakfast $85; ✗), decorated with local Zuni arts and crafts, is the only place to stay on the pueblo. Since each of the eight pleasant rooms is very different, try to check out as many as you can to see which fits your fancy. Full breakfasts are served in the flagstone courtyard in the summer; room service is provided by a grocery store in the back. The inn is located behind Halona Plaza, south from Hwy 53 at the only four-way stop in town.

GALLUP
pop 20,200 / elev 6515ft

This crossroads feels like a real town; walk the downtown suffused with a Native American and wildish West feel. Gallup serves as the Navajo and Zuni peoples' major trading center. Because of that, you'll find many trading posts, pawnshops, jewelry shops, and arts-and-crafts galleries in the historic district. It's arguably the best place in New Mexico for top-quality goods at fair prices. Although Gallup's economy relies on trade and tourism, it's pretty darn quiet (especially in the winter). Gallup grew up in 1881 when the railroad arrived, and when coal was discovered soon thereafter, it remained an important mining town until the mid-20th century.

Developed in 1926, the famous Rte 66 proudly struts its stuff here (p412), serving as the main drag and running parallel to and south of I-40, Rio Puerco and the railway line.

Information
Chamber of Commerce (☎ 505-722-2228; www.gallup chamber.com; 103 W Hwy 66; ⏰ 8am-5pm Mon-Fri) Next to the Gallup Cultural Center. Be sure to check out the permanent exhibit on the Navajo code-talkers of WWII.
Gallup Visitor Information Center (☎ 505-863-3841, 800-242-4282; www.gallupnm.org; 701 Montoya Blvd; ⏰ 8am-5pm Mon-Fri)
Hospital (☎ 505-863-7000; 1901 Red Rock Dr; ⏰ 24hr emergency)
Library (☎ 505-863-1291; 115 W Hill Ave) Free Internet access.
Police (☎ 505-722-2231; 451 State Rd 564)
Post office (☎ 505-863-3491; 950 W Aztec)

Sights & Activities
Gallup is lined with about 20 downtown structures of historic and architectural interest, built between 1895 and 1938. Most are located along 1st, 2nd and 3rd Sts between

Hwy 66 and Hill Ave and are detailed in a brochure found at the visitor center. Among these is the small **Gallup Historical Museum** (☎ 505-863-1363; 300 W Rte 66; admission by donation; ☻ 8:30am-3:30pm Mon-Fri), in the renovated, turn-of-the-19th-century Rex Hotel.

The **Gallup Cultural Center** (☎ 505-863-4131; www.southwestindian.com; 218 E Rte 66; ☻ 8am-5pm) houses a small but well-done museum with Indian art, including excellent collections of both contemporary and old kachina dolls (p186), pottery, sand painting and weaving. A 10ft-tall bronze sculpture of a Navajo code-talker honors the sacrifices made by many men of the Navajo Nation in WWII. A tiny theatre screens films about Chaco Canyon and the Four Corners region.

Six miles east of town, beautiful **Red Rock State Park** (☎ 505-863-1337; ☻ 8am-4:30pm Mon-Fri, trading post 6:30am-5:30pm) has a little museum with modern and traditional Indian crafts, a campground (right) and hiking trails.

Festivals & Events

Thousands of Native Americans and non-Indian tourists throng the streets of Gallup and the huge amphitheater at Red Rock State Park for **Inter-Tribal Indian Ceremonial Gallup** (first week Aug). It includes a professional all-Indian rodeo, beautifully bedecked ceremonial dancers from many tribes and a powwow with competitive dancing. Book accommodations as far ahead as possible during this and several other annual events. Foremost among them is the **Navajo Nation Fair** (first weekend Sep), held in nearby Window Rock, Arizona (p180). The **Lions Club Rodeo** (3rd week Jun) is the most professional and prestigious of several area rodeos. Almost two hundred colorful hot-air balloons take part in demonstrations and competitions at the **Balloon Rally** (first weekend Dec) at Red Rock State Park (p168).

Local Native Americans perform social Indian dances at 7pm nightly from late June to early September, near the Amtrak Station.

Sleeping

It's a seller's market during Ceremonial week and other big events, when hotel and motel prices can double.

El Rancho (☎ 505-863-9311, 800-543-6351; www .elranchohotel.com; 1000 E Hwy 66; s/d $42/55, ste $80) Gallup's most historic hotel opened in 1937 and quickly became known as the 'home of the movie stars.' Many of the great actors of the '40s and '50s stayed here, including Humphrey Bogart, Katharine Hepburn and John Wayne. El Rancho features a superb Southwestern lobby, restaurant (below), bar and an eclectic selection of simple rooms, including suites that sleep up to six. Next door, a modern 24-room **motel** is under the same ownership and has less interesting rooms for a few dollars less.

Red Rock Park Campground (☎ 505-722-3839; tent/RV sites $15/18) This beautiful setting has showers, flush toilets, drinking water and a grocery store.

Eating & Drinking

Oasis Mediterranean Restaurant (☎ 505-722-9572; 100 E Hwy 66; dishes $5-17; ☻ 10am-9pm Mon-Sat) This pleasant gallery excels in conventional Mediterranean cuisine like baba ganoush, falafel and baklava, but they also get much more creative with chicken dishes prepared with blazingly fresh components. It's a breath of fresh air in these parts.

El Rancho Restaurant (☎ 505-863-9311; 1000 E Hwy 66; breakfast & lunch dishes $6-10, dinner dishes $6-19) For real old-world Western atmosphere, this hotel (left) eatery rules. Photos of old-time movie stars plaster the walls; heavy furniture dots the landscape. It's straight out of a movie set. As for the food, it tends toward upscale-diner grub like pancakes, burgers and steaks.

Coffee House (☎ 505-726-0291; 203 W Coal Ave; dishes under $10; ☻ 7am-9:30pm Mon-Thu, to 11pm Fri & Sat, to 4pm Sun) With local art on the walls, over-stuffed couches and newspapers, this place has the feel of a small college-town hang out. But there's no mistaking its Southwestern roots – a pressed-tin ceiling and historic building attest to that. As you might imagine, it serves strong espresso, chicken salads, soups, turkey sandwiches and homemade desserts.

Earl's Restaurant (☎ 505-863-4201; 1400 E Hwy 66; dishes $6-13) Earl's has been serving great green chile and fried chicken (but no alcohol) since the late 1940s. And the locals know it; the fast-food, diner-like place is packed on weekends. Perhaps you'll even get some shopping done here; Navajos sell goods at the eatery to tourists passing through.

Ranch Kitchen (☎ 505-722-2537; 3001 W Hwy 66; dishes $6-13; ☻ 5am-9pm Tue-Sun) Almost everybody seems to stop by this place because of the combination of reasonable prices, good food (barbecued and smoked meats, prime rib and the like) and the availability of beer and wine. Raised knotty pine ceilings and pine furniture set the bar higher than other places in town.

Genaro's Café (☎ 505-863-6761; 600 W Hill Ave; dishes $6-12; ⏱ lunch & dinner Tue-Sun) This small, out-of-the-way place serves large portions of New Mexican food, but no alcohol. If you like your chile hot, you'll feel right at home here. And if you're up for a green-chile cheeseburger, ask for chile on the side or your buns will become soggy really quickly – the burger swims in the green stuff.

Getting There & Around

The **Greyhound bus station** (☎ 505-863-3761), at the Amtrak building next to the cultural center, has four daily buses to Flagstaff, Arizona ($38.50, three hours), Albuquerque ($23, 2½ hours) and beyond.

Amtrak (☎ 800-872-7245; www.amtrak.com; 201 E Hwy 66), which has an 'Indian Country Guide' providing informative narration between Gallup and Albuquerque, runs an afternoon train to Albuquerque and a daily evening train to Flagstaff, Arizona.

NORTHEASTERN NEW MEXICO

East of Santa Fe, the lush Sangre de Cristo Mountains give way to high and vast rolling plains. Dusty grasslands stretch to infinity, and further – to Texas. Cattle and dinosaur prints dot the landscape around Tucumcari and Clayton, as do elk at Vermejo Park Ranch in Raton and boy scouts at the Philmont Scout Ranch in Cimarron. This is a land of extremes, from formerly fiery volcanoes in Capulin to currently hot springs in Montezuma. Ranching is an economic mainstay of this sparsely populated corner and on many stretches of the road, you'll see more cattle than cars.

The Santa Fe Trail (p347), along which pioneer settlers rolled in wagon trains, ran from New Mexico to Missouri. And you can still see the wagon ruts in some places off I-25 between Santa Fe and Raton. Because of this trade route, Las Vegas and

Raton became important centers in the late 1800s, and both towns retain the flavor of that era in their many well-preserved buildings. If you're looking for a bit of the Old West without a patina of consumer hype, this is the place. Another scenic byway, Rte 66 (p412), more or less parallels I-40 east; it's a nice stretch from Santa Rosa to Tucumcari. As if that weren't enough, the region is also dotted with small lakes and beautiful canyons.

SANTA ROSA
pop 2750 / elev 4600ft

Scuba in Santa Rosa? Yup, that's right. Settled in the mid-19th century by Spanish farmers, Santa Rosa's modern claim to fame is, oddly enough, as the scuba-diving capital of the Southwest. There's not much else going on here, though.

Orientation & Information

Due east of Albuquerque, it and Tucumcari (p418) were once key stops along old Rte 66 (p412). Today, three freeway exits have shifted most travelers' experiences of Rte 66. From the western exit 273, the main street begins as Coronado St, then becomes Parker Ave through downtown, before becoming Will Rogers Dr when it passes exits 275 and 277. Most hotels and restaurants lie along the main thoroughfare, part of the celebrated Rte 66.

The **Chamber of Commerce** (☎ 505-472-3763; www.santarosanm.org; 486 Parker Ave; ⏱ 8am-5pm Mon-Fri) has more information.

Sights & Activities

One of the 10 best spots to dive in the country is, surprisingly, here in li'l ol' Santa Rosa. How could that be? Because of the bell-shaped, 81ft-deep **Blue Hole**. Fed by a natural spring flowing at 3000 gallons a minute, the water in the hole is both very clear and pretty cool (about 61°F to 64°F). It's also 80ft in diameter at the surface and 130ft in diameter below the surface. Platforms for diving are suspended about 25ft down; divers get permits ($8) from the **dive shop** (☎ 505-472-3370; ⏱ 8am-5pm Sat & Sun), located right at the hole.

Nine miles south of town along Hwy 91, tiny **Puerto de Luna** was founded in the 1860s and is one of the oldest settlements in New Mexico. The drive there is pretty, winding through arroyos surrounded by eroded

NEW MEXICO

sandstone mesas. In town you'll find an old county courthouse, a village church and a bunch of weathered adobe buildings. It's all quite charming, as long as you're not in a hurry to do something else.

The **Route 66 Auto Museum** (☎ 505-472-1966; 2766 Rte 66; adult $5, child under 12 free; ☺ 7:30am-7pm May-Aug, to 5pm Sep-Apr) pays homage to the mother of all roads. It boasts upwards of 35 cars from the 1920s through the 1960s, all in beautiful condition, and lots of 1950s memorabilia. It's a fun place; enjoy a milkshake at the '50s-style snack shack.

Festivals & Events

In keeping with the Rte 66 theme, the **Annual Custom Car Show** (Aug or Sep) attracts vintage-and classic-car enthusiasts, as well as folks driving strange things on wheels. The **Santa Rosa Fiesta** (third week Aug) is homespun, to say the least, with a beauty-queen contest and the bizarre, annual Duck Drop, for which contestants buy squares and then wait for a duck suspended over the squares to poop – if the poop lands on their square, they win cold cash.

Sleeping & Eating

Budget 10 Motel (☎ 505-472-3454; 120 Hwy 54; s/d $28/32) Lots of inexpensive motels, many of which have been around since before the interstate, cater to I-40 traffic. Of those, this is a good, clean place to stay.

Santa Rosa Lake State Park (☎ 505-472-3110; per car per day $5, tent/RV sites $10/14; ☺ 24hr) The hot showers are handy here. From downtown Santa Rosa, turn north on 2nd St and follow the signs.

Joseph's Restaurant & Cantina (☎ 505-472-3361; 865 Will Rogers Dr; dishes $6-12) Rte 66 nostalgia lines the walls of this popular place, family owned since its inception in 1956. Many of the bountiful Mexican and American recipes have been handed down through the generations. Burgers and steaks are as popular as anything smothered in green chile. Joseph's also mixes the best margaritas on Rte 66.

Comet II Drive-in (☎ 505-472-3663; 239 Parker Ave; dishes $5-10; ☺ 11am-9pm Tue-Sun) This classic drive-in offers options beyond the usual burgers and fries, like *carne adobada* and green-chile enchiladas.

Silver Moon (☎ 505-472-3162; Will Rogers Dr; dishes $5-13) The homemade chile *relents* are tasty here, as is most of the other diner

grub dressed up with a New Mexican twist. There's a reason it's been around since the late 1960s.

TUCUMCARI

pop 6000 / elev 4080ft

The biggest town on I-40 between Albuquerque (173 miles west) and Amarillo (114 miles east), Tucumcari has one of the best-preserved sections of the mythological road. Not surprisingly, it still caters to travelers with inexpensive motels, several classic Rte 66 buildings and souvenir shops like the Tee Pee Curios. A **chamber of commerce** (☎ 505-461-1694; 404 W Tucumcari Blvd) keeps sporadic hours.

Tucumcari lies barely north of I-40. The main west–east thoroughfare between these exits is old Rte 66, called Tucumcari Blvd through downtown. The principal north–south artery is 1st St.

Sights & Activities

Several rooms of the **Tucumcari Historical Museum** (☎ 505-461-4201; 416 S Adams St; admission $2; ☺ 8am-5pm Mon-Sat, to 6pm May-Sep) consist of reconstructions of early Western interiors, such as a sheriff's office, a classroom and a hospital room. It's an eclectic collection, to say the least, displaying a barbed-wire collection alongside Indian artifacts.

Well worth a visit, though, is the **Mesalands Dinosaur Museum** (☎ 505-461-3466; 222 E Laughlin St; adult/child $5/2.50; ☺ noon-5pm Tue-Sat, to 8pm mid-Mar–mid-Nov), which showcases real dinosaur bones and has hands-on exhibits. Casts of dinosaur bones are done in bronze (rather than the usual plaster of Paris), which not only shows fine detail, but also makes them works of art.

At the east end of town, the 770-acre **Ladd S Gordon Wildlife Preserve** (off Tucumcari Blvd) encompasses Tucumcari Lake. Wintering ducks begin arriving mid-October, and geese a month later. To reach it, take the gravel road north when you see the Motel 6.

The **Blue Swallow Motel** (☎ 505-461-9849; 815 E Tucumcari Blvd) is a beautifully restored Rte 66 motel listed on the State and National Registers of Historic Places. It has a great lobby and a classic neon sign that's featured in many articles about Rte 66.

Sleeping & Eating

KOA (☎ 505-461-1841; www.koa.com; 6299 Quay Rd; tent/RV sites $16/23; 'kamping kabins' $25) A quarter mile east of I-40 exit 355, this place has tent sites, RV hookups and one-room log 'kabins' that tend to have a more private feel. Each of the latter has porches with swings so you can drink in views of the Tucumcari Mountains.

Del's Restaurant (☎ 505-461-1740; 1202 E Tucumcari Blvd; dishes $5-15; ☒ Mon-Sat) Del's is popular in these here parts for its hearty salad bar.

Rubees (☎ 505-461-1463; 605 W Tucumcari Blvd; dishes $5-10; ☒ 7am-7pm). If your arteries can take the hardening, *chicarones* (fried pork skins) are a Rubees New Mexican specialty.

Entertainment

Odeon Theater (☎ 505-461-0100; 123 S 2nd St; adult $5, child under 11 $4) This renovated, cool old place screens movies.

Lizard Lounge (☎ 505-461-0500; Best Western Pow Wow Inn, 801 W Tumcumcari Blvd) For weekend drinks and dancing, this lounge has two-steppin' to live country and western.

Getting There & Away

Buses to Albuquerque ($38, three hours) depart three or four times daily from the **Greyhound terminal** (☎ 505-461-1350, 800-229-9424; www.greyhound.com; 2618 S 1st St).

LAS VEGAS & AROUND

pop 14,600 / elev 6470ft

Not to be confused with the glittery, over-the-top city to the west, this Vegas is one of the loveliest towns in New Mexico, and one of the largest and oldest towns east of the Sangre de Cristo Mountains. Architecture and Wild West buffs will be equally enthralled here. Its eminently strollable downtown has a pretty plaza and some 900 historic buildings listed in the National Register of Historic Places. Although they keep company with each other, you'll find far more late-19th-century Victorian and Queen Anne buildings than 16th-century adobe. The classic Western backdrop is the perfect spot for a high noon shootout, an ambiance exploited in cowboy flicks like *Wyatt Earp* and *The Ballad of Gregorio Cortez*.

Home to the Comanche people for some 10,000 years, the Mexican government established Las Vegas in 1835, just in time to serve as a stop along the Santa Fe Trail (p347) and later the Santa Fe Railroad. It quickly grew into one of the biggest, baddest boomtowns in the West, and in 1846 the USA took possession of it. Those days are gone, but Las Vegas still retains a sienna-tinted elegance and lively social swirl, much of which radiates from the city's two small universities. It's also the gateway to two striking wilderness areas: the Pecos Wilderness (p371) and Las Vegas National Wildlife Refuge (p420).

Las Vegas is located on I-25, 65 miles east of Santa Fe. Hwy 85 or Grand Ave, which runs north–south, parallels the interstate and is the main thoroughfare.

Information

Carnegie Public Library (☎ 505-454-1403; 500 National; ☒ 8am-5pm Mon-Fri, to 8pm Thu, 8am-noon Sat) Free Internet access.

Chamber of Commerce (☎ 505-425-8631, 800-832-5947; www.lasvegasnm.org; 701 Grand Ave; ☒ 9am-5pm Mon-Fri)

Hospital (☎ 505-426-3500; 104 Legion Dr; ☒ 24hr emergency)

Police (☎ 505-425-7504; 318 Moreno)

Post office (☎ 505-425-9387; 1001 Douglas Ave)

Santa Fe National Forest Ranger Station (☎ 505-425-3534; 1926 7th St; ☒ 8am-5pm Mon-Fri)

Sights & Activities

IN LAS VEGAS

The Chamber of Commerce publishes walking tours of various historic districts and beautiful neighborhoods surrounding the plaza and Bridge St. Around the historic center, note the lovely **Plaza Hotel** (p420); it was built in 1880 and is still in use.

The small but informative **City of Las Vegas Museum & Rough Rider Memorial Collection** (☎ 505-454-1401; 727 Grand Ave; admission free; ☒ 9am-4pm Mon-Fri, 10am-3pm Sat year-round, noon-4pm Sun Apr-Sep) chronicles the fabled cavalry unit led by future US President Theodore Roosevelt in the 1898 fight for Cuba. More than one-third of the volunteer force came from New Mexico, and in this museum you'll see their furniture, clothes and military regalia.

Santa Fe Trail Interpretive Center (☎ 505-425-8803; 127 Bridge St; admission free; ☒ 10am-4pm Mon-Sat) The local historical society's impressive collection is on display here, including old photos and artifacts from Las Vegas' heyday as a rough-and-tumble trading post along the Santa Fe Trail (p347). Guided tours are available.

NEW MEXICO

NEARBY

Five miles southeast of Las Vegas on Hwys 104 and 67, the 14 sq mile **Las Vegas National Wildlife Refuge** (☎ 505-425-3581; Rte 1; admission free; ◷ dawn-dusk) has marshes, woodlands and grasslands to which upwards of 275 bird species have found their way. Visitors can follow a 7-mile drive and walking trails.

The pretty **Villanueva State Park** (☎ 505-421-2957; per car per day $5, tent/RV sites $10/14), about 35 miles south of Las Vegas, lies in a red rock canyon on the Rio Pecos valley. A small visitor center and self-guided trails explain the area's history – it was once a main travel route for Indians and, in the 1500s, for the Spanish conquistadors. Head south on I-25 for 22 miles, then take Hwy 3 south for 12 miles. Tent and RV sites have showers.

En route along Hwy 3, you'll pass the Spanish colonial villages of **Villanueva** and **San Miguel** (the latter with a fine church built in 1805), surrounded by vineyards belonging to the **Madison Winery** (☎ 505-421-8028; Hwy 3; ◷ 10am-4:30pm Mon, Tue, Thu & Fri, noon-4:30pm Sun), which has a tasting room. While here, don't miss **La Risa** (☎ 505-421-3883; Hwy 3; dishes $5-8; ◷ 8am-8pm Mon-Sat, to 2pm Sun), a gourmet anomaly in the middle of nowhere, with homemade desserts, breads, and pastries.

Montezuma, 5 miles northwest of Las Vegas on Hwy 65, is famous for Montezuma Castle, built in 1886 as a luxury hotel close to local hot springs. (It's now owned by the United World College and is under renovation.) The nearby natural **hot springs** (☎ 505-454-4200; Hwy 65; admission free; ◷ 5am-midnight), just north of the college, reputedly have curative and therapeutic powers.

Festivals & Events

The four-day festivities surrounding the **Fourth of July** here are a colorful mix of Hispanic and Anglo festivities, and include Mexican folk music, dancing and mariachi bands. Other events include the **San Miguel County Fair** (third weekend Aug) and a **Harvest Festival** (third Saturday Sep), with music and food.

Sleeping

Plaza Hotel (☎ 505-425-3591, 800-328-1882; www .plazahotel-nm.com; 230 Old Town Plaza; r incl breakfast $88-116; ▯) This is Las Vegas' most celebrated and historic lodging. It was opened in 1882 and carefully remodeled a century later; plenty of architectural details abound.

The elegant brick building now offers 36 comfortable accommodations in antique-filled rooms.

Carriage House B&B (☎ 505-454-1784; www.new mexicocarriagehouse.com; 925 6th St; r incl breakfast $75, with bathroom $85; ▯) Ensconced in a Victorian home dating back to 1893, this B&B offers five homey rooms as well as afternoon tea (for an extra $10).

Star Hill Inn (☎ 505-425-5605; www.starhillinn.com; 247 Las Dispensas Rd, Sapello; cottages $170-380) The tiny village of Sapello, 13 miles north of Las Vegas on Hwy 518, looms large as 'an astronomers' retreat in the Rockies.' What does that mean? Well, that complimentary telescopes are offered, for instance. Other than that, there are eight comfortable cottages with fireplaces and kitchens; a two-night minimum is required. The inn, sitting high at 7200ft, occupies 195 acres laced with hiking and cross-country skiing trails. Since there are no stores nearby, you should bring along food to fully utilize the kitchens.

El Fidel (☎ 505-425-6761; www.elfidelhotel.com; 500 Douglas St; d/ste $60/85; ✗) This elegant, if faded, 1920s belle of a hotel has character to spare (perhaps too much character for some folks), a worthy lounge with a **coffee bar** (◷ 7am-5pm) and an attractive pub, the **Wolff's Den** (◷ 5pm-2am).

Inn on the Santa Fe Trail (☎ 505-425-6791, 888-448-8438; www.innonthesantafetrail.com; 1133 Grand Ave; s $69-79, d $74-84, incl breakfast; ▯) Along with a good restaurant, central courtyard and shaded grounds, this well-maintained place has 30 large, modern rooms (some with microwaves and refrigerators) decorated in Southwestern hacienda-style decor.

Eating

Estella's Café (☎ 505-454-0048; 148 Bridge St; lunch dishes $5-7, dinner dishes $7-12; ◷ 11am-3pm Mon-Wed, to 8pm Thu-Fri, to 7pm Sat) Estella's devoted patrons treasure their homemade red chile, *menudo* and scrumptious enchiladas. Owned by the Gonzalez family since 1950, this crowded gem is the best place in town for simple and tasty New Mexican food.

Pastime Deli (☎ 505-454-1755; 113 Bridge St; dishes $4-10; ◷ 11am-2:30pm Mon-Fri & 5-7pm Wed-Sat) Need a new pastime? Dropping in here could quickly become it. For some of the healthiest food in the area, this café has no equal. Think along the lines of grilled chicken dressed up with avocado.

Semilla Natural Foods (☎ 505-425-8139; 510 University Ave; ☻ 10am-6pm Mon-Fri, to 5pm Sat) Vegetarians and healthy eaters unite! This natural grocery store has organic treats galore.

Spic 'n Span (☎ 505-426-1921; 715 Douglas St; dishes $5-12; ☻ 6am-6pm Mon-Sat, 7am-3pm Sun) This place is cheerful, casual and usually crowded, thanks to a great bakery and better food.

Hot Rods Deli (☎ 505-426-8612; Douglas Ave at 6th; dishes $5-7; ☻ 11am-6pm) Used as a real life set in the movie, *All the Pretty Horses,* this place serves sandwiches at a classic soda fountain.

Drinking & Entertainment

Cafés and coffee shops on Bridge St may have poetry readings or folk music.

Byron T Saloon (☎ 505-425-3591; 230 Old Town Plaza) Within the Plaza Hotel (opposite), this bar hosts live jazz, blues and country music on weekends.

Fort Union Drive-In (☎ 505-425-9934; 3300 7th St; per car $5; ☻ Mar-Nov) One of New Mexico's few remaining drive-in movie theatres lies just north of town and has great views of the surrounding high desert. But you're supposed to be watching the flicks, remember?

Shopping

Los Artesanos Bookstore (☎ 505-425-8331; 220 N Plaza; ☻ 11am-4pm Tue-Sat) Operational since 1949, this lovely shop has a good selection of used and rare books on Las Vegas as well as the entire Southwest. It's an old-fashioned place; owner Diana Stein still does all the paperwork on an Underwood typewriter.

You'll find other bookstores along Bridge St, tucked away among galleries and antique stores – it's a fun place to browse and shop.

Getting There & Around

TNM&O buses (☎ 505-425-8387, 505-243-4435; www.greyhound.com; 1901 W Grand) stop at Pino's Truck Stop several times a day on their way to Raton and Santa Fe.

Amtrak (☎ 800-872-7245; www.amtrak.com) runs a daily train between Chicago, Illinois, and Los Angeles, California.

CIMARRON

pop 900 / elev 6430ft

Cimarron has a wild past. Once a stop on the Santa Fe Trail (p347), it attracted gunslingers, train robbers, desperadoes, lawmen and other Wild West figures like Kit Carson, Buffalo Bill Cody, Annie Oakley, Wyatt Earp, Jesse James and Doc Holliday. The old St James Hotel alone saw the deaths of 26 men within its walls. Today, Cimarron is a peaceful and serene village with few street signs. Poke around to find what you need, or ask the friendly locals. The town is located on Hwy 64, 41 miles southwest of Raton (p422) and 54 winding miles east of Taos (p391). The **Chamber of Commerce** (☎ 505-376-2417; www.cimarronnm.com; Hwy 64) doesn't adhere to anything remotely resembling consistent hours.

Sights & Activities

Most historic buildings lie south of the Cimarron River on Hwy 21. Find the historic St James Hotel (below) and you'll find the old town plaza, Dold Trading Post, the Santa Fe Trail Inn (which dates to 1854), Schwenk's Gambling Hall, a Wells Fargo Station, the old jail (1872) and the **Old Mill Museum** (Aztec Mill; admission $2; ☻ Jun-Aug), built in 1864 as a flour mill. Today it houses historical photographs and local memorabilia. It keeps irregular hours, so call ahead.

About 4 miles south of Cimarron is the 220 sq mile **Philmont Scout Ranch** (☎ 505-376-2281; www.philmont.com; Hwy 21), at which hundreds of thousands of boy scouts have learned about leadership over the years. Its headquarters is in **Villa Philmonte**, a 1927 Spanish Mediterranean–style mansion filled with antiques and Southwestern art. Guided tours ($4) are offered June through August. Seven miles further south in Rayado, the **Kit Carson Museum** (☎ 505-376-2281; Kit Carson Rd; admission free; ☻ 9am-5pm Jun-Aug, hrs vary Sep-May) is filled with 1850s-style furnishings; daily guided tours are offered by interpreters in period costumes.

Sleeping & Eating

St James Hotel (☎ 505-376-2664, 800-748-2694; www.stjamescimarron.com; Hwy 21; historic rooms $90-120, modern rooms $60-100) A saloon in 1873, this well-known place was converted into a hotel in 1880 and renovated 100 years later. It's a toss up between the 14 simple historical rooms or the modern annex, which has 10 rooms equipped with TVs and phones. Within the hotel, you'll find a decent midrange restaurant and a cozy bar with a pool table. Just for fun, count the bullet holes in the period pressed-tin ceiling. Dorothy, you're not in Kansas anymore.

Casa del Gavilan (☎ 505-376-2246, 800-428-4526; www.casadelgavilan.com; Hwy 21; r incl breakfast $80-110, guesthouse $130; ✗) This magnificent Pueblo Revival–style house, built in 1908 and set on 225 acres, offers four double rooms decorated with Southwestern antiques and art. Complete with high ceilings, vigas and thick adobe walls, the house is a treat. A two-room guesthouse sleeps up to four people.

Cimarron Inn (☎ 505-376-2268, 800-546-2244; www.cimarroninn.com; Hwy 64; s/d $40/69) Operated by friendly hosts, these 12 spotless motel-style rooms (most with microwaves and refrigerators) are decorated with different themes. A few cabins and a casita can sleep up to 12 (a bargain at $75 a night for six people).

Cimarron Art Gallery (☎ 505-376-2614; 9th St; ☼ 8am-6:30pm) Places do what they can in these parts to get by. That said, enjoy an ice cream at this 1937 soda fountain, then wander around the gallery, which offers Southwestern art, souvenirs and fishing licenses.

RATON & AROUND
pop 7300 / elev 6668ft

It's probably time to get out of the car and stretch. Though Raton isn't a big tourist destination, the well-preserved town will hold your attention for a short stroll. If you're passing through, visit the museum, wax nostalgic at the drive-in and spend a night at the historic hotel. Raton was founded with the arrival of the railroad in 1879 and quickly grew into an important railway stop and mining and ranching center. Upwards of 100 of the turn-of-the-19th-century buildings from this era have been preserved.

The stretch of the Santa Fe Trail (p347) that ran through town was tough going for 19th-century travelers, given that Raton Pass (7834ft) lies in the foothills of the Rockies. It's a tad easier now.

Raton lies along I-25, 8 miles south of the Colorado state line. The main north–south thoroughfare is 2nd St, which runs parallel to and just west of I-25. The main east–west street is Hwy 64/87, called Tiger Dr west of 2nd St and Clayton Rd east of 2nd St. The **visitor center** (☎ 505-445-3689, 800-638-6161; www.raton.info; Clayton Rd; ☼ 8am-5pm Mon-Fri) has statewide information.

Sights & Activities

The small **historic district** along 1st, 2nd and 3rd Sts (between Clark and Rio Grande Aves) harbors over two dozen buildings. From the Raton Museum (below), check out the 1903 **Santa Fe Depot**, and across from the railway, note the yellow brick **Marchiondo Building** (1882). It housed a dry-goods store and a post office, and its dusty interior (peer inside) probably looks very similar to what it would have looked like when it was flourishing.

The 1915 **Shuler Theater** (131 N 2nd St) features an elaborate European Rococo interior with excellent acoustics (it's still in operation, see opposite). The foyer contains eight murals which were painted during the New Deal (1930s) by Manville Chapman that depict the region's history from 1845 to 1895. New Deal art also graces the historic 1904 El Portal Hotel (opposite), as well as the post office and library. The latter dates back to 1917 and originally served as the post office.

Note the reversed swastika signs (a Native American symbol of good luck) on top of the **International Bank** building, originally built in 1929 as the Swastika Hotel. The reversed swastika had been the symbol of one of the coal companies in Raton during the late 19th century, and it served as the town's unofficial logo until WWII. During the war, the reversed swastikas were covered with tarp and the hotel finally changed its name in 1943.

The great little **Raton Museum** (☎ 505-445-8979; 2nd St; admission free; ☼ 9am-5pm Tue-Sat late Jun-early Sep, Wed-Sat Sep-May), well worth a visit, is housed in the 1906 Coors Building. Look for great photos, artifacts pertaining to Raton's mining days and illuminating information documenting the history of the Santa Fe Trail (p347).

Sugarite Canyon State Park (☎ 505-445-5607; tent/RV sites $10/14), featuring two lakes stocked with rainbow trout, is situated in the pretty meadows and forests of the foothills of the Rockies, about 10 miles northeast of Raton. In winter, the 7800ft elevation is perfect for cross-country skiing. In summer, there are 15 miles of hiking trails which begin from a half-mile nature trail. To reach it, take Hwy 72 east out of Raton, then turn north onto Hwy 526; it's signposted about 7 miles north of here.

Sleeping & Eating

El Portal Hotel (☎ 505-445-3631; www.elportalhotel
.com; 101 N 3rd St; r $65-75) This wonderful turn-
of-the-19th-century livery stable expanded
in 1904 and turned itself into the Seaburg
European Hotel. An interesting alternative
to a plethora of standard issue motels, El
Portal (as it's now known) offers 18 spacious antique-filled rooms (many with
claw-foot bathtubs) and TVs.

Vermejo Park Ranch (☎ 505-445-3097; www
.vermejoparkranch.com; Hwy 555; per person incl meals
& activities around $300; ☒ ▣) Maintained by
Ted Turner as a premier fishing and hunting lodge, this beautifully situated 920 sq
mile enterprise is about 40 miles west of
Raton and offers fly-fishing clinics from
June through August. As if to balance out
the hunting and fishing aspects, the ranch
also restores prairie dog habitats and en-
courages guests to observe a diverse array
of wildlife – from elk and bison to bears
and birds.

3rd St Cafe (☎ 505-445-9090; 101 N 3rd St; dishes
$6-10; ❤ 7am-4pm Mon-Sat) Despite what you
might guess because of the Naugahyde
booths and swivel stools, this casual and airy
dining room within El Portal Hotel (above)
serves very good food. Creativity spills over
onto good sandwiches, pan seared salmon,
soups (curry chicken with apple), burgers
and breakfasts. It's also quite friendly.

La Cosina Café (☎ 505-445-9675; 745 S 3rd St; dishes
$6-10; ❤ lunch & dinner Mon-Sat) Although they
don't serve beer to wash down basic New
Mexican fare, when you have a hankerin' for
local fare, there's nowhere else to go.

Drinking & Entertainment

During the summer, films are shown at the
classic **drive-in** (2nd St at Kearny Ave), but from
September through June, folks head in-
doors to the 1940s-era **Raton Movie Theater**
(☎ 505-445-3721; 2nd St at Park Ave). The beautiful
Shuler Theater (☎ 505-445-4746; www.shulertheater
.com; 131 N 2nd St) presents a variety of productions, including dances and plays. The **White
House Saloon** (☎ 505-445-9992; 133 Cook Ave; lunch
dishes $8, dinner dishes $15-25; ❤ lunch Tue-Thu, lunch &
dinner Fri, dinner Sat) serves as the local hangout
when you want a beer.

CLAYTON & AROUND

pop 2500 / elev 5050ft

Ranches and prairie grasses surround Clayton, a quiet town with a sleepy Western
feel on the Texas border. Near the Bravo
Dome CO_2 Field (the world's largest natural deposit of carbon dioxide gas), Clayton
is where infamous train robber Black Jack
Ketchum was caught and hanged in 1901.
The **Herzstein Memorial Museum** (☎ 505-374-
2977; Methodist Episcopal Church, 2nd St at Walnut St;
admission free; ❤ 1-5pm Tue-Sun) tells the story.

DETOUR: THE FOLSOM MAN & VOLCANOES

The most important archaeological discovery in America was made near Folsom. In 1908, George
McJunkin, a local cowboy, noticed some strange bones in Wild Horse Arroyo. Cowboy that he
was, he knew that these were no ordinary cattle bones. And so he kept them, suspecting correctly
that they were bones from an extinct species of bison. McJunkin spoke of his find to various
people, but it wasn't until 1926 to 1928 that the site was properly excavated, first by fossil bone
expert Jesse Figgins and then by others.

Until that time, scientists thought that humans had inhabited North America for, at most,
4000 years. With this single find, the facts about the continent's ancient inhabitants had to be
completely revised. Subsequent excavations found stone arrowheads in association with extinct
bison bones dating from 8000 BC, thus proving that people have lived here for at least that long.
These Paleo-Indians became known as Folsom Man.

Recent dating techniques suggest that these artifacts are 10,800 years old, among the oldest discovered on the continent, although it is clear that people have lived in the Americas for
even longer.

The area is also known for its volcanoes. Rising 1300ft above the surrounding plains, **Capulin
Volcano National Monument** is the easiest to visit. From the **visitor center** (☎ 505-278-2201; www
.nps.gov/cavo; per car $5), a 2-mile road winds precariously up the mountain to the crater rim (which
is 8182ft). There, a quarter-mile trail drops into the crater and a mile-long trail follows the rim.
The entrance is 3 miles north of Capulin, which is 30 miles east of Raton on Hwy 87.

If you're moseying about these parts, you'll find over 500 dinosaur footprints of eight different species at **Clayton Lake State Park** (☎ 505-374-8808; Hwy 370; per car per day $5, tent/RV sites $10/14), 12 miles northwest of Clayton. The pretty lake has swimming and camping.

Sometimes when you're in the mood for a detour to nowhere, there's nowhere to go. Not true here. Southwest of Clayton, in the most sparsely populated county in New Mexico, the **Kiowa National Grasslands** consist of high-plains ranch land – open, vast and lonely. Farmed throughout the early 20th century, the soil suffered from poor agricultural techniques and it basically became useless, essentially blowing away during the dust bowl years of the 1930s. The most visited section (though visitors are scarce) is **Mills Canyon**, north of Roy (with only a gas station and grocery store). About 10 miles northwest of Roy on Hwy 39, a signposted dirt road heads west another 10 miles to the **Mills Camping Area**, with free primitive camping, but no drinking water. The river forms a small gorge here and the area is quite scenic.

If you've a hankerin', stop by the historic 1890 **Eklund Hotel Dining Room & Saloon** (☎ 505-374-2551; 15 Main St; r $73-83; dishes $7-10; ☉ 10:30am-9pm) for a meal in the elegant dining room or a beer in the Old West saloon. If you need to stay the night after bellying up to the beautifully carved bar a few too many times, the 26 guest rooms are simple but newly renovated. Some have access to the balcony.

SOUTHWESTERN NEW MEXICO

The Rio Grande Valley unfurls from Albuquerque as it runs by the finger-like Elephant Butte Reservoir to the bubbling hot springs of funky Truth or Consequences. As desert gives way to water, the river attracts wildlife to places like Bosque del Apache National Wildlife Refuge. Crops, while plentiful, grow on a wing and a prayer. Illegal aliens creep across the border with Mexico on the same wing and prayer. Residents are few and far between, except in Las Cruces, the state's second largest city. With the exception of lively Las Cruces and sedate Socorro, most towns are relatively

young, dating to the late 19th century when mining began.

I-10 cuts through the Chihuahuan Desert, dominated by yucca and agave. This is ranching country, though the cattle are sparse. North of the desert and west of I-25, the rugged Gila National Forest is wild with backpacking and fishing adventures. The very wildness of Southwestern New Mexico is perhaps its greatest attraction, but the breadth of attractions may surprise you. Don't overlook the Gila Cliff Dwellings National Monument, superb Mimbres black-on-white pottery at many small area museums, Spanish architecture in Mesilla near Las Cruces, quaint Victorian buildings in Silver City, giant white disks (the Very Large Array) west of Socorro and plenty of ghost towns (and almost-ghost towns) like Chloride.

SOCORRO

pop 8900 / elev 4585ft

A quiet and amiable layover, Socorro's downtown has a good mix of buildings dating from the 1800s to late 20th century. Its standout is a 17th-century mission. Still, most visitors are birders drawn to the nearby Bosque del Apache refuge (opposite).

Socorro means 'help' in Spanish. The town's name supposedly dates to 1598, when Juan de Onate's expedition received help from Pilabo Pueblo (now defunct). The Spaniards built a small church nearby, expanding it into the San Miguel Mission in the 1620s. With the introduction of the railroad in 1880 and the discovery of gold and silver, Socorro became a major mining center and New Mexico's biggest town by the late 1880s. The mining boom went bust in 1893. True to its roots, the New Mexico Institute of Mining and Technology (locally called Tech) offers post-graduate education and advanced research facilities, and runs a mineral museum.

The **Chamber of Commerce** (☎ 505-835-0424; www.socorro-nm.com; 101 Plaza; ☉ 8am-5pm Mon-Fri, 10am-noon Sat) is helpful.

Sights & Activities

Most of the **historic downtown** dates to the late 19th century. Pick up the chamber of commerce's walking tour, the highlight of which is the **San Miguel Mission** (☎ 505-835-1620; San Miguel Rd), three blocks north of the plaza.

Although restored and expanded several times, the mission still retains its colonial feel and parts of the walls date back to the original building.

Most travelers are naturalists who descend on Socorro because of its proximity to the **Bosque Del Apache National Wildlife Refuge** (per car $3; ☺ dawn-dusk). About 8 miles south of town, the refuge protects almost 90 sq miles of fields and marshes, which serve as a major wintering ground for many migratory birds – most notably the very rare and endangered whooping cranes of which about a dozen winter here. Tens of thousands of snow geese, sandhill cranes and various other waterfowl also call this place home, as do bald eagles. The wintering season lasts from late October to early April, but December and January are the peak viewing months and offer the best chance of seeing bald eagles. Upwards of 325 bird species and 135 mammal, reptile and amphibian species have been recorded here. From the **visitor center** (☎ 505-835-1828; ☺ 7:30am-4pm Mon-Fri, 8am-4:30pm Sat & Sun), a 15-mile loop circles the refuge; hiking trails and viewing platforms are easily accessible. To get here leave I-25 at San Antonio (10 miles south of Socorro) and drive 8 miles south on Hwy 1. Refuge visitors often stop by the Owl Bar Cafe (right).

Back in Socorro, the state's largest mineral collection is housed within the **Mineral Museum** (☎ 505-835-5420; www.geoinfo.nmt. edu; Workman Edition Bldg, College St; admission free; ☺ 8am-5pm Mon-Fri, 10am-3pm Sat & Sun), on the Tech campus on the northwestern outskirts of town. Displays include thousands of minerals from around the world, fossils and other geological curiosities.

Festivals & Events

Socorro's **Balloon Rally** (late Nov) is not to be missed; all participating balloonists line up on the street and inflate their balloons prior to a mass ascension. At the **49ers Festival** (3rd weekend Nov), the entire town gets involved in a parade, dancing and gambling, while the **Festival of the Cranes** (3rd weekend Nov) features special tours of Bosque del Apache, wildlife workshops and arts and crafts.

Sleeping & Eating

Economy Inn (☎ 505-835-4666; 400 California NE; r $30-50; ☒) There aren't a lot of options in

town. Clean and reasonably well kept, most rooms here have microwaves and small refrigerators.

Socorro RV Park (☎ 505-835-2234; S Frontage Rd; tent/RV sites $17/20; ☒) This place has a pool, showers and coin laundry.

Socorro Springs Brewing Co (☎ 505-838-0650; 115 Abeyta Ave; dishes $5-9) In the mood for a relatively sophisticated experience? Come to this renovated adobe joint for a really good clay-oven pizza, big calzones, decent pasta dishes and homemade soups. At times, the selection of brews can be on the minimalist side. Whatever they're serving at the moment, though, is always smooth and tasty.

Frank & Lupe's El Sombrero (☎ 505-835-3945; 210 Mesquite; dishes $5-11) Of Socorro's several very local Mexican restaurants, this cheerful and friendly place is a good bet. Try to get a table in the garden room. Fajitas and enchiladas are quite popular, but mostly it's the sauces (like mole and *poblano* chile) that cover them. If only they would bottle the stuff.

Martha's Black Dog Coffeehouse (☎ 505-838-0311; 110 Manzanares Ave; dishes under $10) Martha's serves tasty coffees and desserts, but don't stop there. Make sure you arrive during a mealtime so that you can take advantage of a bountiful breakfast dish (perhaps a burrito), a vegetarian Mediterranean plate at lunchtime, a complex soup or a healthy green salad.

Owl Bar Cafe (☎ 505-835-9946; 215 San Antonio; dishes $6-15; ☺ breakfast, lunch & dinner Mon-Sat) Half a mile east of I-25 near San Antonio, this place is known for its green-chile cheeseburger. San Antonio, by the way, is the childhood home of hotelier Conrad Hilton.

Entertainment

The funky **Loma Theater** (☎ 505-835-0965; 107 Manzanares Ave) shows Hollywood movies in a remodeled Victorian store.

TRUTH OR CONSEQUENCES

pop 7300 / elev 4260ft

Originally called Hot Springs, funky and rustic little T or C (as it's locally known) of the game-show fame (p427) has more character than most New Mexico towns. Wander around the little hole-in-the-wall cafés downtown, and check out the antique, thrift and junk shops. And take a bath, so to speak. Most visitors eventually find time

DETOUR: VERY LARGE ARRAY RADIO TELESCOPE

In some remote regions of New Mexico, TV reception is little more than a starry-eyed fantasy. About 40 miles west of Socorro, though, 27 huge antenna dishes sprout from the high plains like a couch potato's dream-come-true. Actually, the 240-ton dishes comprise the National Radio Astronomy Observatory's **Very Large Array Radio Telescope** (VLA; 4 miles south of US 60 off Hwy 52; www.vla.nrao.edu; admission free; 8:30am-sunset). Together, they combine to form a very large eye-ball peeking into the outer edges of the universe. It would take a 422ft-wide satellite dish to provide the same resolution that this Y-shaped configuration of 82ft-wide antennas offers the observatory.

Sure, the giant 'scope may reveal the relativistic electron movement in the heavens and allow geophysicists to wonder at the wobble of the earth on its axis...But what does it tell the rest of us? Well, without them, Jodie Foster never could have flashed-forward into our future (or was it her past?) in the movie *Contact*, which was filmed here with a little help from Canyon de Chelly (p182). The radio waves collected by these enormous dishes have increased our understanding of the complex phenomena that make up the surface of the sun. They have given us a gander at the internal heating source deep within the interiors of several planets sharing our orbit. They provide us with just enough information to turn our concepts of time and space inside-out as we extrapolate the existence of varieties of matter that, sans satellites, might only exist in our imaginations as we spin through space on the head of this peculiar, little blue-green globe.

to soak in the hot springs or camp and fish at the three state parks nearby.

The **Chamber of Commerce** (☎ 505-894-3536; 400 W 4th St; 9am-5pm Mon-Fri, to 1pm Sat) and **Gila National Forest Ranger Station** (☎ 505-894-6677; 1804 N Date St; 8am-4:30pm Mon-Fri) have detailed information.

Sights & Activities

Geronimo Springs Museum (☎ 505-894-6600; 211 Main St; adult/student $3/1.50; 9am-5pm Mon-Sat) This extensive museum displays minerals, local art and plenty of local historical artifacts ranging from prehistoric Mimbres pots to beautifully worked cowboy saddles. Exhibits also clarify the details of the famous 1950 name change.

Indians, including Geronimo, have bathed in the area's mineral-laden **hot springs** for centuries. Long said to boast therapeutic properties, the waters range in temperature from 98°F to 115°F and have a pH of 7 (neutral). Although the commercial hot baths date from the 1920s and 1930s and look a little worse for wear from the outside, they are acceptably clean inside. Most places charge $5 to $10 per person for a hot bath; private, couple and family tubs are also available. Massages ($50) and other treatments require advance notice.

The swankiest place, by far, is Sierra Grande Lodge & Spa (right). Other places, though, also offer lodging (right) with their

hot springs: **Charles Motel & Bath House** (☎ 505-894-7154; www.charlesspa.com; 601 Broadway; 8am-9am) has the hottest water in town and in- and outdoor tubs, massage, Ayurvedic treatments, sauna, reflexology and holistic healing; **Riverbend Hot Springs** (☎ 505-894-6183; www.nmhotsprings.com; 100 Austin St; 8am-9am) has six outdoor tubs by the river.

Most places in town pump mineral water from wells, but a few have natural springs, including: **Hay-Yo-Kay Hot Springs** (☎ 505-894-2228; www.hay-yo-kay.com; 300 Austin St; 10am-7pm Wed-Sun), with five pools and massage; and **Marshall Hot Springs** (☎ 505-894-9286; www.marshallhotsprings.com; 311 Marr St; 10am-6pm), with five private free-flowing tubs and massage.

Special Events

The **T or C Fiesta** (1st weekend May) celebrates the town's name change from 1950 (see box, opposite) with a rodeo, barbecue, parade and other events. The **Sierra County Fair** (late Aug) has livestock and agricultural displays, and the **Old Time Fiddlers State Championship** (3rd weekend Oct) features country and western, bluegrass and mariachi music.

Sleeping & Eating

Sierra Grande Lodge & Spa (☎ 505-894-6976; www.sierragrandelodge.com; 501 McAdoo St; r $105-135, dinner dishes $15-25; Wed-Sun;) This is an oasis, not a mirage. It's real and refined and occupies a masterfully renovated 1920s lodge.

Guest rooms and suites are luxe and tranquil, furnished with sophisticated touches and attention to detail; mineral bath privileges are included with the room. Spa treatments (for an additional fee) radiate warmth, as does the contemporary kitchen which prepares rack of lamb, stuffed free range chicken and other sophisticated and seasonal dishes. The wine selection is diverse and reasonably priced

Marshall Hot Springs (☎ 505-894-9286; www.marshallhotsprings.com; 311 Marr St; s $45-65, d $70-90; 🖳) Along with 10 rooms and a nice downtown location, guests are allowed unlimited use of hot springs and access to mountain bikes, trampoline and barbecue.

Riverbend Hot Springs (☎ 505-894-6183; 100 Austin St; per person with/without membership $18/20, d $36-47, r with kitchenette $62) Overseen by friendly hosts, this riverside hostel offers dormitory-style accommodations in cabins, trailers and teepees, with discounts to HI and AYH members. Private rooms have kitchenettes, microwaves and coffeepots; several teepees sleep families and small groups. Hot spring tubs are available morning and evening and are free for guests.

Artesian Baths & RV Park (☎ 505-894-2684; 312 Marr St; sites nightly/weekly $10/40) Soaking in their tubs costs $2 per hour when you stay overnight.

Los Arcos (☎ 505-894-6200; 1400 N Date St; dishes $10-23; 🕑 dinner; ✗) T or C's most upscale place serves very good steaks, lobsters and locally caught fish. Dine on the pleasant patio or within the hacienda-like interior. Surprise, surprise, there's also a salad bar.

La Cocina (☎ 505-894-6499; 1 Lakeway Dr; lunch dishes $6-9, dinner dishes $9-16; 🕑 lunch & dinner) For decent Mexican food, fabulous salsa and good steaks, search out the 'Hot Stuff' sign behind the Super 8 motel. Make sure you have enough time; it doesn't have the fastest service in the Southwest.

Getting There & Away

Greyhound/TNM&O (☎ 505-894-3649; www.greyhound.com) run one or two daily buses north and south along I-25.

AROUND TRUTH OR CONSEQUENCES
Elephant Butte Lake

Formed in 1916 by damming the Rio Grande, **Elephant Butte Lake** (☎ 505-744-5421; I-25; per car per day $4, unpowered/powered sites $10/14)

is the state's largest artificial lake (60 sq miles). It's popular for fishing, waterskiing and windsurfing. In addition to camping, you can walk a 1.5-mile loop nature trail. The nearby **marina** (☎ 505-894-2041) rents tackle and boats (for fishing, pontoon and skiing). Spring and fall are best for **fishing**; guides will help you get the most out of your time for about $200 to $325 per day (for one to four anglers). Contact professional angler Randy Snyder, who operates recreational and instructional fishing tours through **Bass Busters** (☎ 505-894-0928; www.zianet.com/bassbusters), or Frank Vilorio, who works through **Fishing Adventures** (☎ 800-580-8992; www.stripersnewmexico.com) to make sure you take home your fill of striped bass.

Caballo Lake State Park

Seventeen miles south of T or C, **Caballo Lake State Park** (☎ 505-743-3942; I-25; per car per day $5) offers fishing (best from mid-March to mid-June), boating, skiing and windsurfing. There are boat ramps, a playground, and several campgrounds with hot showers, 60 RV hookups ($11) and 250 sites without hookups ($7). Also, get out your binoculars because a few dozen bald eagles winter at the lake between October and February.

A TOWN BY ANY OTHER NAME

Seems like there's at least one town named Hot Springs in every state of the union – heck, in California alone, there are more than 30 of 'em. In 1950, TV game-show host Ralph Edwards wished aloud that a town somewhere in the US liked his show so much that they would name themselves after it. That year, there was one fewer town named Hot Springs: by a margin of four to one, the 1294 residents of Truth or Consequences voted to change their town's name. That same year, NBC broadcast the show live for the first time ever from (where else?) Truth or Consequences to celebrate the town and the popular show's 10th anniversary.

Nowadays, T or C residents live among the sandstone bluffs, basking in the healing springs and the renown not only as one of the top retirement destinations, but as one of the quirkiest-named towns in the country – to heck with the consequences.

NEW MEXICO

DETOUR: GHOSTLY MINING TOWNS

South of T or C, Hwy 152 west leads into silver country through **Hillsboro**, **Kingston** and **Santa Rita** (a ghost town). The slow but scenic road has some hairpin bends and crests at the Black Range at 8228-foot Emory Pass, where a lookout gives views of the drier Rio Grande country to the east. A few miles beyond Emory Pass, the almost–ghost town of Kingston had 7000 inhabitants in its 1880s heyday as a silver-mining center, but now only a few dozen residents call it home. Nearby Hillsboro was revived by local agriculture after mining went bust. Today it's known for an **Apple Festival** (Labor Day), when fresh-baked apple pies, delicious apple cider, street musicians and arts and crafts stalls attract visitors. Have a sandwich at the **Barbershop Café** (☎ 505-895-5283; 200 Main St; dishes under $10; ☯ 11am-3pm Wed, Thu & Sun, to 8pm Fri & Sat), which also offers rooms (around $60), or stay at the **Enchanted Villa B&B** (☎ 505-895-5686; ste incl breakfast $55-84), with three rooms and a two-bedroom suite.

It's hard to miss the **Santa Rita Chino Open Pit Copper Mine**, which has an observation point on Hwy 152 about 6 miles from its intersection with Hwy 180. Worked by Indians and Spanish and Anglo settlers, it's the oldest active mine in the Southwest. The open pit mine is a staggering 1.5-miles wide, 1800ft deep and produces 300 million pounds of copper annually.

Winston & Chloride

There's silver in them there hills. In 1879, Englishman Harry Pye, scrapping together a living as a mule-skinner, prospector, and freighter for the US army, discovered silver in a canyon between Hillsboro and Camp Ojo Caliente. It took him two years to garner the resources to return and stake a claim. But stake a claim he did, and it set off a silver-mining boom that gave rise to Chloride and Winston. Many a town began with a tent like Harry's, pitched beside a mother-lode. Few survived as more than rubble and remnants of the alchemal rigging erected to extract riches from stone.

Pye didn't live long enough to suffer the consequences of the silver panic of 1893, brought on by the country opting for the gold standard. That plunged the value of silver to about 10% of its prior value and quickly drained the dreams from the boomtowns that had sprung up along the fruitful veins of silver. Pye was killed by a band of Apache Indians in 1881, his death attributed to the fact that his gun jammed.

Chloride is a ghost town these days, while the population of Winston hovers at around 97 souls, down from about 500 in 1886 when Frank H Winston arrived to settle what was then Fairview. He established a store, became a state legislator and a cattleman, and prospected a bit on the side. He also extended generous credit at his store, even when the chances of being repaid were slim. After his death in 1929,

the town changed its name to Winston to honor his altruism. To reach the little towns, head west on Hwy 52 from I-25 just north of T or C.

SILVER CITY & AROUND

pop 10,500 / elev 5938ft

The city's name tells the story of a mining town founded in 1870 after the discovery of silver. When that went bust, instead of becoming a ghost town like many others in the area, Silver City tapped its copper reserves. It still mines the reserves today. Is there a name change (à la it's northern neighbor T or C) to Copper City in the works? Nah; locals still sometimes call their town, simply, Silver. Downtown streets are dressed with lovely old brick and cast-iron buildings, some Victorian ones, a few adobes and a Wild West air. In fact, Billy the Kid spent some of his boyhood here, and a few of his haunts can be seen. Silver is also the gateway to outdoor activities in the Gila National Forest (p431).

North of Silver City, scenic and mountainous Hwy 15 heads through Pinos Altos and dead-ends at the Gila Cliff Dwellings (p431), 42 miles away. Narrow and winding, the road to Gila Cliffs takes almost two hours.

Information

Chamber of Commerce (☎ 505-538-3785, 800-548-9378; www.silvercity.org; 201 N Hudson St; ☯ 9am-5pm Mon-Sat) With so many area artists, the chamber publishes a map with the city's galleries.

Library (☎ 505-538-3672; 515 W College Ave; ☼ 9am-5pm Tue-Wed & Fri, 9am-8pm Mon & Thu) Free Internet access.

Medical center (☎ 505-538-4000; 1313 E 32nd)

Post office (☎ 505-538-2831; 500 N Hudson St)

Sights & Activities

The heart of this Victorian town is encompassed by Bullard, Texas, and Arizona Sts between Broadway and 6th St. The former Main St, one block east of Bullard, washed out during a series of massive floods in 1895. Caused by runoff from logged and overgrazed areas north of town, the floods eventually cut 55ft down below the original height of the street. In a stroke of marketing genius, it's now called **Big Ditch Park**.

The **Silver City Museum** (☎ 505-538-5921; www .silvercitymuseum.org; 312 W Broadway; admission free; ☼ 9:30am-4:30pm Tue-Fri, 10am-4pm Sat & Sun), ensconced in an elegant 1881 Victorian house, displays Mimbres pottery, as well as mining and household artifacts from Silver City's Victorian heyday. Its shop has a good selection of Southwestern books and gifts.

The **Western New Mexico University Museum** (WNMU; ☎ 505-538-6386; 1000 W College Ave; admission free; ☼ 9am-4:30pm Mon-Fri, 10am-4pm Sat & Sun) boasts the world's largest collection of Mimbres pottery, along with exhibits detailing local history, culture and natural history. The gift shop specializes in Mimbres motifs.

Seven miles north of Silver City along Hwy 15 lies **Pinos Altos**, established in 1859

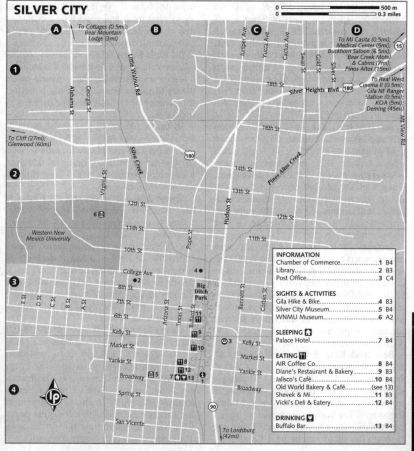

SILVER CITY

INFORMATION
Chamber of Commerce.....................1 B4
Library..2 B3
Post Office......................................3 C4

SIGHTS & ACTIVITIES
Gila Hike & Bike.............................4 B3
Silver City Museum.........................5 B4
WNMU Museum.............................6 A2

SLEEPING
Palace Hotel...................................7 B4

EATING
AIR Coffee Co.................................8 B4
Diane's Restaurant & Bakery...........9 B3
Jalisco's Café.................................10 B4
Old World Bakery & Café..........(see 13)
Shevek & Mi..................................11 B3
Vicki's Deli & Eatery.....................12 B4

DRINKING
Buffalo Bar....................................13 B4

NEW MEXICO

as a gold-mining town. These days, it's almost a ghost town; its few residents strive to retain the 19th-century flavor of the place. Cruise Main St to see the log cabin schoolhouse built in 1866 (it's a teensy museum), an opera house, a reconstructed fort and an 1870s courthouse.

Gila Hike & Bike (☎ 505-388-3222; 103 E College Ave; ☼ 9am-5:30pm Mon-Sat) rents bicycles, snowshoes and camping equipment for exploring the adjacent National Forest. This rugged country is perfect for backpackers, campers, hunters, anglers, birders, cross-country skiers and other outdoor-sports enthusiasts who are looking for challenging solitude.

Sleeping

Palace Hotel (☎ 505-388-1811; www.zianet.com /palacehotel; 106 W Broadway; d $38-49, ste $62, incl breakfast; ☒ ▣) For a sliver of Silver City's history, this restored 1882 hostelry has 18 rooms that vary from small (with a double bed) to two-room suites (with king- or queen-size beds). Suites are outfitted with refrigerators, microwaves, phones and TVs, but they still have old-fashioned Territorial-style decor. If you want to log on, they also have an Internet café.

Bear Mountain Lodge (☎ 505-538-2538, 877-620-2327; www.bearmountainlodge.com; 2251 Cottage San Rd; d incl breakfast $105-200; ☒) This large ranch house, built in 1928 and set on 160 acres, is operated by the Nature Conservancy. There's plenty of area hiking and a lodge naturalist can help with suggestions. In addition to 10 rooms and suites, the lodge also rents a guesthouse with kitchenette. Inquire about other meals that may be arranged.

Cottages (☎ 505-388-3000, 800-938-3001; www .silvercitycottages.com; 2037 Cottage San Rd; ste $129, cottages $169) This quiet getaway surrounded by countryside offers two suites (one of which is the childhood home of astronaut Harrison Schmitt who walked on the moon) and three cottages. All units have stocked kitchens, a private veranda or patio, TV, VCR and phone.

Bear Creek Motel & Cabins (☎ 505-388-4501, 888-388-4515; www.bearcreekcabins.com; 88 Main St, Pinos Altos; cabins $119-149) These 15 cabins – some with two bedrooms and a kitchenette or balcony – have fireplaces or wood-burning stoves. Try your luck at gold prospecting; the managers have gold pans for sifting through the silt at nearby Bear Creek.

KOA (☎ 505-388-3351; www.koa.com; 11824 E Hwy 180; tent/RV sites $16/21, 'kamping kabins' $32; ☒) Five miles east of town, this place has a playground and coin laundry; reservations are encouraged in summer. Jackie, the campground owner, is helpful about where to go hiking, birding and exploring.

Eating

AIR Coffee Co (☎ 505-388-5952; 112 W Yankie St; ☼ 7am-5:30pm Mon-Sat, to 2pm Sun) For easy conversation over a good cuppa (really good) gourmet coffee, AIR has lots of life. It's a sunny, happy place frequented by folks with the same disposition (well, artists and gallery-owners, that is). Hang on the patio in good weather.

Vicki's Deli & Eatery (☎ 505-388-5430; 107 W Yankie St; dishes $7; ☼ 10:30am-3:30pm Mon-Sat) Vicki's has fresh feel-good food, vegetarian dishes, simple sandwiches and light meals. Dine outside in good weather.

Old World Bakery & Cafe (☎ 505-534-9372; 200 N Bullard St; dishes $5-7; ☼ 9am-4pm Mon-Sat) This low-key and friendly place, which offers plenty of salads and sandwiches, is perfect for hanging out a bit. Come for coffee, stay for quiche.

Mi Casita (☎ 505-538-5533; 2340 Bosworth Dr; dishes $5-10; ☼ 11am-7pm Mon-Fri) A local favorite with super-fast and plenty friendly service, Mi Casita serves huge plates of Mexican food with flavorful chile. Try their enchiladas and *chimichangas*.

Shevek & Mi (☎ 505-534-9168; 602 N Bullard St; lunch dishes $5-10, dinner dishes $10-22; ☼ 10:30am-8:30pm Mon-Thu, 8:30am-10:30pm Fri & Sat, 8:30am-8:30pm Sun) Owned by a CIA-trained chef, this delightful eatery is at turns formal, bistro-like and patio-casual. It depends on which room you choose. Sunday brunch is decidedly New York, à la Upper West side; dinners range from Moroccan to Spanish to Italian. Enjoy the excellent selection of beer and wine.

Diane's Restaurant & Bakery (☎ 505-538-8722; 510 N Bullard St; lunch dishes $7-11, dinner dishes $18-28; ☼ 11am-2:30pm & 5pm-8:30pm Tue-Fri, 9am-2pm Sat & Sun) Often referred to as an oasis in the culinary wasteland known as Southwestern New Mexico, Diane's employs elegant touches like white linens to complement her fine eclectic specialties. It's quite popular at lunchtime, but the tempo settles down at dinner which turns more romantic.

Jalisco's Cafe (☎ 505-388-2060; 100 S Bullard St; lunch dishes $4-8, dinner dishes $9-15; ⏱ 11am-8:30pm Mon-Sat) Family owned, this Mexican eatery dishes up large and very good enchiladas and chile *rellenos*. It's a fun place in the historic district. Even if you're in the health-conscious camp that thinks fried *sopaipillas* are trouble, eat one here.

Buckhorn Saloon (☎ 505-538-9911; Main St, Pinos Altos; dishes $12-22; ⏱ dinner Mon-Sat) About 7 miles north of Silver City, this restored adobe eatery offers steaks (a house specialty) and seafood amid 1860s Wild West decor. The big stone fireplaces are warming. Live country music livens up the joint on Friday and Saturday.

Drinking & Entertainment

Catch a flick at **Real West Cinema II** (☎ 505-538-5659; 11585 E Hwy 180) or belly up to the **Buffalo Bar** (☎ 505-538-3201; 201 N Bullard St), which hosts occasional dancing in the adjacent nightclub. Without the dancing it's your basic (not particularly salubrious) Western bar.

GILA NATIONAL FOREST

If you're looking for isolated and undiscovered, not to mention magnificent, these mountains have it in spades. Northwest of Silver City, Hwy 180 crosses the Continental Divide and winds through remote and wild country dotted with a few tiny communities. The Gila National Forest and Mogollon Mountains offer some excellent opportunities for remote and primitive backpacking, hiking, camping and fishing. The **ranger station** (☎ 505-539-2481; Hwy 180; ⏱ 8am-4:30pm) a half-mile south of Glenwood has details.

From Glenwood head 5 miles east on Hwy 174 to the **Catwalk** – a trail enclosed by a wire cage hugging the cliff up narrow Whitewater Canyon. It follows water pipes built by miners in 1893. When the pipes needed repair, the miners walked along them (the 'Catwalk'). It's a short but worthwhile hike with some steep spots.

Mogollon, a semi–ghost town, lies 4 miles north of Glenwood and then 9 miles east on steep and narrow Hwy 159 (inaccessible during the winter). Once an important mining town, it's now inhabited by only a few people offering 'antiques.' Many buildings lie deserted and empty – it's an interesting but slightly spooky place.

The USFS maintains the **Bighorn campground** (free; ⏱ year-round) in Gila National Forest, a quarter-mile north of Glenwood, with no drinking water or fee.

The area around **Reserve** on Hwy 180 is mainly settled by ranchers, cowboys and loggers who particularly loathe federal government interference and environmentalists. It's the kind of place where county officials passed a resolution urging every family to own a gun. This is about as close to the old Wild West as you'll get.

Casitas de Gila Guesthouse (☎ 505-535-4455, 877-923-4827; www.casitasdegila.com; off Hwy 180, near the town of Cliff; casitas $120-160) This private and stunningly sited group of five adobe-style casitas is like a dream come true. If you're stressed out getting here, you won't be within minutes of arriving. Each unit has a fully stocked kitchen, plenty of privacy and one or two bedrooms. Stay a while and use telescopes, an outdoor hot tub and grills. The guest house is about two hours from the Cliff Dwellings, but practically right on top of the National Forest.

Gila Cliff Dwellings

Mysterious, relatively isolated and accessible, these remarkable cliff dwellings look very much like they would have at the turn of the first century. Luckily, the cliffs are not crowded with visitors, so it will be easy for you to step back in time. The influence of the Ancestral Puebloans (p27) on the Mogollon culture is writ large. Take the 1-mile round-trip self-guided trail that climbs 180ft to the dwellings, overlooking a lovely forested canyon. Parts of the trail are steep and involve ladders. The trail begins at the end of Hwy 15, 2 miles beyond the **visitor center** (☎ 505-536-9461; admission $3; ⏱ 8am-5pm). Between the visitor center and trailhead, two small **campgrounds** with drinking water, picnic areas and toilets. They're free on a first-come, first-served basis and often fill on summer weekends. A short trail behind the campground leads to older dwellings.

Gila Hot Springs

Used by Indians since ancient times, these springs are 39 miles north of Silver City, within the **Gila Hotsprings Vacation Center** (☎ 505-536-9551; www.gilahotspringsranch.com; Hwy 15; unpowered/powered sites $12/17, d $60). The center has simple rooms with kitchenettes

A HOT TIME IN THE CHILE CAPITAL OF THE WORLD

Many folks in **Hatch** (☎ 505-267-5050; www.villageofhatch.org; 105 Carr St; ☽ visitor center 9am-3pm Mon-Fri) can tell if a chile was grown north or south of I-40 just by tasting the pod. The epicenter of all things chile, new breeds developed in this sleepy town of 1673 are paraded in the national market with all the fanfare of the latest sports car model. The state even legislated its own spelling of the word, with one 'l.' They take chile-growing seriously here, but not seriously enough to dampen the fiery passions of more than 30,000 chile fans who swarm into town for the annual **chile festival** (www.hatchchilefest.com; Labor Day weekend). They come for food, barn dancing, carnival rides, fiddle contests, and, of course, the chiles. Chile fans waft into town on a current of roasting chiles. The aroma is distinctive. *Ristras*, or strings of dried chiles, festoon buildings. Can't time your visit with the fair? Harvesting begins with the greens when the corn tassels appear (around July 25) and continues with the reds right up until Jack Frost – the only one who can cool the jets of chiles – arrives in town.

and an RV park with a spa and showers fed by hot springs. Primitive camping is adjacent to the **hot pools** (hot pools $3; camping & hot pools $4). You can arrange horseback rides, guided fishing and wilderness pack trips and other outfitting services in advance through the center.

LAS CRUCES & AROUND

pop 74,000 / elev 3890ft

Nicely sited between the Rio Grande Valley and the fluted Organ Mountains, Las Cruces (Spanish for 'crosses') acquired its name through death. In 1787 and again in 1830, Apaches killed bands of travelers camping here, and their graves were marked by a collection of crosses. Settled permanently in 1849, Las Cruces today is New Mexico's second largest city. Although its next-door neighbor, Mesilla, was more important than Las Cruces in the mid-1800s, it's quieter now than it was then. Poke around Mesilla's shady plaza and surrounding streets; it has lovely 19th-century buildings hung with colorful *ristras*, including a stagecoach stop for the Butterfield Overland Mail Company. The plaza is a nice place to people-watch. Shops on the plaza sell souvenirs ranging from cheap and kitschy to expensive and excellent.

Locals get by on small and family owned farms cultivating chiles, corn, fruit and pecans; or they work at the nearby White Sands Missile Range. New Mexico State University (NMSU) keeps things somewhat lively with about 15,000 students. Las Cruces makes a good base for southern exploration.

Information

Chamber of Commerce (☎ 505-524-1968; 760 W Picacho Ave, Las Cruces; ☽ 8am-5pm Mon-Fri)
Convention & Visitors Bureau (☎ 505-541-2444, 800-343-7827; www.lascrucescvb.org; 211 N Water, Las Cruces)
Library (☎ 505-528-4000; 200 E Picacho Ave, Las Cruces; ☽ 10am-9pm Mon-Thu, to 6pm Fri & Sat, to 5pm Sun) Free Internet access.
Medical center (☎ 505-522-8641; 2450 S Telshor Blvd, Las Cruces; ☽ 24hr emergency)
Mesilla Visitor Center (☎ 505-647-9698; www.old mesilla.org; Av de Mesilla, Mesilla ☽ 9:30am-4:30pm Mon-Sat, 11am-3pm Sun)
Police (☎ 505-526-0795; 217 E Picacho Ave, Las Cruces)
Post office (☎ 505-524-2841; 201 E Las Cruces Ave, Las Cruces)

Sights

For many, a visit to neighboring **Mesilla** is the highlight of their time in Las Cruces. Despite the souvenir shops and tourist-oriented restaurants, the Mesilla Plaza and surrounding blocks are a step back in time. Wander a few blocks beyond the plaza to garner the essence of a mid-19th-century Southwestern town of Hispanic heritage.

Back in Las Cruces, the **Branigan Cultural Center** (☎ 505-541-2155; 490-500 N Water St; admission free; ☽ 8:30am-4:40pm Mon-Fri, 9am-1pm Sat) houses both the **Museum of Fine Art & Culture** and the **Las Cruces Historical Museum**, with small collections of local art, sculpture, quilts and historic artifacts.

The **NMSU Museum** (☎ 505-646-3739; www.nmsu .edu/~museum; Kent Hall, cnr Solano Dr & University Ave; admission free; ☽ noon-4pm Tue-Fri) is worth a look because of changing exhibits focusing on local art, history and archaeology. **NMSU Art**

Gallery (☎ 505-646-2545; www.nmsu.edu/~artgal; Williams Hall; admission free; ⏰ 10am-5pm Mon-Sat) has a large collection of contemporary art.

If you're interested in agricultural history, the **Farm & Ranch Heritage Museum** (☎ 505-522-4100; 4100 Dripping Springs Rd; adult/senior/child 6-17 $3/2/1; ⏰ 9am-5pm Mon-Sat, noon-5pm Sun) is for you. From prehistoric Indian farming techniques to the life histories of 20th-century ranchers, the exhibits here are well laid out. Children get a kick out of seeing livestock up close and personal. Call ahead about milking and blacksmithing demonstrations. The museum also features a good restaurant.

Dripping Springs National Recreation Area (☎ 505-522-1219; per car $3; ⏰ 8am-sunset), once called the Cox Ranch and now jointly managed by the BLM and the Nature Conservancy, is a great bird-watching and picnicking place. About 11 miles from town, head east on University Ave, which becomes unpaved Dripping Springs Rd.

White Sands Missile Test Center Museum (☎ 505-678-2250, 505-678-8824; www.wsmr-history.org; Bldg 200, Headquarters Ave; admission free; ⏰ 8am-4pm Mon-Fri, 10am-3pm Sat & Sun), 25 miles east of Las Cruces along Hwy 70, represents the heart of the White Sands Missile Range. A major military testing site since 1945, it still serves as an alternate landing site for the space shuttle. At the gate, tell the guard you are visiting the museum; you'll need to show your driver's license, proof of car insurance and car registration (or rental papers).

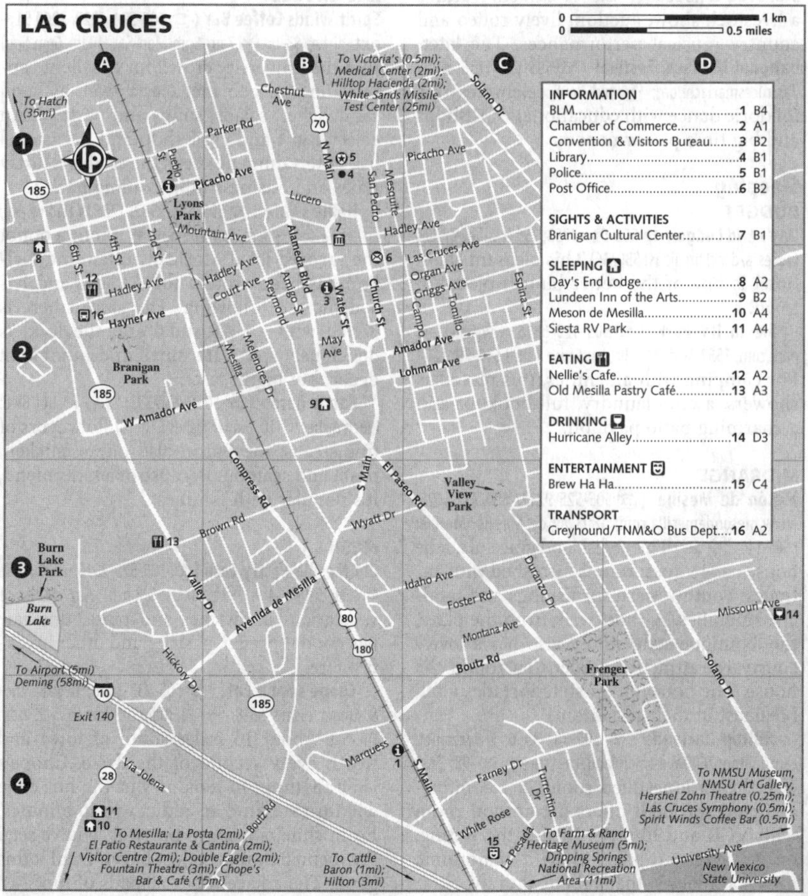
LAS CRUCES
0 1 km
0 0.5 miles
INFORMATION
BLM....1 B4
Chamber of Commerce....2 A1
Convention & Visitors Bureau....3 B2
Library....4 B1
Police....5 B1
Post Office....6 B2
SIGHTS & ACTIVITIES
Branigan Cultural Center....7 B1
SLEEPING
Day's End Lodge....8 A2
Lundeen Inn of the Arts....9 B2
Meson de Mesilla....10 A4
Siesta RV Park....11 A4
EATING
Nellie's Cafe....12 A2
Old Mesilla Pastry Café....13 A3
DRINKING
Hurricane Alley....14 D3
ENTERTAINMENT
Brew Ha Ha....15 C4
TRANSPORT
Greyhound/TNM&O Bus Dept....16 A2
To Victoria's (0.5mi); Medical Center (2mi); Hilltop Hacienda (2mi); White Sands Missile Test Center (25mi)
To Hatch (35mi)
To Airport (5mi) Deming (58mi)
Exit 140
To Mesilla: La Posta (2mi); El Patio Restaurante & Cantina (2mi); Visitor Centre (2mi); Double Eagle (2mi); Fountain Theatre (3mi); Chope's Bar & Café (15mi)
To Cattle Baron (1mi); Hilton (3mi)
To Farm & Ranch Heritage Museum (5mi); Dripping Springs National Recreation Area (11mi)
To NMSU Museum, NMSU Art Gallery, Hershel Zohn Theatre (0.25mi); Las Cruces Symphony (0.5mi); Spirit Winds Coffee Bar (0.5mi)
New Mexico State University
Lyons Park
Branigan Park
Burn Lake Park
Burn Lake
Valley View Park
Frenger Park
Chestnut Ave
Parker Rd
Picacho Ave
Mountain Ave
Hadley Ave
Hayner Ave
Court Ave
W Amador Ave
Amador Ave
Lohman Ave
Las Cruces Ave
Organ Ave
Griggs Ave
Alameda Blvd
Water St
Church St
N Main
S Main
El Paseo Rd
Compress Rd
Brown Rd
Wyatt Dr
Valley Dr
Avenida de Mesilla
Idaho Ave
Foster Rd
Montana Ave
Boutz Rd
Missouri Ave
Solano Dr
Espina St
Duranzo Dr
Hickory Dr
Via Jolena
Marquess
Farney Dr
Turrentine Dr
White Rose
La Pesada
University Ave
Boutz Rd

Festivals & Events

The **Whole Enchilada Fiesta** (☺ late Sep–early Oct), the city's best-known event, features live music, food booths, arts and crafts, sporting events, a chile cook-off, carnival rides and a parade. It culminates in the cooking of the world's biggest enchilada on Sunday morning. The **Fiesta of Our Lady of Guadalupe** (☎ 505-526-8171; ☺ Dec 10-12), held in the nearby Indian village of Tortugas, is different. Late into the first night, drummers and masked dancers accompany a statue of Mary in a procession from the church. On the following day, participants climb several miles to Tortugas Mountain for mass; dancing and ceremonies continue into the night in the village. The **Southern New Mexico State Fair & Rodeo** (☺ late Sep–early Oct) features a livestock show, auction, lively rodeo and country musical performances. The **International Mariachi Festival** (☎ 505-525-1735; www.lascrucesmariachi.org; ☺ mid-Nov) celebrates this folkloric dance with educational workshops and big time performances.

Sleeping

BUDGET

Day's End Lodge (☎ 505-524-7753; 755 N Valley Dr, Las Cruces; s/d incl breakfast $30/36) This pleasant chain hotel is one of the better budget places in town.

Siesta RV Park (☎ 505-523-6816; www.siestarvpark.com; 1551 Av de Mesilla, Las Cruces; sites $18-29; ▢) For camping with amenities, this place has showers, a coin laundry, full hookups and a charming patio pavilion.

MIDRANGE

Mesón de Mesilla (☎ 505-525-9212, 800-732-6025; www.mesondemesilla.com; 1803 Av de Mesilla, Mesilla; r $65-140; ✖ ▣) This stylish and graceful adobe house has 15 guest rooms furnished with antiques, Southwestern furnishings and modern amenities. A short walk from the plaza, the 'boutique-style' house also has a lovely courtyard; attractive gardens surround the house. The honeymoon suite includes a full breakfast in their restaurant.

Hilltop Hacienda (☎ 505-382-3556; www.zianet.com/hilltop; 2600 Westmoreland, Las Cruces; r $85-98; ✖) Yes, the antique-filled rooms are comfortable and the B&B offers a common room with VCR and library. But it's the setting, on 18 acres atop a hill with panoramic mountain views, that's the real draw.

Lundeen Inn of the Arts (☎ 505-526-3326, 888-526-3326; www.innofthearts.com; 618 S Alameda Blvd, Las Cruces; s $58-64, d $75-85, ste incl breakfast $85-105; ✖) This large, turn-of-the-19th-century Mexican Territorial–style inn has 20 guest rooms (all wildly different), an airy living room with soaring ceilings (made of pressed tin) and an art gallery. Some rooms have kitchenettes; some might feature vigas or a kiva fireplace; all have a phone.

Hilton (☎ 505-522-4300; 705 S Telshor Blvd, Las Cruces; r $80; ▢ ▣) The town's best hotel, a seven-story Mexican colonial structure, has 200 spacious rooms, exercise facilities and good city and mountain views.

Eating

LAS CRUCES

Spirit Winds Coffee Bar (☎ 505-521-1222; 2260 S Locust; dishes $3-6; ☺ 7am-8pm Mon-Sat, 10am-6pm Sun) Join the university crowd for excellent cappuccino and gourmet tea, as well as good sandwiches, salads, soups and pastries. An eclectic gift and card shop and occasional live entertainment keeps the students, artsy types and business folks coming back.

Nellie's Cafe (☎ 505-524-9982; 1226 W Hadley Ave; dishes $4-6; ☺ 8am-4pm Tue-Sat) Without a doubt the favored local Mexican restaurant, Nellie's has been around for decades and has a dedicated following. The slogan here is 'Chile with an Attitude' and the food is deliciously spicy. It's small and humble in decor, but big in taste.

Cattle Baron (☎ 505-522-7533; 790 S Telshor Blvd; lunch dishes $5-10, dinner dishes $10-18) Purveyors of fine steaks, the Baron also offers chicken, pasta and seafood. Because of a kid's menu, it's popular with families.

MESILLA

Old Mesilla Pastry Café (☎ 505-525-2636; 2790 Av de Mesilla; dishes $4-9; ☺ breakfast & lunch) An oasis of vegetarian sandwiches and pizza, this café has good espresso, pastries and other breakfast fare.

Chope's Bar & Café (☎ 505-233-3420; Hwy 28; lunch & dinner dishes $5-8; ☺ 11:30am-1:30pm & 5-9:30pm Tue-Sat) About 15 miles south of town and worth every second of the drive, Chope's isn't anything to look at, but the hot chile will turn you into an addict within minutes. From chile *rellenos* to burritos, you've seen the menu before; you just haven't had it this good. The adjacent bar is loads of fun.

Double Eagle Restaurant (☎ 505-523-6700, 505-523-4999; 308 Calle de Guadalupe; lunch dishes $9-16, dinner dishes $14-40; ☯ 11am-10pm Mon-Sat, irregular hr Sun) An upscale eatery offering continental and Southwestern cuisine in an elegant Victorian and Territorial-style setting, Double Eagle doesn't mind if you stroll around to drink in the 19th-century architecture even if you decide not to eat here. It's on the National Register of Historic Places; they don't make' em like this anymore, with central courtyards, chandeliers and 30ft bars.

La Posta (☎ 505-524-3524; 2410 Calle de San Albino; lunch dishes $4-10, dinner dishes $5-16; ☯ lunch & dinner Tue-Sun) The area's most famous Mexican eatery (because of its location more than the quality of food or the table settings) is housed in an early-19th-century adobe house that predates the founding of Mesilla. A Butterfield stagecoach stop in the 1850s, today's restaurant claims to have the largest collection of tequila in the Southwest (with close to 100 varieties). Order enchiladas.

Drinking & Entertainment

The *Bulletin*, a free weekly published on Thursday, has up-to-the-minute entertainment information.

Foreign and art films are screened at the **Fountain Theater** (☎ 505-524-8287; 2469 Calle de Guadalupe, Mesilla; adult/student $6/5). Shoot some pool and down some brews at **Brew Ha Ha** (☎ 505-647-3348; 2500 S Valley Dr; ☯ 3pm-2am daily) or belly up to the bar at **El Patio Restaurante & Cantina** (☎ 505-524-0982; on the plaza, Mesilla; bar ☯ until late). Also housed in an early adobe building and in operation since the 1930s, El Patio is similar to La Posta (above) but also has a bar that attracts jazz lovers. **Hurricane Alley** (☎ 505-532-9358; 1490 Missouri Ave) has live rock or DJs and dancing on weekends. **Victoria's** (☎ 505-523-0440; 2395 N Solano Dr) features weekend dancing with Latin bands.

The American Southwest Theater Company presents plays at the **Hershel Zohn Theater** (☎ 505-646-4515; McFie Circle; tickets $8-13) on the NMSU campus, while the **Las Cruces Symphony** (☎ 505-646-3709; tickets $20) performs at the NMSU Music Center Recital Hall.

Getting There & Away

Greyhound/TNM&O (☎ 505-524-8518; www.greyhound .com; 490 N Valley Dr) has buses traversing the two interstate corridors (I-10 and I-25), as well as buses to Roswell and beyond.

Las Cruces Shuttle Service (☎ 505-525-1784, 800-288-1784; www.lascrucesshuttle.com) runs 12 vans daily to the El Paso Airport ($31 to $38 one-way, $15 to $30 for each additional person) and vans to Deming, Silver City and other destinations on request.

DEMING & AROUND

pop 14,100 / elev 4335ft

The least populous of the state's four corners, Deming (founded in 1881 as a railway junction) is popular with retirees. It's surrounded by cotton fields on the northern edge of the Chihuahuan Desert. But if this is a desert, where does all the water come from for the family farms and ranches? It's tapped from the invisible Mimbres River, which disappears underground about 20 miles north of town and emerges in Mexico. A good museum, nearby state parks and the unique duck races (p436) attract visitors on their way to Arizona.

The **Chamber of Commerce** (☎ 505-546-2674, 800-848-4955; www.demingchamber.com; 800 E Pine St; ☯ 9am-5pm Mon-Fri, 9am-11pm Sat) has more details if you're hanging around a while. **Greyhound** (☎ 505-546-3881; www.greyhound.com; 300 E Spruce St) runs two or three daily buses along the I-10 corridor.

Sights & Activities

Run by the Luna County Historical Society, the **Deming Luna Mimbres Museum** (☎ 505-546-2382; 301 S Silver Ave; admission free; ☯ 9am-4pm Mon-Sat, 1:30-4pm Sun, closed major holidays) has varied, interesting and well-displayed exhibits including a superb doll collection, Mimbres pots, vintage cars, liquor decanters, homemade quilts and, get this, a braille edition of *Playboy*.

Fourteen miles southeast of Deming via Hwys 11 and 141, **Rock Hound State Park** (☎ 505-546-6182; per car per day $4) is known for the semiprecious or just plain pretty rocks that can be collected here (there's a 15lb limit). You'll need a shovel and some rockhounding experience to uncover anything special; local experts suggest walking into the Little Florida Mountains for a while before beginning to look for rocks bearing (perhaps) agate, opal, jasper or quartz crystals. Don't know what you're looking for? Stop at the **Geolapidary Museum & Rock Shop** (☎ 505-546-4021; admission $1; ☯ 9am-5pm Thu-Tue), 2 miles before the park entrance.

NEW MEXICO

Pancho Villa looms large in Southwestern consciousness. And his story is described in a small museum at **Pancho Villa State Park** (☎ 505-531-2711; www.nmparks.com; 400 W Hwy 9; per car per day $5; ⏰ 8am-5pm). On March 9, 1916, the Mexican revolutionary and outlaw, unhappy with the US government's support of his enemies, stormed across the border with several hundred troops. He attacked US Army Camp Furlong and the town of **Columbus** (3 miles north of the Mexican border), killing 18 people and burning several buildings before being pushed back into Mexico, having lost over 100 men. He was chased deep into Mexico by General John 'Black Jack' Pershing, who led US troops using aircraft and motor vehicles – the first time the US used both in warfare. Camp Furlong is long gone, and once-bustling Columbus is now a village of some 1000 inhabitants, but visitors head there because of its unique history. There's a desert botanical garden, picnic area, playground, and a **campground** ($10-14) with about 80 sites and showers, drinking water and fire pits. The small **Columbus Historical Museum** (☎ 505-531-2620; cnr NM 9 & NM 11; admission free, donation accepted; ⏰ 10am-1pm Mon-Thu, to 4pm Fri-Sun), opposite the state park in the 1902 railway depot, includes exhibits on Pancho Villa, the railroad, and farm and ranching culture.

Festivals & Events
Attracting tens of thousands of visitors, the **Great American Duck Races** (4th weekend Aug) is perhaps the most whimsical and popular festival in the state. The main event is the duck races themselves, which offer thousands of dollars in prize money. Anyone can enter for a $10 fee ($5 for kids), which includes 'duck rental.' Other wacky events include the Tortilla Toss (winners toss tortillas over 170ft), Outhouse Races and a Duckling Contest. As if that weren't enough, entertainment ranges from cowboy poets to local musicians, and there's a parade, hot-air balloons and food.

Sleeping & Eating
Room rates rise during duck races and the state fair (early October), when you need to make reservations.
Grand Motor Inn (☎ 505-546-2631; 1721 E Pine St; r $40; 🐾) You can often get a discount at this nice place, surrounded by grassy grounds.

City of Rocks State Park (☎ 505-536-2800; Hwy 61; sites $10-14) Rounded volcanic towers make up this 'city,' and you can camp among the towers in secluded sites with tables and fire pits. A nature trail, drinking water and showers are available. Head 24 miles northwest of Deming along Hwy 180, then 3 miles northeast on Hwy 61.

Si Senor (☎ 505-546-3938; 200 E Pine St; dishes $5-10; ⏰ 9:30am-8pm Mon-Sat, 10am-3pm Sun) Deming has a handful of good and simple Mexican-American restaurants but this is the best. Order *huevos rancheros* in the morning and a big deluxe platter with the works later in the day. Then go take a siesta.

SOUTHEASTERN NEW MEXICO

With the exception of the forests surrounding the resort towns of Cloudcroft and Ruidoso, Southeastern New Mexico is marked by seemingly endless horizons and grassy plains. It's also marked by an awesome expanse of gypsum at White Sands National Monument and a 60-mile cave system at Carlsbad Caverns. Spend dusk at both places if you can. For variety, it just doesn't get any better. Natural and historical attractions range from thousand-year-old rock etchings at Three Rivers Petroglyph National Recreation Area to ground zero where the atomic bomb was first detonated to even more Billy the Kid history at Fort Sumner in Lincoln. Why stop there though? Southeastern New Mexico epitomizes quirky and diverse. You'll also encounter alien sightings in Roswell, painter Peter Hurd in Lincoln, Smokey Bear, a winery and artists near Alamogordo, lava fields at Valley of Fires and cattle and oil rigs the further east you go.

ALAMOGORDO & AROUND
pop 35,500 / elev 4350ft
Despite a dearth of amenities, Alamogordo (Spanish for 'fat cottonwood tree') is the center of one of the most historically important space and atomic research programs. Perhaps more importantly for today's traveler, it's close to La Luz (opposite), an outpost for artists and craftspeople, and Tularosa (opposite), which has a fine winery.

White Sands Blvd (also called Hwy 54, 70 or 82) is the main drag through town and runs north–south. Addresses on North White Sands Blvd correspond to numbered cross-streets (thus 1310 N WSB is just north of 13th); addresses on South WSB are one block south of 1st.

Information

Hospital (☎ 505-439-6100; 2669 N Scenic Dr; ☽ 24hr emergency)

Library (☎ 505-439-4140; 10th St; ☽ 10am-8pm Mon-Thu, 10am-5pm Fri, 11am-5pm Sat, 1-5pm Sun) Free Internet access.

Lincoln USFS National Forest Ranger Station (☎ 505-434-7200; 1101 New York; ☽ 7:30am-4:30pm Mon-Fri)

Police (☎ 505-439-4300; 700 Virginia Ave)

Post office (☎ 505-437-9390; 30 E 12th St)

Visitor center (☎ 505-437-6120, 800-826-0294; www .alamogordo.com; 1301 N White Sands Blvd; ☽ 8am-5pm Mon-Fri, 9am-5pm Sat & Sun)

Sights & Activities

Alamogordo's most important attraction, the four-story **New Mexico Museum of Space History** (☎ 505-437-2840, 877-333-6589; www.spacefame .org; Hwy 2001; adult $2.50, child 4-12 $2; ☽ 9am-5pm), is nicknamed 'the golden cube' and looms over the town. It has excellent exhibits on space research and flight. Its **Tombaugh Imax Theater & Planetarium** (adult/child $6/4.50) shows outstanding films on anything from the Grand Canyon to the dark side of the moon, as well as laser shows and multimedia presentations on a huge wraparound screen.

Established in 1898 as a diversion for railway travelers, the **Alameda Park & Zoo** (☎ 505-439-4290; 1021 N White Sands Blvd; adult $2.20, child 3-11 $1.10; ☽ 9am-5pm) is the oldest zoo west of the Mississippi. Small but well run, it features exotics from around the world, among them the endangered Mexican gray wolf.

Railroad buffs and kids flock to the **Toy Train Depot** (☎ 505-437-2855; 1991 N White Sands Blvd; admission $3; ☽ noon-5pm Wed-Sun), an 1898 railway depot with five rooms of train memorabilia and toy trains, and a 2.5-mile narrow-gauge train.

Wander around the historical center of town, east of N White Sands Blvd along and just off 10th St; the USFS building at 11th and New York houses Peter Hurd's *Sun and Rain* frescoes, painted in the early 1940s as part of the New Deal's WPA art program.

The small and thoroughly local **Tularosa Basin Historical Society Museum** (☎ 505-434-4438; www.alamogordomuseum.org; 1301 N White Sands Blvd; admission free; ☽ 10am-4pm Mon-Fri, 10am-3pm Sat, noon-3pm Sun) focuses on Mescalero Indians and the mining, railroad, and logging industries. The museum's most cherished holding is a 47-star US flag, one of only a handful that exist because Arizona joined the USA just six weeks after New Mexico did.

La Luz, lies 4 miles north of Alamogordo and is worthy of a stroll, as it remains unspoilt by tourism. Ten miles further north on Hwy 54, the attractive village of **Tularosa** is dominated by the 1869 St Francis de Paula Church, built in a simple New Mexican style. **Tularosa Vineyards** (☎ 505-585-2260; www.tularosavineyards.com; Hwy 54; ☽ 9am-5pm Mon-Sat, noon-5pm Sun) is a friendly and picturesque winery about 2 miles north of Tularosa. It offers daily afternoon tours and tastings. **Casa de Suenos** (☎ 505-585-3494; 35 St Francis Dr; breakfast dishes $4-8, lunch & dinner dishes $7-13; ☽ 11am-8pm Mon-Sat, 10:30am-8pm Sun), all done up with folk paintings from South of the Border, is a festive place with a great outdoor patio. Its New Mexican cuisine is some of the best in the area and the lunch-time buffet is bountiful.

Sleeping & Eating

Best Western Desert Aire Motor Inn (☎ 505-437-2110; www.bestwestern.com; 1021 S White Sands Blvd; r $62-109; ☒) Recently remodeled, this chain hotel has standard-issue rooms and suites (some with kitchenettes), along with a sauna and whirlpool.

Satellite Inn (☎ 505-437-8454, 800-221-7690; www .satelliteinn.com; 2224 N White Sands Blvd; d incl breakfast $40; ☒) All these simple and clean double rooms have a microwave and refrigerator. It's your typical (albeit above-average) roadside motel.

Alamogordo Roadrunner Campground (☎ 505-437-3003; 412 24th St; tent sites $21-23, RV sites $24-29, 'kamping kabins' $35-37; ☒ ▢) Great for families, these one-room cabins have bunk beds and a double bed. You'll find a laundry, playground, recreation room and grocery store on the premises.

Oliver Lee State Park (tent/RV sites $10/14) Developed and free dispersed camping is available in the Lincoln National Forest, particularly along forest roads branching off from Hwy 82 east of Alamogordo.

NEW MEXICO

Margo's (☎ 505-434-0689; 504 E 1st St; lunch & dinner dishes $5-9; ◷ 10:30am-9pm Mon-Sat, 11am-8:30pm Sun) There's not much to look at inside but hey, when they offer such good Mexican cuisine at such good prices, who can complain? Family owned since the early 1980s, Margo's has a robust and tasty combo plate.

Compass Rose Brew Pub (☎ 505-434-9633; 2203 E 1st St; dishes $10-20) If you're tired of green chile and beans, and are overcome by a desire for food with a German flair, try this slightly yuppyish place. Both with friendly service and family-friendly, Compass Rose has a great selection of brews, and fresh guacamole and salads.

Plaza Pub (☎ 505-437-9495; cnr White Sands Blvd & 10th St; dishes $4-6) A truly local place to kick back, this pub has good burgers and green-chile stew along with a wide selection of beer. Or come to shoot some pool and ponder the stuffed animal heads that adorn the walls. On weekends, live bands draw locals.

Entertainment

Shooters Pizza & Patio Bar (☎ 505-443-6000; Hwy 70) Shooters has karaoke Monday through Wednesday; the line up the rest of the week is hip-hop, country or top-40.

DETOUR: THREE RIVERS PETROGLYPH NRA

The uncrowded **Three Rivers Petroglyph National Recreation Area** (☎ 505-525-4300; County Rd B30, off Hwy 54; per car $3; tent/RV sites $3/15) showcases 20,000 petroglyphs inscribed 1000 years ago by the Jornada Mogollon people. The 1-mile hike through mesquite and cacti offers good views of the Sacramento Mountains to the east and White Sands Monument on the horizon. Nearby is a pithouse in a partially excavated village. There are six camping shelters with barbecue grills (free), restrooms, water and two hook-ups for RVs. The **BLM** (☎ 505-525-4300; Marquess St, off Valley Dr) in Las Cruces has details.

The site is 27 miles north of Alamogordo on Hwy 54, and then 5 miles east on a signed road. If you want to rough it, a dirt road continues beyond the petroglyphs for about 10 miles to the Lincoln National Forest, where you'll find **Three Rivers Campground** (☎ 505-434-7200).

Getting There & Around

The **TNM&O Bus Station** (☎ 505-437-3050, 800-231-2222; www.greyhound.com; 601 N White Sands Blvd) has several daily buses to Albuquerque ($38, 4½ hours), Roswell ($25, 2½ hours), Carlsbad ($37, 4½ hours) and El Paso ($22, two hours). The **Alamo El Paso Shuttle** (☎ 505-437-1472, 800-872-2701; Best Western Desert Aire Motor Inn) has five buses daily to the El Paso International Airport ($33, 1½ hours).

WHITE SANDS NATIONAL MONUMENT

These captivating windswept dunes are a highlight of any trip to New Mexico. Try to time a visit to the oasis-like and ethereal **White Sands** (www.nps.gov/whsa; 15 miles southwest of Hwy 82/70; adult $3, under child 16 free) with sunrise or sunset (or both) when it's even more magical than normal. It's here that, gypsum, a chalky mineral used in making plaster of Paris, covers 275 sq miles. From the **visitor center** (☎ 505-679-2599; ◷ 8am-7pm Jun-Aug, to 5pm Sep-May), drive the 16-mile scenic loop into the heart of the dazzling white sea of sand – get out of the car and climb, romp, slide and roll in the soft dunes. Hike the Alkali Flat, a 4.5 mile (round-trip) backcountry trail through the heart of the dunes, or the simple 1-mile loop nature trail. **Backcountry campsites**, with no water or toilet facilities, are a mile from the scenic drive. Pick up permits (adult $3, child under 16 $1.50 per night) in person at the visitor center up to one hour before sunset.

CLOUDCROFT & AROUND

pop 750 / elev 9000ft

Pleasant Cloudcroft, which has early-19th-century buildings, offers lots of outdoor recreation options, a good base for exploration and a low-key feel. Situated high in the mountains, it provides welcome relief from the lowlands heat to the east.

Hwy 82 is the main drag through town; most places are on Hwy 82 or within a few blocks of it. Stop at the **Chamber of Commerce** (☎ 505-682-2733; www.cloudcroft.net; Hwy 82; ◷ 10am-5pm Mon-Sat) or **Sacramento Ranger Station** (☎ 505-682-2551; Chipmunk Ave; ◷ 7:30am-4:30pm Mon-Fri).

Sights & Activities

One of the world's largest solar observatories is near Sunspot, 20 miles south of Cloudcroft. Though primarily for scientists,

---

THE BLAST HEARD 'ROUND THE WORLD

Just two days a year (on the first Saturdays in April and October), the public is permitted to tour the **Trinity Site**, where the first atomic bomb was detonated on July 16, 1945. Thirty-five miles west of Carrizozo, the eerie tour includes the base camp, the McDonald Ranch house where the plutonium core for the bomb was assembled, and ground zero itself. The test was carried out above ground and resulted in a quarter-mile-wide crater and an 8-mile-high cloud mushrooming above the desert. The radiation level of the site is 'only' 10 times greater than the region's background level; a one-hour visit to ground zero will result in an exposure of one-half to one millorentgen (mrem), two to four times the estimated exposure of a typical adult on an average day in the USA. Trinitite, a green, glassy substance resulting from the blast, is still radioactive, still scattered around and still must not be touched. Resist the urge to add it to your road-trip rock collection. This desolate area is fittingly called **Jornada del Muerto** (Journey of Death) and is overshadowed by 8638ft **Oscura Peak** (Darkness Peak on state maps). Call the **Alamogordo Chamber of Commerce** (☎ 505-437-6120, 800-826-0294; www.alamogordo.com) for information.

---

tourists can take self-guided tours of the **Sacramento Peak Observatory** (☎ 505-434-7000; visitor center 10am-4pm) on Friday, Saturday and Sunday at 2pm during the summer. The drive to Sunspot, along the **Sunspot Scenic Byway**, is a high and beautiful one, with the mountains to the east and White Sands National Monument (opposite) to the west. From Cloudcroft, take Hwy 130 to Hwy 6563.

Hiking (April to November) is popular here; outings range from short hikes close to town to overnight backpacking trips. Although trails are often fairly flat, the 9000ft elevation can make for some strenuous hiking if you are not acclimatized. The most popular day hike is the 2.6-mile Osha Loop Trail, which leaves Hwy 82 from a small parking area 1 mile west of Cloudcroft.

The Lodge Resort (right) has a beautiful nine-hole **golf course** (☎ 505-682-2098; midweek/weekend $19/25, cart rental per person $7) that is one of the highest and oldest in the USA. In the winter, the course is groomed for cross-country skiing. The Lodge also provides guided snowmobile and horse-drawn sleigh rides.

Trails in the Sacramento Mountains offer great mountain biking and **High Altitude** (☎ 505-682-1229; www.highaltitude.org; 310 Burro Ave; 10am-5pm Sun, Mon, Wed & Thu, 10am-6pm Fri & Sat) can tell you where to go when they rent you bikes. For horseback riding, contact **Chippeway Riding Stables** (☎ 505-682-2565; Hwy 130) 6 miles out of town.

Ski Cloudcroft (☎ 505-682-2333; www.ski-cloudcroft.com; Hwy 8; lift tickets adult $35, child under 12 $25), about 2 miles east of town, has 24 runs de-

signed mostly for beginner and intermediate skiers. Inner-tubing and snowboarding are also possible.

Triple M Mystical Mountain Snow Ski Area (☎ 505-682-2205, 800-766-7529; www.triplemsnowplay.com; Sunspot Hwy, off Hwy 6563; Sat, Sun & holidays), 5 miles south of Cloudcroft, has snowmobile tours, horse-drawn sleigh rides and inner-tubing.

Ski Palace (☎ 505-682-2045; 207 Hwy 82) rents equipment for cross-country and downhill skiing, inner-tubing, snowshoeing and sledding.

Festivals & Events
Autumn is celebrated with **Oktoberfest** (first weekend Oct) and summer is celebrated with an annual **Cherry Festival** (3rd Sun Jun). The nearby hills between Cloudcroft and Alamogordo are rife with cherry orchards.

Sleeping & Eating
Lodge Resort & Spa (☎ 505-682-2566, 800-395-6343; www.thelodgeresort.com; 1 Corona Place; r $109-189, pavilion r $99-129, ste $179-319;) One of the best historic hotels in the Southwest, this grand old Lodge was built in 1899 as a vacation getaway for railroad employees. Try to get a room in the main Bavarian-style hotel; these are furnished with period and Victorian pieces. Pavilion rooms are a few blocks away in a separate, less attractive building. The Lodge also rents four more luxurious suites in a mountain home and has a fine restaurant, Rebecca's (p440).

New Mexico Skies (☎ 505-687-2429; www.nmskies.com; 1-/2-bedroom apt $140-170, 3-bedroom home $210) This B&B rents high-powered star gazing equipment, so amateur astronomers (in particular) will really enjoy this place tucked against a national forest backdrop. Advance reservations required. As for the rooms, they consist of simple knotty pine cottages and simple one- and two-bedroom apartments (with and without separate entrances).

Raven Wind (☎ 505-687-3073;www.ravenwindranch .com; 1234 NM Hwy 24, Weed; r incl breakfast $85; 🖳) Surrounded by the Lincoln National Forest about 28 miles from Cloudcroft, this ranch-style place offers two basic double rooms (don't expect Southwestern style), comfortable rockers on a huge wraparound porch and a complimentary light lunch. Families can settle into an entire guest house.

USFS Camping (☎ 505-682-2551; sites $8-10; 🕒 May–mid-Sep) Several USFS campgrounds are open in the summer only because of the elevation, though some may open earlier or later, with no services or fees, weather permitting. There are no RV hookups.

Rebecca's (☎ 505-682-3131; 1 Corona Place; breakfast $6-11, lunch $7-17, dinner $18-34) Within the Lodge (p439), Rebecca's offers by far the best food in town, especially the Sunday brunch buffet ($17). Kick back on the outside deck that has spectacular views of the mountains and the distant and shimmering White Sands National Monument (p438). All in all, it's elegant with good service and nicely prepared steaks and continental cuisine (and some Mexican dishes of course).

Western Bar & Café (☎ 505-682-2445; Burro Ave; dishes $5-12; 🕒 6am-9pm) This popular place looks like something out of the Wild West.

RUIDOSO & AROUND

pop 8000 / elev 7000ft

You want lively in these parts? You want Ruidoso. Downright bustling in the summer and big with punters at the racetrack, resorty Ruidoso has an utterly pleasant climate thanks to its lofty and forested perch near the Sierra Blanca (12,000ft). Neighboring Texans and local New Mexicans escaping the summer heat of Alamogordo (46 miles to the southwest) and Roswell (71 miles to the east) are happy campers here (or more precisely, happy 'cabiners'). The lovely Rio Ruidoso, a small creek with good fishing, also runs through town. Summertime hiking and wintertime skiing at Ski Apache keep folks busy, as do a smattering of galleries.

Orientation & Information

Ruidoso is very spread-out, with vacation homes tucked away on narrow streets sprawling into the surrounding mountains. Hwy 48 from the north is the main drag through town. This is called Mechem Dr until the small downtown area where it becomes Sudderth Dr, heading east to the Y-intersection with Hwy 70. Six miles north on Mechem Dr is the community of Alto, with more accommodations. The community of Ruidoso Downs is a separate village just east of Ruidoso on Hwy 70.

Both the **Chamber of Commerce** (☎ 505-257-7395, 800-253-2255; www.ruidoso.net; 720 Sudderth Dr; 🕒 8:30am-5pm Mon-Thu, 9am-5pm Fri-Sun) and the **Lincoln National Forest Ranger Station** (☎ 505-257-4095; 901 Mechem Dr; 🕒 7:30am-4:30pm Mon-Fri, 7:30am-4:30pm Sat May-Oct) are helpful.

Sights

The fine **Hubbard Museum of the American West** (☎ 505-378-4142; www.hubbardmuseum.org; 841 Hwy 70 W; admission $6; 🕒 9am-5pm) displays more than 10,000 Western-related items including Old West stagecoaches and American Indian pottery, and works by Frederic Remington and Charles M Russell. An impressive collection of horse-related displays, including a collection of saddles and the Racehorse Hall of Fame, lures horse-lovers.

The **Ruidoso Downs Racetrack** (☎ 505-378-4431; www.ruidosodownsracing.com; Hwy 70; admission free, grandstand seats & boxes $2.50-8.50; 🕒 races Thu-Sun late May-early Sep), one of the major racetracks in the Southwest, hosts the All American Futurity on Labor Day. The world's richest quarterhorse race has a purse of over $2,000,000. A track **casino** (🕒 11am-11pm) features an all-you can eat buffet ($7 to $15).

About 3000 Native Americans live on the 719 sq mile **Mescalero Apache Indian Reservation**, which lies in attractive country 17 miles southwest of Ruidoso on Hwy 70. The nomadic Apache arrived in this area 800 years ago and soon became enemies to local Pueblo Indians. In the 19th century, under pressure from European settlement and with their mobility greatly increased by the introduction of the horse, the Apache became some of the most feared raiders of the West. Despite the name of the Reservation, the Apache here are of three tribes: the Mescalero, the Chiricahua and the Lipan. The

Cultural Center (☎ 505-464-4494; Chiricahua Plaza, off Hwy 70, Mescalero; ☻ irregular) has an interesting exhibit about the Apache peoples and customs. The Inn of the Mountain Gods (p443) is a great place to sleep.

Activities

The best ski area south of Albuquerque is **Ski Apache** (☎ 505-336-4356, snow conditions 505-257-9001; www.skiapache.com; Hwy 48 exit 532; day-pass adult $49-52, child $31-34; ☻ 8:45am-9pm) 18 miles northwest of Ruidoso on the slopes of beautiful Sierra Blanca Peak (about 12,000ft).

Hiking is a popular summertime activity, especially the 4.6-mile day hike from the Ski Apache area to Sierra Blanca Peak, an ascent of 2000ft. Take Trail 15 from the small parking area just before the main lot and follow signs west and south along Trails 25 and 78 to Lookout Mountain (11,580ft). From there an obvious trail continues due south for 1.25 miles to Sierra Blanca Peak. Several other trails leave from the Ski Apache area; the ranger station in Ruidoso (opposite) has maps and information for more adventurous trips, including the beautiful Crest Trail.

Sierra Blanca Peak offers several lookouts with stunning views, especially in the fall – just drive up Ski Area Rd (Hwy 532) from Alto. Along this road, you'll see signs for the Monjeau Lookout via USFS Rd 117.

The Chamber of Commerce has a list of stables offering **horseback riding**; try **Grindstone Stables** (☎ 505-257-2241; Grindstone Resort Dr).

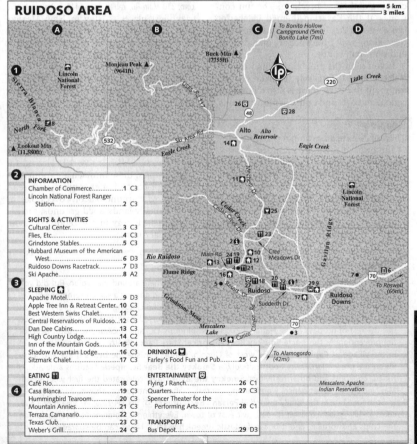

RUIDOSO AREA

INFORMATION	
Chamber of Commerce	1 C3
Lincoln National Forest Ranger Station	2 C3

SIGHTS & ACTIVITIES	
Cultural Center	3 C3
Flies, Etc.	4 C3
Grindstone Stables	5 C3
Hubbard Museum of the American West	6 D3
Ruidoso Downs Racetrack	7 D3
Ski Apache	8 A2

SLEEPING 🏠	
Apache Motel	9 D3
Apple Tree Inn & Retreat Center	10 C3
Best Western Swiss Chalet	11 C2
Central Reservations of Ruidoso	12 C3
Dan Dee Cabins	13 C3
High Country Lodge	14 C2
Inn of the Mountain Gods	15 C4
Shadow Mountain Lodge	16 C3
Sitzmark Chalet	17 C3

EATING 🍴	
Café Rio	18 C3
Casa Blanca	19 C3
Hummingbird Tearoom	20 C3
Mountain Annies	21 C3
Terraza Camanario	22 C3
Texas Club	23 C3
Weber's Grill	24 C3

DRINKING 🍷	
Farley's Food Fun and Pub	25 C2

ENTERTAINMENT 🎭	
Flying J Ranch	26 C1
Quarters	27 C3
Spencer Theater for the Performing Arts	28 C1

TRANSPORT	
Bus Depot	29 D3

NEW MEXICO

Rio Ruidoso offers good **fishing**, as do several lakes in the national forest. **Flies Etc** (☎ 505-257-4968; 2800 Sudderth Dr) offers guided fly-fishing trips for $35 an hour for two people on public water or $450 a day for fishing on private water (only two people are allowed at a time).

Festivals & Events

The top-quality **Ruidoso Art Festival** (last full weekend Jul) attracts thousands of browsing and buying visitors from all over the Southwest, while the **Golden Aspen Motorcycle Rally** (3rd weekend Sep) attracts 30,000 motorcycles riders. **Aspenfest** (1st weekend Oct) features a chile cook-off and a street festival, while the **Lincoln County Cowboy Symposium** (2nd weekend Oct) features cowboy poetry, chuckwagon cooking and horse breaking. The fun continues at the Bavarian-themed **Oktoberfest** (3rd weekend in Oct), with German food and beer, along with professional polka dancing and oom-pah bands.

If you're in the area, the annual Apache **Maidens' Puberty Ceremony** (Jul 4) takes place for about five days; there is also a powwow, rodeo, and arts and crafts demonstrations.

Sleeping

There are lots of area cabin rentals, but some of the ones in town are cramped. Most of the newer cabins are located in the Upper Canyon. Generally, cabins have kitchens and grills, and often fireplaces and decks. **Central Reservations of Ruidoso** (☎ 888-257-7577; www.casasderuidoso.com; 712 Mechem Dr; ☽ 8am-5pm) arranges condominium, cabin and lodge rentals. Although Ruidoso hotels are often referred to as 'lodges' or 'inns,' they're basically your standard motel.

BUDGET

Apache Motel (☎ 505-257-2986, 800-426-0616; www .ruidoso.net/apache; 344 Sudderth Dr; r from $50) These small basic rooms are clean; some have kitchenettes. A family unit is offered with fireplace and dining area.

Bonito Hollow Campground (☎ 505-336-4325; tent sites $16, RV sites $25-30, bunkhouse r & cabins $45; ☽ May–mid-Oct) On the Bonito River in Alto, this campground is so 21st century, offering a laptop modem hookup along with the usual picnic tables and campfire rings.

MIDRANGE

Dan Dee Cabins (☎ 505-257-2165; www.dandeecabins .com; 310 Main Rd; cabins from $119) One of the friendliest places to stay in New Mexico, these 12 woodsy cabins are spread over five grassy and forested acres. Constructed at various times beginning in the 1940s, each one is unique, private and comfy.

Apple Tree Inn & Retreat Center (☎ 505-257-1717, 877-277-5322; www.appletreebb-spa.com; 100 Lower Terrace; r $89-139; ☒ ▢) These 10 suites, with and without kitchens, are comfortable and unpretentious. They all have private entrances and easy access to the spa area.

Shadow Mountain Lodge (☎ 505-257-4886; www .smlruidoso.com; 107 Main St; r $99-135) Geared toward couples, these immaculate rooms feature fireplaces and offer romantic allure. A wooden wraparound balcony overlooks the professionally landscaped grounds; the hot tub is tucked away in a gazebo. Ask about individual cabins.

DETOUR: SMOKEY THE BEAR'S STOMPING GROUNDS

You've seen his likeness in state and national forests everywhere around the region. But did you know that Smokey the Bear was a real, live black bear cub and not just a sketch summoned from some designer's imagination? Once upon a time, he was found clinging to a tree, paws charred from a 17,000-acre forest fire in the Capitan Mountains. Nursed back to health, Smokey lived out the rest of his days in the National Zoo in Washington, DC, and became the poster bear for fire prevention. At the 3-acre **Smokey Bear Historical State Park** (☎ 505-354-2748; per day $1), set in the village of **Capitan**, 12 miles west of Lincoln, visitors can see the bear's grave and learn about fire prevention. Every Fourth of July, a **Smokey the Bear Stampede** features a parade, a rodeo, cookouts and other festivities. **Smokey the Bear Days**, celebrated the first weekend in May, includes a street dance, woodcarving contest, craft and antique car shows.

Stop for a bite at the family-owned **El Paisano Restaurant** (☎ 505-354-2206; 442 Smokey Bear Blvd; dishes $5-10; ☽ lunch & dinner Tue-Sat), just east of town. Everything is homemade here, including the chips and tortillas, and it boasts fantastic green-chile salsa. Hours can be sporadic.

High Country Lodge (☎ 505-336-4321, 800-845-7265; www.highcountrylodge.net; Hwy 48; r Sun-Thu $94, Fri & Sat $124; ☎) Just south of the turnoff to Ski Apache (p441), this older selection of rustic cabins is still among the town's most comfortable. The complex has 32 basic two-bedroom cabins, each with kitchen, fireplace and porch. Other facilities include a sauna, hot tub and tennis courts.

Best Western Swiss Chalet (☎ 505-258-3333; 1451 Mechem Dr; r $69-99; ☎) Convenient to the ski slopes and hugging the forest, this chain motel offers basic rooms. Ask about ski and bike packages.

Sitzmark Chalet (☎ 505-257-4140, 800-658-9694; www.sitzmark-chalet.com; 627 Sudderth Dr; r $65-105; ☐ ☒) These 17 simple but nice rooms have refrigerators and microwaves, perfect for longer stays. The hot tub comes in handy after a day of hiking.

TOP END

Inn of the Mountain Gods (☎ 505-257-5141, 800-545-9011; www.innofthemountaingods.com; 287 Carrizo Rd; r $129-299; ☎) This luxury resort hotel on the Mescalero Apache Reservation (p440), offers a casino and all kinds of activities, including guided fishing, paddleboat rentals and horseback riding. The old Inn of the Mountain Gods was completely leveled in 2003 and a new one sprang up in 2004, complete with a fitness room, several restaurants, a nightclub, sports bar and a championship golf course.

Eating

BUDGET

Cornerstone Bakery (☎ 505-257-1842; 359 Audeth Dr; dishes under $8; ☯ breakfast & lunch) Stay around long enough and the Cornerstone may become your touchstone. Everything on the menu, from omelets to croissant sandwiches, is worthy.

Casa Blanca (☎ 505-257-2495; 501 Mechem Dr; dishes $6-20) Dine on Southwestern cuisine in a renovated Spanish-style house or on the pleasant patio in the summer. The chile *rellenos* are to die for.

Hummingbird Tearoom (☎ 505-257-5100; 2306 Audeth Dr, Village Plaza; dishes $5-7; ☯ lunch Mon-Sat) This homey little place specializes in simple soups, salads and lunchtime sandwiches; delectable desserts and rich teas make a lovely afternoon diversion. The service is particularly attentive.

Terraza Camanario (☎ 505-257-4227; 1611 Sudderth Dr; lunch dishes $5-10, dinner dishes $6-13; ☯ 7am-8:30pm) Ruidoso's best Mexican restaurant has plenty for vegetarians; the guacamole is particularly great. But the service isn't exactly the fastest gun in the West.

MIDRANGE

Café Rio (☎ 505-257-7746; 2547 Sudderth Dr; pizzas $10-25; ☯ lunch & dinner) Thick crust pizza, with your choice of toppings, are wickedly and deservedly popular here, but their stuffed calzones are a good runner-up. Wash it down with a big selection of international and seasonal beer.

Weber's Grill (☎ 505-257-9559; 441 Mechem Dr; lunch dishes $6-10, dinner dishes $13-25; ☯ 11am-9pm Mon-Thu, to 10pm Fri & Sat & to 8pm Sun) A kinda cool and kinda happenin' kinda place that appeals to both families (upstairs) and brewpub crawlers (downstairs), Weber's is a friendly place to nosh on appetizers and burgers or gravitate toward something more serious like rib-eye steaks.

TOP END

Texas Club (☎ 505-258-3325; 212 Metz Dr; dinner dishes $10-30; ☯ dinner Wed-Sun) One of the busiest and best restaurants in town, decorated with all the bigness you'd expect in a place that takes its name from Texas (think longhorn and cowboy hats), this place serves big steaks and has dancing and live entertainment on the weekends. Call for directions – since it's a bit hidden – and reservations, since it's so beloved.

Mountain Annies (☎ 505-257-7982; 2710 Sudderth Dr; dinner dishes $10-25; ☯ dinner) It's a friendly place with a more-than-respectable salad bar that plays second fiddle to steaks and barbecue. Still, vegetarians won't go hungry.

Drinking & Entertainment

At **Farley's Food Fun & Pub** (☎ 505-258-5676; 1200 Mechem Dr; ☯ 11:30am-midnight), the most popular hangout in town, you can enjoy a beer and a game of pool while throwing peanut shells on the floor. The Texas Club (above) is popular for dancing. **Quarters** (☎ 505-257-9535; 2535 Sudderth Dr; ☯ 11am-2pm) provides space for blues and rock acts along with dancing. Hang out at the bar or at comfortable tables.

The **Spencer Theater for the Performing Arts** (☎ 505-336-4800, 888-818-7872; Hwy 220, Alto; performances $20-40), set in a stunning mountain

---

DETOUR: GREEN CHILE & BLACK LAVA

About 30 miles west of Lincoln and just four miles west of **Carrizozo** (☎ 505-648-2732; www.townof carrizozo.org; Hwy 54 & 380; ⊙ 10am-2pm Mon-Fri), the **Valley of Fires Recreation Area** (☎ 505-648-2241; Hwy 380; per car $5) features the most recent lava flows in continental USA. Visitors can walk over a lava flow estimated to be 1500 years old, 47 miles long and up to 160ft thick. **Camping sites** (tent & RV sites $7-18) have hookups, showers and restrooms. In the never-ending quest for New Mexico's best green chile, stop by the **Outpost Bar & Grill** (US 54 S, Carrizozo; ⊙ 10am-2am Mon-Sat, noon-midnight Sun), smack in the middle of nowhere. Along with an impressive gun collection and an obligatory selection of stuffed animal heads adorning the walls, Outpost has a great bar and excellent green-chile stew and green-chile cheeseburgers.

Eleven miles northeast of Carrizozo on Hwy 349, **White Oaks** was a gold-mining center in the 1880s, but now it's a ghost town with a few hearty souls, some interesting old buildings and historic tombstones. Stop in the White Oaks Saloon to cool off and chat with the bartender over a beer.

---

venue, hosts theatrical, musical and dance performances.

If the kids want some entertainment along with their steak, circle the wagons and ride over to **Flying J Ranch** (☎ 505-336-4330; Hwy 48; adult $19, child 4-12 $10; ⊙ nightly May-Aug, Sat Sep-Oct). About 1.5 miles north of Alto, this 'Western village' stages gunfights and offers pony rides with their cowboy-style chuckwagon. Western music tops off the evening.

Getting There & Around

The **bus depot** (☎ 505-257-2660; www.greyhound .com; 138 Service Rd) serves buses heading to Alamogordo ($12, one hour), Roswell ($15.75, 1½ hours) and El Paso, Texas ($30, three hours), several times a day; buses to Carlsbad ($34, four hours) also leave daily.

LINCOLN

pop 70 / elev 5700ft

Fans of Western history won't want to miss little Lincoln. Twelve miles east of Capitan along the **Billy the Kid National Scenic Byway** (p348; www.billybyway.com), this is where the gun battle that turned Billy the Kid into a legend took place. Perhaps surprisingly, modern influences, such as souvenir stands, are not allowed in town.

Only about 70 folks still reside in Lincoln and they're intent on preserving the 1880s buildings; the main street has been designated the **Lincoln State Monument**. You can visit the **Anderson Freeman Visitor Center & Museum** (☎ 505-653-4025; Hwy 380; admission to 4 sites $6; ⊙ 8:30am-4:30pm) where exhibits on the Buffalo soldiers, Apaches and the Lincoln County War explain the town's history. The admission price includes entry to the Tunstall Store (with a remarkable display of late-19th-century merchandise), the courthouse where the Kid escaped imprisonment, and Dr Wood's house, an intact turn-of-the-century doctor's home and office. The Tunstall Store and Dr Wood's house are closed from March to November.

During the **Old Lincoln Days** (1st full weekend Aug) musicians and mountain men, doctors and desperadoes wander the streets in period costume, and there are demonstrations of spinning, blacksmithing and other common frontier skills. In the evening there is the folk pageant, 'The Last Escape of Billy the Kid.'

Sleeping & Eating

Ellis Store Country Inn (☎ 505-653-4609, 800-653-6460; www.ellisstore.com; MM 98, Hwy 380; r $89-99, r incl breakfast $90-$120) This 19th-century adobe offers three antique-filled rooms (complete with wood stove) in the main house; five additional rooms are located in a historic mill on the property. Since dining options are limited in town, the host offers a six-course dinner ($70 per person) served in the cozy dining room Thursday to Saturday. Nonguests are welcome with a reservation.

Casa de Patrón B&B (☎ 505-653-4676, 800-524-5202; www.casapatron.com; r incl breakfast $82-112) This adobe house (c 1860) was purportedly slept in by the Kid. Seven rooms are located in the historic main house, adjoining casitas or a newer addition. Some have a fireplace or kitchenette; pick your preference.

Hurd Ranch Guest Homes (☎ 505-653-4331, 800-658-6912; www.wyethartists.com; 105 La Rinconada, San Patricio; casitas $140-250) This 2500-acre, very rural place in San Patricio, about 14 miles south of Lincoln, rents six lovely casitas by an apple orchard. Furnished with style and grace, and lots of original art, some units sleep up to six people. They are outfitted with modern conveniences. Owner and artist Peter Hurd runs the **Hurd la Rinconada Gallery** on the premises; he also shows the work of his relatives NC and Andrew Wyeth, his mother Henriette Wyeth and his father Michael Hurd.

ROSWELL

pop 45,000 / elev 3649ft

Conspiracy theorists and *X-Files* fanatics descend from other worlds into Roswell. Oddly famous as both the country's largest producer of wool and its UFO capital, Roswell has built a tourist industry around the alleged July 1947 UFO crash (see Identify *This!*, p447). The military quickly closed the area and allowed no more information to filter out for several decades (although later they claimed it was a balloon). Was it a flying saucer? The local convention and visitors bureau suggest that Roswell's special blend of climate and culture attracted touring space aliens who wanted a closer look! Decide for yourself.

If you're driving east on Hwy 70/380 from the Sacramento Mountains, enjoy the view. Roswell sits on the western edge of the dry plains, and these are the last big mountains you'll see for a while.

The 'Staked Plains' extending east into Texas were once home to millions of buffalo and many nomadic Native American hunters. White settlers and hunters moved in throughout the late 19th century, and killed some 3.5 million buffalo during a two-year period. Within a few years, the region became desolate and empty; only a few groups of Comanche mixed with other tribes roaming the plains, hunting and trying to avoid confinement on reservations. Roswell, founded in 1871, served as a stopping place for cowboys driving cattle.

The main west–east drag through town is 2nd St and the main north–south thoroughfare is Main St; their intersection is the heart of downtown.

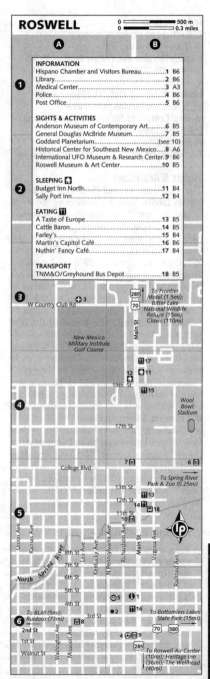

ROSWELL

0   500 m
0   0.3 miles

INFORMATION	
Hispano Chamber and Visitors Bureau............1	B6
Library..2	B6
Medical Center..3	A3
Police..4	B6
Post Office..5	B6

SIGHTS & ACTIVITIES	
Anderson Museum of Contemporary Art........6	B5
General Douglas McBride Museum................7	B5
Goddard Planetarium.........................(see 10)	
Historical Center for Southeast New Mexico.....8	A6
International UFO Museum & Research Center.9	B6
Roswell Museum & Art Center....................10	B5

SLEEPING	
Budget Inn North....................................11	B4
Sally Port Inn...12	B4

EATING	
A Taste of Europe....................................13	B5
Cattle Baron...14	B5
Farley's...15	B5
Martin's Capitol Café...............................16	B6
Nuthin' Fancy Café..................................17	B4

TRANSPORT	
TNM&O/Greyhound Bus Depot...................18	B5

Information

BLM office (☎ 505-627-0272; 2909 W 2nd St; ☺ 7:30am-4:30pm Mon-Fri)

Hispano Chamber and Visitors Bureau (☎ 505-624-0889, 888-767-9355; www.roswell-usa.com; 426 N Main St; ☺ 8am-5pm Mon-Fri)

Library (☎ 505-622-7101; 301 N Pennsylvania Ave; ☺ 5-10pm Wed-Sun) Free Internet access.

Medical Center (☎ 505-622-8170; 405 W Country Club Rd; ☺ 24hr emergency)

Police (☎ 505-624-6770; 128 W 2nd St)

Post office (☎ 505-623-7232; 415 N Pennsylvania Ave)

Sights & Activities

The excellent **Roswell Museum & Art Center** (☎ 505-624-6744; www.roswellmuseum.org; 100 W 11th St; admission free; ☺ 9am-5pm Mon-Sat, 1-5pm Sun) deserves a visit. Seventeen galleries showcase Southwestern artists including Georgia O'Keeffe (p389), Peter Hurd and Henriette Wyeth. An eclectic mix of Native American, Hispanic and Anglo artifacts means there's something for everyone. A major focus of the museum is space research. The **Goddard Planetarium** is the reconstructed lab of Robert H Goddard, who launched the first successful liquid fuel rocket in 1926. Goddard spent more than a decade carrying out rocket research in Roswell. A variety of early rocketry paraphernalia is also on display.

Serious followers of UFO phenomena (not to mention skeptics or the merely curious) will want to check out the **International UFO Museum & Research Center** (☎ 505-625-9495; www.iufomrc.org; 114 N Main St; admission free; ☺ 9am-5pm). Original photographs and witness statements form the 1947 Roswell Incident Timeline and explain the 'great cover-up.' The library claims to have the most comprehensive UFO-related materials in the world. And we have no reason to be sceptical.

Housed in the 1910 mansion of local rancher James Phelp White, the **Historical Center for Southeast New Mexico** (☎ 505-622-8333; 200 N Lea St; admission by donation; ☺ 1-4pm) is well worth seeing. On the National Register of Historic Places, the interior has been carefully restored to its original early-20th-century decor with period furnishings, photographs and art.

The small **Anderson Museum of Contemporary Art** (☎ 505-623-5600; www.roswellcvb.com/anderson .htm; 409 E College Blvd; admission free; ☺ 9am-noon & 1-4pm Mon-Fri, 1-5pm Sat & Sun) exhibits work by past and present Roswell residents.

The **Spring River Park & Zoo** (☎ 505-624-6760; www.roswellcvb.com/zoo.htm; College Blvd at Atkinson St; admission free; ☺ 10am-8pm Jun-Aug, 10am-5:30pm Sep-May), is a good place for younger kids, and has a petting zoo, prairie dogs, miniature train, carousel and kids' fishing pond.

Wintering water birds gather at the 38 sq mile **Bitter Lake National Wildlife Refuge** (☎ 505-622-6755; www.fws.gov/southwest; Pine Lodge Rd; admission free; ☺ sunrise-sunset); many birds remain to nest in the summer. To reach the refuge, about 15 miles northeast of Roswell, follow the signed roads from either Hwy 380 or Hwy 285/70.

The **General Douglas McBride Museum** (☎ 505-624-8220; 101 W College Blvd; admission free; ☺ 8:30am-3pm Tue-Fri, closed during lunch), on the campus of the New Mexico Military Institute, was established in 1891. The military Gothic architecture is quite impressive. The museum has displays on US military history that focus on contributions made by New Mexicans and alumni.

Festivals & Events

As you might imagine, Roswell has a couple of quirky festivals worth checking out. **New Mexico Dairy Day** (early June) features the

---

DETOUR: PORTALES' PEANUTS

The smell of roasting peanuts fills the air at the annual **Peanut Valley Festival** (third or fourth weekend Oct), where residents of Portales, a high-plains college town, have been celebrating their famous crop since the 1970s. Perhaps you didn't know that New Mexico grows 90 percent of the nation's Valencia peanuts? They're among the sweetest in the peanut family and they're big business in these parts. Peanut-based foods of all kinds are available at the festival. Go nuts burying students in a tank full of peanuts (for charity), or go for gold at the Peanut Olympics. You'll swoon over peanut-butter shakes ($2.10) at **Pat's Twin Cronnies** (☎ 505-356-5841; 100 N Chicago Ave), where they have been serving up their secret recipe since 1952. For festival information, contact the **Chamber of Commerce** (☎ 505-356-8541, 800-635-8036; www.portales.com; 200 E 7th St). Portales is 85 miles northeast of Roswell, via Hwy 70.

IDENTIFY *THIS!*

It was a heady time, the summer of 1947. Several UFOs were sighted around the country, but none like the one that fell into the desert near Roswell (p445) sometime during the first week of July, 1947. In a press release, the government identified the object as a crashed disk. A day later it claimed the disk was really just a weather balloon, confiscated all the previous press releases, cordoned off the area as they collected all the debris, and posted armed guards to escort curious locals from the site of the 'weather-balloon' crash. A local mortician fielded calls from the mortuary office at the government airfield inquiring after small, hermetically-sealed coffins for preventing tissue contamination and degeneration after several days of exposure to the elements. To this day, eyewitness accounts, rumor, and misinformation continue to swirl, fueling all manner of speculation over what really happened in the desert that day.

Now Roswell celebrates the assertions and denials, and the mystery and the speculation surrounding the event in an annual **UFO Festival** (July 1 to 4), which attracts upwards of 20,000 visitors from around the planet. Interplanetary-travel celebs such as the Duras sisters (known to Trekkies as Klingon warriors from the TV series *Star Trek*), as well as past astronauts, often make appearances. Besides enough lectures, films, and workshops to make anyone's ears go pointy, the nighttime parade and alien-costume competitions are not to be missed.

Great Milk Carton Boat Race on Lake Van, 20 miles south of Roswell, as well as cheese sculpting contests, 36ft-long ice-cream sundaes, games and sporting events. **UFO Festival** (1 to 4 July; see Identify This!, above) centers around alien-costume competitions and lectures about UFOs. The main annual event, though, is the **Eastern New Mexico State Fair** (☎ 505-623-9411; ☯ early Oct), with rodeo, livestock and agricultural competitions and chile-eating contests.

Sleeping

Heritage Inn (☎ 505-748-2552; www.artesiaheritage inn.com; 209 W Main St, Artesia; r $65-75; ☐ ☒) The nicest place to stay is actually not in Roswell. If you're traveling between Roswell and Carlsbad and in the mood for slightly upscale digs (this is Southeastern New Mexico, don't forget), this c 1900, in-town establishment offers 11 Old West–style rooms about 36 miles south of Roswell.

Sally Port Inn (☎ 505-622-6430, 800-528-1234; 2000 N Main St; r $85-95; ☒ ☯) This is as good as it gets in Roswell. This Best Western has limited spa facilities and standard-issue rooms (some with refrigerators and microwaves).

Budget Inn North (☎ 505-623-6050; 2101 N Main St; r $40; ☯) Similar to Sally Port Inn, with a hot tub.

Frontier Motel (☎ 505-622-1400, 800-678-1401; www.frontiermotelroswell.com; 3010 N Main St; r $32-44; ☒ ☯) Also similar to Sally Port Inn.

Bottomless Lakes State Park (☎ 505-624-6058; Hwy 409; per car per day $5; tent/RV sites $10/14) Seven

popular lakes in the area provide welcome relief from summer heat. These primitive campsites are among the best available. To reach them, drive 10 miles east of Roswell on Hwy 380, then 5 miles south on Hwy 409.

Eating

Nuthin' Fancy Café (☎ 505-623-4098; 2103 N Main St; dishes $9-15; ☯ 6am-9pm) There is truth in advertising after all. For blue-plate specials and diner food, along with an espresso bar and upward of 15 beers on tap, nuthin' much compares.

Wellhead (☎ 505-746-0640; 332 W Main St, Artesia; dishes $6-15; ☯ lunch & dinner Mon-Sat) If you're traveling between Roswell and Carlsbad, you'll find the region's best food and drink at this modern brewpub restaurant and bar. Housed in a 1905 building and reflecting the town's origins, it's decorated with an oil drilling theme. Artesia is about 36 miles south of Roswell.

Cattle Baron (☎ 505-622-2465; 1113 N Main St; dishes $7-15; ☯ 10am-9:30pm Mon-Thu, 11am-10pm Fri & Sat) This efficient and friendly place specializes in consistently good and reasonably priced beef. With a name like that, what-daya expect? And yet, the salad bar would give any vegetarian a run for their money. Hang your spurs at the full bar before or after dinner.

Farley's (☎ 505-627-1100; 1315 N Main St; lunch & dinner dishes $7-12; ☯ 11am-midnight, to 2am Fri & Sat) A boisterous barn-like place, Farley's has something for everyone: burgers, pizza, chicken and ribs. It's family friendly except on Friday and Saturday nights, when kids might grow impatient at the wait.

A Taste of Europe (☎ 505-624-0313; 1201 N Main St; lunch dishes $7-9, dinner dishes $10-20; ☯ lunch & dinner Tue-Fri, dinner Sat, lunch Sun) For a relative united nations of Continental and European cuisine choices, these tastes are a treat. Having said that, the menu leans heavily toward Italian dishes.

Martin's Capitol Café (☎ 505-624-2111; 110 W 4th St; dishes $5-7; ☯ 6am-9pm Mon-Sat) Although several inexpensive New Mexican and Mexican restaurants in town are good, this one is dependable.

Getting There & Around

Mesa Air (☎ 800-637-2247; www.mesa-air.com) flies daily to Albuquerque and Carlsbad from the **Roswell Air Center** (☎ 505-347-5703; south end of Main St). **Pecos Trails Transit** (☎ 505-624-6766) runs local buses throughout the city and to/from the airport.

The **TNM&O/Greyhound Bus Depot** (☎ 505-622-2510; www.greyhound.com; 1100 N Virginia Ave) has daily buses to Carlsbad ($18, 1½ hours), Albuquerque ($37, four hours) and beyond.

From Tuesday to Saturday, a 7am bus heads to Santa Fe ($40, 5¾ hours). Buses also go to El Paso, Texas.

FORT SUMNER
pop 1250 / elev 4030ft

If you have a moment to spare, use it at Fort Sumner. The little village that sprang up around old Fort Sumner gets more than a footnote in the history books for two reasons: the disastrous Bosque Redondo Indian Reservation and Billy the Kid's last showdown with Sheriff Pat Garrett. The area is brimming with Indian and outlaw history.

Hwy 60 (Sumner Ave) is the main thoroughfare and runs east–west through town; most places of interest lie along it. Fort Sumner is 84 miles north of Roswell (p445), 45 miles southwest of Santa Rosa (p417) and 60 miles west of Clovis. The **Chamber of Commerce** (☎ 505-355-770; www.ftsumnerchamber .com; 707 N 4th St; ☯ 9am-4pm Mon-Fri) is helpful.

Sights & Activities

With more than 60,000 privately owned items on display, the **Billy the Kid Museum**

LEGEND OF BILLY THE KID

So much speculation swirls. Even the most basic information about Billy the Kid tends to cast a shadow larger than the outlaw himself. Here's what we know, or don't. Most historians agree that he was born sometime in 1859, most likely in New York City (or Indiana or Missouri). He *may* be buried in **Old Fort Sumner** (above), where his skull *may* have been stolen (and *possibly* recovered) – that is, unless he colluded with his presumed assassin, Sheriff Pat Garrett, and lived to a ripe, old age…somewhere.

The Kid didn't start out as a murderer. His first known childhood crimes included stealing laundry and fencing butter. In the mid-1870s, about the time the teen-aged Billy arrived in New Mexico, the 400 residents of **Lincoln** (p444) shopped at 'Murphy's,' the only general store in the region. In 1877, though, Englishman John Tunstall arrived and built a competing general store.

Within a year, Tunstall was dead, allegedly shot by Murphy and his boys. The entire region erupted in what became known as the **Lincoln County War**. Tunstall's most famous follower was a wild teenager named Henry McCarty, alias William Bonney, aka Billy the Kid. Over the next several months the Kid and his gang gunned down any members of the Murphy faction they could find. The Kid was captured or cornered a number of times but managed brazen and lucky escapes before finally being shot by Sheriff Pat Garrett near Fort Sumner in 1881, where he lies in a grave in a barren yard. Maybe.

Enough controversy still dangles over whether he conspired with Sheriff Garrett to fake his death that there is a movement afoot to exhume the body and do a little DNA testing. Brushy Bill Roberts of Hico, Texas, now deceased, claimed that he was actually the elusive outlaw. A man in his 70s claims that Sheriff Garrett's widow told him at the tender age of nine that the conspiracy was, in fact, the truth. Should they actually perform the tests and discover the truth, not only will it lay some portion of the legend to rest, but also forever cast a shadow of a doubt over the old saying, 'Dead men tell no tales.'

(☎ 505-355-2380; 1601 E Sumner Ave; adult $4, child 6-11 $2; ☯ 8:30am-5pm spring-fall, shorter in winter, closed first 2 weeks Jan) is obviously more than just a museum about the famous outlaw. It's a veritable shrine, almost a research institution. Indian artifacts and items from late-19th-century frontier life fill many rooms.

The **Fort Sumner State Monument** (☎ 505-355-2573; www.nmmonuments.org; Hwy 272; admission $1; ☯ Wed-Mon) is located 2 miles east of town on Hwy 60 and 4 miles south on Hwy 272. The original 1862 Fort Sumner was used as an outpost to fight the Apache tribe and Confederate army. After driving the Confederates south, the troops killed or moved the Apache to a reservation. Shortly thereafter, the wealthy rancher Lucien Maxwell turned the fort into a palatial retreat. Maxwell owned most of New Mexico north of Fort Sumner and east of the Rockies; it was the largest spread ever owned by one individual in the USA. Billy the Kid was visiting here on July 14, 1881, when he was shot and killed by Sheriff Pat Garrett. Unfortunately, the original fort no longer stands, but a visitor center has interpretive exhibits. Several trails, including one to Navajo sites and one to the river, leave from the visitor center.

The **Old Fort Sumner Museum** (☎ 505-355-2942; Billy the Kid Rd; adult $3.50, child 8-14 $2.50; ☯ 10am-5pm), with more local history and an emphasis on Billy the Kid, is located near the state monument. Behind the museum you'll find **Billy the Kid's Grave** and that of Lucien Maxwell. The Kid's tombstone is protected by an iron cage because 'souvenir hunters' kept trying to steal it.

Unusual atmospheric circulation patterns in the spring and fall bring NASA and international scientists to Fort Sumner to launch **weather balloons** carrying scientific research instruments 32 miles into the atmosphere. One inflates to the size of the Houston Astrodome at its highest elevation.

Festivals & Events
Old Fort Days (2nd weekend Jun) features various athletic events. The purse for the winner of the tombstone race, in which contestants must negotiate an obstacle course while lugging an 80lb tombstone, is $2000.

Sleeping & Eating
Sumner Lake State Park (☎ 505-355-2541; per car per day $5, sites $10-14) When the Pecos River was

dammed, this artificial lake was created; primitive camping is available. To reach it, take Hwy 84 north for 11 miles, then Hwy 203 west for 6 miles. There is also free primitive camping near Bosque Redondo Lake, 2 miles south of town.

Sadie's Frontier Restaurant (☎ 505-355-1461; 510 Sumner Ave; dishes $5-10; ☯ 7:30am-8pm Thu-Mon) If you're passing through, pick up a homemade breakfast burrito or other simple but good New Mexican fare.

CARLSBAD
pop 25,600 / elev 3120ft
When Carlsbad Caverns (p452) was declared a national monument in 1923, a trickle of tourists turned into a veritable flash flood. Today, hundreds of thousands of visitors come through annually. Situated on the Pecos River about 30 miles north of the Texas state line, Carlsbad's main thoroughfare is Hwy 285, which becomes Canal St, then S Canal (south of Mermod St) and then National Parks Hwy at the southern end of town.

Information
BLM (☎ 505-234-5972; 620 E Green St; ☯ 7:45am-4:30pm Mon-Fri)

Chamber of Commerce (☎ 505-887-6516, 800-221-1224; www.carlsbadchamber.com; 302 S Canal St; ☯ 9am-5pm Mon, 8am-5pm Tue-Fri, 9am-3pm Sat May-Sep)

Library (☎ 505-885-6776; 101 S Halagueno St; ☯ 10am-8pm Mon-Thu, 10am-6pm Fri & Sat, 2-6pm Sun) Free Internet access.

Medical Center (☎ 505-887-4100; 2430 W Pierce St; ☯ 24hr emergency)

National Parks Information Center (☎ 505-885-8884; 3225 National Parks Hwy; ☯ 8am-4:30pm Mon-Fri) Information on both Carlsbad Caverns National Park and Guadalupe Mountains National Park.

Police (☎ 505-885-2111; 405 S Halagueno St)

Post office (☎ 505-885-5717; 301 N Canyon St)

USFS Ranger Station (☎ 505-885-4181; 114 S Halagueno; ☯ 7:30am-4:30pm Mon-Fri) The Lincoln National Forest Guadalupe ranger station is located in the federal building at Halagueno and Fox Sts.

Sights & Activities
On the northwestern outskirts of town, **Living Desert State Park** (☎ 505-887-5516; 1504 Miehls Dr, off Hwy 285; adult $5, child 7-12 $3; ☯ 8am-8pm May-Aug, 9am-5pm Sep-Apr) is a great place to see and learn about cacti, coyotes and wildlife

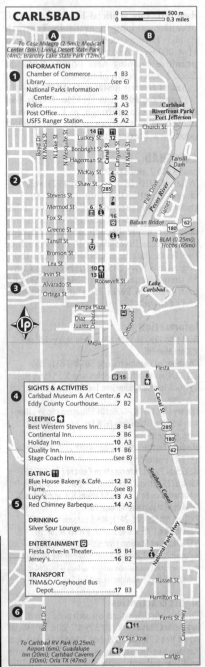

CARLSBAD

0 — 500 m
0 — 0.3 miles

To Casa Milagro (2.5mi); Medical
Center (3mi); Living Desert State Park
(4mi); Brantley Lake State Park (12mi)

INFORMATION
Chamber of Commerce................1 B3
Library..(see 6)
National Parks Information
Center......................................2 B5
Police...3 A3
Post Office..................................4 B2
USFS Ranger Station....................5 A2

Carlsbad
Riverfront Park/
Port Jefferson

SIGHTS & ACTIVITIES
Carlsbad Museum & Art Center..6 A2
Eddy County Courthouse...........7 B2

SLEEPING
Best Western Stevens Inn...........8 B4
Continental Inn..........................9 B6
Holiday Inn................................10 A3
Quality Inn.................................11 B6
Stage Coach Inn.....................(see 8)

EATING
Blue House Bakery & Café.......12 B2
Flume.....................................(see 8)
Lucy's......................................13 A3
Red Chimney Barbeque............14 A2

DRINKING
Silver Spur Lounge..................(see 8)

ENTERTAINMENT
Fiesta Drive-In Theater............15 B4
Jersey's....................................16 B2

TRANSPORT
TNM&O/Greyhound Bus
Depot....................................17 B3

To Carlsbad RV Park (0.25mi);
Airport (6mi); Guadalupe
Inn (20mi); Carlsbad Caverns
(30mi); Orla TX (47mi)

with evocative Southwestern names such
as agave, javelina, ocotillo and yucca. The
park has a good 1.3-mile trail that showcases different habitats of the Chihuahuan
Desert.

The **Carlsbad Museum & Art Center** (☎ 505-
887-0276; www.nmculture.org; 418 W Fox St; admission
free; ❂ 10am-5pm Mon-Sat) displays Apache artifacts, pioneer memorabilia and art from
the renowned Taos School.

Southwestern touches at the 1891 **Eddy
County Courthouse** are also worth a look: the
cattle brands of the most important local
ranches are carved into the door frames,
and the interior ceilings boast heavy beams
and ornate iron chandeliers.

A system of dams and spillways on the
Pecos River creates the 2-mile **Lake Carlsbad**,
which has a pleasant 4.5-mile trail along
its banks. At the north end of Park Dr
(or at the east end of Church St), **Carlsbad
Riverfront Park** has a beach and swimming
area. At nearby **Port Jefferson** (☎ 505-887-8343;
❂ 10am-5pm Mon-Sat late May-early Sep & Sat & Sun
Oct), you can rent a paddlewheel boat to tour
the river.

Sleeping

The nearby national park and mild winters
make this a year-round destination; always
ask for the best rates. Sorry, folks, but it's
mostly chain motels in Carlsbad.

BUDGET

Stage Coach Inn (☎ 505-887-1148; 1819 S Canal St;
r $38-46; ❌ ☢) Of the budget motels on the
main drag, the conventional one is the best,
with an indoor hot tub and in-room refrigerators.

Best Western Stevens Inn (☎ 505-887-2851, 800-
730-2851; 1829 S Canal St; r $75; ☢) Carlsbad's larg-
est hotel has more than 200 rooms, some
with kitchenettes or microwave/refrigerator
combos.

Quality Inn (☎ 505-887-2861; www.qualityinn
carlsbad.com; 3706 National Parks Hwy; r incl breakfast $60;
☢) This place has attractively landscaped
grounds, a courtyard patio and hot tub,
and live entertainment and dancing in the
lounge.

Continental Inn (☎ 505-887-0341; 3820 National
Parks Hwy; r $30-40; ❌ ☢) This brick motel has
60 rooms and suites, including some that
accommodate families willing to use the
sleeper sofa.

Carlsbad RV Park & Campground (☎ 505-885-6333; 4301 National Parks Hwy; tent/RV sites $16.50/22, cabins $32; 🖳) You'll find more than 100 sites, a game room, a grocery store, laundry, playground and showers here.

Brantley Lake State Park (☎ 505-457-2384; per car per day $5, camp & RV sites $14-18) Primitive camping is available ($8) if you head 12

miles north of Carlsbad and 5 miles east of Hwy 285.

MIDRANGE

Casa Milagro (☎ 505-887-2188, 866-332-0743; www .casa-milagro-nm.com; 1612 N Guadalupe St; r $95; ✕) Casa Milagro is a comfortable, turn-of-the-20th-century homestead on the edge

---

DETOUR: WEST TEXAS BOUND

Pull off the highway and scramble to the top of any of the buttes in West Texas, squint your eyes just so, and you'll actually see a waterline: the ghost of an ancient ocean that deposited an eon's worth of corals, skeletons, shells, and sediment that make up this blistering and beautiful landscape. The western reaches of this state are to many native Texans the quintessential Texas experience.

Here's where you'll find **Guadalupe Mountains National Park**, where, in the fall, **McKittrick Canyon** becomes one of the most scenic hiking areas in the park. **Pines Springs Campground** (campsites $8) sits next to the **visitor center** (☎ 915-828-3251; www.nps.gov/gumo; Hwy 62/180; ⏱ 8am-4:30pm Mon-Fri).

Isolated at the state's far-western tip, **El Paso** is an unpretentious, bicultural city with a strong independent streak. Its historic heart is **San Jacinto Plaza**, which could easily pass for Mexico. For a **self-guided walking tour**, head to the **visitor center** (☎ 915-534-0601, 800-351-6024; www .visitelpaso.com; Santa Fe St; ⏱ 8am-5pm Mon-Fri).

Across the Rio Grande lies **Ciudad Juarez**, Mexico's fourth-largest city. Though the US Border Patrol tries to keep the two countries neatly separated, Mexican culture has always been dominant in El Paso and Spanish is the default language. Don't forget your passport.

About 32 miles east of El Paso, off US 62/180, **Hueco Tanks State Historic Site** has abundant wildlife and ancient pictographs. The 860-acre **park** (☎ 915-857-1135; www.tpwd.state.tx.us/park/hueco/) is also a magnet for rock climbers. To minimize impact on the fragile park, a daily visitor quota is enforced; call ahead.

Big Bend National Park is vast enough for a lifetime of discovery. A river-running, mountain-biking and hiking paradise, it's also one of the least visited national parks, and for good reason: it's hot. The area around the park, surprisingly, is home to many artist retreats, historic hotels and quaint mountain villages. Its diverse geography makes for an amazing variety of wildlife. Stop at the main **visitor center** (☎ 432-477-2251; www.nps.gov/bibe; 7-day pass per car $15; ⏱ 8am-6pm). The park's 110 miles of paved road and 150 miles of dirt road make scenic driving the most popular activity.

West of Big Bend you'll find **Terlingua**, one of Willie Nelson's favorite spots. Travelers and artists passing through tend to linger here. There are several excellent restaurants and a nice live-music scene. It's also one of the main jumping-off points for Big Bend.

West of Lajitas, FM 170 hugs the Rio Grande through spectacular and remote scenery. Known as the **Camino del Rio**, it winds its way for 50 miles to **Presidio**, a dreary border town. From there US Hwy 67 heads north to **Marfa**, home to the **Chinati Foundation** (☎ 432-729-4362; adult/child $10/5; ⏱ tours 10am & 2pm Wed-Sun; booked 2 weeks in advance), a sprawling complex of minimalist art founded by New York artist Donald Judd in 1986. The town's original fame came after James Dean, Elizabeth Taylor and Rock Hudson filmed *Giant* here in 1955. Everyone stays at the 1930s-era **Hotel Paisano** (☎ 866-729-3669; 207 N Highland; r $89-200; 🖳). Marfa is also known for the unexplained 'Marfa lights,' which flash across the desert sky on random nights. As yet, no one has figured out where they come from.

East of Marfa, **Marathon** is an artsy hamlet with art galleries, great eateries and the best place to sleep in Texas: the **Gage Hotel** (☎ 432-386-4205, 800-884-4243; www.gagehotel.com; 101 Hwy 90 W; r $69-300; 🅿 🖳). Rooms are straight out of a Wild West pulp novel, with wide wooden blinds, saddles in the rooms and cowhides on the beds.

NEW MEXICO

of town, with five pleasant rooms that are the pride of the owner. Plan your day on the porch or stay a while and read.

Holiday Inn (☎ 505-885-8500; 601 S Canal St; d incl breakfast $75-100; 🖭) This two-story place is the only full-service hotel downtown; rooms are spacious and have a faux Southwestern feel.

Eating

Lucy's (☎ 505-887-7714; 701 S Canal St; dishes under $10; 🕑 lunch & dinner Tue-Sun) The most popular place in Carlsbad, Lucy's is usually packed with devoted locals *and* visitors. Apart from a great Mexican menu, Lucy's serves up tasty margaritas and a good selection of microbrews. (Admittedly that may be one reason the place is jumpin'.) There really is a Lucy and chances are she'll greet you.

Blue House Bakery & Café (☎ 505-628-0555; 609 N Canyon St; dishes under $8; 🕑 7:30am-3:30pm Mon-Sat) This sweet Queen Anne house perks the best coffee and espresso in this quadrant of New Mexico. Its baked goods are pretty darn good too. At lunchtime, the cheery place has good sandwiches made with fresh breads.

Red Chimney Barbeque (☎ 505-885-8744; 817 N Canal St; dishes $7-10; 🕑 11am-2:30pm & 4:30pm-8:30pm Mon-Fri) Barbecue aficionados will agree: Red Chimney has one of the most unusual sauces you'll ever encounter. It just may have you dreaming about secret ingredients.

Flume (☎ 505-887-2851; 1829 S Canal St; lunch dishes $6-8, dinner dishes $14-22; 🕑 6am-10pm) One of Carlsbad's best is known for its steaks, prime rib and chicken.

Drinking & Entertainment

For country music, try the **Silver Spur Lounge** (☎ 505-887-2851; 1829 S Canal St) at the Best Western Stevens Inn (p450) or the Quality Inn (p450). Upstairs at **Jersey's** (☎ 505-234-1546; 222 W Fox) there's live music on weekends.

Head to the **Fiesta Drive-In Theater** (☎ 505-885-4126; San Jose Blvd; $2-8 per person; 🕑 Fri-Mon) to soak up some nighttime desert air and experience a form of American entertainment that has almost disappeared.

Getting There & Away

TNM&O/Greyhound (☎ 505-887-1108; www.greyhound.com; 1000 Canyon St) buses depart daily for Albuquerque ($45, five hours) and El Paso, Texas ($39 to $41, three hours).

CARLSBAD CAVERNS NATIONAL PARK

Drive for hours across the desert just to see a cave? But it's not just any cave; it's a truly astonishing and immense system of caves, one of the world's greatest. Once visitors get a glimpse, even the most skeptical are impressed. A visit is, without a doubt, a highlight of any Southwestern journey. But wait, there's more. The cave's other claim to fame is the 250,000-plus Mexican free-tail bat colony that roosts here from April to October. Visitors flock here at sunset to watch them fly out to feast on a smorgasbord of bugs.

The park covers 73 sq miles and includes almost 100 caves. Visitors can take a 2-mile subterranean walk from the cave mouth to an underground chamber 1800ft-long, 255ft high and over 800ft below the surface. Exploration for experienced spelunkers only continues at the awe-inspiring **Lechugilla Cave**. With a depth of 1567ft and a length of about 60 miles, it's the deepest cave and third-longest limestone cave in North America.

The park entrance is 23 miles southwest of Carlsbad. A three-day pass for self-guided tours to the natural entrance and the Big Room (send a postcard from the lunchroom, 829ft below the surface!) costs $6 for adults and $3 for children. The **park** (☎ 505-785-2232, 800-967-2283; www.nps.gov/cave; 3225 National Parks Hwy; 🕑 8am-5pm, to 7pm late May-mid-Aug) also has a spectrum of ranger-led tours ($7); call for advance reservations. If you want to scramble to lesser known areas, ask about Wild Cave tours. The last tickets are sold 2 to 3½ hours before the visitor center closes. Wilderness backpacking trips into the desert are allowed by permit (free); the visitor center sells topographical maps of the 50-plus miles of hiking trails.

There are no accommodations within the park, but the comfortable, small and resort-like **Guadalupe Inn** (☎ 505-785-2291, 800-228-3767; www.bestwestern.com; 17 Carlsbad Hwy, White's City; r $100; 🖭 🖭 🖭) is the closest, most decent place to stay near the park. It has 63 good-sized rooms in three buildings, the best being Guadalupe.

Directory

CONTENTS

ACCOMMODATIONS

The Southwest provides a vast array of types of accommodations: from tent camping under the stars and budget motels; to midrange Victorian B&Bs, adobe inns and historical hotels; to four-star hotels, luxurious spas, dude ranches and over-the-top casinos. The most comfortable accommodations for the lowest price are usually found in that great American invention, the roadside motel.

For last-minute deals, check www.expedia .com, www.travelocity.com, www.orbitz.com, www.priceline.com, www.hotwire.com and www.hotels.com. For more on discounts, see p18 and p458.

If you're traveling with children, be sure to ask about child-related policies before making reservations (p456).

Our reviews indicate rates for single occupancy (s), double (d) or simply the room (r), when there's no appreciable difference in the rate for one or two people. Unless otherwise noted, breakfast is *not* included, bathrooms are private and all lodging is open year-round. Rates generally don't include taxes, which vary considerably between towns and states (p464).

A double room in our budget category costs $75 or less; midrange rooms for doubles cost $75 to $150; top-end rooms start at $150 (except in Las Vegas, where they generally start at $300 a night).

As for icons (see inside front cover), a parking icon is only utilized in bigger cities. The Internet icon appears where establishments offer access to people not carrying their laptops (or where an innkeeper is okay with people using his/her personal computer for an hour or so). When there is an additional fee for parking or Internet usage, a fee follows the icon.

High season varies depending on the region within the Southwest. In general the peak travel season runs June through August, except in the hottest parts of Arizona, when some places slash their prices in half because it's just too darn hot. The peak travel season for southern Arizona and the ski areas of northern Utah (for different reasons) and other mountainous areas are mid-December to mid-April. Throughout the book, when it is not obvious, we define which months constitute high season. Generally, we only list high season rates. For more seasonal discussions, see p18.

Holidays (p461) command premium prices. When demand peaks (and during special events no matter the time of year, p459), book lodgings well in advance.

B&Bs & Inns

Accommodations in the Southwest vary from small B&Bs to rambling old hostelries that have sheltered travelers for several

PRACTICALITIES

- Voltage is 110/120V, 60 cycles.

- Self-service, coin-operated laundry facilities are located in all but the tiniest towns, most campgrounds and many motels.

- Major newspapers are published in Salt Lake City (*Desert News* and *Salt Lake Tribune*), Albuquerque (*Albuquerque Journal*), Phoenix (*Arizona Republic*), Tucson (*Tucson Citizen*) and Las Vegas (*Las Vegas Sun* and *Las Vegas Review Journal*).

- National Public Radio (NPR) features a level-headed approach to news and talk radio and is found on the lower frequencies of your FM dial. In rural areas, country & western music, Christian programming and Spanish language radio predominates.

- All the major US TV and cable networks are represented and readily available.

- Video systems use the NTSC color TV standard, not compatible with the PAL system.

- Distances are measured in feet, yards and miles; weights are tallied in ounces, pounds and tons.

centuries. In smaller towns, guesthouses with simple rooms may charge $75 to $100 for rooms with shared bathroom, breakfast included. Others are relentlessly charming, with kiva fireplaces, courtyards and helpful hosts. These fancier B&Bs tend to charge $100 to $150 per night with private bathroom. Other places may be ensconced in historical buildings, exquisite haciendas or luxurious urban homes. These tend to be equipped with every conceivable modern amenity and easily cost $200 and up a night. Most inns require a minimum stay of two or three days on weekends and advance reservations. Many don't accept children, pets or smokers. It's always best to call ahead at B&Bs.

Camping

When it's not raining, there's nothing like camping beneath a tapestry of stars in the Southwest's national forests, state and national parks and on Bureau of Land Management (BLM) land. The more developed areas may accept or require reservations; credit cards are needed. For reservations, call **USFS campground** (☎ 877-444-6777; www.reserveusa.com) or **national park camping** (☎ 800-365-2267; http://reservations.nps.gov).

Free camping is permitted on much public land; contact information for local ranger stations is interspersed throughout the book. Developed camping areas usually have toilets, drinking water, fire pits and picnic benches. Some don't have drinking water. At any rate, it is always a good idea to have a few gallons of water in the vehicle if you are going to be out in the boonies.

Basic tenting usually costs $10 to $15 a night. More developed campgrounds may be geared to recreational vehicle (RV) travel and cost $25 to $40 a night. For information on renting an RV, see p475. **Kampgrounds of America** (KOA; ☎ 406-248-7444; www.koa.com) is a national network of private campgrounds with sites averaging $20 per night.

Hostels

US citizens/residents can join **Hostelling International USA** (HI; ☎ 301-495-1240; www.hihostels.com; 8401 Colesville Rd, Suite 600, Silver Spring, MD 20910) by calling and requesting a membership form or by downloading a form from the website and mailing or faxing it. Membership can also be purchased at regional council offices and at many (but not all) youth hostels. Non-US residents should buy an HI membership in their home countries. If you don't, you can still stay in US hostels by purchasing 'Welcome Stamps' for each night you stay in a hostel. When you have six stamps, your stamp card becomes a one-year HI membership card valid throughout the world.

HI has its own toll- and surcharge-free **reservations service** (☎ 800-909-4776), but not all hostels participate in the service. The HI card may be used to get discounts at some local merchants and for local services, including some intercity bus companies.

There are many more independent hostels in the Southwest, which have comparable rates and conditions to HI hostels and may sometimes be better. They often have a few private single/double rooms available, sometimes with private bathrooms.

Kitchen, laundry, notice board and TV facilities are available. **Hostels.com** (www.hostels.com) lists hostels throughout the world.

Southwest hostels are located in:

Arizona Phoenix, Lake Powell, Grand Canyon, Williams, Sedona, Tucson

Colorado Silverton, Crested Butte

Las Vegas Las Vegas

New Mexico Albuquerque, Cedar Crest, Santa Fe, Taos, Chama, Cuba, Truth or Consequences

Utah Torrey, Moab, Salt Lake City

Hotels

Southwest hotels, mostly found in cities, are generally large and lavish, except for a few small, inexpensive 'boutique' hotels (which are small and understatedly lavish). Prices generally start at $200 and shoot straight up; ask about discounts and special packages when making reservations. Las Vegas hotels, though, are an entirely different animal. Attractions in and of themselves, they are as flashy as a sequined dress. Since the hotels expect you to lose (er…spend) money in their casinos, many offer great room deals. Throughout the region, virtually all large hotels have toll-free national numbers for making reservations, but you may find better savings by calling the hotel directly.

Lodges

Normally situated within national parks, lodges are often rustic-looking but are usually quite comfy inside. Rooms generally start at $100, but can easily be double that in high season. Since they represent the only option if you want to stay inside the park without camping, many are fully booked well in advance. Want a room today? Call anyway – you might be lucky and hit on a cancellation. In addition to on-site restaurants, they also offer touring services.

Motels

Budget chain motels ('If you've stayed in one, you've stayed in them all!') are quite prevalent throughout the Southwest. In smaller towns, they will often be your only option. Many motels have at-the-door parking, with exterior doors. These are convenient, though some folks, especially single women, may prefer the more expensive places with safer interior corridors.

Advertised prices are referred to as 'rack rates' and are not written in stone. If you simply ask about any specials that might apply, you can often save quite a bit of money. Children are often allowed to stay free with their parents; call and inquire if traveling with a family.

The Motel 6 chain is generally the cheapest of the lot. Although we generally don't include details on chain motels throughout the book, you may have or develop a favorite franchise.

To that end, here's a handy list with contact information:

Best Western (☎ 800-937-8376; www.bestwestern.com)

Budget Host (☎ 800-283-4678; www.budgethost.com)

Clarion Hotel (☎ 800-252-7466; www.clarionhotel.com)

Comfort Inn (☎ 800-228-5150; www.comfortinn.com)

Courtyard by Marriott (☎ 800-321-2211; www.courtyard.com)

Days Inn (☎ 800-329-7666; www.daysinn.com)

Econo Lodge (☎ 800-553-2666; www.econolodge.com)

Fairfield Inn by Marriott (☎ 800-228-2800; www.fairfieldinn.com)

Hampton Inn (☎ 800-426-7866; www.hampton-inn.com)

Holiday Inn (☎ 800-465-4329; www.holiday-inn.com)

Howard Johnson (☎ 800-446-4656; www.hojo.com)

La Quinta (☎ 800-531-5900; www.laquinta.com)

Motel 6 (☎ 800-466-8356; www.motel6.com)

Quality Inn (☎ 800-228-5151; www.qualityinn.com)

Ramada (☎ 800-272-6232; www.ramada.com)

Red Roof Inn (☎ 800-843-7663; www.redroof.com)

Sleep Inn (☎ 800-753-3746; www.sleepinn.com)

Super 8 Motel (☎ 800-800-8000; www.super8.com)

Travel Lodge (☎ 800-578-7878; www.travelodge.com)

Resorts & Guest Ranches

Luxury resorts and guest ranches (often called dude ranches) really require a stay of several days to be appreciated and are often destinations in themselves. Start the day with a round of golf or a tennis match, then luxuriate with a massage, swimming, sunbathing, hot-tubbing and drinking. You get the idea. Guest ranches are even more like 'whole vacations,' with active schedules of horseback riding and maybe cattle roundups, rodeo lessons, cookouts and other Western activities. Ranches in the desert lowlands may close in summer, while those in the mountains may close in winter or convert into skiing centers. Ski resorts charge upwards of $200 or more for a condo in season; prices drop to less than half that in summer.

ACTIVITIES

For millions of visitors to the Southwest, especially first-time visitors, the sheer scale and grandeur of the place as seen from car windows and scenic overlooks is reward enough. Locals, however, know that the Southwest offers an enormous variety of world-class outdoor activities, some of which, such as skiing or boating, may not be the first things that come to mind when one thinks about desert states.

For a complete discussion of the wealth, depth and breadth of ways to have fun in the Southwest, see p58.

BUSINESS HOURS

Generally speaking, business hours are from 9am to 5pm. In large cities, a few supermarkets and restaurants are open 24 hours a day. In Utah, many restaurants are closed on Sundays; if you find one open, snag a seat and be happy. Unless there are variances of more than a half hour in either direction, the following serve as 'normal' opening hours for entries in this book:

Banks 9am or 10am to 5pm or 6pm Monday to Friday; some are open on Saturday.

Bars and clubs 4pm to 1am, some clubs are open till 2am on Thursday to Saturday.

Businesses 9am to 5pm Monday to Friday.

Post offices 8am to 4pm or 5:30pm Monday to Friday, some open 9am to noon Saturday.

Restaurants Breakfast 7am to 10am; lunch 11am to 2:30pm; dinner 5pm to 9:30pm.

Shops 9am or 10am to 5pm or 6pm Monday to Saturday, some also open noon to 5pm on Sunday; often open until 9pm in shopping malls.

CHILDREN

As parents will be all too aware, successful travel with young children requires a bit of planning and effort. Within the Southwest, in particular, traveling with children presents two destination-specific problems. It's very hot in the summertime for little tykes; guard them against sunburn, make sure they drink plenty of water and get enough rest (especially at higher altitudes). Then there's the little matter of those pesky long-distance drives. Be sure to break them up with frequent stops. Try not to overdo things; even for adults, packing too much into the time available can cause problems. Include children in the trip planning; if they've helped to work out where you will

be going, they will be much more interested when they get there.

Consult Lonely Planet's *Travel with Children*, which has lots of valuable tips and interesting anecdotal stories. Also check p25 for more information.

Practicalities

How welcome are children? At many smaller B&Bs and inns (see p453), they're not welcome. But since establishments are not allowed by law to discriminate, proprietors won't usually say 'no' outright. They'll try to dissuade you gently, so listen carefully to their answers. No one wants to end up where they're not wanted. But in motels and hotels, children under age 17 or 18 can usually stay for free when sharing a room with their parents and using existing bedding. Cots and roll-away beds are usually available (for an additional fee) in hotels and resorts. When places are particularly family friendly, we say so in the review.

Many restaurants have children's menus with significantly lower prices. High chairs are usually available, but it pays to inquire ahead of time.

Most car rental companies (p474) lease child-safety seats, but they don't always have them on hand; reserve in advance if you can.

Sights & Activities

Family-friendly sights abound and we have peppered suggestions throughout the regional chapters where we've ferreted out activities worth your time – even when Junior *isn't* driving you up the wall. For a whole host of suggestions in larger cities, see Albuquerque (p354), Santa Fe (p372), Las Vegas (p88), Phoenix (p123), the Grand Canyon (p139) and Salt Lake City (p293).

CLIMATE CHARTS

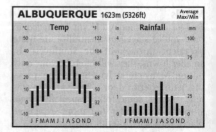

ALBUQUERQUE 1623m (5326ft)				Average Max/Min

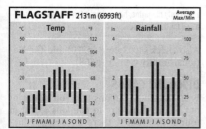

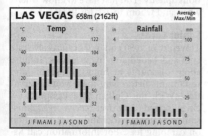

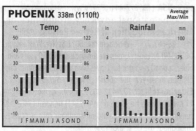

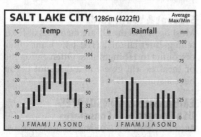

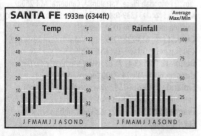

COURSES

Opportunities to educate and enhance yourself while on vacation aren't as endless as the Southwestern sky, but you'll have plenty of choices nonetheless. Take meditation and tai chi classes at Sedona's Center for the New Age (p168), Albuquerque's T'ai Chi Chih Center (p353) or Santa Fe's Yoga Source (p372). With all that relentlessly perfect light, hone your image-making skills with photographic offerings from the Santa Fe Workshops (p372).

Practically every sport has an outfitter who wants to teach you how to enjoy it with confidence; these are listed throughout the guide. For cooking courses, the best of the bunch is the Santa Fe School of Cooking (p372).

CUSTOMS

Each visitor is allowed to bring 1L of liquor and 200 cigarettes duty-free into the US, but you must be at least 21 years old to possess the former and 18 to possess the latter. In addition, each traveler is permitted to bring up to $100 worth of gift merchandise into the US without incurring any duty.

Agricultural inspection stations at the Arizona-California border may ask you to surrender fruit when entering California, in an attempt to halt the spread of pests associated with the fruit.

DANGERS & ANNOYANCES

Southwestern cities generally have lower levels of violent crime than larger cities like New York, Los Angeles and Washington, DC. Nevertheless, violent crime is certainly present, and you should take the usual precautions. For health matters pertaining to dehydration and the like, see p478.

Whether you're in rural or urban areas, follow these safety tips:

- Lock your car doors and don't leave any valuables visible.
- Avoid walking alone on empty streets or in parks at night.
- Try to use ATMs only in well-trafficked areas.
- Avoid being in the open, especially on canyon rims or hilltops, during lightening storms.
- Avoid riverbeds and canyons when storm clouds gather in the distance; flash floods are deadly.

EMERGENCIES

If you need any kind of emergency assistance, such as police, ambulance or firefighters, call ☎ 911. This is a free call from any phone. A few rural phones might not have this service, in which case dial ☎ 0 for the operator and ask for emergency assistance.

- When dust storms brew, pull off to the side of the road, turn off your lights and wait it out. They don't usually last long.
- Drivers should watch for livestock on highways, Indian reservations and in areas marked 'Open Rangelands.' Hitting an animal at 65mph can total your car and kill the creature.
- When camping where bears are present, place your food inside a food box (one is often provided by the campground).
- Watch where you step when you hike – particularly on hot summer afternoons and evenings when rattlesnakes like to bask on the trail.
- Scorpions spend their days under rocks and woodpiles; use caution.

DISABLED TRAVELERS

Travel within the Southwest is getting easier for people with disabilities, but it's still not easy. Public buildings are required to be wheelchair accessible and to have appropriate restroom facilities. Public transportation services must be made accessible to all, and telephone companies have to provide relay operators for the hearing impaired. Many banks provide ATM instructions in braille, curb ramps are common, many busy intersections have audible crossing signals, and most chain hotels have suites for disabled guests. Still, it's best to call ahead to check.

A number of organizations specialize in the needs of disabled travelers:

Mobility International USA (☎ 541-343-1284; www .miusa.org; PO Box 10767, Eugene, OR 97440) Advises disabled travelers on mobility issues but primarily runs an educational exchange program.

Twin Peaks Press (☎ 360-694-2462, 800-637-2256; http://home.pacifier.com/~twinpeak; PO Box 129, Vancouver, WA 98666) Publishes a quarterly newsletter, directories and access guides.

Society for the Advancement of Travel for the Handicapped (SATH; ☎ 212-447-7284; www.sath.org; 347 Fifth Ave, Suite 610, New York, NY 10016) Publishes

a quarterly magazine; has various information sheets on travel for the disabled.

Also check out Splore (p270) and the National Ability Center (p308).

DISCOUNT CARDS

From Internet coupons that you can print out before departure to coupons found in tourist magazines, there are price reductions aplenty. You just have to know where, when and whom to ask for them.

Senior Cards

Travelers aged 50 and older can receive rate cuts and benefits at many places. Inquire about discounts at hotels, museums and restaurants before you make your reservation. With the Golden Age Passport, US citizens aged 62 or over receive free admission to national parks and a 50% reduction on camping fees. For information call **ReserveUSA** (☎ 877-444-6777; www.reserveusa.com).

Some national advocacy groups include:

American Association of Retired Persons (AARP; ☎ 888-687-2277; www.aarp.org; 601 E St NW, Washington, DC 20049) Advocacy group for Americans aged 50 years and older; a good resource for travel bargains. US residents can get one/three-year memberships for $12.50/29.50.

Elderhostel (☎ 877-426-8056; www.elderhostel.org; 11 Ave de Lafayette, Boston, MA 02111) Nonprofit offering seniors the opportunity to attend academic college courses throughout the US and Canada.

Student & Youth Cards

Most hostels in the US are members of Hostelling International (HI; p454) and offer discounts to HI members. Often museums or theatres will give you a discount if you have a student ID.

EMBASSIES & CONSULATES
USA Embassies & Consulates

Australia (☎ 02-6214 5600; http://canberra.usembassy .gov; 21 Moonah Place, Yarralumla, Canberra, ACT 2600)

Austria (☎ 1-31339-0; http://vienna.usembassy.gov/en; Boltzmanngasse 16, A-1090, Vienna)

Canada (☎ 613-238 5335; http://canada.usembassy.gov; 490 Sussex Dr, Ottawa, ON K1N 1G8)

Denmark (☎ 33 41 71 00; www.usembassy.dk; Dag Hammarskjölds Allé 24, 2100 Copenhagen)

Finland (☎ 9-616-250; www.usembassy.fi; Itäinen Puistotie 14 B, 00140 Helsinki)

France (☎ 33 1 43 12 22 22; www.amb-usa.fr; 2 Av Gabriel, 75382 Paris)

Germany (☎ 030-8305 0; www.usembassy.de; Neu-
städtische Kirchstrasse 4-5, 10117 Berlin)
Greece (☎ 30-210-721-2951; www.usembassy.gr;
91 Vasilissis Sophias Blvd, 10160 Athens)
Ireland (☎ 353 1 668 8777; http://dublin.usembassy
.gov; 42 Elgin Rd, Ballsbridge, Dublin 4)
Israel (☎ 3-519-7575; www.usembassy-israel.org.il;
71 Hayarkon St, Tel Aviv 63903)
Italy (☎ 39 06 46741; www.usembassy.it; Via Vittorio
Veneto 119/A, 00187 Rome)
Japan (☎ 03-3224 5000; http://tokyo.usembassy.gov;
1-10-5, Akasaka, Minato-ku, Tokyo)
Mexico (☎ 5-209-9100; www.usembassy-mexico.gov;
Paseo de la Reforma 305, Colonia Cuauhtémoc, 06500
México, DF)
Netherlands (☎ 070-310 9209; http://netherlands
.usembassy.gov; Lange Voorhout 102, 2514 EJ The Hague)
New Zealand (☎ 04-462 6000; www.usembassy.org
.nz; 29 Fitzherbert Terrace, Thorndon, Wellington)
Spain (☎ 91-587-2200, US passport holders call
☎ 91587-2240; http://madrid.usembassy.gov; Calle
Serrano 75, 28006 Madrid)
Sweden (☎ 08 783 53 00; http://stockholm.usembassy
.gov; Dag Hammarskjölds Väg 31, SE-115 89 Stockholm)
Switzerland (☎ 031-357-7011; http://bern.usembassy
.gov; Jubiläumsstrasse 93, CH-3005 Bern)
UK (☎ 020-7499 9000; www.usembassy.org.uk; 24/31
Grosvenor Square, London W1A 1AE)

Embassies & Consulates in Southwest USA

Most nations' main consulates or embas-
sies are in Washington, DC. To find the
telephone number of your embassy or consulate, call Washington, DC, directory assistance (☎ 202-555-1212).

There are few foreign consular offices in
the Southwest. Even the skimpy list here
changes regularly, so it's best to do an Internet search before departing your country
of origin. Once in the Southwest, search the
yellow pages of telephone directories under
'Consulates.'
Germany (Map p350; ☎ 505-872-0800; 8500 Louisiana
Blvd NE, Albuquerque)
Mexico (www.sre.gob.mx) Albuquerque (Map p350;
☎ 505-247-4177; 1610 4th St NW); Nogales (☎ 520-287-
2521; 571 Grand Ave); Phoenix (Map pp120-1; ☎ 801-521-
8502; 1190 W Camelback Rd, Suite 110, 85015); Salt Lake
City (Map pp292-3; ☎ 801-521-8502; 155 S 300 West);
Tucson (Map pp202-3; ☎ 520-882-5595; 553 S Stone Ave)
New Zealand (Map p288; ☎ 801-237-2664; 1379 N
Brookhurst Circle, Centerville, Salt Lake City)
Switzerland (Map p288; ☎ 801-272-7102; 4641 S Hunters
Ridge Cr, Salt Lake City)

FESTIVALS & EVENTS

From arts festivals to country fairs, from
Indian ceremonial dances to chile cook-
offs, from duck races to hot-air balloon
ascents, the Southwest has hundreds of
holidays, festivals and events. In larger cities with diverse cultures, traditional holidays of other countries are also celebrated
with as much, if not more, fanfare. Dates
vary from year to year, so check with tourist
information offices. Regional chapters are
full of details. Also see p19 and p461.

January
Sundance Film Festival (mid–late-Jan) Aspiring filmmakers, actors and industry buffs gather for cutting-edge
indie films; Park City, Utah (p309).
Various dances (1 & 6 Jan) Public dances and performances at most Native American pueblos; New Mexico.
Ouray Ice Festival (mid-Jan) Four days of climbing
competitions, clinics, food and microbrew beer; Ouray,
Colorado (p338).

February
Gem & Mineral Show (early–mid-Feb) Huge expo for
jewelry and lapidary dealers; Tucson, Arizona (p204).
La Fiesta de los Vaqueros (late Feb) The world's largest nonmotorized parade, followed by a rodeo and other
cowboy events; Tucson, Arizona (p204).

March
Territorial Days (mid-March) Mining demonstrations,
firemen's hose cart competitions and a pet parade; Tombstone, Arizona (p216).

April
Gathering of Nations Powwow (late Apr or early
May) Over 3000 indigenous dancers and singers gather to
compete; Albuquerque, New Mexico (p355).

May
Cinco de Mayo (5 May) Celebrates Mexico's 1862 victory
over the French in the Battle of Puebla with parades,
dances, music, arts and crafts, and street fairs; New Mexico.

June
**St Anthony's Feast Day, San Juan Feast Day & St
Pedro's Feast Day** (13, 24 & 29 Jun) Feast days celebrated with an intermixing of Catholic ritual and traditional
dances; New Mexico.

July
Shakespearean Festival (late Jun–late Aug) Dramatic
'Shakespearience' performances, literary seminars and
educational backstage tours; Cedar City, Utah (p241).

DIRECTORY

August
Inter-Tribal Indian Ceremonial (mid-Aug) Extremely popular event draws dozens of tribes with rodeos, dances, powwows, parades, races, food, arts and crafts; Gallup, New Mexico (p416).

San Lorenzo Day (10 Aug) Food and craft booths, dances and races; Laguna and Picuris Pueblos, New Mexico.

Bryce Canyon Rim Run (late Aug) A scenic six-mile run along the canyon rim; Bryce Canyon, Utah (p249).

September
Annual Navajo Nation Fair (mid-Sep) The country's largest Indian fair, with a rodeo, parade, dances, songs, arts and crafts, and food; Window Rock, Arizona (p181).

All American Futurity (Labor Day) A quarter-horse race with a $2 million purse; Ruidoso Downs, New Mexico.

Fiestas (early Sep) One of the oldest annual fiestas in the country, with concerts and a carnival; Santa Fe, New Mexico (p373).

State Fair & Rodeo (mid-Sep) One of the largest state fairs in the country, with a rough 'n' tough rodeo, entertainment, carnival rides, livestock and culinary delicacies often served on a stick; Albuquerque, New Mexico (p355).

October
Whole Enchilada Fiesta (early Oct) A chile cook-off, entertainment, arts and crafts, races and the world's largest enchilada; Las Cruces, New Mexico (p434).

International Balloon Fiesta (mid-Oct) The world's biggest gathering of hot-air balloons, with daily mass ascensions that invoke childlike awe; Albuquerque, New Mexico (see p353).

Arts Festival (late Oct) A juried show overflowing with jewelry, ceramics, glass and sculptures; Sedona, Arizona (p169).

November
San Diego Feast Day (12 Nov) Traditional dancing; Tesuque Pueblo, New Mexico (p383).

Folk Music Festival (mid-Nov) A week of concerts powered 100% by wind-generated electricity; Moab, Utah (p275).

Day of the Dead (2 Nov) A traditional Mexican celebration honoring deceased relatives. Often breads and sweets resembling skeletons are made, and families visit graveyards.

December
Fiesta of Our Lady of Guadalupe (10-12 Dec) A procession from the church and dancing; Tortugas, New Mexico.

Christmas Month-long festivities, including Nativity pageants and festivals of lights; held in many Southwestern towns.

FOOD
Eating sections are broken down into three price categories: budget (with main dishes costing $10 or less), midrange (where most main dishes cost $10 to $20) and top end (where most dinner mains cost more than $20). These price estimates do not include taxes, tips or beverages.

Note that many Utah restaurants are closed on Sunday; when you find one open (even if it's not your first choice), consider you're among the fortunate.

For details about Southwestern specialties and delicacies, see Food & Drink (p66).

GAY & LESBIAN TRAVELERS
Per usual, the most visible gay communities are in major cities. Gay travelers should be careful in the predominantly rural areas – simply holding hands might get you bashed. Between the Mormons in Utah, right-wing Republicans in Arizona and conservative Hispanics in New Mexico, there's no mistaking the region for San Francisco.

The most active gay community in the Southwest is in Phoenix, not surprising considering that metro Phoenix has a larger population than either Utah or New Mexico. Although Santa Fe and Albuquerque have active lesbian communities, including a pride parade (p356), there are still three times more single-sex households in Arizona than in New Mexico. In Santa Fe, no one bothers much about wondering who's a lesbian and who isn't for two reasons: 'everyone' looks like a lesbian and folks are so groovy that no one cares. Perhaps some day there will be a saying, 'As Santa Fe goes, so goes the country.' In response to gay marriage becoming legal in Massachusetts in 2003, Sandoval Community, just north of Albuquerque, began issuing same-sex marriage licenses in early 2004. Las Vegas has an active gay scene, while conservative Utah has almost no visible gay life outside Salt Lake City.

According to www.epodunk.com, here's how the Southwest's big cities fare on a 'gay index,' a comparative score based on the percentage of same-sex households in a state: Las Vegas 123, Albuquerque 140, Phoenix 159, Salt Lake City 193 and Santa Fe 201. A score of 100 is the national norm; the higher the number, the more gays and lesbians there are.

Good national guidebooks include *Damron Women's Traveller*, providing listings for lesbians, *Damron Men's Travel Guide*, for men, and *Damron Accommodations*, with listings of gay-owned or gay-friendly accommodations nationwide. All three are published by the **Damron Company** (☎ 415-255-0404, 800-462-6654; www.damron.com).

Another good resource is the **Gay & Lesbian Yellow Pages** (☎ 800-697-2812, www.glyp.com), with 33 national and regional directories.

National resources include the **National AIDS/HIV Hotline** (☎ 800-232-4636; www.ashastd.org), the **National Gay/Lesbian Task Force** (☎ 202-393-5177; www.thetaskforce.org) in Washington, DC, and the **Lambda Legal Defense Fund** (NYC office ☎ 212-809-8585, LA office ☎ 213-382-7600; www.lambdalegal.org).

In the Southwest, there are few gay organizations compared to coastal cities. They are listed under Gay & Lesbian Organizations in the yellow pages of major cities' telephone directories.

HOLIDAYS

Also see Festivals & Events (p459) and When to Go (p18) for planning your holiday.

New Year's Day 1 January
Martin Luther King Jr Day 3rd Monday of January
Presidents Day 3rd Monday of February
Easter March or April
Memorial Day Last Monday of May
Independence Day 4 July
Labor Day 1st Monday of September
Columbus Day 2nd Monday of October
Veterans Day 11 November
Thanksgiving 4th Thursday of November
Christmas Day 25 December

INSURANCE

It's expensive to get sick, crash a car or have things stolen from you in the US. For rental car insurance see p475 and for health insurance see p477. To insure yourself from theft from your car, consult your homeowner's (or renter's) insurance policy before leaving home.

INTERNET ACCESS

If you usually access your email through your office or school, you'll find it easier to open a free account with Yahoo! (www.yahoo.com) or Hotmail (www.hotmail.com).

In case you're traveling with a laptop or hand-held computer, be aware that your modem may not work once you leave your home country. The safest option is to buy a reputable 'global' modem before you leave home, or buy a local PC-card modem if you're going to spend an extended time in any one country. For more information on traveling with a portable computer, see www.teleadapt.com.

Cyber cafés and business centers like Kinkos offer inexpensive on-line computer access. When hostels or other lodgings provide access, this is noted with an 🖳 . For Internet cafés, see the relevant Internet Access sections (under Information) in individual chapters.

It's always safest to get local access dial-up numbers from your Internet service provider (eg, Earthlink, AOL) before leaving home. In lots of places in the Southwest, dial-up access numbers require long-distance toll calls, which can be problematic for those traveling with a computer.

LEGAL MATTERS

If you are arrested for a serious offence, you are allowed to remain silent, entitled to have an attorney present during any interrogation and presumed innocent until proven guilty. You have the right to an attorney from the very first moment you are arrested. If you can't afford one, the state must provide one for free. All persons who are arrested have the right to make one phone call. If you don't have a lawyer or family member to help you, call your embassy or consulate.

The minimum age for drinking alcoholic beverages in the US is 21; you'll need a government-issued photo ID to prove it (such as a passport or a US driver's license). Stiff fines, jail time and penalties can be

LEGAL AGE				
The legal ages for certain activities around the Southwest varies by state, in this order: Arizona, Colorado, Las Vegas, New Mexico, Utah.				
Driving	16/16/15/16/16			
Voting	18 in every state			
Drinking	21 in every state			
Heterosexual sex	18/17/16/17/18			
Homosexual sex	no age/17/18/13/illegal			

incurred if you are caught driving under the influence of alcohol or providing alcohol to minors.

For information about driving speed limits and other road rules, see p475.

MAPS

The most detailed state highway maps are those distributed free by state governments. Order them from state tourism offices (p465) in advance, or pick up maps at highway tourism information offices when you enter a state on a major highway.

The **Delorme Mapping Company** (☎ 207-846-7100; www.delorme.com) publishes great atlas-style state maps that cost about $20. Nothing compares to these maps for delving into backcountry roads.

Hiking trail maps are available from outdoor equipment stores, local outfitters, outdoors organizations (p58), National Park Service (NPS) visitor centers and USDA Forest Service (USFS) ranger stations.

MONEY

The dollar ($, commonly called a buck) is divided into 100 cents (¢). Coins come in denominations of one cent (penny), five cents (nickel), 10 cents (dime), 25 cents (quarter) and the rare 50-cent piece (half dollar). Notes come in one-, five-, 10-, 20-, 50- and 100-dollar denominations.

See the inside the front cover for exchange rates and p18 for information on costs in this region.

ATMs & Cash

Automatic teller machines (ATMs) are great for quick cash influxes and can negate the need for traveler's checks entirely, but watch out for ATM surcharges. Most banks in the Southwest charge around $1.50 per withdrawal.

The Cirrus and Plus systems both have extensive ATM networks that will give cash advances on major credit cards and allow cash withdrawals with affiliated ATM cards. Look for ATMs outside banks and in large grocery stores, shopping centers, convenience stores and gas stations.

Credit Cards

Major credit cards are widely accepted throughout the Southwest, including at car rental agencies and most hotels, restaurants, gas stations, grocery stores and tour operators. Many B&Bs and some condominiums – particularly those handled through rental agencies – do not accept credit cards, however.

American Express	☎ 800-528-4800
Diners Club	☎ 800-234-6377
Discover	☎ 800-347-2683
MasterCard	☎ 800-826-2181
Visa	☎ 800-336-8472

Moneychangers

Some banks exchange cash or traveler's checks in major foreign currencies, though banks in outlying areas do this infrequently and it may take some time. It's easier to exchange foreign currency in larger cities. Thomas Cook and American Express exchange windows in international airports offer exchange (although you will get a better rate at a bank or at home).

Traveler's Checks

Traveler's checks provide protection from theft and loss. For refunds on lost or stolen traveler's checks, call **American Express** (☎ 800-992-3404) or **Thomas Cook** (☎ 800-287-7362). Keeping a record of the check numbers and those you have used is vital for replacing lost checks, so keep this information separate from the checks themselves.

Foreign visitors carrying traveler's checks will find things infinitely easier if the checks are in US dollars. Most midrange and upscale restaurants, hotels and shops accept US dollar traveler's checks and treat them just like cash.

Tipping

Taxi drivers expect a 15% tip. Waiters and bartenders rely on tips for their livelihoods. Tip $1 per drink to bartenders and 15% to waiters unless the service is terrible (in which case a complaint to the manager is warranted), or about 20% if the service is great. Don't tip in fast food, takeout or buffet-style restaurants where you serve yourself. Baggage carriers in airports and hotels should get $1 or $2 per bag. In hotels with daily housekeeping, leave a few dollars in the room for the staff for each day of your stay when you check out. In budget hotels, tips are not expected, but are always appreciated.

PHOTOGRAPHY & VIDEO

For the traditionalists out there, both print and slide film are readily available in the Southwest. Furthermore, every town of any size has a photo shop that stocks cameras and accessories. With little effort you should be able to find a shop to develop your color print film in one hour, or at least on the same day. Expect to pay about $7 to process a roll of 24 color prints.

With the implementation of high-powered X-ray at many airports, don't pack film into checked luggage or carry-on bags. Instead, carry your film in a baggie to show separately to airport security officials (ask for a hand check). Remember to finish off the roll in your camera and take it out, too, or those photos may end up foggy. Don't leave your film and camera in your car on a hot summer's day, and don't place your camera on your dashboard while you are driving.

For information on photographing reservations and pueblos, see p466. For video information, see Practicalities (p454). For more specific tips, see Top Five Photo Tips (below).

POST

No matter how much people like to complain, the **US postal service** (☎ 800-275-8777; www.usps.gov) provides great service for the price. For 1st-class mail sent and delivered within the US, postage rates are 37¢ for letters up to 1oz (23¢ for each additional ounce) and 23¢ for standard-size postcards. If you have the correct postage, drop your mail into any blue mailbox. However, to send a package weighing 16oz or more, you must bring it to a post office. See the individual Information sections for post office locations.

International airmail rates for letters up to 1oz are 60¢ to Canada or Mexico, 80¢ to other countries. Postcards cost 50¢ to Canada or Mexico, 70¢ to other countries.

You can have mail sent to you c/o General Delivery at most big post offices in the Southwest. When you pick up your mail, bring some photo identification. General delivery mail is usually held for up to 30 days. Most hotels will also hold mail for incoming guests.

Call private shippers like **United Parcel Service** (UPS; ☎ 800-742-5877; www.ups.com) and **Federal Express** (FedEx; ☎ 800-463-3339; www.fedex.com) to send more important or larger items.

SHOPPING

Local arts and crafts top most shopping lists. Often, the dividing line between traditional tribal (p38) or Hispanic crafts and Southwestern art is a hazy one, with the latter often being heavily influenced by the former. Buying Indian crafts on reservations, directly from the makers, is often substantially cheaper than buying it in off-reservation gift shops. However, the latter afford the buyer a much greater selection and, in the best stores, knowledgeable sales staff who have chosen only the finest quality work and can tell you about it. Buying from roadside stands in reservations can be fun, and you know that you are avoiding the middleman, but it's definitely a case of 'buyer beware' – the quality will vary tremendously.

Just about all the tribes make beautiful jewelry; most New Mexico pueblos produce

---

TOP FIVE PHOTO TIPS

For the very complete short course on photographic ins and outs, dos and don'ts, consult Lonely Planet's *Travel Photography*. In the meantime, try these tips:

- Shoot at dusk and dawn. Sure it's hard to wake up and be in the right place at the right time, but the light is more angular and dramatic.
- Include people for perspective. When you get home, your friends won't ask 'How big was that?'
- Shoot street life. Shots of one building after another will test your friends' patience.
- Change perspective. Get low and shoot up; get high and look down.
- Move in closer. Whether it's people or places, there's almost no such thing as too close (and when there, it's called an abstraction!).

DIRECTORY

distinctive ceramics and pots, which vary from tribe to tribe. Look for Navajo items at the Hubbell Trading Post (p182), Hopi crafts at the Hopi Cultural Center (p185), ceramics at many pueblos between Albuquerque and Santa Fe. Taos Pueblo (p400) is always a good bet. Gift shops at major museums are quite reliable outlets for authentic goods, too. Don't miss the Heard Museum in Phoenix (p119), the Millicent Rogers Museum in Taos (p394) and the Museum of Northern Arizona in Flagstaff (p155). Many visitors build entire vacations around shopping at the Indian Market in Santa Fe (p374).

For information on Navajo rugs and Hopi kachinas, see p181 and p186 respectively.

SOLO TRAVELERS

Travel, including solo travel, is generally safe and easy. In general, women need to exercise more vigilance in large cities than in rural areas. Everyone, though, should avoid hiking, cycling long distances or camping alone, especially in unfamiliar places. For more safety advice see p466 and p457.

TAXES

Meal and lodging taxes vary from county to county, but here is a guide:

State	Meal	Lodging	Sales
Arizona	2-4.5%	8-10%	5.6%
Colorado	2.5-7.4%	8.9-9.25%	2.9%
Las Vegas	7.25%	9%	6.5%
New Mexico	6.75-7.3%	9-14.5%	5%
Utah	7.25-8%	9-10%	4.75%

TELEPHONE

Always dial '1' before toll-free (800, 888, etc) and domestic long-distance numbers. Remember that some toll-free numbers may only work within the region or from the US mainland, for instance. But you'll only know if it works by making the call.

All phone numbers in the US consist of a three-digit area code followed by a seven-digit local number.

Pay phones aren't as readily found at shopping centers, gas stations and other public places now that cell phones are more prevalent. But keep your eyes peeled and you'll find them. Calls made within town are local and cost 25¢ or 50¢.

To make international calls direct, dial ☎ 011 + country code + area code + number. (An exception is to Canada, where you dial ☎ 1 + area code + number. International rates apply for Canada.)

For international operator assistance, dial ☎ 0. The operator can provide specific rate information and tell you which time periods are the cheapest for calling.

If you're calling the Southwest from abroad, the international country code for the US is ☎ 1. All calls to the Southwest are then followed by the area code and the seven-digit local number.

Cell Phones

The US uses a variety of mobile phone systems, 99% of which are incompatible with the GSM 900/1800 standard used throughout Europe and Asia. Check with your cellular service provider before departure. Verizon and Cingular have the most extensive cellular network, but you'll find a lot of coverage holes when you're driving in the middle of nowhere. Don't take undue risks thinking you'll be able to call for help from anywhere. Once you get up into the mountains, too, cell phone reception can be sketchy at best.

Phone Cards

These private prepaid phone cards are available from convenience stores, supermarkets and pharmacies. Cards sold by major telecommunications companies such as AT&T may offer better deals than upstart companies.

TIME

Most of the Southwest is on Mountain Time, which is seven hours behind Greenwich Mean Time. Nevada is an hour behind, on Pacific Standard Time. Daylight savings time begins on the first Sunday in April, when clocks are put forward one hour, and ends on the last Sunday in October, when the clocks are turned back one hour.

Arizona does not use daylight savings time, so during that period it's one hour behind the other Southwestern states. The Navajo Reservation, most of which lies in Arizona, uses daylight savings time, but the small Hopi Reservation, which is surrounded by the Navajo Reservation, doesn't. Confused?

TIME ZONES	
Time	**Place**
noon	Southwest USA
1pm	Chicago
11pm	San Francisco
2pm	Montreal
9am	Vancouver
6am	Melbourne (next day)
7pm	London
8pm	Amsterdam

TOURIST INFORMATION

State and regional tourist offices include:
Arizona Office of Tourism (Map pp120-1; ☎ 866-275-5816; www.arizonaguide.com; 1110 W Washington, Suite 155, Phoenix, AZ 85007)
Colorado Travel & Tourism Authority (☎ 800-265-6723; www.colorado.com; PO Box 3524, Englewood, CO 80155)
Las Vegas Convention & Visitors Authority Visitor Information Center (Map pp76-8; ☎ 702-892-0711, 877-847-4858; www.vegasfreedom.com; 3150 Paradise Rd, Las Vegas, NV 89109)
New Mexico Tourism Bureau (Map pp368-9; ☎ 800-545-2040; www.newmexico.org; 491 Old Santa Fe Trail, Santa Fe NM 87503)
Utah Travel Council (Map pp292-3; ☎ 801-538-1030, 800-200-1160; www.utah.com; Council Hall, Capitol Hill, Salt Lake City, UT 84114)

TOURS

For those with a limited amount of time or specialized interests, tours may be the best option. Always read the fine print; tour prices may or may not include airfare, meals, taxes and tips. **Backroads, Inc** (☎ 800-462-2848; www.backroads.com; 801 Cedar St, Berkeley, CA 94710) offers hiking and biking trips for all ages across Arizona, New Mexico and southern Utah.

The sophisticated Washington, DC **Smithsonian Journeys** (☎ 887-338-8687; www.smithsonianjourneys.org) organizes academically inclined, upscale tours such as Santa Fe Opera, National Parks of the West, Las Vegas Art and Architecture, and the Atomic Age in New Mexico.

Elderhostel (☎ 617-426-7788, 877-426-8056; www.elderhostel.org) also offers a whole host of educational programs (p458).

For an alternative to pure tourism, look into **Global Citizens Network** (GCN; ☎ 651-644-0960, 800-644-9292; www.globalcitizens.org; 130 N Howell St, St Paul, MN 55104) where socially conscious visitors can work with the Navajo Nation in both Arizona and New Mexico. Smaller site- or town-specific tour companies are sprinkled throughout the individual chapters of this guidebook.

VISAS

Since the establishment of the Department of Homeland Security following the events of September 11, 2001, immigration now falls under the purview of the **Bureau of Citizenship & Immigration Service** (BCIS; www.uscis.gov).

Getting into the US can be a bureaucratic nightmare, depending on your country of origin. To make matters worse, the rules are rapidly changing. For up-to-date information about visas and immigration, check with the **US State Department** (☎ 202-663-1225; www.travel.state.gov).

Most foreign visitors to the US need a visa. However, there is a Visa Waiver Program in which citizens of certain countries may enter the US for stays of 90 days or less without first obtaining a US visa. This list is subject to continual re-examination and bureaucratic rejiggering. At the time of writing these countries include: Andorra, Australia, Austria, Belgium, Brunei, Canada, Denmark, Finland, France, Germany, Iceland, Ireland, Italy, Japan, Liechtenstein, Luxembourg, Monaco, the Netherlands, New Zealand, Norway, Portugal, San Marino, Singapore, Slovenia, Spain, Sweden, Switzerland and the UK.

Because the Department of Homeland Security is continually modifying its requirements, even those with visa waivers may be subject to enrolment in the US-Visit program. This program may require that visa recipients have a machine-readable passport and/or a digital scan of their fingerprints. Contact the **Department of Homeland Security** (www.dhs.gov) for current requirements.

Nonetheless, your passport should be valid for at least another six months after you leave the US and you'll need to submit a recent photo (50.8mm x 50.8mm) with the visa application. Documents of financial stability and/or guarantees from a US resident are sometimes required, particularly for those from developing countries.

ETIQUETTE ON PUEBLOS & RESERVATIONS

Visitors to pueblos and reservations are generally welcome, but they should behave in an appropriately courteous and respectful manner. Tribal rules are often clearly posted at the entrance to each reservation, but here are a few guidelines.

- **Photography and other recording** Many tribes ban all forms of recording, be it photography, videotaping, audiotaping or drawing. Others permit these activities in certain areas only if you pay the appropriate fee (usually $5 to $10). If you wish to photograph a person, do so only after obtaining his or her permission. A posing tip is usually expected. Photographers who disregard these rules can expect tribal police officers to confiscate their cameras and then escort them off the reservation.

- **Private property** Do not walk into houses or climb onto roofs unless invited. Do not climb on ruins. Kivas are always off-limits to visitors. Do not remove any kind of artifact. Off-road travel (foot, horse or vehicle) is not allowed without a permit.

- **Verbal communication** It is polite to listen without comment, particularly when an elder is speaking. Silent listening does not mean that the listener is ignoring the speaker; to the contrary, intent listening is considered respectful. Be prepared for long silences in the middle of conversations; such silences often indicate that a topic is under serious consideration.

- **Ceremonials and powwows** These are either open to the public or exclusively for tribal members. Ceremonials are religious events. Applauding, chatting, asking questions or trying to talk to the performers is rude. Photography and other recording are rarely permitted. While powwows also hold spiritual significance, they are usually more informal. Many ceremonials and powwows don't have a fixed date and are arranged a couple of weeks ahead of time. The tribal office can inform you of upcoming events.

- **Clothing** Modest dress is customary. Especially when watching ceremonials, you should dress conservatively. Tank tops and short shorts are inappropriate.

- **Alcohol** Most reservations ban the sale or use of alcohol. The Apache reservations are notable exceptions.

- **Eating** There are few restaurants. Especially during public ceremonials, visitors may be invited into a house for a meal. Tipping is not customary.

- **Recreation** Activities such as backpacking, camping, fishing and hunting require tribal permits. On Native American lands, state fishing or hunting licenses are not valid.

Visa applicants may be required to 'demonstrate binding obligations' that will ensure their return home. Because of this requirement, those planning to travel through other countries before arriving in the US are generally better off applying for their US visa while they are still in their home country rather than while on the road.

The validity period for a US visitor visa depends on your home country. The actual length of time you'll be allowed to stay in the US is determined by the BCIS at the port of entry.

WOMEN TRAVELERS

Women travelers everywhere face challenges particular to their gender. Avoiding vulnerable situations and conducting yourself in a common-sense manner will help you to avoid most problems. You're more vulnerable if you've been drinking or using drugs than if you're sober, and you're more vulnerable alone than if you're with company. If you don't want company, most men will respect a firm but polite 'no, thank you.'

If you are assaulted, you do not need to call the police directly in order to get help. The best course of action is often to call a rape-crisis hotline; contact numbers for these are normally listed in the telephone directory. Rape-crisis center staff act as a link between medical, legal and social service systems, advocating on behalf of survivors to ensure their rights are respected and their needs are addressed. They often provide free translation services as well. Outside of urban areas, usually you can go directly to the nearest hospital for help first, then decide later whether or not to call the police. For the telephone number of the nearest center, call directory information (☎ 411 or 1 + area code + 555-1212).

The **National Organization for Women** (NOW; ☎ 202-331-0066; www.now.org; 1100 H St NW, 3rd fl, Washington, DC 20005) is a good resource for a variety of information and can refer you to state and local chapters. **Planned Parenthood** (☎ 212-541-7800; www.plannedparenthood.org; 26 Bleecker St, New York, NY 10012) can refer you to clinics throughout the country and offer advice on medical issues.

WORK

Seasonal work is possible in national parks and other tourist sites, especially ski areas; for information, contact park concessions or local chambers of commerce. These are usually low-paying service jobs filled by young people (often college students) who are happy to work part of the day so they can play the rest. You can't depend on finding a job just by arriving in May or June and looking around.

If you are not a US citizen, you must apply for a work visa from the US embassy in your home country before you leave. The type of visa varies, depending on how long you're staying and the kind of work you plan to do. Generally, you need either a J-1 visa, which you can obtain by joining a visitor-exchange program (issued mostly to students for work in summer camps), or an H-2B visa, when you are sponsored by a US employer.

The latter can be difficult to procure unless you can show that you already have a job offer from an employer who considers your qualifications to be unique and not readily available in the US. There are, of course, many foreigners working illegally in the country. Controversial laws prescribe punishments for employers employing 'aliens' (foreigners) who do not have the proper visas. BCIS officers can be persistent and insistent in their enforcement of the laws.

Transportation

CONTENTS

GETTING THERE & AWAY

Most travelers to the Southwest arrive by air and car, with bus running a distant third place. The train service is little used but available. Major regional hubs include Las Vegas (p109), Phoenix (p131), Albuquerque (p359) and Salt Lake City (p299).

AIR

Unless you live in or near the Southwest, flying in and renting a car is the most time-efficient option. If time is not of the essence, drive. Most domestic visitors fly into Phoenix or Las Vegas. Most international visitors, though, first touch down in Los Angeles, New York, Miami or Dallas/Fort Worth before catching an onward flight to any number of Southwest cities.

> **THINGS CHANGE...**
>
> The information in this chapter is particularly vulnerable to change. Check directly with the airline or a travel agent to make sure you understand how a fare (and ticket you may buy) works, and be aware of the security requirements for international travel. Shop carefully. The details given in this chapter should be regarded as pointers and are not a substitute for your own careful, up-to-date research.

Airports & Airlines

There are many good options for flying into this region from elsewhere in the country, and around the world, for that matter. In addition to the major airports listed here, international visitors might consider flying into San Francisco or Los Angeles and driving. **Los Angeles Airport** (LAX; ☎ 310-646-5252; www.los-angeles-lax.com), busier than any of the airports listed here, is an easy day's drive from western Arizona or southwestern Utah via Las Vegas.

Sky Harbor International Airport (code PHX; p131; ☎ 602-273-3300; www.phxskyharbor.com) Serving Phoenix, AZ, and the Grand Canyon. It's one of the region's two busiest airports, handling over 30 million passengers annually; a hub for America West and Southwest Air.

McCarran International Airport (code LAS; p109; ☎ 702-261-5211; www.mccarran.com) Serving Las Vegas, NV, and southern Utah. The region's other busiest airport, handling over 30 million passengers annually; a hub for America West, Continental and Southwest.

Salt Lake City International Airport (code SLC; p299; ☎ 801-575-2400; www.slcairport.com) Serving Salt Lake City, UT, and northern Utah. Receives about half as many flights as Phoenix; a hub for Delta.

Albuquerque International Sunport (code ABQ; p359; ☎ 505-244-7700; www.cabq.gov/airport) Serving Albuquerque and all of New Mexico. A small and friendly airport that's easy to navigate; a hub for low cost carriers Southwest Airlines and America West.

Tucson International Airport (code TUS; p209; ☎ 520-573-8000; www.tucsonairport.org) Serving Tucson, AZ, and southern Arizona. A small and friendly airport that's easy to navigate; a hub for low cost carriers Southwest Airlines and America West.

Denver International Airport (code DEN; p323; ☎ 303-342-2000; www.flydenver.com) Serving southern Colorado. If you rent a car in Denver, you can be in northeastern New Mexico in four hours; a United and (low-cost) Frontier hub.

El Paso International Airport (code ELP; ☎ 915-780-4749; www.elpaso-elp.com) On the border with southern New Mexico; a possible minor gateway. For a teaser and primer on El Paso and West Texas, see p451.

Airlines flying to and from the Southwest include:

Aer Lingus (EI; ☎ 800-223-6537; www.aerlingus.com)

AeroMexico (AM; ☎ 800-237-6639; www.aeromexico.com.mx)

Air Canada (AC; ☎ 888-247-2262; www.aircanada.ca)

DEPARTURE TAX

Taxes and fees for US airports are normally included in the price of tickets when you buy them, whether they're purchased in the US or abroad.

Air France (AF; ☎ 800-237-2747; www.airfrance.com)
Air New Zealand (NZ; ☎ 800-262-1234; www.airnz.co.nz)
Alaska Airlines (AS; ☎ 800-252-7522; www.alaskaair.com)
America West Airlines (HP; ☎ 800-235-9292; www.americawest.com)
American Airlines (AA; ☎ 800-223-5436; www.aa.com)
ATA (TZ; ☎ 800-225-2995; www.ata.com)
British Airways (BA; ☎ 800-247-9297; www.britishairways.com)
China Airlines (CI; ☎ 800-227-5118; www.china-airlines.com)
Continental Airlines (CO; ☎ 800-523-3273; www.continental.com)
Delta (DL; ☎ 800-221-1212; www.delta.com)
Frontier (F9; ☎ 800-432-1359; www.flyfrontier.com)
Lufthansa (LH; ☎ 800-645-3880; www.lufthansa.de)
Japan Airlines (NQ; ☎ 800-525-3663; www.jal.co.jp)
JetBlue (JB; ☎ 800-538-2583; www.jetblue.com)
Mesa Air (YV; ☎ 800-637-2247; www.mesa-air.com)
Midwest Express (YX; ☎ 800-452-2022; www.midwestairlines.com)
Northwest-KLM (NW; ☎ 800-225-2525; www.nwa.com)
Qantas (QF; ☎ 800-227-4500; www.qantas.com.au)
Spirit Airlines (NK; ☎ 800-772-7117; www.spiritair.com)
Southwest Airlines (SW; ☎ 800-435-9792; www.southwest.com)
Song (SQ; ☎ 800-359-7664; www.flysong.com)
United (UA; ☎ 800-241-6522; www.united.com)
US Airways (US; ☎ 800-428-4322; www.usairways.com)
Virgin Atlantic (VS; ☎ 800-862-8621; www.virginatlantic.com)

Tickets

Airfares to the US and Southwest range from incredibly low to obscenely high. The best deals are often found on the Internet (see p471). **STA Travel** (☎ 800-777-0112; www.statravel.com), which offers on-line booking, also has offices (with real live people!) in major cities nation- and worldwide.

For one-way flights, low-cost airlines such as Southwest, America West, Frontier and JetBlue are the best places to look.

Many domestic carriers offer special fares to visitors who are not US citizens.

Typically, you must purchase a booklet of coupons in conjunction with a flight into the US from a foreign country other than Canada or Mexico. In addition to other restrictions, these coupons typically must be used within a limited period of time.

Round-the-world (RTW) tickets can be a great deal if you want to visit other regions on your way to or from the Southwest. Often they are the same price – or just a tad more expensive – than a simple round-trip ticket to the US, which means you get to visit other places for nothing. RTW itineraries that include stops in South America or Africa, though, can be substantially more expensive. **British Airways** (☎ 800-247-9297; www.britishairways.com) and **Qantas** (☎ 800-227-4500; www.qantas.com.au) offer the best plans through tickets called oneworld Explorer and Global Explorer, respectively.

Asia

Hong Kong is the discount plane ticket capital of the region, but its bucket shops can be unreliable. Ask the advice of other travelers before buying a ticket. China Airlines flies to San Francisco and Los Angeles from Hong Kong. Summertime round-trip fares are around HK$7400 to HK$8970 ($950 to $1150).

There are nonstop flights to the west coast from several Japanese cities with various airlines. Japan Airlines flies to San Francisco and Los Angeles from Tokyo. Summertime round-trip fares are generally around ¥104,200 ($1000) in July and ¥203,200 ($1950) in August.

Connector flights are usually available from the west coast to the Southwest for about $100 (one-way) on Southwest and America West.

STA Travel proliferates in Asia, with branches in **Bangkok** (☎ 02-236 0262; www.statravel.co.th), **Singapore** (☎ 6737 7188; www.statravel.com.sg), **Hong Kong** (☎ 2736 1618; www.statravel.com.hk) and **Japan** (☎ 03 5391 2922; www.statravel.co.jp). Another resource in Japan is **No 1 Travel** (☎ 03 3205 6073; www.no1-travel.com); in Hong Kong try **Four Seas Tours** (☎ 2200 7760; www.fourseastravel.com/english).

Australia

Qantas flies to Los Angeles from Sydney, Melbourne and Brisbane. United flies from Sydney to San Francisco and Los Angeles.

TRANSPORTATION

Summertime round-trip fares are generally around A$2640 to A$3020 ($2100 to $2400) from Melbourne or Sydney to the west coast. Connector flights are available to the Southwest from the west coast for about $100 (one-way) on Southwest and America West.

For the location of **STA Travel** branches call ☎ 1300 733 035 or visit www.statravel.com .au. **Flight Centre** (☎ 133 133; www.flightcentre.com .au) has offices throughout Australia. For online bookings, try www.travel.com.au.

Canada

The Canadian Federation of Students' **Travel CUTS** (www.travelcuts.com) travel agency offers low fares and has offices in major cities throughout Canada. They have good prices for students and deal with the general public as well. The Toronto *Globe and Mail* and *Vancouver Sun* carry travel agents' ads. For online bookings try www.expedia.ca and www.travelocity.ca.

Many connections between Canada and the Southwest are through Vancouver, BC. Air Canada flies from Toronto to Vancouver for a round-trip fare of about C$725 ($600). From Vancouver, there are relatively frequent flights to Phoenix and Salt Lake City. You can expect round-trip summertime airfares from Vancouver to Phoenix for C$540 ($450) and to Salt Lake City for C$600 ($500).

Continental Europe

There are no direct flights to the Southwest from Europe. Flying straight to the west coast is quicker than transferring in a city such as New York or Chicago. Nonstop summertime flights to Los Angeles are available from Amsterdam with Northwest-KLM (costing about €1200, or $1600); from Frankfurt with Delta, United and Lufthansa (costing about €930, or $1250); and from Paris with Air France (costing about €1000, or $1350). Nonstop flights from Europe to San Francisco are priced comparably.

It usually costs about $200 less to fly round-trip to the west coast from London than it does from the Continent.

Recommended travel agencies include:
Airfair (☎ 020 620 5121; www.airfair.nl) In the Netherlands.
Anyway (☎ 0892 893 892; www.anyway.fr) In France.

Barcelo Viajes (☎ 902 116 226; www.barceloviajes.com) In Spain.
CTS Viaggi (☎ 06 462 0431; www.ctsviaggi.it) In Italy.
Just Travel (☎ 089 747 3330; www.justtravel.de) In Germany.
Lastminute France (☎ 0892 705 000; www.lastminute.fr); Germany (☎ 01805 284 366; www.lastminute.de)
STA (☎ 01 44 41 89 80; www.sta.com) In Paris.
Nouvelles Frontières France (☎ 0825 000 747; www .nouvelles-frontieres.fr); Spain (☎ 90 217 09 79)
Voyageurs du Monde (☎ 01 40 15 11 15; www.vdm .com) In France.

New Zealand

United and Air New Zealand both fly to San Francisco and Los Angeles from Auckland (via Sydney) for about NZ$2015 ($1500) round-trip during the summer. Connecting flights are readily available to the Southwest for about $100 (one-way) aboard Southwest and America West.

Both **Flight Centre** (☎ 0800 243 544; www.flight centre.co.nz) and **STA Travel** (☎ 0508 782 872; www .statravel.co.nz) have branches throughout the country. The site www.travel.co.nz is recommended for online bookings.

South & Central America

Most flights from Central and South America to the Southwest fly via Miami, New Orleans, Houston, Dallas/Fort Worth or Los Angeles. Most countries' international flag carriers, as well as US airlines like United Airlines, American Airlines and Continental Airlines, serve these destinations from Latin America, with onward connections to cities in the Southwest. There are infinite permutations of airfares that we could quote here, but we suggest that our South American readers plug their own specifics into an Internet site or consult a local travel agency.

America West, United Airlines, Continental Airlines and AeroMexico have flights from Phoenix and Tucson to numerous Mexican cities. From Mexico City expect to pay M$4200 ($375) to Phoenix and M$6200 ($550) to Tucson.

Recommended agencies include:
ASATEJ (☎ 54-011 4114-7595; www.asatej.com) In Argentina.
IVI Tours (☎ 0212-993 6082; www.ividiomas.com) In Venezuela.
Student Travel Bureau (☎ 3038 1555; www.stb.com.br) In Brazil.

UK & Ireland

London is arguably the world's headquarters for bucket shops specializing in discount tickets, and they are well advertised. Two good, reliable agents for cheap tickets in the UK are **Trailfinders** (☎ 020-7628 7628; www.trailfinders.co.uk; 1 Threadneedle St, London) and **STA Travel** (☎ 020-240 9821; www.statravel.co.uk; 33 Bedford St, Covent Garden, London).

A flight in the summer from London to Phoenix (with one stop) is available on British Airways (£750, $1450). Several carriers fly nonstop to Los Angeles for about £52 less ($100), but then you'll have to add the cost (and time) of getting where you want to go in the Southwest.

Aer Lingus has direct flights from Shannon (one stop) and Dublin (nonstop) to Las Vegas for about €850 ($1100) in summer, from where you can catch a connecting flight to the Southwest.

USA

Competition is high among airlines flying to the Southwest from major US cities. With a little advance planning and some savvy Internet browsing, you can usually get a nonstop summertime flight on a major carrier from Los Angeles to Las Vegas for about $125 round-trip, and from San Francisco for $200. From Washington, DC, fares to these same cities are in the $300 round-trip range. From Chicago, expect to spend about $200 (round-trip).

You have a choice: talk to a live agent or tap the computer keys. Frankly, your odds are better doing it yourself if you have the time.

Atevo (www.atevo.com)
Best Fares (www.bestfares.com)
Cheap Tickets (www.cheaptickets.com)
Expedia (www.expedia.com)
Orbitz (www.orbitz.com)
STA Travel (☎ 800-777-0112; www.statravel.com)
Travelocity (www.travelocity.com)

LAND
Border Crossings

From Yuma, AZ (p197), you can cross into Baja California and Mexico. Nogales, AZ (p220), is also a prime border town. For more information about traveling south of the Southwest, pick up Lonely Planet's *Baja & Los Cabos* and *Mexico* guides. The biggest gateway if you're traveling in New Mexico

is actually El Paso, TX (p451), to reach bustling Ciudad Juarez.

Don't forget your passport if you are crossing the border; see p221.

Bus

If you wish to or must travel by bus, long-distance buses can get you to major points within the region, but then you should really rent a car (see p474). Keep in mind that bus lines don't serve most national parks or some important, off-track tourist towns such as Moab. Additionally, bus terminals are often in poorer or more dangerous areas of town. Having said that, **Greyhound** (☎ 800-231-2222; www.greyhound.com) is the main US bus system. Parts of New Mexico and southern Colorado, though, are served by the TNM&O (Texas, New Mexico & Oklahoma) bus line in conjunction with Greyhound.

To save money on bus travel, plan seven days in advance, travel on weekdays, travel with a companion and avoid holiday travel. Search out special Internet deals. Students, military personnel and seniors receive discounts.

From	To	Duration	Fare*
Los Angeles, CA	Las Vegas, NV	6hr	$55-75
Chicago, IL	Las Vegas, NV	14-18hr	$158-259
Portland, OR	Salt Lake City, UT	18hr	$118-135
Dallas, TX	Albuquerque, NM	13-15hr	$98-149

* Prices are for round-trip

When you've graduated from **Green Tortoise** (☎ 800-867-8647; www.greentortoise.com), a rolling mosh pit of youthful sightseers, but you still want to sleep on a bus and hang with like-minded adventurers, look into **Adventure Bus** (☎ 888-737-5263; www.adventurebus.com). They specialize in travel to the national parks of southern Utah, the Grand Canyon and the Moab area.

Car & Motorcycle

Although the quickest way to get to the Southwest is by plane, the best way to get around is by car. (For information on car rentals, see p474.) If you have time, it's less expensive to drive to the Southwest than fly and rent a car. And then there's the little matter of driving. If you love driving, you'll be in heaven driving to and around the Southwest. Simply put, mile-for-mile, of the 160,000 miles (or so) in the national highway system, the Southwest has more stunning ones than any other region in the country.

Although little compares to the feeling of wind in your hair and the freedom of the open road, long distance motorcycle driving is dangerous because of the fatigue factor that settles in. Please use caution during long hauls.

From	To	Via	Duration
San Diego, CA	Phoenix, AZ	I-8	7hr
Los Angeles, CA	Las Vegas, NV	I-15	5hr
San Francisco, CA	Santa Fe, NM	I-5 & I-40	19hr
Denver, CO	Santa Fe, NM	I-25	6½hr
Dallas, TX	Albuquerque, NM	I-35 & I-40	11½hr

Train

Three **Amtrak** (☎ 800-872-7245; www.amtrak.com) trains cut a swath through the Southwest, but are unconnected with one another. Use them to reach the region, but not for touring around. The *Southwest Chief* offers a daily service between Chicago and Los Angeles, via Kansas City. Significant stations include Albuquerque, New Mexico, and Flagstaff and Williams, Arizona. As an added value, on-board guides provide commentary through Native American regions and national parks. The *California Zephyr* offers a daily service between Chicago and San Francisco (Emeryville) via Denver, with a stop in Salt Lake City, Utah. The *Sunset Limited* runs thrice weekly from Los Angeles to Orlando and stops in Tucson, Arizona.

Book tickets in advance and look for plenty of available deals. Children, seniors and military personnel receive good discounts. Amtrak offers various rail passes to non-US citizens (that must be purchased outside the US; check with a travel agent) as well as to Americans and Canadians.

From	To	Duration	Fare*
Los Angeles, CA	Flagstaff, AZ	$102	11hr
Chicago, IL	Albuquerque, NM	$313	26hr
Chicago, IL	Salt Lake City, UT	$152	35hr
San Francisco	Salt Lake City, UT	$133	20hr
Los Angeles, CA	Tucson, AZ	$66	10hr
* prices are for round-trip			

GETTING AROUND

Once you reach the Southwest, traveling by car is the best way of getting around and allows you to reach rural areas not otherwise served by public transportation. If you do not relish long drives, you can always take buses and trains between select (read: a limited number of) major destinations and then rent a car. But that's both time consuming and more expensive than driving yourself and stopping everywhere along the way. Besides, isn't that why you bought this book?

AIR

Because distances between places in the Southwest are so great, regional airports are located in a number of smaller towns such as Yuma and Flagstaff (both in Arizona), and Carlsbad and Taos (both in New Mexico). But since these places primarily serve residents and business people, and because it is quite expensive and impractical to consider flying between these places, we have emphasized the major air gateways (see p468). Still, you can find information about these smaller airports scattered throughout the regional chapters. If you're flying your own plane, consult **Flyguides** (www.flyguides.com).

Airlines in the Southwest

America West Airlines (HP; ☎ 800-235-9292; www .americawest.com) Major regional and budget carrier with hubs in Las Vegas and Phoenix. Flies to Albuquerque and Farmington (both in NM), El Paso (TX), Durango and Telluride (both in CO), Salt Lake City (UT), and Tucson, Yuma, Prescott, Lake Havasu, Kingman and Flagstaff (all in AZ).

Mesa Air (YV; ☎ 800-637-2247; www.mesa-air.com) Flies to Farmington, Albuquerque, Roswell and Carlsbad (all in NM), and to Kingman, Prescott, Lake Havasu and Phoenix (all in AZ). Also flies to Denver (CO).

Southwest Airlines (SW; ☎ 800-435-9792; www .southwest.com) Major regional and budget carrier; flies to Albuquerque (NM), Tucson and Phoenix (both in AZ), and to Las Vegas, Salt Lake City and El Paso (TX).

BICYCLE

Cycling is a cheap, convenient, healthy, environmentally sound and, above all, fun way of traveling. In the Southwest – because of altitude, distance and heat – it's also a good work-out. Bicyclists should carry at least a gallon of water and refill bottles at every opportunity since dehydration (p478) is a major problem in the arid Southwest.

Airlines accept bicycles as checked luggage. But since each airline has specific requirements, it's best to contact them for details. Bicycle rentals are listed throughout this guide when we've found a desirable place to cycle that also offers rentals. Expect to spend $15 to $20 a day for rental. For more on biking, see p61. Moab (p269) is generally considered the mountain biking capital of the Southwest. The countryside around Sedona is great for biking (p168).

Bicycles are generally prohibited on interstate highways if there is a frontage road. However, where a suitable frontage road or other alternative is lacking, bicyclists are permitted on some interstates. On the road, cyclists are generally treated courteously by motorists. In most states helmets are required by law (in Arizona, New Mexico and Utah under-18s have to wear a helmet, all riders must wear them in Las Vegas, and there are no requirements in Colorado); in any case, they should be worn to reduce the risk of head injury.

Cycling has increased in popularity so much in recent years that concerns have risen over damage to the environment, especially from unchecked mountain biking. Know your environment and regulations before you ride. Bikes are restricted from entering wilderness areas and some designated trails but may be used in National Park Service (NPS) sites, state parks, national and state forests and Bureau of Land Management (BLM) single-track trails.

BUS

Greyhound (☎ 800-231-2222; www.greyhound.com) is the main carrier to and within the Southwest, operating buses several times a day along major highways between large towns. Greyhound only stops at smaller towns that happen to be along the way, in which case, the 'bus terminal' is likely to be a grocery store parking lot or something similar. Under this scenario, boarding passengers usually pay the driver with exact change. If Greyhound serves a town, look for the blue and red Greyhound symbol. The best schedules often involve overnight routes; the best fares often require seven days' advance notice.

In New Mexico, the TNM&O (Texas, New Mexico and Oklahoma) bus line supplement Greyhound routes. Local phone numbers are given throughout the regional chapters.

From	To	Duration	Fare*
Las Vegas, NV	Phoenix, AZ	8-11hr	$39-45
Phoenix, AZ	Tucson, AZ	2hr	$18
Tucson, AZ	Albuquerque, NM	13hr	$49-88
Albuquerque, NM	Santa Fe, NM	1¼hr	$10
Santa Fe, NM	Durango, CO	7hr	$29
Santa Fe, NM	Salt Lake City, UT	19hr	$49-109

* prices are one way

CAR & MOTORCYCLE

You've heard it a few times already: distances are great in this mighty region and car travel is easily the best mode of transport. Betting against that is akin to Las Vegas bookies taking money from children.

The interstate system is thriving in the Southwest, but smaller state roads and fine scenic byways (see the regional chapters for these beauties) offer unparalleled opportunities for exploration. As for the former, you should know that I-10 runs east–west through southern Arizona; I-40 runs east–west through Arizona and central New Mexico; I-70 runs east–west through central Utah, and I-80 runs east–west through northern Utah. As for the north–south interstates, I-15 runs from Las Vegas to Salt Lake City; I-25 runs through central New Mexico to Denver, CO. The oh-so-classic Route 66 more or less parallels the modern day I-40 through Arizona and New Mexico; see p189, p189 and p412 for detailed information.

Automobile Associations

The **American Automobile Association** (AAA; www .aaa.com; ☎ 800-564-6222) provides members with maps and other information. Members also get discounts on car rentals, air tickets, some hotels, some sight-seeing attractions, as well as emergency road service and towing (☎ 800-222-4357). AAA has reciprocal agreements with automobile associations in other countries. Be sure to bring your membership card from your country of origin.

Main offices in the Southwest are located in Phoenix (☎ 602-274-1116), Salt Lake City (☎ 801-364-5615), Las Vegas (☎ 702-870-9171) and Albuquerque (☎ 505-291-6611).

TRANSPORTATION

ROAD DISTANCES (miles)

	Albuquerque, NM	Bryce Canyon NP, UT	Cortez (Mesa Verde NP), CO	Grand Canyon (North Rim), AZ	Grand Canyon (South Rim), AZ	Las Cruces, NM	Las Vegas, NV	Phoenix, AZ	Salt Lake City, UT	Santa Fe, NM
Bryce Canyon NP, UT	620									
Cortez (Mesa Verde NP), CO	279	408								
Grand Canyon (North Rim), AZ	538	126	336							
Grand Canyon (South Rim), AZ	416	285	366	212						
Las Cruces, NM	226	759	505	710	588					
Las Vegas, NV	579	499	488	266	276	743				
Phoenix, AZ	421	506	488	343	221	367	376			
Salt Lake City, UT	884	264	672	390	517	1023	435	770		
Santa Fe, NM	57	677	248	595	473	283	636	475	941	
Tucson, AZ	480	628	554	465	343	336	498	122	892	537

Many other smaller cities like Tucson, Santa Fe and Ogden also have offices; consult the *Yellow Pages*.

Emergency breakdown services are available 24 hours a day.

Driver's License

An international driver's license, obtained before you leave home, is only necessary if your country of origin is a non-English-speaking one.

Fuel

Gas stations are ubiquitous and many are open 24 hours a day. Small-town stations may be open only from 7am to 8pm or 9pm. Plan on spending $2.00 to $2.50 per US gallon.

At some stations, you must pay before you pump; at others, you may pump before you pay. The more modern pumps have credit/debit card terminals built into them, so you can pay with plastic right at the pump. At more expensive, 'full service' stations, an attendant will pump your gas for you; no tip is expected.

Hire

Rental cars are readily available at all airports and many downtown city locations. With advance reservations for a small car, the daily rate with unlimited mileage is about $30 to $40, while typical weekly rates are $150 to $200. Rates for mid-size cars are often only a tad higher. Since deals abound and the business is competitive, it pays to shop around between rental companies. You can often snag great last-minute deals via the Internet; rental reservations made in conjunction with an airplane ticket often yield better rates too. In planning, if you decide to fly into one city and out another (quite likely given the distances and sights), drop off charges for a rental car may not matter much. Nonetheless, don't forget to ask.

Having a major credit card greatly simplifies the car rental process. Without one, some companies simply will not rent vehicles, while others require things such as prepayment, a deposit of $200 per week, pay stubs, proof of round-trip airfare and more.

The following companies operate in the Southwest.

Alamo (☎ 800-327-9633; www.alamo.com)
Avis (☎ 800-831-2847; www.avis.com)
Budget (☎ 800-527-0700; www.budget.com)
Dollar (☎ 800-800-4000; www.dollar.com)
Enterprise (☎ 800-325-8007; www.enterprise.com)
Hertz (☎ 800-654-3131; www.hertz.com)
National (☎ 800-227-7368; www.nationalcar.com)
Rent-A-Wreck (☎ 800-944-7501; www.rent-a-wreck.com)
Thrifty (☎ 800-847-4389; www.thrifty.com)

Insurance

Liability insurance covers people and property that you might hit. For damage to the actual rental vehicle, a collision damage waiver (CDW) is available for about $15 a day. If you have collision coverage on your vehicle at home, it might cover damages to rental cars; inquire before departing. Additionally, some credit cards offer reimbursement coverage for collision damages if you rent the car with that credit card; again, check before departing. Most credit card coverage isn't valid for rentals of more than 15 days or for exotic models, jeeps, vans and 4WD vehicles.

Note that many rental agencies stipulate that damage a car suffers while being driven on unpaved roads is not covered by the insurance they offer. Check with the agent when you make your reservation.

Road Conditions & Hazards

Be extra defensive while driving in the Southwestern states, especially in New Mexico. In fact, New Mexico has one of the highest ratios of fatal car accidents to miles driven in the whole country. Hwy 666 heading north to Shiprock has an especially high accident rate, and Gallup has an unfortunate reputation for careless and drunken drivers.

Distances are great in the Southwest, and there are long stretches of road without gas stations. Running out of gas on a hot and desolate stretch of highway is no fun, so pay close attention to signs that caution 'Next Gas 98 Miles.'

For updates on wintertime road conditions, contact:

Arizona (☎ 888-411-7623)
Southern Colorado (in Colorado ☎ 877-315-7623)
New Mexico (☎ 800-432-4269)
Utah (in Utah ☎ 511)

Road Rules

Driving laws are slightly different in each of the Southwest states, but each requires the use of safety belts. In every state, children under five years of age must be placed in a child safety seat secured by a seat belt. In New Mexico, children under one year old must be properly restrained in a rear-facing seat.

The maximum speed limit on all rural interstates is 75mph, but that drops to 65mph in urban areas in Colorado, Nevada and Utah. New Mexico allows urban interstate drivers to barrel through at 75mph, but Arizona makes drivers crawl through high density areas at 55mph. On undivided highways, the speed limit will vary from 30mph in populated areas to 65mph on stretches where tumbleweeds keep pace with wily coyotes. Police enforce speed limits by patrolling in marked and unmarked cars; fines can be upwards of $300.

Consult p458 for general safety rules regarding driving in the Southwest, and p461 for matters concerning drinking and driving.

HITCHHIKING

Hitching is never entirely safe in any country in the world, and we don't recommend it. Travelers who decide to hitch should understand that they are taking a small but serious risk. You may not be able to identify the local rapist/murderer before you get into the vehicle. People who do choose to hitch will be safer if they travel in pairs and let someone know where they are planning to go. Ask the driver where he or she is going rather than telling the person where you want to go.

LOCAL TRANSPORTATION

Salt Lake City, UT, is the region's only city that has a light-rail system (p299). Most cities and some larger towns have local bus systems that will get you around (albeit slowly), but these buses generally run on very limited schedules on Sunday and at night. For more information on local transport, see the individual Getting Around sections throughout the regional chapters.

MOTOR HOME (RV)

Touring remote canyonlands, sparse deserts and Native American reservations by recreational vehicle can be as low-key or as over-the-top as you are. Rentals range from ultra-efficient VW campers to plush land yachts that resemble suites at the Bellagio in Las Vegas. Whatever mode you choose, what you've bought (or rented) represents freedom (except when you venture in to big cities, when freedom's just another word for a parking nightmare.)

After the size of the vehicle, consider the impact of gas prices, gas mileage, additional mileage costs, insurance and refundable deposits; these can add up quickly. It pays to shop around and read the fine print. Given the myriad of permutations in rental choices, it's incredibly hard to generalize but to get you started, you might expect a four-person vehicle with 1000 'free' miles to run $1100 to $1400 weekly in the summer, plus 32¢ for each additional mile. Get out a good map and a calculator to determine if that's too steep a price for freedom. Perhaps tent camping in a rental car doesn't sound so bad after all?

Before heading out, consult www.rvtravel .com for tips galore, including wi-fi locations. Then purchase a campground guide

from **Woodall's** (www.woodalls.com), which also has a great all-round website, or **KOA** (☎ 406-248-7444; www.koa.com), and hit the road.

For RV rentals contact the following:
Adventure Touring RV Rentals (☎ 866-672-3572; www.adventuretouring.com) Serving Las Vegas.
American RV Rentals (☎ 909-613-0562; www .americanrvrentals.com) Out of Los Angeles, with deliveries to Las Vegas.
Canyondlands RV Rentals (☎ 800-597-3370; www .rentrvutah.com) Serving Utah and Las Vegas.
Cruise America (☎ 800-327-7799; www.cruiseamerica .com)
Vacation RV Rentals (☎ 866-837-4502; www.vacation -rv-rentals.com) Serving Albuquerque.

TRAIN

Several train lines provide services using historic steam trains and are mainly for sightseeing, although the Williams to Grand Canyon (p142) run is a destination in itself. More scenic train rides are detailed in Yuma, AZ (p197), Chama, NM (p409), Santa Fe, NM (p373) and Durango, CO (p332).

For info on Amtrak trains, see p472.

Health David Goldberg MD

CONTENTS

The Southwest encompasses a wide range of climates and temperatures, from the blistering heat of the desert summer to several 12,000ft-plus peaks where snow lingers almost year-round. Because of the high level of hygiene here, as in the rest of the USA, infectious diseases are rarely a significant concern for most travelers.

BEFORE YOU GO

INSURANCE

The US offers possibly the finest health care in the world. The problem is that unless you have good insurance, it can be prohibitively expensive. If you're coming from abroad, you're advised to buy supplemental travel health insurance if your regular policy doesn't cover you for overseas trips. If you are covered, find out in advance if your insurance plan will make payments directly to providers or reimburse you later.

Domestic travelers who have insurance coverage should check with their insurance company for affiliated hospitals and doctors. US citizens who don't have regular health coverage can purchase domestic travel insurance, but be aware that most plans only cover emergencies.

Bring any medications you may need in their original containers, clearly labeled. A signed, dated letter from your physician describing your conditions and medications, including generic names, is a good idea.

INTERNET RESOURCES

There is a wealth of travel health advice on the Internet. The World Health Organization (WHO) publishes the superb *International Travel and Health,* which is revised annually and is available free online at www.who .int/ith/. Another website of general interest is MD Travel Health at www.mdtravel health.com, which provides complete travel health recommendations for every country, updated daily, also at no cost.

IN SOUTHWEST USA

AVAILABILITY & COST OF HEALTH CARE

In general, if you have a medical emergency, the best bet is to find the nearest public hospital and go to its emergency room; these hospitals are committed to providing emergency care to anyone who walks in the door, regardless of ability to pay.

If the problem isn't urgent, you can call a nearby hospital and ask for a referral to a local physician, which is usually cheaper than a trip to the emergency room if you have insurance. You should avoid stand-alone, for-profit urgent care centers, which tend to perform large numbers of expensive tests, even for minor illnesses.

Pharmacies are abundantly supplied, but international travelers may find that some medications which are available over-the-counter at home require a prescription in the US, and, as always, if you don't have insurance to cover the cost of prescriptions, they can be shockingly expensive.

INFECTIOUS DISEASES
Rabies

Rabies is a viral infection of the brain and spinal cord that is almost always fatal. The rabies virus is carried in the saliva of infected animals and is typically transmitted through an animal bite, though contamination of any break in the skin with infected saliva may result in rabies. In the US, most cases of human rabies are related to exposure to bats. Rabies may also be contracted from raccoons, skunks, foxes and unvaccinated cats and dogs.

If there is any possibility, however small, that you have been exposed to rabies, you

HEALTH

should seek preventative treatment, which consists of rabies immune globulin and rabies vaccine and is quite safe. In particular, any contact with a bat should be discussed with health authorities, because bats have small teeth and may not leave obvious bite marks. If you wake up to find a bat in your room, or discover a bat in a room with small children, rabies prophylaxis may be necessary.

Giardiasis

This parasitic infection of the small intestine occurs throughout North America and the world. Symptoms may include nausea, bloating, cramps and diarrhea, and may last for weeks. To protect yourself from giardia, you should avoid drinking directly from lakes, ponds, streams and rivers, which may be contaminated by animal or human feces. The infection can also be transmitted from person-to-person if proper hand washing is not performed. Giardiasis is easily diagnosed by a stool test and readily treated with antibiotics.

HIV/AIDS

As with most parts of the world, HIV infection occurs throughout the Southwest. You should never assume, on the basis of someone's background or appearance, that they're free of this or any other sexually transmitted disease. Be sure to use a condom for all sexual encounters.

Plague

While rare, plague (aka Black Death, the little flea-borne bacterium that killed some 25 million Europeans in the 1350s) still infects about a dozen people in northern New Mexico each year, usually between April and November. Medical technology has improved a bit since the Middle Ages, and prompt diagnosis and treatment almost always means a full recovery.

Plague has an incubation period of two to seven days and rather non-specific symptoms: headache, chills, high fever and painful, swollen lymph nodes in the groin, armpit and/or neck. If you display these symptoms shortly after your vacation, tell your doctor that you've been in a plague area and ask to be tested for the disease.

Plague is usually contracted by hikers and campers bitten by fleas shared with infected rodents and small animals, in particular rock squirrels and gophers. Stay on trails, avoid stirring up the undergrowth in piñon forests and give wide berth to sick, slow-moving or disoriented animals. It cannot be transmitted directly from person to person in the bubonic form.

ENVIRONMENTAL HAZARDS
Altitude Sickness

Visitors from lower elevations undergo rather dramatic physiological changes as they adapt to high altitudes, and while the side-effects are usually mild, they can be dangerous if ignored. Some people – age and fitness level are not predictors of who these will be – will feel the effects of altitude strongly, while others won't even notice.

Symptoms, which tend to manifest after four days and continue for about two weeks, may include headache, fatigue, loss of appetite, nausea, sleeplessness, increased urination and sometimes hyperventilation due to overexertion. More severe cases (usually affecting hikers over 10,000ft who didn't take time to acclimatize) display extreme disorientation, breathing problems and vomiting. These folks should descend immediately and get to a hospital.

To avoid the discomfort characterizing the milder symptoms, drink plenty of water (dehydration exacerbates the symptoms) and take it easy – at 7000ft, a pleasant walk around Santa Fe can wear you out faster than a steep hike at sea level. Schedule a nap if you have a sleepless night and put off serious hiking and biking for a few days, if possible. A mild painkiller like aspirin should take care of the headache.

Dehydration

Visitors to the desert may not realize how much water they're losing, as sweat evaporates almost immediately and increased urination (to help the blood process oxygen more efficiently) can go unnoticed. The prudent tourist will make sure to drink more water than usual – think a gallon a day if you're active. Parents can carry fruit and fruit juices to help keep kids hydrated.

Severe dehydration can easily cause disorientation and confusion, and even day hikers have gotten lost and died because they ignored their thirst. So bring plenty of water, even on short hikes, and drink it!

Heat Exhaustion & Heat Stroke

Dehydration or salt deficiency can cause heat exhaustion. Take time to acclimatize to high temperatures and make sure you get enough liquids. Salt deficiency is characterized by fatigue, lethargy, headaches, giddiness and muscle cramps. Salt tablets may help. Vomiting or diarrhea can also deplete your liquid and salt levels. Anhydrotic heat exhaustion, caused by the inability to sweat, is quite rare. Unlike other forms of heat exhaustion, it may strike people who have been in a hot climate for some time, rather than newcomers. Always use water bottles on long trips. One gallon of water per person per day is recommended if hiking.

Long, continuous exposure to high temperatures can lead to the sometimes-fatal condition of heat stroke, which occurs when the body's heat-regulating mechanism breaks down and body temperature rises to dangerous levels. Hospitalization is essential for extreme cases, but meanwhile get out of the sun, remove clothing, cover the body with a wet sheet or towel and fan continually.

Hypothermia

Skiers and winter hikers will find that temperatures in the mountains or desert can quickly drop below freezing. A sudden soaking or even high winds can lower your body temperature rapidly. Travel with a partner whenever possible.

Seek shelter when bad weather is unavoidable. Woolen clothing and synthetics, which retain warmth even when wet, are superior to cottons. Carry a good-quality sleeping bag and high-energy, easily digestible snacks like chocolate or dried fruit.

The symptoms of hypothermia are exhaustion, numbness, shivering, slurred speech, irrational or violent behavior, lethargy, stumbling, dizzy spells, muscle cramps and violent bursts of energy. Get hypothermia victims out of bad weather and into dry, warm clothing. Give hot liquids (not alcohol) and high-calorie, easily digestible food. In advanced stages place victims in warm sleeping bags and get in with them. Do not rub victims.

Animal Bites

Do not attempt to pet, handle or feed any wild animal, no matter how cuddly it may look; most injuries from animals are directly related to people trying to do just that.

Any bite or scratch by a mammal, including bats, should be promptly and thoroughly cleansed with large amounts of soap and water, followed by application of an antiseptic such as iodine or alcohol. The local health authorities should be contacted immediately for possible post-exposure rabies treatment, whether or not you've been immunized against rabies. It may also be advisable to start an antibiotic, since wounds caused by animal bites and scratches frequently become infected.

Mosquito Bites

When mosquitoes are present, keep yourself covered (wear long sleeves, long pants, hats and shoes rather than sandals) and apply a good insect repellent, preferably one containing DEET, to exposed skin and clothing. Don't overuse the stuff, though, because neurologic toxicity – though uncommon – has been reported from DEET, especially in children. DEET-containing compounds should not be used at all on kids under age two.

Insect repellents containing certain botanical products, including oil of eucalyptus and soybean oil, are effective but last only 1½ to 2 hours. Products based on citronella are not effective.

Tick Bites

Ticks are parasitic arachnids that may be present in brush, forest and grasslands, where hikers often get them on their legs or in their boots. Adult ticks suck blood from hosts by burrowing into the skin and can carry infections such as Lyme disease (rare in the Southwest).

Always check your body for ticks after walking through high grass or thickly forested area. If ticks are found unattached, they can simply be brushed off. If a tick is found attached, press down around the tick's head with tweezers, grab the head and gently pull upwards – do not twist it. (If no tweezers are available, use your fingers, but protect them from contamination with a piece of tissue or paper.) Do not rub oil, alcohol or petroleum jelly on it. If you get sick in the next couple of weeks, consult a doctor.

HEALTH

Snake Bites

There are several varieties of venomous snakes in the USA, but unlike those in other countries they do not cause instantaneous death, and antivenins are available. Rattlesnake bites are fairly common. First aid is to place a light constricting bandage over the bite, keep the wounded part below the level of the heart and move it as little as possible. Stay calm and get to a medical facility as soon as possible. Bring the dead snake for identification if you can, but don't risk being bitten again. Do not use the mythic 'cut an X and suck out the venom' trick, as this causes more damage to snakebite victims than the bites themselves.

The Arizona Poison Control System reports that half of reported snake bites result from people picking up the snake, either out of bravado or mistakenly assuming that the animal was dead. Keep a healthy distance away from snakes and watch where you step.

Spider & Scorpion Bites

Although there are many species of spiders in the Southwest, the main two that cause significant human illness are the black widow and brown recluse. The black widow is black or brown in color, measuring about 15mm in body length, with a shiny top, fat body and a distinctive red or orange hourglass figure on its underside. It's usu-ally found in barns, woodpiles, sheds, harvested crops and bowls of outdoor toilets. The brown recluse spider is brown, usually 10 mm in body length, with a dark violin-shaped mark on the top of the upper section of the body. It's active mostly at night and lives in dark sheltered areas, such as under porches and in woodpiles, and typically bites when trapped.

If bitten by a black widow, you should apply ice or cold packs and immediately go to the nearest emergency room. Complications of a black widow bite may include muscle spasms, breathing difficulties and high blood pressure. The bite of a brown recluse typically causes a large, inflamed wound, sometimes associated with fever and chills. If bitten, apply ice and see a physician.

If stung by a scorpion, you should immediately apply ice or a cold pack, immobilize the affected body part and go to the nearest emergency room. To prevent scorpion stings, be sure to inspect and shake out clothing, shoes and sleeping bags before use, and wear gloves and protective clothing when working around piles of wood or leaves.

Poison Control Centers are staffed 24 hours a day and advise about bites, stings and ingested poisons of all kinds. Call ☎ 800-222-1222 anywhere in the Southwest for the one nearest you.

Behind the Scenes

THIS BOOK

This 4th edition of *Southwest USA* was researched and written by Kim Grant (coordinating author), Becca Blond and John A Vlahides. David Lukas contributed the Environment chapter. Lisa Dunford wrote the 'Mormons, Polygamy & the LDS' boxed text, and Mark Morford penned the 'What Is Burning Man?' boxed text. The Health chapter was adapted from text by Dr David Goldberg. Much of the Las Vegas chapter was adapted from *Best of Las Vegas 2*, by Andrew Dean Nystrom.

The 3rd edition of *Southwest* was written by Jeff Campbell, Jennifer Rasin Denniston and Rob Rachowiecki, who also wrote the 2nd edition.

THANKS from the Author

Kim Grant It takes a pueblo to pull these books together. I'm grateful beyond measure that my world overflows with the kindness and good grace of others. Colby Cedar Smith pulled yeoman's duty during my disappearances; Kim Bolger exhibited laserlike professionalism; Clare Innes jumped in where others feared to tread; Catherine Direen said 'yes' to living in both relativism and absolutism. Thanks to all my Albuquerque friends.

To coauthors John and Becca: your passion is obvious. To Becca, in particular: your contributions to lifestyle and identity are above and beyond. Thanks for making my job as coordinating author a delight. To commissioning editor Suki Gear: your reasonableness and patience are a breath of fresh air. Thanks for making Lonely Planet a better place. And to Barbara Delissen: thanks for caring about rodeos.

Becca Blond Giant thanks goes to my boyfriend, Aaron, for hitting the road with me. Your unwavering enthusiasm and constant support made researching this book a wonderful experience. In Las Vegas, thanks to David Gonzalez at the MGM Grand for all the helpful info. Thanks also to Andrew Nystrom: your excellent writing in the *Best of Las Vegas* guide made my life a lot easier! In Durango I owe a big thanks to Dave at Ska Brewing Company, and Ron and Big John at Second Ave Sports for clueing me in on what was happening around town. In Tucson, thanks to Chris and Coree for the delightful dinners and floor space. Thanks also goes to Ian, Major Freedom and Pascale, who showed Aaron and me a good time on a side trip to the California coast. At Lonely Planet I'm indebted to Suki Gear for giving me the chance to explore some of my favorite places in the USA. Thanks also to Sam Benson for all the computer help and for your awesome *Road Trip: Route 66* text. Finally, I'm forever grateful to my family: David, Patricia, Jessica, Jennie, Vera, John, Spanky and Brittany – you guys are the best!

John A Vlahides Thanks Jim Aloise and Karl Soehnlein, for your wonderful friendship and for reminding me I'm not writing into a void. Kate Brady, Liz Costello and David Booth, thanks for pushing me in the right direction. Jake Torrens, Dan Fronczak, Kevin Clarke, Sondra Hall, Brian Busta and Bill Moore, thanks for reminding me that deadlines pass. Mom, Dad, Chris, Barb, Tere, I love you. Ken Kraus, you're a gentleman. Jason Mathis, you're terrific. Thanks Rick Green for the inside scoop.

THE LONELY PLANET STORY

The story begins with a classic travel adventure: Tony and Maureen Wheeler's 1972 journey across Europe and Asia to Australia. There was no useful information about the overland trail then, so Tony and Maureen published the first Lonely Planet guidebook to meet a growing need.

From a kitchen table, Lonely Planet has grown to become the largest independent travel publisher in the world, with offices in Melbourne (Australia), Oakland (USA) and London (UK). Today Lonely Planet guidebooks cover the globe. There is an ever-growing list of books and information in a variety of media. Some things haven't changed. The main aim is still to make it possible for adventurous travelers to get out there – to explore and better understand the world.

At Lonely Planet we believe travelers can make a positive contribution to the countries they visit – if they respect their host communities and spend their money wisely. Every year 5% of company profit is donated to charities around the world.

Mark Bennett and Hilary Reiter, I appreciate your kindness. Most importantly, thanks Suki Gear, Jay Cooke and Kim Grant for shepherding me through adversity. I dedicate this work to the memory of my grandmother Clio.

CREDITS
Commissioning Editor: Suki Gear
Coordinating Editor: Barbara Delissen
Coordinating Cartographer: David Connolly
Coordinating Layout Designer: Indra Kilfoyle
Managing Cartographer: Alison Lyall
Assisting Editors: Simone Egger, Carly Hall, Piers Kelly
Assisting Cartographer: Lyndell Stringer
Cover Designer: Pepi Bluck
Color Designer: Margaret Jung
Indexer: Evan Jones
Project Manager: Rachel Imeson

Thanks to: Adriana Mammarella, Sally Darmody, Yvonne Bischofberger, Martin Heng, Jay Cooke

THANKS from Lonely Planet
Many thanks to the following travellers who used the last edition and wrote to us with helpful hints, useful advice and interesting anecdotes.

A Scott Alquist, Mary Arnold, Peter Arnold **B** John Baker, Eva Behrens, E Blair, Carol Bouchard **C** FL Clarke, Connie Constan, Arthur Corte, Ken Crago, Russ Crockett **D** Wim de Boer, John Doerr **E** Lynne Earle, Richard Earle, Ruth Eastham **F** Terry Fabiano, Annette Ferguson, Sarah Fleck, Cathy Foster, KL Fuchs **G** Elisabeth Gitter, Jessica Gregory **H** RWJ Hartley, Lawrence Hauser, Lizz Higgins, Norma Jean Hogan, Alyson Hogarth, Alexa Huenges, **J** Kimi Jackson **K** F Karouta, John Kirk, Wayne Kuam **L** Ruth Ann Lebold, Carolyn Lee, Debra Lehrberger, Antje Lindinger, Bob Lipske, Paul Littlefair, Susan Logan **M** Lars Bjoern Madsen, Gina Manning, Liz Marini, Julia Mason, Kate Matthams, Norma McCarty, Iain McCormick, Deborah Meyer, Rich Mick, Karina Montgomery, Frances Morrier, Pat & John Morton **N** David & Rhonda Norbury, **P** Kristin Page, Roberta Paladini, Julie Phillips, John Preece **R** Thomas Reichardt, Chris Reynolds, Andrew Robertson, Virginia & Gilbert Roy **S** Dorothy Savidge, Mary Schantz, Melanie Scholz, Jana Schumann, Vera Schwartzbord, Andrew Sharp, Nick Sisnett, Mark Smalley **T** Julie Talbot **V** Willem van Kempen, Margo & Fred van Roosmalen **W** Barbara Wall, Don Webley, Christine Wegener, Kurt Werle, Toyabe Williams, Derek Wright

SEND US YOUR FEEDBACK
We love to hear from travelers – your comments keep us on our toes and help make our books better. Our well-traveled team reads every word on what you loved or loathed about this book. Although we cannot reply individually to postal submissions, we always guarantee that your feedback goes straight to the appropriate authors, in time for the next edition. Each person who sends us information is thanked in the next edition – and the most useful submissions are rewarded with a free book.

To send us your updates – and find out about Lonely Planet events, newsletters and travel news – visit our award-winning website: **www.lonelyplanet.com/feedback**.

Note: We may edit, reproduce and incorporate your comments in Lonely Planet products such as guidebooks, websites and digital products, so let us know if you don't want your comments reproduced or your name acknowledged. For a copy of our privacy policy visit www.lonelyplanet.com/privacy.

Index

000 Map pages
000 Location of color photographs

INDEX

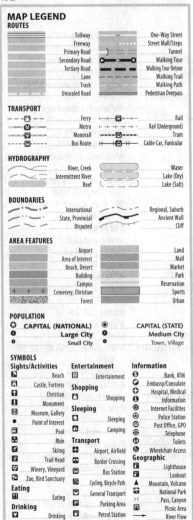

MAP LEGEND

ROUTES

Tollway	One-Way Street
Freeway	Street Mall/Steps
Primary Road	Tunnel
Secondary Road	Walking Tour
Tertiary Road	Walking Tour Detour
Lane	Walking Trail
Track	Walking Path
Unsealed Road	Pedestrian Overpass

TRANSPORT

Ferry	Rail
Metro	Rail (Underground)
Monorail	Tram
Bus Route	Cable Car, Funicular

HYDROGRAPHY

River, Creek	Water
Intermittent River	Lake (Dry)
Reef	Lake (Salt)

BOUNDARIES

International	Regional, Suburb
State, Provincial	Ancient Wall
Disputed	Cliff

AREA FEATURES

Airport	Land
Area of Interest	Mall
Beach, Desert	Market
Building	Park
Campus	Reservation
Cemetery, Christian	Sports
Forest	Urban

POPULATION

◎ CAPITAL (NATIONAL)	◉ CAPITAL (STATE)
● Large City	● Medium City
○ Small City	○ Town, Village

SYMBOLS

Sights/Activities
- Beach
- Castle, Fortress
- Christian
- Monument
- Museum, Gallery
- Point of Interest
- Pool
- Ruin
- Skiing
- Trail Head
- Winery, Vineyard
- Zoo, Bird Sanctuary

Eating
- Eating

Drinking
- Drinking
- Café

Entertainment
- Entertainment

Shopping
- Shopping

Sleeping
- Sleeping
- Camping

Transport
- Airport, Airfield
- Border Crossing
- Bus Station
- Cycling, Bicycle Path
- General Transport
- Parking Area
- Petrol Station
- Taxi Rank

Information
- Bank, ATM
- Embassy/Consulate
- Hospital, Medical
- Information
- Internet Facilities
- Police Station
- Post Office, GPO
- Telephone
- Toilets
- Wheelchair Access

Geographic
- Lighthouse
- Lookout
- Mountain, Volcano
- National Park
- Pass, Canyon
- Picnic Area
- River Flow
- Waterfall

LONELY PLANET OFFICES

Australia
Head Office
Locked Bag 1, Footscray, Victoria 3011
☎ 03 8379 8000, fax 03 8379 8111
talk2us@lonelyplanet.com.au

USA
150 Linden St, Oakland, CA 94607
☎ 510 893 8555, toll free 800 275 8555
fax 510 893 8572, info@lonelyplanet.com

UK
72–82 Rosebery Ave,
Clerkenwell, London EC1R 4RW
☎ 020 7841 9000, fax 020 7841 9001
go@lonelyplanet.co.uk

Published by Lonely Planet Publications Pty Ltd
ABN 36 005 607 983

© Lonely Planet 2005

© photographers as indicated 2005

Cover photographs by Lonely Planet Images: Monument Valley, Andrew Marshall & Leanne Walker (front); the Narrows in Zion National Park, Richard Cummins (back). Many of the images in this guide are available for licensing from Lonely Planet Images: www .lonelyplanetimages.com